W9-AAM-858

Randy J. Larsen
WASHINGTON UNIVERSITY IN ST. LOUIS
David M. Buss
UNIVERSITY OF TEXAS AT AUSTIN

Personality Psychology

Third Edition

DOMAINS
OF
KNOWLEDGE
ABOUT
HUMAN
NATURE

Boston Burr Ridge, IL Dubuque, IA Madison, WI New York San Francisco St. Louis
Bangkok Bogotá Caracas Kuala Lumpur Lisbon London Madrid Mexico City
Milan Montreal New Delhi Santiago Seoul Singapore Sydney Taipei Toronto

PERSONALITY PSYCHOLOGY: DOMAINS OF KNOWLEDGE ABOUT HUMAN NATURE

This book is printed on acid-free paper.

1 2 3 4 5 6 7 8 9 0 DOW/DOW 0 9 8 7 6

ISBN 978-0-07-353190-8
MHID 0-07-353190-1

Vice president and editor in chief: *Emily Barrosse*
Publisher: *Beth Mejia*
Sponsoring editor: *Michael J. Sugarman*
Editorial coordinator: *Katherine C. Russillo*
Marketing manager: *Sarah Martin*
Senior project manager: *Diane M. Folliard*
Designer: *Marianna Kinigakis*
Photo research coordinator: *Sonia Brown*
Media producer: *Stephanie Gregoire*
Supplement development editor: *Meghan Campbell*
Senior production supervisor: *Carol A. Bielski*
Composition: *10/12 Times Roman, by Techbooks-York*
Printing: *45#Pub Matte Plus, R. R. Donnelley & Sons*

Credits: The credits section for this book begins on page 739 and is considered an extension of the copyright page.

Library of Congress Cataloging-in-Publication Data

Larsen, Randy J.
Personality psychology: domains of knowledge about human nature / Randy J. Larsen, David M. Buss.–3rd ed.
p. cm.
Includes bibliographical references (p.) and indexes.
ISBN-13: 978-0-07-353190-8 (alk. paper)
ISBN-10: 0-07-353190-1 (alk. paper)
1. Personality–Textbooks. I. Buss, David M. II. Title.
BF698.L3723 2008
155.2–dc22 2006047327

www.mhhe.com

Dedication

To my children.

RL

To my father and first personality teacher, Arnold H. Buss.

DB

Brief Contents

Contents

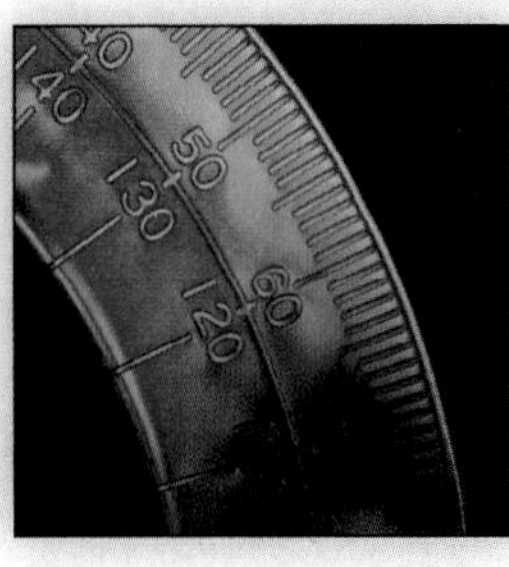

PART I

The Dispositional Domain

PART II
The Biological Domain

Chapter 6
Genetics and Personality 172

Chapter 7
Physiological Approaches to Personality 204

Chapter 8
Evolutionary Perspectives on Personality 242

PART III
The Intrapsychic Domain

Chapter 9
Psychoanalytic Approaches to Personality 284

PART IV

The Cognitive/Experiential Domain

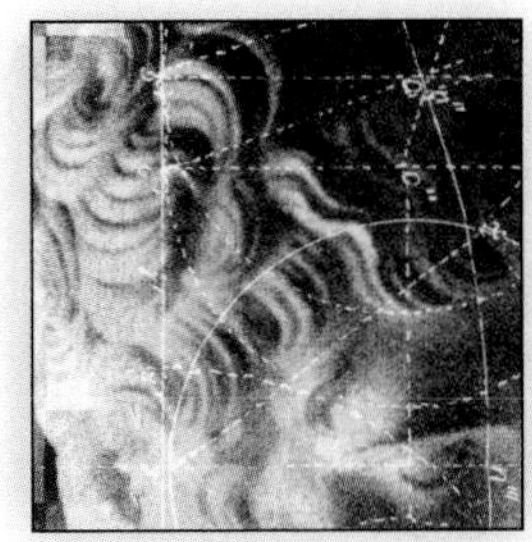

Chapter 12

Chapter 13

Chapter 14

PART V

The Social and Cultural Domain

Chapter 19
Disorders of Personality 620

CONCLUSION

Chapter 20
Summary and Future Directions 660

About the Authors

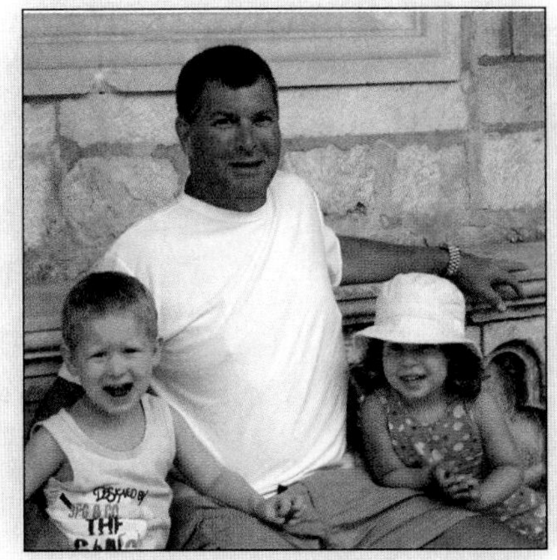

Randy J. Larsen received his Ph.D. in Personality Psychology from the University of Illinois at Champaign-Urbana in 1984. In 1992 he was awarded the Distinguished Scientific Achievement Award for Early Career Contributions to Personality Psychology from the American Psychological Association, and in 1987 he received a Research Scientist Development Award from the National Institute of Mental Health. He has been an associate editor at the *Journal of Personality and Social Psychology* and the *Personality and Social Psychology Bulletin,* and has been on the editorial boards of the *Journal of Research in Personality, Review of General Psychology,* and the *Journal of Personality.* Randy Larsen has served on several Scientific Review Groups for the National Institutes of Mental Health and the National Research Council. He is a Fellow in the Association for Psychological Science and the American Psychological Association. His research on personality has been supported by the National Institute of Mental Health, the National Science Foundation, the McDonnell Foundation for Cognitive Neuroscience, and the Solon Summerfield Foundation. In 2000 he was elected president of the Midwestern Psychological Association. He has served on the faculty at Purdue University and the University of Michigan. Currently Randy Larsen is the chairman of the Psychology Department, and the William R. Stuckenberg Professor of Human Values and Moral Development, at Washington University in St. Louis, where he teaches Personality Psychology and other courses. He lives in St. Louis with his wife and two children.

David M. Buss received his Ph.D. in 1981 from the University of California at Berkeley. He served on the faculties of Harvard University and the University of Michigan before accepting a professorship at the University of Texas at Austin, where he has taught since 1996. Buss received the American Psychological Association (APA) Distinguished Scientific Award for Early Career Contribution to Psychology in 1988; the APA G. Stanley Hall Award in 1990; and the APA Distinguished Scientist Lecturer Award in 2001. Books by David Buss include: *The Evolution of Desire: Strategies of Human Mating* (Revised

Edition) (Basic Books, 2003), which has been translated into 10 languages; *Evolutionary Psychology: The New Science of the Mind* (2nd ed.) (Allyn & Bacon, 2004), which was presented with the Robert W. Hamilton Book Award; *The Dangerous Passion: Why Jealousy Is as Necessary as Love and Sex* (Free Press, 2000), which has been translated into 13 languages; and *The Handbook of Evolutionary Psychology* (Wiley, 2005). Buss has authored more than 200 scientific publications, and has also written articles for the *New York Times* and the *Times Higher Education Supplement*. In 2003, he appeared in the ISI List of Most Highly Cited Psychologists Worldwide, and as the 27th Most Cited Psychologist in Introductory Psychology textbooks. He lectures widely throughout the United States and abroad, and has extensive cross-cultural research collaborations. David Buss greatly enjoys teaching, and in 2001 he won the President's Teaching Excellence Award at the University of Texas.

Preface

We have devoted our lives to the study of personality and believe this field is one of the most exciting in all of psychology. Thus we were enormously gratified to see the volume of e-mails, letters, and comments from satisfied consumers of our First and Second Editions. At the same time, preparing the Third Edition proved to be a humbling experience. The cascade of exciting publications in the field of personality is formidable, requiring not merely an updating, but also the addition of major sections of new material. Moreover, in important ways our First Edition proved prescient.

Rather than organize our text around the traditional grand theories of personality, we instead devised a framework of six important domains of knowledge about personality functioning. These six domains are *the dispositional domain* (traits, trait taxonomies, and personality dispositions over time), *the biological domain* (physiology, genetics, evolution), *the intrapsychic domain* (psychodynamics, motives), *the cognitive-experiential domain* (cognition, emotion, and the self), *the social and cultural domain* (social interaction, gender, and culture), and *the adjustment domain* (stress, coping, health, and personality disorders). We believed these domains of knowledge represented the contemporary state of affairs in personality psychology, and progress in the field since publication of our First Edition has continued to bear out that belief.

Our First and Second Editions differed from other texts in the importance placed on *culture, gender,* and *biology,* and these are areas of personality that have shown substantial growth in recent years. But we have also been fascinated to witness the growth in *each* of the six major domains of personality that form the organizational core of the book.

We have always envisioned our text as a reflection of the field. Our desire has always been to capture the excitement of what the science of personality is all about. For the Third Edition, we did our best to remain true to that vision. We believe that the field of personality psychology is now entering a golden age of sorts, and hope that the changes we've made to the Third Edition convey a discipline that is vibrant in a way it never has been before. After all, no other field is devoted to the study of all that it means to be human.

Chapter 1: Introduction to Personality Psychology

Chapter 2: Personality Assessment, Measurement, and Research Design
- Expanded coverage on ingredients of identity
- Facial expressions during marital conflict as predictors of marital outcomes
- Acts of individuals with a dependent personality

Chapter 3: Traits and Trait Taxonomies
- Act frequencies as predictors of hierarchy negotiation and marital violence
- Conscientiousness as a predictor of workplace achievement
- Neuroticism as a predictor of suicidal ideation and health-impairing coping strategies
- Personality predictors of forgiveness and volunteer work
- Personality traits that fall outside of the Big Five

Chapter 4: Theoretical and Measurement Issues in Trait Psychology
- Expanded coverage of the history and legal issues involved in the use of personality tests in employment settings

- A critical examination of the Myers-Briggs Type Indicator, including a discussion of its utility
- Expanded discussion of personality and integrity testing in business settings
- Expanded discussion of different types of validity
- Description of Hogan Assessment Systems, Inc., a successful personality testing company providing employment screening and selection
- Expanded description of Person-by-Situation interactions, with examples
- Increase in references to gender and culture in personality assessment

Chapter 5: Personality Dispositions over Time: Stability, Change, and Coherence
- New material on personality stability and change
- New section on longevity and personality
- New longitudinal studies of personality development

Chapter 6: Genetics and Personality
- Updated behavioral genetics concepts
- Latest heritability studies reported (e.g., heritability of religiosity)
- New material on genetics of marriage
- New material on gene-environment interactions

Chapter 7: Physiological Approaches to Personality
- Deleted material on Sheldon's theory of body types
- Added "A Closer Look" on personality and gambling
- Corrected description of Eysenck's lemon juice experiment
- Updated references

Chapter 8: Evolutionary Perspectives on Personality
- More details on how evolutionary psychology accounts for individual differences
- Evolution and life-history strategies

Chapter 9: Psychoanalytic Approaches to Personality
- Added "A Closer Look" on examples of the unconscious: blindsight and the deliberation-without-attention effect
- Deleted "Closer Look" on subliminal psychodynamic stimulation
- New factual material on the case of Anna O. and her relevance to Freud's overarching theory of personality
- Expanded coverage of theory on how sexual stages can influence personality
- Reorganized material to achieve better flow in this chapter

Chapter 10: Psychoanalytic Approaches: Contemporary Issues
- Updated contemporary views of the unconscious with material from Bargh, 2005
- Added "A Closer Look" on the controversy surrounding the Rind et al. (1998) article on childhood sexual abuse
- Cut material on divorce

Chapter 11: Motives and Personality
- Distinguish need for affiliation from need for intimacy
- Distinguish state levels from trait levels of motives
- Dewck's theory of competence motivation
- Gender differences in need for achievement

- New table on tips for increasing need for achievement in children
- New material on cultural differences in need for achievement
- Introduce the concept of "flow" in discussion of self-actualization

Chapter 12: Cognitive Topics in Personality
- New studies on field independence and language learning and decoding facial expressions
- Increased coverage of explanatory style and its three dimensions
- New section on social learning theory (e.g., Bandura, Dweck, Higgins, and Mischel)
- Deleted material on the KFA test, some details on Kelly's theory, and much of the material on goals

Chapter 13: Emotion and Personality
- New material on the direction of causality between happiness and successful outcomes in life
- New coverage of brain abnormality findings in aggressive and violent persons

Chapter 14: Approaches to the Self
- Reviewed experiments on self-identification in mirrors
- New material on development of the self-concept
- A new "Closer Look" on six myths of self-esteem

Chapter 15: Personality and Social Interaction
- Personality and conflict resolution tactics
- Personality predictors of relationships satisfaction
- Narcissism and inability to forgive others

Chapter 16: Sex, Gender, and Personality
- Gender differences in temperament in childhood
- Gender differences in valuation of power
- Massive 50-culture study of gender differences in personality
- New findings on real-life correlates of masculinity and femininity

Chapter 17: Culture and Personality
- New section on do cultures have distinct personality profiles?
- New cross-cultural research on the Big Five
- New cross-cultural research on possible factors beyond the Big Five

Chapter 18: Stress, Coping, Adjustment, and Health
- Updated AIDS statistics
- Shortened chapter exercises, converted one to an application
- Inserted brain scans of emotion centers

Chapter 19: Disorders of Personality
- New section distinguishing antisocial personality disorder from psychopathy
- New section distinguishing obsessive-compulsive personality disorder from obsessive-compulsive disorder
- New material on borderline and histrionic personality disorders
- New section on gender differences in personality disorders

Chapter 20: Summary and Future Directions

Acknowledgments

We would like to thank our own mentors and colleagues who, over the years, generated in us a profound interest in psychology. These include Arnold Buss, Joe Horn, Devendra Singh, and Lee Willerman (*University of Texas*); Jack Block, Ken Craik, Harrison Gough, Jerry Mendelsohn, and Richard Lazarus (*University of California, Berkeley*); Roy Baumeister (*Florida State University–Tallahassee*); Brian Little, Harry Murray, and David McClelland (*Harvard University*); Sam Gosling, Bob Josephs, Jamie Pennebaker, and Bill Swann (now at *University of Texas*); Ed Diener (*University of Illinois*); Gerry Clore (*University of Virginia*); Chris Peterson (*University of Michigan*); Hans Eysenck and Ray Cattell (both deceased); Tom Oltmanns, Roddy Roediger, and Mike Strube (*Washington University*); Alice Eagly (*Northwestern University*); Janet Hyde (*University of Wisconsin*); Robert Plomin (*King's College London*) and Lew Goldberg (*Oregon Research Institute*) and Jerry Wiggins (*University of British Columbia—Emeritus*) as mentors from afar. Special thanks again go to Vicki Babbitt (*Washington University*), who handled many special requests along the way to this edition, including many last-minute overnight deliveries. We would also like to thank our team at McGraw-Hill, including executive editor Mike Sugarman, senior project Manager Diane Folliard, and photo research coordinator Sonia Brown. Special thanks go to developmental editor Liz Sugarman for coordinating the developmental aspects of this revision. Liz displayed all the characteristics authors can hope for in an editorial collaborator, including reliability, punctuality, accuracy, resiliency in the face of setbacks, clear communication of expectations, economical use of editorial authority, liberal use of editorial wisdom, and an intelligent sense of humor that we both appreciated.

Finally, RL would like to acknowledge family members who supported him and tolerated his neglect while he concentrated on this book, including his wife, Zvjezdana, and his children, Tommy and Ana. DB would like to thank his ".50" genetic relatives: his parents Arnold and Edith Buss; his siblings Arnie and Laura Buss; and his children Ryan and Tara Buss.

A project of this scope and magnitude requires the efforts of many people. We are greatly indebted to our colleagues who reviewed this manuscript in its various stages. We sincerely appreciate the time and effort that the following instructors gave in this regard:

Timothy Atchison
West Texas A&M University
Nicole E. Barenbaum
University of the South
Michael D. Botwin
California State University–Fresno
Mark S. Chapell
Rowan University
Wayne A. Dixon
Southwestern Oklahoma State University
Barry Fritz
Quinnipiac University
Steven C. Funk
Northern Arizona University
Glenn Geher
State University of New York–New Paltz
Evan Harrington
John Jay College of Criminal Justice
Gail A. Hinesley
Chadron State College
Jill C. Keogh
University of Missouri–Columbia
John E. Kurtz
Villanova University

Brian Little
Harvard University
Todd Nelson
California State University–Stanislaus
Stephen J. Owens
Ohio University
David Pincus
Chapman University
Stephanie Sogg
Massachusetts General Hospital; Harvard Bipolar Research Program
David Harold Zald
Vanderbilt University

We also continue to be grateful to the reviewers of our previous editions for their valuable comments.

Michael Ashton
Brock University
Michael D. Botwin
California State University–Fresno
Fred B. Bryant
Loyola University Chicago
Joan Cannon
University of Massachusetts at Lowell
Scott J. Dickman
University of Massachusetts at Dartmouth
Richard Ely
Boston University
Stephen G. Flanagan
University of North Carolina
Irene Frieze
University of Pittsburgh
Lani Fujitsubo
Southern Oregon State College
Steven C. Funk
Northern Arizona University
Susan B. Goldstein
University of Redlands
Jane E. Gordon
The McGregor School of Antioch College
Marjorie Hanft-Martone
Eastern Illinois University
Marvin W. Kahn
University of Arizona
Carolin Keutzer
University of Oregon
Laura A. King
Southern Methodist University
Alan J. Lambert
Washington University
Michael J. Lambert
Brigham Young University
Mark R. Leary
Wake Forest University
Len B. Lecci
University of North Carolina at Wilmington
Christopher Leone
University of North Florida
Charles Mahone
Texas Tech University
Gerald Matthews
University of Cincinnati
Gerald A. Mendelsohn
University of California at Berkeley
Julie K. Norem
Wellesley College
William Pavot
Southwest State University
Bill E. Peterson
Smith College
Mark E. Sibicky
Marietta College
Jeff Simpson
Texas A&M University
Robert M. Stelmack
University of Ottawa
Steven Kent Sutton
University of Miami
Vetta L. Sanders Thompson
University of Missouri at St. Louis
Forrest B. Tyler
University of Maryland at College Park
Barbara Woike
Barnard College

Supplements for the Instructor

The supplements listed here accompany *Personality Psychology.* Please contact your McGraw-Hill representative for more information.

Instructor's Manual

Todd K. Shackelford, *Florida Atlantic University*
The Instructor's Manual includes chapter outlines, lecture topics and suggestions, ideas for classroom activities and demonstrations, questions for use in classroom discussions, ideas for student research papers, and lists of current research articles. The Instructor's Manual is organized by chapter, and has been designed to assist instructors new to the teaching of personality psychology, as well as more experienced professors.

Test Bank

Todd K. Shackelford, *Florida Atlantic University* and Michael D. Botwin, *California State University–Fresno*
This comprehensive Test Bank includes over 1,500 multiple-choice questions. The test questions are organized by chapter and are designed to test factual, applied, and conceptual understanding. This important instructor resource is accessible on the Instructor Resource CD-ROM and can be ordered in print as well.

Computerized Test Bank CD-ROM

The Computerized Test Bank is compatible for both Macintosh and Windows platforms. This CD-ROM provides a fully functioning editing feature that enables instructors to integrate their own questions, scramble items, and modify questions. The CD-ROM also offers an instructor the option of implanting the following unique features: Online Testing Program, Internet Testing, and Grade Management. Additional information regarding these features can be found in the accompanying CD-ROM documentation.

Online Learning Center for Instructors

This extensive Web site, designed specifically to accompany *Personality Psychology,* offers an array of resources for both instructor and student. Among the features included on the Instructor's side of the Web site, which is password protected, are an online version of the Instructor's Manual, PowerPoint Slides, and links to professional resources. These resources and more can be found by logging onto the text site at www.mhhe.com/larsen3.

PowerPoint™ Presentation Slides

These presentations cover the key points of each chapter, serving as a springboard for your lectures. They can be used as is, or you may modify them to meet your specific needs.

PageOut™

PageOut™ is the easiest way to create a Web site for your course. It requires no prior knowledge of HTML coding or graphic design, and is free with every McGraw-Hill textbook. Visit us at www.pageout.net to learn more about PageOut™.

As a full-service publisher of quality educational products, McGraw-Hill does much more than just sell textbooks to your students. We create and publish an extensive array of print, video, and digital supplements to support instruction on your campus. Orders of new (versus used) textbooks help us to defray the cost of developing such supplements, which is substantial. We have a broad range of other supplements in psychology that you may wish to tap for your course. Ask your local McGraw-Hill representative about the availability of supplements that may help with your course design.

For the Student

Online Learning Center

This extensive Web site, designed specifically to accompany *Personality Psychology,* offers an array of resources for both instructor and student. The student side of the Online Learning Center provides a variety of learning tools, including a chapter outline, learning objectives, multiple-choice questions, true-false questions, essay questions, and Web links for each chapter. These resources and more can be found by logging on to the text site at www.mhhe.com/larsen3.

Personality Psychology

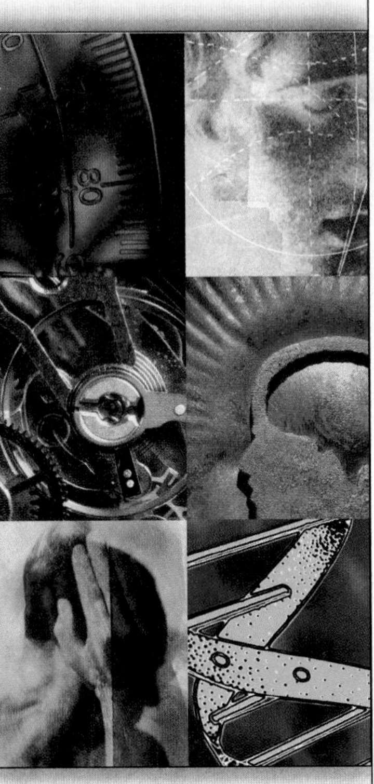

1

Introduction to Personality Psychology

INTRODUCTION

Each person is, in certain respects, like all other persons, like some other persons, and like no other person.

> *Those who carry humor to excess are thought to be vulgar buffoons, striving after humor at all costs, not caring about pain to the object of their fun; . . . while those who can neither make a joke themselves nor put up with those who do are thought to be boorish and unpolished. But those who joke in a tasteful way are called ready-witted and tactful . . . and it is the mark of a tactful person to say and listen to such things as befit a good and well-bred person.*

Aristotle, in *The Nicomachean Ethics,* expressed these wise observations on the subject of humor and people who do and do not indulge in it. In this quote we see Aristotle behaving much as a personality psychologist. Aristotle is analyzing the characteristics of persons who have an appropriate sense of humor, providing some details on what features are associated with a sense of humor. Aristotle adds to this description by comparing people who are extreme, having either too much or too little sense of humor. In his book on ethics, Aristotle described and analyzed many personality characteristics, including truthfulness, courage, intelligence, self-indulgence, anger-proneness, and friendliness.

We might conclude that Aristotle was an amateur personality psychologist. But aren't we all amateur personality psychologists to some extent? Aren't we all curious about the characteristics people possess, including our own characteristics? Don't we all use personality characteristics in describing people? And haven't we all used personality characteristics to explain behavior, either our own or others'?

When we say that our friend goes to a lot of parties because she is outgoing, we are using personality to explain her behavior. When we refer to another friend as conscientious and reliable, we are describing features of his personality. When we characterize ourselves as thoughtful, intelligent, and ambitious, we are describing features of our personalities.

Features of personality make people different from one another, and these features usually take the form of adjectives we use to speak about a particular person, such as John is lazy and unreliable, Mary is optimistic, and Fred is anxiety-ridden. *Adjectives that can be used to describe characteristics of people are called* **trait-descriptive adjectives.** There are more than 20,000 such trait-descriptive adjectives in the English language. This astonishing fact alone tells us that, in everyday life, there are compelling reasons for trying to understand and describe the nature of those we interact with, as well as compelling reasons for trying to understand and describe ourselves.

Notice that the adjectives describing personality refer to several very different aspects of people. Words such as *thoughtful* refer to inner qualities of mind. Words such as *charming* and *humorous* refer to the effects a person has on other people. Words such as *domineering* are relational and signify a person's position, or stance, toward others. Words such as *ambitious* refer to the intensity of desire to reach our goals. Words such as *creative* refer both to a quality of mind and to the nature of the products we produce. Words such as *deceitful* refer to the strategies a person uses to attain his or her goals. All of these features describe aspects of personality.

Exercise

Think of someone you know well—say, a friend, family member, or roommate. Consider the many characteristics that make this person unique. List the five adjectives you think best capture this person's personality. For example, if you were to describe this person to someone, what five adjectives would you use? Now, ask your target person to list the five adjectives *he or she* thinks best describe that person. Compare your lists.

Personality Defined

Establishing a definition for something as complex as human personality is difficult. The authors of the first textbooks on personality—Gordon Allport (1937) and Henry Murray (1938)—struggled with the definition. The problem is how to establish a definition that is sufficiently comprehensive to include all of the aspects mentioned in the introduction to this chapter, including inner features, social effects, qualities of the mind, qualities of the body, relations to others, and inner goals. Because of these complexities, some texts on personality omit a formal definition entirely. Nonetheless, the following definition captures the essential elements of personality: **Personality** *is the set of psychological traits and mechanisms within the individual that are organized and relatively enduring and that influence his or her interactions with, and adaptations to, the intrapsychic, physical, and social environments*. Let's examine the elements of this definition more closely.

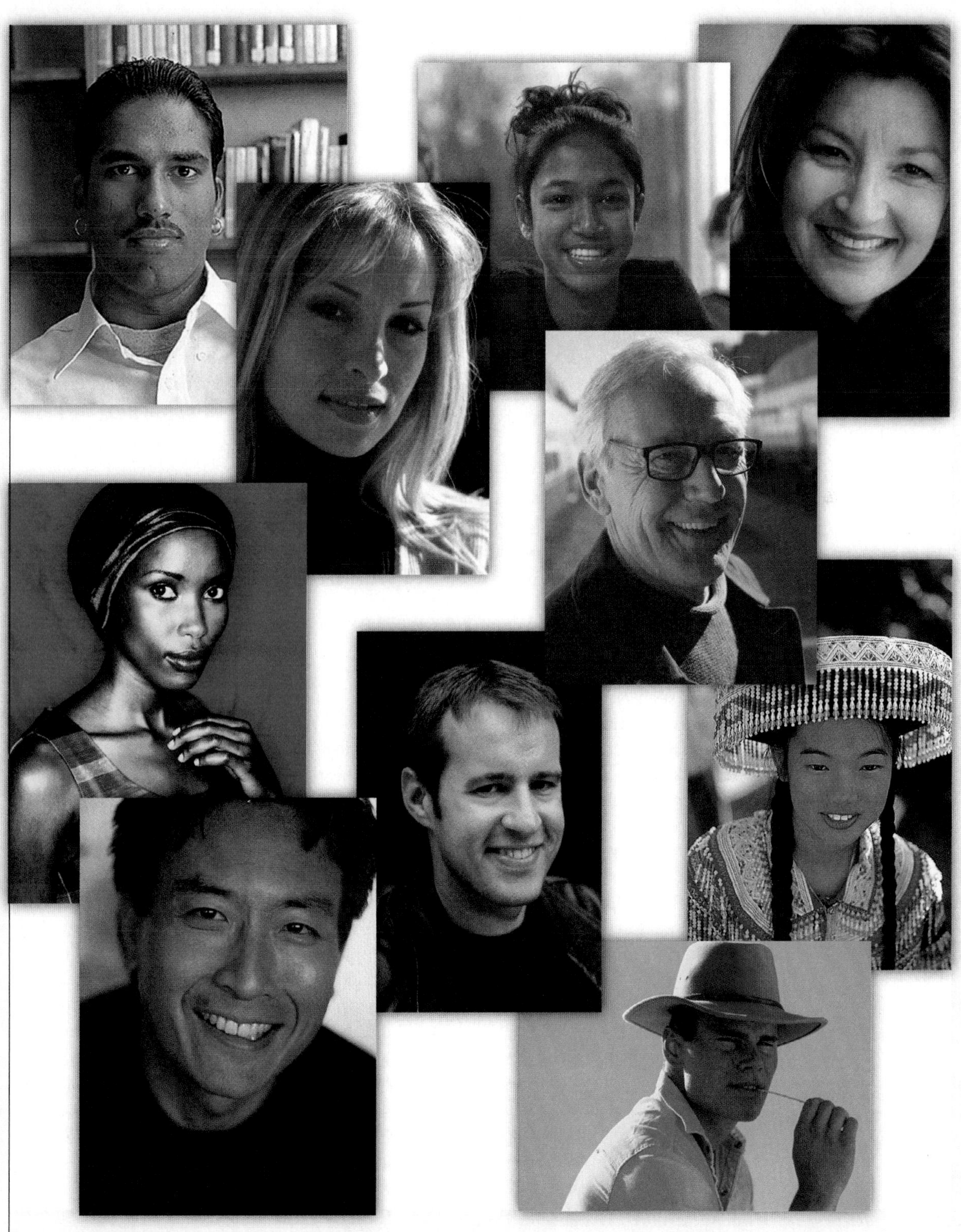

People are different from each other in many ways. The science of Personality Psychology provides an understanding of the psychological ways that people differ from each other.

Personality Is the Set of Psychological Traits . . .

Psychological traits are characteristics that describe ways in which people are different from each other. Saying that someone is *shy* is to mention one way in which he or she differs from others who are more outgoing. Traits also define ways people are *similar*. For example, people who are shy are similar to each other in that they are anxious in social situations, particularly situations in which there is an audience focusing attention on them.

Consider another example—the trait of talkativeness. This characteristic can be meaningfully applied to persons and describes a dimension of difference between them. Typically, a talkative person is that way from day to day, from week to week, and from year to year. Certainly, even the most talkative person can have quiet moments, quiet days, or even quiet weeks. Over time, however, those with the trait of talkativeness tend to emit verbal behavior with greater frequency than those who are low on talkativeness. In this sense, traits describe the **average tendencies** of a person. On average, a high-talkative person starts more conversations than a low-talkative person.

Research on personality traits asks four kinds of questions:

- How many traits are there?
- How are the traits organized?
- What are the origins of traits?
- What are the correlations and consequences of traits?

One primary question is *how many* fundamental traits there are. Are there dozens or hundreds of traits, or merely a few? The second research question pertains to the *organization,* or structure, of traits. For example, how is talkativeness related to other traits, such as impulsivity and extraversion? A third research question concerns the *origins* of traits—where they come from and how they develop. Does heredity influence talkativeness? What sorts of child-rearing practices affect the development of traits such as talkativeness? A fourth key question pertains to the *correlations and consequences* of traits in terms of experience, behavior, and life outcomes. Do talkative persons, for example, have many friends? Do they have a more extended social network to draw upon in times of trouble? Do they annoy people who are trying to study?

The four research questions constitute the core of the research program of many personality psychologists. Psychological traits are useful for at least three reasons. First, they help us *describe* people and help us understand the dimensions of difference between people. Second, traits are useful because they may help us *explain* behavior. The reasons people do what they do may be partly a function of their personality traits. Third, traits are useful because they can help us *predict* future behavior—for example, the sorts of careers individuals will find satisfying, who will tolerate stress better, and who is likely to get along well with others. Thus, personality is useful in *describing, explaining,* and *predicting* differences between individuals. All good scientific theories enable researchers to describe, explain, and predict in their domains. Just as an economic theory might be useful in describing, explaining, and predicting fluctuations in the stock market, personality traits describe, explain, and predict differences between persons.

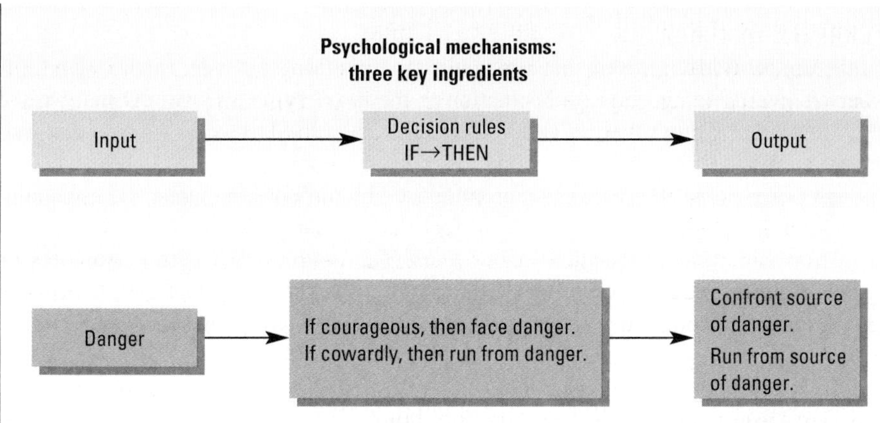

Figure 1.1

Psychological Mechanisms: Three Key Ingredients

And Mechanisms . . .

Psychological mechanisms are like traits, except that the term *mechanisms* refers more to the processes of personality. For example, most psychological mechanisms involve an information-processing activity. Someone who is extraverted, for example, may look for and notice opportunities to interact with other people. That is, an extraverted person is prepared to notice and act on certain kinds of social information.

Most psychological mechanisms have three essential ingredients: *inputs, decision rules,* and *outputs.* A psychological mechanism may make people more sensitive to certain kinds of information from the environment (input), may make them more likely to think about specific options (decision rules), and may guide their behavior toward certain categories of action (outputs). For example, an extraverted person may look for opportunities to be with other people, may consider in each situation the possibilities for human contact and interaction, and may encourage others to interact with him or her. Our personalities contain many psychological mechanisms of this sort—information-processing procedures that have the key elements of inputs, decision rules, and outputs (see Figure 1.1).

This does not mean that all of our traits and psychological mechanisms are activated at all times. In fact, at any point in time, only a few are activated. Consider the trait of courageousness. This trait is activated only under particular conditions, such as when people face serious dangers and threats to their lives. Some people are more courageous than others, but we will never know which people are courageous unless and until the right situation presents itself. Look around next time you are in class; who do you think has the trait of courageousness? You won't know until you are in a situation that activates courageous behavior.

Courage is an example of a trait that is activated only under particular circumstances.

Within the Individual . . .

Within the individual means that personality is something a person carries with him- or herself over time and from one situation to the next. Typically, we feel that we are today the same people we were last week, last month, and last year. We also feel that we will continue to have these personalities into the coming months and years. And, although our personalities are certainly influenced by our environments, and especially by the significant others in our lives, we feel that we carry with us the same personalities from situation to situation in our lives. The definition of personality stresses that the important sources of personality reside within the individual and, hence, are at least somewhat stable over time and somewhat consistent over situations.

That Are Organized and Relatively Enduring . . .

Organized means that the psychological traits and mechanisms, for a given person, are not simply a random collection of elements. Rather, personality is organized because the mechanisms and traits are linked to one another in a coherent fashion. Imagine the simple case of two desires—a desire for food and a desire for intimacy. If you have not eaten for a while and are experiencing hunger pangs, then your desire for food might override your desire for intimacy. On the other hand, if you have already eaten, then your desire for food may temporarily subside, allowing you to pursue intimacy. Our personalities are organized in the sense that they contain decision rules that govern which needs are activated, depending on the circumstances.

Psychological traits are also relatively **enduring** over time, particularly in adulthood, and are generally consistent over situations. To say that someone is angry at this moment is not saying anything about a trait. A person may be angry now but not tomorrow or may be angry in this situation but not in others. Anger is more of a *state* than a trait. To say that someone is anger-prone or generally hot-tempered, however, is to describe a psychological trait. Someone who is anger-prone is *frequently* angry, relative to others, and shows this proneness time and time again in many different situations (e.g., the person is argumentative at work, is hostile and aggressive while playing team sports for recreation, and argues a lot with family members).

There may be some occasions when this generalization about the consistency of personality from situation to situation does not hold. Some situations may be overpowering and suppress the expression of psychological traits. Persons who are generally talkative, for example, may remain quiet during a lecture, at the movies, or in an elevator—although you undoubtedly have experienced someone who could not or would not keep quiet in any of these circumstances!

The debate about whether people are consistent across situations in their lives has a long history in personality psychology. Some psychologists have argued that the evidence for consistency is weak (Mischel, 1968). For example, honesty measured in one situation (say, cheating on a test) may not correlate with honesty measured in another situation (say, cheating on income taxes). We will explore this debate more fully later in the book. For now we will simply say that most personality psychologists maintain that, although people are not perfectly consistent, there is enough consistency to warrant including this characteristic in a definition of personality.

The fact that personality includes relatively enduring psychological traits and mechanisms does not preclude change over time. Indeed, describing precisely the ways in which we change over time is one goal of personality psychologists.

And That Influence . . .

In the definition of personality, an emphasis on the **influential forces** of personality means that personality traits and mechanisms can have an effect on people's lives. Personality influences how we act, how we view ourselves, how we think about the world, how we interact with others, how we feel, how we select our environments (particularly our social environment), what goals and desires we pursue in life, and how we react to our circumstances. Persons are not passive beings merely responding to external forces. Rather, personality plays a key role in affecting how people shape their lives. It is in this sense that personality traits are thought of as forces that *influence* how we think, act, and feel.

His or Her Interactions with . . .

This feature of personality is perhaps the most difficult to describe, because the nature of **person–environment interaction** is complex. In Chapter 15, we will examine interactionism in greater detail. For now, however, it is sufficient to note that interactions with situations include perceptions, selections, evocations, and manipulations. *Perceptions* refers to how we "see," or interpret, an environment. Two people may be exposed to the same objective event, yet what they pay attention to and how they interpret the event may be very different. And this difference is a function of their personalities. For example, two people can look at an inkblot, yet one person sees two cannibals cooking a human over a fire, whereas the other perceives a smiling clown waving hello. As another example, a stranger may smile at someone on the street; one person might perceive the smile as a smirk, whereas another person might perceive the smile as a friendly gesture. It is the same smile, just as it is the same inkblot, yet how people interpret such objective situations can be determined by their personalities.

Selection describes the manner in which we choose situations to enter—how we choose our friends, our hobbies, our college classes, and our careers. And how we go about making these selections is, at least in part, a reflection of our personalities. How we use our free time is especially a reflection of our traits. One person may take up the hobby of parachute jumping, whereas another may prefer to spend time quietly gardening. We select from what life offers us, and such choices are a function of personality.

Evocations are the reactions we produce in others, often quite unintentionally. To some extent, we create the social environment that we inhabit. A child with a high activity level, for example, may evoke in parents attempts to constrain the child, even though these attempts are not intended or desired by the child. A person who is physically large may evoke feelings of intimidation in others, even if intimidation is not the goal. Our evocative interactions are also essential features of our personalities.

Manipulations are the ways in which we intentionally attempt to influence others. Someone who is anxious or frightened easily may try to influence the group he or she is a part of to avoid scary movies or risky activities. Someone who is highly conscientious may insist that everyone follow the rules. Or a man who is very neat and orderly may insist that his wife pick up her things and help with daily cleaning. The ways in which we attempt to manipulate the behavior, thoughts, and feelings of others are essential features of our personalities. All of these forms of interaction—perceptions, selections, evocations, and manipulations—are central to understanding the connections between the personalities of people and the nature of the environments they inhabit.

And Adaptations to . . .

An emphasis on **adaptation** conveys the notion that a central feature of personality concerns adaptive functioning—accomplishing goals, coping, adjusting, and dealing with the challenges and problems we face as we go through life. Few things are more obvious about human behavior than the fact that it is goal-directed, functional, and purposeful. Even behavior that does not appear functional—such neurotic behavior as excessive worrying—may, in fact, be functional. For example, people who worry a lot often receive lots of support and encouragement from others. Consequently, what appears on the surface to be maladaptive (worrying) may, in fact, have some rewarding characteristics for the person (eliciting social support). In addition, some aspects of personality processes represent deficits in normal adaptations, such as breakdowns in the ability to cope with stress, to regulate one's social behavior, or to manage one's own emotions. By knowing the adaptive consequences of such disordered behavior patterns, we begin to understand some of the functional properties of normal personality. Although psychologists' knowledge of the adaptive functions of personality traits and mechanisms is currently limited, it remains a challenging and indispensable key to understanding the nature of human personality.

The Environment

The physical **environment** often poses challenges for people. Some of these are direct threats to survival. For example, food shortages create the problem of securing adequate nutrients for survival. Extremes of temperature pose the problem of maintaining thermal homeostasis. Heights, snakes, spiders, and strangers can all pose threats to survival. Human beings, like other animals, have evolved solutions to these adaptive problems. Hunger pangs motivate us to seek food, and taste preferences guide our choices of which foods to consume. Shivering mechanisms help combat the cold, and sweat glands help fight the heat. At a psychological level, our fears of heights, snakes, spiders, and strangers—the most common human fears—help us avoid or safely interact with these environmental threats to our survival.

Our social environment also poses adaptive challenges. We may desire the prestige of a good job, but there are many other persons competing for the same positions. We may desire interesting friends and mates, but there are many others competing for them. We may desire greater emotional closeness with our significant others, but it may not be immediately clear to us how to achieve this closeness. The ways in which we cope with our social environment—the challenges we encounter in our struggle for belongingness, love, and esteem from others—is central to an understanding of personality.

The particular aspect of the environment that is important at any moment in time is frequently determined by personality. A person who is talkative, for example, will notice more opportunities in the social environment to strike up conversations than will someone who is low on talkativeness. A person who is disagreeable will occupy a social environment where people frequently argue with him or her. A person for whom status is very important will pay attention to the relative hierarchical positions of others—who is up, who is down, who is ascending, who is sliding. In short, from among the potentially infinite dimensions of the environments we inhabit, our "effective environment" represents only the small subset of features that our psychological mechanisms direct us to attend and respond to.

In addition to our physical and social environments, we have an intrapsychic environment. *Intrapsychic* means "within the mind." We all have memories, dreams, desires, fantasies, and a collection of private experiences that we live with each day. This intrapsychic environment, although not as objectively verifiable as our social or physical environment, is nevertheless real to each of us and makes up an important part of our psychological reality. For example, our self-esteem—how good or bad we feel about ourselves at any given moment—may depend on our assessment of the degree to which we are succeeding in attaining our goals. Success at work and success at friendship may provide two different forms of success experience and, hence, form different intrapsychic memories. We are influenced by our memories of such experiences whenever we think about our own self-worth. Our intrapsychic environment, no less than our physical and social environments, provides a critical context for understanding human personality.

Write a one-page essay about a good friend, someone you know well, in which you describe what is characteristic, enduring, and functional about that person. Include in this description those elements of the ways in which he or she interacts with, or adapts to, the physical, social, and intrapsychic environments.

Three Levels of Personality Analysis

Although the definition of personality used in this book is quite broad and encompassing, personality can be analyzed at three levels. These three levels are well summarized by Kluckhohn & Murray, in their 1948 book on culture and personality, in which they state that every human being is, in certain respects,

1. Like all others (the human nature level).
2. Like some others (the level of individual and group differences).
3. Like no others (the individual uniqueness level).

Another way to think of these distinctions is that the first level refers to "universals" (the ways in which we are all alike), the middle level refers to "particulars" (the ways in which we are like some people but unlike others), and the third level refers to "uniqueness" (the ways in which we are unlike any other person) (see Table 1.1).

Human Nature

The first level of personality analysis describes **human nature** in general—the traits and mechanisms of personality that are typical of our species and are possessed by everyone or nearly everyone. For example, nearly every human has language skills, which allow him or her to learn and use a language. All cultures on earth speak a language, so spoken language is part of the universal human nature. At a psychological level, all humans possess fundamental psychological mechanisms—for example, the desire to live with others and belong to social groups—and these mechanisms are

Table 1.1 Three Levels of Personality Analysis

Level of Analysis	Examples
Human Nature	Need to belong
	Capacity for love
Individual and Group Differences	Variation in need to belong (individual difference)
	Men more physically aggressive than women (group difference)
Individual Uniqueness	Letisha's unique way of expressing her love
	Santino's unique way of expressing aggression

part of general human nature. There are many ways in which each person is like *every* other person, and by understanding those ways we may achieve an understanding of the general principles of human nature.

Individual and Group Differences

The second level of personality analysis pertains to individual and group differences. Some people are gregarious and love parties; others prefer quiet evenings reading. Some people take great physical risks by jumping out of airplanes, riding motorcycles, and driving fast cars; others shun such risks. Some people enjoy high self-esteem and experience life relatively free from anxiety; others worry constantly and are plagued by self-doubt. These are dimensions of **individual differences,** ways in which each person is like *some* other people (e.g., extraverts, sensation seekers, and high self-esteem persons).

Personality can also be observed by studying **differences between groups.** That is, people in one group may have certain personality features in common, and these common features make that group of people different from other groups. Examples of groups studied by personality psychologists include different cultures, different age groups, different political parties, and groups from different socioeconomic backgrounds. Another important set of differences studied by personality psychologists concerns those between men and women. Although many traits and mechanisms of humans are common to both sexes, a few are different for men and women. For example, there is accumulated evidence that, across cultures, men are typically more physically aggressive than women. Men are responsible for most of the violence in society. One goal of personality psychology is to understand why certain aspects of personality are differentiated along group lines, such as understanding how and why women are different from men and why persons from one culture are different from persons from another culture.

Personality psychologists sometimes study group differences, such as differences between men and women.

Individual Uniqueness

No two individuals, not even identical twins raised by the same parents in the same home in the same culture, have exactly the same personalities. Every individual has personal qualities not shared by any other person in the world. One of the goals of personality psychology is to allow for individual uniqueness and to develop ways to capture the richness of unique individual lives.

One debate in the field concerns whether individuals should be studied *nomothetically*—that is, as individual instances of general characteristics that are distributed in the population, or should be studied *idiographically,* as single, unique cases. **Nomothetic** *research typically involves statistical comparisons of individuals or groups, requiring samples of subjects on which to conduct research.* Nomothetic research is typically applied to identify universal human characteristics and dimensions of individual or group differences. **Idiographic** (translated literally as "the description of one") *research typically focuses on a single subject, trying to observe general principles that are manifest in a single life over time.* Often, idiographic research results in case studies or the psychological biography of a single person (Runyon, 1983). Sigmund Freud, for example, wrote a psychobiography of Leonardo da Vinci (1916/1947). An example of another version of idiographic research is provided by Rosenzweig (1986, 1997), in which he proposes to analyze persons in terms of the sequence of events in their lives, trying to understand critical life events within the persons' own histories.

The important point is that personality psychologists have been concerned with all three levels of analysis: the universal level, the level of individual and group differences, and the level of individual uniqueness. Each contributes valuable knowledge to the total understanding of the nature of personality.

A Fissure in the Field

Different personality psychologists focus on different levels of analysis. And there is a gap within the field that has not yet been successfully bridged. It is the gap between the human nature level of analysis and the analysis of group and individual differences. Many psychologists have theorized about what human nature is like in general. However, when doing research, psychologists most often focus on individual and group differences in personality. As a consequence, there is a fissure between the grand theories of personality and contemporary research in personality.

Grand Theories of Personality

Most of the grand theories of personality primarily address the human nature level of analysis. That is, these theories attempt to provide a universal account of the fundamental psychological processes and characteristics of our species. Sigmund Freud (1915/1957), for example, emphasized universal instincts of sex and aggression; a universal psychic structure of the id, ego, and superego; and universal stages of psychosexual development (oral, anal, phallic, latency, and genital). Statements about the universal core of human nature typically lie at the center of all such grand theories of personality.

Many of the textbooks used in teaching college courses in personality psychology are structured around grand theories. Such books have been criticized, however, because many of those theories are of historical interest. Only portions of them have stood the test of time and inform personality research today. Although the grand theories are an important part of the history of personality psychology, there is also a lot of interesting personality research going on today that is not directly relevant to the grand theories.

Contemporary Research in Personality

Most of the empirical research in contemporary personality addresses the ways in which individuals and groups differ. For example, the extensive research literature on extraversion and introversion, on anxiety and neuroticism, and on self-esteem all focuses on the ways in which people differ from one another. The extensive research on masculinity, femininity, and androgyny deals with the psychological ways in which men and women differ, as well as the ways in which they acquire sex-typed social roles and behavior patterns. Research on cultures shows that one major dimension of difference concerns the degree to which individuals endorse a collectivistic or an individualistic attitude, with Eastern cultures tending to be more collectivistic and Western cultures more individualistic.

One way to examine personality psychology might be to pick a dozen or so current research topics and explore what psychologists have learned about each. For example, a lot of research has been done on self-esteem—what it is, how it develops, how people maintain high self-esteem, and how it functions in relationships. There are a lot of interesting topics in contemporary personality psychology—for example, shyness, aggression, trust, dominance, hypnotic susceptibility, depression, intelligence, attributional style, goal setting, anxiety, temperament, sex roles, Type A behavior, self-monitoring, extraversion, sensation seeking, agreeableness, impulsivity, sociopathic tendencies, morality, locus of control, personality and occupational choice, optimism, creativity, leadership, prejudice, and narcissism.

A course that just surveys current topics in personality research seems unsatisfactory. It would be like going to an auction and bidding on everything—soon you would have too much and would be overwhelmed. Just picking topics to cover would not result in any sense of the connection among the aspects of personality. Indeed, the field of personality has been criticized for containing too many independent areas of investigation, with no sense of the whole person behind the separate topics of investigation. What holds personality together as a coherent field would be missing in such an approach.

You have probably heard the ancient legend of the three blind men who were presented with an elephant. They tried to figure out what the whole elephant was like. The first blind man approached cautiously; walking up to the elephant and putting his hands and then arms around the animal's leg, he proclaimed, "Why, the whole elephant is much like a tree, slender and tall." The second man grasped the trunk of the elephant and exclaimed, "No, the whole elephant is more like a large snake." The third blind man grasped the ear of the elephant and stated, "You are both wrong; the whole elephant more closely resembles a fan." The three blind men proceeded to argue with one another, each insisting that his opinion of the whole elephant was the correct one. In a sense, each blind man had a piece of the truth, yet each failed to recognize that his perceptions of the elephant captured only a narrow part of the truth. Each failed to grasp the whole elephant. Working together, however, the blind men could have assembled a reasonable understanding of the whole elephant.

The topic of personality is like the elephant, and personality psychologists are somewhat like the blind men who take only one perspective at a time. Psychologists often approach the topic of personality from one perspective. For example, some psychologists study the biological aspects of personality. Others study ways that culture promotes personality differences between people and between groups. Still other psychologists study how various aspects of the mind interact and work together to produce personality. And others study relationships among people and believe that social interaction is where personality manifests its most important effects. Each of these perspectives on personality captures elements of truth, yet each specialty area alone is inadequate to describe the entire realm of human personality—the whole elephant, so to speak.

Six Domains of Knowledge about Human Nature

The various views of researchers in personality stem *not* from the fact that one perspective is right and the others wrong but, rather, from the fact that they are studying different domains of knowledge. A **domain of knowledge** is a specialty area of science and scholarship, in which psychologists have focused on learning about some specific and limited aspects of human nature. A domain of knowledge delineates the boundaries of researchers' knowledge, expertise, and interests.

To a large extent, this degree of specialization is reasonable. Indeed, specialization characterizes many scientific fields. The field of medicine, for example, has heart specialists and brain specialists, focusing in great detail on their own domains. It is likewise reasonable for the field of personality psychology to have intrapsychic specialists, cultural specialists, and biological specialists. Each of these domains of personality (intrapsychic, cultural, biological) has accumulated its own base of knowledge. Nonetheless, it is still desirable at some point to integrate these diverse domains to see how they all fit together.

The whole personality, like the whole elephant, is the sum of the various parts and the connections among them. For personality, each part is a domain of knowledge, representing a collection of knowledge about certain aspects of personality. How are the domains of knowledge defined? For the most part, natural boundaries have developed in the field of personality psychology. That is, researchers have formed natural clusters of topics, which fit together and which are distinct from other clusters of knowledge. Within these identifiable domains, researchers have developed common *methods for asking questions;* have accumulated a foundation of *known facts;* and have developed *theoretical explanations,* which account for what is known about personality from the perspective of each domain.

In this way, the field of personality can be neatly cleaved into six distinct domains of knowledge about human nature: personality is influenced by traits the person is born with or develops (*dispositional domain*); by biological events (*biological domain*); by conflicts within the person's own mind (*intrapsychic domain*); by personal and private thoughts, feelings, desires, beliefs, and other subjective experiences (*cognitive-experiential domain*); by social, cultural, and gendered positions in the world (*social and cultural domain*); and by the adjustments that the person must make to the inevitable challenges of life (*adjustment domain*).

Personality psychologists working within the various domains often use different theoretical perspectives and focus on different facts about human nature. As a consequence, psychologists from different domains can sometimes appear to contradict one another. The psychoanalytic perspective of Sigmund Freud, for example, views the human personality as consisting of irrational sexual and aggressive instincts, which ultimately fuel all human activity. The cognitive perspective on personality developed in the later half of the twentieth century, in contrast, views humans as rational "scientists," calmly trying to anticipate, predict, and control the events that occur in their worlds.

On the surface, these perspectives appear incompatible. How can humans be both irrational and rational? How can humans be driven by desire yet be cool and detached in their quest for accurate prediction? On deeper examination, the contradictions may be more apparent than real. It is entirely possible, for example, that humans have both powerful sexual and aggressive motivations and cognitive mechanisms designed to perceive and predict events with accuracy. It is entirely possible that sometimes basic emotions and motivations are activated and at other times the cool cognitive mechanisms are activated. And it is further possible that the two sets of mechanisms sometimes become linked with one another, such as when the rational mechanisms are used in the service of fulfilling fundamental desires. In short, each theoretical perspective within the domains of personality may be focused on a critically important part of human psychological functioning, but each perspective by itself does not capture the *whole* person. Just as an elephant must be viewed from different angles to comprehend the whole animal, human personality must be viewed from different theoretical perspectives to begin to grasp the whole person.

This book is organized around the six domains of personality functioning—dispositional, biological, intrapsychic, cognitive-experiential, social and cultural, and adjustment. Within each of these domains of personality, we will focus on two key elements: (1) the *theories* that have been proposed within each domain, including the basic assumptions about human nature, and (2) the *empirical research* that has been accumulating within each of these domains. In an attempt to bridge the gap between theory and research in personality, we will focus primarily on the theories that have received the greatest research attention and the topics within each domain for which there is the greatest cumulative knowledge base.

Dispositional Domain

The **dispositional domain** deals centrally with the ways in which individuals differ from one another. As such, the dispositional domain cuts across all the other domains. The reason for this is that individuals can differ in their habitual emotions, in their habitual concepts of self, in their physiological propensities, and even in their intrapsychic mechanisms. However, what distinguishes the dispositional domain is an interest in the number and nature of fundamental dispositions. The central goal of personality psychologists working in the dispositional domain is to identify and measure the most important ways in which individuals differ from one another. They are also interested in the origin of the important individual differences and in how they develop and are maintained.

Biological Domain

The core assumption within the **biological domain** is that humans are, first and foremost, collections of biological systems, and these systems provide the building blocks for behavior, thought, and emotion. As personality psychologists use the term, *biological approaches* typically refers to three areas of research within this general domain: genetics, psychophysiology, and evolution.

The first area of research consists of the genetics of personality. Because of advances in behavioral genetic research, a fair amount is known about the genetics of personality. Some questions this research addresses include the following: Are identical twins more alike than fraternal twins in their personalities? What happens to identical twins when they are reared apart versus when they are reared together? Behavioral genetic research permits us to ask and provisionally answer these questions.

The second biological approach is best described as the psychophysiology of personality. Within this domain, researchers summarize what is known about the basis of personality in terms of nervous system functioning. Examples of such topics include cortical arousal and neurotransmitters, cardiac reactivity, strength of the nervous system, pain tolerance, circadian rhythms (whether you are a morning or night person), and the links between hormones, such as testosterone, and personality.

Identical twins Alvin (left) and Calvin (right) Harrison, age 26, celebrate their first and second place finishes in the 400 meter race in Brisbane, Australia, August 8, 2000. Psychologists are studying twins to determine whether some aspects of personality are influenced by genetics.

The third component of the biological approach concerns how evolution may have shaped human psychological functioning. This approach assumes that the psychological mechanisms that constitute human personality have evolved over thousands of years because they were effective in solving adaptive problems. An evolutionary perspective sheds light on the functional aspects of personality. We will also highlight some fascinating research on personality in nonhuman animals (Gosling, 2001; Vazire & Gosling, 2003).

Intrapsychic Domain

The **intrapsychic domain** deals with mental mechanisms of personality, many of which operate outside of conscious awareness. The predominant theory in this domain is Freud's theory of psychoanalysis. This theory begins with fundamental assumptions about the instinctual system—the sexual and aggressive forces that are presumed to drive and energize much of human activity. Although these fundamental assumptions often lie outside the realm of direct empirical testing, considerable research reveals that sexual and aggressive motives are powerful, and their manifestations in actual behavior can be studied empirically. The intrapsychic domain also includes defense mechanisms, such as repression, denial, and projection—some of which have been examined in laboratory studies. Although the intrapsychic domain is most closely linked with the psychoanalytic theory of Sigmund Freud, there are modern versions as well. For example, much of the research on the power motives, achievement motives, and intimacy motives is based on a key intrapsychic assumption—that these forces often operate outside the realm of consciousness.

Sigmund Freud proposed a comprehensive theory of personality. While some of his more radical ideas have been discarded, many of his concepts have been supported by research.

Cognitive-Experiential Domain

The **cognitive-experiential domain** focuses on cognition and subjective experience, such as conscious thoughts, feelings, beliefs, and desires about oneself and others. The psychological mechanisms involved in subjective experience, however, differ in form and content from one another. One very important element of our experience entails the self and self-concept. Descriptive aspects of the self organize how we view ourselves: our knowledge of ourselves, our images of past selves, and our images of possible future selves. Do we see ourselves as good or as evil? Are our past successes or past failures prominent in our self-views? Do we envision ourselves in the future as married with children or as successful in a career? How we evaluate ourselves—our self-esteem—is another facet of the cognitive-experiential domain.

A somewhat different aspect of this domain pertains to the goals we strive for. Some personality psychologists, for example, view human nature as inherently goal-directed, stressing the organizing influence of fundamental needs, such as the need for affiliation and the need to influence others. Recent research within this tradition includes approaching personality through the personal projects or tasks that individuals are trying to accomplish in their daily lives. These can range from the commonplace, such as getting a date for Saturday night, to the grandiose, such as changing thought in Western civilization.

Another important aspect of subjective experience entails our emotions. Are we habitually happy or sad? What makes us angry or fearful? Do we keep our emotions bottled up inside, or do we express them at the drop of a hat? Joy, sadness, feelings of triumph, and feelings of despair all are essential elements in our subjective experience and are subsumed by the cognitive-experiential domain.

Social and Cultural Domain

One of the special features of this book is an emphasis on the **social and cultural domain** of personality. The assumption is that personality is not something that merely resides within the heads, nervous systems, and genes of individuals. Rather, personality affects, and is affected by, the social and cultural context.

At a cultural level, it is clear that groups differ tremendously from one another. Cultures such as the Yanomamö Indians of Venezuela are highly aggressive; indeed, a Yanomamö man does not achieve full status as a man until he has killed another man. In contrast, cultures such as the !Kung San of Africa are relatively peaceful and agreeable. Overt displays of aggression are discouraged and bring social shame on the perpetrator. Personality differences between these groups are most likely due to cultural influences. In other words, different cultures may bring out different facets of our personalities in manifest behavior. Everyone may have the capacity to be peaceful as well as the capacity for violence. Which one of these capacities we display may depend to a large extent on what is acceptable in and encouraged by the culture.

At the level of individual differences within cultures, personality plays itself out in the social sphere. Whether we are dominant or submissive affects such diverse parts of our lives as the conflicts we get into with our partners and the tactics we use to manipulate others. Whether we tend to be anxious and depressed or buoyant and optimistic affects the likelihood of social outcomes, such as divorce. Whether we are introverted or extraverted affects how many friends we will have and our popularity within the group. Many of the most important individual differences are played out in the interpersonal sphere.

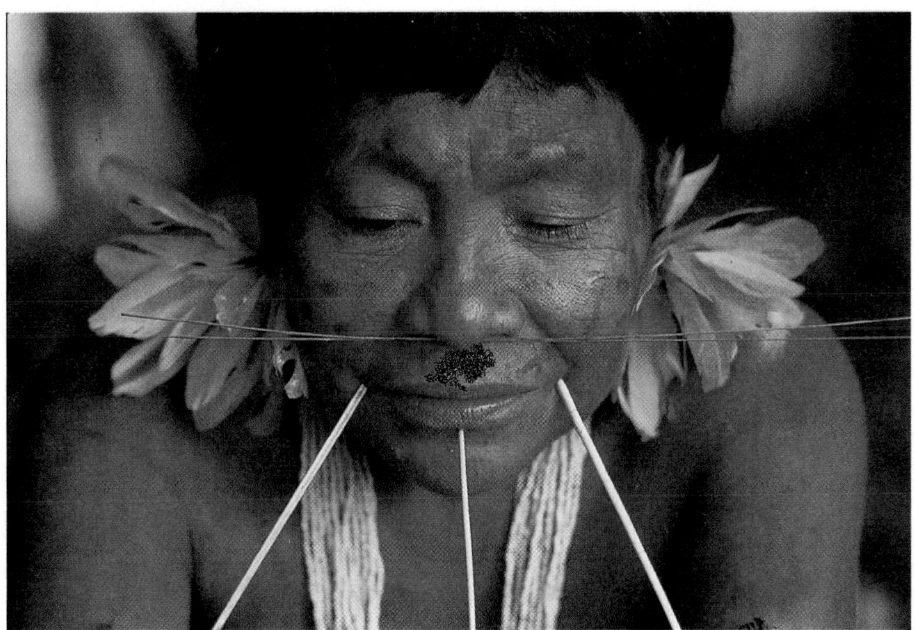

By studying people in different cultures, psychologists are learning how society shapes personality by encouraging or discouraging specific behaviors.

One important social sphere concerns relationships between men and women. At the level of differences between the sexes, personality may operate differently for men than for women. Gender is an essential part of our identities.

Adjustment Domain

The **adjustment domain** refers to the fact that personality plays a key role in how we cope, adapt, and adjust to the ebb and flow of events in our day-to-day lives. Considerable evidence, for example, shows that personality is linked with important health outcomes, such as heart disease. Personality is certainly linked with health-related behaviors, such as smoking, drinking, and risk taking. Some research has even demonstrated that personality is linked with how long we live.

Personality relates to health by influencing health-related behaviors, such as smoking.

In addition to health, many of the important problems in coping and adjustment can be traced to personality. In this domain, certain personality features are related to poor adjustment and have been designated as personality disorders. Chapter 19 is devoted to the personality disorders, such as narcissistic personality disorder, antisocial personality disorder, and avoidant personality disorder. An understanding of "normal" personality functioning can be deepened by examining the disorders of personality, much as in the field of medicine, in which an understanding of normal physiological functioning is often illuminated by the study of disease.

Think of a behavior pattern or characteristic that you find interesting in yourself or someone you know. Such characteristics as procrastination, narcissism, and perfectionism are good examples, but any personality characteristic that catches your interest is good. Then write six sentences about this characteristic, one to represent each of the six domains: dispositional, biological, intrapsychic, cognitive-experiential, social and cultural, and adjustment. Each sentence should make a statement or ask a question about the characteristic from the perspective of a particular domain.

The Role of Personality Theory

One of the central aims of this book is to highlight the interplay between personality theory and research. In each domain of knowledge, there are some prevailing theories, so we will close this chapter with a discussion of theories. Theories are essential in all scientific endeavors, and they serve several useful purposes. A **good theory** is one that fulfills three purposes in science:

- Provides a guide for researchers.
- Organizes known findings.
- Makes predictions.

One of the most important purposes of theories is that they serve as a *guide for researchers,* directing them to important questions within an area of research.

A second useful function of theories is to *organize known findings*. In physics, for example, there is a bewildering array of events—apples fall from trees, planets exert attraction on each other, black holes suck down light. The theory of gravity neatly and powerfully accounts for all these observations. By accounting for known findings, theories bring both coherence and understanding to the known world. The same applies to personality theories. Theories are viewed as powerful if they succeed in accounting for known findings, in addition to guiding psychologists to important domains of inquiry.

A third purpose of theories is to *make predictions* about behavior and psychological phenomena that no one has yet documented or observed. Einstein's theory of relativity, for example, predicted that light will bend around large planets long before we had the technology to test this prediction. When researchers finally confirmed that light does, indeed, bend when going around planets, that finding bore out the power of Einstein's theory.

Finally, we need to distinguish between scientific **theories and beliefs.** For example, astrology is a collection of beliefs about the relationship between personality and the position of the stars at birth. Some people hold that such relationships are true, even in the absence of systematic data supporting such relationships. To date, psychologists have not found reliable factual support, using standard research methods and systematic observations, for the idea that the positions of the stars at a person's birth influence his or her personality. As such, astrology remains a *belief,* not a scientific theory. Of course, maybe someday reliable evidence will be found and astrology will become a scientific theory. But, until then, if you think astrology is true, then you hold to a belief, not a scientific theory. Beliefs are often personally useful and crucially important to some people, but they are based on faith, not on reliable facts and systematic observations. Theories, on the other hand, are tested by *systematic observations that can be repeated by others and that yield similar conclusions.*

In sum, there are three key criteria of personality theories that highlight the interplay of theory and research. They guide researchers to important domains of inquiry, account for known findings, and make predictions about new phenomena. Also, theories are based on systematic and repeatable observations.

Standards for Evaluating Personality Theories

As we explore each of the six domains, it will be useful to bear in mind five **scientific standards for evaluating personality theories:**

- Comprehensiveness.
- Heuristic value.
- Testability.
- Parsimony.
- Compatibility and integration across domains and levels.

The first standard is **comprehensiveness**—does the theory do a good job of explaining all of the facts and observations within its domain? Theories that explain more empirical data within their domains are generally superior to those that explain fewer findings.

A second evaluative standard is **heuristic value**—does the theory provide a guide to important new discoveries about personality that were not known before? Theories that steer scientists to making these discoveries are generally superior to theories that fail to provide this guidance. Plate tectonic theory in geology, for example, guided researchers to discover regions of volcanic activity that were unknown prior to the theory. Similarly, a good personality theory will guide personality researchers to make discoveries that were previously unknown.

A third important standard for evaluating theories is **testability**—does the theory render precise enough predictions that personality psychologists can test them empirically? Some theories, for example certain aspects of Freud's theory of intrapsychic conflict, have been criticized on the grounds that they are difficult or impossible to test; other aspects of Freud's theory are testable (see Chapters 9 and 10). As a general rule, the testability of a theory rests with the precision of its predictions. Precise theoretical predictions aid progress in the science because they allow inadequate theories to be discarded (those whose predictions are falsified) while good theories can be retained (those whose predictions are empirically confirmed). If a theory does not lend itself to being tested empirically, it is generally judged to be a poor theory.

A fourth standard for evaluating personality theories is **parsimony**—does the theory contain few premises and assumptions (parsimony) or many premises and assumptions (lack of parsimony). As a general rule, theories that require many premises and assumptions to explain a given set of findings are judged to be poorer than theories that can explain the same findings with fewer premises and assumptions.

Table 1.2 Five Standards for Evaluating Personality Theories

Standard	Definition
Comprehensiveness	Explains most or all known facts.
Heuristic value	Guides researchers to important new discoveries.
Testability	Makes precise predictions that can be empirically tested.
Parsimony	Contains few premises or assumptions.
Compatibility and integration	Consistent with what is known in other domains; can be coordinated with other branches of scientific knowledge.

Although parsimony is important, bear in mind that this does not mean that simple theories are always better than complex theories. Indeed, simple theories often crash and burn because they fail to meet one or more of the other five standards described here; for example, they may fail to be comprehensive because they explain so little. It is our belief that human personality is genuinely complex, and so a complex theory—one containing many premises—may ultimately be necessary.

A fifth standard is **compatibility and integration across domains and levels.** A theory of cosmology in astronomy that violated known laws of physics, for example, would be incompatible across levels and hence judged to be fundamentally flawed. A theory of biology that violated known principles of chemistry similarly would be judged to be fatally flawed. In the same way, a personality theory in one domain that violated well-established principles in another domain would be judged highly problematic. For example, a theory of the development of personality dispositions that was inconsistent with well-established knowledge in physiology and genetics would be judged to be problematic. Similarly, a theory of evolutionary influences on personality that contradicted what is known about cultural influences, or vice versa, would be similarly problematic. Although the criterion of *compatibility and integration across domains and levels* is a well-established principle in most sciences (Tooby & Cosmides, 1992), it has rarely been used to evaluate the adequacy of personality theories. We believe that the "domains" approach taken in this book highlights the importance of the evaluative criterion of compatibility across levels of personality analysis.

In sum, as you progress through the six domains of personality functioning, keep in mind the five standards by which theories within each domain can be evaluated—comprehensiveness, heuristic value, testability, parsimony, and cross-domain compatibility (see Table 1.2).

Is There a Grand Ultimate and True Theory of Personality?

The field of biology contains a grand unifying theory—the theory of evolution by natural selection, originally proposed by Darwin (1859), and further refined in its neo-Darwinian form as inclusive fitness theory (Hamilton, 1964). This theory is comprehensive, guides biologists to new discoveries, has led to thousands of empirical tests, is highly parsimonious, and is compatible with known laws in adjacent scientific disciplines. Evolutionary theory provides the grand unifying framework within which most or all biologists conduct their work. Ideally, the field of personality psychology would also contain such a grand unifying theory. Alas, at the current time, it does not.

Perhaps Sigmund Freud, the inventor of psychoanalytic theory, provided the most ambitious attempt at a grand unifying theory of personality (see Chapter 9). And there have been many grand theories that have followed in Freud's wake. But over the past several decades, most personality researchers have come to the realization that the field currently lacks a grand unifying theory. Instead, most have focused on more specific domains of functioning. It is precisely for this reason that our book is organized around the six domains—these represent the domains in which progress, scientific findings, and new discoveries are being made.

In our view, an ultimate grand theory of personality psychology will have to unify all these six domains. It will have to explain personality characteristics and how they develop over time (dispositional domain). It will have to explain evolutionary, genetic, and physiological underpinnings of personality (biological domain). It will have to explain deeply rooted motives and dynamic intrapsychic processes (intrapsychic domain). It will have to explain how people experience the world and process information about it (cognitive-experiential domain). It will have to explain how personality affects, and is affected by, the social and cultural context in which people conduct their lives (social and cultural domains). And it will have to explain how people cope and function—as well as how adjustment fails—as they encounter the numerous adaptive problems they face over the inevitably bumpy course of their lives (the adjustment domain).

In this sense, although the field of personality psychology lacks a grand theory, we believe that work in these six domains will ultimately provide the foundations on which such a unified personality theory will be built.

KEY TERMS

Personality Assessment, Measurement, and Research Design

2

INTRODUCTION

Much of the discussion surrounding political candidates involves their personalities.

Imagine that a presidential election is looming. You are faced with a choice between two candidates. The personalities of the candidates may prove to be critical to your decision. How will they hold up under stress? What are their attitudes toward abortion or gun control? Will they stand tough in negotiating with leaders from other countries? This chapter is concerned with the means by which we gain information about other people's personalities—the sources from which we gather personality data and the research designs we use in the scientific study of personality.

When deliberating between the two presidential candidates, you might want to know what they say about their values and attitudes—through a *self-report*. You might want to know what others say about their strengths in dealing with foreign leaders—through an *observer report*. These two sources of data can tell you a lot, but not everything. You also might want to place the candidates in a more controlled situation, such as a debate, and see how each performs—to acquire *test data*. Furthermore, you might want to know about certain events in their lives, such as whether they have ever used illegal drugs, whether they have ever dodged the draft, or whether they have ever been caught in an embarrassing sexual scandal—*life history data*.

Each of these sources of data reveals something about the personalities of the presidential candidates, yet each alone is incomplete and may be biased. (For fascinating personality analyses of presidential candidates, see Immelman, 2002; Post, 2003; and Renshon, 1998, 2005.) The candidate may self-report a tough stance on crime but then fail to follow through on it. Observers may report that the candidate is honest, yet they may be unaware of lies the candidate has told. A debate may show one candidate in a positive light, but perhaps the other candidate happened to have a cold that day. And the public record of serving in the military reserve may not reveal the family connections that enabled the candidate to avoid combat. Each source of data provides important information. But each source, by itself, is of limited value, an incomplete picture.

This chapter covers three topics related to personality assessment and research. The first concerns where we get our information about personality—the sources of personality data and the actual measures that personality psychologists use. The second topic concerns how we evaluate the quality of those measures. The third topic pertains to how we use these measures in actual research designs to study personality.

The first question provides the most basic starting point: what are the key sources of information about an individual's personality?

Sources of Personality Data

Perhaps the most obvious source of information about a person is **self-report data (S-data)**—the information a person reveals. Clearly, individuals may not always provide accurate information about themselves for a variety of reasons, such as the desire to present themselves in a positive light. Nevertheless, the journals that publish the latest research in personality reveal that self-report is the most common method for measuring personality.

Self-Report Data (S-Data)

Self-report data can be obtained through a variety of means, including interviews that pose questions to a person, periodic reports by a person to record the events as they happen, and questionnaires. The questionnaire method, in which individuals respond to a series of items that request information about themselves, is by far the most commonly used self-report assessment procedure.

There are good reasons for using self-report. The most obvious reason is that individuals have access to a wealth of information about themselves that is inaccessible to anyone else. Individuals can report about their feelings, emotions, desires, beliefs, and private experiences. They can report about their self-esteem, as well as their perceptions of the esteem in which others hold them. They can report about their innermost fears and fantasies. They can report about how they relate to others and how others relate to them. And they can report about immediate and long-term goals. Because of this potential wealth of information, self-report is an indispensable source of personality data.

Self-report can take a variety of forms, ranging from open-ended "fill in the blanks" to forced-choice true-or-false questions. Sometimes these are referred to as **unstructured** (open-ended, such as "Tell me about the parties you like the most") and **structured** ("I like loud and crowded parties"—answer "true" or "false") personality tests. A prime example of the open-ended form of self-report is called the Twenty Statements Test (see A Closer Look on the next page for more information). In this test, a participant receives a sheet of paper that is essentially blank, except for the words "I am" repeated 20 times. There is a space after each of these partial statements, and participants

A Closer Look

Who Am I?

The Twenty Statements Test (TST) was published by a pair of sociologists. Manford Kuhn and Thomas McPartland were interested in attitudes people had toward themselves. In 1954, they published the "Who am I?" test. This test asked the participant to simply answer this question by completing the phrase "I am __________" 20 times. Kuhn and McPartland developed a way of scoring the test that involved analyzing the content of the person's responses. In addition, the order of each response was thought to be significant (e.g., something mentioned earlier might be more important to the self-definition than something mentioned later).

Psychologists quickly learned of this test, even though it was published in the *American Sociological Review,* a journal psychologists typically don't read, and began using it in their research. Because the test involved having the participants come up with 20 statements about themselves, it quickly became known in the psychological literature as the Twenty Statements Test.

In the first decade of use by psychologists, the TST was applied mainly to clinical and personality research questions. For example, one study used the TST to see if the self-concepts of persons in "unadjusted" marriages differed from the self-concepts of persons in "well-adjusted" marriages (Buerkle, 1960). Results showed that the persons in adjusted marriages tended to mention their partner, their marriage, and their family more often in their self-definitions than the persons in unadjusted marriages. This finding implies that part of a successful marriage is incorporating the marriage role into one's definition of oneself, so that self-concept includes one's spouse, marital relationship, and family.

In the 1970s, researchers turned a more critical eye on the TST. It is an open-ended questionnaire, so people with low verbal ability do not complete it as quickly or as thoroughly as persons with high verbal ability, leading the test scores to be biased by intelligence differences in participants (Nudelman, 1973). However, if people are given enough time to complete the 20 questions—at least 15 minutes—then it appears that the intelligence bias is eliminated. All in all, the TST survived this decade of questioning and emerged as a measure that the field deemed useful for assessing how people defined themselves.

In the 1980s, the TST was used in the study of timely personality topics, such as the influence of gender and other social roles in people's self-definitions. For example, one study compared married and single women (Gigy, 1980). Married women tended to respond to the "Who am I?" question by mentioning relationships *(I am a mother, I am a wife),* acquired roles in family life *(I am the one who feeds the children),* and household activities *(I am the one who buys groceries).* Clearly, marriage can mean a large change in self-concept, and studies such as this one document the link between social roles and the ways in which individuals see themselves.

There has been a trend toward using culture and ethnicity in self-definitions (Bochner, 1994). This coincides with the sharp increase in interest in cross-cultural research. One example of a cross-cultural study using the TST is a study that compares people from Kenya with people from the United States. Several groups were compared on the percentage of responses that included references to social group categories (e.g., *I am a member of the local school board* or *I am a player on the local softball team*). U.S. college students mentioned social groups in their self-definitions 12 percent of the time. In Kenya, university students mentioned social groups 17 percent of the time. However, for traditional rural Kenyan citizens, results were quite different. Massai tribespersons in Kenya mentioned social groups 80 percent of the time in their responses, and Samburu tribespersons mentioned social groups 84 percent of the time in their TST responses (Ma & Schoeneman, 1997). Results such as these show how the culture in which we are raised may have a strong influence on how we view ourselves and what we consider to be important in defining our identity and in answering the question "Who am I?" The Twenty Statements Test is a useful way to measure how people define themselves and to learn what is important to a person's self-understanding. The TST has proven especially effective at identifying the most important components of a person's identity—the ingredients that provide a person with a sense of self-esteem, meaning in life, and sense of belonging in the world of other people (Vignoles, Regalia, Manzi, Golledge, & Scabini, 2006).

are asked to complete them. For example, a person might say, in this order: *I am a woman; I am 19 years old; I am shy; I am intelligent; I am someone who likes quiet nights at home; I am introverted;* and so on. Personality instruments that use open-ended formats require coding schemes for classifying the responses they obtain. In other words, psychologists must devise a way to score or interpret the participant's open-ended responses. For example, to get an idea of how outgoing the woman in our example is, the psychologist might count how many statements refer to social characteristics.

More common than open-ended questionnaires are structured personality questionnaires, in which the response options are provided. The simplest form of the structured self-report questionnaire involves a series of trait-descriptive adjectives, such as *active, ambitious, anxious, arrogant, artistic, generous, gregarious, greedy, good-natured, xenophobic*, and *zany*. Individuals are asked to indicate whether or not each adjective describes them. The simplest format for presenting these terms is a checklist, such as the Adjective Check List (ACL) (Gough, 1980). In completing the ACL, the individuals merely place a check beside adjectives that they feel accurately describe them and leave blank items that don't describe them. A more complex method involves requesting participants to indicate in numerical form the degree to which each trait term characterizes them, say on a 7-point rating scale of 1 (least characteristic) to 7 (most characteristic). This is called a **Likert rating scale** (after the person who invented it), and it is simply a way for someone to express with numbers the degree to which a particular trait describes him or her. A typical Likert rating scale looks like this:

ENERGETIC

1 2 3 4 5 6 7

Least characteristic Most characteristic

Most commonly, a *personality scale* consists of summing the scores on a series of individual rating scales. A personality scale for activity level, for example, might consist of summing up scores from rating scales on *energetic, active,* and *vigorous.*

Exercise

DIRECTIONS: This list contains a series of adjectives. Please read them quickly and put an X in the box beside each one you consider to be self-descriptive. Try to be honest and accurate.

___	**absent-minded**	___	**cheerful**	___	**dependent**
___	**active**	___	**civilized**	___	**despondent**
___	**adaptable**	___	**clear-thinking**	___	**determined**
___	**adventurous**	___	**clever**	___	**dignified**
___	**affected**	___	**coarse**	___	**discreet**
___	**affectionate**	___	**cold**	___	**disorderly**
___	**soft-hearted**	___	**touchy**	___	**zany**

More common than adjective checklists, however, are self-report questionnaires in the form of statements. Examples of widely used self-report inventories are the NEO Personality Inventory (Costa & McCrae, 1989) and the California Psychological

Inventory (CPI) (Gough, 1957/1987). Sample items from the CPI are *I enjoy social gatherings just to be with people; I looked up to my father as an ideal man; a person needs to "show off" a little now and then; I have a very strong desire to be a success in the world; I am very slow in making up my mind.* Participants read each statement and then indicate on an answer sheet whether they agree with the statement and feel that it is true of them or disagree with the statement and feel that it is false about them. Sample items from the NEO Personality Inventory are *I like most people I meet; I laugh easily; I often get disgusted with people I have to deal with.* Participants indicate the degree to which they agree the item describes them using a 1 to 5 Likert scale, with 1 anchored with the phrase *strongly disagree* and 5 anchored with *strongly agree*.

Exercise

Pick a personality characteristic you would like to measure. Start by writing down a clear definition of that characteristic. For example, you might choose such characteristics as friendly, conscientious, anxious, or narcissistic. Then write a short questionnaire, about five items long, to measure this characteristic. Your items can be statements or adjectives, and they can be open-ended, true-false, or on a Likert response scale. Then give your questionnaire to other people. How easy was it to write items? Do you think your measure accurately assesses the trait?

Self-report measures, like all methods, have limitations and weaknesses. For the self-report method to be effective, respondents must be both willing and able to answer the questions put to them. Yet people are not always honest, especially when asked about unconventional experiences, such as unusual desires, unconventional sex practices, and undesirable traits. Some people may lack accurate self-knowledge. Because of these limitations, personality psychologists often use sources of data that do not rely on the honesty or insight of the participant. One of those sources is observers.

Application

***Experience sampling—a new wrinkle in self-report.* A relatively new source of data in personality research is called experience sampling (e.g., Hormuth, 1986; Larsen, 1989). In this method, people answer some questions, perhaps about their moods or physical symptoms, every day for several weeks or longer. People are usually contacted electronically (paged) one or more times a day at random intervals to complete the measures. In one study, 74 college students reported on their moods every day for 84 consecutive days (Larsen & Kasimatis, 1990). The investigators were interested in discovering the links between the day of the week and mood. Not surprisingly, they found a strong weekly cycle in the moods of the college students, with positive moods peaking on Friday and Saturday and negative moods peaking on Tuesday and Wednesday (Monday was not the worst day of the week). The introverts turned out to have a much more regular weekly mood cycle than extraverts. That is, the moods of the introverts were more predictable from this 7-day rhythm than the moods of the extraverts. This difference was probably due to the fact that extraverts are less likely to wait for the**

Application (*Continued*)

weekend to do things that put them in a good mood—partying, socializing, or going out for a special meal with friends. Extraverts typically avoid routine in their daily lives, and introverts typically lead more predictable lives.

Although experience sampling uses self-report as the data source, it differs from more traditional self-report methods in being able to detect patterns of behavior over time. Thus, experience sampling provides information not readily available using questionnaires taken at just one point in time. It's an excellent method, for example, for obtaining information about how a person's self-esteem may go up and down over time, or how a person reacts to the stress of life day after day.

Observer-Report Data (O-Data)

In everyday life, we form impressions and make evaluations of others with whom we come into contact. For each individual, there are typically dozens of observers who form impressions. Our friends, families, teachers, and casual acquaintances are all potential sources of information about our personalities. **Observer-report data (O-data)** capitalize on these sources and provide tools for gathering information about a person's personality.

Observer reports offer both advantages and disadvantages as sources of personality data. One advantage is that observers may have access to information not attainable through other sources. For example, observers can report about the impressions a person makes on others, his or her social reputation, whether interactions with others are smooth or full of strife, and the person's relative status within the group hierarchy.

A second advantage of observer-reports is that multiple observers can be used to assess each individual, whereas in self-report only one person provides information. The use of multiple observers allows investigators to evaluate the degree of agreement among observers—also known as **inter-rater reliability.** Furthermore, statistical procedures, such as averaging the assessments of multiple observers, have the advantage of reducing the idiosyncratic features and biases of single observers. Typically, a more valid and reliable assessment of personality can be achieved when multiple observers are used.

Observer reports can be used as one source of personality information.

Selection of Observers

A key decision point that researchers face when using observers is how to select them. Personality researchers have developed two strategies. One strategy is to use professional personality assessors who do not know the participant in advance. The other strategy is to use individuals who actually know the target participants. We will discuss each strategy in turn.

One setting in which professional observers are used is the Institute for Personality and Social Research (IPSR) at the University of California at Berkeley. Participants go to the institute for periods of time ranging from one to five days, so that a wide variety of in-depth personality assessments can take place. Participants are invited to go to the IPSR as part of specific studies. For example, one study contacted a set of architects who were judged by their peers to be highly creative, as part of a study to determine the personality predictors of creativity. Another study looked at novelists judged to be creative. A third assessed graduate students in an MBA program to determine the personality predictors of success in business. During studies at the IPSR, trained personality assessors observe the participants in a variety of contexts. Subsequently, each observer provides an independent personality description of the participants.

A second strategy for obtaining observational data is to use individuals who actually know the target participants. For example, close friends, spouses, mothers, and roommates have all been used to provide personality data on participants (e.g., Buss, 1984; Ozer & Buss, 1991). The use of observers who have existing relationships with the participant has advantages and disadvantages when compared with professional assessors. One advantage is that such observers are in a better position to observe the target's natural behavior. In the relatively public context of an IPSR assessment, in contrast, professional observers cannot witness the more private actions of a person and must settle for observing his or her public persona. A spouse or close friend has access to privileged information often inaccessible through other sources.

A second advantage of using intimate observers is that **multiple social personalities** can be assessed (Craik, 1986). Each one of us displays different sides of ourselves to different people—we may be kind to our friends, ruthless to our enemies, loving toward a spouse, and conflicted toward our parents. Our manifest personalities, in other words, vary from one social setting to another, depending on the nature of relationships we have with other individuals. The use of multiple observers provides a method for assessing the many aspects of an individual's personality.

Although there are advantages in using intimate observers in personality assessment, there are also drawbacks. Because intimate observers have relationships with the target person, they may be biased in certain ways. A participant's mother, for example, may overlook the negative and emphasize the positive features of her child.

Naturalistic versus Artificial Observation

In addition to deciding what type of observers to use, personality researchers must determine whether the observation occurs in a natural or an artificial setting. In **naturalistic observation,** observers witness and record events that occur in the normal course of the lives of their participants. For example, a child might be followed throughout an entire day, or an observer may sit in a participant's home. In contrast, observation can take place in contrived or artificial settings, such as occur at the IPSR. Experimenters can instruct participants to perform a task, such as participation in a group discussion, and then observe how individuals behave in these constructed settings. For example, psychologists John Gottman and Robert Levenson have had married couples go to their laboratory and discuss a topic on which they disagree. The psychologists then observe the couple have a small argument. The way in which a couple conducts an argument can predict the likelihood that the couple will remain together or get divorced (Gottman, 1994). Even the facial expressions displayed during these laboratory conflicts predict subsequent marital outcomes (Gottman, Levenson, & Woodin, 2001).

Naturalistic observation offers researchers the advantage of being able to secure information in the realistic context of a person's everyday life, but at the cost of not being able to control the events and behavioral samples witnessed. Observation in experimenter-generated situations has the advantage of controlling conditions and eliciting the relevant behavior. But this advantage comes at a cost—sacrificing the realism of everyday life.

In summary, there are many dimensions along which O-data differ, and personality researchers must take these into account. Decisions about whether to use (1) professional assessors or intimate observers and (2) a naturalistic or an artificial setting for observation must be made on the basis of the specific purposes of the personality study. The strengths and weaknesses of the options must be evaluated with the goals of the investigation in mind. No single method is ideally suited for all assessment purposes.

Test Data (T-Data)

Beyond self-report and observer-report data sources, a third common source of personality-relevant information comes from standardized tests—**test data (T-data)**. In these measures, participants are placed in a standardized testing situation. The idea is to see if different people react differently to an identical situation. The situation is designed to elicit behaviors that serve as indicators of personality variables (Block, 1977). An interesting example is the bridge-building test found in Henry Murray's (1948) classic book *The Assessment of Men*. In this test, the person being assessed is given two assistants and a collection of wood, rope, and tools, and he or she has the task of building a bridge over a small creek. The person being assessed cannot do the work him- or herself but must instruct the two assistants on how to build the bridge. Unbeknownst to the person being assessed, the two assistants are role-playing: one is acting dim-witted and has trouble understanding instructions; the other is a "know-it-all," who has his or her own ideas about how the bridge should be built and often contradicts the person being assessed. These two "helpers" actually are there to frustrate the person being assessed. While the person being assessed thinks he or she is being observed on leadership skills, the person is actually being evaluated on tolerance of frustration and performance under adversity.

One fascinating example of the use of T-data is Edwin Megargee's (1969) study on manifestations of *dominance*. Megargee wanted to devise a laboratory test situation in which he could examine the effect of dominance on leadership. Toward this end, he first administered the California Psychological Inventory Dominance scale to a large group of men and women who might serve as potential research participants. He then selected only those men and women who scored either very high or very low on dominance. On completion of this selection procedure, Megargee took pairs of individuals into the laboratory, in each case pairing a high-dominant participant with a low-dominant participant. He created four conditions: (1) a high-dominant man with a low-dominant man; (2) a high-dominant woman with a low-dominant woman; (3) a high-dominant man with a low-dominant woman; and (4) a high-dominant woman with a low-dominant man.

Megargee then presented each pair with a large box containing many red, yellow, and green nuts, bolts, and levers. Participants were told that the purpose of the study was to explore the relationship between personality and leadership under stress. Each pair of participants was to work as a team of troubleshooters to repair the box as fast as possible—by removing nuts and bolts with certain colors and replacing them with other colors. The participants were told that one person from the team had to be the *leader,* a position which entailed giving instructions to his or her partner. The second person was to be the *follower,* who had to go inside the box and carry out the menial tasks requested by the leader. The experimenter then told the participants that it was up to them to decide who would be the leader and who would be the follower.

The key variable of interest for Megargee was who would become the leader and who would become the follower, so he simply recorded the percentage of high-dominant participants within each condition who became leaders. He found that 75 percent of the high-dominant men and 70 percent of the high-dominant women took the leadership role in the same-sex pairs. When high-dominant men were paired with low-dominant women, however, 90 percent of the men became leaders. But the most startling result occurred when the woman was high in dominance and the man was low in dominance. In this condition, only 20 percent of the high-dominant women assumed the leadership role.

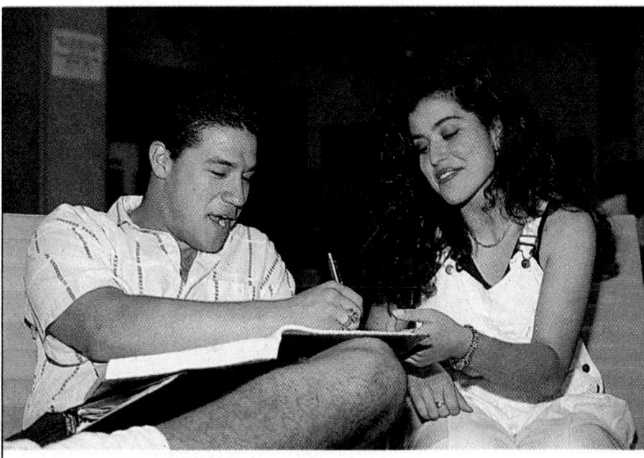

Who takes the leadership role when people work together is often a function of personality.

From these laboratory findings alone, one might conclude that the dominant women in this condition were suppressing their dominance, or that the men in this condition, despite being low in dominance, felt compelled to assume a traditional sex role by taking charge. It turns out, however, that neither of these conclusions was supported. Megargee happened to have tape-recorded the conversations within each pair of participants while they were deciding who would be the leader. When he analyzed these tapes, he made a startling finding: the high-dominant women were *appointing* their low-dominant partners to the leadership position. In fact, the high-dominant women actually made the final decision about the roles 91 percent of the time. This finding suggests that women are *expressing* their dominance in a different manner than the men in the mixed-sex condition.

Megargee's study highlights several key points about laboratory studies. First, it shows that it is possible to set up conditions to reveal key indicators of personality. Second, it suggests that laboratory experimenters should be sensitive to manifestations of personality that occur in incidental parts of the experiment, such as the discussions between the participants. And, third, there are often interesting links between S-data obtained through questionnaires and T-data obtained through controlled testing conditions. Such links enhance the validity of both the questionnaire and the laboratory test of dominance.

Like all data sources, T-data have limitations. First, some participants might try to guess what trait is being measured and then alter their responses to create a specific impression of themselves. A second challenge is the difficulty in verifying that the research participants define the testing situation in the same manner as the experimenter. An experiment designed to test for "obedience to authority" might be misinterpreted as a test for "intelligence," perhaps raising anxiety in ways that distort subsequent responses. Failure to confirm the correspondence between the conceptions of experimenters and those of participants may introduce error.

A third caution in the use of T-data is that these situations are inherently *interpersonal,* and a researcher may inadvertently influence how the participants behave. A researcher with an outgoing and friendly personality, for example, may elicit more cooperation from participants than a cold or aloof experimenter (see Kintz, Delprato, Mettee, Parsons, & Schappe, 1965). The choice of who runs the experiment, in short, including the personality and demeanor of the experimenter, may inadvertently introduce effects that skew the obtained results.

Despite these limitations, T-data remain a valuable and irreplaceable source of personality information. Procedures used to obtain T-data can be designed to *elicit behavior* that would be difficult to observe in everyday life. They allow investigators to *control the context* and to eliminate extraneous sources of influence. And they enable experimenters to *test specific hypotheses* by exerting control over the variables that are presumed to have causal influence. For these reasons, T-data procedures remain an indispensable set of tools for the personality researcher.

Mechanical Recording Devices

Personality psychologists have been enterprising in adapting technological innovations for the study of personality. An example of researcher ingenuity is the use of the "actometer" to assess personality differences in activity or energy level. The actometer is essentially a modified self-winding watch, which can be strapped to the arms or legs of participants (typically, children). Movement activates the winding mechanism, registering the person's activity on the hands of the dial. Of course, day-to-day and even hour-to-hour fluctuations in mood, physiology, and setting limit the usefulness of any single sample of activity level. However, several samples of activity level can be recorded on different days to generate composite scores, reflecting, for each person, whether he or she is hyperactive, normally active, or sedentary (Buss, Block, & Block, 1980).

In one study, preschool children ages 3 and 4 wore actometers on the wrist of the nonfavored hand for approximately two hours (Buss et al., 1980). The dial of each actometer was covered with tape, so that the children would not be distracted. Indeed, in pretesting, the children who could observe the dial became preoccupied with it—sitting in one spot, shaking the device back and forth—a practice that interfered with the usefulness of the measure. The experimenters had to be careful to eliminate data if a child removed the watch during the session or if illness or rainy weather limited the range within which a child's activity level could be expressed. Several separate recording sessions were held, and the actometer readings were aggregated, in order to obtain a more reliable index of each child's activity level.

The experimenters then sought answers to three questions: (1) Does activity level measured with the actometer yield the same results as activity level measured through observation? (2) To what extent is activity level stable over time? (3) Do activity level measurements using this mechanical recording device relate to observer-based judgments of personality functioning? To answer these questions, the children's teachers provided observer evaluations using the children's version of the California Q-Sort—an instrument designed to produce a wide-ranging description of children's personality characteristics (Block & Block, 1980). Examples of items on the Q-Sort are *is a talkative individual; behaves in a giving way toward others; is basically submissive; is guileful and deceitful, manipulative, opportunistic; has a high energy level.* These observations were made when the children were 3, 4, and 7 years old, whereas the actometer measures were recorded at ages 3 and 4.

It turns out that there was a strong correspondence between actometer measures of activity level and the observer-based measures. Activity level also turns out to be moderately stable over time. For example, actometer measures at age 3 showed a moderate correspondence with actometer measures at age 4. Is there any relationship between actometer measurements of activity level and observer-based judgments of personality? The highly active children, as assessed with the actometer, were judged by their teachers to be vital, energetic, and active. In addition, the highly active children were judged to be restless and fidgety—all attributes that are more or less indicative of hyperactivity. Of particular interest is that the active children were also seen by teachers as uninhibited, assertive, competitive, aggressive physically and verbally, attention-getting, and manipulative of others. Thus, actometer-based activity scores are linked to *other* personality characteristics, traits that have important consequences for social interaction.

In sum, some aspects of personality can be assessed through mechanical recording devices, such as the actometer. These forms of T-data have several advantages and disadvantages. Their main advantage is that they provide a mechanical means of assessing personality, one that is not hampered by the biases that might be introduced when a human observer is involved. A second advantage is that they can be obtained in relatively naturalistic settings—such as a children's playground. Their primary disadvantage is that relatively few personality dispositions lend themselves readily to being assessed by mechanical devices. There are no mechanical devices, for example, to directly measure introversion or conscientiousness. Nonetheless, mechanical devices can serve as powerful sources of personality data in the domains in which they can be used. Perhaps future technological advances will expand the range of personality traits amenable to mechanical assessment.

Activity level is stable over time and correlates with teacher ratings of vital, energetic, and active.

Physiological Data

A critical source of personality data enjoying a resurgence of interest is physiological measurement. Physiological measures can provide information about a person's level of arousal, a person's reactivity to various stimuli, and the speed at which a person takes in new information—all potential indicators of personality. Sensors can be placed on different parts of a person's body, for example, to measure sympathetic nervous system activity, blood pressure, heart rate, and muscle contraction. Brain waves, such as reactivity to stimuli, also can be assessed. And even physiological changes associated with sexual arousal can be measured via instruments such as a penile strain gauge (Geer & Head, 1990) or a vaginal bloodflow meter.

In Chapter 7 we go into some detail on physiological measures. For our purposes here—in examining alternative ways of measuring personality—we will look at only one example of using physiological data as a source of personality information. Psychologist Christopher Patrick (1994, 2005) has been studying psychopaths, particularly men in prison who have committed serious crimes against other people, particularly violent crimes. One theory about psychopaths is that they do not have the normal fear or anxiety response that most people have. Things that might make most people anxious may not make the psychopath anxious. To test this idea, Dr. Patrick used a technique called the "eyeblink startle reflex," which had previously been used in studies of fear.

When we are startled, as when a loud noise occurs, we exhibit the startle reflex, which consists of blinking our eyes, lowering our chin toward the chest, and inhaling suddenly. If we are already anxious for some reason, we will exhibit the startle reflex faster than when we are feeling normal. It makes adaptive sense that we will be prepared to have a faster defensive startle if we are already in a fearful or anxious state. You can demonstrate this by showing persons pictures of frightening or unpleasant scenes, such as a snake, a vicious dog, or spiders, which most people find make them a little anxious. If they are startled while looking at these scenes, they will exhibit a faster eyeblink startle response than when they are looking at nonfeared objects, such as a house, a tree, or a table. Interestingly, Patrick found that psychopaths, who were in prison for violent crimes, did not exhibit the faster eyeblink response while viewing the anxiety-producing photographs, suggesting that they were not feeling the same level of fearfulness or anxiety as normal participants viewing these objects. Perhaps psychopaths commit their crimes because they don't have the normal level of anxiety or guilt that prevents most of us from doing anything wrong. This is a good example of how physiological measures can be used to examine and understand various personality characteristics.

A more recent physiological data source comes from **functional magnetic resonance imaging (fMRI),** a technique used to identify the areas of the brain that "light up" when performing certain tasks such as verbal problems or spatial navigation problems. It works by gauging the amount of oxygen that is brought to particular places in the brain. When a certain part of the brain is highly activated, it draws large amounts of blood. The oxygen carried by the blood accumulates in that region of the brain. The fMRI is able to detect concentrations of iron carried by the oxygen contained in the red blood cells and thus determine the part of the brain that is used in performing certain tasks. The colorful images that emerge from fMRI brain scans are often quite dramatic.

In principle, fMRI provides a physiological data source that can be linked with personality dispositions, intelligence, or psychopathology. In practice, however, the method has limitations on what it reveals. Since fMRI must compare the "activated" state with a "resting" state, it becomes critical to know what the resting state really is. If men's resting state turns more to sports and women's resting state turns more to social interactions, for example, it is possible that a comparison of a task such as looking at faces to the resting state would suggest that men and women are performing the task differently, when in fact the difference is due entirely to a sex difference in the resting state (Kosslyn & Rosenberg, 2004).

One of the key benefits of physiological data is that it is difficult for participants to fake responses, particularly on measures of arousal or reflexive responses, such as the eyeblink startle reflex. Nonetheless, physiological recording procedures share most of the same limitations as other laboratory test data. In particular, recording is typically constrained by a relatively artificial laboratory situation, and the accuracy of the recording hinges on whether the participants construe the situation in the manner that the experimenter wants them to construe it.

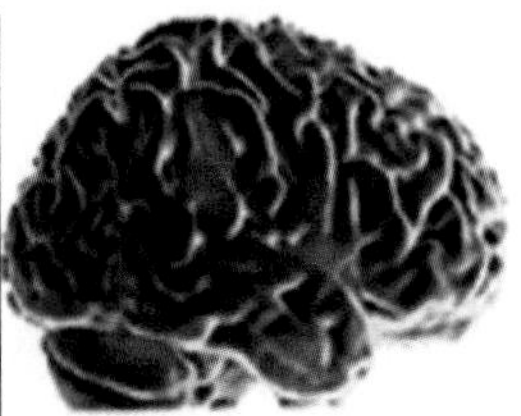

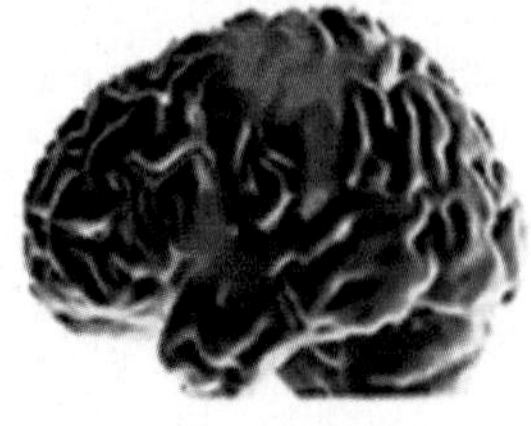

Measures of physiological responses, such as these fMRI brain scans, are a source of data in personality research.

Projective Techniques

Another type of T-data are **projective techniques,** in which the person is given a standard stimulus and asked what he or she sees. The most famous projective technique for assessing personality is the set of inkblots developed by Hermann Rorschach. However, there are others—for example, the hand technique, in which the person is given pictures of hands and is asked to make up a story about what the hands just did and what they are going to do next. The hallmark of any projective technique is that the person is presented with an ambiguous stimulus, such as an inkblot or a picture of a hand. The person is then asked to impose structure on this stimulus by describing what he or she sees—for example, what is in the inkblot or what the hand has just done. The idea behind projective techniques is that what the person sees in the stimulus is directly related to what is on his or her mind. What the person sees in the stimulus is interpreted to reveal something about his or her personality. Presumably, the person "projects" his or her concerns, conflicts, traits, and ways of seeing or dealing with the world onto the ambiguous stimulus.

Projective techniques are considered T-data because all persons are presented with a standard testing situation, all are given the same instructions, and the test situation elicits behaviors that are thought to reveal personality.

To the psychologist interpreting a person's responses to the inkblots, the content of those responses is important. Someone with a "dependent personality," for example, might produce a high frequency of responses such as food, food providers, passively being fed, nurturers, oral activity, passivity, helplessness, and "baby talk" (Bornstein, 2005). In addition to content, the psychologist is interested in how the perceptions are formed. For example, one participant might focus on the lines dividing the ink from the white area, whereas another might focus only on the ink. In sum, all projective measures present the participant with ambiguous stimuli, asking him or her to provide structure by interpreting, drawing, or telling a story about the stimuli. Psychologists who advocate projective measures argue that they are useful for getting at wishes, desires, fantasies, and conflicts that the participants themselves may be unaware of and, so, could not report on a questionnaire. Others are critical of projectives, questioning their validity and reliability as accurate measures of personality (Wood et al., 1996).

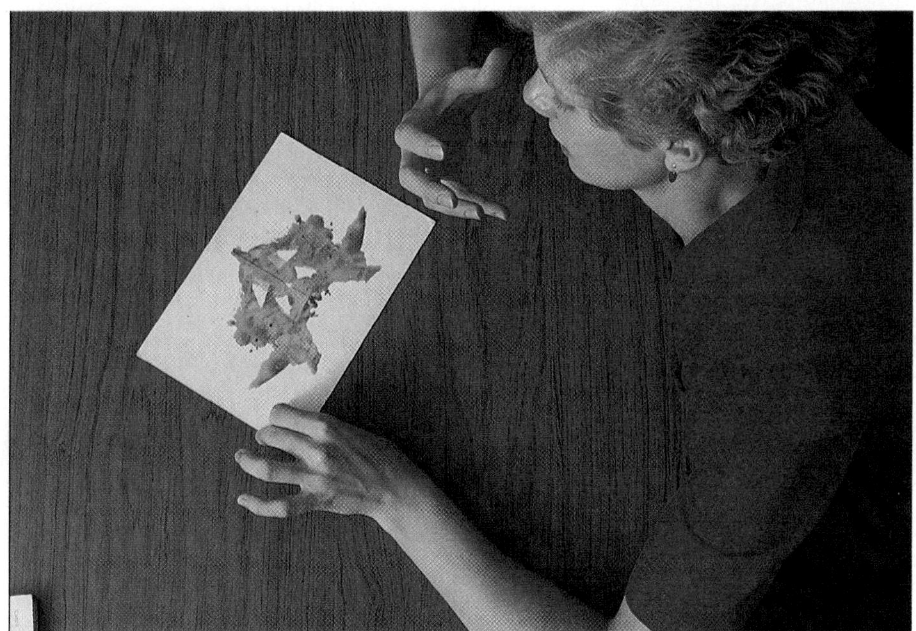

A person interpreting an inkblot may project his or her personality into what is "seen" in the image.

Life-Outcome Data (L-Data)

Life-outcome data (L-data) refers to information that can be gleaned from the events, activities, and outcomes in a person's life that are available to public scrutiny. For example, marriages and divorces are a matter of public record. Personality psychologists can sometimes secure information about the clubs a person joins; how many speeding tickets a person has received; and whether he or she owns a handgun. Whether a person gets arrested for a violent or white-collar crime is a matter of public record. Success at one's job, whether one is upwardly or downwardly mobile, and the creative products one produces, such as books published and music recorded, are often important outcomes in a person's life. These can all serve as important sources of information about personality.

Personality psychologists often use S-data and O-data to predict L-data. An example that illustrates how O-data can be used to predict important life events is provided by Avshalom Caspi and his colleagues (Caspi, Elder, & Bem, 1987). Based on clinical interviews with mothers of children ages 8, 9, and 10, these researchers created two personality scales to measure ill-temperedness. One scale was based on the *severity* of temper tantrums; it noted physical behaviors such as biting, kicking, striking, and throwing things, and verbal expressions such as swearing, screaming, and shouting. The other scale assessed the *frequency* of these temper tantrums. Caspi and his colleagues summed these two scales to create a single measure of temper tantrums. This measure represents O-data, since it is based on the mothers' actual observations. Then, in adulthood, when the participants were 30 to 40 years old, the researchers gathered information about life outcomes, such as education, work, marriage, and parenthood. They then examined whether the personality characteristic of ill-temperedness, measured in childhood as O-data, predicted significant life outcomes two to three decades later, measured as L-data.

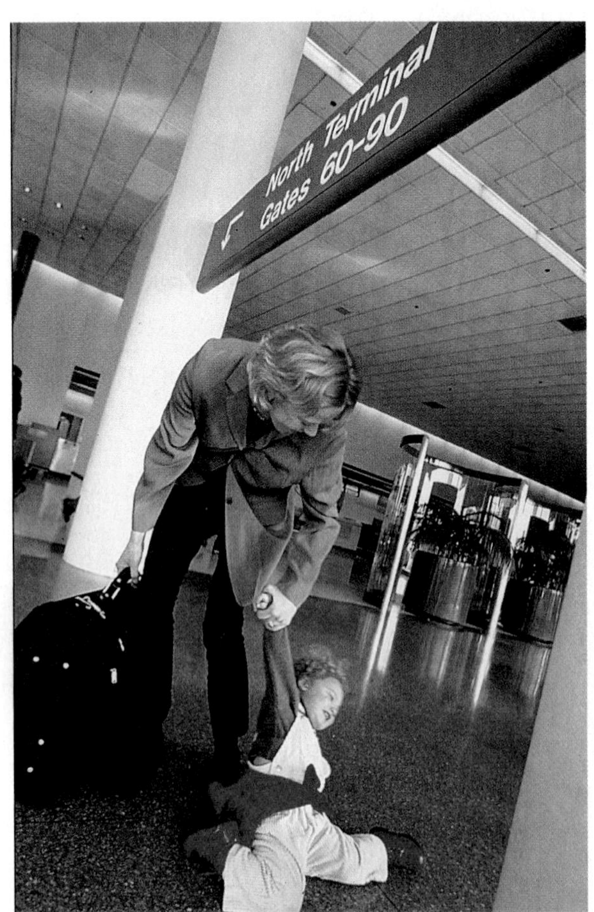

The tendency to have frequent temper outbursts in childhood has been linked with negative adult outcomes, such as increased likelihood of divorce.

The results proved to be remarkable. For the men, early temper tantrums were linked with many negative outcomes in adult life. The men who had exhibited temper tantrums in childhood achieved significantly lower rank in their military service. They tended to have erratic work lives—changing jobs more frequently and experiencing more unemployment than those who had not been judged to be ill-tempered as children. Furthermore, such men were less likely than their even-tempered counterparts to have a satisfying marriage. Fully 46 percent of the ill-tempered men were divorced by age 40, whereas only 22 percent of the men in the low temper-tantrum category were divorced by the age of 40.

For the women, early temper tantrums did not have a bearing on their work lives, in contrast to the men. However, the women who had had temper tantrums as children tended to marry men who were significantly lower than themselves in occupational status; fully 40 percent of the women who had showed temper tantrums as children "married down," compared with only 24 percent of the women who had been even-tempered as children. As with the men, childhood temper tantrums were linked with frequency of divorce for the women. Roughly 26 percent of the women who had had childhood tantrums were divorced by age 40, whereas only 12 percent of the even-tempered women were divorced by that age.

In addition to empirical studies, such as those that predict later divorce from childhood personality, life-outcome data are used in real ways that affect our everyday lives. Our driving records, including speeding tickets and traffic accidents, are used by insurance companies to determine how much we pay for car insurance. Our histories of credit card usage are sometimes tracked by businesses to determine our behavioral preferences, which influence the advertisements we get sent. And more recently, advertisers sometimes track the websites we visit and use e-mail "spam" and pop-up advertisements based on our patterns of Internet surfing. Thus, driving records, credit card usage, and patterns of Internet usage have become modern sources of L-data. Do you think we can predict these patterns of publicly traceable data from personality variables, such as impulsivity (more driving accidents), status striving (credit card purchase of prestige possessions), and sex drive (more frequent visiting of pornography websites)? Future studies of L-data will shortly answer these questions.

In sum, L-data can serve as an important source of real-life information about personality. Personality characteristics measured early in life are often linked to important life outcomes several decades later. In this sense, life outcomes, such as work, marriage, and divorce, are, in part, manifestations of personality. Nonetheless, it must be recognized that life outcomes are caused by a variety of factors, including one's sex, race, and ethnicity and the opportunities to which one happens to be exposed. Personality characteristics represent only one set of causes of these life outcomes.

Exercise

Think of a personality characteristic that you find interesting. For example, you might consider such characteristics as activity level, risk taking, temper, or cooperativeness. Using the four main data sources, think of ways that you might gather information on this characteristic. Give specific examples of how you could assess this characteristic using S-, O-, T-, and L-data as sources of information on people's level of this characteristic. Be specific in providing examples of how and what you might do to assess your chosen personality characteristic.

Issues in Personality Assessment

Now that we have outlined the basic data sources, it is useful to take a step back and consider two broader issues in personality assessment. The first issue involves using two or more data sources within a single personality study. What are the links among the various sources of personality data? The second issue involves the fallibility of personality measurement and how the use of multiple data sources can correct some of the problems associated with single data sources.

Links among Various Data Sources

A key issue that personality psychologists must address is how closely the findings obtained from one data source correspond to findings from another data source. If, for example, a person rates herself as dominant, do observers, such as her friends and spouse, also view her as dominant? Do findings obtained from mechanical recording devices, such as an actometer, correspond to data obtained from observer reports or self-reports of activity level?

Depending on the personality variable under consideration, agreement across data sources tends to range from low to moderate. Ozer and Buss (1991) examined the relationships between self-report and spouse-report for eight dimensions of personality. They found that the degree of agreement varied depending on the particular trait and on the observability of the trait. Traits such as extraversion showed moderate agreement across data sources. The trait of "calculating," on the other hand, showed low self–spouse agreement. Traits that are easily observable (such as extraversion) show a higher degree of self–observer agreement than do traits (such as calculating) that are difficult to observe and require inferences about internal mental states.

One of the central advantages of using multiple measures is that each measure has unique idiosyncrasies that have nothing to do with the underlying construct of interest. By using multiple measures from various data sources, researchers are able to average out these idiosyncrasies and home in on the key variable under study.

A major issue in evaluating linkages among the sources of personality data is whether the sources are viewed as alternative measures of the same construct or as assessments of different phenomena. A person self-reporting about her relative dominance, for example, has access to a wealth of information—namely, her interactions with dozens of other people in her social environment. Any particular observer—a close friend, for example—has access to only a limited and selective sample of relevant behavior. Thus, if the friend rates the woman as highly dominant, whereas the woman rates herself as only moderately dominant, the disagreement may be due entirely to the different behavioral samples on which each person is basing his or her ratings. Thus, lack of agreement does not *necessarily* signify an error of measurement (although it certainly might). It may instead signify that observers are basing their conclusions on different behavioral samples.

In summary, the interpretation of links among the sources of personality data depends heavily on the research question being posed. Strong agreement between two sources of data leads researchers to be confident that their alternative measures are tapping into the same personality phenomenon, as proves to be the case with extraversion and activity level. Lack of strong agreement, on the other hand, may mean that the different data sources are assessing different phenomena, or it may indicate that one or more data sources are fallible or have problems—an issue to which we will now turn.

The Fallibility of Personality Measurement

Each data source has its own problems and pitfalls that limit its utility. This is true of all methods in science. Even so-called objective scientific instruments, such as telescopes, are less than perfect because minor flaws, such as a slight warping in the lens, may introduce errors into the observations. The fallible nature of scientific measures is no less true in personality research.

One powerful strategy of personality assessment, therefore, is to examine results that transcend data sources—a procedure sometimes referred to as *triangulation*. If a particular effect is found—for example, the influence of dominance on the assumption of leadership—does the effect occur when dominance is measured with self-report as well as with observer-reports? If extraverts are more easily driven to boredom than are introverts, does this show up when boredom is assessed with physiological recording devices (e.g., brain waves suggesting the person is almost asleep) as well as via self-report?

Throughout this book, as we discuss the empirical findings that have accumulated within each domain of personality, we will pay special attention to findings that transcend the limitations of single-data-source assessment. If the same results are found with two or more data sources, then researchers can have greater confidence in the credibility of those findings.

Evaluation of Personality Measures

Once personality measures have been identified for research, the next task is to subject them to scientific scrutiny, so that researchers can determine how good the measures are. In general, three standards are used to evaluate personality measures—reliability, validity, and generalizability. Although these three standards will be discussed here in the context of evaluating personality questionnaires, these standards are applicable to all measurement methods within personality research, not merely to those involving self-report personality questionnaires.

Reliability

Reliability can be defined as the degree to which an obtained measure represents the true level of the trait being measured. Assume for a moment that each person has some true amount of the trait you wish to measure, and that you could know this true level. If your measure is reliable then it will correlate with the true level. For example, if a person has a true IQ of 115, then a perfectly reliable measure of IQ will yield a score of 115 for that person. Moreover, a reliable measure of IQ will yield the same score of 115 each time it is administered to the person. A less reliable measure would yield a score, say, in a range of 112 to 118. An even less reliable measure would yield a score in an even broader range, between 100 (which is average) and 130 (which is borderline genius). Personality psychologists prefer reliable measures, so that the scores accurately reflect each person's true level of the personality characteristic.

There are several ways to estimate reliability. One way to estimate reliability is through **repeated measurement.** There are different forms of repeated measurement. A common procedure is to repeat a measurement over time—for example, at intervals of one month—for the same sample of persons. If the two tests are highly correlated, yielding similar scores for most people, the resulting measure is said to have high *test-retest reliability*.

A second way to gauge the reliability of a scale is to examine the relationships among the items themselves at a single point in time. If the items within a test—viewed as a form of repeated measurement—all correlate well with each other, then the scale is said to have high *internal consistency reliability*. The reliability is internal, because it is assessed within the test itself. The rationale for using internal consistency as an index of reliability is that psychologists constructing various measures assume that all items on a scale are measuring the same characteristic. If they are, then the items should be positively correlated with each other.

A third way to measure reliability—applicable only to the use of observer-based personality measures—is to obtain measurements from multiple observers. When different observers agree with each other, the measure is said to have high *inter-rater reliability*. When different raters fail to agree, the measure is said to have low inter-rater reliability.

It is important to demonstrate that a personality measure is reliable, whether through test-retest, internal consistency, or inter-rater reliability. However, this is only the first step in evaluating a personality measure. The next step is to examine whether it is valid.

Validity

Validity refers to the extent to which a test measures what it claims to measure (Cronbach & Meehl, 1955; Wiggins, 2003). Establishing whether a test actually measures what it is designed to measure is a complex and challenging task. There are five types of validity—face validity, predictive validity, convergent validity, discriminant validity, and construct validity. The simplest facet of validity is called **face validity.** *Face validity* refers to whether the test, on the surface, appears to measure what it is supposed to measure. For example, a scale measuring a trait such as manipulativeness might include the following face-valid items: *I made a friend just to obtain a favor; I tricked a friend into giving me personal information; I managed to get my way by appearing cooperative; I pretended that I was hurt to get someone to do me a favor*. Since most people agree that these acts are manipulative, the scale containing them is highly face-valid. Face validity is probably the least important aspect of validity. In fact, some psychologists argue that face validity refers to the assumption of validity, not to evidence for real validity.

A more important component of validity is **predictive validity.** *Predictive validity* refers to whether the test predicts criteria external to the test (thus it is sometimes called **criterion validity**). A scale intended to measure sensation seeking, for example, should predict which individuals actually take risks to obtain thrills and excitement, such as parachute jumping or motorcycle riding. A recent study, for example, found that a measure of sensation seeking indeed successfully predicted a variety of gambling behaviors, such as playing the lottery, betting on sporting events, playing video poker, and using slot machines—attesting to the predictive validity of the sensation-seeking measure (McDaniel & Zuckerman, 2003). A scale created to measure conscientiousness should predict which people actually show up on time for meetings and follow rules. Scales that successfully predict what they should predict have high predictive validity.

A third aspect of validity, called **convergent validity,** refers to whether a test correlates with other measures that it should correlate with. For example, if a self-report measure of tolerance corresponds well with peer judgments of tolerance, then the scale is said to have high convergent validity. Early in this chapter we described a study of "activity level," in which mechanical recordings of activity level correlated highly with observer-based judgments of activity level—another example of convergent validity. Convergent validity is high to the degree that alternative measures of the same construct correlate or converge with the target measure.

A fourth kind of validity, called **discriminant validity,** is often evaluated simultaneously with convergent validity. Whereas *convergent validity* refers to what a measure *should* correlate with, *discriminant validity* refers to what a measure *should not* correlate with. For example, a psychologist might develop a measure of life satisfaction, the tendency to believe one's life is happy, worthwhile, and satisfying. However, there is another trait called social desirability, the tendency to say nice things about oneself; thus, the psychologist might be concerned with the discriminant validity of his or her life-satisfaction measure and try to show that this measure is different from measures of social desirability. Part of knowing what a measure actually measures consists of knowing what it does not measure.

A final type of validity is **construct validity,** defined as a test that measures what it claims to measure, correlates with what it is supposed to correlate with, and does not correlate with what it is not supposed to correlate with. Thus, construct validity is the broadest type of validity, subsuming face, predictive, convergent, and discriminant validity. This form of validity is called construct validity because it is based on the notion that personality variables are **theoretical constructs.** If asked to "show your intelligence" or "show your extraversion," you would be hard-pressed to respond. That is because there is not any one thing you can produce and say, "This is my intelligence" or "This is my extraversion." Intelligence and extraversion, like almost all personality variables, are abstractions. Nevertheless, these theoretical constructs are useful to psychologists in describing and explaining differences between people. Determining whether actual measures can claim to be valid ways of assessing the constructs is the essence of construct validity.

How then do we know if a measure has construct validity? If a measure converges with other measures of the same construct, if it relates to other variables that a theory of the construct says it should, and if it does *not* relate to phenomena that the theory says it should not relate to, then we have the beginnings of construct validity. For example, say that a researcher has developed a questionnaire measure of creativity and is wondering about its construct validity. Do the questionnaire scores correlate with other measures of creativity gathered on the same sample, such as ratings of creativity provided by friends (convergent validity), or awards or grades obtained in fine arts classes (predictive validity)? In addition, do the results correlate with behavioral test data on creativity (e.g., tests in which participants are asked to name creative uses for common objects, such as a hammer and string)?

Finally, if the researcher hypothesizes that creativity is different from intelligence, for instance, it will also be important to prove that the measure of creativity does *not* correlate with measures of intelligence (discriminant validity). When a large number of known relations is built up around a measure, then we begin to believe that the measure is credible as a measure of a specific personality construct. For example, if we know enough about the correlates of a measure of creativity, then we might say that the measure has sufficient construct validity to be useful for making inferences about creativity, for testing theories about creativity, and for measuring creativity in samples of people.

Generalizability

A third criterion for evaluating personality measures is **generalizability** (Cronbach & Gleser, 1965; Wiggins, 1973). Generalizability is the degree to which the measure retains its validity across various contexts. One context of interest might be different groups of *persons*. A personality psychologist, for example, might be interested in whether a questionnaire retains its predictive validity across age groups, genders, cultures, or ethnic groups. Is a particular scale equally valid when used on men versus women? Is a test equally valid for African Americans and European Americans? Is it equally valid among Japanese and Javanese? Does the scale measure the same trait or quality among college students as among middle-aged adults? If the scale is widely applicable across these person and cultural contexts, then the scale is said to have high generalizability across populations of people.

Another facet of generalizability refers to *different conditions*. Does a dominance scale, for example, predict who becomes the leader in business settings as well as in informal, after-work settings? Does a scale designed to measure conscientiousness predict who will show up for class on time, as well as who will keep their bedrooms tidy? Scales have high generalizability to the degree that they apply widely over different persons, situations, cultures, and times.

Research Designs in Personality

In this chapter, we have examined the *types of personality measures* and the *means for evaluating the quality* of those measures. The next step in personality research is to use these measures in actual *research designs*. Although the variations are nearly infinite, there are three basic research designs in the field of personality psychology—experimental, correlational, and case study. Each has strengths and weaknesses. Each provides information that complements the information provided by the others.

Experimental Methods

Experimental methods are typically used to determine causality—that is, to find out whether one variable *influences* another variable. A *variable* is simply a quality that differs, or can take different values, for different people. Height, for example, is a variable because individuals differ from each other in height. Aggressiveness is a variable because individuals differ in their levels of aggressiveness. Personality characteristics, such as extraversion and agreeableness, are other examples of variables. In order to establish the influence of one variable on another, several key requirements of good experimental design must be met: (1) **manipulation** of one or more variables and (2) ensuring that participants in each experimental condition *are equivalent to each other at the beginning of the study*.

In the first requirement, manipulation, the variable thought to be the influence is manipulated as part of the experiment. For example, if a drug is hypothesized to influence memory, then some participants get the drug and other participants get sugar pills; then all participants have their memories tested. The second requirement, equivalence, is accomplished in one of two ways. If the experiment has manipulation between groups, then the **random assignment** of participants to experimental groups is a procedure that helps ensure that all groups are equivalent at the beginning of the study. However, in some experiments, manipulation is within each single group. For example, in the memory experiment, participants might get the drug and have their memories tested, then later take the sugar pills and have their memories tested again. In this case, each participant is in both conditions. In this kind of experiment (called a within-participant design), equivalence is obtained by **counterbalancing** the order of the conditions, with half of the participants getting the drug first and sugar pill second, and the other half getting the sugar pill first and the drug second.

The meaning of each of these features will become clear through an example of a personality experiment. Perhaps you are curious about why some people like to study with an iPod or TV on, whereas others demand total silence for studying. A personality theory predicts that extraverts prefer lots of stimulation and introverts

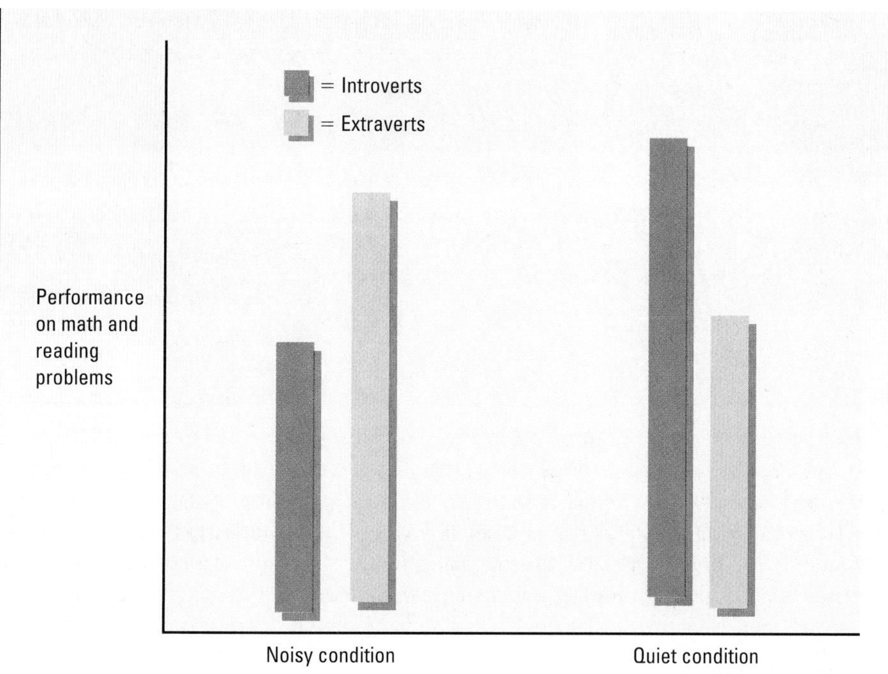

Figure 2.1
Performance on math and reading problems.

prefer very little. Imagine being interested in testing the hypothesis that extraverts function best under conditions of high external stimulation, whereas introverts function best under conditions of low stimulation. To test this hypothesis, you could first give a group of participants a self-report questionnaire that measures extraversion–introversion. Then you could select only those individuals who score at either extreme—as very introverted or very extraverted—to participate in your experiment. Next you would take these participants into the laboratory and have them work on math and sentence comprehension problems under two different conditions—in one condition, a radio would be blaring in the background and, in the other, there would be total silence. Half of each group (that is, half of the extraverts and half of the introverts) should be randomly placed in the noisy condition first and the quiet condition second. The other half should be placed in the quiet condition first and the noisy condition second. Then, you would measure the number of errors each group makes under each of the two conditions. If the personality theory you are testing is correct, you should get a pattern of results like that in Figure 2.1. The hypothetical results in Figure 2.1 show that the extraverts made few errors in the noisy condition and more errors when it was quiet. The introverts showed the opposite pattern—noise hampered their performance, whereas they functioned best under conditions of silence.

This study, although hypothetical, highlights the key features of good experimental design. The first is manipulation. In this case, the external condition (the *independent variable*) was manipulated—whether there was a lot of or a little ambient noise in the laboratory. The second feature is counterbalancing—half of the participants received the noisy condition first, whereas the other half received the quiet

People who study alone in a library are likely to be introverted, whereas those who do their studying in groups tend to be extraverted.

condition first. Counterbalancing is critical because there might be *order effects* as a consequence of being exposed to one condition first. Counterbalancing allows the experimenter to rule out order effects as an explanation for the results. The third feature is random assignment. Through random assignment, all persons have an equal chance of being selected for a given condition. Randomization can occur by flipping a coin or, more commonly, by the use of a table of random numbers. Randomization ensures that there are no predetermined patterns linked with condition assignment that could account for the final results.

In experimental designs, it is desirable to establish whether or not the groups in the different conditions are *significantly* different. In the introversion/extraversion example, we want to know if the performance of introverts and extraverts in the noisy condition is significantly different. Is the performance of the introverts significantly different from that of the extraverts in the quiet condition? To answer these questions, we need to know five things—sample size, the mean, the standard deviation, the t-test, and the p-value (significance of the differences between the conditions).

The *mean* refers to the average—in this case, the average number of errors within each condition. The *standard deviation* is a measure of variability within each condition. Since not all participants make the same average number of errors, we need a way to estimate how much participants within each condition vary; this estimate is the standard deviation. Using these numbers, we can use a statistical formula—called the *t-test*—to calculate the difference between two means.

The next step is to see whether the difference is large enough to be called significantly different (the *p-value*). Although "large enough" is a somewhat arbitrary concept, psychologists have adopted the following convention: if the difference between the means would be likely to occur *by chance alone* (i.e., due to random fluctuations in the data) only 1 time out of 20 or less, then the difference is **statistically significant** at the $p < .05$ level (the .05 refers to 5 percent chance level, or 1 time in 20). A difference between means that is significant at the .05 level implies that the finding would be likely to occur by chance alone only 5 times out of 100. Another way to think about this is to imagine that, if the experiment were repeated 100 times, we would expect to find these results by chance alone only 5 times.

In sum, the experimental method is effective at demonstrating *relationships among variables*. Experiments similar to the one described, for example, have established a link between extraversion–introversion and performance under conditions of high versus low noise. The procedures of manipulating the conditions, counterbalancing the order in which the conditions occur, and randomly assigning participants to conditions help to ensure that extraneous factors are canceled out. Then, after calculating means and standard deviations, t-tests and p-values are used to determine whether the differences between the groups in the two conditions are statistically significant. These procedures determine whether personality influences how people perform.

Correlational Studies

A second major type of research design in personality is the correlational study. In the **correlational method** a statistical procedure is used for determining whether or not there is a relationship between two variables. For example, do people with a high need for achievement in college go on to earn higher salaries in adulthood than persons lower on need for achievement? In correlational research designs, the researcher is attempting to identify directly the relationships between two or more variables, without imposing the sorts of manipulations seen in experimental designs. Correlational designs typically try to determine what goes with what in nature. We might be interested, for example, in the relationship between self-esteem, as assessed through S-data, and the esteem in which a person is held by others, as assessed through O-data. Or we might be interested in how a measure of achievement motivation relates to grade point average. A major advantage of correlational studies is that they allow us to identify relationships among variables as they occur naturally. To continue the extraversion–introversion and performance under noise conditions example, we might measure people's preferences for studying with or without music in real life, then see if there is a correlation with their scores on a measure of introversion–extraversion.

The most common statistical procedure for gauging relationships between variables is the **correlation coefficient.** To understand what correlation coefficients indicate, consider examining the relationship between height and weight. We might take a sample of 100 college students and measure their height and weight. If we chart the results on a scatterplot, we see that people who are tall also tend to be relatively heavy and that people who are short tend to be less heavy. But there are exceptions, as you can see in Figure 2.2.

Correlation coefficients can range from +1.00 through 0.00 to −1.00. That is, the variables of interest can be positively related to each other (+.01 to +1.00), unrelated to each other (0.00), or negatively related to each other (−.01 to −1.00). Height and weight happen to be strongly positively correlated with each other—with a calculated correlation coefficient of +.60, for the data shown in Figure 2.2.

Consider a more psychological example. Suppose we are interested in the relationship between people's self-esteem and the amount of time they are unhappy. We might see a scatterplot as depicted in Figure 2.3. This scatterplot was obtained from a sample of college students, using a standard questionnaire measure of self-esteem. As the second variable, a measure of unhappiness, the participants were asked to keep a diary for two months, noting for each day whether that day was generally good (felt happy) or generally bad (felt unhappy). Then the percentage of days for each participant being unhappy was calculated. As you can see in Figure 2.3, as self-esteem goes up, the percentage of time a person is unhappy tends to go down. In contrast, those with low self-esteem tend to be unhappy a lot. In other words, there is a negative correlation between self-esteem and the percentage of time unhappy—in this case, approximately −.60.

As a final example, suppose we are interested in the relationship between extraversion and emotional stability (the tendency to be calm and secure). The

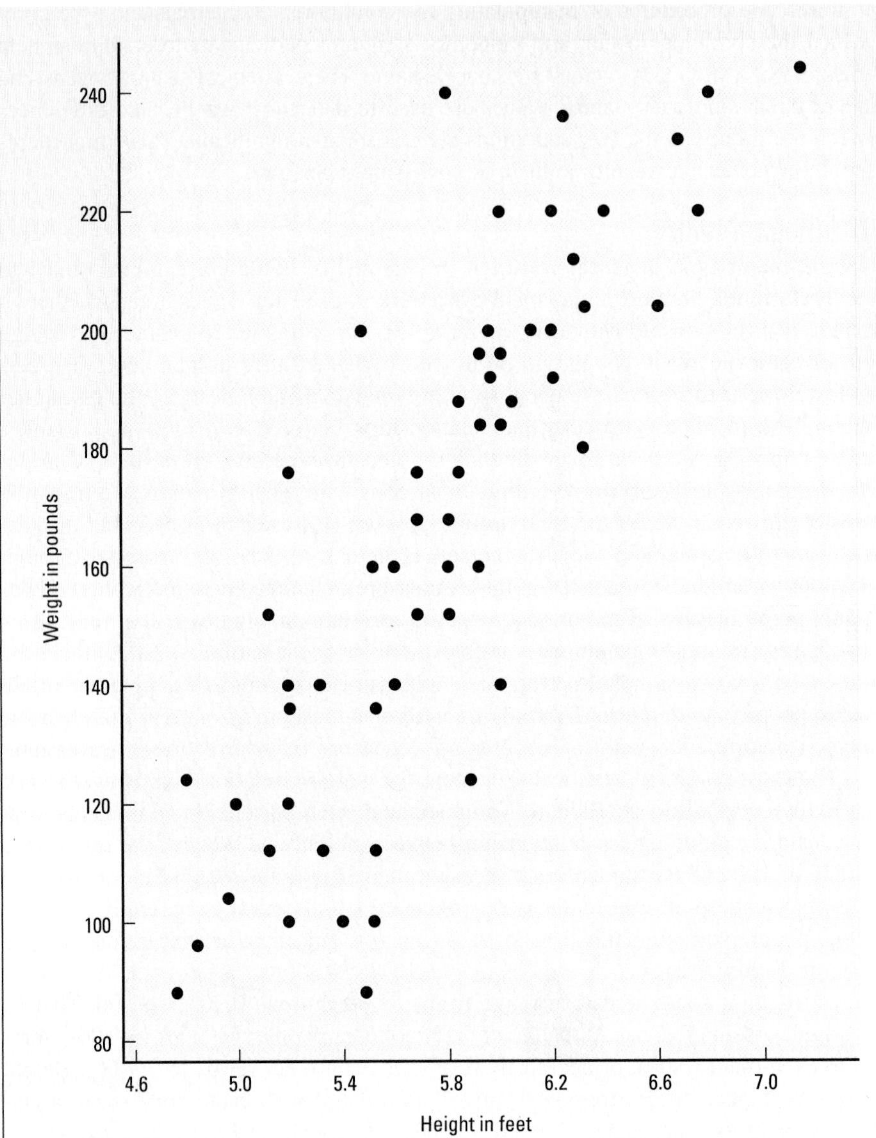

Figure 2.2

Fifty-five cases plotted, showing a strong positive correlation between height and weight. Each symbol (•) represents one person who was measured on both height and weight. Heavier persons tend to be taller; lighter persons tend to be shorter.

relationship is depicted in Figure 2.4. As you can see, there is no relationship between extraversion and emotional stability; as one variable goes up, the other may go up, down, or stay the same. In this case, the correlation coefficient is 0.00. This means that you can find people with all the different combinations of extraversion and emotional stability, such as those who are outgoing and sociable but also highly neurotic and unstable. In sum, relationships between variables can be positive, negative, or neither, as signified by positive, negative, or zero correlations.

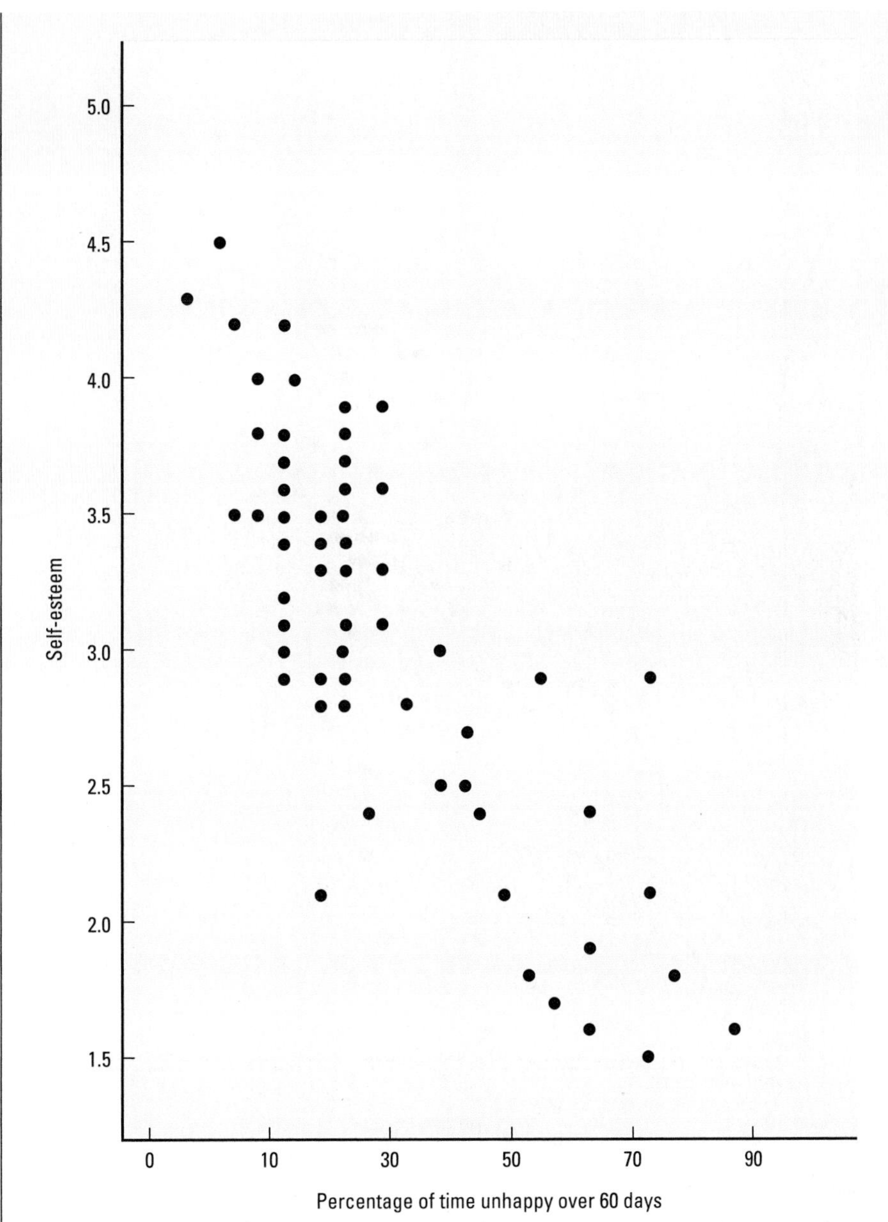

Figure 2.3

Fifty-eight cases plotted to illustrate the negative correlation between self-esteem and the percentage of time reported as being unhappy over two months. The correlation is −.60, indicating that people with higher self-esteem tend to be less unhappy than people with low self-esteem.

Most researchers are not merely interested in the *direction* of the relationship; they are also interested in the *magnitude* of the relationship, or how large or small it is. Although what is considered large or small depends on many factors, social scientists have adopted a general convention. Correlations around .10 are considered small; those around .30 are considered medium; and those around .50 or greater are

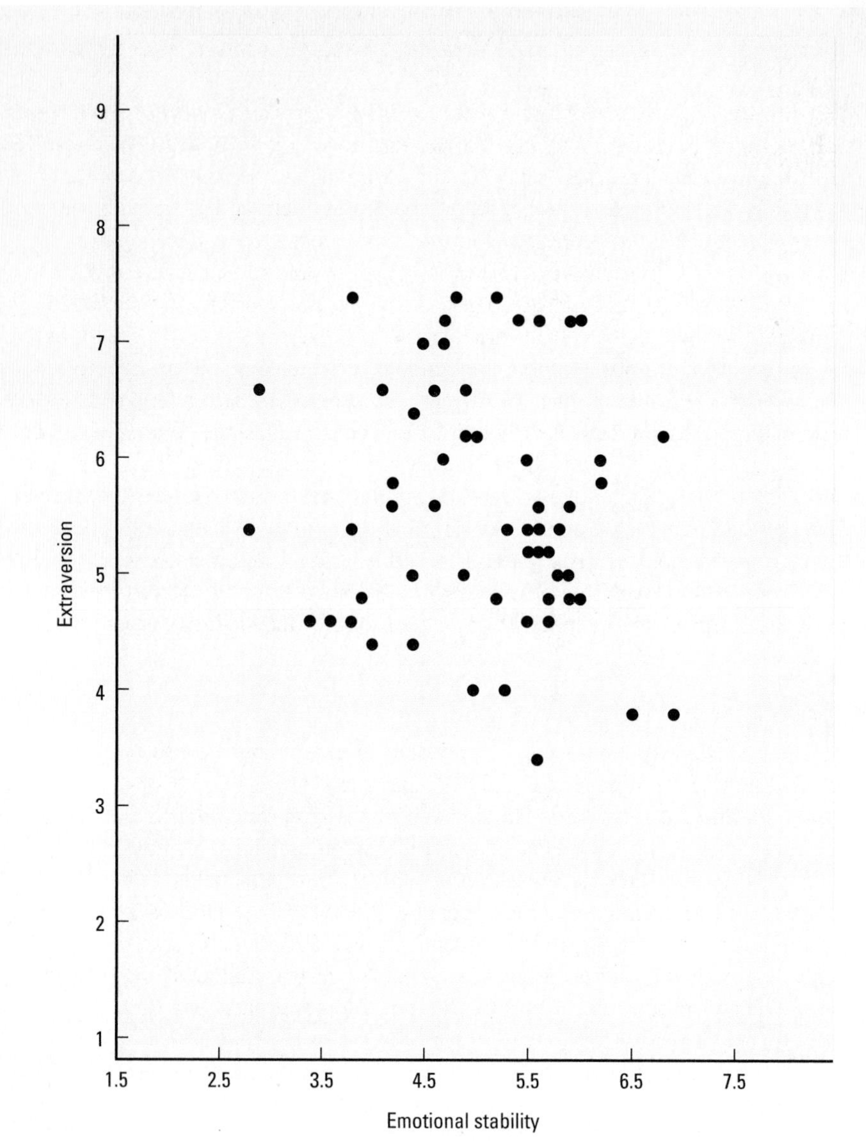

Figure 2.4

Fifty-seven cases plotted to show the relationship between emotional stability and extraversion. The correlation between these two variables is essentially 0.00, meaning that there is no relationship. Consequently, in the scatterplot, we see that people fall fairly equally in all sections of the plot, with no clear pattern.

considered large (Cohen & Cohen, 1975). Using the examples in Figures 2.2–2.4, the +.60 correlation between height and weight is considered large, as is the −.60 correlation between self-esteem and percentage of time unhappy. These correlations are equivalent in magnitude but different in sign.

The concept of statistical significance can also be applied to correlation values. This is basically part of the statistical calculation, and it results in a numerical statement about how likely you are to find a correlation this size by chance, given the variables measured and the size of the sample. Here psychologists also require a probability of .05 or less before referring to a correlation as significant.

It is important to keep in mind that one cannot infer causation from correlations. There are at least two reasons why correlations can never prove causality. One is called the **directionality problem.** If *A* and *B* are correlated, we do not know if *A* is the cause of *B* or if *B* is the cause of *A*. For example, we know there is a correlation between extraversion and happiness. From this fact alone, we do not know if being extraverted causes people to be happy or if being happy causes people to be extraverted.

The second reason that correlations can never prove causality is the **third variable problem.** It could be that two variables are correlated because a third, unknown variable is causing both. For example, the amount of ice cream sold on any given day may be correlated with the number of people who drown on that particular day. Does this mean eating ice cream causes drowning? Not necessarily, since there is most likely a third variable at work: hot weather. On very hot days, many people eat ice cream. Also, on very hot days, many people go swimming who otherwise don't swim very much, so more are likely to drown. Drowning has nothing to do with eating ice cream; rather, these two variables are likely to be caused by a third variable: hot weather. With both correlational and experimental methods, it's important to recognize that not all individuals conform to the generalizations established in the studies that use them.

Case Studies

Sometimes a personality researcher is interested in examining the life of one person in-depth as a case study. There are many advantages to the **case study method.** Researchers can find out about personality in great detail, which rarely can be achieved if the study includes a large number of people. Case studies can give researchers insights into personality that can then be used to formulate a more general theory to be tested on a larger population. They can provide in-depth knowledge of particularly outstanding individuals, such as Mahatma Gandhi or Martin Luther King. Case studies can also be useful in studying rare phenomena, such as a person with a photographic memory or a person with multiple personalities—cases for which large samples would be difficult or impossible to obtain.

One case study occupied an entire issue of the *Journal of Personality* (Nasby & Read, 1997). This study presents the case of Dodge Morgan, who, at the age of 54, completed a nonstop solo circumnavigation of the earth by small boat. The case study reported by Nasby and Read is a highly readable account of this interesting man undertaking an almost impossible task. The focus is on how Mr. Morgan's early life experiences formed a particular adult personality, which led him to undertake the extreme act of going around the world alone in a small boat. The psychologists used Morgan's voyage log book, autobiographical material, interviews, and even standard personality questionnaires in conducting their case study. The report is noteworthy in that the psychologists also discussed the strengths and weaknesses of the case study method for advancing the science of personality psychology. The authors concluded that personality theories provide a language for discussing individual lives; analysis of individual lives, in turn, provides a means for evaluating personality theories on how they help us understand specific individuals.

Dodge Morgan was 54 when he completed a nonstop, solo circumnavigation of the earth in his boat American Promise. *An extensive case study of this fascinating man was conducted by psychologists William Nasby and Nancy Read and reported in their paper "The Voyage and the Voyager" published in the* Journal of Personality, *1997, volume 65, pages 823–852.*

Case study design can use a wide array of tools. One can develop coding systems to be applied to written texts, such as personal letters and correspondence. One can interview dozens of people who know the individual. One can interview the participant for hours and at great depth. One can follow the person around with a video camera and record, with sound and image, the actions in his or her everyday life. In sum, the assessment techniques used in case study designs are limited only by the imagination of the investigator.

Case Study: An Attention-Seeking Boy

One of the strongest advocates of the case study method was Gordon Allport, one of the founders of the field of modern personality psychology. Allport firmly believed that important hypotheses about personality could come from examining single individuals in great depth. He also believed that one could test hypotheses about the underlying personality characteristics of a single individual using case study methods. The following example illustrates this sort of hypothesis formation and testing:

> *A certain boy at school showed exemplary conduct; he was orderly, industrious, and attentive. But at home he was noisy, unruly, and a bully toward the younger children . . .*
>
> *Now the psychologist might make the hypothesis: This boy's central disposition is a craving for attention. He finds that he gains his end best at school by conforming to the rules; at home, by disobeying them.*
>
> *Having made this hypothesis, the psychologist could then actually count the boy's acts during the day (being checked by some independent observer) to see how many of them were "functionally equivalent," i.e., manifested a clear bid for attention. If the proportion is high, we can regard the hypothesis as confirmed, and the p.d. [personality disposition] as established. (Allport, 1961, p. 368)*

Case Study: The Serial Killer Ted Bundy

Although Ted Bundy was convicted of killing three women, he was suspected of raping and killing as many as 36 women during his half-decade murder spree in the states of Oregon, Washington, Colorado, and Florida in the 1970s (Rule, 2000). Case studies have been devoted to explaining what drove Bundy to rape and kill. Some traced it back to the fact that he was adopted and felt a burning shame over the fact that he never knew his biological parents. Some tied it to his failed aspirations as a lawyer—where a status-striving motive was frustrated. Some traced it to the fact that he developed a deep-seated hostility toward women after being rejected by his fiancée—a woman who was considerably higher than he in socioeconomic status and who he felt was impossible to replace. All case studies of Bundy revealed, however, that he shared many traits with other serial killers. He had a "classic" sociopathic personality—characterized by grandiosity, extreme sense of entitlement, preoccupation with unrealistic fantasies of success and power, lack of empathy for other people, a long history of deceitfulness, repeated failures to meet normally expected obligations of school and work, and high levels of interpersonal exploitativeness. Furthermore, Ted Bundy showed early behavior and personality dispositions that are known to be associated with serial killers, the so-called "serial killer triad": (1) torturing animals while young, (2) starting destructive fires, and (3) bedwetting. Case studies such as those of Ted Bundy can reveal unique aspects of his life (e.g., being rejected by a higher status fiancée, failure to achieve status

Ted Bundy, a convicted serial killer, showed the personality characteristics of a classic sociopath.

as an attorney), as well as the common personality dispositions that are often linked with serial killers (e.g., torturing animals, bedwetting; see also the recent case of Keith Hunter Jesperson, who confessed to raping and killing eight women, in Olson, 2002). In Bundy's case, his personality and his life both ended, and he will kill no more. After two successful escapes from jail, Bundy went on to kill his final victims in Florida and was finally captured and convicted. After a decade of legal appeals were eventually exhausted, Ted Bundy was executed in Florida in 1989.

Despite the strengths of the in-depth case study method, it has some critical limitations. The most important one is that findings based on one individual cannot be generalized to other people. A case study is to the other research designs what a study of the planet Mars is to the study of planetary systems. We may find out a great deal about Mars (or a particular person), but what we find out may not be applicable to other planets (or other people). For this reason, case studies are most often used as a *source of hypotheses* and as a *means to illustrate* a principle by bringing it to life. Nonetheless, case studies of personality can be viewed as an exceptionally valuable research method, and often can be intrinsically interesting in illuminating the lives of exceptional individuals.

When to Use Experimental, Correlational, and Case Study Designs

Each of the three major types of research designs has strengths and weaknesses or, more precisely, questions that each is good at answering and questions that each is poor at answering. The experimental method is ideally suited for establishing causal relationships among variables. For example, it can be used to determine whether noisy conditions hamper the performance of introverts but not of extraverts. On the other hand, the experimental method is poor at identifying the relationships among variables as they occur naturally in everyday life. Moreover, it may be impractical or unethical to use the experimental method for some questions. For example, if a researcher is interested in the role of nutrition in the development of intelligence, it is unethical to conduct an experiment in which half of the participants are put on a starvation diet for several years as children to see if it affects their IQs as adults.

Exercise

Think of a question about one aspect of personality. Most questions take the form of "Is variable *A* related to or caused by variable *B*?" For example, are extraverted persons better than introverts at coping with stress? Are people with high self-esteem more likely to be successful than people with low self-esteem? Do narcissistic persons have problems getting along with others? Write down your question about personality. Now think about how you might approach your question using an experiment, using the correlational method, and doing a case study. Briefly describe how you would use each of these three research designs to try to answer your question.

However, there are people who, for whatever unfortunate circumstances, have had several years of very poor nutrition. Thus, a correlational study could be done on whether level of nutrition is related to the development of intelligence. The weakness of the experimental research design is precisely the strength of the correlational design. Correlational designs are ideally suited for establishing the relationships between two or more variables that occur in everyday life, such as between height and dominance, conscientiousness and grade-point average, or anxiety and frequency of illness. But correlational designs are poor at establishing causality. They cannot determine, for example, whether frequent illnesses lead to anxiety, whether anxiety leads to illness, or whether a third variable accounts for being both frequently ill and frequently anxious.

Case studies are ideally suited for generating hypotheses that can be tested subsequently using correlational or experimental methods. Case studies can be used to identify patterns in individual psychological functioning that might be missed by the more rigorous but artificial experimental approach and the limited correlational designs. Furthermore, case studies are wonderful in depicting the richness and complexity of human experience. Despite these strengths, case studies cannot establish causality, as can experimental methods, nor can they identify patterns of covariation across individuals as they occur in nature. Case studies also cannot be generalized to anyone beyond the single individual being studied. Together, all three designs provide complementary methods for exploring human personality.

SUMMARY AND EVALUATION

Personality assessment and measurement start with identifying the sources of personality data—the places from which we obtain information about personality. The four major sources of personality data are self-report (S-data), observer report (O-data), laboratory tests (T-data), and life history outcomes (L-data). Each of these data sources has strengths and weaknesses. In self-report, for example, participants might fake or lie. Observers in the O-data mode may lack access to the relevant information. Laboratory tests may be inadequate for identifying patterns that occur naturally in everyday life. Each source of personality data is extremely valuable, however, and each provides information not attainable through the other sources. Furthermore, new measurement techniques continue to be invented and explored; a recent example is fMRI, or functional magnetic resonance imaging, which detects locations and patterns of brain activity when individuals perform particular tasks.

Once sources of data have been selected for measuring personality, the researcher then subjects them to tests to evaluate their quality. Personality measures, ideally, should be reliable in the sense of attaining the same scores through repeated measurement. They should be valid, measuring what they are supposed to measure. And researchers should establish how generalizable their measures are—determining the people, settings, and cultures to which the measure is most applicable. Scales applicable only to college students in the United States, for example, are less generalizable than scales applicable to people of differing ages, economic brackets, ethnic groups, and cultures.

The next step in personality research involves selecting a particular research design within which to use the measures. There are three basic types of research designs. The first, the experimental research design, which involves controlling or manipulating the variables of interest, is best suited to determining causality between two variables. The second, correlational research design, is best for identifying relationships between naturally occurring variables but is poorly suited to determining causality. The third is the case study method, which is well suited to generating new hypotheses about personality and to understanding single individuals.

Perhaps the most important principle of personality assessment and measurement is that the decisions about data source and research design depend heavily on the purpose of the investigation. There are no perfect methods; there are no perfect designs. But there are data sources and methods that are better suited for some purposes than for others. Thus, as we examine the theories and research findings in this book, bear in mind that different investigators use different data sources and different research designs because they have different purposes in conducting their research.

KEY TERMS

PART ONE

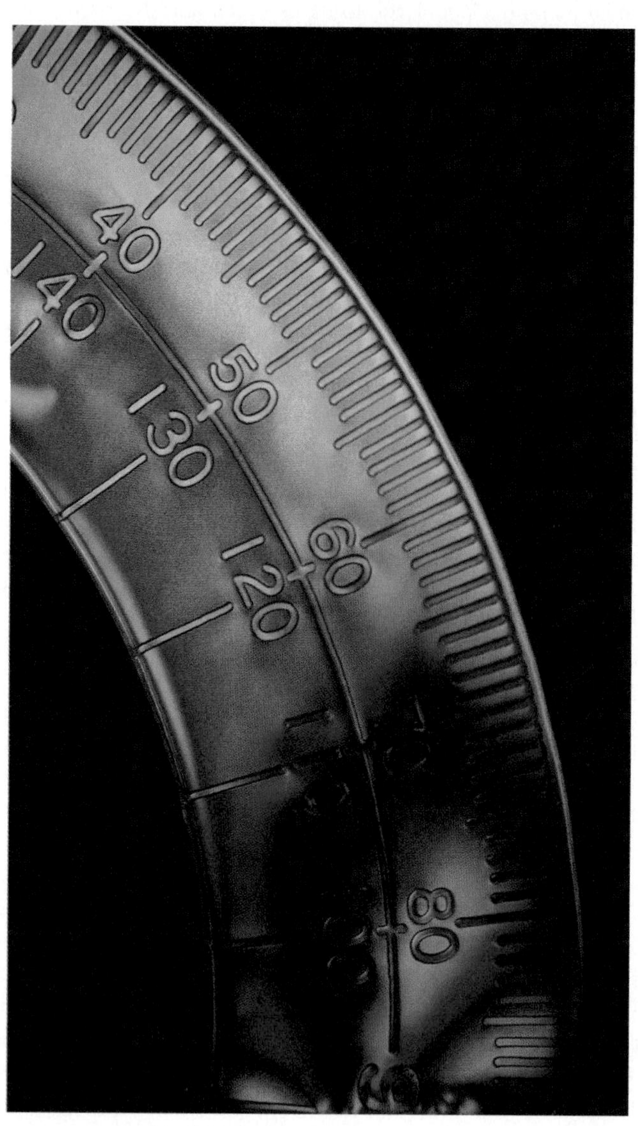

The Dispositional Domain

I

The dispositional domain concerns those aspects of personality that are stable over time, relatively consistent over situations, and make people different from each other. For example, some people are outgoing and talkative; others are introverted and shy. The introverted and shy person tends to be that way most of the time (is stable over time) and tends to be introverted and shy at work, at play, and at school (is consistent over situations). As another example, some people are emotionally reactive and moody; others are calm and cool. Some people are conscientious and reliable; others are unreliable and untrustworthy. There are many ways in which people differ from one another, and these differences are often stable and consistent features of a person's behavior.

The study of traits makes up the dispositional domain. The term *disposition* is used because it refers to an inherent tendency to behave in a specific way. The term *trait* is used interchangeably with the term *disposition*. The major questions for psychologists working in the dispositional domain are: How many personality traits exist? What is the best taxonomy or classification system for traits? How can we best discover and measure these traits? How do personality traits develop? How do traits interact with situations to produce behaviors?

In this domain, traits are seen as the building blocks of personality. A person's personality is viewed as being built out of a set of common traits. Psychologists have been concerned with identifying the most important traits, the ones out of which all differences between people can be formed. Three traditions have developed to achieve this goal. One is to analyze natural language, especially trait terms, to determine which traits are fundamental. The idea here is that, if some individual difference were socially important, such as how reliable a person was, then our ancestors would have developed and added words to the language to describe this difference. A second strategy for identifying personality traits is statistical and relies on various statistical techniques to identify patterns in data that describe fundamental traits. And the final strategy is theoretical, where some prior theory is used to deduce what traits are fundamental. In practical terms, personality psychologists often blend these three strategies together, or use one to validate the results found in another.

The next step is to develop taxonomies or classification systems. Taxonomies are very useful in all areas of science. Currently, the most popular taxonomy of personality has five fundamental traits: extraversion, neuroticism, agreeableness, conscientiousness, and openness to experience. Other taxonomies have also been proposed, ranging from three important traits to 16 important traits. Moreover, some taxonomies posit a structure, whereby the traits in the taxonomy are related to each other. We will discuss an example of this kind of taxonomy that is called the interpersonal circumplex, because the traits all refer to interpersonal behaviors and they are arranged in a circle.

The dispositional domain emphasizes measurement. More than any other domain of knowledge about personality, the dispositional domain uses quantitative techniques for measuring and studying personality traits. And a lot of work in this domain has gone into developing better measures of personality traits, ones that are not easily faked by persons taking the tests.

This domain also has a very applied side, in that personality traits are often used in selecting people for specific careers, for specific educational opportunities, for promotions, or for parole from prison. Personality traits can be useful for prediction. Will a person with this sort of personality like this sort of career? Does this inmate have such a high level of aggressiveness and hostility that he should not be put on parole? Would this person make a good police officer? Dispositional psychologists are thus often involved in selecting or screening people. We will discuss some of the legal issues that are involved when personality tests are used in this manner.

In the dispositional domain there is a unique conception of how people change yet remain stable at the same time. We will discuss how the traits that underlie behavior can remain stable, yet how the traits are expressed in behavior can change over a person's life span. Consider the trait of dominance. Suppose that a girl who is dominant at age 8 grows into a young woman who is dominant at age 20. As an 8-year-old this person might display her high level of dominance by showing a readiness for rough-and-tumble play, referring to her less dominant peers as sissies, and insisting on monopolizing whatever interesting toys are available to the group. By age 20, however, she manifests her dominance in quite different behaviors, perhaps by persuading others to accept her views in political discussions, boldly asking young men out on dates, and deciding on the restaurants they will go to on these dates. Consequently, trait levels can stay the same over long time periods, yet the behaviors expressing those traits change as the person ages.

We will discuss the ways in which personality psychologists have studied the development of dispositions as well as studies of how dispositions can change across the life span.

3

Traits and Trait Taxonomies

THE DISPOSITIONAL DOMAIN

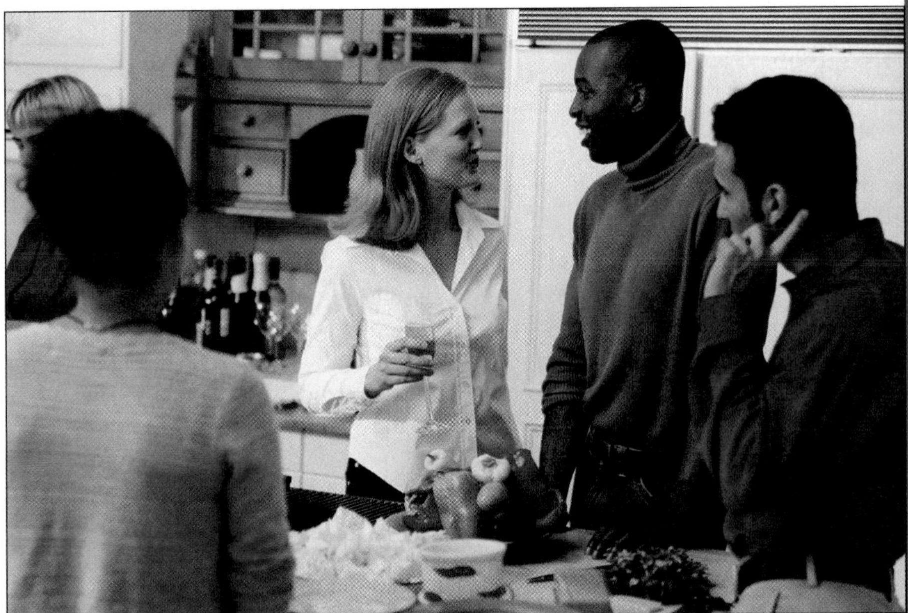

People readily form impressions of others that can be described using a few traits of personality, such as whether or not the person is friendly, generous, and poised.

Suppose that you walk into a party with a friend, who introduces you to the host, an acquaintance of hers. The three of you chat for 10 minutes, and then you mingle with the other guests. Later, as you leave the party with your friend, she asks what you thought of the host. As you mull over the 10-minute interaction, what springs to mind? Perhaps you describe the host as *friendly* (she smiled a lot), *generous* (she told you to help yourself to the bountiful spread of food), and *poised* (she was apparently able to juggle the many demands of her guests as they came and went). These words are all examples of *trait-descriptive adjectives*—words that describe *traits, attributes* of a person that are reasonably *characteristic* of the person and perhaps even *enduring* over time. Just as you might describe a glass as *brittle* or a car as *reliable* (enduring characteristics of the glass and the car), the use of trait-descriptive adjectives when applied to people connotes consistent and stable characteristics. For much of the past century, many psychologists have focused on identifying the basic traits that make up personality and identifying the nature and origins of those traits.

Most personality psychologists hypothesize that traits (also called *dispositions*) are reasonably stable over time and consistent over situations. The host of the party just described, for example, might be friendly, generous, and poised at other parties later on—illustrating stability over time. And she might also show these traits in other situations—perhaps showing friendliness by smiling at people on elevators, generosity by giving homeless persons money, and poised by maintaining her composure when called on in class. However, the actual degree to which traits show stability over time and consistency across situations has been the subject of considerable debate and empirical research.

Three fundamental questions guide those who study personality traits: The first question is *"How should we conceptualize traits?"* Every field needs to define its key terms explicitly. In biology, for example, *species* is a key concept, so the concept of species is defined explicitly (i.e., a group of organisms capable of reproducing with each other). In physics, the basic concepts of mass, weight, force, and gravity are defined explicitly. Because traits are central concepts in personality psychology, they, too, must be precisely formulated.

The second question is "How can we identify which traits are the *most important* traits from among the thousands of ways in which individuals differ?" Individuals differ in many ways that are both characteristic and enduring. Some individuals are extremely extraverted, enjoying loud and crowded parties; others are introverted, preferring quiet evenings spent reading. Some people talk a lot and seek to be the center of attention in most social encounters; some prefer to be quiet and let others do the talking. A crucial goal of personality psychology is to identify the most important ways in which individuals differ.

The third question is "How can we formulate a *comprehensive taxonomy* of traits—a system that includes within it *all* of the major traits of personality?" Once the important traits have been identified, the next step is to formulate an organized scheme—a *taxonomy*—within which to assemble the individual traits. The periodic table of elements, for example, is not merely a random list of all the physical elements that have been discovered. Rather, it is a taxonomy that organizes the elements using a coherent principle—the elements are arranged according to their atomic numbers (which refer to the number of protons in the nucleus of a given atom). Within biology, to use another example, the field would be hopelessly lost if it were to merely list all of the thousands of species that exist, without relying on an underlying organizational framework. Thus, the individual species are organized into a taxonomy—all the species of plants, animals, and microbial species are linked systematically through a single tree of descent. Likewise, a central goal of personality psychology is to formulate a comprehensive taxonomy of all important traits. This chapter describes how personality psychologists have struggled with these three fundamental questions of trait psychology.

What Is a Trait? Two Basic Formulations

When you describe someone as *impulsive, unreliable,* and *lazy,* what specifically are you referring to? Personality psychologists differ in their formulations of what these traits mean. Some personality psychologists view these traits as *internal* (or *hidden*) *properties* of persons that *cause* their behavior. Other personality psychologists make no assumptions about causality and simply use these trait terms to *describe* the enduring aspects of a person's behavior.

Traits as Internal Causal Properties

When we say that Dierdre has a *desire* for material things, that Dan has a *need* for stimulation, or that Dominick *wants* power over others, we are referring to something inside of each that causes him or her to act in particular ways. These traits are presumed to be *internal* in the sense that individuals carry their desires, needs, and wants from one situation to the next (e.g., Alston, 1975). Furthermore, these desires and needs are presumed to be *causal* in the sense that they explain the behavior of the individuals who possess them. Dierdre's desire for material things, for example, might cause her to spend a lot of time at the shopping mall, work extra hard to earn more money, and acquire many household possessions. Her internal desire *influences* her external behavior, presumably causing her to act in certain ways.

Psychologists who view traits as internal dispositions do not equate traits with the external behavior in question. This distinction is most easily explained using a food example. Harry may have a strong desire for a large hamburger and fresh french fries. However, because he is trying to lose weight, he refrains from expressing his desire in behavioral terms—he looks at the food hungrily but resists the temptation to eat it. Similarly, Dominick may have a desire to take charge in most social situations, even if he does not always express this desire. For example, some situations may have an already identified leader, such as in a class discussion with his psychology professor. Note that this formulation assumes that we can measure Dominick's need for power independently of measuring Dominick's actual behavioral expressions.

These examples are analogous to that of a glass, which has the trait of being brittle. Even if a particular glass never shatters (i.e., expresses its brittleness), it still possesses the trait of being brittle. In sum, psychologists who view traits as internal dispositions believe that traits can lie dormant in the sense that the *capacities* remain present even when particular behaviors are not actually expressed. Traits—in the sense of internal needs, drives, desires, and so on—are presumed to exist, even in the absence of observable expressions.

The scientific usefulness of viewing traits as causes of behavior lies in ruling out other causes. When we say that Joan goes to lots of parties *because* she is extraverted, we are implicitly ruling out other potential reasons for her behavior (e.g., that she might be going to a lot of parties simply because her boyfriend drags her to them, rather than because she herself is extraverted). The formulation of traits as internal causal properties differs radically from an alternative formulation that considers traits as merely descriptive summaries of actual behavior.

Traits as Purely Descriptive Summaries

Proponents of this alternative formulation define traits simply as *descriptive summaries* of attributes of persons; they make no assumptions about internality or causality (Hampshire, 1953). Consider an example in which we ascribe the trait of *jealousy* to a young man named George. According to the descriptive summary viewpoint, this trait attribution merely describes George's *expressed behavior*. For example, George might glare at other men who talk to his girlfriend at a party, insist that she wear his ring, and require her to spend all of her free time with him. The trait of jealousy, in this case, accurately *summarizes* the general trend in George's expressed behavior, yet no assumptions are made about what causes George's behavior.

Although it is possible that George's jealousy stems from an internal cause, perhaps deeply rooted feelings of insecurity, his jealousy might instead be due to *social situations*. George's expressions of jealousy might be caused by the fact that other men are flirting with his girlfriend and she is responding to them (a situational cause), rather than because George is intrinsically a jealous person. The important point is that those who view traits as descriptive summaries do not prejudge the cause of someone's behavior. They merely use traits to describe, in summary fashion, the trend in a person's behavior. Personality psychologists of this persuasion (e.g., Saucier &

Goldberg, 1998; Wiggins, 1979) argue that we must first identify and describe the important individual differences among people, then subsequently develop causal theories to explain them.

The Act Frequency Formulation of Traits—An Illustration of the Descriptive Summary Formulation

A number of psychologists who endorse the descriptive summary formulation of traits have explored the implications of this formulation in a program of research called the "act frequency approach" (Amelang, Herboth, & Oefner, 1991; Angleiter, Buss, & Demtroder, 1990; Buss & Craik, 1983; Romero et al., 1994).

The act frequency approach starts with the notion that *traits are categories of acts*. Just as the category "birds" has specific birds as members of the category (e.g., robins, sparrows), trait categories such as "dominance" or "impulsivity" have specific acts as members. The category of dominance, for example, might include specific acts such as the following:

He issued orders that got the group organized.
She managed to control the outcome of the meeting without the others being aware of it.
He assigned roles and got the game going.
She decided which programs they would watch on TV.

Dominance is thus a trait category with these and hundreds of other acts as members. A dominant person, according to the act frequency approach, is someone who performs a large number of dominant acts relative to other persons. For example, if we were to videotape Mary and a dozen of her peers over a period of three months and then count up how many times each person performed dominant acts, Mary would be considered dominant if she performed more dominant acts than her peers. Thus, in the act frequency formulation, a trait such as dominance is a descriptive summary of the general trend in a person's behavior—a trend that consists of performing a large number of acts within a category relative to other persons.

Act Frequency Research Program

The act frequency approach to traits involves three key elements: act nomination, prototypicality judgment, and the recording of act performance.

Act Nomination

Act nomination is a procedure designed to identify which acts belong in which trait categories. Consider the category of impulsive. Now think of someone you know who is impulsive. Then list the specific acts or behaviors this person has performed that exemplify his or her impulsivity. You might say, "He decided to go out with friends at the spur of the moment, even though he had to study," "He immediately accepted the dare to do something dangerous, without thinking about the consequences," or "He blurted out his anger before he had time to reflect on the situation." Through act nomination procedures such as this one, researchers can identify hundreds of acts belonging to various trait categories.

Prototypicality Judgment

The second step in the research process involves identifying which acts are most central to, or *prototypical* of, each trait category. Consider the category of "bird." When you think of this category, which birds come to your mind first? Most people think of birds such as *robins* and *sparrows*. They do not think of *turkeys* and *penguins*. Even though penguins and turkeys are members of the category "bird," robins and sparrows are considered to be more prototypical of the category—they are better examples, more central to what most people mean by "bird" (Rosch, 1975).

In a similar way, acts within trait categories differ in their prototypicality of the trait. Panels of raters judge how prototypical each act is as an example of a particular concept. For example, raters find the acts *She controlled the outcome of the meeting without the others being aware of it* and *She took charge after the accident* to be more prototypically dominant than the act *She deliberately arrived late for the meeting*.

Recording of Act Performance

The third and final step in the research program consists of securing information on the actual performance of individuals in their daily lives. As you might imagine, obtaining information about a person's daily conduct is difficult. Most researchers have used self-reports of act performance or reports from close friends or spouses. As shown in Table 3.1 you can provide your own responses to this measure.

Table 3.1 Self-Report of Impulsive Acts

Instructions. Following is a list of acts. Read each act and circle the response that most accurately indicates how often you typically perform each act. Circle "0" if you never perform the act; circle "1" if you occasionally perform the act; circle "2" if you perform the act with moderate frequency; and circle "3" if you perform the act very frequently.

Circle	Acts
0 1 2 3	1. I say what I think without thinking about the possible consequences.
0 1 2 3	2. I react quickly and aggressively to verbal threats.
0 1 2 3	3. I bought a new car without giving it much thought.
0 1 2 3	4. I decide to live with somebody without due reflection.
0 1 2 3	5. I make hasty decisions.
0 1 2 3	6. I speak without thinking about what I am going to say.
0 1 2 3	7. I am led by the feelings of the moment.
0 1 2 3	8. I spend my money on whatever strikes my fancy.
0 1 2 3	9. Having made definite plans, I suddenly change them and do something totally different.
0 1 2 3	10. I do the first thing that comes into my head.

Source: Adapted from Romero et al. (1994), from among the most prototypical impulsive acts. According to the act frequency approach, you would be judged to be "impulsive" if you performed a high overall frequency of these impulsive acts, relative to your peer group.

Critique of the Act Frequency Formulation

The formulation of traits as purely descriptive summaries, as in the act frequency approach, has been criticized on several grounds (see, Angleitner & Demtroder, 1988; Block, 1989). Most of the criticisms have been aimed at the technical implementation of the approach. For example, the act frequency approach does not specify how much context should be included in the description of a trait-relevant act. Consider the following dominant act: *He insisted that the others go to his favorite restaurant.* To understand this act as a dominant act, we might need to know (1) the relationships among the people involved, (2) the occasion for going out to eat, (3) the history of restaurant going for these people, and (4) who is paying for the dinner. How much context is needed to identify the act as a dominant act?

Another criticism of the approach is that it seems applicable to overt actions, but what about *failures* to act and covert acts that are not directly observable? For example, a person may be very courageous, but we will never know this under ordinary life circumstances in which people have no need to display courageousness. Still another challenge to the approach is whether it can successfully capture complex traits, such as the tendency of narcissistic individuals to oscillate between high and low self-esteem (Raskin & Terry, 1988).

Despite these limitations, the act frequency approach has produced some noteworthy accomplishments. It has been especially helpful in making explicit the *behavioral phenomena* to which most trait terms refer—after all, the primary way that we know about traits is through their expressions in actual behavior. As noted by several prominent personality researchers, "Behavioral acts constitute the building blocks of interpersonal perception and the basis for inferences about personality traits" (Gosling, John, Craik, & Robins, 1998). Thus, the study of behavioral manifestations of personality remains an essential and, indeed, indispensable part of the agenda for the field, despite the difficulties entailed by their study. The act frequency approach is also helpful in identifying behavioral regularities—phenomena that must be explained by any comprehensive personality theory. And it has been helpful in exploring the *meaning* of some traits that have proven difficult to study, such as impulsivity (Romero et al., 1994) and creativity (Amelang et al., 1991).

Explorations of the act frequency approach have helped to identify the domains in which it provides insight into personality. One study, for example, examined the relationship between self-reported act performance and observer codings of the individual's actual behavior (Gosling et al., 1998). Some acts showed high levels of self-observer agreement, such as "Told a joke to lighten a tense moment," "Made a humorous remark," "Took charge of things at the meeting." Acts that reflect the traits of extraversion and conscientiousness tend to show high levels of self-observer agreement. Acts that reflect the trait of agreeableness, on the other hand, tend to show lower levels of self-observer agreement. As a general rule, the more observable the actions, the higher the agreement between self-report and observer codings.

Other research has demonstrated that the act frequency approach can be used to predict important outcomes in everyday life such as job success, salary, and how rapidly individuals are promoted within business organizations (Kyl-Heku & Buss, 1996; Lund et al., 2006). Others have used the act frequency approach to explore topics such as *acts of deception* in social interaction (Tooke & Camire, 1991) and acts of *"mate guarding"* that predict violence in dating and marital relationships (Shackelford et al., 2005).

In sum, there are two major formulations of traits. The first considers traits to be internal causal properties of persons that affect overt behavior. The second considers traits to be descriptive summaries of overt behavior, with the causes of those trends in conduct to be determined subsequently. However traits are formulated, all personality psychologists must confront the next vexing challenge—identifying the most important traits.

Identification of the Most Important Traits

Three fundamental approaches have been used to identify important traits. The first is the **lexical approach.** According to this approach, all traits listed and defined in the dictionary form the basis of the natural way of describing differences between people (Allport & Odbert, 1936). Thus, the logical starting point for the lexical strategy is the natural language. The second method of identifying important traits is the **statistical approach.** This approach uses factor analysis, or similar statistical procedures, to identify major personality traits. The third method is the **theoretical approach.** With this method, researchers rely on theories to identify important traits. As we discuss these approaches, keep in mind that some personality researchers use them in combinations.

Lexical Approach

The lexical approach to identifying important personality traits starts with the **lexical hypothesis:** *all important individual differences have become encoded within the natural language*. Over time, the differences among people that are important are noticed, and words are invented to talk about those differences. People invent words such as *dominant, creative, reliable, cooperative, hot-tempered,* or *self-centered,* to describe these differences. People find these trait terms helpful in describing people and for communicating information about them. And, so, usage of these trait terms spreads and becomes common among the group. The trait terms that are not useful to people in describing and communicating with others get banished to the scrap heap of terms that fail to become encoded within the natural language.

Consider the many words that baseball players have invented over the years for different kinds of pitches. There are fast balls, curve balls, sliders, knuckle balls, and so on. Words for all these types of pitches have been invented, and have been found useful by others, so they have become encoded within the baseball lexicon. By analogy, the differences among people that have been especially important in navigating the social environment have been noticed, have been talked about, and have become part of the natural language (Goldberg, 1981).

If we consider the English language, we find an abundance of trait terms codified as adjectives, such as *manipulative, arrogant, slothful,* and *warm.* A perusal of the dictionary yields about 2,800 trait-descriptive adjectives (Norman, 1967). The key implication of this finding, according to the lexical approach, is clear: trait terms are extraordinarily important for people in communicating with others.

The lexical approach yields two clear criteria for identifying important traits—**synonym frequency** and **cross-cultural universality.** The criterion of synonym frequency means that, if an attribute has not merely one or two trait adjectives to describe it but, rather, six, eight, or nine words, then it is a more important dimension of individual difference. "The more important is such an attribute, the more synonyms and subtly distinctive facets of the attribute will be found within any one language" (Saucier & Goldberg, 1996, p. 24). Consider individual differences in *dominance*. There are many terms to describe this dimension: *dominant, bossy, assertive, powerful, pushy, forceful, leaderlike, domineering, influential, ascendant, authoritative,* and *arrogant*. The prevalence of so many synonyms, with each term conveying a subtle but importantly nuanced difference in dominance, suggests not only that dominance is an important difference but also that different shades of dominance are important in social communication. Thus, synonym frequency provides one criterion of importance.

Cross-cultural universality is the second key criterion of importance within the lexical approach: "the more important is an individual difference in human transactions, the more languages will have a term for it" (Goldberg, 1981, p. 142). Furthermore, "the most important phenotypic [observable] personality attributes should have a corresponding term in virtually every language" (Saucier & Goldberg, 1996, p. 23). The logic is that, if a trait is sufficiently important in all cultures that its members have codified terms to describe the trait, then the trait must be universally important in human affairs. In contrast, if a trait term exists in only one or a few languages, but is entirely missing from most, then it may be of only local relevance. Such a term is unlikely to be a candidate for a universal taxonomy of personality traits (McCrae & Costa, 1997).

The Yanomamö Indians of Venezuela, for example, have the words *unokai* and "*non-unokai*," which mean, roughly, "a man who has achieved manhood by the killing of another man" (*unokai*) and "a man who has not achieved manhood status by the killing of another man" (*non-unokai*) (Chagnon, 1983). In Yanomamö culture, this individual difference is of critical importance, for the unokai have elevated status, are widely feared, have more wives, and are looked to for leadership. In mainstream American culture, by contrast, there is the generic *killer,* but there is no single word that has the specific connotations of *unokai*. Thus, although this individual difference is of critical importance to the Yanomamö, it is unlikely to be a candidate for a universal taxonomy of personality traits.

According to the cross-cultural criterion of the lexical approach, the critical task for researchers is to examine the natural language and trait usage across cultures. The lexical approach faces some formidable problems. To start with, there are many trait terms that are ambiguous or metaphorical, such as *elliptical, snaky,* and *stygian*. There are also many terms that are obscure or difficult, such as *clavering* (inclined to gossip or idle talk), *davering, gnathonic,* and *theromorphic* (Saucier & Goldberg, 1998). These terms must be identified and excluded because most people don't know what they mean.

Another problem with the lexical strategy concerns the fact that personality is conveyed through different parts of speech, including adjectives, nouns, and adverbs. For example, there are also dozens of noun terms encoded within the English language to describe someone who is not too smart: *birdbrain, blockhead, bonehead, chucklehead, cretin, deadhead, dimwit, dolt, dope, dullard, dumbbell, dummy, dunce, jughead, lunkhead, moron, peabrain, pinhead, softhead, thickhead,* and *woodenhead*. Although they have not been explored much, personality nouns remain a viable source of potential information about important dimensions of individual differences. Nonetheless, lexical researchers have justifiably focused primarily on adjectives because most personality descriptions are encoded as trait-adjectives.

The lexical strategy has proven to be a remarkably generative starting point for identifying important individual differences (Ashton & Lee, 2005). To discard this information "would require us needlessly to separate ourselves from the vast sources of knowledge gained in the course of human history" (Kelley, 1992, p. 22). A reasonable position is that the lexical approach represents a good starting point for identifying important individual differences but should not be used exclusively. Two other commonly used approaches are the statistical and theoretical strategies, which we will examine next.

Statistical Approach

The statistical approach to identifying important traits starts with a pool of personality items. These can be trait words, such as those discovered through the lexical approach, or a series of questions about behavior, experience, or emotion. In fact, most researchers using the lexical approach turn to the statistical approach to distill self-ratings of trait adjectives into basic categories of personality traits. However, the starting point can also be self-ratings on a large collection of personality-relevant sentences (e.g., *I find that I am easily able to persuade people to my point of view*). Once a large and diverse pool of adjectives, items, or sentences has been assembled, the statistical approach is applied. It consists of having a large number of people rate themselves on the items, then using a statistical procedure to identify groups or clusters of items. The goal of the statistical approach is to identify the major dimensions, or "coordinates," of the personality map, much the way latitude and longitude provide the coordinates of the map of the earth.

The most commonly used statistical procedure to identify these dimensions is **factor analysis.** Although the complex mathematical procedures underlying factor analysis are beyond the scope of this text, the essential logic of this approach can be conveyed simply. Factor analysis essentially identifies groups of items that *covary* (i.e., go together) but tend not to covary with other groups of items. Consider, as a spatial metaphor, the office locations of physicists, psychologists, and sociologists on your campus. Although these may be spread out, in general the offices of the psychologists tend to be in closer proximity to one another than they are to the offices of the physicists or sociologists. And the physicists are closer to one another than they are to the sociologists or psychologists. Thus, a factor analysis might reveal three clusters of professors.

Similarly, a major advantage of identifying clusters of personality items that covary is that it provides a means for determining which personality variables have some common property. Factor analysis can also be useful in reducing the large array of diverse personality traits into a smaller and more useful set of underlying factors. It provides a means for organizing the thousands of personality traits.

Let's examine how factor analysis works in an example shown in Table 3.2. This table summarizes the data obtained from a sample of 1,210 subjects who were asked to rate themselves on a series of trait-descriptive adjectives. Among the adjectives rated were *humorous, amusing, popular, hard-working, productive, determined, imaginative, original,* and *inventive.*

The numbers in Table 3.2 are called **factor loadings**—which are indexes of how much of the variation in an item is "explained" by the factor. Factor loadings indicate the degree to which the item correlates with, or "loads on," the underlying factor. In this example, three clear factors emerge. The first is an "extraversion" factor, with high loadings on *humorous, amusing,* and *popular*. The second is an "ambition" factor, with high loadings on *hard-working, productive,* and *determined.* The third is a "creativity" factor, with high loadings on *imaginative, inventive,* and *original.* Factor analysis, in this case, is quite useful in identifying three distinct groups of trait terms that covary with each other but are relatively independent of (tend not to covary with) other groups. Without this statistical procedure, a researcher might be forced to

Table 3.2 A Sample Factor Analysis of Personality Adjective Ratings

Adjective Rating	Factor 1 (Extraversion)	Factor 2 (Ambition)	Factor 3 (Creativity)
Humorous	**.66**	.06	.19
Amusing	**.65**	.23	.02
Popular	**.57**	.13	.22
Hard-working	.05	**.63**	.01
Productive	.04	**.52**	.19
Determined	.23	**.52**	.08
Imaginative	.01	.09	**.62**
Original	.13	.05	**.53**
Inventive	.06	.26	**.47**

Note: The numbers refer to factor loadings, which indicate the degree to which an item correlates with the underlying factor (see text).

Source: Adapted from Matthews & Oddy (1993).

consider the nine traits as all separate from each other. Factor analysis tells us that *hard-working, productive,* and *determined* all covary sufficiently that they can be considered a single trait, rather than three separate traits.

A cautionary note should be made about using factor analysis and the statistical approach in general in identifying important traits: *you get out of it only what you put into it.* In other words, if an important personality trait happens to be left out of a particular factor analysis, it will not show up in the subsequent results. Thus, it is critical that researchers pay close attention to their initial selection of items to be included in a study.

Factor analysis and similar statistical procedures have been extremely valuable to personality researchers. Perhaps their most important contribution has been the ability to reduce a large, cumbersome array of diverse personality adjectives or items into a smaller, more meaningful set of broad, basic factors.

Theoretical Approach

The theoretical approach to identifying important dimensions of individual differences, as the name implies, starts with a theory that determines which variables are important. In contrast to the statistical strategy, which can be described as atheoretical in the sense that there is no prejudgment about which variables are important, the theoretical strategy dictates in a highly specific manner which variables are important to measure.

To a Freudian, for example, it is critical to measure "the oral personality" and "the anal personality," because these represent important, theory-driven constructs. Or, to a self-actualization theorist, such as Maslow (1968), it is critical to measure individual differences in the degree to which people are motivated to self-actualize (see Williams & Page, 1989, for one such measure). The theory, in short, strictly determines which variables are important.

As an example of the theoretical strategy, consider the theory of **sociosexual orientation,** developed by psychologists Jeff Simpson and Steve Gangestad (1991). According to the theory, men and women will pursue one of two alternative sexual relationship strategies. The first entails seeking a single committed relationship characterized by monogamy and tremendous investment in children. The second sexual strategy is characterized by a greater degree of promiscuity, more partner switching, and less investment in children. (When applied to men, one easy way to remember these two strategies is to label them as "dads" and "cads.") Because the theory of sociosexual orientation dictates that the mating strategy one pursues is a critical individual difference, Gangestad and Simpson have developed a measure of sociosexual orientation (see the Exercise following).

Exercise

INSTRUCTIONS: Please answer all of the following questions honestly. For the questions dealing with behavior, *write* your answers in the blank spaces provided. For the questions dealing with thoughts and attitudes, *circle* the appropriate number on the scales provided.

1. **With how many different partners have you had sex (sexual intercourse) within the past year? ____________________**
2. **How many different partners do you foresee yourself having sex with during the next five years? (Please give a *specific, realistic* estimate.)**

   ____
3. **With how many different partners have you had sex on *one and only one* occasion? ____________________**
4. **How often do you fantasize about having sex with someone other than your current partner? (circle one).**
   1. **never**
   2. **once every two or three months**
   3. **once a month**
   4. **once every two weeks**
   5. **once a week**
   6. **a few times a week**
   7. **nearly every day**
   8. **at least once a day**
5. **Sex without love is OK.**

   1 2 3 4 5 6 7 8 9

   I strongly disagree — I strongly agree
6. **I can imagine myself being comfortable and enjoying "casual" sex with different partners.**

   1 2 3 4 5 6 7 8 9

   I strongly disagree — I strongly agree
7. **I would have to be closely attached to someone (both emotionally and psychologically) before I could feel comfortable and fully enjoy having sex with him or her.**

   1 2 3 4 5 6 7 8 9

   I strongly disagree — I strongly agree

Source: From Simpson and Gangestad (1991).

Evaluating the Approaches for Identifying Important Traits

In sum, the theoretical approach lets the theory determine which dimensions of individual differences are important. Like all approaches, the theoretical approach has strengths and limitations. Its strengths coincide with the strengths of the theory. If we have a powerful theory that tells us which variables are important, then it saves us from wandering aimlessly, like a sailor without a map or compass. A theory charts the course to take. At the same time, its weaknesses coincide with the weaknesses of the theory. To the extent that the theory contains gaps and imprecision, the subsequent identification of important individual differences will reflect omissions and distortions.

The current state of the field of personality trait psychology is best characterized as "letting a thousand flowers bloom." Some researchers start with a theory and let their measurement of individual differences follow from that theory. Others believe that factor analysis is the only sensible way to identify important individual differences. Still other researchers believe that the lexical strategy, by capitalizing on the collective wisdom of people over the ages, is the best method of ensuring that important individual differences are captured.

In practice, many personality researchers use a combination of the three strategies. Norman (1963) and Goldberg (1990), for example, started with the lexical strategy to identify their first set of variables for inclusion. They then applied factor analysis to this initial selection of traits in order to reduce the set to a smaller, more manageable number (five). This solved two problems that are central to the science of personality (Saucier & Goldberg, 1996): the problem of identifying the domains of individual differences and the problem of figuring out a method for describing the order or structure that exists among the individual differences identified. The lexical strategy can be used to sample trait terms, and then factor analysis supplies a powerful statistical approach to providing structure and order to those trait terms.

Taxonomies of Personality

Over the past century, dozens of taxonomies of personality traits have been proposed. Many have been merely lists of traits, often based on the intuitions of personality psychologists. As personality psychologist Robert Hogan observed, "the history of personality theory consists of people who assert that their private demons are public afflictions" (Hogan, 1983). Indeed, two editors of a book on personality traits (London & Exner, 1978) expressed despair at the lack of agreement about a taxonomy of traits, so they simply listed the traits alphabetically. Clearly, however, we can develop a firmer basis for organizing personality traits. Thus, the taxonomies of traits presented in the rest of this chapter are not random samplings from the dozens available. Rather, they represent taxonomies that have solid empirical and theoretical justification.

Eysenck's Hierarchical Model of Personality

Of all the taxonomies of personality, the model of Hans Eysenck, born in 1916, is most strongly rooted in biology. Eysenck was raised in Germany at the time when Hitler was rising to power. Eysenck showed an intense dislike for the Nazi regime, so at age 18 he migrated to England. Although intending to study physics, Eysenck lacked the needed prerequisites, so almost by chance he began to study psychology at the

University of London. He received his Ph.D. in 1940 and after World War II became director of the psychology department at the Maudsley Hospital's new Institute of Psychiatry in London. Eysenck's subsequent productivity was enormous, with more than 40 books and 700 articles to his name. Hans Eysenck was the most cited living psychologist until he died in 1998.

Hans Eysenck at his London office. Photo by Randy J. Larsen, 1987.

Eysenck developed a model of personality based on traits that he believed were highly heritable (see Chapter 6) and had a likely psychophysiological foundation. The three main traits that met these criteria, according to Eysenck, were *extraversion–introversion* (E), *neuroticism–emotional stability* (N), and *psychoticism* (P). Together, they can be easily remembered by the acronym PEN.

Description

Let us begin by describing these three broad traits. Eysenck conceptualizes each of them as sitting at the top of its own hierarchy, as shown in Figure 3.1. *Extraversion,* for example, subsumes a large number of narrow traits—sociable, active, lively, venturesome, dominant, and so forth. These narrow traits are all subsumed by the broader trait of extraversion because they all covary sufficiently with each other to load on the same large factor. Extraverts typically like parties, have many friends, and seem to require having people around them to talk to (Eysenck & Eysenck, 1975). Many extraverts love playing practical jokes on people. They also display a carefree and easy manner. They tend also to have a high activity level.

Introverts, in contrast, like to spend more time alone. They prefer quiet time and pursuits such as reading. Introverts are sometimes seen as aloof and distant, but they often have a small number of intimate friends with whom they share confidences. Introverts tend to be more serious than extraverts and to prefer a more moderate pace. They tend to be well organized, and they prefer a routine, predictable lifestyle (Larsen & Kasimatis, 1990).

"You should get out more."

Introverts prefer to spend more time alone than extraverts.

Source: By Richard Jolley. Used by permission of Cartoonstock, Ltd.

(a) The hierarchical structure of psychoticism (P).

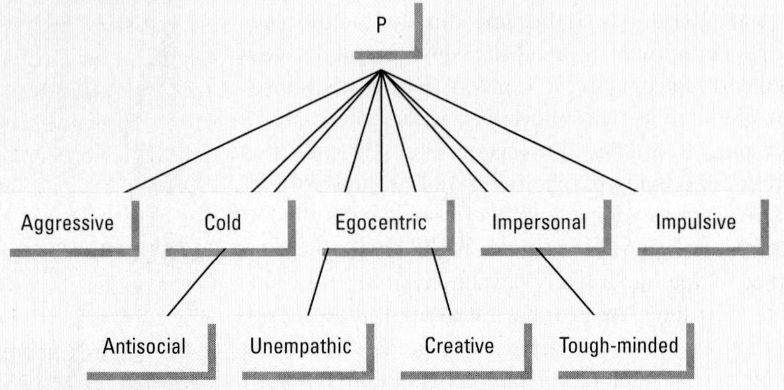

(b) The hierarchical structure of extraversion–introversion (E).

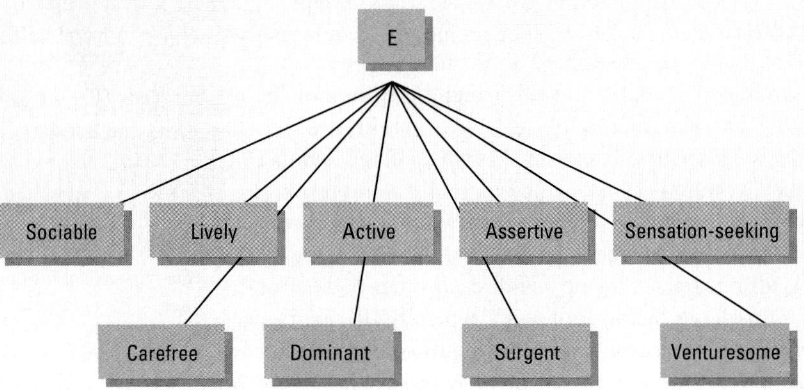

(c) The hierarchical structure of neuroticism (N).

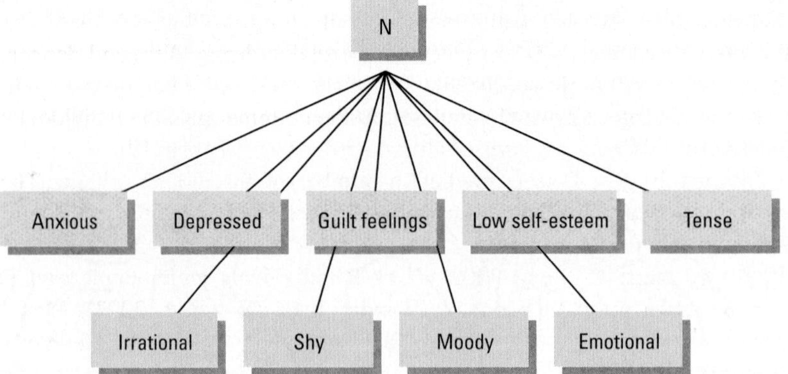

Figure 3.1

Eysenck's hierarchical structure of major personality traits. Each "super-trait" (P, E, and N) occupies the highest level in the hierarchy, representing broad personality traits. Each of these broad traits subsumes more narrower traits in the hierarchy. (a) The hierarchical structure of psychoticism (P); (b) the hierarchical structure of extraversion–introversion (E); (c) the hierarchical structure of neuroticism–emotional stability (N).

The trait of *neuroticism* (N) consists of a cluster of more specific traits, including anxious, irritable, guilty, lacking self-esteem, tense, shy, and moody. Conceptually, narrow traits such as anxious and irritable might be viewed as very different from each other. Empirically, however, men and women who feel anxious also tend to get irritated. Thus, factor analysis has proven to be a valuable tool in showing that these two narrow traits are actually linked together, tending to co-occur in people.

The typical high scorer on neuroticism (N) tends to be a worrier. Frequently anxious and depressed, the high-N scorer has trouble sleeping and experiences a wide array of psychosomatic symptoms. Indeed, a national study of 5,847 individuals found that those high on neuroticism tend to be especially prone to the disorders of depression and anxiety (Weinstock & Whisman, 2006). One of the hallmarks of the high-N scorer is overreactivity on the negative emotions. That is, the high-N scorer experiences a greater degree of emotional arousal than the low-N scorer in response to the normal stresses and strains of everyday life. He or she also has more trouble returning to an even keel after such an emotionally arousing event. The low-N scorer, on the other hand, is emotionally stable, even-tempered, calm, and slower to react to stressful events; moreover, such an individual returns to his or her normal self quickly after an upsetting event.

The third large trait in Eysenck's taxonomy is *psychoticism* (P). As shown in Figure 3.1, P consists of the constellation of narrower traits that includes aggressive, egocentric, creative, impulsive, lacking empathy, and antisocial. Factor analysis proves valuable in grouping together narrower traits. Factor analyses show, for example, that impulsivity and lack of empathy tend to co-occur in individuals. That is, people who tend to act without thinking (impulsivity) also tend to lack the ability to see situations from other people's perspectives (lack of empathy).

The high-P scorer is typically a solitary individual, often described by others as a "loner." Because he or she lacks empathy, he or she thus may be cruel or inhumane (men tend to score twice as high as women on P). Often, such people have a history of cruelty to animals. The high-P scorer may laugh, for example, when a dog gets hit by a car or when someone accidentally gets hurt. The high-P scorer shows insensitivity to the pain and suffering of others, including that of his or her own kin. He or she is aggressive, both verbally and physically, even with loved ones. The high-P scorer has a penchant for the strange and unusual and may disregard danger entirely in pursuit of novelty. He or she likes to make fools of other people and is often described as having antisocial tendencies. In the extreme case, the individual may display symptoms of antisocial personality disorder (see Chapter 19).

Empirically, the P-scale predicts a number of fascinating criteria. Those who score high on P tend to show a strong preference for violent films and rate violent scenes from films more enjoyable and even more comical than those who score low on P (Bruggemann & Barry, 2002). High-P individuals prefer unpleasant paintings and photographs more than do low-P individuals (Rawling, 2003). Men, but not women, who score high on Machiavellianism (which is highly correlated with P) endorse promiscuous and hostile sexual attitudes—they are more likely than low scorers to divulge sexual secrets to third parties, pretend to be in love when they are not in love, ply potential sex partners with alcoholic drinks, and even report trying to force others into sex acts (McHoskey, 2001). Those who are low in P tend to be more deeply religious, whereas high-P scorers tend to be somewhat cynical about religion (Saroglou, 2002). Finally, high-P scorers are predisposed to getting into severe and life-threatening events, such as violence and criminal activity (Pickering, Farmer, Harris, Redman, Mahmood, Sadler, & McGuffin, 2003).

As you might imagine, the labels Eysenck has given to these super-traits, especially P, have generated some controversy. Indeed, some suggest that more accurate and appropriate labels for psychoticism might be "antisocial personality" and "psychopathic personality." Regardless of the label, P has emerged as an important trait in normal-range personality research.

Let's look more closely now at two aspects of Eysenck's system that warrant further comment—its hierarchical nature and its biological underpinnings.

Hierarchical Structure of Eysenck's System

Figure 3.1 shows the levels in Eysenck's hierarchical model—with each super-trait at the top and narrower traits at the second level. Subsumed by each narrow trait, however, is a third level—that of *habitual acts*. For example, one habitual act subsumed by sociable might be talking on the telephone; another might be taking frequent coffee breaks to socialize with other students. Narrow traits subsume a variety of habitual acts.

At the very lowest level in the hierarchy are *specific acts* (e.g., *I talked on the telephone with my friend* and *I took a coffee break to chat at 10:30 A.M.*). If enough specific acts are repeated frequently, they become habitual acts at the third level. Clusters of habitual acts become narrow traits at the second level. And clusters of narrow traits become super-traits at the tops of the hierarchy. This hierarchy has the advantage of locating each specific personality-relevant act within a precise nested system. Thus, the fourth-level act *I danced wildly at the party* can be described as extraverted at the highest level, sociable at the second level, and part of a regular habit of party-going behavior at the third level.

Biological Underpinnings

There are two aspects of the biological underpinnings of Eysenck's personality system that are critical to its understanding—*heritability* and *identifiable physiological substrate*. For Eysenck a key criterion for a "basic" dimension of personality is that it has reasonably high heritability. The behavioral genetic evidence confirms that all three super-traits in Eysenck's taxonomy—P, E, and N—do have moderate heritabilities, although this is also true of many personality traits (see Chapter 6 for more discussion of heritability of personality).

The second biological criterion is that basic personality traits should have an identifiable physiological substrate—that is, that one can identify properties in the brain and central nervous system that correspond to the traits and are presumed to be part of the causal chain that produces those traits. In Eysenck's formulation, extraversion is supposed to be linked with central nervous system arousal or reactivity. Eysenck predicted that introverts would be more easily aroused (and more autonomically reactive) than extraverts (see Chapter 7). In contrast, he proposed that neuroticism was linked with the degree of *lability* (changeability) of the autonomic nervous system. Finally, high-P scorers were predicted to be high in testosterone levels and low in levels of MAO, a neurotransmitter inhibitor.

In sum, Eysenck's personality taxonomy has many distinct features. It is hierarchical, starting with broad traits, which subsume narrower traits, which in turn subsume specific actions. The broad traits within the system have been shown to be moderately heritable. And Eysenck has attempted to link these traits with physiological functioning—adding an important level of analysis not included in most personality theories.

Despite these admirable qualities, Eysenck's personality taxonomy has several limitations. One is that many other personality traits also show moderate heritability, not just extraversion, neuroticism, and psychoticism. A second limitation is that

Eysenck may have missed some important traits in his taxonomy—a point argued by other personality psychologists, such as Raymond B. Cattell, and more recently by authors such as Lewis Goldberg, Paul Costa, and Robert McCrae. Since he was a contemporary of Eysenck's, we'll turn first to a discussion of Cattell's taxonomy.

Cattell's Taxonomy: The 16 Personality Factor System

Cattell was born in England in 1905. A precocious student, he entered the University of London at age 16, where he majored in chemistry. He pursued graduate study in psychology to gain an understanding of the social problems of the times. During his graduate education, Cattell worked closely with Charles Spearman, the inventor of factor analysis. Cattell viewed factor analysis as a powerful new tool for developing an objective, scientifically derived taxonomy of personality. He devoted much of his career to developing and applying factor analytic techniques to understanding personality.

Cattell came to the United States in 1937 to become the research associate of Edward Thorndike (a famous psychologist) at Columbia University in New York. Cattell retired from University of Illinois in 1973, moved to Hawaii, and continued to write books and articles. Cattell, similar to Eysenck in many ways, also died in 1998.

Early in his career, Cattell established as one of his goals the identification and measurement of the basic units of personality. He took as an example the biochemists who were, at that time, discovering the basic vitamins. Cattell followed vitamin researchers by naming with letters the personality factors he discovered. Just as the biochemists named the first vitamin vitamin A, the second vitamin B, and so on, Cattell named the personality factors A, B, and so forth in the order in which he was convinced of their existence.

Raymond Cattell produced one of the most extensive taxonomies of personality traits.

Cattell believed that true factors of personality should be found across different types of data, such as self-reports (S-data) and laboratory tests (T-data) (see Chapter 2). In contrast to Eysenck, who developed one of the smallest taxonomies of personality, as judged by the number of factors (3), Cattell's taxonomy of 16 is among the largest in the number of factors identified as basic traits. Much research has been conducted on the personality profiles of persons in various occupational groups, such as police officers, research scientists, social workers, and janitors. Descriptions of the 16 PF (personality factors) are presented in Table 3.3 and include information about occupational groups that score high or low on those scales.

Cattell, like Eysenck, published an extensive volume of work on personality, including over 50 books and 500 articles and chapters (e.g., Cattell, 1967, 1977, 1987). During his most productive period (the mid-1960s), there were times when he published over 1,000 pages a year. Cattell can be credited with developing a strong empirical strategy for identifying the basic dimensions of personality and with stimulating

Table 3.3 The 16 Personality Factor Scales

1. *Factor A: interpersonal warmth.* Warmhearted, personable, easy to get along with, likes being with other people, likes helping others, adapts well to the needs of others rather than has others adapt to his or her needs; this is similar to Eysenck's extraversion.
2. *Factor B: intelligence.* A rough indicator of intellectual functioning or efficiency of processing information.
3. *Factor C: emotional stability.* A high level of emotional resources with which to meet the challenges of daily life, able to work toward goals, not easily distracted, good emotional control, able to "roll with the punches," tolerates stress well; this is similar to Eysenck's neuroticism factor (reverse scored).
4. *Factor E: dominance.* Self-assertive, aggressive, competitive, forceful and direct in relations with others, likes to put own ideas into practice and have things own way; occupational groups scoring high on this dimension include athletes and judges, and low-scoring groups include janitors, farmers, and cooks.
5. *Factor F: impulsivity.* Happy-go-lucky, lively, enthusiastic, enjoys parties, likes to travel, prefers jobs with variety and change; occupational groups scoring high on this dimension include airline attendants and salespersons; adults scoring high on impulsivity tend to leave home at an earlier age and to move more often during their adult lives.
6. *Factor G: conformity.* Persistent, respectful of authority, rigid, conforming, follows group standards, likes rules and order, dislikes novelty and surprises; military cadets score above average, along with airport traffic controllers; university professors, however, tend to be below average on conformity.
7. *Factor H: boldness.* Likes being the center of attention, adventurous, socially bold, outgoing, confident, able to move easily into new social groups, not socially anxious, has no problems with stage fright.
8. *Factor I: sensitivity.* Artistic, insecure, dependent, overprotected, prefers reason to force in getting things done; high scorers are found among groups of employment counselors, artists, and musicians, whereas low scorers are found among engineers.
9. *Factor L: suspiciousness.* Suspecting, jealous, dogmatic, critical, irritable, holds grudges, worries much about what others think of him or her, tends to be critical of others; accountants are one group scoring high on this dimension.
10. *Factor M: imagination.* Sometimes called the "absent-minded professor" factor; unconventional, impractical, unconcerned about everyday matters, forgets trivial things, not usually interested in mechanical activities; high-scoring groups include artists and research scientists; high scorers are more creative than low scorers but also tend to have more automobile accidents.
11. *Factor N: shrewdness.* Polite, diplomatic, reserved, good at managing the impression made on others, socially poised and sophisticated, good control of his or her own behavior; high scorers may appear "stiff" and constrained in their social relations.
12. *Factor O: insecurity.* Tends to worry, feels guilty, moody, has frequent episodes of depression, often feels dejected, sensitive to criticism from others, becomes upset easily, anxious, often lonely, self-deprecating, self-reproaching; extremely low scorers come across as smug, self-satisfied, and overly self-confident; low-scoring persons may not feel bound by the standards of society and may not operate according to accepted social conventions, (i.e., may be somewhat antisocial).
13. *Factor Q1: radicalism.* Liberal attitudes, innovative, analytic, feels that society should throw out traditions, prefers to break with established ways of doing things; high scorers

(continued)

Table 3.3 (continued)

tend to be effective problem solvers in group decision-making studies; however, high scorers, because they tend to be overly critical and verbally aggressive, are not well liked as group leaders.

14. *Factor Q2: self-sufficiency.* Prefers to be alone, dislikes being on committees or involved in group work, shuns support from others; social workers tend to be below average on this dimension; accountants and statisticians tend to be high, with Antarctic explorers among the highest groups ever tested on self-sufficiency.
15. *Factor Q3: self-discipline.* Prefers to be organized, think before talking or acting, is neat, does not like to leave anything to chance; high-scoring persons have strong control over their actions and emotions; airline pilots score high on this dimension.
16. *Factor Q4: tension.* Anxious, frustrated, takes a long time calming down after being upset, irritated by small things, gets angry easily, has trouble sleeping.

Source: Adapted from Krug, 1981.

and shaping the entire trait approach to personality. Nonetheless, Cattell's work, especially the model of 16 factors of personality, has been criticized. Specifically, some personality researchers have failed to replicate the 16 separate factors, and many argue that a smaller number of factors capture the most important ways in which individuals differ.

Circumplex Taxonomies of Personality

People have been fascinated with circles for centuries. There is something elegant about circles. They have no beginning and no end, and they symbolize wholeness and unity. Circles have also fascinated personality psychologists as possible representations of the personality sphere.

In the twentieth century, the two most prominent advocates of circular representations of personality have been Timothy Leary (also known for his LSD experiments at Harvard) and Jerry Wiggins, who formalized the circular model with modern statistical techniques. (Circumplex is simply a fancy name for circle.)

Wiggins (1979) started with the lexical assumption—the idea that all important individual differences are encoded within the natural language. But he went further in his efforts at taxonomy by arguing that trait terms specify different *kinds* of ways in which individuals differ. One kind of individual difference pertains to what people do to and with each other—**interpersonal traits.**

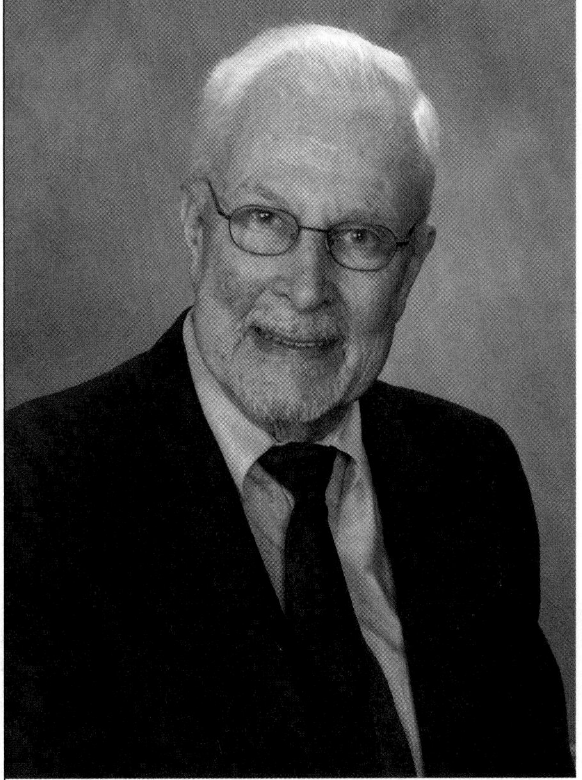

Jerry Wiggins developed measurement scales to assess the traits in the circumplex model.

Other kinds of individual differences are specified by the following types of traits: *temperament* traits, such as nervous, gloomy, sluggish, and excitable; *character* traits, such as moral, principled, and dishonest;

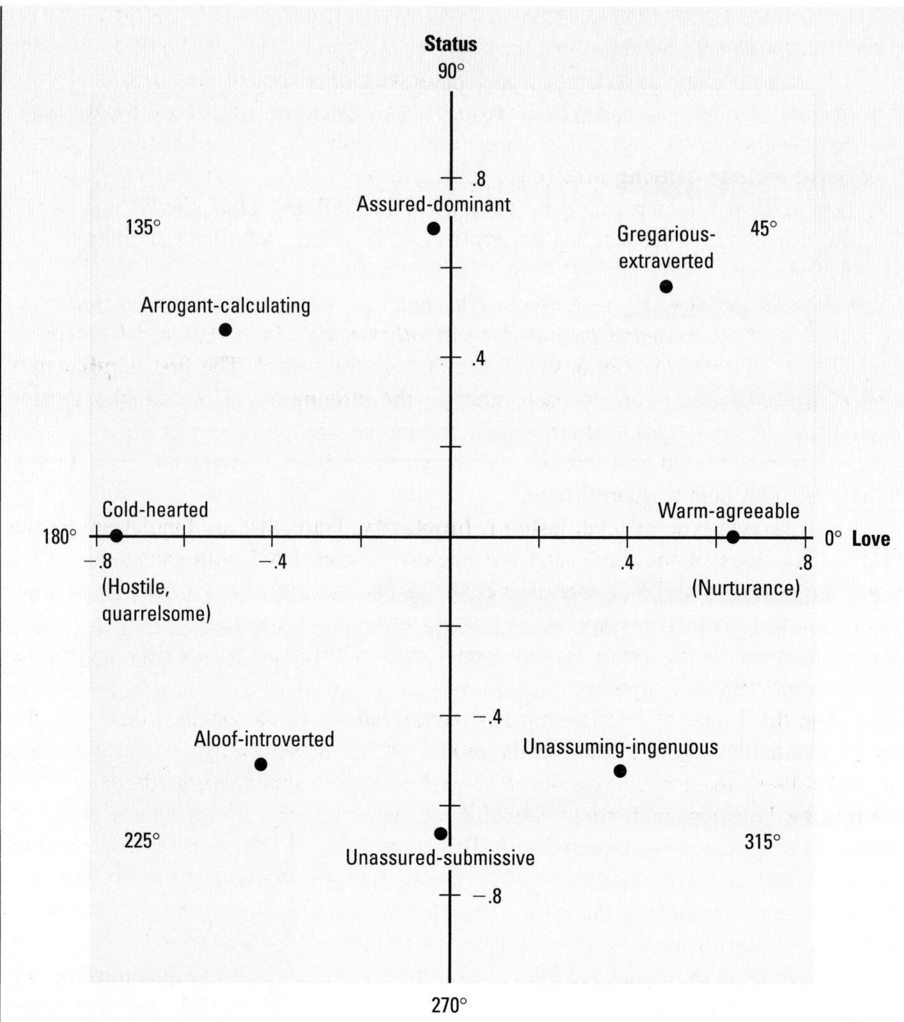

Figure 3.2

The circumplex model of personality.

Source: Adapted from "Circular Reasoning About Interpersonal Behavior" by J. S. Wiggins, 1989, *Journal of Personality & Social Psychology*, 56, p. 297. Copyright 1989 by the American Psychological Association. Reprinted with permission.

material traits, such as miserly and stingy; *attitude* traits, such as pious and spiritual; *mental* traits, such as clever, logical, and perceptive; and *physical* traits, such as healthy and tough.

Because Wiggins was concerned primarily with *interpersonal* traits, he carefully separated these from the other categories of traits. Then, based on the earlier theorizing of Foa and Foa (1974), he defined *interpersonal* as interactions between people involving exchanges. The two resources that define social exchange are *love* and *status:* "interpersonal events may be defined as *dyadic interactions that have relatively clear-cut social (status) and emotional (love) consequences for both participants*" (Wiggins, 1979, p. 398, italics original). Hence, the dimensions of status and love define the two major axes of the Wiggins circumplex, as shown in Figure 3.2.

There are three clear advantages to the Wiggins circumplex. The first is that it provides an *explicit definition* of interpersonal behavior. Thus, it should be possible to locate any transaction in which the resources of status or love are exchanged within a specific area of the circumplex pie. These include not just giving love (e.g., giving a friend a hug) or granting status (e.g., showing respect or honor to a parent). They also include denying love (e.g., yelling at one's boyfriend) and denying status (e.g., dismissing someone as too inconsequential to talk to). Thus, the Wiggins model has the advantage of providing an explicit and precise definition of interpersonal transactions.

The second advantage of Wiggins's model is that the circumplex *specifies the relationships between each trait and every other trait within the model.* There are basically three types of relationships specified by the model. The first is **adjacency**, or how close the traits are to each other in the circumplex. The variables that are adjacent, or next, to each other within the model are positively correlated. Thus, gregarious-extraverted is correlated with warm-agreeable. Arrogant-calculating is correlated with hostile-quarrelsome.

The second type of relationship is **bipolarity.** Traits that are bipolar are located at opposite sides of the circle and are negatively correlated with each other. Thus, dominant is the opposite of submissive, so the two are negatively correlated. Cold is the opposite of warm, so they are negatively correlated. Specifying this bipolarity is useful because nearly every interpersonal trait within the personality sphere has another trait that is its opposite.

The third type of relationship is **orthogonality,** which specifies that traits that are perpendicular to each other on the model (at 90° of separation, or at right angles to each other) are entirely unrelated to each other. In other words, there is a zero correlation between such traits. Dominance, for example, is orthogonal to agreeableness, so the two are uncorrelated. This means that dominance can be expressed in a quarrelsome manner (e.g., *I yelled in order to get my way*) or in an agreeable manner (e.g., *I organized the group in order to get help for my friend*). Similarly, aggression (quarrelsome) can be expressed in an active/dominant manner (e.g., *I used my position of authority to punish my enemies*) or in an unassured/submissive way (e.g., *I gave him the silent treatment when I was upset*). Thus, orthogonality allows one to specify with greater precision the different ways in which traits are expressed in actual behavior.

The third key advantage of the circumplex model is that it *alerts investigators to gaps* in investigations of interpersonal behavior. For example, whereas there have been many studies of dominance and aggression, personality psychologists have paid little attention to traits such as unassuming and calculating. The circumplex model, by providing a map of the interpersonal terrain, directs researchers to these neglected areas of psychological functioning.

In sum, the Wiggins circumplex model provides an elegant map of major individual differences in the social domain. Despite these positive qualities, the circumplex also has some limitations. The most important limitation is that the interpersonal map is limited to two dimensions. Some have argued that other traits, not captured by these two dimensions, also have important interpersonal consequences. The trait of conscientiousness, for example, may be interpersonal in that persons high on this trait are very dependable in their social obligations to friends, mates, and children. Even a trait such as neuroticism or emotional stability may show up most strongly in interpersonal transactions with others (e.g., *He overreacted to a subtle interpersonal slight when the host took too long to acknowledge his presence, and he insisted that he and his partner leave the party*). A more comprehensive taxonomy of personality that includes these dimensions is known as the five-factor model, to which we now turn.

Five-Factor Model

In the past two decades, the taxonomy of personality traits that has received the most attention and support from personality researchers has been the **five-factor model**—variously labeled the five-factor model, the Big Five, and even in a humorous vein The High Five (Costa & McCrae, 1995; Goldberg, 1981; McCrae & John, 1992; Saucier & Goldberg, 1996). The broad traits composing the Big Five have been provisionally named: I. *surgency* or *extraversion,* II. *agreeableness,* III. *conscientiousness,* IV. *emotional stability,* and V. *openness-intellect.* This five-dimensional taxonomy of personality traits has accrued some persuasive advocates (e.g., John, 1990; McCrae & John, 1992; Saucier & Goldberg, 1998; Wiggins, 1996), as well as some strong critics (e.g., Block, 1995b; McAdams, 1992).

The five-factor model was originally based on a combination of the lexical approach and the statistical approach. The lexical approach started in the 1930s, with the pioneering work of Allport and Odbert (1936), who laboriously went through the dictionary and identified some 17,953 trait terms from the English language (which then contained roughly 550,000 separate entries). Allport and Odbert then divided the original set of trait terms into four lists: (1) *stable traits* (e.g., *secure, intelligent*), (2) *temporary states, moods, and activities* (e.g., *agitated, excited*), (3) *social evaluations* (e.g., *charming, irritating*), and (4) *metaphorical, physical, and doubtful terms* (e.g., *prolific, lean*).

The list of terms from the first category, consisting of 4,500 presumably stable traits, was subsequently used by Cattell (1943) as a starting point for his lexical analysis of personality traits. Because of the limited power of computers at the time, however, Cattell could not subject this list to a factor analysis. Instead, he reduced the list to a smaller set of 171 clusters (groups of traits) by eliminating some and lumping together others. He ended up with a smaller set of 35 clusters of personality traits.

Fiske (1949) then took a subset of 22 of Cattell's 35 clusters and discovered, through factor analysis, a five-factor solution. However, this single study of relatively small sample size was hardly a robust foundation for a comprehensive taxonomy of personality traits. In historical treatments of the five-factor model, therefore, Fiske is noted as the first person to discover a version of the five-factor model, but he is not credited with having identified its precise structure.

Tupes and Christal (1961) made the next major contribution to the five-factor taxonomy. They examined the factor structure of the 22 simplified descriptions in eight samples and emerged with the five-factor model: *surgency, agreeableness, conscientiousness, emotional stability,* and *culture*. This factor structure was subsequently replicated by Norman (1963), then by a host of other researchers (e.g., Botwin & Buss, 1989; Goldberg, 1981; Digman & Inouye, 1986; McCrae & Costa, 1985). The key markers that define the Big Five, as determined by Norman (1963), are shown in Table 3.4.

The past 20 years have witnessed an explosion of research on the Big Five. Indeed, the big five taxonomy has achieved a greater degree of consensus than any other trait taxonomy in the history of personality trait psychology. But it has also generated some controversy. We consider three key issues: (1) What is the empirical evidence for the five-factor taxonomy of personality? (2) What is the identity of the

Table 3.4 Norman's Markers for the Big Five

I. Surgency Talkative–silent Sociable–reclusive Adventurous–cautious Open–secretive	**IV. Emotional stability** Calm–anxious Composed–excitable Not hypochondriacal–hypochondriacal Poised–nervous/tense
II. Agreeableness Good-natured–irritable Cooperative–negativistic Mild/gentle–headstrong Not jealous–jealous	**V. Culture** Intellectual–unreflective/narrow Artistic–nonartistic Imaginative–simple/direct Polished/refined–crude/boorish
III. Conscientiousness Responsible–undependable Scrupulous–unscrupulous Persevering–quitting Fussy/tidy–careless	

Source: Norman (1963).

fifth factor? (3) Is the Big Five taxonomy really comprehensive, or are there major trait dimensions that lie beyond the Big Five?

What Is the Empirical Evidence for the Five-Factor Model?

The five-factor model has proven to be astonishingly replicable in studies using English language trait words as items (Goldberg, 1981, 1990; John, 1990). The five factors have been found by more than a dozen researchers using different samples. It has been replicated in every decade for the past half-century. It has been replicated in different languages and in different item formats.

In its modern form, the Big Five taxonomy has been measured in two major ways. One way is based on self-ratings of single-word trait adjectives, such as *talkative, warm, organized, moody*, and *imaginative* (Goldberg, 1990), and one way is based on self-ratings of sentence items, such as "My life is fast-paced" (McCrae & Costa, 1999). We will discuss these in turn.

Lewis R. Goldberg has done the most systematic research on the Big Five using single-word trait adjectives. According to Goldberg (1990), key adjective markers of the Big Five are as follows:

1. Surgency or extraversion: *talkative, extraverted, assertive, forward, outspoken* versus *shy, quiet, introverted, bashful, inhibited.*
2. Agreeableness: *sympathetic, kind, warm, understanding, sincere* versus *unsympathetic, unkind, harsh, cruel.*
3. Conscientiousness: *organized, neat, orderly, practical, prompt, meticulous* versus *disorganized, disorderly, careless, sloppy, impractical.*
4. Emotional stability: *calm, relaxed, stable* versus *moody, anxious, insecure.*
5. Intellect or imagination: *creative, imaginative, intellectual* versus *uncreative, unimaginative, unintellectual.*

In addition to measures of the big five that use single trait words as items, the most widely used measure using a sentence-length item format has been developed by Paul T. Costa and Robert R. McCrae. It's called the NEO-PI-R: the neuroticism-extraversion-openness (NEO) Personality Inventory (PI) Revised (R) (Costa &

McCrae, 1989). Sample items from the NEO-PI-R are neuroticism (N): *I have frequent mood swings;* extraversion (E): *I don't find it easy to take charge of a situation* (reverse scored); openness (O): *I enjoy trying new and foreign foods;* agreeableness (A): *Most people I know like me;* and conscientiousness (C): *I keep my belongings neat and clean.*

Your job is to develop a way to measure the Big Five traits in someone you know, such as a friend, a roommate, or a family member. Read the adjectives in Table 3.4 carefully until you have an understanding of each of the Big Five traits. Then, consider the different sources of personality data described in Chapter 2:

1. **Self-report—typically, asking questions on a questionnaire.**
2. **Observer-report—typically, asking someone who knows the subject to report what the subject is like.**

	Very low	Somewhat low	Average	Somewhat high	Very high
Surgency					
Agreeableness					
Conscientiousness					
Emotional stability					
Intellect-openness (culture)					

3. **Test data—typically, objective tasks, situations, or physiological recordings that get at manifestations of the trait in question.**
4. **Life-outcome data—aspects of the person's life that may reveal a trait, such as introverted people selecting careers in which there is little contact with others.**

Your job is to assess your target person on each of the Big Five traits, using a combination of data sources. In your report, you should first list, for each of the five traits, the way in which you measured that trait, such as the items on your questionnaire or interview or the life-outcome data you think indicates that trait. Then, in the second part of your report, indicate how high or low you think your examinee is on each of the five traits.

You might be thinking at this point that five factors may be too few to capture all of the fascinating complexity of personality. And you may be right. But consider this. Each of the five global personality factors has a host of specific "facets," which provide a lot of subtlety and nuance. The global trait of conscientiousness, for example, includes these six facets: competence, order, dutifulness, achievement striving, self-discipline, and deliberation. The global trait of neuroticism has these six facets: anxiety, angry hostility, depression, self-consciousness, impulsivity, and vulnerability. These facets of each global factor go a long way toward adding richness, complexity, and nuance to personality description.

Note that, although the NEO-PI-R traits are presented in a different order (N, E, O, A, C) than the Goldberg order, and in a few cases the traits are given different names, the underlying personality traits being measured are nearly identical to those found by Goldberg. This convergence between the factor structures of single-trait item formats and sentence-length item formats provides support for the robustness and replicability of the five-factor model.

What Is the Identity of the Fifth Factor?

Although the five-factor model has achieved impressive replicability across samples, investigators, and item formats, there is still some disagreement about the content and replicability of the fifth factor. Different researchers have variously labeled this fifth factor as *culture, intellect, intellectance, imagination, openness, openness to experience,* and even *fluid intelligence* and *tender-mindedness* (see Brand & Egan, 1989; De Raad, 1998). A major cause of these differences is that different researchers start with different item pools to factor analyze. Those who start with the lexical strategy and use adjectives as items typically endorse *intellect* as the meaning and label of the fifth factor (Saucier & Goldberg, 1996). In contrast, those who use questionnaire items tend to prefer *openness* or *openness to experience,* because this label better reflects the content of those items (McCrae & Costa, 1997; 1999).

One way to resolve these differences is to go back to the lexical rationale to begin with and to look *across cultures* and *across languages.* Recall that, according to the lexical approach, traits that emerge universally in different languages and cultures are deemed more important than those that lack cross-cultural universality.

What do the cross-cultural data show? In a study conducted in Turkey, a clear fifth factor emerged that is best described as *openness* (Somer & Goldberg, 1999). A different Dutch study found a fifth factor marked by *progressive* at one end and *conservative* at the other (DeRaad et al., 1998). In German, the fifth factor represents *intelligence, talents,* and *abilities* (Ostendorf, 1990). In Italian, the fifth factor is *conventionality,* marked by the items *rebellious* and *critical* (Caprara & Perugini, 1994). Looking across all these studies, the fifth factor has proven extremely difficult to pin down.

In summary, although the first four factors are highly replicable across cultures and languages, there is uncertainty about the content, naming, and replicability of the fifth factor. Perhaps some individual differences are more relevant to some cultures than to others—intellect in some cultures, conventionality in other cultures, and openness in yet other cultures. Clearly, more extensive cross-cultural work is needed, particularly in African cultures and in more traditional cultures that are minimally influenced by Western culture.

What Are the Empirical Correlates of the Five Factors?

Over the past 15 years, a tremendous volume of research has been conducted on the empirical correlates of each of the five factors. This section summarizes some of the most recent interesting findings.

Surgency or extraversion. Extraverts love to party—they engage in frequent social interaction, take the lead in livening up dull gatherings, and enjoy talking a lot. Indeed, recent evidence suggests that **social attention** is the cardinal feature of extraversion (Ashton, Lee, & Paunonen, 2002). From the perspective of the extravert, "the more the merrier." Extraverts have a greater impact on their social environment, often assuming leadership positions, whereas introverts tend to be more like wallflowers (Jensen-Campbell & Graziano, 2001). Extraverted men are more likely to be bold with women they don't know, whereas introverted men tend to be timid with women (Berry & Miller, 2001). Extraverts tend to be happier, and this positive affect is experienced most intensely when a person acts in an extraverted manner (Fleeson, Malanos, & Achille, 2002). But there are also downsides—extraverts like to drive fast, listen to music while driving, and as a consequence, tend to get into more car accidents, and even road fatalities, than their more introverted peers (Lajunen, 2001).

Agreeableness. Whereas the motto of the extravert might be "let's liven things up," the motto of the highly agreeable person might be "let's all get along." Those who score high on agreeableness favor using negotiation to resolve conflicts; low-agreeable persons try to assert their power to resolve social conflicts (Graziano & Tobin, 2002; Jensen-Campbell & Graziano, 2001). The agreeable person is also more likely to withdraw from social conflict, avoiding situations that are unharmonious. Agreeable individuals like harmonious social interaction and cooperative family life. Agreeable children tend to be less often victimized by bullies during early adolescence (Jensen-Campbell et al., 2002). As you might suspect, politicians, at least in Italy, tend to score high on scales of agreeableness (Caprara, Barbaranelli, Consiglio, Picconi, & Zimbardo, 2003).

At the other end of the scale of agreeableness lies aggressiveness. In a fascinating study of daily acts, Wu and Clark (2003) found that aggressiveness was strongly linked to many everyday behaviors. Examples include: *hitting someone else in anger; blowing up when things don't work properly; slamming doors; yelling; getting into arguments; clenching fists; raising voices; being intentionally rude; damaging someone's property; pushing and hitting others;* and *slamming down the phone*. So the next time you think about getting into an argument with someone, you might want to find out where they are on the agreeable–aggressiveness disposition.

Agreeable individuals, in short, get along well with others, are well liked, avoid conflict, strive for harmonious family lives, and may selectively prefer professions in which their likeability is an asset. Disagreeable individuals are aggressive and seem to get themselves into a lot of social conflict.

Conscientiousness. If extraverts party up and agreeable people get along, then conscientious individuals are industrious and get ahead. The hard work, punctuality, and reliable behavior exhibited by conscientious individuals result in a host of life outcomes such as a higher grade point average, greater job satisfaction, greater job security, and more positive and committed social relationships (Langford, 2003).

Those who score low on conscientiousness, in contrast, are likely to perform more poorly at school and at work. The fact that highly conscientious individuals succeed in the work domain is likely due to two key correlates. They do not procrastinate, in contrast to their low-conscious peers whose motto might be "never put off until tomorrow what you can put off until the day after tomorrow" (Lee, Kelly, & Edwards). And those high in conscientiousness are exceptionally industrious, putting in the long hours of diligent hard work needed to get ahead (Lund et al., 2006). Furthermore, low C is linked with risky sexual behaviors such as failing to use condoms (Trobst, Herbst, Masters, & Costa, 2002), and being more responsive to other potential partners while already in an existing romantic relationship (Schmitt & Buss, 2001). Among a sample of prisoners, low-C scorers tend to have frequent arrests (Clower & Bothwell, 2001). The high-C individual, in sum, tends to perform well in school and work, avoids breaking the rules, and has a more stable and secure romantic relationship.

Emotional stability. Life poses stresses and hurdles that everyone must confront. The dimension of emotional stability taps into the way people cope with these stresses. Emotionally stable individuals are like boats that remain on course through choppy waters. Emotionally unstable people get buffeted about by the waves and wind and are more likely to get knocked off course. The hallmark of emotional instability or neuroticism is variability of moods over time—such people swing up and down more than emotionally stable individuals (Murray, Allen, & Trinder, 2002). Perhaps as a consequence, emotionally unstable individuals experience more fatigue over the course of the day (De Vries & Van Heck, 2002). Psychologically, emotionally unstable individuals are more likely to have dissociate experiences such as an inability to recall important life events, feeling disconnected from life and other people, and feeling like they've woken up in a strange or unfamiliar place (Kwapil, Wrobel, & Pope, 2002). Have you ever had thoughts about committing suicide? Those high on neuroticism also tend to have more frequent suicidal ideation than those low on neuroticism (Chioqueta & Stiles, 2005). Those high on neuroticism report poorer physical health, more physical symptoms, and fewer attempts to engage in health-promoting behaviors (Williams, O'Brien, & Colder, 2004). They also engage in health-impairing behaviors, such as drinking alcohol as a means of coping with, and attempting to forget about, their problems (Theakston et al., 2004).

Interpersonally, those high on neuroticism or emotional instability have more ups and downs in their social relationships. In the sexual domain, for example, emotionally unstable individuals experience more sexual anxiety (e.g., worried about performance) as well as a greater fear of engaging in sex (Heaven, Crocker, Edwards, Preston, Ward, & Woodbridge, 2003; Shafer, 2001). And with highly stressful events, such as an unwanted loss of a pregnancy, emotionally unstable individuals are more likely to develop "post-traumatic stress disorder," in which the psychological trauma of the loss is experienced profoundly and for a long time (Englelhard, van den Hout, & Kindt, 2003).

Emotional instability augers poorly for professional success. This may be partly due to the fact that emotionally unstable people are thrown off track by the everyday stresses and strains that we all go through. It may be partly due to their experience of greater fatigue. But it may also be attributable to the fact that they engage in a lot of "self-handicapping" (Ross, Canada, & Rausch, 2002). Self-handicapping is defined as a tendency to "create obstacles to successful achievement in performance or competitive situations in order to protect one's self-esteem" (Ross et al., 2002, p. 2). Those high on neuroticism seem to undermine themselves, creating roadblocks to their own achievement. Nonetheless, one study found that those high on neuroticism actually outperformed their more emotionally stable counterparts in performance in an office setting when changes in the work needs created an unusually busy work environment (Smillie, Yeo, Furnham, & Jackson, 2006). In sum, the affective volatility that comes with being low on emotional stability affects many spheres of life, from sexuality to achievement.

Openness. Would you agree or disagree with the following statements? *"Upon awakening during the night, I am unsure whether I actually experienced something or only dreamed about it," "I am aware that I am dreaming, even as I dream," "I am able to control or direct the content of my dreams," "A dream helped me to solve a current problem or concern"* (Watson, 2003). If you tend to agree with these statements, the odds are that you score high on the personality disposition of openness. Those who are high on openness tend to remember their dreams more, have more waking dreams, have more vivid dreams, have more prophetic dreams (dreaming about something that later happens), and have more problem-solving dreams (Watson, 2003).

The disposition of openness has been linked to experimentation with new foods, a liking for novel experiences, and even "openness" to having extramarital affairs (Buss, 1993). One possible cause of openness may lie in individual differences in the processing of information. A recent study found that those high in openness had more difficulty in ignoring previously experienced stimuli (Peterson, Smith, & Carson, 2002). It's as though the perceptual and information processing "gates" of highly open people are literally more "open" to receiving information coming at them from a variety of sources. Less-open people have more tunnel vision and find it easier to ignore competing stimuli. Those high in openness exhibit less prejudice against minority groups, and are less likely to hold negative racial stereotypes (Flynn, 2005). In sum, the disposition of openness has been correlated with a host of other fascinating variables from intrusive stimuli to possible alternative sex partners.

Combinations of Big Five variables. Many life outcomes, of course, are better predicted by combinations of personality dispositions than by single personality dispositions. Here are a few examples.

- *Good grades* are best predicted by Conscientiousness (high) and Emotional Stability (high) (Chamorro-Premuzic & Furnham, 2003). One reason might be that emotionally stable and conscientious people are less likely to procrastinate (Watson, 2001).
- *Risky sexual behaviors,* such has having many sex partners and not using condoms, are best predicted by high Extraversion, high Neuroticism, low Conscientiousness, and low Agreeableness (Miller et al., 2004; Trobst et al., 2002).
- *Alcohol consumption* is best predicted by high Extraversion and low Conscientiousness (Paunonen, 2003). A study of more than 5,000 workers in Finland found that low Conscientiousness also predicts *increases* in alcohol consumption over time, that is, who ends up becoming a heavy drinker (Grano et al., 2004).

- *Mount Everest mountain climbers* tend to be extraverted, emotionally stable, and high on Psychoticism (Egan & Stelmack, 2003).
- *Happiness* and experiencing positive affect in everyday life are best predicted by high Extraversion and low Neuroticism (Cheng & Furnham, 2003; Steel & Ones, 2003; Stewart, Ebmeier, & Deary, 2005; Yik & Russell, 2001).
- *Proclivity to engage in volunteer work,* such as campus or community services, is best predicted by a combination of high Agreeableness and high Extraversion (Carlo et al., 2005).
- *When you join the workforce, do you think you will join the voluntary union organization or decline to become a member of the union?* Those low on Extraversion and high on Emotional Stability have been shown to have a disproportionately low rate of joining work unions (Parkes & Razavi, 2004).
- *Forgiveness,* the proclivity to forgive those who have committed some wrong, characterizes individuals who are high on Agreeableness and high on Emotional Stability (Brose, Rye, Lutz-Zois, & Ross, 2005).
- *Leadership effectiveness* in business settings is best predicted by high Extraversion, high Agreeableness, high Conscientiousness, and high Emotional Stability (Silverthorne, 2001).

We should not be surprised that combinations of personality variables often do better than single variables in predicting important life outcomes, and we can expect future research to focus increasingly on these combinations.

Is the Five-Factor Model Comprehensive?

Critics of the five-factor model argue that it leaves out important aspects of personality. Almagor, Tellegen, and Waller (1995), for example, present evidence for seven factors. Their results suggest the addition of two factors—*positive evaluation* (e.g., *outstanding* versus *ordinary*) and *negative evaluation* (e.g., *awful* versus *decent*). Goldberg, one of the proponents of the five-factor model, has discovered that factors such as *religiosity* and *spirituality* sometimes emerge as separate factors, although these are clearly smaller in size (accounting for less variance) than those of the Big Five (Goldberg & Saucier, 1995).

Lanning (1994), using items from the California Adult Q-set, has found a replicable sixth factor, which he labels *attractiveness,* including the items *physically attractive, sees self as attractive,* and *charming*. In a related vein, Schmitt and Buss (2000) have found reliable individual differences in the sexual sphere, such as *sexiness* (e.g., *sexy, stunning, attractive, alluring, arousing, sensual,* and *seductive*) and *faithfulness* (e.g., *faithful, monogamous, devoted,* and *not adulterous*). These individual difference dimensions are correlated with the five factors: *sexiness* is positively correlated with *extraversion,* and *faithfulness* is positively correlated with both *agreeableness* and *conscientiousness*. But these correlations leave much of the individual variation unaccounted for, suggesting that these individual differences in sexuality are not completely subsumed by the five-factor model.

Paunonen and colleagues have identified 10 personality traits that appear to fall outside of the five-factor model: Conventionality, Seductiveness, Manipulativeness, Thriftiness, Humorousness, Integrity, Femininity, Religiosity, Risk Taking, and Egotism (Paunonen, 2002; Paunonen et al., 2003). Other researchers have confirmed that these traits are not highly correlated with the Big Five, and that they highlight many interesting facets of personality at a more specific level than the "global" factors represented by the five-factor model (Lee, Ogunfowora, & Ashton, 2005).

Proponents of the five-factor model are typically open-minded about the potential inclusion of factors beyond the five factors, if and when the empirical evidence warrants it (Costa & McCrae, 1995; Goldberg & Saucier, 1995). Nonetheless, these researchers have not found the evidence for additional factors beyond the Big Five to be compelling. *Positive* and *negative evaluation,* some have argued, are not really separate factors but, rather, false factors that emerge simply because raters tend to evaluate all things as either good or bad (McCrae & John, 1992). With respect to the *attractiveness* factor found by Lanning (1994), Costa and McCrae (1995) argue that *attractiveness* is not ordinarily considered to be a personality trait, although the *charming* item that loads on this factor surely would be considered part of personality.

One approach to personality factors beyond the Big Five has been to explore **personality-descriptive nouns,** rather than adjectives. Saucier (2003) has discovered eight fascinating factors within the domain of personality nouns such as: *Dumbbell* (e.g., dummy, moron, twit), *Babe/Cutie* (e.g., beauty, darling, doll), *Philosopher* (e.g., genius, artist, individualist), *Lawbreaker* (e.g., pothead, drunk, rebel), *Joker* (e.g., clown, goof, comedian), and *Jock* (e.g., sportsman, tough, machine). A study of personality nouns in the Italian language revealed a somewhat different organization than that of the Big Five, discovering factors such as Honesty, Humility, and Cleverness (Di Blas, 2005). As Saucier concludes, "Personality taxonomies based on adjectives are unlikely to be comprehensive, because type-nouns have different content emphases" (Saucier, 2003, p. 695).

A second approach to personality factors beyond the Big Five has been to use the lexical approach, focusing on large pools of trait adjectives in different languages. In an exciting development, several studies have converged on six rather than five factors. One study of seven languages (Dutch, French, German, Hungarian, Italian, Korean, and Polish) found variants of the Big Five, plus a sixth factor *Honesty–Humility* (Ashton et al., 2004). At one end of the Honesty–Humility factor lies trait adjectives such as honest, sincere, trustworthy, and unselfish; the other end is anchored by adjectives such as arrogant, conceited, greedy, pompous, self-important, and egotistical. Independent investigators have also found versions of this sixth factor in Greece (Saucier, Georgiades, Tsaousis, & Goldberg, 2005) and Italy (Di Bias, 2005). These findings point to an exciting expansion of the basic factors of personality within the dispositional domain.

In addition to the possibility of discovering dimensions *beyond* the Big Five, some researchers have had excellent success in predicting important behavioral criteria from *within* the Big Five using the *facets* of the Big Five (Paunonen & Ashton, 2001a, b). For example, in predicting course grades in a college class, Paunonen and Ashton (2001a) found significantly greater predictability from the facet subscales of *Need for Achievement* (a facet of Conscientiousness) and *Need for Understanding* (a facet of Openness) than from the higher-level factor measures of Conscientiousness and Openness themselves. Similarly, although job performance is well predicted by global measures of Conscientiousness, even better prediction of job performance is attained by including the facet measures such as achievement, dependability, order, and cautiousness (Dudley et al., 2006). Paunonen and Ashton conclude that "the aggregation of narrow trait measures into broad factor measures can be counterproductive from the point of view of both behavioral prediction and behavioral explanation" (Paunonen & Ashton, 2001a, p. 78).

Thus, we are left with an important question: does the five-factor model provide a comprehensive description of personality? On the yes side, the five-factor model has proven to be more robust and replicable than any other taxonomy of personality that claims to be comprehensive. Four of the five factors have proven to be highly replicable across investigators, data sources, item formats, samples, languages, and cultures. Furthermore, the five-factor model has been discovered to be the major structure underlying many existing personality inventories. On the no side, claims that the five-factor model is comprehensive may be premature, as the proponents of the five-factor model readily admit. Indeed, the quest for factors beyond the Big Five and the discovery of a replicable sixth factor makes the field of personality psychology such an exciting and vibrant discipline (Ashton, Lee, & Goldberg, 2004).

The model has also drawn articulate critics, such as McAdams (1992) and Block (1995b). Block, for example, argues that these five factors, although perhaps useful for laypersons in everyday life, fail to capture the underlying causal personality processes that researchers are really interested in. Describing someone as high on *neuroticism,* for example, may be useful in social communication or global character descriptions, but it does not capture the underlying psychological processes involved in such things as feeling guilty, obsessing over worst-case scenarios, and worrying excessively when someone fails to respond to an e-mail message.

Proponents of the five-factor model respond to these criticisms by suggesting that the Big Five taxonomy has been proposed merely as a framework for the phenotypic attributes of personality that have become encoded within the natural language and makes no claims about the underlying personality processes (Goldberg & Saucier, 1995). Debates such as these are the essence of the scientific enterprise and indicate a healthy and thriving field. These controversies can be expected to continue as personality psychologists struggle to develop better, more adequate, and more comprehensive taxonomies of personality.

SUMMARY AND EVALUATION

This chapter focused on three fundamental issues for a personality psychology based on traits: how to conceptualize traits, how to identify the most important traits, and how to formulate a comprehensive taxonomy of traits.

There are two basic conceptualizations of traits. The first views traits as the internal properties of persons that cause their behavior. In the internal property conception, traits cause the outward behavioral manifestations. The second conceptualization views traits as descriptive summaries of overt behavior. The summary view does not assume that traits cause behavior but, rather, treats the issue of cause separately, to be examined after the behavioral summaries are identified and described.

There have been three major approaches to identifying the most important traits. The first is the lexical approach, which views all the important traits as captured by the natural language. The lexical approach uses synonym frequency and cross-cultural universality as the criteria for identifying important traits. The second approach, the statistical approach to identifying important traits, adopts statistical procedures, such as factor analysis, and attempts to identify clusters of traits that covary. The third approach, the theoretical approach, uses an existing theory of personality to determine which traits are important. In practice, personality psychologists sometimes use blends of these three approaches—for example, by starting with the lexical approach to identify the universe of traits and then applying statistical procedures, such as factor analysis, to identify groups of traits that covary and form larger factors.

The third fundamental issue—formulating an overarching taxonomy of personality traits—has yielded several solutions. Eysenck developed a hierarchical model, in which the broad traits *extraversion, neuroticism,* and *psychoticism* subsume more narrow traits, such as activity level, moodiness, and egocentricity. Eysenck's taxonomy is based on a factor analysis but is also explicitly anchored in biological underpinnings, including a heritable basis for the traits and the identification of the underlying physiological basis for the traits.

Cattell's taxonomy of 16 personality traits, also based on factor analysis, contains more than five times the number of traits found in Eysenck's taxonomy. Cattell's taxonomy is anchored in the usage of multiple data sources, including questionnaire data, test data, and life-record data. Eysenck argued, however, that Cattell's 16-trait taxonomy can be reduced to his 3-trait taxonomy through factor analysis.

Circumplex taxonomies of personality have been more narrowly targeted toward the domain of interpersonal traits, as opposed to the entire personality sphere. Circumplex models are circular arrangements of traits organized around two key dimensions—status (dominance) and love (agreeableness).

The five-factor model of personality is a taxonomy that subsumes the circumplex in that the first two traits in the model—*surgency* and *agreeableness*—are roughly the same as the circumplex dimensions of *dominance* and *agreeableness.* In addition, however, the five-factor model includes *conscientiousness, emotional stability,* and *openness-intellect* (sometimes called "culture"). The five-factor model has been criticized for not being comprehensive and for being inadequate for understanding underlying psychological processes. Nonetheless, the five-factor model remains heavily endorsed by many personality psychologists and continues to be used in a variety of research designs and applied settings. Recent evidence points to the exciting discovery of a sixth factor—*Honesty–Humility*—that necessitates an expansion of the Big Five.

KEY TERMS

Lexical Approach 67
Statistical Approach 67
Theoretical Approach 67
Lexical Hypothesis 67
Synonym Frequency 67
Cross-Cultural Universality 67
Factor Analysis 69
Factor Loadings 69
Sociosexual Orientation 70
Interpersonal Traits 79
Adjacency 81
Bipolarity 81
Orthogonality 81
Five-Factor Model 82
Surgency or Extraversion 86
Social Attention 86
Agreeableness 86
Conscientiousness 86
Emotional Stability 87
Openness 88
Combinations of Big Five Variables 88
Personality-Descriptive Nouns 90

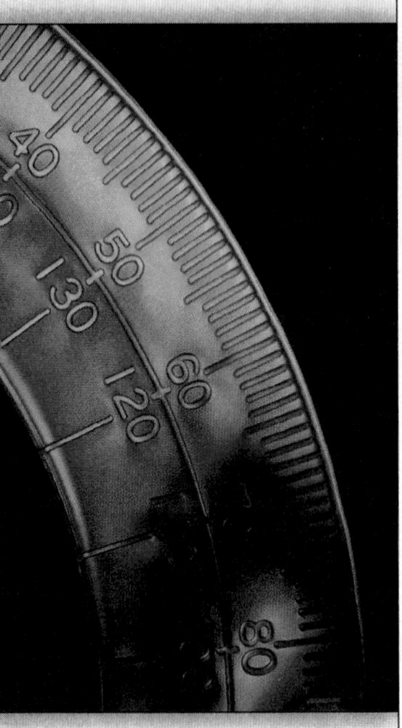

Theoretical and Measurement Issues in Trait Psychology

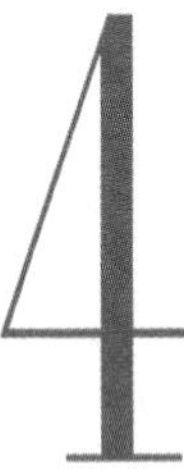

THE DISPOSITIONAL DOMAIN

Signing up for an Internet dating service often involves answering a personality trait questionnaire.

Sarah was a junior in college with a double major in math and computer science, which left her little time to socialize. She was a bit shy, especially with men her own age. Although she wanted to date more, she was very particular about the characteristics she looked for in a man. She decided that a Web-based dating service might be an efficient way to find someone to date. She signed up with an Internet dating service and discovered that the first step was to complete an extensive personality inventory. She answered a lot of questions, about her likes and dislikes, her habits, traits, and what others thought of her. She even answered questions about the kind of car she owned and her driving style. After this, the site returned the personality profiles of a few men who, the site claimed, would be good matches for her. One looked particularly interesting to her, so she spent a couple of hours with him in online chat sessions. As these went well, Sarah decided to call him a couple of times on the phone. They had a lot in common and Sarah found it easy to talk to him. She enjoyed the conversations, as did he, so they decided to take the next step and meet in person for a dinner date. When they made arrangements to meet, she was surprised to learn that they lived in the same apartment complex and that they had probably already seen one another, perhaps had even spoken to one another. But it took an Internet dating service, using a program that matches people according to personality, for them to actually find each other.

There are many Internet-based dating services, and many of these use personality psychologists to help them do a better job of matching people. For

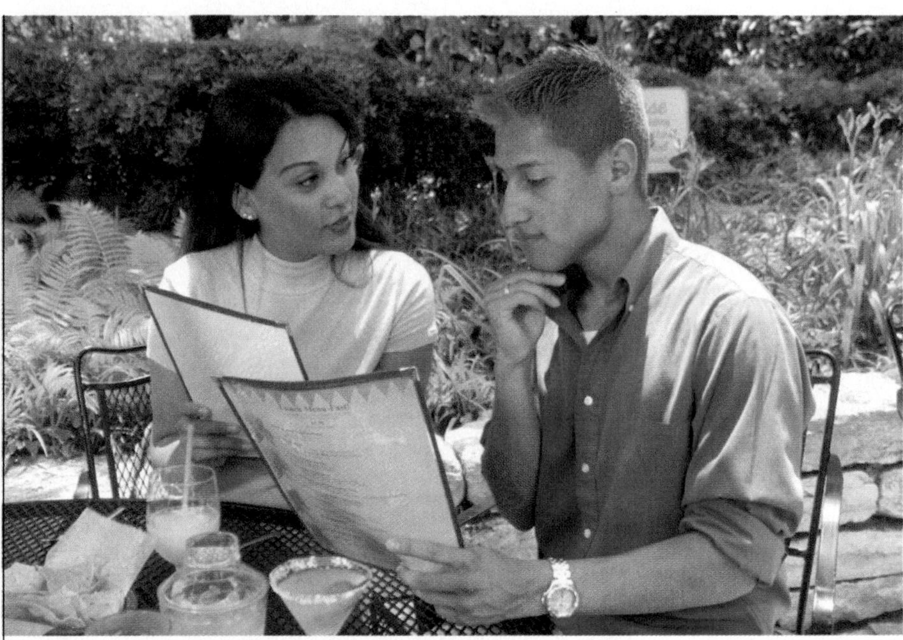

A key task for a first date is determining what you have in common with the other person—that is, how similar your personalities are.

example, if a person is introverted and sensitive, will he or she get along with someone who is practical and conscientious? Psychologists are also using the Web to gather data on what makes two people become good companions for each other. What they are learning then enters into quantitative software programs that run through a complex matching procedure for the online dating services.

For example, the website eHarmony.com uses a 480-item personality questionnaire. The site also presents the applicant with a list of "bad behaviors" and asks them to check off those they "absolutely cannot stand" in someone they date. This dating service uses a combined matching system that relies on selecting matches on major personality traits and then deselecting based on what the applicant says he or she cannot tolerate in another. Other Internet dating services, such as Matchmaker.com and Emode.com, also gather extensive personality data and engage in sophisticated matching routines.

Matching on personality traits sounds like a great idea, but it works only to the extent that people are telling the truth about themselves when they answer the questionnaires. People can represent themselves falsely in terms of physical characteristics (e.g., say they are petite when they are not, say they have thick, wavy hair when they are in fact bald), and they may represent themselves falsely in terms of their personality. They may, for example, try to cover up an aggressive, abusive personality. Consequently, some of these dating services are very concerned about safety and are using techniques from personality assessment to detect potential problem clients. For example, some sites ask about minor misbehaviors, such as "I never resent being asked to return a favor" or "I have, on occasion, told a white lie." People who deny a lot of these common faults raise a red flag, since they are probably misrepresenting themselves on all the questionnaires. In fact, eHarmony.com claims that 16 percent of its clients are asked to leave the site based on their answers to such questionnaires (reported in *U.S. News & World Report,* September 29, 2003).

This use of personality testing brings into focus several questions about measurement of traits. Do traits represent consistent behavior patterns, such that we could make accurate predictions about a person's future based on her or his trait standings? How do personality traits interact with situations, particularly social situations? Are there ways to detect if someone is not telling the truth on a personality questionnaire? Are some people motivated to fake good or to fake bad on questionnaires?

Personality measures are also used in other selection situations, such as for jobs or for prison parole or for placement within an organization. What are some of the legal issues in using personality measures to make such decisions? Are there some common problems with selection procedures? Can an employer use a measure of "integrity" to screen out potentially dishonest employees? What about selecting people for admission into college, law school, or medical school on the basis of aptitude tests or other so-called intelligence tests?

Although many of these questions seem abstract, they are important for how we think about personality traits. They are important for understanding controversial issues, such as the use of personality measures in business, industry, and education for the selection, training, and promotion of candidates.

Theoretical Issues

Trait theories of personality offer a collection of viewpoints about the fundamental building blocks of human nature. As we saw in Chapter 3, there are differences among the various theories concerning what constitutes a trait, how many traits exist, and what are the best methods for discovering basic traits. Despite their differences, trait theories share three important assumptions about personality traits. These assumptions go beyond any one theory or taxonomy of personality traits and, so, form the basic foundation for trait psychology. These three important assumptions are

- Meaningful individual differences.
- Stability or consistency over time.
- Consistency across situations.

Meaningful Differences between Individuals

Trait psychologists are primarily interested in determining the ways in which people are *different from each other.* Any meaningful way in which people differ from each other may potentially be identified as a personality trait. Some people like to talk a lot; others don't. Some people are active; others are couch potatoes. Some people enjoy working on difficult puzzles; others avoid mental challenges. Because of its emphasis on the study of differences among people, trait psychology has sometimes been called **differential psychology** in the interest of distinguishing this field from other branches of personality psychology (Anastasi, 1976). Differential psychology includes the study of other forms of individual differences in addition to personality traits, such as abilities, aptitudes, and intelligence. In this chapter, however, we will focus mainly on personality traits.

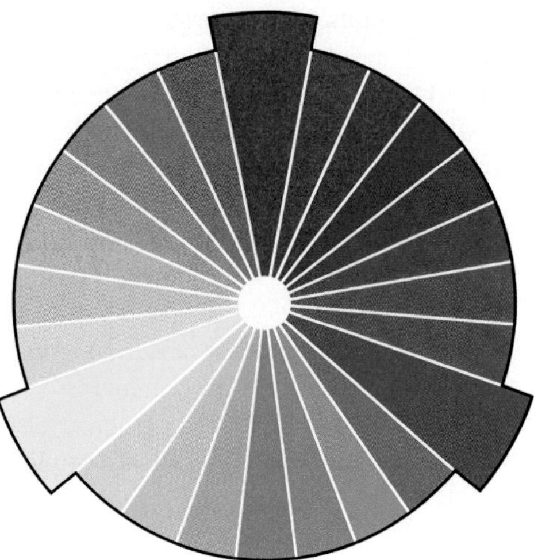

The Color Wheel. The infinite hues of color are created from a combination of three primary colors. Similarly, trait psychologists hold that the infinite variety of personalities are created from a combination of a few primary traits.

The trait perspective historically has been concerned with accurate measurement. It takes a quantitative approach, which emphasizes how much a given individual differs from an agreed-upon average. Of all the perspectives and strategies for studying personality, the trait approach is the most mathematically and statistically oriented, due to its emphasis on amount. After all, people differ from each other in the *amounts* of the various traits.

You might be wondering how the vast differences among people could be captured and represented by a few key personality traits. How is it that the uniqueness of every individual can be portrayed by just a few traits? Trait psychologists are somewhat like chemists. They argue that, by combining a few primary traits in various amounts, they can distill the unique qualities of every individual. This process is analogous to that of combining the three primary colors. Every visible color in the spectrum, from dusty mauve to burnt umber, is created through various combinations of the three primary colors: red, green, and blue. According to trait psychologists, every personality, no matter how complex or unusual, is the product of a particular combination of a few basic and primary traits.

Consistency over Time

The second assumption made by all trait theories is that there is a degree of **consistency** in personality over time. If someone is highly extraverted during one period of observation, trait psychologists tend to assume that he or she will be extraverted tomorrow, next week, a year from now, or even decades from now. The view that many broadbased personality traits show considerable stability over time has been supported by a large number of research studies, which we will review in Chapter 5. Traits such as intelligence, emotional reactivity, impulsiveness, shyness, and aggression show high test-retest correlations, even with years or decades between measurement occasions. Personality traits that are thought to have a biological basis, such as extraversion, sensation seeking, activity level, and shyness, also show remarkable consistency over time. Attitudes, however, are much less consistent over time, as are interests and

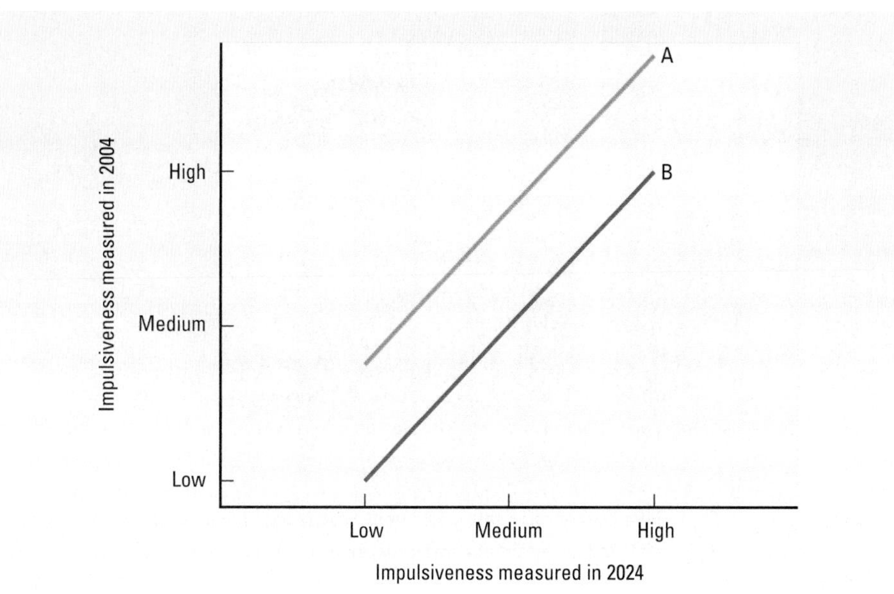

Figure 4.1

Hypothetical regression lines between impulsiveness measured 20 years apart. Line A represents an age change in impulsiveness, with all persons scoring as less impulsive in later life. Line B represents no change in impulsiveness over twenty years. Both lines represent rank order consistency, however, and thus test-retest correlations.

opinions (Conley, 1984a, 1984b). Of course, people do change in important behavioral ways throughout adulthood, whether in terms of their political involvement, their attitudes toward social issues, or their participation in social change movements or perhaps through psychotherapy (Stewart, 1982). When it comes to broad personality traits, consistency over time is more often the rule than the exception (Izard et al., 1993).

Although a trait might be consistent over time, the way in which it manifests itself in actual behavior might change substantially. Consider the trait of disagreeableness. As a child, a highly disagreeable person might be prone to temper tantrums and fits of breath holding, fist pounding, and undirected rage. As an adult, a disagreeable person might be difficult to get along with and hence might have trouble sustaining personal relationships and holding down a job. Researchers have found, for example, a correlation of −.45 between throwing temper tantrums in childhood and being able to hold a job as an adult 20 years later (Caspi, Elder, & Bem, 1987). This finding is evidence of consistency in the underlying trait (disagreeableness), even though the *manifestation* of that trait changes over time.

What about traits that decrease in intensity with age, such as activity level, impulsiveness, or sociopathy? How can there be consistency in a trait if it is known to change with age? For example, criminal tendencies usually decrease with age, so that a 20-year-old sociopath becomes much less dangerous to society as he or she ages. The answer to this question lies in the concept of **rank order.** If all people show a decrease in a particular trait at the same rate over time, they might still maintain the same rank order relative to each other. Accounting for general change with age can be compared to subtracting or adding a constant to each participant's score on the trait measure. Figure 4.1

The Hartshorne and May study examined cross-situational consistency in academic and play situations in children. While they found little evidence for consistency in such traits as honesty, the study has been criticized for measuring behavior on one occasion in each situation. Studies that aggregate measurements over several occasions in each situation find much higher levels of cross-situational consistency.

illustrates how a general decrease in impulsiveness with age might have no real effect on the correlation between measures obtained 20 years apart. People in general can show a decrease in impulsiveness as they get older, yet those individuals who were the most impulsive at an earlier age are still the ones who are most impulsive at a later age. We will revisit the idea of rank order consistency, as well as the whole notion of stability and change, in Chapter 5.

Consistency across Situations

The third assumption made by trait psychologists is that traits will exhibit some consistency across situations. Although the evidence for consistency in traits *over time* is substantial, the question of consistency in traits *from situation to situation* has been more hotly debated. Trait psychologists have traditionally believed that people's personalities show consistency from situation to situation. For example, if a young man is "really friendly," he is expected to be friendly at work, friendly at school, and friendly during recreation activities. This person might be friendly toward strangers, friendly toward people of different ages, and friendly toward authority figures.

Even though someone is really friendly, there are, of course, situations in which the individual will not act friendly. Perhaps a particular situation exerts an influence on how friendly most people will be. For example, people are more likely to start conversations with strangers if they are at a party than if they are at a library. If situations mainly control how people behave, then the idea that traits are consistent across situations holds less promise as an approach to explaining behavior.

The issue of cross-situational consistency has a long and checkered history in personality psychology. Hartshorne and May (1928) studied a large group of elementary school students at summer camp, focusing especially on the trait of honesty. They observed honest and dishonest behavior in several situations. For example, they observed which children cheated while playing field games at summer camp and which children cheated during some written exams in school. The correlation between honesty measured in each of these two situations was rather low. Knowing that a child cheated one night while playing kick-the-can at summer camp tells us very little about whether this child is likely to copy from a neighbor during a test at school. Hartshorne and May (1928) reported similar low cross-situational correlations for the traits of helpfulness and self-control.

Forty years later, in 1968, Walter Mischel published a groundbreaking book entitled *Personality and Assessment.* In it, he summarized the results of the Hartshorne and May (1928) study, as well as the results of many other studies reporting low correlations between personality scores obtained in different situations. After reviewing many such findings, Mischel concluded that "behavioral consistencies have not been demonstrated, and the concept of personality traits as broad predispositions is thus untenable" (p. 140).

Mischel suggested that personality psychologists should abandon their efforts to explain behavior in terms of personality traits and recommended that they shift their focus to situations. If behavior differs from situation to situation, then it must be situational differences, rather than underlying personality traits, that determine behavior. This position, called **situationism,** can be illustrated with the following examples. A young woman may be friendly at school with people she knows but reserved with strangers. Or a young man may want to achieve good grades at school but may not care whether he excels in sports. The situationist position is that the situation, not personality traits, determines, for example, how friendly a person will behave or how much need for achievement a person displays. Mischel proposed that behavior was more a function of the situation than of broad personality traits.

Mischel's challenge to the trait approach preoccupied the field of trait psychology for the 20 years following the publication of his 1968 book. Many researchers responded to Mischel's situationist approach by formulating new theoretical perspectives and gathering new data designed to rescue the idea of traits (e.g., A. H. Buss, 1989; Endler & Magnusson, 1976). Mischel, in turn, countered with new ideas and new data of his own, intended to reinforce his position that the trait concept was limited in its usefulness (e.g., Mischel, 1984, 1990; Mischel & Peake, 1982).

Although the dust is still settling from this long-running debate, it is safe to say that both trait psychologists *and* Mischel have modified their views as a result. Mischel has tempered his position that situations are always the strongest determinants of behavior. However, he still maintains that trait psychologists have been guilty of overstating the importance of broad traits. Prior to Mischel's critique, it was common for trait psychologists to make statements about the predictability of people's behavior from their scores on personality tests. Mischel points out that psychologists simply are not very good at predicting how *an individual* will behave *in particular situations.* Trait psychologists, too, have modified their views. Two of the most lasting changes that trait psychologists have embraced have been the notion of **person-situation interaction** and the practice of **aggregation,** or averaging, as a tool for assessing personality traits.

Person-Situation Interaction

We first looked at the topic of person-situation interaction in Chapter 1. In this section, we will examine this topic in a bit more detail, focusing on interactionism as a response to Mischel's challenge to trait consistency. As Mischel's debate with trait psychologists made clear, there are two possible explanations for behavior, or why people do what they do in any given situation:

1. Behavior is a function of personality traits, $B = f(P)$.
2. Behavior is a function of situational forces, $B = f(S)$.

Clearly, there is some truth in both of these statements. For example, people behave differently at funerals than they do at sporting events, illustrating that situational forces direct behavior in certain ways, as Mischel emphasized. Some people, however, are consistently quiet, even at sporting events, whereas other people are talkative and sociable, even at funerals. These examples lend support to the traditional trait position, which stresses that personality determines why people do what they do.

The obvious way to integrate these two points of view is to declare that both personality and situations interact to produce behavior, or

$$B = f(P \times S)$$

This formula suggests that behavior is a function of the *interaction* between personality traits and situational forces. Consider, for example, the trait of having a hot temper, a tendency to respond aggressively to minor frustrations. Acquaintances of a person high on this trait might be unaware of it as long as they did not encounter the person attempting to deal with a frustrating situation. The trait of having a short temper might be expressed only under the right situational conditions, such as in frustrating situations. If a person is frustrated by a situation (e.g., a vending machine takes the person's money but does not give him or her the product) *and* the person happens to have a quick temper (personality forces), then he or she will become upset and perhaps strike out at the source of the frustration (e.g., kick the vending machine repeatedly while cursing loudly). Any explanation of why such people get so upset would have to take into account both particular situations (e.g., frustration) and personality traits (e.g., hot temper). This point of view is called person-situation interaction, and it has become a fairly standard view in modern trait theory. Another way to view this is in the form of "If . . . . , if . . . . , then . . . . " statements (Shoda, Mischel, & Wright, 1994)—for example, "If the situation is frustrating, and if the person has a hot temper, then aggression will be the result."

In the interactional view, differences between people are understood to make a difference only under the right circumstances. Some traits are specific to certain situations. Consider the trait of test anxiety. A young man might be generally easygoing and confident. However, under a set of *very specific* situational conditions, such as when he has to take an important exam, he becomes very anxious. In these particular circumstances, someone who is otherwise easygoing might become distressed, anxious, and quite upset. This example illustrates how certain very specific situations can provoke behavior that is otherwise out of character for the individual. This is referred to as **situational specificity,** in which a person acts in a specific way under particular circumstances.

Some trait-situation interactions are rare because the kinds of situations that elicit behavior related to those traits are themselves rare. For example, you would find it difficult to identify which of your classmates were high in courageousness. It would take a certain kind of *situation,* such as a hostage situation at your school, for you to find out just who is courageous and who is not.

The point is that personality traits interact with situational forces to produce behavior. Personality psychologists have given up the hope of predicting "all of the people all of the time" and have settled on the idea that they can predict "some of the people some of the time." For example, given the trait of anxiety, we might be able to predict who is likely to be anxious in some situations (e.g., evaluation situations, such as tests), but not anxious in other situations (e.g., when relaxed at home with family).

An interesting example of person X situation interaction is provided in a study by Debbie Moskowitz (1993). It has long been thought that the personality traits of dominance (the disposition to try to influence others) and friendliness (the degree to which a person is cordial and congenial) show large gender differences, with men being more dominant than women, and women being more friendly than men (Eagly, 1987). However, the study by Moskowitz showed that these traits interact with situation variables. Specifically, a person's level of dominance or friendliness may depend on who they are interacting with at the time, for example, whether they are interacting with a same-sex or opposite sex person, and whether that person is someone they know or a stranger. Moskowitz's (1993) study showed that women are more friendly than men, but only when they are interacting with other women; when interacting with opposite sex strangers, women were not more friendly than men. As for dominance, the men were more dominant than women, but only when interacting with a same-sex friend; when interacting with strangers, the men were not more dominant than women. This study shows that who a person is interacting with will influence the expression of the personality traits of dominance and friendliness, and that this expression may or may not differ for men and women depending on the social setting.

Some situations are so strong, however, that nearly everyone reacts in the same way. For example, in a study of emotional reactions to life events, Larsen, Diener, and Emmons (1986) were interested in finding out who tended to overreact emotionally to everyday events. Participants in this study kept a daily diary of life events every day for two months. They also rated their emotions each day. Based on a trait measure of emotional reactivity, these researchers were able to predict who would overreact to a minor or moderately stressful event, such as getting a flat tire, being stood up for a date, or having an outdoor event get rained out. When *really* bad things happened, such as the death of a pet, virtually everyone reacted with strong emotion. Researchers have coined the term **strong situation** to refer to situations in which nearly all people react in similar ways.

Certain strong situations, such as funerals, religious services, and crowded elevators, seem to pull for uniformity of behavior. By contrast, when situations are weak or ambiguous, personality has its strongest influence on behavior. The Rorschach inkblot cards are a classic example of a weak or ambiguous situation. A person being asked to interpret these inkblots is, in effect, being asked to provide structure by describing what he or she sees in the inkblot. Many situations in real life are also somewhat ambiguous. When a stranger smiles at you, is it a friendly smile or is there a bit of a sneer in the smile? When a stranger looks you right in the eye and holds the stare for a bit too long, what does it mean? Many social situations, like these two, require us to interpret the actions, motives, and intentions of others. As with interpretations of inkblots, how we interpret social situations may reveal our personalities. For example, people with a Machiavellian character (e.g., the tendency to use others, to be manipulative and cold), often think others are out to get them (Golding, 1978). Especially in ambiguous social interactions, Machiavellian persons are likely to see others as threatening.

Situational Selection

There are three other ways in which personality traits interact with situations. We will discuss each of these in general terms here. The first form of interactionism is **situational selection,** the tendency to choose the situations in which one finds oneself (Ickes, Snyder, & Garcia, 1997; Snyder & Gangestad, 1982). In other words, people typically do not find themselves in random situations. Instead, they select the situations

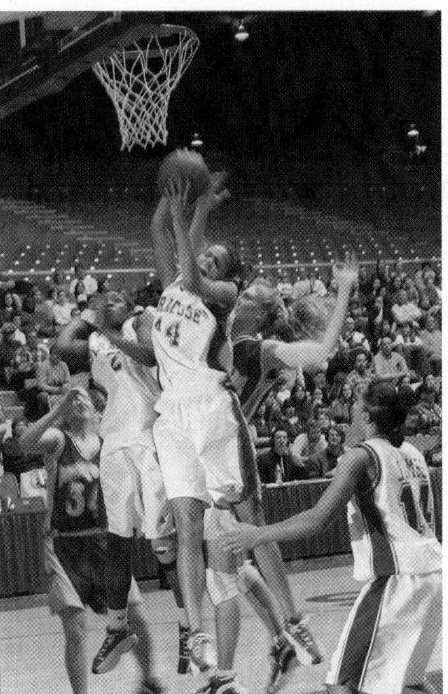

Personality plays a role in determining which situations a person chooses to enter. For example, whether one chooses team activities for recreation, such as basketball, or individual activities, such as long-distance running, is a function of one's level of extraversion. Studies show that extraverts prefer team activities and introverts prefer solitary activities for recreation.

in which they will spend their time. Snyder (1983) states this idea concisely: "Quite possibly, one's choice of the settings in which to live one's life may reflect features of one's personality; an individual may choose to live his or her life in serious, reserved, and intellectual situations precisely because he or she is a serious, reserved, and thoughtful individual" (p. 510).

Researchers have examined whether specific personality traits predict how often people enter into specific situations (Diener, Larsen, & Emmons, 1984). These researchers had participants wear pagers, so that the participants could be signaled electronically throughout the day. The participants wore the pagers every day for six weeks as they went about their normal routines. They were paged twice each day, resulting in a sample of 84 occasions for each participant. Each time the pager went off, the participants had to complete a brief questionnaire. One question inquired about the kind of situation each participant was in when the pager went off. Over the 84 times when the participants were "caught," the researchers predicted that certain personality traits would predict how many times they were caught in certain situations. For example, the researchers found that the trait of need for achievement correlated with spending more time in work situations, the need for order with spending time in more familiar situations, and extraversion with choosing social forms of recreation (e.g., team sports, such as baseball or volleyball, rather than solitary sports, such as long-distance running or swimming).

The idea that personality influences the kinds of situations in which people spend their time suggests that we can investigate personality by studying the choices people make in life. When given a choice, people typically choose situations that fit their personalities (Snyder & Gangestad, 1982). The personality effect does not have to be large to result in substantial life-outcome differences. For example, choosing to enter into work situations just 10 percent more of the time (e.g., studying 10 percent longer, or working 10 percent more hours) may result in very large differences in real-life outcomes, such as achieving a degree or a higher salary. Think, for example, about how you choose to spend your free time and about whether your choices reflect your own personality, to a degree.

The relationship between persons and situations goes in both directions. So far, we have been emphasizing how personality affects situational selection. However, once in the situation, that situation can affect the person's personality. A fascinating study illustrating this notion was done by Bolger and Schilling (1991) on neuroticism and stressful life events. People high on the trait of neuroticism report higher levels of distress in their lives than people low on neuroticism. Bolger and Shilling hypothesized that this increased level of distress could come about because high neuroticism subjects get themselves more frequently into stressful situations, or because high neuroticism subjects respond to ordinary stressful situations with greater reactivity. To test these two hypotheses, they followed 339 people every day for 42 consecutive days, having the subjects keep detailed daily records of their life events and their self-reported levels of distress. They discovered that both hypotheses were true: high neuroticism subjects did indeed have more frequent stressful life events (e.g., arguments, tension with others) than low neuroticism subjects, *and* they reacted to such stressful life events with more subjective distress than low neuroticism subjects. In this case, the trait of neuroticism related to more frequent stressful life events, and greater reactivity to stressful life events.

A recent study by psychologist Will Fleeson and colleagues (Fleeson, Malanos, & Achille, 2002) also illustrates how situations can influence personality. It has long been known that the trait of extraversion is related to positive emotions. We will discuss this more in the chapter on emotion, but for now it is important simply to know that a strong correlation exists between extraversion and feeling high levels of positive emotions. In their study, Fleeson and colleagues had subjects come to the lab in groups of three to participate in a group discussion. They were randomly assigned to an "introverted" or an "extraverted" condition. Instructions for the extraverted condition emphasized that they should behave in a talkative, bold, and energetic manner for the group discussion. Instructions for the introverted condition emphasized that they should behave in a reserved, compliant, and unadventurous manner for the group discussion. They were then asked to have a discussion of either the 10 most important items needed after an airplane crash or to come up with 10 possible solutions to the parking problem on their campus.

During the discussion, observers rated how positive each participant appeared. Also, following the discussion, each participant self-reported how positive they felt during the discussion. For both of these variables—observed positivity and self-reported positive feelings—the subjects in the extraverted condition were substantially higher than persons in the introverted condition. Moreover, this effect did not depend on the person's actual levels of trait extraversion. This study shows that being in an extraverted situation (being with a group of energetic, talkative people) can raise a person's level of positive affect. The study clearly illustrates that, when it comes to person X situation interactions, situations can influence persons just as much as persons can influence situations.

Evocation

Another form of person-situation interaction discussed by Buss (1987) is **evocation,** the idea that certain personality traits may evoke specific responses from the environment. For example, people who are disagreeable and manipulative may evoke certain reactions in others, such as hostility and avoidance. In other words, people may create their own environments by eliciting certain responses from others. Consider the case of a male patient who had trouble sustaining relationships with women, such that he was divorced three times (Wachtel, 1973). He complained to his therapist that every woman with whom he became involved turned out to be bad-tempered, vicious, and spiteful. He complained that his relationships started out satisfying but always ended with the women becoming angry and leaving him. Wachtel (1973) speculated that *the man* must have been doing something to *evoke* this response from the women in his life.

The idea of evocation is similar to the idea of transference, discussed in Chapter 9 on psychoanalysis. Transference occurs when a patient in psychoanalysis re-creates, with the analyst, the interpersonal problems he or she is having with significant others. In doing so, the patient may evoke in the therapist the reactions and feelings that he or she typically evokes in other persons. Malcomb (1988) reported on a male psychoanalyst who found one female patient to be particularly boring. The analyst could hardly stay awake during the therapy sessions because the patient and her problems seemed so dull and trivial to him. After experiencing this reaction for a few weeks, however, the analyst realized that the patient was making him feel bored, just as she made other men in her life feel bored. She made herself dull, he concluded, in order to avoid the attentions of men and drive them away. However, she was in therapy, in part, because she complained of being lonely. This case illustrates how people can evoke reactions in others—creating and re-creating certain kinds of social situations in their everyday lives.

Manipulation

A third form of person-situation interaction is **manipulation,** which can be defined as the various means by which people influence the behavior of others. Manipulation is the intentional use of certain tactics to coerce, influence, or change others. Manipulation changes the social situation. Manipulation differs from selection in that selection involves choosing existing environments, whereas manipulation entails altering those environments already inhabited. Individuals differ in the tactics of manipulation they use. Researchers have found, for example, that some individuals use a charm tactic—complimenting others, acting warm and caring, and doing favors for others in order to influence them. Other people use a manipulation tactic sometimes referred to as the silent treatment, ignoring or failing to respond to the other person. A third tactic is coercion, which consists of making demands, yelling, criticizing, cursing, and threatening the other to get what one wants (Buss et al., 1987).

Interestingly, these forms of manipulation are linked with personality traits. Extraverts, for example, tend to deploy the charm tactic more than introverts do. Those high on neuroticism tend to use the silent treatment to get their way. And those high on quarrelsomeness tend to use the coercion tactic to get their way. In summary, the enduring personality traits of individuals are linked in interesting ways with the tactics they use to manipulate their social environment.

Aggregation

We've seen how their debate with Mischel led trait psychologists to appreciate that behavior is an outcome of the interaction between personality traits and situations. Another important lesson learned by trait psychologists is the value of aggregation when it comes to measuring personality traits. Aggregation is the process of adding up, or averaging, several single observations, resulting in a better (i.e., more reliable) measure of a personality trait than a single observation of behavior. This approach usually provides psychologists with a better measure of a personality trait than does using a single observation. Consider the concept of batting average, which is seen as a measure of a baseball player's batting ability (a trait). It turns out that batting average is not a very good predictor of whether or not a player will get a hit during any *single* time at bat. In fact, psychologist Abelson (1985) analyzed single batting occasions over the whole season. He found that batting average accounted for only .3 percent of the variance in getting a hit. This is a remarkably poor relationship, so why do people pay such close attention to batting average, and why do players with a good batting average earn so much more money? Because what matters is how a player performs *over the long run,* over an entire season. This is the principle of aggregation in action.

To draw an analogy between batting average and personality, let's say you decide to marry someone, in part, because of that person's cheerful disposition. Clearly, there will be days when your spouse is not going to be cheerful. However, what matters to you is your spouse's behavior over the long term (i.e., how cheerful your spouse will be in general) and not his or her mood on any given day or occasion.

Imagine taking an intelligence test that has only one item. Do you think that this one-item test would be a good measure of your overall intelligence? You would be right if you concluded that a single question was probably not a very accurate or fair measure of overall intelligence. A related example might be if the instructor in your personality course were to decide that your entire grade for a course would be determined by asking you only one question on the final exam. Surely one question could not possibly measure your knowledge of the course material. Single questions or single observations are rarely good measures of anything.

Recall the Hartshorne and May (1928) study in which the researchers measured honesty by assessing whether or not a child cheated during a game on one occasion during summer camp. Do you think that this one-item measure of honesty was an accurate reflection of the participants' true levels of honesty? It probably was not. This is one reason that Hartshorne and May found such small correlations between their various measures of honesty (that is, because they were all single-item measures).

Personality psychologist Seymour Epstein published several papers (1979, 1980, 1983) showing that aggregating several questions or observations results in better trait measures. Longer tests are more reliable than shorter ones (reliability was introduced in Chapter 2) and hence are better measures of traits. If we want to know how conscientious a person is, we should observe many conscientious-related behaviors (e.g., how neat he or she is or how punctual) on many occasions and aggregate, or average, the responses. Any single behavior on any single occasion may be influenced by all sorts of extenuating circumstances unrelated to personality.

Imagine that a trait psychologist is developing a questionnaire to measure how helpful, caring, and conscientious respondents are. She includes the following item on the questionnaire: "How often in the past few years have you stopped to help a person whose car was stuck in the snow?" Imagine further that you live in a place where it rarely snows. You answer "never," even though you are a generally helpful person. Now imagine being asked a whole set of questions, such as how often you donate money to charity, participate in blood donation programs, and do volunteer work in your community. Your answers to that whole series of questions provides a better indicator of your true level of helpfulness than does your answer to any single question.

Psychologists "rediscovered" aggregation in the 1980s. Charles Spearman published a paper back in 1910, explaining that tests with more items are generally more reliable than tests with fewer items. Spearman provided a formula—now called the Spearman-Brown prophesy formula—for determining precisely how much a test's reliability will increase as it is made longer. Although this formula appears in all the major textbooks on measurement and statistics, personality psychologists seemed to have forgotten about the principle of aggregation until Epstein (1980, 1983) published his reminders in the early 1980s. Since then, other researchers have provided ample demonstrations of how the principle of aggregation works to increase the strength of correlations between measures of personality and measures of behavior. For example, according to a study by Diener and Larsen (1984), measures of activity level on one day correlated with activity level on another day at a correlation of only .08. However, when activity level was averaged over a three-week period and then correlated with activity level averaged over another three-week period, that correlation went up to .66. Clearly, aggregation provides a more stable and reliable measure of a person's average standing on a trait than any single observation can.

Aggregation is a technique designed to improve trait measures by adding items to a questionnaire or adding observations to obtain an overall score. Aggregation implies that traits are only one influence on behavior. That is, at any given time, for any given behavior, many factors influence why a person does one thing and not another. Aggregation also implies that traits refer to a person's average level. Traits are similar to the set-point concept in weight; a person's weight will fluctuate from day to day, but there is a set point, or average level, to which they typically return. An otherwise cheerful woman, for example, might be irritable on one occasion because she has a stomachache. If you were to observe this person on many occasions, however, you would be apt to conclude that, on average, she is generally cheerful.

This example illustrates that personality traits are **average tendencies** to behave in certain ways. Personality psychologists will *never* be very good at predicting single acts on single occasions. We may know, for example, that there is a strong negative correlation between conscientiousness and an aggregate measure of being late for class, yet, even if we know everyone's conscientiousness score in your class, are we able to predict on which particular day a specific person will be late? That's not likely. We can, for example, predict who is likely to be late over the whole semester, but we are not able to predict, from that person's personality scores alone, which *specific days* he or she will be late. Situational forces (e.g., a failed alarm clock or a flat tire) may determine why a person is late on any specific day. But personality may play a role in determining why a person is frequently late (e.g., low on conscientiousness).

Measurement Issues

More than any other approach to personality, the trait approach relies on self-report questionnaires to measure personality. Although trait psychologists *can* use other measurement methods (e.g., projective techniques, behavioral observation), questionnaires are the most frequently used method for measuring traits (Craik, 1986). Personality psychologists assume that people differ from each other in the *amounts* of various traits they possess, so the key measurement issue is determining *how much* of a particular trait a person possesses.

Traits are often represented as dimensions along which people differ from each other. Consider the trait of conscientiousness. At one end of the conscientiousness dimension are people who are responsible, dependable, reliable, trustworthy, and scrupulous in their appearance and personal habits. Perhaps you know someone who fits this description. At the other end of the dimension are people who are irresponsible, unconcerned about details, untidy, careless, and perhaps even disorderly and unreliable in their personal affairs. One of the most efficient ways to assess people's standing on this or any other personality trait dimension is simply to ask them about their characteristics—how neat they are, whether they are usually on time for appointments, and so on. If the right questions are asked, as the trait view holds, an accurate assessment of a person's standing on the trait dimension will be obtained.

As compelling as this view of trait assessment is, it assumes that people generally are willing and able to report accurately on their behavior. However, some people may be unwilling to disclose information about themselves or may be motivated for some reason to distort or otherwise falsify their self-reports, such as during an employment interview or a parole hearing. Trait psychologists have long concerned themselves with the circumstances that affect the accuracy, reliability, validity, and utility of trait measures. We will now consider some important measurement issues in trait research.

Carelessness

Some participants filling out a trait questionnaire might not be motivated to answer carefully or truthfully. For example, some colleges and universities require introductory psychology students to participate in psychology experiments, many of which involve personality questionnaires. These volunteer participants may not be motivated to complete the questionnaires carefully; they may rush through the questionnaire answering randomly. Other participants may be motivated to answer correctly but might accidentally invalidate their answer sheets. For example, when participants are asked to put their answers on optical scanning sheets by filling in circles with a number 2 lead pencil, it is not uncommon for participants to inadvertently neglect to fill in a circle or two, which means that all subsequent answers are then incorrect as well. Another problem arises when, for some reason, the participant is *not* reading the questions carefully but is nevertheless providing answers. Perhaps the participant has difficulty reading, is tired, or even is hallucinating.

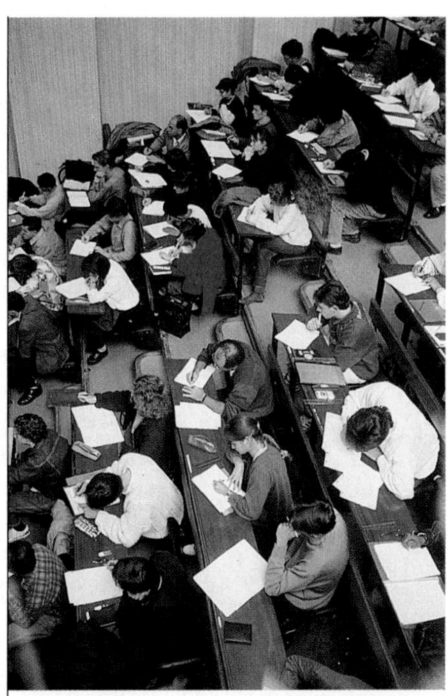

Personality tests are frequently administered in large group settings. In such settings, some people may be careless or even fake their responses. Psychologists have developed ways of detecting faking and carelessness, as well as response sets, in the answers from individual test takers.

A common method for detecting these problems is to use an **infrequency scale** embedded within the set of questionnaire items. The infrequency scale contains items that all or almost all people will answer in a particular way. Using such items, if a person endorses more than one or two of these items in the "wrong" direction, then his or her test is flagged as suspicious. For example, on the Personality Research Form (Jackson & Messick, 1967), the infrequency scale contains items such as the following: "I do not believe that wood really burns," "I make all my own clothes and shoes," and "Whenever I walk up stairs, I always do so on my hands." These questions are answered "False" by over 95 percent of the people in samples from the United States and Canada. If a participant answers more than one or two of these as "True," we may begin to suspect that his or her answers do not represent valid information. Such a participant may be answering randomly, may have difficulty reading, or may be marking his or her answer sheet incorrectly.

Another technique used to detect carelessness is to include duplicate questions spaced far apart in the questionnaire. The psychologist can then determine the number of times the participant answered identical questions with different responses. If this happens often, the psychologist might suspect carelessness or another problem that invalidates the person's answers.

Faking on Questionnaires

Faking involves the motivated distortion of answers on a questionnaire. When personality questionnaires are used to make important decisions about people's lives (e.g., hire them for a job, promote them, decide that they are not guilty by reason of insanity, or allow prisoners to be paroled), then there is always the possibility of faking. Some people may be motivated to "fake good" in order to appear to be better off or better adjusted than they really are. Others may be motivated to "fake bad" in order to appear to be worse off or more maladjusted than they really are. For example, a worker suing a company for mental anguish caused by a poor working condition might be motivated to appear very distressed to the court-appointed psychologist.

Questionnaire developers have attempted to devise ways to detect faking good and faking bad. In constructing the 16 Personality Factor Questionnaire, for example, Cattell, Eber, and Tatsouoka (1970) had groups of participants complete the questionnaire under specific instructions. One group of participants was instructed to fake good, to appear to be as well adjusted as possible. Another group of participants was instructed to fake bad, to try to appear as maladjusted as possible. The data for these two groups were then used to generate a "faking good profile" and a "faking bad profile." The data from real participants can then be compared with those in these two faking profiles, and the psychologist can calculate just how much a person's responses fit the profile of the groups asked to fake their answers. This approach offers psychologists an imperfect but nevertheless reasonable method for determining the likelihood that a person is faking his or her responses to the questionnaire.

There are two ways for psychologists to make a mistake when seeking to distinguish between genuine and faked responses. They may conclude that a truthful person was faking and reject that person's data (called a **false negative**). Or they may decide that a person who was faking was actually telling the truth (called a **false positive**). Psychologists do not know for certain how well their faking scales perform when it comes to minimizing the percentages of false positives and false negatives. Because of this problem of undetected faking, many psychologists are suspicious of self-report questionnaire measures of personality.

Response Sets

When participants answer questions, psychologists typically assume that they are responding to the content of the questionnaire items. For example, when participants are confronted with the question "I have never felt like smashing things," psychologists assume that participants think of all the times when they were angry or frustrated and then recall whether on those occasions they have ever felt like smashing or actually did smash something. Psychologists also assume that participants make a

		The person being tested really is being . . .	
		Honest	Dishonest
The psychologist concludes he or she is . . .	Honest	Correct	False positive "incorrect"
	Dishonest	False negative "incorrect"	Correct

Two ways to make a mistake when deciding whether a person was faking his or her responses to a personality questionnaire.

deliberate and conscious effort to consider the content of the question and then answer "True" or "False" to honestly reflect their behavior. This assumption may sometimes be incorrect.

The concept of **response sets** refers to the tendency of some people to respond to the questions on a basis that is unrelated to the question content. Sometimes this is also referred to as **noncontent responding.** One example is the response set of **acquiescence,** or yea saying. This is the tendency to simply agree with the questionnaire items, regardless of the content of those items. Psychologists counteract acquiescence by intentionally reverse-scoring some of the questionnaire items, such as an extraversion item that states, "I frequently prefer to be alone." **Extreme responding** is another response set, which refers to the tendency to give endpoint responses, such as "strongly agree" or "strongly disagree" and to avoid the middle part of response scales, such as, "slightly agree" or "slightly disagree."

Many personality psychologists worry about the effects of response sets on the validity of questionnaire information. If a participant is responding not to the content of the questions but on another basis, then his or her answers do not reflect the aspect of personality being measured. Response sets may invalidate self-report measures of personality, so psychologists have looked for ways to detect and counteract the effects of noncontent responding.

The response set known as **social desirability** has received the greatest amount of research and evaluation by personality psychologists. Socially desirable responding is the tendency to answer items in such a way as to come across as socially attractive or likable. People responding in this manner want to make a good impression, to appear to be well adjusted, to be a good citizen. For example, imagine being asked to answer "True" or "False" to the statement "Most of the time I am happy." A person might actually be happy only 45 percent of the time yet answer "True" because this is the well-adjusted thing to say in our culture. People like happy people, so the socially desirable response is "Yes, I am happy most of the time." This is an example of responding not to the content of the item but to the kind of impression a "True" or "False" answer would create, and it represents a response set.

Some rare individuals, like the late Mother Teresa of Calcutta, might score high on social desirability because they are in fact truly good, not because they want to create a good impression of themselves by lying on a personality questionnaire.

There are two views regarding the interpretation of social desirability. One view is that it represents distortion or error and should be eliminated or minimized. The other view is that social desirability is a valid part of other desirable personality traits, such as happiness, conscientiousness, or agreeableness. We will first consider how psychologists have viewed social desirability as distortion.

Viewing social desirability as distortion does not assume that the person is consciously trying to create a positive impression. A social desirability response set may not actually be an outright effort to distort responses and, so, is different from outright faking or lying. Some people may simply have a distorted view of themselves or have a strong need to have others think well of them. For this reason, most psychologists have resisted calling this response set "lying" or "faking" (cf. Eysenck & Eysenck, 1972, for a different opinion). Nevertheless, many personality psychologists believe that socially desirable responding introduces inaccuracies into test scores and should be eliminated or controlled. If you wanted to know how happy a person perceives him- or herself to be, for example, you would want to have an accurate measure of his or her true level of happiness, not one that is contaminated by a need to create a good impression.

One approach to the problem of socially desirable responses is to assume that they are erroneous or deceptive, to measure this tendency, and to remove it statistically from the other questionnaire responses. There are several social desirability measures available to the personality psychologist. Several items from a popular measure developed by Crowne and Marlowe (1964) are presented in Table 4.1. Crowne and Marlowe thought of social desirability as reflecting a need for approval,

Table 4.1 Crowne/Marlowe Scale for Measuring Social Desirability

Instructions: Listed below are a number of statements concerning personal attitudes and traits. Read each item and decide whether the statement is true or false as it pertains to you personally.

	True	False
1. I'm always willing to admit it when I make a mistake.	___	___
2. I always try to practice what I preach.	___	___
3. I never resent being asked to return a favor.	___	___
4. I have never been irked when people expressed ideas very different from my own.	___	___
5. I have never deliberately said something that hurt someone's feelings.	___	___
6. I like to gossip at times.	___	___
7. There have been occasions when I took advantage of someone.	___	___
8. I sometimes try to get even rather than forgive and forget.	___	___
9. At times I have really insisted on having things my own way.	___	___
10. There have been occasions when I felt like smashing things.	___	___

Source: from Crowne & Marlowe, 1964.

and they published the social desirability scale in their book *The Approval Motive*. Looking at the items on their scale, you can see that they typically refer to minor transgressions that most of us have committed, or inadequacies that many if not most of us suffer from. In addition, some items refer to almost saintlike behavior. To the extent that a person denies common faults and problems and endorses a lot of perfect and well-adjusted behaviors, he or she will get a high score on social desirability. A person's score on social desirability can be used to statistically adjust his or her scores on other questionnaires, thereby controlling for this response set.

A second way to deal with the problem of social desirability is by developing questionnaires that are less susceptible to this type of responding. For example, in selecting questions to put on a questionnaire, the researcher may select only the items that have been found *not* to correlate with social desirability. This approach allows the test maker to build in a defense against the problem of social desirability during the process of constructing a questionnaire.

A third approach to minimizing the effects of socially desirable responding is to use a **forced-choice questionnaire** format. In this format, test takers are confronted with pairs of statements and are asked to indicate which statement in each pair is more true of them. Each statement in the pair is selected to be similar to the other in social desirability, forcing participants to choose between statements that are equivalently socially desirable (or undesirable). The following items (see bottom of page 115) from the Vando Reducer Augmenter Scale (Vando, 1974) illustrate the forced-choice format: Which would you most prefer (a or b)?

A Closer Look

Integrity Testing

Throughout history, employers have been concerned about employee theft. Such thefts could be avoided or at least minimized if there were a way to tell whether a person was generally honest or dishonest before hiring him or her. Over two centuries ago, the Chinese developed a test to determine whether a person was lying. The test consisted of asking the suspect a question, waiting for the answer, and then placing rice powder in the suspect's mouth. If the suspect could not swallow the rice powder, it was viewed as a sure sign that he or she was lying. This may sound like superstition, but, if you think of the dry mouth that usually accompanies nervousness, then there might be some face validity to this early lie detection technique.

The modern lie detector, a polygraph, is a mechanical device that relies on psychophysiological measures, such as heart rate, respiration, and skin conductance (see Chapter 7). The use of physiological measures for lie detection started early in the 1900s in the United States. The idea behind this approach is that physiological measures may be useful in detecting the nervous arousal (e.g., guilt feelings) that often accompanies lying. The origin of the modern lie detection machine is shrouded in mystery. Some attribute it to a police officer from Berkeley, California, named Larson, who constructed the prototype of the multichanneled polygraph between 1917 and 1921 and also published a manual on how to use the machine. Others trace the idea of using psychophysiological recordings—in particular, systolic blood pressure—to measure deception in laboratory and legal settings to William Moulton Marston, who worked on this problem while he was a graduate student at Harvard University from 1915 to 1921.

The lie detector gained widespread attention in the 1930s when it was introduced in the trial of Bruno Hauptman, who was accused of murdering the Lindbergh baby. Businesses began using the polygraph widely in the 1970s.

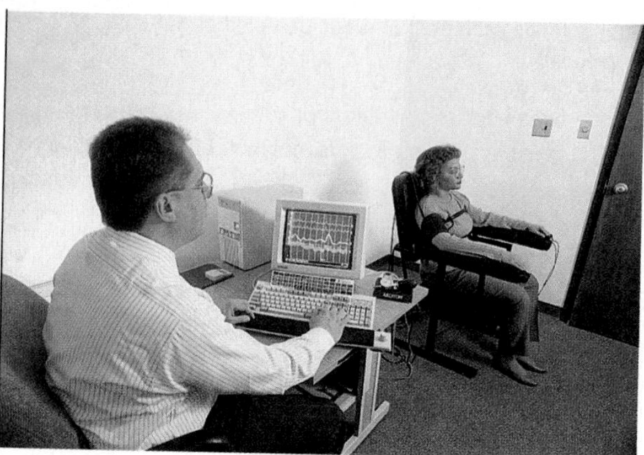

Polygraph exams formerly were widely used in employment screening until they were banned by Congress in 1988 from use in private sector employment settings. The government, however, still uses polygraphs in employment screening as well as periodic honesty verification of persons in sensitive positions. In fact, the U.S. government runs several training institutes that certify persons to administer standard polygraph exams.

The polygraph was originally designed to detect guilt reactions arising from denying specific criminal acts. However, many employers began to use polygraph and other so-called lie detector tests to screen potential employees for general *honesty*. That is, the original purpose was to assess a state (guilt), whereas the polygraph was often pressed into usage to assess a trait (honesty). At any rate, participants were connected to these devices and asked various incriminating questions, such as whether they had ever taken anything that did not belong to them. If they showed any signs of nervousness or arousal (e.g., increased heart rate or shallower breathing) they might not have been hired. Employers also routinely used lie detector tests to question employees who were already on the job. Fast-food chains were among the largest users of polygraph tests in employment settings during this era (1970 to 1988). Managers hired polygraphers to connect employees to these devices, then ask questions such as whether they had taken any hamburgers or money in the past few months. If the polygraphs indicated any signs of nervousness, the employee might have been fired.

Through the 1970s and 1980s, more than 3 million polygraph tests were administered each year in the United States alone (Murphy, 1995). If you went into a large class of college students in the 1980s and asked if anyone had ever taken a polygraph exam, it was common to see at least a couple of hands go up for every hundred or so persons. Most said that they took the polygraph test as part of an employment screening procedure, often when applying for jobs in fast-food outlets.

A scientific evaluation of the polygraph as a lie detector was undertaken in 1983 by the U.S. federal government's Office of Technology Assessment. Its report concluded that there was no such device as a lie detector. Technically, this is true, as the polygraph detects physiological arousal, and sometimes lying is not accompanied by physiological arousal. In addition, sometimes physiological arousal is not accompanied by lying. The government evaluators also concluded that none of the methods used for lie detection were foolproof and that there were several effective ways to beat the device. Moreover, the polygraph's use in employment settings to screen for honesty trait may have resulted more in employment discrimination than in honesty detection.

In 1988, the U.S. Congress banned the use of the polygraph for most employment purposes in the private sector. Interestingly, the government still uses polygraphs for employee selection in several government service branches, such as the Secret Service, the CIA, the FBI, the DEA, Customs, and even the Postal Service. The government also maintains several polygraph schools, where people go to be trained in the use of the polygraph. In the private sector, however, the use of the polygraph in employment settings is highly restricted at this time.

This leaves the private sector employer with no mechanical means for detecting whether potential employees are honest or not. However, since the ban on polygraphs, many publishing companies have developed and promoted questionnaire measures to use in place of the polygraph (DeAngelis, 1991). These questionnaires, called **integrity tests,** are designed to assess whether a person is generally honest or dishonest. Many of these tests are considered to be reasonably reliable and valid and, so, may be legally used for employment screening (DeAngelis, 1991). Integrity tests measure attitudes related to one or more of the following psychological constructs: tolerating others who steal, beliefs that many others engage in theft, rationalizations that theft may be acceptable, interthief loyalty, antisocial beliefs and behaviors, and admission to stealing in the past. These tests typically consist of two parts. The first part measures attitudes toward theft, e.g., beliefs concerning the frequency and extent of theft, whether or not theft should be punished and how severely, and ruminations about theft. The second part concerns admissions regarding theft and other wrongdoing. Applicants are asked to describe the frequency and amount of theft and other illegal or counterproductive activity they engaged in on past jobs. Test items that make up integrity tests are clearly assessing job-related content (e.g., "Will everyone steal at work if the conditions are right?"; "Do you believe you are too honest to steal at work?"; "Do you think it is humanly possible for the average person to be completely honest on the job?" etc.).

A recent review of integrity questionnaires (Ones & Viswesvaran, 1998) looked at the use of these tests in organizations. They concluded that the measures are reliable (have test-retest correlations in the range of .85). There has been a great deal of validity research showing that integrity test scores can predict theft behavior. Questionnaire integrity tests have been found to predict the following theft criteria: (a) supervisors' ratings of employees' dishonesty, (b) applicants who are likely to get caught stealing once hired, (c) applicants who have a criminal history, and (d) applicants who are likely to admit theft in an anonymous testing situation. Longitudinal studies also demonstrate the impact of integrity tests. In one study, a group of convenience stores started using an integrity test to select employees and experienced a 50 percent reduction in inventory shrinkage due to theft over an 18-month period. A home improvement center chain also reported similar reductions in inventory loss after starting an integrity testing program.

When assessed against the big five traits—a widely accepted theory of personality known as the Big Five model (see Chapter 3, p. 82)—integrity appears to be a combination of high conscientiousness, high agreeableness, and low neuroticism. Moreover, these researchers found that integrity tests showed good predictive validity for absenteeism, counterproductive behavior on the job, violence at work, and theft on the job. They concluded that the concept of integrity has an important role to play in theories of job performance and counterproductivity in organizations, and that integrity tests can be valuable additions to typical measures used in employee selection (e.g., background checks, letters of reference).

1. a. to read the book
b. to see the movie
2. a. eat soft food
b. eat crunchy food
3. a. continuous anesthesia
b. continuous hallucinations
4. a. a job that requires concentration
b. a job that requires travel

If one answers all *b*s, this scale measures the preference for arousing or strong stimulation. The two choices presented in each item are of approximately the same value in terms of social desirability. Consequently, participants must decide on an answer based on something other than social desirability. They should respond to the *content* of the item and hence provide accurate information about their personalities. Other scales that use the forced-choice format to control for social desirability have been developed by Crandall (1991) and Buss et al. (1992).

Although many psychologists view socially desirable responding as error and as something to be avoided or eliminated, others see it as valid responding. Psychologists who subscribe to this point of view consider social desirability to be a trait in itself, one that is correlated with other positive traits, such as happiness, adjustment, and conscientiousness. These psychologists have argued that being mentally healthy may, in fact, entail possessing an overly positive view of oneself and one's abilities. In her book *Positive Illusions,* social psychologist Shelly Taylor (1989) summarizes a good deal of research suggesting that positive and self-enhancing illusions about the self, the world, and one's future can promote psychological adjustment and mental health. In a recent summary of this position, Taylor et al. (2000) review research that finds that unrealistic beliefs about the self (positive illusions) are related to better physical health, such as slower progression of disease in men infected with HIV. If psychologists were to measure such positive illusions in the form of social desirability, and remove them from other personality measures, they might, in effect, be throwing the baby out with the bathwater. That is, social desirability may be part of being high on various trait measures of adjustment and positive mental health.

Work on social desirability has attempted to disentangle self-deceptive optimism from impression management. Psychologist Delroy Paulhus has developed a social desirability inventory, called the Balanced Inventory of Desirable Responding, which contains two separate subscales (Paulhus, 1984, 1990). The Self-deceptive Enhancement subscale was designed to tap self-deceptive overconfidence and contains items such as "My first impressions of other people are always right." The Impression Management subscale was designed to measure the tendency to present oneself favorably, as in the distortion interpretation of social desirability, and contains items such as "I don't gossip about other people's business." This subscale was intended to be sensitive to self-presentation motives, such as those that lead someone to want to create a good impression in others. In one study, the Impression Management subscale was strongly affected by instructions to the participants to fake good or bad, whereas the Self-deceptive Enhancement subscale, the part that measures overconfidence and positive illusions, was hardly affected at all by these instructions (Paulhus, Bruce, & Trapnell, 1995). The Impression Management subscale might thus be sensitive to changes in self-presentation strategies, as might occur in job application settings or parole hearings (Paulhus, Fridhandler, & Hayes, 1997).

Beware of Barnum Statements in Personality Test Interpretations

"We have something for everyone."

—P. T. Barnum

Barnum statements are generalities—statements that could apply to anyone—though they often appear to the readers of astrology advice columns to apply specifically to them. Astrology predictions are very popular in newspapers and magazines. For example: "You sometimes have doubts about whether you have done the right thing" or "You have a need for others to like or admire you" or "Although you are able to deal with confrontation in a pinch, you typically like to avoid it if you can." These are Barnum statements. People read such statements and think, "Yes, that's me all right," when in fact such statements could apply to anyone.

Personality test interpreters also sometimes offer interpretations that consist of Barnum statements. To illustrate this, one of the authors of this textbook completed an online version of the Meyers-Briggs Type Indicator, a very popular personality test. He then submitted his answers to three different online interpretation services, to get feedback about his personality. Reading the results of the first interpretation, he felt it had it right: "You advance toward good and retreat from evil . . . , you hate to miss out on what is going on around you . . . , you always try to tell the truth to those around you . . . , you strive to be authentic and genuine and you communicate well with others . . ." The second interpretation also sounded accurate: "You want to be liked and admired by others . . . , you are interested in new ideas . . . , you have a great deal of charm and others genuinely like you . . . , at times your attention span can be short . . . , you dislike bureaucracy . . ." The third interpretation, too, seemed to apply: "You are fun to be around . . . , while you can be intellectual, serious, and all business, you are also capable of flipping the switch and becoming childlike, interested in fun . . . , you enjoy learning new things and have good self-discipline . . ."

These interpretations all sounded personally relevant. The only problem was that the answers to the questionnaire were filled in at random. That is, the author of this book did not read the questions, but merely clicked "true" or "false" randomly. How then did these test interpretations seem to apply so personally and directly? Read the interpretations again and you will see that they are Barnum statements. They could apply to just about anyone.

This example is not meant to suggest that the MBTI is not a good test. Rather, it is the personality feedback or test interpretations that can sometimes not be accurate. Recall that these interpretations were obtained from free online services. So this example could also be an illustration of the advice, "you get what you pay for." Most reliable test interpretation services charge a fee for this service.

Reliable test interpretation services typically make statements that are quantitative or that provide information about a person's standing on a trait relative to others. So, for example, an interpretation might state: "Your scores on extraversion put you in the highest or most extraverted 10% of the population." Or the statement might refer to research results, such as: "Persons with extraversion scores such as yours were found to be extremely satisfied in careers that involved frequent social contact, such as salespersons, teachers, or public relations work." Also, reliable test interpretation services typically include checks for careless responding, as discussed earlier in this chapter. They typically provide an assessment of how suspicious one should be regarding the validity of the person's responses. None of the free test interpretation services used in this example provided such checks, and so none of them detected that the responses were random.

So far we have discussed some of the theoretical and measurement issues in trait psychology. Trait psychologists do not only concern themselves with these somewhat esoteric and academic issues. Trait psychology also has some real-world applications. We turn now to a consideration of some of the practical uses to which personality trait measures have been put.

Personality and Prediction

Personality measures have a long history of use in industry and government. They are used in the federal and state prison systems to make decisions about inmates. They are also widely used in industry to match people with particular jobs, to help screen people for employment, and to select people for promotion. An employer may feel that emotional stability is a requirement for a specific job (e.g., firefighter) or that the personality trait of honesty is especially important (e.g., for a clerk in a jewelry store or for a driver for a money delivery truck). Other jobs may require strong organizational or social skills or the ability to work in a distracting environment. Whether someone does well in employment settings may be determined, in part, by whether the individual's personality traits mesh with the job requirements. In short, personality traits may predict who is likely to do well in a particular job, so it makes some sense to try to select people for employment based on measures of these traits.

Applications of Personality Testing in the Workplace

In an increasingly competitive business environment, many employers resort to employment testing to improve their workforce. The majority of the Fortune 100 companies use some form of employment selection that includes psychological testing. A survey by the American Management Association revealed that 44 percent of its responding members used testing to screen or select employees. While cognitive ability testing (e.g., comprehension, reading speed) is the most commonly used form of psychological testing in the workplace, personality tests are being used more and more frequently.

The personality tests used in the workplace are mostly self-report measures of specific traits or dispositions. A very large number of personality measures are available. Some personality measures characterize people within the normal range of personality functioning, while others focus on the identification of psychopathology or abnormal levels of functioning. Many personality tests, such as the Minnesota Multiphasic Personality Inventory (MMPI) or the California Personality Inventory (CPI), assess a large number of personality characteristics; others measure single traits in which the employer is specifically interested.

Employers use different types of personality tests for different purposes. There are three main reasons why employers use personality assessment in the workplace:

Personnel Selection

Employers sometimes use personality tests to select people especially suitable for a specific job. For example, an insurance company might use a measure of extraversion–introversion to select applicants high on extraversion for a sales job so that their characteristics match successful incumbents in their sales department. Alternatively, the employer may want to use personality assessments to de-select, or screen out, people with specific traits. For example, a police department might use the MMPI or a similar test to screen out applicants that have high levels of mental instability or psychopathology. Next we will describe several specific tests and applications of **personnel selection** using personality tests.

Integrity Testing

Personality tests that assess honesty or integrity are probably the most widely used form of personality assessment in the business world. They are commonly used in the retail and financial services industries in selecting people for low-paying entry level jobs where the employee handles money or merchandise in an unsupervised setting. Integrity tests are designed to predict a tendency toward theft or other forms of counterproductive behaviors in work settings, such as absenteeism.

The annual economic losses to American business from employee theft are estimated at between $15 billion to $25 billion per year. Moreover, a substantial proportion of annual business failures have been blamed on employee theft. Because of this, many employers are interested in any technique that could detect those employees most likely to commit theft on the job. Because of the frequency and importance of integrity testing in the workplace, we have dedicated a "Closer Look" box to this topic.

Concerns over Negligent Hiring

A third reason some employers use personality testing arises from the fact that, should an employee assault a customer or another coworker on the job, the employer may be held accountable in a court case. In such a case, the employer could be charged with **negligent hiring,** that is, hiring someone who is unstable or prone to violence. With cases of negligent hiring now being tried in the courts of most states, employers are defending themselves against a growing number of suits seeking compensation for crimes committed by their employees. In such cases, the employer is charged with negligently hiring an applicant with traits that posed a threat of injury to others. Such cases hinge on whether the employer should have discovered those traits ahead of time, before hiring such a person into a position where he or she posed a threat to others. Personality testing may provide evidence that the employer did in fact try to reasonably investigate an applicant's fitness for the workplace. Companies that do engage in some form of pre-employment personality testing to screen job applicants may reduce their chances of being charged with a negligent hiring claim. Personality testing may be particularly important in states where it is difficult to conduct criminal or other background checks on applicants.

Legal Issues in Personality Testing in Employment Settings

Legal issues surrounding the use of personality and other tests in employment settings can be traced to the Civil Rights Act of 1964, which barred racial discrimination in public places, including theaters, restaurants, hotels, and polling places. **Title VII of the Civil Rights Act** also required employers to provide equal employment opportunities to all persons. The first test of the Civil Rights Act in employment law occurred in the case of ***Griggs v. Duke Power.*** Prior to 1964 the Duke Power Company had used clearly discriminatory practices in hiring and work assignment, including barring blacks from certain jobs. After passage of the Civil Rights Act, Duke Power instituted various requirements for such jobs, including passing certain aptitude tests. The effect was to perpetuate discrimination. In 1971 the Supreme Court ruled that the seemingly neutral testing practices used by Duke Power were unacceptable because they operated to maintain discrimination. Moreover, the court ruled that any selection procedure could not produce disparate impact for a group protected by the Act (e.g., racial groups, women). This Supreme Court decision put the burden of proof on the employer to demonstrate that selection procedures were not discriminatory and did not produce disparate impact on specific groups, for example, were not biased to select fewer people from specific groups.

The next major event in employee selection occurred in 1978 when the Department of Labor released the **Uniform Guidelines on Employee Selection Procedures.**

These guidelines were widely adopted and are still in use today by the Department of Justice. The purpose of the guidelines is to provide a set of principles for employee selection that meet the requirements of all Federal laws, especially those that prohibit discrimination on the basis of race, color, religion, sex, or national origin. They provide details on the proper use of personality tests and other selection procedures in employment settings. The guidelines define discrimination and adverse impact, describe how to evaluate and document the validity evidence for tests, and instruct employers on what records to keep. Most good companies that provide psychological testing services for employment selection will also provide consultation on how to make sure all employment practices conform to the Uniform Guidelines. Indeed, an employer who subcontracts testing to a psychological services company would want to make sure not only that the testing company conforms to the Uniform Guidelines, but that they would also assist in any court case brought against the original company on the basis of their hiring practices.

Another important legal case in employment law is that of ***Ward's Cove Packing Co. v. Atonio.*** Ward's Cove Packing Co. was a salmon cannery operating in Alaska. Cannery jobs were filled predominantly by non-Whites. Noncannery jobs were filled predominantly with White workers. Virtually all of the noncannery jobs paid more than cannery positions. In 1974 the non-White cannery workers started legal action against the company, alleging that a variety of the company's hiring and promotion practices—for example, nepotism, a rehire preference, a lack of objective hiring criteria, separate hiring channels—were responsible for the racial stratification of the workforce. The claim was advanced under the disparate impact portion of Title VII of the Civil Rights Act. In 1989 the Supreme Court decided that employees filing discrimination lawsuits must expose specific hiring practices that led to disparities in the workplace. However, the court also decided that, even if the employees can prove discrimination, the hiring practices may still be considered legal if they serve "legitimate employment goals of the employer."

The *Ward's Cove* case watered down the effects of the *Griggs* decision, and allowed companies a loophole to continue with discriminatory employment practices as long as they could prove such practices served the needs of the company. For example, if a test excluded most black applicants, yet the company could prove that the test was job relevant, then the company could continue using this test. This case prompted Congress to pass the Civil Rights Act of 1991, which contained several important modifications to Title VII of the original act. The 1991 act expanded protected groups to include those based on race, color, religion, sex, or national origin. The new Act also prohibited use of different cutoff scores based on race in employment tests. Most importantly, however, the new Act shifted the burden of proof onto the employer by requiring that it must prove a close connection between disparate impact and the ability to actually perform the job in question.

Another important case, one with clear personality connections, was the case of ***Price Waterhouse v. Hopkins,*** also decided in 1989 by the Supreme Court. Ann Hopkins was a senior manager at an accounting firm who was being considered for promotion to partnership in the firm. Following its usual promotion practice, the firm asked each existing partner to evaluate Ms. Hopkins. Many of the evaluations came in as negative, criticizing her interpersonal skills and accusing her of being abrasive and too masculine for a woman (they felt she needed to wear more makeup, to walk and talk more femininely, etc.). She sued the company, charging that they had discriminated against her on the basis of sex, on the theory that her evaluations had been based on sexual stereotyping. The case eventually rose to the Supreme Court. Price Waterhouse acknowledged discrimination, but maintained that sexual stereotypes were just one factor and argued that there were other reasons to deny partnership to Hopkins. They argued that, even without any sex discrimination, Hopkins still would have been passed over.

The other legal issue, the one that won the case for Hopkins, was that she had been passed over for partner because of gender stereotyping within the company. In essence, she argued, the voting partners compared her to a cultural stereotype of how a woman is supposed to behave in the workplace and they decided that Hopkins did not fit that image. The American Psychological Association joined the case and provided expert evidence that such stereotypes do exist and that women who deviate from the cultural expectations are often penalized for violating these standards. The Supreme Court accepted the argument that gender stereotyping does exist and that it can create a bias against women in the workplace that is not permissible. By court order Ann Hopkins was made a full partner in her accounting firm. She went on to describe her long court case, both from a legal and personal perspective, in a book titled *So Ordered: Making Partner the Hard Way* by Ann Branigar Hopkins (Amherst: University of Massachusetts Press, 1996).

Disparate Impact

To prove a case of **disparate impact,** a plaintiff must show that an employment practice disadvantages people from a protected group. The Supreme Court has not defined the size of the disparity necessary to prove disparate impact. Most courts define disparity as a difference that is sufficiently large enough that it is unlikely to have occurred by chance. Tests of statistical significance are generally used to establish this. Some courts, however, have preferred the 80 percent rule contained in the Uniform Guidelines on Employee Selection Procedures. Under this rule, adverse impact is established if the selection rate for any race, sex, or ethnic group is less than four-fifths (or 80 percent) of the rate for the group with the highest selection rate.

Once the court accepts that adverse impact has occurred, the burden shifts to the employer to prove that the selection practice is job-related and consistent with business necessity. The Uniform Guidelines suggests three methods by which an employer can show job-relatedness: content validity, criterion validity, and construct validity. Content validity is used when the test closely approximates the job, as in a typing exam for a typist position. This form of validation is not generally applicable to personality testing because such tests measure general traits not specific abilities. Criterion validity compares performance on the test with performance on critical or important job behaviors. It is the preferred method of validation under the Uniform Guidelines but is not always technically feasible. Construct validity establishes relationships between aspects of satisfactory job performance and a specific trait, then measures of that trait are used for selection. For example, the job of customer service representative may require a specific interpersonal style to function effectively. This form of validation is the most appropriate for personality testing, because it focuses on the link between a particular trait and different aspects of job performance. If a test is job-related and satisfies the validity requirements of the Uniform Guidelines, then, in most cases, the disparate impact claim is dropped by the court. Table 4.2 lists the key kinds of validities that can be considered for any personality test.

Table 4.2 Types of Validity for Personality Tests

Content Validity—The test samples all the important features that are relevant to the trait being measured.

Criterion (or Concurrent) Validity—The test correlates with another measure of the trait in question. Often this other measure is too difficult or expensive to obtain routinely (e.g., performance in a standardized stress setting). Nevertheless, it defines a criterion that should be related to the test, if that test is valid.

Predictive Validity—The test predicts important future behaviors (e.g., outcomes) that are relevant to the trait being measured, e.g., supervisor ratings after a year on the job.

Discriminant Validity—The test is a relatively pure measure of the trait, in that it is not contaminated by other psychological characteristics. For example, a test of creativity measures primarily creativity, not intelligence or some other trait unrelated to creativity.

Incremental Validity—The test adds to our assessment-based knowledge above and beyond other information gathered, e.g., other tests. For example, the test performs in predictive or criterion validity studies at a better level than other known tests.

Construct Validity—When multiple relationships are established between a test and other measures and manifestations of the trait in question, then we say the test has construct validity for making inferences about that trait. Construct validity is a product of establishing many other kinds of validity, e.g., content validity, criterion validity, predictive validity, and discriminant validity.

Sources: Myers et al. (1988); Hirsch & Kummerow (1990).

There have been relatively few disparate impact cases involving personality tests, because such tests generally do not disadvantage any protected group. Integrity tests may have the best record of any selection technique in demonstrating freedom from adverse impact. Moreover, integrity test publishers typically have extensive statistical evidence demonstrating the validity of integrity tests in predicting theft and job-relevant counterproductive behavior, which would satisfy the employer's burden. Similar data supporting the job-relevance for other personality tests also exists. In some cases, however, an employer may need to perform their own validity studies.

Race or Gender Norming

The Civil Rights Act of 1991 forbids employers from using different norms or cutoff scores for different groups of people. For example, it would be illegal for a company to set a higher threshold for women than men on their selection test. A few personality test publishers, including versions of the Myers-Briggs Type Indicator (MBTI), recommend different scoring practices based on **race or gender norming.** This practice is clearly illegal and employers should avoid tests of this sort in favor of personality tests with standard norms applied equally to all applicants.

Americans with Disabilities Act (ADA)

The **American with Disabilities Act** states that an employer cannot conduct a medical examination, or even make inquiries as to whether an applicant has a disability, during the selection process. Moreover, even if a disability is obvious, the employer cannot ask about the nature or severity of that disability. Consequently, employers should be careful when they administer psychological testing to job applicants to make sure that the testing is not a medical examination. Psychological testing can be considered a medical examination if it provides evidence that would lead to a diagnosis or the identification of mental disorder or impairment.

Consider the following example: A psychological test (like the MMPI) is constructed to diagnose mental illnesses, but a particular employer says she does not use the test to disclose mental illness. Instead, the employer says she uses the test to disclose preferences and habits of job applicants. However, the test also is interpreted by a psychologist working for the company. In addition, the test is routinely used in clinical settings to provide evidence that would lead to a diagnosis of a mental disorder or impairment (for example, whether a person has paranoid tendencies, or is depressed). Under these conditions, this test might be considered a medical examination and may violate the ADA laws.

The use of clinically oriented personality measures designed primarily to diagnose psychopathology, such as the MMPI, would probably violate the ADA's prohibition on medical examinations. Consequently, employers should avoid the MMPI and similar measures for selection purposes. Tests of normal-range personality functioning, and measures of integrity, have never been considered equivalent to a medical examination.

Right to Privacy

Perhaps the largest issue of legal concern for employers using personality testing is privacy. The **right to privacy** in employment settings grows out of the broader concept of the right to privacy. Cases that charge an invasion-of-privacy claim against an employer can be based on the federal constitution, state constitutions and statutes, and common law.

In the case of *McKenna v. Fargo* a federal district court in New Jersey upheld the right of a city fire department to use personality testing to select applicants for the position of firefighter. The case was based on an invasion-of-privacy claim. The court determined that, although the test did infringe on the applicant's right to privacy, the city's interest in screening out applicants who would be unstable under the pressures of the job was sufficient to justify the intrusion. The *McKenna* ruling establishes that personality test questions that inquire about an applicant's sexual, religious, or political attitudes may intrude on an applicant's right to privacy. However, the ruling also recognizes that a government can justify this intrusion if it has a compelling need, such as the need for firefighters who can protect the safety of the public.

In another case, a California Court of Appeals found that certain items on a personality test administered to security guard applicants violated the state constitutional right to privacy. In *Saroka v. Dayton Hudson* the plaintiff had applied for a security guard position with the Target Stores chain and was required to complete both the MMPI and the California Psychological Inventory (CPI). The two tests are widely used to assess personality traits and adjustment, and they contain items asking about very personal topics such as religion, sexual behavior, and political beliefs. The plaintiff argued that the questions required him to reveal very private thoughts and highly personal behaviors and were not job-related. The court agreed, finding that certain questions invaded the applicants' privacy because they asked about sexual and religious preferences. Target tried to mount a defense by arguing that they had a compelling business interest in the outcome of the selection process. The court acknowledged that Target had an interest in employing emotionally stable persons as store security officers. However, the court ruled that Target did not show how questions about an applicant's religious beliefs or sexual orientation would have any bearing on their emotional stability. Because Target Stores could not provide evidence on the construct or criterion validity of the specific items in question, they lost the case.

A Closer Look

Fit for the Job?

Harvey Horowitz applied for the job of probation officer in New York City. He had an excellent record of employment as a social worker with the New York Department of Social Services. Becoming a probation officer would have been a real step up in his career. When he applied for the probation officer position, he was given the Minnesota Multiphasic Personality Inventory (MMPI). Officials in the New York City personnel office decided not to hire Mr. Horowitz because the test suggested that he was "possibly prone to worry" and that he "may be passive and dependent."

Mr. Horowitz joined forces with the New York Civil Liberties Union and filed a complaint against the city's personnel office. Horowitz's complaint to the State Division of Human Rights argued that the city had denied him employment on the basis of "psychiatric unsuitability" and that this violated the state's human rights law. The complaint also questioned the interpretation of the test. The Division of Human Rights ruled that using the test to determine whether Horowitz was suitable for that particular job was inappropriate and Horowitz received damages. The test was deemed inappropriate because it was designed to be used for diagnosing psychiatric disorders, not for selecting people for employment.

Rob Levy, chair of the mental patients' rights project of the New York Civil Liberties Union, who handled the Horowitz case, indicated in an interview with the American Bar Association that he receives many complaints each year about employment selection procedures involving testing. He asserted that most complainants argue that the test questions are not related to the job or to performance on the job. Others believe that the test results are improperly evaluated or that they do not accurately measure potential for job success. Still others argue that the tests are a violation of privacy or that they discriminate on an inappropriate or illegal basis (e.g., sexual preference, religion).

This concern with test validity and nondiscriminatory hiring practices sometimes conflicts with a company's desire to take steps to assure that the workers they hire actually succeed on the job. Even a clerical worker can cost a company $20,000 to recruit, hire, train, dismiss, and replace. A middle- or upper-level manager can cost several times that amount. With these amounts of money on the line, businesses are motivated to try to find the right person for the job. They are also motivated to avoid lawsuits by making efforts to avoid the mistake of rejecting the wrong people or rejecting people for the wrong reasons. Businesses with such concerns in mind sometimes turn to industrial and personality psychologists for help in making the best hiring decisions.

When assisting a business in hiring for a particular job, a psychologist typically starts by analyzing the requirements of that job. The psychologist might interview the employees who currently work in that job or might interview the supervisors who are involved in managing the people in that particular job. The psychologist might then observe workers in that job, noting any particular verbal, written, performance, and social skills needed to perform the job. He or she might also take into account both the physical and social aspects of the work environment in an effort to identify any special pressures or responsibilities associated with the job.

Based on this thorough **job analysis,** the psychologist develops some hypotheses about the kinds of abilities and personality traits that would best equip a person to perform well in that job. This is a good example of the person-by-situation interaction concept. Ideally, the psychologist then gathers personality and ability data on people in those jobs, along with measures of job performance. Such data can then be used to see if there is a correlation between the traits and skills and the performance on the job. Such data would also be useful if the employer were called into court to prove that the selection tests used to hire employees do predict job performance.

Source: Adapted from Silas, 1984.

Personnel Selection—Choosing the Right Person for the Job

Imagine giving a person a badge, a powerful car, and several guns and telling that person to drive around the community and uphold the law. It would be beneficial if you could make sure that you were not giving all this power to the wrong person. Personality tests are frequently used to screen out the wrong individuals from the pool of applicants for police officers. One of the most frequently given tests is the revised

Minnesota Multiphasic Personality Inventory (MMPI II), which was designed to detect various mental illnesses. The MMPI II has 550 items, and its primary use is to identify persons with significant psychological problems. Individuals with elevated scores indicating mental or emotional difficulties can be screened out of the pool of potential officers (Barrick & Mount, 1991).

Until recently, little was known about which personality traits contribute to the successful performance of the job of police officer. Then Hargrave and Hiatt (1989) examined the California Personality Inventory (CPI) in relation to police officer performance. In their study, they found that 13 percent of the cadets in training were found to be "unsuitable" by their instructors. Moreover, these unsuitable cadets differed from the "suitable" group on 9 scales of the CPI, including the conformity and social presence scales. In another sample of 45 officers on the job who were having serious problems, Hargrave and Hiatt (1989) found that the CPI also discriminated this group from other police officers who were not having problems. These findings provided evidence that the CPI is useful in the selection of police officers, and it, as well as other personality questionnaires, are being used for this purpose (e.g., Black, 2000; Coutts, 1990; Grant & Grant, 1996; Lowry, 1997; Mufson & Mufson, 1998).

The personality profile that characterizes police officers emphasizes boldness and self-confidence (qualities which facilitate the direction or control of others), a heightened need for adventure, and a low need for support from others (suggestive of self-assurance). The personality traits associated with being a good police officer are distributed equally among men and women (Krug, 1981).

The 16 Personality Factor (16 PF) questionnaire, described in Chapter 3, is also being used in vocational advising and selection. The 16 PF profile that best matches police officers is one that emphasizes boldness and self-confidence, qualities that facilitate one's abilities to direct or control others and to achieve goals (Krug, 1981). A heightened need for adventure and a strong need to influence others are linked with the enjoyment of careers that provide challenge and opportunities to take charge. The police officer personality profile is low on the need for support from others, which suggests a very self-assured personality. All of these personality characteristics appear to combine into a "masculine" profile. Nevertheless, the profile that matches the police prototype occurs equally often among "normal" men and women in U.S. samples (Krug, 1981). Psychologically, men and women appear about equally equipped with the personality traits that most match the police officer prototype.

Selection in Business Settings—The Myers-Briggs Type Indicator (MBTI)

Businesses confront critical decisions on which success or failure hinge. Different jobs pose different demands, and it's likely that personality plays a critical role in determining success in different positions. By far the most widely used personality assessment device in business settings is the **Myers-Briggs Type Indicator (MBTI)** (Myers, McCaulley, Quenk, & Hammer, 1998). The test was developed by a mother-daughter team, Katherine Briggs and Isabel Myers, anchored in Jungian concepts (see Chapter 10). The test provides information about personality by testing for eight fundamental preferences. A sample item: "Do you usually value sentiment more than logic, or value logic more than sentiment?" This type of item is an example of a "forced-choice" format, in which individuals must respond in one way or another, even if they feel that their preferences might be somewhere in the middle. The eight fundamental preferences are shown in Table 4.3.

Table 4.3 Eight Fundamental Preferences Measured by the Myers-Briggs Type Indicator

Extraversion Draws energy from the outside; involved with people; likes action and activity	**Introversion** Draws energy from internal world of thoughts and ideas
Sensing Prefers taking in information through all five senses; attends to what actually exists	**Intuition** Prefers information derived from a "sixth sense"; notices what's possible rather than what is
Thinking Prefers logic, organization, and clean objective structure	**Feeling** Prefers a person- and value-oriented way of processing information
Judging Prefers living a well-ordered and controlled life	**Perceiving** Prefers to live spontaneously, with room for flexible spur-of-the-moment activities

Sources: Myers et al. (1998); Hirsh & Kummerow (1990).

These eight fundamental preferences reduce to four scores—you are either extraverted OR introverted; sensing OR intuitive; thinking OR feeling; judging OR perceiving. These four scores are then combined to yield *types*. Indeed, each person is placed into one of the 16 types yielded by their four scores. For example, you could be an *ESTP* type: Extraverted, Sensing, Thinking, and Perceiving. This type, according to the MBTI authors, has a distinctive leadership style in business settings. She likes to take charge when a crisis occurs; she's good at persuading others to adopt her point of view; she is assertive and leads the group to the most direct route to the goal; and she wants to see immediate results.

Contrast this with another type, an *INFJ:* Introverted, Intuitive, Feeling, and Judging. This type, according to the authors of the instrument, has a fundamentally different leadership style. Rather than take charge and assert, INFJs are more likely to develop a *vision* for the organization; get others to cooperate rather than demand cooperation; work to inspire others rather than command others; and work solidly and with integrity and consistency to achieve business goals. One can readily imagine that different types of business leaders would be better in different organizational settings. In a time of crisis, for example, an ESTP might be better at organizing others to deal with immediate threats. On a plateau in business, an INFJ might be better at pausing to reflect on a long-term vision for the organization.

It is estimated that over 3 million people a year take the MBTI (Gardner & Martinko, 1996). Although it was developed for applications in education, counseling, career guidance, and workplace teambuilding, it is also widely used in personnel selection settings (Pittenger, 2005). Its wide use most likely comes from its intuitive appeal; people can readily understand the relevance of the personality traits supposedly measured by this test.

There are, however, several problems with the MBTI. The first problem is that the theory on which it is based—Jung's theory of **psychological types**—is not widely endorsed by academic or research-oriented psychologists. For one thing, people don't come in "types," such as extraverted types and introverted types. Instead, most personality traits are normally distributed. Figure 4.2 illustrates the difference between

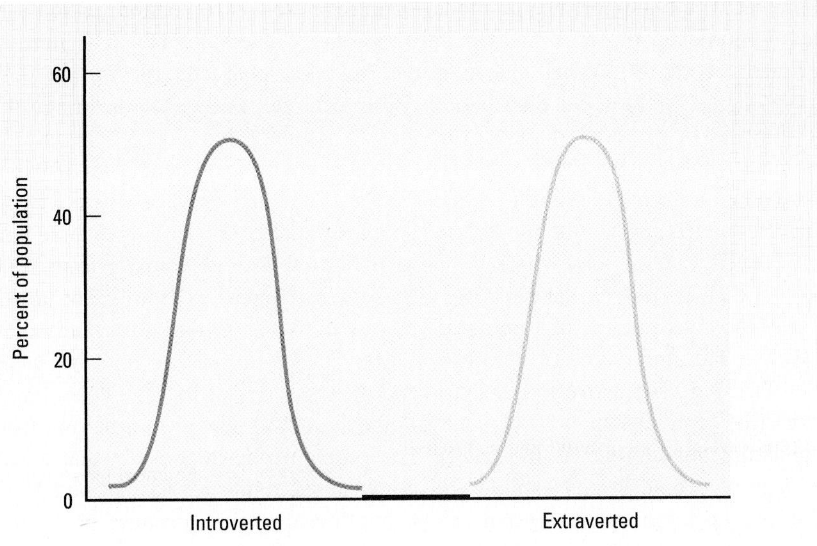

A. Hypothetical data on the trait of introversion–extraversion if it followed a truly type-like distribution in the population. There would be a large number of introverts, a large number of extraverts, and few people in between.

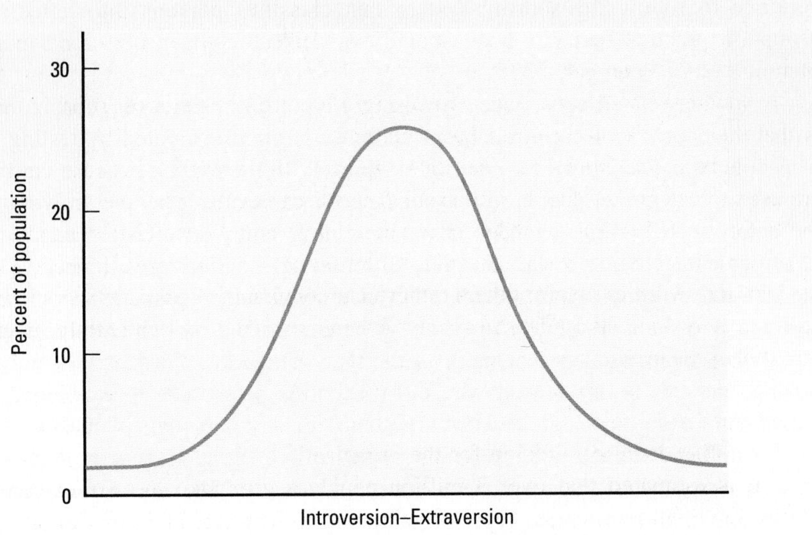

B. Typical data on the trait of introversion–extraversion, which follows a bell-curve or normal distribution in the population. There are a large number of people in between the relatively rare extreme introverts and extreme extraverts.

Figure 4.2

Examples illustrating what the trait of introversion–extraversion would look like in terms of distributions in the population if it followed a type model (Panel A) or a normal distribution model (Panel B). Real data support the normal distribution model, not the type model.

data that would support a type model of introversion–extraversion (called a bimodal distribution) and the real data on introversion–extraversion, which is normally distributed according to a bell-shaped curve. Very few characteristics of persons follow a typological or bimodal distribution. Biological sex is one characteristic that does conform to a bimodal distribution; there are many female-type people, as well as many male-type people, and very few people in between. The distribution of extraversion–introversion is not like this at all; it has only one peak, right in the middle, suggesting that the majority of people are neither purely introverted nor purely extraverted, but are somewhere in between. Virtually all personality traits follow this normal distribution, so the concept of personality "types" is simply not justified.

One consequence of forcing a typology onto a trait that is normally distributed concerns the importance of cutoff scores for classifying people into one category or the other, e.g., as introverted or extraverted. Most users of the MBTI use the median score (the score at which 50 percent fall above and 50 percent fall below) from some standardization sample as the cutoff. The problem lies in the fact that a large percentage of people in any sample will be clustered right around the median score. If that median score moves a point or two in either direction, because of differences in sample characteristics used to determine the cutoff score, a very large number of people will be reclassified into their opposite category. In fact, a person with an introversion–extraversion score of 20 might be classified as an introvert in one sample (if it had a median of 21), or classified as an extravert in another sample (if it had a median of 19). So, the same individual score (a 20) will be interpreted very differently depending on the median used to perform the cutoff for classification. Despite this problem with cutoff scores and typologies, the majority of users of the MBTI continue to follow the scoring system that classifies persons into letter category groups, a practice that has been soundly criticized in the professional consulting literature (e.g., Pittenger, 2005).

Another related consequence of using a typology scheme for scoring the MBTI is that the scores will be unreliable. Reliability is often estimated by testing a group of people twice, separated by a period of time. With the MBTI, because cutoff scores are used to categorize people into groups, and because many people are very close to the cutoff scores, slight changes in peoples' raw scores on retesting can result in a large percentage being reclassified into different personality types. Indeed, a study of the test–retest reliability of the MBTI (McCarley & Clarskadon, 1983) showed that, across a five-week test–retest interval, 50 percent of the participants received a different classification on one or more of the type categories. These results are not surprising, and this is one reason why most scientific personality psychologists do not recommend using typological scoring systems for any personality measure.

Another problem with typological scoring systems is that it assumes large between-category differences, and no within-category differences, between people. For example, all extraverted types are assumed to be alike, and introverted types are assumed to be very different from extraverted types. This, however, is not necessarily the case. Imagine two people who score as "extraverted types," yet one of these is just one point above the median and the other is 31 points above the median. These two "extraverted types" are likely to be very different from each other (they differ by 30 points on the scale yet are given the same type category). Now imagine an "introverted type" who scored one point below the median, and an "extraverted type" who scored one point above the median. This "introvert" and this "extravert" are likely to be indistinguishable from each other (they differ by only 2 points on the scale yet are given different type categories). This is another reason why psychologists who know about measurement issues avoid using type scoring systems for any personality test.

Dozens of validity studies of the MBTI have been published, mostly relating type categories to occupational preferences. These studies have been criticized, however, because most fail to report statistical details necessary to determine if the differences are significant. For example, Gardner and Martinko (1996) review 13 studies that examined the distribution of MBTI types in managerial professions. All of these studies reported the frequencies of types in different categories yet none reported scale score means that would have allowed strong statistical tests of mean personality differences between the different managerial categories. Moreover, other recent reviewers (e.g., Hunsley, Lee, & Wood, 2003) point out that no adequate tests have been done on the predictive validity of the MBTI (e.g., that the MBTI can predict *future* career choices or job satisfaction). Also, virtually no studies have been done examining the incremental validity of the MBTI (e.g., whether the MBTI can add meaningfully to the prediction of career choice or job satisfaction above and beyond that obtained with more traditional personality measures). Table 4.2 lists the major elements of validity for personality tests, and we see from this discussion that the research base on the MBTI does not cover many aspects of validity. The conclusion is that the evidence for the validity and utility of the MBTI is weak at best.

Every few years psychologists take a fresh look at the evidence for the MBTI and summarize what they find. In 1991 Bjork and Druckman reviewed the evidence and concluded: "At this time, there is not sufficient, well-designed research to justify the use of the MBTI in career counseling programs" (p. 99). A few years later, Boyle (1995) also reviewed the literature and found no strong scientific evidence supporting the utility of the MBTI. In 2003 Hunsley, Lee, and Wood reviewed the latest evidence and summarized their findings: "One can only conclude that the MBTI is insufficient as a contemporary measure of personality" (pp. 63–64). And in an even more recent review paper, Pittenger (2005) evaluated all of the scientific literature on the MBTI and concluded that, "Using the MBTI to select employees, to assign employees to work groups or assignments, or for other forms of employment evaluation are not justified for the simple reason that there are no available data to recommend such decisions" (p. 219).

Given the highly negative reviews on the scientific merit of the MBTI, why does it continue to be a hugely popular tool in consulting and career counseling? There are probably several reasons. First, the popularity of the MBTI may reflect the success of the publisher's marketing campaign. In addition, the test comes with rather simple scoring and interpretation instructions, making it usable and understandable by people without advanced training in personality psychology. Moreover, the interpretations the test offers are readily translated into seemingly sensible predictions about work and interpersonal relations. Like the popularity of horoscopes, people like hearing about themselves and their futures, even if little or no scientific evidence exists for those descriptions and predictions.

Is there any legitimate use for the MBTI? While it should definitely not be used as the single piece of evidence on which to base employment selections or career decisions, it may have a role in such areas as team-building, career exploration, or relationship counseling. The test can get people thinking about differences between people. People with vastly different personalities see the world differently, and if the test fosters an appreciation for this diversity, then it may be useful. The test might also be useful if it gets people thinking about the relationship between personality and behavior. If we understand that how we act toward others, and they toward us, is influenced in part by our personalities, then this increases our ability to understand and relate well to others. For example, if a teacher takes the MBTI as part of a "teacher development workshop" he or she may think about their own teaching style, or may gain an awareness that not all pupils are alike in how they relate to teachers. The test may even act as a catalyst for group exercises or team building that foster esprit de corps among group members. For example, at a "corporate retreat" a group of managers may take the test and then explore ways that they can work better as a team given the differences in their personalities. So the test may indeed have some utility for getting people to think about personality, even though the test does not appear adequate as an instrument for selection.

Selection in Business Settings—The Hogan Personality Inventory

Because of the problems noted earlier, the Myers-Briggs Type Indicator test should probably not be used to select employees. Which tests are good alternatives? There are literally thousands of published personality tests (Spies & Plake, 2005) and hundreds of companies that use personality tests to help companies select employees. We have chosen one of these companies, and one of their personality tests, to describe here, mainly because the procedures they use are based on a solid scientific foundation. The company is called Hogan Assessment Systems, and its main personality test is called the Hogan Personality Inventory.

The founder of this assessment company, Robert Hogan, was a professor of psychology at the University of Tulsa for many years. He had been teaching and doing research in personality psychology through the 1970s and 1980s, even becoming the head editor of the most prestigious scientific journal in personality psychology, the *Journal of Personality and Social Psychology.* During this time, Hogan's own research concerned efforts to identify aspects of personality important in contemporary business settings. He started with the big five model of personality, but focused on how these traits might work in the business world. He developed a theory about the social aspects of personality that are important to business, and concluded that the dominant themes in social life are the motive to get along with others and the motive to get ahead of others.

In most business settings, people work in groups, and every group has a status hierarchy. The theory states that, within such groups, people want three things: (1) acceptance, including respect and approval, (2) status and the control of resources, and (3) predictability (Hogan, 2005). Some of Hogan's research showed that business problems often occur when a manager violates one or more of these motives within a workgroup, for example, by treating staff with disrespect, by micromanaging in a way that takes away the staff's sense of control, or by not communicating or providing feedback, thereby making the workplace unpredictable.

Hogan developed a questionnaire measure of personality, called the **Hogan Personality Inventory (HPI),** that measures aspects of the big five traits that are relevant to the above three motives important to business. The traits this inventory measures are described in Table 4.4. Hogan and his wife, Joyce Hogan, also a research psychologist, started using this inventory in research on the effectiveness of people working in a variety of businesses. They began to look at how specific job requirements fit with specific combinations of these personality traits. Soon they were doing validity studies, exploring how the personality test predicted how well people fit into specific business cultures. They also conducted outcome studies, to see how well the personality inventory predicted occupational performance in a wide variety of jobs.

Table 4.4 The Hogan Personality Inventory (HPI) Contains Seven Primary Scales and Six Occupational Scales

Primary Scales	Occupational Scales
Adjustment—self-confidence, self-esteem, and composure under pressure. The opposite of neuroticism.	***Service Orientation***—being attentive, pleasant, and courteous to customers.
Ambition—initiative, competitiveness, and the desire for leadership roles.	***Stress Tolerance***—being able to handle stress, remaining even-tempered and calm under fire.
Sociability—extraversion, gregariousness, and a need for social interaction.	***Reliability***—honesty, integrity, and positive organizational citizenship.
Interpersonal Sensitivity—warmth, charm, and the ability to maintain good relationships.	***Clerical Potential***—following directions, attending to detail, and communicating clearly.
Prudence—self-discipline, responsibility, and conscientiousness.	***Sales Potential***—energy, social skills, and the ability to solve customers' problems.
Inquisitiveness—imagination, curiosity, vision, and creative potential.	***Managerial Potential***—leadership ability, planning, and decision-making skills.
Learning Approach—enjoying learning, staying current on business and technical matters.	

Across a large number of studies, the test achieved high levels of reliability and acceptable levels of validity for predicting a number of important occupational outcomes, including organizational fit and performance. Joyce Hogan and J. Holland (2003) provide a meta-analysis of 28 validity studies on the Hogan Personality Inventory, the results of which strongly support the validity of the personality scales for predicting several important job-relevant criteria.

In 1987 Robert and Joyce Hogan started their own company, Hogan Assessment Systems, to consult with businesses that wanted to use personality measures to select employees. Soon afterward, Robert Hogan left his position at the University of Tulsa to devote his full effort toward helping companies successfully use personality measures in business applications. The Hogans continue to use a scientific approach to improve and validate the use of their personality inventory in the business community. Their focus is mainly on determining the statistical personality profiles of people who perform well in specific job categories, and how these personality profiles fit with specific business cultures.

Why is the Hogan Personality Inventory (HPI) a better choice than the MBTI when it comes to employee selection? First, the HPI is based on the big five model, which has been modified specifically for applications to the workplace. The construction and development of the HPI followed standard statistical procedures, resulting in an inventory with a high level of measurement reliability (test–retest correlations range from .74 to .86). To date, there have been more than 400 validity studies of the HPI. These studies have examined the ability of the test to predict a wide variety of important business results in a large number of job categories, such as employee turnover, absenteeism, improved sales performance, customer service, employee satisfaction, customer satisfaction, and overall business performance. The test has been able to predict occupational success in a wide variety of job categories. Personality profiles on the HPI are available for over 200 different work categories that span the range of jobs in the U.S. economy. The company maintains a database from over a million people who have taken the HPI.

The HPI itself consists of true–false items and takes about 20 minutes to administer. None of the items are invasive or intrusive, and none of the scales show adverse impact on the basis of gender or race or ethnicity. The test is also available in a number of foreign languages. Hogan Assessment Systems maintains a research archive and record-keeping practice that scrupulously follows the procedures outlined by the Uniform Guidelines on Employee Selection Procedures discussed earlier. If a company using the HPI is sued by a job applicant, Hogan Assessment Systems will provide reports and records on test development and validity necessary to defend the case. The selection procedures and validation research on the HPI have never been successfully challenged in court. The test authors are members of the American Psychological Association and the Society of Industrial/Organizational Psychology, both of which mandate professional levels of ethical, legal, and scientific standards with regard to assessment practices.

Because of all these positive qualities, including the research base and demonstrated effectiveness of the test, use of the HPI in business and industry has grown tremendously in the last 20 years. Hogan Assessment Systems has consulted with 60 percent of the Fortune 100 companies, and has provided assessment services to more than a thousand other customers around the world. Currently, in any given month, between 300 and 500 companies utilize their services to select or develop employees.

While Hogan Assessment Systems provides other services, such as employee development, we will focus on a couple of case studies of the use of the HPI in employee selection applications. In one case, a large national bank approached Hogan Assessment Systems wanting to improve customer services by hiring better bank tellers. The bank hired hundreds of tellers per year from thousands who applied for those jobs. A personality profile was determined for the teller position and used to select employees. Soon after this selection procedure was put into effect, the bank assessed customer satisfaction at their regional banks, which was found to have increased substantially. In addition, the routine evaluations of tellers done by bank managers showed a significant improvement in quality ratings of the local tellers.

In another case example, a leading financial services company approached Hogan Assessment Systems to develop a pre-employment assessment procedure to select financial consultants. The job requirements were analyzed and compared to known validity research on performance in related jobs, and a personality selection profile was determined. After new people were hired and on the job for a few years, the company evaluated the effectiveness of the selection procedure by comparing the performance of financial consultants hired before and after the selection procedure went into effect. They found that those financial consultants hired on the basis of their personality profiles earned 20 percent more in commissions annually, conducted 32 percent more volume in dollar terms annually, and made 42 percent more trades annually. Obviously, selecting those applicants with the "right stuff" was beneficial to this company. Other business examples of the use of the HPI in selecting employees can be found at www.hoganassessments.com.

It is clear that personality factors can play an important role in predicting who does well in specific employment settings. When it comes to using personality tests to select employees for specific positions, one should realize that not all personality

A Closer Look

Personnel Selection in Other Cultures

At a recent meeting of the Society for Industrial and Organizational Psychology (SIOP), there was a panel discussion of issues in cross-national employee selection, chaired by psychologists from Hogan Assessment Systems. The discussion focused on how, as corporations shift from domestic to global markets, the frequency of interactions across borders and countries expands. Knowledge of international business practices and employment laws become important, as do basic principles in employee selection. Some companies facing the issue of selecting employees in new countries have simply translated their selection test from English into the required language, and started using it in the new country in which they were setting up business. However, people from different cultures do not just speak a different language. Many of their customs and traditions differ, as do their styles of interacting, the expectations they have for each other, and even their basic concepts, such as what is considered just and right, may differ. We cannot assume that American concepts and theories about personality and work can be transported and applied to new cultures without modification. As Triandis (1994) said over a decade ago, "much more needs to be done to examine how people and cultural variables affect management systems or job designs" (p. 156).

Research is just getting started on understanding how employment selection tools developed in one culture can be applied in another culture. Ryan et al. (1999) surveyed international business organizations about how they implement selection procedures when transporting them to new countries. The most successful ones modified their selection procedures based on a careful scrutiny of the local cultural standards. It is clear that cultural values permeate business organizations. For example, in America our culture values individualism, and we admire people who work hard to achieve individual success. However, in many Eastern cultures individualism is frowned upon, and even punished in the workplace, where the valued behavior is not individual success, but helping the group or team succeed. It is quite possible that a personality test that predicts occupational achievement in America will not predict that outcome in a different culture.

The panel discussion concluded that globalization is opening an important new frontier for research on how culture affects employment selection. The panel acknowledged that the issue is complicated by many variables, including differences between countries in terms of employment law, politics, or the existence of different kinds of discrimination from culture to culture. Nevertheless, the most successful companies are likely to be those who pay attention to cultural norms as they set up business in a new country. This also represents exciting employment opportunities for future psychologists interested in personality and culture.

tests do the job equally well. Clearly those assessment systems with a strong scientific base, grounded in an accepted theory of personality, with acceptable reliability and strong evidence of validity relative to the needs of the company, will have the best potential for helping business users achieve positive results.

SUMMARY AND EVALUATION

This chapter described some important issues and concepts that the various trait theories have in common. The hallmark of the trait perspective is an emphasis on differences between people. Trait psychology focuses on the study of differences, the classification of differences, and the analysis of the consequences of differences between people. Trait psychology assumes that people will be relatively consistent over time in their behavior because of the various traits they possess. Trait psychologists also assume a degree of cross-situational consistency for traits. Psychologists assume that people will be *more or less* consistent in their behavior, depending on the particular trait being studied and the situations in which it is observed. Nevertheless, some situations are very strong in terms of their influence on behavior. Some situations are so strong that they overpower the influence of personality traits. One important lesson is that traits are more likely to influence a person's behavior when situations are weak and ambiguous and don't push for conformity from all people.

Most trait psychologists agree that personality trait scores refer primarily to average tendencies in behavior. A score on a trait measure refers to how a person is likely to behave, on average, over a number of occasions and situations. Trait psychologists are better at predicting average tendencies in behavior than specific acts on specific occasions. For example, from a person's high score on a measure of trait hostility, a personality psychologist could not predict whether this person was likely to get into a fight tomorrow. However, the psychologist could confidently predict that such a person was more likely to be in more fights in the next few years than a person with a lower score on hostility. Traits represent average tendencies in behavior.

Trait psychologists are also interested in the accuracy of measurement. More than any other personality perspective, trait psychology has occupied itself with efforts to improve the measurement of traits, particularly through self-report questionnaire measures. Psychologists who devise questionnaires work hard at making them less susceptible to lying, faking, and careless responding.

A particularly important measurement issue is social desirability, or the tendency to exaggerate the positivity of one's personality. Currently, trait psychologists hold that one motive for socially desirable responding is the test taker's desire to convey a certain impression (usually positive). This behavior is sometimes referred to as impression management. Many psychologists worry about social desirability as a response set, thinking that it lowers the validity of the trait measure. However, another view on social desirability is that socially desirable responding is a valid response by some people who simply view themselves as better or more desirable than most, or who actually have deceived themselves into thinking they are better off psychologically than they probably are. As is typical, trait psychologists have devised measures to identify and distinguish between these two types of socially desirable responding.

Finally, their interest in measurement and prediction has led trait psychologists to apply these skills to the selection and screening of job applicants and other situations in which personality might make a difference. There are legal issues employers must keep in mind when using trait measures as a basis for making important hiring or promotion decisions. For example, tests must not discriminate unfairly against protected groups, such as women and certain minorities. In addition, the tests must be shown to be related to important real-life variables, such as job performance. We considered a number of important legal cases in employment law that are relevant to personality testing. We also considered two specific instruments that are popular in employment selection settings. One instrument, the Myers-Briggs Type Indicator, is widely used but also widely criticized in the scientific literature for its low levels of measurement reliability and unproven validity. The other instrument, the Hogan Personality Inventory, can be considered a "best practice" case when it comes to the use of personality in employee selection.

KEY TERMS

Differential Psychology 97
Consistency 98
Rank Order 99
Situationism 101
Person-Situation Interaction 101
Aggregation 101
Situational Specificity 102
Strong Situation 103
Situational Selection 103
Evocation 106
Manipulation 106
Average Tendencies 108
Infrequency Scale 109
Faking 110
False Negative 110
False Positive 110
Response Sets 111
Noncontent Responding 111
Acquiescence 111
Extreme Responding 111
Social Desirability 111
Forced-Choice Questionnaire 113
Integrity Tests 115
Barnum Statements 116
Personnel Selection 118
Negligent Hiring 119
Title VII of the Civil Rights Act of 1964 119
Griggs v. Duke Power 119
Uniform Guidelines on Employee Selection Procedures 119
Ward's Cove Packing Co. v. Atonio 120
Price Waterhouse v. Hopkins 120
Disparate Impact 121
Race or Gender Norming 122
Americans with Disabilities Act (ADA) 122
Right to Privacy 123
Job Analysis 124
Myers-Briggs Type Indicator (MBTI) 125
Psychological Types 126
Hogan Personality Inventory (HPI) 130

Personality Dispositions over Time: Stability, Change, and Coherence

THE DISPOSITIONAL DOMAIN

5

Even though people change and develop as they age, each person still has a sense of themselves as the same person, the same "self," from year to year. As we will see in this chapter on development, when it comes to personality, some things change and some things stay the same.

Think back to your days in middle school. Can you remember what you were like then? Try to recall what you were most interested in, how you spent your time, what things you valued most and were most important to you at that time of your life. If you are like most people, you probably feel that, in many ways, you are a different person now than you were in middle school. Your interests have probably changed somewhat. Different things may be important to you. Your attitudes about school, family, and relationships have probably all changed at least a bit. Perhaps now you are more mature and more articulate and have a more experienced view of the world.

As you think about what you were like then and what you are like now, you probably also feel that there is a core of "you" that is essentially the same over the years. If you are like most people, you have a sense of an enduring part of you, a feeling that you are "really" the same person now as then. Sure, you are older, more experienced, and more mature. But certain inner qualities seem the same over these several years.

In this chapter, we will explore the psychological continuities and changes over time, which define the topic of personality development. When it comes to personality, a common saying is "Some things change; some things stay the same." In this chapter, we will discuss how psychologists think about personality development, with a primary focus on personality traits or dispositions.

Conceptual Issues: Personality Development, Stability, Change, and Coherence

This section defines personality development, examines the major ways of thinking about personality stability over time, and explores what it means to say that personality has changed. The study of personality development has attracted increasing research attention, with an entire issue of the *Journal of Personality* recently devoted to the topic (Graziano, 2003).

What Is Personality Development?

Personality development can be defined as the continuities, consistencies, and stabilities in people over time *and* the ways in which people change over time. Each of these two facets—stability and change—requires definitions and qualifications. There are many forms of personality stability and, correspondingly, many forms of personality change. The three most important forms of stability are rank order stability, mean level stability, and personality coherence. We will discuss each of these in turn. Then we examine personality change.

Rank Order Stability

Rank order stability is the maintenance of individual position within a group. Between ages 14 and 20, most people become taller, but the rank order of heights tends to remain fairly stable because this form of development affects all people pretty much the same, adding a few inches to everyone. The tall people at 14 fall generally toward the tall end of the distribution at age 20. The same can apply to personality traits. If people tend to maintain their positions on dominance or extraversion relative to the other members of their group over time, then there is high rank order stability

Exercise

To illustrate the phrase "Some things change; some things stay the same," consider the period just before high school (your middle school years) and compare that with the period just after high school—typically, your college years. Identify three characteristics that have changed noticeably during that period. These characteristics might be your interests, your attitudes, your values, and what you like to do with your time. Then list three characteristics about you that have not changed. Again, these characteristics could reflect certain traits of your personality, your interests, your values, or even your attitudes about various topics. Write them down in the following format:

	What I was like in middle school:	What I was like after high school:
Characteristics that have changed	1. ________	1. ________
	2. ________	2. ________
	3. ________	3. ________
Characteristics that have not changed	1. ________	
	2. ________	
	3. ________	

to that personality characteristic. Conversely, if people fail to maintain their rank order—if the submissive folks rise up and put down the dominants, for example—then the group is displaying rank order instability, or rank order change.

Mean Level Stability

Another kind of personality stability is constancy of level, or **mean level stability.** Consider political orientation as an example. If the average level of liberalism or conservatism in a population remains the same with the increasing age of that population, the population exhibits high mean level stability on that characteristic. If the average degree of political orientation changes—for example, if people tend as a group to get increasingly conservative as they get older—then that population is displaying **mean level change.**

Personality Coherence

A more complex form of personality development involves changes in the *manifestations* of a trait. Consider the trait of dominance. Suppose that the people who are dominant at age 8 are the same people who are dominant at age 20. The 8-year-old boys, however, manifest their dominance by showing toughness in rough-and-tumble play, calling their rivals "sissies," and insisting on monopolizing the video games. At the age of 20, they manifest their dominance by persuading others to accept their views in political discussions, boldly asking someone out on a date, and insisting on the restaurant at which the group will eat.

This form of personality development—maintaining rank order in relation to other individuals but changing the manifestations of the trait—is called **personality coherence.** Notice that this form of personality coherence does not require that the precise behavioral manifestations of a trait remain the same. Indeed, the manifestations may be so different that there is literally no overlap between age 8 and age 20. The act manifestations have all changed, but something critical has remained the

The manifestation of disagreeableness may differ across the life span, ranging from temper tantrums in infancy to being argumentative and having a short temper in adulthood. Even though the behaviors are different at the different ages, they nevertheless express the same underlying trait. This kind of consistency is called personality coherence.

A Closer Look

A Case of Personal Stability

Mohandas Karamchan Gandhi was born in 1869 into a family of modest means in India. His mother was devoutly religious, and she impressed young Mohandas with her beliefs and practices. The Gandhi family not only practiced traditional Hinduism but also practiced Buddhist chants, read from the Koran, recited verses from Zoroastrianism, and even sang traditional Christian hymns. Young Mohandas developed a personal philosophy of life that led him to renounce all personal desires and to devote himself to the service of his fellow human beings.

After studying law in England, and a few years practicing in South Africa, Gandhi returned to India. At that time, India was under British rule, and most Indians resented the oppression of their colonial rulers. Gandhi devoted himself to the ideal of Indian self-rule and to freedom from British oppression. When the British decided to fingerprint all Indians, for example, Gandhi came up with an idea he called passive resistance—he encouraged all Indians to simply refuse to go in for fingerprinting. During the period of 1919–1922, Gandhi led widespread but nonviolent strikes and boycotts throughout India. He coordinated campaigns of peaceful noncooperation with anything British—he urged Indians not to send their children to the British-run schools, not to participate in the courts, even not to adopt the English language. In their frustration, British soldiers sometimes attacked crowds of boycotting or striking Indians, and many Indians were killed, but others stepped up to take their places. The people of India loved Gandhi so much that they followed him in droves, recording everything he did and said. Eventually, this ongoing record of his words and acts filled more than 90 volumes with the record of his life. He became a living legend, and the people referred to him as Maha Atma, or the Great Soul. We know him today as Mahatma Gandhi.

Mahatma Gandhi lived in a tumultuous period and led one of the largest social revolutions in human history. Despite the changing conditions of his life, his personality remained remarkably stable. For example, he practiced self-denial and self-sufficiency throughout his adult life, preferring a simple loincloth and shawl to the suit and tie worn by most leaders of the world's great nations.

In 1930, Gandhi led the Indian people in nonviolent defiance of the British law forbidding Indian people from making their own salt. He started out with a few of his followers on a march to the coast of India, intending to make salt from seawater. By the time Gandhi had reached the sea, several thousand people had joined him in this act of civil disobedience. By this time, the British had jailed more than 60,000 Indians for disobedience to British law. The jails of India were bursting with native people put there by foreign rulers for breaking foreign laws. The British rulers were finally coming to some sense of embarrassment and shame for this situation. In the eyes of the world, this frail man Gandhi and his nonviolent followers were shaking the foundation of the British Empire in India.

Gandhi was not an official of the Indian government, nor was he ever elected to any office. Nevertheless, the British began negotiations with him to free India from British rule. During negotiations, the British played tough and put Gandhi in jail. The Indian people demonstrated and nearly a thousand of them were killed by the British, again bringing shame on the colonial rulers in the eyes of the world. Gandhi was finally freed and a few years later, in 1947, Britain handed India its independence. Gandhi's leadership of nonviolent resistance and noncooperative pacifism forced the more powerful British to relinquish their colonial rule of India.

During his adult life, Gandhi became the popular leader of one of the largest nations on earth. He negotiated a mostly peaceful transition from British rule to self-rule for the people of India. He was admired and respected by millions of people, who happily put their lives in his hands. In his lifetime, he was one of the most influential leaders in the world. His ideas have influenced the struggles of many oppressed groups since.

In 1948, an assassin fired three bullets into Gandhi at point blank range. The assassin was a Hindu fanatic who believed that Gandhi should have used his position to preach hatred of the Muslims of India. Gandhi instead preached tolerance and trust, urging Muslims and Hindus to participate together in the new nation of India. This most nonviolent and tolerant man became a victim of violence.

Even though Gandhi became the "Father of India," he remained essentially the same person throughout his adult life. Each day of his life, he washed himself in ashes instead of expensive soap, and he shaved with an old, dull straight razor rather than with more expensive blades. He cleaned his own house and swept his yard almost every day. Each afternoon he spun thread on a handwheel for an hour or two. The thread was then made into cloth for his own clothes and for the clothes of his followers. He practiced the self-denial and self-sufficiency he learned early in his life. In most ways, his personality was remarkably stable over his life, even though he was at the center of one of the most tumultuous social revolutions in history.

same—the overall level of dominant acts. Thus, personality coherence includes both elements of continuity and elements of change—continuity in the underlying trait but change in the outward manifestation of that trait.

Personality Change

The notion of personality development in the sense of change over time also requires elaboration. To start with, not all change qualifies as development. For instance, if you walk from one classroom to another, your relationship to your surroundings has changed. But we do not speak of your "development" in this case, since the change is external to you and not enduring.

And not all internal changes can properly be considered development. When you get sick, for example, your body undergoes important changes—your temperature may rise, your nose may run, and your head may ache. But these changes do not constitute development, since the changes do not last—you soon get healthy, your nose stops running, and you spring back into action. In the same way, temporary changes in personality—due to taking alcohol or drugs, for example—do not constitute personality development unless they produce more enduring changes in personality.

If you were to become consistently more conscientious or responsible as you aged, however, this would be a form of personality development. If you were to become gradually less energetic as you aged, this also would be a form of personality development. And, if you were to become progressively more concerned with politics, this would be a form of personality development.

In sum, personality change has two defining qualities. First, the changes are typically *internal* to the person, not merely changes in the external surroundings, such as walking into another room. Second, the changes are relatively *enduring* over time, rather than being merely temporary.

Three Levels of Analysis

We can examine personality over time at three levels of analysis—the population as a whole, group differences within the population, and individual differences within groups. As we examine the empirical research on personality development, it is useful to keep these three levels in mind.

Population Level

Several personality psychologists have theorized about the changes that we all go through in navigating from infancy to adulthood. Freud's theory of psychosexual development, for example, contained a conception of personality development that was presumed to apply to *everyone* on the planet. All people, according to Freud, go through an invariant stage sequence, starting with the oral stage and ending with the mature genital stage of psychosexual development (see Chapter 9).

This level of personality development deals with the changes and constancies that apply more or less to everyone. For example, almost everyone in the population tends to increase in sexual motivation at puberty. Similarly, there is a general decrease in impulsive and risk-taking behaviors as people get older. This is why auto insurance rates go down as people age, because a typical 30-year-old is much less likely than a typical 16-year-old to drive in a risky manner. This change in impulsivity is part of the population level of personality change, describing a general trend that might be part of what it means to be human and go through life.

Group Differences Level

Some changes over time affect different groups of people differently. Sex differences are one type of group differences. In the realm of physical development, for example, females go through puberty, on average, two years earlier than males. At the other end of life, men in the United States tend to die seven years earlier than women. These are sex differences in development.

Analogous sex differences can occur in the realm of personality development. As a group, men and women suddenly develop differently from one another during adolescence in their average levels of risk taking (men become more risk taking). Men and women also develop differently in the degree to which they show empathy toward others (women develop a stronger awareness and understanding of others' feelings). These forms of personality development are properly located at the group differences level of personality analysis.

Some changes affect different groups of people differently. For example, European American women tend to be, as a group, much less satisfied with their bodies than are African American women with theirs. Consequently, European American women have a higher risk for developing eating disorders, such as anorexia or bulimia, compared with women in other groups.

Other group differences include cultural or ethnic group differences. For example, in the United States, there is a large difference in body image satisfaction between European American women and African American women. European American women tend to be, as a group, much less satisfied with their bodies than are African American women with theirs. Consequently, European American women are much more at risk for developing eating disturbances, such as anorexia or bulimia, compared with women in other groups. This group difference emerges primarily around puberty, when a larger proportion of white women develop feelings of dissatisfaction with their physical appearance, compared with African American women.

Individual Differences Level

Personality psychologists also focus on individual differences in personality development. For example, can we predict, based on their personalities, which individuals will go through a midlife crisis? Can we predict who will be at risk for a psychological disturbance later in life based on earlier measures of personality? And perhaps most interesting, can we predict which individuals will change over time and which ones will remain the same? These are all issues located at the individual differences level of personality analysis.

Personality Stability over Time

Perhaps no issue in personality development has been more extensively examined than the question of whether personality traits remain stable over time. One reason for this focus is that personality psychologists tend to be interested in what people carry with them from one decade of life to the next. This section examines the research and findings on the stability of personality over the lifetime. We will first examine stability in infancy, then explore stability during childhood, and finally look at stability during the decades of adulthood.

Stability of Temperament during Infancy

Many parents of two or more children will tell you that their children had distinctly different personalities the day they were born. For example, Albert Einstein, the Nobel prize–winning father of modern physics, had two sons with his first wife. These two boys were quite different from each other. The older boy, Hans, was fascinated with puzzles as a child and had a gift for mathematics. He went on to become a distinguished professor of hydraulics at the University of California at Berkeley. The younger son, Eduard, enjoyed music and literature as a child. As a young adult, however, he ended up in a Swiss psychiatric hospital, where he died. Although this is an extreme example, many parents notice differences between their children, even as infants. Do the intuitions of parents square with the scientific evidence?

By far the most commonly studied personality characteristics in infancy and childhood fall under the category of temperament. Although there is some disagreement about what the term means, most researchers define **temperament** as the individual differences that emerge very early in life that are likely to have a heritable basis (see Chapter 6) and that are often involved in behaviors linked with emotionality or arousability.

Researcher Mary Rothbart (1981, 1986) studied a group of infants at different ages, starting at 3 months of age. She examined six factors of temperament, using a measure completed by the infants' caregivers:

1. *Activity level:* the infant's overall motor activity, including arm and leg movements.
2. *Smiling and laughter:* How much does the infant smile or laugh?
3. *Fear:* the infant's distress and reluctance to approach novel stimuli.
4. *Distress to limitations:* the child's distress at being refused food, being dressed, being confined, or being prevented access to a desired object.
5. *Soothability:* the degree to which the child reduces stress, or calms down, as a result of being soothed.
6. *Duration of orienting:* the degree to which the child sustains attention to objects in the absence of sudden changes.

The caregivers, mostly mothers, completed observer-based scales designed to measure these six aspects of temperament. Table 5.1 shows the cross-time correlations over different time intervals. If you scan the correlations in the table, you will notice first that they are all positive. This means that infants who tend to score high at one time period on activity level, smiling and laughter, and the other personality traits, also tend to score high on these traits at later time periods.

Next, notice that the correlations in the top two rows of Table 5.1 tend to be higher than those in the bottom four rows. This means that activity level and smiling and laughter tend to show higher levels of stability over time than the other personality traits.

Now notice that the correlations in the right-most two columns in Table 5.1 are generally higher than those in the left-most columns. This suggests that personality traits tend to become more stable toward the end of infancy (from 9 to 12 months), compared with the earlier stages of infancy (from 3 to 6 months).

Like all studies, this one has limitations. Perhaps most important, the infants' caregivers may have developed certain conceptions of their infants, and it may be their conceptions rather than the infants' behaviors that show stability over time. After all, the correlations are based on ratings from the caregivers. Nonetheless, these findings reveal four important points. First, stable individual differences appear to emerge very early in life, when they can be assessed by observers. Second, for most temperament variables, there are moderate levels of stability over time during the first

Table 5.1 Stability Correlations for Temperament Scales

	MONTHS					
Scale	**3–6**	**3–9**	**3–12**	**6–9**	**6–12**	**9–12**
AL—activity level	.58	.48	.48	.56	.60	.68
SL—smiling and laughter	.55	.55	.57	.67	.72	.72
FR—fear	.27	.15	.06	.43	.37	.61
DL—distress to limitations	.23	.18	.25	.57	.61	.65
SO—soothability	.30*	.37*	.41	.50	.39	.29
DO—duration of orienting	.36*	.35*	.11	.62	.34	.64

*Correlations based on only one cohort.

year of life. Third, the stability of temperament tends to be higher over short intervals of time than over long intervals of time—a finding that occurs in adulthood as well. And, fourth, the level of stability of temperament tends to increase as infants mature (Goldsmith & Rothbart, 1991).

Stability during Childhood

Longitudinal studies, examinations of the same groups of individuals over time, are costly and difficult to conduct. As a result, there are precious few of such studies to draw on. A major exception is the Block and Block Longitudinal Study, which initiated the testing of a sample of more than 100 children from the Berkeley-Oakland area of California when the children were merely 3 years old (see, e.g., Block & Robbins, 1993). Since that time, the sample has been followed and repeatedly tested at ages 4, 5, 7, 11, and into adulthood.

One of the first publications from this project focused on individual differences in activity level (Buss, Block, & Block, 1980). When the children were 3 years old, and then again at 4, their activity levels were assessed in two ways. The first was through the use of an **actometer,** a recording device attached to the wrists of the children during several play periods. Motoric movement activated the recording device—essentially a self-winding wristwatch. Independently, the children's teachers completed ratings of their behavior and personalities. The behavioral measure of activity level contained three items that were directly relevant: "is physically active," "is vital, energetic, active," and "has a rapid personal tempo." These items were summed to form a total measure of teacher-observed activity level. This observer-based measure was obtained when the children were 3 and 4 and then again when they reached age 7.

Table 5.2 shows the correlations among the activity level measures, both at the same ages and across time to assess the stability of activity level during childhood. The correlations between the same measures obtained at two different points in time are called **stability coefficients** (these are also sometimes called test-retest reliability coefficients). The correlations between different measures of the same trait obtained at the same time are called **validity coefficients.**

Several key conclusions about validity and stability can be drawn from Table 5.2. First, notice in Table 5.2 that the actometer-based measurements of activity level have significant positive validity coefficients with the judge-based measurements of activity

Table 5.2 Intercorrelations among Activity Measures

	ACTOMETER		JUDGE-BASED		
	Age 3	**Age 4**	**Age 3**	**Age 4**	**Age 7**
Actometer:					
Age 3	. . .	.44*	.61***	.56***	.19
Age 4	.43**	. . .	.66***	.53***	.38**
Judge-based:					
Age 3	.50***	.36**	. . .	.75***	.48***
Age 4	.34*	.48***	.51***	. . .	.38**
Age 7	.35*	.28*	.33*	.50***	. . .

*$p < .05$. **$p < .01$. ***$p < .001$ (two-tailed). Correlations above the ellipses (. . .) are based on boys' data, those below the ellipses (. . .) are based on girls' data.

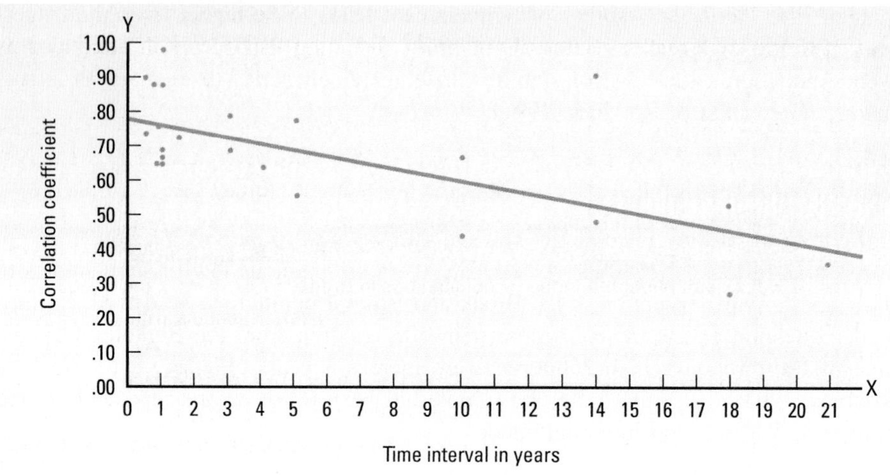

Figure 5.1

The figure shows the stability of aggression in males over different time intervals. Aggression shows the highest levels of stability over short time intervals such as from one year to the next. As the time interval between testings increases, however, the correlation coefficients decline, suggesting that aggressiveness changes more over long time intervals than over short time intervals.

level. Activity level in childhood can be validly assessed through both observational judgments and activity recordings from the actometers. The two measures are moderately correlated at each age, providing cross-validation of each type of measure.

Second, notice that the correlations of the activity level measurements in Table 5.2 are all positively correlated with measurements of activity level taken at later ages. We can conclude from these correlations that activity level shows moderate stability during childhood. Children who are highly active at age 3 are also likely to be active at ages 4 and 7. Their less active peers at age 3 are likely to remain less active at ages 4 and 7.

Finally, notice that the size of the correlations in Table 5.2 tend to decrease as the time interval between the different testings increases. This finding parallels the finding about infancy made by Rothbart (1986). As a general rule, the longer the time between testings, the lower the stability coefficients. In other words, measures taken early in life can predict personality later in life, but the predictability decreases with the length of time between the original testing and the behavior being predicted.

These general conclusions apply to other personality characteristics as well. Aggression and violence have long been a key concern of our society. In recent years in the United States, violence has captured the attention of the whole country. For example, the startling killings by two students at Columbine High School shocked the country. These and other similar shootings have prompted many to ask, "What causes some children to act so aggressively?"

As it turns out, numerous studies of childhood aggression have been conducted by personality psychologists. Dan Olweus (1979) reviewed 16 longitudinal studies of aggression during childhood. The studies varied widely on many aspects, such as age at which the children were first tested (2–18), length interval between first testing and final testing (half a year to 18 years), and the specific measures of aggression used (e.g., teacher ratings, direct observation, and peer ratings).

Figure 5.1 shows a summary graph of the results of all these studies. The graph depicts the stability coefficients for aggression as a function of the interval between first

A Closer Look

Bullies and Whipping Boys from Childhood to Adulthood

The individual differences that emerge early in life sometimes have profound consequences, both for the life outcomes of individuals and for the impact on the social world. Norwegian psychologist Dan Olweus has conducted longitudinal studies of "bullies" and "whipping boys" (Olweus, 1978, 1979). The meanings of these terms are precisely what they sound like. Bullies are those who pick on and victimize other children. They do such things as tripping their victims in the hallway, pushing them into lockers, elbowing them in the stomach, demanding their lunch money, and calling them names.

Although the victims, or "whipping boys," do not have any external characteristics that appear to set them apart, they do have certain psychological characteristics. Most commonly, victims tend to be anxious, fearful, insecure, and lacking in social skills. They are emotionally vulnerable and may be physically weak as well, making them easy targets who don't fight back. The victims suffer from low self-esteem, lose interest in school, and often show difficulties establishing or maintaining friendships. They seem to lack the social support that might buffer them against bullies. It has been estimated that 10 percent of all schoolchildren are afraid of bullies during the school day, and most children have been victimized by bullies at least once (Brody, 1996).

In one longitudinal study, bullies and victims were identified through teacher nominations in Grade 6. A year later, the children attended different schools in different settings, having made the transition from elementary school to junior high school. At this different setting during Grade 7, a different set of teachers categorized the boys on whether they were bullies, victims, or neither. The results are shown in Table 5.3. As you can see from looking at the circled numbers in the diagonal in Table 5.3 the vast majority of the boys received similar classifications a year later, despite the different school, different setting, and different teachers doing the categorizing.

The bullying, however, does not appear to stop in childhood. When Olweus followed thousands of boys from grade school to adulthood, he found marked continuities. The bullies in childhood were more likely to become juvenile delinquents in adolescence and criminals in adulthood. An astonishing 65 percent of the boys who were classified by their Grade 6 teachers as bullies ended up having felony convictions by the time they were 24 years old (Brody, 1996). Many of the bullies apparently remained bullies throughout their lives. Unfortunately, we don't know the fate of the victims, other than that they tended not to get involved in criminal activities.

A study of 228 children, ranging in age from 6 to 16, found several fascinating personality and family relationship correlates of bullying (Connolly & O'Moore, 2003). A total of 115 children were classified as "bullies" based on both their own self-ratings and on the basis of at least two of their classmates categorizing them as bullies. These were then compared with 113 control children, who both did not nominate themselves as bullies and were not categorized as bullies by any of their classmates. The bullies scored higher on the Eysenck scales of Extraversion, Neuroticism, and Psychoticism (see Chapter 3). Bullies, in short, tended to be more outgoing and gregarious (extraversion); emotionally volatile and anxious (neuroticism); and impulsive and lacking in empathy (psychoticism). In addition, the bullies, relative to the controls, expressed more ambivalence and conflict with their family members, including their brothers, sisters, and parents. Conflicts in the home, in short, appear to be linked to conflicts these children get into during school, pointing to a degree of consistency across situations.

Table 5.3 Longitudinal Classification of Boys in Aggressive Behaviors

	GRADE 7		
Grade 6	**Bully**	**Neither**	**Victim**
Bully	(24)	9	2
Neither	9	(200)	15
Victim	1	10	(16)

and final testing. As you can see, marked individual differences in aggression emerge very early in life, certainly by the age of 3 (Olweus, 1979). Individuals retain their rank order stability on aggression to a substantial degree over the years. And, as we have seen with infant temperament and childhood activity level, the stability coefficients tend to decline as the interval between the two times of measurement increases.

In sum, we can conclude that individual differences in personality emerge very early in life—most likely in infancy for some traits and certainly by early childhood for other traits, such as aggression. These individual differences tend to be moderately stable over time, so that the persons who are high on a particular trait tend to remain high on that dimension. Indeed, childhood personality at age 3 turns out to be a good predictor of adult personality at age 26 (Caspi et al., 2003). And, finally, the stability coefficients gradually decline over time as the distance between testings increases.

Rank Order Stability in Adulthood

Many studies have been conducted on the stability of adult personality. Longitudinal studies have been conducted spanning as many as four decades of life. Furthermore, many age brackets have been examined, from age 18 through older cohorts ranging up to age 84.

A summary of these data is shown in Table 5.4, assembled by Costa and McCrae (1994). This table categorizes the measures of personality into the five-factor model of traits, described in Chapter 3. The time intervals between the first and last personality assessments for each sample range from a low of 3 years to a high of 30 years. The results yield a strong general conclusion: across self-report measures of personality, conducted by different investigators, and over differing time intervals of adulthood, the traits of neuroticism, extraversion, openness, agreeableness, and conscientiousness all show moderate to high levels of stability. The average correlation across these traits, scales, and time intervals is roughly +.65.

These studies all rely on self-report. What are the stability coefficients when other data sources are used? In one six-year longitudinal study of adults using spouse ratings, stability coefficients were +.83 for neuroticism, +.77 for extraversion, and +.80 for openness (Costa & McCrae, 1988). Another study used peer ratings of personality to study stability over a seven-year interval. Stability coefficients ranged from +.63 to +.81 for the five-factor taxonomy of personality (Costa & McCrae, 1992). In sum, moderate to high levels of personality stability, in the individual differences sense, are found whether the data source is self-report, spouse-report, or peer-report.

Recent studies continue to confirm the rank order stability of personality during the adult years. In one study, Richard Robins and his colleagues (Robins, Fraley, Roberts, & Trzesniewski, 2001) examined 275 college students during their freshman year, and then again four years later in their senior year. They used the NEO-PI scales to measure the Big Five. Across the four years of college, the rank order stability obtained was: .63 for Extraversion, .60 for Agreeableness, .59 for Conscientiousness, .53 for Neuroticism, and .70 for Openness, all of which were highly statistically significant. In sum, the moderate levels of rank order stability of the Big Five found earlier by Costa and McCrae appear to be highly replicable across different populations and investigators.

Similar findings emerge for personality dispositions that are not strictly subsumed by the Big Five. In a massive meta-analytic study of the stability of self-esteem—how good people feel about themselves—Trzesniewski, Donnellan, and Robins (2003) found high levels of continuity over time. Summarizing 50 published studies involving 29,839 individuals and four large national studies involving 74,381 individuals, they found

Table 5.4 Stability Coefficients for Selected Personality Scales in Adult Samples

Factor/Scale	Interval	r
Neuroticism		
NEO-PI N	6	.83
16PF Q4: Tense	10	.67
ACL Adapted Child	16	.66
Neuroticism	18	.46
GZTS Emotional Stability (low)	24	.62
MMPI Factor	30	.56
	Median:	.64
Extraversion		
NEO-PI E	6	.82
16PF H: Adventurous	10	.74
ACL Self-Confidence	16	.60
Social Extraversion	18	.57
GZTS Sociability	24	.68
MMPI Factor	30	.56
	Median:	.64
Openness		
NEO-PI O	6	.83
16PF I: Tender-Minded	10	.54
GZTS Thoughtfulness	24	.66
MMPI Intellectual Interests	30	.62
	Median:	.64
Agreeableness		
NEO-PI A	3	.63
Agreeableness	18	.46
GZTS Friendliness	24	.65
MMPI Cynicism (low)	30	.65
	Median:	.64
Conscientiousness		
NEO-PI C	3	.79
16PF G: Conscientious	10	.48
ACL Endurance	16	.67
Impulse Control	18	.46
GZTS Restraint	24	.64
	Median:	.67

Note: Interval is given in years; all retest correlations are significant at $p < .01$. NEO-PI = NEO Personality Inventory, ACL = Adjective Check List, GZTS = Guilford Zimmerman Temperament Survey, MMPI = Minnesota Multiphasic Personality Inventory.

stability correlations ranging from the .50s to the .70s. How people feel about themselves—their level of self-confidence—appears very consistent over time. Similar findings have been obtained with measures of prosocial orientation and interpersonal empathy (Eisenberg, Guthrie, Cumberland, Murphy, Shepard, Zhou, & Carlo, 2002). In sum, personality dispositions, whether the standard Big Five or other dispositions, show moderate to considerable rank order stability over time in adulthood.

Researchers have posed an intriguing question about rank order personality stability in the individual differences sense—when does personality consistency peak? That is, is there a point in life when people's personality traits become so firm that

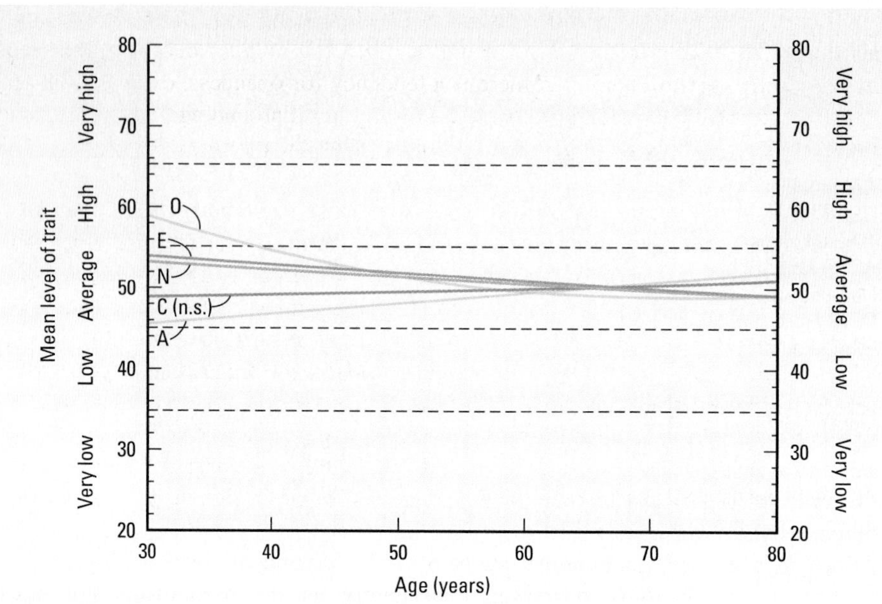

Figure 5.2

The figure shows the mean level of five traits over the life span. Although the average scores on each trait are quite stable over time, Openness, Extraversion, and Neuroticism show a gradual decline from age 30 to 50. In contrast, Agreeableness shows a gradual increase over these ages.

they don't change much relative to those of other people? To address this fascinating question, Roberts and DelVecchio (2000) conducted a meta-analysis of 152 longitudinal studies of personality. Recall that a meta-analysis is a set of statistical procedures for discovering trends across a large number of independent empirical studies. The key variable Roberts and DelVecchio (2000) examined was "personality consistency," which was defined as the correlation between Time 1 and Time 2 measures of personality (e.g., the correlation between a personality trait at age 15 and the same trait at age 18). Only time intervals of at least one year were included in the study.

Roberts and DelVecchio (2000) found two key results when they looked across all these studies. First, personality consistency tends to increase in a stepwise fashion with increasing age. For example, the average personality consistency during the teenage years was +.47. This jumped to +.57 during the decade of the twenties and +.62 during the thirties. Personality consistency peaked during the decade of the fifties at +.75. As the authors conclude, "trait consistency increases in a linear fashion from infancy to middle age where it then reaches its peak after age 50" (Roberts & DelVecchio, 2000, p. 3). As people age, apparently, personality appears to become more and more "set."

Mean Level Stability in Adulthood

The five-factor model of personality also shows fairly consistent mean level stability over time, as shown in Figure 5.2. Especially after age 50, there is little change in the average level of stability in openness, extraversion, neuroticism, conscientiousness, and agreeableness.

Little change, however, does not mean no change. In fact, there are small but consistent changes in these personality traits, especially during the decade of the twenties. As you can see in Figure 5.2, there is a tendency for openness, extraversion, and neuroticism to gradually decline with increasing age until around age 50. At the same time, conscientiousness and agreeableness show a gradual increase over time. The magnitude of these age effects is not large.

Recent studies have confirmed that mean-level personality traits change in slight, but nonetheless important, ways during adulthood. By far the most consistent change is a good one—people score lower on Neuroticism or Negative Affect as they grow older. From freshman to senior years in college, for example, students show a decrease in Neuroticism corresponding to roughly half a standard deviation ($d = -.49$) (Robins et al., 2001). Even a smaller longitudinal study from freshman year to 2.5 years later showed the same finding—students reported experiencing less negative affect and more positive affect over time (Vaidya, Gray, Haig, & Watson, 2002). A longitudinal study from adolescence to mid-life found a consistent decrease in the experience of Negative Affect—individuals feel less anxious, less distressed, and less irritable as they move into mid-life (McCrae et al., 2001). Similar findings were obtained in a massive longitudinal study of 2,804 individuals over a 23-year time span—negative affectivity decreased consistently as the participants got older (Charles, Reynolds, & Gatz, 2001). A massive meta-analysis of 92 different samples found that both women and men gradually become more emotionally stable as they grow older, with the largest changes occurring between the ages of 22 and 40 (Roberts, Walton, & Viechtbauer, 2006). In sum, most people become less emotionally volatile, less anxious, and generally less neurotic as they mature—a nice thing to look forward to for people whose current lives contain a lot of emotional turmoil.

Some people, however, change more than others. Do people know how their personality may have changed? In a fascinating study, researchers assessed the Big Five personality traits in a sample of students right when they entered college (Robins et al., 2005). Four years later they assessed them on the Big Five, and then asked them to evaluate whether they believed that they had changed on each of these personality dimensions. Interestingly, people actually show some awareness of the changes—perceptions of personality change show moderate correspondence with actual personality change.

While neuroticism and negative affect are declining with age, people also score higher on agreeableness and conscientiousness as they grow older. One study found an increase in agreeableness of nearly half a standard deviation ($d = +.44$), while conscientiousness increased roughly one-quarter of a standard deviation ($d = +.27$) (Robins et al., 2001). Similar findings have been discovered by other researchers: College students become more agreeable, extraverted, and conscientious from freshman year to two and a half years later (Vaidya et al., 2002); agreeableness and conscientiousness increase throughout early and middle adulthood (Srivastava, John, Gosling, & Potter, 2003); positive affect increases from the late teen years through the early fifties (Charles et al., 2001). Perhaps a good summary of the mean level personality changes comes directly from the longitudinal researchers: "The personality changes that did take place from adolescence to adulthood reflected growth in the direction of greater maturity; many adolescents became more controlled and socially more confident and less angry and alienated" (Roberts, Caspi, & Moffitt, 2001, p. 670).

Finally, the Big Five personality dispositions may be changeable through therapy. In a unique study, Ralph Piedmont (2001) evaluated the effects of an outpatient drug rehabilitation program on personality dispositions, as indexed by the Big Five. The therapy, administered to 82 men and 50 women over a six-week period, revealed fascinating findings. Those who went through the program showed a decrease in Neuroticism, and increases in Agreeableness and Conscientiousness (d = .38). These personality changes were largely maintained in a follow-up assessment 15 months later, although not as dramatically (d = 28).

In sum, although personality dispositions generally show high levels of mean stability over time, predictable changes occur with age and perhaps also with therapy—lower Neuroticism and Negative Affect, higher Agreeableness, higher Conscientiousness.

Exercise

Each person's personality is, in some ways, stable over time; however, in other ways, it changes over time. In this exercise, you can evaluate yourself in terms of what describes you now and how you think you will be in the future (Markus & Nurius, 1986). Following is a list of items. For each one, simply rate it on a 1 to 7 scale, with 1 meaning "does not describe me at all" to 7 meaning "is a highly accurate description of me." Give a rating for each of two questions: (1) Does this describe me now? and (2) Will this describe me in the future?

Items	Describes Me Now	Will Describe Me in the Future
Is happy		
Is confident		
Is depressed		
Is lazy		
Travels widely		
Has lots of friends		
Is destitute (poor)		
Is sexy		
Is in good shape		
Speaks well in public		
Makes own decisions		
Manipulates people		
Is powerful		
Is trusted		
Is unimportant		
Is offensive		

Now compare your answers to the two questions. Any items you gave the same answers to indicate that you believe that this attribute will remain stable for you over time. The items that change, however, may reflect the ways in which your personality will change over time.

You can view your possible self in a number of ways, but two are especially important. The first pertains to the *desired self*—the person you wish to become. Some people wish to become happier, more powerful, or in better physical shape. The second pertains to your *feared self*—the sort of person you do not wish to become, such as poor or rigid. Which aspects of your possible self do you desire? Which aspects of your possible self do you fear?

Personality Change

Global measures of personality traits, such as those captured by the five-factor model, give us hints that personality can change over time. But it is also true that researchers who have focused most heavily on personality stability have generally not explicitly designed studies and measures to assess personality change. Thus, it is important to remember that knowledge about personality change is sparse.

One reason for the relative lack of knowledge about change is that there might be a bias among researchers against even looking for personality change (Helson & Stewart, 1994). As Block (1971) notes, even the terms used to describe stability and change are laden with evaluative meaning. Terms that refer to absence of change tend to be positive: *consistency, stability, continuity,* and *constancy* all seem like good things to have. On the other hand, *inconsistency, instability, discontinuity,* and *inconstancy* all seem undesirable or unpredictable.

Changes in Self-Esteem from Adolescence to Adulthood

In a unique longitudinal study, Block and Robbins (1993) examined self-esteem and the personality characteristics associated with those whose self-esteem had changed over time. **Self-esteem** was defined as "the extent to which one perceives oneself as relatively close to being the person one wants to be and/or as relatively distant from being the kind of person one does not want to be, with respect to person-qualities one positively and negatively values" (Block & Robbins, 1993, p. 911). Self-esteem was measured by use of an overall difference between a *current* self-description and an *ideal* self-description: the researchers hypothesized that, the smaller the discrepancy, the higher the self-esteem. Conversely, the larger the discrepancy between current and ideal selves, the lower the self-esteem.

The participants were first assessed on this measure of self-esteem at age 14, roughly the first year of high school. Then they were assessed again at age 23, roughly five years after high school.

For the sample as a whole, there was no change in self-esteem with increasing age. However, when males and females were examined separately, a startling trend emerged. Over time, the sexes departed from each other, with men's self-esteem tending to increase and women's self-esteem tending to decrease. The males tended, on average, to increase in self-esteem by roughly a fifth of a standard deviation, whereas the females tended, on average, to decrease in self-esteem by roughly a standard deviation. This is an example of personality change at the group level—the two subgroups (women and men) changed in different directions over time.

Furthermore, there were interesting personality correlates of those whose self-esteem tended to change over time. The females whose self-esteem tended to increase over time were judged by observers to have an excellent sense of humor, to be protective of others, and to be giving and talkative persons. The females whose self-esteem tended to go down over time, on the other hand, tended to be judged to be moody, hostile, irritable, negativistic, unpredictable, and condescending.

The males whose self-esteem increased over time were observed to be socially at ease, to regard themselves as physically attractive, and to have a calm and relaxed manner. The males whose self-esteem decreased over time tended to be anxious, easily stressed, self-defensive, and ruminative.

In sum, the transition from early adolescence to early adulthood appears to be harder on women than on men, at least in terms of the criterion of self-esteem. As a whole, females tend to decrease in self-esteem, showing an increasing gap between their current self-conceptions and their ideal selves. As a whole, males tend to show a smaller discrepancy between their real and ideal selves over the same time period.

Flexibility and Impulsivity

Another example of personality change can be found in a study of creative architects. In this study, researchers measured personality twice, with the testings separated by 25 years (Dudek & Hall, 1991). Two large personality inventories were administered at each testing—the CPI (California Psychological Inventory) and the ACL (Adjective Check List). The architects were tested at the beginning of their careers and again 25 years later. Some of the architects turned out to be very successful and creative, whereas others were just average architects. At both testings, the highly creative architects displayed personalities consisting of high scores on spontaneity, intensity of motivation, and independence. The less creative architects, on the other hand, started out with mainly high scores on conformity and continued to show higher scores on conformity 25 years later. The participants as a whole, however, showed a marked *decrease* in impulsivity and flexibility as they aged. These findings correspond with our intuitions about older people—they tend to reign in their impulses and perhaps become a bit more fixed in their ways and more rigid as they age.

Autonomy, Dominance, Leadership, and Ambition

Another longitudinal study examined 266 male managerial candidates at the business AT&T (Howard & Bray, 1988). The researchers first tested these men when they were in their twenties (in the late 1950s) and then followed them up periodically over a 20-year time span when they were in their forties (in the late 1970s). One of the key personality measures was the Edwards Personal Preference Schedule (Edwards, 1959), a broad personality inventory designed to capture a wide range of personality characteristics.

Several dramatic personality changes were observed for the sample as a whole. The most startling change was a steep drop in the *ambition* score. This drop was steepest during the first eight years but continued to drop over the next 12 years. The drop was steepest for the college men, less so for the noncollege men, although it should be noted that the college men started out higher on ambition than did the noncollege men. Supplementary interview data suggested that the men had become more realistic about their limited possibilities for promotion in the company. It is not that these men lost interest in their jobs or became less effective. Indeed, their scores on *autonomy, leadership motivation, achievement,* and *dominance* all increased over time (see Figure 5.3). The men seemed to become less dependent on others as they assumed the individual responsibilities of supporting their families.

Sensation Seeking

Conventional wisdom has it that people become more cautious and conservative with age. Studies of sensation seeking confirm this view. The general trait of sensation seeking is described, mostly from a biological point of view, in Chapter 7. The Sensation-Seeking Scale (SSS) contains four subscales, each containing items and phrases as a forced-choice between two distinct options. First is *thrill and adventure seeking,* with items such as "I would like to try parachute jumping" versus "I would never want to try jumping out of a plane, with or without a parachute." The other scales are *experience seeking* (e.g., "I am not interested in experience for its own sake" versus "I like to have new and exciting experiences and sensations even if they

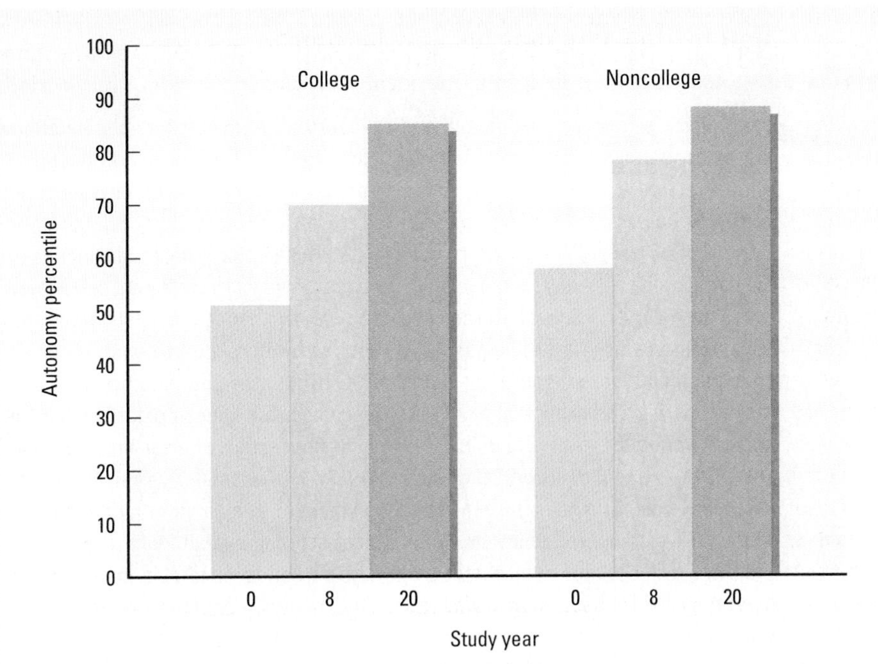

Figure 5.3

The figure shows change with age in autonomy scores of men in the AT&T study. Both college-educated and noncollege-educated men tend to become more autonomous or independent as they grow older.

are a little frightening, unconventional, or illegal"); *disinhibition* (e.g., "I like wild, uninhibited parties" versus "I prefer quiet parties with good conversation"); and *boredom susceptibility* (e.g., "I get bored seeing the same old faces" versus "I like the comfortable familiarity of everyday friends").

Sensation seeking increases with age from childhood to adolescence and peaks in late adolescence around ages 18–20; then it falls more or less continuously as subjects get older (Zuckerman, 1974). The average correlation between sensation seeking and age is −.30, suggesting a modest or gradual decline with increasing age beyond adolescence. Parachute jumping and wild, uninhibited parties seem to be less appealing to older folks.

Femininity

In a longitudinal study of women from Mills College in the San Francisco bay area, Helson and Wink (1992) examined changes in personality between the early forties and early fifties. They used the California Psychological Inventory at both time periods. The most dramatic change occurred on the *femininity* scale (now called the femininity/masculinity scale). High scorers on femininity tend to be described by observers as dependent, emotional, feminine, gentle, high-strung, mild, nervous, sensitive, sentimental, submissive, sympathetic, and worrying (Gough, 1996). Low scorers (i.e., those who score in the masculine direction), in contrast, tend to be described as aggressive, assertive, boastful, confident, determined, forceful, independent, masculine, self-confident, strong, and tough. In terms of acts performed (recall the Act Frequency Approach from Chapter 3), as reported by the spouses of these women,

A Closer Look

Day-to-Day Changes in Self-Esteem

Most personality psychologists who study self-esteem focus on a person's average level, whether the person is generally high, low, or average in terms of his or her self-esteem. A few studies have been done on changes in self-esteem over long time spans in people's lives—for example, in the years from adolescence to adulthood. However, with some reflection, most of us would realize that we often change from day to day in how we feel about ourselves. Some days are better than other days when it comes to self-esteem. Some days we feel incompetent, that things are out of our control, and that we even feel a little worthless. Other days we feel satisfied with ourselves, that we are particularly strong or competent and that we are satisfied with who we are and what we can become. In other words, it seems that feelings of self-esteem can change, not just from year to year but also from day to day.

Psychologist Michael Kernis has become interested in how changeable or variable people are in their self-esteem in terms of day-to-day fluctuations. *Self-esteem variability* is the magnitude of short-term changes in ongoing self-esteem (Kernis, Grannemann, & Mathis, 1991). Self-esteem variability is measured by having people keep records of how they feel about themselves for several consecutive days, sometimes for weeks or months. From these daily records, the researchers can determine just how much each person fluctuates, as well as his or her average level of self-esteem.

Researchers make a distinction between level and variability of self-esteem. These two aspects of self-esteem turn out to be unrelated to each other and are hypothesized to interact in predicting important life outcomes, such as depression (Kernis, Grannemann, & Barclay, 1992). For example, variability in self-esteem is an indicator that the person's self-esteem, even if high, is fragile and the person is vulnerable to stress. Consequently, we can think of level and variability as defining two qualities of self-esteem as in the following figure:

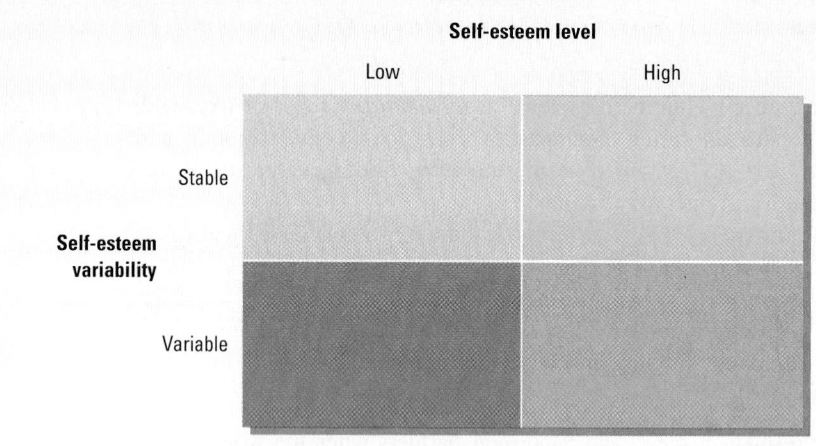

Level of self-esteem (whether one is high or low) and variability in self-esteem (whether one is stable or variable from day to day) are unrelated to each other. This makes it possible to find people with different combinations, such as a person who has a high level of self-estem, but is also variable.

high scorers on the femininity scale tend to do such things as send cards to friends on holidays and remember an acquaintance's birthday, even though no one else did. Low scorers, in contrast, tend to take charge of committee meetings and take the initiative in sexual encounters (Gough, 1996).

A fascinating change occurred in this sample of educated women—they showed a consistent drop in femininity as they moved from their early forties to their early

Kernis et al. (1991, 1992) have suggested that self-esteem variability is related to the extent to which one's self-view can be influenced by events, particularly social events. Some people's self-esteem is pushed and pulled by the happenings of life more than is other people's self-esteem. For example, for some people, self-esteem might soar with a compliment and plummet with a social slight, whereas others, who can better roll with the punches of life, might be more stable in their self-esteem, weathering both the slights as well as the uplifts of life without much change in their self-view. This stability versus changeability of self-esteem is the psychological disposition referred to as self-esteem variability.

Several studies have been conducted to examine whether self-esteem variability predicts life outcomes, such as depressive reactions to stress, differently than does self-esteem level. In one study (Kernis et al., 1991), self-esteem level was related to depression, but this relation was much stronger for persons higher in self-esteem variability than for persons lower in self-esteem variability. In other words, at all levels of self-esteem, the participants who were low in variability showed less of a relation between self-esteem and depression than did the participants who were high in variability. Similar results were obtained by Butler, Hokanson, and Flynn (1994), who showed that self-esteem variability is a good predictor of who would become depressed six months later, especially when there was life stress in the intervening months. These authors also concluded that variability indicates that the person may have a fragile sense of self-value and that, with stress, he or she may become more chronically depressed than someone whose self-esteem is more stable.

Based on findings from studies like these, researchers have come to view self-esteem variability as a vulnerability to stressful life events (Roberts & Monroe, 1992). That is, variability is thought to result from a particular sensitivity in one's sense of self-worth. Psychologists Ryan and Deci (2000) have suggested that variable persons are dependent for their self-worth on the approval of others. Variable persons are very sensitive to social feedback and they judge themselves primarily through the eyes of others. High-variability persons show (1) an enhanced sensitivity to evaluative events, (2) an increased concern about their self-concept, (3) an overreliance on social sources for self-evaluation, and (4) reactions of anger and hostility when things don't go their way.

fifties—a group level change in this personality variable. It is not known precisely why this drop in femininity occurs. Perhaps it is linked with the known decreases in levels of the hormone estrogen during this decade.

Competence

Another key finding from the longitudinal study of Mills College women (Helson & Wink, 1992) pertained to self-assessments of competence. Competence was measured with the Adjective Check List (ACL) scale, which contained these items: goal-oriented, organized, thorough, efficient, practical, clear-thinking, realistic, precise, mature, confident, and contented (Helson & Stewart, 1994). High scorers tend to endorse many of these items as self-descriptive, whereas low scorers endorse few. Figure 5.4 shows the results for the women and their partners when the women were at age 27 and then again at age 52.

The women in this sample showed a sharp increase in self-assessments of competence. Their husbands showed fairly constant scores across the two time periods. Furthermore, the women's increases in self-described competence did not depend on whether or not they had children. Both those who had and those who did not have children showed comparable increases in competence.

Independence and Traditional Roles

The longitudinal study of Mills College women (Helson & Picano, 1990) yielded another fascinating finding. The women were divided into four distinct groups: (1) homemakers with intact marriages and children, (2) working mothers with children (neotraditionals), (3) divorced mothers, and (4) nonmothers (Helson & Picano,

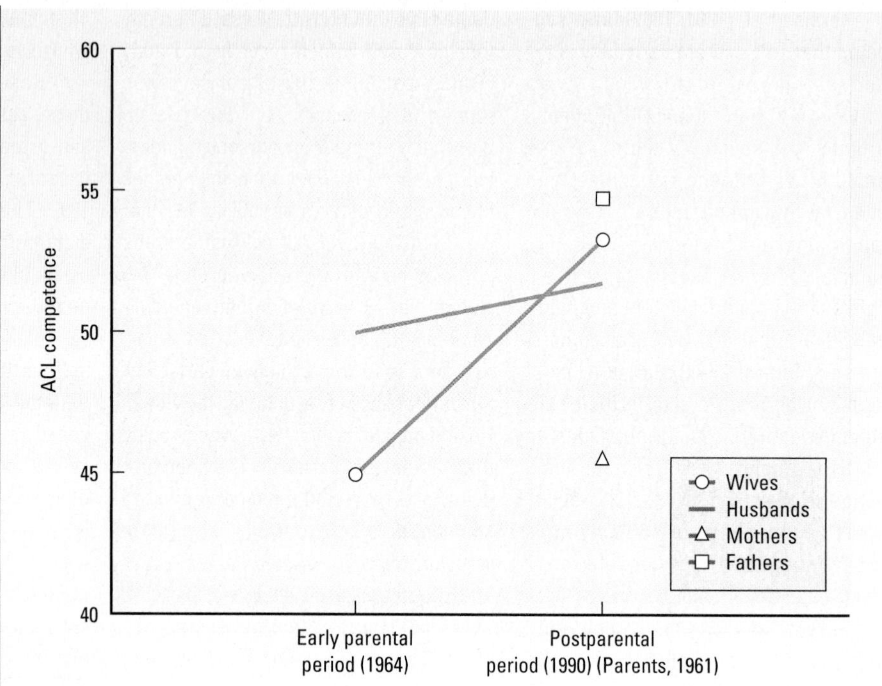

Figure 5.4

Means on the Competence cluster of the Adjective Check List (ACL) for women and their partners at the early parental (n = 65) and postparental (n = 48) periods, and for a subsample of the women's parents (n = 29 couples) at the postparental period.

1990). Figure 5.5 shows the results for the CPI Independence scale, which measures two related facets of personality. The first is self-assurance, resourcefulness, and competence. The second is distancing self from others and not bowing to conventional demands of society. The act frequency correlates of this scale reflect these themes (Gough, 1996). Those high on the independence scale tend to set goals for groups they are in, talk to many people at parties, and take charge of the group when the situation calls for it. High scorers also tend to interrupt conversations and do not always follow instructions from those who are in a position to lead (hence, distancing themselves from others in these ways).

For the divorced mothers, nonmothers, and working mothers, independence scores increased significantly over time. Only the traditional homemakers showed no increase in independence over time. These data, of course, are correlational, so we cannot infer causation. It is possible that something about the roles affected the degree to which the women became more independent. It is also possible that the women who were less likely to increase in independence were more content to remain in the traditional homemaking role. Regardless of the interpretation, this study illustrates the utility of examining subgroups within the population. Personality change may be revealed in specific subgroups, whereas such change may be obscured when the entire group is examined in an undifferentiated manner.

In sum, although the evidence is sparse, there are enough empirical clues to suggest that personality traits show some predictable changes with age. First, impulsivity and sensation seeking show predictable declines with age. Second, men tend to

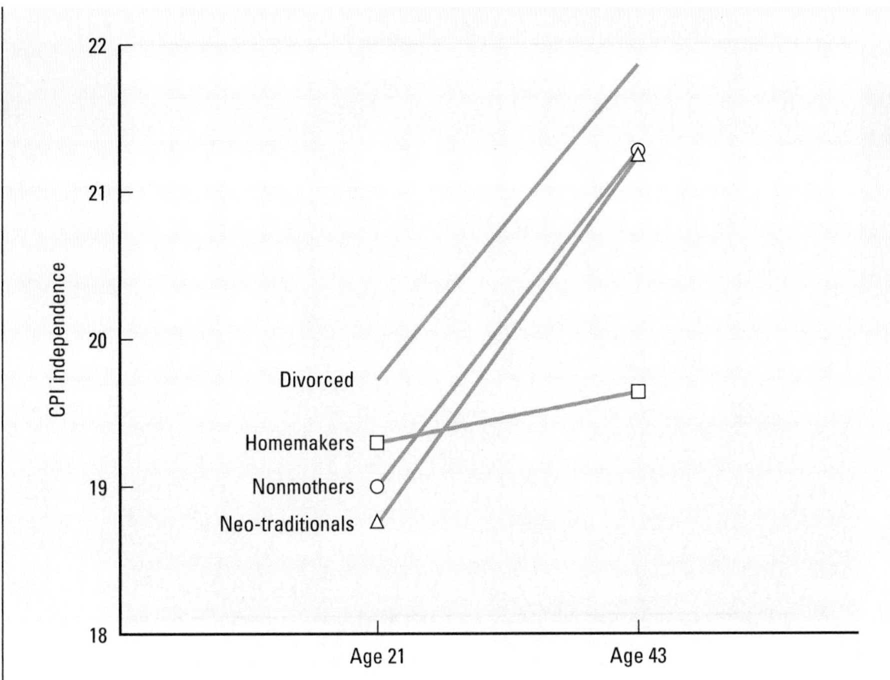

Figure 5.5

Means on the CPI Independence scale at ages 21 and 43 for homemakers (n = 17) and three groups of women with less traditional role paths: neotraditional, n = 35; divorced, n = 26; and nonmothers, n = 26.

decline in psychological flexibility and to become somewhat less ambitious with age. There are indications that both men and women become somewhat more competent and independent with increasing age. Finally, there are hints that changes in independence are linked with the role and lifestyle adopted, with traditional homemaking women changing less on independence than women who get divorced or lead less traditional work lives.

Personality Changes across Cohorts: Women's Assertiveness in Response to Changes in Social Status and Roles

One of the fascinating issues in exploring personality change over time is trying to determine whether the changes observed are due to true personal change that all people undergo as they age, as can be determined by longitudinal studies of the sort just presented, or, conversely, changes in the **cohort effects**—the social times in which they lived. Jean Twenge (2000, 2001a, 2001b) has been at the forefront in exploring personality change that is likely to be caused by cohort. She argues that American society has changed dramatically over the past seven decades. One of the most dramatic changes centers on women's status and roles. During the depression era of the 1930s, for example, women were expected to be self-sufficient, but during the 1950s and 1960s, women assumed a more domestic role. Then from 1968 through 1993, women surged into the workforce and American society increasingly adopted norms of sexual equality. For example, from 1950 to 1993, the number of women obtaining

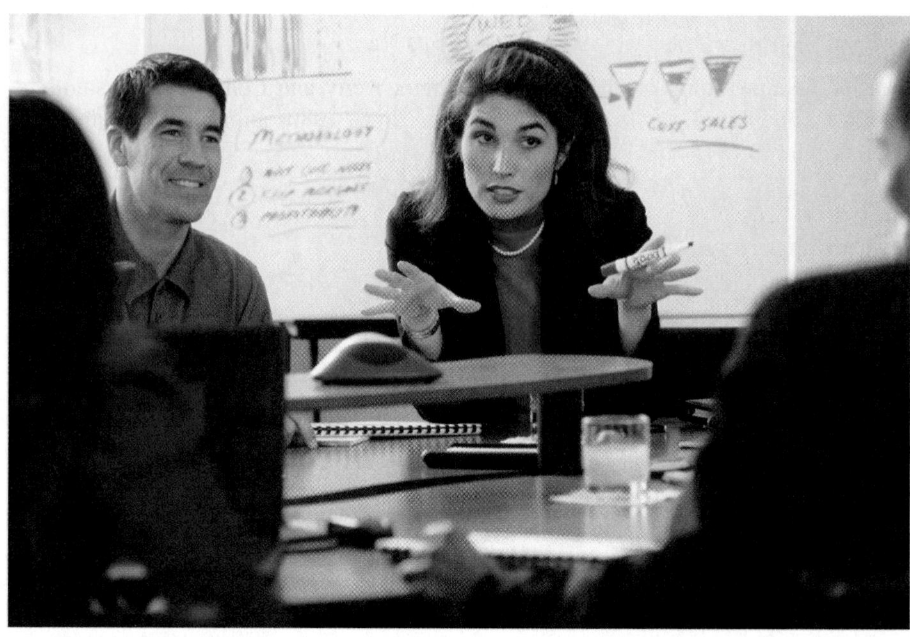

Women's assertiveness scores rose from 1968 to 1993, pointing to a cohort effect.

bachelor's degrees doubled from roughly 25 percent to roughly 50 percent. And the number of women obtaining Ph.D.s, medical degrees, and law degrees all more than tripled. It would be astonishing if these dramatic societal changes had absolutely no impact on women's personality.

Twenge (2001a) discovered that women's trait scores on assertiveness rose and fell dramatically, depending on the cohort in which the woman was raised. Women's assertiveness scores generally rose half a standard deviation from 1931 to 1945; fell by roughly that amount from 1951 to 1967; and then rose again from 1968 to 1993. On measures such as the California Psychological Inventory scale of Dominance, for example, women increased +.31 of a standard deviation from 1968 to 1993. Men, in contrast, did not show significant cohort differences in their levels of assertiveness or dominance. Twenge (2001a) concludes that "social change truly becomes internalized with the individual . . . girls absorb the cultural messages they received from the world around them, and their personalities are molded by these messages" (p. 142). Studies of current and future generations will determine the degree to which these interesting cohort effects remain or change (see the recent book by Jean Twenge, 2006).

Personality Coherence over Time: The Prediction of Socially Relevant Outcomes

The final form of personality development we will examine is called personality coherence, defined as predictable changes in the *manifestations* or *outcomes* of personality factors over time, even if the underlying characteristics remain stable. In particular, we will focus on the consequences of personality for socially relevant outcomes, such as marital stability and divorce, alcoholism and emotional disturbance, and job outcomes later in life.

Marital Stability, Marital Satisfaction, and Divorce

In a longitudinal study of unprecedented length, Kelly and Conley (1987) studied a sample of 300 couples from their engagements in the 1930s all the way through their status later in life in the 1980s. At the final testing, the median age of the subjects was 68 years. Within the entire sample of 300 couples, 22 couples broke their engagements and did not get married. Of the 278 couples who did get married, 50 ended up getting divorced sometime between 1935 and 1980.

During the first testing session in the 1930s, acquaintances provided ratings of each participant's personality on a wide variety of dimensions. Three aspects of personality proved to be strong predictors of marital dissatisfaction and divorce—the neuroticism of the husband, the lack of impulse control of the husband, and the neuroticism of the wife. High levels of neuroticism proved to be the strongest predictors. Neuroticism was linked with marital dissatisfaction of both the men and the women in the 1930s, again in 1955, and yet again in 1980.

Furthermore, the neuroticism of both the husband and the wife, as well as the lack of impulse control of the husband, were strong predictors of divorce. The three major aspects of personality accounted for more than half of the predicable variance in whether or not the couples split up. This is a particularly strong effect in personality research. The couples who had a stable and satisfying marriage had neuroticism scores that were roughly half a standard deviation lower than the couples who subsequently got divorced. Furthermore, in the emotionally stable couples, the husbands tended to score roughly half a standard deviation higher on impulse control, compared with the husbands in unstable marriages.

The reasons for divorce themselves appear to be linked to the personality characteristics measured earlier in life. The husbands with low impulse control when first assessed, for example, tended later in life to have extramarital affairs—breaches of the marital vows that loomed large among the major reasons cited for the divorce. The men with higher impulse control appear to have been able to refrain from having sexual flings, which are so detrimental to marriages (Buss, 2003).

These results, spanning a 45-year period consisting of most of the adult lives of the participants, point to an important conclusion about personality coherence. Personality may not be destiny, but it leads to some predictable life outcomes, such as infidelity, marital unhappiness, and divorce.

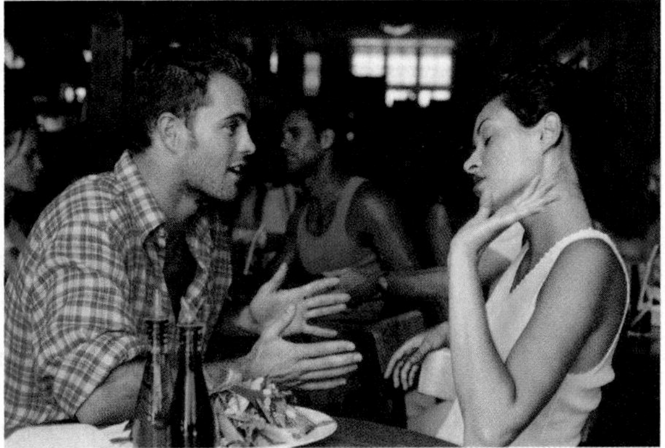

Psychologists have identified personality variables that predict whether a marriage will turn out to be happy and satisfying or whether it will end in divorce. Although personality is not destiny, it does relate to important life outcomes, such as marital unhappiness and divorce.

Interestingly, neuroticism also plays a role in another important life outcome—resilience after losing a spouse. A fascinating longitudinal study showed that one of the best predictors of coping well with the death of a spouse was the personality disposition of emotional stability (Bonanno, Wortman, Lehman, Tweed, Haring, Sonnega, Carr, & Nesse, 2002). A total of 205 individuals were assessed several years prior to the death of their spouse, and then 6 and 18 months after their spouse's demise. Those high on emotional stability grieved less, showed less depression, and displayed the quickest psychological recovery. Individuals low on emotional stability (high on neuroticism) were still psychologically anguished half a year and even a year and a half later. Personality, in short, affects many aspects of romantic life: who is likely to get involved in a successful romantic relationship (Shiner, Masten, & Tellegen, 2002); which marriages remain stable and highly satisfying (Kelly & Conley, 1987); which people are more likely to get divorced (Kelly & Conley, 1987); and how people cope following the loss of a spouse (Bonanno et al., 2002).

Alcoholism and Emotional Disturbance

One longitudinal study found that early personality predicts the later development of alcoholism and emotional disturbance (Conley & Angelides, 1984). Of the 233 men in the study, 40 were judged to develop a serious emotional problem or alcoholism. These 40 men had earlier been rated by their acquaintances as high on neuroticism. Specifically, they had neuroticism scores roughly three-fourths of a standard deviation higher than men who did not develop alcoholism or a serious emotional disturbance.

Furthermore, early personality characteristics were useful in distinguishing between the men who had become alcoholic and those who had developed an emotional disturbance. Impulse control was the key factor. The alcoholic men had impulse control scores a full standard deviation lower than those who had an emotional disturbance. These personality traits proved to be more predictive of these later adult problems than were measures of stress experienced early in life, or even stresses that occurred subsequently. Recent studies have continued to find that those high on personality traits such as sensation seeking and impulsivity, and low on traits such as Agreeableness and Conscientiousness, tend to use and abuse alcohol more than their peers (Cooper, Wood, Orcutt, & Albino, 2003; Hampson, Severson, Burns, Slovic, & Fisher, 2001; Markey, Markey, & Tinsley, 2003; Ruchkin, Koposov, Eisemann, & Hagglof, 2002). In sum, neuroticism and impulsivity early in life are coherently linked with socially relevant outcomes later in life.

Education, Academic Achievement, and Dropping Out

Impulsivity also appears to play a key role in education and academic achievement. Kipnis (1971) had a group of individuals self-report on their levels of impulsivity. He also obtained their SAT scores, which are widely regarded as measures of academic achievement and potential. Among those with low SAT scores, there was no link between impulsivity and subsequent grade-point average. Among those with high SAT scores, however, the impulsive individuals had consistently lower GPAs than did their less impulsive peers. Furthermore, the impulsive individuals were more likely to flunk out of college than were those who were less impulsive. Another researcher found a similar link, showing a correlation of −.47 between peer ratings of impulsivity before entry into college and GPA subsequently (Smith, 1967). Impulsivity (or lack of self-control) continues to affect performance in the workplace. One longitudinal study looked at personality dispositions at age 18 and work-related outcomes at age 26 (Roberts, Caspi, & Moffitt, 2003). They found that those who were high on Self-Control at age 18 had higher occupational attainment, greater involvement with their work, and superior financial security at age 26. Conversely, the impulsive 18-year-olds were less likely to progress in their work, showed less psychological involvement, and experienced lower financial security.

The personality trait of *conscientiousness* turns out to be the single best predictor of successful achievement in school and work. High conscientiousness at age three predicts successful academic performance nine years later (Abe, 2005). Observer-based assessment of children's conscientiousness at ages 4 to 6 predict school grades nine years later (Asendorpf & Van Aken, 2003). Conscientiousness of children assessed between the ages of 8 and 12 predict academic attainment two decades later (Shiner, Masten, & Roberts, 2003). Although other personality traits also predict successful academic performance, such as emotional stability (Chamorro-Premuzic & Furnham, 2003), and agreeableness and openness (Hair & Graziano, 2003), conscientiousness is the most powerful longitudinal predictor of success in school and work.

Interestingly, work experiences also have an effect on personality change (Roberts et al., 2001). Those who attain high occupational status at age 26 have become happier, more self-confident, less anxious, and less self-defeating since they were 18 years old. Those who attain high work satisfaction also become less anxious and less prone to stress in their transition from adolescence to young adulthood. Finally, what about people who attain financial success in the workplace? These individuals not only become less alienated and better able to handle stress, but they also increase their levels of social closeness—they like people more, turn to others for comfort, and like being around people. In sum, just as personality at age 18 predicts work outcomes at age 26 (e.g., self-control predicts income), work outcomes predict personality change over time. We see again that impulsivity is a critical personality factor, which is linked in meaningful ways with later life outcomes.

Health and Longevity

How long people live and how healthy or sickly they become during their years of life are exceptionally important developmental outcomes. It may come as a surprise to you that your personality actually predicts how long you are likely to live. The most important traits conducive to living a long life are *high conscientiousness, positive emotionality (extraversion),* and *low levels of hostility* (Danner et al., 2001; Friedman et al., 1995; Miller et al., 1996). There are several paths through which these personality traits affect longevity (Ozer & Benet-Martinez, 2006). First, conscientious individuals engage in more health-promoting practices, such as maintaining a good diet and getting regular exercise; they also avoid unhealthy practices such as smoking and becoming a "couch potato." Conscientious children in elementary school, for example, end up smoking less and drinking less alcohol when they are adults fully 40 years later (Hampson, Goldberg, Vogt, & Dubanoski, 2006). Conscientiousness at age 17 also predicts refraining from engaging in legal (nicotine, alcohol) and illegal drug use three years later (Elkins, King, McGue, & Iacono, 2006). Those low on conscientiousness in adolescence are more likely to get addicted in young adulthood to drugs of all sorts. Moreover, conscientious individuals are more likely to follow doctor's orders and adhere to the treatment plans they recommend.

A Closer Look

Adult Outcomes of Children with Temper Tantrums

In a longitudinal study spanning 40 years, Caspi et al. (1987) explored the implications of childhood personality for adult occupational status and job outcomes. He identified a group of explosive, undercontrolled children, using interviews with their mothers as the data source. When the children were 8, 9, and 11, their mothers rated the frequency and severity of their temper tantrums. Severe tantrums were defined as behaviors involving biting, kicking, striking, throwing things, screaming, and shouting. From the sample, 38 percent of the boys and 29 percent of the girls were classified as having frequent and uncontrolled temper tantrums.

These children were followed throughout life, and the adult manifestations of childhood personality for men were especially striking. The men who, as children, had had frequent and severe temper tantrums achieved lower levels of education in adulthood. The occupational status of their first job was also consistently lower than that of their calmer peers. The explosive children who had come from middle-class backgrounds tended to be downwardly mobile, and by midlife their occupational attainment was indistinguishable from that of their working-class counterparts. Furthermore, they tended to change jobs frequently, showed an erratic work pattern with more frequent breaks from employment, and averaged a higher number of months being unemployed.

Since 70 percent of the men in the sample served in the military, their military records could also be examined. The men who, as children, had been classified as having explosive temper tantrums attained a significantly lower military rank than their peers. Finally, nearly half (46 percent) of these men were divorced by the age of 40, compared with only 22 percent of the men without a childhood history of temper tantrums. In sum, early childhood personality shows coherent links with important adult social outcomes, such as job attainment, frequency of job switching, unemployment, military attainment, and divorce.

It is easy to imagine why explosive, undercontolled individuals tend to achieve less and get divorced more. Life consists of many frustrations, and people deal with their frustrations in different ways. Explosive undercontrollers are probably more likely to blow up and yell at the boss, for example, or to quit their jobs during an impulsive moment. Similarly, explosive undercontrollers are probably more likely to vent their frustrations on their spouses, or perhaps even to impulsively have an extramarital affair. All of these events are likely to lead to lower levels of job attainment and higher levels of divorce.

Second, extraverts are more likely to have lots of friends, leading to a good social support network—factors linked with positive health outcomes. And third, low levels of hostility put less stress on the heart and cardiovascular system—a topic explored in greater detail in Chapter 18. In sum, the personality traits of conscientiousness, positive emotionality (extraversion), and low hostility predict both positive health outcomes and longevity.

Prediction of Personality Change

Can we predict who is likely to change in personality and who is likely to remain the same? In a fascinating longitudinal study, Caspi and Herbener (1990) studied middle-aged couples over an 11-year period. The couples were tested twice, once in 1970 and again in 1981. All the subjects had been born in either 1920–21 or 1928–29 and were part of a larger longitudinal project.

The question that intrigued Caspi and Herbener was this: Is the choice of a marriage partner a cause of personality stability or change? Specifically, if you marry someone who is similar to you, do you tend to remain more stable over time than if you marry someone who is different from you? They reasoned that similarity between spouses would support personality stability, since the couple would tend to reinforce one another on their attitudes, to seek similar external sources of stimulation, and perhaps even to participate together in the same social networks. Marrying someone

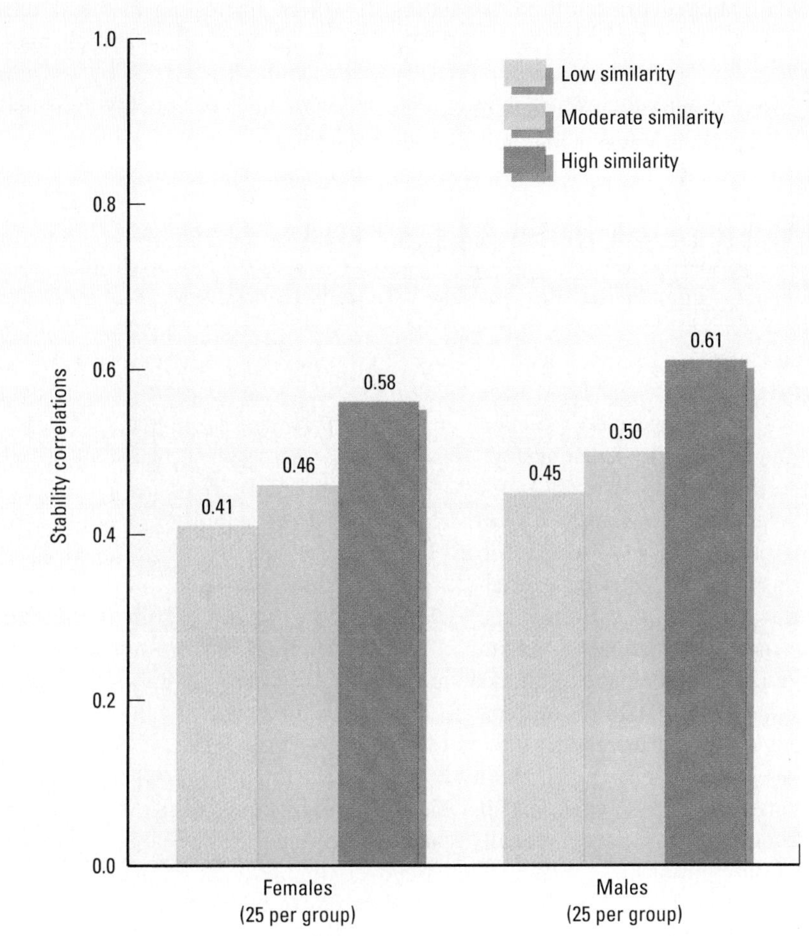

Figure 5.6

The figure shows the stability of personality over time as a function of the similarity (low, medium, or high) of the person to his or her spouse. Men and women who are married to someone similar to themselves in personality show the highest levels of personality stability over time.

who is unlike oneself, in contrast, may offer attitudinal clashes, exposure to social and environmental events that one might not otherwise seek alone, and generally create an environment uncomfortable to maintaining the status quo.

Using personality measures obtained on both husbands and wives, Caspi and Herbener divided the couples into three groups: those who were highly similar in personality, those who were moderately similar in personality, and those who were low in similarity. Then they examined the degree to which the individuals showed stability in personality over the 11-year period of midlife in which they were tested. The results are shown in Figure 5.6.

As you can see in Figure 5.6, the people married to spouses who were highly similar to themselves showed the most personality stability. Those married to spouses least similar to themselves showed the most personality change. The moderate group fell in between. This study is important in pointing to a potential source of personality stability and change—the selection of spouses. It will be interesting to see whether future research can document other sources of personality stability and change—perhaps by examining the selection of similar or dissimilar friends, or by selecting college or work environments that show a good "fit" with one's personality traits upon entry into these environments (Roberts & Robins, 2004).

SUMMARY AND EVALUATION

Personality development includes both the continuities and changes in personality over time. There are three forms of personality stability: (1) rank order stability is the maintenance of one's relative position within a group over time, (2) mean level stability is the maintenance of the average level of a trait or characteristic over time, and (3) personality coherence is predictable changes in the manifestations of a trait. We can examine personality development at three levels of personality analysis—the population level, the group differences level, and the individual differences level.

There is strong evidence for personality rank order stability over time. Temperaments such as activity level and fearfulness show moderate to high levels of stability during infancy. Activity level and aggression show moderate to high levels of stability during childhood. Bullies in childhood tend to become juvenile delinquents in adolescence and criminals in adulthood. Personality traits, such as those captured by the five-factor model, show moderate to high levels of stability during adulthood. As a general rule, the stability coefficients decrease as the length of time between the two periods of testing increases.

Personality also changes in predictable ways over time. With respect to the Big Five, a consensus is now emerging that Neuroticism generally decreases over time; people become a bit more emotionally stable as they age. Furthermore, Agreeableness and Conscientiousness tend to increase over time. All these changes suggest increased maturity, as the sometimes tumultuous times of adolescence settle out into the maturity of adulthood. From early adolescence to early adulthood, men's self-esteem tends to increase, whereas women's self-esteem tends to decrease. In adulthood, there is some evidence from a study of creative architects that flexibility and impulsivity decline with increasing age. Sensation seeking also declines predictably with age. And, in women, femininity tends to decrease over time, notably from the early forties to the early fifties. On the other hand, several studies suggest that the personality characteristics of autonomy, independence, and competence tend to increase as people get older, especially among women.

In addition to personality change due to age, there is also evidence that mean personality levels can be affected by the social cohort in which one grows up. Jean Twenge has documented several such effects, most notably on women's levels of assertiveness or dominance. Women's assertiveness levels were high following the 1930s in which women had to be extremely independent; they fell during the 1950s and 1960s when women were largely homemakers and fewer became professionals. From 1967 to 1993, however, women's levels of assertiveness increased, corresponding to changes in their social roles and increasing participation in professional occupations.

Personality also shows evidence of coherence over time. Early measures of personality can be used to predict socially relevant outcomes later in life. High levels of neuroticism in both sexes and impulsivity in men, for example, predict marital dissatisfaction and divorce. Neuroticism early in adulthood is also a good predictor of later alcoholism and the development of emotional problems. Impulsivity plays a key role in the development of alcoholism and the failure to achieve one's academic potential. Highly impulsive individuals tend to get poorer grades and drop out of school more than their less impulsive peers. Children with explosive temper tantrums tend to manifest their personalities as adults through downward occupational mobility, more frequent job switching, lower attainment of rank in the military, and higher frequencies of divorce. People who are impulsive at age 18 tend to do more poorly in the workplace—they attain less occupational success and less financial security. Work experiences, in turn, appear to affect personality change. Those who attain occupational success tend to become happier, more self-confident, and less anxious over time.

Although little is known about what factors maintain these forms of personality stability and coherence over time, one possibility pertains to our choices of marriage partners. There is evidence that we tend to choose those who are similar to us in personality, and, the more similar our partners, the more stable our personality traits remain over time.

How can we best reconcile the findings of considerable personality stability over time with evidence of important changes? First, longitudinal studies have shown conclusively that personality traits, such as those subsumed by the Big Five, show substantial rank order stability over time. These personality traits also show evidence of coherence over time. Bullies in middle school, for example, tend to become criminals in adulthood. Those with self-control and conscientiousness in adolescence tend to perform well academically and well in the workplace later in life. In the context of these broad-brush strokes of stability, it is also clear that people show mean level changes with age—as a group people become less neurotic, less anxious, less impulsive, lower in sensation seeking, more agreeable, and more conscientious. Some changes are more pronounced in women—they become less feminine and more competent and autonomous over time. And some personality change affects only some individuals, such as those who succeed in the workplace. In short, although personality dispositions tend to be stable over time, they are not "set in plaster" in the sense that some change in some individuals some of the time.

KEY TERMS

Personality Development 138
Rank Order Stability 138
Mean Level Stability 139
Mean Level Change 139
Personality Coherence 139
Temperament 143
Longitudinal Studies 145
Actometer 145
Stability Coefficients 145
Validity Coefficients 145
Self-Esteem 153
Cohort Effects 159

PART TWO

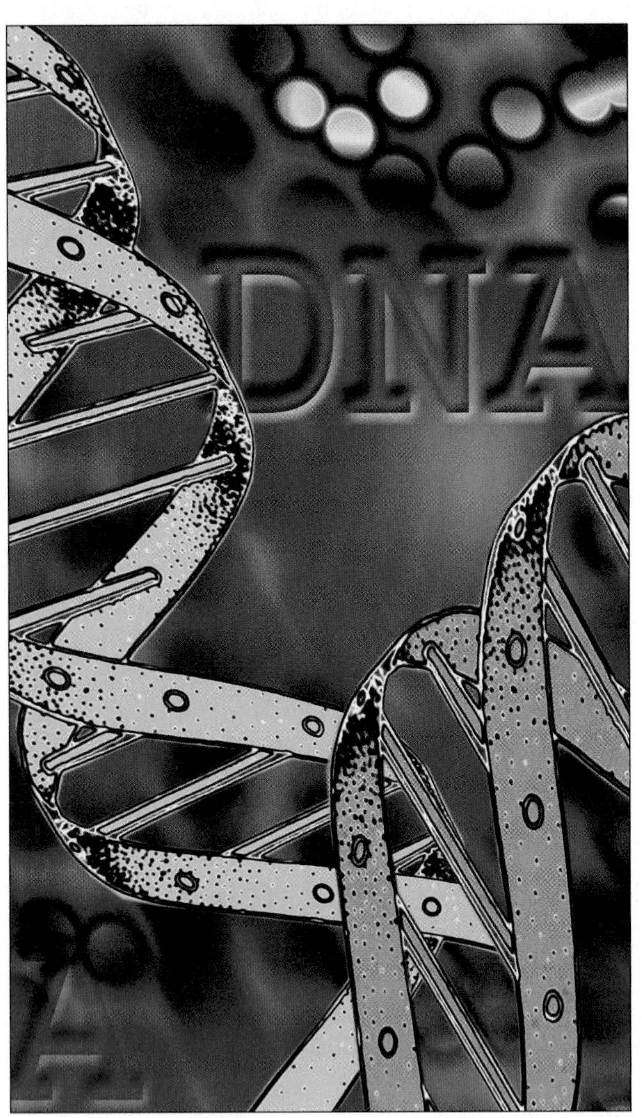

The Biological Domain

II

The biological domain concerns those factors within the body that influence or are influenced by personality. This domain is not any more fundamental than the other domains, nor is knowledge about this domain any closer to the "truth" about personality than knowledge in other domains. This domain simply represents one perspective on the nature and consequences of personality.

There is a long history of speculation and theorizing about the relation between the body and the mind. Some of this speculation has led to dead ends. For example, less than a century ago, people believed that the bumps on a person's head revealed his or her personality. This so-called science of phrenology has been discredited and abandoned. Nevertheless, many modern personality psychologists believe that differences between people in other bodily systems (such as activity in the brain and peripheral nervous system) are related to their personalities. People who like a lot of stimulation and thrills in their lives, for example, might differ from those who don't in terms of certain blood chemicals that influence nerve transmission. Or shy people might have a more reactive sympathetic nervous system compared to socially confident people.

The biological domain refers to those physical elements and biological systems within our bodies that influence or are influenced by our behaviors, thoughts, and feelings. For example, one type of physical element within our bodies that may influence our personalities is our genes. Our genetic makeup determines whether our hair is curly or straight, whether our eyes are blue or brown, and whether we have large, heavy bones or a slight build. It also appears that our genetic makeup influences how active we are, whether we are hot-tempered and disagreeable, and whether we like to be with others or prefer solitude. Understanding if and how genetics contribute to personality falls squarely within the biological domain. This is our subject in Chapter 6.

Another area in which biology and personality intersect is in the physiological systems, such as the brain or peripheral nervous system, where subtle differences between people might contribute to personality differences. For example, some people might have more activity in the right half than in the left half of their brains. Based on recent evidence, we know that such an imbalance of activation between the brain hemispheres is associated with a tendency to experience distress and other negative emotions more strongly. Here, physical differences between persons are associated with differences in emotional style. Because such differences represent enduring and stable ways that people differ from one another, and otherwise conform to our definition of personality laid out in Chapter 1, these physiological features represent aspects of personality. We'll cover physiological approaches to personality in Chapter 7.

In some areas of research a physiological response is viewed as a *correlate* or indicator of a trait. It is not viewed as a causal mechanism that serves as the physiological basis of the trait in question. Rather, the physiological response is considered a *biological correlate* of a particular trait.

The literature in personality psychology contains many examples of physiological measures that are considered to be correlates of personality. The finding that shy children show elevated heart rates when in the presence of strangers, compared to nonshy children, is one such example (Kagan & Snidman, 1991). Would eliminating the heart rate reactivity make the shy child less shy? Probably not. This is because the physiological response is a *correlate* of the traits in question, rather than an underlying substrate that *produces* or *contributes* to the personality trait.

This is not to say that studying physiological correlates of personality is a worthless endeavor. On the contrary, physiological measures often reveal important *consequences* of personality. For example, the high cardiovascular reactivity of Type A persons may have serious consequences in terms of developing heart disease. For this reason identifying physiological measures that are correlates of personality is also a scientifically useful and important task.

On the other hand, there are several modern theories of personality in which underlying physiology plays a more central role in *generating* or forming the substrate of specific personality differences. In Chapter 7 we will consider several of these theories in detail. Each shares the notion that specific personality traits are based on underlying physiological differences. Each theory also assumes that if the underlying physiological substrate is altered, the behavior pattern associated with the trait will be altered as well.

The third biological approach we will cover is based on Charles Darwin's theory of evolution. Support for evolution comes mainly from fossil evidence that species developed physical adaptations to their environment. Adaptations that helped members of the species to survive and reproduce were passed on as evolved characteristics. For example, primates who could walk upright could colonize open fields and their hands were freed for using tools. Evidence for the evolution of such physical characteristics is solid. Psychologists are now considering evidence for the evolution of psychological characteristics. They are taking the principles of evolution, such as natural selection, and applying them to an analysis of psychological traits. For example, natural selection may have operated on our ancestors to select for group cooperation; those early humans who were able to cooperate and work in groups were more likely to survive and reproduce, and those who preferred not to cooperate were less likely to become an ancestor. Consequently, the desire to be part of a group may be an evolved psychological characteristic that is present in today's population of humans. Evolutionary perspectives on personality are discussed in Chapter 8.

The biological domain differs from all the other domains in that it is concerned with those factors within the person that are based upon physical aspects of bodily functioning. The French philosopher Merleau-Ponty stated that the body is our "entry into the world." By this he meant that we are, first and foremost, physical creatures dependent on our bodies for all information about, and interactions with, the world around us. The world we come to know and experience is thus influenced by the functioning and status of our physical bodies. For example, a person with an overactive sympathetic nervous system might experience his or her world as a place that is anxiety producing and might be seen by others as being a person who is "on edge" and prone to nervousness.

In this part of the book we describe some of the major ideas and findings from the domain of biology as it applies to personality. As you read, it is important to keep in mind that biology is not destiny. Rather, the best way to think about the biological domain, as well as any of the other domains, is that it refers to one set of factors that influence or are related to personality. Personality is best thought of as multiply determined, as the collection of influences from all six of the broad domains of knowledge to be considered in this book.

Genetics and Personality

THE BIOLOGICAL DOMAIN

6

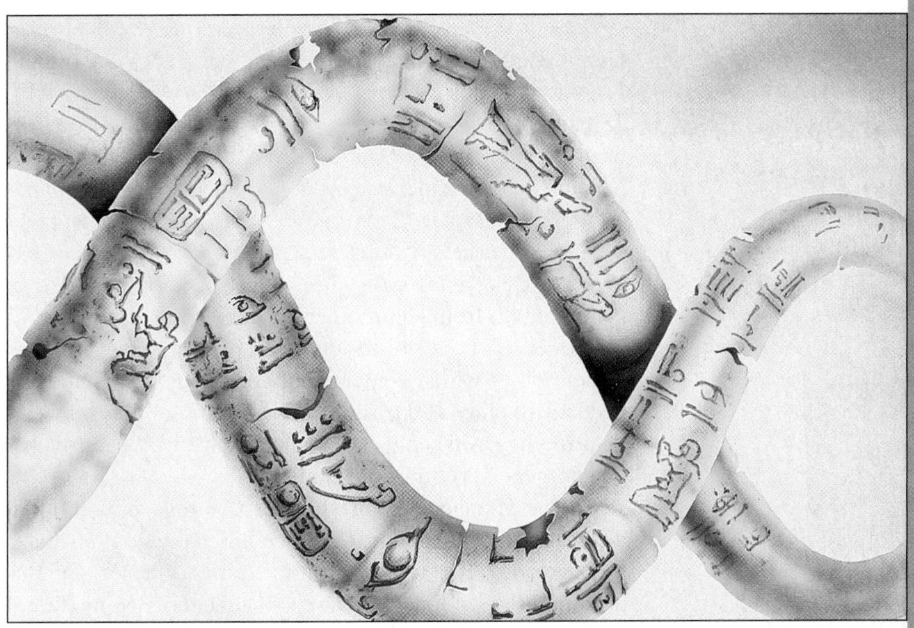

The past as well as the future is written in the genetic blueprint for life.

The Jim twins are identical twins separated at birth and raised in different adoptive families. They met for the first time when they were 39 years old, having been apart for their entire lives. One of the twins, Jim Springer, made the first phone call on February 9, 1979, after learning that he had a twin brother, Jim Lewis, who was living in the Midwest. They had an instant connection; three weeks after the phone call, Jim became the best man at his brother's wedding.

When they first met, the Jim twins displayed an astonishing set of similarities. Both weighed 180 pounds. Both were 6 feet tall. They had each been married twice, and, in each case, their first wives were named Linda and their second wives named Betty. Each had a son named James. Their jobs were also similar—each worked part-time as a sheriff. Both smoked Salem cigarettes and drank Miller Lite beer. Both suffered from the same kind of headache syndrome, and both had a habit of biting their fingernails. Both left love notes for their wives scattered around the house. And both had remarkably similar personality scores on standardized tests (Segal, 1999).

The Jim twins were not identical in all ways, of course. One was a better writer, the other a better speaker. They wore their hair differently; one combed his hair down over his forehead, and the other combed his hair back. But, overall, the similarities were striking, especially since they had grown up from infancy in entirely different families. This is a single twin pair, and, of course, no conclusions can be drawn from one case. But the case of the Jim twins raises the intriguing question, "What is the role of genetics in influencing personality?"

The Human Genome

Genome refers to the complete set of genes an organism possesses. The human genome contains between 30,000 and 40,000 genes. All these genes are located on 23 pairs of chromosomes. Each person inherits one set of each pair of chromosomes from the mother and one set from the father. One way to think about the human genome is to consider it to be a book containing 23 chapters, with each chapter being a chromosome pair. Each one of the chapters contains several thousand genes. And each gene consists of long sequences of DNA molecules. One astonishing fact is that the nucleus of each cell within the body contains two complete sets of the human genome, one from the mother and one from the father. The only exceptions are red blood cells, which do not contain any genes, and female egg cells and male sperm cells, each of which contains only one copy of the human genome. Because the body contains roughly 100 trillion cells (a million times a million), each of which is smaller than the head of a pin, in essence each of us has roughly 100 trillion copies of the human genome within our bodies.

The Human Genome Project is a multibillion-dollar research endeavor that is dedicated to sequencing the entire human genome—that is, to identify the particular sequence of DNA molecules in the human species. On June 26, 2000, scientists made headlines by announcing that they had completed the first draft of the complete human genome. Identifying the sequence of DNA molecules does not mean identifying all the functions of these DNA molecules. Scientists now have the "book" of life, but they must still figure out what role the gene sequences play in the body, the mind, and behavior.

Indeed, recent findings appear to be turning standard assumptions about the human genome on its head. Two findings are especially noteworthy. First, although the number of genes humans possess is similar to the number of genes estimated for mice and worms (30,000 to 40,000), the *manner* in which human genes get decoded into proteins turns out to be far more variable than in other species. These alternative forms of decoding create a tremendous variety of proteins—many more than seen in mice or worms—and may account for the complex differences we observe between rodents and humans (Plomin, 2002). Second, these protein-coding genes, making up roughly 2 percent of the human genome, are only part of the story. Many parts of the other 98 percent of the DNA in the human chromosomes used to be chalked up as **"genetic junk"** because scientists believed that these parts were functionless residue that served no purpose. Recently genetic researchers are discovering that this "junk DNA" is not junk at all. Rather, parts of these chunks of DNA have an impact on humans, potentially affecting everything from a person's physical size to personality (Gibbs, 2003; Plomin, 2002). These hidden layers of complexity in the human genome—given names such as "pseudogenes" and "riboswitches"—mean that we have a long way to go before understanding the complex and mysterious links between genes and human behavior.

Most of the genes within the human genome are the same for each individual on the planet. That is why all normally developing humans have many of the same characteristics—2 eyes, 2 legs, 32 teeth, 10 fingers, a heart, a liver, 2 lungs, and so on. A small number of these genes, however, are different for different individuals. Thus, although all humans have 2 eyes, some people have blue eyes, some have brown eyes, and a few even have violet eyes. Some of the genes that differ from individual to individual influence physical characteristics, such as eye color, height, and bone width. What is more controversial, but at the same time exciting, is whether some genes that differ across individuals influence the behavioral characteristics that define human personality.

Controversy about Genes and Personality

Perhaps no other area of personality psychology has been fraught with as much controversy as the study of behavioral genetics. Researchers in this field attempt to determine the degree to which individual differences in personality are caused by genetic and environmental differences. Scientific reports on behavioral genetic studies often make headlines and cover stories. On January 2, 1996, for example, *The New York Times* caused a stir with reports of a scientific breakthrough: "Variant Gene Is Connected to a Love of the Search for New Thrills." It reported the discovery of a specific gene for novelty seeking—the tendency to be extraverted, impulsive, extravagant, quick-tempered, excitable, and exploratory. Some popular media sources are proposing "designer babies," where parents select from a genetic checklist the characteristics they would like in their children. Ideas such as these are controversial because they suggest that genetic differences between individuals, rather than differences in parental socialization or personal experience, are responsible for shaping the core features of human personality. Reports such as these, however, often become sensationalized and accounts become simplified.

The Human Genome Project promises to map human DNA sequences; in so doing, some proponents hope to show links between specific genes and everything from alcoholism to attitudes. Such fascinating new developments in molecular genetics have revived excitement and rekindled the promise of genetic approaches to personality psychology. However, at the same time, genetic ideas have ignited controversy surrounding the study of genes and their influence on human behavior and personality.

Part of the reason for the controversy is ideological. Many people worry that findings from behavioral genetics will be used (or misused) to support particular political agendas. If individual differences in thrill seeking, for example, are caused by specific genes, then does this mean that we should not hold juvenile delinquents responsible for stealing cars for joy rides? If scientists trace a behavior pattern or personality trait to a genetic component, some people worry that such findings might lead to pessimism about the possibilities for change. If criminal behavior is influenced by genetics, so the argument goes, then attempts at rehabilitation may be doomed to failure.

Another part of the controversy concerns the idea of eugenics. **Eugenics** is the notion that we can design the future of the human species by fostering the reproduction of persons with certain traits and by discouraging the reproduction of persons without those traits. Many people in society are concerned that findings from genetic studies might be used to support programs intended to prevent some individuals from reproducing or, even worse, to bolster the cause of those who would advocate that some people be eliminated in order to create a "master race."

However, modern psychologists who study the genetics of personality are typically extremely careful in their attempts to educate others about the use and potential misuse of their findings (Plomin, 2002). Knowledge is better than ignorance, they argue. If people believe that hyperactivity, for example, is caused by parenting behaviors when, in fact, hyperactivity turns out to be primarily influenced by genes, then attempts to influence hyperactive behavior by altering parental practices could cause frustration and resentment on the part of the parents. Furthermore, psychologists maintain that genetic findings need not lead to the evil consequences that some worry about. Finding that a personality characteristic has a genetic component, for example, does not mean that the environment is powerless to modify that characteristic. Thus, let's now turn to the field of genetics and personality and discover what lies beneath the swirling controversy.

Goals of Behavioral Genetics

To understand the primary goals of the field of behavioral genetics, let's look at a concrete example—individual differences in height. Some individuals are tall, such as basketball player Shaquille O'Neal (over 7 feet). Other individuals are short, such as actor Danny DeVito (around 5 feet). Geneticists focus on the key question, "What causes some individuals to be tall and others to be short?" In other words, what are the causes of individual differences in height?

In principle, there can be a variety of causes of individual height differences. Differences in diet while growing up, for example, can cause differences in height among people. Genetic differences can also account for some of the differences in height. One of the central goals of genetic research is to determine the percentage of an individual difference that can be attributed to genetic differences and the percentage that is due to environmental differences.

In the case of height, both environmental and genetic factors are important. Clearly, children tend to resemble their parents in height—generally, tall parents have taller than average children and short parents have shorter than average children. And

In determining height, genetics accounts for 90 percent of the variation, while environmental factors, such as diet, account for 10 percent of the variation. The actor Danny DeVito (left) is about 2 feet shorter than basketball player Shaquille O'Neal (right).

genetic research has confirmed that roughly 90 percent of the individual differences in height are indeed due to genetic differences. The environment, which contributes 10 percent to individual differences in height, is far from trivial. In the United States, average adult height has increased in the entire population by roughly 2 inches over the past century, most likely due to increases in the nutritional value of the food eaten by U.S. citizens. This example brings home an important lesson: even though some observed differences between people can be due to genetic differences, this does not mean that the environment plays no role in modifying the trait.

Exercise

Can you think of some human characteristics that you consider mostly under genetic influence? Consider, for example, individual differences in eye color. Can you think of other characteristics that are not very much influenced by genetic factors? Consider, for example, individual differences in eating with forks versus eating with chopsticks. How might you go about proving that some individual differences are, or are not, influenced by genetic differences?

The methods used by behavioral geneticists, which we will examine in this chapter, can be applied to any individual difference variable. They can be used to identify the causes of individual differences in height and weight, differences in intelligence, differences in personality traits, and even differences in attitudes, such as liberalism or conservatism, and preferences for particular styles of art. The methods have been applied to all of these phenomena.

However, behavioral geneticists are typically not content simply with figuring out the **percentage of variance** due to genetic and environmental causes. *Percentage of variance* refers to the fact that individuals vary, or are different from each other, and this variability can be partitioned into percentages that are due to different causes. Behavioral geneticists also are interested in determining the ways in which genes and the environment interact and correlate with each other. And they are interested in figuring out precisely where in the environment the effects are taking place—in parental socialization practices, for example, or in the teachers to which children are exposed. We will turn to these more complex issues toward the end of this chapter. But, first, we must examine the fundamentals of behavioral genetics: What is heritability, and what methods do geneticists use to get their answers?

What Is Heritability?

Heritability is a statistic that refers to the proportion of observed variance in a *group* of individuals that can be accounted for by genetic variance (Plomin, DeFries, McClearn, & McGuffin, 2001). It describes the degree to which genetic differences between individuals cause differences in an observed property, such as height, extraversion, or sensation seeking. Heritability may be one of the most frequently misunderstood concepts in psychology. If precisely defined, however, it provides useful information in identifying the genetic and environmental determinants of personality.

Heritability has a formal definition: *the proportion of phenotypic variance that is attributable to genotypic variance.* **Phenotypic variance** refers to observed individual differences, such as in height, weight, or personality. **Genotypic variance** refers to individual differences in the total collection of genes possessed by each person. Thus, a heritability of .50 means that 50 percent of the observed phenotypic variation is attributable to genotypic variation. A heritability of .20 means that only 20 percent of the phenotypic variation is attributable to genotypic variation. In these examples, the environmental component is simply the proportion of phenotypic variance that is *not* attributable to genetic variance. Thus, a heritability of .50 means that the environmental component is .50. A heritability of .20 means that the environmental component is .80. These examples illustrate the simplest cases and assume that there is no correlation or interaction between genetic and environmental factors.

The environmental contribution is defined in a similar way. Thus, the percentage of observed variance in a *group* of individuals that can be attributed to environmental (nongenetic) differences is called **environmentality.** Generally speaking, the larger the heritability, the smaller the environmentality. And vice versa—the smaller the heritability, the larger the environmentality.

Discuss the meaning of the following statement: "All normally developing humans have language, but some people speak Chinese, others French, and others English." To what degree is variability in the language spoken due to variability in genes or variability in the environment in which one is raised?

Misconceptions about Heritability

One common misconception about heritability is that it can be applied to a single individual. It can't. It is meaningful to say that individual differences in height are 90 percent heritable, but it makes absolutely no sense to say, "Meredith's height is 90 percent heritable." You cannot say, for example, that the first 63 inches of her height are due to genes and the other 7 inches are due to the environment. For an individual, genes and environment are inextricably intertwined. Both play a role in determining height, and they cannot be separated. Thus, *heritability* refers only to differences in a sample or population, not to an individual.

Another common misconception about heritability is that it is constant. In fact, it is nothing of the sort. Heritability is a statistic that applies only to a population at one point in time and in a particular array of environments. If the environments change, then heritability can change. For example, in principle, heritability can be high in one population (e.g., among Swedes) but low in another (e.g., among Nigerians). And heritability can be low at one time and high at another time. Heritability always depends on both the range of genetic differences in the population and the environmental differences in that population. To draw on a concept from Chapter 2, heritability does not always generalize across persons and places.

A final common misconception is that heritability is an absolutely precise statistic (Plomin et al., 2001). Nothing could be further from the truth. Error or unreliability of measurement, for example, can distort heritability statistics. And, because heritability statistics are typically computed using correlations, which themselves fluctuate from sample to sample, further imprecision creeps in. In sum, heritability is best regarded as merely an *estimate* of the percentage of phenotypic differences due to genetic differences. It is not precise. It does not refer to an individual. And it is not eternally fixed.

Nature-Nurture Debate Clarified

Clarifying the meaning of the term *heritability*—what it is and what it is not—allows us to think more clearly about the **nature-nurture debate** (the arguments about whether genes or environments are more important determinants of personality), even before we examine the methods and findings from the field of behavioral genetics. The clarification comes from clearly distinguishing between two levels of analysis—the level of the individual and the level of a population of individuals.

At the level of an individual, there is no nature-nurture debate. Every individual contains a unique constellation of genes. And those genes require environments during one's life to produce a recognizable individual. At this moment, each person reading these pages is the product of an inseparable intertwining of genes and environment. It makes no sense to ask "Which is more important, genes or environment, in accounting for Sally?" At the individual level of analysis, there is simply no issue to debate. As an analogy, consider baking a cake. Each particular cake consists of flour, sugar, eggs, and water. It makes no sense to ask whether the finished cake is "caused" more by the flour or more by the water. Both are necessary ingredients, inextricably combined and inseparable in the finished cake. Genes and environment for one individual are like flour and water for one cake—both ingredients are necessary, but we cannot logically disentangle them to see which is more important.

At the level of the population, however, we can disentangle the influence of genes and environments. This is the level of analysis at which behavioral geneticists operate; it makes perfectly good sense to ask, "Which is more important in accounting for individual differences in trait *X*—genetic differences or environmental differences?" This is analogous to asking "If you bake 100 cakes, and these cakes turn out to taste a little different from each other, what accounts for the *differences* among the cakes?"

At the population level, we can partition the differences into these two sources—differences in genes and differences in environments. And, for a particular population at a given point in time, we can make sensible statements about which is more important *in accounting for the differences*. Consider the cake example. If you have 100 cakes, it makes sense to ask whether the differences among the cakes in, say, sweetness are more caused by differences in the amount of flour used or by differences in the amount of sugar used.

Now consider physical differences among people. Individual differences in height, for example, show a heritability of roughly .90. Individual differences in weight show a heritability of roughly .50. And individual differences in mate preferences—the qualities we desire in a marriage partner—show very low heritabilities of roughly .10 (Waller, 1994). Thus, it is meaningful to say that genetic differences are indeed more important than environmental differences when it comes to height. Genetic and environmental factors are roughly equal when it comes to weight. And environmental differences are overwhelmingly important when it comes to mate preferences.

Thus, the next time you get into a debate with someone about the nature-nurture issue, be sure to ask, "Are you asking the question at the level of the individual or at the level of individual differences within a population?" Only when the level of analysis is specified can the answers make any sense.

Behavioral Genetic Methods

Behavioral geneticists have developed an array of methods for teasing apart the contributions of genes and environments as causes of individual differences. Selective breeding with animals is one method. Family studies provide a second method. A third, and perhaps the most well-known, method is that of twin studies. Adoption studies provide a fourth behavioral genetic method. We will briefly discuss the logic of each of these methods, exploring where heritability estimates come from.

Selective Breeding—Studies of Humans' Best Friend

Artificial selection—as occurs when dogs are bred for certain qualities—can take place only if the desired characteristics are under the influence of heredity. **Selective breeding** occurs by identifying the dogs that possess the desired characteristic and having them mate only with other dogs that also possess the characteristic. Dog breeders have been successful precisely because many of the qualities they wish specific dog breeds to have are moderately to highly heritable.

Some of these heritable qualities are physical traits, characteristics that we actually see, such as size, ear length, wrinkled skin, and coat of hair. Other characteristics we might try to breed for are more behavioral and can even be considered personality traits. Everyone knows, for example, that some dogs, such as pit bulls, are, on average, more aggressive than most other dogs. Other breeds, such as the Labrador, are, on average, very sociable and agreeable. And others, such as the Chesapeake Bay

The Labrador Retriever (left) and the Chesapeake Bay Retriever (right) have been selectively bred for certain physical characteristics. Both have webbed feet, for example, which make them strong swimmers and excellent water retrievers. They have also been selectively bred for certain "personality" characteristics. The Labrador was bred to be sociable and friendly, whereas the Chesapeake Bay dog was bred to be loyal to only one owner and suspicious of strangers. Consequently, the Chesapeake Bay Retriever makes a good watch-dog in addition to its skills as a sporting dog. The Labrador, however, is the most popular family dog in America, most likely due to the unrestrained friendliness and cheerful disposition of this breed. Photos by Randy Larsen.

retriever, have a strong desire to please their owners by retrieving objects. All of these behavioral traits—aggressiveness, agreeableness, and the desire to please—are characteristics that have been established in these animals through selective breeding.

If the heritability for these personality traits in dog breeds is literally zero, then attempts to breed dogs selectively for such traits will be doomed to fail. On the other hand, if the heritability of these personality traits is high (e.g., >80 percent), then selective breeding will be highly successful and will occur rapidly. The fact that selective breeding has been so successful with dogs tells us that heredity must be a factor in the personality traits, such as aggressiveness, agreeableness, and desire to please, that were successfully selected.

The selective breeding studies of dogs conducted over the course of several decades by Scott and Fuller (1965) were critical in informing the scientific world that personality characteristics, no less than physical characteristics, can be heritable in this species. The heritability of behavioral traits in dogs, however, tells us nothing about the heritability of personality traits in humans. For obvious reasons, we cannot do selective breeding experiments on people. Fortunately, however, there are other methods of behavioral genetics that can be used to study humans.

Family Studies

Family studies—studies that correlate degree of genetic relatedness among family members with degree of personality similarity—capitalize on the fact that there are known degrees of genetic overlap among family members. Parents are usually not related to each other genetically. However, each parent shares 50 percent of his or her genes with each of the children. Similarly, siblings share 50 percent of their genes, on average. Grandparents and grandchildren share 25 percent of their genes, as do uncles and aunts with their nieces and nephews. First cousins share only 12.5 percent of their genes.

If a personality characteristic is highly heritable, then family members with greater genetic relatedness should be more similar to each other than are family members with less genetic relatedness. If a personality characteristic is not at all heritable, then even family members who are closely related genetically, such as parents and children, should not be any more similar to each other than are family members who are less genetically related to each other.

The Family Study method assumes that, for traits with a large genetic component, the degree of similarity between relatives on that trait will be in proportion to the amount of genetic overlap, or degree of kinship, between them.

If you have been following the logic of the argument thus far, you may have noticed a potential flaw, or confound, in family studies—namely, members of a family who share the same genes also typically share the same environment. In other words, two members of a family might be similar to each other not because a given personality characteristic is heritable but, rather, because of a shared environment. For example, certain brothers and sisters may be similar on shyness not because of shared genes but because of shared parents. For this reason, results from family studies alone can never be viewed as definitive. Finding that family members become increasingly similar to each other as the percentage of genetic overlap increases is certainly compatible with a genetic hypothesis. But it cannot be regarded as conclusive evidence. A more compelling behavioral genetic method is that of twin studies.

Twin Studies

Twin studies estimate heritability by gauging whether identical twins, who share 100 percent of their genes, are more similar to each other than are fraternal twins, who share only 50 percent of their genes. Twin studies, and especially studies of twins reared apart, have received tremendous media attention. The Jim twins, described at the beginning of this chapter, are identical twins given up for adoption at birth. Because they were adopted into different families, they were unaware that they had a twin. When they met for the first time, to everyone's astonishment, these men shared many behavioral habits—having the same favorite TV shows, using the same brand of toothpaste, owning a Jack Russell terrier dog, and so on. They also shared many personality traits, such as being highly conscientious and emotionally stable, as measured by valid personality scales. Is this coincidence? Perhaps, but these coincidences seemed to happen with unusual regularity in the course of studying twins, even those who have been reared apart by different sets of parents (Segal, 1999). Of course, these single examples prove nothing about heritability. It is always possible to find similarities even between two randomly chosen individuals if you look hard enough (e.g., "they both hate broccoli"). Only by using the logic of the twin method can firmer conclusions be drawn.

Twin studies take advantage of a fascinating quirk of nature. Nearly all individuals come from a single fertilized egg, and humans—as contrasted with some other mammals, such as mice—typically give birth to a single child at a time. Occasionally, however, twins are born, occurring only once in 83 births (Plomin et al., 1990). But twins come in two distinct types—identical and fraternal.

Identical twins, technically called **monozygotic (MZ) twins,** come from a single fertilized egg (or zygote—hence, *monozygotic*), which divides into two at some point during gestation. No one knows why fertilized eggs occasionally divide. They just do. Identical twins are remarkable in that they are genetically identical, like clones, coming from the same single source. They share literally 100 percent of their genes. In contrast, the odds of being genetically identical to someone else if you are not a twin are about one in several billion.

The other type of twin is not genetically identical to the co-twin; instead, such twins share only 50 percent of their genes. They are called fraternal twins, or **dizygotic (DZ) twins,** because they come from two eggs that were separately fertilized (*di* means "two," so *dizygotic* means "coming from two fertilized eggs"). Fraternal twins can be same sex or opposite sex. In contrast, identical twins are always the same sex because they are genetically identical. Dizygotic twins are no more alike than regular siblings, at least in terms of genetic overlap. They just happen to share the same womb at the same time and have the same birthday; otherwise, they are no more similar than are ordinary brothers and sisters. Of all the twins born, two-thirds are fraternal, or dizygotic, and one-third are identical, or monozygotic.

The twin method capitalizes on the fact that some twins are genetically identical, sharing 100 percent of their genes, whereas other twins share only 50 percent of their genes. If fraternal twins are just as similar to each other as identical twins are, in terms of a particular personality characteristic, then we can infer that the characteristic under consideration is not heritable: the greater genetic similarity of identical

Twins come in two varieties; monozygotic and dizygotic. Can you identify which of these two pairs of twins is more likely to be monozygotic? Which pair is definitely dizygotic? What is the clue that helps you answer these questions?

twins, in this case, is not causing them to be more similar in personality. Conversely, if identical twins are substantially *more similar* to each other than are fraternal twins on a given characteristic, then this provides evidence that is compatible with a heritability interpretation. In fact, studies have shown that identical twins are more similar than fraternal twins in dominance, height, and the ridge count on their fingertips (Plomin et al., 1990), suggesting that heritability plays a causal role in influencing these individual differences. For dominance, identical twins are correlated +.57, whereas fraternal twins are correlated only +.12 (Loehlin & Nichols, 1976). For height, identical twins are correlated +.93, whereas fraternal twins are correlated only +.48 (Mittler, 1971).

There are several formulas for calculating heritability from twin data, each with its own problems and limitations. One simple method, however, is to double the difference between the MZ correlation and DZ correlation:

$$\text{heritability}^2 = 2(r_{mz} - r_{dz})$$

In this formula, r_{mz} refers to the correlation coefficient computed between pairs of monozygotic twins, and r_{dz} refers to the correlation between the dizygotic twins. Plugging in the correlations for height, for example, leads to the following heritability estimate: heritability of height $= 2(.93 - .48) = .90$. Thus, according to this formula, height is 90 percent heritable (and 10 percent environmental, as the total has to add up to 100 percent). The basic logic of this method can be applied to any phenotypic characteristic—personality traits, attitudes, religious beliefs, sexual orientation, drug use habits, and so on. We must first note two important assumptions of the twin method. If either of these assumptions is not met, then the results from twin studies might be called into question.

The first assumption is known as the **equal environments assumption.** The twin method assumes that the environments experienced by identical twins are no more similar to each other than are the environments experienced by fraternal twins. If they are more similar, then the greater similarity of the identical twins could plausibly be due to the fact that they experience more similar environments, rather than the fact that they have more genes in common. If identical twins are treated by their parents as more similar than fraternal twins are treated by their parents—for example, if the parents of identical twins dress them in more similar clothing than do the parents of fraternal twins—then the resulting greater similarity of the identical twins might be due to this more similar treatment.

Behavioral geneticists have been worried about the validity of the equal environments assumption and, so, have designed studies to test it. One approach is to examine twins who have been misdiagnosed as identical or fraternal (Scarr, 1968; Scarr & Carter-Saltzman, 1979). That is, some twins who were believed to be identical by their parents were really just fraternal. And some twins whose parents believed them to be fraternal turned out to be identical. These mistakes in labeling allowed the researchers to examine whether fraternal twins who were *believed* to be identical were, *in fact,* more similar to each other than accurately labeled fraternal twins. Similarly, it allowed the researchers to examine whether the identical twins, believed to be fraternal, were, in fact, less similar to each other than identical twins correctly labeled as identical. The findings on a variety of cognitive and personality tests supported the validity of the equal environments assumption. The parents' beliefs and labeling of the twins did not affect their actual similarity on the personality and cognitive measures. This means that, however twins are labeled, the environments experienced by identical twins do not seem to be functionally more similar to each other than the environments experienced by fraternal twins.

Studies such as this one cannot definitively rule out other possible confounds. For example, parents may treat identical twins more similarly than they treat fraternal twins because they look more alike, regardless of the parents' beliefs about their twin status. Nonetheless, additional studies over the years have continued to support the equal environments assumption (e.g., Loehlin & Nichols, 1976; Lytton, Martin, & Eaves, 1977). Although it is true that identical twins do tend to dress more alike than fraternal twins, spend more time together, and have more friends in common, there is no evidence that these environmental similarities cause them to be any more similar in their personalities than they are to begin with (Plomin et al., 1990).

A second potential problem with twin studies is the possibility that twins are not *representative* of the general population from which they come. As a rule, twins tend to be born a few weeks prematurely and tend to weigh less than nontwins (MacGillivray, Nylander, & Corney, 1975). If twins are not representative of the general population, then this could limit generalizations about heritability based on twin studies. Most behavioral genetic researchers have concluded, however, that twins are reasonably representative of the general populations from which they come. One way to overcome some of the potential biases of the twin method is to use the adoption method—the final behavioral genetic method—to which we now turn.

Adoption Studies

Adoption studies may be the most powerful behavioral genetic method available. In an adoption study, one can examine the correlations between adopted children and their adoptive parents, with whom they share no genes. If one finds a positive correlation between adopted children and their adoptive parents, then this provides strong evidence for environmental influences on the personality trait in question.

Similarly, we can examine the correlations between adopted children and their genetic parents, who had no influence on the children's environments. If we find a zero correlation between adopted children and their genetic parents, again this is strong evidence for a lack of heritable influence on the personality trait in question. Conversely, if we find a positive correlation between parents and their adopted-away children, with whom they have had no contact, then this provides evidence for heritability.

Adoption studies are especially powerful because they allow us to get around the equal environments assumption, which must be made in twin studies. In twin studies, because parents provide both genes and environments to their children, and may provide more similar environments for identical than for fraternal twins, there is a potential compromise of the equal environments assumption. In adoption studies, however, genetic parents provide none of the environmental influences on their children, thus unconfounding genetic and environmental causes.

Adoption studies, however, are not without potential problems of their own. Perhaps the most important potential problem is the assumption of representativeness. Adoption studies assume that adopted children, their birth parents, and their adoptive parents are representative of the general population. For example, these studies assume that couples who adopt children are not any different from couples who do not adopt children. Fortunately, the assumption of representativeness can be tested directly. Several studies have confirmed that the assumption of representativeness holds for cognitive abilities, personality, education level, and even socioeconomic status (Plomin & DeFries, 1985; Plomin, DeFries, & Fulker, 1988).

Another potential problem with adoption studies is **selective placement.** If adopted children are placed with adoptive parents who are similar to their birth parents, then this may inflate the correlations between the adopted children and their adoptive parents. In this case, the resulting inflated correlations artificially inflate estimates of environmental influence, since the correlation appears to be due to the environment provided by the adoptive parent. Fortunately, there does not seem to be selective placement, so this potential problem is not a problem in actual studies (Plomin et al., 1990).

Without a doubt, one of the most powerful behavioral genetic designs is one that combines the strengths of twin and adoption studies at the same time, by studying twins reared apart. In fact, the correlation between identical twins reared apart can be interpreted directly as an index of heritability. If identical twins reared apart show a correlation of +.65 for a particular personality characteristic, then that means that 65 percent of the individual differences are heritable. Unfortunately, identical twins reared apart are exceedingly rare. Only more recently have painstaking efforts been undertaken to find such twins and study them (Segal, 1999). The effort has been well worth it, as such studies have yielded a bounty of fascinating results, to which we now turn. A summary of the behavioral genetic methods, along with their advantages and limitations, is shown in Table 6.1.

Table 6.1 Summary of Behavioral Genetic Methods

Method	Advantages	Limitations
Selective breeding studies	Can infer heritability if selective breeding works	Are unethical to conduct on humans
Family studies	Provide heritability estimates	Violate equal environments assumption
Twin studies	Provide both heritability and environmentality estimates	Sometimes violate equal environments assumption; may violate assumption of representativeness
Adoption studies	Provide both heritability and environmentality estimates; get around the problem of equal environments assumption	Adopted kids might not be representative of population; problem of selective placement

Major Findings from Behavioral Genetic Research

This section summarizes what is known about the heritability of personality. The results may surprise you.

Personality Traits

The most commonly studied personality traits in behavioral genetic designs have been extraversion and neuroticism. Recall that extraversion is a dimension containing people who are outgoing and talkative at one end and people who are quiet and withdrawn at the other (introverted) end. Neuroticism is a dimension with one end characterized by people who tend to be anxious, nervous, and emotionally volatile and the other end having people who tend to be calm and emotionally stable. Henderson (1982) reviewed the literature on more than 25,000 pairs of twins. He found substantial heritability for both traits. In one study involving 4,987 twin pairs in Sweden, for example, the correlations for extraversion were +.51 for identical twins and +.21 for fraternal twins (Floderus-Myrhed, Pedersen, & Rasmuson, 1980). Using the simple rule-of-thumb formula of doubling the difference between the two correlations yields a heritability of .60.

The findings for neuroticism were similar (Floderus-Myrhed et al., 1980). The identical twin correlation for neuroticism was +.50, whereas the fraternal twin correlation was only +.23. This suggests a heritability of .54. Twin studies have yielded very similar results, suggesting that extraversion and neuroticism are traits that are approximately half due to genetics. The most recent large-scale twin study, conducted in Australia, found a heritability for neuroticism of 47 percent (Birley, Gillespie, Heath, Sullivan, Boomsma, & Martin, 2006).

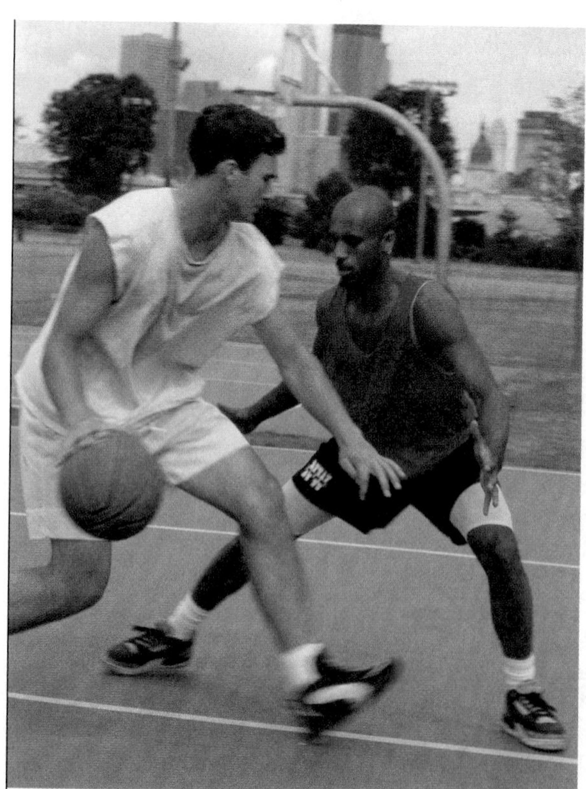

The trait of activity level—how vigorous and energetic a person is—shows a moderate degree of heritability.

The findings for extraversion and neuroticism from adoption studies suggest somewhat lower heritabilities. Pedersen (1993), for example, found heritability estimates based on comparisons of adoptees and their biological parents of about 40 percent for extraversion and about 30 percent for neuroticism. Correlations between adoptive parents and their adopted children tend to be around zero, suggesting little *direct* environmental influence on these traits.

Individual differences in *activity level* have also been subjected to behavioral genetic analysis. You may recall from Chapter 5 that individual differences activity level, measured with a mechanical recording device called an "actometer," emerges early in life and show stability in children over time. Recently, activity level was assessed in an adult sample of 300 monozygotic and dizygotic twin pairs residing in Germany (Spinath, Wolf, Angleitner, Borkenau, & Riemann, 2002). The researchers measured the physical energy each individual expended through body movements, recorded mechanically with motion recorders analogous to self-winding wristwatches. Movement of a person's limbs activates the device, which records the frequency and intensity of body activity. Activity level showed a heritability of .40, suggesting that a moderate proportion of the individual differences in motor energy expended are due to genetic differences.

Activity level is one among several temperaments that show moderate heritability. A study of 1,555 twins in Poland found 50 percent heritability, on average, for all temperaments, including activity, emotionality, sociability, persistence, fear, and distractibility (Oniszczenko et al., 2003). A study of Dutch twins, at ages 3, 7, and 10, found even higher heritabilities for aggressiveness, ranging from 51 to 72 percent (Hudziak, van Beijsterveldt, Bartels, Rietvelt, Rettew, Derks, & Boomsma, 2003).

Behavioral genetic studies have also been carried out on a wide array of other personality dispositions. Using 353 male twins from the Minnesota Twin Registry, researchers explored the heritability of so-called "psychopathic" personality traits (Blonigen, Carlson, Krueger, & Patrick, 2003). These include traits such as Machiavellianism (e.g., enjoys manipulating other people), Coldheartedness (e.g., has a callous emotional style), Impulsive Nonconformity (e.g., indifferent to social conventions), Fearlessness (e.g., a risk taker; lacks anticipatory anxiety concerning harm), Blame Externalization (e.g., blames others for one's problems), and Stress Immunity (e.g., lacks anxiety when faced with stressful life events). All of these "psychopathic" personality traits showed moderate to high heritability. For example, for Coldheartedness, the r_{mz} was +.34, whereas the r_{dz} was −.16; for Fearlessness, the r_{mz} was +.54, whereas the r_{dz} was only .03. Using the method of doubling the difference between the MZ and DZ correlations suggests *substantial* heritability to all of these psychopathic-related personality dispositions.

Interestingly, heritability of personality might not be limited to our own species. In an innovative study of chimpanzees, Weiss, King, and Enns (2002) explored the heritability of dominance (high extraversion, low neuroticism) and well-being (e.g., seems happy, contented, and enjoying itself), as indexed by trained observer judgments. Individual differences in chimpanzee well-being showed a moderate heritability of .40, whereas individual differences in chimpanzee dominance showed an even stronger heritability of .66. These findings suggest that the importance of genes in influencing personality may not be restricted to humans, but instead may extend to other primates.

Behavioral genetic studies using more comprehensive personality inventories have also been carried out in many different countries as personality research expands to include more and more cross-cultural work. A study of 296 twin pairs in Japan revealed moderate heritability for Cloninger's Seven-Factor model of temperament and character, which includes dispositions such as novelty seeking, harm avoidance, reward dependence, and persistence (Ando, Ono, Yoshimura, Onoda, Shinohara, Kanba, & Asai, 2002). A study of 168 MZ and 132 DZ twins in Germany, using observational methodology, revealed a 40 percent heritability to markers of the Big Five (Borkenau, Reimann, Angleitner, & Spinath, 2001). Similar findings for the Big Five personality traits have been documented in Canada and Germany using self-report measures (Jang, Livesley, Angleitner, Reimann, & Vernon, 2002).

Perhaps the most fascinating study to examine personality traits is the Minnesota Twin Study (Bouchard & McGue, 1990; Tellegen et al., 1988). This study examined 45 sets of identical twins reared apart and 26 sets of fraternal twins reared apart. The researchers found the correlations shown in Table 6.2 between identical twins reared apart. These findings startled many people. How could traditionalism,

Table 6.2 Correlations between Identical Twins Reared Apart

Personality Trait	Twin Correlation
Sense of well-being	.49
Social potency	.57
Achievement orientation	.38
Social closeness	.15
Neuroticism	.70
Sense of alienation	.59
Aggression	.67
Inhibited control	.56
Low risk taking	.45
Traditionalism	.59
Absorption or imagination	.74
Average twin correlation	**.54**

Sources: Bouchard & McGue, 1990; Tellegen et al., 1988.

for example, which reflects an attitude or a preference for the established ways of doing things, show such strong heritability? And how could neuroticism have such a high heritability, given the traditional view that it is parents who make their children neurotic by their inconsistency of reinforcement and improper attachment? These behavioral genetic findings caused some researchers to question long-held assumptions about the origins of individual differences—a topic we will consider later in this chapter under the heading "Shared versus Nonshared Environmental Influences: A Riddle."

Summaries of the behavioral genetic data for many of the major personality traits—extraversion, agreeableness, conscientiousness, neuroticism, openness to experience—yield heritability estimates of approximately 50 percent (Bouchard & Loehlin, 2001; Caspi, Roberts, & Shiner, 2005). Furthermore, it is clear that the heritability of personality is heavily responsible for the fact that personality traits remain fairly stable over time (Blonigen et al., 2006; Caspi, Roberts, & Shiner, 2005; Johnson, McGue, & Krueger, 2005; van Beijsterveldt, Bartels, Hudziak, & Boomsma, 2003). Overall, it is clear that major personality traits show a modest degree of heritability, at least for the samples that have been studied so far. The same studies, however, also suggest that a substantial portion of the variance in personality traits is environmental in origin.

Attitudes and Preferences

Stable attitudes are generally regarded to be part of personality—they show wide individual differences, they tend to be stable over time, and at least sometimes they are linked with actual behavior. Behavioral geneticists have also examined the heritability of attitudes. The Minnesota Twin Study showed that traditionalism—as evidenced by attitudes favoring conservative values over modern values—showed a heritability of .63. One study of more than 2,000 twin pairs living in Australia found an identical twin pair correlation of .63 and a fraternal twin pair correlation of .46 for the attitude of traditionalism (Martin et al., 1986). This yields a heritability of roughly .34.

A longitudinal study of 654 adopted and nonadopted children from the Colorado Adoption Project revealed significant genetic influence on conservative attitudes (Abrahamson, Baker, & Caspi, 2002). Markers of conservative attitudes included whether participants agreed or disagreed with specific words or phrases such as "death penalty," "gay rights," "censorship," and "Republicans." Significant genetic influence emerged as early as 12 years of age in this study.

Genes also appear to influence occupational preferences. Occupational preferences are not mere whims, but can have extremely important effects on a person's life work, wealth, and eventual social status attained. In a massive study of 435 adopted and 10,880 genetic offspring residing in Canada and the United States, Ellis and Bonin (2003) had participants respond to 14 different aspects of prospective jobs using a scale ranging from 1 (not at all appealing) to 100 (extremely appealing). The 14 job aspects were high income, competition, prestige, envied by others, taking risks, element of danger, controlling others, feared by others, little supervision, independence, job security, part of a team, clear responsibilities, and help others. These occupational preferences were then correlated with seven measures of parental social status, including mother's and father's education level, occupational status, and income. A full 71 percent of the correlations were statistically significant for the genetic children, whereas only 3 percent were significant for the adopted children (suggesting that rearing environment does not create the effect). The authors conclude that "this study not only suggests that the genes influence various preferences related to occupations, but that these preferences have an effect on the social status attainment" (Ellis & Bonin, 2003, p. 929). In short, occupational preferences such as desire for competition and wealth can lead to choosing occupations in which more status and income are actually achieved. The jobs in which we spend a large portion of our lives and the prestige and income that comes from those jobs are at least partly influenced by the genes we inherit from our parents.

Not all attitudes and beliefs show these levels of moderate heritability, however. One study of 400 twin pairs yielded heritabilities of essentially zero for beliefs in God, involvement in religious affairs, and attitudes toward racial integration (Loehlin & Nichols, 1976). A recent study of adopted and nonadopted children confirmed that there is no evidence of a heritable influence on *religious* attitudes (Abrahamson et al., 2002). A more recent study also found extremely low heritability—12 percent—for religiousness, as measured by items such as "frequency of attending religious services," during adolescence (Koenig, McGue, Krueger, & Bouchard, 2005). In adulthood (average age of 33), however, the heritability of religiousness had increased to 44 percent. These findings are particularly interesting, in that they suggest that genes have an increasingly important role in religiousness as people move from adolescence into adulthood. The causes of individual differences in attitudes depend on the attitudes being studied. They range from moderate (30 to 60 percent) in the case of traditionalism down to 12 percent in the case of religiosity during adolescence, and even 0 for some specific attitudes.

At this time, no one knows *why* some attitudes appear to be partly heritable. Are there specific genes that predispose people to be more conservative? Or are these heritabilities merely incidental by-products of genes for other qualities? Future research in behavioral genetics might be able to address these questions and provide an answer to the mystery of why some attitudes appear to be partly heritable.

A Closer Look

Sexual Orientation

Sexual orientation refers to the object of a person's sexual desires, whether the person is sexually attracted to those of the same sex or of a different sex. Although not all personality researchers consider individual differences in sexual orientation to be part of personality, a reasonable case can be made that this is an important way in which individuals differ from each other. And these differences tend to be relatively stable over time. Moreover, these differences are associated with a host of important life outcomes, such as the social groups with which one affiliates, the leisure activities one pursues, and the lifestyle one adopts. By the definition of personality provided in Chapter 1, sexual orientation clearly falls well within the scope of personality.

Behavioral genetic studies of sexual orientation have been in the newspaper headlines. Is homosexuality inherited? Psychologist Michael Bailey has conducted the most extensive studies of this issue. Bailey and his colleagues examined the twin brothers of a sample of homosexuals, as well as the adoptive brothers of another sample of homosexuals. Heritability estimates from all studies, depending on various assumptions, ranged from 30 percent to a strikingly high 70 percent. Similar heritabilities were found in a sample of lesbians and their adoptive sisters (Bailey et al., 1993).

These heritability findings come on the heels of another startling discovery, which was published in *Science* magazine (LeVay, 1991). Brain researcher Simon LeVay discovered that homosexual and heterosexual men differ in a specific area of the brain known as the hypothalamus. One area of the hypothalamus, the medial preoptic region, appears to be partially responsible for regulating male-typical sexual behavior (LeVay, 1993, 1996). LeVay obtained the brains of gay men who had died of AIDS and compared them with the brains of heterosexual men who had died of AIDS or other causes. He found that the size of the medial preoptic region of the hypothalamus—the region believed to regulate male-typical sexual behavior—to be two to three times *smaller* in the gay men, compared with that of the heterosexual men. Unfortunately, given the extremely expensive nature of brain research, the samples in this study were quite small. Moreover, no one has yet replicated these findings.

Behavioral geneticist Dean Hamer has published some evidence that male sexual orientation is influenced by a gene on the X chromosome (Hamer & Copeland, 1994). However, this finding also needs to be replicated, and several researchers have debated its validity (e.g., see Bailey, Dunne, & Martin, 2000).

Obviously, this research area is controversial, and the findings are hotly debated. Moreover, the genetic studies of homosexuality have attracted their share of critics. The studies have been challenged on the grounds that the samples, which were secured from advertisements in lesbian and gay publications, were unrepresentative (Baron, 1993). For example, gays are probably more likely to respond to an advertisement looking for gays with twins only if each is actually gay, inflating the estimate of heritability.

Another weakness in past studies was a neglect of the correlates of sexual orientation. For example, childhood gender nonconformity is strongly related to adult sexual orientation. Gay men as adults recall having been feminine boys, and lesbian women as adults recall being masculine girls. This association is strong and has been established with many sources of data (e.g., using peer reports of childhood gender nonconformity). Regarding the importance of gender nonconformity in childhood, a leading researcher has remarked that "it is difficult to think of other individual differences that so reliably and so strongly predict socially significant outcomes across the life span, and for both sexes, too" (Bem, 1995, p. 323). In fact, Bem has proposed his own theory of the source of adult sexual orientation, that biological factors may cause childhood gender nonconformity and that early gender nonconformity causes children to feel different from other children of their own sex and, as a result, to be attracted to people who are "different" from themselves (even though they are of the same gender).

Bailey and his colleagues set out to clear up these two weaknesses—unrepresentative samples and lack of accounting for childhood gender nonconformity—by conducting one of the largest twin studies of adult sexual orientation to date (Bailey et al., 2000). The participants were from a sample of almost 25,000 twin pairs in Australia, out of which approximately 1,000 MZ and 1,000 DZ twins participated. Their average age at time of participation was 29 years. The participants completed a questionnaire about childhood (before age 12) participation in a variety of sex-stereotyped activities and games. They also completed a detailed questionnaire on adult sexual orientation and activity, such as "when you have sexual daydreams, how often is your sexual partner male? how often female?"

Results showed that approximately 92 percent of the men and 92 percent of the women were exclusively heterosexual in orientation. An interesting sex difference was found, however, in the distribution of sexual behaviors. The women were more likely than the men to have slight homosexual feelings without being exclusively homosexual, whereas the men tended to be more either exclusively heterosexual or exclusively homosexual. Just over 3 percent of the men, but only 1 percent of the women, were predominantly or exclusively homosexual in sexual attraction and sexual fantasy. This finding suggests that sexual behavior and orientation should be analyzed separately for men and for women, with researchers prepared to develop a different theoretical account for each group.

Regarding whether homosexual orientation runs in families, this study found lower rates than previous studies, at 20 percent concordance for the identical twin men and 24 percent concordance for the identical twin women. Concordance is the probability that one twin is gay if the other is also gay. Previous studies typically found concordance rates ranging between 40 and 50 percent. Bailey argues that previous studies overestimate genetic contributions due to selecting participants by advertising in gay and lesbian magazines.

In the Bailey et al. (2000) study, participants were randomly selected from a large pool of twins, so there was no selection bias. It seems likely that the real rate of genetic contribution to sexual orientation is much lower than previously thought. Childhood gender nonconformity did, however, show significant heritability for both men (50 percent heritability) and women (37 percent heritability). This finding provides some support for Bem's (1995) theory that childhood gender nonconformity may be the inherited component of adult sexual orientation. And the link from gender nonconformity in childhood to adult homosexual orientation, although statistically significant, is far from perfect. Clearly, the most recent evidence suggests that genes provide a relatively modest and indirect influence on adult sexual orientation.

Results of recent, well-controlled studies, find concordance rates for homosexual orientation to be about 20 percent, much lower than previously thought.

A recent twin study explored a phenomenon known as **gender identity disorder (GID)** (Coolidge, Thede, & Young, 2002). A diagnosis of GID requires that two aspects be present simultaneously: (1) cross-gender identification that is strong and persists over time, and (2) persistent psychological discomfort with one's biological sex (American Psychological Association, 1994). In the twin study, clinically significant GID was present in roughly 2.3 percent of his sample of 314 twins. The results showed a strong genetic component in whether or not the individuals were diagnosed with GID—62 percent of the variance was due to heritability. The authors conclude that "gender identity may be much less a matter of choice and much more a matter of biology" (Coolidge et al., 2002, p. 251).

In summary, the findings from behavioral genetics and brain research point to the fascinating possibility that sexual orientation—an individual difference that is linked with the social groups one associates with, the leisure activities one pursues, and the lifestyle one adopts—may be partly heritable. However, exactly which part is heritable and how this indirectly affects adult sexual orientation are questions for future research.

Drinking and Smoking

Drinking and smoking are often regarded as behavioral manifestations of personality dispositions, such as sensation seeking (Zuckerman & Kuhlman, 2000), extraversion (Eysenck, 1981), and neuroticism (Eysenck, 1981). Individuals differ widely in their smoking and drinking habits, and, although consumers sometimes quit for good and abstainers sometimes start, these differences tend to be stable over time.

Individual differences in drinking and smoking habits also show evidence of heritability. In one study of Australian twins, an MZ twin who smoked was roughly 16 times more likely than an MZ twin who did not smoke to have a twin who smoked (Hooper et al., 1992). The comparable figures for DZ twins were only a sevenfold increase, suggesting evidence of heritability. Similar findings were obtained in a sample of 1,300 Dutch families of adolescent Dutch twins (Boomsma et al., 1994). Studies that separate the various components of smoking behavior—initiation, persistence, and quitting—also find moderate heritability. These studies also point simultaneously to the importance of environmental factors—a point to be taken up in the following section.

Heritability studies of alcohol drinking are more mixed. Some studies find heritability for boys but not for girls (Hooper et al., 1992). Other studies find heritability for girls but not for boys (Koopmans & Boomsma, 1993). Most studies, however, show moderate heritability for both sexes, ranging from .36 to .56 (Rose, 1995). As summarized by Rose (1995), "Alcohol consumption patterns in adults are stable, and the genetic contributions are largely responsible" (p. 640).

Heritability studies of alcoholism, as opposed to everyday drinking habits, show even stronger heritabilities. Indeed, nearly all behavioral genetic studies of alcoholism show heritabilities of .50 or greater (Kendler et al., 1992). In one study, the heritabilities of alcoholism were 67 percent in women and 71 percent in men (Heath et al., 1994). Interestingly, the same study found a genetic linkage between alcoholism and "conduct disorder" (antisocial behavior), suggesting that the genes for both occur in the same individuals.

Marriage

A fascinating recent study revealed that genes can even influence the propensity to marry or stay single (Johnson, McGue, Krueger, & Bouchard, 2004). The heritability estimate for propensity to marry turned out to be an astonishing 68 percent! One causal path through which this could work is through personality characteristics. Men who got married, compared to their single peers, scored higher on social potency and achievement—traits linked with upward mobility, success in careers, and financial success. These traits are also highly valued by women in selecting marriage partners (Buss, 2003). Thus, a genetic proclivity to marry occurs, at least in part, through heritable personality traits that are desired by potential marriage partners.

Genes also play an interesting role in marital satisfaction. First, individual differences in women's marital satisfaction are roughly 50 percent heritable (Spotts et al., 2004) (this study could not evaluate the heritability of a husband's marital satisfaction). Second, the personality characteristics of wives, notably dispositional optimism, warmth, and low aggressiveness accounted for both their own marital satisfaction and their husband's marital satisfaction (Spotts et al., 2005). Thus, the marital satisfaction of both women and men seems partly to depend on the moderately heritable personality dispositions of the wives. Interestingly, husbands' personality did not explain as much of their own or their wives' marital satisfaction. Taken together, these results suggest that genes play a role in the quality of marriages, in part through heritable personality characteristics.

Shared versus Nonshared Environmental Influences: A Riddle

With all of the findings on the moderate heritability of so many personality characteristics, it is important not to lose sight of one important fact: the same studies that suggest moderate heritability also provide the best evidence for the importance of environmental influences. If many personality characteristics show heritabilities in the range of 30 to 50 percent, this means that the same characteristics show a substantial degree of environmentality—as much as 50 to 70 percent. This conclusion must be tempered, however, by the fact that all measures are flawed, containing errors of measurement; some of the differences in personality might be attributable to *neither* environmental nor genetic differences but, rather, to error of measurement. Nonetheless, because behavioral genetic evidence points to the importance of environmental influences on personality, behavioral geneticists have turned increasingly to the issue of how their methods can be used to provide insights into the nature of environmental influences.

One critical distinction behavioral geneticists make is between **shared** and **nonshared environmental influences.** Consider siblings—brothers and sisters in the same family. Some features of their environment are shared—the number of books in the home, the presence or absence of a TV, DVD player, or computer, the quality and quantity of food in the home, the parents' values and attitudes, and the schools, church, synagogue, or mosque the parents send the children to. All of these are features of the shared environment. On the other hand, the same brothers and sisters do not share *all* features of their environment. Some children might get special treatment from their parents. They might be labeled differently by their parents. They might have different groups of friends. They might occupy different rooms in the house. One might go to summer camp, whereas the others stay home each summer. All of these features are called nonshared because they are experienced differently by different siblings.

Exercise

Make a list of five shared environmental influences you have in common with your siblings (or, if you are an only child, what things might be shared environmental influences if you had siblings?). Then list five nonshared environmental influences. Which had the strongest influence on your personality, attitudes, or behavior?

We know that the environment exerts a major influence on personality—it accounts for a substantial share of the variance. But which environment matters most—the shared or the nonshared environment? Some behavioral genetic designs allow us to figure out whether the environmental effects come more from shared or from nonshared sources. The details of how this is done are too technical to examine in this book, but, if you are interested, you can check out the fascinating article by Plomin and Daniels (1987) for more details.

The bottom line is this: for most personality variables, the shared environment has either little or no discernible impact. Adoption studies, for example, show that the average correlation for personality variables between adopted siblings who share much of their environment, but who share no genes, is only .05. This suggests that, even though these siblings are growing up together—with the same parents, same schools, same religious training, and so on—whatever is happening in their shared environment (e.g., parenting, rearing practices, values education) is not causing them to be similar in personality.

Instead, most environmental causes appear to stem from the aspects of the environment that siblings experience differently. Thus, it's not the number of books in the home. It's not parental values or parental attitudes toward child rearing. In fact, it's not what most psychologists have long believed it is. Rather, the critical environmental influences on personality appear to lie in the unique experiences of individual children.

These findings should not be surprising. Identical twins, and even nontwin siblings who grow up together, may work to create their own identities, cultivate their own skills, and forge their unique paths in life. In the case of identical twins reared together, people may have a vested interest in telling them apart and, so, create an environment that emphasizes the differences between them. The key point is that environments matter tremendously in the development of personality, but not the environmental features that siblings share. Their unique environments and experiences, instead, appear to be critical for the development of personality.

Which unique experiences are important? Well, here we run into a brick wall. The discovery of the importance of the nonshared environment is recent, coming to the attention of the scientific community only within the past few years. Most theories of socialization over the decades have focused exclusively on the shared environment, such as parental attitudes toward child rearing. Thus, it is only recently that psychologists have begun to study nonshared environments.

There are two possibilities of what they will find. One possibility is a major breakthrough—a discovery of a critically important environmental variable that has been overlooked by psychologists who for years focused only on the shared environment. The other possibility is less satisfying. It is conceivable that there are so many environmental variables that exert an impact on personality that each one alone might account only for a tiny fraction of the variance (Willerman, 1979). If this is the case, then we are stuck with the discovery of many small effects.

Does this mean that the shared environment accounts for nothing? Have psychologists been entirely misguided in their thinking by their focus on shared effects? The answer is no. In some areas, behavioral genetic studies have revealed tremendously important shared environmental influences: attitudes, religious beliefs, political orientations, health behaviors, and to some degree verbal intelligence (Segal, 1999). As an example, adoptive siblings reared together but genetically unrelated correlated .41 (girls) and .46 (boys) in their patterns of smoking and drinking (Willerman, 1979). Thus, although smoking and drinking have a substantial genetic component, there is also a large shared environmental component.

Another recent study found that shared environments accounted for several personality clusters in the "adjustment" domain (Loehlin, Neiderhiser, & Reiss, 2003). These include antisocial behavior (e.g., showing behavior problems and breaking rules), depressive symptoms (e.g., moody, withdrawn), and autonomous functioning (e.g., being able to care for self in basic needs and recreational activities). And a study of adult twins using observational measurement—trait ratings of videotaped behaviors—suggests that shared environment might be more important in explaining Big Five personality traits than is typically revealed by studies using self-report (Borkenau, Reimann, Angleitner, & Spinath, 2001). If this study is replicated by future research, it may have the far-reaching consequence of challenging the now-conventional wisdom that shared environments have little effect on personality traits.

Exercise

Discuss what you think might represent shared environmental influences that contribute to the tendency to smoke. That is, what in the environment might have influenced most people who smoke to start and maintain their smoking habit?

In summary, environments shared by siblings are important in some domains. But, for many personality traits, such as extraversion and neuroticism, shared environments do not seem to matter. Instead, it is the unique environment experienced by each sibling that carries the causal weight.

Genes and the Environment

As important as it is to identify sources of environmental and genetic influence on personality, the next step requires an understanding of how genetic and environmental factors interact. More complex forms of behavioral genetic analysis involve notions such as *genotype-environment interaction* and *genotype-environment correlation.* We will address these briefly in turn.

Genotype-Environment Interaction

Genotype-environment interaction refers to the differential response of individuals with different genotypes to the same environments. Consider introverts and extraverts, who have somewhat different genotypes. Introverts tend to perform well on cognitive tasks when there is little stimulation in the room, but they do poorly when there are distractions, such as a radio blaring or people walking around. In contrast, extraverts do just fine with the stereo blasting, the phone ringing, and people walking in and out. But the same extraverts make a lot of errors in these cognitive tasks when there is little stimulation, when the task they are working on is boring or monotonous.

Extraversion–introversion is a perfect example of genotype-environment interaction, whereby individuals with different genotypes (introverts and extraverts) respond differently to the same environment (e.g., noise in the room). Individual differences *interact* with the environment to affect performance. You may want to take this into consideration when you arrange your studying environment. Before turning on the stereo, first determine whether you lie on the introverted or extraverted end of the continuum. If you are an introvert, you would likely do better studying in a quiet environment with few interruptions. The notion that people with different genotypes (introverts versus extraverts) respond differently to specific environments (e.g., a noisy setting) is what is meant by genotype-environment interactions.

Recent developments have begun to identify genotype-environment interactions. One study examined the effects of abusive parenting on whether children developed antisocial personalities (Caspi et al., 2002). Abused children who had a genotype that produced low levels of the brain neurotransmitter monoamine oxidase A (MAOA) frequently developed conduct disorders, antisocial personalities, and violent dispositions. In contrast, maltreated children who had high levels of MAOA were far less likely to develop aggressive antisocial personalities. This study provides an excellent example of genotype-environment interaction—exposure to the same environment (abusive parenting) produces different effects on personality, depending on the differences in genotype. Interestingly, this suggests that violent parents may create violent children *only* if the children have a genotype marked by low levels of MAOA. The empirical study of genotype-environment interactions represents one of the most exciting new developments in the behavior genetics of personality (Jang, Dick, Wolf, Livesley, & Paris, 2005; Moffitt, 2005).

Genotype-Environment Correlation

Perhaps even more interesting than genotype-environment interaction is the concept of **genotype-environment correlation,** the differential exposure of individuals with different genotypes to different environments. Consider, for example, a child who has a genotype for high verbal ability. Her parents may notice this and provide her with lots of books to read, engage in intellectual discussions with her, and give her word games and crossword puzzles. Parents of children with less verbal skill, who presumably have different genotypes than those with high verbal abilities, may be less inclined to provide this stimulation. This is an example of genotype-environment correlation—whereby individuals with different genotypes (e.g., those with high versus low verbal abilities) are exposed to different environments (e.g., high versus low stimulation). In another example, parents might promote sports activities for athletically inclined children more than for less athletically inclined children.

Plomin, DeFries, and Loehlin (1977) describe three very different kinds of genotype-environment correlation: passive, reactive, and active. **Passive genotype-environment correlation** occurs when parents provide both genes and the environment to children, yet the children do nothing to obtain that environment. Suppose, for example, that parents who are verbally inclined pass on genes to their children that make them verbally inclined. However, because the parents are highly verbal, they buy a lot of books. Thus, there is a correlation between the children's verbal ability and the number of books in their home, but it is passive in the sense that the child has done nothing to cause the books to be there.

In sharp contrast, the **reactive genotype-environment correlation** occurs when parents (or others) respond to children differently, depending on the child's genotypes. A good example is cuddlers versus noncuddlers. Some babies love to be touched—they giggle, smile, laugh, and show great pleasure when they are handled. Other babies are more aloof and simply do not like to be touched very much. Imagine that a mother starts out touching and hugging each of her two children a lot. One child loves it; the other hates it. Over the course of several months, the mother reacts by continuing to hug the cuddler but cuts down on hugging the noncuddler. This example illustrates the reactive genotype-environment correlation, which is achieved because people react to children differently, based in part on the children's heritable dispositions, such as a liking for being cuddled.

Active genotype-environment correlation occurs when a person with a particular genotype creates or seeks out a particular environment. High sensation seekers, for example, expose themselves to risky environments—skydiving, motorcycle jumping, and drug taking. Highly intellectual individuals are likely to attend lectures, read books, and engage others in verbal discourse. This active creation and selection of environments has also been called "niche picking" (Scarr & McCartney, 1983). Active genotype-environment correlation highlights the fact that we are not passive recipients of our environments; we mold, create, and select the environments we subsequently inhabit, and some of these actions are correlated with our genotypes.

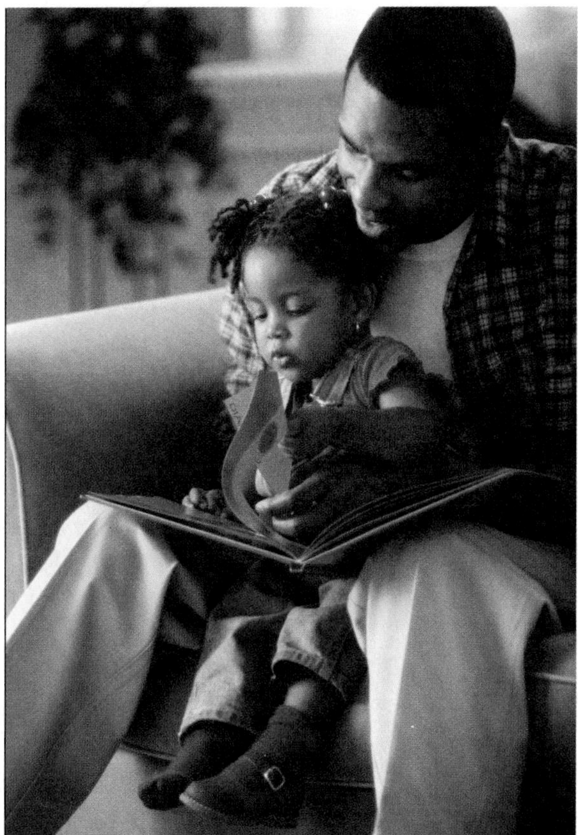

Modern views on the nature-nurture debate suggest more complex answers to the question of the origins of personality. One view is that genes and environments interact in determining personality.

These genotype-environment correlations can be positive or negative. That is, the environment can encourage the expression of the disposition, or it can discourage its expression. For example, parents of highly active children may try to get them to sit still and calm down, and parents of less active children may try to get them to perk up and be more lively, in which case there is a negative genotype-environment correlation because the parents' behavior opposes the children's traits (Buss, 1981). Another example of negative genotype-environment correlation occurs when people who are too dominant elicit negative reactions from others, who try to "cut them down" (Cattell, 1973). The key point is that environments can go against a person's genotype, resulting in a negative genotype-environment correlation, or they can facilitate the person's genotype, creating a positive genotype-environment correlation.

A recent study of 180 twins reared apart points to an intriguing potential example of genotype-environment correlation (Krueger, Markon, & Bouchard, 2003). The study assessed personality traits through the Multidimensional Personality Questionnaire (MPQ), which identifies three major factors of personality: Positive Emotionality (happy, content), Negative Emotionality (anxious, tense), and Constraint (controlled, conscientious). Then they evaluated each individual's *perceptions* of the family environments in which they were raised, which yielded two main factors: Family Cohesion (e.g., parental warmth, absence of family conflict) and Family Status (e.g., parents provided intellectual and cultural stimulation, active recreational activities, and financial resources). The intriguing results were that the correlations between personality and perceptions of family environment were genetically mediated. In other words, the perceived environment in which the individuals were raised was largely due to heritable personality traits. Specifically, experiencing a cohesive family upbringing was explained by genetic influence on the two personality traits of Constraint and lack of Negative Emotionality. In contrast, recalling a family environment high in cultural, intellectual, and economic status was explained by the heritable personality trait of Positive Emotionality.

These results may be subject to several interpretations. One interpretation is that personality affects the subjective manner in which people remember their early environments. Perhaps calm, controlled individuals are more likely to forget about real family conflict that was present during their childhood, and so may simply recall greater family cohesion than actually existed. An alternative interpretation is in terms of genotype-environment correlation: Individuals with calm, controlled personalities (high Constraint, low Negative Emotionality) may actually *promote* cohesion among family members—in essence, creating a family environment that further fosters their calm, controlled personality. Future studies of personality, parenting, and perceived family environments offer the promise of unraveling the subtle and complex ways in which genes interact and correlate with environments (Spinath & O'Connor, 2003).

The concepts of genotype-environment interaction and correlation are intriguing in providing a more complex picture of human personality functioning. It is clear from behavioral genetic studies that both heredity and shared and nonshared environments influence personality. It will be exciting to follow these lines of research over the next decade as they document the precise nature of these interactions and correlations.

Molecular Genetics

The most recent development in the science of behavioral genetics has been the exploration of **molecular genetics.** The methods of molecular genetics are designed to identify the specific genes associated with personality traits. The details are quite technical, but the most common method, called the association method, is to identify whether individuals with a particular gene (or allele) have higher or lower scores on a particular trait than individuals without the gene. These methods have been applied to the study of personality traits only fairly recently, with the first publications appearing in 1996 (Benjamin et al., 1996; Ebstein et al., 1996).

The most frequently examined gene is called **D4DR,** which is located on the short arm of chromosome 11. This gene codes for a protein called a dopamine receptor. The function of this dopamine receptor, as you might guess, is to respond to the presence of dopamine, which is a neurotransmitter. When the dopamine receptor encounters dopamine from other neurons in the brain, it discharges an electrical signal, activating other neurons.

The most frequently examined association between the D4DR gene and a personality trait has involved novelty seeking, the tendency to seek out new experiences, especially those considered risky, such as drug experiences, risky sexual experiences, gambling, and high-speed driving (Zuckerman & Kuhlman, 2000). Individuals with so-called long repeat versions of the D4DR gene were found to be higher on novelty seeking than individuals with so-called short repeat versions of this gene (Benjamin et al., 1996). The researchers hypothesized that the reason for this association is that people with long D4DR genes tend to be relatively unresponsive to dopamine. This causes them to seek out novel experiences, which gives them a "dopamine buzz." In contrast, those with the short D4DR genes already tend to be highly responsive to whatever dopamine is already present in their brains, so they tend not to seek out novel experiences, which might boost their dopamine to uncomfortable levels.

Although the association between D4DR and novelty seeking has been replicated several times, there have also been several failures to replicate (Plomin & Crabbe, 2000). One study, for example, found that the D4DR was *not* at all associated with measures of novelty seeking (Burt, McGue, Iacono, Comings, & MacMurray, 2002). A second study of preschool children found that D4DR *was* significantly linked with mothers' reports of their children's problems with aggression (a possible precursor to novelty seeking), but was *not* significantly linked with observed behavioral measures of aggression (Schmidt, Fox, Rubin, Hu, & Hamer, 2002). And a third study found that high novelty seeking was linked with a different allele of a *different* gene—the A1 allele of the D2 dopamine receptor gene (D2DR) (Berman, Ozkaragoz, Young, & Noble, 2002).

Part of the problem is that the size of the association is small. The original researchers (Benjamin et al., 1996) estimate that the D4DR gene explains only 4 percent of the variation in novelty seeking. It has also been speculated that there may be 10 other genes that are equally important in novelty seeking, none of which has yet been explored. And perhaps there are 500 genes that vary with other aspects of human personality (Ridley, 1999). It seems unlikely, therefore, that any single gene will ever be found to explain more than a small percentage of variation in personality.

As exciting as the results are from these molecular genetic methods, it is important to exercise caution when interpreting them. In several cases, researchers have found an association between a particular gene and personality-related traits, such as anxiety and attention deficit disorder, but subsequent researchers have failed to replicate these associations (Plomin & Crabbe, 2000). Research over the next decade, however, should reveal the degree to which specific genes for specific personality traits can be found. Although the initial enthusiasm over the possible link between D4DR and novelty seeking has waned as failures to replicate have come in, vigorous research on the molecular genetics of aggression, shyness, and neuroticism appears promising (Plomin, 2002; Benjamin, Ebstein, & Belmaker, in press). Neuroticism, for example, has been linked to genes involved in the serotonin system, which involves neurotransmitters implicated in mood, emotion, sleep, and appetite (Jang, Hu, Livesley, Angleitner, Reimann, Ando, Ono, Vernon, & Hamer, 2001; Lesch, in press).

In summary, some scientists remain pessimistic about the promise of molecular genetic techniques in the realm of personality. Meta-analyses show that failure to replicate links between specific genes and personality is a pervasive problem (Munafo, Clark, Moore, Payne, Walton, & Flint, 2003). Other scientists remain optimistic that new scientific techniques will eventually lead to uncovering the molecular genetic architecture of human personality (Ebstein, 2006).

Now that we have examined some of the basic concepts and findings from the behavioral genetics of personality, it is appropriate to take a step back and examine these findings from the perspectives of science, politics, and values.

Behavioral Genetics, Science, Politics, and Values

The history of behavioral genetic research has taken some fascinating twists and turns, which are worth noting (see Plomin et al., 1990, for an excellent summary of this history). During the past century in the United States, behavioral genetic research received what can be phrased as a "frosty reception." Findings that some personality traits were moderately heritable seemed to violate the dominant paradigm, which was environmentalism (and, especially, behaviorism). The prevailing **environmentalist view** was that personality was determined by socialization practices, such as parenting style. Furthermore, people worried about the potential misuse of findings emerging from behavioral genetics. Images of Nazi Germany sprang to mind, with the evil notions of a master race. Of course, there is the notion of ethnic cleansing, which has strong genetic overtones.

A large part of the controversy over genetic research on personality has centered around studies of intelligence, which has often been considered to be a personality variable. Many people have worried that findings from these studies will be misused to label some people intrinsically superior or inferior to others (e.g., see Herrnstein & Murray, 1994). Others worry that findings will be misused to give some people preferential treatment in education or job placement. Still others are concerned that standard tests of intelligence fail to capture many of the multiple facets of intelligence, such as social intelligence, emotional intelligence, and creativity. All of these are legitimate concerns, and they suggest that the findings from the field of behavioral genetics must be viewed with caution and interpreted responsibly, in terms of the larger picture of human nature and society.

In the past decade, attitudes have shifted somewhat, and the field of psychology now considers the findings from behavioral genetics as fairly mainstream. Behavioral genetic studies tend not to generate the intense controversy that they did in prior decades. One recent exception to this are the studies on the heritability of sexual orientation, which generated some media controversy. For example, if homosexuality is more environmental and learned than was previously thought, then some groups have suggested that homosexuality could be unlearned, or "cured."

The links between science and politics, between knowledge and values, are complex, but they need to be confronted. Because scientific research can be misused for political goals, scientists bear a major responsibility for presenting findings carefully and accurately. Some argue that science and values cannot be separated and that even science itself is a political tool used to oppress certain people. There may be no subdiscipline for which these complex issues of the mingling of science and values is more relevant than the field of behavioral genetics.

Science can be separated from values. Science is a set of methods for discovering what exists. Values are notions of what people *want* to exist—to be desired or sought after. Although scientists clearly can be biased by their values, the virtue of the scientific method is that it is self-correcting. The methods are public, so other scientists can check the findings, discover errors in procedure, and, hence, over time correct any biases that creep in. This does not imply, of course, that scientists are unbiased. Indeed, the history of science is filled with cases in which values influenced the nature of the questions posed and the acceptance or rejection of particular findings or theories. Nonetheless, the scientific method provides a method for correcting such biases in the long run.

SUMMARY AND EVALUATION

The behavioral genetics of personality has a fascinating history in the twentieth century. Early on, when behavioral genetic methods were being developed, the field of psychology was dominated by the behaviorist paradigm. In this context, findings from behavioral genetic research were not warmly received. Furthermore, social scientists worried that findings from behavioral genetic research might be misused for ideological purposes.

Over the past two decades, the empirical evidence on heritability has become stronger and stronger, in part because of the convergence of evidence across behavioral genetic methods. There are four major behavioral genetic methods: selective breeding studies, family studies, twin studies, and adoption studies. Selective breeding studies cannot be ethically conducted on humans. Family studies are problematic because the genetic and environmental factors are often confounded. Twin studies have potential problems, such as violations of the equal environments assumption (the assumption that identical twins are not treated any more alike than fraternal twins) and the assumption of representativeness (the notion that twins are just like nontwins). Adoption studies also have potential problems, such as the nonrandom placement of adopted-away children in particular families and, like twin studies, the assumption of representativeness (the notion that adopted children are like nonadopted children in all key respects). Empirical tests of these assumptions suggest that they are not violated much or are violated in ways that do not seem to make much difference. However, the most compelling evidence on the heritability of personality comes from looking across methods that do not share methodological problems. Thus, if the findings from twin studies *and* adoption studies converge on the same result, then we can have more confidence in the results than we can when just a single method is used.

The study of large samples of twins reared together, the study of smaller samples of identical twins reared apart, and sound adoption studies have added greatly to the credibility of behavioral genetic research. The empirical findings clearly show that personality variables, such as extraversion and neuroticism, as well as the other dimensions of the Big Five, have moderate heritability. Perhaps even more striking are the findings that drinking, smoking, attitudes, occupational preferences, and even sexual orientation appear to be moderately heritable. Equally important, however, is the finding that the same studies provide the best evidence for the importance of environmental influences. Overall, personality characteristics are 30 to 50 percent heritable and 50 to 70 percent environmental.

Perhaps most interesting, the environmental causes appear to be mostly of the nonshared variety—that is, the different experiences that siblings have even though they are in the same family. This finding is so startling because nearly all theories of environmental influence—such as those that posit the importance of parental values and child-rearing styles—have been of the shared variety. Thus, behavioral genetic research may have provided one of the most important insights into the nature of nurture—the location of the most important environmental influences on personality. The next decade of personality research should witness progress in identifying the precise locations of these nonshared environmental influences. Separating perceived environments from objective environments will be an important part of this research program.

In interpreting the research findings, it is important to keep in mind the meaning of heritability and the meaning of environmentality. Heritability is the proportion of observed individual differences that are caused by genetic differences in a particular population or sample. It does not pertain to an individual, since genetic and environmental influences are inextricably interwoven at the individual level and cannot be separated. Heritability does not mean that the environment is powerless to alter the individual differences. And heritability is not a fixed statistic—it can be low in one group and high in another, low at one time and high at another. Environmentality is the proportion of observed individual differences that is caused by environmental differences. Like heritability, environmentality is not a fixed statistic. It, too, can change over time and across situations. The discovery of a powerful environmental intervention, for example, could, in principle, dramatically increase environmentality while lowering heritability. The key point is that neither heritability nor environmentality is fixed in space and time.

In addition to providing estimates of heritability and environmentality, some behavioral genetic research examines the interactions and correlations between genetic and environmental variables. There are three major types of genotype-environment correlations—passive, reactive, and active. Passive genotype-environment correlation occurs when parents provide both genes and environment to their children in ways that just happen to be correlated—for example, parents who pass on genes for verbal ability and stock their houses with a lot of books. Books and verbal ability become correlated, but in a passive way, since the children did not have to do anything for the correlation to occur. Reactive genotype-environment correlation occurs when parents, teachers, and others respond differently to some children than to others. Parents generally tickle and coo at smiley babies more than at nonsmiley babies, creating a correlation between genotypes for smiling and a cuddly social environment. The correlation occurs because parents react to babies differently. Active genotype-environment correlation occurs when individuals with certain genotypes seek out environments nonrandomly. Extraverted individuals, for example, might throw a lot of parties, thus surrounding themselves with a different social environment than that of the more reclusive introverts. The correlation occurs because individuals actively create it.

The more complex and interesting behavioral genetic concepts such as genotype-environment correlation have received relatively little research attention. A recent possible exception is the fascinating finding that individuals low on Negative Emotionality and high on Constraint recall their early family environment as being extremely cohesive. One interpretation is in terms of genotype-environment correlation: Calm, nonneurotic individuals may actually promote calmness and cohesion in their family environment, thus creating an upbringing that further fosters their calm, controlled personality. Now that some of the basic estimates of heritability and environmentality have been established, however, the next wave of research may reveal the more complex nature of the causes of individual differences in personality.

Molecular genetics represents the most recent development in the realm of personality psychology. The research techniques attempt to establish an association between specific genes and scores on personality traits. Initial findings of a link between the D4DR gene and novelty seeking, however, have not been successfully replicated. More recent work has focused on possible genes underlying neuroticism—specifically, genes involved in the serotonin system.

KEY TERMS

Genome 174
Genetic Junk 174
Eugenics 175
Percentage of Variance 177
Heritability 177
Phenotypic Variance 178
Genotypic Variance 178
Environmentality 178
Nature-Nurture Debate 179
Selective Breeding 180
Family Studies 181
Twin Studies 182
Monozygotic (MZ) Twins 182
Dizygotic (DZ) Twins 182
Equal Environments Assumption 183
Adoption Studies 184
Selective Placement 185
Gender Identity Disorder (GID) 191
Shared Environmental Influences 193
Nonshared Environmental Influences 193
Genotype-Environment Interaction 195
Genotype-Environment Correlation 196
Passive Genotype-Environment Correlation 196
Reactive Genotype-Environment Correlation 196
Active Genotype-Environment Correlation 197
Molecular Genetics 198
D4DR Gene 198
Environmentalist View 199

Physiological Approaches to Personality

THE BIOLOGICAL DOMAIN

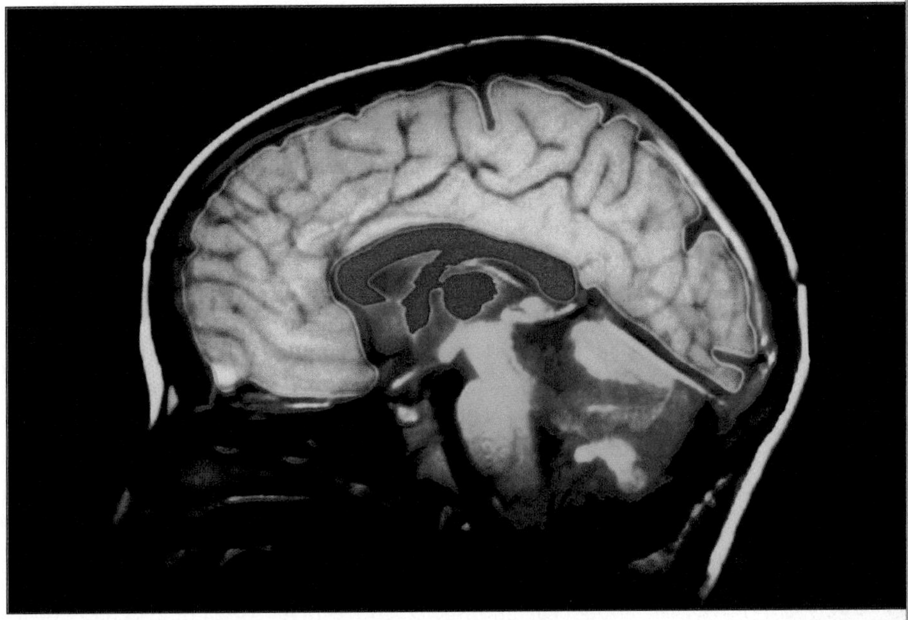

Brain imaging techniques have enabled researchers to learn more about the brain's role in behavior and personality than previously thought possible.

Elliot was a successful businessman, a proud father, and a good husband. At his firm, he was a role model for his younger colleagues. Personally, he was charming and pleasant. His social skills were such that he often was called on to settle disputes at work. Elliot was respected by others. His position in the community, his satisfying personal life, and his prosperity and professional status were all enviable.

One day Elliot began to have severe headaches. After a few days, he went to his doctor, who suspected a brain tumor. This suspicion was confirmed when a small tumor was found growing, not on his brain, but on the lining of tissue that covers the brain. The location was just above his eyes, behind his forehead. The tumor was, however, pushing against his brain and had damaged a small portion of the front of his brain, part of the prefrontal cortex, which had to be removed with the tumor.

The operation went smoothly and Elliot recovered quickly, with no apparent lasting damage, at least none that could be found with ordinary tests. Elliot's IQ was tested after the operation and was found to be superior, as it was before his operation. His memory was tested and was found to be excellent. His ability to use and understand language was also unaffected by the operation. His ability to do arithmetic, to memorize lists of words, to visualize objects, to make judgments, and to read a map all remained unaffected by the operation. All his cognitive functions remained normal or above normal, completely unaffected by the removal of a small portion of his prefrontal cortex.

Elliot's family, however, reported that his personality had changed. He began to behave differently at work as well. He could not seem to manage his time properly. He needed lots of prompting from his wife to get going in the morning. Once at work, he had problems finishing tasks. If he was interrupted in a task, he had difficulty starting back up where he had left off. Often he would get captivated by one part of a task and get side-tracked for hours. For example, in refiling some books, which should have taken 15 minutes, he stopped to read one of the books and returned to his desk hours later. He knew his job but just had trouble putting all the actions together in the right order.

Soon Elliot lost his job. He tried various business schemes on his own and finally took his life savings and started an investment management business. He teamed up with a disreputable character, against the advice of many of his friends and family members. This business went bankrupt, and he lost all his savings. To his wife and children Elliot appeared to be behaving impulsively, and they had trouble coping with the difficulties he was getting into. A divorce followed. Elliot quickly remarried, but to a woman whom none of his friends or family approved of. This marriage ended quickly in another divorce. Without a source of income, and without a family to support him, Elliot became a drifter.

Elliot came to the attention of Dr. Antonio Damasio, a neurologist at the University of Iowa, who later wrote a book about Elliot's condition (Damasio, 1994). It seems that the small bit of brain matter destroyed by Elliot's tumor was essential in transmitting emotional information to the higher reasoning centers of the brain. Elliot reported that the only change in himself that he noticed was that, after his operation, he did not feel any strong emotion, or much of any emotion for that matter.

The case of Elliot shows us that the body and the mind are intimately connected. Indeed, after Elliot's operation, the biggest change in him was in his personality, not in his memory, his reasoning, or his knowledge.

Studies have shown that traumatic brain injury can lead to large changes in personality (Tate, 2003). One of the most common changes in personality following brain injury is a diminished ability to inhibit or control one's impulses. This has been found in children who experienced brain trauma during birth (Christ, White, Brunstrom, & Abrams, 2003), in adults with traumatic brain injuries (Kim, 2002), and in elderly persons whose brains have been injured by stroke (Freshwater & Golden, 2002). This increased impulsivity and lack of self-control is most likely due to disruptions between the frontal lobes, which serve as the executive control center of the brain, and other parts of the brain. As a result, persons with extensive brain injury can retain most of their cognitive abilities, yet lose some degree of self-control (Lowenstein, 2002). Persons with personality changes following traumatic brain injuries often have spontaneous outbursts, sudden changes in mood, and episodes of aggression and can become quite disruptive to their families. Indeed, this is the personality profile of one of the most famous brain injury patients, Phineas Gage, who was injured by an iron rod that was blasted through his brain while he was working as a railway builder in the early 1900s (see A Closer Look).

The idea that elements of personality are the products of biological processes is an old one. In A.D. 170 ancient Roman physician Galen, building on even earlier work by Greek physician Hippocrates, wrote that personality or character was influenced by biology. Galen taught that the amounts of four fluids present in the body determined personality: an abundance of phlegm made a person passive, calm, and thoughtful (phlegmatic); an abundance of blood made a person happy, outgoing, and lively (sanguine); too much yellow bile made a person unstable, aggressive, and excitable

A Closer Look

The Brain Injury of Phineas Gage

Phineas Gage was a nineteenth-century rail worker, serving as foreman on a construction gang preparing the way for the Rutland and Burlington Railroad in Vermont. His work involved blasting large rocks with dynamite, and one day he was injured in a serious accident. Prior to his accident, Phineas was an industrious worker, highly agreeable and conscientious, and seen by his employers as one of their most capable and efficient foremen. On September 13, 1848, he was tamping dynamite into a hole in a rock using an iron rod. The dynamite accidentally ignited and the explosion shot the iron rod out of the hole like a bullet. Phineas was bending over the work area. The iron rod he was working with was 1¼ inches in diameter, 3-feet, 7-inches long, and weighed almost 14 pounds. It was tapered at one end almost to a point. The heavy iron rod came out of the tamping hole point first. It shot up through Gage's left cheek, just below the cheek bone, passed behind his left eye and exited the top of his skull, landing approximately 75 feet away. Gage was knocked off his feet but did not lose consciousness. The iron rod destroyed a large portion of the front part of his brain. Remarkably, Gage survived this accident. He spent 10 weeks under a doctor's care, then returned to his home in New Hampshire. Even more remarkably, most of his intellectual functions remained intact. However, his personality changed dramatically. His doctor, John Harlow, described the new Phineas Gage as "obstinate, capricious, and vacillating, devising many plans of future operations which are no sooner arranged than they are abandoned, a child, yet with the passions of a strong man" (cited in Carter, 1999). He lacked the ability to direct himself nor could he devise plans to achieve goals. He was impulsive and aggressive. He started using profane language and disregarded social conventions, behaving impolitely toward those around him. Women were advised to avoid him. He never worked as a foreman again. Instead, he had various farm jobs, mostly caring for horses and cleaning stables. He died on May 21, 1860, almost 12 years after his devastating accident. His skull and the iron rod are on display at Harvard's Countway Library of Medicine. See Macmillan (2000) for a modern perspective on this famous case.

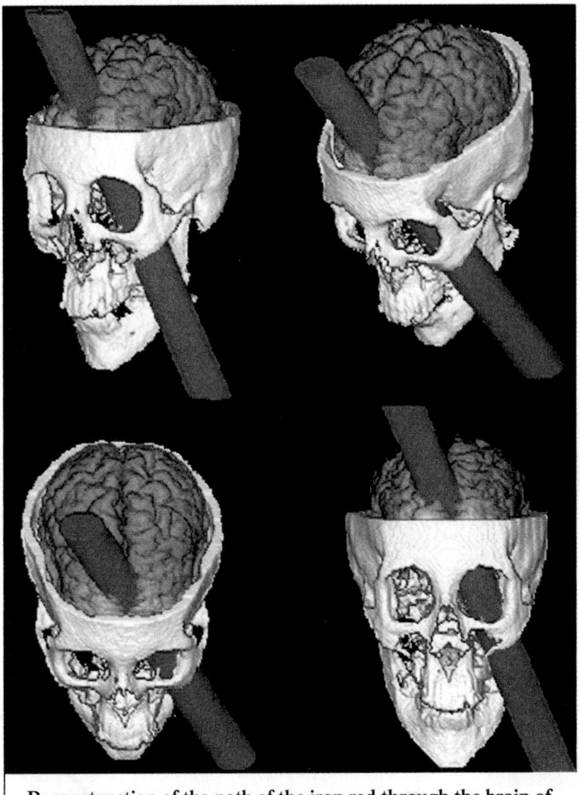

Reconstruction of the path of the iron rod through the brain of Phineas Gage.

(choleric); and an abundance of black bile made a person unhappy, pessimistic, and somber (melancholic). Galen wrote that "the melancholic . . . shows fear and depression, discontent with life and hatred of all people. [F]ear of death is the principle concern . . . [T]he black humour [bile] . . . brings about the fear . . . All people call this affliction . . . melancholis, indicating by this term that the black humour is responsible" (from Siegel, 1973, p. 195). The **bodily-fluid theory** of personality remained in favor for centuries, influencing both philosophers (e.g., Immanuel Kant) and early psychologists (e.g., Wilhelm Wundt). Although antiquated by today's understanding of both physiology and medicine, Galen's theory is noteworthy as one of the first to take a physiological approach to personality (Stelmack & Stalkas, 1991).

Physiologically oriented approaches are based on the premise that psychological characteristics, such as friendliness and thoughtfulness, are due to an underlying physiological system.

An advantage of the physiological approach is that physiological characteristics can be measured mechanically and reliably. The term *physiological characteristics* refers to the functioning of organ systems within the body. Examples of **physiological systems** are the nervous system (including the brain and nerves), the cardiac system (including the heart, arteries, and veins), and the musculoskeletal system (including the muscles and bones, which make all movements and behaviors possible). To get an idea of the importance of these physiological systems, imagine the result of removing any one of them. Without a brain, a person could not think or respond to the environment; without the musculoskeletal system, a person could not move or act on the environment; and, without a cardiac system, the result is obvious. All of the physiological systems are important to the maintanence of life, and their study has resulted in the fields of medicine, anatomy, and physiology.

From the perspective of personality psychology, physiology is important to the extent that differences in physiology create, contribute to, or indicate differences in psychological functioning. For example, people differ from one another in how sensitive their nervous systems are to stimulation. Given exposure to loud noise, for example, some people find it quite irritating, whereas other people are not bothered at all. A person who is particularly sensitive might frequent quiet environments (e.g., the library), avoid crowds (e.g., not go to loud parties), and limit the amount of stimulation in their environments (e.g., never play loud rock-and-roll music). The physiologically oriented personality psychologist would say that this person is introverted (a psychological characteristic) because he or she has an overly sensitive nervous system (a physiological characteristic). Thus, this approach assumes that differences in physiological characteristics are related to differences in important personality characteristics and behavior patterns. In this chapter, we will discuss several physiology-personality relationships.

Another characteristic of the physiological approach to personality is simplicity or parsimony. Physiological theories often propose to explain a good deal of behavior with a few constructs. Often the theories simply state that a physiological difference results in a given personality difference or a difference in an important behavior pattern. Why, for example, do some people take up skydiving, race car driving, and other high-risk behaviors? One theory states that they do so because they have a deficiency of a certain chemical in their nervous systems. Despite the obvious simplicity of theories such as these, human nature is actually more complicated. For example, two people could be equally high on sensation seeking, yet one of them has satisfied this need in a socially approved matter (for instance, by becoming an emergency room doctor), while the other satisfies it in a socially unacceptable manner (for example, through various exciting but illegal behaviors, such as illegal gambling or drug use). Most physiologically oriented psychologists would *not* argue that "physiology is destiny." Most would agree that physiology is only one cause among many for explaining behavior.

As you know from Chapter 1, Gordon Allport wrote one of the first textbooks in personality (1937), and in it he argued that "the organization (of personality) entails the operation of both body and mind, inextricably fused into a personal unity" (p. 48). Because personality consists of both bodily and mental aspects, its study can be approached from either direction. In this chapter, we will focus on several physiological systems that contribute to our understanding of personality.

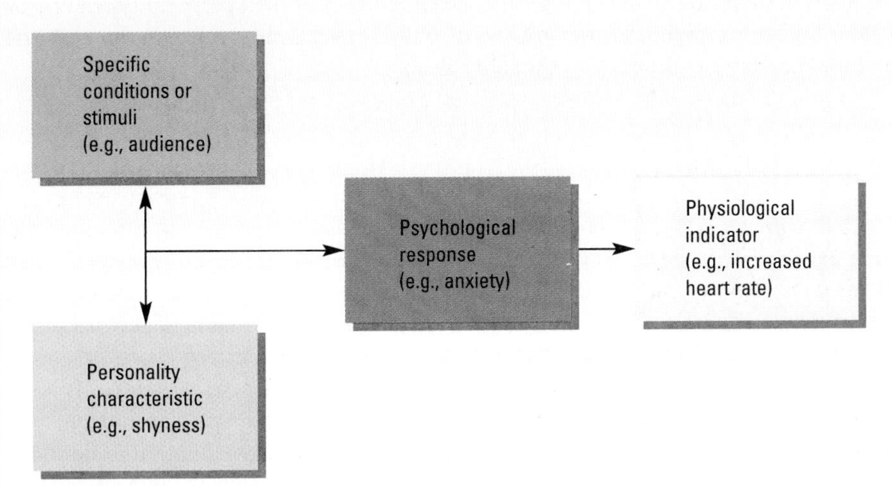

Figure 7.1

Building a theoretical bridge that links personality to specific situations in terms of evoking a certain psychological response, which can be identified and measured using specific physiological measures. A theory specifies which conditions or stimuli will interact with which personality traits to produce specific responses, which can be observed physiologically.

A Physiological Approach to Personality

Early notions that personality is based in biology often implicated global physiological systems, such as the bodily fluid theory mentioned earlier. Another global example can be found in the idea that gross body type influenced personality. A strong proponent of this idea was a man named Sheldon, who wrote a number of books on how specific body types (e.g., whether one was skinny, muscular, or fat) promoted specific personality traits (Sheldon & Stevens, 1940, 1942). However, controlled research failed to support Sheldon's findings (Eysenck, 1970) and so the theory of body types and personality is of historical interest only.

Most physiological personality psychologists today do not focus on global variables, such as gross body type. Instead, the majority of researchers in this area use measures of distinct physiological systems, such as heart rate or brain waves. The typical research question posed by contemporary psychologists concerns whether some people will exhibit more or less of a specific physiological response than others under certain conditions. For example, are shy people likely to show a higher level of anxiety, as exemplified by large increases in heart rate, when called on to perform a difficult task in front of an audience, compared with persons who are not shy? Notice that this question involves the specific conditions (audience) under which a specific personality characteristic (shyness) will produce a specific psychological response (anxiety), which will show up in a specific physiological indicator (heart rate). These connections are depicted in Figure 7.1.

Specific statements—about which traits are connected to which psychological reactions under which conditions or in response to which stimuli—are now the way personality psychologists talk about physiology. Researchers must be able to build such a **theoretical bridge** between the personality dimension of interest and physiological variables in order to use physiological concepts to help explain personality (Levenson, 1983). Let's turn now to a brief review of physiological variables, with an emphasis on how they are measured in personality research.

Physiological Measures Commonly Used in Personality Research

Most of the common physiological measures in personality research are obtained from **electrodes,** or sensors placed on the surface of a participant's skin. They are noninvasive in that they do not penetrate the skin, and these electrodes cause practically no discomfort. One drawback to such measures is that the participant is literally wired to the physiological recording machine (often called a polygraph), so movement is constrained. A new generation of electrodes will, however, overcome this limitation through the use of **telemetry,** a process by which electrical signals are sent from the participant to the polygraph through radio waves instead of by wires. This is already being used with astronauts, in which their physiological systems are being monitored constantly on earth. Three physiological measures of particular interest to personality psychologists are electrodermal activity (skin conductance of electricity), cardiovascular measures, and activity in the brain. Other biological measures, such as the amounts of hormones in the blood are also of interest. We will discuss each of these in turn.

Electrodermal Activity (Skin Conductance)

The skin on the palms of the hands (and the soles of the feet) contains a high concentration of sweat glands. These sweat glands are directly influenced by the sympathetic nervous system, the branch of the **autonomic nervous system** that prepares the body for action—that is, the fight-or-flight mechanism. When the sympathetic nervous system is activated (such as during episodes of anxiety, startle, or anger), the sweat glands begin to fill with salty water. If the activation is sufficiently strong or prolonged, the sweat may actually spill out onto the palms of the hands, causing the person to develop sweaty palms. Interestingly, all mammals have a similarly high concentration of sweat glands on the friction surfaces of their hands/paws.

Even before the sweat is visible, however, it can be detected by the clever application of a small amount of electricity, since water (i.e., sweat) conducts electricity. The more water that is present in the skin, the more easily the skin carries, or conducts, electricity. This bioelectric process, known as **electrodermal activity** (*dermal* means "of the skin"), or **skin conductance,** makes it possible for researchers to directly measure sympathetic nervous system activity.

In this technique, two electrodes are placed on the palm of one hand. A very low voltage of electricity is then put through one electrode into the skin, and the researcher measures how much electricity is present at the other electrode. The difference in the amount of electricity that is passed into the skin at one electrode and the amount detected at the other electrode tells researchers how well the skin is conducting electricity. The more sympathetic nervous system activity there is, the more water is produced by the sweat glands in the skin, and the better the skin conducts the electricity. The levels of electricity involved are so small that the participant does not feel anything.

Electrodermal responses can be elicited by all sorts of stimuli, including sudden noises, emotional pictures with charged content, conditioned stimuli, mental effort, pain, and emotional reactions such as anxiety, fear, and guilt (as in the so-called lie detector test, which uses skin conductance). One phenomenon of interest to personality psychologists is the observation that some people show skin conductance responses in the *absence* of any external stimuli. Imagine a participant sitting quietly in a dimly lit room who is instructed to just relax. Most people in this situation exhibit very little in the way of autonomic nervous system activity. However, some participants in this situation exhibit spontaneous electrodermal responses, even though there is nothing objectively causing these responses. Not surprisingly, the personality traits most consistently associated with nonspecific electrodermal responding are anxiety and neuroticism (Cruz & Larsen, 1994). A person who is rated as high in anxiety and neuroticism appears to have a sympathetic nervous system that is in a state of chronic activation. This is just one example of how electrodermal measures have been used by personality psychologists to ascertain differences in personality between people.

Cardiovascular Activity

The cardiovascular system involves the heart and associated blood vessels, and examples of measures of cardiovascular activity include blood pressure and heart rate. Blood pressure is the pressure exerted by the blood on the inside of the artery walls, and it is typically expressed with two numbers: diastolic and systolic pressure. The systolic pressure is the larger number, and it refers to the maximum pressure within the cardiovascular system produced when the heart muscle contracts. The diastolic pressure is the smaller number, and it refers to the resting pressure inside the system between heart contractions. Blood pressure can increase in a number of ways—for example, the heart may pump with larger strokes generating more volume or through a narrowing of the artery walls. Both of these actions occur through activation of the sympathetic nervous system in the fight-or-flight response. While blood pressure is responsive to a number of conditions, personality researchers have been especially interested in blood pressure response to stress.

Another easily obtained cardiovascular measure is heart rate, often expressed in beats-per-minute (BPM). Heart rate can change beat by beat, so a technique with a degree of sophistication is needed to ensure accurate measurement. One approach is to measure the time interval between successive beats. If that interval is exactly one second, then the heart rate is 60 BPM. As the time interval between beats becomes shorter, the heart is beating faster, and vice versa. By measuring the intervals between successive heartbeats, the psychologist can get a readout of heart rate on a beat-by-beat basis. Heart rate is important because, as it increases, it indicates that the person's body is preparing for action—to flee or to fight, for example. It tells us that the person is distressed, anxious, fearful, or otherwise more aroused than normal. Heart rate also increases with cognitive effort, as when people try to solve a difficult math problem. People differ from each other in heart rate responses, with some showing large increases and others only minor increases, in response to the same stimuli or task.

Researchers have been interested in what happens to a person's cardiovascular system when he or she is challenged by having to perform a stressful task in front of an audience. One technique used to induce temporary stress is to have participants perform backwards serial subtraction (e.g., "take the number 784 and subtract 7, take the result and subtract 7, and keep doing so until you are told to stop"). Having to carry out a serial subtraction task is stressful, especially if the experimenter is standing there, writing down the answers and telling the participant to "work faster, come on, I know you can try harder." Not surprisingly, everyone's blood pressure and heart rate goes up during this task, but some people show much larger increases than others. This phenomenon has been called **cardiac reactivity** and has been associated with the **Type A personality**—a behavior pattern characterized by impatience, competitiveness, and hostility. Evidence suggests that chronic cardiac reactivity contributes to coronary artery disease, which may be why the Type A personality trait, especially the hostility part of being Type A, is associated with a higher likelihood of heart disease and heart attacks. The relation between cardiovascular reactivity and Type A is one example of how physiological measures have been used in the study of personality.

Brain Activity

The brain spontaneously produces small amounts of electricity, which can be measured by electrodes placed on the scalp. This measure is called the electroencephalogram (EEG), and EEG recordings can be obtained for various regions of the brain while the participant is asleep, is relaxed but awake, or is doing a task. Such measures of regional brain activity can provide useful information about patterns of activation in various regions of the brain, which may be associated with different types of information-processing tasks (e.g., processing verbal versus spatial information, as in receiving directions from someone verbally or being shown a map of where to go). Personality psychologists have been especially interested in whether different regions of the brain show different activity for different people (e.g., introverts versus extraverts).

Another technique in measuring brain activity is called the evoked potential technique, in which the brain EEG is measured but the participant is given a stimulus, such as a tone or a flash of light, and the researcher assesses the participant's brain responsiveness to the stimulus. Several examples of how measurement of brain activity has contributed to our understanding of personality differences will be presented in the section on brain asymmetry in this chapter.

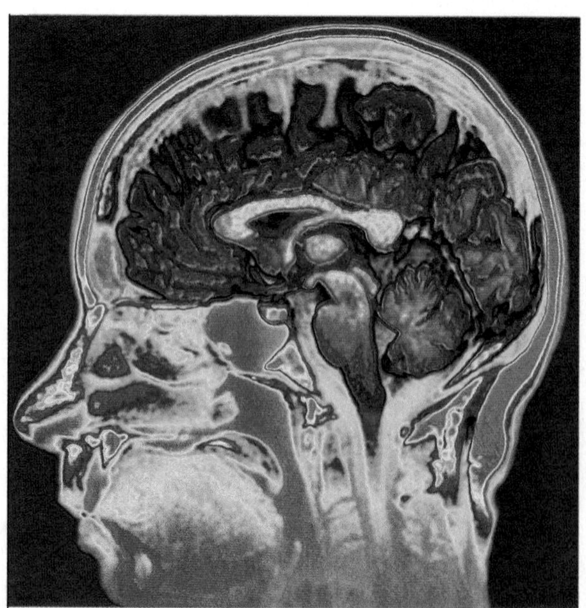

Regions of the brain communicate with each other, and with other parts of the body, using electrical signals. Brain imaging techniques enable researchers to listen in on these communications.

The powerful brain imaging techniques currently being developed and perfected are another class of physiological measures useful in personality research. For example, positron emission tomography (PET) and functional magnetic resonance imaging (fMRI) are noninvasive imaging techniques used for mapping the structure and function of the brain. In fact, the 2003 Nobel prize for medicine was awarded to two researchers—Paul C. Lauterbur and Sir Peter Mansfield—for their discoveries leading to the development of fast **functional magnetic resonance imaging (fMRI).** This powerful imaging tool, which was developed primarily for medical diagnosis, allows physicians and researchers to look inside the working brains of their patients and subjects. This tool can show which portions of the brain are active while the person is performing a particular task. For example, if we wanted to know what part of the brain is involved in memory, we would have a sample of people perform a memory task (such as remember a phone number for 5 minutes) while their brains were scanned by fMRI.

Powerful brain imaging techniques are now being applied to the study of personality. An important study was published by Canli and colleagues (2001) in which they used fMRI to scan the brains of people as they looked at 20 negative pictures (e.g., spiders, people crying) and 20 positive pictures (a happy couple, cute puppies). They found specific brain changes associated with viewing the different emotion-inducing photographs. More important, however, they found that personality correlated with the degree of brain activation in response to the positive and negative images. Specifically, neuroticism correlated with increased frontal brain activation to the negative images, and extraversion correlated with increased frontal brain activation to the positive images. Correlations between personality and other brain structures were also found, and the pattern of findings is consistent with the notion that personality is associated with brain reactivity to emotional stimuli. The full report is posted on the Web by the American Psychological Association, at http://www.apa.org/journals/bne/bne115133.html. Brain imaging tools are very likely to revolutionize what we know about the brain and personality over the next few years, making this a particularly exciting area of research (Canli & Amin, 2002).

Other Measures

Although skin conductance, heart rate, and brain activity are the most commonly used measures in physiological studies of personality, other biological measures have also proven useful. One important class of measures includes biochemical analyses of blood and saliva. For example, from saliva samples, biochemists can extract indicators of how competently a person's immune system is functioning (Miller & Cohen, 2001). The quality of immune system functioning may go up and down with stress or emotions and thereby may relate to personality. Hormones, such as testosterone, that play a role in important behaviors can also be extracted from saliva samples. Testosterone has been linked to uninhibited, aggressive, and risk-taking behavior patterns (Dabbs & Dabbs, 2000). Cortisol, a by-product of the hormone noradrenaline, can be readily assessed from saliva samples. Researchers have found, for example, that shy children have high levels of cortisol in their systems (Kagan & Snidman, 1991), suggesting that they experience more stress than less shy children. Monoamine oxidase (MAO) is an enzyme found in the blood that is known to regulate neurotransmitters, the chemicals that carry messages between nerve cells. MAO may be a causal factor in the personality trait of sensation seeking. Other theories of personality are based directly on different amounts of neurotransmitters in the nervous system, and we will briefly touch on these in the section on sensation seeking.

Physiologically Based Theories of Personality

Now that we have covered some of the basic physiological measures used in personality research, we will turn to some of the theories that have generated interest and attention among personality psychologists. We will begin with what is perhaps the most widely studied physiological theory of personality—the theory that proposes a biological explanation for why some people are introverted and others extraverted.

Extraversion–Introversion

Among the people you know, someone probably fits the following description: is talkative and outgoing, likes meeting new people and going new places, is active, is sometimes impulsive and venturesome, gets bored easily, and hates routine and monotony. Such a person would score as an extravert on an extraversion–introversion questionnaire. See Table 7.1 for items from a popular extraversion–introversion questionnaire—the Eysenck Personality Inventory.

You probably also know someone who is just the opposite, someone who is quiet and withdrawn, who prefers being alone or with a few friends to being in large crowds, who prefers routines and schedules, and who prefers the familiar to the unexpected. Such a person would score in the introverted direction on an extraversion–introversion questionnaire. If you are wondering *why* introverts and extraverts are so different from

Table 7.1 Items from the Eysenck Personality Questionnaire Extraversion Scale

Extraversion Items

For every question, circle just one response.

YES	NO	Are you a talkative person?
YES	NO	Are you rather lively?
YES	NO	Can you usually let yourself go and enjoy yourself at a lively party?
YES	NO	Do you enjoy meeting new people?
YES	NO	Do you tend to keep in the background on social occasions? (reversed)
YES	NO	Do you like going out a lot?
YES	NO	Do you prefer reading to meeting people? (reversed)
YES	NO	Do you have many friends?
YES	NO	Would you call yourself happy-go-lucky?
YES	NO	Do you usually take the initiative in making new friends?
YES	NO	Are you mostly quiet when you are with other people? (reversed)
YES	NO	Can you easily get some life into a rather dull party?
YES	NO	Do you like telling jokes and funny stories to your friends?
YES	NO	Do you like mixing with people?
YES	NO	Do you nearly always have a "ready answer" when people talk to you?
YES	NO	Do you like doing things in which you have to act quickly?
YES	NO	Can you get a party going?
YES	NO	Do you like plenty of bustle and excitement around you?
YES	NO	Do other people think of you as very lively?

Scoring directions: reverse your answers to the items marked "reversed"; then count how many questions you endorsed with a "yes." The average college student scores about 11 on this questionnaire.

Source: Eysenck, S. B. G., Eysenck, H. J., & Barrett, P. (1985). A revised version of the Psychoticism scale. *Personality & Individual Differences,* 6, 21–29.

Are you a talkative person? Do you like mixing with people? Do you like plenty of bustle and excitement around you? Answering "No" to such questions suggests an introverted personality.

Do you like telling jokes and funny stories to your friends? Do you like mixing with people? Can you get a party going? Answering "Yes" to such questions suggests an extraverted personality. Interestingly, Eysenck's extraversion–introversion theory is based not on a need to be with people, but rather on a need for arousal and stimulation.

each other, physiologically minded personality psychologists have an intriguing explanation: Eysenck's theory.

A classic example of a physiologically based theory of personality was put forward by H. J. Eysenck (1967) in his book *The Biological Basis of Personality*. Eysenck proposed that introverts are characterized by higher levels of activity in the brain's **ascending reticular activating system (ARAS)** than are extraverts. The ARAS is a structure in the brainstem thought to control overall cortical arousal. In the 1960s, the ARAS was thought of as a gateway through which nervous stimulation entered the cortex. If the gate was somewhat closed, then the resting **arousal level** of the cortex would be lower, and if the gate was more open, then the resting arousal level would be higher. Introverts, according to this theory, have higher resting levels of cortical arousal because their ARAS lets in too much stimulation. Introverts engage in introverted behaviors (are quiet and seek low-stimulation settings, such as libraries) because they need to keep their already heightened level of arousal in check. Conversely, extraverts engage in extraverted behaviors because they need to increase their level of arousal (Claridge et al., 1981).

Eysenck also incorporated Hebb's (1955) notion of "optimal level of arousal" into his theory. By optimal level of arousal, Hebb meant a level that is just right for any given task. For example, imagine going into a final exam in an underaroused state (e.g., sleepy, tired). Being sleepy and underaroused would be just as bad for your performance as going into the exam in an overaroused state (e.g., extremely anxious and agitated). There is an optimal level of arousal for taking an exam, one in which you are focused, alert, and attentive, but not aroused to the point of anxiety. Figure 7.2 presents a graph of the optimal arousal curve, also known as the Yerkes-Dodson law.

If introverts have a higher baseline level of arousal than extraverts (i.e., level of arousal while at rest), then introverts are above their optimal level of arousal more often than extraverts. According to the theory, the generally overaroused condition of introverts leads them to be more restrained and inhibited. They avoid active social interactions that might aggravate their already overstimulated condition. Extraverts, on the other hand, need to get their arousal level higher and, so, seek out stimulating

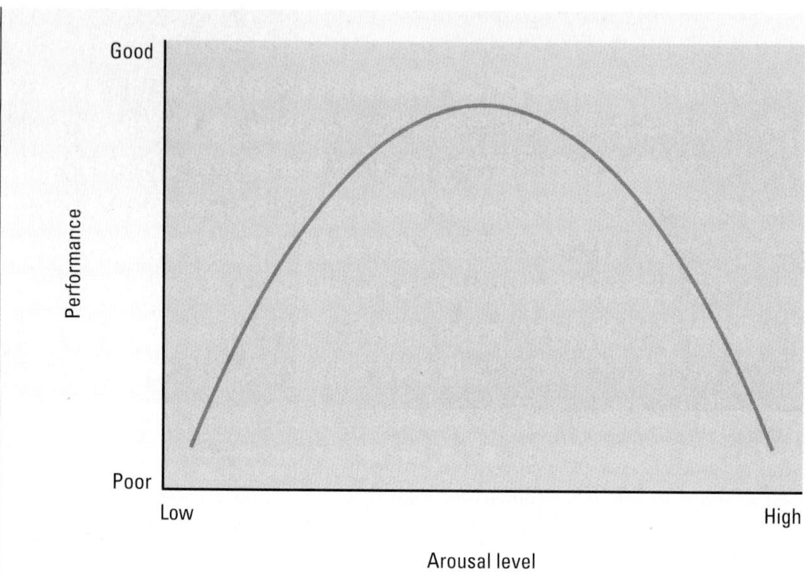

Figure 7.2
Optimal arousal curve.

activities and engage in more unrestrained behaviors. The qualities that typically characterize introverts (e.g., quiet, withdrawn) and extraverts (e.g., outgoing, engaging) are understood to be attempts to regulate arousal downward (in the case of introverts) or upward (in the case of extraverts) to maintain an optimal level of arousal.

In the decades following the publication of Eysenck's theory, many studies were conducted to test it (see reviews by Eysenck, 1991; Matthews & Gilliland, 1999; and Stelmack, 1990). If it is true that introverts are more cortically aroused than extraverts, then introverts should display enhanced responsiveness on measures of cortical activity, such as the electroencephalogram (EEG), as well as on measures of autonomic nervous system activity, such as electrodermal response. Studies designed to test this hypothesis typically have taken the form of comparing introverts with extraverts on physiological measures gathered under conditions of various degrees of stimulation (Gale, 1986). In conditions where participants were presented with either no stimulation or very mild stimulation, differences between introverts and extraverts turned out to be small or nonexistent. However, in studies that looked at nervous system responsiveness to moderate levels of stimulation, introverts showed larger or faster responses than extraverts, as predicted by Eysenck's theory (Bullock & Gilliland, 1993; Gale, 1983).

The fact that introverts and extraverts are not different at resting levels, but *are* different under moderate levels of stimulation, led Eysenck to a revise his arousal theory (Eysenck & Eysenck, 1985). When he first stated his theory in 1967, Eysenck did not distinguish between resting, or *baseline,* levels of arousal and arousal *responses* to stimulation. A good deal of evidence now suggests that the real difference between introverts and extraverts lies in their **arousability,** or arousal response, not in their baseline arousal level. Extraverts and introverts do not differ in their level of brain activity while sleeping, for example, or while lying quietly in a darkened room with their eyes shut (Stelmack, 1990). However, when presented with moderate levels of stimulation, introverts show enhanced physiological reactivity, compared with extraverts (Gale, 1987).

Imagine that an introvert and an extravert have to do a monotonous task, such as monitoring a computer display of the operating status of a nuclear power plant. The display does not change much, so the stimulation level is very low, and the situation is rather monotonous and boring. Eysenck's theory would predict that the introvert would remain more alert and perform better in this situation and that the extravert would be relatively underaroused and most likely bored to sleep. However, now imagine an emergency at the nuclear power plant, with sirens blasting, lights flashing, and people running and shouting. In such a high arousal situation, it is likely that the extravert would perform better, due to the introvert's tendency toward overarousal in response to stimulation.

Exercise

***The Lemon Juice Demonstration:* This demonstration is designed to illustrate that introverts are more reactive to stimulation than extraverts. While some teachers have tried this in the classroom, it can be a bit messy and so might best be done as a thought experiment to illustrate the point in individual differences in reactivity. Here is how it would go: Take a double-tipped cotton swab and tie a thread exactly in its center so that it hangs perfectly in balance (i.e., is horizontal). Swallow three times and put one end on your tongue for exactly 20 seconds. After removing the swab, place 4 drops of lemon juice under your tongue. Place the other end of the cotton swab on your tongue for 20 seconds. Remove the swab and let it hang by the thread. If you are an extravert it is likely that the swab will remain horizontal, indicating that you did not react strongly to the lemon juice by producing more saliva. If you are an introvert, it is likely that the swab will no longer balance horizontally and will instead be heavier on the end placed on the tongue following the lemon juice. This would indicate that you produced more saliva in response to the lemon juice. Eysenck conducted a similar experiment (Eysenck & Eysenck, 1967) as did Corcoran, 1964.**

An important corollary of the theory is that, when given a choice, extraverts should prefer higher levels of stimulation than do introverts. Indirect evidence supports this prediction. For example, laboratory studies have shown that extraverts will press a button at a higher rate than introverts when the button pressing produces changes in the visual environment (such as change the channel on a TV, change the slide on a projector) (e.g., Brebner & Cooper, 1978). In a more naturalistic study, done in a university library, persons studying in a noisy reading room scored as more extraverted than did students studying in the quieter rooms (Campbell & Hawley, 1982). Findings such as these suggest that, when given a choice, extraverts tend to seek greater levels of stimulation than introverts.

A clever study designed by psychologist Russell Geen (1984) tested the hypothesis that, although introverts should choose lower levels of stimulation than extraverts, these two groups should nevertheless be equivalent in physiological arousal when performing under their chosen levels of stimulation. However, when extraverts are given the level of stimulation chosen by introverts, they should be underaroused and bored and should perform poorly on the task. When introverts are given the level of stimulation chosen by extraverts, they should be overaroused and distressed and perform poorly on the task. The predictions are complex—take a look at this study on pages 218–219, A Closer Look.

A Closer Look The Geen Study

Participants in the Geen (1984) study were selected on the basis of their answers to the extraversion scale of the Eysenck Personality Inventory (the items presented in Table 7.1 in the text). Thirty high-scoring participants formed the extraverted group, and 30 low-scoring participants formed the introverted group. Participants reported to the laboratory one at a time, whereupon they were told they would be participating in an experiment on the effects of noise on learning. Each participant was given a difficult paired-associates learning task, in which they guessed which word, from a pair of words, was selected by the experimenter according to some rule, and he or she had to learn the rule. The rules were "all words referring to animals," "all words that begin with a vowel," or "all words that are names of colors." During the time they were engaged in this task, the participants were having their heart rate and skin conductance measured.

Before starting the experiment, however, the participants were told they would have to perform the learning task while listening to random bursts of noise over headphones. One-third (10 introverts and 10 extraverts) were allowed to select the level of noise that they would hear over the headphones. Participants in this *choice* condition listened to the noise and turned a dial to adjust the volume of the noise. They were instructed to adjust the volume control upward until the intensity was "just right" for them in terms of working on the difficult task. Participants were told that they were not allowed to choose a perfectly quiet noise setting, although two participants (both introverts) inquired about this possibility before the complete instructions were given.

There were two control conditions in this study. In one control condition, called the *assigned-same* condition, one-third of the introverts and extraverts were subjected to the noise levels selected by previous introvert or extravert participants, respectively. In the other control condition, called the *assigned-other* condition, the final one-third of the introverts and extraverts experienced the noise levels selected by previous extraverts and introverts, respectively. Participants in this condition had to perform under the noise level selected by the most recently run participant from the *other* personality group. These two control conditions make this experiment an unusually strong one.

The results concerning the choice of noise intensity were as predicted, with extraverted participants choosing significantly louder levels of noise than introverts. The noise level chosen by the extraverts averaged 72 decibels, and the noise level chosen by the introverts averaged 55 decibels. The results for heart rate and skin conductance are displayed in Figure 7.3. When working under the noise levels selected by themselves or by someone from their personality group, there were no differences between introverts and extraverts.

Personality differences are seen, however, when we look at introverts working under conditions selected by extraverts and extraverts working under conditions selected by introverts. Under these conditions, the introverts showed evidence of greater arousal, compared with the extraverts. At the introvert-selected noise level, the extraverts were least aroused—in fact, probably bored. When subjected to the noisier, extravert-selected level of loudness, the extraverts' arousal level went up, but the introverts' went up to an even higher level. What the extraverts found just right, the introverts found overarousing.

As far as performance on the learning task was concerned, the introverts assigned to the noisy, extravert-selected volume had the poorest performance. Introverts in the noisy, extravert-selected condition took an average of 9.1 trials to learn the association, but only 5.8 trials to learn it in the quieter, introvert-chosen condition. This decrease in performance was probably due to the fact that the louder noise levels overstimulated the introverts. The extraverts, on the other hand, performed quite well under the noisy conditions, averaging only 5.4 trials to learn the association. Under the quieter, introvert-selected noise levels, the extraverts performed only somewhat worse, averaging 7.3 trials to learning.

This study is important because it clearly demonstrates that the extraverts preferred more intense stimulation than did the introverts. What the extravert finds just right is overarousing to the introvert and leads to poorer performance. Similarly, what the introvert finds just right leads to decreases in arousal and performance in the extravert. The best performance for both introverts and extraverts occurs when stimulation is provided at the appropriate level of intensity for each group.

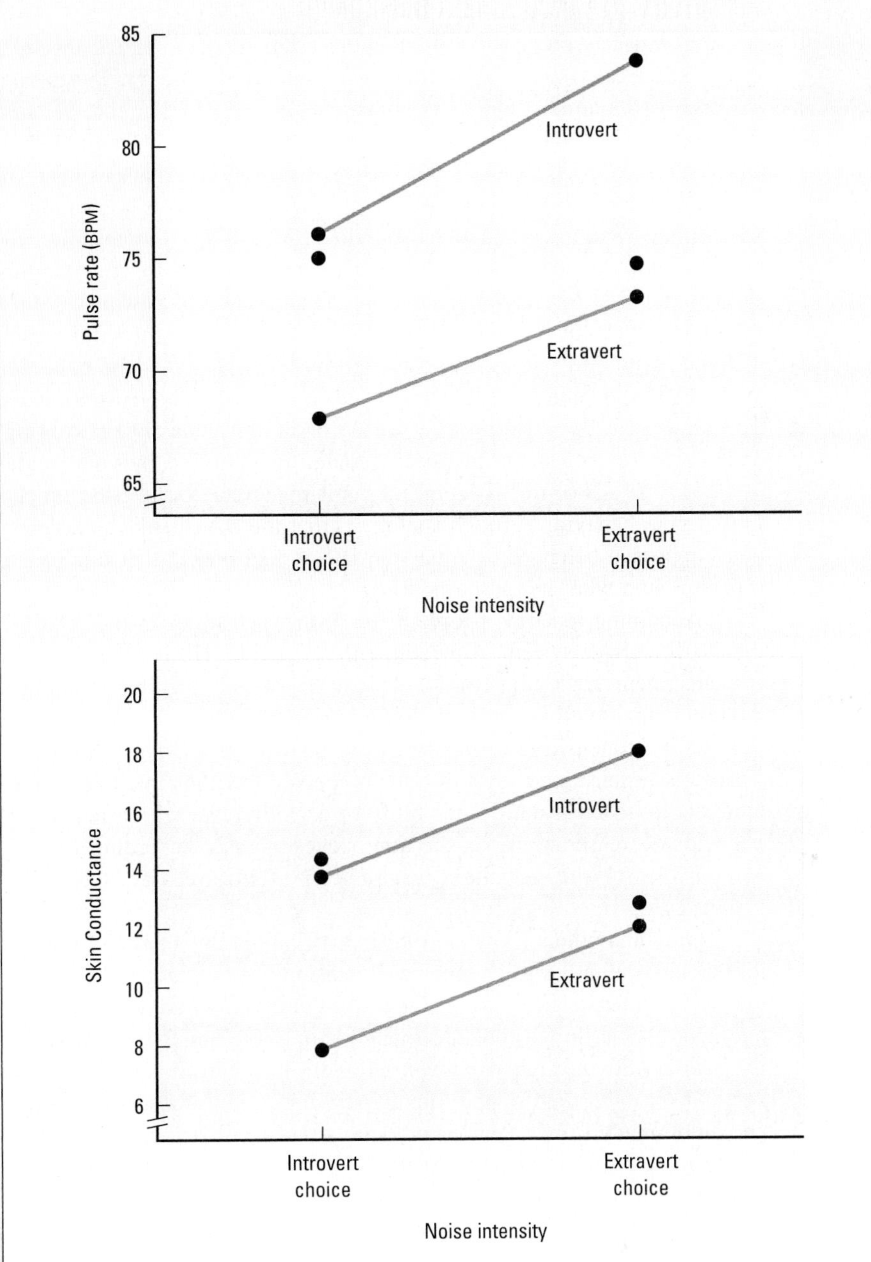

Figure 7.3

Results from Geen's study of preferred stimulation levels in introverts and extraverts. Unconnected dots are the Assigned-Same Conditions.

Sensitivity to Reward and Punishment

Jeffrey Gray has proposed an influential alternative biological theory of personality (Gray, 1972, 1990), called **reinforcement sensitivity theory.** Based on brain function research with animals, Gray has constructed a model of human personality based on two hypothesized biological systems in the brain. The first is the **behavioral activation system (BAS),** which is responsive to incentives, such as cues for reward, and regulates approach behavior. When the BAS recognizes a stimulus as potentially rewarding, it triggers approach behavior. For example, as a child, you might have learned about an ice cream truck that made deliveries to your neighborhood while playing music. When you heard that music (cues of reward), your BAS created the urge to run out into the street to find the ice cream truck (approach motivation). The other system in the brain postulated by Gray (1975) is the **behavioral inhibition system (BIS),** which is responsive to cues for punishment, frustration, and uncertainty. The effect of BIS activation is to cease or inhibit behavior or to bring about avoidance behavior. You may have been scolded or punished by your mother for running into the street. The street becomes a punishment cue to the BIS, which causes you to inhibit your behavior. A rough analogy is that the BAS is like an accelerator that motivates approach behavior, whereas the BIS is like brakes that inhibit behavior or help a person stop what he or she is doing.

According to Gray, people differ from each other in the relative sensitivity of their BIS or BAS system. A person with a reactive BIS is especially sensitive to cues of punishment, frustration, or novelty. He or she is vulnerable to unpleasant emotions, including anxiety, fear, and sadness. According to Gray, the BIS is responsible for the personality dimension of **anxiety.** A person with a reactive BAS, on the other hand, is especially sensitive to reward. Such a person is vulnerable to positive emotions and tends to approach stimuli. The ability of an individual with a reactive BAS to inhibit behavior decreases as he or she approaches a goal. According to Gray, the BAS is responsible for the personality dimension of **impulsivity,** the inability to inhibit responses.

Gray and others (Fowles, 1987) have framed this model of impulsivity and anxiety as an alternative to Eysenck's dimensions of extraversion and neuroticism. This alternative interpretation is presented in Figure 7.4. In Gray's model, the extraversion and neuroticism dimensions are rotated about 30 degrees from anxiety and impulsivity. Those who are highly extraverted and a bit neurotic are seen as the most impulsive. At the other end of the impulsivity dimension are persons who are introverted and emotionally stable. Persons who are a bit introverted and highly neurotic are seen as the most prone to anxiety. At the other end of the anxiety dimension are persons who are extraverted and emotionally stable.

Some debate has focused on exactly where to locate BAS (impulsivity) and BIS (anxiety) in the conceptual space defined by Eysenck's dimensions of extraversion and introversion (Gomez, Cooper, & Gomez, 2000; Zuckerman et al., 1999). In fact, one of the authors of this book has had a series of exchanges with Gray and his colleagues about this issue (Pickering, Corr, & Gray, 1999; Rusting & Larsen, 1997, 1999). It appears that the relation between Gray's constructs and Eysenck's constructs is direct, with BAS being equivalent to extraversion and BIS being equivalent to neuroticism. In fact, the Canli et al. (2001) study cited earlier showed that the brains of extraverts (compared to introverts) were more reactive to pleasant, rewarding images and the brains of persons high on neuroticism are more reactive (than those low on neuroticism) to images associated with negative emotions. Many researchers

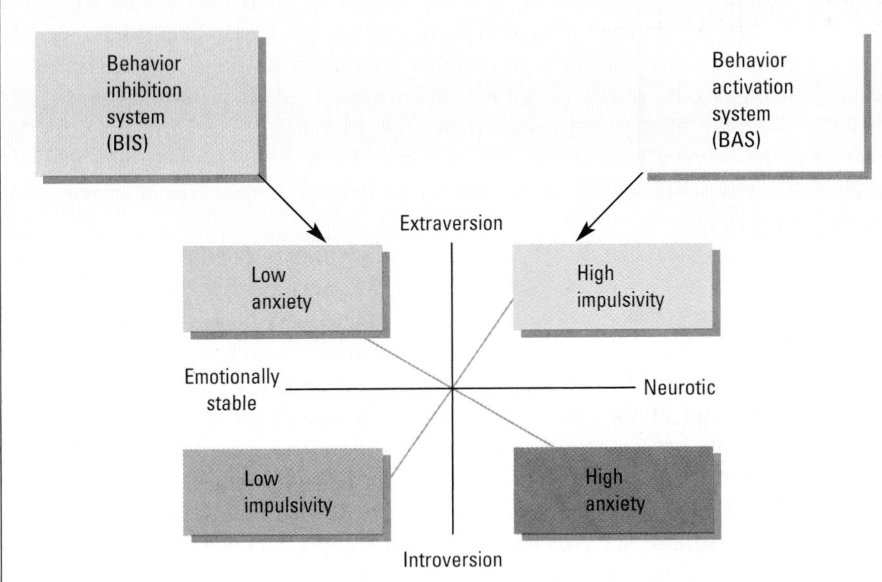

Figure 7.4

Relation between Eysenck's dimensions of extraversion and neuroticism and Gray's dimensions of impulsivity and anxiety.

view the BIS and BAS constructs as similar to neuroticism and extraversion in that both refer to dispositional tendencies to withdraw from punishment or to approach reward, respectively (e.g., Davidson, 2003; Kosslyn et al., 2002; Sutton, 2002). Gray has revised his model and now locates BIS much closer to neuroticism and locates BAS much closer to extraversion (Pickering et al., 1999).

Gray believes that differences between people in sensitivity to reward and punishment are responsible for generating the varieties of behavior associated with being anxious/neurotic and with being impulsive/extraverted. If we ask why some people are more susceptible than others to anxiety attacks, fears, worry, depressions, phobias, obsessions, or compulsions, Gray would argue that their susceptibility is due to an overly sensitive behavioral inhibition system. Such people tend to notice and are sensitive to punishment and other frustrations. Moreover, they are distressed by uncertainty and novelty. Then, if we ask why some people are more susceptible than others to positive emotions, to approach behaviors, to seeking out and interacting with others, Gray would argue that this is due to an overly sensitive behavioral activation system.

One team of researchers, stimulated by Gray's theory, constructed a questionnaire to measure BIS sensitivity—a tendency toward anxiety and fearfulness and the avoidance of uncertainty and risk (MacAndrew & Steele, 1991). The researchers identified a high and a low fearful group and determined which questions discriminated between the groups. Some examples of questions on this questionnaire are "I have been quite independent and free from family rule," "I am entirely self-confident," and "I do not blame a person for taking advantage of someone who lays himself open to it." For the high BIS group, the researchers selected a group of female psychiatric patients who had a history of anxiety and panic attacks. The low BIS group called for a sample of persons who had little regard for their own safety, who took risks and disregarded danger. To represent this group, the researchers used a sample of convicted prostitutes—persons who regularly engaged in illegal, high-risk sexual and drug-taking behavior. The prostitutes and anxiety patients were found to be significantly different in their responses to the questionnaire. The prostitutes scored lower than the anxiety patients on this measure. Such a finding indicates that the questionnaire has some validity as a measure of tolerance for risky situations, danger, and fearlessness.

A second research group making use of Gray's theory consists of psychologist Charles Carver and his colleagues (Carver, Sutton, & Scheier, 1999; Carver & White, 1994). Carver and White (1994) developed and validated a scale to measure individual differences in the strength of the BIS and BAS. Other researchers are adding to the validity evidence behind this scale. For example, Zelenski and Larsen (1999) found this scale to be one of the best measures of BIS and BAS. Carver et al. (1999) reviewed Gray's theory, emphasizing individual differences in approach or incentive motivation (extraversion or impulsivity) and individual differences in withdrawal or aversive motivation (neuroticism or anxiety). They showed how several programs of research can be integrated into the theme that humans appear to possess separate systems for responding to incentives and threats. For example, these systems show reliable individual differences, they relate to major affective dispositions, they may be lateralized in our cerebral architecture, and they may relate differently to learning by punishment and learning by reward. Carver and his colleagues consider these the "Big Two" personality dimensions. This review paper shows the remarkable integrating power of Gray's theory of personality.

Gray has primarily conducted research with animals. With animals, you can use drugs or surgery to eliminate certain areas of the brain, then test whether this affects the animal's ability to learn through punishment or reward. Gray's theory relates anxiety and impulsivity to the two principles of learning: reinforcement (both positive and negative) and punishment (and the loss of reinforcement). There is some evidence that these two forms of learning are under separate neural control. It appears likely that different brain mechanisms may be involved when a person or an animal learns through reinforcement or through punishment (Gray, 1991). Thus, there should be people with varying degrees of sensitivity (high, medium, or low) to punishment and to reward.

In a study of reward and punishment, participants were required to complete hundreds of trials of a difficult reaction time task (Larsen, Chen, & Zelenski, 2003). They had to name the colors of words that popped up on a computer screen as quickly and accurately as possible. It is a difficult task, and people can get only about half the trials correct given that they have to respond in less than one second on each trial. One group was rewarded for each correct and fast response, and they earned 5 dollars during the course of a 20-minute experiment. Another group was punished after incorrect or slow responses and, though they started the experiment with 10 dollars, proceeded to lose 5 dollars. As such, everyone finished the experiment with 5 dollars, but one group was rewarded on a trial-by-trial basis whereas the other group was punished on a trial-by-trial basis. It turned out that BAS scores predicted better performance in the reward condition, with high BAS persons working faster and becoming more accurate when they were working for reward. BIS scores, on the other hand, predicted performance in the punishment condition, with high-BIS persons responding with better performance when they were being punished, compared to low BIS participants.

Much of the work carried out to test Gray's theory has focused on impulsivity (the inability to inhibit responses). Our jails are full of people who are deficient in the ability to control their behavior, especially behavior that may be immediately rewarding. For example, a 17-year-old male sees an expensive sports car parked on the street. As he looks at the car and thinks about how much fun it would be to drive, he notices that the keys are in the ignition. The owner appears nowhere in sight and the street is fairly deserted. He starts to reach for the door handle. The ability to stop this approach behavior, even though it is immediately rewarding, separates the average person from the impulsive person.

Impulsive individuals can be characterized as having stronger approach than avoidance tendencies and are less able to inhibit approach behavior, especially in the presence of desirable goals or rewards. You probably know someone who often says things that get them into trouble or who hurts other people's feelings without even thinking. Even though they know they might hurt someone's feelings and feel bad themselves (i.e., are "punished" by feelings of remorse), why can't they control what they do and say?

According to Gray's theory, impulsive people do not learn well from punishment because they have a weak behavioral inhibition system. If this is true, then researchers should be able to demonstrate that, in a task that involves learning from punishment, impulsive persons do less well than nonimpulsive persons. Studies have been conducted on impulsive college students, juvenile delinquents, psychopaths, and criminals in jail (Newman, 1987; Newman, Widom, & Nathan, 1985). The typical finding is that such persons are, in fact, deficient in learning through punishment. For example, when impulsive persons play a game of chance and are *punished* for wrong responses, they learn more slowly than when playing the same game but are *rewarded* for correct responses. Impulsive persons, it seems, do not learn as well from punishment as from reward.

Let's say you have a roommate and would like to teach her to clean her part of the apartment. You could try rewarding with candy and praise every time she picked something up. Or you could try punishing by yelling and scolding every time she left something out of place. If your roommate is an impulsive person, chances are that you would do better using the reward strategy than the punishment strategy. On the other hand, if your roommate is an anxious person, it might be more effective to use punishment than reward.

Exercise

Think of a situation in which you are trying to teach someone something new. Discuss an example of how you might use reward to teach that behavior. Then discuss how you might use mild punishment to teach the same behavior.

Sensation Seeking

Sensation seeking is another dimension of personality postulated to have a physiological basis. Sensation seeking is the tendency to seek out thrilling and exciting activities, to take risks, and to avoid boredom. Research on the need for sensory input grew out of studies on **sensory deprivation.** Let's begin, then, with a description of sensory deprivation research.

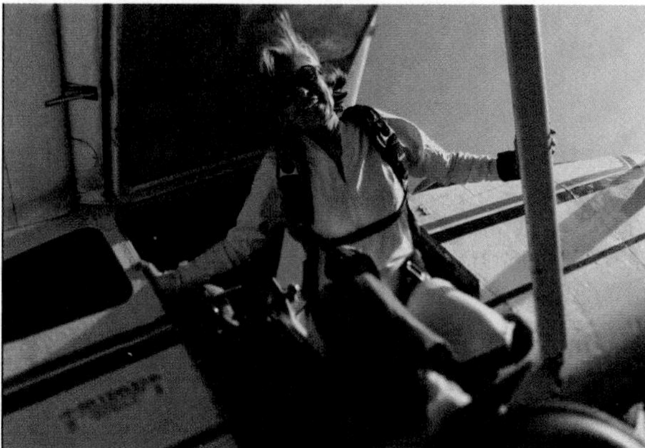
The theory of sensation seeking was proposed to explain why some people routinely seek out thrilling experiences, even though such experiences may come with certain risks.

Imagine volunteering for a study in which you are put into a small chamber, where there is no light, no sound, and only minimal tactile sensations. Imagine further that you agree to do this for 12 hours straight. What would this experience be like? Research suggests that at first you would feel relaxed, then bored, then anxious as you started to hallucinate and have delusions. Early research by Hebb (1955) showed that, in such a situation, college students chose to listen over and over to a taped lecture intended to convince 6-year-olds about the dangers of alcohol. Other participants in these early sensory deprivation experiments who were offered a recording of an old stock market report opted to listen to it over and over again, apparently to avoid the unpleasant consequences of sensory deprivation. Persons in sensory deprived environments appear motivated to acquire *any* sensory input, even if ordinarily such input would be perceived as boring.

Hebb's Theory of Optimal Level of Arousal

Hebb developed the theory of **optimal level of arousal,** which was used by Eysenck in his theory of extraversion. Hebb's theory states that people are motivated to reach an optimal level of arousal. If they are underaroused, relative to this level, an increase in arousal is rewarding; conversely, if they are overaroused, a decrease in arousal is rewarding. For its time, Hebb's theory was controversial, since most researchers thought that tension *reduction* was the goal of all motives, yet Hebb was saying that we are motivated to *seek out* tension and stimulation. How else can we explain the fact that people *like* to work on puzzles, enjoy mild frustration, and occasionally take risks or do something to arouse mild fears, such as going on a roller coaster ride. Hebb's belief that people need stimulation and sensory input is consistent with the results of sensory deprivation research. The nervous system appears to need at least some sensory input.

Zuckerman's Research

Early on in sensory deprivation research, Zuckerman and Haber (1965) noted that some people were not as distressed as others by the sensory deprivation experience. In these early experiments, some people found sensory deprivation extremely unpleasant. These participants requested lots of sensory material (tapes, reading material) during the experiment and quit the experiment relatively early. Zuckerman believed that such persons had a particularly *high need for sensation* because they were the least tolerant of deprivation. He called them sensation seekers because they appeared to seek out stimulation, not just in the sensory deprivation experiment but in their everyday lives as well.

Zuckerman developed a questionnaire designed to measure the extent to which a person needs novel or exciting experiences and enjoys the thrills and excitement

Table 7.2 Items from the Sensation-Seeking Scale

There are several aspects of sensation seeking that are reflected in the items on this scale.

Thrill and adventure seeking—reflected in items that ask about desire for outdoor sports or activities involving elements of risk, such as flying, scuba diving, parachute jumping, motorcycle riding, and mountain climbing—for example, "I sometimes like to do things that are a little frightening" (high) versus "A sensible person avoids activities that are dangerous" (low).

Experience seeking—reflected in items that refer to the seeking of new sensory or mental experiences through unconventional or nonconforming lifestyle choices—for example, "I like to have new and exciting experiences and sensations even if they are frightening, unconventional, or illegal" (high) versus "I am not interested in experience for its own sake" (low).

Disinhibition—reflected in items indicating a preference for getting "out of control" or an interest in wild parties, gambling, and sexual variety—for example, "Almost everything enjoyable is illegal or immoral" (high) versus "The most enjoyable things are perfectly legal and moral" (low).

Boredom susceptibility—reflected in items that refer to a dislike for repetition, routine work, monotony, predictable and dull people, and a restlessness when things become unchanging—for example, "I get bored seeing the same old faces" (high) versus "I like the comfortable familiarity of everyday friends" (low).

All of the items on the Sensation-Seeking Scale, as well as scoring instructions, can be found in Zuckerman (1978).

associated with them. He called the questionnaire the Sensation-Seeking Scale, and items from it appear in Table 7.2. Zuckerman hypothesized that some people (high sensation seekers) require a lot of stimulation to reach their optimal level of arousal. Moreover, when deprived of stimulation and sensory input (as in a sensory deprivation chamber), such persons find that experience particularly unpleasant.

As it turned out, Zuckerman's questionnaire about preferences for stimulation in everyday life predicted how well people tolerated the sensory deprivation sessions. High sensation seekers found sensory deprivation to be particularly unpleasant, whereas low sensation seekers were able to tolerate it for longer periods of time. In the early 1960s, Zuckerman left the sensory deprivation laboratory and began to study the other unique characteristics associated with the personality dimension of sensation seeking. Notice that this theoretical explanation of sensation seeking is very similar to that Eysenck offered for extraversion. In fact, there is a moderately strong positive correlation between extraversion and sensation seeking.

In the 30-plus years that Zuckerman and his colleagues and others have been doing research on sensation seeking, many interesting findings have emerged. A number of these findings are consistent with the idea that high sensation seekers have a need for high levels of stimulation in their daily lives (reviewed in Zuckerman, 1978). Police officers who volunteer for riot duty have higher sensation-seeking scores on Zuckerman's scale than officers who do not volunteer for riot duty. Skydivers score higher on sensation-seeking measures than nonskydivers. Among college students who volunteered to be in psychology experiments, the students with high sensation-seeking scores volunteered to participate in the more unusual studies (studies on ESP, hypnosis, or drugs) than in the typical studies (on learning, sleep, or social interaction). In studies of gambling behavior, the participants with high sensation-seeking scores tended to make riskier bets. High sensation seekers also report having a larger

A Closer Look

Personality and Problem Behaviors: Gambling

Greg Hogan, age 19, was president of his sophomore class at Lehigh University in Pennsylvania and the son of a Baptist pastor. He played cello in the Lehigh orchestra, was a member of Sigma Phi Epsilon fraternity, and acted as an assistant to the university chaplain. On Dec. 9, 2005, Hogan walked into the Wachovia Bank in Allentown, PA, and passed a note to the teller, saying he was armed and wanted money. He walked out with $2,871. He then went to a movie, *The Chronicles of Narnia*, with two friends. Later that day, while preparing to go to rehearsal with his university orchestra, seven police cars surrounded his fraternity house. Greg Hogan never made it to rehearsal that evening. Instead, he was charged with bank robbery, arrested, and taken away in handcuffs. If convicted, he faces up to five years in jail.

Greg Hogan had run up over $5,000 in gambling debt, mostly at Internet gambling sites. Due to his gambling compulsion, he was in a desperate, but not unique, situation. A study done by PokerPlus.com estimates that more than 1.8 million people play online poker each month, wagering an average total of $200 million a day. Considering all forms of card gambling, more than 3 million students a week engage in gambling for money, according to the National Council on Problem Gambling estimates. This study also estimates that, out of every 10 college students who play poker regularly, two will develop an addiction. Of these gambling addicts, about 80 percent will commit a crime to fund their gambling debt. Many will contemplate suicide as a way out of their situation.

On Dec. 14, 2005, in a follow-up to the Greg Hogan story in the Lehigh student newspaper, *The Brown and White*, a reporter described the prevalence of gambling among Lehigh students. The story is probably similar at other universities. Several of the Lehigh fraternities have hosted gambling parties for years, but lately the gambling parties are more frequent and the stakes are higher: $40 to get into a poker game, with pots typically rising to $500 and higher. Internet gambling is rampant, especially among the male Lehigh students.

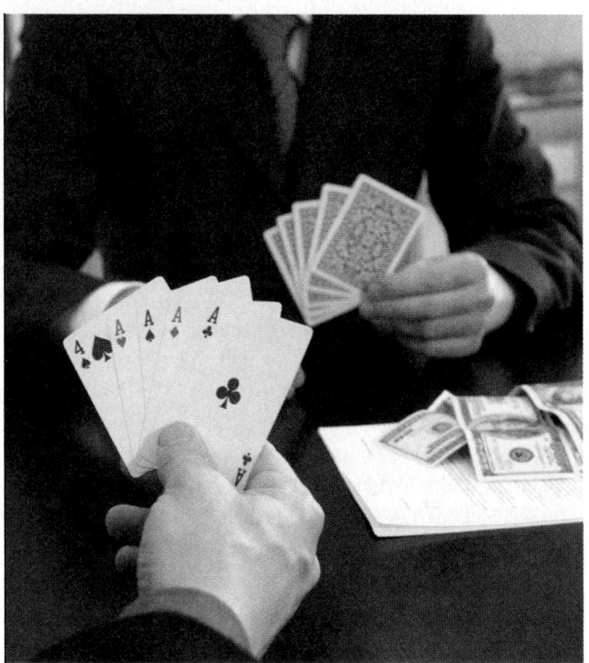

For some people playing cards is a form of recreation. For others, however, it can result in compulsive gambling.

The story describes Andrew, a student who bets on sports games over the Internet. Andrew often skips classes to watch sporting events he has bet on, and ignores homework in order to spend time juggling accounts on various betting sites. Like many students, Andrew also spends a vast amount of time playing online poker. On Nov. 6 he was up $250, but only briefly; he quickly lost that and more with continued gambling.

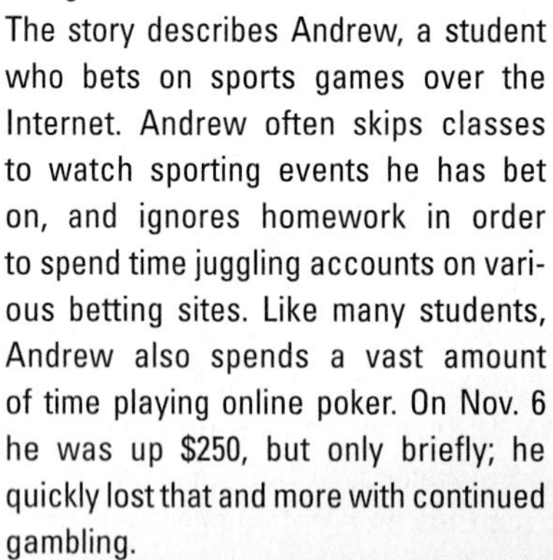

"I just have an addictive personality," Andrew says.

Is there any evidence for an "addictive personality"? Are certain people more prone than others to get hooked on gambling? Before answering this question, we briefly review the scope of the gambling problem in the United States. Pathological gambling disorder (PGD) is characterized by gambling behavior that is persistent over time and that causes significant problems in the person's life, such as with family members, or at school or work. The diagnosis of PGD is made when at least 5 out of 10 criteria are present (American Psychiatric Association, 1994). These criteria include a preoccupation with or inability to control or stop gambling, the need to gamble more often or to make larger bets to obtain a level of excitement, continuing to gamble despite problems, lying to conceal gambling involvement, committing illegal acts to obtain gambling money, "withdrawal" symptoms of restlessness irritability when unable to gamble, and gambling to escape negative moods. These criteria look very similar to criteria for drug and alcohol addictions.

Other gambling specific criteria include "chasing losses" (i.e., continuing to bet in an attempt to recover losses) and relying on others for financial help following gambling losses.

Studies in the United States report that the proportion of the population that will be diagnosable with PGD at some point in their lifetime is between 1 percent and 2.5 percent, with more recent studies obtaining percentages in the higher ranges (Cunningham-Williams et al., 2004). Problem gambling can be defined as meeting between 1 and 4 of the above criteria. The rate of problem gambling in the United States is 12.4 percent. However, 42 percent of the population has never or rarely (less than 5 times) gambled. So, if we take the 58 percent of Americans who do gamble at least recreationally, of these 4.3 percent will develop PGD and 21 percent will develop some problems with gambling (Cunningham-Williams et al., 2004). If all you know about someone is that they regularly gamble, then that person has at least a 4 percent chance of having PGD and a 21 percent chance of developing problems from gambling.

Pathological gambling behavior often co-occurs with other addictions, including nicotine dependence, cannabis use, drug addiction, and alcohol dependence (Slutske et al., 2000). In fact, persons with pathological or problem gambling are 2 to 4 times more likely to develop alcohol dependence than nongamblers. This is an example of **comorbidity,** where two or more disorders simultaneously occur within the same individual.

We return now to the question of whether any specific personality traits are associated with problem gambling. Several correlational studies have found that measures of impulsiveness and sensation seeking correlate with problem gambling (McDaniel & Zuckerman, 2003; Vitaro, Arsenault, & Tremblay, 1997). From correlational data, we don't really know if the personality traits are causing the gambling, or if gambling is causing people to become more impulsive and sensation seeking. In a recent longitudinal study, however, the psychologist Wendy Slutske and her colleagues (2006) found that problem gambling at age 21 was associated with the personality traits of risk taking and impulsivity at age 18. This study strengthens the conclusion that the personality traits of high impulsivity and risk taking (or sensation seeking) put a person at risk for developing problem gambling. Risk taking is a trait that refers to the desire for novelty, for thrills and excitement, and for experiences that provide a good deal of excitement. Impulsivity is a trait that refers to lowered self-control, especially in the presence of potentially rewarding fun activities, the tendency to act before one thinks, and a lowered ability to anticipate the consequences of one's behavior. These two traits also are associated with the risk of developing alcohol, drug, and nicotine dependence (Slutske et al., 2006).

Genetic studies suggest that the risk for developing problem gambling and the risk for developing other addictions (e.g., alcohol) may be explained by largely overlapping genetic risk factors. These genetic factors may give rise to the specific personality traits related to low behavioral control (impulsivity and risk taking), and these traits may in turn be responsible for the comorbidity of pathological gambling and other addictive disorders.

The Iowa Gambling Task is a laboratory procedure developed to study impulsivity and insensitivity to consequences. In this task, the subject is confronted with various decks of cards, from which they can choose. Some of the decks have very high initial rewards but also high punishments, such that over time the person drawing from these decks would lose money. Other decks have lower initial rewards, but also lower and less frequent punishments, such that if choices were made from these decks, the person would ultimately win money. Most people pick up on the pattern and learn to avoid the risky decks and select from the safer decks (less rewarding but also fewer losses). People with high levels of impulsive sensation seeking (Crone, Vende, & van der Molen, 2002), as well as people with alcohol and drug addictions (Bechara et al., 2001), often stay with the riskier decks and end up losing money. Interestingly, people with specific damage to their brains (in the region of the prefrontal cortex) also will stick with the riskier decks and not learn to avoid the frequent losses that come with the infrequent gains (Bechara, Tranel, & Damasio, 2000). Studies of age changes in the Iowa Gambling Task show that performance continues to improve through adolescence, consistent with findings that the prefrontal cortex continues to develop through adolescence (Hooper, Luciann, Conklin, & Yarger, 2004). By implication, adolescence is not a time one should be experimenting with gambling, since the brain centers that help one appreciate consequences are still developing.

In summary, even casual or recreational gambling can reach problem proportions for certain individuals. The personality traits of impulsivity and sensation seeking appear to put people at risk for developing gambling problems. Moreover, these traits also put people at risk for developing other addictions, such as alcohol, nicotine, and drug dependence. It may be that both the personality traits and addictive behaviors are expressions of a common genetic pathway. Moreover, this pathway may also be expressed in a specific brain area—the prefrontal cortex—that has been associated with the ability to anticipate consequences and to engage in self-regulation.

number of sex partners, engaging in a wider variety of sex acts, and beginning to have sex at an earlier age than low sensation seekers. The list of correlates of sensation seeking is quite long, and you may consult various reviews to learn more about this personality trait (e.g., Zuckerman, 1984, 1991).

According to Zuckerman, there is a physiological basis for sensation-seeking behavior. Zuckerman's more recent work (1991) focuses primarily on the role played by neurotransmitters in bringing about differences in sensation seeking. **Neurotransmitters** are chemicals in the nerve cells that are responsible for the transmission of a nerve impulse from one cell to another. As you may recall from your introductory psychology class, nerve cells are separated from one another by a slight gap, called a synapse. A nerve impulse must jump across this gap if it is to continue toward its destination. Neurotransmitters are the chemicals released by the nerves that allow nerve impulses to jump across the synapse and continue on their way.

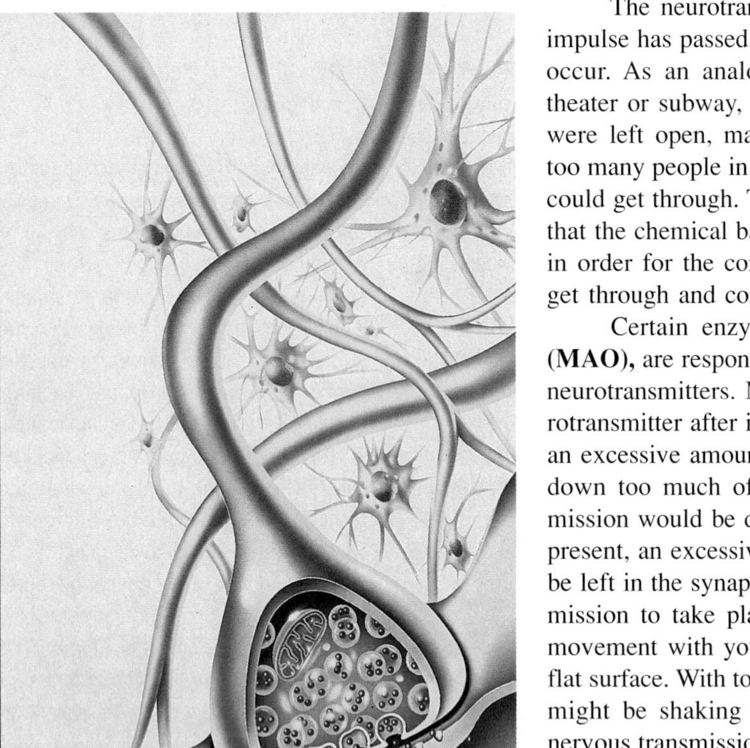

Illustration of a synapse, the junction between two nerve cells. Synapses transmit electrical signals from one nerve cell to the next. When an electrical signal reaches a synapse it triggers the release of chemicals called neurotransmitters (red) from vesicles (pink). The vesicles burst through the membrane, and neurotransmitters cross a microscopic gap called the synaptic cleft and bind to the receptor nerve cell, causing it to propagate an electrical impulse.

The neurotransmitter must be broken down after the impulse has passed, or too many nerve transmissions would occur. As an analogy, think of the turnstyle at a movie theater or subway, which lets in one person at a time. If it were left open, many people could run through, allowing too many people in. If it were stuck closed, however, no one could get through. The neurotransmitter system is similar in that the chemical balance in the synapse has to be just right in order for the correct amount of nervous transmission to get through and continue on.

Certain enzymes, particularly **monoamine oxidase (MAO),** are responsible for maintaining the proper levels of neurotransmitters. MAO works by breaking down the neurotransmitter after it has allowed a nerve impulse to pass. If an excessive amount of MAO were present, it would break down too much of the neurotransmitter, and nerve transmission would be diminished. If there were too little MAO present, an excessive amount of the neurotransmitter would be left in the synapse, allowing for too much nervous transmission to take place. Suppose that you had to do a fine movement with your fingers, such as pick up a dime off a flat surface. With too little MAO in your system, your fingers might be shaking and your movements jerky (too much nervous transmission). With too much MAO, however, your fingers might be clumsy because of dulled sensation and lethargic movement control. When MAO levels are just right, neurotransmitter levels are regulated appropriately and the nervous system works properly to control the muscles, thoughts, and emotions.

High sensation seekers tend to have low levels of MAO in their bloodstream, compared with low sensation seekers. Across studies, the correlation tends to be small to moderate but is consistently negative (Zuckerman, 1991). If high sensation seekers tend to have low MAO levels, and low MAO means more neurotransmitter available in the nerve cells, then perhaps sensation seeking is caused by or is maintained by having high levels of neurotransmitters in the nervous system. MAO acts like the brakes of the nervous system, by decomposing neurotransmitters and thereby inhibiting neurotransmission. With low MAO levels, sensation seekers have less inhibition in their nervous systems and therefore less control over behavior, thoughts, and emotions. According to Zuckerman's (1991) theory and research, sensation-seeking behaviors (e.g., illicit sex, drug use, wild parties) are due not to seeking an optimal level of arousal but to having too little of the biochemical brakes in the synapse.

Neurotransmitters and Personality

Whereas Zuckerman's theory concerns levels of MAO, which breaks down neurotransmitters, other researchers hypothesize that levels of neurotransmitters themselves are responsible for specific individual differences. Neurotransmitters are receiving a great deal of attention as possible sources of personality differences. One neurotransmitter, **dopamine,** appears to be associated with pleasure. For example, animals will work to obtain doses of dopamine, much as they would work to obtain food. As such, dopamine appears to function like a reward system and has even been called the feeling good chemical (Hamer, 1997). Drugs of abuse, such as cocaine, mimic dopamine in the nervous system, which accounts for the pleasure associated with taking them. However, such drugs deplete a person's natural levels of dopamine, leading to unpleasant feelings after the drug leaves the nervous system, creating a drive or urge to obtain more of the drug.

A second important neurotransmitter is **serotonin.** Researchers have documented the role of serotonin in depression and other mood disorders, such as anxiety. Specifically, drugs such as Prozac, Zoloft, and Paxil block the reuptake of serotonin, leaving it in the synapse longer, leading depressed persons to feel less depressed. In one study, Prozac was given to nondepressed subjects. Over several weeks of observation, they reported less negative affect and engaged in more outgoing and social behavior than did those in a control group (Knutson et al., 1998). In studies of monkeys, the monkeys that were higher in dominance and that engaged in more grooming had higher levels of serotonin. The monkeys low in serotonin were frequently fearful and aggressive (Rogness & McClure, 1996). In summarizing animal studies, Depue (1996) notes that low serotonin is associated with irritable behavior.

A third important neurotransmitter, **norepinephrine,** is involved in activating the sympathetic nervous system for fight-or-flight. Not surprisingly, personality theories have been proposed based on the neurotransmitters dopamine, serotonin, and norepinephrine. Probably the most comprehensive is Cloninger's **Tridimensional Personality model** (Cloninger, 1986, 1987; Cloninger, Svrakic, & Przybeck, 1993), in which three personality traits are tied to levels of the three neurotransmitters. The first trait, **novelty seeking,** is based on low levels of dopamine. Recall that low levels of dopamine create a drive state to obtain substances or experiences that increase dopamine. Novelty, thrills, and excitement can make up for low levels of dopamine, so novelty-seeking behavior is thought to result from low levels of this neurotransmitter.

The second personality trait identified in Cloninger's model is **harm avoidance,** which he associates with abnormalities in serotonin metabolism. Although various descriptions of the theory indicate increased or decreased serotonin levels are associated with increased harm avoidance, Cloninger himself (personal communication, October 2003) states that it is unwise to suggest a simple linear correlation between harm avoidance and absolute levels of serotonin. Very low levels of the principal serotonin metabolite 5-HIAA in cerebrospinal fluid are associated with risk of severe depression, but serotonin levels can also be elevated in states of anxiety or stress. The selective serotonin uptake inhibitors (like the antidepressants Prozac, Zoloft, or Paxil) result in increased levels of serotonin at synapses, which may increase anxiety initially, but then lead to decreased vulnerability to overreact to stress, probably by down-regulating sensitivity to serotonin when it is released in response to stress. So we have to distinguish the acute role of serotonin, which is increased in states of acute stress, and the role of serotonin down-regulation over the life span, which is associated with lower levels of harm avoidance. People low in harm avoidance are described as energetic, outgoing, and optimistic, whereas people high in harm avoidance are described as cautious, inhibited, shy, and apprehensive. They seem to expect that harmful and unpleasant events will happen to them, so they are constantly on the lookout for signs of such threatening events. And, like a dog that bites out of fear rather than anger, such a person can be irritable, snappy, and hostile.

The third trait in Cloninger's model is **reward dependence,** which Cloninger sees as related to low levels of norepinephrine. People high on this trait are persistent; they continue to act in ways that produce reward. They work long hours, put a lot of effort into their work, and often continue striving after others have given up.

Genes Work through Neurotransmitter Systems to Influence Personality

Although we discussed behavior genetics in more detail in Chapter 6, it is worth mentioning here that many researchers interested in personality and genetics are focusing on the genes involved in regulating our neurotransmitter systems. For example, if low levels of dopamine are related to novelty seeking, then perhaps the genes involved in dopamine transmission would be a good place to start in the search for the genetic basis of this personality trait. Keltikangas-Järvinen and her colleagues in Finland (2003) have found that the type 4 dopamine receptor gene **(D4DR)** is associated with heightened levels of novelty seeking. However, other studies have not found these particular genetic differences associated with novelty seeking (Azar, 2002). A meta-analysis of genetic studies of novelty seeking has suggested that very specific types of repeated genetic codes on the D4DR gene (Schinka, Letsch, and Crawford, 2002) are reliably associated with novelty seeking. These findings imply that many genes will be involved in the creation of any single personality trait. So, while looking for one gene as the basis of a personality trait is like looking for the proverbial needle in the haystack, now the researchers are looking for many different needles in the same big haystack. That is, they are looking for multiple genes that interact in complex ways to influence neurotransmitter systems. A prominent researcher in this area, Dean Hamer, recently commented, "After 10 years, it is quite clear to me that at least for most traits there are a very large number of genes involved" (quoted in Azar, 2002). As new technology for analyzing gene sequences is developed, the search will likely become more tractable. Nevertheless, any answers that are found in the future are likely to reveal complicated and multiple interacting genetic contributions, possibly requiring environmental triggers, for the expression of any biologically based personality trait.

Cloninger's theory has had some impact in psychiatry, where it has been used to help explain various types of addictions. For example, alcoholics do not all become addicted for the same reasons. Cloninger argues that some alcoholics began drinking due to high novelty seeking, that they drink to make up for low levels of dopamine, and that they drink primarily for the pleasure afforded by boosting dopamine. Other alcoholics began drinking because they are high in harm avoidance, and they drink to relieve the stress and anxiety they chronically feel. These drinkers are motivated primarily for the relief from anxiety that alcohol provides (Cloninger, Sigvardsson, & Bohman, 1988). Understanding people's motivations for abusing substances may play a large role in helping them overcome their addictions. For example, some people may enjoy smoking because it relieves stress, whereas others enjoy smoking because it enhances pleasurable activities, such as drinking coffee and socializing.

It is probably clear that Cloninger's model has much in common with Gray's, Eysenck's, and Zuckerman's. For example, novelty seeking seems a lot like the reward sensitivity associated with the BAS of Gray's theory. All of these theories have different explanatory bases for the traits (Depue & Collins, 1999). For example, Gray suggests that brain systems involved in learning through reward and punishment are important in determining these traits. Eysenck also implicates the brain and nervous system. Zuckerman focuses on the synapse and the neurochemicals found there. And Cloninger specifies particular neurotransmitters. All are perhaps describing the same behavioral traits but focusing on different levels of explanation within the body, ranging from the synapse to the brain.

Let's turn now to a consideration of two other personality dimensions, which appear to have a biological base that is not related to physiological reactivity—morningness–eveningness and brain asymmetry.

Morningness–Eveningness

Perhaps you are the kind of person who likes to sleep late and stay up late, saving your important schoolwork for late afternoon or evening, when you are feeling at your peak. Or perhaps you are more of a morning person, regularly getting up early without the aid of an alarm clock. Moreover, perhaps you tend to do all your important work early in the day, when you are feeling at your best, and get to sleep fairly early in the evening. Being a morning type or an evening type of person appears to be a stable characteristic. Personality psychologists have become interested in such stable differences between persons in preferences for different times of the day and have coined the term **morningness–eveningness** to refer to this dimension (Horne & Ostberg, 1976).

Differences between morning and evening types of persons, sometimes called "larks" and "owls," appear to be due to differences in underlying biological rhythms. Many biological processes have been found to fluctuate around an approximate 24- to 25-hour cycle. These have been called **circadian rhythms** (*circa* means "around," *dia* means "day," or "24 hours"). Of particular interest have been circadian rhythms in body temperature and endocrine secretion rates. For example, on average, body temperature shows a peak around mid-evening (between 8 and 9 P.M.) and a trough in the early morning (around 6 A.M.). Figure 7.5 presents a graph of body temperature by time of day.

Researchers use a temporal-isolation design to study such circadian rhythms. In this design, participants volunteer to live in an environment totally controlled by the experimenter with respect to time cues. There are no windows, so the participants do not know if it is day or night. There are no regularly scheduled meals, so the participants do not know if it is breakfast-, lunch-, or suppertime. Participants are given food whenever they ask for it. There is no access to live television or radio. Instead, the participants have a large collection of videotapes and audiotapes for entertainment. Volunteers live in this environment for several weeks or longer. Often, the participants are students who want to use the time in

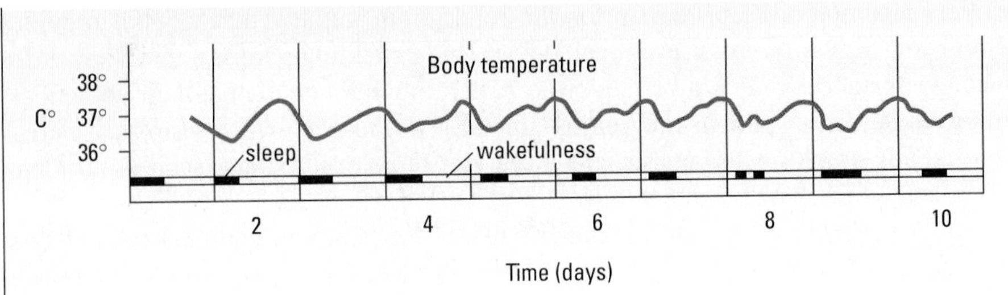

Figure 7.5
Circadian rhythm in body temperature.

isolation as an opportunity to study for an important exam or who need to write a Ph.D. thesis.

Imagine being a participant in such a study. You would go to sleep whenever you wanted, sleep as long as you wanted, eat whenever you felt like it, work or watch movies as the inclination struck, and so on. This is called **free running** in time, in which there are no time cues to influence your behavior or biology. If you were in such a situation and your temperature were taken every hour, and if you were like the average person, you would find that your temperature followed an approximate 24- to 25-hour cycle, starting to rise before waking up and falling before going to sleep (Aschoff, 1965; Finger, 1982; Wever, 1979).

Note that 24- to 25-hour rhythms are the average; there are wide differences between persons in the actual length of their biological rhythms (Kerkhof, 1985). Circadian rhythms in temporal-isolation studies have been found to be as short as 16 hours in one person and as long as 50 hours in another person (Wehr & Goodwin, 1981). While free running in a temporal-isolation experiment, the first person would complete a sleep-wake cycle every 16 hours, whereas the second person's sleep-wake cycle would last 50 hours.

Such wide differences between persons are only evident in a temporal isolation situation. In real life, there are time cues all around us that fluctuate in a 24-hour rhythm—most notably, the light-dark cycle. These cues entrain us and make us fit into the 24-hour day. Even though people with short and long biological cycles entrain quite well to the 24-hour cycle, there nevertheless are differences between those people in terms of the timing of peaks and valleys in their biological rhythms. Imagine someone with a slightly long circadian rhythm (such as 26 hours) and someone with a slightly short rhythm (such as 22 hours). They both may entrain to the same 24-hour day, but the peak in body temperature might occur relatively late for the first person (perhaps at 10 P.M.), whereas the peak would occur relatively early for the second person (perhaps around 6 P.M.).

Individuals with short biological rhythms hit their peak body temperature and alertness levels earlier in the day and, thus, begin to get sleepy earlier than do persons with longer circadian rhythms (Bailey & Heitkemper, 1991). A person with a 26-hour rhythm, would have a harder time getting up at 6 in the morning, because his or her 26-hour biological rhythm still has 2 hours to go, even though the 24-hour clock is telling him or her to start a new day. A person with a 22-hour rhythm would have an easier time getting up early because he or she has completed a biological "day" in 22 hours and is ready to start another day even *before* the 24-hour clock is up.

Exercise

Do you know someone who you think is a morning type of person? What specific evidence makes you come to this conclusion? Do you think people with a morning type of rhythm are different in other ways from evening-type people? For example, are there other personality characteristics associated with being a morning type? Benjamin Franklin is quoted as saying that "early to bed, early to rise, makes a person healthy, wealthy, and wise." Do you think it is possible that morning types are actually wiser or that they have better outcomes in life? How would you design a study to answer this question?

Research on individual differences in circadian rhythms provides the groundwork for understanding why some people are morning types and others are evening types. As you know, those with *shorter* biological rhythms tend to be morning persons, and those with *longer* biological rhythms tend to be evening persons. Horne and Ostberg (1976, 1977) developed a 19-item questionnaire to measure morningness–eveningness (see Table 7.3). The items ask about preferences for activities earlier or later in the day. In a sample of 48 participants, who took their body temperature every hour for several days, the researchers found that the scores on this questionnaire correlated −.51 with time of day that peak body temperature was reached. While the original study was done in Sweden, the negative correlation between self-reported preferences for activities in the morning and timing of peak body temperature has been replicated in the United States (Monk et al., 1983), Italy (Mecacci, Scaglione, & Vitrano, 1991), Spain (Adan, 1991, 1992), Croatia (Vidacek et al., 1988), and Japan (Ishihara, Saitoh, & Miyata, 1983).

These cross-cultural replications are consistent with the idea that preferences for morning or evening activities, and the time of day people are at their best, is a stable disposition with a biological basis. Scores on the Horne and Ostberg measure of morningness–eveningness are stable over time. Croatian researchers tested 90 college students on this measure and then tested them again seven years later, when they had finished college (Sverko & Fabulic, 1985). They found a significant positive correlation, suggesting that the morningness–eveningness characteristic is fairly stable over time. There was, however, a general shift in the whole sample toward morningness, which might be expected in a group that moves from being college students to persons having jobs.

Many studies have been done on the validity of the morningness–eveningness construct. In one study (Larsen, 1985), college students completed a report every day for 84 consecutive days, stating what time they felt at their best each day and what time they got up and went to bed each day. The Horne and Ostberg questionnaire correlated strongly with average rise and retire times, as well as with the time of day the participants reported feeling at their best. The morning persons got up earlier, went to bed earlier, and reportedly felt at their best earlier, on average, than the evening persons.

What would happen if people who had to live together, such as college roommates, were mismatched on morningness–eveningness? One person likes to stay up late and sleep late, whereas the other likes to get up early, even on weekends, as well as go to bed early. How happy do you think these people would be with their rooming situation? This was the topic of a study by Watts (1982), who selected first-year

Table 7.3 Items from the Morningness–Eveningness Questionnaire

Instructions

Please read each question carefully before answering. Each question should be answered independently of others. Do *not* go back and change or check your answers.

All questions have a selection of answers. For each question, circle the number in front of only one answer. Please answer each question as honestly as possible.

1. Considering only your "feeling best" rhythm, at what time would you get up if you were entirely free to plan your day?
   1. between 11:00 A.M. and noon
   2. between 9:30 A.M. and 11 A.M.
   3. between 7:30 A.M. and 9:30 A.M.
   4. between 6:00 A.M. and 7:30 A.M.
   5. before 6:00 A.M.
2. Considering only your "feeling best" rhythm, at what time would you go to bed if you were entirely free to plan your evening?
   1. after at least 1:30 in the morning
   2. between midnight and 1:30 A.M.
   3. between 10:30 P.M. and midnight
   4. between 9:00 P.M. and 10:30 P.M.
   5. before 9:00 P.M.
3. On the average, how easy do you find getting up in the morning?
   1. not at all easy
   2. not very easy
   3. fairly easy
   4. very easy
4. How alert do you feel during the first half-hour after having awakened in the morning?
   1. not at all alert
   2. not very alert
   3. fairly alert
   4. very alert
5. How is your appetite during the first half-hour after having awakened in the morning?
   1. very poor
   2. fairly poor
   3. fairly good
   4. very good
6. When you have no commitments the next day (e.g., on weekends), at what time do you go to bed, compared with your usual bedtime?
   1. more than two hours later
   2. between one and two hours later
   3. less than one hour later
   4. seldom or never later
7. You wish to be at your peak performance for a test that you know is going to be mentally exhausting and lasting for two hours. You are entirely free to plan your day and, considering your own "feeling best" rhythm, which *one* of the four testing times would you choose?
   1. 7:00 to 9:00 P.M.
   2. 3:00 to 5:00 P.M.
   3. 11:00 A.M. to 1:00 P.M.
   4. 8:00 to 10:00 A.M.

(continued)

Table 7.3 Continued

8. If you went to bed at 11:00 in the evening, at what level of tiredness would you be at that time?
   1. not at all tired
   2. a little tired
   3. fairly tired
   4. very tired
9. For some reason, you have gone to bed several hours later than usual, but there is no need to get up at any particular time the next morning. Which one of the following events are you most likely to experience?
   1. will not wake up until much later than usual
   2. will wake up at my usual time but will fall asleep again
   3. will wake up at my usual time and will doze on and off for awhile
   4. will wake up at my usual time and will not fall back asleep at all
10. Suppose that you can choose your own work hours. Assume that you worked a *five*-hour day and that your job was interesting and was paid by results. Circle the five consecutive hours you would work (circle five consecutive hours):

    midnight 1 2 3 4 5 6 7 8 9 10 11 noon 1 2 3 4 5 6 7 8 9 10 11
11. At what single hour of the day do you think you reach your "feeling best" peak (circle one)?

    midnight 1 2 3 4 5 6 7 8 9 10 11 noon 1 2 3 4 5 6 7 8 9 10

Source: Adapted from Horne, J. A., & Ostberg, O. (1976). A self-assessment questionnaire to determine morningness–eveningness in human circadian rhythms. *International Journal of Chronobiology,* 4, 97–110.

college students living on the campus of Michigan State University. The participants had to have only one roommate. The roommate pairs completed the Morningness–Eveningness Questionnaire (MEQ), and they rated various aspects of their roommate relationship. Watts found that, the greater the difference between the roommates' MEQ scores, the lower ratings they gave to the quality of their relationship. Roommates who were very different on morningness–eveningness said that they did not get along very well with each other, that they did not enjoy their relationship and were not good friends, and that they were unlikely to continue living together. Differences on other personality dimensions, such as achievement motivation and competitiveness, did not predict such dissatisfaction with the roommate relationship. It appears that differences in morningness–eveningness are especially related to interpersonal compatibility problems.

Other studies of morningness–eveningness have looked at cognitive performance at different times of the day in relation to this personality disposition. Monk and Leng (1986) measured performance on a serial search task and a logical reasoning task at different times of day for participants classified as morning or evening types by the Horne and Ostberg questionnaire. Between the hours of 8 and 11 A.M., the morning types performed their best. Between the hours of 5 and 11 P.M., the evening types showed their best performance. Such differences might be lessened through the use of stimulants, such as caffeine, as implied in the research of Revelle and colleagues (1980). Caffeine may help the performance of evening types most if taken in the morning, whereas it may help the performance of morning types most if taken in the evening. Persons can time their coffee consumption to give them the greatest benefit, given their morningness–eveningness disposition.

Being a morning type or evening type refers to preferences for time of day that may have a biological basis; however, sometimes situations occur that go against such preferences. Imagine a college student who is definitely an evening type, yet a class he or she needs to take is offered only at 8 A.M. or a morning type of person who takes a job in a factory and is assigned to the late shift (4 P.M. to midnight). Going against one's natural circadian preferences is difficult but not impossible. People do adjust to shift work and changes in sleep-wake schedule, and there is some evidence that evening types adjust to disruptions in sleep-wake cycles better than morning types (Ishihara et al., 1992). Such disruptions as transmeridian airline flights (which create jet lag) or working all night without sleeping (i.e., pulling an all-nighter) may be better tolerated by an evening type than a morning type of person.

In summary, the preference for being active and doing important or demanding work earlier or later in the day may be rooted in the length of a person's inherent biological circadian temperature rhythm. This is a good example of a physiological approach to personality because it highlights the notion of a behavior pattern (i.e., preference for different times of the day) being based on an underlying physiological mechanism (i.e., circadian rhythms).

Brain Asymmetry and Affective Style

As you are probably aware, the left and right sides of the brain are specialized, with asymmetry in the control of various psychological functions. One type of asymmetry that is receiving research attention is the relative amount of activity in the front part of the left and right brain hemispheres. The brain constantly produces small amounts of electrical activity, which can be measured on the scalp with sensitive electrical recording equipment. A recording of such electrical activity is called an **electroencephalograph,** or **EEG.** Moreover, such electrical activity is rhythmic and exhibits waves that are fast or slow, depending on neurological activation in the brain. One particular type of brain wave, called an **alpha wave,** oscillates at 8 to 12 times a second. The amount of alpha wave present in a given time period is an inverse indicator of brain activity during that time period. The alpha wave is given off when a person is calm and is relaxed and is feeling a bit sleepy and not attentive to the environment. In a given time period of brain wave recording, the *less* alpha wave activity present, the *more* we can assume that part of the brain was active.

EEG waves can be measured over any region or part of the brain. In emotion research, particular attention has been directed toward the frontal part of the brain, comparing the amount of activation in the right and left hemispheres. Study results suggest that the left hemisphere is relatively more active than the right when a person is experiencing pleasant emotions and vice versa, that the right frontal hemisphere is more active than the left when the person is experiencing unpleasant emotions. For example, in a study by Davidson and colleagues (1990), they showed film clips to the participants in an attempt to amuse some of the participants and disgust the others. The participants were also videotaped while they watched the funny or disgusting films. EEGs were taken while the participants looked at the films. When the participants were smiling at the amusing films, they had relatively more activation in their left than right frontal hemispheres. Similarly, when the participants were exhibiting a facial expression of disgust (lower lip pulled down, tongue protruding, nose wrinkled), their brains were more active in the right than left hemispheres. These results are shown in Figure 7.6.

Similar results have also been obtained in very young children. Instead of using films, Fox and Davidson (1986) used sweet and bitter solutions placed in the mouths

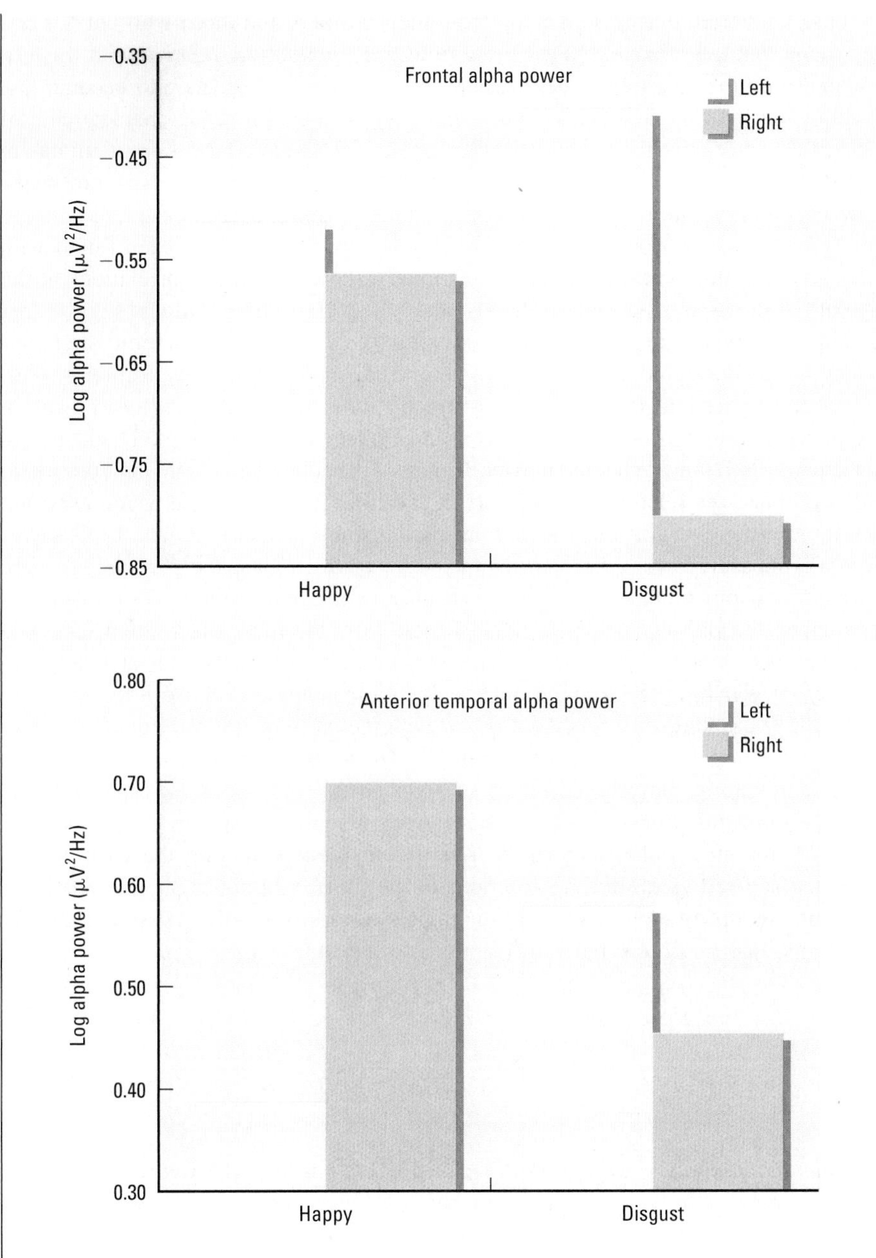

Figure 7.6
Results of Davidson et al. (1990) study.

of 10-month-old infants to produce pleasant and unpleasant affective reactions. The infants showed relatively more left- than right-brain activation to the sweet solution and more right- than left-brain activation to the bitter solution. In another study of 10-month-old infants, the infants' mothers left them alone in the testing room, whereupon a stranger entered the room (Fox & Davidson, 1987). In this standard anxiety-producing procedure, some infants become distressed but some do not; some infants cry and fuss but others do not. The researchers divided their sample of infants into those who cried during separation from their mothers and those who did not cry. They found that the criers exhibited more right-brain activation, relative with the left, compared with the noncriers. These results suggest that this tendency to become distressed or not (and the associated brain EEG asymmetry) is a stable characteristic of infants. Fox and colleagues (Fox, Bell, & Jones, 1992) studied a group of infants at age 7 months and again at age 12 months and found that the EEG measures of hemisphere asymmetry taken at those two time periods were highly correlated, suggesting stability over time in frontal brain asymmetry. Similar results have been found with adults, showing that measures of EEG asymmetry show test-retest correlations in the range of .66 to .73 across studies (Davidson, 1993, 2003). These findings suggest that individual differences in **frontal brain asymmetry** exhibit enough stability and consistency to be considered as indicative of an underlying biological disposition or trait.

Other studies suggest that EEG asymmetry indicates a vulnerability to pleasant or unpleasant affective states. Tomarken and colleagues (Tomarken, Davidson, & Henriques, 1990) and Wheeler and colleagues (Wheeler, Davidson, & Tomarken, 1993) examined the relation between individual differences in frontal asymmetry and reactions to affective film clips in normal participants. In these studies, EEG asymmetry was measured while the participants were resting. Then the participants were shown either happy and amusing films or disgusting and fearful films. For the dependent variable, the participants were asked to rate how the films made them feel. The hypothesis was that the participants with greater right-side activation at rest (measured before watching the films) would report more intense *negative* affective reactions to the fear and disgust films, compared with the participants with relatively more left-side activation. The opposite prediction was made for the participants with greater left-side activation—they should report stronger *positive* emotions in response to the happy and amusing films. The predictions were essentially supported, with frontal asymmetry measures taken *before* the films were seen predicting the participants' *subsequent* self-reported affective reactions to the films, with the right-side-dominant participants reporting more distress to the unpleasant films and the left-side-dominant participants reporting more pleasant reactions to the films.

Application

Assessing brain assymetry without an EEG. **An EEG is not the only way to obtain an index of asymmetry in brain activation. Research suggests that a person's characteristic level of left- or right-sided activation may be indicated by the direction in which their eyes drift as they concentrate on answering difficult questions. When answering a difficult question (for example, "Make up a sentence using the words *rhapsody* and *pleasure*"), people's eyes drift one way or the other as they reflect on their answer (Davidson, 1991). Among right-handed persons, eyes drifting to the right signify left-sided activation, and eyes drifting to the left signify right-sided activation. If you ask a person several difficult questions (e.g., "How many turns do you make from your house or apartment to the nearest store?") and note which way his or her eyes usually drift, you may get an indication of whether they tend to be right- or left-sided asymmetric. Of course, this quick measure is not as reliable as an EEG. It nevertheless may be a rough gauge of whether a person is left- or right-side asymmetric.**

Application (*Continued*)

Perhaps you could make some observations of a few friends or acquaintances, asking them several difficult questions and observing which way they move their eyes as they think through their answers. Most people will not show completely consistent patterns of going one way or the other. That is why it is important to ask several questions and see which way they *usually* move their eyes. You will also need to decide whether they are more vulnerable to positive or negative emotions. Persons who glance frequently to the right are more likely to be left-hemisphere dominant and should be more vulnerable to the pleasant emotions (e.g., happiness, joy, enthusiasm). Persons who frequently glance to the left while engaging in reflective thought are more likely to be right-hemisphere dominant and, by implication, should be more vulnerable to the negative emotions (e.g., distress, anxiety, sadness).

Certainly, many factors influence how people feel and which emotions they experience. The findings reviewed here suggest that the characteristic pattern of brain activation is one factor that may influence our affective lives by contributing to the likelihood that we will experience certain emotions.

Similar results have also been found with monkeys. Because monkeys cannot tell you how positive or negative they are feeling, researchers have used measures of **cortisol** to assess emotional reactivity. Cortisol is a stress hormone that prepares the body to fight or flee, and increases in cortisol mean that the animal has recently experienced stress. Davidson and his colleagues (reviewed in Kosslyn et al., 2002) have found that monkeys with greater right-sided activation had higher levels of cortisol. Identical results have recently been found with 6-month-old children. These researchers induced fear in the infants by having a male stranger enter the room, slowly approach the infant, and stare at the infant for two minutes. Those infants who had greater right-sided activation at baseline showed increased cortisol responses to the stranger. Also, those infants who showed the most right-sided activation during the stranger approach phase also displayed more crying and facial expressions of fear, and tried to escape more, compared to infants with less right-sided activation (Buss et al., 2003).

A study by Sutton and Davidson (1997) showed that dispositionally positive persons (assessed by Carver and White's (1994) BIS/BAS inventory) showed greater relative left frontal EEG asymmetry at baseline, in the absence of emotional stimulation. Sutton and Davidson (1997) explicitly draw on Gray's theory to organize the literature on affective dispositions and brain function, illustrating the utility of Gray's BAS and BIS concepts (e.g., approach motivation and withdrawal motivation, respectively) and their distinct activation. These results have recently been replicated using functional brain imaging techniques (Canli et al., 2001).

The importance of brain asymmetry research is that different portions of the brain may respond with pleasant or unpleasant emotions, given the appropriate affective stimulus. Fox and Calkins (1993) discuss this notion in terms of thresholds for responding. The person who displays a right-frontal-activation pattern may have a lower threshold for responding with negative emotions when an unpleasant event happens. It may take less of an affective event to evoke negative feelings for right-dominant persons. For an individual who displays a left-frontal-activation pattern, the threshold for experiencing pleasant emotions in response to positive events is lowered. The concept of thresholds implies that persons with a left- or right-sided pattern require less of the affective stimulus to evoke the corresponding emotion. A person's affective lifestyle may have its origins in, or at least may be predicted by, his or her pattern of asymmetry in frontal brain activation.

Recently, an unlikely collaboration has emerged between the psychologist Richard Davidson, who runs the Laboratory for Affective Neuroscience at the University of Wisconsin, and Tenzin Gyatso, who is also known as the fourteenth Dalai Lama, the supreme leader of Tibetan Buddhism and winner of a Nobel peace prize. Dr. Davidson and other psychologists and researchers met with the Dalai Lama for five days in Dharamsala, India, in March 2000. Dr. Davidson measured the brain waves of one senior Tibetan monk, who turned out to have the most left-sided asymmetry that has ever been recorded. Was this a quirk, or is there something about the training of these monks that produces more left-sided brain activity?

To answer this question Davidson teamed up with Jon Kabat-Zinn, who founded the Stress Reduction Clinic at the University of Massachusetts Medical School. Dr. Kabat-Zinn uses a form of mindfulness meditation to teach people how to reduce stress. This form of meditation is loosely based on Buddhist meditation techniques. In this research, they obtained a sample of 41 workers employed in high-stress jobs in the biotechnology industry. Twenty-five of the workers were taught mindfulness meditation and practiced it for eight weeks. A control group consisted of 16 workers from the same company in the same kinds of jobs. All subjects had their brain waves assessed before and after the eight-week period.

Before the mindfulness training, subjects tended toward a slightly right-sided asymmetry, suggesting chronic stress. After the training, these subjects, compared to the control group, showed a significant shift toward left-sided asymmetry. They also reported less stress, feeling more energized, more engaged in their work, and less anxiety. In a surprising finding, mindfulness meditation appeared to give the workers' immune systems a boost. This was determined by the amount of flu antibodies they produced in response to a flu shot, with the mindfulness meditators showing a more robust immune response to the flu shot (Davidson et al., 2003).

The Dalai Lama wrote a column in the *New York Times* (Gyatso, 2003) describing mindfulness meditation as a nonsectarian technique involving "a state of alertness in which the mind does not get caught up in thoughts or sensations, but lets them come and go, much like watching a river flow by . . . these methods are not just useful, but inexpensive. You don't need a drug or an injection. You don't have to become a Buddhist, or adopt any particular religion. Everybody has the potential to lead a peaceful, meaningful life." Indeed, it appears that practicing such mindfulness can bring about changes in biology, and that these changes in turn appear to promote more positive emotional traits.

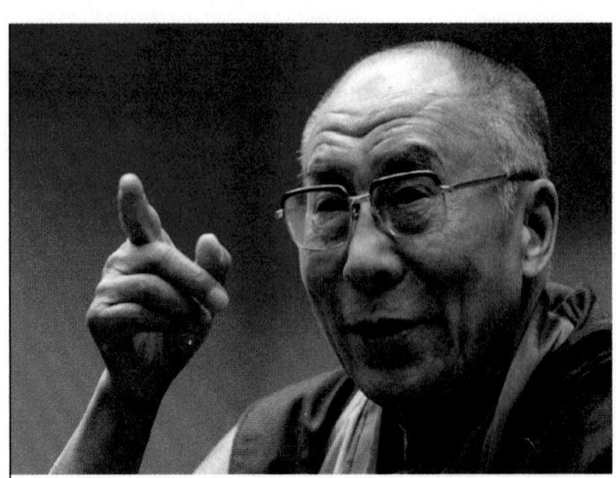

The Dalai Lama has been working with neuroscientists in an effort to understand the human mind.

In 2005 the Dalai Lama attended the annual meeting of the Society for Neuroscience, where he charmed an audience of 14,000 with a talk presenting meditation as an empirical way to investigate the mind. While many neuroscientists argued that a religious leader should not be given time at a meeting of scientists, most of those attending agreed with the Dalai Lama's view that scientific evidence will persuade more people than religious dogma. After his remarks, a symposium of several research papers examined the question of whether meditation can alter brain physiology and offer health benefits. For example, Sara Lazar, a psychologist at

Harvard Medical School, reported that areas of the brain associated with attention and sensory processing were thicker in persons who had been practicing meditation for many years than in subjects with no meditation experience. By encouraging scientific investigations of the brain, the Dalai Lama provides an interesting and current example of a physiological perspective on the mind.

SUMMARY AND EVALUATION

The study of personality can be approached biologically. There is a long history of theorizing about the biological influences on personality, and there are two ways to think about how physiological variables can be useful in personality theory and research. One way to view physiological measures is as variables that may be correlated with personality traits. For example, in a sample of college students, there may be a negative correlation between resting heart rate and scores on a neuroticism questionnaire (perhaps due to the heightened level of chronic anxiety associated with neuroticism). Here a physiological variable is seen as a correlate of a personality dimension, as something that is associated with being neurotic. Does an elevated heart rate cause a person to become neurotic? Probably not. Instead, a pounding heart goes along with, or is a correlate of, being neurotic.

A second way to think about physiological approaches to personality is to view physiological events as contributing to or providing the physiological substrate for the personality characteristic. This chapter covered six such examples of theories about the biological underpinnings of specific personality dimensions: extraversion (and neuronal excitability or arousability), sensitivity to cues of reward and punishment (based on brain circuits of the BIS and BAS systems), sensation seeking (and level of MAO and hormones in the bloodstream), Tridimensional Personality theory (based on neurotransmitters), morningness–eveningness (and circadian rhythms in body temperature), and affective style (and hemispheric asymmetry in the frontal cortex of the brain). In these theories, the physiological variables are assumed to be more than just correlates of the personality traits; they are assumed to be substrates of the biological underpinnings for the behavior pattern that defines the personality trait.

KEY TERMS

Evolutionary Perspectives on Personality

THE BIOLOGICAL DOMAIN

How much of human nature today is the result of behavior patterns that evolved as our ancestors solved the problems of surviving and reproducing?

Imagine living as our ancestors did a million years ago. You awaken at dawn and shrug off the coldness of night. A few warm embers are still glowing in the fire, so you stoke it with kindling. The others in your group gather around the fire as the sun breaks the horizon. Stomachs start growling and your thoughts turn to food. Small groups form to set off in search of berries, edible plants, and small game animals.

After a long day of hunting and gathering, the members converge back at their temporary home site. As night begins to fall, the group again gathers around the fire. The day's hunting and gathering have been successful and the mood is warm and animated. Tales of the hunt are reenacted, the bounty of gathered goods admired. With the group's bellies full, discussion turns to whether the group should move the next day or stay a bit longer. A successful hunter makes eye contact with his young lover, but she shyly looks away. Others notice this flirtation but do not remark on it. Mating universally draws interest. As people grow sleepy and babies are put to sleep, the young lovers quietly slip away from the group to be alone. Their warm embrace echoes events recurring millions of times as people partake of life's cycle.

Evolutionary psychology is a new and rapidly growing scientific perspective, and it offers important insights into human personality. In this chapter, we will look at some of these insights in three areas: human nature, sex differences, and individual differences. We will see how theories of evolutionary psychology fit with the discoveries of personality psychologists and generate new lines of research in personality psychology. We will see why human mating and sexual behavior, being close to the engine of the evolutionary process, is central to personality psychology. We begin by reviewing some basic information about the theory of evolution.

Evolution and Natural Selection

All of us come from a long and unbroken line of ancestors who accomplished two critical tasks: they survived to reproductive age, and they reproduced. If any one of your ancestors had failed at reproduction, you would not be here today to contemplate their existence. In this sense, every living human is an evolutionary success story. As descendants of these successful ancestors, we carry with us the genes for the adaptive mechanisms that led to their success. From this perspective, our human nature—the collection of mechanisms that defines us as human—is the product of the evolutionary process. Nonetheless, humans are rarely aware of these mechanisms.

Long before Charles Darwin, the originator of evolutionary theory, it was known that change takes place over time in organic structures. The fossil record showed the bones of long extinct dinosaurs, suggesting that not all species in the past are with us today. The paleontological record showed changes in animals' body forms, suggesting that nothing remains static. Moreover, the structures of species seemed extraordinarily well adapted to their environments. The long necks of giraffes enabled them to eat leaves from tall trees. The turtle's shell seemed designed for protection. The beaks of birds seemed suited for cracking nuts to get at their nutritious meat. What could account for the dual observations of change over time and apparent adaptation to environmental conditions?

THE FAR SIDE® By GARY LARSON

"And now, Randy, by use of song, the male sparrow will stake out his territory ... an instinct common in the lower animals."

Natural Selection

Darwin's contribution was not in observing change over time, nor in noticing the adaptive design of mechanisms. Rather, Darwin revolutionized the field of biology by proposing a theory of the *process* by which adaptations are created and change takes place over time. He called it the theory of **natural selection.**

Darwin noticed that species seemed to produce many more offspring than could possibly survive and reproduce. He reasoned that changes, or *variants,* that better enabled an organism to survive and reproduce would lead to more descendants. The descendants, therefore, would inherit the variants that led to their ancestors' survival and reproduction. Through this process, the successful variants were selected and unsuccessful variants weeded out. Natural selection, therefore, results in gradual changes in a species over time, as successful variants increase in frequency and eventually spread throughout the gene pool, replacing the less successful variants. Over time, these successful variants come to characterize the entire species, whereas unsuccessful variants decrease in frequency and vanish from the species.

This process of natural selection, sometimes called *survival selection,* led Darwin to focus on the events that impede survival, which he called the **hostile forces of nature.** These hostile forces included food shortages, diseases, parasites, predators, and extremes of weather. Whatever variants helped organisms survive these hostile forces of nature would lead to an increased likelihood of successful reproduction. Food preferences for substances rich in fat, sugar, and protein, for example, would help organisms survive food shortages. An immune system teeming with antibodies would help organisms survive diseases and parasites. Fear of snakes and spiders would help them survive these dangers. These mechanisms, resulting from a long and repeated process of natural selection, are called **adaptations,** inherited solutions to the survival and reproductive problems posed by the hostile forces of nature.

Even after Darwin came up with his theory of natural selection, there remained many mysteries in the organic world that puzzled him. He noticed that many mechanisms seemed to fly in the face of survival. The elaborate plumage, large antlers, and other conspicuous features displayed by the males of many species seemed costly in terms of survival. He wondered how the brilliant plumage of peacocks could evolve, and become common, when it posed such an obvious threat to survival, acting as a blatant advertisement to predators. In response to anomalies of this sort, Darwin proposed a second evolutionary theory—the theory of sexual selection.

Sexual Selection

Darwin's answer to the mysteries of the peacock's tail and the stag's antlers was that they evolved because they contributed to an individual's mating success, providing an advantage in the competition for desirable mates. The evolution of characteristics because of their mating benefits, rather than because of their survival benefits, is known as **sexual selection.**

Sexual selection, according to Darwin, takes two forms. In one form, members of the same sex compete with each other, and the outcome of their contest gives the winner greater sexual access to members of the opposite sex. Two stags locking horns in combat is the prototypical image of this **intrasexual competition.** The characteristics that lead to success in contests of this kind, such as greater strength, intelligence, or attractiveness to allies, evolve because the victors are able to mate more often and, hence, pass on more genes.

In the other type of sexual selection—**intersexual selection**—members of one sex choose a mate based on their preferences for particular qualities in a mate. These characteristics evolve because animals that possess them are chosen more often as mates, and their genes thrive. Animals that lack the desired characteristics are excluded from mating, and their genes perish. Since peahens prefer peacocks with plumage that flashes and glitters, dull-feathered males get left in the evolutionary dust. The leading theory is that peacocks today possess brilliant plumage because, over evolutionary history, peahens have preferred to mate with dazzling and colorful males (Trivers, 1985). The most likely explanation for why peahens prefer luminous plumage is because it's a signal of healthiness; peacocks that have a high prevalence of parasites look dull by comparison.

Success at same-sex competition leads to success at mating; traits that help to win these battles are passed on in greater numbers, and hence evolve in the population

Genes and Inclusive Fitness

Genes are packets of DNA that are inherited by children from their parents in distinct chunks. Genes are the smallest discrete units that are inherited by offspring intact, without being broken up. According to modern evolutionary biologists, evolution operates by the process of **differential gene reproduction,** defined by reproductive success relative to others. The genes of organisms that reproduce more than others get passed down to future generations at a relatively greater frequency than do the genes of those that reproduce less. Since survival is usually critical for reproductive success, characteristics that lead to greater survival get passed along. Since success in mating is also critical for reproductive success, the qualities that lead to success in same-sex competition or to success at being chosen as a mate get passed along. Successful survival and successful mate competition, therefore, are both part of differential gene reproduction.

The characteristics that lead to the greater reproduction of genes that code for them are selected and, hence, evolve over time. In this sense, survival is important only inasmuch as it is necessary for reproduction. Nonetheless, many biologists maintain the distinction between natural, or survival, selection and sexual selection because it helps clarify two important types of adaptations—those that help organisms survive (e.g., fear of snakes) and those that help organisms reproduce (e.g., large antlers for same-sex combat).

The modern evolutionary theory based on differential gene reproduction is called **inclusive fitness theory** (Hamilton, 1964). The "inclusive" part is the fact that the characteristics that facilitate reproduction need not affect the personal production of offspring. They can affect the survival and reproduction of genetic relatives as well. For example, if you take a personal risk to defend or protect your sister or another relative, then this might enable her to better survive and reproduce. Since you share genes with your sister—50 percent on average in the case of siblings—

then helping her survive and reproduce will also lead to the spread of your genes (successful gene reproduction).

A critical condition for such helping to evolve is that the cost to your reproduction as a result of the helping must be less than the benefits to the reproduction of your genes that reside in your relative. If helping your sister survive—for example, by jumping into rushing rapids to save her from drowning—puts your own life at risk, the odds of saving her must exceed twice the odds of your dying in order for evolution to select for mechanisms underlying this helping behavior. Thus, inclusive fitness can be defined as one's personal reproductive success (roughly, the number of children you produce) *plus* the effects you have on the reproduction of your genetic relatives, weighted by the degree of genetic relatedness. Inclusive fitness leads you to take some risks for the welfare of your genetic relatives, but not too great a risk. Inclusive fitness theory, as an expansion and elaboration of Darwin's theory, represented a major advance in understanding human traits, such as altruism.

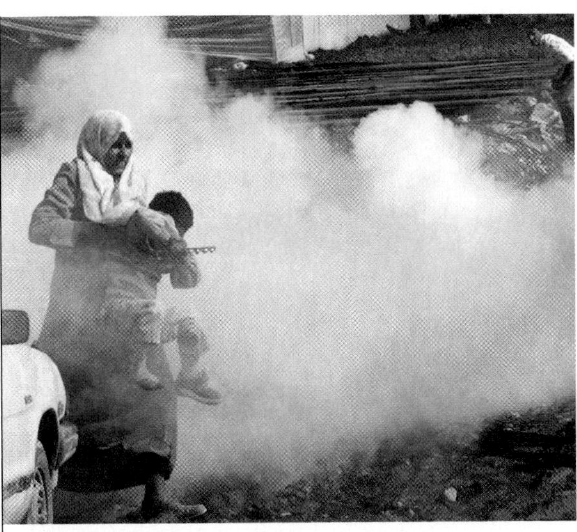

Traits for helping can evolve through inclusive fitness.

Products of the Evolutionary Process

All living humans are products of the evolutionary process, the descendants of a long line of ancestors who succeeded in surviving, reproducing, and helping their genetic relatives. The evolutionary process acts as a series of filters. In each generation, only a small subset of genes passes through the filter. The recurrent filtering process lets only three things pass through—adaptations; by-products of adaptations; and noise, or random variations.

Adaptations

Adaptations are the primary product of the selective process. An adaptation can be defined as a "reliably developing structure in the organism, which, because it meshes with the recurrent structure of the world, causes the solution to an adaptive problem" (Tooby & Cosmides, 1992, p. 104). Adaptations might include a taste for sweet and fatty foods, the drive to defend one's close relatives, and preferences for specific mates, such as those that are healthy.

Let's examine the components of the definition of adaptation. The focus on reliably developing structure means that an adaptation tends to emerge with regularity during the course of a person's life. The mechanisms that allow humans to see, for example, develop reliably. But this does not mean that vision develops invariantly. The development of the eye can be perturbed by genetic anomalies or by environmental trauma. The emphasis on reliable development suggests that evolutionary approaches are *not* forms of "genetic determinism." Environments are always needed for the development of an adaptation, and environmental events can always interfere with or enhance such development.

The emphasis on meshing with recurrent structures of the world means that adaptations emerge from, and are structured by, the selective environment. Features of the environment must be recurrent over time for an adaptation to evolve. The

For most of our evolutionary past, humans lived in small, close-knit groups, usually of less than 100 people. This form of group living is relatively rare today.

venomous snakes must be recurrently dangerous, ripe fruit must be recurrently nutritious, and enclosed caves must be recurrently protective before adaptations to them can emerge.

Finally, an adaptation must facilitate the solution to an adaptive problem. An **adaptive problem** is anything that impedes survival or reproduction. Stated more precisely, all adaptations must contribute to fitness during the period of time in which they evolve by helping an organism survive, reproduce, or facilitate the reproductive success of genetic relatives. In sum, adaptations emerge from and interact with recurrent structures of the world in a manner that solves adaptive problems and, hence, aids in reproductive success.

The hallmark of adaptation is *special design*. That is, the features of an adaptation are recognized as components of specialized problem-solving machinery. Factors such as *efficiency* in solving a specific adaptive problem, *precision* in solving the adaptive problem, and *reliability* in solving the adaptive problem are key criteria in recognizing the special design of an adaptation. Adaptations are like keys that fit only specific locks. The tines of the key (adaptation) show special design features, which mesh with the specific mirror-image elements within the lock (adaptive problem).

All adaptations are products of the history of selection. In this sense, we live with a stone-age brain in a modern world, which is in some ways different from the world in which we evolved. For example, ancestral humans evolved in relatively small groups of 50 to 150, using both hunting and gathering as methods of acquiring food (Dunbar, 1993). In the modern world, by contrast, many people live in large cities surrounded by thousands or millions of people. Characteristics that were probably adaptive in ancestral environments—such as **xenophobia,** or fear of strangers—are not necessarily adaptive in modern environments. Some of the personality traits that make up human nature may be vestigial adaptations to an ancestral environment that no longer exists.

By-products of Adaptations

The evolutionary process also produces things that are not adaptations—such as **by-products of adaptations.** Consider the design of a lightbulb. A lightbulb is designed to produce light—that is its function. But it also may produce heat, not because it is designed to produce heat but, rather, because heat is an incidental by-product, which occurs as a consequence of design for light. In the same way, human adaptations can also have **evolutionary by-products,** or incidental effects that are not properly considered to be adaptations. The human nose, for example, is clearly an adaptation designed for smelling. But the fact that we use our noses to hold up our eyeglasses is an incidental by-product. The nose was designed for smelling odors, not for holding up glasses. Notice that the hypothesis that something is a by-product (e.g., by holding up eyeglasses) requires specifying the adaptation (e.g., the nose) of which it is a by-product. Thus, both sorts of evolutionary hypotheses—adaptation and by-product hypotheses—require a description of the nature of the adaptation.

Noise, or Random Variations

The third product of the evolutionary process is **evolutionary noise,** or random variations that are neutral with respect to selection. In the design of a lightbulb, for example, there are minor variations in the surface texture of the bulb, which do not affect the functioning of the design elements. Neutral variations introduced into the gene pool through mutation, for example, are perpetuated over generations if they do not hinder the functioning of adaptations.

An example of noise, or a random variation, is the shape of the human earlobe. Some people have long earlobes; others have short earlobes. Some lobes are thin; others are plump. These variations represent random noise—they do not affect the basic functioning of the ear.

In sum, there are three products of the evolutionary process—adaptations, by-products, and noise. Adaptations are the primary product of the selective process, so evolutionary psychology is primarily focused on identifying and describing human psychological adaptations. The hypothesis that something is a by-product requires specifying the adaptation of which it is a by-product. The analysis of by-products, therefore, leads us back to the need to describe adaptations. And noise is the residue of nonfunctional variation that is selectively neutral.

Evolutionary Psychology

The basic elements of the evolutionary perspective apply to all forms of life on earth, from slime molds to people. We will turn now to the specific application of this perspective to human psychology. This branch of psychology is referred to as evolutionary psychology.

Premises of Evolutionary Psychology

Evolutionary psychology involves three key premises—domain specificity, numerousness, and functionality.

Domain Specificity

Adaptations are presumed to be **domain-specific** in the sense that they are designed by the evolutionary process to solve a particular adaptive problem. Consider the problem of food selection—choosing the right foods to eat from among a large array of possible objects in the world. A general decision rule, such as "eat the first thing you encounter," would be highly maladaptive, since it would fail to guide you to choose the small subset of objects that are edible and nutritious. Such a general rule would result in the consumption of poisonous plants, twigs, dirt, or feces, which would interfere with successful survival. The mechanisms favored by the evolutionary process are more specialized. In the area of food selection, domain specificity is seen in our preferences for calorically rich fat and in our evolved sweet tooth, which leads us to objects rich in sugar, such as ripe fruit and berries. General mechanisms cannot guide us to the small islands of successful adaptive solutions that are surrounded by oceans of maladaptive solutions.

Another reason for domain specificity is that different adaptive problems require different sorts of solutions. Our taste preferences, which guide us to successful food choices, do not help us solve the adaptive problem of choosing successful mates. If we were to use our food preferences as a general guide to the choice of mates, we would select strange mates indeed. Successful mate choices require different mechanisms. Domain specificity implies that selection tends to fashion specific mechanisms for each adaptive problem.

Numerousness

Since our ancestors faced many sorts of adaptive problems in the course of human evolution, we have numerous adaptive mechanisms. If you look at a textbook on the body, for example, you will discover a large number of physiological and anatomical mechanisms. We have a heart to pump our blood, a liver to detoxify poisons, a larynx to prevent us from choking, and sweat glands to keep the body thermally regulated.

Evolutionary psychologists suggest that the human mind, our evolved psychology, also contains a large number of mechanisms—psychological mechanisms. Consider the most common fears and phobias. We tend to be scared of snakes, heights, darkness, spiders, cliff edges, and strangers. Just in the domain of fears, we have a large number of psychological mechanisms because the number of hazardous hostile forces of nature has been so large. We are also likely to have psychological mechanisms for the selection of mates, the detection of cheaters in social exchanges, the favoring of habitats, the rearing of children, and the formation of strategic alliances. Evolutionary psychologists expect there to be a large number of domain-specific psychological mechanisms to correspond to the large number of distinct adaptive problems humans have recurrently confronted.

Functionality

The third key premise of evolutionary psychology is **functionality,** the notion that our psychological mechanisms are designed to accomplish particular adaptive goals. If you were a medical researcher studying the liver, you could not get very far in your understanding unless you understood the functions of the liver (e.g., in filtering out toxins). Evolutionary psychologists suggest that understanding adaptive function is also critical to insight into our evolved *psychological* mechanisms. We can't understand our preferences for certain mates, for example, without inquiring about the function of such preferences (e.g., to select a healthy or fertile mate). The search for function involves identifying the specific adaptive problem for which the mechanism is an evolved solution.

Empirical Testing of Evolutionary Hypotheses

In order to understand how evolutionary psychologists test hypotheses, it is necessary to consider the hierarchy of levels of evolutionary analysis depicted in Figure 8.1. At the top of the hierarchy is evolution by selection. The theory has been tested directly in many cases. New species can be formed in the laboratory by its application, and dogs can be selectively bred using its principles. Since there has never been a single case in which the general theory has been proved to be incorrect, most scientists take the general theory for granted and proceed with a more specific form of hypothesis testing.

At the next level down are middle-level evolutionary theories, such as the theory of parental investment and sexual selection. According to this theory, the sex (male or female) that invests more in offspring is predicted to be more discriminating or "choosy" about its mating partners. And the sex (male or female) that invests less in offspring is predicted to be more competitive with members of its own sex for sexual access to the high-investing sex. From these hypotheses, a number of specific predictions can be derived and tested empirically. In the human case, for example, women bear the heavy parental investment burdens of internal fertilization and nine-month pregnancy. Women are the high-investing sex; thus, according to the theory, they should exert more selectivity in their choice of mates than should men, who require

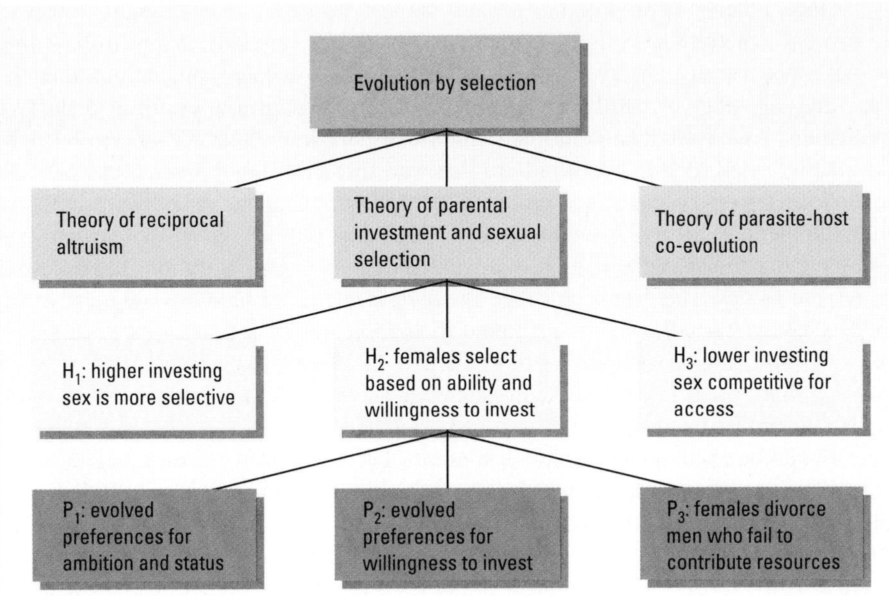

Figure 8.1

Evolutionary analysis hierarchy, depicting the conceptual levels of evolutionary analysis. At the top of the hierarchy is natural selection theory. At the next level down are middle-level evolutionary theories from which specific hypotheses and predictions can be derived. Each level of the hierarchy is evaluated by the cumulative weight of the empirical evidence from tests of the predictions derived from it. Source: Adapted from Buss, 1995a.

only the contribution of sperm in order to reproduce. Two specific predictions can be derived from this hypothesis: (1) women will choose as mates men who are willing to invest resources in them and their children and (2) women will divorce men who fail to continue providing resources to them and their children.

Using this method of deriving specific testable predictions, researchers can carry out the normal scientific business of empirical research. If the data fail to support the predictions and hypotheses, then the middle-level theory from which they were derived is called into question. If the findings, when tested many times by independent researchers, support the predictions and hypotheses, then the middle-level theory from which they were derived increases in credibility.

The **deductive reasoning approach,** or the "top down," theory-driven method of empirical research is one approach to scientific investigation. Another method, which is equally valid, is called the **inductive reasoning approach,** or the "bottom-up," data-driven method of empirical research. In the inductive reasoning approach, a phenomenon is first observed, and then the researchers look for or develop a theory to fit the observations. Just as astronomers observed the galaxies in the universe expanding before they had a theory to explain why, psychologists notice and empirically document a number of phenomena before they have theories to explain them. In the domain of personality, for example, we might notice that men tend to be more physically aggressive than women. Although nothing in the theory of evolution by selection would have predicted this sex difference in advance, it is fair game for subsequent theorizing. The dual inductive and deductive approaches, of course, can apply to all theories in personality psychology, not just evolutionary theories.

Once a theory is proposed to explain the sex difference in aggression, however, we can ask, "If the theory is true, then what *further* predictions follow from it that we have not already observed?" It is in these further deduced predictions that the value and tenability of the theory rest. If the theory generates a wealth of deductive predictions, which are then confirmed empirically, we know that we are on the right explanatory track. If the theory fails to generate further testable predictions, or if its predictions fail to be confirmed empirically, then the theory is called into question. For example, one theory of sexual aggression against women has proposed that men who have experienced deprivation of sexual access to women are more likely to use aggressive tactics. This has been called the *mate deprivation theory* (Lalumiere et al., 1996). The evidence, however, has failed to support this hypothesis—men who have difficulty attracting women are no more likely to use sexual aggression than are men who are highly successful at attracting women. The mate deprivation theory, in short, appears to be false.

Evolutionary hypotheses have sometimes been criticized as being vague, speculative "just-so stories," implying that they are like fairy tales that have little scientific value. There is some justification for this criticism, and, in the early days of evolutionary psychology, there were more armchair speculators than empirical scientists. Recently, however, evolutionary hypotheses have been framed in a precise and testable manner, so this criticism is no longer valid (Buss, 2004; Buss, 2005; Kenrick & Luce, 2004). All the standards of normal science hold in evaluating evolutionary psychological hypotheses. Individual scientists bear a responsibility to formulate the evolutionary hypotheses in as precise and testable manner as possible.

With this theoretical background in mind, let's now turn to the implications of an evolutionary perspective for the three key levels of personality analysis—human nature, sex differences, and individual differences.

Human Nature

In the history of psychology, "grand" theories of personality were proposed about the universal contents of human nature. Sigmund Freud's theory of psychoanalysis, for example, proposed that humans had the core motives of sex and aggression. Alfred Adler, one of Freud's disciples, proposed that humans had the striving for superiority as a core motive. A more contemporary personality theorist, Robert Hogan, suggests that humans are driven by the desire for status and acceptance by the group—getting ahead and getting along, respectively. Even the most radical behaviorist, B. F. Skinner, had an implicit theory of human nature, consisting of a few domain-general learning mechanisms. Thus, all personality theories attempt to answer the following question: If humans have a nature that is different from the nature of gorillas, dogs, rats, or praying mantises, what are its contents and how can we discover them?

The perspective of evolutionary psychology offers a set of tools for discovering the human nature component of personality. From this perspective, human nature is the primary product of the evolutionary process. Psychological mechanisms that are successful in helping humans survive and reproduce tend to out-replicate those that are less successful. Over evolutionary time, these successful mechanisms spread throughout the population and come to characterize a species. Let's examine a few evolutionary hypotheses about the contents of human nature.

Need to Belong

Hogan (1983) argues that the most basic human motivators are status and acceptance by the group. According to Hogan, the most important social problems early humans had to solve in order to survive and reproduce involved establishing cooperative relations with other members of the group and negotiating hierarchies. Achieving status and popularity likely conferred a host of reproductively relevant resources on an individual, including better protection, more food, and more desirable mates.

According to Hogan's theory, being ostracized from a group would have been extremely damaging. Therefore, it can be predicted that humans have evolved psychological mechanisms to prevent being excluded. Baumeister and Tice (1990) propose that this is the origin and function of **social anxiety,** which is defined as distress or worry about being negatively evaluated in interpersonal situations. They propose that social anxiety is a species-typical adaptation that prevents social exclusion. People who were indifferent to being excluded by others may have suffered in the currency of survival by lacking the protection of the group. They may also have suffered by failing to find mates as a result of being excluded. These individuals may have experienced lower reproductive success than those whose psychological mechanisms caused them to maintain inclusion in the group by avoiding doing things that elicit criticism.

If this hypothesis is correct, what testable predictions might follow from it? One set of testable predictions pertains to the *events* that elicit social anxiety (Buss, 1990). Groups can be expected to shun those who inflict costs on others within the group in the currencies of survival and reproduction. Thus, showing cowardice in the face of danger, displaying aggression toward in-group members, trying to lure away the mates of in-group members, stealing from in-group members, and murdering in-group members would all have inflicted costs on particular members of the group.

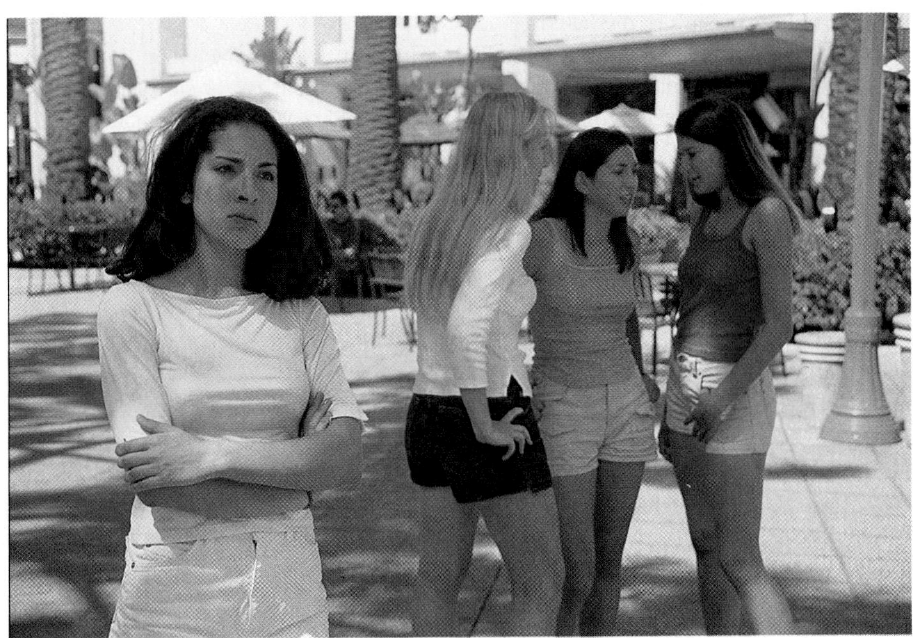

Humans evolved to live in groups. Consequently, an individual who is shunned by a group will feel anxious.

Baumeister and Leary (1995) present empirical evidence that the need to belong may be a central motive of human nature. They argue that the group serves several key adaptive functions for individuals. First, groups can share food, information, and other resources. Second, groups can offer protection from external threat, or defense against rival groups. Third, groups contain concentrations of mates, which are needed for reproduction. And, fourth, groups usually contain kin, which provide opportunities to receive altruism and to invest in genetic relatives.

Several lines of empirical research support Baumeister and Leary's theory about the need to belong. First, external threats have been shown repeatedly to increase group cohesion (Stein, 1976). In one study, World War II veterans were examined for enduring social ties (Elder & Clipp, 1988). Remarkably, their strongest social ties 40 years after the war were with comrades who had experienced combat together. This effect was intensified among the units in which some comrades had died, suggesting that, the more intense the external threat, the greater the social bonding.

The opportunity to acquire resources also seems to be a powerful context for triggering group cohesion. In one study, participants were randomly assigned to two groups (Rabbie & Horwitz, 1969). The assignment to groups alone produced no increase in group cohesion. When one group was given a prize—a transistor radio—based on the flip of a coin, however, both the rewarded group and the deprived group showed an increase in in-group preference. Apparently, when resources are linked with group membership, people become increasingly bonded with their groups.

Interestingly, researchers have begun to make progress in identifying the underlying brain circuitry for the pain caused by social exclusion (MacDonald & Leary, 2005; Panksepp, 2005). Social rejection or exclusion has often been described as literally painful. Brain research suggests that social exclusion is mediated by components of the physical pain system, such as the anterior cingulated cortex. The fact that people use words like *hurt, wounded,* and *damaged* when they are socially excluded may reflect the shared brain circuitry through which physically induced pain and socially induced pain are mediated.

Since humans have always been intensely group living, and lack of a group almost surely would have meant death in ancestral environments, it is not surprising that we have a strong need to belong, which may represent a key part of our human nature.

Helping and Altruism

An evolutionary perspective provides a relatively straightforward set of predictions about the human nature of helping and altruism (Burnstein, Crandall, & Kitayama, 1994). One group of authors proposed a set of hypotheses directly derived from Hamilton's theory of inclusive fitness. Specifically, they hypothesized that helping others is a direct function of the recipients' ability to enhance the inclusive fitness of the helpers. Helping should decrease, according to this hypothesis, as the degree of genetic overlap decreases between the helper and the recipient. Thus, you should be more likely to help your sibling, who shares 50 percent of your genes, on average, than your nieces and nephews, who share only 25 percent of their genes, on average. Helping is expected to be lower still between individuals who share only 12.5 percent of their genes, such as first cousins. No other theory in psychology generates this precise helping gradient as a function of genetic relatedness or specifies kinship as one underlying principle for altruism.

The results of a series of studies in the United States and Japan support these predictions. In one condition, participants were asked to imagine different individuals asleep

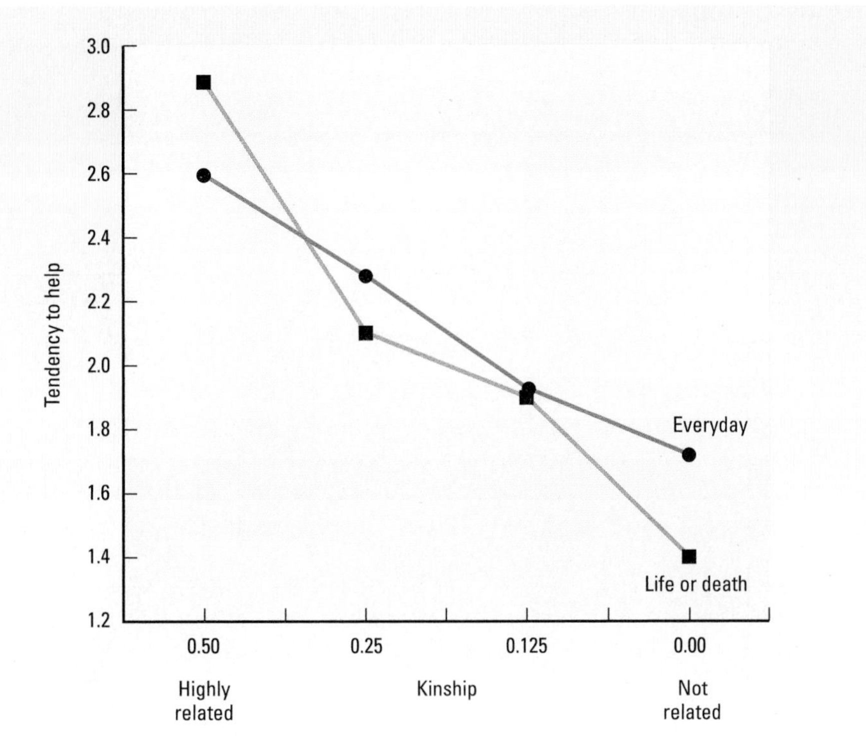

Figure 8.2

Tendency to help kin under life-or-death versus everyday conditions. Genetic overlap predicts the tendency to help, especially under life-or-death conditions. Source: Adapted from Burnstein, E., Crandall, C., & Kitayama, S. (1994). "Some neo-Darwinian decision rules for altruism: Weighing cures for inclusive fitness as a function of the biological importance of the decision," *Journal of Personality & Social Psychology*, 67, 773–789, figure 2, p. 778. Copyright © 1994 by the American Psychological Association. Reprinted with permission.

in different rooms of a rapidly burning building. The participants were further asked to imagine that they had time to rescue only one of them. The participants were instructed to circle the target they were most likely to help and to cross out the target they were least likely to help. As shown in Figure 8.2, the tendency to help is a direct function of the degree of genetic relatedness. This is especially true in a life-or-death context.

Mere genetic relatedness, however, represents just the start of an evolutionary analysis of the altruistic component of human nature. Burnstein et al. (1994) predicted that people should help younger relatives more than older relatives, since helping older kin would have less impact, on average, on his or her reproductive success than would helping a younger person. Furthermore, individuals of higher reproductive value (ability to produce children) should be helped more than individuals of lower reproductive value.

In one study, 1-year-olds were helped more than 10-year-olds, who in turn were helped more than 45-year-olds (Burnstein et al., 1994). Least helped were 75-year-old individuals. These findings, replicated across both Japanese and American samples, provide further support for the hypothesis that life-or-death helping decreases as the kin member gets older. Interestingly, these results were strongest in the life-or-

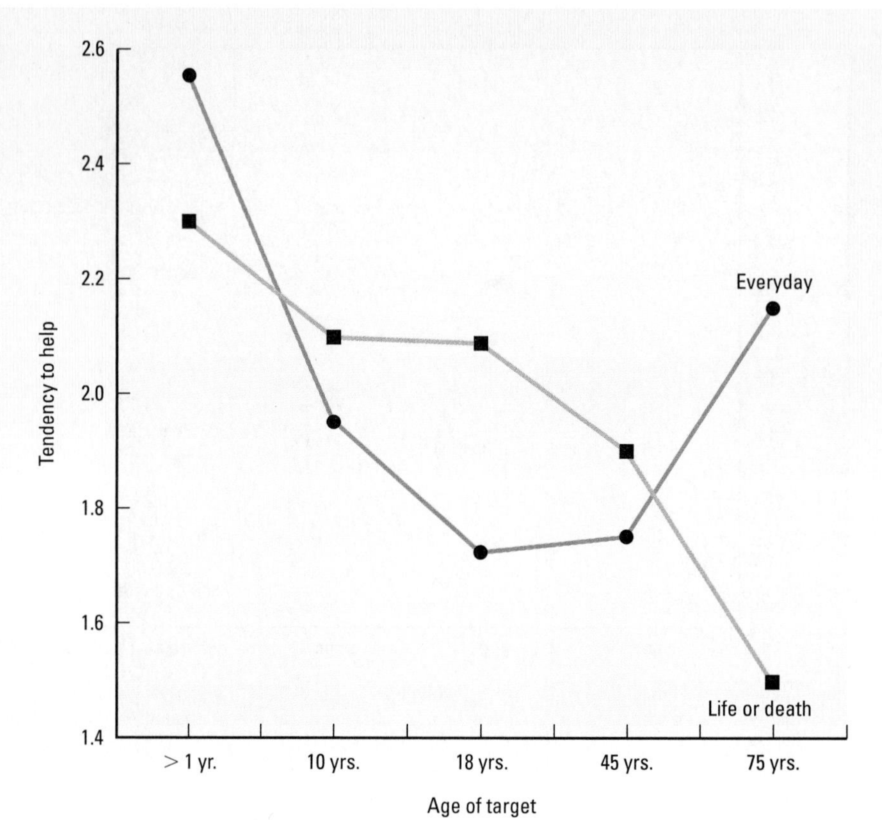

Figure 8.3

Tendency to help as a function of the recipient's age under life-or-death versus everyday conditions. When helping is relatively trivial, people tend to help those most in need, such as the young and the elderly. Under costly forms of help, however, the young are helped more than the old. Source: Adapted from Burnstein, E., Crandall, C., & Kitayama, S. (1994). "Some neo-Darwinian decision rules for altruism: Weighing cures for inclusive fitness as a function of the biological importance of the decision," *Journal of Personality & Social Psychology,* 67, 773–789, figure 3, p. 779. Copyright © 1994 by the American Psychological Association. Reprinted with permission.

death situation but showed a reversal in a trivial helping condition. For everyday helping, such as running a small errand for someone, the 75-year-olds were helped more than the 45-year-olds (see Figure 8.3).

In yet one more interesting twist, the tendency to help younger people depended on a critical survival context—famine conditions (Burnstein et al., 1994). When the participants were asked to imagine themselves living in a sub-Saharan African country that suffered widespread famine and disease, they reported a curvilinear relationship between age and helping (see Figure 8.4). Infants in this condition were helped *less* than 10-year-olds, who were helped the most. But then helping began to drop, with the least helped being the 75-year-olds.

These studies suggest that a central component of human nature is helping other people, but in a highly domain-specific way. The ways in which humans help others—the distribution of helping acts across individuals—is highly predictable from

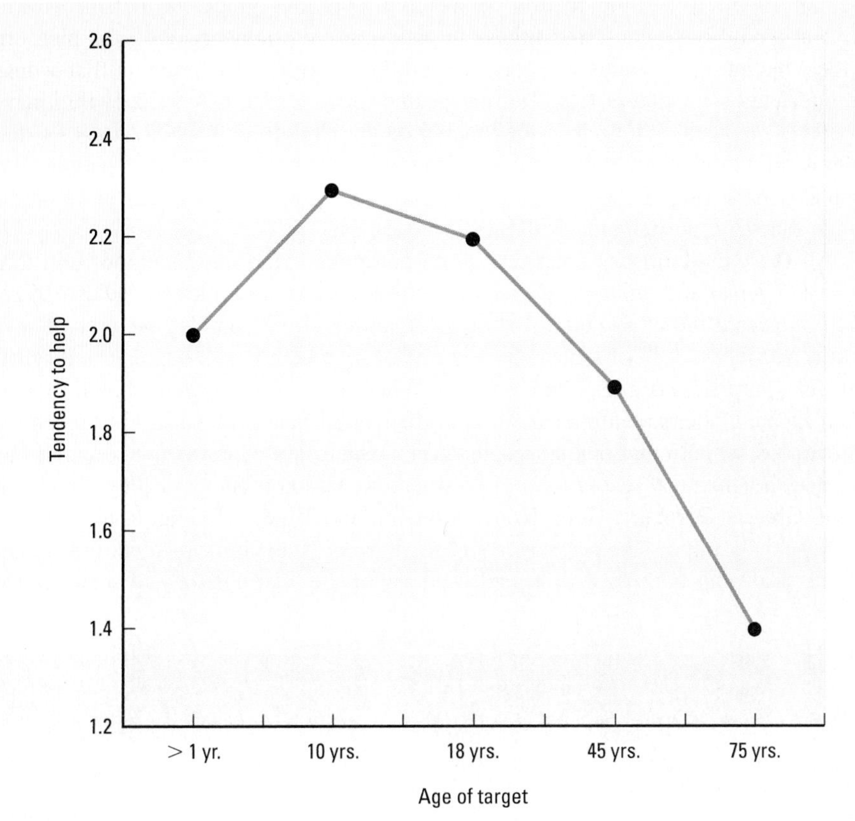

Figure 8.4

Tendency to help under famine conditions. Under conditions of possible starvation, the young and the old are left to die, whereas those most able to use the help—from ages 10 to 45 years—are helped most. Source: Adapted from Burnstein, E., Crandall, C., & Kitayama, S. (1994). "Some neo-Darwinian decision rules for altruism: Weighing cures for inclusive fitness as a function of the biological importance of the decision," *Journal of Personality & Social Psychology,* 67, 773–789, figure 6, p. 780. Copyright © 1994 by the American Psychological Association. Reprinted with permission.

an evolutionary perspective. The importance of genetic relatedness on helping others has even been documented for patterns of grandparental investment (Laham, Gonsalkorale, & von Hipple, 2005).

Universal Emotions

Evolutionary psychologists have taken three distinct perspectives on the study of emotions, such as fear, rage, and jealousy. One view, represented by the work of Paul Ekman, is to examine whether facial expressions of emotion are interpreted in the same ways across cultures, on the assumption that universality is one criterion for adaptation (Ekman, 1973, 1992a, 1992b). In other words, if all humans share an adaptation, such as smiling to express happiness, that adaptation is likely to be a core part of human nature. A second evolutionary view is that emotions are adaptive psychological mechanisms that signal various "fitness affordances" in the social environment

(Ketelaar, 1995). According to this perspective, emotions guide the person toward goals that would have conferred fitness in ancestral environments (e.g., the pleasure one feels having one's status rise within a group) or to avoid conditions that would have interfered with fitness (e.g., getting beaten up or abused). A third evolutionary perspective on social emotions is the "manipulation hypothesis," which suggests that emotions are designed to exploit the psychological mechanisms of other people. For example, expressions of rage might be designed to make a verbal threat more credible than the same threat made without displaying rage.

All these evolutionary perspectives on emotions hinge on the proposition that they are universal and universally recognized in the same way. Ekman (1973, 1992a, 1992b) pioneered the cross-cultural study of emotions. He assembled pictures of several different faces, each of which showed one of seven emotions: happiness, disgust, anger, fear, surprise, sadness, and contempt. When these pictures were shown to subjects in Japan, Chile, Argentina, Brazil, and the United States, all showed tremendous agreement on which emotions corresponded to which face. Subsequent research has confirmed the universal recognition of these emotional expressions in Italy, Scotland, Estonia, Greece, Germany, Hong Kong, Sumatra, and Turkey (Ekman et al., 1987).

Especially impressive is the study of the Fore of New Guinea—a cultural group with practically no contact with outsiders. They spoke no English, had seen no TV

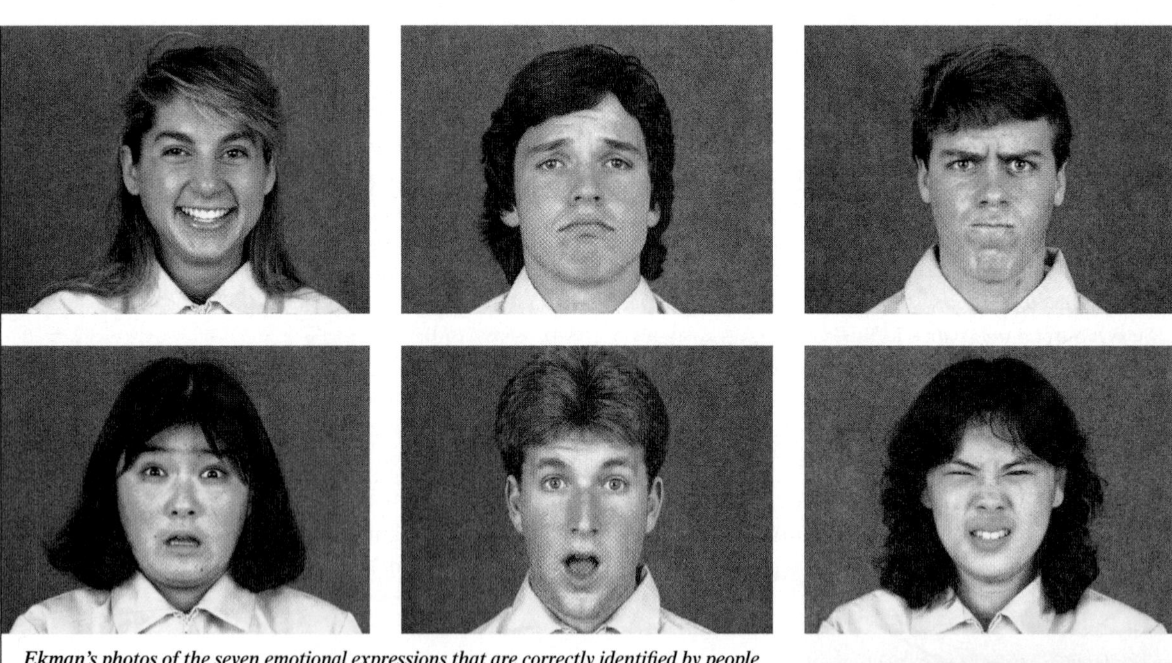

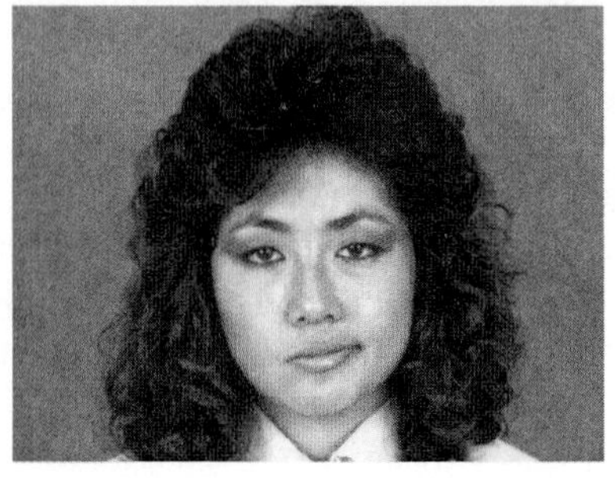

Ekman's photos of the seven emotional expressions that are correctly identified by people from many diverse cultures. Can you identify which photo is associated with the following emotions: happiness, disgust, anger, fear, surprise, sadness, and contempt?

or movies, and had never lived with Caucasians. Nonetheless, the Fore also showed the universal pairing of emotions and faces. Subsequent research has also shown the universality of the facial expression of contempt (Ekman et al., 1987). Although only the most preliminary aspects of the evolutionary psychology of emotions have been studied, Ekman's work suggests that emotions, as central components of personality, are universally expressed and recognized, thus fulfilling an important criterion for adaptation. They are good candidates for evolved components of human nature.

We have reviewed only a few hypotheses about the components of human nature from an evolutionary perspective—the need to belong, social anxiety about ostracism, the urge to help, and the universality of emotions. An evolutionary perspective may shed light on many other possible components of human nature, such as childhood fears of loud noises, darkness, spiders, and strangers; emotions such as anger, envy, passion, and love; the universality of play among children; retaliation and revenge for perceived personal violations; status striving; psychological pain on the loss of status and reputation; and perhaps many more. Human nature, however, represents only one level of personality analysis. We now turn to the second level—sex differences.

Sex Differences

Evolutionary psychology predicts that males and females will be *the same* or *similar* in all the domains in which the sexes have faced the same or similar adaptive problems. Both sexes have sweat glands because both sexes have faced the adaptive problem of thermal regulation. Both sexes have similar (although not identical) taste preferences for fat, sugar, salt, and particular amino acids because both sexes have faced similar (although not identical) food consumption problems.

In other domains, men and women have faced substantially different adaptive problems over human evolutionary history. In the physical realm, for example, women have faced the problem of childbirth; men have not. Women, therefore, have evolved particular adaptations that are lacking in men, such as mechanisms for producing labor contractions through the release of oxytocin into the bloodstream.

Men and women have also faced different information-processing *problems* in some adaptive domains. Because fertilization occurs internally within the woman, for example, men have faced the adaptive problem of uncertainty of paternity in their offspring. Men who failed to solve this problem risked investing resources in children who were not their own. We are all descendants of a long line of ancestral men whose characteristics led them to behave in ways that increased their likelihood of paternity and decreased the odds of investing in children who were presumed to be theirs but whose genetic fathers were other men.

This does not imply, of course, that men were or are consciously aware of the adaptive problem of compromised paternity. A man does not think, "Oh, if my wife has sex with someone else, then my certainty that I'm the genetic father will be jeopardized, and this will endanger the replication of my genes; I'm really mad." Or, if a man's wife is taking birth-control pills, he does not think, "Well, because Joan is taking the pill, it doesn't really matter whether she has sex with other men; after all, my certainty in paternity is secure." Instead, jealousy is a blind passion, just as our hunger for sweets and craving for companionship are blind passions. The blind "wisdom" of jealousy is passed down to us over millions of years by our successful forebears (Buss, 2000a).

Women faced the problem of securing a reliable or replenishable supply of resources to carry them through pregnancy and lactation, especially when food resources were scarce (such as during droughts and harsh winters). We are all descendants of a long and unbroken line of women who successfully solved this adaptive challenge—for example, by preferring mates who showed the ability to accrue resources and the willingness to channel them toward particular women (Buss, 2003). The women who failed to solve this problem failed to survive, imperiled the survival chances of their children, and hence failed to become our ancestors.

Evolutionary-predicted sex differences hold that the sexes will differ in precisely those domains where women and men have faced different sorts of adaptive problems (Buss, 2004). To an evolutionary psychologist, the likelihood that the sexes are psychologically identical in domains in which they have recurrently confronted different adaptive problems over the long expanse of human evolutionary history is essentially zero (Symons, 1992). The key question, therefore, is not "Are men and women different psychologically?" Rather, the key questions about sex differences, from an evolutionary psychological perspective, are the following:

1. In what *domains* have women and men faced different adaptive problems?
2. What are the *sex-differentiated psychological mechanisms* of women and men that have evolved in response to these sex-differentiated adaptive problems?
3. Which social, cultural, and contextual inputs affect the magnitude of expressed sex differences?

This section reviews some of the key domains in which the sexes have been predicted to differ: aggression, jealousy, desire for sexual variety, and mate preferences.

Sex Differences in Aggression

The earliest known homicide victim was a Neanderthal man who died 50,000 years ago (Trinkaus & Zimmerman, 1982). He was stabbed in the left front of his chest, indicating a right-handed attacker. As paleontological detective work has become increasingly sophisticated, evidence of prehistoric violence among our forebears has mushroomed (Daly & Wilson, 1988). Ancient skeletal remains contain cranial and rib fractures that appear inexplicable except by the force of clubs and weapons that stab. Weapon fragments are occasionally found lodged in skeletal rib cages. Humans apparently have a long evolutionary history of violence (Buss, 2005).

In a sample of homicides committed in Chicago from 1965 through 1980, 86 percent were committed by men (Daly & Wilson, 1988). Of these, 80 percent of the victims were also men. Although the exact percentages vary from culture to culture, cross-cultural homicide statistics reveal strikingly similar findings. In all cultures studied to date, men are overwhelmingly more often the killers, and most of their victims are other men. Any reasonably complete theory of aggression must provide an explanation for both facts—why men engage in violent forms of aggression so much more often than women do, and why men comprise the majority of their victims.

An evolutionary model of intrasexual competition provides the foundation for such an explanation. It starts with the theory of parental investment and sexual selection (Trivers, 1972). In species in which females invest more heavily in offspring than males do, females become the valuable limiting resource on reproduction for males. Males become constrained in their reproduction not so much by their own ability to survive but, rather, by their ability to gain sexual access to the high-investing females. In other words, in a species in which females can bear only a small number of offspring, such as the human species, females will express great care in their choice of mates, and males will be forced to compete for access.

Because female mammals bear the physical burden of gestation and lactation, there is a considerable sex difference in minimum obligatory parental investment. Therefore, males can have many more offspring than females can. Stated differently, the ceiling on reproduction is much higher for males than for females. This difference leads to differences in the *variances* in reproduction between the sexes. The differences between the haves and have-nots, therefore, become greater for males than for females: most females will have some offspring. Among males, however, a few males will sire many offspring, whereas some will have none at all. This is known as **effective polygyny.**

Men tend to engage in riskier tactics of competition, such as aggression and violence.

As a general rule, the greater the variance in reproduction, the more ferocious the competition within the sex that shows higher variance. In an extreme case, such as the elephant seals off the coast of northern California, 5 percent of the males sire 85 percent of all offspring produced in a given breeding season (Le Boeuf & Reiter, 1988). Species that show high variance in reproduction within one sex tend to be highly **sexually dimorphic,** highly different in size and structure. The more intense the effective polygyny, the more dimorphic the sexes are in size and form (Trivers, 1985). Elephant seals are highly size dimorphic: males are four times larger than females (Le Boeuf & Reiter, 1988). Chimpanzees are less sexually dimorphic: males are roughly twice as large as females. Humans are mildly dimorphic, with males roughly 12 percent larger than females. Within primate species, the greater the effective polygyny, the more the sexual dimorphism, and the greater the reproductive variance between the sexes (Alexander et al., 1979).

Effective polygyny means that some males gain more than their fair share of copulations, whereas other males are shut out entirely, banished from contributing to the ancestry of future generations. Such a system leads to ferocious competition within the high-variance sex. In essence, polygyny selects for risky strategies, including those that lead to violent combat with rivals and those that lead to increased risk taking to acquire the resources needed to attract members of the high-investing sex.

Violence can occur at the top as well as the bottom of the hierarchy. Given an equal sex ratio, for each man who monopolizes two women, another man is forced to be a bachelor (Daly & Wilson, 1996). For those facing reproductive oblivion, a risky, aggressive strategy may represent a last resort. The homicide data reveal that men who are poor and unmarried are more likely to kill, compared with their more affluent and married counterparts (Wilson & Daly, 1985). This finding is correlational, of course, so we cannot know with certainty that being poor and unmarried is a cause of violence (a third variable, such as the personality trait of aggressiveness, might be responsible for being poor, unmarried, and violent).

This account provides an explanation for both facts revealed in the cross-cultural homicide record. Males are more often the perpetrators of violence because they are the products of a long history of effective polygyny. Throughout human evolution, male sexual strategies have been characterized by risky intrasexual competition for females, or for the social status and resources that attract females. The fact that men die, on average, seven years earlier than women is but one of the many markers of this aggressive and risk-taking intrasexual strategy (Promislow, 2003).

Men are the victims of aggression far more than women because men are in competition primarily with other men. It is other men who block any given man's access to women. With increased aggression comes a greater likelihood of injury and early death. The patterns of aggression, in summary, are well predicted by the evolutionary theory of intrasexual competition (Buss & Duntley, in press). Even psychologists who argue that most psychological and behavioral sex differences are due to social roles concede that sex differences in aggression are most likely caused by a long evolutionary history in which women and men have confronted different adaptive problems.

Sex Differences in Jealousy

Another difference between the sexes in the nature of the adaptive problems they have faced stems from the fact that fertilization occurs internally (and unseen) within women. This means that, over human evolutionary history, men have risked investing in children who were not their own. Few women, however, have ever been uncertain about which children were their own. From this perspective, the most reproductively damaging act, from an ancestral man's point of view, would have been if his mate had had a pregnancy through sexual intercourse with another man. That is the act that would have jeopardized his certainty of passing on his genes.

From an ancestral woman's point of view, however, the fact that her mate was having sex with another woman, by itself, would not jeopardize her certainty in that she is the mother of her own children. Such an infidelity, however, could be extremely risky to the woman's reproductive success: she could risk losing her mate's resources, time, commitment, and investment, all of which could be diverted to another woman.

For these reasons, evolutionary psychologists have predicted that men and women should differ in the weighting they give to cues that trigger jealousy. Specifically, men have been predicted to become more jealous than women in response to cues to a sexual infidelity. Women have been predicted to become more jealous than men in response to cues to the long-term diversion of a mate's commitment, such as emotional involvement with someone else. To test these predictions, participants were put in an agonizing dilemma, which you can participate in as well. Take a look at the Exercise that follows.

Exercise

Think of a serious, committed romantic relationship that you had in the past, that you currently have, or that you would like to have. Imagine that you discover that the person with whom you've been seriously involved has become interested in someone else. Of the following, what would distress or upset you more?

1. **Imagining your partner forming a deep emotional attachment to that person.**
2. **Imagining your partner enjoying passionate sexual intercourse with that other person.**

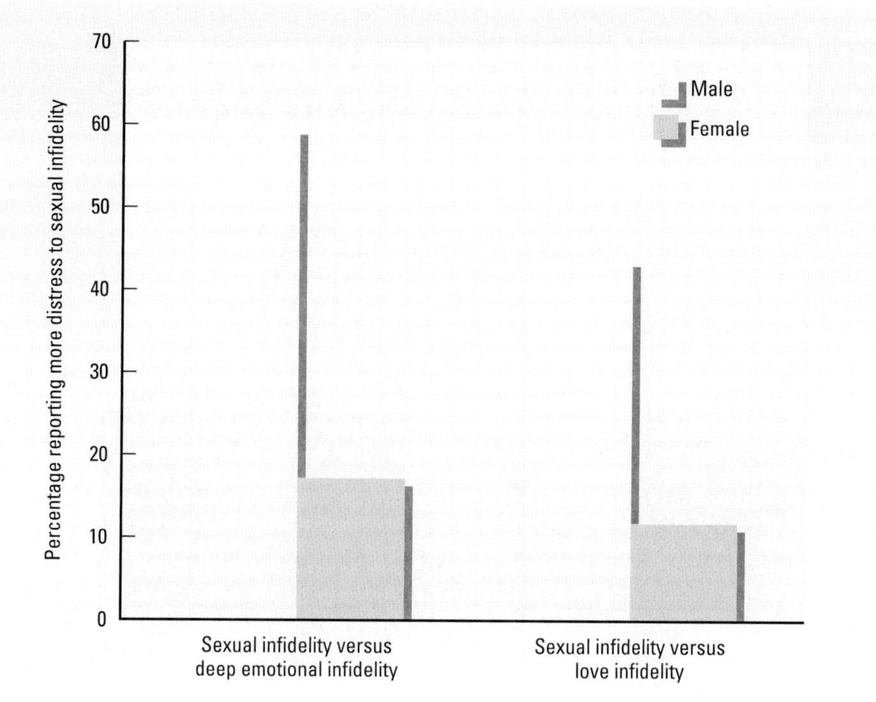

Figure 8.5

Percentage reporting more distress to sexual infidelity than to emotional or love infidelity. A large sex difference is found, with far more men than women reporting more distress to sexual infidelity, and the overwhelming majority of women reporting more distress to emotional or love infidelity. Source: From Buss, D. M., Larsen, R., Westen, D., & Semmelroth, J. (1992). "Sex differences in jealousy: Evolution, physiology, and psychology," *Psychological Science,* 3, 251–255, fig. 1, top panel, p. 252. Copyright © 1992 Blackwell Publishers UK. Reprinted by permission.

As shown in Figure 8.5, men are far more distressed than women when imagining their partners having sexual intercourse with someone else (Buss et al., 1992). The overwhelming majority of women, in contrast, are more distressed when imagining their partners becoming emotionally involved with someone else. This does not mean that women are indifferent to their partners' sexual infidelities or that men are indifferent to their partners' emotional infidelities—far from it. Both events upset both sexes. However, when forced to choose which one is more upsetting, a large sex difference emerges, precisely as predicted by the evolutionary hypothesis of sex differences in the nature of the adaptive problems. These results also show up in measures of physiological distress (Buss et al., 1992; Pietrzak, Laird, Stevens, & Thompson, 2002). When imagining partners having sex with someone else, men's heart rate goes up five beats per minutes, which is like drinking three cups of coffee at one time. Their skin conductance increases, and their frown response is visible. Women, in contrast, show greater physiological distress at imagining their partners becoming emotionally involved with someone else.

Are these sex differences found across cultures? Thus far, researchers have replicated these sex differences in Germany, the Netherlands, and Korea (Buunk et al., 1996),

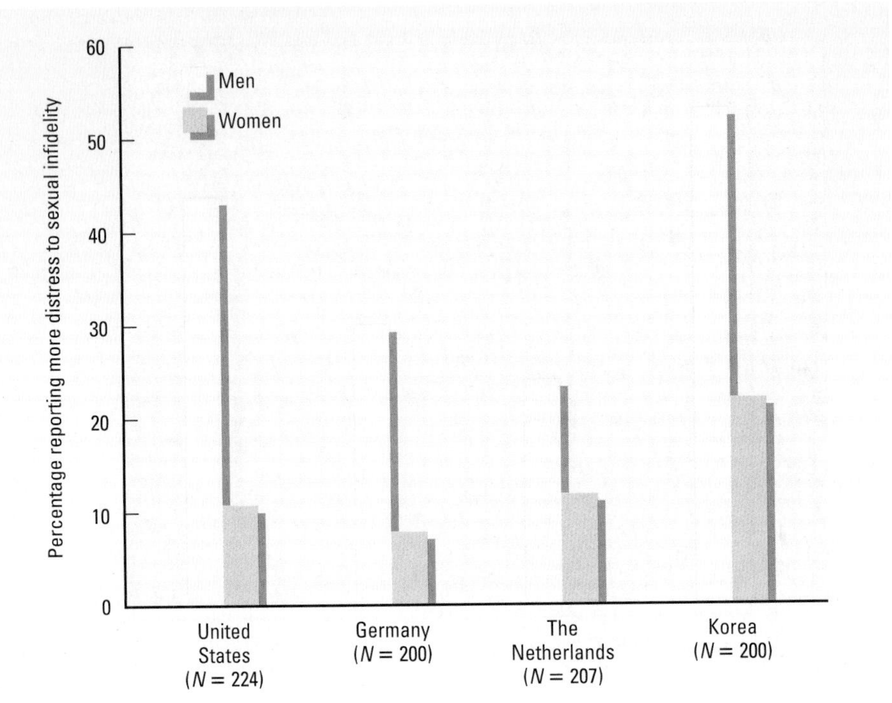

Figure 8.6

Sex differences in jealousy across four cultures. In all four cultures, more men than women are distressed about imagining a partner's sexual infidelity; most women are more distressed by a partner's emotional infidelity. Source: From Buunk, A. P., Angleitner, A., Oubaid, V., & Buss, D. M. (1996). "Sex differences in jealousy in evolutionary and cultural perspective: Tests from the Netherlands, Germany, and the United States," *Psychological Science*, 7, 359–363, fig. 1, p. 361. Copyright © 1996 Blackwell Publishers UK. Reprinted by permission.

as shown in Figure 8.6. Other researchers have replicated these sex differences in Korea and Japan (Buss et al., 1999). The sex differences in jealousy appear to be robust across a range of cultures.

Not every psychologist agrees with the evolutionary explanation. DeSteno and Salovey (1996) have proposed that men and women differ in their "beliefs" about sexual and emotional involvement. When a man thinks that his partner is becoming sexually involved with a rival, for example, he might also think that his partner will also be getting emotionally involved with him—a so-called double shot of infidelity. The reason men get more upset about sexual rather than emotional infidelity, DeSteno and Salovey argue, is not because men are really more jealous about sexual infidelity—it's because men "believe" that a sexual infidelity will result in the double shot of infidelity, which includes emotional infidelity.

Women, DeSteno and Salovey argue, have different beliefs, although they fail to explain why. Women believe in a reverse double-shot, that if their partners become emotionally involved with a rival, they will also become sexually involved. It's women's beliefs about this double shot of infidelity that upsets them, DeSteno and Salovey argue, and not that women really are more upset about an emotional betrayal.

The evolutionary explanation opposes the double-shot explanation. Given the large sex differences stemming from fundamental differences in reproductive biology, according to evolutionary psychologists, it would be unlikely for selection to have failed to produce psychological sex differences about the two forms of infidelity. The hard hand of data, however, usually settles scientific disagreements. Buss and his colleagues (1999) conducted four empirical studies in three different cultures to pit the predictions of evolutionary theory against the predictions of the double-shot hypothesis. One of the studies involved 1,122 participants from a liberal arts college in the southeastern United States. The researchers asked them to imagine their partners becoming interested in someone else and asked: What would upset or distress you more: (a) imagining your partner forming a deep emotional *(but not sexual)* relationship with that person? or (b) imagining your partner enjoying a sexual *(but not emotional)* relationship with that person? The men and women differed by roughly 35 percent in their responses, precisely as predicted by the evolutionary model. The women continued to express greater upset about a partner's emotional infidelity, even if it did not involve sex. The men continued to show more upset than the women about a partner's sexual infidelity, even if it did not involve emotional involvement. If the double-shot hypothesis were the correct explanation for the initial sex differences that were found, then the sex difference should have disappeared when the sexual and emotional components of infidelity were isolated. It did not.

In a second study of 234 women and men (Buss et al., 1999), the researchers used a different strategy for pitting the competing hypotheses against each other. They asked participants to imagine that their worst nightmare had occurred—that their partners had become both sexually *and* emotionally involved with someone else. They then asked the participants to state *which aspect* they found more upsetting. The results were conclusive. The researchers found large sex differences, precisely as predicted by the evolutionary explanation—63 percent of the men but only 13 percent of the women found the sexual aspect of the infidelity to be most upsetting. In contrast, 87 percent of the women, but only 37 percent of the men, found the emotional aspect of the infidelity to be most upsetting. No matter how the questions were worded, no matter which method was used, the same sex difference emerged in every test. Several other scientists have now confirmed these results using somewhat different methods and different cultures, such as Sweden (e.g., Wiederman & Kendall, 1999). Wiederman and Kendall concluded that, "contrary to the double-shot explanation, choice of scenario was unrelated to attitudes regarding whether the other gender was capable of satisfying sexual relations outside of a love relationship" (p. 121).

These and similar sex differences have now been replicated in China, Germany, the Netherlands, Korea, Sweden, Japan, England, and Romania (Brase, Caprar, & Voracek, 2004). The cross-cultural findings provide support for the theory that these are universal sex differences. The double-shot theory cannot explain why these sex differences are universal. Based on the available evidence, the double-shot theory has failed to be supported both from the cross-cultural findings and from the studies that test its predictions in direct competition with those from the evolutionary theory.

Despite the fact that the sex differences in the weighting given to the triggers of jealousy have been well documented across cultures using a variety of methods ranging from memorial recall of jealous episodes (e.g., Schutzwohl & Koch, 2004) to physiological recordings (Pietrzak et al., 2002), the findings continue to be challenged (e.g., Harris, 2000; De Steno, Bartlett, Salovey, & Braverman, 2002). After the belief theory of sex differences in jealousy was repeatedly disproved, however, its original authors appear to have abandoned it entirely. Instead, they've changed their position and now argue not for an alternative theory, but rather for the idea that sex differences in jealousy are merely an artifact of experimental conditions (DeSteno et al., 2002). These researchers placed participants under conditions of "high cognitive load" with an extremely distracting task and then found that under these conditions, the usual sex differences failed to appear. This is like dangling a hungry person over a cliff with the threat of a drop to death and then discovering that "humans don't experience hunger." All effects can be made to disappear by providing overwhelming distracting experimental stimuli. Indeed, researchers have concluded that "cognitive load" manipulations are poor methods for testing evolutionary hypotheses about jealousy using the scenario paradigm (Barrett, Frederick, & Haselton, in press).

The new attempt to dismiss the sex differences in jealousy as "experimental artifact" does not hold up when faced with the many studies that have found the sex differences using a variety of different methods. In a recent ingenious study, for example, Schutzwohl and Koch (2004) used an entirely new method that has never been used in jealousy research. They had participants listen to a story about their own romantic relationship in which an infidelity was said to have occurred. Embedded within the story were five cues that had been previously determined to be cues highly diagnostic of *sexual infidelity* (e.g., He suddenly has difficulty becoming sexually aroused when you and he want to have sex) and five cues highly diagnostic of *emotional infidelity* (e.g., He doesn't respond any more when you tell him that you love him). In a surprise recall test a week later, men spontaneously remembered more cues to sexual than to emotional infidelity (42 percent versus 29 percent), whereas women remembered more cues to emotional than to sexual infidelity (40 percent versus 24 percent). These findings support the hypothesis that sex differences in jealousy are quite real, and cannot be dismissed as an "experimental artifact" (Schutzwohl & Koch, 2004).

The gold standard in science is independent replication, and by this criterion, the evolutionary explanation has fared well. After each challenge, additional research by independent scientists has continued to find support for the existence of sex differences in jealousy and the evolutionary explanations for them (e.g., Brase, Caprar, & Voracek, 2004; Buss & Haselton, 2005; Cann, Mangum, & Wells, 2001; Dijkstra & Buunk, 2001; Fenigstein & Pelz, 2002; Geary et al., 2001; Murphy et al., 2006; Pietrzak et al., 2002; Sagarin, 2005; Sagarin et al., 2003; Schutzwohl & Koch, 2004; Shackelford, Buss, & Bennett, 2002; Shackelford et al., 2004; Strout, Laird, Shafer, & Thompson, 2005).

Sex Differences in Desire for Sexual Variety

Another sex difference predicted by evolutionary psychological theories is a difference in the desire for sexual variety (Figure 8.7). This prediction stems from parental investment and sexual selection theory. The members of the sex that invests less in offspring, according to this theory, are predicted to be less discriminating in their selection of mates and more inclined to seek multiple mates. In ancestral times, men could increase their reproductive success by gaining sexual access to a variety of women.

If you were given your ideal wish, how many sex partners would you like to have in the next month? How about the next year? How about over your entire lifetime? When unmarried college students were asked these questions, the women indicated that they wanted about 1 in the next month and 4 or 5 in their entire lifetimes (see Figure 8.7) (Buss & Schmitt, 1993). The men, in contrast, thought that 2 would be about right in the next month, 8 over the next couple of years, and 18 in their lifetimes. In terms of expressed desires, men and women differ in the ways predicted by the evolutionary account.

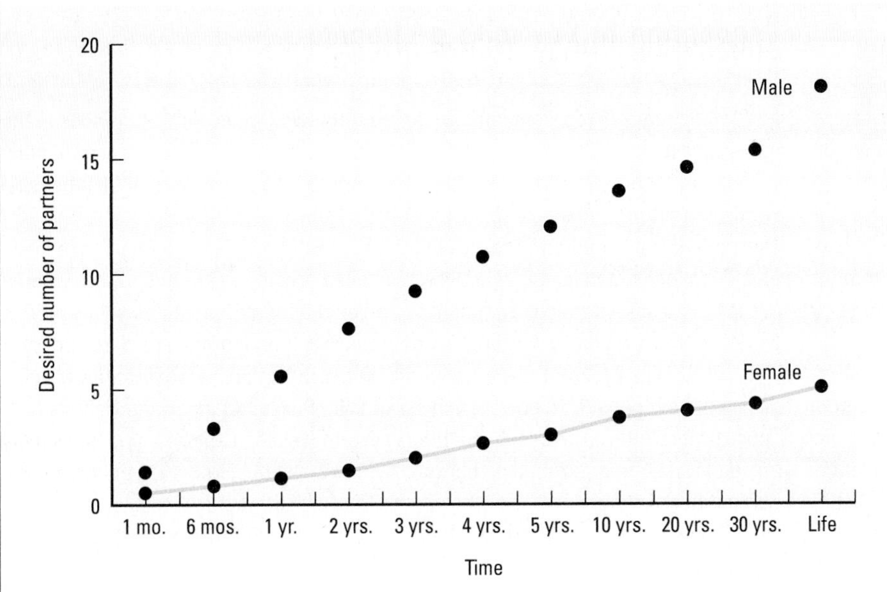

Figure 8.7

Number of sex partners desired at different time intervals, ranging from one month to a lifetime. Men and women differ at every time interval, showing the largest difference in lifetime partners desired. Source: From Buss, D. M., & Schmitt, D. P. (1993). "Sexual strategies theory: An evolutionary perspective on human mating," *Psychological Review,* 100, 204–232, figure 2, p. 211. Copyright © 1993 by the American Psychological Association. Reprinted with permission.

The sex differences in number of partners desired has now been replicated in a massive cross-cultural study. David Schmitt and his colleagues (2003) studied 16,288 individuals from 10 world regions, representing 52 different nations from Argentina to Slovakia to Zimbabwe. They used instruments identical to those used for Figure 8.7, translated into the appropriate language for each culture. For the time interval of the next 30 years, men worldwide expressed a desire for roughly 13 sex partners, whereas women expressed a desire for roughly 2.5 partners. The sex difference in the desire for sexual variety, in short, appears to be large and universal. The sex difference extends to how often men and women think about sex. One study found that women, on average, think about sex 9 times per week; men, on average, think about sex 37 times per week (Regan & Atkins, 2006). This sex difference in desire deserves a closer look.

Sex Differences in Mate Preferences

Evolutionary psychologists have also predicted that men and women will differ in the qualities they desire in a long-term mate. Specifically, because women bear the burdens of the heavy obligatory parental investment, they are predicted to place more value on a potential mate's financial resources and the qualities that lead to such resources. Men, in contrast, are predicted to place greater value on a woman's physical appearance, which provides cues to her fertility. In a sample of college students, the men ranked physical attractiveness an average of 4.04, whereas the women

A Closer Look

Consenting to Sex with a Stranger

The sex difference in desire for sexual variety shows up in behavioral data. In one study conducted at a university in Florida, experimental confederates approached people of the opposite sex (Clark & Hatfield, 1989). After introducing themselves, they said, "Hi, I've been noticing you around campus lately, and I find you very attractive. Would you go out on a date with me tonight?" A different group was asked, "Would you go back to my apartment with me tonight?" And a third group was asked, "Would you have sex with me tonight?"

Experimenters simply recorded the percentage of people approached who agreed to the request. Of the women who were approached by the male confederate, 55 percent agreed to the date, 6 percent agreed to go back to the man's apartment, and 0 percent agreed to have sex with him. Of the men approached by the female confederate, 50 percent agreed to go out on the date, 69 percent agreed to go back to her apartment, and 75 percent agreed to have sex with her.

The reactions of the two sexes were very different in the sex condition. The women approached for sex were often insulted, and many thought the request was simply strange. The men, in contrast, were typically flattered. And some of the 25 percent of the men who declined the request for sex were apologetic. Others offered excuses, such as the fact that their parents or fiancée was in town visiting.

These studies and many others support the evolutionary hypothesis that men and women differ in their desire for sexual variety. Men tend to have more sexual fantasies than do women, and they engage more often in "partner switching" during the course of those fantasies—that is, they fantasize about two or more sex partners during the course of a single fantasy episode (Buss, 2003). In fact, one meta-analysis found that attitudes toward casual sex was one of the two largest sex differences in the sexual domain, with men typically much more positive than women about casual sex (Oliver & Hyde, 1993).

Journalist Natalie Angier questions these results, arguing that women would hop into bed as easily as men in these situations but are deterred by a concern for their personal safety (Angier, 1999). Russell Clark, of the University of North Texas, explored this possibility (Clark, 1990). First, he replicated the "sex with strangers" study on a different sample in a different part of the country, and the results were virtually identical—more men than women were willing to have sex with a virtual stranger. Second, Clark noted that roughly half of the women in each study were quite willing to go out on a date with the strangers, which seemed puzzling if they were concerned about their safety. Third, when Clark's experimenters asked the participants to describe the reason for their refusal (if they refused),

ranked it lower, giving it 6.26 (the highest possible rank would be a "1," whereas the lowest possible rank would be "13"). On the dimension of good earning capacity, the women ranked it 8.04, whereas the men ranked it 9.92 (Buss & Barnes, 1986). Thus, it is clear that women and men both place many qualities above looks and resources. In particular, "kind and understanding" (rank: 2.20) and having an "exciting personality" (rank: 3.50) are more valued by both sexes. Personality, in short, plays a key role in what people want in a marriage partner. Nonetheless, in the study, the men and women differed in their rankings of looks and resources in the predicted direction. Indeed, these sex differences have been found across 37 cultures (Buss, 1989). Zambian, Chinese, Indonesian, and Norwegian men rank physical attractiveness as more important than do their female counterparts, just like the American samples. Similarly, worldwide, women rank a potential partner's good financial prospects to be more important than do their male counterparts. Perhaps even more important, the personality characteristics that contribute to financial women's and men's answers were nearly identical—both mentioned that they had a boyfriend or girlfriend or that they did not know the person well enough.

Perhaps a date seems safer than sex and women really do want sex with strangers, if only they could be assured of their safety. To explore this possibility, Clark (1990) conducted yet another experiment. Men and women participants were contacted by close personal friends, who testified about the integrity and character of the stranger. The participants were assured by their friends that the stranger was warm, sincere, trustworthy, and attractive. The participants were then asked one of two questions: "Would you be willing to go on a date?" or "Would you be willing to go to bed?" After being debriefed, the participants were asked for their reasons for their decisions.

The overwhelming majority of both sexes agreed to the date—91 percent of the women and 96 percent of the men. In the sex condition, however, a large sex difference emerged—50 percent of the men but only 5 percent of the women agreed. Not a single woman indicated a concern for safety. Clearly, making conditions safer for women increases the odds that they will consent to sex with a stranger—from 0 percent to 5 percent—so safety concerns are not irrelevant, but the sex difference remains large. Most women agree to date strangers when a close friend vouches for the man's warmth and integrity, but 95 percent still refuse to consent to sex.

The difference is *not* that "women are coy," which would imply a false shyness, a pretense of lack of interest, or a childlike coquettishness. And it's not that women lack interest in sex. The evidence is compelling, however, that most women are careful about whom they choose to sleep with and, for the most part, avoid jumping into bed with total strangers. Men are more willing. Most men responded to the sexual request by saying, "What time?" or "Why not?" and then asking for the requester's telephone number and directions to her house.

These differences hold with equal force in lust for affairs. In one study by Ralph Johnson (1970) of Sacramento State College, 48 percent of American men, but only 5 percent of American women, expressed a desire to engage in extramarital sex. In a classic older study by Lewis Terman (1938) of 769 American men and 770 American women, 72 percent of the men, but only 27 percent of the women, admitted that they sometimes desired sex with someone outside of their marriage. Germans revealed similar tendencies—46 percent of married men but only 6 percent of married women admit that they would take advantage of a casual sexual opportunity with someone else if the chance arose (Sigusch & Schmidt, 1971). Studies by David Wyatt Seal and his colleagues at the University of New Mexico show similar sex differences (Seal, Agosinelli, & Hannett, 1994).

Women, of course, may be more reluctant to confide their sexual desires to a surveyor, so the figures are likely to underestimate women's adulterous impulses. Nonetheless, the sex difference proves so robust across studies and methods of inquiry that there is no reason to doubt that men and women differ in desire.

success—ambition, industriousness, and dependability—are also highly valued by women worldwide.

Some psychologists have proposed alternative explanations for these sex differences. Indeed, Buss and Barnes (1986) have proposed the "structural powerlessness hypothesis" (SPH). According to this hypothesis, women value income in a mate not because of any evolved preferences but, rather, because men tend to control resources, so the primary route women traditionally have had to obtain needed resources has been through marriage. In essence, women are forced to value resources in men because they've been shut out of getting resources themselves. Eagly and Wood (1999) have argued along similar lines, suggesting that sex differences are due to men and women being assigned different social roles, with men assigned the breadwinning role and women the homekeeping role. This is an exciting area of research, in which competing theories are currently being pitted against each other—one of the hallmarks of cutting-edge science. In the next few years, there will likely be an empirical resolution of this debate.

Exercise

Following is a list of characteristics that might be present in a potential mate or marriage partner. Rank them on their desirability in someone you might marry. Give a 1 to the most desirable characteristic in a potential mate, a 2 to the second most desirable characteristic in a potential mate, a 3 to the third most desirable characteristic, and so on down to 13 for the 13th most desirable characteristic in a potential mate.

___ kind and understanding
___ religious
___ exciting personality
___ creative and artistic
___ easygoing
___ good housekeeper
___ intelligent
___ good earning capacity
___ wants children
___ good heredity
___ college graduate
___ physically attractive
___ healthy

In summary, personality plays a key role in mate preferences across the globe, and on a few dimensions there are universal sex differences in what people want in a marriage partner. Although the evolutionary hypotheses for these sex differences have so far received support in cross-cultural research, competing hypotheses have been proposed to explain them, and these are currently being tested.

Individual Differences

The study of individual differences, which is central to personality psychology, has been the most challenging and difficult level of analysis for evolutionary psychologists. Unlike sex differences, for which scientists have accumulated a large empirical foundation, there is far less of a foundation for adaptive individual differences. Thus, this section must necessarily be more speculative and preliminary than the previous sections.

There are a variety of ways in which individual differences can be explained from the vantage point of evolutionary psychology. The most common is explaining individual differences as a result of environmental differences acting on species-typical (human nature) psychological mechanisms (these are sometimes called *facultative traits*). An analogy is the phenomenon of calluses that people sometimes develop on their hands and feet. Individual differences in calluses can be explained by suggesting that different individuals are exposed to different amounts of repeated friction to their skin. All humans are presumed to have essentially the same callus-producing mechanisms, so individual differences are the result of the environmental differences that activate the mechanisms to differing degrees. Evolutionary psychologists invoke a similar form of explanation to account for psychological individual differences.

Second, individual differences can emerge from *contingencies among traits* (Bouchard & Loehlin, 2001). For example, "a hair-trigger temper may be advantageous if one is big and strong but not if one is small and weak" (Bouchard & Loehlin, 2001, p. 250). These individual differences are a kind of facultative trait. Rather than the trait's expression being contingent on the environment, however, its expression is contingent on other traits the person has—in this case, the size and strength of one's body.

A third source of individual difference stems from *frequency-dependent selection:* the process whereby the reproductive success (fitness) of a trait depends on its frequency relative to other traits in the population. For example, in a large population of people with a cooperative disposition, selection may favor those with a cheating disposition as long as they do not get too common. As the frequency of cheaters gets more common, cooperators evolve defenses to punish cheaters, and so the success of cheating goes down. Thus, heritable individual differences can be created through frequency-dependent selection.

A fourth source of individual differences comes from the fact that *the optimum level of a personality trait can vary over time and space.* Consider as an example differences over evolutionary time (or space) in the abundance of food, perhaps due to droughts or ice-ages. In times of food scarcity, selection favors a risk-taking personality trait—one that prompts a person to risk encountering predators in order to venture widely to get food and prevent starvation. In times of food abundance, selection favors a more cautious personality disposition to reduce the risk of venturing widely in the environment. Variations over time and space in the optimum level of a trait can create heritable individual differences in personality that are maintained in the population.

In sum, the evolutionary framework identifies several sources of individual differences: (1) those that arise from individuals possessing universal adaptations whose expression is contingent on the environment; (2) those that arise from contingencies with other traits; (3) those due to variation over time and space in the optimum value of a trait; and (4) those due to frequency-dependent selection. Below we explore some examples of these individual differences.

Environmental Triggers of Individual Differences

According to one theory, the critical event of early father presence versus father absence triggers specific sexual strategies in individuals (Belsky, Steinberg, & Draper, 1991). Children who grow up in father-absent homes during the first five years of life, according to this theory, develop expectations that parental resources will not be reliably or predictably provided. Furthermore, these children come to expect that adult pair bonds will not be enduring. Such individuals cultivate a sexual strategy marked by early sexual maturation, early sexual initiation, and frequent partner switching—a strategy designed to produce a larger number of offspring. Extraverted and impulsive personality traits may accompany and facilitate this sexual strategy. Other individuals are perceived as untrustworthy and relationships as transitory. Resources sought from brief sexual encounters are opportunistically attained and immediately extracted.

In contrast, individuals who experience a reliable, investing father during the first five years of life, according to the theory, develop a different set of expectations about the nature and trustworthiness of others. People are seen as reliable and trustworthy, and relationships are expected to be enduring. These early environmental experiences shunt individuals toward a long-term mating strategy, marked by delayed sexual maturation; a later onset of sexual activity; a search for long-term, securely attached adult relationships; and heavy investment in a small number of children.

There is some empirical support for this theory. Children from divorced homes, for example, are more sexually promiscuous than children from intact homes (Belsky et al., 1991). Furthermore, girls from father-absent homes reach menarche (age of first menstruation) earlier than girls from father-present homes (Kim, Smith, & Palermiti, 1997). Nonetheless, these findings are correlational, so causation cannot be inferred. It may be the case, for example, that men who are genetically predisposed to pursue a short-term mating strategy are more likely to get divorced and more likely to pass on to their children genes for that strategy (Bailey, Kirk, Zhu, Dunne, & Martin, 2000). However, despite the current lack of conclusive data, this theory nicely

According to reactive heritability, a man with a slim, wiry build is less likely than a stocky man to engage in aggressive behavior.

illustrates an evolutionary approach to the emergence of consistent individual differences—in this case, the effects of different environments on species-typical mechanisms.

Heritable Individual Differences Contingent on Other Traits

Another type of evolutionary analysis of personality involves evaluating one's personal strengths and weaknesses. Suppose, for example, that men could pursue two different strategies in social interaction—an aggressive strategy marked by the use of physical force and a nonaggressive strategy marked by cooperativeness. The success of these strategies, however, hinges on an individual's size, strength, and fighting ability. Those who happen to be muscular in body build can more successfully carry out an aggressive strategy than those who are skinny or chubby. If humans have evolved ways to evaluate themselves on their physical formidability, they can determine which social strategy is the most successful to pursue—an aggressive strategy or a cooperative strategy. Adaptive self-assessments, therefore, can produce stable individual differences in aggression or cooperativeness. In this example, the tendency toward aggression is not directly heritable. Rather, it is **reactively heritable:** it is a secondary consequence of heritable body build (Tooby & Cosmides, 1990). There is some evidence to support this idea that body build enters into a man's decision of whether to pursue an aggressive strategy (Buss, 2004).

Studies have shown that men with muscular, or mesomorphic, body builds are more likely to become juvenile delinquents than are those with either an ectomorphic (skinny) or endomorphic (fat) body build (Glueck & Glueck, 1956; Stewart, 1980). Nonetheless, these are correlational data, so causation from body build to self-assessment to aggression cannot be shown unambiguously. The notion of self-assessment of heritable qualities, however, remains a fascinating avenue for understanding the adaptive patterning of individual differences.

Frequency-Dependent Strategic Individual Differences

The process of evolution by selection tends to use up heritable variation. In other words, heritable variants that are more successful tend to replace those that are less successful, resulting in species-typical adaptations that show little or no heritable variation. The universal human design is to have two eyes, for example.

In some contexts, two or more heritable variants can evolve within a population. The most obvious example is biological sex itself. Within sexually reproducing species, the two sexes exist in roughly equal numbers because of **frequency-dependent selection.** If one sex becomes rare relative to the other, evolution will produce an increase in the numbers of the rarer sex. Frequency-dependent selection, in this example, causes the frequency of men and women to remain roughly equal.

Gangestad and Simpson (1990) argue that human individual differences in women's mating strategies have been caused by frequency-dependent selection. They start with the observation that competition tends to be most intense among individuals who are pursuing the same mating strategy (Maynard Smith, 1982). This lays the groundwork for the evolution of alternative strategies.

According to Gangestad and Simpson, women's mating strategies should center on two key qualities of potential mates—the parental investment a man could provide and the quality of his genes. A man who is able and willing to invest in a woman and her children can be an extraordinarily valuable reproductive asset. Similarly, independent of a man's ability to invest, women could benefit by selecting men who have high-quality genes, which can be passed down to her children. Men may carry genes for good health, physical attractiveness, or sexiness, which are then passed on to the woman's sons or daughters.

There may be a trade-off, however, between selecting a man for his parenting abilities and selecting a man for his genes. Men who are highly attractive to many women, for example, may be reluctant to commit to any one woman. Thus, a woman who is seeking a man for his genes may have to settle for a short-term sexual relationship without parental investment.

These various selection forces, according to Gangestad and Simpson (1990), gave rise to two alternative female mating strategies. A woman seeking a high-investing mate would adopt a **restricted sexual strategy** marked by delayed intercourse and prolonged courtship. This would enable her to assess the man's level of commitment, detect the existence of prior commitments to other women or children, and simultaneously signal to the man her sexual fidelity and, hence, assure him of his paternity of future offspring.

A woman seeking a man for the quality of his genes, on the other hand, has less reason to delay sexual intercourse. A man's level of commitment to her is irrelevant, so prolonged assessment of his prior commitments is not necessary. Indeed, if the man is pursuing a short-term sexual strategy, any delay on her part may deter him from seeking sexual intercourse with her, thus defeating the main adaptive reason for her mating strategy. This is referred to as an **unrestricted mating strategy.**

According to Gangestad and Simpson's theory, the two mating strategies of women—restricted and unrestricted—evolved and are maintained by frequency-dependent selection. As the number of unrestricted females in the population increases, the number of "sexy sons" in the next generation also increases. As the number of sexy sons increases, however, the competition between them also increases. Then, because there are so many sexy sons competing for a limited pool of women, their average success declines.

Now consider what happens when the number of restricted females seeking investing men increases in the population. Because there are now so many women seeking investment, they end up competing with each other for men willing to invest. Therefore, as the number of women seeking investment increases, the average success of their strategy declines. In short, the key idea behind frequency-dependent selection is that the success of each of the two strategies depends on how common each strategy is in the population. As a given strategy becomes more common, it becomes less successful; when it becomes less common, it becomes more successful.

There is some evidence for this theory. Individual differences in female mating strategy (restricted versus unrestricted) have been shown to be heritable (Gangestad

& Simpson, 1990). Furthermore, there is some evidence to suggest the existence of two distinct female mating strategies. Finally, women who pursue an unrestricted sexual strategy have been shown to place more value on qualities of men linked with good genes, such as physical attractiveness and good health (Greiling & Buss, 2000). Additional research is needed on these important individual differences in mating strategies, for they have important implications for social issues, such as father absence and single motherhood.

Another hypothesized example of personality differences originating from frequency-dependent selection centers on **psychopathy**—a cluster of personality traits marked by irresponsible and unreliable behavior, egocentrism, impulsivity, an inability to form lasting relationships, superficial social charm, and a deficit in social emotions such as love, shame, guilt, and empathy (Cleckley, 1988; Lalumiere, Harris, & Rice, 2001). Psychopaths pursue a deceptive "cheating" strategy in their social interactions. Psychopathy is more common among men than women, but psychopaths occur among both sexes (Mealey, 1995). Psychopaths pursue a social strategy of exploiting the cooperative proclivities of other people. After feigning cooperation, psychopaths typically defect, cheat, or violate the presumed relationship. This cheating strategy might be pursued by those who are unlikely to out-compete others in more mainstream or traditional social hierarchies (Mealey, 1995).

According to one evolutionary theory of this individual difference, a psychopathic strategy can be maintained by frequency-dependent selection. As the number of cheaters increases, and hence the average cost to the cooperative hosts increases, adaptations will evolve in cooperators to detect and punish cheating, thus lowering its overall effectiveness (Price, Cosmides, & Tooby, 2002). As psychopaths get detected and punished, the average success of the strategy declines. As long as the frequency of psychopaths is not too large, however, it can be maintained amidst a population composed primarily of cooperators.

There is some empirical evidence consistent with this theory of the evolution of this individual difference cluster. First, behavioral genetic studies suggest that psychopathy is moderately heritable (Willerman, Loehlin, & Horn, 1992). Second, psychopaths often pursue an exploitative sexual strategy, which could be the primary route by which genes for psychopathy increase or are maintained (Rowe, 2001). Psychopathic men, for example, tend to be more sexually precocious, have sex with higher numbers of women, have more illegitimate children, and are more likely to get divorced if they marry than nonpsychopathic men (Rowe, 2001). This short-term exploitative sexual strategy would increase in populations marked by high geographic mobility, in which the costs to reputation associated with this strategy are muted (Buss, 2004). This leads to the alarming idea that we may be witnessing an increase in psychopaths in modern times, as society becomes increasingly geographically mobile. Recent evidence supports the frequency-dependent theory of this individual difference cluster—that it is part of normal personality variation, and is not due to "pathology" (Lalumiere et al., 2001). In sum, individual differences in this cluster of personality traits—unreliability, egocentrism, impulsivity, superficial social charm, and a deficit in empathy and other social emotions—may originate evolutionarily from frequency-dependent selection (see also Millon, 1990, 1999, for additional explorations of personality from an evolutionary perspective).

The most recent effort to explore individual differences from the perspective of frequency-dependent selection focuses on *life history strategy* (Figueredo et al., 2005a, 2005b). According to this approach, individuals have evolved differences in the effort they allocate to reproductively relevant problems, such as survival, mating, and parenting. The core idea is that there are trade-offs among these problems. Effort allocated to mating, for example, is effort taken away from parenting. On one end of the continuum, individuals favor what is called a *K-strategy*—greater effort is allocated to survival and heavy parenting over effort allocated to obtaining many mates. These high-K individuals are hypothesized to have formed strong attachments to their biological parents, avoid risk-taking that would imperil survival, pursue long-term mating rather than short-term mating, and invest heavily in children. Low-K individuals, at the other end, are hypothesized to have formed weaker attachments to their biological parents, have a risk-taking personality, pursue short-term mating, and invest little in their children. One study thus far supports the hypothesis that these variables do indeed covary or cluster together (Figueredo et al., 2005b). Future studies will be needed to determine whether individual differences in K-strategy represent evolved frequency-dependent individual differences, but the approach appears promising.

In sum, we have examined several ways in which evolutionary psychologists study individual differences that might be adaptively patterned. First, different environments can direct individuals into different strategies, as in the case of father absence directing individuals toward a short-term sexual strategy. Second, there can be adaptive self-assessment of heritable traits, as is the case when individuals who are mesomorphic in body build pursue a more aggressive strategy than those who are ectomorphs. Third, two heritable strategies can be supported by frequency-dependent selection.

Fourth, the forces of selection can be different in different places, for example, or different times. This can result in evolved individual differences that are due to different evolutionary selection pressures in different local ecologies. We know, for example, that individual differences in the presence or absence of "sickle cells" in the blood, an adaptation to protect against mosquito-borne malaria, have been caused by different selection pressures in different local ecologies. Although no individual differences in personality have yet been empirically traced to this particular evolutionary source, it remains a viable theoretical possibility in the evolutionary arsenal of explanatory options.

The Big Five and Evolutionarily Relevant Adaptive Problems

Evolutionary psychologists have attempted to understand the importance of the Big Five personality dispositions within an evolutionary framework (Buss, 1991b, 1996; Buss & Greiling, 1999; Ellis, Simpson, & Campbell, 2002). The basic thrust of these approaches has been to pose the question: What are the most adaptively consequential individual differences? Accordingly, the Big Five personality traits are conceptualized as clusters of the most important features of the "adaptive landscape" of other people (Buss, 1991b). Humans, according to this perspective, have evolved "difference-detecting mechanisms" designed to notice and remember those individual differences that have the most relevance for solving social adaptive problems. Specifically, the five factors may provide important answers to questions such as these:

- Who is likely to rise in the social hierarchy, and hence gain access to status and position in the social hierarchy? *(Surgency, Dominance, Extraversion)*
- Who is likely to be a good cooperator and reciprocator, who will be a loyal friend or romantic partner? *(Agreeableness)*

- Who will be reliable and dependable in times of need and work industriously to provide resources? *(Conscientiousness)*
- Who will be a drain on my resources, encumber me with their problems, monopolize my time, and fail to cope well with adversity? *(Neuroticism)*
- Who can I go to for sage advice? *(Openness, Intellectance)*

In an ingenious study, Ellis and his colleagues (Ellis et al., 2002) developed a theoretical synthesis of the Big Five and evolutionary psychology, and conducted studies to see whether positioning on the five factors was correlated with these adaptively relevant individual differences. They also included two additional individual differences that are highly relevant to the evolutionary psychology of romantic relationships—physical attractiveness (a sign of health and fertility) and physical prowess (a sign of the ability to protect a friend or romantic partner from danger). Using factor analysis, they discovered that the Big Five were indeed closely linked with solutions to these critical adaptive problems. In the context of romantic relationships, those who were high on Agreeableness, for example, were also judged to be highly cooperative, devoted to their partners, and in love with their partners. Those who were high on Surgency were also judged to be socially ascendant, taking leadership roles in the group and showing proclivities to elevate themselves in social hierarchies. Those who were highly responsible and efficient (signs of Conscientiousness) could be depended on in times of need, were well organized, and showed good potential for future earning.

This study is just the start of exploring the five-factor model within an evolutionary framework. But it does highlight the important point that individual differences of people who inhabit one's social environment are adaptively consequential. It's reasonable to hypothesize that humans have evolved psychological sensitivities to noticing, detecting, naming, and remembering precisely those individual differences that are most relevant to solving critical social adaptive problems—problems that are ultimately linked to survival and reproduction.

Limitations of Evolutionary Psychology

Like all approaches to personality, the evolutionary perspective carries a number of important limitations. First, adaptations are forged over the long expanse of thousands or millions of generations, and we cannot go back in time and determine with absolute certainty what the precise selective forces on humans have been. Scientists are forced to make inferences about past environments and past selection pressures. Nonetheless, our current mechanisms provide windows for viewing the past. Our fear of snakes and heights, for example, suggests that these were hazards in our evolutionary past. Humans seem to come into the world prepared to learn some things quite easily (e.g., fear of snakes, spiders, and strangers) (Seligman & Hager, 1972). Intense male sexual jealousy suggests that uncertain paternity was an adaptive problem in our evolutionary past. The intense pain we feel on being ostracized from a group suggests that group membership was critical to survival and reproduction in our evolutionary past. Learning more and more about our evolved mechanisms is thus a major tool for overcoming the limitation of sparse knowledge of the environments of our ancestors.

A second limitation is that evolutionary scientists have just scratched the surface of understanding the nature, details, and design features of evolved psychological mechanisms. In the case of jealousy, for example, there is a lack of knowledge about the range of cues that trigger it, the precise nature of the thoughts and emotions that are activated when a person is jealous, and the range of behaviors, such as vigilance and violence, that are manifest outcomes. As more research is conducted, this limitation can be expected to be circumvented.

A third limitation is that modern conditions are undoubtedly different from ancestral conditions in many respects, so that what was adaptive in the past might not be adaptive in the present. Ancestral humans lived in small groups of perhaps 50 to 150 in the context of close extended kin (Dunbar, 1993). Today we live in large cities in the context of thousands of strangers. Thus, it's important to keep in mind that selection pressures have changed. In this sense, humans can be said to live in the modern world with a stone-aged brain.

A fourth limitation is that it is sometimes easy to come up with different and competing evolutionary hypotheses for the same phenomena. To a large extent, this is true of all of science, including personality theories that do not invoke evolutionary explanations. In this sense, the existence of competing theories is not an embarrassment but, rather, is an essential element of science. The critical obligation of scientists is to render their hypotheses in a sufficiently precise manner so that specific empirical predictions can be derived from them. In this way, the competing theories can be pitted against each other, and the hard hand of empirical data can be used to evaluate the competing theories.

Finally, evolutionary hypotheses have sometimes been accused of being untestable and, hence, unfalsifiable. The specific evolutionary hypotheses on aggression, jealousy, and so on presented in this chapter illustrate that this accusation is certainly false for some of them. Nonetheless, there is no doubt that some evolutionary hypotheses (like some standard "social" hypotheses) have indeed been framed in ways that are too vague to be of much scientific value. The solution to this problem is to hold up the same high scientific standards for all competing theories. To be scientifically useful, theories and hypotheses should be framed as precisely as possible, along with attendant predictions, so that empirical studies can be conducted to test their merits.

SUMMARY AND EVALUATION

Selection is the key to evolution, or change in life forms over time. Variants that lead to greater survival, reproduction, or the reproductive success of genetic relatives tend to be preserved and spread through the population.

Evolutionary psychology starts with three fundamental premises. First, adaptations are presumed to be domain-specific; they are designed to solve specific adaptive problems. Adaptations good for one adaptive problem, such as food selection, cannot be used to solve other adaptive problems, such as mate selection. Second, adaptations are presumed to be numerous, corresponding to the many adaptive problems humans have faced over evolutionary history. Third, adaptations are functional. We cannot understand them unless we figure out what they were designed to do—the adaptive problems they were designed to solve.

The empirical science of testing evolutionary hypotheses proceeds in two ways. First, middle-level evolutionary theories, such as the theory of parental investment and sexual selection, can be used to derive specific predictions in a top-down method of investigation. Second, one can observe a phenomenon and then develop a theory about its function in a process known as bottom-up investigation. Using this method, specific predictions are then derived based on the theory about phenomena that have not yet been observed.

Evolutionary psychological analysis can be applied to all three levels of personality analysis—human nature, sex differences, and individual differences. At the level of human nature, there is suggestive evidence that people have evolved the need to belong to groups; to help specific others, such as genetic relatives; and to possess basic emotions, such as happiness, disgust, anger, fear, surprise, sadness, and contempt. At the level of sex differences, men and women diverge only in domains in which they have faced recurrently different adaptive problems over human evolutionary history. Examples include proclivities toward violence and aggression, the desire for sexual variety, the events that trigger jealousy, and specific mate preferences for qualities such as physical appearance and resources.

Individual differences can be understood from an evolutionary perspective using one of three approaches. First, individual differences can result from different environmental inputs into species-typical mechanisms. Second, individual differences can be contingent on other traits, such as when being large and strong inclines one to an aggressive disposition, whereas being small and weak inclines one to be less aggressive. Third, individual differences can result from frequency-dependent selection. Fourth, individual differences can be caused by variations over time or space in the optimum value for a trait.

The Big Five personality dispositions have begun to be examined through the lens of evolutionary psychology. Recent empirical evidence suggests that positioning on the five factors may provide adaptively relevant information to solving key problems of social living: Whom can I trust for cooperation, devotion, and reciprocation (those high on Agreeableness)? Who is likely to ascend social hierarchies (those high on Surgency or Extraversion)? Who will be likely to work hard, be dependable, and accrue resources over time (those high on Conscientiousness)? Future evolutionary research will undoubtedly explore individual differences as they relate to the important social adaptive problems humans face in the context of group living.

Evolutionary psychology has several critical limitations at this stage of scientific development. The first is the lack of precise knowledge about the environments in which humans evolved and the selection pressures our ancestors faced. We are also limited in our knowledge about the nature, details, and workings of evolved mechanisms, including the features that trigger their activation and the manifest behavior that they produce as output. Nonetheless, the evolutionary perspective adds a useful set of theoretical tools to the analysis of personality at the levels of human nature, sex differences, and individual differences.

KEY TERMS

Natural Selection 244
Hostile Forces of Nature 245
Adaptations 245
Sexual Selection 245
Intrasexual Competition 245
Intersexual Selection 245
Genes 246
Differential Gene Reproduction 246
Inclusive Fitness Theory 246
Adaptive Problem 248
Xenophobia 248
By-products of Adaptations 248
Evolutionary By-products 248
Evolutionary Noise 248
Domain-Specific 249
Functionality 250
Deductive Reasoning Approach 251
Inductive Reasoning Approach 251
Social Anxiety 253
Evolutionary-Predicted Sex Differences 260
Effective Polygyny 261
Sexually Dimorphic 261
Reactively Heritable 272
Frequency-Dependent Selection 272
Restricted Sexual Strategy 273
Unrestricted Mating Strategy 273
Psychopathy 274

PART THREE

The Intrapsychic Domain

III

We now turn to the intrapsychic domain. This domain concerns the factors within the mind that influence behavior, thoughts, and feelings. The pioneer of this domain was Sigmund Freud. Freud was a medical doctor and neurologist and was highly influenced by biology. He often applied biological metaphors to the mind—for example, proposing that the mind had separate "organ systems," which operated independently from each other yet that influenced each other. His goal was to analyze the elements within the mind and describe how the elements worked together. He named this enterprise psychoanalysis, which refers both to his intrapsychic theory of personality and his method of helping people change.

In this domain, we will devote two chapters to psychoanalysis. In Chapter 9, we will cover the foundations of classical psychoanalysis, primarily in terms of Freud's original ideas and formulations. We will present Freud's most influential ideas, including the notion that the human mind is divided into two parts, the conscious part and the unconscious part. Moreover, Freud proposed three forces in the human mind—the id, the ego, and the superego—and these forces were constantly interacting over taming the twin motives of sex and aggression, or the life and death instincts. We will also present Freud's ideas on personality development and how he stressed the importance of childhood events in determining the adult personality.

Some of Freud's ideas, such as repression, unconscious processing, and recalled memories, have stood the test of time and are active research topics in personality today. However, many students of Freud have modified some of his ideas, so we will devote Chapter 10 to a discussion of contemporary topics in psychoanalytic theory. These include the idea of personality development as continuing through adulthood rather than stopping in childhood as Freud originally proposed. Another key development in contemporary psychoanalysis concerns the importance of a child's attachments to caregivers in influencing his or her subsequent relationships.

The intrapsychic domain differs from all the other domains in that it is concerned with the forces within the mind that work together and interact with each other and the environment. To some extent, this domain is similar to the biological domain in that the biological domain also emphasizes forces within the person. However, in the intrapsychic domain, the concern is with aspects of *psychic* functioning. In the biological domain, we are concerned with aspects of *physical* functioning, such as the brain, genes, and the chemicals in the bloodstream.

A fundamental assumption of psychologists working in the intrapsychic domain is that there are areas of the mind that are outside awareness. Within each person, there is a part of him- or herself that even he or she does not know about.

This is called the unconscious mind. Moreover, the unconscious mind is thought to have a life of its own, with its own motivation, its own will, and its own energy.

Another assumption within the intrapsychic domain is that most things do not happen by chance. That is, every behavior, every thought, and every experience means something or reveals something about the person's personality. A slip of the tongue, for example, occurs not by accident but because of an intrapsychic conflict. A person forgets someone's name not by accident but because of something about the person whose name cannot be remembered. Or a person dreams of flying, not because dreams are random but because of an unconscious wish or desire being expressed in the dream. Everything a person does, says, or feels has meaning and can be analyzed in terms of intrapsychic elements and forces.

We will also examine some of the main ideas of a few of Freud's students, including Carl Jung and Karen Horney. Jung developed the idea of a collective unconscious, common to all people. Horney was among the first to apply a feminist interpretation of Freud's ideas.

In Chapter 11, we examine work on motivational aspects of personality. Here psychologists emphasize the common motives that most people have to varying degrees. Individual differences in motives help psychologists answer the question: "Why do people do what they do?" The three most common motives studied in this domain are: the desire to achieve, the need to have close relationships with other people, and the motive to have power and influence over others. We will present some of the basic findings on each of these three motives, as well as describe a projective technique that has been developed for assessing these needs. We will also describe a contemporary notion that suggests that motives can be conscious or unconscious and that unconscious motives affect different kinds of behavior than conscious motives.

Most of the research on motives emphasizes deficit motives, that is, motives that arise because something is lacking. There is, however, the notion that one particular motive is not based on a deficit, but rather is based on growth and change. This motive refers to the more abstract need to become who we are, to actualize our potential as the persons we were meant to be. The need to self-actualize can also operate outside awareness, and we may engage in certain behaviors, not because we have thought everything through, but because it just feels like the right thing to be doing at the moment.

In Part Three of this book, we will explore some of the major ideas and findings from the intrapsychic domain of personality. As you read this part, it is important to keep in mind that the intrapsychic domain, as well as all the other domains, refers to just one set of factors that influence personality. Personality is determined by many factors; like a jigsaw puzzle, it is made up of many parts. Let's now consider the part that dwells in the deeper reaches of the human mind.

Psychoanalytic Approaches to Personality

THE INTRAPSYCHIC DOMAIN

Professor Cheit, whose case of recovered memories has stimulated the debate over the intrapsychic source of everyday behavior, thoughts, and emotions.

Dr. Ross Cheit is a professor of political science and public policy at Brown University. In 1992, he received a phone call from his sister, saying that his nephew had joined a boys' choir, just as Professor Cheit had done when he was a boy. Instead of being happy at the news that his nephew was following in his footsteps, Professor Cheit was strangely unhappy. Over the next few weeks, Professor Cheit became increasingly depressed and irritable and began to have marital difficulties. He did not connect any of his troubles to the phone call from his sister.

Shortly thereafter, Professor Cheit recalled a memory of a man he had not seen or thought about for 25 years. The man he remembered was William Farmer. Mr. Farmer had been the administrator of the San Francisco Boys Chorus summer camp, which Professor Cheit had attended between the ages of 10 and 13. Professor Cheit was now 38, and for the first time in 25 years he was recalling how Mr. Farmer would come into his cabin at night, sit on his bed, and begin stroking his chest and then his stomach, and then reach into his pajamas.

Intent on gathering objective information about his abuse, Professor Cheit hired a private investigator. The director of the boys' chorus at the time Professor Cheit was there, Madi Bacon, now 87 years old, was located in Berkeley. When Professor Cheit first talked to her and mentioned Farmer's name, she spontaneously remarked how she had almost had to fire Farmer for "hobnobbing" with the boys. For the first time, Professor Cheit felt that his memory of being molested was authentic. Moreover, after talking with Madi Bacon, he realized that he might not have been the only young boy abused by Farmer.

Using chorus records, Professor Cheit located dozens of the 118 boys who had been at camp with him 25 years earlier. In contacting them, he soon found that others had been molested by Mr. Farmer but had kept quiet. A professor at a university in Michigan, a librarian in the Midwest, and a homeless man living in San Francisco—all had allegedly been abused by Mr. Farmer. The camp nurse at the time recalled catching Mr. Farmer in bed with a sick child in the camp infirmary. The nurse claims to have reported the incident to the camp director, Madi Bacon, who took no action. Professor Cheit obtained documentation that, on at least four occasions, the camp director was informed of molestation of the boys by staff members but took no steps to address the problem.

Now more sure than ever that his memory of abuse was authentic, Professor Cheit wanted to talk directly with Mr. Farmer, who was finally located in the tiny town of Scio, Oregon. Professor Cheit phoned him. Mr. Farmer had no trouble remembering Professor Cheit as one of the boys in summer camp 25 years earlier. "What can I do for you?" Farmer inquired. "You can tell me whether you have any remorse for what you did to me and the other boys at summer camp," replied Professor Cheit. With a tape recorder running, Professor Cheit kept Mr. Farmer on the phone for nearly an hour. Mr. Farmer admitted molesting Professor Cheit in his cabin at night, he acknowledged that the camp director had known of the abuse but had allowed him to stay on at the camp, admitted that he had since lost other jobs for molesting children, and conceded that he knew the acts he had committed with children were criminal.

On August 19, 1993, Professor Cheit and his parents filed a lawsuit against the San Francisco Boys Chorus, charging that the chorus had "negligently or intentionally" allowed staff members to molest children in its care. Lawyers for the chorus at first denied the charges. Professor Cheit's lawsuit asked the boys chorus to meet three conditions: to apologize, thereby admitting guilt; to institute protective measures for current campers; and to pay $450,000 to Professor Cheit as financial compensation. During the litigation, Professor Cheit produced five corroborating witnesses and the tape-recorded admission from Mr. Farmer himself. Just over a year later, the lawsuit was settled. The boys chorus agreed to apologize to Professor Cheit, to put safeguards in place to protect present chorus members from possible molestation, and to pay Professor Cheit $35,000. Professor Cheit is currently writing a book on the law and politics of childhood sexual abuse.

Professor Cheit was fortunate in that the state of California had just changed its statute of limitations laws, allowing for criminal charges of child abuse to be filed anytime within three years of the time that the alleged victim *remembered* the abuse, with independent corroboration. On July 12, 1994, Mr. Farmer was arrested at his home, then in Texas, and extradited to Plumas County, California, the site of the boys chorus camp. According to the county district attorney, Mr. Farmer was charged with six counts of child molestation involving three boys, including Professor Cheit, in 1967 and 1968. Mr. Farmer was charged with committing crimes over a quarter of a century earlier. He pleaded not guilty. The details of this fascinating case are discussed in several books, including Chu (1998) and Schachter (1997).

Is it possible that a person can forget something as traumatic as sexual abuse? Can a forgotten memory lie dormant for years, only to be aroused later by an event, such as a chance phone call? Once aroused, can such a memory cause a person to start having difficulties, such as feelings of depression and irritability, without his or her knowing the cause of those difficulties? Some psychologists believe that people sometimes are unaware of the reasons for their own problematic behaviors. When treating a person for a psychological problem, some therapists believe that the cause of the problem resides in the person's unconscious, the part of the mind outside the person's immediate awareness. They contend that a memory of a past traumatic event can be completely forgotten yet nevertheless cause a psychological problem years later (Bass & Davis, 1988). This reasoning has led many states, such as California, to place the statute of limitations on child abuse at three years from when the abuse is *remembered* by the person. Furthermore, such therapists believe that, if they can help make this unconscious memory conscious—that is, if they can help the patient recall a forgotten traumatic memory—they can put the patient on the road to recovery (Baker, 1992).

This perspective on the causes and cures of psychological problems has its origin in a theory of personality developed by Sigmund Freud (1856–1939), commonly called psychoanalysis. In this chapter, we will examine the basic elements of classical psychoanalytic theory and will explore some of the empirical studies conducted to test certain aspects of the theory. We will consider the scientific evidence for the repression of childhood memories, for the concept of unconscious motivation, and for other aspects of psychoanalytic theory. Whereas many of Freud's ideas have not stood the test of time, other ideas are still with us and are topics of contemporary research. Because this theory is so much the result of one person's thinking, let's first look at a brief biographical sketch of Freud.

Sigmund Freud: A Brief Biography

Although Freud was born in Freiberg, Moravia, in 1856 (now part of the Czech Republic), his family moved to Vienna when he was 4 years old, and he spent virtually the remainder of his life there. Freud excelled in school and obtained his medical degree from the University of Vienna. Although he started out as a researcher in neurology, he realized that he could make more money to support his wife and growing family if he entered into private medical practice. After studying hypnosis with Jean-Martin Charcot in Paris, Freud returned to Vienna and started a private practice, treating patients with "nervous disorders." During that time, Freud began developing the idea that portions of the human mind were outside conscious awareness. The unconscious is the part of the mind about which the conscious mind has no awareness. Freud sought to study empirically the implications of the unconscious for understanding people's lives and their problems with living. From his early contact with patients, Freud began to surmise that the unconscious mind operated under its own power, subject to its own motivations and according to its own logic. Freud devoted the rest of his career to exploring the nature and logic of the unconscious mind.

Sigmund Freud at age 82. He most likely insisted this photo be taken from the side in order not to show the ravages of his jaw and throat cancer, and the many operations he underwent in an unsuccessful attempt to cure that disease. He died in 1939, less than a year after this photo was taken.

Freud's first solo-authored book, *The Interpretation of Dreams,* was published in 1900. In it, he described how the unconscious mind was expressed in dreams, and how dreams contained clues to our innermost secrets, desires, and motives. The analysis of dreams became a cornerstone of his treatment. This book sold poorly at first but nevertheless attracted the attention of other medical doctors seeking to understand psychological problems. By 1902, there was a small group of followers (e.g., Alfred Adler) who met with Freud every Wednesday evening. At these meetings, Freud talked about his theory, shared insights, and discussed patients' progress, all the while smoking one of the 20 or so cigars he smoked each day. During this period, Freud was systematically building his theory and testing its acceptance by knowledgeable peers. By 1908, the membership of the Wednesday Psychological Circle had grown significantly, prompting Freud to form the Vienna Psychoanalytic Society (Grosskurth, 1991).

In 1909, Freud made his only visit to the United States, to present a series of lectures on psychoanalysis at the invitation of psychologist G. Stanley Hall, who was then president of Clark University. Rosenzweig (1994) describes Freud's trip to the United States in fascinating detail. In 1910, the International Psychoanalytic Association was formed. Freud's theories were gaining recognition around the world.

Freud and his work drew both praise and criticism. Whereas some accepted his ideas as brilliant insights into the workings of human nature, others opposed his views on various scientific and ideological grounds. To some, his treatment approach (the so-called talking cure) was absurd. Freud's theory that the adult personality was a result of how the person as a child coped with his or her sexual and aggressive urges was considered politically incorrect by the standards of Victorian morality. Even some of the founding members of his Vienna Psychoanalytic Society grew to disagree with developments in his theory. Nevertheless, Freud continued to refine and apply his theory, writing 20 books and numerous papers during his career.

Germany invaded Austria in 1938, and the Nazis began their persecution of the Jews there. Freud, who was Jewish, had reasons to fear the Nazis. The Nazi party burned his books and the books of other modern intellectuals. With the assistance of wealthy patrons, Freud, his wife, and their six children fled to London. Freud died the following year after a long, painful, and disfiguring battle with cancer of the jaw and throat.

Freud's London house continued to be occupied by his daughter, Anna Freud, herself a prominent psychoanalyst, until her death in 1982. The house is now part of the Freud Museum in London. Visitors can walk through Freud's library and study, which remain largely as he left them when he died. The study, which is where Freud treated his patients, still contains his celebrated couch, covered with an Oriental rug. It also contains the many ancient artifacts and small statues and icons that seemed to fascinate him and reveal his secret passion for archeology. Freud has been referred to as the original archeologist of the human mind.

Fundamental Assumptions of Psychoanalytic Theory

Freud's model of human nature relied on the notion of **psychic energy** to motivate all human activity. What were the forces that motivated people to do one thing and not another or that motivated people to do anything at all? Freud proposed a source of energy that is within each person and used the term *psychic energy* to refer to this wellspring of motivation. Freud believed that psychic energy operated according to the law of conservation of energy: The amount of psychic energy an individual possessed remained constant throughout his or her lifetime. Personality change was viewed as a redirection of a person's psychic energy.

Basic Instincts: Sex and Aggression

What was the basic source of psychic energy? Freud believed that there were strong innate forces that provided *all* the energy in the psychic system. He called these forces **instincts.** Freud's original theory of instincts was profoundly influenced by Darwin's theory of evolution. Darwin had published his book on evolution just a few years after Freud was born. In Freud's initial formulation, there were two fundamental categories of instincts: self-preservation instincts and sexual instincts. Curiously, these corresponded exactly to two major components of Darwin's theory of natural selection: selection by survival and selection by reproduction. Thus, Freud's initial classification of instincts could have been borrowed from Darwin's two forms of evolution by selection (Ritvo, 1990).

In his later formulations, however, Freud collapsed the self-preservation and sexual instincts into one, which he called the life instinct. And, due in part to his witnessing the horrors of World War I, he developed the idea of a death instinct. Freud postulated that humans had a fundamental instinct toward destruction and that this instinct was often manifest in aggression toward others. The two instincts were usually referred to as **libido** for the life instinct and **thanatos** for the death instinct. Although the libido was generally considered sexual, Freud also used this term to refer to any need-satisfying, life-sustaining, or pleasure-oriented urge. Similarly, thanatos was considered to be the death instinct, but Freud used this term in a broad sense to refer to any urge to destroy, harm, or aggress against others or oneself. Freud wrote more about the libido early in his career, when this issue was perhaps relevant to his own life. Later in his career, Freud wrote more about thanatos, when he faced his own impending death.

Although Freud initially believed that the life and death instincts worked to oppose one another, he later argued that they could combine in various ways. Consider the act of eating. Eating obviously serves the life instinct, entailing the consumption of nutrients necessary for survival. At the same time, eating also involves acts of tearing, biting, and chewing, which Freud thought could be seen as aggressive manifestations of thanatos. As another example, Freud viewed rape as an expression of extreme death instinct, directed toward another person in a manner that is fused with sexual energy. The combination of erotic and aggressive instincts into a single motive is a particularly volatile mixture.

Because each person possesses a fixed amount of psychic energy, according to Freud, the energy used to direct one type of behavior is not available to drive other types of behaviors. The person who directs his or her death instinct into a socially acceptable channel, such as competitive sports, has less energy to expend toward more destructive manifestations of this instinct. Because psychic energy exists in a fixed and limited amount within each person, it can be directed and redirected in various ways.

Unconscious Motivation: Sometimes We Don't Know Why We Do What We Do

According to Freud, the human mind consists of three parts. The **conscious** mind is the part that contains all the thoughts, feelings, and perceptions that you are presently aware of. Whatever you are currently perceiving or thinking about is in your conscious mind. These thoughts represent only a small fraction of the information available to you.

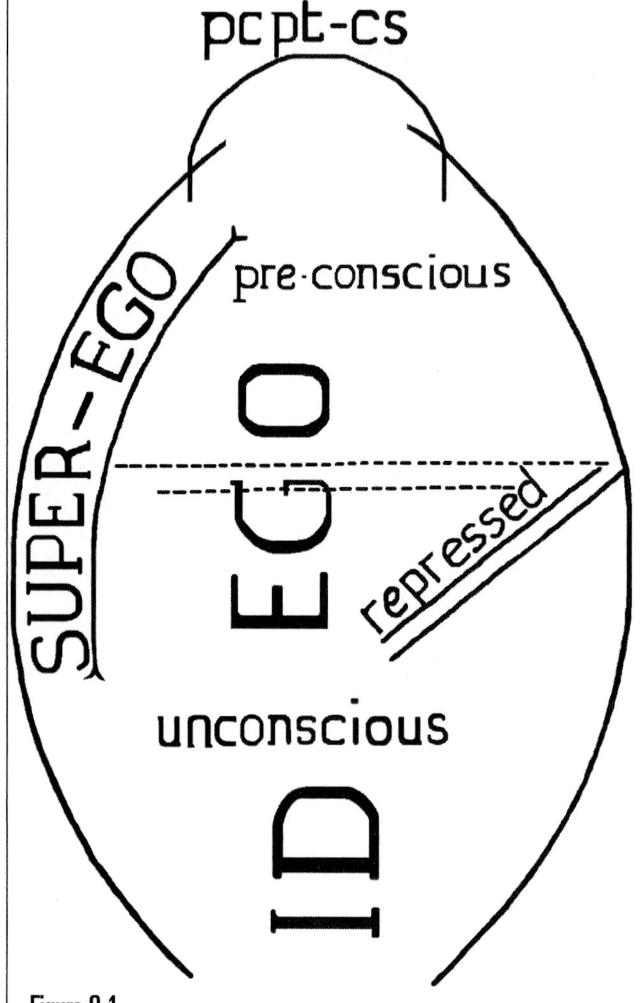

Figure 9.1

Freud's original drawing depicting the structure of personality and the levels of consciousness, from LECTURE XXXI (1932), "The Anatomy of the Mental Personality," is reproduced in "Introductory Lectures on Psycho-analysis," published in 1933 by Hogarth Press. Freud's main dissatisfaction with the diagram is that the space taken by the unconscious id ought to be much greater than that given to the ego or the preconscious. "You must, if you please, correct that in your imagination," Freud advised his readers.

You also have a vast number of memories, dreams, and thoughts that you could easily bring to mind if you so desired. What were you wearing yesterday? What was the name of your best friend in seventh grade? What is the earliest memory you have of your mother? This information is stored in the **preconscious** mind. Any piece of information that you are not presently thinking about, but that could easily be retrieved and made conscious, is found in the preconscious mind.

The **unconscious** is the third and, according to Freud, largest part of the human mind. The metaphor of an iceberg is often used to describe the topography of the mind. The part of the iceberg above the water represents the conscious mind. The part that you can see just below the water surface is the preconscious mind. And the part of the iceberg totally hidden from view (the vast majority of it) represents the unconscious mind. In Figure 9.1 we reproduce a drawing made by Freud in 1932, in which he graphically presented the three levels of consciousness. The top level is perception and consciousness, which he abbreviated "pcpt-cs." The middle level is the preconscious, and the lower level is the unconscious. Residing in the unconscious mind is unacceptable information, hidden from conscious view so well that it cannot even be considered preconscious. Those memories, feelings, thoughts, or urges are so troubling or even distasteful that being aware of them would make the person anxious. Many of the cases reported in the psychoanalytic literature involve distressing unconscious themes—such as incest; hatred toward siblings, parents, or spouses; and memories of childhood traumas.

Society does not allow people to express freely all of their sexual and aggressive instincts. Individuals must learn to control their urges. One way to control these urges, according to Freud, is to keep them from entering conscious awareness in the first place. Consider a child who has gotten extremely angry with a parent. This child might have a fleeting wish that the parents die. Such thoughts would be very distressing to a child—so distressing that they might be held back from conscious awareness and banished instead to the unconscious—the part of the mind holding thoughts and memories about which the person is unaware. All kinds of unacceptable sexual and aggressive urges, thoughts, and feelings might accumulate in the unconscious during the course of a typical childhood.

One of Freud's Famous Students: Carl Gustav Jung

Carl Gustav Jung (1875–1961) was a Swiss psychiatrist who became interested in Freud's theories of personality and the unconscious. He went to Vienna to see Freud and their first meeting lasted 13 hours! After this, they carried on a very active correspondence and their letters to each other have been published (McGuire, 1974). Jung accompanied Freud on his only trip to America (described in Rosenzweig, 1994). The long boat trip to America gave them plenty of time to talk and to analyze each other's dreams. This proved to be the beginning of the end of their relationship, when Freud held back from discussing certain of his dreams. He chose to maintain his authority rather than give in to unrestricted associations to his dreams (Rosen, 1993).

Jung began to feel that Freud's theories put too much emphasis on sexuality and aggression, and he also disagreed with Freud about the inherently negative role of unconscious conflicts. Jung went on to develop his own version of how the mind works and, while he drew on Freud's basic notions, he produced a theory that has taken on a life of its own. Jung contributed many ideas to personality psychology. For example, his theory of traits resulted in the Myers-Briggs Type Indicator, a widely used personality inventory we described in Chapter 3. Jung also developed the word association test, the basic idea of which (that emotional reactions to words interfere with the cognitive processing of those words) is still being investigated by research psychologists in the emotional Stroop test (which we describe in Chapter 13).

One of Jung's most famous ideas concerned the presence in each person of a **collective unconscious,** which complemented the **personal unconscious.** The personal unconscious grew out of the person's own unique experiences, very much like Freud's version of the unconscious. The collective unconscious, on the other hand, was thought to be much more prehistoric, the inherited unconscious content that is passed on from previous generations and contains the collected primordial images common across the human species. This repository of core human feelings and experience is represented in the common symbols that turn up in myths and stories across vastly different cultures. He called these **archetypes,** expressions or images of basic human needs and instincts that we are all born with. Newborns, for example, all react to their mothers in a similar way because they are born with an archetype of the "good mother" in their collective unconscious. Most cultures share a fear of the dark because we have an archetype of evil hiding in the shadows. Two other important archetypes are the anima, which represents the feminine side of human nature, and the animus, which represents the masculine side of human nature. Jung taught that all persons have the masculine and the feminine archetypes in their collective unconscious.

The collective unconscious is one of Jung's most controversial ideas, and his only argument for its existence was in noting recurring images and symbols in the myths and stories of different cultures. For this reason, most personality psychologists have rejected the idea as unsupported. But is the notion of a collective past, one that we are unaware of but that influences our present behavior, really such a far-fetched idea? In some ways, the idea of evolved psychological mechanisms, which we described in Chapter 8 on evolutionary approaches to personality, is a lot like Jung's notion of the collective unconscious. If we think of the collective unconscious as growing out of the common experiences of our ancestors, and as containing predispositions to perceive and process information in certain ways, then it seems to fit the notion of evolved psychological mechanisms. Both Jung and evolutionary psychology share the common view that we are not born as blank slates, but rather that we enter the world with predispositions inherited from our ancestors.

Exercise

Think back to the first house or apartment you lived in as a child. If you are like most people, you can probably remember as far back as your fourth or fifth year of age. Try to recall the structure of the house or apartment, the location of the rooms relative to each other. Draw a floor plan, starting with the basement if there was one, then the first floor, then the upstairs rooms (if the house had a second floor). On your floor plan, label each room. Now think about each room, letting the memories of events that happened in each of them come back to you. It is likely that you will recall some people and events that you have not thought about for a decade or more. You also might notice that many of your memories have an emotional quality; some memories are pleasant, whereas others are unpleasant. The memories that you can bring to conscious awareness are in your preconscious. You may have memories of events that occurred that do not come back to you during this exercise because they are in your unconscious.

Freud believed that unconscious thoughts, feelings, and urges could take on a life of their own. He therefore called this part of the mind the **motivated unconscious.** Many psychological researchers agree with Freud that one part of the human mind can contain information about which another part of the mind is unaware. As we will see in Chapter 10, not every psychologist who believes in the unconscious believes in the *motivated* unconscious (Shevrin & Dickman, 1980). Freud taught that material in the motivated unconscious is dynamic in the sense that it can produce particular behaviors, thoughts, and feelings. Once in the unconscious, an urge might later surface in any of the following ways: in the disguise of a dream or a recurring nightmare, as a slip of the tongue, as seemingly irrational feelings toward someone else (e.g., unexplained attraction, anger, or jealousy), as a physical symptom (such as paralysis or an eating disorder), or as inexplicable anxiety.

Psychic Determinism: Nothing Happens by Chance

Freud maintained that nothing happens by chance or by accident. There is a reason behind every act, thought, and feeling. Everything we do, think, say, and feel is an expression of the mind—the conscious, preconscious, or unconscious mind. In his book *The Psychopathology of Everyday Life,* Freud introduced the idea that the little "accidents" of daily life are often expressions of the motivated unconscious, such as calling someone by the wrong name, missing an appointment, and breaking something that belongs to another. Texas Republican Dick Armey once referred to the openly homosexual congressman from Massachusetts, Barney Frank, as "Barney Fag." Once, a psychology professor referred to Sigmund Freud as "Sigmund Fraud." Such mix-ups can often be embarrassing, but, according to Freud, they represent the motivated activity of the unconscious. There is a reason for every slip of the tongue, for being late, for forgetting a person's name, and for breaking something that belongs to another. The reasons can be discovered if the contents of the unconscious can be examined.

Freud taught that most symptoms of mental illnesses are caused by unconscious motivations. Freud provided detailed case histories of 12 patients, as well as dozens of shorter discussions of specific patients. In these case studies, he found support for his theory that psychological problems were caused by unconscious memories or desires. For example, Freud wrote about the case of Anna O. Although Freud did not directly treat or even meet Anna O., her physician, Joseph Breuer, consulted with Freud.

At the time, Anna O. was a 21-year old woman who had fallen ill while taking care of her sick father who eventually died of tuberculosis. Anna's illness began with a severe cough, and later included the loss of movement in her right side, disturbances of vision, hearing, and the inability to drink liquids. Dr. Breuer diagnosed Anna O's illness as hysteria, and developed a form of therapy that appeared effective in relieving her symptoms. This form of therapy consisted of Breuer talking with Anna O. about her symptoms, and in particular about her memories of events that happened before the onset of the symptoms. For example, in talking about her severe cough, they talked about her memories of caring for her father, and the severe cough he had from his tuberculosis. As she explored these memories, and especially her feelings toward her father and about his death, her own cough lessened and disappeared. Similarly, when talking about her inability to drink liquids (she had been quenching her thirst with fruit and melons), she suddenly recalled the memory of seeing a dog drink from a woman's glass, an incident that completely disgusted her at the time but about which she had forgotten. Soon after describing this memory, she asked for a drink of water and immediately regained her ability to drink liquids.

To Breuer, and to Freud, hysterical symptoms did not occur by chance. Rather, they were physical expressions of repressed traumatic experiences. From the experience treating Anna O., Breuer concluded that the way to cure hysterical symptoms was to help the person recall the memory of the incident that had originally led to the symptoms. By the patient's recalling the traumatic incident (e.g., her father's death), an emotional catharsis or release can be achieved by having she or he express any feelings associated with that memory. This then removes the cause of the symptom and hence the symptom disappears.

Freud adopted and refined the technique developed by Breuer for effecting the "talking cure." Freud believed that for a psychological symptom to be cured, the unconscious cause of the symptom must first be discovered. Often the process involves discovering a hidden memory of an unsettling, disagreeable, or even repulsive experience that has been repressed or pushed into the unconscious (Masson, 1984). Freud always acknowledged the importance of the case of Anna O. on his thinking, and gave credit to the careful observations of Dr. Breuer:

> *If it is a merit to have brought psychoanalysis into being, that merit is not mine. I had no share in its earliest beginnings. I was a student and working for my final examinations at the time when another Viennese physician, Dr. Josef Breuer first made use of this procedure on a girl who was suffering from hysteria. (From Freud's lectures presented at Clark University in Massachusetts, 1909.)*

Freud is uncharacteristically immodest in the above quote. He adapted the notions of symptom formation and the talking cure from Breuer, and combined these with other ideas about the unconscious, about repression, about stages of development and many other notions, and, from these, he formulated a grand theory of personality that has yet to be rivaled by a single unitary theory of personality.

A Closer Look

Examples of the Unconscious: Blindsight and Deliberation-without-Attention

Following an injury or stroke that damages the primary vision center in the brain, a person will lose some or all of their ability to see. In this kind of blindness the eyes still work to bring information into the brain; it is just that the brain center responsible for object recognition fails. People who suffer this kind of "cortical" blindness often display an interesting capacity to make judgments about objects that they truly cannot see. This phenomenon is termed **blindsight** and it has fascinated psychologists since it was first documented in the 1960s.

Imagine having a person with cortical blindness as a subject. You could hold a red ball in front of her open eyes and ask if she can see it. She would reply no, which is consistent with the fact that she is blind. Now you ask her to point to the red ball (which she has just denied seeing). What happens? She points directly to the red ball even though she does not have the ability to see it!

Blindsight is taken as evidence of the unconscious. Here one part of the mind knows about something that another part of the mind does not know about. There are many demonstrations of people with blindsight. For example, when an object is placed in front of a person with blindsight—that is, a person who does not know for sure whether it is there or not—that person can guess the color of that object at levels much better than merely by chance. In other words, such a condition illustrates that information that is unconscious (whether an object is or is not in front of the person) is actually being processed somewhere in the mind (because they know the color of objects that are presented).

An explanation for such "unconscious" perception has been offered in terms of nerve pathways from the eyes into the brain. The optic nerve carries information from the eye into the brain, and the majority of this information is transferred to the primary visual center in the striate cortex. However, pathways split off of the optic nerve before getting to the visual center and carry some of this visual information to other parts of the brain. These other centers may be involved in movement recognition or color recognition or even emotional evaluation. If the vision center were completely destroyed, the person would not recognize *what* the object was, but they might know if it was moving or how they felt about it.

One of the most interesting and robust examples of blindsight concerns the perception of the emotional significance of something that one does not see. In one study, a person with blindsight underwent a conditioning procedure, where a visual cue which they could not see (a picture of a circle) was accompanied by an unpleasant shock whereas other visual cues (pictures of squares, rectangles, etc.) were not paired with shock. Following a period of conditioning, the stimuli shapes were later "shown" to the blind subject, and the subject exhibited a fear response to the circle but not the squares or rectangles (Hamm, Weike, Schupp, Treig, Dressel, & Kessler, 2003). These researchers argue that emotional conditioning does not require a conscious representation in the mind of the subject. Other studies of people with cortical blindness demonstrate that, when "shown" pictures of facial expressions, they can "guess" the emotions expressed in the faces even when they cannot see the faces being

Structure of Personality

Psychoanalytic personality theory describes how people cope with their sexual and aggressive instincts within the constraints of a civilized society. Sexual and aggressive instincts often lead to drives and urges that conflict with society and with reality. One part of the mind creates these urges, another part has a sense of what civilized society expects, and another part tries to satisfy the urges within the bounds of reality and society. How is it that the mind can have so many parts, and how do these parts work together to form personality?

A metaphor may be helpful in answering this question. Think of the mind as a plumbing system, which contains water under pressure. The pressure is the metaphor presented. Obviously, a lot of emotional processing occurs at some level in the brain that does not involve the primary visual center. People could have feelings about (i.e., like or dislike) something that they are not even aware of.

Another example of the unconscious at work concerns the phenomenon of **deliberation-without-awareness,** or the "let me sleep on it" effect. The notion here is, if a person confronted with a difficult decision can put it out of their conscious mind for a period of time, then their unconscious mind will continue to deliberate on it outside of their awareness, helping them to arrive at a "sudden" and often correct decision sometime later. This is sometimes called "unconscious decision-making."

The phenomenon of unconscious decision-making was the topic of several clever studies recently published in the prestigious journal *Science* by a team of Dutch researchers (Dijksterhuis, Bos, Nordgren, and van Baaren, 2006). These researchers hypothesized that, for simple decisions, conscious deliberation would work best, but when decisions were complex, involving many factors, then unconscious deliberation would work best. They presented subjects with the task of deciding on the best car out of four different cars. Subjects in the simple condition considered four attributes of the cars, whereas subjects in the complex condition considered 12 attributes of the cars. In all cases, one car was characterized by 75 percent positive attributes (i.e., the best car), two by 50 percent positive attributes, and one by 25 percent positive attributes. After reading all the information about the cars, half of the subjects were assigned to the conscious deliberation condition and the other half were assigned to the unconscious deliberation condition. In the conscious deliberation condition subjects were asked to think about the information for four minutes before deciding on the best car. In the unconscious deliberation condition, subjects were distracted for four minutes by being asked to solve anagram puzzles, then immediately asked to decide on the best car.

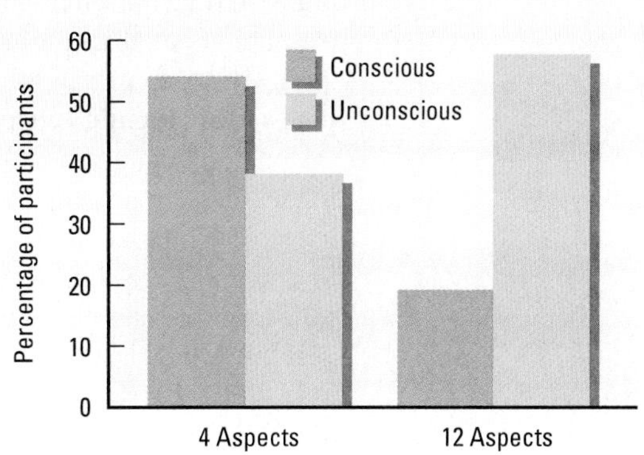

Figure 9.2

Percentage of participants who chose the most desirable car as a function of complexity of decision and mode of thought.

As shown in Figure 9.2, in the simple decision condition, with only four attributes to consider on each car, subjects who consciously deliberated made the best decisions. However, when the decision was complex, involving 12 different attributes of the cars, subjects in the "unconscious" deliberation condition made the best decisions. The authors demonstrate similar effects in three additional studies. Even though the studies concern consumer items (e.g., cars), there is reason to believe that the unconscious deliberation effect might apply to any type of decision, e.g., what career path to pursue, who to vote for, who to marry, etc. The authors (Dijksterhuis et al., 2006) argue that, with any decision, it would "benefit the individual to think consciously about simple matters and to delegate thinking about more complex matters to the unconscious" (p. 1007).

for the psychic energy from the sexual and aggressive instincts, which builds up and demands release. According to Freud's theory, when it comes to this internal pressure, there are three schools of plumbing: one plumber suggests that we open all the valves at the slightest pressure, another offers ways to redirect the pressure so that the strain is relieved without making much of a mess, and the third plumber wants to keep all the valves closed. Let's discuss each of these "psychic plumbers" in some detail, using Freud's terminology.

Id: Reservoir of Psychic Energy

Freud taught in the beginning there was id, the most primitive part of the human mind. Freud saw the **id** as something we are born with and as the source of all drives and urges. Using the plumbing metaphor, the id is the plumber who wants to let off all pressure at the slightest hint of strain or tension. The id is like a spoiled child—selfish, impulsive, and pleasure-loving. According to Freud, the id operates according to the **pleasure principle,** which is the desire for immediate gratification. The id cannot tolerate any delays in satisfying its urges. During infancy, the id dominates. When an infant sees an attractive toy, it will reach for the toy and will cry and fuss if it cannot get it. Infants can sometimes appear unreasonable in their demands. Because the id operates according to the pleasure principle, it does not listen to reason, does not follow logic, has no values or morals (other than immediate gratification), and has very little patience.

The id also operates with **primary process thinking,** which is thinking without logical rules of conscious thought or an anchor in reality. Dreams and fantasies are examples of primary process thinking. Although primary process thought does not follow the normal rules of reality (e.g., in dreams, people fly and walk through walls), Freud believed that there were principles at work in primary process thought and that these principles could be discovered. If an urge from the id requires an external object or person, and that object or person is not available, the id may create a mental image or fantasy of that object or person to satisfy its needs. Mental energy is invested in that fantasy, and the urge is temporarily satisfied. This process is called **wish fulfillment,** whereby something unavailable is conjured up and the image of it is temporarily satisfying. Someone might be very angry, for example, but the target of the anger is too powerful to attack. In this case, engaging in wish fulfillment might produce an imagined fantasy of revenge for past wrongs. This strategy of wish fulfillment works only temporarily to gratify the id, since the need is not satisfied in reality. A person must find other ways to gratify id urges or hold them in check.

In the psychoanalytic theory of personality, conflicts between children and parents are normal, necessary, and an important part of personality development.

Ego: Executive of Personality

The ego is the plumber who works to redirect the pressure produced by the id instincts into acceptable or at least less problematic outlets. The **ego** is the part of the mind that constrains the id to reality. According to Freud, it develops within the first two or three years of life (after the "terrible 2s"). The ego operates according to the **reality principle.** The ego understands that the urges of the id are often in conflict with social and physical reality. A child cannot just grab a candy bar off the shelf at the grocery store or hit his sister whenever she makes him angry. Although such acts might reduce immediate tension in the child, they conflict with society's and parents' rules about stealing and beating up little sisters. The ego understands that such actions can lead to problems and that *direct* expression of id impulses must therefore be avoided, redirected, or postponed.

The ego works to postpone the discharge of id urges until an appropriate situation arises. The ego engages in **secondary process thinking,** which is the development of strategies for solving problems and obtaining satisfaction. Often this process involves taking into account the constraints of physical reality, about when and how to express a desire or an urge. For example, teasing one's sister is more acceptable than hitting her, and this can perhaps satisfy the id's aggressive urge almost as well. There may be some urges, however, that simply remain unacceptable according to social reality or conventional morality, *regardless* of the situation. The third part of the mind, the superego, is responsible for upholding social values and ideals.

Superego: Upholder of Societal Values and Ideals

Around the age of 5, a child begins to develop the third part of the mind, which Freud called the superego. The **superego** is the part of the mind that internalizes the values, morals, and ideals of society. Usually, these are instilled into the child by society's various socializing agents, such as parents, schools, and organized religions. Freud emphasized the role of parents in particular in children's development of self-control and conscience, suggesting that the development of the superego was closely linked to a child's identification with his or her parents.

To return to the plumbing metaphor, the superego is the plumber who wants to keep the valves closed all the time and even wants to add more valves to keep the pressure under control. The superego is the part of personality that makes us feel guilty, ashamed, or embarrassed when we do something "wrong" and makes us feel pride when we do something "right." The superego determines what is right and what is wrong: it sets moral goals and ideals of perfection and, so, is the source of our judgments that some things are good and some are bad. It is what some people refer to as conscience. The main tool of the superego in enforcing right and wrong is the emotion of guilt.

Like the id, the superego is not bound by reality. It is free to set standards for virtue and for self-worth, even if those standards are perfectionistic, unrealistic, and harsh. Some children develop low moral standards and, consequently, do not feel guilty when they hurt others. Other children develop very powerful internal standards, due to a superego that demands perfection. The superego burdens them with almost impossibly high moral standards. Such persons might suffer from a chronic level of shame because of their continual failures to meet their unrealistic standards.

Interaction of the Id, Ego, and Superego

The three parts of the mind—id, ego, and superego—are in constant interaction. They have different goals, provoking internal conflicts within an individual. Consequently, one part of a person can want one thing, whereas another part wants something else. For example, imagine that a young woman is last in line at a fast-food counter. The man in front of her unknowingly drops a $20 bill from his wallet and does not notice. The woman sees the money on the floor in front of her. The situation sets off a conflict between the three parts of her personality. The id says, "Take it and run! Just grab it; push the person out of the way if you have to." The superego says, "Thou shalt not steal." And the ego is confronted with the reality of the situation as well as the demands from the id and the superego, saying "Did the clerk see the $20 fall? Do any of the other customers see the $20 on the floor? Could I put my foot over it without being noticed? Maybe I should just pick it up and return it to the person; perhaps he will even give me a reward." The young woman in this situation is bound to experience some **anxiety.** Anxiety is an unpleasant state, which acts as a signal that things are not right and something must be done. It is a signal that the control of the ego is being threatened by reality, by impulses from the id, or by harsh controls exerted by the superego. Such anxiety might be expressed as physical symptoms, such as a rapid heart rate, sweaty palms, and irregular breathing. A person in this state might also feel herself on the verge of panic. Regardless of the symptoms displayed, a person whose desires are in conflict with reality or with internalized morals will appear more anxious in such a situation.

A well-balanced mind, one that is free from anxiety, is achieved by having a strong ego. It is the ego that balances the competing forces of the id, on the one hand, and the super-ego on the other. If either of these two competing forces overwhelms the ego, then anxiety is the result.

Dynamics of Personality

Because it is unpleasant, people try to resolve the conditions that give rise to anxiety. These efforts to defend oneself from anxiety are called **defense mechanisms,** and they are used to defend against all forms of anxiety.

Types of Anxiety

Freud identified three types of anxiety; objective, neurotic, and moral anxiety.

Objective anxiety is fear. Such anxiety occurs in response to a real, external threat to the person. For example, being confronted by a large, aggressive-looking man with a knife while taking a shortcut through an alley would elicit objective anxiety (fear) in most people. In this case, the control of the ego is being threatened by an external factor, rather than by an internal conflict. In the other two types of anxiety, the threat comes from within.

The second type of anxiety, **neurotic anxiety,** occurs when there is a direct conflict between the id and the ego. The danger is that the ego may lose control over an unacceptable desire of the id. For example, a woman who becomes anxious whenever she feels sexually attracted to someone, who panics at even the thought of sexual arousal, is experiencing neurotic anxiety. As another example, a man who worries excessively that he might blurt out an unacceptable thought or desire in public is also beset by neurotic anxiety.

The third type of anxiety, **moral anxiety,** is caused by a conflict between the ego and the superego. For example, a person who suffers from chronic shame or feelings of guilt over not living up to "proper" standards, even though such standards might not be attainable, is experiencing moral anxiety. A young woman with bulimia, an eating disorder, might run 3 miles and do 100 sit-ups in order to make up for having eaten a "forbidden" food. People who punish themselves, who have low self-esteem, or who feel worthless and ashamed most of the time are most likely suffering from moral anxiety, from an overly powerful superego, which constantly challenges the person to live up to higher and higher expectations.

The ego faces a difficult task in attempting to balance the impulses of the id, the demands of the superego, and the realities of the external world. It is as if the id is saying, "I want it now!" The superego is saying, "You will never have it!" And the poor ego is caught in the middle, saying, "Maybe, if I can just work things out." Most of the time, this conversation is going on outside a person's awareness. Sometimes the conflicts between the id, ego, and superego are expressed in a disguised way in various thoughts, feelings, and behaviors. According to Freud, such conflicts often are expressed in dreams. They can also be elicited through hypnosis, free association (saying whatever comes to mind), and projective assessment instruments (e.g., the inkblot test).

Defense Mechanisms

In all three types of anxiety, the function of the ego is to cope with threats and to defend against the dangers they pose in order to reduce anxiety. The ego accomplishes this task through the use of various defense mechanisms, which enable the ego to control anxiety, even objective anxiety. Although intrapsychic conflicts frequently evoke anxiety, people can successfully defend themselves from conflict and never consciously feel the anxiety. For example, in conversion reaction, where a conflict is converted to a symptom, the conflict is expressed in the form of physical symptoms, an illness or weakness in a part of the body. Curiously, such people may be indifferent to the symptom, not anxious about losing feeling in a leg or having a headache that will not go away. The symptoms help them avoid the anxiety, and even the symptoms do not make them anxious. Defense mechanisms serve two functions: (1) to protect the ego and (2) to minimize anxiety and distress. Let's turn now to a discussion of one of the defense mechanisms that Freud wrote about extensively and that has received a good deal of attention from researchers in personality psychology.

Repression

Early in his theorizing, Freud used the term **repression** to refer to the process of preventing unacceptable thoughts, feelings, or urges from reaching conscious awareness. Repression was the forerunner of all other forms of defense mechanisms. Repression is defensive in the sense that, through it, a person avoids the anxiety that would arise if the unacceptable material were made conscious. From his clinical practice, Freud learned that people often tended to remember the pleasant circumstances surrounding an event more easily than the unpleasant ones. He concluded that unpleasant memories were often repressed.

Freud first developed the concept of repression as a global strategy that the ego uses to maintain forbidden impulses in the unconscious. The term is still used today to refer to "forgotten" wishes, urges, or events—recall the account of "repressed" traumatic memories with which the chapter opened. Later, Freud articulated several more specific kinds of defense mechanisms. All of these specific forms involved a degree of repression, in that some aspect of reality is denied or distorted in the service of reducing anxiety and protecting the control of the ego over the psychic system.

Other Defense Mechanisms

Freud's daughter Anna, herself an accomplished psychoanalyst, played a large role in identifying and describing other mechanisms of defense (A. Freud, 1936). She believed that the ego could muster some very creative and effective mechanisms to protect against blows to self-esteem and threats to psychic existence. A few of these defense mechanisms will be described in detail in this section.

A student of Freud's named Fenichel (1945) revised the idea of defense to focus more on how these mechanisms function to protect self-esteem. That is, people have a preferred view of themselves, and they will defend against any unflattering changes or blows to that self-view. Obviously, realizing that one has unacceptable sexual or aggressive wishes might be a blow one's self-view, especially for persons in the Victorian era. However, in today's society there may be other events that threaten self-esteem, such as failure, embarrassment, and being excluded from a group. Most modern psychologists believe that people defend themselves against these threats to their self-esteem (Baumeister & Vohs, 2004). Much of the contemporary research on self-esteem maintenance can thus be thought of as having roots in the psychoanalytic concept of defense mechanisms. Baumeister and his colleagues (Baumeister, Dale, & Sommer, 1998) reviewed a good deal of modern research linking self-esteem protection to defense mechanisms, and we will provide some examples from their review where appropriate.

Denial When the reality of a situation is extremely anxiety-provoking, a person may resort to the defense mechanism of **denial.** In contrast to repression, which involves keeping an *experience* out of memory, a person in denial insists that things are not the way they seem. Denial involves refusing to see the facts. A man whose wife has left him might still set a place at the dinner table for her and insist that she is supposed to come home at any time. Playing out this scenario night after night might be more acceptable than acknowledging that she is, in reality, gone. Denial can also be less extreme, as when someone reappraises an anxiety-provoking situation so that it seems less daunting. For example, a man might convince himself that his wife *had* to leave him for some reason, that it really was *not* her fault, and that she *would* return if only she could. In this case, he is denying that his wife freely chose to leave him instead of acknowledging the whole reality of the situation.

A common form of denial is to dismiss unflattering feedback as wrong or irrelevant. When people are given a poor evaluation, say by a supervisor, some will reject the evaluation rather than change their view of themselves. They might blame their difficulties on bad luck or problems with the situation, anything but accept personal responsibility and have to alter their view of themselves. Indeed, the tendency to blame events outside one's control for failure but to accept responsibility for success is so common that psychologists refer to this as the **fundamental attribution error.** It may be interpreted, however, as a specific form of denial.

Health psychologists are also interested in denial. How can a person smoke two packs of cigarettes a day and not worry about his or her health? One answer would be to deny one's personal vulnerability, or to deny the evidence linking smoking to illness, or to deny that one wants to live a long and healthy life. Baumeister et al. (1998) review evidence that people often minimize the risks they see in various unhealthy behaviors.

Denial often shows up in daydreams and fantasies. Daydreams are frequently about how things might have been. To some extent, daydreams deny the present situation by focusing on how things could have been otherwise. In doing so, they may lessen or defend against the potentially anxiety-provoking circumstances of one's present situation. For example, a person who has done something embarrassing might daydream about how things might have gone had he or she not done that stupid, embarrassing thing.

Displacement In **displacement,** a threatening or an unacceptable impulse is channeled or redirected from its original source to a nonthreatening target. Consider, for example, a woman who has an argument with her supervisor at work. She is really angry with the supervisor, but her ego keeps her in check because, after all, the supervisor is the boss and can make her work life difficult, so she goes home and displaces her anger onto her husband, perhaps yelling and nagging at him or belittling him. Although this approach may contribute to marital problems, it will most likely avoid the difficulties associated with losing one's temper at one's boss. Sometimes displacement has a domino effect, whereby one spouse berates another, who in turn yells at the children, who then abuse the family dog. Moreover, although displacement is often thought of as a defense mechanism involving the redirection of aggressive instincts, it can also involve sexual urges that are redirected from a less acceptable to a more acceptable target. For example, a man may have a strong sexual attraction toward a woman who is subordinate to him at work, but this woman has no interest in him. Rather than harass the woman, he may redirect this sexual energy toward his wife and rediscover that he is still attracted to her. Freud also noted that sometimes even fears are redirected through displacement and cited as an example the case of a boy who feared his father but who redirected that fear toward horses.

Although these examples seem to involve conscious awareness and a calculating choice of how to express the unacceptable emotion, the process of displacement takes place outside of awareness. *Deliberately* redirecting one's anger, for example, is not displacement, even though someone might do this to manage a situation. Real displacement is an unconscious means of avoiding the recognition that one has certain inappropriate or unacceptable feelings (e.g., anger or sexual attraction) toward a specific other person or a specific object. Those feelings then are displaced onto another person or object that is more appropriate or acceptable.

Researchers have tried to study the displacement of aggressive impulses. In one study, student participants were frustrated (or not, if they were in the control group) by the experimenter. Later they had the opportunity to act aggressively toward the experimenter, the experimenter's assistant, or another participant. The frustrated participants were more aggressive, but they were equally aggressive toward the experimenter, the assistant, or the other student (Hokanson, Burgess, & Cohen, 1963). The target did not matter. Other studies have replicated this finding. In one study subjects were angered, not by the experimenter, but by another participant, then given an opportunity to act aggressively toward that subject or toward a friend of that participant. Again, angered participants were more aggressive, but it did not seem to matter who the target was.

Are these results evidence for displacement? Baumeister et al. (1998) conclude they are not. Angered people act aggressively, they argue, and there is no evidence that it is defensive. They argue that, while displacement is an interesting dynamic concept, there is little empirical support for the idea that urges are like hydraulic fluid in a closed system being shunted this way or that depending on displacement.

Rationalization Another common defense mechanism, especially among educated persons, such as college students, is **rationalization.** It involves generating acceptable reasons for outcomes that might otherwise appear socially unacceptable. In rationalization, the goal is to reduce anxiety by coming up with an explanation for an event that is easier to accept than the real reason. For example, a student who receives a failing grade on a term paper might explain it away by insisting that the teacher did not give clear directions for how to write the paper. Or perhaps a woman whose boyfriend has broken up with her explains to her friends that she never really liked him that much to begin with. These reasons are a lot more emotionally acceptable than the alternatives that one is not as smart or as desirable as one thinks.

Reaction Formation In an attempt to stifle the expression of an unacceptable urge, a person may continually display a flurry of behavior that indicates the opposite impulse. Such a tactic is known as **reaction formation.** For example, imagine the woman who is angry with her supervisor, described in the discussion of displacement. If, instead of displacing her anger, her ego unconsciously resorts to reaction formation, then she might go out of her way to be overly kind to her boss, to show the boss special courtesy and consideration.

A Closer Look

Empirical Studies of Repression

Although psychoanalysts have been interested in repression since Freud introduced the concept, empirical research on this topic has been relatively sparse until recent years (Holmes, 1990). Perhaps this has been due to the difficulty of defining repression in such a way that it may actually be measured for research purposes. Researchers have developed questionnaires to identify individuals who typically use repression as a mechanism for coping with threatening, stressful, or anxiety-producing situations.

Freud held that the essential aspect of repression was the motivated unavailability of unpleasant, painful, or disturbing emotions (Bonanno, 1990). He wrote that repression was a process whereby unpleasant emotions are turned away and kept "at a distance from the conscious" (Freud, 1915/1957, p. 147). Almost 65 years later, Weinberger, Schwartz, and Davidson (1979) were the first to propose that repression, as a style of coping with unpleasant emotions, can be measured by examining various combinations of scores on questionnaires of anxiety and defensiveness. These researchers administered a questionnaire measure of anxiety and a questionnaire measure of defensiveness to a group of subjects. The anxiety questionnaire contained items that inquired about whether or not one has strong symptoms of anxiety (e.g., heart pounding) when engaging in various behaviors, such as public speaking. The defensiveness questionnaire contained items inquiring about common faults, such as whether respondents had ever gossiped, had ever become so angry that they wanted to break something, or had ever resented someone's asking them for a favor. Clearly, almost everyone is guilty of these minor offenses at one time or another. Therefore, subjects who consistently deny engaging in these somewhat undesirable behaviors score high on defensiveness. The researchers combined the subjects' anxiety and defensiveness scores, which resulted in the four-fold typology portrayed in Figure 9.3. Most of the subsequent research on repression involved comparing the repressor group to the other three groups on a dependant measure.

In the initial study, after subjects had completed the questionnaires, Weinberger et al. (1979) had the subjects engage in a phrase association task, where they match up phrases in one list with phrases in another list that have similar meaning; several phrases contained angry and sexual overtones. As the subjects attempted to match up the phrases, the researchers measured their physiological reactions. The researchers also measured the subjects' self-reported levels of distress immediately after their performance. They found that the repressors reported the lowest levels of subjective distress yet were found to exhibit the highest levels of physiological arousal (heart rate, skin conductance). In short, repressors *verbally* say they are not distressed yet *physiologically* appear to be very distressed. Other researchers have obtained similar findings (e.g., Asendorpf & Scherer, 1983; Davis & Schwartz, 1987). These experimental results are consistent with Freud's view that repression keeps unpleasant experiences out of conscious awareness. Moreover, the results are consistent with Freud's ideas that such repressed unpleasant experiences still affect the individual, in spite of being outside of awareness (in this case, the repressed experiences affect the person's level of physiological arousal, even though the person is not consciously aware of being anxious).

Another way to examine repression is to ask subjects to recall childhood experiences associated with pleasant and unpleasant emotions. This is exactly what psychologists Penelope Davis and Gary Schwartz did in 1987. They asked their subjects to recall and describe childhood experiences that they associated with happiness, sadness, anger, fear, and wonder. The researchers' findings showed that the repressors, defined as high defensive–low anxious persons, did recall fewer negative emotional experiences than the other subjects and that the repressors were substantially older at the time of their earliest negative emotional memories. Somewhat surprisingly, the repressors also had limited access to positive memories. This finding illustrates what may be one of the costs of repression—pleasant as well as unpleasant emotional memories may be diminished or lost to conscious recall.

Penelope Davis (1987) expanded on the general idea that repressors have limited access to emotional memories. First, she found that the effect is strongest for memories about the *self*. The repressors in her study had no trouble remembering bad things that had happened to *other* people (e.g., siblings), but they did have limited recollection about unpleasant events that they themselves had experienced. Second, the effects of repression appeared to be strongest for the memories associated with feelings of fear and self-consciousness. Although Freud (1915/1957) wrote "the motive and purpose of repression was nothing else than the

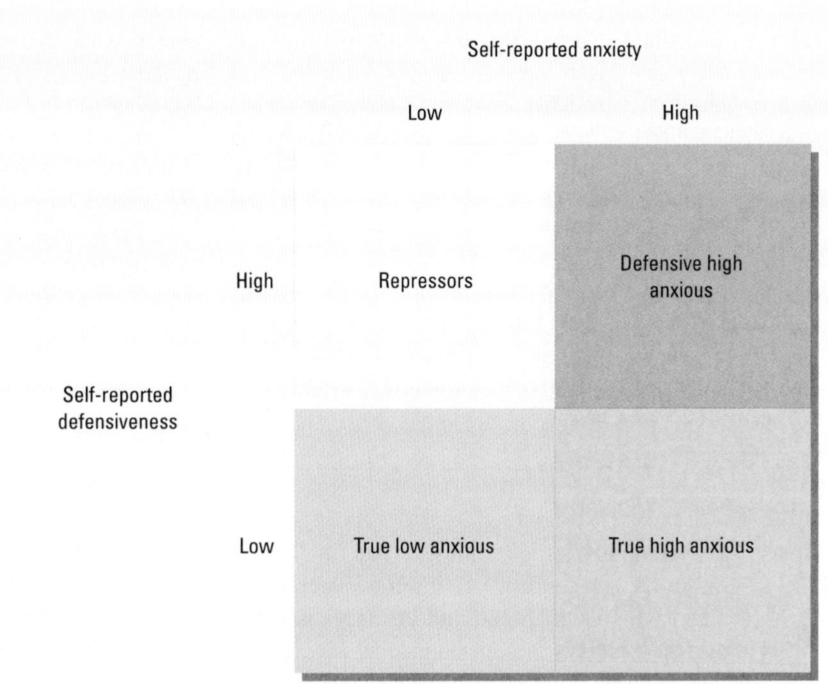

Figure 9.3

Finding repressors by measuring anxiety and defensiveness. The subjects who deny being anxious, but who are high on defensiveness, are most likely repressors.

avoidance of unpleasure" (p. 153), according to Davis, the motive to repress is particularly strong for experiences associated with fear and self-consciousness. Why might this be the case? These emotions are often evoked in situations where the focus of attention is on the self in an evaluative or threatening way. In fear, for example, there is a threat to the very existence of the self. In self-consciousness, the threat of being negatively evaluated by others looms large, leading a person to feel exposed and vulnerable.

Hansen and Hansen (1988) found that repressors' memories are relatively less elaborate when it comes to emotion than are those of nonrepressors. That is, repressors have memories for emotional events that are less developed, less refined, and less rich than those of nonrepressors. These authors raise the intriguing question of what might account for this impoverished emotional memory on the part of repressors. It could come about in one of two ways. First, repressors may have limited *recall* of their emotional experiences. That is, repressors may have actually *had* varied emotional experiences and those experiences may actually be *in* their memories, but they just have trouble retrieving or recalling them. Alternatively, repressors could actually have blocked certain emotional experiences from entering into their memories in the first place. The effect of repression could have occurred at the *encoding* rather than the recall stage.

Although most studies of repression have examined memory for past events, a few studies (e.g., Hansen, Hansen, & Shantz, 1992) suggest that the effect of repression may occur not only as diminished *memory* for negative events but also in the person's actual reaction to negative events when they occur. This is what Freud would have predicted, that repressors actually do not experience negative emotions as strongly as nonrepressors do. We can ask whether repressors simply have poor memories for bad events or whether, when bad events happen, they actually experience less negative emotion than nonrepressors do, or both.

In a study by Cutler, Larsen, and Bunce (1996), repressors and nonrepressors kept daily diaries of 40 different

A Closer Look (*Continued*)

emotions for 28 consecutive days. After reporting on their emotions every day for a month, the subjects were then asked to think back over the month and to rate how much of each emotion they recalled experiencing, on average, during the course of that month. The researchers, thus, had a measure of actual day-to-day emotion, recorded close to the time when the subjects experienced the emotions, as well as a measure of recalled emotion. This approach allowed the researchers to test whether the repressors reported less negative emotion, recalled less negative emotion, or both. The results showed that the repressors, compared with the nonrepressors, actually reported *experiencing* fewer and less intense unpleasant emotions on a day-to-day basis. The repressors' memories for unpleasant emotions, however, were only slightly less accurate than the memories of the nonrepressors. The effect of repression seems to occur during the *experience* of unpleasant events, whereby repressors somehow dampen their emotional reactions to bad events.

Freud said that the function of repression was to keep unpleasant experiences out of conscious awareness. We now know more specifically that the blunting effect of repression occurs primarily during the reaction to bad events. Repressors do not have bad memories; rather, somehow they keep unpleasant events from entering into their memories in the first place.

An interesting example of reaction formation is provided by Copper (1998), who discusses the concept of "killing someone with kindness." Consider a man who is angry with his girlfriend, but the anger is not conscious; he is not aware of how angry he really is. It is raining outside so he offers her his umbrella. She refuses to take it, but he insists. She keeps refusing, and he keeps insisting that she take it. Here he is replacing his hostility with apparent kindness. However, his aggression is coming out in his persistent insistence and his ignoring her wishes not to take the umbrella. According to psychoanalysis, this dynamic can often be found when defenses are being used; people may try to cover up their wishes and intention and yet unwittingly express them.

The mechanism of reaction formation makes it possible for psychoanalysts to predict that sometimes people will do exactly the opposite of what you might otherwise think they would do. It also alerts us to be sensitive to instances when a person is doing something in excess, such as when someone is being overly nice to us for no apparent reason. Perhaps in such cases the person really means the opposite of what he or she is doing. One of the hallmarks of reaction formation is excessive or persistent behavior.

Projection Another type of defense mechanism, **projection,** is based on the notion that sometimes we see in others the traits and desires we find most upsetting in ourselves. We literally "project" (i.e., attribute) our own unacceptable qualities onto others. We can then hate them, instead of hating ourselves, for having those unacceptable qualities or desires. At the same time, we can disparage the tendencies or characteristics in question without admitting that we possess them. Other people become the target by virtue of their having qualities that we intensely dislike in ourselves. For instance, a thief is often worried about the prospect of others stealing from him and claims that others are not to be trusted. Or a woman denies having any interest in sexuality yet insists that all the men she knows "have nothing but sex on their minds." Married men who have affairs are more suspicious than other husbands that their wives are unfaithful. What a person intensely dislikes in or gets upset about with others is often revealing of his or her innermost insecurities and conflicts. A person who always insults others by calling them "stupid" may, in fact, harbor some insecurity about his or her own intelligence.

As another example, consider people who become involved in antihomosexuality campaigns. Some people publicly express moral outrage or even propose violence against persons with this sexual orientation. Trent Lott was Senate Majority Leader in June 1998, when he stated on television that homosexuals had an illness similar to alcoholism or kleptomania. At the same time, Christian fundamentalists were airing TV advertisements stating that homosexuality was a disease and that gay persons should be cured. Pat Robertson, a fundamentalist preacher on the Christian Broadcasting Network, said that a hurricane might strike Orlando, Florida, because of a recent gathering of homosexual persons there. Could it be that homophobic persons are engaging projection as a defense mechanism against their own questionable sexual orientation?

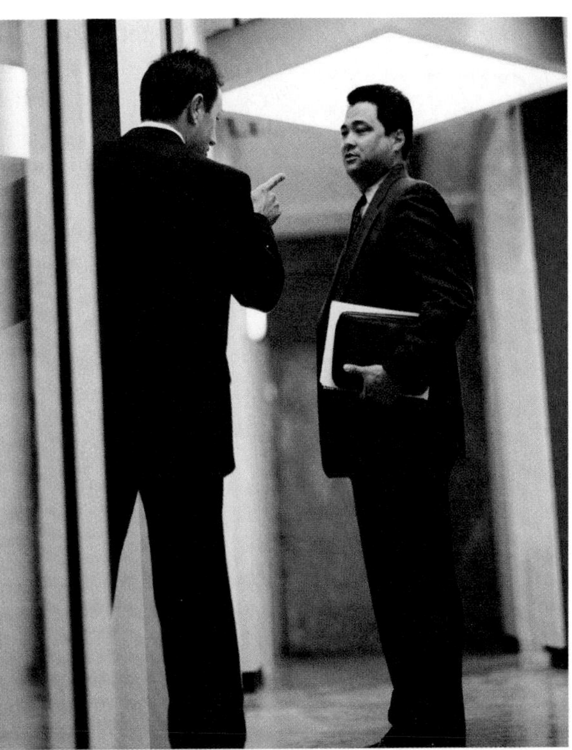

In projection, we see in others those traits or desires we find most upsetting in ourselves. We can then disparage them for having the undesirable characteristic, without admitting that we have that very characteristic.

In modern psychological research there is an effect, similar to projection, called the **false consensus effect.** This was first described by Ross, Greene, and House in 1977. It refers to the tendency many people have to assume that others are similar to them. That is, extraverts think many other people are extraverted, and conscientious persons think many other people are conscientious. To think that many other people share your own preferences, motivations, or traits is to display the false consensus effect.

Baumeister and colleagues (1998) argue that having a false consensus about one's unflattering traits could be ego defensive. For example, to be the only person whose credit card is over the limit would imply that one is unique in this moral deficiency. But if one believes that many people are over their credit limits, or close to it, then this false consensus belief might be protective of one's self-concept. The adolescent who explains some misbehavior with the phrase, "Gee, everyone else was doing it," is perhaps engaging in defensive false consensus, essentially saying, "I'm not so bad because everyone is bad too."

Sublimation According to Freud, **sublimation** is the most adaptive defense mechanism. Sublimation is the channeling of unacceptable sexual or aggressive instincts into socially desired activities. A common example is going out to chop wood when you are angry rather than acting on that anger or even engaging in other less adaptive defense mechanisms, such as displacement. Watching football or boxing is more desirable than beating someone up. Mountain climbing or volunteering for combat duty once in the army might be forms of sublimating a death wish. Freud once reportedly remarked about all the sublimated sexual energy that must have gone into building the skyscrapers of New York City. One's choice of occupation (e.g., athlete, mortician, and emergency room nurse) might be interpreted as the sublimation of certain unacceptable urges. The positive feature of sublimation is that it allows for some limited expression of id tendencies, so the ego does not have to invest energy in holding the id in check. Freud maintained that the greatest achievements of civilization were due to the effective sublimation of sexual and aggressive urges.

Defense Mechanisms in Everyday Life

Life provides each of us with plenty of psychological bumps and bruises. We don't get a job we badly wanted, an acquaintance says something hurtful, we realize something about ourselves that is not flattering. In short, we must face unexpected or disappointing events all the time. Defense mechanisms may be useful in coping with these occurrences and the emotions they generate (Larsen, 2000a, 2000b; Larsen & Prizmic, 2004). We all have to deal with stress, and, to the extent that defense mechanisms help, so much the better (see Valliant, 1994, for a discussion and categorization of defense mechanisms).

It is not too difficult, however, to imagine circumstances that are made worse by the use of defense mechanisms (Cramer, 2000, 2002). Others may avoid a person who projects a lot. A person who displaces frequently may have few friends. Moreover, the use of defense mechanisms takes psychic energy that is therefore not available for other pursuits. How do you know when the use of defense mechanisms is becoming a problem? The answer is twofold: you know a behavior is becoming a problem if it begins inhibiting the ability to be *productive* or if it begins limiting the ability to *maintain relationships*. If either one of these areas in life is negatively affected—work or relationships—then you might wonder about a psychological problem. Moreover, there is much to be said in favor of directly confronting difficult issues and taking action directed at solving problems. Nevertheless, sometimes problems simply cannot be solved or a person does not have the energy or resources to directly confront a problem. Under these temporary circumstances, defense mechanisms may be very useful. When used occasionally, defense mechanisms most likely will not interfere with work or social life. According to Freud, the hallmark of mature adulthood was the ability to work productively and to develop and maintain satisfying relationships. Reaching mature adulthood, however, involves passing through several stages of personality development.

Psychosexual Stages of Personality Development

Freud believed that all persons passed through a set series of stages in personality development. Each of these stages involves a conflict, and how the person resolves this conflict gives rise to various aspects of his or her personality. So, in psychoanalytic theory, the source of individual differences lies in how the child comes to resolve conflicts in each of the stages of development. The end result, after going through all the stages, is a fully formed personality. Because all of this happens in childhood, the famous phrase, "The child is father to the man," captures a key Freudian idea.

At each of the first three stages, young children must face and resolve specific conflicts. The conflicts revolve around ways of obtaining a type of sexual gratification. For this reason, Freud's theory of development is called the **psychosexual stage theory.** According to the theory, children seek sexual gratification at each stage by investing libidinal energy in a specific body part. Each stage in the developmental process is named after the body part in which sexual energy is invested.

If a child fails to fully resolve a conflict at a particular stage of development, he or she may get stuck in that stage, a phenomenon known as **fixation.** Each successive stage represents a more mature mode of obtaining sexual gratification. If a child is fixated at a particular stage, he or she exhibits a less mature approach to obtaining sexual gratification. In the final stage of development, mature adults obtain pleasure from healthy intimate relationships and from work. The road to this final stage, however, is fraught with developmental conflicts and the potential for fixation. Let's examine these stages and discuss the conflicts that arise, as well as the consequences of fixation at each stage.

The first stage, which Freud called the **oral stage,** occurs during the initial 18 months after birth. During this time, the main sources of pleasure and tension reduction are the mouth, lips, and tongue. You don't have to be around many babies to realize how busy they are with their mouths (e.g., whenever they come across something new, such as a rattle or toy, they usually put it into their mouths first). The main conflict during this stage is weaning, withdrawing from the breast or bottle. This conflict has both a biological and a psychological component. From a biological standpoint, the id wants the immediate gratification associated with taking in nourishment and obtaining pleasure through the mouth. From a psychological perspective, the conflict is one of excessive pleasure versus dependency, with the fear of being left to fend for oneself. Sometimes a child has a painful or traumatic experience during the weaning process, resulting in a degree of fixation at the oral stage. Adults who still obtain pleasure from "taking in," especially through the mouth, might be fixated at this stage (e.g., people who overeat or smoke). Problems with nail biting, thumb sucking, or pencil chewing might also occur. At a psychological level, people who are fixated at the oral stage may be overly dependent: they may want to be babied, to be nurtured and taken care of, and thus to have others make decisions for them. Some psychoanalysts also believe that drug addiction (because it involves pleasure from "taking in") is a sign of oral fixation.

There is another possible conflict of the oral stage that is associated with biting. This conflict can occur after the child grows teeth and finds that he or she can obtain pleasure from biting and chewing. Parents typically discourage a child from biting, particularly if the child bites other children or adults. Thus, the child has the conflict between the urge to bite and parental restrictions. People who fixate during this stage might develop adult personalities that are hostile, quarrelsome, or mocking. They continue to draw gratification from being psychologically "biting" and verbally attacking.

The second stage of development is the **anal stage,** which typically occurs between the ages of 18 months and 3 years of age. At this stage, the anal sphincter is the source of sexual pleasure. During this time, the child obtains pleasure from first expelling feces and then, during toilet training, from retaining feces. At first, the id desires immediate tension reduction whenever there is any pressure in the rectum. This is achieved by defecating whenever and wherever the urge arises. Parents, however, work to instill in the child a degree of self-control through the process of toilet training. Many conflicts arise around this issue of the child's ability to achieve some self-control. Some children achieve too little control and grow up to be sloppy and dirty. Other children have the opposite problem: they develop too much self-control and begin to take pleasure in little acts of self-control. Adults who are compulsive, overly neat, rigid, and never messy are, according to psychoanalysts, likely to be fixated at the anal stage. After all, toilet training usually presents a child with the first opportunity to exercise choice and willpower. When a parent puts the child on the potty seat and says, "Now, do your business," the child has the opportunity to say, "No!" and to withhold. This might signal the beginnings of being stingy, holding back, not giving others what they want, and being overly willful and stubborn.

The third stage, which occurs between 3 and 5 years of age, is called the **phallic stage,** because the child discovers that he has (or she discovers that she does not have) a penis. In fact, the major event during this stage is children's discovery of their own genitals and the realization that some pleasure can be derived from touching them. This is also the awakening of sexual desire directed outward and, according to Freud, it is first directed toward the parent of the opposite sex. Little boys fall in love with their mothers, and little girls fall in love with their fathers. But children feel more than just parental love, according to Freud's theory. A little boy lusts for his mother and wants to have sex with her. His father is seen as the competitor, as the one who is preventing the little boy from possessing his mother and receiving *all* of her attention. For the boy, the main conflict, which Freud called the **Oedipal conflict,** is the unconscious wish to have his mother all to himself by eliminating the father. (Oedipus is a character in Greek mythology who unknowingly kills his father and marries his mother.) Daddy is the competitor for Mommy's attention, and he should be beaten and driven from the home or killed. But killing or beating Daddy is wrong.

Part of the Oedipal conflict, then, is that the child loves, yet is competing with, the parent of the same sex. Moreover, the little boy grows to fear his father because, surely, this big and powerful person could prevent this all from happening. In fact, Freud argued that little boys come to believe that their fathers might make a preemptive strike by taking away the thing that is at the root of the conflict: the boy's penis. This fear of losing his penis, called **castration anxiety,** drives the little boy into giving up his sexual desire for Mommy. The boy decides that the best he can do is to become like the guy who has Mommy—in other words, like his father. This process of wanting to become like Daddy, called **identification,** marks the beginning of the resolution of the Oedipal conflict and the successful resolution of the phallic stage of psychosexual development for boys. Freud believed that the resolution of the Oedipal conflict was the beginning of both the superego and morality, as well as the male gender role.

For little girls, the situation is at once similar and different. One similarity is that the conflict centers on the penis, or actually the lack thereof, on the part of the little girl. According to Freud, a little girl blames her mother for the fact that she lacks a penis. She desires her father yet, at the same time, envies him for his penis. This is called **penis envy,** and it is the counterpart of castration anxiety. Penis envy is different in that the little girl does not necessarily fear the mother, as the boy fears the father. Thus, for girls, there is no strong motivation to give up her desire for her father.

Freud's student Carl Jung termed this stage the **Electra complex,** for girls. Electra was also a character in a Greek myth. Electra convinced her brother to kill their mother, after the mother had murdered the father. Freud actually rejected the idea of the Electra complex, and he was vague about how the phallic stage is resolved for girls. He wrote that it drags on later in life for girls and may never fully be resolved. Since successful resolution results in the development of the superego, Freud believed that women must therefore be morally inferior to men. This aspect of Freud's developmental theory is not widely accepted today, and Freud has been strongly criticized for his beliefs about sex differences (e.g., Helson & Picano, 1990).

The next stage of psychosexual development is called the **latency stage.** This stage occurs from around the age of 6 until puberty. Little psychological development is presumed to occur during this time. It is mainly a period when the child is going to school and learning the skills and abilities necessary to take on the role of an adult. Because of the lack of specific sexual conflicts during this time, Freud believed that it was a period of psychological rest, or latency. Subsequent psychoanalysts have argued, instead, that much development occurs during this time, such as learning to make decisions for oneself, learning to interact and make friends with others, developing an identity, and learning the meaning of work. Because this is a more contemporary modification of Freud's theory, we will examine it in Chapter 10.

The latency period ends with the sexual awakening brought about by puberty. If the Oedipus or Electra complex has been resolved, the person goes on to the next and final stage of psychosexual development, the **genital stage.** This stage begins around puberty and lasts through one's adult life. Here the libido is focused on the genitals, but not in the manner of self-manipulation associated with the phallic stage. This differs from the earlier stages in that it is not accompanied by a specific conflict. People reach the genital stage only if they have resolved the conflicts at the prior stages. It is in this sense that personality development, according to Freud, is largely complete at around the age of 5 or 6: the adult personality is dependent on how the conflicts that arise during infancy and childhood are resolved.

Freud's psychosexual stage theory is a theory about personality development, both normal and abnormal. In a nutshell, the theory states that we are all born with a drive for sexual pleasure (the id) but that the constraints of civilized society limit the ways we can satisfy that drive. We all go through a series of predictable clashes or conflicts between our desire for pleasure and the demands placed on us by our parents and by society in general. The nature of the conflicts and the stages we go through are universal, but the specific instances and outcomes are each unique. Parts of our personalities are shaped at each stage by the particular ways we resolve the conflict. If, for example, at the oral stage, a person did not receive enough gratification (was weaned early) or received too much gratification (was weaned too late), then he or she might continue to have inappropriate demands for oral gratification throughout the rest of his or her life (perhaps in the form of being a dependent personality or developing an eating disorder or developing an alcohol or drug problem).

Freud developed the metaphor of an army whose troops are called into battle during each stage of psychosexual development. If the resolution of a stage is incomplete, then some soldiers must be left behind to monitor that particular conflict. It is as if some psychic energy must stand guard, lest the psychosexual conflict break out again. The poorer the resolution at a particular stage, the more psychic soldiers have to be left behind. One consequence of this is that less psychic energy is available for the subsequent tasks of maturity. The more soldiers brought forward to the genital stage, the more psychic energy that can be invested in mature intimate and productive relationships and the better the adult personality adjustment. It is interesting to note that neither happiness nor life satisfaction was directly a part of Freud's conception of successful personality development. Successful personality development, instead, was defined by the ability to be productive and to maintain loving relationships.

Personality and Psychoanalysis

Psychoanalysis, besides being a theory of personality, is also a method of psychotherapy, a technique for helping individuals who are experiencing a mental disorder or even relatively minor problems with living. Psychoanalysis can be thought of as a method for deliberately restructuring the personality. The connection between the psychoanalytic theory of personality and psychoanalytic therapy is very strong. Principles of psychoanalytic therapy are based directly on the psychoanalytic theory about the structure and functioning of personality. Freud developed his theory of personality while treating patients in therapy. Similarly, many modern psychoanalysts, even those in academic settings, maintain a practice of seeing patients. Most psychoanalysts have themselves undergone psychoanalytic psychotherapy, which Freud held to be a requirement for becoming a psychoanalyst.

Techniques for Revealing the Unconscious

The goal of psychoanalysis is to make the unconscious conscious. Mental illness, problems with living, and unexplained physical symptoms can all be viewed as the result of unconscious conflicts. Thoughts, feelings, urges, or memories have been forced into the unconscious, because of their disturbing or threatening nature. Due to the dynamic nature of the human mind, these conflicts or restrained urges may slip out of the unconscious in ways that cause trouble. They often obtain expression as psychological or physical symptoms.

The first aim of psychoanalysis is to identify these unconscious thoughts and feelings. Once the patient can be made aware of this material, the second aim is to enable the person to deal with the unconscious urges, memories, or thoughts realistically and maturely. The major challenge facing the psychoanalyst is determining how to penetrate the unconscious mind of the patient. By its very definition, the unconscious mind is the part of which the person has no awareness. How can one person (the therapist) come to know something about another person (the patient) which that other person does not know? Freud and other psychoanalysts have developed a set of standard techniques that can be used to dredge up material from the unconscious minds of patients.

Free Association

If you were to relax, to sit back in a comfortable chair, to let your mind wander, and then to say whatever came into your mind, you would be engaging in **free association.** Chances are, you would say some things that would surprise even yourself, and you might even be embarrassed by what comes out. If you were able to resist the urge to censor your thoughts before speaking, then you would have an idea of how a patient spends much of his or her time in psychoanalysis. The typical psychoanalytic session lasts 50 minutes and may be repeated several times a week; the sessions may continue for years. The goals of the sessions are to enable patients to identify unconscious material that might be causing unwanted symptoms and to help them cope with that material in an adult fashion.

By relaxing the censor that screens our everyday thoughts, the technique of free association allows potentially important material into conscious awareness. This takes some practice. Patients are encouraged to say whatever comes to mind, no matter how absurd, trifling, or obscene. The technique is a bit like looking for a needle in a haystack, in that the psychoanalyst is likely to be subjected to a barrage of trivial material before stumbling on an important clue to an unconscious conflict.

In free association, the psychoanalyst must be able to recognize the subtle signs that something important has just been mentioned—a slight quiver in the way a word is pronounced, a halting sentence, the patient's immediate discounting of what he or she has just said, a false start, a nervous laugh, or a long pause. An effective psychoanalyst will detect such signs and intervene to ask the patient to stick with that topic for awhile, to free associate further on that issue. Archeology is a good metaphor for this type of work, as the psychoanalyst is digging through all sorts of ordinary material in search of clues to past conflicts and trauma.

Dreams

Thinkers have always speculated about the meaning of dreams, and it has long been thought that dreams are messages from deep regions of the mind that are not accessible during waking life. In 1900, Freud published his book *The Interpretation of Dreams,* in which he presented his theory of the meaning and purpose of dreaming. He held that the purpose of dreaming was to satisfy urges and to fulfill unconscious wishes and desires, all within the protection of sleep. But aren't most dreams absurd and nonsensical? How, then, can they have anything to do with desires and wishes? For example, a person might have a dream about riding a white horse that suddenly begins to fly. Does this mean the person wishes to have a flying horse? No, Freud would argue, because the dream contains wishes and desires in *disguised* form. **Dream analysis** was a technique Freud taught for uncovering the unconscious material in a dream by *interpreting* the dream's content. Freud maintained that we must distinguish between the **manifest content** of a dream (what the dream actually contains) and the **latent content** (what the elements of the dream represent). He believed that the direct expression of desires and wishes would be so disturbing that it would waken the dreamer. The ego is still somewhat at work during sleep, and it succeeds in disguising the disturbing content of our unconscious. The wishes and unacceptable impulses have to be disguised in order to allow the person to keep sleeping, which is necessary, yet must be expressed in order to satisfy desires. Having a dream about killing one's father, for example, might be so disturbing that it would awaken a young boy who has an Oedipal fixation. However, a dream about a king who has a garden containing a fountain that is disabled by a small animal, so that it no longer shoots its plume of water up into the air, might make the same psychological point yet allow the sleeper to remain asleep.

Thus, although our dreams often appear to be ridiculous and incomprehensible to us, to a psychoanalyst, a dream may contain valuable clues to the unconscious. Freud called dreams "the royal road to the unconscious." The psychoanalyst interprets dreams by deciphering how the unacceptable impulses and urges are transformed by the unconscious into **symbols** in the dream. Parents may be represented as a king and queen. Children may be represented as small animals. Hence, a dream about a king whose fountain is broken by a small animal can be interpreted as wish fulfillment with an Oedipal overtone.

According to Freud, dreaming serves three functions. First, it allows for wish fulfillment and the gratification of desires, even if only in symbolic form. Second, dreams provide a safety valve by allowing a person to release unconscious tension by expressing his or her deepest desires, although in disguised form. And, third, dreams are guardians of sleep. Even though a lot is going on in dreams, such as the expression of wishes and desires, the person remains asleep. Although tension is being released, no anxiety is being aroused, and the person sleeps without interruption.

In many of his writings, Freud provided interpretations or translations of common dream symbols. Not surprisingly, most symbols have sexual connotations. This may be because Freud was influenced by the Victorian era in which he lived, when most people were very inhibited about sexual matters. Freud believed that, because people repressed their sexual feelings and desires, these inhibited urges came out in symbolic form in dreams. Many later thinkers have been critical of Freud's seeming preoccupation with sex, which they have attributed to the historical period during which he was developing his theory.

Exercise

For a few days, keep a pencil and pad of paper by your bedside. Immediately on awakening each morning, write down anything you can remember about the dreams you had the night before. After a few days, read over your dream diary and look for themes. Do you see any recurring themes or elements in your collection of dreams? What are some of the common symbols in your dreams, and what do you think they represent? To help you answer these questions, try free associating to your dream content. That is, find a quiet place and relax. Start by describing your dream aloud, and then just keep talking, saying anything that comes to mind, no matter how foolish or trivial. After doing this exercise, have you learned anything about yourself or about what is important to you?

Projective Techniques

You've undoubtedly seen drawings that can be interpreted in two or more ways (e.g., the picture of a vase that, when looked at differently, looks like two faces). Or maybe you've seen the children's games in which, within a larger drawing, there are hidden images that you are supposed to find. Imagine that you give a person a picture of something totally ambiguous, such as an inkblot, and ask him or her what he or she sees. A person might see all sorts of things in the shapes created by the ink splatter: a rocketship, two fish swimming, a clown. The idea that what a person sees in an ambiguous figure, such as an inkblot, reflects his or her personality is called the **projective hypothesis.** People are thought to *project* their own personalities into what they report seeing in an ambiguous stimulus. A hostile and aggressive person might

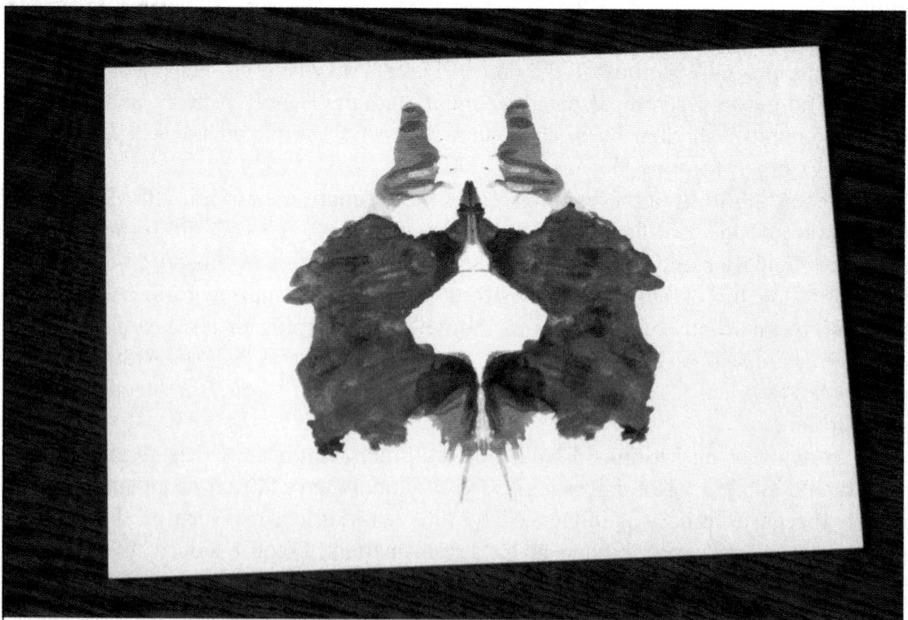

Projective techniques, such as the inkblots developed by the Swiss psychiatrist Hermann Rorschach, are popular methods for assessing unconscious aspects of personality, such as repressed desires, wishes, or conflicts.

see teeth, claws, and blood in an inkblot. Someone with an oral fixation might see food or people eating. The inkblot technique, as well as other projective measures, is often criticized by research psychologists for the scant scientific evidence as to its validity or reliability (Wood, Nezworski, Lilienfeld, & Garb, 2003).

Another type of projective technique involves asking the person to produce something, such as a drawing of a person. What someone draws might be a projection of his or her own conflicts. Consider a young man whom, when asked to draw a person, draws only a head. When asked to draw another person, but this time of someone of the opposite sex, he draws another head. Finally, when asked to draw a picture of himself, he again draws only a head. We might presume that this person has an unconscious conflict about his body image. As with dreams and free association, the goal of projective techniques is to bypass the patient's conscious censor and reveal his or her unconscious conflicts and repressed urges and desires.

The Process of Psychoanalysis

With the help of free association, dream analysis, and projective techniques, the psychoanalyst gradually comes to understand the unconscious source of the patient's problems. The patient must also come to understand the unconscious dynamics of his or her situation. Toward this end, the psychoanalyst offers the patient **interpretations** of the psychodynamic causes of the problems. The patient is led to view problematic thoughts, dreams, behaviors, symptoms, or feelings as all having unconscious roots and as expressions of unconscious conflicts or repressed urges. The psychoanalyst might say, "Could it be that the reason you feel so sleepy when you go out with your boyfriend is that you are afraid of being sexually attractive to him?" The patient is confronted with an explanation of something she has been keeping from herself. Through many interpretations, the patient is gradually led to an understanding of the unconscious source of her problems. This is the beginning of **insight.** Insight, in psychoanalysis, is more than a simple cognitive understanding of the intrapsychic basis of one's troubles, though this certainly is a part of insight. Insight refers to an intense emotional experience that accompanies the release of repressed material. When this material is reintegrated into conscious awareness, and the person experiences the emotions associated with that previously repressed material, then we say that some degree of insight has been achieved.

As you might imagine, none of this is easy. The patient, or at least the patient's ego, has expended much energy to repress the root of the problem in order to keep anxiety at bay. As the therapist pokes at the unconscious material through free association and dream analysis, and begins to offer interpretations, the patient typically feels threatened. The forces that have worked to repress the disturbing impulse or trauma now work to resist the psychoanalytic process, in a stage of psychoanalysis called **resistance.** As the patient's defenses are threatened by the probing psychoanalyst, the patient may unconsciously set up obstacles to progress. The patient may come up with all sorts of clever ways to misdirect or derail the psychoanalyst. The patient may forget appointments, not pay the analyst's bill, or go very late to a session. Sometimes during a session, a patient in resistance might spend a great deal of time on trivial matters, thereby avoiding important issues. A patient might waste lots of time recalling the names of and other details about every classmate he or she knew in grade school, a process that could take weeks of session time. Or a patient who is being pressed by the analyst and confronted with interpretations might become angry and insult the analyst.

When an analyst detects a patient's resistance, it is usually a welcome sign that progress is being made. Resistance signifies that important unconscious material is coming to the fore. The resistance itself then becomes an integral part of the interpretations the analyst offers to the patient. For example, the analyst might say, "Perhaps you are insulting me because you want to avoid discussing the various ways in which you have been trying to make yourself sexually unattractive to men. Let's talk some more about what you are trying to avoid by starting an argument with me."

Another important step in most analyses is called **transference.** In this stage, the patient begins reacting to the analyst as if he or she were an important figure from the patient's own life. The patient displaces past or present feelings toward someone from his or her own life onto the analyst. For example, a patient might feel and act toward his analyst the way he felt or acted toward his father. The feelings that the patient transfers onto the analyst can be either positive or negative. For example, a patient may express her admiration for the analyst's powerful intellect and keen mind and offer the sort of adoration that a child is likely to have toward a parent. Old conflicts and old reactions then are played out during the therapy sessions.

The idea behind transference is that the interpersonal problems between a patient and the important people in his or her life will be reenacted in the therapy session with the analyst. Freud called this the "repetition compulsion," whereby the person reenacts his or her interpersonal problems with new people, including the psychoanalyst. Transference may be one source of clues about the person's unconscious conflicts, and it provides the analyst with opportunities for offering interpretations about the patient's behavior.

Exercise

Transference can occur in everyday life as well as in psychoanalysis. The nature of our everyday interactions with others can be influenced by past relationship patterns. For example, a student might work hard on a paper to please a favorite professor. Earning less than a perfect grade on that paper—say, a B+—might cause distress, a tearful scene with the professor, or a temper tantrum. The surprised professor might wonder what this person is really reacting to. Perhaps the student is replaying a childhood pattern of reacting immaturely whenever he or she disappoints a person from whom he or she desperately seeks approval, such as a demanding parent.

Think of a time when you or someone you know overreacted to an event. Once you have identified such a situation, can you think of any similarities it has to past situations, particularly from childhood? Are there any reasons to suppose that you or someone you know who is overreacting is repeating a conflict from the past?

Movies and other modern media often portray psychoanalysis as resulting in a flash of insight, in which the patient is suddenly and forever cured. Real life is not so simple. A thorough psychoanalysis can take years, sometimes a decade or longer. The analyst provides interpretation after interpretation, illustrating to the patient the unconscious source of his or her problems. Along the way, the patient may exhibit resistance. Transference also typically becomes an issue for interpretation. Through long and laborious work by both patient and analyst, the patient gradually gains insight. The successfully analyzed patient then has available the psychic energy that his or her ego has formerly been expending in repressing conflicts. This energy may be directed into those twin pursuits Freud said were the hallmarks of adult personality development—to love and to work.

Why Is Psychoanalysis Important?

Throughout much of the twentieth century, Freud's ideas had a profound influence on how the mind was understood to operate. His continuing influence can be seen in several areas. First, psychoanalytic ideas influence the practice of psychotherapy even today. The second largest division of the American Psychological Association is the Division of Psychoanalysis. The basic idea of the "talking cure" can be traced back to Freud. Even if a psychotherapist does not engage in classic psychoanalysis, many rely on a few psychoanalytic ideas, such as free association (saying whatever comes to mind as a part of therapy) or transference (that the patient will re-create interpersonal problems with the therapist) in their practice of therapy.

Another area of influence concerns the resurgence of interest in some Freudian ideas on the part of research psychologists. Research psychologists are showing a revival of interest in such topics as the unconscious (e.g., Bornstein, 1999) and defense mechanisms (Cramer & Davidson, 1998). While they may not endorse the whole of Freudian theory, such researchers are nevertheless finding empirical support for several of his ideas, either in their original form or as they have been modified by others.

A third area of influence can be found in our popular culture, where many of Freud's ideas have been incorporated into everyday language and the logic of understanding our own and others' behavior. For example, if someone says, "He cannot get along with his teacher because he has a conflict with authority," this comment draws on Freudian ideas. Or if someone explains a person's current problems as being the result of poor parenting, this is a Freudian interpretation. Or if you think a person is avoiding dating and putting all her time into needlepoint work because she is conflicted over sexuality, then you are following a Freudian theme. Many of Freud's ideas have made it into everyday explanations of behavior and everyday forms of speech, such that you probably know more about Freud's theory than you actually realize.

A final reason that Freud's ideas are important is because he laid the foundation for many of the topics and questions that psychologists are still addressing. He proposed a developmental sequence in the growth of personality. He devised a method to resolve internal conflicts. He proposed a structure of the basic elements of personality and described what he thought were the main dynamic relationships between these elements. He noted that the mind has regions about which it does not itself have awareness. All these ideas have continued to be areas of inquiry among contemporary psychologists.

Freud started one of the more interesting, influential, and even controversial approaches to understanding human nature. Consequently, no student of personality should skip over this theory, even if the theory does not play a large role in contemporary studies of personality. Pieces of it have survived and inform various parts of current personality research and theory and so it is worth taking a good look at Freud's classic theory as well as the contemporary modifications of it.

Evaluation of Freud's Contributions

Among contemporary personality psychologists, Freud's theory of personality remains controversial. Some personality psychologists (e.g., Eysenck, 1985; Kihlstrom, 2003) suggest that psychoanalysis be abandoned. Others contend that psychoanalysis is alive and well (Westen, 1992, 1998; Weinberger, 2003). Opinions among personality psychologists differ dramatically on the accuracy, worth, and importance of psychoanalytic theory, and discussions about the merits of psychoanalysis often provoke passionate debate among those on both sides of the issue (Barron, Eagle, & Wolitsky, 1992).

Proponents of psychoanalysis argue that it is the first and perhaps only comprehensive theory of human nature. Freud's voluminous writings offer a sweeping view of human nature and how the mind works. Even those who disagree with psychoanalysis would have to concede that the theory is impressive in its scope and influence.

Proponents of psychoanalysis point to the major impact that Freud's theory has had on Western thought. Many psychoanalytic terms—id, ego, superego, oedipal conflict—have entered our everyday language. In addition to their influence in psychology, Freud's writings have played a significant role in sociology, literature, fine arts, history, anthropology, and medicine, to name only a few disciplines. Within psychology, Freud's works are among the most frequently cited sources in the literature. Many subsequent developments in the discipline of psychology have borrowed or built on the foundation laid by Freud. Freud shaped modern personality psychology and set the course of advancement for perhaps half a century, and Freud's ideas on psychosexual development played a significant role in initiating the field of developmental psychology. His views on anxiety, defense, and the unconscious show up in modified forms across many areas of modern clinical psychology. The psychotherapy techniques he pioneered are frequently practiced, even if sometimes in modified form. Although many modern therapists have done away with the couch, they still inquire about their patients' dreams, ask their patients to free associate, identify and interpret forms of resistance, and work through transference. Moreover, if we think Freud overemphasized sex and aggression, we need merely to look at the popular movies, books, and TV shows.

Critics of psychoanalysis also have strong arguments (e.g., Kihlstrom, 2003). They maintain that Freud's theory is primarily of historical value, that it does not inform much of the contemporary research in personality psychology. If you were to look in the pages of mainstream personality journals that publish research, you would find very little that had direct relevance to classical psychoanalysis. Critics insist that, without holding psychoanalysis up to scrutiny from outsiders, its merits cannot be fairly evaluated on scientific grounds. Freud himself did not believe in the value of experimentation or hypothesis testing in establishing the validity of psychoanalysis (Rosenzweig, 1994). The scientific method is self-correcting, in that experiments are conducted to try to disprove theories. If psychoanalysis is not examined scientifically, is not subjected to tests of disproof, then it is simply not supported by scientific fact. Consequently, in the view of some psychologists, psychoanalysis is more a matter of belief than scientific fact.

Another criticism of psychoanalysis pertains to the nature of the evidence on which it was built. Freud relied primarily on the case study method, and the cases he studied were his patients. Who were his patients? They were primarily wealthy, highly educated, and highly verbal women who had lots of free time to spend in frequent sessions with Freud and lots of disposable income to pay his bills. His observations were made during the therapy sessions only. These are limited observations, obtained on a narrow segment of humanity. However, from these observations, Freud constructed a universal theory of human nature. In his writings, he provided as evidence, not original observations but his *interpretations* of those observations. Unlike scientists, who make their raw data available so that the results of their experiments can

In the **Kill Bill** *movies* **(Volume I and Volume II)** *actress Uma Thurman plays a character with extremely violent and aggressive urges. The popularity of such movies suggests an almost universal fascination with themes of aggression, revenge, and death.*

be checked and verified by others, Freud wrote about his interpretations of the patients' behavior, rather than reporting or describing their behavior per se. If the actual raw observations were made available, it would be interesting to see if readers would come to the same conclusions that Freud did. Psychoanalysts today could tape therapy sessions for use as evidence. This is rarely done, however, as analysts argue that patients who know they are being taped do not respond naturally.

There are other specific disagreements with Freudian theory. For example, many believe that Freud's emphasis on sexual drives in his theory of childhood development is inappropriate and perhaps reflects more of a preoccupation of Freud, and the times in which he lived, than an actual topic of childhood development. Others disagree with the notion that personality development pretty much ends at around the age of 5, as Freud held. Those psychologists point to the sometimes profound changes in personality that can occur in adolescence and even throughout adulthood. In Chapter 10, we will take up alternative conceptions of personality development that build on, but significantly extend, Freud's ideas. We will examine other issues in contemporary psychoanalytic thought as well, including a modern view of the unconscious and the importance of relationships in determining personality development (Kihlstrom, Barnhardt, & Tataryn, 1992).

Some personality psychologists take issue with Freud's generally negative view of human nature. At heart, Freud's theory suggests that human nature is violent, self-centered, and impulsive. Freud suggested, in effect, that, without the inhibiting influence of society, mediated by the superego, humans would self-destruct. Other personality psychologists suggest a more neutral or even positive core to human nature, which we will cover in Chapter 11. Finally, Freud's view of women, when he wrote about them at all, implied that they were inferior to men (Kofman, 1985). He suggested that women developed weaker superegos than men (making them more primitive, with weaker moral character), that women's problems were more difficult to cure than men's, and even that women universally had an unconscious wish to become like men (the penis envy component of the Electra complex). Feminist writers have criticized Freud for confusing women's true capacities and potential with the role they were assigned in an oppressive, male-dominated society, an idea we discuss further in Chapter 10. For a strong feminist critique of Freud, see *Feminism and Psychoanalytic Theory* (Chodorow, 1989).

SUMMARY AND EVALUATION

Freud proposed a theory of human nature that has become highly influential. The theory is unique in its emphasis on how the psyche is compartmentalized into conscious and unconscious portions. Freud's theory holds that there are three main forces in the psyche—the id, ego, and superego—which constantly interact in taming the two motives of sex and aggression. These motives may generate urges, thoughts, and memories that arouse so much anxiety that they are banished to the unconscious. Keeping these unacceptable thoughts, desires, and memories out of conscious awareness requires defense mechanisms, such as repression. Several of these defense mechanisms are topics of contemporary research by academic personality psychologists. Freud also theorized about a series of developmental stages that all persons went through, with each stage involving a conflict over expressions of sexuality. How the person resolves these conflicts and learns to satisfy his or her desires within the constraints of a civilized society is the development of personality. That is, adults are different from each other because, as children, they learned different strategies for dealing with specific kinds of conflicts.

Freud also developed a theory and technique of psychotherapy, also called psychoanalysis. The goals of this form of therapy are to make the patient's unconscious conscious and to help the patient understand the traumatic basis of his or her problems. There has been a lively debate in the field about the value of psychoanalysis. However, as psychoanalytic ideas undergo more scientific examination, and as researchers undertake tests on psychoanalytic hypotheses using controlled laboratory experiments, they will undoubtedly learn more about the value and validity of Freud's theory.

The theory of personality proposed by Freud is one of the most comprehensive views on the working of human nature ever proposed; however, most modern personality psychologists do not totally and uncritically accept the entire theory as it was proposed, word for word, by Freud. Instead, most psychologists accept portions of the theory or agree with modifications to Freud's theory. For example, many psychologists agree that there is an unconscious mind that exists outside awareness, yet many disagree that it is motivated in the way Freud proposed. In Chapter 10, we will discuss how this influences the debate over repressed memories.

KEY TERMS

Psychic Energy 288
Instincts 289
Libido 289
Thanatos 289
Conscious 289
Preconscious 290
Unconscious 290
Collective Unconscious 291
Personal Unconscious 291
Archetypes 291
Motivated Unconscious 292
Blindsight 294
Deliberation-without-Awareness 295
Id 295
Pleasure Principle 296
Primary Process Thinking 296
Wish Fulfillment 296
Ego 296
Reality Principle 296
Secondary Process Thinking 296
Superego 297
Anxiety 297
Defense Mechanisms 298
Objective Anxiety 298
Neurotic Anxiety 298
Moral Anxiety 298
Repression 299
Denial 300
Fundamental Attribution Error 300
Displacement 300
Rationalization 301
Reaction Formation 301
Projection 304
False Consensus Effect 305
Sublimation 305
Psychosexual Stage Theory 306
Fixation 306
Oral Stage 307
Anal Stage 307
Phallic Stage 307
Oedipal Conflict 308
Castration Anxiety 308
Identification 308
Penis Envy 308
Electra Complex 308
Latency Stage 308
Genital Stage 309
Psychoanalysis 309
Free Association 310
Dream Analysis 311
Manifest Content 311
Latent Content 311
Symbols 311
Projective Hypothesis 312
Interpretations 313
Insight 313
Resistance 313
Transference 314

Psychoanalytic Approaches: Contemporary Issues

10

THE INTRAPSYCHIC DOMAIN

Gary Ramona, left, and his attorney walk to Napa County Superior Court on March 24,1994, for the start of a trial accusing his daughter's therapist of implanting molestation memories using improper suggestion and drugs.

The following information is drawn from a case decided in a California court in 1994 (*Ramona v. Isabella,* California Superior Court, Napa, C61898). The case is described in detail in Johnston, 1999.

Holly Ramona was a 23-year-old woman being treated through counseling for bulimia. One of her counselors, Marche Isabella, acknowledges telling Holly Ramona that an overwhelming majority of women with bulimia were sexually abused during childhood. During the course of therapy, which included sessions during which a hypnotic drug (sodium amytal) was administered, Holly Ramona began recalling incidents of sexual abuse that had occurred during her childhood. More specifically, in response to leading questions from her therapists, Holly began "recovering" memories of her father repeatedly raping her between the ages of 5 and 8. The therapist admitted telling Holly that, since sodium amytal is a "truth serum," if she recalled sexual abuse while under its influence it *must* have really taken place.

Holly's father, Gary Ramona, was severely affected by his daughter's accusations. When Holly went public with the allegations of incest, his wife divorced him, the rest of his family left him, he lost his well-paying job as an executive at a large winery, and his reputation in the community was ruined. Mr. Ramona claimed he was innocent and accused his daughter's therapists of implanting false memories of incest in her mind.

In an unprecedented legal case, Gary Ramona decided to sue the therapists for the damage they had caused him and his family. He charged that his daughter's recovered memories of being raped by him were, in fact, created by the therapists through repeated suggestions that this was the cause of her bulimia and that she wouldn't get better until she actually remembered having been abused. Mr. Ramona held that implanting these false memories was a form of negligence on the part of the therapists, so he filed a malpractice suit against them.

The therapists claimed that Gary Ramona had no legal grounds on which to sue for malpractice, since he was not their patient. In an important landmark decision, however, the trial judge held that, as a family member of the patient, and especially as one who had been substantially affected by the therapists' alleged malpractice, Mr. Ramona *did* have the right to file a malpractice suit against the defendants.

During the trial, which lasted seven weeks, Mr. Ramona denied abusing his daughter, whereas Holly repeated her allegations that he had raped her many times during her childhood. It appeared to be a classic case of one person's word against another's. As often happens in such cases, expert witnesses were called in to try to clarify the issues. Psychologist Elizabeth Loftus, a prominent memory researcher, testified during the trial that "there is no support for the idea that you can be raped . . . over a period of years and totally forget about it." A psychiatrist specializing in legal issues, Park Dietz, testified that, although Holly Ramona recalled being abused, she could not at first recall who the abuser was. It was only after the sodium amytal session, during which the therapists suggested to Holly that the abuser was her father, that she "remembered" it was her father. Martin Orne, a psychiatrist, psychologist, and authority on hypnosis, also testified that sodium amytal interviews are "inherently untrustworthy and unreliable" and that "Holly Ramona's memory is so distorted that she no longer knows what the truth is." Finally, Harvard psychiatry professor Harrison Pope offered his opinion that Holly Ramona had been "grossly and negligently treated, with catastrophic results."

The jury decided that the therapists were guilty of malpractice and awarded Mr. Ramona $475,000 in damages. The jury foreman was quoted in media sources as having said that the verdict was intended to "send a message about false child abuse memories." Mr. Ramona's attorney saw the verdict as a warning to other therapists, especially to those who believe that adult psychological problems are the result of repressed childhood traumas. One defendant, therapist Marche Isabella, described the verdict as a blow to the mental health profession, adhering to the position that "repressed memories are a reality."

Why did this case turn out so differently from the case of Professor Cheit, described at the start of Chapter 9? The major difference between the two cases is that Ross Cheit provided substantial corroborating evidence in support of his recovered memory. Unlike Holly Ramona, Ross Cheit's memory fragment was corroborated by many other persons, and even by a tape-recorded confession from the abuser himself.

But what do these cases tell us about the psychoanalytic idea of the motivated unconscious, the idea that the mind can bury memories of horrifying events and then, decades later, accurately retrieve those memories? By themselves, single cases do not prove anything for or against unconsciously motivated repression. People forget all sorts of things. Can you remember what you ate for dinner last Tuesday? With the right cues, however, could you be led to remember accurately? With other cues, could you be led to inaccurately remember what you had for dinner last Tuesday?

What is the difference between ordinary forgetting and motivated repression? Is there good scientific evidence for motivated repression? Could people be motivated to "remember" events that did not actually happen, as apparently was the case with Holly Ramona? To answer these questions we will examine contemporary revisions to classical psychoanalysis, collectively known as the Neo-Analytic movement.

The Neo-Analytic Movement

As proposed by Freud, classical psychoanalysis is a detailed and comprehensive theory, developed in the early 1900s, of the totality of human nature. Many of Freud's ideas are out of date; however, contemporary psychoanalyst Drew Westen (1998) argues that they *should* be out of date; after all, Freud died in 1939 and "he has been slow to undertake further revisions" (p. 333) of his theory. Westen goes on humorously to note that "Freud, like Elvis, has been dead for a number of years but continues to be cited with some regularity" (p. 333). Whereas many of Freud's ideas have not stood the test of time, others have and have been incorporated into a contemporary version of psychoanalysis. Today, psychoanalysis is probably best thought of as a theory containing ideas variously inspired by Sigmund Freud but modified and advanced by others.

Westen (e.g., 1990, 1998) is one of the most active proponents of contemporary psychoanalysis. Writing on the scientific legacy of Freud, Westen notes that contemporary psychoanalysts no longer write much about ids, superegos, and repressed sexuality; nor do they liken treatment to an archaeological expedition in search of forgotten memories. Instead, most contemporary psychoanalysts focus their attention on childhood relationships and adult conflicts with others, such as difficulties becoming intimate or readily becoming intimate with the wrong kinds of persons (Greenberg & Mitchell, 1983). Westen (1998) defines contemporary psychoanalysis as being based on the following five postulates:

1. The unconscious still plays a large role in life, although it may not be the ubiquitous influence that Freud held it was.
2. Behavior often reflects compromises in conflicts between mental processes, such as emotions, motivations, and thoughts.
3. Childhood plays an important part in personality development, particularly in terms of shaping adult relationship styles.
4. Mental representations of the self and relationships guide our interactions with others.
5. Personality development involves not just regulating sexual and aggressive feelings but also moving from an immature, socially dependent way of relating to others to a mature, independent relationship style.

This neo-analytic viewpoint has wider currency and better empirical support, in some cases, than Freud's original ideas. To start our coverage of contemporary issues in psychoanalysis, we will begin with a discussion of repression and memory.

Repression and Contemporary Research on Memory

It is easy to find conflicting opinions among respected psychologists on the issue of motivated repression. One review of the clinical literature on motivated repression concluded "the evidence for repression is overwhelming and obvious" (Erdelyi & Goldberg, 1979, p. 384). Another review of the same literature concluded "the concept of repression has not been validated with experimental research" (Holmes, 1990, p. 97).

Professor Elizabeth Loftus testified in the Ramona trial and has contributed a good deal of scientific information to the debate over repressed memories.

Elizabeth Loftus, a professor of psychology and world-renowned memory researcher, has perhaps conducted the most research on the authenticity of recovered memories. In her article entitled "The Reality of Repressed Memories" (Loftus, 1993), she discusses many cases of individuals who suddenly recover memories of important events: some of these turn out to be true memories, whereas others are false or inaccurate accounts, which are later recanted. However, she argues that we should not conclude that *all* recovered memories are **false memories,** just because some, such as Holly Ramona's, have turned out to be apparently false. Similarly, we should not assume that *all* recovered memories are true, just because some, such as Ross Cheit's that we explored in Chapter 9, have turned out to be true. Loftus believes that what is important is being aware of the processes that may contribute to the possible creation of inaccurate or false memories. Loftus (1992, 1993) suggests that many variables contribute to the construction of false memories.

One factor that might influence people to have false memories is the popular press. There are many books currently on the market that purport to be guides for survivors of abuse; these are undoubtedly of some comfort to people who have been living with painful memories of abuse. For those who have no such memories, these books often provide strong suggestions that abuse could have happened, even if there is no memory of the abuse. For example, a popular book in this category is *The Courage to Heal* (Bass & Davis, 1988), which states:

> *You may think you don't have memories. . . . To say, "I was abused," you don't need the kind of recall that would stand up in a court of law. Often the knowledge that you were abused starts with a tiny feeling, an intuition. . . . Assume your feelings are valid. . . . If you think you were abused and your life shows the symptoms, then you were. (p. 22)*

This quote is a powerful suggestion that may lead some persons to conclude falsely that they must have been abused. A person who starts with this idea may embellish this suggestion by filling in details to make a convincing or consistent story of abuse. If he or she is led further along these lines by a questioning therapist, his or her false memories may become more and more convincing. Loftus (1993) has demonstrated in the lab that subjects questioned in a leading manner after watching a video of a car accident can be led to conclude that one car ran a stop sign, even though there was no stop sign in the video. And, with more leading questioning, subjects increase their confidence that one car is to blame because it ran the stop sign. The quote from *The Courage to Heal* can act as a powerful suggestion to the person to conclude that psychological symptoms are the result of memories of abuse that have been forgotten.

What are some of the symptoms *The Courage to Heal* suggests indicate a person is likely to have been abused? The book lists, among other things, low self-esteem, self-destructive thoughts, depression, and sexual dysfunction. This book, and others like it, provides a strong message that, even in the absence of a specific memory, many people should conclude that they have been abused. However, there are many causes of low self-esteem, depression, and sexual dysfunction. In addition, these symptoms are associated with many other psychological disorders, such as phobias and anxieties, and these disorders certainly can occur without a history of abuse.

Another factor that may contribute to false memories is the behavior of some therapists. Loftus tells of a woman who wrote to her after the woman's therapist had concluded that her depression was caused by childhood sexual abuse. The patient stated that her therapist was certain of that diagnosis, even though the patient had no memory of the abuse. The patient further stated that she could not understand how something so terrible could have happened without her being able to remember the event. Loftus tells of another case of a man who went to a therapist because he was distraught over his father's suicide. The patient talked about painful events in his life, but the therapist kept suggesting that there must be something else. Not knowing what this "something else" was, the patient became even more depressed. Then, during a therapy session, the therapist stated that "you display the same kinds of characteristics as some of my patients who are victims of . . . ritualistic abuse" (cited in Loftus, 1993, p. 528).

A variety of techniques are used in therapy that encourage patients to reflect on their childhoods. Hypnosis is one technique used to get patients to recall freely childhood experiences within the protection of a relaxed, suggestion-induced, trance-like state. An extensive scientific literature, however, shows that hypnosis does not improve memory (Nash, 1987, 1988). This explains why hypnotizing witnesses is not allowed in courts of law; hypnotized witnesses do not recall facts with any greater accuracy than nonhypnotized witnesses (Wagstaff, Vella, & Perfect, 1992). In fact, hypnosis may be associated with increased distortions in memory (Spanos & McLean, 1986). In one case, a highly suggestible man was led under hypnosis to develop "memories" for crimes that had not even been committed (Ofshe, 1992). Under hypnosis, people are often more imaginative, more spontaneous, and more emotional and they often report unusual bodily sensations (Nash, 1988). After being taken back to childhood through hypnosis, people have been known to recall being abducted by alien creatures with fantastic spaceships (Loftus, 1993). It is unknown to what extent hypnosis allows fantasy and imagination to creep into consciousness and be interpreted as memories.

Loftus and colleagues have recently pointed to specific techniques in psychotherapy that can contribute to the creation of false memories (Loftus, 2000; Lynn, Lock, Loftus, Krackow, & Lilienfeld, 2003). These include the use of hypnosis, suggestive interviewing, the interpretation of symptoms as signs of past trauma, pressure from an authority figure to recall trauma, and dream interpretation. Such practices can be used to foster the recollection of events that did not actually happen (Tsai, Loftus, & Polage, 2000). In laboratory studies, Loftus and colleagues have shown that having persons imagine various events can lead them to later rate those events as more familiar, leading subjects to have a more elaborate memory representation, which in turn leads them to rate those imagined events as likely to have happened (Thomas, Bulevich, & Loftus, 2003). This effect is called the **imagination inflation effect,** and it occurs when a memory is elaborated upon through imagination, leading the person to confuse the imagined event with events that actually happened. For example, by showing people an advertisement suggesting that they shook hands with Mickey Mouse as a child, those people later had higher confidence that they had personally shaken hands with Mickey as a child. Another study had persons imagining shaking hands with Bugs Bunny and produced a similar effect (Braun, Ellis, & Loftus, 2002). Having persons imagine something, even something as unusual as shaking hands with Bugs Bunny, can lead them to have a false confidence that it actually may have happened. Loftus and others have pointed out the implications of this research for the admissibility of allegedly repressed memories in courts (Hyman & Loftus, 2002; Loftus, 2003).

Why would some therapists suggest false memories to their patients? Many therapists believe that effective treatment must result in a patient's overcoming repressed memories and reclaiming a traumatic past. They believe that the road to wellness requires bringing traumatic memories into consciousness and having the patient

A Closer Look

So, You Want to Have a False Memory

Imagine you are a subject in a psychology experiment in which you are assigned to listen carefully to a list of 15 words, knowing that you will later be tested on these words. The words are *bed, rest, awake, tired, dream, wake, snooze, blanket, doze, slumber, snore, nap, peace, yawn,* and *drowsy.* Now cover the list of words and indicate whether or not each of the following words was on the list:

	On the List? Yes	No
snooze	——	——
mother	——	——
bed	——	——
television	——	——
sleep	——	——
chair	——	——

If you are like most people, you checked yes following the word *sleep.* Indeed, many people are so certain that *sleep* was on the first list that they argue with the experimenter when they are told that, in fact, it was not. Thus, if you checked yes indicating that sleep was on the list during the recall phase of the task, and you really remember seeing the word *sleep,* then you just had a false memory. Approximately 80 percent of normal subjects are induced to have this false memory—that is, they believe that *sleep* was on the original list (Roediger, Balota, & Watson, 2001; Roediger, McDermott, & Robinson, 1998).

The procedure you just completed was developed by psychologists Henry Roediger and Kathleen McDermott (1995). They devised the technique based on the **spreading activation** model of memory. This model of memory holds that mental elements (such as words or images) are stored in memory along with associations to other elements in memory. For example, *doctor* is associated with *nurse* in most people's memories, because of the close connection or similarity between these concepts. The mental association between these two concepts can be demonstrated easily; the speed of deciding that a letter string *(doctor)* is a word or not is faster if it is preceded by an associated concept *(nurse)* relative to an unrelated word *(table).* The explanation is that the activation of *nurse* in your memory spreads through an association network and activates other related concepts, such as *doctor,* allowing them to be recognized faster.

How does this explain the false memory for *sleep* in the exercise? Like any concept, *sleep* is stored in your memory in a network of associations to other words, such as *bed, rest, awake, tired, dream, wake, snooze, blanket,* and *doze.* This network of associations is depicted in Figure 10.1.

Activation from the multiple words on the first list spreads or primes the critical concept on the recall list *(sleep)* in the memory network of the person studying the list. The activation from all the words related to sleep (e.g., *bed, rest,* and *tired*) sums up and makes the concept of *sleep* more likely to be recalled or recognized later, even though the actual word *sleep* was not on the original list.

Researchers have also shown that the probability of a false memory in this task is a function of the number of words on the first list that are associated with the critical word (e.g., *sleep*). That is, the sum of the association strength from the list items to the critical item determines false recall of the critical item. Association strength is determined by how frequently the critical word (e.g., *sleep*) is named when people are asked for the first word that comes to mind from some other word (e.g., *bed*). In fact, psychologists have determined lists of common associates to a whole variety of words, and the sum of association strength of the listed items to the critical item is what determines the probability of false recall (Roediger et al., 2001).

How is this material related to the psychoanalytic idea of false memories? First, this material highlights how most cognitive psychologists, even those with strong scientific values, believe that false memories can occur. It is accepted as fact that humans have a **constructive memory;** that is, memory contributes to or influences in various ways (adds to, subtracts from, and so on) what is recalled. Rather than referring to pristine and objective retrieval of facts from the past, human memory is fallible and open to error and corruption. Moreover, the corruption is most likely to occur when elements with strong associations to each other converge repeatedly in experience. In this condition, the person is likely to recognize or recall something associated to those elements, even if that new element never occurred. For example, during interrogation, imagine that a person is repeatedly asked about an event in many different leading ways. After some time, the person is asked something that is new but related to the first information. The person may then be more likely to recall this new event as happening, not because it did happen but because it is associated with the previously presented information. This is how innocent mistakes of recognition on word lists might help us understand the larger and more dramatic false memories that have been documented in certain legal cases, such as that of Holly Ramona.

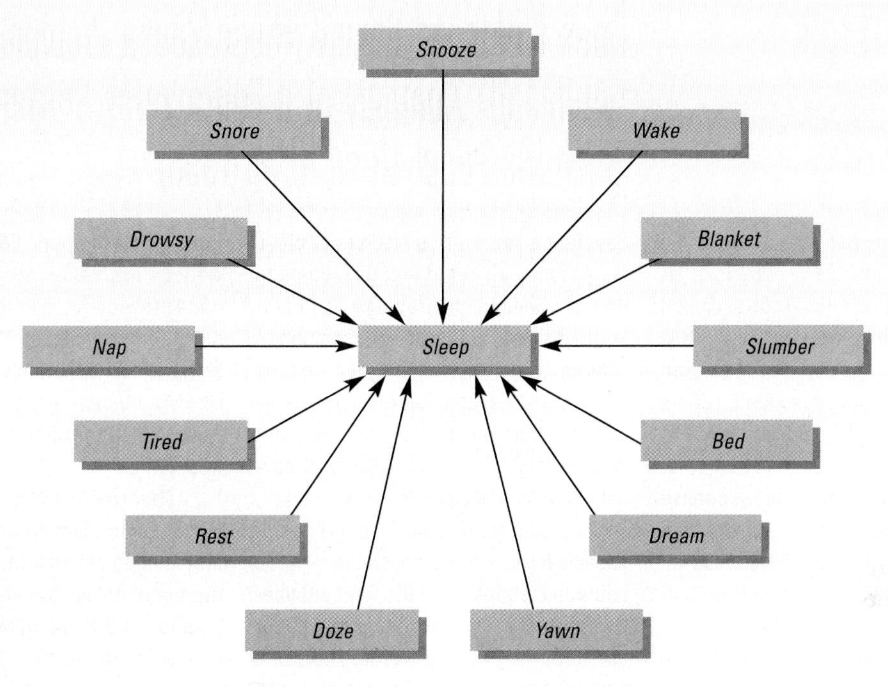

Figure 10.1

Hypothetical network of concepts related to the word *sleep*. Source: Adapted from Roediger, Balota, & Watson, 2001.

acknowledge and overcome them or at least deal with them in a mature, adult fashion. Therapists, like many other people, can also suffer from a **confirmatory bias**—the tendency to look only for evidence that confirms their previous hunch and to not look for evidence that might disconfirm their belief. If a therapist believes that childhood trauma is the cause of most adult problems, he or she will most likely probe for memories of childhood trauma. Compliant and suggestible patients are then often induced to spend long periods of time trying to imagine what events must have happened in their childhoods to produce their current difficulties. Meanwhile, the therapist relates stories of other patients with similar problems who were helped by recalling and coping with memories of childhood abuse. The therapist, as an "authority" on how to get better, stands ready to authenticate any possible memory of trauma that the patient might produce. These are the ideal conditions for constructing a shared reality that, even though both parties are confident of its authenticity, is not true.

However, this position must be balanced with some known facts about the rates of various forms of child abuse. Recent surveys suggest that a remarkable amount of trauma is inflicted on children. For example, in 1998 there were approximately 903,000 child victims of maltreatment in the United States. Of these, 54 percent were for neglect, 23 percent involved physical abuse, 12 percent were sexual abuse cases, and approximately 5.5 percent each involved psychological abuse and medical neglect. In this reporting year, an estimated 1,100 children died of abuse and neglect. Of these fatalities, 77 percent were under the age of five years! (All statistics are from U.S. Department of Health and Human Services, 2000.)

A Closer Look

Does Childhood Sexual Abuse Cause Problems in Adulthood? Anatomy of a Controversy Started by a Scientific Paper (Rind et al. 1998)

In 1998 a scientific paper appeared in the journal *Psychological Bulletin* titled: "A meta-analytic examination of assumed properties of child sexual abuse (CSA) using college samples," and authored by psychologists Bruce Rind, Philip Tromovitch, and Robert Bauserman. The authors' goal was to determine whether child sexual abuse (CSA) causes intense or long-term psychological harm for both genders. They reviewed 59 studies on this topic, all conducted on college students. By meta-analyzing these studies Rind et al. (1998) found that students with a history of CSA were, on average, slightly less well adjusted than students without a history of CSA. However, poor family environment also correlated with a history of CSA, making it impossible to argue that CSA in itself causes adjustment problems (independent from poor family environment). In general, the authors concluded that CSA does not appear to cause as much intense or long-lasting psychological harm as might be assumed.

This paper ignited a firestorm of controversy that took several years to play out. Most people assume that the sexual abuse of children is bad because of the long-term harm such abuse holds for children. Yet here was a study saying that it was difficult to document any substantial harm over the long run for childhood sexual abuse. Consequently, many people entered the debate because they were simply outraged over the conclusions that childhood sexual abuse was not so bad.

Other groups were outraged by the Rind et al. (1998) paper for other reasons. Psychologists with a psychoanalytic bent start with the critical assumption that psychological problems in adulthood often have their roots in childhood trauma. The Rind paper goes against this critical assumption by purportedly showing that the link between adult adjustment difficulties and history of sexual abuse in childhood is weak.

Organizations that endorse pedophilia (sexual contact between children and adults) applauded the Rind publication on their websites, citing this paper as supporting their moral position that sexual relations between children and adults is acceptable. In 1999 the publisher of the *Psychological Bulletin*—The American Psychological Association—issued a statement saying that they do not endorse pedophilia, and that "the sexual abuse of children is wrong and harmful to its victims." In 1999 the U.S. House of Representatives passed a resolution condemning the Rind et al. (1998) study, declaring that child–adult sex was inherently "abusive and destructive" and the resolution was passed unanimously in the Senate.

What can we say about the Rind et al. (1998) study in light of this controversy? The authors attacked a common assumption that CSA causes harm and leads to long-term problems. Most cultures around the world consider it wrong for adults to have sexual contact with children. However, Rind et al. (1998) argued that the "wrongfulness" of CSA may be in question because its "harmfulness" is in dispute. In other words, because the act may not produce harmful *consequences,* we might question whether CSA is actually *wrong.* Moreover, the authors were quite provocative in interpreting their results, for example, arguing that discussions of CSA should not include such terms as *victim* or *perpetrator* or even *abuse* since these are moral, not scientific, terms.

The rebuttals of the Rind et al. (1998) paper fall into two categories, methodological and interpretational. On the methodological side, one important concern is that the data were based on college students. Such a sample would exclude victims of CSA that were so traumatized that they did not go on to attend college. Also, it could be that, for example, people with a history of CSA are more likely to drop out of college than people without such a history. It may be that, by excluding noncollege attending persons from their research, Rind et al. (1998) may have severely underestimated the effect of CSA on adult adjustment. Another methodological concern is the broad definition they used of CSA, which included acts ranging from forced sexual intercourse to being verbally propositioned. By including such "mild" abuses as being verbally propositioned (without sexual contact) in their definition of CSA, it could be that Rind diluted the effects of real CSA on adjustment.

A final methodological concern involves the fact that most of the studies analyzed by Rind et al. (1998) relied completely on retrospective self-report of college students as the only source of data. A much better (though also much more difficult) approach would be a prospective design, where children identified as having been recently abused would be followed over the years until they are adults and then adjustment is assessed and compared with a control group that was not abused.

One can also disagree with how Rind et al. (1998) interpret their findings. For example, they argue that, because poor family environment correlates with CSA, one cannot know that it is CSA that is causing the poorer adjustment outcomes. It could be that people from poor family backgrounds (those that have other forms of abuse or neglect, high levels of conflict, mental illness, etc.) are at risk of poor adjustment outcomes regardless of whether CSA occurs. However, Rind et al. (1998) never seriously consider whether poor family background is caused by, or is a consequence of, the child sexual abuse. Because most of the studies are based on retrospective self-report, we cannot know which of these possibilities is the correct interpretation for the relationship between poor family background and CSA.

Another interpretation issue concerns the meaning of "small" when the authors describe the relation between CSA and such adjustment outcomes as anxiety, depression, suicide, divorce, or paranoia. It is true that the effect sized conform to the statistical definition of small (e.g., effect sizes less than .30). However, even small effects can reflect very important consequences for people and impact large percentages of persons. Moreover, individuals may exhibit elevated levels of one type of symptom, but the symptoms may differ from person to person, such that any one symptom may not be very elevated in the CSA population as a whole, even though individuals themselves suffer greatly. In certain ways, statistical effect sizes do not convey clinical significance and, in this regard, can be misleading.

A final interpretation issue concerns the fact that, because their data suggest that CSA is not intensely harmful, Rind et al. (1998) go on to allude that CSA is morally benign. However, this is a slippery slope. Such a position holds that, in order for something to be wrong, it must be shown to be harmful. It replaces a moral standard with a scientific standard, and science can only document relations, not decide on what is right or wrong. Ultimately, the question boils down to how do we decide if something is wrong? Legally, the definition of most wrongs is given by society's norms, by what most people feel is wrong or inappropriate. Ultimately we need to rely on the wisdom of societal beliefs to help us determine what is wrong. When it comes to children, society generally believes that they are incapable of making rational and informed life decisions. For example, in U.S. society, children are not allowed to enter into financial contracts, to decide whether or not they want to attend school, to consent to medical procedures, to participate in research, or to consume tobacco or alcohol. In addition, add to this list the sociological belief that children cannot consent to sexual relations. The real moral basis for deeming sexual acts with children inappropriate is based on the social belief that children cannot give consent to sex because they have little knowledge about what is being consented to and, when it is an adult forcing the issue, they may not have the absolute freedom to accept or decline. Because society believes that children lack the maturity to make important life decisions, they need to be protected from those who would exploit their immaturity. In this sense, the data from the Rind et al. (1998) article are irrelevant to whether CSA is wrong. The huge controversy surrounding the article was not so much an attempt to censure unpopular results, though there were methodological problems with the study. Much of the controversy can be traced to the authors' use of science to replace morality, their confusing "harmfulness" with "wrongness."

Contemporary Views on the Unconscious

The idea of a motivated unconscious is at the core of classical psychoanalytic theory. Most contemporary psychologists also believe in the unconscious, although it is a different version of the unconscious than that found in classical psychoanalytic theory. Consider the views of psychologist John Bargh, a social psychologist whose research on unconscious processes has had a large impact on psychology: "People are often unaware of the reasons and causes of their own behavior. In fact, recent experimental evidence points to a deep and fundamental dissociation between conscious awareness and the mental processes responsible for one's behavior" (2005, p. 38). This can be illustrated with one of Bargh's own experiments in which college student subjects took part in what they thought was an experiment on language, where they were presented with many different words. Half of the participants were presented with words synonymous with rudeness; for the other half they were presented with words synonymous with politeness. After finishing the language experiment they went to another experiment in another room where they encountered a staged situation where it was possible to act in either a rude or polite way. While the participants showed no awareness of the possible influence of the language experiment, they nevertheless behaved in the staged situation in a manner that was consistent with the kinds of words they were exposed to in the "previous" experiment (Bargh, 2005). Most psychologists believe that the unconscious can influence our behavior, but not all agree with Freud that the unconscious can have its own autonomous motivation.

We can term these two differing views on the unconscious the **cognitive unconscious** view and the **motivated unconscious** view. Those with the cognitive unconscious view readily acknowledge that information can get into our memories without our ever being aware of the information (Kihlstrom, 1999). For example, in the phenomenon of **subliminal perception,** some information—such as the phrase "Buy a Coke"—is flashed on a screen so quickly that you don't recognize the actual words. That is, you would say that you had seen a flash but were not able to distinguish what was written. Indeed, you could not even guess that the word *Coke* was presented better than chance compared to guessing that some other nonpresented word, say *House,* was presented. However, if you were asked to judge whether a string of letters is a word or not a word, and the dependent variable were reaction time (how quickly you can make this judgment), then you would judge *Coke* as a word faster than words unrelated to Coke or soft drinks in general. Thus, subliminal information primes associated material in memory. **Priming** makes that associated material more accessible to conscious awareness than is material that is not primed. Results such as these using subliminal primes clearly demonstrate that information can get into the mind and have some influence, without going through conscious experience.

If someone were given the subliminal message "Buy a Coke," would they be more likely to spontaneously go out and do so? After all, this is consistent with the psychoanalytic idea of the motivated unconscious—that something in the unconscious can motivate behavior. Can advertisers use subliminal messages to unconsciously motivate consumers? Similar questions arise concerning the influence of subliminal rock music messages that supposedly advocate suicide or violence. The vast majority of research on subliminal perception, however, suggests that unconscious information does not influence people's motivations. That is, the average teen exposed to subliminal messages of violence in a song is unlikely to go out and commit a violent act. Similarly, the average person subliminally exposed to the phrase "Buy a Coke" is unlikely to do so.

In the cognitive view of the unconscious, the content of the unconscious mind is assumed to operate just like thoughts in consciousness. Thoughts are unconscious because they are not in conscious awareness, not because they have been repressed or because they represent unacceptable urges or wishes. For example, we might say that buttoning a shirt is unconscious because we can do it without focusing any conscious attention on the act. Typing can also be unconscious for the person who is good at it. Other kinds of mental content, such as beliefs and values, might also be unconscious. Such elements are not in our unconscious because they are threatening; nor are they there to exert influence on our behavior. And, although unconscious material can influence subsequent thoughts or behavior, as in the priming examples, these influences are not consistent with the motivated unconscious of classical psychoanalytic theory (Kihlstrom, 2003; Nash, 1999). As such, the cognitive unconscious as viewed by contemporary psychologists is quite different from that put forward by Freud a hundred years ago. According to Freud, the unconscious was a torrid and fuming caldron of anger and eroticism. It operated

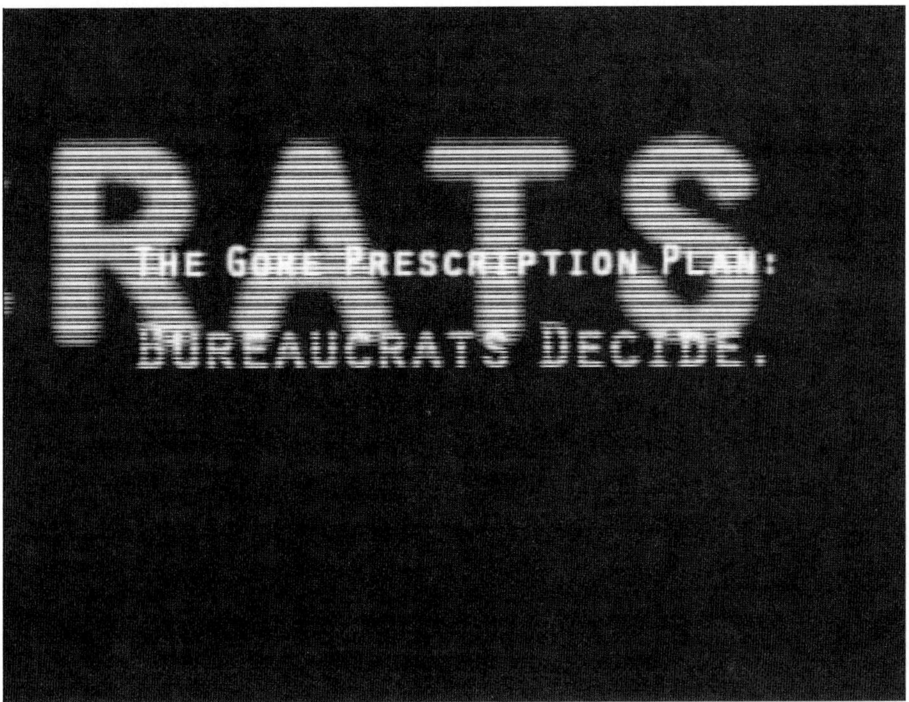

In the 2000 U.S. presidential election campaign, a Republican team released a commercial describing some of the questionable fund-raising efforts of Al Gore, the Democratic opponent. During the commercial, the word RATS was subliminally presented, along with information about Gore. When the Gore campaign team discovered this, they responded with outrage and a public denouncement of this subliminal attempt to influence voter opinion on the part of the Bush campaign. The Bush campaign quickly pulled the commercial, with Bush himself denying he had had any role in ordering subliminal propaganda. The fact that both campaign teams believed that such subliminal messages would have a wide impact on voter motivation shows that many people believe in unconscious motivation. Researchers, however, have found little evidence for the power of subliminal messages in advertising.

according to its own primitive and irrational rules, and it had broad, sweeping influence over our conscious behavior, thoughts, and feelings. In contemporary psychology, the unconscious is peaceful, gentle, and much more rational than Freud's version. Moreover, although the unconscious is still viewed as having an influence on behavior, thoughts, and feelings, that influence is seen as more bounded, rule-governed, and specific, as in unconscious priming, than was taught by Freud (Greenwald, 1992).

Ego Psychology

Another major modification to psychoanalysis concerns a shift in focus from id to ego. Freud's version of psychoanalysis focused on the id, especially the twin instincts of sex and aggression, and how the ego and superego respond to the demands of the id. We might characterize Freudian psychoanalysis as **id psychology.** Later psychoanalysts felt that the ego deserved more attention, that it performed many constructive functions. Indeed, Freud's own daughter—Anna Freud—focused on the strengths of the ego as it defended the person against anxiety. One prominent student of Freud—Erik Erikson—emphasized the ego as a powerful, independent part of personality. Moreover, Erikson noted that the ego was involved in mastering the environment, achieving one's goals, and, hence, establishing one's identity. It is no wonder, then, that the approach to psychoanalysis started by Anna Freud and continued by Erikson is called **ego psychology.**

Establishing a secure identity is seen as the primary function of the ego. Identity can be thought of as an inner sense of who we are, of what makes us unique, and a sense of continuity over time and a feeling of wholeness. You have probably heard the term **identity crisis.** This term comes from Erikson's work, and it refers to the desperation and confusion a person feels when he or she has not developed a strong sense of identity. Maybe you have even felt such feelings when you were uncertain about yourself, uncertain about who you were or how you wanted others to view you, what you valued and wanted out of life, and where you were going in terms of the direction of your life. A period of identity crisis is a common experience during adolescence, but for some people it occurs later in life or lasts for a longer period. The so-called midlife crisis, discussed more in Chapter 11, often begins with an identity crisis (Sheldon & Kasser, 2001).

One of Erikson's lasting contributions was developing the notion of identity as an important developmental achievement in everyone's personality. Identity has been thought of as a story that a person develops about himself or herself (McAdams, 1999). The story answers the following questions: Who am I? What is my place in the adult world? What are the unifying themes of my life? What is the purpose of my existence? McAdams (e.g., 1999) sees identity as a narrative story that a person constructs. Although a person may rearrange and reconstruct the plot of his or her life story, it nevertheless takes on importance as the person's unique story. According to McAdams, once the story has evolved to have coherent themes, the person may make very few changes to his or her story. However, certain events can cause large changes to identity, and are incorporated into the narrative, such as graduation, marriage, birth of a child, turning 40, or retirement. Unexpected events can become a part of the story too, such as the death of a marriage partner, loss of a job, or unexpected wealth. In an illuminating quote, Erikson (1978) describes how all of us construct a life story, and that part of becoming an adult is taking ownership of this story:

> *To be an adult means, among other things, to see one's own life in continuous perspective, both in retrospect and prospect. By accepting some definition as to who he is, usually on the basis of a function in an economy, a place in the sequence of generations, and a status in the structure of society, the adult is able to selectively reconstruct his past in such a way that, step for step, it seems to have planned him, or better, he seems to have planned it. In this sense, psychologically we do choose our parents, our family history, and the history of our kings, heroes, and gods. By making them our own, we maneuver ourselves into the inner position of proprietors, of creators. (Erikson, 1978, pp. 111–112)*

Erikson's Eight Stages of Development

Whereas Freud taught that our personalities were formed by around the age of 5 years, Erikson disagreed and felt that important periods of development occurred throughout the life span. For example, Freud called the period between the ages of 6 to puberty

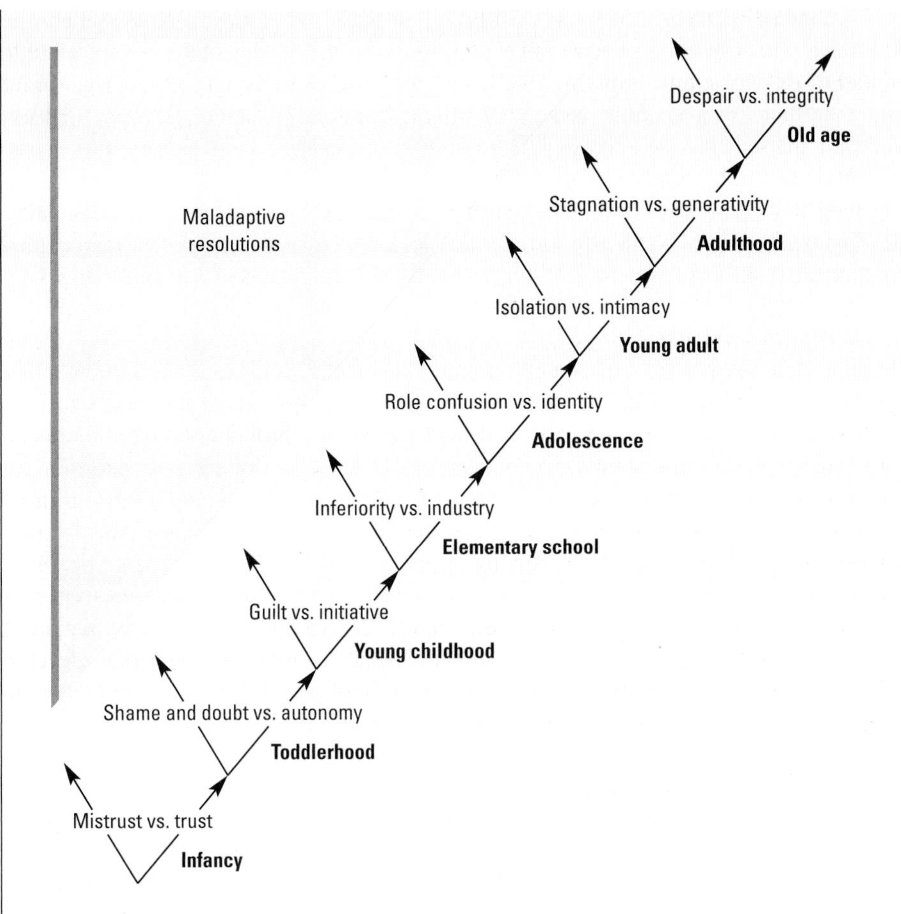

Figure 10.2

Erikson's eight stages of development.

the latency period because he believed not much psychologically was going on. However, this is a period when children are starting to go to school; they are learning to work and to gain satisfaction from success and from accomplishments; they are learning to be sociable, to share, and to cooperate with peers; and they are learning about social structures, such as the fact that teachers are in charge and represent authorities. Erikson (1963, 1968) argued that much development occurred during the years that Freud thought were quiet. Indeed, Erikson believed that the development of personality lasted well into adulthood and even old age (Erikson, 1975). He outlined **eight stages of development,** through which we all pass (Figure 10.2).

Not only did Erikson disagree with Freud about the time span of development, but he also disagreed with Freud about the conflict, or crisis, that occurs at each stage. Whereas Freud felt that the crises were inherently sexual, Erikson believed that the crises were of a social nature. After all, he argued, the persons with whom we have our first social relationships are our parents. Thus, there could be crises of learning to trust our parents, learning to be autonomous from them, learning from them how to act as an adult. He called these **psychosocial conflicts** rather than the psychosexual conflicts that formed Freud's developmental stages.

Although Erikson disagreed with Freud on these two issues of development, he did agree with Freud on several other points. First, like Freud, Erikson kept a **stage model of development,** implying that people go through the stages in a certain order and that there is a specific issue that characterizes each stage. Second, Erikson believed that each stage represented a conflict, or perhaps a **developmental crisis,** which needed to be resolved. Third, Erikson maintained the notion of **fixation,** meaning that, if the crisis was not successfully and adaptively resolved, then personality development could become arrested and the person would continue to be preoccupied by that crisis in development. Let's now briefly consider each of the eight stages.

Trust versus Mistrust

When children are born, they are completely dependent on those around them. Their first questions would most likely be "Who's going to take care of me, and will they do a good job? Can I trust that they will feed me when I am hungry, clothe me when I am cold, comfort me when I cry, and generally take care of me?" If children are well taken care of, if their basic needs are met, then they will develop a sense of trust in their caregivers. This sense of trust, according to Erikson, forms the basis of future relationships, with such children growing up believing that other people are approachable, trustable, and generally good and loving. However, some infants are not well taken care of, for various reasons, and they never receive the love and care they need. Such infants may develop a sense that others are not to be trusted and may develop a lifelong pattern of mistrust in others, suspiciousness, and feelings of estrangement, isolation, or just plain social discomfort when around others.

Autonomy versus Shame and Doubt

Around the second year, most children are on their feet and on the go. This is the stage many parents call the "terrible 2s." Children begin experimenting with their new abilities, including running when the parents tell them to walk, screaming when the parents tell them to be quiet, and generally just testing their powers. They are trying to answer the question "How much of the world do I control?" A good outcome is when a child feels a sense of control and mastery over things and develops self-confidence and a sense of autonomy that lets them explore and learn. If parents inhibit such autonomy, perhaps by being strict, restrictive, or punishing when the child is independent, then the child may feel shame and doubt over the goals he or she is contemplating. Overly protective parents can also cause problems, in that they can hinder the child's natural urge to explore and to encounter a wide variety of life events and experiences. For example, parents who prevent their child from rough-and-tumble play with other children may cause their child to grow up doubting his or her ability to get along with others.

Initiative versus Guilt

Children at this stage—around 3 years of age—often imitate adults, dressing in adult clothes, playing adults, and acting as adults. Children at this stage receive their first practice in adult tasks during play. As adults, we must learn how to work together, to follow leaders, and to resolve disputes. When children play, they practice these skills by organizing games, choosing leaders, and forming goals. Then, during school activities they also take the initiative to accomplish goals and to work with a distinct purpose in mind. If all goes well, children at this stage develop a sense of initiative, which translates into ambition and goal seeking. If things do not go well, children may become resigned to failure or to not even take the initiative to pursue goals.

Industry versus Inferiority

It is good to have experiences of success, but we all have limits, and there is a lot of competition. Starting around age 4, children begin comparing themselves to each other, especially those their own age, and many (although not all) develop a sense of competence and achievement. If people have enough success experiences, then they believe in their strength and abilities and assume that, if they just work hard enough, they can do most things they desire to do. This sense of industry—feeling as if they can work to achieve what they want—sets children on their way to being productive members of society. However, with enough failure experiences, children might develop a sense of inferiority, feeling that they don't have the talent or ability to get ahead in life.

Identity versus Role Confusion

During adolescence, people go through a whole series of drastic physical changes. This can be an especially difficult time of life, in which people emerge from childhood into adulthood, whether they are ready or not. Erikson gave this period special attention in his work, referring to identity achievement as one of the most important goals of development.

At this stage, adolescents begin to ask themselves the questions "Who am I?" and "Do others recognize me for who I think I am?" Many people do a lot of experimentation at this stage, trying on many different identities. One semester, a high school student might try on the role of athlete; the next semester, the role of punk rocker; the next semester, born-again Christian; and the next semester, Goth. Experimenting with identities is common at this time of life, with teenagers searching for identity in all sorts of ways and places. One student said he was going to Hawaii to "find himself." In actuality, no matter where you go, there you are, so the search for identity really has no special place. But many people at this stage join groups, drift around the country, commit themselves to various causes or ideals, or experiment with drugs, politics, or religion, all in an effort to find the true "me." Eventually, most people make some decisions about what is important and what they value and want out of life, and they acquire a sense of "who they are," achieving some degree of consistent self-understanding. People who fail in this stage develop role confusion and enter adulthood without a solid sense of who they are or what they think is the meaning of their lives. Such people bounce around between all sorts of roles, and are generally unstable in their relationships, in their jobs, and in their goals and values.

People differ from one another in the extent to which they commit themselves to their values, careers, relationships, and ideologies (Marcia, 2002). Most people will pass through a period of **identity confusion,** which refers to not having a strong sense of who one really is. Some cultures institute a **rite of passage** ritual, usually around adolescence, which typically is a ceremony that initiates a child into adulthood. For example, some southwestern American Indians send adolescent males to be alone in the wilderness, fasting, until they have a vision. After such ceremonies, the adolescent is sometimes given a new name, bestowing a new adult identity. Secular American culture does not provide common rite of passage rituals, though certain religions do, such as the Confirmation ritual in Roman Catholicism or Bar/Bat Mitzvah in Judaism.

In resolving the identity crisis, some persons develop a **negative identity,** an identity founded on undesirable social roles, such as street gang member. Unfortunately, modern culture provides many undesirable role models. Because this is a time of life when youngsters are looking for models, most are very impressionable. This is one reason most states keep their juvenile court system separate from the adult court system, so that young persons do not come into contact with adult criminals.

Lee Malvo and John Muhammad were arrested for the sniper murders of several people in the Washington, DC, area in 2002. Lee Malvo, who was 17 years old at the time of the crimes, pled that he was so much under the influence of the older man, John Muhammad, that he, Lee Malvo, should not be held responsible for any of the shootings. Malvo was most likely in a period of identity confusion.

Identity is something that must be achieved. If a person commits to an identity that they did not work for or that was handed to them, then that identity is likely to be shallow or changeable (Marcia, 1966). Indeed, Marcia (2002) holds that mature identity development involves going through a crisis and emerging with a firm sense of commitment to one's values, relationships, or career. If a person does not have a crisis, or if he or she forms an identity without exploring alternatives, such as accepting the values of parents, then this is called **identity foreclosure.** People in identity foreclosure are often moralistic and conventional, but when asked to back up their positions, often cannot provide a good rationale for their beliefs and opinions.

A final concept relevant to identity development, especially to college students, concerns the notion of a **moratorium.** This refers basically to taking time to explore options before making a commitment to an identity. In some ways, college can be thought of as a socially approved period in which a young person is able to explore a variety of roles and responsibilities, before taking any one set on "for real." One can change majors, change social groups, explore different relationships, meet people from diverse backgrounds, spend a semester studying abroad, and learn about a variety of fields of study before having to settle on any ideals and values to commit to. Erikson himself emphasized exploring alternatives before making a commitment to a particular identity (1968). He held that, only after considering alternatives, and spending time "shopping around," was a person ready to make commitments and to spend the rest of his or her life honoring those commitments. This is what it means to say that the development of an identity takes work (Newman & Newman, 1988).

Intimacy versus Isolation

Connecting with others, both in terms of friendships and intimate relationships, becomes a prime concern toward the latter half of the teenage years. People at this stage appear to have a need to develop relationships that are mutually satisfying and intimate. In such relationships, people grow emotionally and develop into caring, nurturing, and providing adults. For many people, this takes the form of making a commitment to one person through marriage. But many others find intimacy without the social contract of marriage. And, of course, marriage is no guarantee of intimacy, as it is certainly possible to have a marriage that is devoid of intimate feelings.

Isolation is the result of a failure to find or maintain intimacy. In the United States, the percentage of married people has dropped, from 72 percent in 1970 to 62 percent in 2000. The total number of divorced persons in the United States was 4.3 million in 1970, but that number had risen to 20 million by 2000. Approximately 49 percent of marriages in the United States today end in divorce. Clearly, for many people, the primary struggle in their lives is the crisis of finding intimacy versus isolation. Certainly, being single has its benefits; however, most people report that a satisfying intimate relationship is something they desire. Failing to achieve this level of relationship is often a serious impairment to one's happiness and life satisfaction.

Generativity versus Stagnation

At this stage, occupying most of the adult years, the main question concerns whether or not the person has generated something that he or she really cares about in life. Often this takes the form of a career that one cares about. Other times, it is a family that has generated children that the parent cares about. Sometimes caring is achieved in a hobby or a volunteer activity that is particularly generative and that gives the person something to care about. The crisis at this stage is that, when people step back and look at their adult years, they might get the feeling they are just spinning their wheels, stagnating. In other words, without anything to really care about, people may feel that their lives really don't matter, that they are just "going along to get along," and that they really don't care how it all works out. The people who don't really care about what they are doing, who are just going through the motions, are easily seen as phonies. For example, maybe you've had a teacher who really didn't care about the course material, who just came in, lectured blandly, and left. You have probably also had teachers who cared deeply about their topic, whose lectures were enlivened by their interest and enthusiasm, and who obviously drew satisfaction and meaning from their role as teacher or professor. This is the difference between generativity and stagnation.

Integrity versus Despair

This is the last stage of development, occurring toward the end of life, and even this stage contains a crisis, an issue to face. This occurs when we let go of the generative role; maybe we retire from the jobs we loved, maybe the children we loved and raised leave home and start their own lives, or maybe the hobbies or volunteer activities we found so meaningful are no longer possible for us. We start the process of withdrawing from life, pulling back from our adult roles, and preparing to face death. At this stage, we look back on our lives and pass judgment—"Was it all worth doing?" "Did I accomplish most of what I wanted to do in life?" If we can take some satisfaction in

Late in life there is still one more developmental stage, one more set of questions to be faced: "Was it all worthwhile? Did I accomplish most of what I wanted out of life?" How one answers these questions determines whether the remaining time is filled with bitterness and despair or satisfaction and integrity.

our lives, then we can face the inevitability of our passing with a measure of integrity. However, if we are dissatisfied with our lives, if we wish we had more time to make changes, to repair relationships, and to right wrongs, then we experience despair. People who have a lot of regrets at the end of their lives become bitter old people who have a lot of contempt and irritation. On the other hand, if people feel that their one go-around was acceptable, that they pretty much did it all up right and have no regrets, then they face their end with integrity.

Fredrick Nietzsche, a German philosopher, wrote a story in his book *Thus Spoke Zarathustra* about a person walking on a mountain trail. Along the trail, a troll suddenly jumps out and kills the person. The person, however, is immediately reborn to the same parents, is given the same name, and lives the same life as before. Then one day, again the person is walking on a mountain trail and a troll suddenly jumps out and slays the person, who is reborn to the same parents, is given the same name as before, and lives the same life. And once again the person is walking along a mountain trail when a troll jumps out and slays the person. Once again the person is reborn and so on. The point, Nietzsche says, concerns what a person would think about this eternal return of our lives. If you would not want to live your life over and over again, then perhaps you should make some changes in it now, as you are living it. The person who says, "Yes, I wouldn't mind another go-around of my life, even if it were all the same," is someone who would go through Erikson's last stage and achieve integrity. That is, if a person is satisfied with his or her life as a whole, then they can approach the ending of life with integrity.

Karen Horney and a Feminist Interpretation of Psychoanalysis

Karen Horney (pronounced Horn-eye) was another early proponent of ego psychology. She was a medical doctor and a psychoanalyst at a time when most doctors and practically all psychoanalysts were men, practicing from the 1930s up to about 1950. She questioned some of the more paternalistic notions of Freudian psychoanalysis and reformulated some of the ideas to generate a more feminist perspective on personality development. For example, she reacted against Freud's notion of penis envy. Recall that Freud interpreted the phallic stage for women as a sexual conflict, starting when a little girl realizes she does not have a penis. She blames her mother for this deficient state of affairs and desires to be like her father and have a penis, according to Freud. Horney taught that the penis was a symbol of **social power,** rather than an organ women actually desired. Horney wrote that girls realize, at an early age, that they are being denied social power because of their gender. She argued that girls did not really have a secret desire to become boys. Rather, she taught, girls desired the social power and preferences given to boys in the culture at that time. **Culture** is a set of shared standards for many behaviors. For example, whether a person should feel ashamed about promiscuous sexual behavior is determined by a cultural norm. Moreover, culture might contain different standards for males and females, such that girls should be ashamed if they engage in promiscuous sex, whereas boys should be proud of such behavior, with it being culturally acceptable for them even to brag about such behavior.

Freud's original theory was harsh toward women. Because girls realize they don't have a penis, he argued, they are bound to become dependent, submissive, sensitive, and vain. In Freud's position on the role of women, biology determined outcome. Horney pointed out that it was not so much biology, but culture, that influenced different life outcomes for men and women. For example, in Horney's time, it was common or even expected that a woman would sacrifice her career, if she even had one, for her husband's career, even if the wife had more talent and potential than the husband.

Horney was among the first psychoanalysts to stress the cultural and historical determinants of personality, which we will explore in more detail in Chapters 16 and 17. Horney noted that many gender roles were defined by culture. For example, she coined the phrase **fear of success** to highlight a gender difference in response to competition and achievement situations. Many women, she argued, felt that if they were to succeed they would lose their friends. Consequently many women, she thought, harbored an unconscious fear of success. She held that men, on the other hand, believed they would actually gain friends by being successful, and hence were not at all afraid to strive and pursue achievement. This points to an important cultural influence on behavior.

Horney stressed the point that, although biology determines sex, cultural norms are used to determine what is acceptable for a typical male and female in that culture. Partly because of Horney, today we use the terms **masculine** and **feminine** to refer to traits or roles typically associated with being male or female in a particular culture, and we refer to differences in such culturally ascribed roles and traits as **gender differences,** not *sex differences.* This distinction, so important to modern feminism, can be traced back to Karen Horney. It is unfortunate that Horney died in 1952 and did not see the progress made by the women's movement, of which she can truly be counted as an early leader.

Horney had very personal knowledge of the social and cultural forces that oppressed women in her era. Colleagues in the male-dominated profession of psychoanalysis were disapproving of her skeptical attitudes toward classical Freudian ideas. In 1941, the members of the New York Psychoanalytic Institute voted to remove Horney from her position as instructor there. Horney left immediately and went on to establish her own American Institute for Psychoanalysis, which was very successful. Indeed, she went on to develop a major reconceptualization of psychoanalysis, which stressed social influences over biology and which gave special attention to interpersonal processes in the creation and maintenance of mental disorders and other problems with living. Her intriguing theories were laid out in a series of highly readable books (Horney, 1937, 1939, 1945, 1950).

Emphasis on Self and the Notion of Narcissism

Ego psychology generally emphasizes the role of identity, which is experienced by the person as a sense of self. Contemporary psychoanalysts Otto Kernberg (1975) and Heinz Kohut (1977) are important contributors to the psychoanalytic conception of the role of the self in normal personality functioning and in disorders. In normal personality functioning, most people develop a stable and relatively high level of self-esteem, they have some pride in what they have so far accomplished, they have realistic ambitions for the future, and they feel that they are getting the attention and affection from others that they deserve. Most of us have a healthy level of self-esteem; we consider ourselves worthwhile, we like ourselves, and we believe that others like us as well. And most of us engage in **self-serving biases,** which refer to the common tendency for people to take credit for successes, yet to deny responsibility for failure.

Some take self-esteem too far, however, trying to increase their self-worth in various problematic ways. For example, they may constantly try to appear more powerful than others, more independent, or more liked by others. This style of inflated self-admiration and constant attempts to draw attention to the self and to keep others focused on oneself is called **narcissism.** Sometimes narcissism is carried to extremes and becomes narcissistic personality disorder (see Chapter 19). However, narcissistic tendencies can be found in normal range levels, characterized as an extreme self-focus, a sense of being special, feelings of entitlement (that one deserves admiration and attention without earning it), and a constant search for others who will serve as one's private fan club.

There is a paradox, however, commonly called the **narcissistic paradox:** although a narcissist appears high in self-esteem, he or she actually has doubts about his or her worth as a person. Although the narcissist appears confident and sure of him- or herself, the person needs constant praise, reassurance, and attention from others. Although the narcissist appears to have a grandiose sense of self-importance, he or she is nevertheless very vulnerable to blows to his or her self-esteem and cannot handle criticism very well. In contemporary psychoanalysis, narcissism is seen as disturbance in the sense of self that has many implications for creating problems with living and relating to others.

An example of one problem associated with narcissism is that, when narcissists are criticized or challenged, they may behave aggressively, trying to achieve some respect by belittling their critics. The *Diagnostic and Statistical Manual IV* suggests that persons with narcissistic personality disorder can become at risk for violence following blows to their self-esteem, such as getting reprimanded at work and having been left by a spouse. This tendency toward violence in response to criticism was illustrated in a laboratory study conducted by psychologists Brad Bushman and Roy Baumeister (1998). The subjects went to the laboratory and wrote a short essay on a topic given to them. Another person then commented on the essays they had just written, providing strong criticism of the subjects' opinions. Later in the experiment, the subjects were given the opportunity to play a computer game with their critic and were allowed to "blast" their opponent with loud bursts of noise during the game; that is, subjects could distract their opponents with irritating blasts of noise during the competition. The narcissistic subjects who had been insulted blasted the critic much more aggressively than did either the nonnarcissistic persons or the narcissistic persons who had not received criticism. This finding suggests that narcissism can lead to aggression when the narcissist is provoked or criticized. People with secure and normally high levels of self-esteem, however, do not become distressed and aggressive when insulted (Rhodenwalt & Morf, 1998).

A questionnaire measure of narcissism. The following items are from the Narcissistic Personality Inventory (NPI) (Raskin & Hall, 1979).

1. I think I am a special person. True or False
2. I expect a great deal from other people. True or False
3. I am envious of other people's good fortune. True or False
4. I will never be satisfied until I get all that I deserve. True or False
5. I really like to be the center of attention. True or False

In one interesting study of narcissism, it was found that the number of first-person pronouns a person used in an essay *(I, mine, me)* was correlated positively with narcissism scores (Emmons, 1987). In another study it was found that when given the opportunity to watch themselves on videotape or to watch a tape of someone else, the narcissists spent more time watching the tape of themselves (Robins & John, 1997). This study also showed that narcissists rate their performance on the videotape much more positively than it is rated by others, implying an inflated sense of their own abilities.

In sum, although an interest in narcissism started in ego psychology as a style of defending against poor self-esteem, studies have confirmed the theoretical notions that narcissists are preoccupied with self, are vulnerable to criticism and blows to their self-worth, and respond to such challenges with anger and aggression. While narcissists appear to have high self-esteem their internal or private self representations are fragile and vulnerable. Clearly, an important notion from contemporary psychoanalytic thought is that one's internal representation of self plays an important role in how one interacts with and reacts to the social environment. In the next section, "Object Relations Theory," we will see how contemporary psychoanalysis also focuses on the internal representation of other persons, and how this influences social interactions.

Object Relations Theory

Other changes to Freud's original ideas have been so sweeping that one new approach drops the term "analytic" altogether: object relations theory. Recall that Freud emphasized sexuality in the development of personality. He viewed the adult personality as the result of how people accommodate the inevitable conflicts between their desires for sexual pleasure from various body parts and the constraints of parents, social institutions, and civilized society. Freud's emphasis on sexuality has been completely rethought by recent generations of psychoanalysts. This new movement—**object relations theory**—emphasizes social relationships and their origins in childhood.

Consider the oedipal phase of development. Freud stressed the sexual attraction for the parent of the opposite sex, and the accompanying fear, rage, anger, and jealousy toward the parent of the same sex. Psychoanalysts after Freud looked at the same childhood situation and saw, instead, the importance of forming social relationships to the developing personality. Later analysts emphasized not sexuality but, instead, the development of meaningful social relationships as the task that occurs at this stage of development. After all, the first persons with whom we have a meaningful relationship are our parents.

Although object relations theory has several versions, which differ from each other in emphasis, all the versions have at their core a set of basic assumptions. One assumption is that the internal wishes, desires, and urges of the child are not as important as his or her developing relationships with significant external others, particularly parents. A second assumption is that the others, particularly the mother, become **internalized** by the child in the form of mental objects. The child creates an unconscious mental representation of the mother. The child, thus, has an unconscious "mother" within, to whom he or she can relate. This allows the child to have a relationship with this internalized object, even in the absence of the real mother—hence the term *object relations* theory.

The relationship object the child internalizes is based on his or her developing relationship with the mother. If things are going well between the mother and the infant, the infant internalizes a caring, nurturant, trustworthy mother object. This image then forms the fundamentals for how children come to view others with whom they develop subsequent relationships. If the child internalizes a mother object who is not trustworthy, perhaps because the real mother has left the child alone too often or has not fed the child regularly, then he or she might have difficulty learning to trust other people later in life. The first social attachments that the infant develops form the templates for all meaningful relationships in the future. This is consistent with the classic psychoanalytic idea that the "child is father to the man," in the sense that what develops in childhood determines the outcomes in adulthood. However, in the neo-analytic case, it is early childhood experience with caregivers, especially attachment to the primary caregiver, that determines adult personality.

Early Childhood Attachment

Work on early childhood attachment has drawn on a couple of lines of research in developmental psychology. The first line of research was the work by Harry Harlow and others on infant monkeys. Harlow's well-known experiments involved taking infant monkeys away from their real mothers and raising them with models of mother monkeys made of wire or cloth. These fake mothers did not provide the grooming, cuddling, holding, or social contact of the real mothers. The infant monkeys raised with the fake mothers developed problems in adolescence and adulthood, growing into adults that were socially insecure, that were generally anxious, and that did not develop normal sexual relations as adults (Harlow, 1958; Harlow & Suomi, 1971; Harlow & Zimmerman, 1959). Moreover, the infant monkeys preferred their real mothers to the fake mothers, and they preferred the cloth mother to the wire mother when given the choice. Harlow concluded that **attachment** between infant and primary caregiver required physical contact with a warm and responsive mother and that it is vitally important to the psychological development of the infant.

Attachment to the mother during the first six months of life appears crucial to all primates, including humans. Attachment in the human infant begins when he or she develops a preference for people over objects. For example, the child prefers to look at a human face rather than at a toy. Then the preference begins to narrow to familiar persons, so that the child prefers to see people he or she has seen before, compared with strangers. And finally the preference narrows even further, so that the child prefers the mother or primary caregiver over anyone else.

The strong bond between infant and primary caregiver, called attachment, is important in the development of all primates, including humans.

The ways in which young children develop attachments to their parents and caregivers was the primary topic of research for British psychologist John Bowlby (1969a, 1969b, 1980, 1988). Bowlby focused on the attachment relationship with the mother and how that relationship meets the needs of the infant for protection, nurturance, and support. Bowlby studied what happens when this attachment relationship is temporarily broken, as when the mother has to leave the infant alone for a short time. He noticed that some infants seem to trust that the mother will return and provide uninterrupted care—these infants are happy when the mother returns. Other infants, in contrast, react negatively to separation and become agitated and distressed when the mother leaves. They can be calmed only by the return of the mother. Bowlby said these infants experience **separation anxiety.** Bowlby also observed a third type of infants, who seem to become depressed when their mothers leave. Even when the mother returns, these infants seem to remain detached from, or angry at, their mothers.

Psychologist Mary Ainsworth and her colleagues developed a 20-minute procedure for studying separation anxiety—a procedure also used for identifying differences between children in how they react to separation from their mothers. This is called the **strange situation procedure.** In this procedure, a mother and her baby enter the laboratory room, which is like a comfortable living room. The mother sits down, and the child is free to explore the toys and other things in the room. After a few minutes, a stranger, an unfamiliar but friendly adult, enters the room. The mother then gets up and leaves the baby alone with this unfamiliar adult. After a few minutes, the mother returns to the room and the stranger leaves. The mother is alone with the baby for several more minutes. All the while, the infant is being videotaped, so that his or her reactions can later be analyzed.

Across many studies, Ainsworth and her colleagues (e.g., Ainsworth et al., 1972; 1979) found essentially the same three patterns of behavior noted by Bowlby. One group of infants, called **securely attached,** stoically endured the separation and went about exploring the room, waiting patiently or even approaching the stranger and sometimes wanting to be held by the stranger. When the mothers returned, these infants were glad to see them, typically interacted with them for a while, then went back to exploring the new environment. They seemed confident the mothers would return, hence the term *secure*. This group of infants was the largest of the three (66 percent fell into this group).

The second group, called the **avoidantly attached** group, consisted of infants who avoided the mothers when they returned. The infants in this group typically seemed unfazed when the mothers left and typically did not give them much attention when they returned, as if aloof from their mothers. Approximately 20 percent of the babies fell into this category.

Ainsworth called the third category of infant response to separation the **ambivalently attached** group. The infants in this group were very anxious about the mothers' leaving. Many started crying and protesting vigorously before the mothers even got out of the room. When the mothers were gone, these infants were difficult to calm. On the mothers' return, however, the infants behaved ambivalently. Their behavior showed both anger and a desire to be close to the mothers; they approached their mothers but then resisted by squirming and fighting against being held.

Mothers of babies in these three groups appear to behave differently. According to subsequent research, reviewed by Ainsworth and Bowlby (1991), mothers of securely attached infants provide more affection and stimulation to their babies, and are generally more responsive, than mothers of infants in the other groups. These studies have provided clear evidence that a caregiver's responsiveness to infants leads to a more harmonious relationship later in life between the child and parents. For example, in one study, responsiveness to infant crying in the early months of life was associated with less (not more) crying at 1 year of age. Although this finding was greeted with disbelief at first, especially by learning theorists, it eventually influenced recommendations for parenting practices (Bretherton & Main, 2000).

Mothers of babies from both the ambivalent and the avoidant groups tend to be less attentive to their children, less responsive to their needs. Such mothers appear to be less in tune or less engaged with their babies. Some children react to these less responsive mothers by becoming angry themselves (the ambivalent infants) or by trying to become emotionally detached (the avoidant infants).

These early experiences and reactions of the infant to the parents, particularly the mother, become what Bowlby called **working models** for later adult relationships. These working models are internalized in the form of unconscious expectations about relationships. If children experience that they are not wanted, or that their mothers cannot be trusted to take care of them, then they may internalize the expectation that probably no one else wants them, either. On the other hand, if children's needs are met, and they are confident that their parents really love them, then they will expect that others will find them lovable as well (Bowlby, 1988). These expectations about relationships, which are developed in our first contacts with our caregivers, are thought to become part of our unconscious and thereby exert a powerful influence on our adult relationships.

We might think that the "strange situation" paradigm is useful only for thinking about how children cope with the temporary separation from their caregivers. However, some researchers are studying an adult analogue of this paradigm, where married couples are temporarily separated by life circumstances (Cafferty, Davis, Medway, O'Hern, & Chappell, 1994). These researchers conducted a longitudinal study on members of the National Guard and other military reserve units who were separated from their spouses and deployed overseas during Operation Desert Storm. They found that attachment styles predicted individual differences in emotional reactions to the separation (securely attached persons were not as distressed) and to postreunion marital adjustments (ambivalently attached persons had the most difficulty). When adult marital relationships are temporarily disrupted, it may be that the persons in those relationships will react and adjust in ways that resemble how they coped with their earliest separations, both of which may be influenced by the style of attachment they developed early in life with their primary caregiver.

Adult Relationships

Research on attachment has tested object relations ideas by examining whether the attachment style developed in childhood is related to the kind of later adult relationships. Psychologists Cindy Hazan and Philip Shaver (1987) have shown that there are patterns of adult relationships that look similar to the secure, avoidant, and ambivalent childhood attachment patterns. In the adult **secure relationship style,** the person has few problems developing satisfying friendships and relationships. Secure people trust others and develop bonds with them. The adult **avoidant relationship style** is characterized by difficulty in learning to trust others. Avoidant adults remain suspicious of the motives of others, and they are afraid of making commitments. They are afraid of depending on others because they anticipate being disappointed, being abandoned, or being separated. Finally, the adult **ambivalent relationship style** is characterized by vulnerability and uncertainty about relationships. Ambivalent adults become overly dependent and demanding on their partners and friends. They display high levels of neediness in their relationships. They are high maintenance, in the sense that they need constant reassurance and attention.

Exercise

Determining which adult attachment style a person has can be accomplished by having them report which style is most like them. Consider the following statements, and choose which is most descriptive of you:

1. **I am typically comfortable with others and find it easy to become close friends with people. I can easily come to rely on others and enjoy it when they rely on me. I don't worry about being left out or abandoned and find it easy to let others get close to me.**
2. **I am sometimes tense when I get too close to others. I don't like to trust other people too much, plus I don't like it when people have to depend on me for something. It makes me anxious when people get close or want me to make an emotional commitment to them. People often want me to be more personal and intimate than I feel like being.**
3. **In relationships, I often worry that the other person does not really want to stay with me or that he or she doesn't really love me. I often wish that my friends would share more and be more of a confidante than they seem willing to be. Maybe I scare people away with my readiness to become close and make them the center of my world.**

The first description is associated with a secure relationship style, the second with an avoidant relationship style, and the third with an ambivalent relationship style. It is possible that you have different styles with different people, or that none of these descriptions applies perfectly to your relationships.

Psychologist Philip Shaver and his colleagues have shown that there is a positive correlation between the parent–infant attachment style and the later relationship style developed in adulthood. In one study, for example, adults with an avoidant relationship style more frequently reported that their parents had unhappy marriages compared to adults with a secure relationship style (Brennan & Shaver, 1993). The adults with a secure relationship style, on the other hand, tended to report coming from a trusting and supportive family, with parents who were happily married. Those with an avoidant relationship style tended to report that their family members were aloof and distant, and that they did not feel very much warmth or trust either from or toward their parents.

Object relations theorists believe that the characteristics and quality of adult relationships are determined, in part, by relationships experienced in early childhood.

A dominant theme of attachment theory is that a person's romantic attachments in adulthood will be a reflection of his or her attachment patterns in the past, especially with their earliest relationships. Representations of the earliest relationships can serve as prototypes for later relationships, with the early experiences retaining their influential role in attachment behaviors throughout the life span. The psychologist Chris Fraley has recently published meta-analyses of studies examining the long-term influence of attachment styles (Fraley, 2002a, 2002b). After reviewing a great deal of research, and evaluating different models of change and stability, Fraley concludes that the data are consistent with a moderate degree of stability in attachment security from infancy to adulthood. His best estimate of the correlation between early attachment security and attachment security at any later point in time is approximately .39, which can be described as significantly larger than zero, but moderate in magnitude.

Adult relationship styles may be most important for understanding romantic relationships. What do people look for in a romantic relationship? What do people expect from their romantic partners? How do people cope with abandonment by and separation from their romantic partners either real or imagined? Research suggests that individuals with different attachment styles will answer these questions very differently from each other (e.g., Hazan & Shaver, 1987). Those with an avoidant attachment style tend to shun romance, believing that real love is rare and never lasts. They fear intimacy and rarely develop deep emotional commitments. They tend not to be very supportive of their partners, at least not emotionally.

Adults with an ambivalent attachment style tend to have frequent, but short-lived, romantic relationships. They fall in and out of love easily but rarely say that they are happy with their relationships. They develop a sort of desperation in their adult relationships and show fear of losing their partners. Their focus is often on keeping the other happy and, so, are quick to compromise, to change themselves for the sake of avoiding conflict with the other. As you might guess, ambivalent adults report that being separated from their partners is very stressful.

Adults with a secure attachment style can be separated from their partners without stress, just as secure attachment children can remain calm when their mothers leave the room. Secure adults are generally more warm and supportive in their romantic relationships, and their partners report more satisfaction with the relationship than do the partners of avoidant or ambivalent adults (Hazan & Shaver, 1994). Secure adults are also more likely to give emotional support to their partners when it is needed. Secure adults seek support when they need it more than do ambivalent or avoidant adults. In general, secure adults do a good job of navigating through the treacherous waters of adult romantic relationships.

An interesting study by psychologist Jeff Simpson illustrates the working of attachment styles in adult relationships (Simpson, Rholes, Orinea, & Grich, 2002). In this study they had heterosexual dating couples serve as subjects. The couple was told that the male would undergo a stressful and unpleasant experience as part of the experiment. They were separated and the male was taken to a room where an experimenter recorded his pulse while saying the following:

> *"In the next few minutes you are going to be exposed to a situation and set of experimental procedures that arouse considerable anxiety and distress in most people. Due to the nature of these procedures, I cannot tell you any more at this moment. Of course, I'll answer any questions or concerns you have after the experiment is over."*

The purpose of this statement was to make the male subject anxious. Moreover, he was taken to a darkened, windowless room that contained some polygraphs. The experimenter remarked that the equipment was "not quite ready yet" and that the subject would have to wait a few minutes before the "stress phase" could start. Meanwhile, the female was told that her partner was going to be involved in a "stress and performance session" which would start in five or ten minutes. The couple was brought together to wait, and during this time they were unobtrusively videotaped for five minutes. After five minutes the experimenter entered the room and told the subjects the experiment was over, explained the purpose of the experiment, and told the subjects that they could erase the videotape if they so desired (none did).

The experimenters coded the videotape for a number of behaviors. Mostly they were interested in the degree to which the women offered support to their partners, and the degree to which the men asked for support from their partners. Prior to the start of the experiment, the experimenters used an interview method to assess childhood recollections of experiences with parents and other attachment figures. From these interviews the experimenters rated the degree to which each subject was avoidantly or securely attached to his or her primary caregivers in early childhood.

Results showed that women who had avoidant attachment experiences with their parents were significantly less likely to offer support and encouragement to their male partners, even if the male asked for that. The securely attached women did provide support if the partner asked for it, but provided less if he did not ask for it. This is a contingent pattern of support, what some researchers consider ideal in relationships (George & Solomon, 1996). Regarding help seeking from the men, none of the attachment style variables predicted this behavior in this study. However, this was not a very intense or long-lasting stressor. Studies of real, intense, and chronic stress (persons under missile attacks, persons undergoing combat training) have found that attachment styles do relate to help seeking (Mikulincer, Florian, & Weller, 1993; Mikulincer & Florian, 1995). Specifically, secure men and women seek support from others when distressed, whereas avoidantly attached persons try to distance themselves from others, want to spend time alone when under stress, and distract themselves from the stressors. When stress is severe or chronic, it appears that a person's attachment style might relate to their pattern of support seeking.

Individual differences in attachment style may have implications beyond those for relationships. Any area of life that involves closeness, getting along with others, confiding in others, and exploring relationships might be negotiated differently by persons with different attachment styles (Elliot & Reis, 2003). One study of adults examined attachment styles in relation to satisfaction with work, with family, with one's social role, and with stressful life events (Vasquez, Durik, & Hyde, 2002). These researchers found that those persons with the secure attachment style showed the best adjustment across these domains. Persons with avoidant/fearful attachment styles reported difficulties in many of the domains of family life and in several domains of work life. Other research has shown that, among men, the avoidant/fearful attachment style was related to a collection of traits that is related to abusiveness toward women (Dutton, Saunders, Starzomski, & Bartholomew, 1994).

If a person develops a particular childhood attachment style, is he or she destined to live out the adult version of that style? This important question has been the topic of much theoretical debate and empirical research (Cassidy & Shaver, 1999; Simpson & Rholes, 1998). Attachment theorists believe that even the poorest childhood experiences with relationships can be overcome. Ainsworth and Bowlby (1991) argued that children were not necessarily damaged forever because of unfortunate parenting experiences in infancy. They felt that subsequent positive experiences could compensate for earlier negative relationships. Despite a bad start in life, a person exposed to a loving, nurturant relationship as an adult can revise his or her working model of object relations. If the relationship is positive and supportive enough, Ainsworth and Bowlby argued, the person could internalize a new mental version of relationships, one that was more secure and trusting, with positive expectations about how people would relate to the person.

SUMMARY AND EVALUATION

In this chapter, we explored alternative versions of some of Freud's original ideas. We began with an evaluation of repressed memories, examining a case in which the recalled memory turned out not to be true, at least as determined in a court of law. This case should not put doubt on the possibility of real cases of abuse and trauma causing memories to be forgotten or repressed. Indeed, such cases do exist and conform to the notion that traumatic experiences can be pushed out of consciousness. However, the material in this chapter is meant to lead you to a more balanced approach to the topic of repressed memories. Although repressed memories can occur, not all cases are truly of forgotten memories. Some memories can be implanted by well-meaning therapists and others interrogating a subject about an event. We also discussed how to discriminate real from false memories. The crucial element is corroboration, finding someone who can support the subject's version of the remembered event.

The view of repressed memories also highlights a more contemporary version of the unconscious. Although most modern cognitive psychologists believe in the unconscious, they do not believe in the motivated version of the unconscious proposed by Freud. Certainly, material can get into the mind without conscious experience, as through subliminal perception, but that material does not have the kind of sweeping motivational effects suggested by Freud.

Another reconstruction of Freud's theory concerns the emphasis on the role of the ego relative to the id. Modern theorists have stressed the psychological importance of ego functions, which include planning, developing strategies for achieving goals, developing a stable identity, and achieving mastery over the environment. This is in stark contrast to Freud's emphasis on aggressive and sexual id urges as the twin engines powering psychic life. We discussed two proponents of ego psychology. The first, Erik Erikson, was well known for his alternative theory of personality development, which differed from Freud's in several important ways, including an emphasis on social tasks and an extension of development through the entire life span. A second important figure in ego psychology was Karen Horney, who was among the first psychoanalysts to consider the role of culture and social roles as central features in personality development. Horney also started a feminist reinterpretation of Freud's theories, which continues to this day. Ego psychology also generated an interest in the development of sense of self and the protection of self through various strategies. Narcissism is one problematic way that some people go about defending themselves. The narcissistic paradox suggests that, although narcissists appear strong and confident, they are dependent on the praise and admiration of others.

Object relations theory is another major new development in this area, having been called the most important theoretical development in psychoanalysis since Freud's death. The term *object relations* is used to refer to enduring patterns of behavior in relationships with intimate others, as well as to the emotional, cognitive, and motivational processes that generate those patterns of behavior. The theory is about how relationship behaviors are determined by mental representations laid down in childhood through experiences with caregivers. This theory began with studies of attachment between children and primary caregivers—typically, mothers. This bond may set a pattern that continues into adulthood. Also important are the experiences the growing child has with the relationship he or she observes between the parents. This is also internalized in the form of a mental representation for how people get along and what is appropriate behavior in a relationship.

Object relations theorists focus on the development and maintenance of relationships as the key psychological goal in life. They note that most problems and mental disorders involve a disturbance in relationships. People who have difficulty with relationships often have a pessimistic image in their minds, often expecting mistreatment and abuse as part of what relationships are all about. These people also often have difficulty maintaining a constant representation, such as keeping in their minds the positive view of the people they love, even during the unavoidable disagreements that occur as part of normal relationships. Consequently, such persons often overreact and damage or even sever important relationships when they are temporarily angry.

There are parts and versions of Freud's psychoanalytic theory that are alive and well today. However, instead of focusing on unconscious conflicts over id urges, contemporary psychoanalysts are more likely to focus on interpersonal patterns of behavior and the emotions and motives that accompany those. Instead of seeing personality as the result of a sequence of sexual conflicts with the parents, contemporary psychoanalysts are more likely to see personality as the result of solving a series of social crises and the ensuing movement toward increasingly more mature forms of relating to others. And, finally, unlike much of classical psychoanalytic theory, which was based on one man's views, much of contemporary psychoanalytic theory is connected to empirical studies and corroborated observations of many persons working to improve and expand on some of Freud's lasting contributions.

KEY TERMS

Motives and Personality

11

THE INTRAPSYCHIC DOMAIN

Olympic Gold-medalist Michael Johnson, who uses different strategies to motivate himself before a 200-meter race and a 400-meter race.

One hot August night in 1996, a gun went off in Atlanta. It started the final of the 200-meter Olympic race. Michael Johnson, who had won a gold medal in the 400-meter race just a few days earlier, exploded from the starting blocks. Would he become the first man in history to win both the 400- and 200-meter races at the Olympics? Michael stumbled slightly at the start of the race but soon assumed the upright style that had come to characterize his running technique. As he went around the turn, his trademark golden shoes flashing, it became obvious to the crowd that he was running for more than just the gold medal. As Michael widened his lead over his opponents, people knew they were witnessing something special. Michael finished a full 5 meters ahead of his nearest competitor, and as he crossed the finish line the timer read 19.32 seconds. People who knew the significance of that time, including Michael himself, gasped in disbelief. He had beaten the previous world record, which he had set earlier, by almost three-tenths of a second, a remarkable gap in short-distance running. No runner has since been able to break Michael's incredible 200-meter record.

How did Michael motivate himself to set a world record in the 200-meter race and win a gold medal in the 400-meter race? The 400- and 200-meter races are very different, according to runners. In the 400-meter race, the runners can be strategic and take some time to plan a tactic. The 200, on the other hand, demands that the runners run flat-out and aggressively.

Before the 400-meter race, Michael reportedly listens to jazz on his headset; before the 200, he listens to gangsta rap. He tries to make himself feel aggressive before the 200-meter race. He tries to get into what he calls the "danger zone." In warming up for the 200-meter race at Atlanta, Michael pulled on a T-shirt that read DANGER ZONE. "Now I have to think about the 200," he said. "I've got to get into the danger zone. I've got to get more aggressive. The other 200-meter runners are saying that I'm vulnerable. That's a mistake!" He approached the 200-meter race with a fighting instinct, taking the offense by running not just to beat his competitors but to beat them badly. His coach also helped Michael feel aggressive by filling his head with tough and fast imagery. As Michael approached the finish line in the 200-meter race, the aggression could be seen in his face, an expression that looked as if he could assault his opponents. The only thing he assaulted, however, was the world record. As the shock of his finish time faded from his face, the aggression melted away also. Michael came out of the danger zone. He had just motivated himself to run faster than any other living person.[1]

We saw in Chapter 1 that personality psychologists ask, "Why do people do what they do?" Motivational psychologists phrase the question a bit differently—"What do they want?" All personality psychologists seek to explain behavior. Personality psychologists interested in motivation, however, look specifically for a desire or motive that propels people to do the things they do (Cantor, 1990).

In this chapter, we will cover some of the major theories on human motivation, and we will examine some research findings on these theories. Some theories that we will look at are quite different from each other, such as the theories of Henry Murray and Abraham Maslow. In fact, most texts in personality cover these two theories in different chapters. However, all the theories we will examine have two features in common. First, all view personality as consisting of a few general motives, which all people have or are capable of having. Second, these motives may operate mainly through mental processes, either inside or outside of awareness, generating an intrapsychic influence on a person's behavior (King, 1995).

Basic Concepts

Motives are internal states that arouse and direct behavior toward specific objects or goals. A motive is often caused by a deficit, a lack of something; for example, if a person has not eaten for many hours, he or she is motivated by hunger. Motives differ from each other in both type and amount. Hunger differs from thirst, for example, and both of these differ from the motive to achieve and excel. Motives differ in intensity, depending on the person and his or her circumstances. For example, the strength of the hunger motive varies considerably, depending on whether a person has merely skipped a meal or has not eaten for several days. Also, motives are often based on **needs,** states of tension within a person. As a need is satisfied, the state of tension is reduced. The state of tension is caused by a deficit—for instance, lack of food causes a need to eat. The need to eat creates the motive of hunger. The motive of hunger, in turn, causes the person to seek out food, to think about food constantly, and perhaps even to see food in objects not normally thought of as food. For example, a hungry

[1] In the 2000 Olympics at Sydney, Michael Johnson again won the gold medal in the 400-meter race but had to drop out of competition in the 200-meter race.

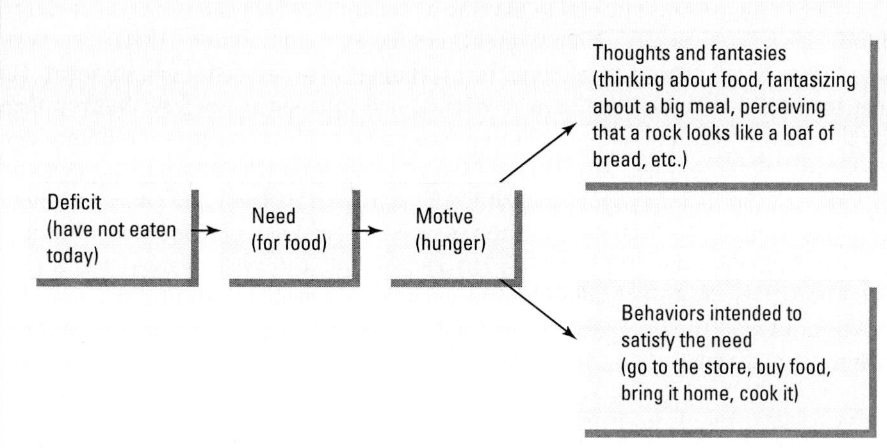

Figure 11.1

Deficits lead to a need, which leads to a motive to satisfy that need, either in reality, by fostering specific actions, or in fantasy, by creating thoughts that are satisfying.

person gazing at the sky might exclaim, "Wow, that cloud looks just like a hamburger." Motives propel people to perceive, think, and act in specific ways that satisfy the need. Figure 11.1 illustrates the relation between needs and motives. As you will see in the section on self-actualization later in this chapter, some motives are not based on deficit needs, but rather are based on growth needs.

Motives belong in the intrapsychic domain for several reasons. First, researchers who study motives have stressed the importance of *internal* psychological needs and urges that propel people to think, perceive, and act in certain predictable ways. Motives can be unconscious, in the sense that the person does not know explicitly what he or she wants. Just as people may not be fully aware of why they engage in particular fantasies, they may not be consciously aware of what compels them to act in certain ways. This similarity leads to another feature shared by psychologists interested in motives and other intrapsychic constructs—the reliance on projective techniques. Motive psychologists, like psychoanalysts, believe that fantasies, free associations, and responses to projective techniques reveal the unconscious motivation behind many thoughts, feelings, and behaviors (Barenbaum & Winter, 2003).

Motive psychologists also share some core ideas with dispositional psychologists, whose work we covered in Part One of this book. Like dispositional psychologists, motive psychologists stress that (1) people differ from one another in the type and strength of their motives; (2) these differences are measurable; (3) these differences cause or are associated with important life outcomes, such as business success or marital satisfaction; (4) differences between people in the relative amounts of various motives are stable over time; and (5) motives may provide one answer to the question "Why do people do what they do?" The motive approach can be thought of as a halfway point between the intrapsychic domain and the dispositional domain (Winter, John, Stewart, Klohnen, & Duncan, 1998). We will discuss motives as we examine the intrapsychic domain because of the view that motives exist within the psyche and can operate outside of conscious awareness to affect everyday behaviors, thoughts, and feelings.

One of the first researchers to develop a modern theory of motivation was Henry Murray, a psychologist active in research from the 1930s through the 1960s. The path that ultimately led Murray to a career in psychology was decidedly untraditional. He went to medical school, became a physician, and interned in surgery. Murray then pursued research in embryology, followed by a Ph.D. in biochemistry from Cambridge University. While studying in England, Murray went to Zurich during spring break in 1925 to visit the famous psychoanalyst Carl Jung (see Chapter 9). He met with Jung every day for three weeks, meetings from which he "emerged a reborn man" (Murray, reprinted in Shneidman, 1981, p. 54). His encounter with psychoanalysis had a profound impact on Murray, leading him to abandon his medical practice and research and to turn his attention entirely to psychology. Murray was then trained in psychoanalysis and accepted a position at Harvard, where he remained until his retirement (Murray, 1967).

Need

Murray began by defining the term *need,* a concept he viewed as similar to the analytic concept of drive. In a nutshell, according to Murray, a need is a "potentiality or readiness to respond in a certain way under certain given circumstances. . . . It is a noun which stands for the fact that a certain trend is apt to recur" (Murray, 1938, p. 124). Needs organize perception, guiding us to see what we want (or need) to see. For example, someone who has a high need for power, a need to influence others, may see even everyday social situations as opportunities to boss others around.

A need also organizes action by compelling a person to do what is necessary to fulfill the need. A person who has a need to achieve, for example, often makes sacrifices and works hard at the task in which he or she wants to excel. Murray believed that needs referred to states of tension and that satisfying the need reduces the tension. According to Murray, however, it was the *process* of reducing tension that the person found satisfying, not the tensionless state *per se*. Murray believed that people might actually seek to increase tension (e.g., by going on a roller-coaster ride or viewing a horror movie) in order to experience the pleasure of reducing that tension (i.e., to end the roller coaster ride or the horror movie).

Based on his research with the Office for Strategic Services (a forerunner of the Central Intelligence Agency), Murray proposed a list of fundamental human needs, some of which are described in Table 11.1. Each need is associated with (1) a specific desire or intention, (2) a particular set of emotions, and (3) specific action tendencies, and each need can be described with trait names. Consider the need for affiliation, which is the desire to win and maintain associations with people. The primary set of emotions associated with this need are interpersonal warmth, cheerfulness, and cooperativeness, and the associated action tendencies are accepting people, spending time with others, and making efforts to maintain contact with others. The associated traits that characterize people with a strong need for affiliation are attributes such as agreeableness, friendliness, loyalty, and goodwill.

Murray believed that each person had a unique **hierarchy of needs.** An individual's various needs can be thought of as existing at different levels of strength—for instance, a person might have a high need for dominance, an average need for affiliation, and a low need for achievement. Each need interacts with the various other needs within each person. This interaction is what makes the concept of motive **dynamic.** The term *dynamic* is used to refer to the mutual influence of forces within a person—in this case, the interaction of various motives within a person. To return

Table 11.1 A Brief Description of Several of Murray's Needs, Organized into Five Higher-Level Categories

Ambition Needs

- **Achievement:** To master, manipulate, or organize others, objects, or ideas. To accomplish difficult tasks, and to do this as rapidly and independently as possible. To overcome obstacles and excel. To surpass rivals by exercising talent.
- **Exhibition:** To be seen and heard, to be the center of attention. To make an impression on others. To excite, fascinate, entertain, intrigue, amuse, entice, or amaze others.
- **Order:** To put things in orderly arrangement, to desire cleanliness, organization, balance, neatness, and precision.

Needs to Defend Status

- **Dominance:** To seek to influence or direct the behavior of others by persuasion, command, suggestion, or seduction. To control one's environment, particularly the social environment. To restrain or prohibit others.

Needs Related to Social Power

- **Abasement:** To accept injury, criticism, and blame. To submit passively to external force, to resign oneself to fate. To admit inferiority, error, or wrongdoing. To confess and atone and seek pain and misfortune.
- **Aggression:** To overcome opposition forcefully. To avenge an injury. To attack, injure, or kill another. To forcefully punish or oppose another.
- **Autonomy:** To shake off restraint, break out of confines. To get free, to resist coercion and restriction. To avoid being domineered. To be free to act according to one's wishes and to remain unattached.
- **Blame-avoidance:** To avoid humiliation at all costs. To avoid situations that may lead to embarrassment or belittlement. To refrain from action because of fear of failure or worry over the scorn, derision, or indifference from others.

Social Affection Needs

- **Affiliation:** To enjoy cooperation or reciprocal interaction with similar others. To draw near to others. To please and win affection of those you like. To remain loyal to friends.
- **Nurturance:** To take care of others in need, to give sympathy and gratify the needs of helpless others, such as a child, or someone who is weak, disabled, inexperienced, infirm, humiliated, lonely, dejected, or confused. To assist persons in danger. To help, support, console, protect, comfort, nurse, feed, and heal others.
- **Succor:** To receive aid from others. To have one's needs gratified by another, to be nursed, supported, protected, advised, indulged, loved, and consoled. To always have a supporter or a devoted protector.

Source: Adapted from Murray, H. A. (1938). *Explorations in personality.* New York: Oxford University Press.

to our person with a high need for dominance, it would make a big difference in her overall behavior if her need for dominance were accompanied with a high or low need for affiliation. If her high need for dominance were coupled with a high need for affiliation (e.g., a strong desire to develop and maintain relationships), then she would most likely develop the social and leadership skills to make others comfortable with her dominance. If her high need for dominance were combined with a weak need for affiliation, in contrast, then she might simply exercise power over others without regard to their feelings. She might impress others as argumentative, quarrelsome, and just plain disagreeable and bossy.

Press

Another important contribution of Murray to personality psychology was a specific way of thinking about the environment. According to Murray, elements in the environment affected a person's needs. For example, a person with a high need for affiliation might be sensitive to the social aspects of his or her environment, such as how many people are present, whether they are interacting, and whether or not they look approachable and outgoing. Murray used the term **press** to refer to need-relevant aspects of the environment. A person's need for affiliation, for example, won't affect that person's behavior without an appropriate environmental press (such as the presence of friendly people). People with a high need for affiliation would be more likely to notice other people, and to see more opportunities for interaction with others, than someone with a low need for affiliation.

Murray also introduced the notion that there is a so-called real environment (which he called **alpha press,** or objective reality) and a perceived environment (called **beta press,** or reality-as-it-is-perceived). In any given situation, what one person sees may be different from what other people see. Consider what might happen if two people are walking down the street and a third person approaches and smiles at each of them. One person who is high on the need for affiliation might see the smile as a sign of friendliness and a nonverbal invitation to start a conversation. The other person who is low on the need for affiliation might see the same smile as a smirk and consequently become suspicious that the stranger is laughing at them. Objectively (alpha press), it was the same smile. Subjectively (beta press), it was a very different event for these two persons, due to their differences in the need for affiliation. The need for affiliation can be distinguished from the need for intimacy. People high on the need for affiliation seek out relationships, build social networks, and find approval from others very satisfying. They tend to prefer being part of a team rather than acting as an individual. The need for intimacy, on the other hand, refers specifically to the need for close, warm, and loving relationships with others.

Apperception and the TAT

Murray held that a person's needs influenced how he or she perceived the environment, especially when the environment is ambiguous (as when a stranger smiles at the person). The act of interpreting the environment and perceiving the meaning of what is going on in a situation is termed **apperception** (Murray, 1933). Because our needs and motives influence apperception, if we want to know about a person's primary motives, we might ask that individual to interpret what is going on in a variety of situations, especially ambiguous situations.

The simple insight that needs and motives influence how we perceive the world led Murray and his research associate Christiana Morgan to develop a formal technique for assessing these two constructs (Morgan & Murray, 1935). They called this the **Thematic Apperception Test** (or TAT, for short). The TAT consists of a set of black-and-white drawings, which are ambiguous. The person is then asked to make up a story about what is happening in the picture. For example, in the drawing of a person on a windowsill, the person may be going in (to rob the house?) or going out (jumping to commit suicide?). Some pictures contain no people at all, such as a picture of a rowboat on the shore of a small creek. Such pictures are perhaps the most ambiguous: Who put the rowboat there? Are they coming or going? Why are they not in the picture right now? It is easy to make up a story because the picture is so ambiguous with respect to what is happening.

This photo, obtained from U.S. Government archives, was used by Morgan and Murray as one of the TAT pictures. Can you make up a story about the child in this photo? What do you think happens next?

In administering the TAT, a person is shown each picture and told to be creative and make up a short story, interpreting what is happening in each picture. He or she is encouraged to tell a story that has a beginning, a middle, and an end. The psychologist then codes the stories for the presence of various types of imagery associated with particular motives. For example, a subject might write the following: "The boat in the picture is being used by a young boy to take produce to market. The boy has stopped to gather some wild berries to take to the market to sell, along with his farm produce. This boy works very hard and eventually grows up, puts himself through college, and become a famous scientist, specializing in the study of plants, primarily agricultural crops." This story has a lot of achievement imagery, so the subject who wrote it would be seen to have a high need for achievement.

Morgan and Murray published the TAT in 1935. Since then, many researchers have modified its administration (e.g., using fewer cards, selecting other drawings, and using a slide projector to show the pictures to large groups). Because the pictures in the original TAT are dated (e.g., clothing and hair are styles from the 1950s), newer versions of TAT-type pictures have been developed and found to function similarly to the original set in terms of soliciting need-relevant themes (Schultheiss & Brunstein, 2001). The essential features of the TAT and similar projective techniques are that (1) the subject is given an *ambiguous* stimulus, usually a picture, and (2) he or she is asked to describe and *interpret* what is going on.

Morgan and Murray did not derive a formal scoring system for the TAT, and instead preferred simply to interpret a person's level on the various needs. Other researchers worked to develop and validate objective scoring strategies for the TAT (Winter, 1998a, 1999). Take the need for achievement motive, which can be scored

A Closer Look

TAT and Questionnaire Measures of Motives: Do They Measure Different Aspects of Motives?

Psychologist David McClelland and his colleagues focused primarily on the TAT. Critics have argued that the TAT demonstrates poor test-retest reliability and that responses to one picture may not correlate with responses to other pictures—that is, the TAT has poor internal reliability (Entwisle, 1972). Moreover, when the TAT is used to predict actual motive-related behaviors (such as when TAT need for achievement scores are used to predict overall college grade-point averages or performance on an achievement test), the correlations are frequently low and inconsistent (Fineman, 1977). Smith and Atkinson (1992) have reviewed the major criticisms of the TAT, as well as responses from its proponents.

These undesirable properties of the TAT have led some researchers to develop questionnaire measures of motives (Jackson, 1967). These questionnaires simply ask people directly about their motives and desires and about whether they engage in the kinds of behaviors that indicate high levels of the motives. These questionnaires turn out to have desirable measurement properties, such as adequate test-retest reliability and predictive validity (Scott & Johnson, 1972). A troubling finding, however, is that TAT measures of motives and questionnaire measures of the same motives are often uncorrelated (Fineman, 1977; for an exception see Thrash & Elliot, 2002). Many researchers, therefore, suggest that the TAT measure and other projective measures should be abandoned.

McClelland and his colleagues did not silently accept these criticisms (McClelland, 1985; Weinberger & McClelland, 1990; Winter, 1999). In response, McClelland argued that, when the TAT is properly administered and scored, the motive scores *do* show acceptable test-retest reliability. In addition, he asserted that the TAT predicts long-term real-life outcomes, such as business success, better than questionnaire measures do. He argued that the questionnaire measures are better at predicting short-term behaviors, such as how competitive a person will behave while playing a game in a psychology laboratory. McClelland argued that the TAT measure and the questionnaire measures are uncorrelated because they measure *two different types of motivation.* Let's discuss each in turn.

One type of motive is called **implicit motivation.** These motives are based on needs, such as the need for achievement (nAch), the need for power (nPow), and the need for intimacy (nInt), as they are measured in fantasy-based (i.e., TAT) measures. When the TAT is used to measure these motives, they are called implicit because the persons writing the stories are not explicitly telling the psychologist about themselves. Instead, they are telling stories about other people. The stories are thought to reflect the *implied* motives of the persons writing the stories—their unconscious desires and aspirations, their unspoken needs and wants. The TAT is based on the premise that individuals' *real* motives will be projected into the pictures, and they will then tell stories that actually reflect their own desires. What people write in response to the TAT pictures is presumed to reflect their real, although unconscious, motivations. People may not express these motivations directly in outward behaviors, but the motivations influence people's perceptions of what they see in the TAT.

by counting up the number of references in the person's story to wanting to do things better, anticipating success, feeling positive about succeeding, and overcoming obstacles (Schultheiss & Brunstein, 2001). Validational studies have often taken the form of arousing the motive in some way, then having subjects respond to the TAT. So, for example, people who were instructed to imagine engaging in a challenging competition might write more achievement themes in TAT stories than persons who did not just undergo such an imaginative exercise (e.g., Zurbriggen & Sturman, 2002). Recent studies of the TAT suggest that people do respond differentially to the themes of the picture, with, for example, high need for achievement people responding to the achievement pictures differently than low need for achievement people (Kwon, Campbell, & Williams, 2001; Tuerlinckz, DeBoeck, & Lens, 2002).

The other type of motivation is called explicit, or **self-attributed motivation,** which McClelland argued reflects primarily a person's self-awareness of his or her own conscious motives or "normative beliefs about desirable goals and modes of conduct" (McClelland, Koestner, & Weinberger, 1989, p. 690). These self-attributed motivations reflect a person's conscious *awareness* about what is important to him or her. As such, they represent part of the individual's conscious self-understanding (e.g., "I'm a person who doesn't really care about influencing others and being the boss [low self-attributed nPow], even though I want terribly to succeed in all my classes [high self-attributed nAch] and have a steady boy/girlfriend and lots of other friends [high self-attributed nInt]").

McClelland argued that implicit and self-attributed motives represent fundamentally different aspects of motivation and that they should predict different life outcomes. Implicit motives predict long-term, spontaneous behavioral trends over time. For example, compared with questionnaire measures, TAT-assessed need for achievement is the better predictor of long-term entrepreneurial success, and TAT-assessed need for power is the better predictor of long-term success as a business manager (McAdams, 1990). Self-attributed motives, on the other hand, are better predictors of responses to immediate and specific situations and to choice behaviors and attitudes (because they measure the person's conscious desires and wants). For example, questionnaire-assessed need for achievement is the better predictor of how hard a person will work to obtain a reward in a psychology experiment, and questionnaire-assessed need for power is the better predictor of a person's self-reported attitudes about social inequality (Koestner & McClelland, 1990; Woike, 1995).

The research literature supports a distinction between implicit and explicit motives, at least for achievement motivation (Spangler, 1992; Thrash & Elliot, 2002). Spangler examined more than 100 studies of need for achievement and performed a meta-analysis of these studies. (In a meta-analysis, many studies are grouped together and analyzed statistically to see if there is an average effect and what might influence the size of that effect.) Half the studies meta-analyzed by Spangler used TAT measures (implicit motives), and the other half used questionnaire measures (self-attributed motives) of the achievement motive. Spangler then looked carefully at the variables being predicted by achievement. He sorted the studies into those that looked at short-term responses to specific tasks (e.g., grades in college courses, performance on ability tests, and performance in laboratory achievement tests) and those that looked at long-term achievements (e.g., lifetime income, job level attained in an organization, number of publications achieved, and participation in community organizations). Spangler found that the TAT-based measure was a better predictor of the long-term outcomes than was the questionnaire measure, whereas the questionnaire was a better predictor of the short-term responses.

Spangler argued that these results support McClelland's view that questionnaire and TAT measures appear to be measuring different aspects of motivation. Spangler's meta-analysis suggests that both the TAT and questionnaire measures may play important roles in helping psychologists understand the short- and long-term effects of motives. If you want to know how someone will react to achievement demands today or tomorrow, you might be best advised to use a questionnaire or to just ask the person about his or her achievement needs. However, if you want to make a prediction about who, in a group of people, will earn the largest lifetime income or climb the highest in an organizational setting, you might be better off using the TAT measure of need for achievement.

We can make a distinction between using the TAT to assess state levels of needs and trait levels of needs. **State levels** of a need refer to a person's momentary amount of a specific need, which can fluctuate with specific circumstances. For example, a person who is failing at a task (e.g., a player on a baseball team that is down 5 to 4 in the ninth inning) might experience a sharp increase in the state of achievement motivation. The assessment of state levels of needs can be useful in determining what aspects of a situation bring about changes in specific needs. The TAT has been shown to be sensitive to changes in state levels of various motives, particularly the needs for achievement, power, and intimacy (Moretti & Rossini, 2004). The assessment of **trait levels** of a need refers to measuring a person's average tendency, or their set-point, on the specific trait. The idea is that people differ from each other in their typical or average amount of specific needs. The TAT and other such instruments have multiple pictures or items, and the amount of imagery related to a particular need is then averaged across the pictures to get at their trait level. The assessment of trait levels is most useful in determining differences between individuals in their average tendencies toward particular needs. Assessing trait levels of needs is the most frequent goal of personality psychologists who use such measures.

A newer form of assessing motives is the **Multi-Motive Grid,** which combines features of the TAT with features of self-report questionnaires (Schmalt, 1999). In this test, 14 pictures are selected to arouse one of the big three motives (achievement, power, or intimacy). The pictures are presented with questions about important motivational states, and the person then answers those questions. The idea is that the photo will arouse the motive, which then will influence how the person will answer the questions. While this technique is relatively new, initial results show promising levels of reliability (Sokolowski, Schmalt, Langens, & Puca, 2000). Initial validity data are also promising, for example, showing that motive grid assessment of need for achievement predicted persistence and performance in laboratory tasks (Schmalt, 1999).

The TAT remains a popular personality assessment technique today, even though some researchers argue that it has low test-retest reliability (see, however, Smith & Atkinson, 1992). In addition, several researchers have reported extremely low correlations between TAT measures of certain needs and questionnaire measures of the same needs, leading them to question whether the TAT is a valid measure. This is the topic of our A Closer Look section on pages 358–359.

The Big Three Motives: Achievement, Power, and Intimacy

Although Murray proposed several dozen motives, researchers have focused most of their attention on a relatively small set. These motives are based on the needs for achievement, power, and intimacy. Research with the TAT, and on motives in general, has tended to focus on these three primary motives. Let's review what we know about each of these fundamental human motives.

Need for Achievement

Behavior that is motivated by the need for achievement has long interested psychologists. Because it has received the most research attention we will begin with this motive.

Doing Things Better

Following Murray at Harvard, psychologist David McClelland carried on the tradition of motive research. McClelland was best known for his research on the **need for achievement,** defined as the desire to do better, to be successful, and to feel competent. Like all motives, we assume that the need for achievement will energize behavior in certain (achievement-related) situations. It is energized by the incentives of challenge and variety, it is accompanied by feelings of interest and surprise, and it is associated with the subjective state of being curious and exploratory (McClelland, 1985). People motivated by a high need for achievement obtain satisfaction from accomplishing a task or from the anticipation of accomplishing a task.

They cherish the process of being engaged in challenging activities.

Many researchers have demonstrated that state need for achievement can be aroused and that stories written in these aroused conditions contain more achievement imagery. For example, in one experiment, subjects are led to believe that they are taking a test of general intelligence and leadership ability. After the test, some are told they scored very high, some are told they scored very low, and some are given no feedback whatsoever. The experimenters assume that success and failure feedback on a test of intelligence and ability would arouse state need for achievement. After a short period, the subjects complete the TAT. The stories written by the subjects who received feedback on the earlier test (either the success or the failure feedback) contain more achievement imagery than the stories written by the people who did not get any feedback.

As the leader of two successful companies, Apple Computer and Pixar Animation, Steve Jobs is constantly striving to do things better. He is a good example of someone high in achievement motivation.

The effect of achievement arousal on TAT scores has been successfully demonstrated on both men and women and on people from such diverse cultures as Germany, India, Japan, Poland, and Brazil (reviewed in Koestner & McClelland, 1990). An extensive study of racial influences on TAT scores found no differences between African American and white subjects in their need for achievement (nAch) scores (Lefkowitz & Frazer, 1980). Neither the race of the TAT administrator nor the race of the figures in the TAT had an impact on nAch scores. These cross-cultural and cross-racial replications are important, because they demonstrate that the effects of arousing state achievement needs, as evidenced by the fantasy content provided by subjects, are the same for people from different cultures, despite differences in the social, linguistic, or cultural definitions of the concepts of achievement and success. This finding exemplifies the concept of generalizability discussed in Chapter 2.

In terms of trait levels, high nAch individuals prefer moderate levels of challenge, neither too high nor too low. This preference makes sense, given that the high nAch person is motivated to do better than others. A task that is almost impossible to accomplish will not be attractive because it will not provide the opportunity to do better if everyone does poorly. A task that is too easy will be easy for everyone; the high nAch person will not do better if everyone is successful. Theoretically, we expect high nAch persons to have a preference for *moderately* challenging tasks. Dozens of studies have found support for this idea. One study examined children's preference for challenge in a variety of games (e.g., the ring-toss game, in which children attempt to toss rings around sticks that are placed at varying distances). Children high in nAch preferred a moderate challenge (e.g., tossed their rings at the sticks in the middle), whereas children low in nAch tried either the very easy levels of the games (closer sticks) or the levels at which success was almost impossible (McClelland, 1958). This relationship has also been demonstrated outside the laboratory. Young adults high in nAch have been found to choose college majors that are of intermediate difficulty and to pursue careers that are of moderate difficulty (reviewed in Koestner & McClelland, 1990).

To summarize the characteristics of persons high in nAch, (1) they prefer activities that provide some, but not too much, challenge, (2) they enjoy tasks in which they are personally responsible for the outcome, and (3) they prefer tasks for which feedback on their performance is available.

Have a look at the TAT picture presented earlier, on page 357. Write a short story about what is happening in this picture. However, instead of writing off the top of your head, try to write a story that would score high on the need for achievement. What themes would you put in such a story? What actions and outcomes might be interpreted as indicating high nAch? What you consciously try to put into such a story are the themes and acts that psychologists look for in the stories of people writing naturally. Some put plenty of such themes and acts into their stories quite naturally and, so, seem to see achievement-related behaviors all around. Others reveal that their stories, and the characters therein, act in very nonstriving, nonachieving ways. And this comes perfectly naturally to them when they make up a story about an ambiguous situation.

Increasing the Need for Achievement

Research on the achievement motive typically takes the form of correlating TAT need for achievement (nAch) scores with other measures thought to be related to achievement. Demonstrating the relationship between nAch and success in entrepreneurial activities is one example of this type of research. Starting and managing a small business appears to offer a high degree of satisfaction for the person with a strong need to achieve. It provides an opportunity to engage in a challenging pursuit, to assume responsibility for making decisions and taking action, and to obtain swift and objective feedback about the success of one's performance. Studies in several countries have found that men with a high nAch are more attracted to business occupations than are their peers who have a low nAch (McClelland, 1965). A study of farmers (who are, in effect, small business operators) showed that those with a high need to achieve were more likely than low nAch farmers to adopt innovative farming practices and to show improved rates of production over time (Singh, 1978).

Research on entrepreneurial talent has not been limited to business activities. Some studies have examined the work habits of college students. Students with high nAch appear to be more deliberate in their pursuit of good grades: they are more likely to investigate course requirements before enrolling in a class, to speak with a professor prior to exams, and to contact the professor about the exam after it was given to obtain feedback about their performance (Andrews, 1967). In a very different subject sample, blue-collar workers with high nAch engaged in more problem-solving activities after being laid off than did unemployed workers lower in nAch: they started looking for a new job sooner and used a greater number of job-seeking strategies (Koestner & McClelland, 1990).

More recent studies on entrepreneurial orientation examined achievement motives in a group of students of small business (a major considered to have high entrepreneurial potential) and compared them to a group of students of economics (considered to have much less entrepreneurial potential). Results showed that small business students were significantly higher on achievement motivation than the economics students (Sagie & Elizur, 1999). A study by Langens (2001) also supports the notion that training for high need for achievement can promote success in business. It seems that persons with high achievement motives are drawn to careers that have more potential risk and uncertainty, where success is a matter of personal responsibility and where emergency problem solving is routine.

There are also cultural differences in how the need for achievement is expressed. In the United States, most high achieving high school students strive for good grades for themselves. Many students, and their parents, go to great lengths to achieve. Cheating can be common, and some students do not view cheating as wrong. The psychologist Demerath (2001) even reports that some parents of high achieving students sought to have them classified as special-education students, which would entitle them to extra time on standardized tests. When he went to Papua New Guinea, Demerath found a very different norm among students. There school is seen as a noncompetitive place where it is important for all to do well. Doing well as an individual, especially if it is at the expense of others, is frowned upon. In fact, New Guineans call this "acting extra" and view it as a form of vanity. Given the cultural differences between New Guinea and the United States, such differences in how the need for achievement is expressed make sense. People in Papua, New Guinea, make their living at farming and fishing, and they need to know that if they get sick or something happens and they cannot work their fields or nets that others will pitch in and help. In collectivist cultures, individual achievement is less valued than the person who helps his or her group achieve.

Determining Sex Differences

Much of the research on nAch, particularly that done in the 1950s and 1960s, was conducted on males only. Perhaps this was due to the fact that Harvard (where both Murray and McClelland did much of their research) was primarily a male institution at that time. Or it might have been due to the biased belief of that period that achievement was important only in the lives of men. Whatever the reason, little was known about achievement strivings in women until the 1970s and 1980s. Since then, some similarities and some differences have been found between men and women. Men and women high in nAch are similar in their preference for moderate challenge, personal responsibility for the outcome, and tasks with feedback. The major differences between such men and women occurs in two areas: the life outcomes predicted by nAch and childhood experiences. Let's consider each of these in turn.

Research on men has focused primarily on achievement in business as a typical life outcome predicted by nAch. Research on women, however, has identified different "achievement trajectories," depending on whether the women value having a family or value having both family and work goals. Among women who value both work and family, nAch is related more to achieving better grades and to completing college, marrying, and starting a family later than it is among women low in nAch with career and family interests. Among women who are more exclusively focused on family, nAch is seen in the women's investment in activities related to dating and courtship, such as placing greater emphasis on physical appearance and talking with friends about their boyfriends more frequently (Koestner & McClelland, 1990). Such findings underscore researchers' need to know the subjects' goals before they can make predictions about success in particular areas.

The second major difference between men and women has been in the childhood experiences associated with nAch. Among women, nAch is associated with a stressful or difficult early family life. The mothers of girls high in nAch were found to be critical of their daughters and to be aggressive and competitive toward them (Kagan & Moss, 1962). The mothers of high-achieving schoolgirls were also less nurturant and affectionate toward their daughters than the mothers of less academically successful girls (Crandall et al., 1964). In contrast, the early lives of males high in nAch are characterized by parental support and care. An interesting related finding

Condoleezza Rice was a straight-A student in grade school, began studying classical piano at age 10, and was a competitive ice skater, rising at 4:30 to practice for two hours before school each day. At age 38 she became provost at Stanford University, then became a National Security Advisor, and currently is the Secretary of State.

concerns the levels of nAch in children who come from families in which the parents have divorced or separated. A nationally representative study found that women whose parents had divorced or separated when they were children had higher nAch scores than women whose parents had stayed together. The opposite outcome was found for men (Veroff et al., 1960). Living with a single mom may provide an achieving role model for young girls, whereas for boys it may demonstrate that men are unnecessary to family life and perhaps even to be resented.

Several recent studies have examined gender differences in competitive achievement settings. In one study the researchers had 40 men and 40 women solve simple addition problems as quickly as they could, paying them 50 cents for each correct answer (Niederle & Vesterlund, 2005). In one condition the participants simply played against the clock, trying to solve as many problems as they could. In another condition the game was changed to a tournament, where subjects were divided into teams of two women or two men each, and they played against each other. The winning team received $2.00 for each problem they solved and the losing team received nothing. They found that men and women performed equally well in both conditions: the tournament setting and the individual setting. The experimenters then had a third round, where each person could choose whether they wanted to play individually or in a tournament setting. Interestingly, only 35 percent of the women chose the tournament setting, whereas 75 percent of the men chose the tournament setting. The authors concluded that, even in settings where women perform just as well as men, they are less likely to want to engage in direct competition with others. Women may be more selective in how they express their achievement strivings, especially when winning for oneself means that others lose.

Promoting Achievement Motivation in Children

Despite the sex differences in childhood antecedents of achievement, McClelland believed that certain parental behaviors could promote high achievement motivation in children. One of these parenting practices is placing an emphasis on **independence training.** Parents can behave in ways that promote autonomy and independence in their children. For example, a young child who is taught to feed him- or herself becomes independent of the parents during feeding time; a child who is toilet trained early no longer relies on his or her parents for assistance with this task. One longitudinal study found that strict toilet training in early childhood is associated with high need for achievement 26 years later (McClelland & Pilon, 1983). Training a child to be independent in various tasks of life promotes a sense of mastery and confidence in the child. This may be one way that parents can promote a need for achievement in their children.

A second parental practice associated with need for achievement is setting challenging *standards* for the child (Heckhausen, 1982). Parents need to let the child know what is expected of him or her. These expectations should not exceed the child's abilities, however, or else the child may give up. The idea is for parents to provide goals that challenge the child, support the child in working toward these goals, and reward

Table 11.2 Raising High Need for Achievement Children

- Set tough but realistic standards
- Applaud successes and celebrate accomplishments
- Acknowledge but don't dwell on failures. Stress that failures are part of learning
- Avoid instilling a fear of failure, and instead emphasize the motive to succeed
- Stress effort over ability: instead of saying "You can do it because you are smart" say "You can do it if you really try"

the child when the goal is attained. Positive and frequent success experiences appear to be part of the prescription for developing a heightened need for achievement. For example, learning the ABCs is a challenging task for a 4-year-old; parents might encourage a young child to undertake this task, enthusiastically sing the ABC song with the child, and reward the child with praise and hugs when he or she recites the alphabet independently for the first time.

Finally, a recent study has shown that persons with a secure attachment style, as described in Chapter 10, typically develop a higher level of adult achievement motivation than persons with avoidant or ambivalent attachment styles (Elliot & Reis, 2003). These researchers hypothesized that children with secure attachments were more likely to explore their environments and to thereby learn new skills. Over time, learning to be effective leads to higher achievement motivation and to valuing one's own competencies and seeing life's difficulties as challenges to be overcome rather than as opportunities to fail.

A recent developmental theory of achievement motivation has been proposed by the psychologist Carol Dweck (2005). This theory emphasizes the beliefs that people develop about their abilities and competencies. Briefly, the theory holds that the most adaptive belief system is that abilities are not fixed but that they are malleable and can be developed through effort. Dweck (2002) argues that sometimes even "smart" people succumb to the belief that their abilities are fixed or given or genetically determined, that their current performance reflects their long-term potential, and that truly gifted persons do not need effort to achieve. She argues that this set of beliefs is "dumb" in the sense that people who hold such beliefs will consequently have a low need for achievement. It is more adaptive, Dweck holds, to believe that abilities are changeable, that one's performance is a temporary indicator of where one is, not where one will ultimately be, and that one's true potential will only be realized through sustained effort. This new theory is having an impact on schools and other educational settings (Elliot & Dweck, 2005).

Need for Power

Another motive of interest to psychologists is based on the need for power—the desire to have an impact on others.

Impact on Others

Although McClelland was known primarily for his studies of the achievement motive, both he and several of his students went on to study other motives. One of his students—David Winter—focused a good deal of his research on the **need for power** (nPow). Winter (1973) defines the need for power as a readiness or preference for having an impact on other people. As with the need to achieve, the need for power is assumed to energize and direct behavior when the person is in opportune situations for exerting power. The TAT has likewise been the predominant assessment tool for research on nPow. The subjects' stories are scored for the presence of images related to themes of power. These include descriptions of strong or vigorous actions, behaviors that bring about strong reactions in others, and statements that emphasize the importance of a character's status or reputation.

Research Findings

Many studies have examined the correlates of individual differences in nPow. The need for power correlates positively with having arguments with others, being elected to student office in college, taking larger risks in gambling situations, behaving assertively and actively in a small-group setting, and acquiring more of what Winter calls "prestige possessions," such as sports cars, credit cards, and nameplates for dormitory doors (Winter, 1973).

It appears that an individual high in nPow is interested in control—control of situations and other people (Assor, 1989). Men high in nPow rate their "ideal wives" as those who are under the men's control and dependent on them, perhaps because such relationships offer them a sense of superiority (Winter, 1973). Men high in nPow are also more likely to abuse their spouses (Mason & Blankenship, 1987). A person with a high need for power prefers as friends people who are not well known or popular, perhaps because such people do not pose a threat to the person's prestige or status (Winter, 1973).

Sex Differences

Research on the power motive has found no sex differences in average levels of nPow or in the kinds of situations that arouse the power motive. Men and women also do not differ in the life outcomes that are associated with nPow, such as having formal social power (e.g., holding office), having power-related careers (e.g., being a manager), or gathering prestige possessions (e.g., sports cars).

The largest and most consistent sex difference is that high nPow men, but not women, perform a wide variety of impulsive and aggressive behaviors. Men high in nPow are more likely than men low in nPow to have dissatisfying dating relationships, arguments with others, and higher divorce rates. Men high in nPow are also more likely to engage in the sexual exploitation of women, have more frequent sex partners, and engage in sex at an earlier age than do their counterparts who are lower in nPow. Men with a strong need for power also abuse alcohol more than those with a low need for power (feelings of power often increase under the influence of alcohol). None of these correlates have been found for women.

"Profligate impulsive" behaviors (drinking, aggression, and sexual exploitation) are less likely to occur if an individual has had **responsibility training** (Winter & Barenbaum, 1985). Taking care of younger siblings is an example of responsibility training. Having one's own children provides another opportunity to learn to behave responsibly. Among people who have had such responsibility training, nPow is not related to profligate impulsive behavior (Winter, 1988). These findings have led Winter and others (e.g., Jenkins, 1994) to assert that socialization experiences, not biological sex per se, determine whether nPow will be expressed in these maladaptive behaviors.

Health Status and the Need for Power

As you might imagine, people high in nPow do not deal well with frustration and conflict. When these people do not get their way, or when their power is challenged or blocked, they are likely to show strong stress responses. McClelland (1982) called such obstacles **power stress** and hypothesized that people high in nPow were vulnerable to various ailments and diseases because of the stresses associated with inhibited power. A study of college students found that, when power motives were inhibited or stressed, the subjects' immune function became less efficient and they reported more frequent illnesses, such as colds and the flu (see McClelland & Jemmott, 1980). A later study of male prisoners found similar results, with prisoners high in nPow showing the highest levels of illness and the lowest levels of immune antibodies (McClelland, Alexander, & Marks, 1982). Other studies have demonstrated that inhibiting the power motive among people high in nPow is linked with high blood pressure. This relationship was also found in a longitudinal study, which revealed that the inhibited power motive measured in men in their early thirties significantly predicted elevated blood pressure and signs of hypertension 20 years later (McClelland, 1979).

An interesting laboratory study induced power stress by having people lead a group discussion without knowing that the group's members were coached ahead of time to disagree with the leader and to display a lot of conflict (Fodor, 1985). The group leader was assessed for muscle tension. Consistent with McClelland's theory, the greatest tension responses were found for those leaders in the group conflict condition who were high in nPow.

War and Peace and Power

In a fascinating line of research, Winter investigated nPow on a national level and related it to the broad areas of war and peace. Traditionally, nPow is measured by evaluating stories written in response to TAT pictures. However, nPow (as well as any motive) can be determined by assessing just about any written document, ranging from children's fairy tales to presidential speeches. Winter analyzed the content of 300 years of State of the Parliament speeches given by the prime ministers of England. Each of the speeches was rated for the presence of power images. He then used these image scores to predict warfare activity in these three centuries of British history. Winter found that wars were started when power imagery in the parliamentary speeches was high. Once under way, wars ended only after the levels of power imagery in the speeches ended. Similar analyses were done on the British–German communications during World War I, as well as on U.S.–Soviet communications during the Cuban missile crisis of the 1960s (Winter, 1993). In these cases, increases in power images preceded military actions, whereas decreases in power imagery preceded decreases in military threat.

Speeches delivered by national leaders can be analyzed for themes of power. The presence of power imagery may predict the onset of war (Winter, 2002).

Winter (2002) has recently conducted research on the motivational dimensions of effective leadership. He analyzes the motive profiles of various contemporary political leaders (e.g., President Bush) to examine how their motives influenced their leadership style and success. Winter shows how different motives can have both strengths and weaknesses, but ultimately he comes up with a motivational prescription for effective leadership: the key is balance between motives, with power motivation balanced by affiliation, and achievement balanced by power concerns. Overall, the responsible leader should want to achieve much, be willing to exercise a good deal of power to attain those goals, yet want to maintain good relationships with all other important persons or governments.

In an extension of this research, Winter and his students examined how power images in communications may lead to escalation in conflict (Peterson, Winter, & Doty, 1994). Subjects were asked to write replies to letters taken from real conflict situations. The letters the subjects were responding to were altered to create two versions: one with high power imagery and the other with low power imagery. Otherwise, the content of the letters remained the same. The subjects' responses were then analyzed for themes of power. Subjects responded to power imagery with power images of their own. Assuming that the other side would similarly respond with more power images, it is easy to see how conflicts might escalate to violence. Misconceptions about the other side's motives, including the assumption that the motive guiding the opponents' behavior does not exert a comparable influence on one's own, can lead to unfortunate consequences, such as the perpetuation of prejudice between members of different groups (Miller & Prentice, 1994).

More recent studies of communications between governments involved in crises have revealed similar motive patterns (Langner & Winter, 2001). Analyzing official documents during four international crises, Langner and Winter found that making concessions was associated with affiliative motives expressed in the communications, whereas power images were associated with making fewer concessions. In a laboratory study, they found that power or affiliative motives could be primed by having the subjects read different communications from their negotiation partner, and that these primed motives predicted the likelihood that they would make a concession during the negotiation. Such personality research may have wide implications for understanding how governments could respond to each other to avoid crises.

To summarize, the need for power is the desire to have an impact on others. It can be measured from the TAT and from other verbal documents, such as speeches and other forms of communication, by looking for evidence of themes related to status seeking, to concerns about reputation, or to attempts to make others do what one wants. For example, Winter (1988) provides an interesting analysis of Richard Nixon's speeches in terms of the needs for achievement, power, and intimacy. Winter (1998b) applies a similar analysis to the speeches of former president Bill Clinton, linking Clinton's motives to some of his problems as well as to his popularity.

Need for Intimacy

The last of the "Big Three" motives is based on the desire for warm and fulfilling relationships with others.

Intimacy

The third motive receiving a good deal of research attention is the need for intimacy (nInt). The researcher most closely associated with this motive is Dan McAdams, another student of McClelland. McAdams defines the **need for intimacy** as the "recurrent preference or readiness for warm, close, and communicative interaction with others" (McAdams, 1990, p. 198). People high in nInt want more intimacy and meaningful human contact in their day-to-day lives than do those who are low in nInt.

Research Findings

McAdams and others have conducted a number of studies of nInt over the years in an effort to determine how people high and low in nInt differ from each other. As with the other motives, the TAT is often used to measure the strength of the intimacy motive. People high in nInt (compared to those who are low) have been found to (1) spend more time during the day thinking about relationships; (2) report more pleasant emotions when they are around other people; (3) smile, laugh, and make more eye contact; and (4) start up conversations more frequently and write more letters. We might think that the people high in nInt are simply extraverts, but the findings do not support this interpretation. Rather than being the loud, outgoing, life-of-the-party extravert, the person high in nInt is more likely to be someone with a few very good friends, who prefers sincere and meaningful conversations over wild parties. When asked to describe a typical time with a friend, people high in nInt tend to report one-on-one interactions instead of group interactions. When they get together with friends, people high in nInt are likely to listen to their friends and to discuss intimate or personal topics with them, such as their feelings, hopes, beliefs, and desires. Perhaps this is why people who are high in nInt are rated by their peers as especially "sincere," "loving," "not dominant," and "not self-centered" (McAdams, 1990).

A few studies have examined the relationship between nInt and well-being. In a longitudinal study, nInt measured at age 30 in a sample of male Harvard graduates was significantly related to overall adjustment (e.g., having a satisfying job and family life, coping well with life's stress, being free from alcohol problems) 17 years later (McAdams & Vaillant, 1982). Other studies have shown that nInt is associated with certain benefits and positive life outcomes, for both men and women. Among women, nInt is associated with happiness and satisfaction with life. Among men, nInt is associated with less strain in life. Unlike the motives for power and achievement, for which no sex differences have been found as far as level of need is concerned, there does exist a consistent sex difference in need for intimacy—women have, on average, a higher need than men (McAdams, 1990; McAdams & Bryant, 1987).

To summarize, the need for intimacy is the desire for warm and intimate relationships with others. Individuals with a strong nInt enjoy the company of others and are more expressive and communicative toward others, compared with people low in nInt. The intimacy motive is distinguished from extraversion in that persons high in nInt prefer having a few close friends to being a member of a rowdy group. In contrast to the need for achievement and power, for which men and women show comparable levels, women's need for intimacy tends to be higher than men's.

The motives we have covered so far—the needs for power, intimacy, and achievement—all fall within the tradition of academic personality psychology. There is, however, another motivational tradition, one that is rooted more in clinical psychology than in academic personality research. This tradition has come to inform the field of personality psychology, and concepts from this tradition are present or implied in several areas of contemporary research. We turn now to the humanistic tradition within personality psychology.

Humanistic Tradition: The Motive to Self-Actualize

In 1995, an American legend passed away—Jerry Garcia, lead guitarist of the Grateful Dead, reportedly of heart failure, at the age of 53. In the many newspaper stories recounting his life and times, reporters often suggested that Garcia lived longer than he should have, given his lifestyle. His band was constantly on the road for three decades, and Garcia was known to have abused a multitude of drugs, including cocaine, heroin, and alcohol, on a regular basis.

Other entertainers from the past have also abused drugs and alcohol—and died as a result—at much younger ages than Garcia, such as John Belushi (died at 33), Kurt Cobain (died at 27), Jimi Hendrix (died at 27), Janis Joplin (died at 27), Jim Morrison (died at 27), Keith Moon (died at 31), and Elvis Presley (died at 42). With each such death, the public engages briefly in an age-old debate about personal responsibility and the self-destructiveness often seen in artists. Some people argue that such artists are victims of their times or their culture. Garcia, for example, was thought to carry the burden of representing the best (and worst) of the 1960s counterculture; he and his band were often viewed as a time capsule from that era.

Another view of the same situation is that Garcia did kill himself, that he slowly but willfully self-destructed. This view implies that Garcia was responsible for his own demise. In an MTV interview the week of Garcia's death, then-President Bill Clinton represented this view: "While he had great talent, he also had a terrible problem [heroin addiction]. . . . You don't have to have a destructive lifestyle to be a genius." The implication is that Garcia's genius and his self-destructive tendencies were two separate parts of his personality and that one did not necessarily produce the other. Garcia killed himself by his own free will, in President Clinton's perspective, and he was responsible for his own death due to the lifestyle choices he had made over the years.

Jerry Garcia of the Grateful Dead, who died in a drug rehabilitation center in 1995. Some argue he was a victim of his times and his mission to maintain a vision of the 1960s counterculture. Others argue that Garcia was a musical genius who also chose a very destructive lifestyle. The issue of personal responsibility is important in the humanistic approach to motivation.

Was Garcia a victim of his culture, or was he responsible for his own self-destruction? The answer depends on how one views free will in relation to motivation. Earlier, in our A Closer Look section we discussed unconscious (implicit) motives. These are motives that a person is largely unaware of yet guide his or her behavior, life choices, and responses to projective tests such as the TAT. Choices based on unconscious motives are, in most respects, made without free will. The Garcia question really becomes whether or not he was aware of his motives, whether he knew what he was doing when he made his many self-destructive life choices.

An emphasis on conscious awareness of needs, choice, and personal responsibility is one of the characteristics of the **humanistic tradition** approach to motivation. Humanistic psychologists emphasize the role of *choice* in human life, as well as the influence of *responsibility* on creating a meaningful and satisfying life. The meaning of any person's life, according to the humanistic approach, is found in the choices that person makes and the responsibility he or she takes for those choices. In midlife, for example, some people conclude that they are not exercising much choice in their daily lives, that they have fallen into a rut in their careers, their personal relationships, or both. For example, the 2000 Oscar-winning movie *American Beauty* portrays the desperation of a man who has realized he is living a life he has not chosen and his extreme attempts to reclaim and take responsibility for his life. Some people respond to such a realization with drastic efforts to resume responsibility for creating their own lives. Career changes, divorce, moves across the country, and other drastic choices are often symptoms of, and sometimes solutions to, the midlife crisis of responsibility for one's life.

A second major characteristic of the humanistic tradition is an emphasis on the human need for growth and the realization of one's full potential. Human nature, according to this view, is positive and life-affirming. This view stands in marked contrast to psychoanalysis, which takes a rather pessimistic view of human nature, one that views humans as seething cauldrons of primitive and destructive instincts. The humanistic tradition provides an optimistic counterpoint, one that stresses the process of positive growth toward a desired or even an idealized human potential. That human potential is summed up in the concept of the self-actualization motive.

We will define self-actualization shortly. First, we must note a third characteristic of the humanistic tradition that distinguishes it from other motivational approaches. The humanistic tradition views much of motivation as being based in a need to *grow,* to become what one is meant to be. The other traditions, including those of Freud, Murray, and McClelland, view motivation as coming from a specific *deficit,* or lack. This is a subtle but important distinction, and it represents a historical break in motivation theory and research. All the motives we have discussed—achievement, power, and intimacy—are deficiency motives. In the humanistic tradition, the most human of all motivations—the motive to self-actualize—is seen as *not* based on a deficiency. Rather, it is a growth-based motive, a motive to develop, to flourish, and to become more and more what one is destined to become. In the words of Abraham Maslow (1968), who coined the term in the 1960s, **self-actualization** is the process of becoming "more and more what one idiosyncratically is, to become everything that one is capable of becoming" (p. 46).

Maslow's Contributions

Any discussion of the motive to self-actualize has to include Maslow's contributions (see Maslow & Hoffman, 1996). Several of his ideas form the foundation for theory and research in this area.

Hierarchy of Needs

Maslow (1908–1970) began with the concept of need but defined needs primarily by their goals. Maslow believed that needs were hierarchically organized, with more basic needs found toward the bottom of the hierarchy and the self-actualization need at the top (see Figure 11.2). He divided the hierarchy of needs into five levels.

At the base of the need hierarchy are the **physiological needs.** These include needs that are of prime importance to the immediate survival of the individual (the need for food, water, air, and sleep), as well as to the long-term survival of the species (e.g., the need for sex). At the next highest level are the **safety needs.** These have to do with shelter and security, such as having a place to live and being free from the threat of danger. Maslow believed that building a life that was orderly, structured, and predictable also fell under safety needs. Having your automobile inspected prior to a long trip might be seen as an expression of your safety needs.

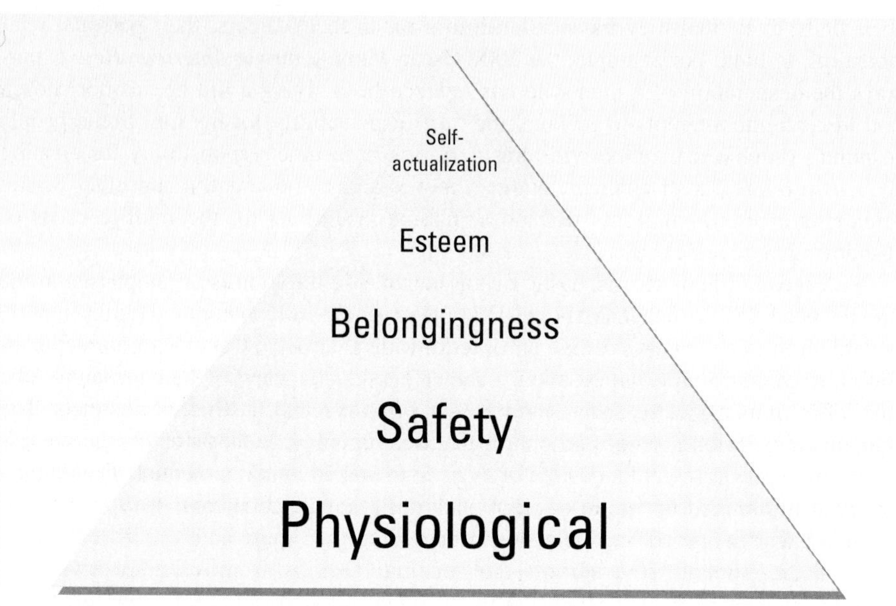

Figure 11.2

Maslow's hierarchy of needs in his theory of motivation. The needs are organized hierarchically into levels. Lower-level needs are more pressing (indicated by larger, bolder fonts) than are higher-level needs.

With only two levels mentioned so far, we can make a few important observations. One is that we typically must satisfy the lower needs before we proceed to satisfy the higher needs. One of Maslow's enduring contributions is that he assembled the needs in a specific order, providing an understanding of how they relate to one another. Obviously, we have to have enough food and water before we will worry about earning esteem and respect from our peers. It is possible, of course, to find examples of people who do not follow the hierarchy (e.g., starving artists, who frequently go without adequate food to continue expressing themselves in their art). Maslow's theory, like most personality theories, is meant to apply to the average person or to describe human nature in general. Although there are always exceptions to the rule, people appear, on average, to work their way up Maslow's hierarchy, from the lowest to the highest level. Maslow also taught that the need hierarchy emerges during the course of human development, with the lower-level needs emerging earlier in life than the higher-level needs.

A second observation is that needs lower in the hierarchy are more powerful or more pressing, when not satisfied, than the needs toward the top of the hierarchy. The higher-level needs are less relevant to survival, so they are less urgent when not satisfied than the lower needs. Another way to put this is that, when people are working on satisfying their higher needs, their motivation is weak and easily disrupted. Maslow (1968) stated that "this inner tendency [toward self-actualization] is not strong and overpowering and unmistakable like the instincts of animals. It is weak and delicate and subtle and easily overcome by habit, cultural pressures, and wrong attitudes toward it" (p. 191).

People typically work at satisfying multiple needs at the same time. It is easy to find examples of people engaging in a variety of tasks that represent different needs in a given period of time (e.g., eating, installing a new lock on the front door, going to a family reunion, and studying for an exam to earn a better grade). At any given time, however, we can determine the level at which a person is investing most of his or her energy. The point is that, even if we are working primarily on self-actualization needs, we need to do certain things (e.g., buy groceries) to make sure the lower needs continue to be satisfied.

In the movie The Edge, *the plot involves two high esteem men who are suddenly knocked several steps down on Maslow's hierarchy of needs by a large and persistent grizzly bear.*

The plots of many movies, particularly adventure movies, involve people who find themselves in situations that force them to take a step downward on the hierarchy of needs—circumstances that require a sudden shift in focus to safety or even physiological needs. The series of *Alien* and *Die Hard* movies are examples of films that illustrate this phenomenon. In the film *The Edge,* actors Anthony Hopkins and Alec Baldwin take a few steps down the hierarchy of needs when their plane crashes in the wilderness and they are pursued by a large, hungry, and very persistent grizzly bear.

The third level in Maslow's hierarchy consists of **belongingness needs.** Humans are a very social species, and most people possess a strong need to belong to groups (families, sororities/fraternities, churches, clubs, teams, etc.) (Baumeister & Leary, 1995). Being accepted by others and welcomed into a group represents a somewhat more psychological need than the physiological needs or the need for safety. Some observers have argued that modern society provides fewer opportunities for satisfying our need to belong than it did in the past, when ready-made groups existed and people were automatic members (e.g., multigenerational extended families and small towns in which virtually everyone felt like a member of the community). Loneliness is a sign that these needs are not being satisfied; alienation from one's social group is another. The popularity of so-called street gangs is a testament to the strength of belongingness needs. Gangs provide group membership to people who might otherwise feel alienated or excluded from groups available to members of the dominant culture.

The fourth level of need in Maslow's hierarchy contains **esteem needs.** There are really two types of esteem—esteem from others and self-esteem, the latter often depending on the former. We want to be seen by others as competent, as strong, and as able to achieve. We want to be respected by others for our achievements and our abilities. We also want this respect to translate into self-esteem; we want to feel good about ourselves, to feel that we are worthwhile, valuable, and competent. Much of the activity of adult daily life is geared toward achieving recognition and esteem from others and bolstering self-confidence.

The pinnacle of Maslow's need hierarchy is the **self-actualization need,** the need to develop one's potential, to become the person one was meant to be. You might think this is difficult, as it assumes that one must first figure out who one was meant to be. However, self-actualizers seem to just know who they are and have few doubts about the direction their lives should take.

Application

Why do people work if they are not paid? When Eastern Europe was under the control of communism, everyone had a job. Although the pay was not good by Western standards, at least most people had their basic needs met; they could buy food and clothing, live in an apartment or house, and have some level of financial, social, and personal security. When communism fell apart across Eastern Europe in the late 1980s and early 1990s, many of the state-supported factories could no longer pay their workers, at least not on a regular basis. Oddly enough, however, many of these workers continued to regularly come to work in their factories. Why did they continue to work even if they were not paid for a long time?

This question was addressed in a case study of a textile factory in Eastern Europe conducted by organizational psychologist Irina Zinovieva (2001). She interviewed almost 200 employees and found that they continued to put a good deal of effort into work even during periods when they were not being paid. She argued that the work itself provided the opportunity to satisfy Maslow-type needs for earning esteem from others, and hence self-esteem. While most psychologists focus on the incentive for work being monetary pay, Zinovieva's research highlights another incentive: that work can provide an arena for self-development, need satisfaction, and movement toward self-actualization. Sometimes, this second incentive can act as a substitute for monetary incentives, at least for a while (most state factories in Eastern Europe have been privatized and now operate on capitalistic, i.e., for-profit, principles).

Research Findings

Maslow developed his theory based on his ideas and thoughts about motivation, not on empirical research. He never, for example, developed a measure of self-actualization, though others did (Flett & Blankstein, 1991; Jones & Crandall, 1986). How has his theory fared in the hands of researchers? Although not all the studies support Maslow's theory (e.g., Wahba & Bridwell, 1973), some recent studies support its main tenets (e.g., Hagerty, 1999). One group of researchers tested the idea that lower-level needs in the hierarchy are stronger than the higher-level needs when deprived (Wicker et al., 1993). These researchers presented subjects with a variety of goals that mapped onto Maslow's theory: having enough to eat and drink, feeling safe and unafraid, being part of a special group, being recognized by others as an outstanding student, and being mentally healthy and making full use of one's capabilities. They then asked subjects several questions about each goal, including "How good would you feel if you attained it?" and "How bad would you feel if you did not attain it?" What the researchers found is that the negative reactions were strongest when subjects thought about not attaining the lower goals. Subjects were more upset when they contemplated their safety needs not being met than they were when they thought about not meeting their self-actualization needs. Just the opposite pattern was found for the positive reaction ratings. When subjects were asked about attaining goals, they reported more positive emotions in response to contemplating the attainment of goals higher in the hierarchy. For example, acquiring esteem from others makes one feel better about oneself than having enough to eat and drink. This study supports Maslow's hierarchical arrangement of motives, while highlighting differences in how people react to the attainment or frustration in the various need levels. Maslow's idea that the lower needs are "prepotent"—imperative for sheer survival—and therefore stronger than the higher needs when unfulfilled was supported. In addition, his belief that people value gratifying the higher needs more than they do the lower needs was also supported by the finding that people rated the attainment of higher goals as more satisfying than the attainment of lower goals.

One study compared groups defined in terms of where they stood on Maslow's need hierarchy in terms of overall happiness (Diener, Horowitz, & Emmons, 1985). All the subjects were asked "What is it that most makes you happy?" The researchers assumed that the answer to this question would reveal each subject's level of need in Maslow's hierarchy. For example, one subject said, "A good meal, and the ability to digest it," which was scored as being at the physiological level. The results showed no relationship between level of need and overall happiness (which was gauged in this study by a questionnaire measure). For happiness, it does not appear to matter what level of need a person is working on. People working on self-actualization needs are not any more likely to be happier than people working on other needs. Maslow also notes in his book that happiness does not necessarily come with working on the self-actualizing need.

Given these findings, we might ask, "What *are* the characteristics that distinguish self-actualized persons from others?" Let's turn to a discussion of Maslow's research on the particular traits that best describe self-actualizing persons.

Characteristics of Self-Actualizing Persons

Most people are not self-actualizers. Instead, most are working on satisfying the lower-level needs, trying perhaps to acquire esteem from others to bolster our status, prestige, and egos or trying to satisfy belongingness needs through our relationships with family members or people in other primary groups. Some are preoccupied with safety needs.

In order to learn more about self-actualization, Maslow conducted case studies of a number of people who he thought were self-actualizers. Maslow estimated about 1 percent of the population are growth motivated and are working on becoming all that they can become. Maslow's list of self-actualizing people whom he investigated included several living persons whom he kept anonymous. He also studied several historical figures through their writings and other biographical information, including Albert Einstein, Eleanor Roosevelt, and Thomas Jefferson. Maslow then looked for common characteristics that could be identified in this group. From this study, he produced a list of 15 characteristics that he suggested are commonly found among self-actualizers (see Table 11.3). Most of the people Maslow studied were famous, and many had made great contributions to science, politics, or the humanities. When reading over the list of characteristics in Table 11.3, bear in mind that the theory does not say "you must make great contributions" to become self-actualized. Students of personality often make this misinterpretation because of the special nature of the people studied by Maslow. It is possible for ordinary as well as extraordinary people to achieve self-actualization.

A notion related to self-actualization is the concept of flow, proposed by psychologist Mihaly Czikszentmihalyi (e.g., 2005). **Flow** is defined as a subjective state that people report when they are completely involved in something to the point of forgetting time, fatigue, and everything else but the activity itself. In states of flow, a person is functioning at his or her fullest capacity. While flow experiences are

Table 11.3 Characteristics of Self-Actualizers from Maslow's Case Studies

1. *Efficient perception of reality.* They do not let their own wishes and desires color their perceptions. Consequently, they are able to detect the deceitful and the fake.
2. *Acceptance of themselves, others, and nature or fate.* They realize that people, including themselves, make mistakes and have frailties, and they accept this fact. They accept natural events, even disasters, as part of life.
3. *Spontaneity.* Their behavior is marked by simplicity and honest naturalness. They do not put on airs or strain to create an effect. They trust their impulses.
4. *Problem-focus.* They have an interest in the larger philosophical and ethical problems of their times. Petty issues hold little interest for them.
5. *Affinity for solitude.* They are comfortable with being alone.
6. *Indepedence from culture and environment.* They do not go in for fads. They prefer to follow their self-determined interests.
7. *Continued freshness of appreciation.* They have a "beginner's mind," for which every event, no matter how common, is experienced as if for the first time. They appreciate the ordinary and find pleasure and awe in the mundane.
8. *More frequent peak experiences.* A peak experience is a momentary feeling of extreme wonder, awe, and vision, sometimes called the "oceanic feeling." They are special experiences that appear to be very meaningful to the person who has one.
9. *Genuine desire to help the human race.* All self-actualizers tend to have a deep and sincere caring for their fellow humans.
10. *Deep ties with relatively few people.* Although they care deeply about others, they have relatively few very good friends. They tend to prefer privacy and allow only a few people to really know them.
11. *Democratic values.* They respect and value all people and are not prejudiced in terms of holding stereotypes about people based on superficial characteristics, such as race, religion, sex, and age. They treat others as individuals, not as members of groups.
12. *Ability to discriminate between means and ends.* They enjoy doing something for its own sake, rather than simply doing something for the goals the activity can fulfill.
13. *Philosophical sense of humor.* Most humor is an attempt to make fun of a perceived inferiority of a person or group of people. Self-actualizers do not think such jokes are funny. Instead, what they find funny are examples of human foolishness in general.
14. *Creativity.* Creativity can be thought of as the ability to see connections between things—connections that no one has seen before. They are more likely to be creative because of their fresh perception of even ordinary things.
15. *Resistance to enculturation.* Cultures tell us how to behave, how to dress, and even how to interact with each other. Self-actualizers remain detached from culture-bound rules. They often appear different from and act differently from the crowd.

Source: Adapted from Maslow, A. H. (1987). *Motivation and personality* (3rd ed.). New York: Harper & Row (original work published 1954).

somewhat rare, they occur under specific conditions; there is a balance between the person's skills and the challenges of the situation, there is a clear goal, and there is immediate feedback on how one is doing. The experience of flow itself can be a powerful motivating force and can be an indication that, at least for the moment, one is experiencing self-actualization.

Exercise

Think of a person you know or have met who impresses you. Try to identify someone who you think might be a self-actualizer. Review Maslow's list of the 15 characteristics he associated with self-actualized individuals (Table 11.3), and identify the characteristics that the person you've chosen appears to possess. Try to provide concrete examples from the person's life to illustrate the 15 characteristics.

Rogers's Contributions

Whereas Maslow focused on the characteristics of self-actualizing individuals, psychologist Carl Rogers (1902–1987) focused on the ways to foster and attain self-actualization. During the four decades of his productive career, Rogers developed a theory of personality and a method of psychotherapy (client-centered therapy). Like Maslow, Rogers believed that people were basically good and that human nature was fundamentally benevolent and positive. He felt that the natural human state was to be fully functioning, but under certain conditions people become stalled in their movement toward self-actualization. His theory explains how people lose their direction. Moreover, he proposed techniques for helping people get back on track toward achieving their potential. His general approach to self-actualization—the person-centered approach—has been expanded and applied to groups, to education, to corporate organizations, and even to government (see Rogers, 2002, for his posthumously published autobiography).

At the core of Rogers's approach is the concept of the **fully functioning person,** the person who is on his or her way toward self-actualization. The fully functioning person may not actually *be* self-actualized yet, but he or she is not blocked or sidetracked in moving toward this goal. Several characteristics describe the fully functioning person. Such persons are open to new experiences, and they enjoy diversity and novelty in their daily lives. Fully functioning individuals are also centered in the present. They do not dwell on the past or their regrets. Neither do they live in the future. Fully functioning individuals also trust themselves, their feelings, and their own judgments. When faced with a decision, they don't automatically look around to others for guidance (e.g., "What would make my parents happy?"). Instead, they trust themselves to do the right thing. Fully functioning individuals are often unconventional, setting their own obligations and accounting to themselves.

How does someone become fully functioning? This is where Rogers's theory of the development of the self comes into play. An entire chapter of this book is devoted to an exploration of the self (Chapter 14). Much of the work covered in Chapter 14 can be traced back to Carl Rogers, who strongly believed that there was one primary motive in life—the motive to self-actualize, to develop the self that was meant to be.

Journey into Selfhood: Positive Regard and Conditions of Worth

According to Rogers, all children are born wanting to be loved and accepted by their parents and others. He called this in-born need the desire for **positive regard.**

Parents frequently make their positive regard contingent on conditions, such as the conditions expressed in the statements, "Show me you are a good child and earn all *A*s on your report card" and "I will really like it if you earn the star role in your school play." In another example, parents push children into sports, and the children might stay in the sports, not because they like sports, but to earn the love and positive regard of the parents. Of course, it is good for parents to have expectations for their children, but not to make their love contingent on the child's meeting those expectations.

The requirements set forth by parents or significant others for earning their positive regard are called **conditions of worth.** Children may become preoccupied with living up to these conditions of worth, rather than discovering what makes them happy. They behave in specific ways to earn the love, respect, and positive regard of parents and other significant people in their lives. Positive regard, when it must be earned by meeting certain conditions, is called **conditional positive regard.**

Children who experience many conditions of worth may lose touch with their own desires and wants. They begin living their lives in an effort to please others. They become what others want them to become, and their self-understanding contains only qualities that others condone. They are moving away from the ideals of a fully functioning person. What matters most is pleasing others. "What will *they* think?"—not "What do I really want in this situation?"—is a question such people ask themselves repeatedly.

As they reach adulthood, they remain preoccupied with what others think of them. They work primarily for approval from others, not out of their own sense of self-direction. They are dependent on others for positive regard and are constantly looking for the conditions of worth, which must be satisfied. They hide their weaknesses, distort their shortcomings, and perhaps even deny their faults. They act in ways that make everybody, except themselves, happy. They have been working to please others for so long that they have forgotten what they want out of life. They have lost self-direction and are no longer moving toward self-actualization.

How can one avoid this outcome? Rogers believed that positive regard from parents and significant others should have no strings attached. It should be given freely and liberally without conditions or contingencies. Rogers called this **unconditional positive regard**—when the parents and significant others accept the child without conditions, communicating that they love and value the child because the child just is. Parents need to show unconditional acceptance of the child, even when providing discipline or guidance. For example, if a child has done something wrong, the parent can still provide correction in combination with unconditional positive regard: "You have done something bad. *You* are not bad, and I still *love* you; it's just that the thing you have done is bad and I don't want you to do that anymore."

With enough unconditional positive regard, children learn to accept experiences rather than deny them. They don't have to engage in efforts to distort themselves for others or alter their behaviors or experiences to fit a mold or model of what others want. Such persons are free to accept themselves, even their own weaknesses and shortcomings, because they have experienced unconditional **positive self-regard.** They are able to give themselves unconditional positive regard and accept themselves for who they are. They trust themselves, follow their own interests, and rely on their feelings to guide themselves to do the right thing. In short, they begin to take on the characteristics of a fully functioning person and begin to actualize the selves that they were meant to be.

Application

Paul Gauguin is most famous for his paintings of South Pacific islanders using lush color, the denial of perspective, and the use of flat, two-dimensional forms. His powerfully expressive yet stylistically simple paintings helped form the basis of modern art. Gauguin was not always an artist, however. In 1872, Gauguin started a very successful career as a stockbroker in Paris. His marriage to his Danish wife Mette produced five children, and they led a content, upper-middle-class life in Paris. Gauguin always wanted to paint, however. He felt he could be a great painter, but his job as a stockbroker consumed all of his time (Hollmann, 2001).

In 1874, Gauguin attended the first Impressionist painting exhibition in Paris. He was entranced with this style of painting. He had a strong desire to become a painter, but instead he put all of his energy into his stockbroker's job and used the proceeds to purchase some paintings by Monet, Pissarro, and Renoir. This was the closest he could come, he felt, to realizing his potential as an artist.

Fortunately or unfortunately, the bank that employed Gauguin began having difficulties in 1884. Gauguin began to take time away from work and started painting. His income went down, and he had to move his family from expensive Paris to the town of Rouen, where the cost of living was lower. As Gauguin devoted more time to painting and less time to stockbrokering, his income went even lower and his marriage started to suffer. Neither Paul nor his wife were happy with their current situation, but

A painting by Paul Gauguin entitled "Self-portrait with Yellow Christ" (1890), from a private collection. The life of Paul Gauguin raises several complicated questions about responsibility, choice, and self-actualization.

Application (*continued*)

for different reasons; Paul wanted more of the new life of painting he was discovering, and his wife wanted more of the old life and for him to return to the Paris life of stockbrokers, banks, and the upper middle class.

After a period of some marital discord, Paul Gauguin left his wife and five children and, with absolute sincerity and clarity of purpose, began to realize his potential as an artist. He fell in with the likes of van Gogh, Degas, and Pissarro, who mentored him in impressionism. In 1891, he decided to flee civilization in search of a new way of life, one that more matched his painting style: primitive, bold, and sincere. He sailed to Tahiti and the islands of the South Pacific, where, except for a brief visit back to France, he remained until his death in 1903 (Gauguin, 1985). In Tahiti, his paintings of indigenous people grew more powerful and distinctive, and on a large scale he achieved his potential as one of the modern world's greatest artists.

The ethical questions in Gauguin's life concern the competing responsibilities that are so evident; he had one life as a responsible banker and stockbroker, complete with a loving wife and five dependent children. On the other hand, Gauguin felt (correctly) that he had the potential to become a truly outstanding artist. Should he have been true to this inner calling, or should he have been true to his responsibilities as husband, father, and provider for his family? How should we judge his decision to abandon his family to pursue his self-actualization? What role does his success as an artist have in our judgment? What if, for example, he had abandoned his family then failed miserably as an artist? What should get priority in life when there is a conflict between one's immediate responsibilities and one's inner calling to become someone else? These are the difficult ethical questions of choice and responsibility that sometimes come to people on their way toward self-actualization.

Promotion of Self-Actualization in Self and Others

People who are not moving forward in terms of self-actualization experience frequent episodes of anxiety. **Anxiety,** according to Rogers, is the result of having an experience that does not fit with one's self-conception. Imagine a young woman who worked hard all through grade school and high school to earn good grades in an effort to make her parents happy. Part of her self-concept is that she "is smart and gets good grades." Then she enters college and obtains some less than perfect grades in some of her courses. This experience is alien; it does not fit with her self-concept as a person who is smart and gets good grades, so it makes her anxious. "What will *they* think," she says to herself, referring to her parents, "when they find out about these grades?" This new experience is a threat to her self-image, and that self-image is vitally important to her because in the past it brought her the positive regard of her parents. Rogers believed that people needed to defend themselves against anxiety, to reduce the discrepancy between one's self-concept and one's experiences. A fully functioning person could change his or her self-concept to incorporate the experience (e.g., "Perhaps I'm not so smart after all, or perhaps I don't always need to get perfect grades").

A less functional response to anxiety is to alter the experience by using a defense mechanism. Rogers emphasized the defense mechanism of **distortion.** Persons who engage in distortion modify their experience, rather than their self-image, in order to reduce the threat. For example, a person might say, "The professors in these classes are unfair," or "The grades really don't reflect how well I did," or in another way distort the experience. Or perhaps the person decides to take only "easy" classes, in which she is likely to earn high grades. Her decisions about which classes to take are based not on her own interests and desires (as would be the case for a self-actualizing reason) but on which classes are more likely to result in better grades to make her parents happy (a condition-of-worth reason). Taking classes merely to obtain easy grades is at odds with her self-concept of someone who is smart, and she may become anxious over the fact that so many of her experiences do not fit exactly with the way she would like to see herself.

A recent study found a relationship between the self-actualizing tendency and emotional intelligence (Bar-On, 2001). **Emotional intelligence** is a relatively new construct that has five components: the ability to know one's own emotions, the ability to regulate those emotions, the ability to motivate oneself, the ability to know how others are feeling, and the ability to influence how others are feeling. This may be an especially adaptive form of intelligence, which we will describe in more detail in the chapter on cognitive approaches (Chapter 12). In the Bar-On (2001) study, the self-actualizing tendency was defined as working on actualizing one's talents and skills, and it was found that emotional intelligence correlated with this tendency. The author argues that emotional intelligence may be more important for self-actualizing than IQ, or mere cognitive intelligence. People may get off the path toward self-actualization, not because they lack IQ or education, but because they have gotten out of touch with their emotions.

Rogers's approach to therapy is designed to get a person back on the path toward self-actualization. Rogers's therapy, sometimes called **client-centered therapy,** is very different from Freudian psychoanalysis. In client-centered therapy, the client (a term Rogers preferred over *patient*) is never given an interpretation of his or her problem. Nor is a client given any direction about what course of action to take to solve the problem. The therapist makes no attempts to change the client directly. Instead, the therapist tries to create the right conditions in which the client can change him- or herself.

There are three **core conditions** for client-centered therapy (Rogers, 1957). These conditions must be present in the therapy context in order for progress to occur. A film of Carl Rogers conducting a therapy session with "Gloria" is widely available and is sometimes used in training therapists. In this film, Rogers expertly sets up these three conditions in his conversation with Gloria (see the analysis of this film by Wickman and Campbell, 2003). The first core condition is an atmosphere of *genuine acceptance* on the part of the therapist. The therapist must be genuinely able to accept the client. Second, the therapist must express *unconditional positive regard* for the client. This means that the therapist accepts everything the client says without passing judgment on the client. Clients trust that the therapist will not reject them if they say the "wrong" thing, or if something unflattering comes out in the course of therapy. The atmosphere is safe for clients to begin exploring their concerns.

The third condition for therapeutic progress is *empathic understanding*. The client must feel that the therapist understands him or her. A client-centered therapist attempts to know the client's thoughts and feelings as if they were his or her own. **Empathy** is understanding the other person from his or her point of view (Rogers, 1975). The therapist conveys empathic understanding by restating the content and feelings for the client. Instead of interpreting the meaning behind what the client says (e.g., "You have a harsh superego, which is punishing you for the actions of your id"), the client-centered therapist simply listens to what the client says and reflects it back. It is analogous to looking in a mirror; a good Rogerian therapist reflects back the person's feelings and thoughts, so that the person can examine them in full and undistorted detail. The client comes to understand him- or herself better by making the therapist understand. The therapist expresses this understanding by restating the content ("What I heard you say is . . .")

and by reflecting back the person's feelings ("It sounds as if you are feeling . . ."). This may sound simple, but it is a very effective approach to helping people understand themselves and helping them change how they think about themselves.

Exercise

Empathic listening is a technique of conversation that can be rather easily developed. You might practice with a friend. Find someone to role-play with you, and ask the person to start by describing a small problem from his or her life. Your job is to role-play a client-centered approach to the conversation. That is, you will try to do the two activities involved in reflecting back: first, try to just restate the content of what your friend says. That is, repeat what the person has said, exactly as you understand it (e.g., "What I hear you saying is . . ."). The second reflecting-back action is to restate your friend's feelings. That is, take any feelings the friend mentions and state them back to him or her exactly as you understand those feelings (e.g., "It seems you are feeling . . . about this situation"). The friend will correct you or elaborate on the situation or feelings. After a few minutes, switch the roles and have your friend be the empathic listener while you describe a small problem. If done correctly, you should feel that your friend is really understanding you and that you are encouraged to explore your problem situation and your feelings about that situation.

Ever since Rogers published his classic article describing empathy as one of the necessary conditions for therapeutic change (Rogers, 1957), many psychologists have attempted to understand the nature of empathy. Are some people natural-born empathizers, or is empathy a skill that can be acquired and improved with training? A study of 839 twin pairs suggests that the ability to take the perspective of another person is not significantly heritable (Davis, Luce, & Kraus, 1994). This finding implies that people are not necessarily born with a predisposition to be good at the empathic understanding of others' points of view. Other studies have demonstrated that empathy can be taught effectively. For example, in one study the researchers measured empathic ability both before and after training in peer counseling (Hacher et al., 1994). They found that the training program, which emphasized listening skills, produced significant increases in overall empathy scores. The training especially helped college and high school students improve their abilities to take the perspectives of other people and understand the others' concerns. Interestingly, these researchers found that, although college women initially had higher starting levels of empathic ability, men and women were equally teachable.

In another study, empathic ability increased with practice (Marangoni et al., 1995). College students watched videotapes of three individuals undergoing an interview about a personal problem (e.g., a recent divorce or the difficulties of being both a wife and a career woman). The researchers' hypothesis was supported; the subjects with more empathy were more accurate in their hunches about what the videotaped person was thinking and feeling, compared with the subjects who had less empathic ability. Moreover, the more practice the subjects had, the better they became at discerning what the videotaped individual was thinking and feeling. Finally, some subjects were simply better than others at empathic understanding. Even though everyone's performance could improve with practice, some subjects

Application

The metaphor of a mirror is a useful one that can help us appreciate how the client-centered techniques work. Imagine that you want to adjust your outward appearance, so you look in a mirror to examine your appearance and see how the adjustment looks. Similarly, if you want to change your inner self, you can use the positive atmosphere and empathic understanding of a client-centered therapist to examine yourself and to contemplate changes. The following example demonstrates the technique of reflecting back:

Client: I just don't know which classes to take next year. I wish someone could make those decisions for me.
Therapist: You are looking for someone to tell you what to do.
Client: Yes, but I know that's impossible [*sigh*]. Nobody can decide what's right for me if even I don't have a clue.
Therapist: You find it exasperating that you are having so much trouble deciding on a class schedule.
Client: Well, none of my friends have this much trouble making decisions.
Therapist: You feel that your situation is not normal; it's not like the experience of your friends.
Client: Yeah, and it makes me mad. I should just be able to pick four or five courses and stick with my decision, but I can't seem to. I know it's silly.
Therapist: You think it is a trivial thing, yet it makes you angry that you cannot seem to make the decision.
Client: Well, you know, it really is trivial, isn't it? I know I can always change classes if they don't work out. I guess I just need to try them out.
Therapist: You see some options, that you can get out of a class if it isn't right for you.

The therapist never directs the client or offers an interpretation of the problem. This is why Rogerian therapy is sometimes called nondirective therapy—the focus is on the client's understanding of the situation, not the therapist's interpretation. The client works to clarify the therapist's understanding and, in so doing, increases his or her self-understanding. The client may come to accept that he or she has been denying or distorting experiences, such as taking classes for grades rather than for their own intrinsic interest. In helping the therapist understand why she is having so much trouble deciding on a class schedule, the person in the example may come to the realization that she has been taking classes primarily to make her parents happy. In an accepting atmosphere, she may come to this unflattering realization, and she might go on to explore how she can change her self-concept to accept this new understanding.

were consistently better than others. Trying to understand the characteristics that make someone particularly adept at empathic understanding is an important topic for future research.

Rogers's theory is important to personality psychology for a number of reasons. His theory concerns the development of the self over the life span and includes specific processes that can interrupt or facilitate that development. He offers a new perspective on the importance of early experiences, similar to secure attachment, but which he calls unconditional positive regard. As in psychoanalysis, he assigns an important role to anxiety as a signal that things are not going well with the psychological system. Also as in classical psychoanalysis, he offers a system of psychotherapy for helping persons overcome personal setbacks on the road toward actualizing their full potential. His work has had a large impact on the practice of psychotherapy over the last half century (see Patterson, 2000).

SUMMARY AND EVALUATION

Motives can be used to explain why people do what they do. Motive explanations are unique in that they imply a goal that pulls people to think, act, and feel in certain ways. Many motives grow out of deficits. For example, someone motivated to achieve must feel that he or she has not yet achieved enough in life. The three motives discussed in detail—achievement, power, and intimacy—are all deficit motives. The fourth major motive—the motive to self-actualize—is not a deficit motive but, rather, a growth motive because it refers to the desire to become more and more what one is destined to become.

Henry Murray was among the first to catalog the variety of human needs. He assumed that individuals differed in the strength of these needs and that the intensity of the needs also fluctuated over time and in different situations. Murray's emphasis was on how individuals differ from each other in terms of the basic needs, such as how some people have a more intense and lasting need for achievement than do other people.

Individual differences in the need for achievement have received a good deal of systematic attention from researchers. The need for achievement is the need to do things better and to overcome obstacles in the quest to attain one's goals. Those with high levels of the need for achievement differ from those low in this need in many important ways, such as the preference for moderate levels of challenge, the tendency to do well in situations where they have control and responsibility, and the interest in receiving feedback on their performance.

The need for power, another deficit motive, has also received research attention. This motive is the desire to have an impact on other people, to make other people respond, and to dominate others. Individuals who have a high need for power seek out positions in which they can influence others and acquire possessions that have all the markings of power, such as sports cars and expensive stereo equipment. They prefer friends who are not particularly powerful or popular. Men with a high need for power may sometimes engage in social influence tactics that are irresponsible or unethical.

The need for intimacy is the motive to acquire warm and communicative relationships. People high in this need tend to think about, and spend more time with, other people. Communication and self-disclosure characterize their interactions, and they prefer one-to-one interactions to large group activities.

The TAT is a projective technique for assessing levels of motivation in people. The technique is based on the idea that what people see is influenced by their needs. For example, a lonely person might see all situations as opportunities to be with people. The TAT was validated by showing that arousing a need in a person influences them to write TAT stories consistent with that aroused need. Recent reviews of the literature suggest that the TAT assesses implicit motives, and it might be best suited for predicting long-term consequences of motives rather than short-term behaviors. Newer measures of motives, including the Multi-Motive Grid, are being developed.

The need to self-actualize represents a distinct tradition in the psychology of motivation, fundamentally different from the tradition that emphasizes deficit motivation. This humanistic approach emphasizes taking responsibility for decisions and making efforts to move and grow in a positive direction. The humanistic tradition assumes that human nature is positive and life-affirming and that most people would become fully functioning human beings if left to their own devices.

Abraham Maslow developed a hierarchical theory of motivation, the pinnacle of which is self-actualization, ranging from lower-level needs (physiological needs and safety needs) to higher-level needs (need for esteem and self-actualization). Maslow also studied the characteristics of self-actualizing persons and developed a list of the traits and behavior patterns that are common among the small percentage of the population working on becoming more of who they were meant to be.

Psychologist Carl Rogers theorized about obstacles to self-actualization and the therapeutic techniques that help people overcome those obstacles. Client-centered therapy is designed to help people regain their potential for growth and positive change. The therapist creates an atmosphere of unconditional positive regard and communicates empathic understanding to the client in order to enhance therapeutic effectiveness. It is clear from research that empathy is a skill that can be learned, supporting Rogers's theory.

Within the field of personality, the motivational approach has a long and fruitful history of helping us understand why people do what they do. Within this approach, people are viewed as having relatively stable amounts of specific needs. Although the level of a given need may fluctuate with the circumstances, a person with a high need for power is likely to exhibit the manifestations of this need (e.g., trying to influence others) more than someone low on this need. That is, the person with a high level of a particular need is disposed to behave in certain ways. The term *disposition* refers to the tendency to behave or react in certain predictable ways. In fact, there is a large part of personality psychology that focuses on dispositions as tendencies to act in certain ways. Because most psychologists interested in dispositions do not infer unconscious motives or intrapsychic dynamics, this part of personality psychology belongs to another domain.

KEY TERMS

PART FOUR

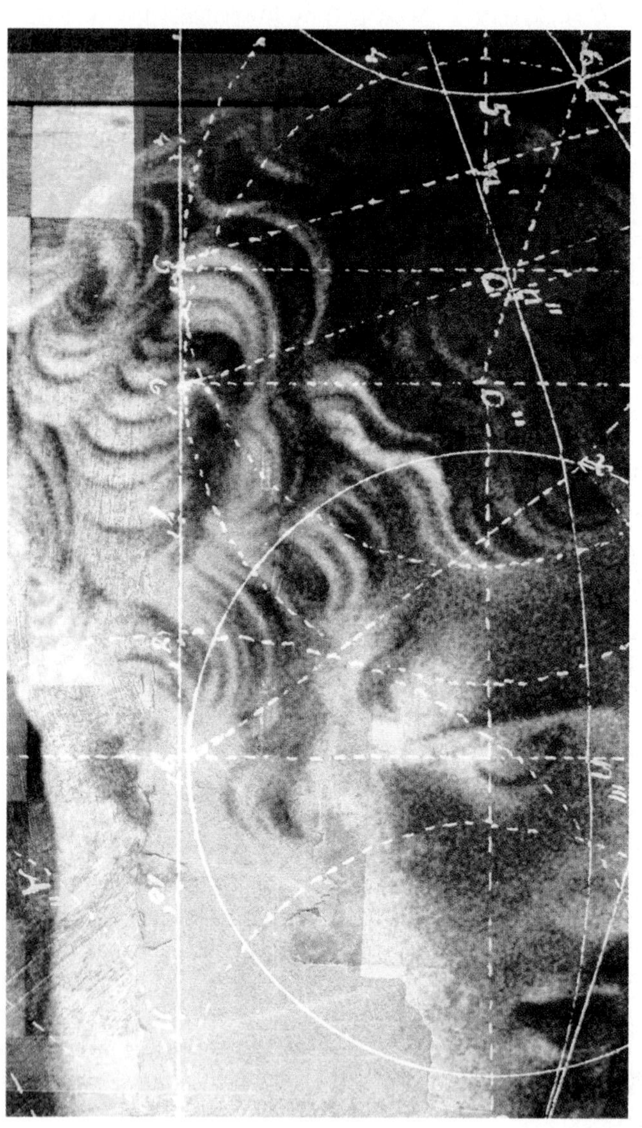

The Cognitive/ Experiential Domain

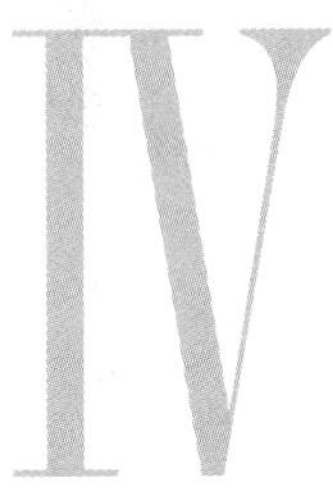

Part Four covers the cognitive/experiential domain, which emphasizes an understanding of people's perceptions, thoughts, feelings, desires, and other conscious experiences. The focus here is on understanding experience, especially from the person's point of view. However, distinctions can be made in terms of the kinds of experiences that people have.

One kind of experience that people have concerns cognitive experiences; what they perceive and pay attention to, how they interpret the events in their lives, and their goals and strategies and plans for getting what they want in the future. All of these kinds of cognitive experiences refer to how people process information.

Humans do not process information the way computers do, accurately reflecting in their minds what is "objectively" given by reality. Instead, even at the level of perception, humans show interesting differences from each other in terms of what they perceive when they process information from the world.

People also differ from each other when it comes to cognitively interpreting or making sense out of life events. We introduce a theory based on the idea that people construct their experiences by applying personal constructs to their sensations. A related theory concerns how people decide on the causes of life events. Often people interpret events by making attributions of responsibility for those events. That is, "why did this happen?" and "whose fault is this?" Personality psychologists have extensively studied how people make attributions of responsibility, and how there may be stable individual differences in the tendency to blame oneself for bad events.

Cognitive experiences can also be studied in terms of the plans and goals that people formulate for themselves, and for the strategies they develop for reaching their goals. People anticipate different futures in terms of having different goals that they strive for. Understanding people's goals, and how their goals are expressions of personality as well as social standards, also forms a part of the cognitive/experiential domain of knowledge about human nature.

A topic related to cognitive experience, and included in this part of the book, is intelligence. Currently there are several controversies about the concept of intelligence. For example, what is the best definition of intelligence—the accumulation of what a person has learned, or the ability to learn new information? Is intelligence one quality, or are there several different kinds of intelligence? While we don't pretend to resolve any of these controversies, it is important that students know the issues in this area and the ways in which personality psychologists are contributing to the debate.

A second broad but important category of experience, one that is associated with, but distinct from, cognition, is emotion. Psychology has seen a sharp rise in research on emotion in the past few decades.

We can ask a straightforward question about emotional lifestyle: Is a person generally happy or generally sad? What makes a person anxious or fearful? Why is it that some people become enthusiastic so easily? What makes people angry, and why can some people control their anger whereas others cannot?

Emotional experiences are often thought of as states that come and go; now you are anxious, now you are not, or now you are angry, now you are not. However, emotions can also be thought of as traits, as the frequent experiences of specific states. For example, a person may become anxious frequently, or have a lower threshold for experiencing anxiety. And so we might talk of anxiety proneness as a personality trait—the tendency to easily and frequently become anxious.

When it comes to emotions as traits, we can divide the main topics into variables that refer to the content, the what of emotional life, and variables that refer to the style of emotional life, or how those emotions are typically experienced. When it comes to content, we are referring to the kinds of emotions a person is likely to experience. The content of emotional life can be divided into pleasant and unpleasant emotions. In terms of pleasant emotions, the typical personality-relevant trait is happiness. Psychologists have recently become very interested in happiness. We will discuss some of this recent research on happiness.

When it comes to unpleasant emotion traits, the research can be divided into three different dispositional emotions: anger, anxiety, and depression. Depression is a syndrome that is experienced by a large portion of the population, and is of great importance in terms of public mental health implications. Trait anxiety has many different names in the personality literature, including neuroticism, negative affectivity, and emotional instability. Anger-proneness is also a trait-like tendency but this one refers to the tendency to easily or frequently become angry, a characteristic personality psychologists are keenly interested in. In this part of the book we will discuss some of what psychologists know about these important emotion-relevant personality characteristics.

Besides content, people differ from each other in the style of their emotional lives. Emotional style refers to how their emotions are typically experienced. Some people, for example, tend to experience their emotions at a higher intensity than other persons. For such high affect-intensity persons, a positive event makes them very, very happy, and a negative event makes them very, very unhappy. Consequently such people experience wider emotional swings from day to day or even within days.

A third major category of experience is distinct from cognition and emotion, yet is a category of experience that is very important to the average person. This category of experience refers to experiences of the self. These experiences are unique in that a person can focus on themselves as an object, pay attention to themselves, come to know themselves. The experience of self is unlike all of our other experiences, because in the experience of the self the knower and the known are one and the same. Psychologists have paid a great deal of attention to this unique object of our experience, self-knowing, and research and theorizing on the self has a long and rich tradition in personality psychology.

There are some useful distinctions between types of self-experiences. First there are descriptive aspects of the self: who are we, what are the important images we have of our past self, and what are the images of possible future selves? A second main component of the experience of self is evaluative: do we like or dislike who we are? This is called self-esteem and it is a central organizing force in much of what we do. And a third component of our self experience concerns the social roles we inhabit, the social selves we show to others, which we call identity. For example, many college students show one identity to their parents and another identity to their companions at school. And people sometimes go through identity crises, especially during transitions in life, such as starting college, getting married, or starting a new job. Understanding how people develop and maintain identities is part of the cognitive/experiential domain.

IV

12 Cognitive Topics in Personality

THE COGNITIVE/EXPERIENTIAL DOMAIN

Mourners in New York City after the shooting of Amadou Diallo. Protests erupted over the killing of an unarmed African male by the police. The court ruled that what occurred the night Mr. Diallo was shot was a series of terrible accidents, errors in perception and cognition on the part of the police officers.

On February 4, 1999, just past midnight, Amadou Diallo, a 22-year-old immigrant from West Africa, was standing on the front stoop of his Bronx home after putting in a full day at work. An unmarked car carrying four plainclothes officers from the NYPD Street Crime Unit cruised by. The police officers were investigating crimes that had plagued that particular area, including a series of gunpoint rapes. This South Bronx neighborhood was one of the most dangerous in New York City. As they passed Mr. Diallo, he backed into the open doorway. On noticing this, the officer driving put the car into reverse and backed up to a point directly in front of Mr. Diallo.

As Mr. Diallo stood on the top step of the stoop, the plainclothes officers exited their vehicle, and two approached Mr. Diallo saying, "Police Department. We'd like to have a word with you." At this point, Mr. Diallo started to back into the vestibule and the two officers then added the commands "Stay where you are," and "Keep your hands where we can see them."

Mr. Diallo reached his right hand into his front pocket. He turned toward the officers while pulling a black object out of his pocket and going into a crouching stance, bringing his hands toward each other. One officer yelled, "Gun!" Two officers fired. The closest officer, trying to back away from Mr. Diallo, fell backwards down the steps. The other officers thought he had been shot.

In the next four seconds, the police officers fired a total of 41 bullets, 19 of which struck Mr. Diallo, killing him almost instantly. When the officers approached Mr. Diallo's body, they found him holding not a gun, but his wallet.

The details of this tragic and controversial case were made public during the subsequent trial of the police officers. Key documents from this trial, as well as news articles on which the above description is based, can be found at http://www.courttv.com/trials/diallo. The jury concluded that what occurred that night was a series of terrible accidents, errors in perception and cognition that had catastrophic results. The officers "saw" a gun, they "thought" one of their own had been shot, and they "thought" Mr. Diallo was returning gunfire, when, in fact, it was their own ricocheting bullets. Their behavior then followed these cognitive errors. Many police academies now analyze the Diallo case during the training of new officers, to understand what factors contributed to such misunderstandings and to avoid similar misperceptions in the future. The final chapter in this case closed in January of 2004 when the City of New York settled a civil rights lawsuit by paying Mr. Diallo's family $3 million and offering an apology for the tragic misunderstanding.

The case of Mr. Diallo illustrates the connection between cognitive factors and behavior. People perceive and think and then act. Sometimes this all happens very quickly; sometimes we take our time thinking things through. We are processing information all the time and using this information to guide our actions. Most of the time, our information processing is fairly accurate, resulting in appropriate actions. Sometimes errors of information processing occur, and mistakes are made. Psychologists are very interested in understanding how humans process information, as well as in how errors occur. Personality psychologists take this interest a step further; they are interested in how people differ from each other in processing information. They are interested in different styles of perceiving and thinking and in different strategies people use to solve problems.

The following case illustrates individual differences in perception. It is not as dramatic as the Diallo case, but it nevertheless illustrates how two people can look at the same object and see two very different things. There were several women from the same sorority in one class. The professor had heard that the sorority had adopted a dog. Curious, he asked one sorority member what kind of dog it was. She said, "He is big and friendly and loves to go for walks and likes to jump up and lick my face. I just love him." The next day, he had an opportunity to ask a different sorority member the same question. She responded, "Our new dog is a 3-year-old male golden retriever. He weighs about 90 pounds, is tall for the breed, and is rusty-red colored." It is interesting that the same question elicited such different information from these two people. The first student offered no information about the breed of dog; instead, she told how she *felt* about the dog. The second student gave details about the dog but said nothing about what she thought of the dog. These two women obviously processed quite different information when asked about the new dog. And it is also quite likely that they think very differently from each other about many things in life. Such differences in how people think are the focus of **cognitive approaches** to personality.

Several years ago, a study was done on what people think about when they are exposed to emotion-provoking stimuli (Larsen, Diener, & Cropanzano, 1987). The researchers showed people slides of emotion-provoking scenes, then asked the participants what they thought about when they looked at each slide (a technique called thought sampling). For example, one picture was of a mother holding a child who was bleeding from a severe head wound. In this study, the researchers were interested not in what the participants felt but in what they thought about—in the information that went through their minds—when exposed to such emotional scenes. One participant said, "My brother once had a bad gash on his head just like that, and I remember all the blood, and how upset my mother became, and my brother screaming and my mother trying to stop the bleeding, and me feeling helpless and confused." The next participant looked at the same picture and said, "Head wounds bleed quite a bit because, in the head, there is a high concentration of blood vessels close to the surface of the skin. I was thinking about the major artery groups in the head when I looked at that photo." The first person who looked at the picture engaged in what is called **personalizing cognition.** That is, the scene prompted him to recall a similar event from his own life. The second subject looked at the same picture and engaged in what is called **objectifying cognition.** That is, the scene prompted her to recall objective facts about the distribution of blood vessels in the human head. The difference between these two persons is a difference in cognition.

Cognition is a general term referring to awareness and thinking, as well as to specific mental acts such as perceiving, attending to, interpreting, remembering, believing, and anticipating. All these mental behaviors add up to what is called **information processing,** or the transformation of sensory input into mental representations and the manipulation of such representations. If you have ever wondered whether other people think about things the same way you do, then you are a budding cognitive personality psychologist. Perhaps you have wondered if other people see colors the same as you do. Is the perception of green, for example, the same for everyone?

An interest in cognitive topics, ranging from perception to problem solving, represents an information-processing approach to personality. This approach to personality grew rapidly during the 1970s and 1980s, during which time psychology in general saw a large upsurge in interest in cognition. It is perhaps no coincidence that an emphasis on information processing in personality psychology took hold during an era commonly known as the Information Age. Humans, in some ways, are like computers, in that we spend a great deal of our time processing information. Unlike computers, however, humans are not always accurate or unbiased in how they process information. Moreover, unlike computers, humans differ greatly from each other in terms of their information processing—in how they perceive, think about, and construe themselves, the world, and other people. Cognitive differences in how people process information represent one domain of human nature that has been investigated in some detail by personality psychologists.

In this chapter, we will cover three levels of cognition that are of interest to personality psychologists. The first level is **perception,** or the process of imposing order on the information our sense organs take in. You might think that there are few, if any, differences in how people perceive the world, since our sensory and perceptual systems are all the same and what we perceive is an accurate representation of what is out there. But this is not true; two people can look at the same situation and actually see very different things.

Consider Figure 12.1. If you look at this illustration, you can see it in three dimensions. That is, instead of being a two-dimensional, flat drawing, you perceive it as having depth, as coming out of the page. This is because your perceptual system interprets cues of depth as representing a three-dimensional object. Another aspect of this figure—known as the Necker Cube—is that you may perceive the cube as extending out and upward to the right of the base, whereas others perceive the cube as extending outward and downward toward the left. Thus, not everyone sees the same object, even though the drawing is objectively the same. An especially interesting feature of the Necker Cube is that most people can actually see the cube reverse directions. If you stare at the cube long enough, you will see the two different three-dimensional cubes, and you should be able to see the two cubes flip back and forth, from up and rightward to down and leftward.

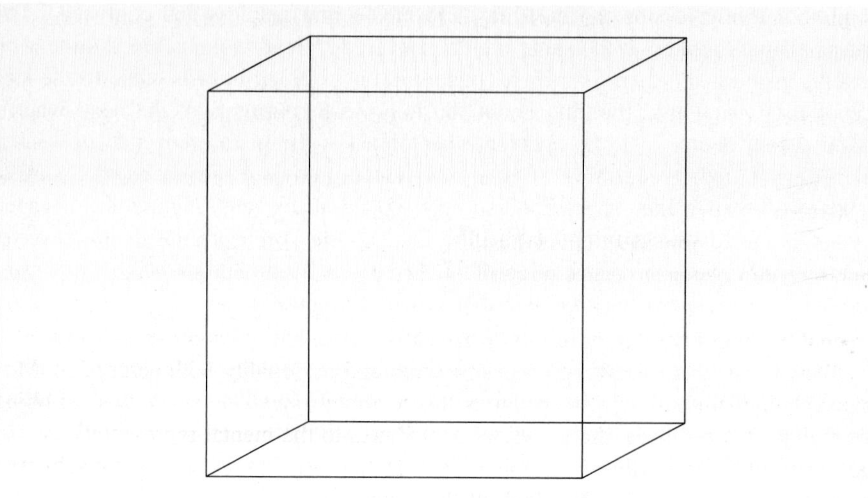

Figure 12.1
The Necker Cube.

Imagine how people might differ in what they see when they look at the much more complicated social world. Even at the level of perception, what we see in the world can be quite different from person to person. Moreover, these differences in what people see may be related to their personalities. It is this reasoning that underlies the rationale for such projective assessment techniques as the Rorschach inkblots. As we discussed in Chapters 2 and 9, what people see in the inkblots can be a function of their personalities. When looking at the same inkblot, one person might see a family of butterflies landing on a garden of flowers, and another person, looking at the same inkblot, might see a dog that has been hit by a car, with blood splattered all over the street. Do you think these two people might have dramatically different personalities?

The second level of cognition of interest to personality psychologists is **interpretation,** or the making sense of, or explaining of, various events in the world. Interpretation concerns the giving of meaning to events. When you are confronted with an event and you are asked, "What does this mean?" or "How did this happen and how will it turn out?" you are likely to engage in the act of interpretation. For example, suppose you have a small mishap while driving your car, driving up a curb and scratching your fender. Someone might ask you, "Why did this happen?" You quickly and automatically make an interpretation and offer it to your inquisitor as a fact: "The street there is poorly laid out. It's too narrow and the curve is too sharp, and lots of people jump the curb there. It's the fault of the road department." However, maybe you offer a different interpretation, equally certain that it represents a fact: "I'm really a clumsy driver; I just can't handle the car. Maybe I should quit driving."

These are two of many possible interpretations, and which ones people offer may reveal aspects of their personalities. This notion of differences in interpretation underlies the rationale for such projective techniques as the Thematic Apperception Test (TAT), discussed in Chapter 11. In the TAT, participants are shown an ambiguous drawing and asked to interpret what is going on, to explain what is happening in the picture and how it will work out. People differ dramatically in how they interpret the TAT pictures, and some evidence suggests that such interpretations reveal aspects of people's personalities, particularly their long-term motives, such as the needs for achievement, power, and intimacy.

The third level of cognition that is of interest to personality psychologists is people's **conscious goals,** the standards that people develop for evaluating themselves and others. People develop specific beliefs about what is important in life and which tasks are appropriate to pursue. These tasks may be age-specific and culture-specific, such as, in Western cultures, establishing independence from one's family in early adulthood. Individuals transform these cultural beliefs about which life tasks are appropriate and important into personal desires or goals. A final topic in cognitive approaches is intelligence. Although this is a large and controversial topic in psychology, the student of personality should have some grasp of the basic issues and concepts in this area.

We will begin our exploration of cognition and personality with perception. Most nonpsychologists think of perception as the accurate mental representation of objective reality. As you'll see, the perceiver contributes to the mental representations such that, even in the perception of simple objects, there may be differences between people in what they see when they look at the same scene.

Personality Revealed through Perception

Most people assume there is reality out there and that the representation we have of it in our minds is a precise duplicate, a flawless perception of the facts. This is simply not true; the perceiver contributes to the mental representations such that, even in perception, there are differences between people in what they see when they look at a scene. In this chapter, we will expand on this notion and cover two topics that explore individual differences in perception. These topics show how perceptual differences can be stable, consistent, and meaningfully related to other areas of life.

Field Dependence

Have you ever heard the phrase that someone "can't see the forest for the trees"? This usually refers to the fact that someone cannot look beyond the details to get the big picture about a situation, that he or she cannot disengage his or her perception from the particular details to get a grasp of the general gist of the situation. Psychologist Herman Witkin studied such differences in perceptual style for almost 30 years. He came to call this topic *field dependence versus field independence.* Witkin's first book was titled *Personality Through Perception* (Witkin et al., 1954), and this title captures the idea that personality can be revealed through differences in how people perceive their environment.

Witkin was first interested in the cues that people use in judging orientation in space. If you see an object that is tilted, how do you know it is the object, and not your body, that is tilted? To make such judgments, some people rely on cues from the environment surrounding the object (are other things tilted as well?), whereas other people rely more on bodily cues that tell them that *they* are upright and therefore it must be the object that is tilted. To investigate this individual difference, Witkin devised an apparatus called the **Rod and Frame Test (RFT).** Using this apparatus, the participant sits in a darkened room and is instructed to watch a glowing rod surrounded by a square frame, which is also glowing. The experimenter can adjust the tilt of the rod, the frame, and the participant's chair. The participant's task is to adjust the rod by turning a dial, so that the rod is perfectly upright. To do this accurately, the participant has to ignore cues in the visual field in which the rod appears (i.e., the square frame surrounding the rod, which the experimenter tilts). If the participant adjusts the rod so that it is leaning in the direction of the tilted frame, then that person is said to be dependent on the visual field, or **field-dependent.** Other people disregard the external cues and, instead, use information from their bodies in adjusting the rod to upright. Such participants are said to be independent of the field, or **field-independent;** they appear to rely on their own sensations, not the perception of the field, to make the judgment.

The Rod and Frame Test is a difficult and time-consuming way to measure field dependence-independence, so Witkin sought new ways to measure this perceptual difference (Witkin et al., 1962). One clever way of measuring field dependence-independence is to create a complex figure that contains many simple figures or shapes. You may have seen children's puzzles that consist of a large drawing with several smaller, hidden figures within it. The goal of such puzzles is to find as many of the hidden figures within the larger drawing as possible. An example of a hidden figures test is given in Figure 12.2. Witkin devised a similar test, called the Embedded Figures Test (EFT), which can be used to measure field dependence without relying on the cumbersome Rod and Frame Test. Some people, when given the EFT, have trouble locating the simple figures embedded within the more complex surrounding figure, apparently being bound up in the "forest" and unable to see the "trees." These people are said to be field-dependent. Other people quickly spot many or all of the embedded figures and, so, are able to see objects independently from the background. Such people are said to be field-independent. Performance on the EFT correlates strongly with performance on the RFT (Witkin, 1973). Moreover, scores on measures of field independence-dependence are stable over time. Witkin and others have extended research on field dependence-independence by investigating its consequences for various domains of life, such as education and social relations.

Field Dependence-Independence and Life Choices

Are differences in perception related to other differences in personality functioning? Just before his death in 1979, Witkin wrote several papers summarizing his research in two broad domains in which field dependence-independence appears to have consequences: education and interpersonal relations. In one large study, 1,548 students were followed from their entry into college until several years after graduation. Choice of major in college was found to be related to field independence-dependence: the field-independent students tended to favor the natural sciences, math, and engineering, whereas the more field-dependent students tended to favor the social sciences and education (Witkin, 1977; Witkin et al., 1977).

A second major area of research reviewed by Witkin and Goodenough (1977) concerns the interpersonal correlates of field independence-dependence. Field-dependent people, as might be predicted, tend to rely on social information and frequently ask other people for their opinions. They are attentive to social cues and, in general, are oriented toward other people. They show a strong interest in others, prefer to be physically close to other people, gravitate to social situations, and get along well with others. Field-independent people, on the other hand, function with more autonomy and display a more impersonal or detached orientation toward others. They are not very interested in others' opinions, keep their distance from others, and show a preference for nonsocial situations.

Current Research on Field Dependence-Independence

After Witkin's death, little research was done on field independence-dependence for about a decade. However, starting in the 1990s, new research began to appear in the

Figure 12.2

An Embedded Figures Test, in which the objective is to find as many of the smaller figures hidden in the larger figure as possible.

literature (Messick, 1994). One new area of research concerns how people react to situations that are rich in sensory stimulation and whether field-independent people can focus on a task and screen out distracting information from the field. For example, one study of 100 police officers examined their ability to disregard noise and distractions in simulated, though naturalistic, shooting situations. Similarities can be drawn between this study and the Diallo case presented at the beginning of this chapter. That night in the Bronx, the officers were trying to focus on Mr. Diallo. However, the light was dim, other people were around, the four officers needed to be aware of each other and aware of the commands being given, and so on. In short, they were in a stimulus-rich environment. Field-independent persons are predicted to be better at ignoring distracting information and focusing on the important details of the event. The researchers conducting the study of 100 police officers in simulated high-stimulation settings (Vrij, van der Steen, & Koppelaar, 1995) made exactly this prediction—that the more field-independent officers would perform better by noticing details more accurately, would be less distracted by the noise and activity, and would be more accurate in deciding when to shoot. Results showed that the field-independent officers performed better on the shooting task under these high-stimulation conditions and were able to give a better description of the witnessed event, compared with the field-dependent officers. Presumably, the field-independent officers could better focus on the target without being distracted by the noise and activity going on in the field around them. In another study, when presented with complex photographs of people, field-independent persons were better at noticing and decoding the facial expressions in the photographs, compared with field-dependent persons (Bastone & Wood, 1997).

Another area of high stimulation is in hypermedia- and multimedia-based computer instruction, such as educational materials on the World Wide Web, which come with sound and streaming video. With the growing popularity of the World Wide Web in education, and the capacity of desktop computers to run multimedia applications, hypermedia-based instruction is taking root in mainstream elementary and secondary schools. This form of instruction involves the presentation of information in multiple media formats (text on a computer screen, graphics, moving video, sound), while students navigate through this maze of sensory and cognitive information at their own pace.

The trait of field independence predicts better performance in simulated shooting tasks among police officers (Vrij et al., 1995). The field-independent officers presumably are better able to focus on the suspect without being distracted by the activity and noise going on around them.

In a study of eighth-graders, the researchers found that the field-independent students learned more effectively than the field-dependent subjects in a hypermedia-based instructional environment. Presumably, the field- independent students more easily found the thread that ran through the various media presentations of information. The experimenters concluded that field-independent students are able to get the points embedded within the various sources of media faster and are able to switch between educational media or sensory fields faster, compared with field-dependent students (Weller et al., 1995). Many studies of this perceptual style suggest that it leads to different styles of learning—for example, field-independent persons are good at selective attention in stimulus-rich environments (at processing specific information while blocking out what is not important), whereas field-dependent persons tend to process information in chunks and are good at seeing connections between categories of information (Oughton & Reed, 1999; Richardson & Turner, 2000).

Some interesting research has also been done on the relation between field dependence and the ability to "read" or decode emotional facial expressions. On the one hand, because field-dependent people tend to be more socially oriented, we might think they should do especially well in reading emotional expressions. On the other hand, if we think of facial expressions as complex arrays of information, then maybe the field-independent persons would be better at analyzing and interpreting such patterns. In a study on this topic, psychologists Linda Bastone and Heather Wood (1997) had subjects indicate the emotion expressed in 72 different faces. However, to make the task difficult, some emotion displays showed only the eyes, and some showed only the mouth. The field-independent subjects were significantly better at interpreting facial expressions than the field-dependent subjects, but only when the tasks were difficult. This finding reinforces the notion that field-independent persons are good at tasks that require finding and interpreting patterns and making generalizations.

The trait of field independence may correlate with the ability to learn in hypermedia-based instructional environments, where the flow of information is fast in a stimulus-rich environment.

Another area that requires skill at seeing patterns, organizing information, and making generalizations is the learning of a second language. Psychologists interested in second language acquisition have examined the role of personality, and several studies have identified field-independent persons as making better progress than field-dependent persons when learning a second language. One study looked at American college students learning a foreign language (Hansen & Stansfield, 1982) and another looked at college students from foreign countries enrolled in English as a Second Language courses at American universities (Jamieson, 1992). Both studies concluded that field-independent persons have an easier time acquiring a second language, most likely because they are better able to perceive patterns within a complex stream of information, e.g., a foreign language.

Is it better to be field-independent or field-dependent? Like most personality dimensions, there are pros and cons associated with both tendencies (and remember, we are describing points along a continuum, not two categories of people). Field-independent people are skillful at analyzing complex situations and extracting information from the clutter of background distractions. However, they are somewhat low on social skills and prefer to keep their distance from others. Field-dependent people, on the other hand, have strong social skills, gravitate toward others, and are more attentive to the context than are field-independent persons. It appears that each of these contrasting perceptual styles is adaptive in particular situations, making it impossible to state which orientation is more valuable (Collins, 1994).

Pain Tolerance and Sensation Reducing-Augmenting

The way in which people perceive their surroundings and navigate through information—whether they tend to focus on the whole or tend to notice the particulars—is a perceptual style. What about other individual differences in perception? One commonly noticed difference between people is in **pain tolerance,** in which people undergo the same physical stimulus (e.g., having to get an injection from the doctor) but react quite differently from each other in terms of the pain they report experiencing. You probably know people who cannot tolerate the slightest pain, who complain about minor discomforts, and who are distressed by even the *thought* of having an injection. Perhaps you know other people who can easily tolerate pain, who don't notice, or at least don't complain about, little discomforts, and who don't even wince when given an injection. This difference between people in their pain tolerance attracted the interest of psychologist Aneseth Petrie, whose book *Individuality in Pain and Suffering* describes her research on and theory of individual differences in tolerance for sensory stimulation (Petrie, 1967).

Petrie's Research

Petrie studied people in hospitals undergoing painful operations, as well as normal subjects in whom she induced pain—through applying heat or by piling weights on the middle joint of her subjects' fingers. In these studies, she was able to quantify how well each subject could tolerate pain. She developed a theory that people with low pain tolerance had a nervous system that amplified, or augmented, the subjective impact of sensory cues. In contrast, people who could tolerate pain well were thought to have a nervous system that dampened, or reduced, the effects of sensory stimulation. For these reasons, her theory came to be called the **reducer-augmenter theory.** This term refers to the dimension along which people differ in their reaction to sensory stimulation; some appear to reduce sensory stimulation, whereas some appear to augment stimulation.

Petrie developed an ingenious method for measuring a person's tendency to either augment or reduce the impact of sensory stimulation. In this task, subjects are blindfolded and presented with different-sized wooden blocks. One block is a long wedge, and the subject can slide the fingers of one hand up and down the wedge. Using the other hand, the participant is presented with wooden rectangular blocks of different size. The participant is asked to feel the width of the rectangular block with the other hand and slide his or her other hand up the wooden wedge until he or she judges that the width of the wedge is equal to the width of the wooden block in the other hand. Participants who consistently overestimate the size of the rectangular blocks are termed "augmenters" because they perceive the blocks to be larger than they really are. Participants who underestimate the size of the test blocks are called "reducers" because they perceive the test blocks to be subjectively smaller than they really are. This task is called the **kinesthetic figural aftereffect,** or **KFA** (Herzog, Williams, & Weintraub, 1985; Petrie, 1967).

The KFA measure has high face validity, since it clearly measures how a person subjectively estimates the magnitude of sensory stimulation. However, it also has construct validity as a measure of pain tolerance. In a number of studies, Petrie found that the KFA augmenters were much less tolerant of pain than the KFA reducers. Indeed, it seems logical that people who reduce the effect of sensory stimulation are able to tolerate more pain than those who amplify sensory stimulation. For instance, Petrie (1967) found that women who were reducers on the KFA task reported relatively less pain during childbirth than did women who were KFA augmenters. Other researchers have replicated and extended these results.

Petrie believed that individual differences in pain tolerance originated in the nervous system. A few studies have examined nervous system reactivity directly in relation to augmenting-reducing. For example, researchers reported that reducers show relatively small brain responses to flashes of lights (Spilker & Callaway, 1969) as well as smaller brain responses to bursts of noise (Schwerdtfeger & Baltissen, 1999), in comparison with augmenters. In this last study, conducted in Germany, reducers also reported that the noise was less loud, compared with augmenters, though the noise was, in fact, identical for all the participants.

The brain evoked response increases with increasing stimulus intensity, but the rate of change differs for different individuals, with augmenters showing a steeper rate of change with increasing stimulus intensity (Schwerdtfeger & Baltissen, 2002). Moreover, the brain evoked potential augmenting-reducing measure shows high test-retest reliability, similar to other personality traits (Beauducel, Debener, Brocke, & Kayser, 2000). Individual differences in brain augmenting-reducing have also been studied in other animals, including cats and rats (Siegel, 1997). In fact, rats that have been bred to be sensation seeking or sensation avoiding have been shown to display brain evoked responses that indicate reducing and augmenting, respectively (Siegel & Driscoll, 1996).

Reducers should be motivated to seek strong stimulation in order to compensate for their lower sensory reactivity, related to optimal level of arousal, discussed in Chapter 6. Supporting this prediction, reducers have been found to drink more coffee, smoke more, and have a lower threshold for boredom, compared with augmenters (Clapper, 1990, 1992; Larsen & Zarate, 1991). Other studies have shown that reducers tend to start smoking at an earlier age and to engage in more minor delinquencies as adolescents, compared with augmenters (Herzog, Williams, & Weintraub, 1985). One study found that smokers were more reducing than augmenting (Patton, Barnes, & Murray, 1993), and another study found that scores of a group of alcohol-abusing persons on a measure of reducing-augmenting were more in the reducing direction (Milin, Loh, & Wilson, 1992). Findings such as these are consistent with the notion that reducers may use substances to artificially obtain a lift in their arousal level.

Exercise

Because the KFA is a difficult measure to obtain, researchers have developed questionnaire measures to assess people's standing on the reducing-augmenting dimension. One example is the questionnaire developed by Vando (1974) and modified by Clapper (1992), called the Revised Reducer Augmenter Scale (RRAS). This measure is based on the notion that, if reducers dampen down stimulation, then they have a relatively high need for stimulation, compared with augmenters. Items on Clapper's RRAS questionnaire present test takers with a choice between a relatively stimulating and a nonstimulating experience. The test taker indicates his or her preference for either the stimulating or the nonstimulating experience. Subjects who prefer many of the stimulating choices are assumed to be reducers. Examples of these items follow. For each pair of activities or events, circle a number that best indicates your preference:

Hard-rock music	1	2	3	4	5	6	Soft pop music
Action movies	1	2	3	4	5	6	Comedy movies
Contact sports	1	2	3	4	5	6	Noncontact sports
A drum solo	1	2	3	4	5	6	A flute solo
Too much exercise	1	2	3	4	5	6	Too little exercise

Many researchers see a strong similarity between the augmenting-reducing construct and other personality constructs related to individual differences in how people respond to stimulation, such as those covered in Chapter 6 (e.g., sensation seeking), as well as Eysenck's theory of extraversion, covered in Chapters 3 and 6. For our purposes here, the reducer-augmenter research illustrates how personality psychologists have studied individual differences in perception, the most basic form of cognition. Let's turn now to a consideration of how people differ from one another in a higher level of cognition—interpretation.

Personality Revealed through Interpretation

Trial lawyers are familiar with the fact that two or more people can witness the same event yet offer differing interpretations of that event. Trials often hinge on having the jury arrive at a particular interpretation of the facts, such as whether the suspect *intended* to harm someone, whether the suspect had *planned* the crime ahead of time, or whether the suspect is capable of *appreciating the consequences* of his or her behavior at the time of the criminal act. Many defense lawyers do not dispute that their clients committed their acts but, rather, argue that the clients did not possess the required intention to be found guilty of a crime. For example, the Menendez brothers confessed to killing their parents with a shotgun. Their lawyers argued that the brothers acted in self-defense and therefore were not guilty of murder, which legally requires intent. The jury interpreted the facts to suggest that the brothers did not intend to murder their parents but did, in fact, act in self-defense.

Everyday life may not be as dramatic as the cases that make their way to courtrooms. Nevertheless, we often find ourselves interpreting everyday events: Why did I get a poor grade on my test? Can I really do anything to lose weight? Whose fault is it that I can't seem to get along with my girlfriend/boyfriend? Such interpretations often concern responsibility or blame—such as whose fault it is when someone gets a poor grade. Other times, such interpretations inquire about expectations for the future—such as if someone can lose weight. Both of these kinds of interpretations—about responsibility and about expectations for the future—have been studied by personality psychologists. However, before covering these topics, let's examine the theory that started the cognitive revolution in personality psychology: the work of George Kelly.

Kelly's Personal Construct Theory

Psychologist George Kelly (1905–1967), who spent most of his career at Ohio State University, played an important role in starting the cognitive tradition within personality psychology. Although a clinical psychologist, Kelly believed that all people are motivated to understand their circumstances and to be able to predict what will happen to them in the near future. He viewed psychoanalysis as effective because it provided people with a system for explaining psychological problems (e.g., "You are depressed because you have a hostile and sadistic superego, probably as the result of an improper anal stage resolution"). Kelly believed that the content of explanations was not as important as the fact that people believed them and could use them to understand their circumstances. Kelly felt that a primary motivation for all people was to find meaning in their life circumstances, and to use this meaning to predict their own future, to anticipate what is likely to happen (Francella & Neimeyer, 2003).

Kelly's view of human nature was that of humans-as-scientists. He felt that, just like scientists, people in general engage in efforts to understand, predict, and control the events in their lives. When people do not know why some event happened (e.g., "Why did my girlfriend break up with me?"), they experience greater distress than if they had an explanation. Thus, people seek explanations for the events in their lives just the way scientists seek explanations for phenomena in the laboratory.

Scientists employ **constructs** to interpret observations. A construct does not exist in itself, but rather is a word that summarizes a set of observations and conveys the meaning of those observations. Gravity, for example, is a scientific construct. We cannot show you gravity, but we can demonstrate the effects of gravity by observing other things, such as an apple falling from a tree. There are lots of constructs that could be applied to people: smart, outgoing, arrogant, shy, deviant. Like scientists interpreting the physical world, we use constructs all the time to give meaning to, or to interpret, the social world.

The constructs a person routinely uses to interpret and predict events are called, in Kelly's theory, **personal constructs.** Kelly's idea was that people have a few key constructs that they habitually apply in interpreting their world, particularly the social world. No two people have the same personal construct system, and so have their own unique interpretation of the world. For Kelly, personality consisted in differences in the way people construe the world, particularly the social world. These differences were the result of differences in the personal constructs that people habitually employed. What do you tend to notice when you meet a person for the first time? For you, it might be important how athletic-versus-non-athletic a person is, and this plays a large role in how you first construe the person. Another person, however, might apply the construct of intelligent-versus-non-intelligent to the same target person. As a result, that person will have a different construal of the target person than you have because you are each viewing the target person through the unique "lens" of your preferred construct systems.

For Kelly all constructs are bipolar. That is, they consist of some characteristic understood against its opposite, or what the person takes to be its opposite. So, a few typical constructs might be smart-not smart, cooperative-uncooperative, tall-short, and boring-interesting. People develop characteristic sets of constructs that they frequently use in interpreting the world. A person might apply smart-not smart to most people they meet and use this construct to parse up their social world into groups. Moreover, they then behave differently toward people in the smart category compared to the not-so-smart category. However, it is the person's own construal that puts the acquaintances into those categories to begin with. Personal constructs are used to create the social groupings.

In many ways, Kelly was ahead of his times. He was post-modern before post-modernism became popular. **Post-modernism** is an intellectual position grounded in the notion that reality is constructed, that every person and certainly every culture has a version of reality that is unique, and that no single version of reality is any more privileged than another (Gergen, 1992). Kelly's emphasis on how personal constructs serve to create each person's psychological reality puts him in the post-modern camp (Raskin, 2001).

Kelly presented a highly complex but systematic theory of personality and personal constructs, which the interested student can pursue in Kelly's own work (e.g., 1955) or in recent summaries of his work (e.g., Fransella, 2003). We will present some of the basic ideas here. His most basic idea was the Fundamental Postulate, which refers to the statement that "a person's processes are psychologically channelized by the ways in which he anticipates events" (1955, p. 46). To this fundamental postulate, Kelly added a number of corrolaries. For example, if two people have similar construct systems, they would be psychologically similar (the commonality corollary). Some couples might be quite different in many ways, but if their personal construct systems are similar, then they are likely to get along quite well.

Like many personality theorists, Kelly also devoted a special place in his theory to the concept of anxiety. For Kelly, anxiety was the result of not being able to understand and predict life events. In his terms, anxiety is the result of our personal constructs failing to make sense of our circumstances. People are anxious when they don't understand what is happening to them and when they feel that events are unpredictable, outside of their control. How do constructs fail? Sometimes they are too rigid and impermeable to new experiences. Something comes along that they just cannot understand. Imagine a woman who, after raising the children and shipping them off to college, decides she wants to work. Her husband, whose conception of a good marriage is one in which "the wife does not have to work," cannot understand this experience. His construct of good-versus-bad marriage cannot make sense out of his wife's new-found desire for employment. Another way that constructs fail is if they are too permeable, if the person applies them too liberally. If a person categorizes everyone she encounters as either smart or not smart, and, once categorized, refuses to change her mind about them, even in the face of contradictory information, then her construct is too rigidly applied. A person knows that her construct system is in trouble when she starts having experiences that she cannot understand ("I just can't understand why you are leaving") or cannot anticipate ("That caught me by surprise").

Kelly's ideas about how people construct their experiences based on construct systems that they "carry" through life was part of a cognitive revolution within personality psychology. Another example of this cognitive emphasis can be seen in a development in learning theory, which occurred about the same time that Kelly was formulating his theory. We turn now to this other important development in the cognitive approach to personality.

Locus of Control

Locus of control is a concept that describes a person's perception of responsibility for the events in his or her life. More specifically, *locus of control* refers to whether people tend to locate that responsibility internally, within themselves, or externally, in fate, luck, or chance. For example, when you see a person who gets good grades, do you think it is because she is just plain lucky, or because of her personal efforts? When you see someone in poor health, do you think it is because of fate, or is it because he does not take care of himself? Your answers to such questions may reveal your standing on the personality dimension of locus of control—the tendency to believe that events are or are not under one's personal control and responsibility.

Locus of control research started in the mid-1950s, when psychologist Julian Rotter was developing his social learning theory. Rotter was working within traditional learning theory, which emphasizes that people learn because of reinforcement. Rotter expanded these notions to suggest that learning also depended on the degree to which the person *valued* the particular reinforcer—its reinforcement value. Rotter's insight was that not all reinforcements are equal. Some reinforcers—for example, social praise and appreciation—are not valued by some people, and such people will not respond well to them. Besides what reinforcements they most value, people also differ in terms of their *expectations* for reinforcement. Some people expect that certain behaviors will result in obtaining a reinforcer. In other words, they believe that they are in control of the outcomes of life. Other people fail to see the link between their behavior and reinforcement. This is Rotter's "expectancy model" of learning behavior. Interestingly, the expectation part involves characteristics that the individual brings to each situation. That is, *the expectancy of reinforcement* refers to characteristics that distinguish specific individuals. For example, suppose a person expects that acting in an assertive and demanding manner will get her what she wants. She wants a raise at work, so she expects that, if she is assertive and demanding toward her boss, she will get her raise. Another person may have the opposite expectation, that acting in such a manner will be counterproductive, so he believes that being assertive will not produce the desired raise. These two individuals have different expectations for the outcome associated with the same assertive behavior pattern. She thinks she can do something to obtain a raise; he thinks he must just wait for the boss to make the decision. Differences in the subsequent behavior of these two people—for example, she is demanding and he is submissive at work—may be due to differences in their expectations of whether a certain behavior (assertiveness) will bring reinforcement (the desired raise).

Rotter published a questionnaire measure of internal versus external locus of control in 1966. Some items from that questionnaire are presented in Table 12.1.

Table 12.1 Sample Items from the Locus of Control Scale

Yes	No	
____	____	1. Do you believe that most problems will solve themselves if you just don't fool with them?
____	____	2. Do you believe that you can stop yourself from catching a cold?
____	____	3. Are some people just born lucky?
____	____	4. Most of the time do you feel that getting good grades means a great deal to you?
____	____	5. Are you often blamed for things that just aren't your fault?
____	____	6. Do you believe that if somebody studies hard enough he or she can pass any subject?
____	____	7. Do you feel that most of the time it doesn't pay to try hard because things never turn out right, anyway?
____	____	8. Do you feel that if things start out well in the morning it's going to be a good day no matter what you do?
____	____	9. Do you feel that most of the time parents listen to what their children have to say?
____	____	10. Do you believe that wishing can make good things happen?

Source: Adapted from Rotter, 1982.

Rotter emphasized that a person's expectations for reinforcement held across a variety of situations, what he called **generalized expectancies** (Rotter, 1971, 1990). When people encounter a new situation, they base their expectancies about what will happen on their generalized expectancies about whether they have the abilities to influence events. For example, if a young man generally believes that he can do little to influence events, then in a new situation, such as entering college, he would have a generalized expectancy that things are outside of his control. He may, for example, assume that his grades will be due to luck or chance or fate, not to anything that he can actually control.

Such a generalized expectancy that events are outside of one's control is called an **external locus of control.** An **internal locus of control,** on the other hand, is the generalized expectancy that reinforcing events are under one's control and that one is responsible for the major outcomes in life. People high on internal locus of control believe that outcomes depend mainly on their own personal efforts, whereas people who have a more external locus of control believe that outcomes largely depend on forces outside of their personal control.

Research on *generalized* locus of control has waned in recent years. Instead, researchers have become interested in specific areas of life, where people might be internal in one area and external in another. This approach is referred to as **specific expectancies,** in which the emphasis is on locus of control in discrete areas of life. One specific area of life concerns locus of control expectations for health and whether or not people believe that their health depends on their own actions (Wallston & Wallston, 1978; Wallston et al., 1989). Another specific area concerns expectations about academic outcomes in young children and the extent to which children expect that their behavior in the classroom influences whether the teacher

Can you think of situations in which having an internal locus of control is a disadvantage? Under what circumstances would a person with an internal orientation experience relatively more stress than someone with an external orientation? What characteristics or situations would match the external locus of control person's expectations? When might it be healthy to have an external locus of control?

Some situations are truly beyond our control and cannot be influenced by us, no matter what we do. For example, a loved one may be dying from an incurable disease. This is not anyone's fault, and there is nothing anyone can do to prevent the outcome. However, even in such situations some people, particularly close relatives, can feel that they are somehow to blame. In such situations, an internal locus of control might be a handicap to personal coping with the outcome.

Another example is the "survivor syndrome" often reported by persons who have lived through a tragedy in which many other persons were severely injured or killed, such as in war or an airplane crash. Often, survivors report feeling that "if only" they had done something differently they could have helped others make it to safety. They often report some feelings of personal responsibility for the outcome, even though the event was horrifically outside of their control.

praises them and gives them good grades (Crandall, Katkovsky, & Crandall, 1965). Another scale was developed to examine locus of control expectations in marriage and whether people believe that their actions can influence the quality and outcome of their marital relationships (Miller, Lefcourt, & Ware, 1983). In all of these areas—health, academic behavior, and marriage—the general finding is that people with an internal locus of control tend to be more active in taking charge, and they take more responsibility for the outcomes in these areas, compared with more externally oriented individuals.

Learned Helplessness

We now turn to another individual difference in how people interpret the world—**learned helplessness.** Research on this topic also had its start in learning theory, similar to Rotter's start. Work on learned helplessness began when psychologists were studying avoidance learning in dogs and subjected the dogs to foot shocks from which the dogs could not escape. During the first few shocks, the dogs would pull at their harnesses, jump and twist, and try to escape. Eventually, however, they seemed to accept the shocks and did not try to escape anymore. The dogs, apparently knowing that they could not escape, would passively accept the shocks.

The dogs were then put into a different cage, a cage where they *could* escape the foot shocks by simply jumping over a small barrier into a different part of the cage. However, the dogs that had received inescapable shocks earlier did not even try to escape in this new situation. It was as if they had learned that their situation was hopeless, and they gave up seeking to avoid their painful circumstance. Other dogs that had not been shocked earlier quickly learned to avoid the shocks by jumping over the barrier. The researchers were surprised that the learned helplessness dogs did not even try to escape and, so, turned off the shock after one minute.

Next, the researchers tried lifting the dogs over the barrier to the safe part of the cage. After being shown how to reach safety, the dogs quickly learned to jump over and avoid the shocks. However, without such coaching, the learned helplessness dogs simply accepted their painful fates without attempting to remove themselves from the unpleasant situation.

Numerous studies document the learned helplessness phenomenon with humans (Seligman, 1992, 1994). Using unpleasant noise rather than shock, researchers set up the following learned helplessness situation. Participants are told that they will be given problems to solve, and they can avoid or turn off the blasts of unpleasant noise by solving the problems (for example, by pressing buttons in a correct order) (Garber & Seligman, 1980; Hiroto & Seligman, 1975). Some participants (the learned helplessness subjects) are given problems without solutions. Consequently, for these participants, the unpleasant blasts of noise are inescapable—nothing they can do will control the irritating and aversive blasts of noise. But do these participants generalize their helplessness to new situations?

Participants are then taken to a new situation and given a new set of problems to solve. This time there is no unpleasant noise. The researchers tell the participants that they are simply interested in how the participants will work on these new problems. Participants who were exposed to the learned helplessness condition in the earlier trials usually perform much worse on the subsequent problems. It is as if they are saying, "What's the use in trying to solve these problems? They are too difficult."

Such participants appear to generalize their experiences of helplessness from one problem-solving situation to another.

Both learned helplessness theory and locus of control theory are about expectancies. In locus of control theory, people who have an external perspective believe that life events are outside of their control, similar to people who have gone through helplessness training. A fascinating study by Hiroto (1974) documented the combined effects of external locus of control and helplessness training to produce impaired escape behavior in humans. Participants who were selected to be either highly internal or highly external on the locus of control scale were run through a standard learned helplessness experiment. In the helplessness condition, participants were repeatedly exposed to a loud and unpleasant sound while they solved problems, and nothing they did would stop the bursts of aversive noise. Later they were given another set of problems to solve, where correct answers would stop the noise bursts. Results replicated the learned helplessness effect (those subjects exposed to the uncontrollable noise during training did not catch on that they could stop the noises in the second phase). However, participants who were high on internal locus of control exhibited less of this helplessness behavior and a higher proportion of them learned to escape the noises in the second phase, despite helplessness training. This important study illustrates the connection between locus of control and learned helplessness, and also shows that the effects of a helplessness experience may depend on the person's general level of locus of control.

In real life, learned helplessness can result whenever people are stuck in an unpleasant situation that is apparently outside of their control. For example, imagine a woman who tries everything she knows to get her husband to stop abusing her. She tries being nice to him, and it works for a while, but soon he is abusive again. She threatens to leave, and this works for a while, but he starts abusing her again. No matter what she does, nothing seems to solve the problem. A woman in such circumstances may develop learned helplessness. She may give up even trying to solve the problem: "What's the use," she may say, "nothing I do seems to help, so maybe I just have to take it."

However, people in learned helplessness don't have to "take it." They need an outside perspective and a new source of optimism. They need someone who can see the situation objectively and who can recommend strategies for solving the problem. Whenever a problem situation looks as if it has no solution or is inescapable, that is the time to ask others for help, to seek an outside opinion (Seligman & Csikszentmihalyi, 2000).

The original model of learned helplessness began with experiments on dogs and was generalized to humans through experimental studies. Humans are more complex than dogs, at least when it comes to thinking about the events in their lives, analyzing situations, and forming new expectancies for behavior. What factors determine whether feelings of helplessness in one situation will spill over to other situations? Under what circumstances do people become motivated to take control of their lives? What factors influence people to decide that they do or do not have the ability to take control of a situation? In seeking answers to these questions, psychologists began to study what was going on in the minds of people who underwent learned helplessness conditioning (Peterson, Maier, & Seligman, 1993). The efforts to answer these questions about humans resulted in a reformulation of the learned helplessness model. The reformulated model focuses on how people think about and interpret the events in their lives (see the following A Closer Look).

A Closer Look

Reformulated Learned Helplessness: Explanatory Style

The reformulation of learned helplessness theory focuses on the cognitions, or thoughts, a person has that may lead to feelings of helplessness. More specifically, the focus is on the *explanations* that people give for events in their lives, particularly the *unpleasant events* (Peterson et al., 1993). Imagine that you had submitted a paper in your class and that you received a surprisingly low grade on that paper. A common question you might ask yourself is "What *caused* the low grade on my paper?" Your explanation for the cause of the low grade might reveal something about your explanatory style. When things go wrong, who or what typically gets the blame? Psychologists prefer the term **causal attribution** to refer to a person's explanation of the cause of an event. To what cause would you attribute your paper's low grade? Was it because you happened to be in a rush and submitted a quickly written paper? Was it because you are simply a poor writer? Was it because the professor who graded it was unduly harsh in her grading? Or was it because your dog ate your original paper, so you quickly wrote another, which was not nearly as good as the one your dog ate? All of these explanations are causal attributions for the event.

Psychologists use the term **explanatory style** to refer to tendencies some people have to frequently use certain explanations for the causes of events. Explanations for the causes of events can be broken down along three broad dimensions. First, explanations for events can be either *internal* or *external.* The poor paper grade could be due to something pertaining to *you* (internal, such as your lack of skill) or something pertaining to the *environment* (external, such as the professor's being unduly harsh). Some people blame themselves for all sorts of events and are constantly apologizing for events that are outside their control. This is called the internal vs. external dimension of explanatory style. The more internal your explanation, the more likely you are to blame yourself for unpleasant events, even those events over which you have little or no control.

A second dimension concerns whether the cause of the event is *stable* or *unstable.* For example, if you were temporarily set back by your dog eating the original version of your paper, then that would be an unstable cause (assuming your dog does not eat all of your papers). However, an explanation that concerns your lack of writing skill is a more or less *permanent,* or stable, characteristic. When bad events happen, some people tend to think that the causes of such situations are permanent, that the causes are stable and long-lasting. This is called the stable vs. unstable dimension of explanatory style.

The third important dimension of causes of events concerns whether the cause is *global* or *specific.* A specific cause is one that affects only the particular situation (e.g., writing papers), whereas a global cause affects many situations in life (all areas involving intellectual skills). For example, you might have explained the cause of your poor paper grade like this: "I am just unable to write; I can hardly put a noun and a verb together to form a sentence." This is a global explanation and might imply that you would be expected to do poorly in whatever task required writing. Using global explanations is like blowing things out of proportion. For example, a person may be robbed while walking through a park at night. He or she might then develop the view that all people are bad—"People are rotten at the core and cannot be trusted." Tendencies such as these and their opposite, the tendency to explain events in terms of very specific causes (e.g., "That person who robbed me is bad"), are referred to as the specific vs. global dimension of explanatory style.

Whenever someone offers an explanation for an event, that explanation can be analyzed in terms of the three dimensions: internal-external, stable-unstable, and global-specific. Most people use different combinations of explanations—sometimes blaming themselves, sometimes blaming external causes, sometimes blaming specific causes, and so forth. However, some people develop a consistent explanatory style. For example, suppose someone consistently blames herself whenever *anything* goes wrong. After arriving at her destination on a plane that was late, the woman apologizes to her friend who picked her up at the airport, saying, "I'm sorry I'm late," when, in fact, *she* was not at all responsible for being late. She might say to her friend instead, "I'm sorry that *the plane I was on was late* and that you had to be inconvenienced. Next time I'll use a different airline." This might be a more appropriate external explanation for the real cause of being late.

Explanatory style can be assessed in a variety of ways. The Attributional Style Questionnaire, published by psychologist Chris Peterson (1991), presents the person taking the questionnaire with several scenarios representing various common good and bad events. It asks

A Closer Look (*Continued*)

participants to imagine such events happening to them. They are then asked a series of questions about the likely causes of each event. The questions refer to internal versus external causes, stable versus unstable causes, and global versus specific causes. While this questionnaire asks about the causes of both good and bad events, researchers typically find that explanatory style for bad events is what matters most. In fact, when using the term "explanatory style" psychologists imply "for bad events."

Another way to score explanatory style is to obtain a person's descriptions of the causes of various bad events. Attributional style can actually be scored from diaries, from letters, or even from TAT stories (Peterson, 1995; Peterson & Ulrey, 1994).

The explanatory style that most puts a person at risk for feelings of helplessness and poor adjustment is one that emphasizes internal, stable, and global causes for bad events. This has been called the **pessimistic explanatory style.** This style is in contrast to the **optimistic explanatory style** which emphasizes external, temporary, and specific causes of events. For example, one scenario on the Attributional Style Questionnaire asks you to imagine being on a date that goes badly, in which both you and your date have a lousy time. You are then asked why this might happen to you. If your explanation involves an external attribution to an unstable and highly specific cause (e.g., "I happened to choose a movie that neither one of us liked, then we went to a resturant where the service was poor, and afterwards my car got stuck in the mud"), then you are scored as more optimistic than someone who offers an internal, stable, and global interpretation (e.g., "I just have trouble relating to people, I cannot keep a conversation going, and I am completely shy when it comes to the opposite sex"). (See Figure 12.3.)

Is explanatory style a stable characteristic? One study examined explanatory style over the life span (Burns & Seligman, 1989). A group of participants, whose average age was 72 years, completed a questionnaire on explanatory style and provided diaries or letters written in their youth, an average of 52 years earlier. The diaries and letters were content analyzed for explanatory style. The correlation between these two measures of explanatory style for negative life events that were generated five decades apart, was .54, indicating a significant amount of stability in explanatory style.

What are some of the correlates and consequences of pessimistic versus optimistic explanatory styles? In Chapter 13, we discuss the role of explanatory style in depression, and, in Chapter 18, we will return to the topic of

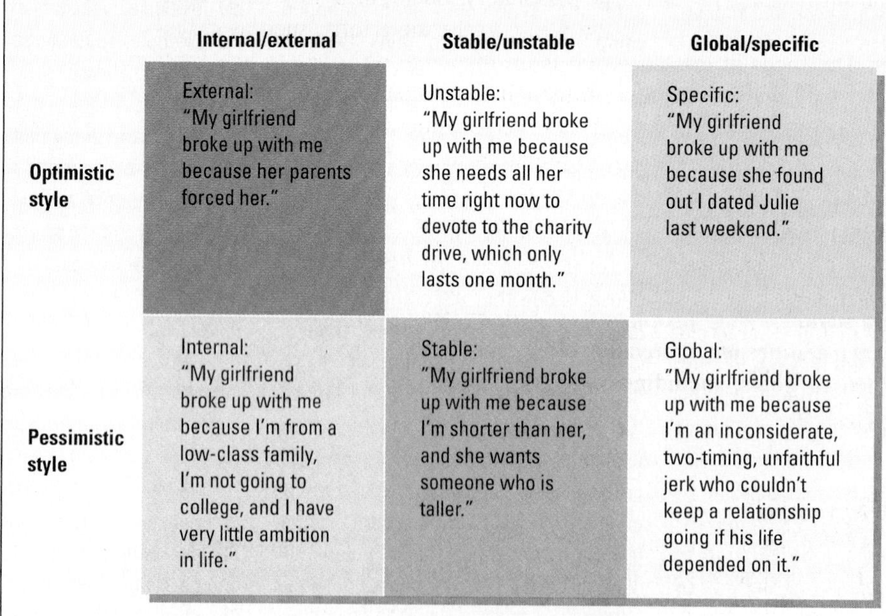

Internal/external
Stable/unstable
Global/specific
Optimistic style
External: "My girlfriend broke up with me because her parents forced her."
Unstable: "My girlfriend broke up with me because she needs all her time right now to devote to the charity drive, which only lasts one month."
Specific: "My girlfriend broke up with me because she found out I dated Julie last weekend."
Pessimistic style
Internal: "My girlfriend broke up with me because I'm from a low-class family, I'm not going to college, and I have very little ambition in life."
Stable: "My girlfriend broke up with me because I'm shorter than her, and she wants someone who is taller."
Global: "My girlfriend broke up with me because I'm an inconsiderate, two-timing, unfaithful jerk who couldn't keep a relationship going if his life depended on it."

Figure 12.3

The three dimensions underlying explanatory style, with their pessimistic and optimistic versions.

explanatory style again in some detail, with reference to health. However, in this chapter we will examine two intriguing studies relating explanatory style to health and early death.

In one study, researchers obtained data on 99 Harvard University undergraduates from the classes of 1942–1944. Explanatory style was scored from questionnaires obtained when the students were age 25, on average. Physical health was then measured several decades later, at ages 45 to 60, using data obtained from physical exams. Pessimistic explanatory style in college predicted poorer health 20 to 35 years later. Indeed, among the subjects who had died by age 60, a larger proportion of the deaths was found among subjects with a pessimistic explanatory style. The authors concluded that a pessimistic style in the college years is a risk factor for poor health and mortality in middle and late adulthood (Peterson, 2000; Peterson, Seligman, & Vaillant, 1988).

How does explanatory style exert its negative influence on health? Researchers have speculated about many different pathways. Pessimistic feelings may lead a person to be passive and to act helplessly rather than to engage in appropriate health behaviors. Or pessimistic persons may have a smaller social support network; they may withdraw from social relations or may be deficient in social skills. One pathway that has been investigated concerns differences in physiological responses to stress among pessimistic and optimistic persons. A study of older adults (ages 62 to 82 years) found that a pessimistic explanatory style was related to lowered competence of the immune system (measured by number of T-helper cells and T-lymphocyte response to a small infection). The relationship between pessimistic style and lowered immunocompetence held even when researchers controlled for such factors as health history, medication, sleep patterns, and alcohol use. A pessimistic explanatory style may be an important psychological risk factor in the early course of immune-related diseases, at least among older people (Kamen-Siegel et al., 1991).

Personality Revealed through Goals

So far in this chapter, we have considered aspects of personality related to how a person perceives and interprets the world. We turn now to a third aspect of cognition, a person's goals and how these are related to personality. Such goals may range from minor ones, such as buying groceries for the week, to the more lofty, such as reducing world hunger. The focus in this approach is on intention, on *what persons want to happen,* on what they want to achieve in their lives. People differ in their goals, and these differences are part of and reveal their personalities.

Different psychologists have offered different terms, such as personal strivings (Emmons, 1989), current concerns (Klinger, 1977a; 1977b), personal projects (Little, 1999) and life tasks (Cantor, 1990). All of these constructs emphasize what people believe is worth pursuing in life, as well as the kinds of goal-directed behaviors they enact to achieve these desires. Other personality theories in this section emphasize self-guides, or the standards that people strive to meet (Higgins, 1996), their understanding of their own abilities and motivations (Dweck, Chiu, & Hong, 1995), or internal abilities related to goals, including people's expectations, beliefs, plans, and strategies (Mischel, 2004).

Personal Projects Analysis

A **personal project** is a set of relevant actions intended to achieve a goal that a person has selected. Psychologist Brian Little believes that personal projects make natural units for understanding the workings of personality, because they reflect how people face up to the serious business of navigating through daily life. Most people, if asked, are able to make a list of the important projects that they work on in their daily lives, such goals as to lose weight, to do homework, to make new friends, to start and maintain an exercise program, to send away for graduate school applications, to develop a better relationship with God, and to find some principles to live by. People typically have many goals which come and go in their day-to-day lives—one project is more important today, a different one is important tomorrow—as well as other projects that are more ongoing.

Little developed the Personal Projects Analysis method for assessing personal projects. Participants first generate a list of their personal projects, as many or as few as they deem relevant. Most participants list an average of 15 personal projects that are currently important in their daily lives. Next, participants rate each project on several scales, such as how important the project is to them, how difficult it is, how much they enjoy working on it, how much progress they have made on it, and the negative and positive impacts it has had in their lives.

Personal Projects Analysis has a number of interesting implications for understanding personality. Researchers have investigated the relation between the Big Five personality traits (discussed in Chapter 3) and aspects of personal projects. Little (1999) reports several interesting relationships. For example, people who score high on the trait of neuroticism are also likely to rate their personal projects as stressful, difficult, likely to end in failure, and outside of their control. Such people are also likely to state that they have made little progress toward achieving their goals. Apparently, part and parcel of being high on the neuroticism dimension is experiencing difficulty and dissatisfaction in accomplishing one's personal projects (Little, Lecci, & Watkinson, 1992).

Researchers have also been interested in which specific aspects of personal projects are most closely related to overall reports of life satisfaction and happiness. Little (1999) summarizes research suggesting that overall happiness is most related to feeling in control of one's personal projects, feeling unstressed about those projects, and being optimistic that projects will end successfully. These aspects of Personal Project Analysis (low stress, high control, high optimism) do indeed predict overall levels of happiness and life satisfaction (Palys & Little, 1983). Such findings have led Little to conclude that "bringing our personal projects to successful completion . . . seems to be a pivotal factor in whether we thrive emotionally or lead lives of . . . quiet desperation" (Little, 1999, p. 25).

Cognitive Social Learning Theory

A number of modern personality theories have expanded on the notion that personality is expressed in goals and in how people think about themselves relative to their goals. Collectively these theories form what has been called the **cognitive social learning approach** to personality, an approach that emphasizes the cognitive and social processes whereby people learn to value and strive for certain goals over others.

Albert Bandura and the Notion of Self-Efficacy The psychologist Albert Bandura was trained in classical behavioral psychology popular in the 1940s, which views humans, and all organisms, as passive responders to the external environment, completely determined by external reinforcements. Bandura helped change this view by emphasizing the active nature of human behavior. He argued that people have intentions and forethought, they are reflective and can anticipate future events, they monitor their behavior and evaluate their own progress, plus they learn by observing others. Because he expanded on classical learning theory by adding cognitive and social variables, the movement he helped start is called cognitive social learning theory. Bandura referred to these distinctly human cognitive and social activities under the rubric of the self-system. The self-system exists for the self-regulation of behavior in the pursuit of goals (Bandura, 1997).

In Bandura's theory, one of the most important concepts is that of **self-efficacy,** which refers to the belief that one can execute a specific course of action to achieve a goal. For example, a child learning to bat a baseball may believe she can hit most balls pitched to her. We would say she has high self-efficacy beliefs for batting. A child who doubts his hitting ability, on the other hand, has low self-efficacy beliefs in this area. As it turns out, high self-efficacy beliefs often lead to effort and persistence on tasks, and to setting higher goals, compared to people with low self-efficacy beliefs (Bandura, 1989). As another example, college students who have higher self-efficacy beliefs about their studies are more persistent in their academic work and perform better in their classes than students with lower self-efficacy (Multon, Brown, & Lent, 1991).

Self-efficacy and performance mutually influence one another. Self-efficacy leads to better performance; then better performance leads to further increases in self-efficacy. As such, high self-efficacy is most important when starting out on some particular task. If the task is complex, it can be broken down into parts or subgoals, which can be accomplished. For example, in learning to dive from a diving board, a child can practice jumping in from the side of the pool, then going in head first from the side of the pool, then going on the diving board and jumping, then finally diving from the diving board. Accomplishing each subgoal along the way can increase overall self-efficacy. Self-efficacy can also be influenced by **modeling,** by seeing others engage in the performance with positive results.

In summary, self-efficacy beliefs can have far-reaching effects on people's behavior. People's beliefs about what they can accomplish will influence the goals they select for themselves. Self-efficacy beliefs will also lead to greater effort and persistence on relevant tasks, often resulting in better performance. People with high self-efficacy beliefs approach their goals with the more positive feelings associated with challenge, rather than the negative feelings associated with threat. And even in the event of failure, people with high self-efficacy beliefs are better able to adjust to disappointments.

Carol Dweck and the Theory of Mastery Orientation We introduced the work of psychologist Carol Dweck in Chapter 11. Her early research focused on helpless and mastery-oriented behaviors in schoolchildren (Deiner & Dweck, 1978, 1980). She noted that some students persist in the face of failure while others quit as soon as they encounter difficulties or their first failure. She started investigating the cognitive beliefs, particularly beliefs about ability, that lie behind these behavior patterns. For example, she discovered that students' implicit beliefs about the nature of intelligence had a significant impact on the way they approach challenging intellectual tasks: Students who view their intelligence as an unchangeable and fixed internal characteristic (what Dweck calls an "entity theory" of intelligence) tend to shy away from academic challenges, whereas students who believe that their intelligence can be increased through effort and persistence (what Dweck calls an "incremental theory" of intelligence) seek them out (Dweck, 1999a, 2002; Dweck, Chiu, & Hong, 1995).

Persons who hold an "entity" theory of intelligence agree with statements such as "Your intelligence is something about you that you can't change very much." Even having to work very hard to achieve success may be perceived as evidence of low intelligence. Therefore, people with entity beliefs may make academic choices that maximize the chances that they will perform well. For example, a student may choose to enroll in lower-level courses because it will be easier to earn good grades with less effort. In contrast, people who have an "incremental" theory of intelligence are not threatened by failure and do not view having to work hard as a sign of low intelligence. Because they believe that intelligence can be increased through effort and persistence, persons with "incremental" views will set mastery goals and seek academic challenges that they believe will help them to grow intellectually (Dweck, 1999b).

Dweck's theory also has implications for how the praise of teachers and parents may unwittingly lead children to accept an entity view of intelligence. Praising a child for his or her intelligence may reinforce the notion that success and failure depend on something beyond the child's control. Comments such as "I'm so happy you got an A+ on your biology test, Mary! You are such a smart girl!" are interpreted by the child as "If good grades means that I'm intelligent, then poor grades must mean I am dumb." When children with an entity view of intelligence perform well they have high self-esteem, but self-esteem diminishes as soon as they hit academic challenges that make them falter. Children who are admired for their effort are much more likely to view intelligence as changeable, and their self-esteem remains stable regardless of how hard they have to work to succeed. Children with an incremental view of intelligence and ability are more likely to work through frustrations and setbacks and reach their full academic potential (Dweck, 1999a; 2002).

E. Tory Higgins and the Theory of Regulatory Focus Psychologist E. Tory Higgins has also developed a motivational theory concerning goals. His theory adds the notion that people regulate their goal-directed behaviors in two distinct ways that serve two different needs. One focus of regulation is called **promotion focus,** where the person is concerned with advancement, growth, and accomplishments. Behaviors with a promotion focus are characterized by eagerness, approach, and "going for the gold." The other focus of regulation is called **prevention focus,** where the person is concerned with protection, safety, and the prevention of negative outcomes and failures. Behaviors with a prevention focus are characterized by vigilance, caution, and attempts to prevent negative outcomes.

When examined from a trait perspective, promotion focus correlates with such traits as extraversion and behavioral activation (which we discussed in Chapter 7). Prevention focus correlates with such traits as neuroticism and harm avoidance and (negatively) with impulsivity (Grant & Higgins, 2003). However, the concepts of prevention and promotion focus are more concerned with motivation and goal behaviors than the standard personality traits with which they correlate. For example, in a study of decision-making and goal striving, subjects participated in a decision task that involved the possibility of making either errors of "commission" (making an incorrect choice) or errors of "omission" (not making a correct choice). Participants high in promotion focus were less likely to make errors of omission; that is they appeared motivated to not miss any possible opportunities for being correct, even if some choices were incorrect. Participants high in prevention focus, on the other hand, were less likely to make errors of commission; that is, they appeared motivated to make sure they did not make incorrect responses (Higgins, Friedman, Harlow, Idson, Adyuk, & Taylor, 2001). Higgins and his colleagues are investigating several other ways that people high in prevention focus differ from those high in promotion focus, such as the kinds of information each finds persuasive, or in terms of how they react to life events.

Walter Mischel and the Cognitive-Affective Personality System (CAPS) Psychologist Walter Mischel had a huge impact on personality psychology when he wrote a book in 1968, entitled *Personality and Assessment,* that was highly critical of the evidence for personality traits. In a nutshell, he argued that people's behavior was more strongly influenced by the situations they were in than by the personality traits they brought to those situations. In more recent years, Mischel has proposed a theory that personality variables (thought not necessarily traits) do have an influence on behavior, mainly by interacting with and modifying the psychological meaning of situations.

In Mischel's cognitive-affective personality system (CAPS), he reconceptualizes personality not as a collection of traits, but as an organization of cognitive and affective activities that influence how people respond to certain kinds of situations (Mischel, 2000, 2004). His emphasis is more on personality processes than on static traits. These cognitive and affective processes consist of such mental activities as construals (how one views a situation), goals, expectations, beliefs, feelings, as well as self-regulatory standards, abilities, plans, and strategies. According to this theory, each individual is characterized by a relatively stable network of such mental activities. Individuals acquire their specific set of these mental abilities through their learning history, their particular culture and subculture, their genetic endowment, and their biological history.

In this theory, Mischel argues that people differ from each other in the distinct organization of their cognitive and affective processes, as well as in the accessibility of these processes. As people move through the different situations in their lives, different cognitive and affective processes will be activated and mediate the impact of specific situations. Some people, due to their cognitive-affective system, will be sensitive to certain situations, and other people, with other cognitive-affective systems, will be sensitive to other situations. For example, if a situation engenders frustration (e.g., being blocked from a goal), and the person has a specific cognitive-affective system (e.g., high expectations for success, the belief that aggression is permissible to obtain what you want), then he or she may respond with hostility. So, it is not the case that aggressive people would be aggressive in all situations (the trait view) but that aggressive people are sensitive to certain kinds of situations (e.g., frustration) and only then will they behave aggressively.

Mischel presents a contextualized view of personality as expressed in **"if . . . then . . . " propositions:** If situation A, then the person does X, but if situation B, then the person does Y. Personality leaves its signature, Mischel argues, in terms of the specific situational ingredients that prompt behavior from the person. To illustrate his approach, Mischel (2004) presents data gathered at a summer camp for delinquent children. All of the children had impulse control problems and had been aggressive in the past. The children were observed over many days and in many different situations in the summer camp. The researchers were interested in verbal aggression. They broke down the situations into five categories: when the child was "teased by a peer," "warned by an adult," "punished by an adult," "praised by an adult," and "approached by a peer." The children showed distinct profiles of verbal aggression across these different situations. For example, some children were aggressive only after being warned by an adult. Other children were aggressive only when approached by a peer. Mischel points out that verbal aggression was not consistent across all five situations, but rather that specific "if . . . then . . ." profiles could be discerned for each child. These profiles were consistent, however, in the sense that kids who were aggressive when warned by an adult behaved that way repeatedly (Mischel, Shoda & Mendoza-Denton, 2002).

Mischel's theory offers an important new way to think about personality, a way that emphasizes cognitive and affective processes that influence a person's behaviors relative to specific situational characteristics. We present this theory in the chapter on cognitive approaches because it emphasizes the internal processes that people engage in to regulate their behavior. It is interesting that Mischel still argues that situations exert the most control over people's behavior, but now believes that it is the psychological situation, that is the meaning of the situation from the individual's perspective, that organizes behavior (Mischel, 2004).

Intelligence

No discussion of individual differences in cognition and information processing would be complete without at least some mention of intelligence. Intelligence has been defined in many ways, and there may be many different kinds of intelligence. One definition of intelligence is associated with educational attainment, how much knowledge a person has acquired, relative to others in his or her age cohort. This is an **achievement view of intelligence.** Other definitions view intelligence less as the product of education and more as an ability to become educated, as the ability or aptitude to learn. This is the **aptitude view of intelligence.** Traditional measures of intelligence—so-called IQ tests—have been often used and interpreted as aptitude measures. For much of the past century, IQ tests were used to predict school performance and to select persons for educational opportunities. They are still used in this fashion today. For example, one study on college undergraduates found that general intelligence predicted 16 percent of the variability in grades, which translates into a correlation of about .40 between IQ and grades. Interestingly, need for achievement, which we discussed in Chapter 11, accounted for 11 percent of the variability in grades, beyond the variability accounted for by IQ (Lounsbury, Sundstrom, Loveland, & Gibson, 2003).

Early in the study of intelligence, most psychologists thought of this characteristic in traitlike terms, as a property of the individual. And individuals were thought to differ from each other in amount, in how much intelligence they possessed. Moreover, intelligence was thought of as a single broad factor—often called *g* for **general intelligence.** As tests were developed, however, researchers began to identify separate abilities—such as verbal ability, memory ability, perceptual ability, and arithmetic ability. The Scholastic Aptitude Test, or SAT, is one example that most college students are familiar with because they have taken this test. The SAT gives two scores—a verbal score and a mathematical score—and is an example of two differentiated kinds of intelligence. As the name implies, many believe the SAT is an aptitude measure, that it measures the ability to learn and acquire new information. However, the SAT contains questions that only persons already with an education can answer and, so, is really, some argue, an achievement test. Nevertheless, the SAT predicts college grade-point average and, so, is useful in selecting persons who are likely to do well in higher education settings.

Other intelligence tests yield even more than two scores. For example, the Wechsler Intelligence Scale for Children—Revised (revised in 1991, originally published by Wechsler, 1949) yields 11 subtest scores, 6 of which require or depend on verbal ability and 5 of which are nonverbal, such as finding missing elements in a picture and assembling a puzzle. Also, the test yields 2 broad scores to represent verbal and performance intelligence. Psychologists use the multiple scores to evaluate a person's strengths and weaknesses, as well as to understand how the individual uniquely approaches and solves problems.

A widely accepted definition of intelligence, proposed by Gardner (1983), is that it is the application of cognitive skill and knowledge to solve problems, learn, and achieve goals that are valued by the individual and the culture. With intelligence defined this broadly, it is obvious that there are many kinds of intelligence, perhaps several more beyond the traditional verbal, mathematical, and performance distinctions. Howard Gardner has proposed a theory of **multiple intelligences,** which includes seven forms, such as interpersonal intelligence (social skills, ability to communicate and get along with others) and intrapersonal intelligence (insight into oneself, one's emotions, and one's motives). Gardner also includes kinesthetic intelligence—describing the abilities of athletes, dancers, and acrobats—and musical intelligence (Gardner, 1999). Other experts are adding to the growing list of forms of intelligence, such as the concept of emotional intelligence, proposed by psychologists Peter Salovey and Jack Mayer (1990) and popularized by journalist Dan Goleman (1995). The concept of emotional intelligence is receiving a great deal of attention from researchers (see Zeidner, Matthews, Roberts, & MacCann, 2003, for a review).

Exercise

The concept of emotional intelligence has been proposed to explain why some people with a lot of academic intelligence do not appear to have a lot of practical intelligence, people skills, or what might be called street smarts. Goleman (1995), in his highly readable book *Emotional Intelligence,* presents many cases of people who have high levels of traditional intelligence yet fail in various areas of their lives, such as in relationships. Goleman also reviews the psychological literature and comes to the conclusion that traditional measures of intelligence, although predicting school performance fairly well, actually do a rather poor job of predicting later life outcomes, such as occupational attainment, salary, professional status, and quality of marriage (e.g., Vaillant, 1977). *Emotional intelligence,* Goleman argues, is more strongly predictive of these life outcomes.

Emotional intelligence is proposed as a set of five specific abilities:

- Awareness of one's own feelings and bodily signals and an ability to identify one's own emotions and to make distinctions (such as realizing the fear that lies behind anger)
- Ability to manage and regulate emotions, especially negative emotions, and to manage stress
- Control of one's impulses—directing one's attention and effort, delaying gratification, and staying on task toward goals
- Ability to decode the social and emotional cues of others, to listen, and to take the perspective of others (empathy)
- Leadership, the ability to influence and guide others without their becoming angry or resentful, the ability to elicit cooperation, and skill in negotiation and conflict resolution

It is easy to see how these skills and abilities relate to positive life outcomes and how they are so different from traditional concepts of intelligence, such as scholastic achievement and scholastic ability. Can you think of someone you know who is very high on scholastic ability yet deficient in one or more of the aspects of emotional intelligence? Such a person might be successful in school yet have problems in other areas of life, such as making friends or becoming independent from his or her family. Alternatively, can you think of someone you know who is high on emotional intelligence yet low on scholastic ability?

Gardner's concept of multiple intelligences is controversial. Some intelligence researchers feel that these separate abilities are correlated enough with each other (implying that they tend to co-occur in the same persons) to justify thinking of intelligence as *g*, a general factor (e.g., Hernstein & Murray, 1994; Petrill, 2002; Rammsayer & Brandler, 2002). Other experts acknowledge a few broad distinctions, such as the verbal and mathematical intelligences that are so much a part of school systems in the United States. Other experts, including many educators, are examining the implications of the multiple intelligences notion. Some schools are making curriculum changes designed to develop and strengthen various forms of intelligence in their students. For example, some schools are teaching units in emotional intelligence. Other schools offer classes for those high on nonverbal intelligence. Other schools are fostering character education, which can be thought of as a form of civic intelligence. These modern educational efforts are the direct outcomes of research being conducted by personality psychologists exploring the basic nature of intelligence.

We cannot leave the concept of intelligence without looking at the **cultural context** of this construct. What is defined as "intelligent behavior" will obviously differ across cultures. For example, among the people who live on the islands of Micronesia, the ability to navigate the ocean and other maritime skills are considered superior forms of intelligence. Among Eskimos who hunt along the shores in their kayaks, the ability to develop a cognitive map of the complex shoreline in Alaska is a valued ability. Many psychologists define culture, in part, as the shared notions about what counts as efficient problem solving (Wertsch & Kanner, 1992). These skills then become part of the way successful people think in that culture. Western cultures, for example, emphasize verbal skills, both written and oral, as well as the mathematical and spatial skills necessary in a technologically advanced culture. Other cultures, however, might guide their members to develop different problem-solving skills, such as developing a sense of direction or a knowledge of animal behavior.

Because of these considerations, we should always view intelligence as comprised of the skills valued in a particular culture. However, Western culture—along with its economic, social, and political systems—is proliferating into countries around the world. Will the world become a monoculture? If so, will there become one form of intelligence, which is universally valued? Or will cultures maintain separate identities and define differences in what counts as intelligent behavior? For example, currently most people in Europe speak more than one language, and many speak three or more, because of the problem-solving advantage a multilingual person has in Europe. Many Europeans consider Americans to be linguistically challenged or, less charitably, verbally unintelligent because most Americans know only one language. Just try traveling in countries shielded from Western influence, such as formerly communist countries, and you will experience how it feels to be verbally unintelligent.

A new variable in intelligence research is called **inspection time,** which refers to the time it takes a person to make a simple discrimination between two displayed objects. For example, two lines appear on a computer screen and the subject's task is to say which one is longer. The time it takes the subject to inspect the two lines, measured in milliseconds (thousandths of a second), before making the discrimination is the measure of inspection time. This variable is highly related to standard measures of general intelligence (Osmon & Jackson, 2002). Another similar measure is the ability to discriminate auditory intervals that differ only in the range of a few milliseconds, which also is related to general intelligence (Rammsayer & Brandler, 2002). Findings such as these suggest that brain mechanisms specifically involved in discriminations of extremely brief time intervals represent a sensitive indicator of general intelligence.

There are many debates about intelligence that are beyond the scope of an introductory personality text. If you are interested, you can go to advanced sources, such as the journal *Intelligence,* or to books, such as Neisser's (1998) or Hernstein and Murray's controversial *The Bell Curve* (1994) and the direct responses to the controversy created by *The Bell Curve*—such as Fraser (1995) and Jacoby and Glauberman (1995). Other alternatives to the Hernstein and Murray position include works by Sternberg (1985), Gardner (1983), and Simonton (1991). You should know that there are several current debates about intelligence, including whether it can be measured accurately, whether measures of intelligence are biased to favor persons from the dominant majority group in the culture, the extent to which intelligence is heritable and the implications of heritability, whether different racial groups differ with respect to intelligence, and whether race differences should be interpreted as social class differences. These issues are politicized and have many implications for social and government policy, and so are generating much heated debate. Personality psychologists are playing an important role by doing the research necessary to provide a scientific approach to these issues.

SUMMARY AND EVALUATION

Cognitive topics in personality psychology are a broad class of subject matter. People differ from each other in many ways, in how they think as well as in how they perceive, interpret, remember, want, and anticipate the events in their lives. In this chapter, we organized the coverage into four broad categories: perception, interpretation, goals, and intelligence.

We began by examining some ways in which personality is related to perceptual differences between people. Field independence-dependence concerns the ability to see the trees despite the forest. This individual difference in perceptual style has to do with the ability to focus on the details, despite the clutter of background information. This style of perceiving may have important implications for learning styles and career choices.

The second perceptual difference we discussed was sensory reducing-augmenting. This dimension originally referred to the tendency to reduce or augment painful stimuli and was first related to individual differences in pain tolerance. It is now more generally used to refer to individual differences in sensitivity to sensory stimulation, with some individuals (augmenters) being more sensitive than others (reducers). This individual difference may have important implications for the development of problem behaviors associated with seeking stimulation, such as smoking or other forms of drug abuse.

Another aspect of cognition is how people interpret events in their lives. This approach to personality has its roots in the work of George Kelly. His personal construct theory emphasizes how people construct their experiences by using their constructs to make sense out of the world. Another general difference between people is in locus of control, the tendency to interpret events either as under one's control or as not under one's control. Many researchers now apply the locus of control concept in particular life domains, such as health locus of control or relationship locus of control.

Learned helplessness is the feeling engendered when a person experiences an inescapable aversive situation. The feeling of helplessness may also generalize to new situations, so that the person continues to act helplessly and fails to seek solutions to his or her problems. The theory of learned helplessness was reformulated to incorporate how people think about events in their lives, particularly unpleasant events. Psychologists have focused on specific dimensions of people's explanations, such as whether the cause is internal or external to the person, whether it is stable or unstable, and whether it is global or specific. A pessimistic explanatory style is internal, stable, and global.

Personality can also be revealed by how people select projects and tasks to pursue in life. If you know what a person really wants out of life, then you probably know that person fairly well. Our goals define us, and the strategies with which we pursue those desires illustrate the active aspects of personality in our daily lives.

Cognitive social learning theory was introduced and several specific examples of this approach were described. All of the example theories incorporate the concept of goals and related cognitive activities, such as expectancies, strategies, and beliefs about one's abilities. These theories are important new additions to the psychology of personality because they emphasize how the psychological situation is a function of characteristics of the person, e.g., their self-efficacy beliefs, etc.

Intelligence was also discussed in this chapter, along with different views on intelligence (as academic achievement versus an aptitude for learning). We reviewed the historical development of intelligence as starting with the view of this as a single and general trait up to today's trend toward a multiple intelligences view. We also noted that culture influences which skills and achievements contribute toward intelligence and presented some results on a biological interpretation of intelligence. In addition, we noted the important and controversial debates currently center stage in the area of intelligence.

KEY TERMS

Cognitive Approaches 392
Personalizing Cognition 393
Objectifying Cognition 393
Cognition 393
Information Processing 393
Perception 393
Interpretation 394
Conscious Goals 395
Rod and Frame Test (RFT) 395
Field-Dependent 396
Field-Independent 396
Pain Tolerance 399
Reducer-Augmenter Theory 400
Kinesthetic Figural Aftereffect (KFA) 400
Constructs 403
Personal Constructs 403
Post-Modernism 403
Locus of Control 404
Generalized Expectancies 406
External Locus of Control 406
Internal Locus of Control 406
Specific Expectancies 406
Learned Helplessness 407
Causal Attribution 409
Explanatory Style 409
Pessimistic Explanatory Style 410
Optimistic Explanatory Style 410
Personal Project 411
Cognitive Social Learning Approach 412
Self-Efficacy 413
Modeling 413
Promotion Focus 414
Prevention Focus 414
If . . . Then . . . Propositions 415
Achievement View of Intelligence 416
Aptitude View of Intelligence 416
General Intelligence 416
Multiple Intelligences 417
Emotional Intelligence 417
Cultural Context 418
Inspection Time 418

13

Emotion and Personality

THE COGNITIVE/EXPERIENTIAL DOMAIN

The emotion of fear is characterized by a distinct facial expression. Fear also has a distinctly unpleasant subjective feeling. There are also the associated changes in physiology, such as heart rate increases and increased blood flow to the large muscles of the legs and arms. These changes prepare the frightened person for the intense action tendency associated with fear, e.g., to flee or to fight.

Imagine you are traveling to visit a friend in a city to which you've never been before. You've taken a train to this city and are walking to your friend's apartment from the station. The train was late, so it is dark as you begin to make your way in the unfamiliar neighborhood. Your directions seem a little vague, and after 20 minutes of walking you are beginning to think they are incorrect. It is late and there are not many people on the street. You are certain that the directions are wrong, and now you just need to find a phone to call your friend. You decide to take a shortcut through an alley and head back to the train station. The alley is dark, but short, and it will get you back to the train station faster, so you start down the alley. You are alert, a bit on edge, as you are really out of your element. You look over your shoulder and notice that someone has followed you down the alley. Your heart is pounding. You turn and look ahead, and you see that someone has entered the alley in front of you as well. You suddenly feel trapped and you freeze. You are in a real predicament, as your way is blocked in both directions. Your breathing is rapid and you feel confused, light-headed. Your mind is racing, but you are not sure what to do as the two people are closing in on you from both directions. Your palms are sweating and you feel the tension in your neck and throat, as if you might scream any second. The two people are getting closer and closer to you. You feel nervousness in your stomach as you look first in front, then behind. You want to run but cannot decide which way to go. You are paralyzed with fear, you stand there, trembling, not knowing whether you can run away or whether you will have to fight for your life. Suddenly, one of the persons calls out your name. You realize it is your friend, who has come with his roommate to look for you between the train station and the apartment. You breathe a sigh of relief, and quickly your state of fear subsides, your body calms, your mind clears, and you greet your friend with an enthusiastic, "Am I glad to see you!"

In this example, you experienced the emotion of fear. You also experienced the emotion of relief, and perhaps even elation, at being rescued by your friend. **Emotions** can be defined by their three components. First, emotions have distinct subjective feelings, or affects, associated with them. Second, emotions are accompanied by bodily changes, mostly in the nervous system, and these produce associated changes in breathing, heart rate, muscle tension, blood chemistry, and facial and bodily expressions. And, third, emotions are accompanied by distinct **action tendencies,** or increases in the probabilities of certain behaviors. With the emotional feeling of fear, there are subjective feelings of anxiety, confusion, and panic. There are also associated changes in bodily function, such as heart rate increases, decreased blood flow to the digestive system (making for stomach queasiness), and increased blood flow to the large muscles of the legs and arms. These changes prepare you for the intense activity sometimes associated with fear. The activity, or action tendency, associated with fear is to flee or to fight.

Why are personality psychologists interested in emotions? People differ from each other in their emotional reactions, even to the same events, so emotions are useful in distinguishing among persons. For example, imagine losing your wallet, which contains a large sum of money, your credit card, and all your identification, including your driver's license. What emotions do you think you would feel—anger, embarrassment, hopelessness, frustration, panic, fear, shame, guilt? Different people would have different emotional reactions to this life event, and understanding how and why people differ in their emotional reactions is part of understanding personality.

Other theories of emotion emphasize the functions that emotions play, such as generating short-term adaptive actions that help us survive. For example, the emotion of disgust has the adaptive value of prompting us to quickly spit out something that is not good for us. Interestingly, the expression of disgust, even when the feeling is evoked by a thought or something that is only psychologically distasteful, is to wrinkle the nose, open the mouth, and protrude one's tongue as if spitting something out.

In his 1872 book *The Expression of the Emotions in Man and Animals,* Charles Darwin proposed a **functional analysis** of emotions and emotional expressions. His analysis focuses on the "why" of emotions and expressions, in particular in terms of whether they increase the fitness of individuals (see Chapter 8 of this textbook). In his book he describes his observations of animals, his own children, and other people, linking particular expressions with specific emotions. He recognized that evolution by natural selection applied not only to anatomic structures but also to the "mind," including the emotions and their expressions. How do emotions increase evolutionary fitness? Darwin concluded that emotional expressions communicate information from one animal to another about what is likely to happen. The dog baring its teeth and bristling the hair on its back is communicating to others that he is likely to attack. If others recognize this communication, they may choose to back away, thereby avoiding the attack. While many modern emotion theorists accept this functional emphasis, most personality psychologists approach emotion with an interest in how and why people differ from each other in terms of emotions.

Issues in Emotion Research

There are several major issues which divide the field of emotion research (Davidson, Scherer, & Goldsmith, 2003). Psychologists typically hold an opinion on each of these issues. We will consider two of these issues, begining with the distinction between emotional states and emotional traits.

Emotional States versus Emotional Traits

We typically think of emotions as states that come and go. A person gets angry, then gets over it. A person becomes sad, then snaps out of it. **Emotional states** are *transitory.* Moreover, emotional states depend more on the situation a person is in than on the specific person. A man is angry *because* he was unfairly treated. A woman is sad *because* her bicycle was stolen. Most people would be angry or sad in these situations. Emotions as states are transitory, they have a specific cause, and that cause typically originates outside of the person (something happens in the environment).

We can also think of emotions as dispositions, or traits. For example, we often characterize people by stating what emotions they *frequently* experience or express: "Mary is cheerful and enthusiastic," or "John is frequently angry and often loses his temper." Here we are using emotions to describe dispositions, or persistent emotional traits, that a person has. Emotional traits are consistencies in a person's emotional life. Traits, as you'll recall from Chapter 3, are patterns in a person's behavior or experience that are at least somewhat consistent from situation to situation and that are at least somewhat stable over time. Thus, an **emotional trait** is a pattern of emotional reactions that a person consistently experiences across a variety of life situations. This pattern of emotional experiences is stable over time and characteristic for each person. To continue with the case of Mary, we might expect her to be cheerful at home, at school, and at work. Moreover, by referring to cheerfulness as an emotional trait, we would expect that she was cheerful last year and will most likely be cheerful next year, barring any major changes to her personality.

Traits are considered to be internal to the person, and we think of traits as causing people to behave or feel in certain ways. If Mary's cheerfulness is a trait, then we assume that her enthusiastic behavior and pleasant manner is a reflection of this internal disposition and is not totally due to an external event. In a sense, Mary carries her cheerfulness with her from situation to situation and over time.

Categorical versus Dimensional Approach to Emotion

Emotion researchers can be divided into two camps based on their answers to the following question: What is the best way to think about emotions? Some suggest emotions are best thought of as a small number of primary and distinct emotions (anger, joy, anxiety, sadness). Others suggest that emotions are best thought of as broad dimensions of experience (e.g., a dimension ranging from pleasant to unpleasant). Those who think that primary emotions are the key are said to take the **categorical approach.** Hundreds of terms describe different categories of emotions. Averill (1975), for example, compiled a list of 550 terms that describe different feeling states. This is similar to the situation with basic trait terms, in which psychologists started with thousands of trait adjectives and searched for the fundamental factors that

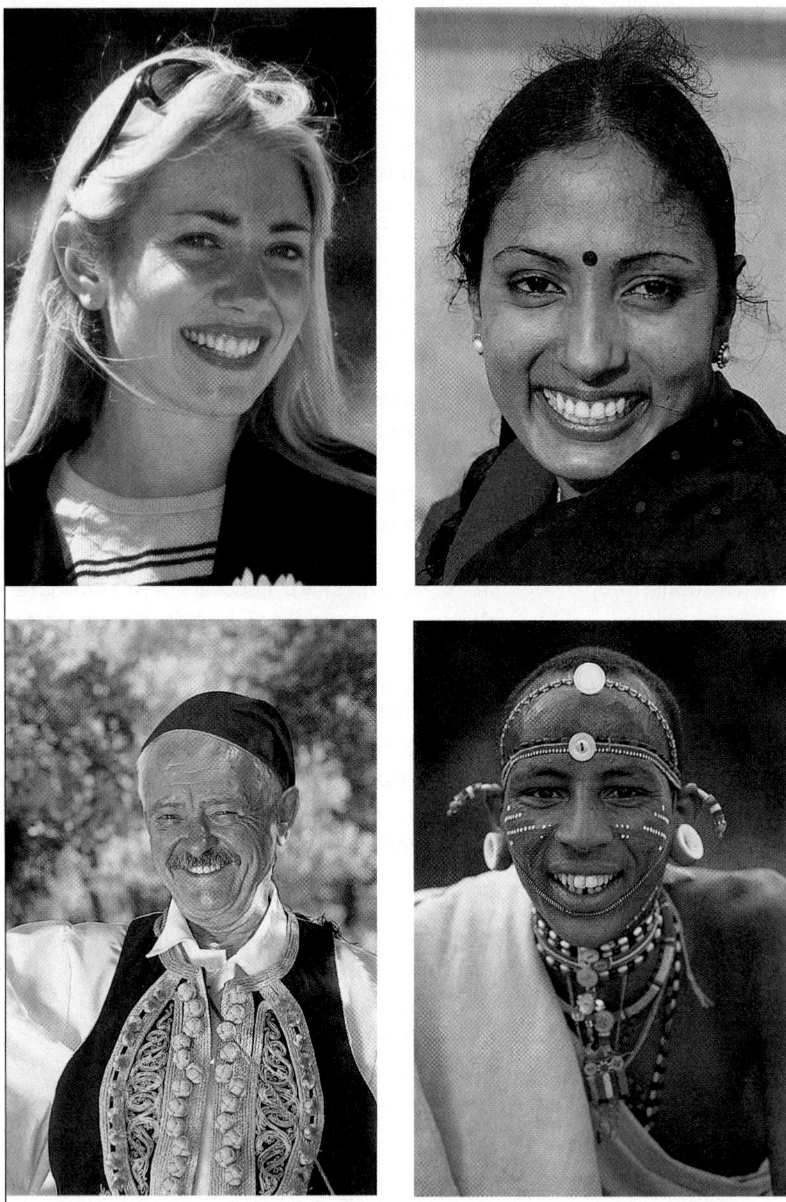

Happiness can be thought of as a state or as a trait. People high in trait happiness experience frequent happiness states, or have a lower threshold for becoming happy. Moreover, happiness is recognized around the world through the expression of smiling. People from all cultures smile when they are happy.

underlie those many variations, concluding that there are probably about five primary personality traits that underlie the huge list of trait adjectives.

Emotion researchers who take the categorical approach have tried to reduce the complexity of emotions by searching for the primary emotions that underlie the great variety of emotional terms (Levenson, 2003). They have not reached the kind of consensus that is found in the personality trait domain, however. The lack of consensus found in this area of psychology results from different criteria that researchers use for defining an emotion as primary. Primary emotions are thought to be the irreducible set of emotions, combinations of which result in the huge variety of experienced emotions. This is similar to the primary trait issue discussed in Chapter 3. Various researchers have proposed criteria for determining which emotions are primary emotions. For example, Ekman (1992a) requires that a primary emotion have a distinct facial expression that is recognized across cultures. For example, sadness is accompanied by frowning and knitting the brow. This facial expression is universally recognized as depicting the emotion of sadness. Similarly, clenching and baring the teeth is associated with anger and is universally recognized as anger. In fact, people who are blind from birth frown when sad, clench and bare their teeth when angry, and smile when they are happy. Because persons blind from birth have never seen the facial expressions of sadness, anger, or joy, it not likely that they learned these expressions. Rather, it seems likely that the expressions are part of human nature. Based on these criteria of distinct and universal facial expressions, Ekman's list of primary emotions contains disgust, sadness, joy, surprise, anger, and fear.

Other researchers hold different criteria for counting emotions as primary. For example, Izard (1977) suggests that the primary emotions are distinguished by their unique motivational properties. That is, emotions are understood to guide behaviors by motivating a person to take specific adaptive actions. Fear is included as a primary emotion on Izard's list because it motivates a person to avoid danger and seek safety. Interest is similarly a fundamental emotion because it motivates a person to learn and acquire new skills. Izard's criteria result in a list of 10 primary emotions. In Table 13.1 are various lists of primary emotions based on various criteria.

Another approach to understanding the complexity of emotion has been based on empirical research rather than on theoretical criteria. In the **dimensional approach,** researchers gather data by having subjects rate themselves on a wide variety of

Table 13.1 A Selection of Theorists Who Provide Lists of Primary Emotions

Theorists	Basic Emotions	Criteria
Ekman, Friesen, & Ellsworth, 1972	Anger, disgust, fear, joy, sadness, surprise	Universal facial expression
Frijda, 1986	Desire, happiness, interest, surprise, wonder, sorrow	Motivation to take specific actions
Gray, 1982	Rage, terror, anxiety, joy	Brain circuits
Izard, 1977	Anger, contempt, disgust, distress, fear, guilt, interest, joy, shame, surprise	Motivation to take specific actions
James, 1884	Fear, grief, love, rage	Bodily involvement
Mower, 1960	Pain, pleasure	Unlearned emotional states
Oatley & Johnson-Laird, 1987	Anger, disgust, anxiety, happiness, sadness	Little cognitive involvement
Plutchik, 1980	Anger, acceptance, joy, anticipation, fear, disgust, sadness, surprise	Evolved biological processes
Tomkins, 1984	Anger, interest, contempt, disgust, fear, joy, shame, surprise	Density of neural firing

Source: Adapted from Ortony & Turner, 1990.

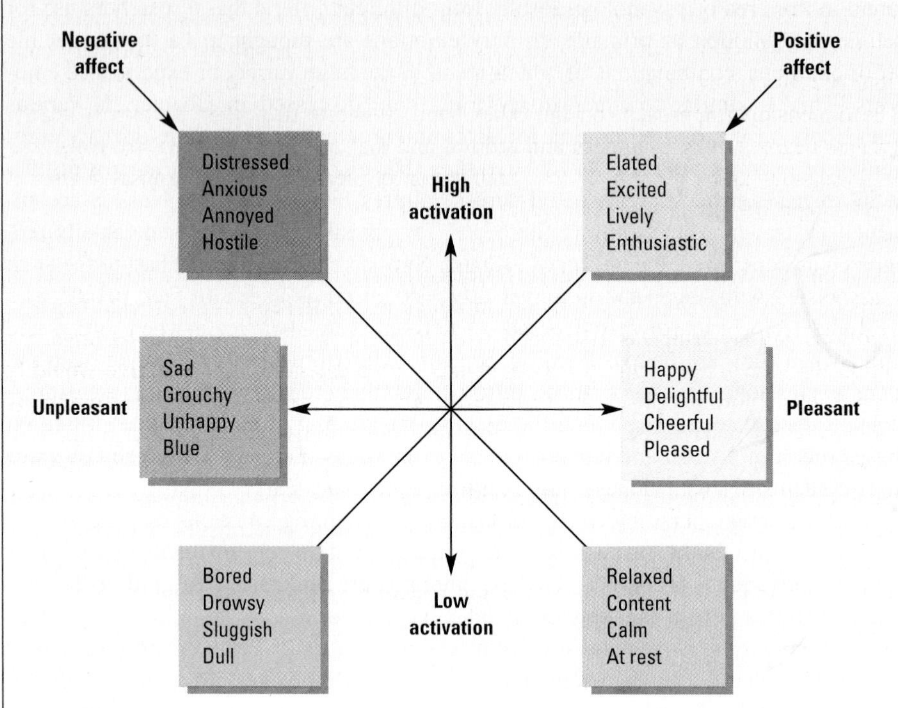

Figure 13.1

The dimensional approach to emotion, showing two primary dimensions: high to low activation and pleasantness to unpleasantness.

emotions, then apply statistical techniques (usually factor analysis) to identify the basic dimensions underlying the ratings.

There is remarkable consensus among researchers on the basic dimensions that underlie self-ratings of affect (Judge & Larsen, 2001; Larsen & Diener, 1992; Watson, 2000). Most of the studies suggest that people categorize emotions using just two primary dimensions: how pleasant or unpleasant the emotion is and how high or low on arousal the emotion is. When these two dimensions are arrayed as axes in a two-dimensional coordinate system, the adjectives that describe emotions fall in a circle around the two dimensions, as shown in Figure 13.1.

This model of emotion suggests that every feeling state can be described as a combination of pleasantness/unpleasantness and arousal. For example, a person can feel unpleasant feelings in a very high-arousal way (nervous, anxious, terrified) or in a very low-arousal way (bored, fatigued, tired). Similarly, a person can feel pleasant feelings in a high-arousal way (excited, enthusiastic, elated) or in a low-arousal way (calm, relaxed). Thus, the two dimensions of pleasantness and arousal are seen as fundamental dimensions of emotion.

The dimensional view of emotion is based on research studies in which subjects rate their emotional experiences. Emotions that occur together, which are experienced as similar to each other, are understood as defining a common dimension. For example, the emotions of distress, anxiety, annoyance, and hostility are very similar in terms of experience and, thus, seem to anchor one end of a dimension of negative affect. The dimensional approach to emotion, thus, refers more to how people *experience* their emotions than to how they think about their emotions. In contrast, the categorical approach relies more on conceptual distinctions between emotions: the primary emotions are those that have distinct facial expressions or distinct motivational properties. The dimensional approach, on the other hand, suggests that what we experience are various degrees of pleasantness and arousal and that every emotion we are capable of experiencing can be described as a combination of pleasantness and arousal (Larsen & Fredrickson, 1999; Larsen & Prizmic, in press).

Some researchers prefer the categorical perspective, finding it useful to think about emotions as distinct categories rather than dimensions. For example, the emotions of anger and anxiety, although similar in terms of being high-arousal negative emotions, are nevertheless associated with different facial expressions, feelings, and action tendencies. Personality psychologists with a categorical perspective would be interested in how people differ from each other with respect to primary emotions, such as anger and anxiety. For example, are there individual or group differences in anxiety, sadness, or aggression? There are also personality psychologists who prefer to think about how people differ with respect to the primary dimensions of emotion. For example, who are the people who have a good deal of pleasantness in their lives? Who are the people who have frequent bouts of high-arousal unpleasant emotions? In this chapter, we will cover the research and findings from both of these perspectives.

Content versus Style of Emotional Life

Another distinction that is useful to personality psychologists is that between the content of a person's emotional life and the style with which that person experiences and expresses emotion. **Content** is the specific kind of emotion that a person experiences, whereas **style** is the way in which an emotion is experienced. For example, saying that someone is cheerful is to say something about the content of the person's emotional life, because this refers to the specific kind of emotions a person frequently experiences. However, to say that someone is high on mood variability is to say something about the style of his or her emotional life—that his or her emotions change frequently. Each of these facets of emotion—content and style—exhibits trait-like properties (stable over time and situations and meaningful for making distinctions between people). Content and style provide an organizational theme for discussing personality and emotion. We will first discuss the content of emotional life, focusing on various pleasant and unpleasant emotions. We will then consider emotional style, focusing on individual differences in the intensity and variability of emotional life.

Content of Emotional Life

Content of emotional life means the typical emotions a person is likely to experience over time. For example, someone characterized as an angry or hot-tempered person should have an emotional life that contains a good deal of anger, irritability, and hostility. Someone else whose emotional life contains a lot of pleasant emotions is someone we might characterize as happy, cheerful, and enthusiastic. Thus, the notion of content leads us to consider the *kinds* of emotions that people are likely to experience over time and across situations in their lives. We will begin with a discussion of the pleasant emotional dispositions.

William James defined happiness as the ratio of one's accomplishments to one's aspirations.

Pleasant Emotions

In lists of primary emotions, happiness or joy are typically the only pleasant emotions mentioned (though some theorists include interest as a pleasant emotion). In trait approaches to emotion, the major pleasant disposition is happiness and the associated feelings of being satisfied with one's life. We begin with these concepts.

Definitions of Happiness and Life Satisfaction Over 2,000 years ago, Greek philosopher Aristotle wrote that happiness was the supreme good and that the goal of life was to attain happiness. Moreover, he taught that happiness was attained by living a virtuous life and being a good person. Countless other scholars and philosophers have offered many other theories on the sources of human happiness. For example, unlike Aristotle, eighteenth-century French philosopher Jean-Jacques Rousseau speculated that the road to happiness lies in the satisfaction of one's desires and the hedonistic pursuit of pleasure. In the late nineteenth century, the founder of psychology in America, William James, taught that happiness was the ratio of one's accomplishments to one's aspirations. One could achieve happiness, James thought, in one of two ways: by accomplishing more in life or by lowering one's aspirations.

Although many philosophers and psychologists have speculated about the roots of happiness for centuries, the scientific study of happiness is relatively recent. Psychologists began the serious study of happiness (also called subjective well-being or life satisfaction) in the mid-1970s. Since then, scientific research on the topic has grown by leaps and bounds. In recent years, hundreds of scientific articles on happiness are published annually in the psychological literature (Diener & Seligman, 2002).

One way to define **happiness** is to examine how researchers measure it. Several questionnaire measures are widely used in surveys and other research. Because happiness is a subjective quality—it depends on an individual's own judgment of his or her life—researchers almost *have* to rely on questionnaires. Some of these questionnaires focus on judgments about one's life, such as "How satisfied are you with your life as a whole these days? Are you very satisfied, satisfied, not very satisfied, or not at all satisfied?" Other questionnaires focus on emotion, particularly on the balance between pleasant and unpleasant emotions in a person's life. An example of this type of questioning was proposed by Fordyce (1978), in which the subject is asked the following questions:

What percent of the time are you happy? __________
What percent of the time are you neutral? __________
What percent of the time are you unhappy? __________
Make sure your percents add up to 100%.

Among college students, data indicate that the average person reports being happy 65 percent of the time, neutral 15 percent, and unhappy 20 percent (Larsen & Diener, 1985). The percent happy scale is one of the better measures of happiness in terms of construct validity. For example, it predicts a wide range of other happiness-related aspects of a person's personality, such as day-to-day moods and peer reports of overall happiness (Larsen, Diener, & Lucas, 2002).

Researchers conceive of happiness in two complementary ways: (1) in terms of a judgment that life is satisfying and (2) in terms of the predominance of positive compared with negative emotions in one's life (Diener, 2000). It turns out, however, that people's emotional lives and the judgments of how satisfied they are with their lives are highly correlated. People who have a lot of pleasant emotions in their lives tend to judge their lives as satisfying, and vice versa (Diener, Lucas, & Larsen, 2003).

Can it be that happy people are just deluding themselves, that most people are really miserable and happy people just don't know it or are denying it? It would be easy to lie on a questionnaire and to portray oneself as being happy and satisfied. This is the idea of social desirability, as discussed in Chapter 4. It turns out that measures of happiness *do* correlate with social desirability scores. In other words, people who score high on social desirability also score high on self-reported happiness scales. Moreover, social desirability measures also correlate with nonself-report happiness scores, such as peer reports of happiness. This finding suggests that having a positive view of oneself is part of being a happy person. Said differently, part of being happy is to have **positive illusions** about the self, an inflated view of one's own characteristics as a good, able, and desirable person, as this characteristic appears to be part of emotional well-being (Taylor, 1989; Taylor et al., 2000).

Despite the correlation of self-report measures of happiness with social desirability, other findings suggest that these happiness measures are valid (Diener, Oishi, & Lucas, 2003). These findings concern the positive correlations found between self-report and nonself-report measures of happiness. People who report that they are happy tend to have friends and family members who agree (Sandvik, Diener, & Seidlitz, 1993). In addition, studies of the daily diaries of happy people find that they report many more pleasant experiences than do unhappy people (Larsen & Diener, 1985). When different clinical psychologists interview a sample of people, the psychologists tend to agree strongly about which are happy and satisfied and which are not (Diener, 2000). And, in an interesting experiment, Seidlitz and Diener (1993) gave the participants five minutes to recall as many happy events in their lives as possible and then gave them five minutes to recall as many unhappy events in their lives as possible. They found that the happy people recalled more pleasant events, and fewer unpleasant events, than did the unhappy people.

Questionnaire measures of happiness and well-being also predict other aspects of people's lives that we would expect to relate to happiness (Diener, Lucas, & Larsen, 2003). For example, compared with unhappy people, happy people are less abusive and hostile, are less self-focused, and report fewer instances of disease. They also are more helpful and cooperative, have more social skills, are more creative and energetic, are more forgiving, and are more trusting (Myers, 1993, 2000; Myers & Diener, 1995; Veenhoven, 1988). In summary, self-reports of happiness appear to be valid and trustworthy (Larsen & Prizmic, in press). After all, who but the persons themselves are the best judge of their subjective well-being? See Table 13.2 for a sample "life satisfaction" questionnaire.

What Good Is Happiness? It has long been known that happiness correlates with many positive outcomes in life, such as marriage, longevity, self-esteem, and satisfaction with one's job (Diener, Suh, Lucas, & Smith, 1999). These correlations between desirable outcomes in life and happiness are often interpreted to mean that success in some area of life (e.g., a good marriage) will make a person happy. As another example, the very small correlation between personal wealth and happiness is often interpreted as meaning that having money can make one (slightly more) happy. The majority of researchers in this area have gone on the assumption that successful outcomes foster happiness and that the causal direction goes from being successful leading to increased happiness.

Table 13.2 Satisfaction with Life Scale*

Below are five statements with which you may agree or disagree. Using the scale below, indicate your agreement with each item by placing the appropriate number on the line preceding that item. Please be open and honest in your responses.

Strong Disagreement	Moderate Disagreement	Slight Disagreement	Slight Agreement	Moderate Agreement	Strong Agreement
1	2	3	4	5	6

1. ______ In most ways my life is close to my ideal.
2. ______ If I could live my life over, I would change almost nothing.
3. ______ I am satisfied with my life.
4. ______ So far I have gotten the important things I want in life.
5. ______ The conditions of my life are excellent.

*From Diener, Emmons, Larsen, & Griffin, 1985.

Recently, a group of researchers (Lyubomirsky, King, & Diener, 2005) questioned this assumption about the causal direction going from success to happiness. They suggested that there may be areas of life where the causality goes in the opposite direction, from happiness to success. For example, it could be that being happy leads one to get married, or to have a better marriage, instead of having a good marriage leading one to become happy.

In an extremely large meta-analysis of the happiness and well-being literature, Lyubomirsky et al. (2005) reviewed many studies that might be used to disentangle the causal direction between happiness and several different outcomes. There are two kinds of studies that are most useful in assessing causal direction. One type of study is longitudinal, where people are measured on at least two occasions separated in time. If happiness precedes success in life, then we have some evidence that the causal direction might go from happiness to the outcome. A second type of study is experimental, where happiness is manipulated (people are put in a good mood) for half the sample (the other half is the control group), and some outcome is measured. If the outcome is higher in the group undergoing the happiness induction than in the control group, then we have some evidence that the causal direction might go from happiness to the outcome.

Lyubomirsky et al. (2005) found that longitudinal studies provided evidence that happiness leads to, or at least comes before, positive outcomes in many areas of life. They found that happiness preceded many important positive outcomes, including fulfilling and productive work, satisfying relationships, and superior mental and physical health and longevity. Experimental studies also provide evidence that happiness can lead to several positive outcomes, including being more helpful and altruistic, wanting to be with others, increases in self-esteem and liking of others, a better functioning immune system, more effective conflict resolution skills, and more creative or more original thinking.

While happiness has been shown to lead to many positive outcomes in life, the situation with some outcomes might be more complex and involve **reciprocal causality,** which refers to the idea that causality can flow in both directions. For example, we know that happy people are more likely to help others who are in need. Also, from the experimental literature, we know that helping someone in need can lead to increases in happiness. This kind of reciprocal causality may apply to many areas of

Does having a good marriage cause a person to be happy? Or does being happy cause one to have a good marriage?

life, including having a satisfying marriage or intimate relationship, having a fulfilling job, or having high self-esteem.

What Is Known about Happy People In an article entitled "Who Is Happy?" psychologists David Myers and Ed Diener (1995) reviewed what is known about happy people. For example, are women happier than men, or are men the happier gender? In the United States, women are diagnosed with depression twice as often as men. This might suggest that men are happier than women. However, men are at least twice as likely as women to become alcoholics. The use of alcohol may be one way men medicate themselves for depression, so the real rate of depression may be more similar for men and women. Researchers need to examine actual studies of happiness to address the gender difference question. Fortunately, an excellent and thorough review of the studies on gender and happiness has already been done. Haring, Stock, and Okun (1984) analyzed 146 studies on global well-being and found that gender accounted for less than 1 percent of the variation in people's happiness. This finding of practically no difference between men and women appears across cultures and countries as well. Michalos (1991) obtained data on 18,032 university students from 39 countries. He found that roughly equal proportions of men and women rated themselves as being satisfied with their lives. Diener (2000) also reports gender equality in overall happiness.

Is happiness more likely among young, middle-aged, or older people? We often think that certain age periods are more stressful than others, such as the midlife crisis or the stress of adolescence. This might lead us to believe that certain times of life are happier than others. Inglehart (1990) addressed this question in a study of 169,776 people from 16 nations. It was found that the circumstances that make people happy change with age. For example, financial security and health are important for happiness later in life, whereas, for younger adults, success at school or work and satisfying intimate relationships are important for happiness. However, in looking at overall levels of happiness, Inglehart concluded that there was no evidence to suggest that any one time of life was happier than any other.

Is ethnicity related to happiness? Are some ethnic groups happier than others? Many surveys have included questions about ethnic identity, so a wealth of data exists on this question. Summarizing many such studies, Myers and Diener (1995) conclude that ethnic group membership is unrelated to subjective well-being. For example, African Americans report roughly the same amount of happiness as European Americans and, in fact, have slightly lower levels of depression (Diener et al., 1993). Crocker and Major (1989) suggest that people from disadvantaged social groups maintain their happiness by valuing the activities they are good at, by comparing themselves with members of their own group, and by blaming their problems on events that are outside of their control.

What about national differences in well-being? Are people from certain nations happier than people from other nations? The answer here seems to be yes. An impressive study by Diener, Diener, and Diener (1995) examined well-being scores obtained using probability surveys in 55 nations. The nations sampled in this study represented 75 percent of the earth's population. The results are portrayed in Table 13.3, where

Table 13.3 Country Scores of Average Subjective Well-Being

Country	Subjective Well-Being	Country	Subjective Well-Being
Iceland	1.11	Bangladesh	−.29
Sweden	1.03	France	−.38
Australia	1.02	Spain	−.41
Denmark	1.00	Portugal	−.41
Canada	.97	Italy	−.44
Switzerland	.94	Hungary	−.48
U.S.A.	.91	Puerto Rico	−.51
Colombia	.82	Thailand	−.62
Luxembourg	.82	South Africa	−.63
New Zealand	.82	Jordan	−.77
N. Ireland	.78	Egypt	−.78
Norway	.77	Yugoslavia	−.81
Finland	.74	Japan	−.86
Britain	.69	Greece	−.89
Netherlands	.68	Poland	−.90
Ireland	.57	Kenya	−.92
Brazil	.57	Turkey	−1.02
Tanzania	.51	India	−1.13
Belgium	.51	S. Korea	−1.15
Singapore	.43	Nigeria	−1.31
Bahrain	.36	Panama	−1.31
W. Germany	.18	E. Germany	−1.52
Austria	.15	U. S. S. R.	−1.70
Chile	.13	China	−1.92
Philippines	.10	Cameroon	−2.04
Malaysia	.08	Dominican Republic	−3.92
Cuba	.00		
Israel	−.18	Average	0.00
Mexico	−.28	Standard deviation	1.00

Source: Diener, Diener, & Diener, 1995.

the nations are rank-ordered on the well-being measure. Looking at the rankings, what do you think might account for the differences between the countries that were high and low on well-being?

The researchers were able to assemble a broad array of other environmental, social, and economic information on each of these countries, and they tested whether any of these variables correlated with average national happiness. At the national level, the poorer countries appeared to possess less happiness and life satisfaction than the countries that were wealthier. The nations also differed in the rights they provided their citizens. The researchers found that the countries that provided few civil and political rights tended to have lower well-being than did the countries where civil rights and individual freedoms were well protected by laws. Other national variables, such as population density and cultural homogeneity, showed only minor correlations with well-being. Diener et al. (1995) concluded that differences in the economic development of nations may be the primary source of differences in the subjective well-being of societies. Researchers who have conducted similar but smaller-scale national surveys have offered similar findings (Easterlin, 1974; Veenhoven, 1991a, 1991b).

Such findings might lead us to think that money or income makes people happy. People often think that, if they made a bit more money or if they had a few more material goods, they would be happier. Some believe that if they win the lottery they will be happy for the rest of their lives. Researchers have found that there is no simple answer to the question about whether money makes people happy (Diener & Biswas-Diener, 2002).

Research on the objective circumstances of a person's life—age, sex, ethnicity, income, and so on—shows that these matter very little to overall happiness, yet we know that people differ from each other and that, even through life's struggles and disappointments, some people are consistently happier than others. Costa, McCrae, and Zonderman (1987) found, in a study of 5,000 adults, that the people who were happy in 1973 were also happy 10 years later, in spite of undergoing many changes in life. What else might explain why some people are consistently happier than others?

Personality and Well-Being In 1980, psychologists Paul Costa and Robert McCrae concluded that demographic variables, such as gender, age, ethnicity, and income, accounted for only about 10 to 15 percent of the variation in happiness, an estimate confirmed by others (Myers & Diener, 1995). This leaves a lot of the variance in subjective well-being unaccounted for. Costa and McCrae (1980) proposed that personality might have something to do with disposing certain people to be happy and, so, looked into that research. The few studies existing at that time suggested that happy people were outgoing and sociable (Smith, 1979), emotionally stable, and low on neuroticism (Wessman & Ricks, 1966).

Costa and McCrae used such information to theorize that there may be two personality traits that influence happiness: extraversion and neuroticism. Moreover, Costa and McCrae made specific predictions about exactly how extraversion and neuroticism influenced happiness. Their idea was both simple and elegant. They began with the notion that happiness was the presence of relatively high levels of positive affect, and relatively low levels of negative affect, in a person's life over time. Extraversion, they held, influenced a person's positive emotions, whereas neuroticism determined a person's negative emotions.

Costa and McCrae (1980; McCrae & Costa, 1991) found that their model was supported by further research. Extraversion and neuroticism predicted the amounts of

A Closer Look

Does Money Make People Happy?

Pop singer Madonna, also known as "the Material Girl," has sung the praises of materialism. Americans are often thought of as materialistic. In fact, in surveys, the goal of being very well off financially is often rated as the top goal in life by first-year college students, surpassing other goals, such as being helpful to others, realizing potential as a person, and raising a family (Myers, 2000). This attitude is summarized by a bumper sticker seen on an expensive car towing a large boat, which read, "When the game is over, the person with the most toys wins." Does having more make one a winner? Does money lead to happiness?

Looked at in terms of national data, the answer seems to be that wealthier countries do indeed have higher average levels of life satisfaction than poorer countries. Myers and Diener (1995) report that the correlation between a nation's well-being score and its gross national product (adjusted for population size) is +.67. However, national wealth is confounded with many other variables that influence well-being, such as health-care services, civil rights, care for the elderly, and education. This is a classic example of how potential third variables might explain why two variables are related (see discussion of this problem in Chapter 2). For example, wealthier countries may have higher well-being *because* they also provide better health care for their citizens.

To counteract this research problem, we must look at the relationship between income and happiness within specific countries. Diener and Diener (1995) report that, in very poor countries, such as Bangladesh and India, financial status is a moderately good predictor of well-being. However, once people can afford life's basic necessities, it appears that increasing one's financial status matters very little to one's well-being. In countries that have a higher standard of living, where most people have their basic needs met (such as in Europe or the United States), income "has a surprisingly weak (virtually negligible) effect on happiness" (Inglehart, 1990, p. 242).

What if we were to look within a country and examine changes in affluence over time, within a single economy, to see if people become happier as the country becomes more affluent? The United States, for example, has undergone huge increases in national wealth, income, and affluence over the past half-century. For example, from 1957 to the late 1990s, the average person's after-tax income (in constant 1995 dollars) has more than doubled, going from $8,000 to $20,000 annually. Are Americans happier today than they were in 1957? Myers (2000) reports that Americans are *not* any happier today. This is illustrated by Figure 13.2, which shows that the percentage of Americans who describe themselves as very happy has stayed fairly constant over the decades, fluctuating right around 30 percent. This constant rate of personal happiness stands in contrast to the corresponding steep increase in personal wealth experienced during those decades. Easterlin (1995) reports similar results for certain European countries and Japan, where increases in average per-person wealth were not accompanied by increases in average per-person happiness. Such findings suggest that, at least within affluent societies, further boosts in economic growth are not necessarily accompanied by rises in life satisfaction among the population.

This finding of a lack of relation between income and happiness contradicts the views of many politicians, economists, and policymakers. Moreover, it seems to run counter to common sense, as well as data on poverty and poor life outcomes. For example, people in the lowest levels of the economy have the highest rates of depression (McLoyd, 1998). Economic hardship takes a toll on people, increasing stress and conflict in people's lives. Poverty is associated with elevations in a variety of negative life outcomes, ranging from infant mortality to increased violent crimes, such as homicide (Belle et al., 2000). How can poverty be associated with such unfortunate circumstances yet income not be related to happiness? The answer, it seems, lies in the notion of a threshold of income, below which a person is very unlikely to be happy, at least in the United States (Csikszentmihalyi, 2000). Once a person is above this threshold, however, the notion that having more money would make one happier does not seem to hold (Diener & Biswas-Diener, 2002).

Myers and Diener (1995) make the analogy between wealth and health: the absence of either health or wealth can bring misery, but their presence is no guarantee that happiness will follow. An interesting experiment to test this assertion for wealth would be to take a sample of people and randomly assign them to two groups. In Group 1, you give each member $1 million. In Group 2 you give each member $1. Then you see whether, six months later, the people in Group 1 (the new millionaires) are happier than

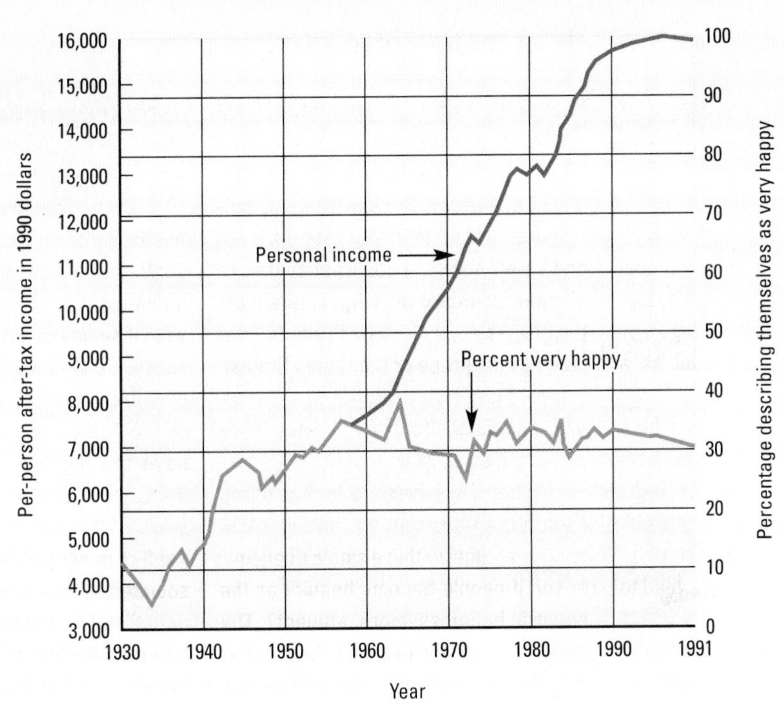

Figure 13.2

Has the large growth in average income been accompanied by an increase in average happiness within the United States? Source: Adapted from Myers, D. G. (2000). "The Funds, Friends, and Faith of Happy People," *American Psychologist*, 55–57, figure 1. Copyright © 2000 by the American Psychological Association. Reprinted with permission.

the people in Group 2. Of course, this experiment would be impossible to conduct, right? Wrong. With the advent of state lotteries in the United States, many people become millionaires overnight. Brickman, Coates, and Janoff-Bulman (1978) conducted a study of lottery winners, comparing their happiness levels with those of people from similar backgrounds who had not won large amounts of money. Within six months of winning, the newly rich lottery winners were found to be no more happy than the subjects in the control group. Apparently, winning the lottery is not as good as it sounds, at least not in terms of making a person permanently happy. In a related study, Diener, Horwitz, and Emmons (1985) had 49 of the wealthiest people in the United States (according to the list published annually in *Forbes* magazine) complete happiness questionnaires. They found that this group of extremely privileged people was not significantly happier than a control group of people with modest incomes. In fact, 37 percent of these extremely wealthy persons were less happy than the average American.

What can we conclude about money and happiness? Probably the most reasonable conclusion is that, below a very low income level, a person is very unlikely to be happy. Being able to meet the basic needs of life (food, shelter, security) appears crucial. However, once those needs are met, research suggests that there is little to the notion that further wealth will bring increased happiness. Diener et al. (1995), for example, found that the correlation between personal income and happiness is +.12 in the United States. Although this correlation is not negative, it is hardly large enough to think that having a huge income, in itself, will make you happy. What wealthy people choose to do with their money may have more to do with their potential happiness than does the mere fact of having a lot of money.

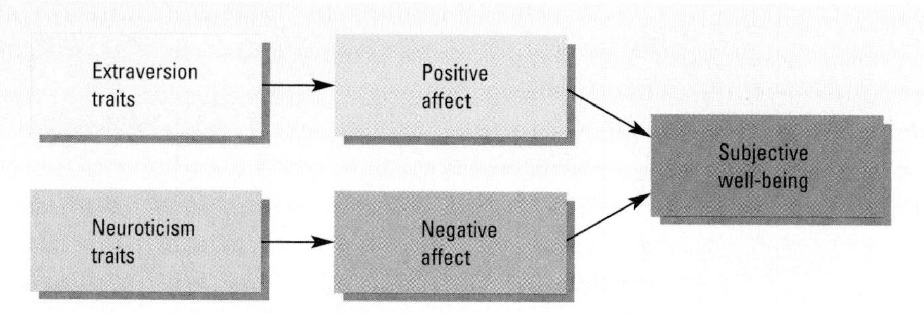

Figure 13.3

The influence of extraversion and neuroticism on subjective well-being, by making a person susceptible to positive and negative affect. Source: Adapted from Costa and McCrae, 1980.

positive and negative emotions in people's lives and hence contributed greatly to subjective well-being. In fact, extraversion and neuroticism accounted for up to three times as much of the variation in happiness between people compared with *all* of the common demographic variables (e.g., age, income, gender, education, ethnicity, religion) put together. It appears that having the right combination of personality traits (high extraversion and low neuroticism) may contribute much more to happiness than gender, ethnicity, age, and all the other demographic characteristics. Their model of well-being is portrayed in Figure 13.3.

Since Costa and McCrae's original study in 1980, more than a dozen studies have replicated the finding that extraversion and neuroticism are strong personality correlates of well-being (summarized in Rusting & Larsen, 1998b). All of these studies have been correlational, however, usually taking the form of administering personality and well-being questionnaires, then examining the correlations.

Correlational studies cannot determine whether there is a direct causal connection between personality and well-being, or whether personality leads one to live a certain lifestyle and that lifestyle, in turn, makes one happy. For example, being neurotic may lead one to be a worrier and complainer. Other people dislike being around someone who worries a lot and is always complaining, so people may avoid the person who is high on neuroticism. Consequently, that person may be lonely and unhappy; however, that unhappiness may be due to the fact that the person drives people away by complaining all the time. The person's neuroticism leads him or her to create certain life situations, such as making others uncomfortable, and these situations in turn make the person unhappy (Hotard et al., 1989).

We can contrast this with a different view of the causal relation between personality and well-being, in which personality is viewed as directly causing people to react to the same situations with different amounts of positive or negative emotions, hence directly influencing their well-being. A neurotic person may respond with more negative emotion, even to the identical situation, than a person low in neuroticism. These two different models of the relation between personality and well-being—the direct and the indirect models—are portrayed in Figure 13.4. In the indirect model (Panel b), personality causes the person to create a certain lifestyle, and the lifestyle, in turn, causes the emotional reaction. In the direct model (Panel a), even when exposed to identical situations, certain people respond with more positive or negative emotions, depending on their level of extraversion and neuroticism.

Application (*Continued*)

3. *Look for ways to be helpful to others.* Helping others can make you feel good about yourself and give you the feeling that your life is meaningful. Helping others thereby provides a boost in self-esteem. Helping has a second benefit as well; helping someone else can take your mind off your own problems or can make your problems seem little by comparison. There are plenty of worthy causes and plenty of organizations that welcome volunteers.
4. *Take time out for yourself; enjoy the activities that give you pleasure.* Don't wait to find time for your favorite hobby or activity. Instead, make time. Many people learn to keep a calendar while in college to schedule work and other obligations. Use it to schedule fun things as well. Set aside time to read a book, take in a movie, exercise regularly, or do whatever else you enjoy. Think about what gives you pleasure, and build time into your busy schedule for those activities.
5. *Stay in shape.* Exercise is positively associated with emotional well-being. Exercise need not be intense or all that frequent to provide the emotional benefit. Playing on team sports, dancing, biking, swimming, gardening, or even walking, if done at a brisk pace, is about all it takes. It doesn't seem to matter what the activity is, as long as you move around enough to keep in shape.
6. *Have a plan, but be open to new experiences.* Having an organized life allows a person to accomplish much. However, sometimes the most fun moments in life are unplanned. Be open to trying different things or having different experiences—try going somewhere you have never been, try doing a routine activity a little differently, or try doing something on the spur of the moment. Be flexible, rather than rigid, and try to avoid getting stuck in any ruts.
7. *Be optimistic.* Put on a smiling face, whistle a happy tune, look for the silver lining in every cloud. Sure, it sounds too good to be true, but acting happy and trying to look on the bright side of things can go a long way toward making you feel happy. Try to avoid negative thinking. Don't make pessimistic statements, even to yourself. Convince yourself that the cup *really is* half full.
8. *Don't let things get blown out of proportion.* Sometimes when something bad happens, it seems like the end of the world. Happy people have the ability to step back and see things in perspective. Happy people think about their options and about the other things in their lives that *are* going well. They think about what they can do to work on their problems or what to avoid in the future. But they *don't* think it is the end of the world. Often asking yourself "What's the worst that can come of this?" will help put things in perspective.

Just wishing for happiness is not likely to make it so. Psychologists agree that people have to work at being happy; they have to work at overcoming the unpleasant events of life, the losses and failures that happen to everyone. The strategies in the previous list can be thought of as a personal program for working on happiness.

Unpleasant Emotions

Unlike pleasant emotion, the unpleasant emotions come in several distinct varieties. We will discuss three important unpleasant emotions that are viewed by psychologists as having dispositional characteristics: anxiety, depression, and anger.

Trait Anxiety and Neuroticism Recall that people who exhibit the trait of neuroticism are vulnerable to negative emotions. **Neuroticism** is one of the Big Five dimensions of personality, and it is present, in some form, in every major trait theory of personality.

Different researchers have used different terms for neuroticism, such as emotional instability, anxiety-proneness, and negative affectivity (Watson & Clark, 1984). Adjectives useful for describing persons high on the trait of neuroticism include moody, touchy, irritable, anxious, unstable, pessimistic, and complaining. Hans Eysenck (1967, 1990; Eysenck & Eysenck, 1985) suggested that individuals high on the neuroticism dimension tend to overreact to unpleasant events, such as frustrations or problems, and that they take longer to return to a normal state after being upset. They are easily irritated, worry about many things, and seem to be constantly complaining. You may have heard the phrase "She is not happy unless she has something to worry about." Well, it is unlikely that worrying actually makes a person happy. But the fact that some people worry almost all the time might suggest that worrying fulfills a need for them. Some people worry about their health ("Is this nagging cough really a sign that I have lung cancer? Could this headache really be a brain tumor?"). Others worry about their social relations ("When that person smiled at me, was it really a smirk?"). And still others worry about their work ("Why can't I seem to get as much work done as my friends do?").

In addition to worry and anxiety, the person high on the neuroticism dimension frequently experiences episodes of irritation. An interesting way to illustrate this is to ask people to list all the things that have irritated them in the past week. Perhaps seeing someone spit in public is irritating to many people. Or seeing someone with a pierced nose and eyebrows might be mentioned as irritating. Or seeing a couple kissing in public might be mentioned. If people were to write down all the things that irritated them, you would find that people high on neuroticism would have much longer lists than people low in neuroticism. Persons high in neuroticism are frequently annoyed, even by the smallest transgressions ("I went to the store and someone was parked in the fire lane. That really irritates me. Then my mathematics professor wore the same suit and tie for two days in a row. What a jerk; he can't even change his tie each class"). The person high on neuroticism is a complainer, and others quickly learn that such a person will complain about practically anything—"That person driving in front of us changed lanes without using his turn signal; what a complete idiot!"

People high on the personality trait of neuroticism tend to worry frequently. They may worry about their health, their social interactions, their work, their future, or just about anything. Worrying and complaining takes up a great proportion of their time.

Eysenck's biological theory As briefly discussed in Chapter 3, Eysenck (1967, 1990) argues that neuroticism has a biological basis. In his theory of personality, neuroticism is due primarily to a tendency of the **limbic system** in the brain to become easily activated. The limbic system is the part of the brain responsible for emotion and the fight-or-flight reaction. If someone has a limbic system that is easily activated, then that person probably has frequent episodes of emotion, particularly emotions associated with flight (such as anxiety, fear, and worry) and with fight (such as anger, irritation, and annoyance). High-neuroticism persons are anxious, irritated, and easily upset, so the theory goes, because their limbic systems are more easily aroused to produce such emotions. They are also prone to get irritated easily, sometimes to the point of anger.

There have been no direct tests of Eysenck's limbic theory of neuroticism, in which direct measures of limbic activity have been obtained and related to neuroticism. Because the limbic system is located deep within the brain, its activity is not easily measured by EEG electrodes, which are placed on the surface of the scalp. Newer brain imaging technologies, such as MRI or PET, are allowing personality researchers to test this theory directly (Canli et al., 2001). Nevertheless, Eysenck (1990) has made several logical arguments in favor of a biological basis for neuroticism. First, many studies have shown a remarkable level of stability in neuroticism. For example, Conley (1984a, b, 1985) found that neuroticism showed a high test-retest correlation after a period of 45 years. Although this does not prove a biological basis for neuroticism, stability is nevertheless consistent with a biological explanation. A second argument is that neuroticism is a major dimension of personality that is found in many different kinds of data sets (e.g., self-report, peer report) in many different cultures and environments by many different investigators. Again, although this ubiquity does not prove a biological basis, the fact that neuroticism is so widely found across cultures and data sources is consistent with a biological explanation. And a third argument in favor of a biological explanation, put forward by Eysenck (1990), is that many genetic studies find that neuroticism shows one of the higher heritability values. Trait negative affect shows relatively high levels of heritability, whereas trait positive affect shows a significant shared environment component (Goldsmith et al., 2001). That is, a predisposition to be neurotic appears to be somewhat inherited. Most behavior geneticists believe that what is heritable in the heritability of emotion traits is individual differences in neurotransmitter function, such as in dopamine transport or serotonin re-uptake (Grigorenko, 2002).

Other biologically based research on emotion traits concerns which areas of the brain are active when processing emotion information, such as looking at sad pictures or thinking about something that makes one anxious or angry (Sutton, 2002). Most of the studies reveal that emotion is associated with an increased activation of the anterior cingulate cortex (Bush, Luu, & Posner, 2000; Whalen et al., 1998). The **anterior cingulate** is the portion of the brain located deep inside toward the center of the brain, and it most likely evolved early in the evolution of the nervous system. A recent study demonstrated increased cingulate cortex activation during social rejection (Eisenberger, Lieberman, & Williams, 2003). In this cleaver study, the subject was in an fMRI machine playing a computer game of catch with two other persons. After a while, the two other persons quit throwing the ball to the subject and instead played catch with themselves for 40 passes in a row. While this was happening, the poor subject's brain was scanned and that was when the researchers discovered that social rejection, which often accompanies feelings of sadness and distress, caused increased activity in the anterior cingulate.

Other researchers have focused on the biological basis of the self-regulation of negative emotions. For example, Levesque and colleagues (2003) had subjects watch a sad film. Half of them were told to do whatever they could to stop or prevent the sad feelings and to not show any emotional reactions during the film. Subjects who were successful at this exhibited increased activity in the right ventral medial **prefrontal cortex,** part of the so-called executive control center of the brain. Other studies have also identified this area as highly active in the control of emotion

(Beauregard, Levesque, and Bourgouin, 2001). As we will see in the section on anger regulation below, many people who have committed violent acts exhibit a neurological deficit in the frontal areas, the areas assumed to be responsible for the regulation of negative emotions.

Cognitive theories Another way to look at neuroticism is as a cognitive phenomenon. Some personality psychologists have argued that the cause of neuroticism lies not so much in the biology of the limbic brain but in the psychology of the person's overall cognitive system. These theorists have argued that neuroticism is caused by certain styles of information processing (such as attending, thinking, and remembering). Lishman (1972), for example, found that high-N (neuroticism) subjects were more likely to recall unpleasant information than were low-N subjects. There was no relation between neuroticism and the recall of pleasant information. After studying lists of pleasant and unpleasant words, high-N subjects also recalled the unpleasant words *faster* than the pleasant words. Martin, Ward, and Clark (1983) had subjects study information about themselves and about others. When asked to recall that information, the high-N subjects recalled more negative information about themselves but did not recall more negative information about others. There appear to be very specific information-processing characteristics associated with neuroticism: it appears to relate to the preferential processing of negative (but not positive) information about the self (but not about others). Martin et al. (1983) state that "high-N scorers recall more self-negative words than low-N scorers because memory traces for self-negative words are stronger in the high-N scorers" (p. 500).

As a related explanation for the relation between neuroticism and selective memory for unpleasant information, researchers use a version of spreading activation concept, which was discussed in Chapter 10. Recall that this notion suggests that material is stored in memory by being linked with other, similar pieces of material. Many psychologists hold that emotional experiences are also stored in memory. Moreover, some individuals—those high in neuroticism—have richer networks of association surrounding memories of negative emotion. Consequently, for them, unpleasant material is more accessible, leading them to have higher rates of recall for unpleasant information.

One type of unpleasant information in memory concerns memory for illnesses, injuries, and physical symptoms. If high-N subjects have a richer network of associations surrounding unpleasant information in memories, then they are also likely to recall more instances of illness and bodily complaints. Try asking a high-N person the following question: "So, what's your health been like the past few months?" Be prepared for a long answer, with a litany of complaints and many details about specific symptoms. Study after study has established a link between neuroticism and self-reported health complaints. For example, Smith and colleagues (1989) asked subjects to recall whether they had experienced each of 90 symptoms within the past three weeks. Neuroticism correlated with the self-reported frequencies of symptoms, usually in the range of $r = .4$ to $.5$. This means that roughly 15 to 25 percent of the variation in health symptoms could be attributed to the personality variable of neuroticism.

Larsen (1992) examined the sources of bias in neurotics' reports of physical illnesses. He asked participants to report every day on whether or not they experienced any physical symptoms, such as a runny nose, cough, sore throat, backache, stomachache, sore muscles, headache, loss of appetite, and so on. The participants made daily reports for two months, providing the researcher with a day-by-day running report of physical symptoms. After the daily report phase was complete, Larsen then asked the participants to recall, as accurately as they could, how many times they reported each symptom during the two months of daily reporting. This unusual research design allowed the researcher to calculate the subjects' "true" total number of symptoms, as reported on a daily basis, as well as their remembered number of symptoms. It turned out that both of these scores were related to neuroticism. That is, the high-N participants reported more daily symptoms, *and* they recalled more symptoms, than did the stable low-N subjects. Moreover, even when controlling for the number of day-to-day symptoms reported, neuroticism was *still* related to elevated levels of recalled symptoms.

High-neuroticism persons recall and report more symptoms, but are they more likely than stable low-N individuals to actually *have* more physical illnesses? This is a tricky question to address, as even medical doctors rely on a person's self-reports of symptoms to establish the presence of physical disease. The answer is to look at objective indicators of illness and disease and to see if those are related to neuroticism. Major disease categories, such as coronary disease, cancer, or premature death, appear to have little, if any, relation to neuroticism (Watson & Pennnebaker, 1989). Costa and McCrae (1985) reviewed this literature and concluded that "neuroticism influences perceptions of health, but not health itself" (p. 24). Similar conclusions were reached by Holroyd and Coyne (1987), who wrote that neuroticism reflects "a biased style of perceiving physiological experiences" (p. 372).

Recent research on the immune system, however, is showing that neuroticism does appear to be related to diminished immune function during stress (Herbert & Cohen, 1993). In a fascinating study by Marsland et al. (2001), subjects underwent vaccination for hepatitis B, and their antibody response to the injection was measured (this is a measure of how well the immune system responds to antigens in a vaccine). It was found that the subjects low in neuroticism mounted and maintained the strongest immune response to the vaccine. This finding suggests that persons high in neuroticism may, in fact, be more susceptible to immune-mediated diseases. In other words, they may not be just remembering more illness but may actually have more symptoms than subjects low in neuroticism. We will return to personality and health in Chapter 18, but for now we will get back to the topic of neuroticism and emotional reactivity and will examine one final theory that suggests a cognitive explanation of negative emotional reactivity in neuroticism.

Psychologists have proposed a theory that high-neuroticism subjects pay more attention to threats and unpleasant information in their environments (e.g., Dalgleish, 1995; Matthews, 2000; Matthews, Derryberry, & Siegle, 2000). High-N subjects are thought to have a stronger behavioral inhibition system, compared to low-N persons, making them particularly vulnerable to cues of punishment and frustration and prompting them to be vigilant for signs of threat. These researchers argue that high-N subjects are on the lookout for threatening information in their environment, constantly scanning for anything that might be menacing, unsafe, or negative.

Researchers have incorporated a version of the Stroop effect into investigations of attentional bias and neuroticism. The Stroop effect (Stroop, 1935) describes the increased time it takes to name the color in which a word is written when that word names a different color, relative to when it is a matching color word or a patch of color. For example, if the word *blue* is written in red ink, then it takes longer to name the color of the ink (red) than it would take if the word *red* were written in red ink. Researchers agree that the relevant dimension (color of ink) and the irrelevant dimension (name of the word) produce a conflict within the attentional system. If a person's attentional system can efficiently suppress the irrelevant dimension (the word), then he or she should be faster in naming the color than someone who cannot suppress the word information.

The Stroop task has been modified to study individual differences in attention to emotion words. In the so-called emotion Stroop task, the content of the words is typically anxiety- or threat-related, such as *fear, disease, cancer, death, failure, grief,* or *pathetic*. The words are written in colored ink, and the subject is asked to name the color of the ink and ignore the content of the words. Emotional interference is assumed when the time it takes to name the colors of the threat words is longer than the time it takes to name the colors of neutral words (Algom, Chajut, & Lev, 2004). Applied to neuroticism, the idea is that high-N persons have an attentional bias such that certain stimuli (the threat words) are more salient, or attention-grabbing. The threat words should be more difficult for them to ignore when naming the colors. Therefore, neuroticism should correlate with response time to name the colors, when the words refer to threat (e.g., *disease, failure*).

A thorough review of this literature was published by Williams, Mathews, and MacLeod 1996. These researchers reviewed more than 50 experiments that have used a version of the emotion Stroop task. Many of the studies show that high-N groups (or participants with anxiety disorder) are often slower to name colors of anxiety- and threat-related words, compared with the color naming of control, nonemotion words. The explanation given for this effect is that the emotion words capture the attention of the high-N participants, but not of the low-N participants.

In summary, neuroticism is a trait that relates to a variety of negative emotions, including anxiety, fear, worry, annoyance, irritation, and distress. Persons high in neuroticism are unstable in their moods, are easily upset, and take longer to recover after being upset. There are both biological and cognitive theories about the causes of negative emotions in neuroticism, and each has some supportive evidence in the scientific literature. One particularly well-known finding concerns the tendency of persons high in neuroticism to complain of health problems. In addition, high-N persons are thought to be on the lookout for threatening information; they pay more attention to negative cues and events in life, however minor, compared with more emotionally stable persons.

Depression and Melancholia **Depression** is another traitlike dimension. In this chapter, we will cover only a small part of what is known about depression. There is a huge body of literature on the topic of depression, as is befitting a psychological disorder that is estimated to strike 20 percent of the people in the United States at some time in their lives (American Psychiatric Association, 1994). There are entire books on depression, graduate courses devoted to this topic, and clinicians who specialize primarily in the treatment of depression. There are thought to be many varieties of depression (e.g., Rusting & Larsen, 1998a), and researchers are attempting to categorize the kinds of depression and are looking for ways to help people who suffer from the debilitating effects of depression. See Table 13.4 for a list of symptoms that define depression.

Diathesis-stress model One way to view depression is through a **diathesis-stress model.** This model suggests that there is a pre-existing vulnerability, or diathesis, that is present among people who later become depressed. In addition to this vulnerability, a stressful life event must occur in order to trigger the depression, such as the loss of a loved one, a career failure, or another major negative life event. Neither element alone—the diathesis or the stress—is sufficient to trigger depression. Rather,

Table 13.4 Signs of Depression

The signs of depression include having five or more of the following symptoms during the same two-week period:

- Depressed mood most of the day, nearly every day
- Diminished interest or pleasure in most activities
- Change in weight: significant weight loss when not dieting or a weight gain
- Change in sleep pattern: insomnia or sleeping much more than usual
- Change in movements: restlessness and agitation or feeling slowed down
- Fatigue or loss of energy nearly every day
- Feelings of worthlessness or guilt nearly every day
- Diminished ability to concentrate or make decisions nearly every day
- Recurrent thoughts of death or suicide

Source: Adapted from American Psychiatric Association, 1994.

they must occur together—something bad or stressful must happen to a person who has a vulnerability to depression.

Beck's cognitive theory Many researchers have emphasized certain cognitive styles as one type of pre-existing condition that makes people vulnerable to depression (Larsen & Cowan, 1988). One of these researchers is Aaron Beck (1967), who has written extensively on his cognitive theory of depression. He suggests that the vulnerability lies in a particular **cognitive schema,** or way of looking at the world. A schema is a way of processing incoming information, a way of organizing and interpreting the facts of daily life, as mentioned in Chapter 12. The cognitive schema involved in depression, according to Beck, distorts the incoming information in a negative way, a way that makes the person depressed.

According to Beck, there are three important areas of life that are most influenced by the depressive cognitive schema. This **cognitive triad** includes information about the self, about the world, and about the future. Information about these important aspects of life is distorted in specific ways by the depressive cognitive schema. For example, after doing poorly on a practice exam, a depressive person might say to himself, "I am a total failure." This is an example of the *overgeneralizing* distortion applied to the self. Overgeneralizing is taking one instance and generalizing to many or all other instances. The lay term for this is "blowing things out of proportion." The person might have failed at one exam, but that does not mean he is a total failure. The same overgeneralizing style can be applied to the world ("If anything can go wrong, it will") and the future ("Why bother trying, when everything I do is doomed to fail?"). In Beck's (1976) theory, there are many other cognitive distortions, such as making *arbitrary inferences* (jumping to a negative conclusion, even when the evidence does not support it), *personalizing* (assuming that everything is your fault), and *catastrophizing* (thinking that the worst will always happen). These cognitive elements are portrayed in Figure 13.5.

According to Beck's influential theory (1976), depression is the result of applying these cognitive distortions to the information from daily life. These distortions are applied quickly and outside of immediate awareness, resulting in a stream of automatic negative thoughts, which deeply affect how the person feels and acts ("I'm no good. The world is against me. My future is bleak"). The person who thinks he is a total failure will often act like a total failure and may even give up trying to do better,

Information processing about:

	The self	The world	One's future
Overgeneralizing	"I received a bad grade on this paper . . . , I just can't seem to do anything right."	"If anything can go wrong with this project, it probably will."	"Why bother trying, everything I do turns out to be a failure."
Arbitrary inferences	"The teacher didn't have time to see me today. She probably doesn't like me."	"This teacher doesn't care . . . , probably none of the teachers care about students."	"I'm sure all the teachers I'll have will be lousy, just like this one."
Personalizing	"My softball team lost today . . . , and it's all my fault."	"This reminds me of all the times my team lost when I was in grade school."	"I'll probably never be on a winning team . . ."
Catastrophizing	"Failing this exam means I'm incapable of learning."	"Failing this exam probably means I won't get into medical school . . ."	"Since I probably won't get into medical school, I should just quit college right now."

Figure 13.5

Beck's cognitive model of depression, showing how distortions are applied to processing information about the self, the world, and one's future. These cognitive distortions promote depression.

creating a **self-fulfilling prophecy.** Moreover, depressive feelings lead to more distortions, which in turn lead to more bad feelings, and so on, in a self-perpetuating cycle. Beck devised a form of therapy for changing people's cognitive distortions. In a nutshell, this involves challenging the person's distortions, such as by asking, "Does it really mean that you are a *total failure* because you flunked just this one exam?"

Explanatory style Another cognitive theory of depression focuses specifically on how people explain the causes of events in their lives. As we saw in Chapter 12, this theory focuses on differences in explanatory style among depressed and nondepressed persons. Studies of depression often find that depressed persons maintain an internal, stable, and global explanatory style. This is the so-called pessimistic pattern of explanatory style, and it puts a person at risk for depression (Peterson, 1991; Peterson & Seligman, 1984). Life provides everyone with occasional bumps, bruises, and setbacks. Most people interpret these as momentary problems or as minor, isolated obstacles in the greater scheme of things and, so, work to overcome them. However, if such events are interpreted as enduring personal failures that generalize to other domains of life, then the person is bound to feel hopeless, helpless, and depressed.

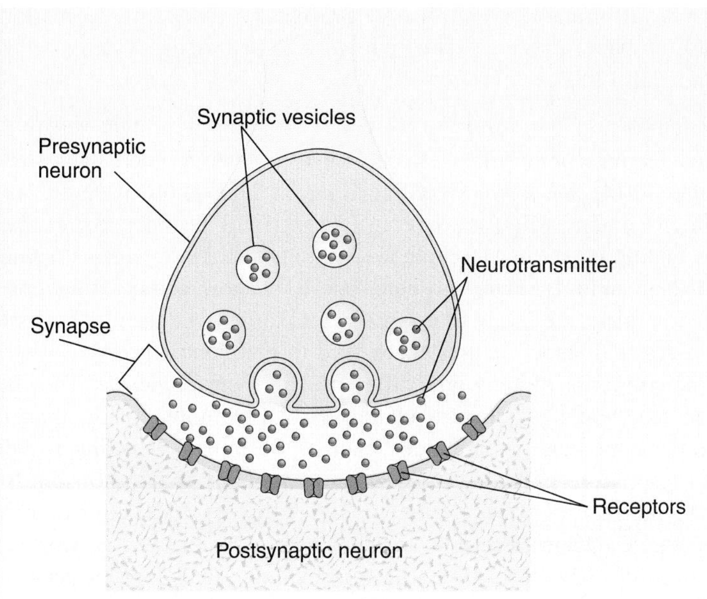

Figure 13.6

Diagram of synapse between two neurons, illustrating how neurotransmitters must be released, cross the synapse, and bond with the receptors on the postsynaptic neuron in order for a nerve impulse to pass on its way to completion.

Biology of Depression Nerve cells in the brain communicate with each other by way of chemical messengers called neurotransmitters (Chapter 6). These neurotransmitters are broken down and delivered from one neuron across a gap—called the synapse—to another neuron (Figure 13.6). The first neuron is called the presynaptic neuron and the second neuron is called the postsynaptic neuron. If the neurotransmitter reaches the other postsynaptic neuron in sufficient strength, the nerve signal continues on its way toward completing the action for which it is intended, for instance, changing the channel on the remote, reading another sentence in a book, casting a flirting glance at someone you like. When someone is depressed, it is thought that there are imbalances in the levels of neurotransmitters in the brain. Depressed persons often describe feeling slowed down, as if they don't have energy to do what they want to do. The **neurotransmitter theory of depression** holds that this emotional problem may be the result of neurotransmitter imbalance at the synapses of the nervous system. The neurotransmitters thought to be most involved in depression include norepinephrine (also called noradrenaline), serotonin, and, to a lesser degree, dopamine. Many of the drugs used to treat depression target exactly these neurotransmitters. For example, Prozac, Zoloft, and Paxil inhibit the re-uptake of serotonin in the synapse, resulting in increased levels of this neurotransmitter in the nervous system. The medication Tofranil works to maintain a better balance between levels of both serotonin and norepinephrine. Not all persons with depression are successfully treated with these kinds of medications, suggesting that there may be varieties of depression, some more biologically based, others more reactive to stress or cognitively based.

Recent studies suggest that exercise might be usefully applied to the treatment of depression, at least for some persons (Dubbert, 2002). In his 1996 annual report, Surgeon General of the United States David Satcher documented the benefits of exercise for health promotion and disease prevention—including depression prevention. The use of exercise in counseling people with depression is described by Pixon, Mauzey, and Hall (2003).

Anger-Proneness and Potential for Hostility Another important negative emotion is anger and feelings of hostility. Psychologists have long been interested in what makes people hostile and aggressive. Social psychologists, for example, have examined conditions under which the average person will become aggressive (Baron, 1977). One finding is that most people are willing to strike out against someone who has treated them unfairly. Here the emphasis is on how certain situations, such as being treated unfairly, are likely to evoke aggression in *most* people. Personality psychologists agree that some circumstances tend to make most people angry, but their interest is more in terms of individual differences in anger-proneness. They begin with the position that some people are characteristically more hostile than others in response to the same kinds of situations, such as frustration. **Hostility** is defined as a tendency to respond to everyday frustrations with anger and aggression, to become irritable easily, to feel frequent resentment, and to act in a rude, critical, antagonistic, and uncooperative manner in everyday interactions (Dembrowski & Costa, 1987).

The scientific objectives, from the personality psychologist's perspective, are (1) to understand how hostile people became that way, what keeps them that way, and in what other ways they differ from nonhostile people and (2) to examine the consequences of hostility in terms of important life outcomes.

Type A personality and heart disease Recent research on the **Type A personality** has focused on hostility and anger-proneness as the toxic component, as that part of the Type A pattern that is most related to heart disease (Contrada, Leventhal, & O'Leary, 1990). We will discuss the Type A personality and health link in more detail in Chapter 18; however, in this section, we will briefly describe the relations between the personality dimension of Type A and the experience and expression of anger and hostility. We will begin with a brief introduction to the concept of Type A personality.

In the 1960s, two cardiologists, Meyer Friedman and Ray Rosenman, began to notice that many of their coronary heart disease (CHD) patients were competitive, aggressive workaholics and ambitious overachievers, were often hostile, were almost always in a hurry, and rarely relaxed. Friedman and Rosenman referred to this pattern of behavior as the *Type A personality* (Friedman & Rosenman, 1974, p. 37). To measure Type A personality, they developed a structured interview consisting of 25 questions asking subjects how they typically responded to situations involving competition, frustration, or a need to hurry. The interviewer also attempted to bring out hostility by intentionally frustrating the subject during the interview. For example, the interviewer tried to make the person angry by deliberately slowing down, by hesitating before asking the next question, and by pretending not to understand what the person was trying to say. Some people may find this behavior quite irritating and react in a hostile or aggressive manner (Dembrowski & MacDougall, 1985; Dembrowski & Williams, 1989).

As research accumulated, consensus grew that Type A is actually not a single personality trait but rather a **syndrome,** or cluster of several traits, which includes achievement strivings, impatience, competitiveness, and hostility. Moreover, these characteristics do not always occur together in the same people. Out of the collection of traits that defines Type A, researchers began to guess that perhaps only one trait is the real pathogenic agent. It became clear that the hostility component, more than any other, was the one factor most related to CHD (Wright, 1988). Table 13.5 presents a widely used questionnaire for assessing trait anger.

Table 13.5 Multidimensional Anger Inventory

INSTRUCTIONS: Everyone gets angry from time to time. A number of statements that people have used to describe the times that they get angry are included below. Read each statement and place a number from the following scale in front of the item to best describe yourself. There are no right or wrong answers. (Items are grouped according to the scales they are scored on; numbers are the original item numbers.)

1 = completely undescriptive of me
2 = mostly undescriptive of me
3 = partly undescriptive and partly descriptive of me
4 = mostly descriptive of me
5 = completely descriptive of me

Frequency of Anger[1]

1. _____ I tend to get angry more frequently than most people.
6. _____ It is easy to make me angry.
9. _____ Something makes me angry almost every day.
14. _____ I am surprised at how often I feel angry.
17. _____ At times, I feel angry for no specific reason.

Duration of Anger

22. _____ When I get angry, I stay angry for hours.
25. _____ When I get angry, I calm down faster than most people.*

Magnitude of Anger

2. _____ Other people seem to get angrier than I do in similar situations.*
10. _____ I often feel angrier than I think I should.
18. _____ I can make myself angry about something in the past just by thinking about it.
26. _____ I get so angry, I feel like I might lose control.

Anger-in

3. _____ I harbor grudges that I don't tell anyone about for a long time.
20. _____ When I hide my anger from others, I think about it for a long time.
23. _____ When I hide my anger from others, I forget about it pretty quickly.*
24. _____ I try to talk over problems with people without letting them know I'm angry.*
27. _____ If I let people see the way I feel, I'd be considered a hard person to get along with.
29. _____ It's difficult for me to let people know I am angry.

Anger-out

4. _____ I try to get even when I'm angry with someone.
7. _____ When I am angry with someone, I let that person know.
12. _____ When I am angry with someone, I take it out on whoever is around.
15. _____ Once I let people know I'm angry, I can put it out of my mind.
19. _____ Even after I have expressed my anger, I have trouble forgetting about it.

(Continued)

Table 13.5 Continued

Guilt

11. _____ I feel guilty about expressing my anger.

29. _____ It's difficult for me to let people know I am angry.

Brooding

15. _____ Once I let people know I'm angry, I can put it out of my mind.*

19. _____ Even after I have expressed my anger, I have trouble forgetting about it.

20. _____ When I hide my anger from others, I think about it for a long time.

23. _____ When I hide my anger from others, I forget about it pretty quickly.*

Anger-discuss

24. _____ I try to talk over problems with people without letting them know I'm angry.

Hostile outlook

5. _____ I am secretly quite critical of others.

8. _____ I have met many people who are supposed to be experts who are no better than I.

13. _____ Some of my friends have habits that annoy and bother me very much.

16. _____ People talk about me behind my back.

21. _____ People can bother me just by being around.

28. _____ I am on my guard with people who are friendlier than I expected.

Range of anger-eliciting situations

30. I get angry when:

a. _____ someone lets me down.

b. _____ people are unfair.

c. _____ something blocks my plans.

d. _____ I am delayed.

e. _____ someone embarrasses me.

f. _____ I have to take orders from someone less capable than I.

g. _____ I have to work with incompetent people.

h. _____ I do something stupid.

i. _____ I am not given credit for something I have done.

Source: Adapted from Siegel, J. M. (1986), "The Multidimensional Anger Inventory," *Journal of Personality and Social Psychology, 51,* 191–200. Copyright © 1986 by the American Psychological Association. Reprinted with permission.

[1]Items cluster into 10 subscales of trait anger. The numbers in front of each item indicate the item placement on the original questionnaire. The items are grouped into their subscales here so that the student may see which items assess the components of trait anger.

*Indicates that this item is reversed before scoring. Recall from Chapter 4 that reversed items are frequently used to control for acquiescence. Students may score their own responses by reversing their answers to these items and totaling their responses to each cluster of items.

Anger is an emotion that causes some people to lose control. Most of the violent inmates in our prisons have trouble with the self-regulation of this potent emotion. Researchers have long speculated that there may be biological differences, particularly in brain function, between violent and nonviolent persons. The psychologist Adrian Raine has spent many years examining some of the most violent and aggressive members of our society (e.g., Raine, 2002; Brennan & Raine, 1997). In one study of especially violent murderers, Raine and his colleagues (1998) found that these persons showed decreased activity in the prefrontal areas of their brains, those areas mentioned earlier that are associated with normal emotional regulation. Psychologist Jonathan Pincus has also specialized in the study of violent criminals. In a review of his work, Pincus (2001) presents information on the lives of numerous serial killers and in virtually all cases these murderers suffered from some damage to their brains, either through violence, accidental injuries, or excessive drug or alcohol abuse. In addition, practically all of these murderers came from severely abusive families. In another chapter, Pincus presents data that the presence of brain damage in violent criminals is most often in the prefrontal areas. Again, these are the areas involved in self-control. Interestingly, this is also the area that was severely damaged in the case of Phineas Gage, discussed in Chapter 6.

In large studies not every violent or sadistic person is found to have brain abnormalities. However, the rates of brain abnormalities are much higher in violent persons than in those persons without a history of violence. For example, in a study of 62 criminals in Japan the researchers divided the inmates into those convicted of murder and those convicted of nonviolent offenses. Brain abnormalities were much more frequent among the murderers than the nonviolent offenders (Sakuta & Fukushima, 1998). In a study done in Austria, a group of high-violence offenders were compared to a group of low-violence offenders. In the high-violence group, 66 percent were found to have brain abnormalities, whereas in the low-violence group only 17 percent were found to have the same brain abnormalities (Aigner, Eher, Fruehwald, Frottier, Gutierrez-Lobos, & Dywer, 2000). In a study of sexual offenders, criminals were divided into those who physically harmed their victims (e.g., committed murder or sadistically violent acts) and those who did not physically harm their victim (e.g., exposed themselves). In the group of violent sex offenders 41 percent were found to have brain abnormalities, a rate significantly higher than in the nonviolent sex offenders (Langevin, Bain, Wortzman, & Hucker, 1988). In a particularly strong longitudinal study, a group of 110 hyperactive and 76 normal boys had their brain activity assessed when they were between 6 and 12 years of age. They were followed up between the ages of 14–20 years, with special attention to arrest records. Those adolescent boys with a history of delinquency turned out to have had unusual brain patterns in childhood compared to those adolescents without subsequent delinquency (Satterfield & Schell, 1984).

In the movie A History of Violence, *the title foreshadows a characteristic of the main character. Would a person with a long history of extreme violence be able to change completely into a gentle, loving father and pillar of his community?*

The kind of brain damage most often observed in hostile aggressive persons involves areas in the frontal lobe and, to a lesser extent, the temporal lobe. These areas are important in regulating impulses, particularly aggressive impulses, and fear conditioning. The damage may be developmentally caused or caused by injury. For example, sniffing glue or inhaling butane gas, which can induce intoxication similar to alcohol, can cause the kind of brain damage that has been related to antisocial behavior (Jung, Lee, & Cho, 2004). Another example is a case report where a man developed a cyst in his brain. Prior to this development he was not a violent person. However, after the cyst grew, and presumably caused damage to his brain, he strangled his wife to death after she scratched his face (Paradis, Horn, Lazar, & Schwartz, 1994). The kind of brain abnormalities found in violent persons appears to involve decrements in the person's ability to inhibit or control aggressive impulses.

Style of Emotional Life

So far in this chapter, we have discussed people's emotional lives in terms of emotional content, or the various characteristic emotions that define how one person is different from others. Now we turn to a discussion of emotional style. As a quick distinction, we might say that content is the *what* of a person's emotional life, whereas style is the *how* of that emotional life.

Affect Intensity as an Emotional Style

When we think about how emotions are experienced, probably the major stylistic distinction is one of intensity. You know from experience with your own emotional reactions that emotions can vary greatly in terms of magnitude. Emotions can be weak and mild, or strong and almost uncontrollable. To characterize a person's emotional style, we must inquire about the typical intensity of his or her emotional experiences. For emotional intensity to be useful to personality theory, we must establish that it describes a stable characteristic useful for making distinctions between persons.

Affect intensity can be defined by a description of persons who are either high or low on this dimension. Larsen and Diener (1987) describe *high affect intensity* individuals as people who typically experience their emotions strongly and are emotionally reactive and variable. High affect intensity subjects typically go way up when they are feeling up and go way down when they are feeling down. They also alternate between these extremes more frequently and rapidly than do low affect intensity individuals. Low affect intensity individuals, on the other hand, typically experience their emotions only mildly and with only gradual fluctuations and minor reactions. Such persons are stable and calm and usually do not suffer the troughs of negative emotions. But they also tend not to experience the peaks of enthusiasm, joy, and other strong positive emotions.

Note that these descriptions of high and low affect intensity persons make use of the qualifying terms typically and usually. This is because certain life events can make even the lowest affect intensity person experience relatively strong emotions. For example, being accepted into one's first choice of schools can cause intense positive emotions in almost anyone. Similarly, the death of a loved pet can cause strong negative emotions in almost everyone. However, because such events are fairly rare, we want to know what people are usually or typically like: how they characteristically react to the normal sorts of everyday emotion-provoking events.

Figure 13.7 presents daily mood data for two subjects from a study by Larsen and Diener (1985). These subjects kept daily records of their moods for 84 consecutive days. Note that Subject A's emotions were fairly stable and did not depart too far from her baseline level of mood over the entire three-month reporting period. Actually, she had a bad week at the beginning of the semester, which is denoted by the

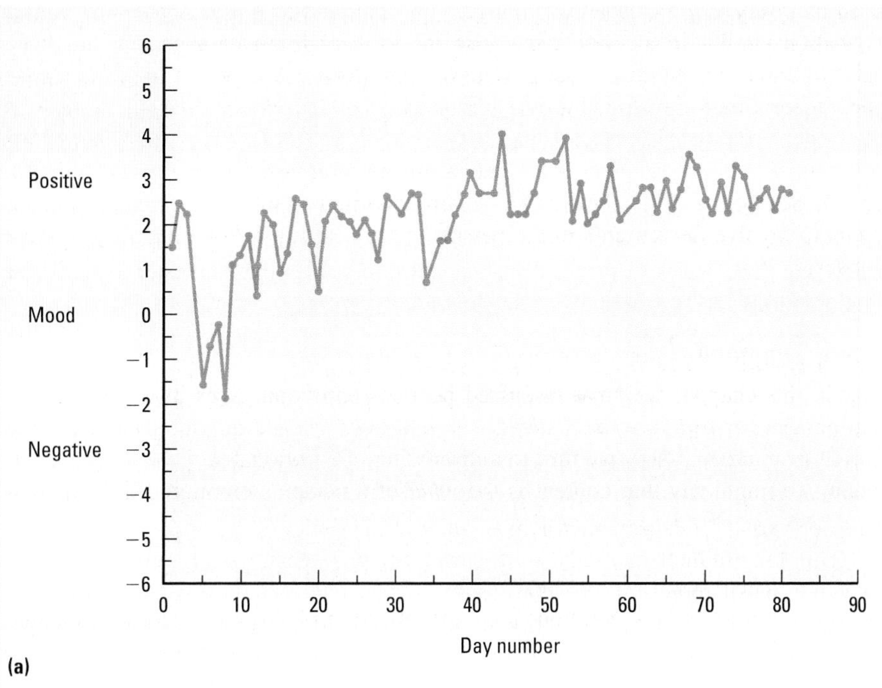

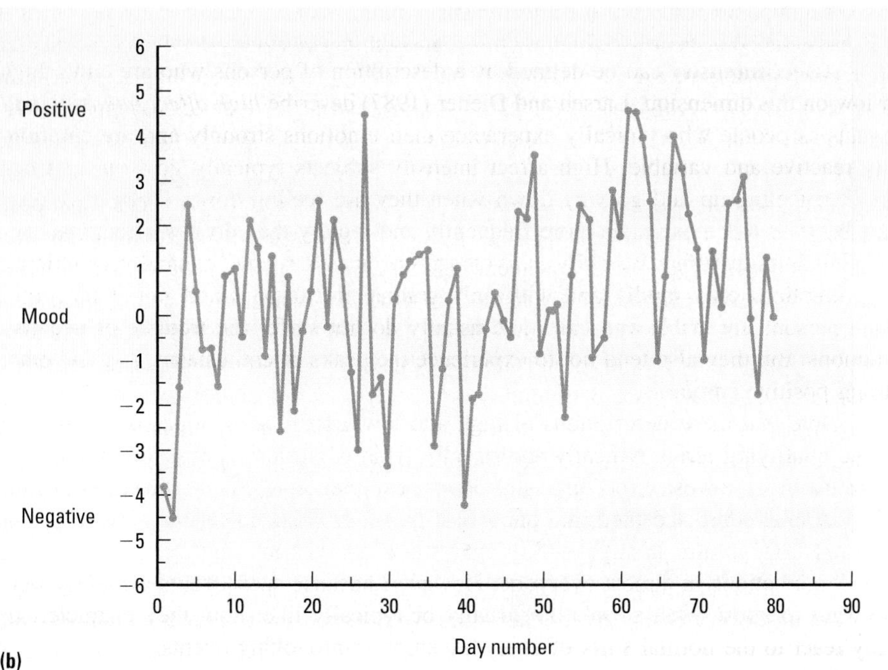

Figure 13.7

Data from individual subjects who kept a mood diary every day for three consecutive months. (a) Data from subject A. (b) Data from Subject B, who has much more intense moods and larger day-to-day mood swings than Subject A. Source: Adapted from Larsen, 1991.

several low points at the left side of the graph. Otherwise, things were pretty stable for this subject.

Subject B, on the other hand, exhibited extreme changes in mood over time. This subject was hardly ever near his baseline level of mood. Instead, Subject B appears to have experienced both strong positive and strong negative affect frequently and to alternate between these extremes frequently and rapidly. In other words, this high affect intensity person exhibited a good deal of variability in his daily moods, fluctuating back and forth between positive and negative affect from day to day. Interestingly, Subject B was in the student hospital three times that semester, once for an infection and twice for feeling run down.

Assessment of Affect Intensity and Mood Variability

In early studies of affect intensity (e.g., Diener, Larsen et al., 1985) this characteristic of emotional life was assessed using a daily experiential sampling method. That is, data were gathered much like that presented in Figure 13.7, panels a and b. Researchers would then compute a total score for each subject to represent how intense or variable that person was over the time period.

This longitudinal method of measuring affect intensity is straightforward and face valid, and it represents the construct of affect intensity quite well. However, it takes several weeks or longer of daily mood reporting to generate a reliable composite affect intensity score for each individual. Consequently, a questionnaire measure of affect intensity has been developed that allows a relatively quick assessment of a person's emotional style in terms of intensity. Table 13.6 lists 20 items from this questionnaire, called the Affect Intensity Measure (AIM) (Larsen & Diener, 1987).

An important aspect of the affect intensity trait is that we cannot really say whether it is bad or good to be low or high on this trait. Both positive and negative consequences are related to scoring either high or low. High-scoring persons, for example, get a lot of zest out of life, enjoying peaks of enthusiasm, joy, and positive emotional involvement. On the other hand, when things are not going well, high-scoring persons are prone to strong negative emotional reactions, such as sadness, guilt, and anxiety. In addition, because high-scoring persons have frequent experiences of extreme emotions (both positive and negative), they tend to suffer the physical consequences of this emotional involvement. Emotions activate the sympathetic nervous system, making the person aroused. Even strong *positive* emotions activate the sympathetic nervous system and produce wear and tear on the nervous system. High-scoring persons tend to exhibit physical symptoms that result from their chronic emotional lifestyles, such as muscle tension, stomachaches, headaches, and fatigue. An interesting finding is that, even though they report more of these physical symptoms, high-scoring persons are not particularly unhappy or upset by them (Larsen, Billings, & Cutler, 1996). Interviews with high-scoring persons usually show that they have no desire to change their level of emotional intensity. They seem to prefer the emotional involvement, the ups and downs, and the physiological arousal that accompanies their highly emotional lifestyle (Larsen & Diener, 1987).

Low affect intensity individuals, on the other hand, are stable and do not typically get upset very easily. Even when negative events happen, they maintain an even emotional state and avoid the troughs of negative affect. The price such people pay for this emotional stability, however, is that they fail to experience their positive emotions very strongly. They lack the peaks of zest, enthusiasm, emotional engagement, and joy that energize the lives of high affect intensity individuals. Low affect intensity individuals, however, do not pay the price of the physical and psychosomatic symptoms that go along with the high affect intensity personality.

Table 13.6 AIM Questionnaire

INSTRUCTIONS: The following statements refer to emotional reactions to typical life events. Please indicate how *you* react to these events by placing a number from the following scale in the blank space preceding each item. Please base your answers on how *you* react, *not* on how you think others react or how you think a person should react.

Never	Almost Never	Occasionally	Usually	Almost Always	Always
1	2	3	4	5	6

1. _____ When I accomplish something difficult, I feel delighted or elated.
2. _____ When I feel happy, it is a strong type of exuberance.
3. _____ I enjoy being with other people very much.
4. _____ I feel pretty bad when I tell a lie.
5. _____ When I solve a small personal problem, I feel euphoric.
6. _____ My emotions tend to be more intense than those of most people.
7. _____ My happy moods are so strong that I feel as if I were in heaven.
8. _____ I get overly enthusiastic.
9. _____ If I complete a task I thought was impossible, I am ecstatic.
10. _____ My heart races at the anticipation of an exciting event.
11. _____ Sad movies deeply touch me.
12. _____ When I'm happy, it's a feeling of being untroubled and content, rather than being zestful and aroused.
13. _____ When I talk in front of a group for the first time, my voice gets shaky and my heart races.
14. _____ When something good happens, I'm usually much more jubilant than others.
15. _____ My friends might say I'm emotional.
16. _____ The memories I like the most are of those times when I felt content and peaceful, rather than zestful and enthusiastic.
17. _____ The sight of someone who is hurt badly affects me strongly.
18. _____ When I'm feeling well, it's easy for me to go from being in a good mood to being really joyful.
19. _____ "Calm and cool" could easily describe me.
20. _____ When I'm happy, I feel as if I'm bursting with joy.

Research Findings on Affect Intensity

In a daily study of mood, Larsen, Diener, and Emmons (1986) had subjects record the events in their daily lives. Sixty-two subjects recorded the best and the worst events of the day for 56 consecutive days, resulting in almost 6,000 event descriptions. The subjects also rated these events each day in terms of how subjectively good or bad the events were for them. The same event descriptions were rated later by a team of raters for how objectively good or bad they would be for the average college student. Results showed that the subjects high on the affect intensity dimension rated their life events as significantly *more severe* than did the low affect intensity subjects. That is, events that were rated as only "moderately good" by the objective raters (such as receiving a compliment from a professor) were rated as "very good" by the high affect intensity subjects. Similarly, events that were rated as only "moderately bad" by the objective raters (such as losing a favorite pen) tended to be rated as "very bad" by the high affect intensity subjects. Thus, the high affect intensity subjects tended to evaluate the events in their lives—both good and bad events—as having significantly more emotional impact than did the low affect intensity subjects. High affect intensity individuals are, thus, more emotionally reactive to the emotion-provoking events in their lives, both the good and the bad events.

An aspect of these findings worth emphasizing is that high affect intensity individuals are more reactive to *both* positive and negative events in their lives. This may be due to the fact that affect intensity correlates positively with both extraversion and neuroticism. These aspects of affect intensity make high-scoring persons look like neurotic extraverts; they respond with strong positive emotion to good events and with strong negative emotion to bad events. However, if we assume that good and bad events happen fairly randomly in life, then we should expect the daily emotions of high affect intensity individuals to go up and down randomly with those events. In other words, high affect intensity individuals should exhibit more **mood variability,** or more frequent fluctuations in their emotional lives over time. Larsen (1987) found that individuals high on the affect intensity dimension do, in fact, exhibit more frequent changes in their moods and that these changes tend to be larger in magnitude than are the mood changes of low affect intensity individuals.

The concept of affect intensity, containing as it does the notion of mood variability, is a general and broad characteristic of emotional life. Affect intensity has been found to relate to a variety of standard personality variables. For example, Larsen and Diener (1987) reported that affect intensity relates to the personality dimensions of high activity level, sociability, and arousability. High affect intensity individuals tend to have a vigorous and energetic lifestyle, tend to be outgoing and enjoy being with others, and tend to seek out stimulating and arousing things to do in their daily lives. During an interview, a high affect intensity subject reported that, to her, the worst thing in life was to be bored. She reported that she often did things to liven up her life, such as playing practical jokes on her roommates. Although such activities sometimes got her into trouble, she felt that it was worth it to obtain the stimulation. Another high affect intensity subject described himself as an "intensity junkie," hooked on the need for an emotionally stimulating lifestyle.

Interaction of Content and Style in Emotional Life

People differ from each other both in terms of the relative amounts of positive and negative emotional *content* in their lives over time, as well as in terms of the *stylistic* intensity of their emotional experiences. In trying to understand emotional life as an aspect of personality, it appears that the hedonic balance—the degree of pleasantness in a person's life over time—represents the content of emotional life. For example, Larsen (2000b) reported that the average college student had a positive hedonic balance on 7 out of 10 days. That is, out of every 10 days, 7 of them contained predominantly positive emotions, and 3 of them contained a predominance of negative emotions. However, there were wide individual differences, so that some people had as few as 20 percent positive days, whereas others had as many as 95 percent positive

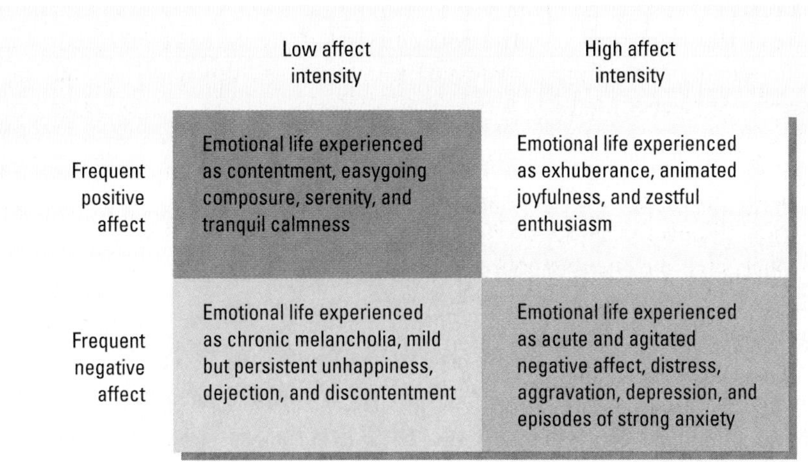

Low affect intensity
High affect intensity
Frequent positive affect
Emotional life experienced as contentment, easygoing composure, serenity, and tranquil calmness
Emotional life experienced as exhuberance, animated joyfulness, and zestful enthusiasm
Frequent negative affect
Emotional life experienced as chronic melancholia, mild but persistent unhappiness, dejection, and discontentment
Emotional life experienced as acute and agitated negative affect, distress, aggravation, depression, and episodes of strong anxiety

Figure 13.8

Quality of emotional life as a function of content (hedonic balance) and style (affect intensity).

days. This hedonic balance between positive and negative affect, between the good and bad days in a person's life over time, best represents the content of emotional life (Zelenski & Larsen, 2000).

Affect intensity represents the style of emotional life and refers to the magnitude of a person's typical emotional reactions. Together, these two characteristics—content and style—provide a good deal of descriptive and explanatory power. An interesting aspect of these two dimensions is that hedonic balance and affect intensity are unrelated to each other (Larsen & Diener, 1985). This means that there are people who have frequent positive affect of low intensity and others who have frequent positive affect of high intensity. Similarly, there are people who have frequent negative affect of low intensity and others who have frequent negative affect of high intensity. In other words, hedonic balance interacts with affect intensity to produce specific types of emotional lives that may characterize different personalities. The effects of this interaction of hedonic balance and affect intensity in creating emotional life are illustrated in Figure 13.8.

In Figure 13.8, you can see that individuals high and low on the affect intensity dimension typically experience the content of their emotional lives in very different ways. A person low in affect intensity has an emotional life that is characterized by its enduringness, evenness, and lack of fluctuation. If such a person also happens to be a happy person (more positive than negative emotional content in life), then he or she experiences this happiness as a tranquil sort of enduring contentment. If he or she happens to be an unhappy person (less positive than negative emotional content in life), then his or her emotional life consists of a chronic and somewhat annoying or irritating level of negative affect over time. On the other hand, a person high on the affect intensity dimension has an emotional life characterized by abruptness, changeableness, and volatility. If this kind of person also happens to be a happy person, then he or she experiences this happiness as enlivened and animated spikes of enthusiasm and exhilaration. If this high affect intensity person is, instead, an unhappy person, then he or she experiences troughs of a variety of negative emotions, such as anxiety, guilt, depression, and loneliness.

SUMMARY AND EVALUATION

Emotions can be thought of either as states or as traits, and both of these are patterns of experience, physiological changes, and changes in behavior, or action tendencies. Emotional states are short-lived and are typically caused by an event in the environment. As traits, however, emotions are consistent and stable patterns of experience in a person's life, where these patterns are due mostly to the person's personality. In this chapter, we looked at emotions as traits. For example, people differ from each other in how often they are angry, happy, or depressed. Such differences can be useful in describing aspects of personality.

Emotional content is the types of emotional experiences that a person is likely to have. If we know, for example, the typical content of a person's emotional life, then we know the kinds of emotions he or she is likely to experience over time.

Emotional content can be broadly divided into the pleasant and the unpleasant emotions. In the pleasant emotion category are happiness and the associated judgment of life satisfaction. On most people's lists of primary emotions, there is only one major pleasant emotion, whereas there are many varieties of unpleasant emotions. From a trait perspective, under pleasant emotions we discussed dispositional happiness. Some people are happier than others, and psychologists are developing theories and gathering data to understand why people differ on happiness and how people might increase their level of trait happiness.

Under the content approach to dispositional unpleasant emotions, we discussed three dispositions: anxiety, depression, and anger. Trait anxiety has many names in the personality literature, including neuroticism and negative affectivity. This trait emotion appears to have distinct cognitive components and is related to ongoing health, especially self-reported health. Depression is also defined as a syndrome of associated experiences and behaviors, and we examined several cognitive theories of depression. Anger-proneness and hostility were also discussed as a trait affect, and we examined the health and well-being implications of this disposition. Anxiety, depression, and anger are currently topics of intense interest for neuroscientists, and data are accumulating on the brain centers involved in the experience, as well as the regulation, of each of these emotions.

Emotional style is the typical way in which a person experiences emotions. We focused on the stylistic component of affect intensity, or the typical magnitude with which people experience emotions. Persons who score high on the affect intensity dimension have larger emotional reactions to the events in their lives, are reactive to both pleasant and unpleasant events, and are more variable in their day-to-day moods. Content and style interact within persons to produce distinct varieties of emotional lives.

KEY TERMS

Emotions 424
Action Tendencies 424
Functional Analysis 424
Emotional States 425
Emotional Traits 425
Categorical Approach 425
Dimensional Approach 427
Content 429
Style 429
Happiness 430
Positive Illusions 431
Reciprocal Causality 432
Mood Induction 440
Neuroticism 442
Limbic System 442
Anterior Cingulate 443
Prefrontal Cortex 443
Depression 446
Diathesis-Stress Model 446
Cognitive Schema 447
Cognitive Triad 447
Self-Fulfilling Prophesy 448
Neurotransmitter Theory of Depression 449
Hostility 450
Type A Personality 450
Syndrome 450
Affect Intensity 454
Mood Variability 458

Approaches to the Self

14

THE COGNITIVE/EXPERIENTIAL DOMAIN

There are many aspects to the self: the ways we see and define our selves, or our self-concept, the evaluation we make of that self-concept, which is called self-esteem, and our social identities, which are the outward reflections we show other people.

"Know thyself!" was the advice given by the Greek Oracle at Delphi. Do you know yourself? Who are you? How would you answer this question? Would you define yourself first as a student, as a son or daughter, or as someone's spouse or boy- or girlfriend? Or would you define yourself by listing your various characteristics: "I am smart, optimistic, and confident"? Or would you instead give a physical description: "I am a male, 6′ 6″ tall, about 200 pounds, with red hair and a ruddy complexion"? No matter how you respond to this question, your answer is an important part of your **self-concept,** your understanding of yourself. Moreover, some people are satisfied with who they are, whereas others are dissatisfied with their self-concept. How you feel about who you are is your **self-esteem.** On top of this, you have a **social identity,** as you present yourself to others. Sometimes social identity does not match our self-concept, and the selves we present to others are not the selves we know our selves to be, leading some of us to feel false or phony in our relationships.

In this chapter, we will explore how psychologists have approached the notion of the self. We will do this by considering the three main components of the self: self-concept, self-esteem, and social identity.

Why might we want to learn about the self? To most people, the sense of self is their anchor, their starting point for interpreting everything around them. For example, when you pick up some group photos from the developer (or download them from your digital camera), whom in the group do you look at first? If you are like most people, you will say that you look at yourself first. And, when looking at the photo of yourself, you immediately engage in an evaluation. You might think the picture is not a good representation, that it does not show you in the best light. Maybe you think that you have a nicer smile than that and that you are, in fact, a happier person than this picture portrays. Or you might think that you have put on a few pounds lately, that you are heavier than your friends in the photo. Maybe you dislike the fact that you have gotten heavier, and a small blow to your self-esteem occurs when you look at the photo. Or maybe you wonder how certain other people would view this photo of you. Would your parents like to see you this way? For example, would they approve of the self you portray in this group photo of your college friends?

Our sense of self is changing all the time. In infancy, we first distinguished ourselves from the world around us and began the life-long process of constructing, evaluating, and presenting to others our sense of who we are. During this process, we constantly undergo challenges and changes to our self-concept. For example, in high school, a young man might try out for the basketball team and do poorly. His sense of himself as an athlete is challenged by this experience of failure. He will have to search for other ways of defining himself. Maybe he will dye his hair purple and start wearing a trench coat to school, beginning to define himself in terms of an alternative teen lifestyle. High school and college are years in which many people struggle with defining their self-concept, and it is a time when people are especially sensitive to events that challenge their sense of self.

Once people have a fairly stable sense of themselves, they begin to use that to evaluate events and objects in the world. For example, when something happens to a person, such as a young woman's breakup with a boyfriend, she evaluates that event from the perspective of her self-concept, and whether the event is good or bad for who she thinks she is. If having this boyfriend was an important part of her self-concept ("I'm nothing without him") (Aron, Aron, Tudor, & Nelson, 2004), then she evaluates the breakup as devastating. On the other hand, if the young woman has a sense of herself that is mostly independent of her relationship with the young man, then the breakup is less devastating.

Our sense of who we are leads us to evaluate events in the world in certain ways. Only events that are important to our sense of self will have any strong impact either way, as very good or very bad. If something does not matter to our sense of self, then it will not bother us one way or the other. For example, if doing well in school is not part of your self-concept (maybe you are in college for other reasons), then doing poorly on an academic assignment will not affect you much. Who we are, our self-concept, determines how we relate to and evaluate the events in the world.

People do not always like or value what they see when they turn inward and assess their self-concept. That liking or value is self-esteem. For example, two people may both tend to save money rather than spend it, to not leave tips at restaurants, and to always buy the cheapest things. One of these persons views herself as frugal and conservative, and she evaluates these to be positive characteristics. She has positive self-esteem, at least as far as these attributes go. The second person may see himself as stingy, ungenerous, and without compassion. He views these characteristics as negative. Consequently, he has low self-esteem, at least as far as these attributes go. Both have the same self-concept, of being thrifty and hoarding their money, but differ in how they evaluate those characteristics and, hence, in their self-esteem.

Finally, social identity is the self that is shown to other people. This is the relatively enduring part of ourselves that we use to create an impression, to let other people know who we are and what can be expected from us. For instance, your driver's license, which is often used for social identification purposes, contains information about your social identity: your family name, your first name, your date of birth, your address, your physical description, such as height, weight, and eye color, and whether or not you smoke in public. These characteristics differentiate you from other people and form some of the more visible and socially available aspects of your identity. Other, less available aspects of your social identity include how you like to be perceived by others and the impression that you want others to have of your personality. Maybe you are the kind of person who wants to be taken seriously, so it is important to you to have a very businesslike social identity. Maybe you are the kind of person who wants to be liked by most people, so you strive to have a social identity as a friendly and agreeable person.

The three components of the self—self-concept, self-esteem, and social identity—are all vitally important in our day-to-day lives. Personality psychologists have studied these aspects of the self and have generated a good deal of knowledge about them. We will begin this chapter with a focus on the descriptive component of the self—the self-concept.

Application

Identity theft: It can happen to anyone. Imagine one night a collection agency calls and informs you of several past-due credit card accounts in your name and demands that you pay up immediately. The problem is, you never opened these accounts. The supermarket now refuses to accept checks because recently several have bounced. The problem is, you did not write those checks that bounced. What is going on?

Recent surveys estimate that there are 7–10 million identity theft victims per year. Using a variety of methods, criminals steal Social Security Numbers (SSN), driver's license numbers, credit card numbers, ATM cards, telephone calling cards, and other pieces of individuals' identities such as date of birth and mother's maiden name. They use this information to impersonate their victims, spending as much money as they can in as short a time as possible.

There are two types of identity theft. One type occurs when a thief acquires a person's *existing* account information and purchases products or services using either the actual credit card or simply the account number and expiration date. This type of identity theft is called "Account takeover." The second type, called "Application fraud," is true identity theft. The thief uses someone else's Social Security Number and other identifying information to open *new* accounts in that person's name. Because the monthly account statements are mailed to an address used by the impostor, the true victims are unlikely to learn of application fraud for some time, long after the damage has been done.

Most credit card companies and banks limit a person's liability to $50 for losses incurred through identity theft. However, victims are often left with bad credit reports and must spend months or even years regaining their credit status. In the meantime, they often have difficulty obtaining loans, renting apartments, obtaining a bank account, or even getting hired.

Application (*Continued*)

There are several websites devoted to identity theft, especially how to avoid it and what to do if it happens to you. See for example, www.privacyrights.org. The major way to prevent identity theft is to carefully guard all personal identifying information, especially your SSN. For example, do not carry extra credit cards, your Social Security card, birth certificate, or passport in your wallet or purse, except when needed. Never give out your SSN, credit card number, or other personal information over the phone, by mail, or on the Internet unless you have a trusted business relationship with the company and *you* have initiated the call. Always take credit card receipts with you. Never toss them in a public trash container. Order your credit report once or twice a year from one or more of the major credit bureaus to check for errors and fraudulent use of your accounts.

Descriptive Component of the Self: Self-Concept

Knowledge of the self does not happen all at once. It develops over years, starting in infancy, accelerating in adolescence, and reaching completion in old age. The self-concept is the basis for self-understanding, and it forms the answer to the question "Who am I?"

Development of the Self-Concept

The first glimmer of a self-concept occurs in infancy, when the child learns that some things are always there (e.g., its body) and some things are there only sometimes (e.g., the mother's breast). The child makes a distinction between its own body and everything else: it discovers that boundaries exist between what is "me" and what is "not me." Gradually, the infant comes to realize that it is distinct from the rest of the world. This distinction forms the rudimentary sense of self, awareness of one's body.

Have you ever seen a dog bark at its own reflection in a mirror? The dog barks because it does not recognize that the image is a reflection of itself. Dogs soon get bored with mirrors and ignore their reflections. Humans and some primates do recognize that the mirror is a self-reflection. Psychologists have devised a clever technique for studying whether a monkey or a human recognizes their own reflection. They place a small mark on the face that cannot be seen without a mirror. Then, when faced with the mirror, they look to see if the monkey or child uses the reflection to touch the mark on their own face. Chimpanzees and orangutans do exhibit self-recognition with mirrors, and will find the mark after about two to three days with the mirror (Gallup, 1977a). Studies of lower primates, such as the macaque, do not find that they exhibit self-recognition with mirrors, even after 2,400 hours of exposure to the mirror (Gallup, 1977b).

In normal children, self-recognition with mirrors occurs on average at age 18 months (Lewis & Ramsay, 2004). There is, however, some variability in age of onset of self-recognition, with 15 months being the earliest documented case, and age 24 months being the point at which all or almost all children demonstrate self-recognition. Interestingly, pretend play appears to require self-recognition (Lewis & Ramsay, 2004). A child pretending to feed a doll imaginary food or a child drinking an imaginary liquid from a cup must know that what he or she is doing is not real.

Pretending behavior requires that the child distinguish "this is what I pretend to be doing" from "this is what I actually am doing." In a study of children aged 15 to 21 months, only those children who exhibited self-recognition to a mirror were capable of pretend play (Lewis & Ramsay, 2004). Moreover, children do not begin using personal pronouns (I, me, mine) until they gain self-recognition abilities in the mirror test. Self-recognition is therefore an important developmental achievement that allows the child to go on to more complex manifestations of self-awareness, such as engaging in pretend play and representing the self in language with personal pronouns.

Although very young children are fascinated with their reflections, it takes a while for a child to be able to recognize photographs of him- or herself in a group. A child needs to be about 2 years old before he or she can pick his or her picture out of a crowd (Baumeister, 1991). Around this time, the second year of life, children begin to grasp the idea that other people have expectations for them. For example, this is about the time when children can follow rules set up by parents. Children learn that some behaviors are good and other behaviors are bad, and they evaluate their own behavior against these standards. They will smile when they do something good and frown when something bad occurs. They clearly are developing a sense of themselves relative to standards. This is the beginning of self-esteem.

Among the first aspects of the self that people learn to identify and associate with themselves are sex and age. This typically occurs between 2 and 3 years of age, when a child begins to call himself a boy or herself a girl and to refer to other children as boys or girls. A rudimentary knowledge of age also develops, with a child often learning to hold up the number of fingers that designate age. Children at this age also expand their self-concept to include reference to a family. "I'm Sarah's brother," a child might say, implying that part of his self-concept includes being in the same family as Sarah.

From age 3 to about 12, children's self-concepts are based mainly on developing talents and skills. The child thinks of him- or herself as someone who can do this or cannot do that, such as recite the alphabet, tie his own shoes, read, walk to school by herself, tell time, or write in cursive handwriting. At this age, the self-concept is defined mainly in terms of sex, age, family of origin, and what the child believes he or she can or cannot do.

Starting with the school years, ages 5 or 6 onward, children increasingly begin to compare their skills and abilities with those of others. They are now either better than or worse than other children. This is the beginning of **social comparison,** which most people engage in to varying degrees and do so for the rest of their lives (Baumeister, 1997). Social comparison is the evaluation of oneself or one's performance in terms of a comparison with a reference group. "Am I faster, smarter, more popular, more attractive, and so on than my friends?" is the question that children repeatedly ask themselves during this period of development.

Also during this time, children learn that they can lie and keep secrets. This is based on the realization that there is a hidden side to the self, a side that includes private attributes, such as thoughts, feelings, and desires. The realization that "Mommy doesn't know everything about me" is a big step. The development of an inner, **private self-concept** is a major but often difficult development in the growth of the self-concept. It may start out with children developing an imaginary friend, someone only they can see or hear. This imaginary friend may actually be the children's first attempt to communicate to their parents that they know there is a secret part, an inner part, to their understanding of the self. Later, children develop the full realization that only they have access to their own thoughts, feelings, and desires and that no one else can know this part of themselves unless they choose to tell others. It is the children's privilege to decide whether to tell others about these aspects of themselves. This is a big step in the developing self-concept.

As children grow from childhood to adolescence their self-concept changes from one based on such concrete characteristics as physical appearance and possessions to one that is based on more abstract psychological terms. We illustrate this below with examples drawn from Montemayor and Eisen (1977). The statements are from children of different ages all answering the question "Who am I?"

The following is from a 9-year-old boy in the fourth grade. Notice how concrete his description is, and that he uses mostly tangible concepts such as age, sex, name, address, and other aspects of his physical self:

> *My name is Bruce. I have brown eyes and brown hair. And I have brown eyebrows. I am nine years old. I LOVE sports. I have seven people in my family. I have great eyesight and I have lots of friends. I will be 10 in September. I live at 1923 Pinecrest. I am a boy. I have an uncle that is almost 7 feet tall. My school is Pinecrest and my teacher is Mrs V. I play Hockey.*

The next statement is from a girl aged $11^1/_2$ in the sixth grade. Notice that she frequently refers to her likes, and also emphasizes more abstract personality and social characteristics:

> *My name is Alice. I am a human being. I am a girl. I am a truthful person. I am not pretty. I do so-so in my studies. I am a very good cellist and a very good pianist. I am a little bit tall for my age. I like several boys and girls. I am old-fashioned. I play tennis and am a very good swimmer. I try to be helpful. I am always ready to be friends with anybody. Mostly I am good, but I lose my temper. I am not well-liked by some girls. I don't know if I'm liked by boys or not.*

The final example is from a 17-year-old girl in the twelfth grade. Notice how she emphasizes interpersonal characteristics, her typical mood states, and several ideological and belief references in her self-description:

> *I am a human being. I am a girl. I am an individual. I don't know who I am. I am a Pisces. I am a moody persona. I am an indecisive person. I am an ambitious person. I am a very curious person. I am not an individual. I am a loner. I am an American (God help me). I am a Democrat. I am a liberal person. I am a radical. I am a conservative. I am a pseudoliberal. I am an atheist. I am not a classifiable person (i.e., I don't want to be classified).*

When asked for a self-description, young children describe themselves in terms of where they live, their age and gender, what they look like, and what they do. Adolescents, however, describe themselves in terms of their personality characteristics and their beliefs, qualities that produce a picture of the self that is unique. Self-concepts undergo transformations as children age, based mainly on the child's ability to infer characteristics that underlie their behavior. For example, a young child might say that he likes to play basketball, hockey, or baseball, whereas an older child might say "I am an athlete." Adolescents infer from their own behavior the existence of underlying personality traits, abilities, and motives.

A final unfolding of the self-concept, during the teen years, involves **perspective taking:** the ability to take the perspectives of others, or to see oneself as others do, to step outside of oneself and imagine how one appears to other people. This is why many teenagers go through a period of extreme self-consciousness during this time, focusing much of their energy on how they appear to others. You might vividly recall this period of your life, the strong emotions involved in episodes of **objective self-awareness,** of seeing oneself as an object of others' attention. Remember going to gym class in your funny gym uniform, or that first trip to the beach in your new swimming suit? Often, objective self-awareness is experienced as shyness, and for some people this is a chronic problem.

In the development of the self, children learn to compare themselves to others. "I'm faster than you" is a phrase commonly heard whenever a group of young children gather. This is the beginning of social comparison, where people define and evaluate themselves in comparison to others.

The self-concept is a distinct knowledge structure, made up of many different elements and stored in our memories much as we might store a cognitive map of our home town.

Self-Schemata: Possible Selves, Ought Selves, and Undesired Selves

So far, we have considered some of the main steps in the development of a self-concept. Once formed, the self-concept provides a person with a sense of continuity and a framework for understanding the past and present and for guiding future behavior. In adults, the self-concept is a structure made up of building blocks of knowledge about the self, a multidimensional collection of knowledge about the self: "Am I responsible, athletic, cooperative, attractive, caring, and assertive?"

The self-concept is like a network of information in memory, which organizes and provides coherence to the ways in which we experience the self (Markus, 1983). The self-concept also guides how each person processes information about him- or herself (Markus & Nurius, 1986). For example, people more easily process information that is consistent with their self-concepts; if you see yourself as highly masculine, then you will quickly agree with statements such as the following: "I am assertive" and "I am strong."

The term **self-schema** (*schema* is singular; *schemata* is plural) refers to the specific knowledge structure, or cognitive representation, of the self-concept. Self-schemata are the networks of associated building blocks of the self-concept. For example, a person might have a schema about what it means to be masculine, and this schema might include such attributes as assertiveness, strength, and independence. A person with a masculine self-schema would then apply this to understanding himself, using it to make sense out of his past experiences and to organize current, self-relevant information. Such a self-schema would guide this person to pay attention to certain kinds of information, such as evidence that he is assertive, strong, and independent. In conversations, for example, he might enjoy when others comment on his assertiveness or say something about his being strong and independent. As such, self-schemata are cognitive structures that are built on past experiences and that guide the processing of information about the self, particularly in social interaction.

Self-schemata usually refer to past and current aspects of the self. However, there are also schemata for future selves, which people are able to imagine. The term **possible selves** describes the many ideas people have about who they might become, who they hope to become, or who they fear they will become (Markus & Nurius, 1987). People often have specific desires, anxieties, fantasies, fears, hopes, and expectations about their own futures selves. Although possible selves are not based on actual past experiences, they nevertheless are part of the overall self-concept. That is, possible selves are some of the building blocks of the general self-concept. For example, are you the kind of person who could become a movie actor—that is, is this a possible self for you?

Because they play a role in defining the self-concept, possible selves may influence a person's behavior in certain ways. For example, a high school student may have no idea what it would be like to be an astronaut. Nevertheless, because this is one of her possible selves, she has many thoughts and feelings about this image of herself as astronaut. Information about astronauts, the space agency, aviation science, and so forth has personal significance for her, and she seeks it out every chance she gets. Thus, this possible self will influence her here and now in terms of her current decisions (e.g., to take an extra math course). Possible selves are like bridges between our present and our future, they are our working models of ourselves in the future (Oyserman & Markus, 1990). Such a working model might lead to problem behaviors, however, as when the possible self is a poor role model. In studying a group of juvenile delinquents, Oyserman and Saltz (1993) found that a high proportion had a possible self of *criminal,* and relatively few had such conventional possible selves as *having a job* or *getting along well in school.*

Possible selves allow us to stay on schedule, to work toward self-improvement. Behaviors that stem from possible selves (desired or undesired) can activate a host of intense feelings and emotions. For example, to a person who does not have a possible self with coronary artery disease, missing a few days of an exercise program will not be as distressing as it is to a person who has such a possible self.

Psychologist Tory Higgins (1987, 1997, 1999) has elaborated on the possible selves notion by distinguishing the **ideal self,** which is what persons themselves want to be, from the **ought self,** which is persons' understanding of what others want them to be. The ought self is built on what people take as their responsibilities and commitments to others, what they ought to do. The ideal self is built on one's own desires and goals, what one wants to become. Higgins refers to the ought and the ideal selves as **self-guides,** standards that one uses to organize information and motivate appropriate behavior. The self-guides get their motivating properties from emotions. Higgins argues that these two types of possible selves are at the root of different emotions. If one's real self does not fit one's ideal self, then one will feel sad, despondent, and disappointed. If, on the other hand, one's real self does not fit one's ought self, then one will feel guilty, distressed, and anxious.

Self-guides also influence our motivation by changing what we pay attention to (Higgins, Shah, & Friedman, 1997). The ideal self guides us to focus our attention on achievement and goal accomplishment, what Higgins calls a promotion focus. Alternatively, a prevention focus is motivated by the ought self-guide, shifting our attention to avoiding harm and seeking safety. Achieving goals associated with the promotion focus results in pleasure, and achieving goals associated with the prevention focus is associated with relief. Some people are more intent on promotion focus; they guide their behavior according to which goals they want to achieve. Other people are more prevention focused; they guide their behavior according to what they do not want to happen.

To summarize, self-schemata are cognitive knowledge structures about the self-concept, and they consist of past, present, and future aspects of the self. The self-concept is the sum of people's self-schemata, what they know and believe about themselves. An important part of the self-concept concerns possible selves, which can be ideals that people desire or undesired selves that people strive to avoid. Who have I been, what am I like now, and what do I want to be like in the future—the answers to these questions define the self-concept.

There are two ways to conceptualize the self. One way is to focus on the content, on what it is that makes up the self-concept for each person—the person's self-schemata and possible selves. The other way to conceptualize the self is in terms of the person's own evaluation of self-concept. Does she like who she has been and who she is now? Is he generally satisfied with himself? Does she feel worthwhile? Does he generally value the attributes he has? These questions all pertain to self-esteem, an important topic to which we now turn.

Evaluative Component of the Self: Self-Esteem

The first glimmer of self-esteem occurs when children identify standards or expectations for behavior and live up to them. For example, parents have expectations for toilet training. When children finally master these expectations, it is a source of pride and self-esteem, at least until larger challenges are encountered. In later childhood, the next shift in the source of self-esteem occurs when children begin to engage in social comparison; children compare themselves to others and, if they are doing better than others, then they feel good about themselves. And, later, people develop a set of internal standards, part of what they hold to be important to their self-concept. Behavior or experiences inconsistent with these internal standards can lead to decreases in self-esteem. In all cases, self-esteem results from an evaluation of oneself.

Evaluation of Oneself

Self-esteem is a general evaluation of self-concept along a good–bad or like–dislike dimension: Do you generally like yourself and feel you are a worthwhile, good person? Do you feel that others respect you? Do you feel you are basically a decent, fair person? Do you take pride and satisfaction in what you have done, in who you are, and in who you would like to become? Self-esteem is the sum of your positive and negative reactions to all the aspects of your self-concept.

Most of us have a mixed reaction to ourselves; we have to take the bad with the good, and we acknowledge that we have both strengths and weaknesses. How we feel about ourselves can change from day to day and even from hour to hour. When we do something that is not consistent with our self-concept, such as hurt someone's feelings, but we do not think of ourselves as uncaring, then we may experience a dip in self-esteem. Such fluctuations, however, occur around our average level of self-esteem. Most personality psychologists are interested in self-esteem in terms of our average level of self-esteem, our characteristic standing on the self-esteem dimension. For example, do we generally have a positive, a neutral, or a negative evaluation of ourselves?

Personality researchers have begun to acknowledge that people can evaluate themselves positively or negatively in different areas of their lives. For example, you

Table 14.1 Items in a Global Self-Esteem Questionnaire

1.	True	False	I feel good about myself.
2.	True	False	I feel I am a person of worth, the equal of other people.
3.	True	False	I am able to do things as well as most other people.
4.	True	False	On the whole, I am satisfied with myself.
5.	True	False	I certainly feel useless at times.
6.	True	False	At times I think I am no good at all.
7.	True	False	I feel I do not have much to be proud of.

Source: Adapted from Marsh, 1996.

may feel pretty good about your intellectual abilities, but perhaps you are shy with members of the opposite sex. Consequently, you may have high academic self-esteem but lower self-esteem when it comes to dating or feeling attractive to others. Global self-esteem may be a composite of several individual areas of self-evaluation. Each of these subareas can be assessed separately, and researchers can examine self-esteem about various areas of life. For example, there is a scale for measuring three aspects of self-esteem: performance self-esteem, appearance self-esteem, and social self-esteem (Heatherton & Polivy, 1991).

Although there are distinct areas of life in which people can feel more or less confident of themselves—such as friendships, academics, and appearance—self-esteem measures of these content areas are moderately correlated. This means that people who tend to have high self-esteem in one area also tend to have high self-esteem in the other areas. Sometimes researchers find it useful to examine specific areas of self-esteem, such as appearance self-esteem in persons at risk for eating disorders. However, the majority of researchers find it useful to think of self-esteem as the person's global or average evaluation of their whole self-concept. Table 14.1 shows a global self-esteem questionnaire that is widely used by researchers in this area. This measure assesses a person's overall self-esteem, and by reading and answering the items for yourself you will get an idea of what self-esteem means in terms of the measures used to assess this construct. High scores on self-esteem are obtained by answering items 1–4 as "True" and items 5–7 as "False."

Research on Self-Esteem

Much of the research on self-esteem concerns how people respond to evaluation. Being evaluated is a very common occurrence, especially during the school years. Homework is evaluated, tests are given, and children receive regular reports on their performance. Even outside school, a lot of play in childhood also involves evaluation, such as occurs with competitive games. In adulthood, the games change but the evaluation continues. At most jobs, there is usually some form of evaluation done on a regular basis, and the workers receive feedback on their performance at least in the form of the size of the raise they get that year. There is also competition and evaluation in many other areas of adult life, such as finances, marriage, and children, where people often compare how they are doing with their neighbors. Because self-esteem is linked to evaluation, much of the research on this topic concerns how people react to criticism and negative feedback.

Reactions to Criticism and Failure Feedback

Many laboratory studies have been conducted on how people high and low on self-esteem react to failure and criticism. In general, participants are taken into the laboratory and instructed to complete an important task. For example, they may be given an intelligence test and told that norms are being developed and that they should try to do the very best they can, since they are representing their school in this norming project. Usually this gets the participants very involved and motivates them to want to perform well. The researcher then scores the test when the subjects are finished, and the researcher is critical of the participants' performance, saying that they did very poorly. The research question is "How are high and low self-esteem persons affected by this criticism and personal failure?" The research has looked mainly at how failure feedback affects subsequent performance on similar tasks, and whether failure affects high and low self-esteem persons differently (Brown & Dutton, 1995; Stake, Huff, & Zand, 1995). The participants are offered the opportunity to work on a similar intelligence test after the failure feedback. The researcher then looks at how hard the participants try, how well they do, and whether they give up on the subsequent difficult tasks. The findings suggest that, following failure, low self-esteem persons are more likely to perform poorly and to give up earlier on subsequent tasks. For high self-esteem persons, on the other hand, failure feedback seems to spur them into action on subsequent tasks, and they are less likely to give up and more likely to work just as hard on the second task as they did on the first (Brown & Dutton, 1995).

Why is it that failure seems to incapacitate low self-esteem persons but seems to encourage high self-esteem persons into renewed effort? Researchers think that people readily accept feedback that is consistent with their self-concept, so, for low self-esteem persons, failure feedback on the first task is consistent with their self-concept, and it confirms their views that they are the kind of people who fail more than succeed. And, so, when confronted with the second task, low self-esteem persons, who have just had their negative self-view confirmed with failing on the first task, believe they will also fail on the second task and, so, do not try so hard or just give up. For high self-esteem persons, however, failure is not consistent with their existing self-concept, so they are more likely *not* to accept this feedback. Also, it is likely that they will discount the feedback, perhaps thinking that failure on the first task must have been an accident or a mistake. Consequently, they are motivated to try just as hard the second time, and to not give up, because they do not see their self-concept as the kind of people who fail. Psychologist Roy Baumeister and his colleagues (e.g., Baumeister, Tice, & Hutton, 1989) argue that high self-esteem persons are concerned with projecting a successful, prosperous, and thriving self-image. Low self-esteem persons, on the other hand, are most concerned with avoiding failure. It is a difference of emphasis: high self-esteem persons fear not succeeding; low self-esteem persons fear failure.

Self-Esteem and Coping with Negative Events

Other research on high self-esteem persons has examined the strategies these people use to get through life. Unpleasant events can happen to everyone. High self-esteem persons appear to maintain their positive evaluation through the ups and downs of everyday life. Have high self-esteem persons somehow figured out how to cope more effectively with these challenges of life? How do high self-esteem persons overcome the disappointments, shortcomings, losses, and failures that are a normal part of being human?

One strategy identified by Brown and Smart (1991) is that, following failure in one area of life, the high self-esteem person often will focus on other areas of life in

A Closer Look

Shyness: When Objective Self-Awareness Becomes Chronic

Garrison Keillor, the popular host of the *Prairie Home Companion* radio show, suffers from acute shyness and has openly discussed this in articles and in interviews. He says that, when shy persons have to be in an interaction, they just want to become invisible. They dislike conversation because they lack social confidence, are made terribly anxious by the interaction, and are not good at promoting themselves. Because of these feelings, the shy person withdraws from social interaction.

Many accomplished people are shy, including singer Barbra Streisand, writer J. D. Salinger, and painter Andrew Wyeth (Stocker, 1997). What shy persons have in common is that they desire friendships and social interactions but are held back by their insecurities and fears. Consequently, they avoid the spotlight, avoid face-to-face interaction, and ruminate excessively after conversations, worrying about whether they said the right things, made a good impression, or sounded stupid. The inner experience of a shy person in an interaction is quite different from that of someone else in the same interaction who is not shy.

Shy people are not necessarily introverts (Cheek, 1989). Introverts prefer to be alone; they enjoy the peace and quiet of solitude. Shy people, on the other hand, want to have contact with others, to be socially involved, and to have friends and be part of the group. But shy persons' self-doubt and self-consciousness prompts them to pass up opportunities to socialize (Henderson & Zimbardo, 2001a, b; see www.shyness.com). They handicap themselves; by not entering groups, not speaking to unfamiliar people, not approaching others, they deny themselves the opportunities to learn and practice the very social skills they need to overcome their shyness.

Psychologist Jerome Kagan has been studying shyness for decades (Kagan, 1981, 1994, 1999). In his studies of infants, he found that about 20 percent of 4-month-old babies exhibit signs of shyness—they flail their arms and legs and cry when presented with an unfamiliar object or person. Following up these infants for several years, Kagan found that most of them exhibited signs of shyness as young children. For example, in play situations they often did not move very far from their parents, and some even clung to their parents, not leaving their sides at all when there were unfamiliar children around. Following them a few more years, Kagan found that roughly half of the shy children were transformed and were no longer shy in later childhood. In looking at parenting practices, Kagan found that the parents of these formerly shy children had encouraged their children to socialize. That is, they often had pushed their children to join groups and to talk to other children, and they had given their children lots of praise for socializing. Often this had been "tough love," in that the parents had had to push the reluctant and complaining children to play with peers. However, a few years later, the result was children who were much less shy. The parents of the children who remained shy often had given in to the children's reluctance to join groups. That is, when the children complained or resisted joining a group, the parents often had given in, not pushing the children away. As a result, such children apparently never learned that they could overcome their self-doubt and lack of social confidence (Kagan, 1999). Other research has shown that parents who are too controlling and protective toward their children often have children who are shy and anxious (Wood et al., 2003).

Psychologists studying shyness sometimes prefer the term **social anxiety**, which is defined as discomfort related to social interactions, or even to the anticipation of social interactions (Chavira, Stein, & Malcarne, 2002). Adults with social anxiety report that they are nervous or that they feel awkward when talking to others, especially people with whom they are unfamiliar (Cheek & Buss, 1981). Socially anxious persons appear to be overly concerned about what others will think. After a conversation, they often conclude that they said something wrong, sounded foolish, or looked stupid (Ritts & Patterson, 1996). Sometimes the social anxiety is so strong that it shows in various outward signs, such as a trembling voice or jittery movements. Other people interacting with a socially anxious person often interpret their behavior as unfriendliness, rather than as shyness (Cheek & Buss, 1981). Sometimes shy persons are so overcome with anxiety that it hinders their ability to carry on a conversation. They may spend time staring at their shoes, rather than talking, because they cannot think of a thing to say. Pauses in a conversation can be very discomforting to shy persons.

In an interesting study, researchers asked participants to work on a unique task, one that could not be completed without having to ask another person for help (DePaulo et al., 1989). The researchers deliberately created this task so they could investigate whether shy persons would reach out to others when they really needed to. They found that the socially anxious participants were reluctant to ask for help from another person, presumably because the shy person is anxious that the other may rebuff a request for help.

Shy people also tend to interpret social interactions negatively; they are more likely to interpret a comment as a criticism than as a helpful suggestion. For example, DePaulo et al. (1987) had students work in groups, then write reports on each other's performance. They were then individually interviewed about what they thought the others had said about them. It turns out that the shy participants thought that the others liked them less and that the others thought they were less competent. It seems that shy people are not only reluctant to enter into social interaction but also expect that others will dislike them. These expectations may lead them to avoid interactions or cut conversations short, losing the very opportunities they need to overcome their shyness.

What makes shy people so socially anxious? Kagan believes that some of it is due to genetics. After all, it shows up in some infants very early in life. However, some of this social anxiety must also be learned. What most researchers believe is that shy persons have learned to put too much stock in other people's judgments of them. This is called evaluation apprehension, the idea that shy persons are apprehensive about being evaluated by others. For example, shy persons believe that a person with whom they are talking will think they are dull, silly, or childish. They fear that others will evaluate them negatively. As a consequence, just the thought of going out on stage or leading a group meeting fills them with dread. And, so, they avoid such situations. When forced into interaction, they try to limit it or cut it short. They avoid eye contact, which indicates to others that they prefer to end the conversation. When forced into conversation, they try to keep it impersonal and nonthreatening. They do a lot of agreeing, nodding their heads, without getting too involved in the conversation. They try not to give too much in the way of opinions or personal information, which can be evaluated by others. In sum, researchers believe that at the root of shyness is a fear of being evaluated negatively by others (Leary & Kowalski, 1995), which translates into a lack of confidence in social interactions and a feeling like they lack the social skills necessary to navigate social situations (Cheek & Melchior, 1990).

Recent surveys estimate that 7–13 percent of persons in Western countries will experience social phobia, or extreme shyness, during their lifetime (Furmark, 2002). This suggests that shyness is not uncommon in the general population. Schmidt and Fox (2002) provide a review of the developmental course of shyness, as well as the varieties of shyness. For example, some shy persons are high in sociability, and are distinguished by being especially anxious and fearful. Another type is shy persons who are low in sociability, who simply avoid others because of their excessive self-consciousness (Cheek & Krasnoperova, 1999). Empirically, however, it is difficult to distinguish owing to the overlap in the characteristics. Self-reports of shyness do correlate strongly with peer reports of shyness, suggesting that this characteristic can be well measured with questionnaires (Zarevski, Bratko, Butkovic, & Lazic, 2002).

Psychologists studying the brain have suggested that shy persons have a more reactive **amygdala,** which is a section of the limbic or emotional system of the brain that is most responsible for fear. A study by Kagan and colleagues followed up a group of adults who, at age 2 years, had been assessed for shyness. They found that the adults who were shy as children showed a greater fMRI response within the amygdala to novel versus familiar faces, compared to the nonshy adults (Schwartz, Wright, Shin, Kagan, & Rauch, 2003). In another interesting study, researchers assessed cortisol (the stress hormone described in Chapter 6) on the first and fifth days of school among 35 first-graders (Bruce, Davis, & Gunnar, 2002). They found that most children showed an elevated cortisol response on the first day of school. However, the shy children showed an elevated and extended cortisol response even on the fifth day of school.

Whatever its causes, shyness can have problematic social implications for the shy person. Several studies have examined how shy persons use the Internet to avoid face-to-face social interaction (e.g., Caplan, 2002). One study found that shy persons were more likely to use the Internet for recreation rather than interact with others in face-to-face recreational settings (Scealy, Phillips, & Stevenson, 2002).

Stocker (1997) reviewed much of what is known about helping shy persons overcome their difficulties. She offers seven concrete steps a shy person can take:

1. *Show up.* Shy persons want to avoid the situations that make them anxious. However, if you really want to overcome shyness, you've got to enter those uncomfortable situations: go to a party or strike up a conversation with a stranger. Often, shy persons overestimate how uncomfortable they will feel; however, once they engage in an interaction, they find that it is not as bad as they had expected.

A Closer Look (*Continued*)

2. *Give yourself credit.* Stop being your own worst critic. In scorning or deriding their own social performance after the fact, shy persons are often very hard on themselves. If they make one little social faux pas, they often blow that misstep out of proportion, ignoring the fact that 99 percent of the interaction went well.
3. *Take baby steps.* It is useful to take big goals and break them into smaller steps. Instead of wanting to "become an engaging conversationalist," maybe try to set some smaller goals, such as going to a meeting of a group you've been wanting to join. The first time, you don't have to talk; just go and listen. The second time, maybe your goal will be to talk, not during the meeting but maybe to someone after the meeting is over. At the third meeting, try to ask a question during the actual meeting by speaking up. The point is to set small goals and experience some small successes along the way.
4. *Give unto others.* Shy people, because they are nervous, are focused on themselves during conversations. Shift your attention to others; look at them when they talk, listen carefully to what they say, try to find something interesting and connect to that, ask questions, and give a compliment or a word of support. Paying attention outwardly, toward other people, will also get your attention off yourself and your own nervousness.
5. *Exude warmth.* The nervousness that shy people feel is often interpreted by others as unfriendliness or tension. Try to create a more positive nonverbal impression by smiling, making eye contact, and staying relaxed.
6. *Anticipate failure.* Overcoming shyness is a learning process. It will take practice, and small failures are inevitable. If you say something wrong in a conversation, chalk it up to the learning process and get on with more practice.
7. *Join the crowd.* Nobody is perfect all the time. There are lots of people who are not perfect conversationalists. Also, you might think that making small talk is a big deal. However, when you really listen to other people's small talk, you'll realize that it really is just that—small talk, nothing more.

Table 14.2 The Henderson/Zimbardo Shyness Questionnaire

INSTRUCTIONS: Rate each item using a number from the following scale to indicate how characteristic that statement is of you.

Not at all characteristic	Somewhat characteristic	Often characteristic	Very characteristic	Extremely characteristic
1	2	3	4	5

1. I am afraid of looking foolish in social situations.
2. I often feel insecure in social situations.
3. Other people appear to have more fun in social situations than I do.
4. If someone rejects me I assume that I have done something wrong.
5. It is hard for me to approach people who are having a conversation.
6. I feel lonely a good deal of the time.
7. I tend to be more critical of other people than I appear to be.
8. It is hard for me to say "no" to unreasonable requests.
9. I do more than my share on projects because I can't say no.
10. I find it easy to ask for what I want from other people.
11. I do not let others know I am frustrated or angry.

12. I find it hard to ask someone for a date.
13. It is hard for me to express my real feelings to others.
14. I tend to be suspicious of other people's intentions toward me.
15. I am bothered when others make demands on me.
16. It is easy for me to sit back in a group discussion and observe rather than participate.
17. I find myself unable to enter new social situations without fearing rejection or not being noticed.
18. I worry about being a burden on others.
19. Personal questions from others make me feel anxious.
20. I let others take advantage of me.
21. I judge myself negatively when I think others have negative reactions to me.
22. I try to figure out what is expected in a given situation and then act that way.
23. I feel embarrassed when I look or seem different from other people.
24. I am disappointed in myself.
25. I blame myself when things do not go the way I want them to.
26. I sometimes feel ashamed after social situations.
27. I am usually aware of my feelings, even if I do not know what prompted them.
28. I am frequently concerned about others' approval.
29. I like taking risks in social situations.
30. If someone is critical of me I am likely to assume that they are having a bad day.
31. If I let people know too much about me they will gossip about me.
32. I think it is important to please others.
33. People feel superior when someone is socially anxious.
34. I spend a lot of time thinking about my social performance after I spend time with people.
35. I am satisfied with my level of social support.

which things are going well. Larsen (2000a; Larsen & Prizmic, 2004) identifies this strategy as one of the most effective but least used strategy for overcoming feelings of failure. For example, imagine you are a research psychologist and you are evaluated in this job by the number of research articles you publish each year. Imagine then that one of your articles is rejected by a publisher. This represents a small failure in your life. If you were a low self-esteem person, this failure would have a large effect, confirming your view that you are generally a failure in most things that you do, that this is just one more instance of how you are unworthy and inadequate. On the other hand, if you were a high self-esteem person, you would likely remind yourself that you are still a good teacher, you are still a good faculty member at your university, you are still a good spouse and a good parent to your children, that you still play a good game of squash, and that your dog still loves you. Larsen and Prizmic (2004) have suggested that, in order to cope with such failures, people should make a list of all the things in their lives that are going well and that they keep this list in their wallets. Then, if a failure occurs in one area of life—for instance, at work—they can take this list out and review it, just as a high self-esteem person might do naturally. This can help people cope with the inevitable bumps, bruises, and failures of everyday life.

This idea of compartmentalizing the self is consistent with the research on **self-complexity** by psychologist Patricia Linville (1987). She holds the view that we have many roles and many aspects to our self-concept. However, for some of us, our self-concept is rather simple, being made up of just a few large categories, such as when a man says, "I am nothing without her," meaning that his whole self-concept is wrapped up in this one relationship. Other people may have a more complex, or differentiated, self-concept. Such a person would say he or she has many parts to his or her self-concept: relationships, family, work, hobbies, friends, and so forth. For people with high self-complexity, a failure in any one aspect of the self (such as a relationship that breaks apart) is buffered because there are many other aspects of the self that are unaffected by that event. However, if a person is low in self-complexity, the same event might be seen as devastating, since the person defines him- or herself mainly in terms of this one aspect. The old phrase "Don't put all your eggs into one basket" seems to apply to the self-concept as well.

Protecting versus Enhancing the Self

Imagine you are a graduating college senior; you have majored in computer science and have a lot of expertise in web-based programming. You are being recruited by a hot Internet start-up company for a job managing its information technology department. You know there is a lot of potential for you in this company. In fact, it could make you a millionaire within a few years if the company were to go public. However, you also know that it will be a lot of hard work. You will have to put in lots of hours and dedicate yourself almost entirely to the company for several years. You know you will also need to have some luck to get the right team together, to have some successes on your first few projects. It is a high-stakes but also a high-risk position. You know you have a lot of skill in this area, but you also know it is quite possible for you to fail miserably. What would you do? Would you take this job?

Some people may decline this opportunity to try for a big success because they are motivated to protect their self-concept. That is, they are concerned with *not failing*, and, in situations in which failure is a good possibility, they prefer not to take the risk. In other words, for some people, not failing is much more important than succeeding wildly. It turns out that people low in self-esteem are like this, in that they are motivated to protect their self-concept by avoiding failure much more than they are motivated to enhance it with success (Tice, 1991, 1993).

Research support for this notion has been found in several studies. For example, in one study (Taylor et al., 2000), the participants took an intelligence test and then were given their scores, plus the scores of the other participants. The participants were led to believe they had done much better (false success feedback) or much worse (false failure feedback) than the others. They then had the opportunity to receive more feedback on how they compared with the others, feedback that was likely to be in the same direction as their test scores. The low self-esteem participants asked for more feedback only when they knew it would be good news, when they were sure that they already were doing above average. When they thought they were below average, the low self-esteem persons did not want any more feedback. This is consistent with the idea that low self-esteem persons are motivated to protect their self-concept; they wanted more feedback only if they were certain it would be positive. The high self-esteem persons, on the other hand, did not avoid more feedback after learning they were below average.

Low self-esteem persons sometimes put a lot of energy into evading any new negative information about themselves. One strategy is to simply expect to fail; then, when it happens, it is not anything new. **Defensive pessimism** is a strategy in which a person facing a challenge, such as an upcoming test, expects to do poorly. Defensive pessimists are motivated by their fear of failure, but they take this gloomy outlook because the impact of failure can be lessened if it is expected in advance. For example, a little boy who strikes out at bat is not so upset with himself if he expects to strike out in the fist place. Psychologist Julie Norem, who has done most of the research on defensive pessimism, sees a positive side to this characteristic: defensive pessimists use their worry and pessimism in a constructive way, to motivate themselves to work on the thing they are pessimistic about. She gives the example of a man who must give a public speech (Norem, 1995). Even though he has done a lot of public speaking, and all his speeches have gone well, he nevertheless is anxious and convinces himself that, this time, he is surely going to make a fool of himself. Thus, he decides to work extra hard on this speech; he rehearses and rehearses, prepares and prepares. When it comes time to give the speech, he does great, as usual. By reflecting on the worst outcome, defensive pessimists work through ways to keep that worst case from happening. The downside to defensive pessimism is that the negativity of defensive pessimists annoys others (Norem, 1998, 2001).

Sometimes people go to great lengths to set up their failure. This is called self-handicapping (e.g., Tice & Baumeister, 1990). **Self-handicapping** is a process in which a person deliberately does the things that increase the probability that he or she will fail (Tice & Bratslavsky, 2000). For example, a young woman may have a pessimistic attitude toward her upcoming exam, so she uses this as an excuse for not studying. However, not studying for the exam provides a handicap, an excuse to fail. By not studying, she increases the chances that she will fail, but it also gives her an excuse for that failure. When she fails, she can then say that she was simply unprepared, not that she is unintelligent or lacks the ability to do well in her classes. For low self-esteem persons, failing is bad, but failing without an excuse is worse.

Self-Esteem Variability

Most of the research on self-esteem concerns the average level, or what people's evaluations of themselves are like, on average. But we also know from Chapter 5 that people fluctuate on their self-esteem from day to day and even from hour to hour. **Self-esteem variability** is an individual difference characteristic; it is the magnitude of short-term fluctuations in ongoing self-esteem (Kernis, Grannemann, & Mathis, 1991). In this section, we will stress only two main points. First, researchers make a distinction between level and variability of self-esteem. These two aspects of self-esteem are unrelated to each other. Moreover, level and variability in self-esteem are hypothesized to be based on different psychological mechanisms and are

A Closer Look The Six Myths of Self-Esteem

Most people naturally try to enhance and protect their self-esteem, believing that it is important to psychological health. In America in the past decade there has been a growing national concern with developing self-esteem, believing it is related to all manner of good things in life. For example, the State of California set up a task force on self-esteem, which ultimately produced a report entitled "The Social Importance of Self-Esteem." In it the task force argued that "many if not most of the major problems plaguing society have roots in the low self-esteem of many of the people who make up society." As a result, self-esteem courses found their way into the grade schools and high schools around the country, fostering a "feel-good" version of self-esteem, e.g., feel good about yourself.

Recently the Association of Psychological Science set up a task force charged with reviewing the scientific literature on self-esteem, particularly with respect to objective behaviors and outcomes. The report was published in 2003 (Baumeister, Campbell, Krueger, & Vohs, 2003). We have taken this report and distilled the findings into a series of myths about self-esteem that are not supported by scientific research.

Myth One: High self-esteem is correlated with all manner of positive characteristics, such as being physically attractive, smart, kind, generous, etc. It is true that, for example, when both self-esteem and physical attractiveness are assessed using self-report (e.g., rate how attractive you are, rate your self-esteem), then strong correlations are typically found. However, when objective measures of attractiveness are used, such as having raters rate photographs of people in terms of attractiveness, then the correlation between self-reported self-esteem and other-rated physical attractiveness drops to zero. Those with high self-esteem may be gorgeous in their own eyes, but they are not necessarily gorgeous in the eyes of others. These kinds of findings are also obtained with a variety of other positive characteristics. For example, high self-esteem people may rate themselves as smart or high in kindness or generosity as well, yet others do not necessarily see them as being this way. In a sense, persons high in self-esteem may have an inflated or unrealistic view of their positive characteristics, a view that is not necessarily supported by those who know the person well.

Myth Two: High self-esteem promotes success in school. The issue here is really one of causality and causal direction; does self-esteem cause people to achieve success or does achieving success lead to self-esteem? Many of the educational movements imply that if only we could raise children's self-esteem then we would help them on their way to achieving success in life. Consequently teachers are sometimes taught to praise students all the time, even if they are not successful. However, there is very little empirical science to support the idea that self-esteem leads to academic success. For example, Baumeister et al. (2003) review a study which tested more than 23,000 high school students, first in the tenth grade, then again in the twelfth grade. They found that self-esteem in the tenth grade only weakly predicted academic achievement in the twelfth grade. Academic achievement in the tenth grade correlated higher with self-esteem in the twelfth grade. Many studies show similar results, and none of them indicate that improving self-esteem offers students much benefit. In fact, some studies show that artificially boosting self-esteem (through unconditional praise, for example) may actually lower subsequent performance (Baumeister et al., 2003).

Myth Three: High self-esteem promotes success on the job. The same basic issues about causality apply here; does self-esteem promote success on the job, or vice versa? When people rate their own job performance, there is often a modest correlation with self-esteem, but when job performance is assessed objectively (e.g., supervisor ratings) the correlations drop to close to zero.

Myth Four: High self-esteem makes a person likeable. Again, if we use self-reports of popularity (e.g., how much do other people like you?) then these self-ratings of likability do correlate with self-esteem, i.e., high self-esteem persons regard themselves as being popular and believe they have many friends. However, these self-perceptions do not reflect reality. Baumeister et al. (2003) report on a study of high-school students who were asked to nominate their most-liked peers. The person in the class receiving the most votes was ranked as most popular, the person with the second most votes was ranked as second most popular, and so on. When self-esteem scores were correlated with the objective peer-ranking of popularity, that correlation was approximately zero. Similar findings have been found with college students. In another study reported by Baumeister et al. (2003) college students self-reported their own interpersonal skills in several domains, e.g., initiating relationships, self-disclosure, being assertive when necessary, providing emotional support to their friends, and managing interpersonal conflict. The researchers also had the subject's roommates report what the subject was like on each of the above interpersonal skill domains. While the subject's self-esteem scores correlated with all of the self-reported interpersonal skill domains, the correlations between self-esteem and the roommates' ratings were essentially zero for four out of five of the interpersonal skills. The only interpersonal skill area that the roommates noticed that was associated with self-esteem was the subject's ability to initiate new social contacts and friendships. This does seem to be the one area in which the confidence associated with self-esteem really matters. People who think that they are desirable and attractive should be good at striking up conversations with strangers. Persons with low self-esteem may shy away from trying to make new friends, perhaps fearing rejection. In most other areas of interpersonal skills, however, self-esteem is not associated with having an advantage over other people.

Myth Five: Low self-esteem puts a person at risk for drug and alcohol abuse and premature sexual activity. The scientific studies reviewed by Baumeister et al. (2003) do not support the idea that low self-esteem predisposes young people to more or earlier sexual activity. If anything, persons with high self-esteem are less inhibited, more willing to disregard risks, and more prone to engage in sex. There is, however, evidence that unpleasant sexual experiences and unwanted pregnancies appear to lower self-esteem. As for alcohol and illicit drugs, preventing these behaviors has been a major rationale for those calling for programs to promote self-esteem. The data, however, do not conclusively show that low self-esteem causes, or even correlates with, the abuse of illicit drugs or alcohol. For example, in a longitudinal study, no correlation was found between self-esteem at age 13 and drinking or drug abuse at age 15. A few other studies have found small correlations between low self-esteem and drinking, but other studies have found the opposite. All in all, the results are not conclusive to make any statements about self-esteem protecting people from the dangers of drug and alcohol use or unwise sexual behavior.

Myth Six: Only low self-esteem people are aggressive. For decades many psychologists thought that low self-esteem was an important factor underlying aggressive behavior. Under their tough exteriors, aggressive people were thought to suffer from insecurities and self-doubt. However, recent research has shown that aggressive persons often have quite favorable views of themselves. In fact, extremely high self-esteem can blend into narcissism, which has been associated with bouts of anger and aggression when the narcissist does not get his or her way. If self-esteem is threatened or disputed by someone or some event, especially among high self-esteem persons, then they may react with hostility or violence. People with a highly inflated view of their own superiority, those with narcissistic tendencies, may be the most prone to violent reactions. After a challenge to self-esteem (e.g., getting beaten at a game), a person might protect their self-concept by directing their anger outward, attacking the victor. Baumeister et al. (2003) review the literature on bullying and conclude that bullies are often very self-confident and less socially anxious than average. The general pattern in these studies and those on adults is that even high self-esteem, especially when it blends into narcissism, can be associated with interpersonal aggression. In several empirical studies, Baumeister and Bushman and colleagues have demonstrated that, when their self-esteem is threatened, persons who are narcissistic are more likely to retaliate or aggress against the source of the threat (e.g., Baumeister, Bushman, & Campbell, 2000; Bushman & Baumeister, 1998). In a study of men in prison, Bushman and Baumeister (2002) found that those prisoners who had a history of violent offenses were significantly higher on narcissism than those prisoners with no history of violence. All of these findings run counter to the notion that low self-esteem causes aggression, and instead point to the counterintuitive notion that threatened egotism is a likely cause of aggression and violence.

After crushing these myths about self-esteem, we can ask the question: So, what good is self-esteem? As described elsewhere in this chapter, self-esteem improves persistence in the face of failure. Persons high in self-esteem perform better in groups than those with low self-esteem. Also, having a poor self-image is a risk factor for developing certain eating disorders, especially bulimia. Low self-esteem is also related to depression, and high self-esteem is related to happiness. High self-esteem also is related to social confidence and taking the initiative in making new friends. It is most likely the case that successes in academics, in the interpersonal domain or in one's career, lead to both happiness and to self-esteem. Consequently, efforts to artificially boost children's self-esteem (through unconditional praise, for example) might fail. Rather we should encourage and praise children when they put effort into learning or achieving the skills necessary to succeed in the various areas of life.

often found to interact in predicting important life outcomes (Kernis, Grannemann, & Barclay, 1992).

A second point is that self-esteem variability is related to the extent to which one's self-evaluation is changeable. That is, some people's self-esteem is pushed and pulled by the events of life much more than other people's self-esteem. Psychologist Michael Kernis, who has written extensively about this characteristic, believes that self-esteem variability is high in some people because they

- Have an enhanced sensitivity to social evaluation events.
- Have an increased concern about their self-view.
- Overrely on social sources of evaluation.
- React to evaluation with anger and hostility.

Several studies have been conducted to examine whether self-esteem variability moderates the relation between self-esteem level and other variables, such as depression (Gable & Nezlak, 1998). In one study (Kernis et al., 1991), self-esteem level was related to depression, but this relation was much stronger for persons higher in self-esteem variability. Based on such findings researchers have come to view variability as a susceptability to depression (Roberts & Monroe, 1992). That is, depression is thought to be a result of a person's vulnerability to the self-deprecating events of everyday life (Butler, Hokanson, & Flynn, 1994).

Social Component of the Self: Social Identity

Social identity is the self that is shown to other people. This is the part of ourselves that we use to create an impression, to let other people know who we are and what they can expect from us. Social identity is different from self-concept because identity contains elements that are socially observable, publicly available outward expressions of the self. Gender and ethnicity are aspects of social identity. This may or may not figure into a person's self-concept, but gender and ethnicity are parts of one's social self, one's identity that is available to others.

Identity has an element of continuity because many of its aspects, such as gender and ethnicity, are constant. People are recognized as being the same from day to day, week to week, and year to year. If you were asked for your "identification," you might produce a passport or a driver's license. These documents contain socially available facts about you, such as your height, weight, age, and eye color. They also contain your family name and your address. All of these pieces of information are aspects of your identity, and they provide others with a brief sketch of who you are.

The Nature of Identity

Identity has two important features: continuity and contrast. **Continuity** means that people can count on you to be the same person tomorrow as you are today. Obviously, people change in various ways, but many important aspects of social identity remain relatively stable, such as gender, surname (though some women elect to change this when they marry), language, ethnicity, and socioeconomic status.

Other aspects of identity can change, but do so gradually, lending some sense of continuity, e.g., education, occupation, and marital status. Other aspects of identity refer to behavior patterns that are public, such as being an athlete, a delinquent, or a "party animal," which also contribute to a sense of continuity (Baumeister & Muraven, 1996).

Contrast means that your social identity differentiates you from other people. An identity is what makes you unique in the eyes of others. The combination of characteristics that make up your identity differentiates you from everyone else. For example, there may be other students who speak the way you do and work where you do, but you are the only one who likes a particular type of music and has your ethnic background and eye color. Some characteristics are more important to social identity for some people than others. We now turn to how people develop identity by selecting what they choose to emphasize about themselves in their social identities.

Identity Development

Although anything that provides a sense of sameness can potentially become part of identity, people have some latitude to choose what they want to be known for. For example, a student may try out for the swimming team, thereby choosing the identity of an athlete. Another might break a lot of rules, thereby choosing the identity of a delinquent. People also differ from each other in the strength of their identities. Some people feel a strong sense of reputation, whereas others feel adrift in their social relations, not knowing who they are expected to be. In fact, most people go through a period, usually in high school or college, in which they experiment with various identities. For many people, this is an uncomfortable time. They may feel socially insecure or sensitive while developing their social identity.

As mentioned in Chapter 10, the term *identity* was popularized in the 1960s by the psychoanalyst Erik Erikson (1968). He believed that identity resulted from efforts to separate oneself from one's parents, to stop relying on one's parents to make decisions about what values to hold and what goals to pursue in life. Erikson believed that achieving an identity took effort and work and that there was always a risk that an identity achieved could come undone, resulting in what he called role confusion. People need to continually work on achieving and maintaining their identity, Erikson taught.

Identity can be achieved in several ways, according to Erikson (1968). Many people struggle with identities, particularly during late adolescence and early adulthood. Experimenting with various identities can be compared to trying on different hats to see which one fits. In trying on identities, a young man in college might one semester be an athlete and the next semester join the debate and chess clubs; the following semester, he gets a tattoo, has some body parts pierced, and starts hanging with a crowd of similarly mutilated persons. People actively struggle to find a social identity that fits, one they are comfortable with. Usually, after a period of experimentation, most people settle into a comfortable social identity and attain some stability.

For other people, the route to identity is not through experimentation. Instead, some people attain an identity by accepting and adopting a ready-made social role. Typically, such people adopt an identity that is practiced and provided by their parents or significant others. For example, they may take over the family business, buy a house in their hometown, and join the same church as their parents. Such people appear stable and mature in their identities and have mature values, plans, and objectives even when they are teenagers. Another identity adoption example is arranged marriages, in which the parents decide whom their children will marry and the children accept this decision willingly, a practice still common in India today.

These kinds of instant identity adoptions can be risky, however, as they may be achieved with a certain amount of rigidity, making the person closed to new ideas or lifestyles. Such people may be inflexible and stubborn in their social roles, especially when they are under stress. Nevertheless, for many people, this route to identity is an acceptable and reasonably healthy alternative.

Application

The true story of the return of Martin Guerre is so interesting that several film depictions have been made. In the real story, which took place in medieval sixteenth-century France, a peasant, Martin Guerre, leaves his wife to fight in the "One Hundred Years War." His wife waits patiently for him, but after nine years without word, she presumes that Martin is dead. Believing herself a widow, she is astonished when Martin returns suddenly after being away so long. Although the neighbors have a big homecoming celebration for Martin, several are suspicious that the man is an impostor, that he is not really Martin but someone who knew Martin well enough to steal his identity. To the lonely wife, however, he looks like her Martin, sounds like her Martin, and has a working knowledge of the intimate details of their prior relationship. In addition, the man in her house now is nicer, gentler, more loving, and more responsible than the man who went to war almost a decade earlier. And so she very much wants this man to be her Martin.

The French movie The Return of Martin Guerre, *starring Gerard Depardieu, portrays a true story from medieval times about the theft of social identity. The scene here shows the "new" Martin, who has just returned from a nine-year absence, embracing the "old" Martin's wife. The film won three French Academy Awards.*

Telltale signs of a forged identity emerge bit by bit and unravel the clever facade around Martin's social self. The neighbors get the local magistrate involved. His wife tries to defend Martin as her husband and, even if he is not, she wants him to stay anyway. Nevertheless, the case is made that he is an impostor, that this Martin is not really Martin Guerre. The impostor is believed to have forced the real Martin to reveal details of his self-concept and social identity and then to have used this knowledge to create a self-concept and social identity so similar to Martin's that he fooled even Martin's wife into believing he was truly her returning husband. The magistrate, convinced that this is not the "real" Martin, charges the impostor with adultery, a crime punishable by death. Martin's wife is not similarly charged because she believed this was her husband.

The 1993 French film based on this story, *The Return of Martin Guerre*, starring Gerard Depardieu, won three French Academy Awards. It is a stunningly filmed study in the portrayal of the self and social identity. In it, we see the small details that go into making a social identity. It shows how people form expectations for social behavior from others based on identity and how small violations of those expectations can create doubts and suspicions.

Identity Crises

A person's identity is challenged from time to time. The answer to the question "Who do others think I am?" can change. For example, when a woman gets divorced, her social identity changes from "I am married" to "I am divorced and newly single." Or a man gives up a career as a business executive to pursue a vocation in small-scale farming, so his identity changes from "I am an executive" to "I am a farmer." Other challenges to identity would be events that change one's reputation, change one's family life, or change one's economic status.

Erikson (1968) coined the phrase **identity crisis,** meaning the feelings of anxiety that accompany efforts to define or redefine one's own individuality and social reputation. For most people, the process of going through an identity crisis is an important and memorable phase of life. Sometimes it happens early, in adolescence; sometimes it happens later, in midlife. And some people have identity crises multiple times in their lives. Psychologist Roy Baumeister suggests that there are two distinct types of identity crises, identity deficit and identity conflict (Baumeister, 1986, 1997).

Identity Deficit

An **identity deficit** arises when a person has not formed an adequate identity and thus has trouble making major decisions: Should I go to college or not? If I go to college, what major should I choose? Should I join the military service? Should I get married? A person without a secure, established identity would have trouble making such major decisions because he or she has no inner foundation. When facing a tough decision, many people turn inward to find the answer. In doing so, many people arrive at a course of action right away, because they know their own values and preferences very well; they know what "a person like me" would do in such situations. When people who have an identity deficit turn inward however, they find little in the way of a foundation on which to base such life choices.

Identity deficits often occur when a person discards old values or goals. For example, college students often reject old opinions in favor of new ideas and new values to which they are exposed in college. In fact, some college courses are designed to encourage students to doubt or challenge their previous assumptions about themselves or the world. A popular bumper sticker, often seen on college campuses, is "Question Authority." But rejecting old beliefs and assumptions creates a void or an identity deficit, which is accompanied by feelings of emptiness and uncertainty. Such feelings prompt people to search for new beliefs, for new values and goals. People who are trying to fill this identity deficit may try on new belief systems, explore new relationships, and investigate new ideas and values. They may be alternatively depressed and confused at one point in time, then euphoric about the possibilities in their lives.

People in identity deficit are particularly vulnerable to the propaganda of various groups. They are often very curious about other belief systems, so they are very vulnerable to influence from other people. Because of their feelings of emptiness and their search for new values and ideas, they tend to be very persuadable during this period. As Baumeister (1997) points out, recruiters for cults are often especially successful at enlisting persons who are undergoing identity deficit crises.

Identity Conflict

An **identity conflict** involves an incompatibility between two or more aspects of identity. This kind of crisis often occurs when a person is forced to make an important and difficult life decision. For example, a person who emigrates to the United States may have an identity conflict between wanting to assimilate into the majority culture and wanting to maintain his or her ethnic identity. A similar identity conflict arises in working persons who also want to have a family. A person with a strong commitment to building a family might experience an identity conflict if he or she were offered a promotion at work that involved longer hours or frequent out-of-town travel. Whenever two or more aspects of identity clash (such as career woman and dedicated mother) there is a potential for an identity conflict crisis.

Identity conflicts are "approach-approach" conflicts, in that the person wants to reach two mutually contradictory goals. Although these conflicts involve wanting two desirable identities, not much pleasure is experienced during identity conflicts. Identity conflicts usually involve intense feelings of guilt or remorse over perceived unfaithfulness to an important aspect of the person's identity. People in an identity conflict may feel as if they are letting themselves and others down.

Overcoming an identity conflict is often a difficult and painful process. One course of action is to put aside a part of one's identity, to abandon a formerly important aspect of the self. Some people are able to strike a balance in their lives. For example, a college professor may accept a lighter teaching load to have more time with his children; a business executive may telecommute to her job two days a week in order spend more time with her children. Some people partition their lives in ways that prevent such conflicts from arising. For example, some people keep their work lives and their private lives entirely separate.

Resolution of Identity Crises

Identity crises—both deficits and conflicts—commonly occur during adolescence, though not all adolescents experience identity crises. Those who do find that resolution involves two steps (Baumeister, 1997). First, they decide which values are most important to them. Second, they transform these abstract values into desires and actual behaviors. For example, a person might arrive at the conclusion that what is really important is to have a family. The second step is to translate this value into actions, such as finding the right spouse, someone who also wants a family; working hard to maintain this relationship; preparing a career with which to support a family; and so forth. As the person begins working toward these goals, he or she assumes a secure identity and is unlikely to experience an identity crisis, at least during this early phase of life.

A second phase of life in which identity crises commonly occur is during middle age. For some people, this is a period in which they experience dissatisfaction with their existing identities, perhaps at work or in a marriage. Whatever the reason, people undergoing a midlife identity crisis begin to feel that things are not working out as they wished. They may feel that their lives are inauthentic. People in the midlife identity crisis begin to doubt that they made the right choices early in life, and they reconsider those commitments: "If only I had done . . ." is a frequent complaint. It is a period of regret over time spent pursuing goals that turned out to be unsatisfying or impossible. Many people in this predicament decide to abandon their goals and experience an identity deficit because they give up the principles that have guided their lives so far.

Application

The movie character Lester, played by Kevin Spacey in the Oscar-winning film *American Beauty,* undergoes an acute midlife identity crisis. In fact, the movie is about the havoc Lester wreaks on his family, neighbors, and co-workers during his identity crisis. Lester goes from being a complacent husband, a neglecting but "good-enough" father, and a submissive worker to someone who wants things his own way at home and at work. One day, Lester decides that he does not like what he has become and decides to make drastic changes in his life. During his transformation, Lester ruins his marriage, drives his daughter to contemplate running away, loses his job, experiments with drugs, pushes an unstable neighbor over the brink, and contributes to the delinquency of two minor children. Clearly, Lester's attempts to redefine himself are adolescent and dysfunctional throughout most of the movie. However, toward the end, Lester appears to be starting on the right track; he has finally found some integrity and is heading in a positive direction. It is the scene in which Lester decides not to have sex with his daughter's girlfriend that he acknowledges that his new identity will at least be that of a mature adult.

In the Oscar-winning movie American Beauty, *actor Kevin Spacey plays Lester, a man undergoing a severe midlife identity crisis. In his effort to transform his social identity, Lester changes the way he interacts with his wife, his boss, his child, and even his neighbors. While he makes some rash decisions along the way, toward the end of the movie we get a sense that Lester is finally forming a positive new identity.*

People who undergo midlife crises often act as adolescents again. That is, an identity crisis often looks the same, whether it occurs at adolescence or at midlife: the person experiments with alternative lifestyles, forms new relationships and abandons old ones, and gives up previous ambitions and responsibilities. In midlife crises, people often change their careers, change their spouses, change their religions, change where they live, or do various combinations of these. Sometimes they simply change their priorities—for example, a woman might keep her job and her spouse but decide to spend more time with her spouse and less time working. A midlife identity crisis can be just as much of an emotional roller-coaster ride as an adolescent identity crisis.

To summarize, a social identity consists of the social or public aspects of yourself, the impression that you typically create in others. Many of your more visible characteristics—such as gender, ethnicity, and occupation—contribute to your identity. Other characteristics, including those that make up reputation, also go into the formation of identity. Your identity is what gives you and others a sense of continuity, of being the same person tomorrow as today. It also makes you unique in the eyes of others.

SUMMARY AND EVALUATION

This chapter presented an outline of what personality psychologists know about the self. This knowledge is neatly divided into three broad areas: self-concept, self-esteem, and social identity. These aspects of the self are important to understanding personality. The notion of a self makes sense in terms of our everyday lives and our experience. We frequently use terms such as *selfish, self-worship, selfless, self-conscious,* and *self-esteem* in everyday life. In the evolution of language, we developed a rich vocabulary for talking about the self. This reflects people's general preoccupation with themselves. Another reason psychologists are interested in the self is that it plays an important role in organizing a person's experiences of the world. What a person deems important, for example, are the things that are relevant to his or her self-concept. Moreover, people behave differently when they are self-involved than when they are not, so the concept of the self is important for understanding how people construe their world, their experiences, and their actions. The self is a major organizing force within the person.

Self-concept is a person's self-understanding—their story of themselves. The self-concept has its start in infancy, when the child first makes a distinction between its body and everything else. This glimmer of self-concept goes on to develop, through repeated experiences of self-awareness, into a collection of characteristics that the child uses for self-definition, such as gender, age, and membership in a particular family. Children acquire skills and talents and start comparing themselves with others and refining their self-concept. They also develop a sense of privacy and a sense of their ability to keep secrets, so they begin to develop a private self-concept, things they know about themselves that no one else knows. Cognitive schemata then develop around aspects of the self; these knowledge structures are collections of characteristics associated with the self-concept. People also develop views of themselves in the future, their possible selves, which include both desirable (ideal self) and undesirable features. All in all, the self-concept is the person's answer to the questions "Who have I been, what am I like now, and who do I want to be in the future?"

Self-esteem is the evaluation a person makes of his or her self-concept along a good–bad dimension. People differ from each other in terms of whether they see themselves as worthwhile, valuable, and good. Research on self-esteem has emphasized how people respond to failure, and findings suggest that high self-esteem persons persevere in the face of failure, whereas low self-esteem persons often give up following failure. High self-esteem people seem particularly good at deflecting the bumps and bruises of everyday life. One strategy they seem particularly adept in using is, when something bad happens in one area of their lives, to remind themselves that other areas in their lives are going well. This puts negative events in perspective and helps them cope. Extremely high self-esteem, associated with narcissistic tendencies, can sometimes result in aggressive responses to threats to that self-esteem. Researchers have shown that narcissistic persons often retaliate following negative feedback. Another clinical problem associated with self-esteem is extreme shyness. While shyness does have some biological correlates, it is also associated with an over-controlling parenting style. Shyness can often be changed through treatment efforts. Another area of research shows that high self-esteem people are often concerned with enhancing their self-concept, whereas low self-esteem persons are often concerned with protecting what they have from insult. Finally, in terms of self-esteem variability, variable persons seem especially sensitive to evaluative life events, such as social slights and public failures.

The final aspect of the self discussed in this chapter was social identity, as a person's outward manifestation or the impression he or she gives others. Identity develops over time through relations with others. For many people, the development of an identity follows a period of experimentation, but for others it happens more easily by adopting ready-made social roles. There are periods in life when some people undergo identity crises and have to redefine their social identities. Developing an identity is a life-long task, as identity changes with the changing social roles that come with age.

Erikson coined the term *identity crisis* to refer to the anxiety that comes with having to redefine one's social reputation. There are two kinds of crises: identity deficit, not forming an adequate identity, and identity conflict, in which two or more aspects of identity come into conflict. Despite crises and challenges, most people develop a solid identity and other people know them for their unique characteristics.

KEY TERMS

Self-Concept 463
Self-Esteem 463
Social Identity 463
Social Comparison 467
Private Self-Concept 467
Perspective Taking 469
Objective Self-Awareness 469
Self-Schema 469
Possible Selves 470
Ideal Self 470
Ought Self 470
Self-Guides 470
Social Anxiety 474
Amygdala 475
Self-Complexity 478
Defensive Pessimism 479
Self-Handicapping 479
Self-Esteem Variability 479
Continuity 482
Contrast 483
Identity Crisis 485
Identity Deficit 485
Identity Conflict 486

PART FIVE

The Social and Cultural Domain

In the social and cultural domain of knowledge, there is an emphasis on the public aspects of personality. The assumption here is that personality is not something that is only in the heads of people, or residing only in their nervous systems or carried in their genes. In this domain, the emphasis is on personality as it is affected by and expressed through social institutions, social roles and expectations, and through relationships with other people in our lives.

We saw in Chapter 3 that several taxonomies of traits emphasize interpersonal traits, or traits that pertain to styles of interacting, such as dominance versus submissiveness, or love versus hate. Indeed, most of the important trait adjectives in language are important for describing how people behave with others, whether a person is cooperative or not, whether a person is reliable, easy to get along with, and so forth. Individuals differ greatly in how they interact with each other. Moreover, such interpersonal traits have long-term outcomes in our lives. For example, whether a person is controlling or easygoing affects such different aspects of his life as the conflicts he gets into with his spouse and work partners and the strategies he uses to achieve his goals. Whether a person tends to be nervous and depressed or optimistic and cheerful affects the likelihood of diverse social outcomes, such as divorce or success in a sales career. Many of the most important individual differences and personality traits are played out in our interpersonal relationships.

We will describe three key processes whereby personality affects social interactions. The first process is through selection, in which people may choose specific social environments according to their personalities. An example of this is assortative mating, where people look for specific kinds of people to marry, often people who have similar personality traits. A second process whereby personality affects social interactions is through the reactions we evoke in others. For example, in arguments between married couples, there are specific ways that men tend to upset their wives, and other ways in which women tend to upset their husbands. We will examine how people evoke distress, as well as positive feelings, in others. A final process whereby personality affects social interactions is through manipulations for influencing others. What are the strategies that people use to get what they want from others? How do people go about influencing others? We will discuss research on strategies for social influence, and focus on a particular style called machiavellianism, named after a medieval advisor to kings, who wrote a book on how to take advantage of others.

One very important interpersonal context concerns relationships between men and women. An essential part of our social identity is our gender. Differences between men and women in terms of personality have long been of interest to personality psychology. And indeed, much of the work by personality psychologists on gender

V

differences has been incorporated into feminist theories in various ways. This is an area in which politics and values intermingle with the science of personality. Some researchers prefer to minimize the differences between men and women, emphasizing that sex differences are small and that the variability within sex (e.g., between women) far exceeds the variability between the sexes (e.g., between men and women). Other researchers focus on the differences between the sexes and emphasize that some are rather large and are found in different cultures. For example, women tend to have slightly higher verbal ability than men, and men tend to have somewhat better spatial visual ability than women. In terms of personality, men tend to score higher on measures of assertiveness and aggressiveness, whereas women tend to score higher on measures of trust and nurturance. Where do such differences come from?

Much of what we call gender may have its origins in culture, that is, in how society makes up different rules and expectations for men and women. The title of a popular book, *Men Are from Mars, Women Are from Venus,* by John Gray, suggests that men and women are so different from one another that it is like they are from different planets, or that they are different species. While men and women are not different species, one can argue that they are from different cultures. The culture of growing up as a boy may be very different from the culture of growing up as a girl. For example, parents tend to hold and cuddle infant girls longer than they do infant boys. So, differences in how people interact with boys and girls start very early in life, and such differences may accumulate and result in differences in personalities between adult men and adult women.

While there is clear support for how social factors contribute to gender differences, there are also findings that show such differences across many different societies and cultures. Men, for example, are the more aggressive gender in all societies studied to date. Consequently, some theories are emphasizing differences between men and women that may be due to hormones. Testosterone levels, for example, differ greatly between men and women, and testosterone has been reliably associated with the personality traits of dominance, aggression, and sexuality.

At the level of difference between the sexes, personality may operate differently for men than for women. One answer to why men and women are different may lie in evolved behavior patterns that represent adaptations to different pressures that faced men and women in the distant past of human history. That is, as men and women faced different challenges (e.g., childbearing, competition for mates) there may have evolved solutions to these different challenges, and such solutions resulted in differences between how men and women behave. Whatever their origins, gender differences have long been of interest to personality psychologists and are clearly part of the social and cultural domain because they refer to and are played out in interpersonal relations.

Another socially important difference between people derives from their culture, the system of social rules, expectations, and rituals in which a person is raised. For example, in one culture it might be expected that a crying baby is always picked up and comforted by its parents, whereas in another culture crying babies are left to cry. Could it be that being raised in these two different cultures results in differences in adult personality? Indeed, do people in different cultures have different personalities? Even within a country do people from different regions differ from others in that country? Are people raised on the East Coast of the United States different from the average American? Are southerners different from northerners?

It might be assumed that people from different cultures have different personalities because of the cultural forces that shape personality. It has often been said that there are more similarities than differences between individuals from diverse cultures. However, it is also a truism that small differences are magnified when people from different cultures live close together. For example, in recent years in several large U.S. cities, there have been tensions between recent Asian immigrants to the United States and African Americans who already occupy neighborhoods where the immigrants settle. Many of these tensions arise because of misunderstandings about behavior between these two groups of people who grew up in distinctly different cultures.

The world is becoming an increasingly smaller place, in the sense that people from different cultural backgrounds often live and work in the same communities. Small cultural differences—for example, in conversational style, in privacy, in dress, in the use of space, in attention, in what counts as being polite, in how emotions are expressed or not expressed, and in our expectations for friends and acquaintances—become large differences when there is a misunderstanding. An important goal of personality psychology is to understand how cultures shape personality and how specific cultures are different from, or similar to, each other. People from different cultures have different experiences, which have taught them different lessons about the social and physical world. It is of compelling importance that we seek to understand one another and the forces that shape differences between persons from different cultures.

One personality variable that has been the topic of much cross-cultural research concerns individualistic versus collectivistic values. The U.S. culture, as well as much of Europe, tends to be more individualistic, emphasizing autonomy and individual striving and self-enhancement. The Asian cultures, as well as many formerly communist countries, tend to endorse more collectivistic values with higher priority given to group goals, or the common good, than to personal desires or wants. People from more collectivistic cultures focus more on the social context and are more self-effacing than people from individualistic cultures.

In many ways, the culture in which a person was raised has a profound effect on the person's self-concept. For example, persons raised in the United States tend to describe themselves with abstract concepts, such as "I am reliable" or "I am friendly." Persons from Asian cultures, on the other hand, tend to describe themselves through their social relations, such as "I am Liu's friend" or "I am the daughter of Hong Lee." Differences such as these are examples of transmitted culture, that is, what is handed down from generation to generation. It is also important to know that such differences are always a matter of degree, since even in Eastern cultures it is possible to find individualistic persons.

Besides identifying ways in which people from different cultures differ, cultural personality psychologists have also looked for similarities between cultures. One example of a cultural universal appears to be the expression of specific emotions. For example, people in all cultures smile when they are happy, frown when they are sad, bare their teeth when they are angry, and protrude their tongue when they are disgusted. Moreover, people from around the world recognize these expressions as indicating the person is experiencing the specific emotion. People from Dubuque, Iowa, to Calcutta, India, recognize the expression of teeth clenched and bared, nostrils flared, and eyebrows brought down and together as an expression of anger. Another aspect of personality that appears to show cultural universality is described by the five-factor model of traits. Analyzing adjectives from many different languages, personality psychologists have found strong evidence that five factors can be uncovered. This structure of personality, at least as it is described in natural language, may be highly similar across cultures.

In this part of the book we focus on the broader social and interpersonal aspects of personality. This side of personality many students find interesting. After all, part of understanding why people behave the way they do involves understanding their social behavior, why they interact with others in certain ways, how they do or do not maintain friendships, why they can or cannot cooperate in a group. Many important personality traits refer to styles of interacting with others. Narcissism, as an example, refers to the style of a person who needs lots of attention, recognition, and praise from others. We will begin our exploration of this fascinating domain of psychological knowledge with a chapter on the interpersonal aspects of personality.

15 Personality and Social Interaction

The advertisements in personals columns often mention personality characteristics that the person is seeking in a mate (e.g., caring, sense of humor, affectionate). This highlights the fact that personality plays an important role in social interaction.

Sue and Joan sipped coffee while discussing their dates from the previous evening. "Michael seemed like a nice guy, at least at first," Sue noted. "He was polite, asked me what kind of food I liked, and seemed genuinely interested in knowing me as a person. But I was a little turned off by the rude way he talked to the waitress. He barked at her like she was his servant. He also insisted in choosing the food for me and selected a pork dish I didn't like. I think he was trying to show off, but it really turned me off. Then, over dinner, he talked about himself the whole time. At the end of the evening, he tried to invite himself back to my room, but I told him that I was tired and wanted to call it a night." "Did you kiss him?" asked Joan. "Well, yes, I started to give him a good-night kiss, but he began to get really aggressive with me, and I had to push him away. All the politeness disappeared, and he stormed off angry. I guess he wasn't such a nice guy after all. He seemed really immature. How did your date go?"

In the course of this conversation, Sue revealed a treasure trove of information about her date, Michael—information that figures prominently in the social decisions we make. Michael displayed aggressiveness, both toward the waitress and toward Sue during the good-night kiss. He displayed self-centeredness, focusing on himself during the course of the dinner. He showed a lack of empathy, as illustrated by his uncaring attitude toward the feelings of the waitress and his abrupt sexual aggressiveness. The thin veneer of politeness quickly gave way over the evening, revealing an abrasive interpersonal disposition that turned Sue off.

The episode above illustrates several key ways in which personality plays an important role in social interaction. As we discussed in Chapter 4, personality interacts with situations in three ways: through selection, through evocation, and through manipulation of the situation. These three mechanisms can be applied to an understanding of how personality affects interpersonal situations. First, the personality characteristics of others influence whether we *select* them as our dates, friends, and even marriage partners. In this episode, Sue was turned off by Michael's aggressive and self-centered personality characteristics. People's personality characteristics also play a role in the kinds of interpersonal situations they select to enter and stay in. For example, someone with a personality different from Sue's might actually be attracted to a guy like Michael and could put up with his self-centeredness and brash behavior.

Second, the personality qualities of others *evoke* certain responses in us, and us in them. Michael's aggressive displays upset Sue, evoking an emotional response in her that would not have been evoked if he had behaved in a kinder, more caring manner. Furthermore, behaviors related to personality can evoke all sorts of responses in others, ranging from aggression to social support, and even to marital satisfaction in close relationships.

Third, personality is linked to the ways in which we try to influence or *manipulate* others. In this episode, Michael first tried the charm tactic. Then he pulled out the boasting tactic. Finally, he used coercion, trying to force himself on Sue. A man with a different constellation of personality attributes would have used different tactics of social influence, such as reason or reward.

These three processes—selection, evocation, and manipulation—are three key ways in which personality interacts with the social environment. Individuals in everyday life are not exposed to all possible social situations; individuals with certain personality dispositions seek out and avoid social situations selectively. Personality also influences how we evoke different reactions from other people and how others, in turn, evoke different responses from us, sometimes quite unintentionally. And personality affects how we purposefully influence, change, exploit, and manipulate the others with whom we have chosen to be associated. Among these three processes, selection is the first, since it determines the people to whom we are exposed.

Selection

In everyday life, people choose to enter some situations and avoid other situations. These forms of **situation selection** can hinge on personality dispositions and how we view ourselves. The following story illustrates the process of selection. In this example a couple inadvertently entered a situation and then chose a rapid exit from it.

> *Chip and Priscilla, a Yuppie couple from Chicago, have just moved to Dallas and are sampling some of the trendier nightspots on Lower Greenville Avenue. As they push through the swinging doors of what appears to be a quaint little Western saloon right out of the TV series Gunsmoke, they are confronted by six huge bikers from the motorcycle gang Los Diablos, who turn on their barstools to glare at them. The bikers have an average of more than two tattoos and three missing teeth. The fumes they emit smell flammable. Two of them stare with contempt at Chip, and one leers evilly at Priscilla. "This doesn't look like our kind of place," Chip says to Priscilla, as they prepare to beat a hasty retreat. (Ickes, Snyder, & Garcia, 1997, p. 165)*

Social selections permeate daily life. These choices range in importance from the seemingly trivial ("Should I attend this party tonight?") to the profound ("Should I select this person as my marriage partner?"). Social selections are decision points that direct us to choose one path and avoid another. These decisions, which determine the nature of our social environments and social worlds, are often based on the personality characteristics of the selector.

Mate selection provides a dramatic example of this mechanism. When you select a long-term mate, you place yourself into close and prolonged contact with one particular other. This alters the social environment to which you are exposed and in which you will reside. By selecting a mate, you are simultaneously selecting the social acts you will experience and the network of friends and family in which those acts will be carried out.

In terms of personality characteristics, who do people seek as potential mates? Are there common personality characteristics that are highly desired by everyone? Do we look for potential mates who have personalities similar to our own or different from our own? That is, do birds of a feather flock together, or do opposites attract? And how is the choice of a mate linked to the likelihood that a couple will stay together over time? These questions have been the focus of a series of investigations over the past few decades. In this section, we will consider how personality affects choice of a mate and whether couples stay together.

Personality Characteristics Desired in a Marriage Partner

What do people want in a long-term partner? This was the focus of an international investigation of 10,047 individuals located on six continents and five islands from around the world (Buss et al., 1990). A total of 37 samples were chosen from 33 countries, representing every major racial group, religious group, and political system. Samples ranged from the coastal dwelling Australians to the South African Zulu people. The economic status of the samples varied from middle- and upper-middle class college students to lower socioeconomic groups, such as the Gujarati Indians and Soviet Estonians. Fifty researchers were involved in the data collection. Standard questionnaires were translated into the native language of each culture and then were administered to the samples by native residents of each culture. This study, the most massive ever conducted on what people want in a long-term mate, revealed that personality characteristics play a central role in the selection of a mate. In the Exercise that follows and then in Table 15.1, you can complete this questionnaire yourself and see how your selection preferences compare with those of the worldwide sample.

INSTRUCTIONS: Evaluate the following factors in choosing a mate or marriage partner. If you consider the factor to be

indispensable, give it	**3 points**
important, but not indispensable, give it	**2 points**
desirable, but not very important, give it	**1 point**
irrelevant or unimportant, give it	**0 points**

Exercise (*Continued*)

___ 1. Good cook and housekeeper
___ 2. Pleasing disposition
___ 3. Sociability
___ 4. Similar educational background
___ 5. Refinement, neatness
___ 6. Good financial prospect
___ 7. Chastity (no prior intercourse)
___ 8. Dependable character
___ 9. Emotional stability
___ 10. Desire for home and children
___ 11. Favorable social status
___ 12. Good looks
___ 13. Similar religious background
___ 14. Ambition and industriousness
___ 15. Similar political background
___ 16. Mutual attraction or love
___ 17. Good health
___ 18. Education and intelligence

Now compare your ratings with the ratings given by the international sample of 10,047 men and women, shown in Table 15.1.

Table 15.1 Summary of Ratings by Sex Using Entire International Sample

	RATINGS BY MALES			RATINGS BY FEMALES		
Ranked Value	**Variable Name**	**Mean**	**Std. Dev.**	**Variable Name**	**Mean**	**Std. Dev.**
1.	Mutual Attraction—Love	2.81	0.16	Mutual Attraction—Love	2.87	0.12
2.	Dependable Character	2.50	0.46	Dependable Character	2.69	0.31
3.	Emotional Stability and Maturity	2.47	0.20	Emotional Stability and Maturity	2.68	0.20
4.	Pleasing Disposition	2.44	0.29	Pleasing Disposition	2.52	0.30
5.	Good Health	2.31	0.33	Education and Intelligence	2.45	0.25
6.	Education and Intelligence	2.27	0.19	Sociability	2.30	0.28
7.	Sociability	2.15	0.28	Good Health	2.28	0.30
8.	Desire for Home and Children	2.09	0.50	Desire for Home and Children	2.21	0.44
9.	Refinement, Neatness	2.03	0.48	Ambition and Industriousness	2.15	0.35
10.	Good Looks	1.91	0.26	Refinement, Neatness	1.98	0.49
11.	Ambition and Industriousness	1.85	0.35	Similar Education	1.84	0.47
12.	Good Cook and Housekeeper	1.80	0.48	Good Financial Prospect	1.76	0.38
13.	Good Financial Prospect	1.51	0.42	Good Looks	1.46	0.28
14.	Similar Education	1.50	0.37	Favorable Social Status or Rating	1.46	0.39
15.	Favorable Social Status or Rating	1.16	0.28	Good Cook and Housekeeper	1.28	0.27
16.	Chastity (no previous experience in sexual intercourse)	1.06	0.69	Similar Religious Background	1.21	0.56
17.	Similar Religious Background	0.98	0.48	Similar Political Background	1.03	0.35
18.	Similar Political Background	0.92	0.36	Chastity (no previous experience in sexual intercourse)	0.75	0.66
	Mean	1.87	0.57	Mean	1.94	0.63

Source: Adapted from Buss et al. (1990), p. 19, Table 4.

As you can see in Table 15.1, mutual attraction or love was the most favored characteristic, viewed as indispensable by almost everyone in the world. Perhaps the famous rock group, the Beatles, were right—"all you need is love." After mutual attraction or love, personality characteristics loom large in people's mate selection preferences. Viewed as almost as important as love are the personality factors of dependable character, emotional stability, and pleasing disposition. You may recall that these are quite close to the labels given to three of the factors in the five-factor model of personality (see Chapter 3). Dependability is close to conscientiousness. Emotional stability is identical to the fourth factor on the five-factor model. And pleasing disposition is quite close to agreeableness, the second factor in the model. Other personality factors rated highly by the international sample included sociability, refinement and neatness, and ambition and industriousness.

Note that the respondents' top choices, except for love, were personality characteristics. Thus, personality factors play a central role in what people worldwide are looking for in a long-term mate (see also Fletcher et al., 2004).

Assortative Mating for Personality: The Search for the Similar

Over the past century, two fundamentally competing scientific theories have been advanced for who is attracted to whom. **Complementary needs theory** postulates that people are attracted to those who have different personality dispositions than they have (Murstein, 1976; Winch, 1954). People who are dominant, for example, might have a need to be in a relationship with someone whom they can control and dominate. People who are submissive, according to complementary needs theory, have a need to choose a mate who can dominate and control them. One easy way to think about complementary needs theory is with the phrase "opposites attract."

In contrast, **attraction similarity theory** postulates that people are attracted to those who have similar personality characteristics. People who are dominant might be attracted to those who are also dominant, because they like someone who "pushes back." People who are extraverted, to take another example, might like partners who are also extraverted so that they can party together. One easy way to remember this theory is with the phrase "birds of a feather flock together." Although there have been many proponents of both theories over the past century, the results are now in. They provide overwhelming support for the attraction similarity theory and no support for the complementary needs theory (Buss, 2003). Indeed, the only characteristic on which "opposites attract" that has been reliably documented is biological sex: Men tend to be attracted to women and women tend to be attracted to men. Although of course there will always be individual exceptions to the rule, the research shows that people are generally drawn to those who share their personalities.

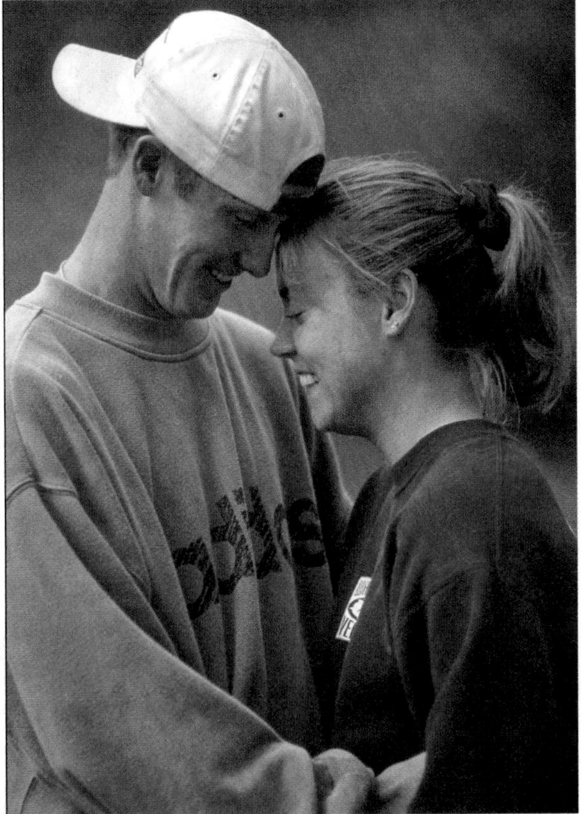

People often are attracted to others who are similar to themselves. This refers to the concept of assortative mating.

One of the most common findings in the mate selection literature—that people are married to people who are similar to themselves—is a phenomenon known as **assortative mating.** For nearly every variable that has been examined—from single actions to ethnic and racial status—people seem to select mates who are similar to themselves. Even for physical characteristics such as height, weight, and, astonishingly, nose breadth and earlobe length, couples show positive correlations. Even the perceived personality of individuals based on faces—personality trait assessment based solely on judgments of photographs—shows assortative mating (Little, Burt, & Perrett, 2006). Couples who have been together the longest appeared most similar in personality—a finding that may result from couples growing more similar in personality over time or from dissimilar couples breaking up more often.

But are these positive correlations caused by the active selection of mates who are similar? Or are these positive correlations merely by-products of other causal processes? Sheer proximity, for example, could, in principle, account for some of the positive correlations. It is known that people tend to marry those who are close by. It has even been noted that, notions of romantic love aside, the "one and only" typically lives within driving distance. It is naturally easier to meet and become intimate with someone who is close by. And, since people in close proximity may have certain common characteristics, the positive correlations found between married couples may be merely a side effect of mating with those who are close by, rather than the active selection of partners who are similar. Cultural institutions, such as colleges and universities, may promote assortative mating by preferentially admitting those who are similar with respect to certain variables, such as intelligence, motivation, and social skills.

To test these competing predictions, Botwin and colleagues (Botwin, Buss, & Shackelford, 1997) studied two samples of subjects—dating couples and newlywed couples. The participants were asked to express their preferences for the personality characteristics in a potential mate on 40 rating scales, which were scored on five dimensions of personality: extraversion, agreeableness, conscientiousness, emotional stability, and intellect–openness. The next step was to assess the subjects' personality dispositions on these dimensions using the same 40 rating scales. Three data sources were used for this second stage: self-reports; reports by their partners, who had no knowledge of the preference scores of the target subjects; and independent reports by interviewers, who also had no knowledge of the preference scores of the target subjects. Then, correlations were computed between two sets of personality ratings: the ones made by the subject (self) and the average of the peer and interviewer ratings of the subject (aggregate). The subjects' expressed mate preferences to determine whether they wanted mates who were similar to themselves.

As shown in Table 15.2, these correlations were consistently positive. Those who scored high on extraversion wanted to select an extraverted person as a mate. Those who scored high on conscientiousness desired a conscientious mate. The conclusions from this study, of course, must be qualified by one important consideration—perhaps the preferences people express for the personalities of their ideal mates might be influenced by the mates they already have. If an emotionally stable person is already mated to an emotionally stable person, perhaps they justify their choice by claiming that they are truly attracted to the one they are with. This could result in positive correlations between one's own personality and the personality people express for a desired mate. Nonetheless, studies of individuals who are not mated already find the same pattern of results—people prefer those who are similar to themselves (e.g., Buss, 1984, 1985, 1987)—supporting the attraction similarity theory.

Table 15.2 Personality Correlated with Mate Preferences

	DATING COUPLES				MARRIED COUPLES			
	MEN		WOMEN		MEN		WOMEN	
Trait	**Self**	**Aggregate**	**Self**	**Aggregate**	**Self**	**Aggregate**	**Self**	**Aggregate**
Surgency	.33*	.42**	.59***	.35**	.20*	.15	.30**	.25**
Agreeableness	.37*	.17	.44***	.46***	.30**	.12	.44***	.31**
Conscientiousness	.34**	.45***	.59***	.53***	.53***	.49***	.61***	.53***
Emotional Stability	.29*	.36**	.52***	.30*	.27**	.21*	.32***	.27**
Intellect–Openness	.56***	.54***	.63***	.50***	.24*	.31**	.48***	.52***

*$p < .05$
**$p < .01$
***$p < .001$.
Note: Each correlation in the table refers to the relationship between the personality trait of the individual and the corresponding personality trait desired in a mate. Thus, under Men, Self-Report column, the .33* indicates that men who are highly surgent tend to prefer mates who are also surgent. The fact that all the correlations in the table are positive, many significantly so, indicates that people generally want mates who are similar to themselves in personality.
Source: *Personality and Mate Preferences: Five Factors in Mate Selection and Marital Satisfaction.* Botwin, M. D., Buss, D. M., & Shackelford, T. K. (1997).

These data provide evidence that positive correlations on personality variables between husbands and wives are due, at least in part, to direct social preferences, based on the personality characteristics of those doing the selecting. In sum, personality characteristics appear to play a pivotal role in the social mechanism of selection.

Do People Get the Mates They Want?

A fact of human life is that we do not always get what we want, and this is true of mate selection. You may want a mate who is kind, understanding, dependable, emotionally stable, and intelligent, but such desirable mates are always in short supply, compared with the numbers of people who seek them. Therefore, many people end up mated with individuals who fall short of their ideals. It is reasonable to predict, therefore, that individuals whose mates deviate from their ideals will be less satisfied than those whose mates embody their desires.

Table 15.3 shows the correlations between the preferences that individuals express for the ideal personality characteristics of their mates and the actual personality characteristics of their obtained mates (Botwin et al., 1997, p. 127). Across three of the four subsamples—women who are dating, women who are married, and men who are married—there are modest but consistently positive correlations between the personality desired in a partner and the actual personality characteristics displayed by the partner. The correspondence between what one wants and what one gets is especially strong for surgency and intellect–openness. In short, as a general rule, people seem to get the mates they want in terms of personality.

These correlations suggest individual differences, however. Are people who get what they want happier with their marriages than people who do not? To examine this issue, Botwin et al. (1997) created difference scores between the preferences each individual expressed for the ideal personality of a mate and assessments of the spouse's actual personality. These difference scores were then used to predict satisfaction with the marriage, after first controlling for the main effects of the spouse's

Table 15.3 Personality Mate Preferences and Personality of Partner Obtained

	DATING COUPLES				MARRIED COUPLES			
	WOMEN'S PREFERENCES		MEN'S PREFERENCES		WOMEN'S PREFERENCES		MEN'S PREFERENCES	
Partner's Personality	**Self**	**Aggregate**	**Self**	**Aggregate**	**Self**	**Aggregate**	**Self**	**Aggregate**
Surgency	.25	.39**	.28*	.24	.39***	.49***	.31***	.32**
Agreeableness	.28*	.32	.24	.02	.20*	.40***	.03	.25
Conscientiousness	.28*	.29*	.24	.26	.36***	.46***	.13	.24
Emotional Stability	.36**	.12	.40**	.10	.27**	.37**	.07	.12
Intellect–Openness	.33**	.41**	.40**	.11	.24**	.39***	.14	.39***

*$p < .05$
**$p < .01$
***$p < .001$.
Source: *Personality and Mate Preferences: Five Factors in Mate Selection and Marital Satisfaction.* Botwin, M. D., Buss, D. M., & Shackelford, T. K. (1997).

personality. The results were consistent—one's partner's personality had a substantial effect on marital satisfaction. Specifically, people were especially happy with their relationships if they were married to partners who were high on the personality characteristics of agreeableness, emotional stability, and openness. But the difference scores between the partner's personality and one's ideal for that personality did *not* predict marital satisfaction. In other words, the key to marital happiness is having a partner who is agreeable, emotionally stable, and open, regardless of whether the partner departs in specific ways from what one wants.

The correlations between the participants' marital satisfaction scores and the partners' personality scores, obtained through the partners' self-reports, are shown in Table 15.4. Having a partner who is agreeable is an especially strong predictor of being happy with one's marriage for both men and women. People married to agreeable partners are more satisfied with their sex lives, view their spouses as more loving and affectionate, as a source of shared laughter, and as a source of stimulating conversation. People married to disagreeable partners are the most unhappy with the marriage and perhaps are most at risk of getting divorced.

The other personality factors that are consistently linked with marital satisfaction are conscientiousness, emotional stability, and openness. Men whose wives score high on conscientiousness are significantly more sexually satisfied with the marriage than are other husbands. Women whose husbands score high on conscientiousness are generally more satisfied, as well as happier with their spouses as sources of stimulating conversation. Both men and women whose spouses score high on emotional stability are generally more satisfied, view their spouses as sources of encouragement and support, and enjoy spending time with their spouses. Similarly, both men and women whose spouses score high on openness are generally satisfied with the marriage and perceive that a lot of love and affection are expressed in the marriage. Women whose husbands score high on intellect–openness view their husbands as sources of stimulating conversation.

In summary, the personality of one's spouse plays an important role in marital satisfaction. Those who select mates high on agreeableness, conscientiousness, emotional stability, and openness show the greatest happiness with their marriages. Those who select mates low on these personality factors are the most unhappy with

Table 15.4 Facet of Marital Satisfaction and Spouse's Self-Reported Trait Ratings

	SPOUSE'S SELF-REPORTED TRAIT RATINGS				
Marital Satisfaction	**S**	**A**	**C**	**ES**	**I–O**
Husband's marital satisfaction					
General	.12	.32***	.06	.27**	.29**
Spouse as someone to confide in	−.05	.27**	.07	.11	.05
Sexual	−.08	.31**	.32***	.25**	.04
Spouse as source of encouragement and support	.03	.29**	.11	.26**	.18
Love and affection expressed	.07	.31**	.14	.21*	.26**
Enjoyment of time spent with spouse	.11	.30**	.13	.28**	.08
Frequency of laughing with spouse	.19*	.23*	.19	.11	.24**
Spouse as source of stimulating conversation	.06	.12	−.04	.21*	.17
Wife's marital satisfaction					
General	.07	.37***	.20*	.23*	.31***
Spouse as someone to confide in	.06	.25**	.15	.24**	.27**
Sexual	.08	.19*	.14	.09	.13
Spouse as source of encouragement and support	.04	.47***	.06	.20*	.31***
Love and affection expressed	−.04	.29**	.14	.28**	.33***
Enjoyment of time spent with spouse	.06	.27**	.06	.33***	.18
Frequency of laughing with spouse	−.02	.27**	−.02	.10	.08
Spouse as source of stimulating conversation	.23*	.24**	.25**	.18	.45***

Note: S = Surgency; A = Agreeableness: C = Conscientiousness: ES = Emotional Stability; I–O = Intellect–Openness.
*$p < .05$
**$p < .01$
***$p < .001$.
Source: *Personality and Mate Preferences: Five Factors in Mate Selection and Marital Satisfaction.* Botwin, M. D., Buss, D. M., & Shackelford, T. K. (1997).

their marriages. Differences from each person's individual ideal, however, do not appear to contribute to marital satisfaction.

Personality and the Selective Breakup of Couples

We have examined two ways in which personality plays a role in the mate selection process. First, there appear to be universal selection preferences—personality characteristics that everyone desires in a potential mate, such as dependability and emotional stability. Second, beyond the desires shared by everyone, people prefer partners who are similar to themselves in personality—dominant people prefer other dominant people, conscientious people prefer other conscientious people, and so on. But there is a third role that personality plays in the process of selection—its role in the selective breakup of marriages.

According to one theory of conflict between the sexes, breakups should occur more when one's desires are violated than when they are fulfilled (Buss, 2003). Following this so-called **violation of desire** theory, we would predict that people married to others who lack desired characteristics, such as dependability and emotional stability, will more frequently dissolve the marriage. We would also predict, based on people's preferences for those who share their personality attributes, that the couples who are dissimilar on personality will break up more often than those who fulfill desires for similarity. Are these predictions borne out in the research findings?

Across a wide variety of studies, emotional instability has been the most consistent personality predictor of marital instability and divorce, emerging as a significant predictor in nearly every study that has included a measure of it (Kelly & Conley, 1987). Low impulse control, or low conscientiousness (i.e., being impulsive and unreliable), particularly as exhibited by husbands, also emerges as a good predictor of marital dissolution (Bentler & Newcomb, 1978; Kelly & Conley, 1987). Finally, low agreeableness predicts marital dissatisfaction and divorce, although this result is less consistent and less powerful than that found for emotional instability and low conscientiousness (Burgess & Wallin, 1953; Kelly & Conley, 1987).

These results suggest that being married to someone who lacks the personality characteristics that are most widely desired—dependability, emotional stability, and pleasing disposition—puts one most at risk for breakup. Thus, people actively seek mates who are dependable and emotionally stable, and those who fail to choose such mates are more at risk for termination of the marriage. Recent studies also point to two other influences of personality on relationship satisfaction or dissatisfaction. One is *similarity in overall personality profile,* rather than similarity in individual personality traits (Luo & Klohnen, 2005). The second is closeness of match between an *individual's conception of an ideal mate* and their partner's actual personality (Zentner, 2005). Both personality profile similarity and congruence between ideal and actual partner are linked with positive relationship outcomes, such as marital quality.

Another study examined the fate of 203 dating couples over the course of two years (Hill, Rubin, & Peplau, 1976). Over that time, roughly half of the couples broke up and half stayed together. An important predictor of which couples stayed together was their similarity in personality and values. Those who were most dissimilar were more likely to break up. These findings provide further support for the violation of desire theory. Those who fail to get what they want—in this case, mates who are to themselves similar—tend to break up more often than those who do get what they want.

In summary, personality plays two key roles in the selection of mates. First, as part of the initial selection process, it determines the mates to whom we are attracted and the mates whom we desire. Second, personality affects satisfaction with one's mate and therefore determines the selective breakup of couples. Those who fail to select partners who are similar to themselves, as well as agreeable, conscientious, and emotionally stable, tend to break up more often than those who succeed in selecting such mates.

Shyness and the Selection of Risky Situations

Although mate selection provides a dramatic example of the effects of personality on social choices, several other domains of selection have also been explored by personality researchers. One important domain pertains to the effects of the personality disposition of shyness. **Shyness** is defined by a tendency to feel tense, worried, or anxious during social interactions or even when anticipating a social interaction (Addison & Schmidt, 1999). Shyness is a common phenomenon, and more than 90 percent of the population reports experiencing shyness at some point during their lives (Zimbardo, 1977). Some people, however, seem to be dispositionally shy—they tend to feel awkward in most social situations and, so, tend to avoid situations in which they will be forced to interact with people, as described in Chapter 14.

The effects of shyness on the selection of situations have been well documented. During high school and early adulthood, shy individuals tend to avoid social situations, resulting in a form of isolation (Schmidt & Fox, 1995). Shy women are also more likely to avoid going to the doctor for gynecological exams, and hence they put themselves at greater health risk (Kowalski & Brown, 1994). They are less likely to bring up the awkward issue of contraception with their partners before sexual intercourse and, so, put themselves in potentially dangerous sexual situations (Bruch & Hynes, 1987).

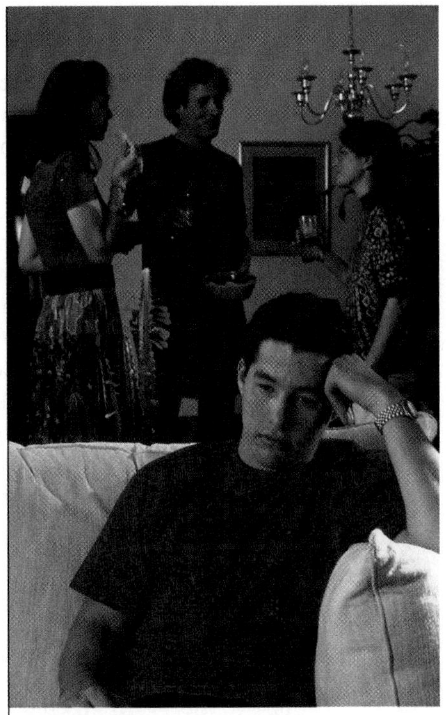

Shy individuals often feel tense or anxious in social situations and often avoid entering situations in which they would be forced to interact with others.

Perhaps most interesting, shyness appears to affect whether a person is willing to select risky situations in the form of gambles (Addison & Schmidt, 1999). In one experiment, shy people were identified through the Cheek (1983) shyness scale, which contains items such as "I find it hard to talk to strangers" and "I feel inhibited in social situations." On entry into the laboratory, each participant received the following instructions: "During this part of the experiment, you have a chance to win some money by picking a poker chip out of this container. There are 100 poker chips in this box that are numbered from 1 to 100. . . ." The participants were given a choice to pick a gamble that they would most likely win (95 percent odds of winning), but from which they would receive only a small amount of money (e.g., 25¢), or to pick a riskier gamble, perhaps with only a 5 percent chance of winning, but from which, if they won, they would receive $4.75. The experimenters also recorded the heart rate of the participants during their choice of gambles.

The results were striking. The shy women differed substantially from their nonshy counterparts in choosing the smaller bets that were linked with a higher likelihood of winning. The nonshy women, in contrast, chose the riskier bets with a lower likelihood of winning but with a larger payoff if they did win. During the task, the shy participants showed a larger increase in heart rate, suggesting that fearfulness might have led them to avoid the risky gambles.

These studies illustrate the importance of the personality disposition of shyness in the selection of, or avoidance of, certain situations. Shy women tend to avoid others, creating social isolation, and to avoid choosing risky gambles. Perhaps paradoxically, they also avoid going to the doctor for gynecological exams and avoid obtaining condoms, thus putting them at greater health risk than less shy women. Shyness, in short, appears to have a substantial impact on the selective entry into, or avoidance of, situations.

Other Personality Traits and the Selection of Situations

A wide variety of other personality traits have been shown to affect selective entry into, or avoidance of, certain situations (Ickes, Snyder, & Garcia, 1997). Those who are characteristically more empathic, for example, are more likely to enter situations such as volunteering for community activities (Davis et al., 1999). And those high on psychoticism seem to choose more volatile and spontaneous situations more than formal or stable ones (Furnham, 1982). Those high on Machiavellianism prefer face-to-face situations, perhaps because these offer a better chance to ply their social manipulative skills to exploit others (Geis & Moon, 1981).

One of the most thoroughly explored personality variables in the context of situation selection has been sensation seeking. High sensation seekers are more likely to volunteer for unusual experiments, such as studies involving drugs or sex (Zuckerman, 1978). Furthermore, high sensation seekers, even during high school, have been found to more frequently choose to enter risky situations (Donohew et al., 2000). High school students high in sensation seeking, more than their low sensation-seeking peers, more frequently attend parties where alcohol or marijuana is available to be consumed. They also more often have unwanted sex when drunk. Those who are high in sensation seeking also tend to select social situations characterized by high-risk sexual behavior (McCoul & Haslam, 2001). In a study of 112 heterosexual men, those who scored high on sensation seeking were more likely than their low-scoring peers to have unprotected sex more frequently ($r = .21$, $p < .05$). Even more striking, high sensation seekers had sexual intercourse with many more different partners than low sensation seekers ($r = .45$, $p < .001$). Interestingly, there were no links between sensation seeking and choosing risky sexual behaviors among the sample of 104 homosexual men. Personality, in sum, affects the situations to which people are exposed through their selective entry into, or avoidance of, certain kinds of activities.

Evocation

Once we select others to occupy our social environment, a second class of processes is set into motion—the evocation of reactions from others. **Evocation** may be defined as the ways in which features of personality elicit reactions from others. Recall from Chapter 3 the study of highly active children (Buss, Block, & Block, 1980). Compared with their less active peers, highly active children tend to elicit hostility and competitiveness from others. Both parents and teachers tend to get into power struggles with these active children. The social interactions of less active children are more peaceful and harmonious. This is a perfect example of the process of evocation at work—a personality characteristic (in this case, activity level) evokes a predictable set of social responses from others (hostility and power struggles).

This form of evocation occurs for a wide variety of personality characteristics, not just activity level. Imagine that you were walking down a long hallway on your way to class, when suddenly someone bumps into you. You interpret the intentions behind this behavior depending on your personality. If you have an aggressive personality, you are more likely to interpret this bump as hostile and intentional. If you have a more agreeable personality, you are more likely to interpret the bump as an accident.

Aggression and the Evocation of Hostility

It is well known that aggressive people evoke hostility from others (Dodge & Coie, 1987). Essentially, people who are aggressive expect that others will be hostile toward them. One study has shown that aggressive people chronically interpret ambiguous behavior from others, such as being bumped into, as intentionally hostile (Dill et al., 1999). This is called a **hostile attributional bias,** the tendency to infer hostile intent on the part of others in the face of uncertain or unclear behavior from them.

Because they expect others to be hostile, aggressive people tend to treat others in an aggressive manner. People who are treated in an aggressive manner often aggress back. In this case, the aggressive reactions of others confirm what the aggressive person suspected all along—that others have hostility toward him. But what the aggressive person fails to realize is that the hostility from others is a product of his or her own making—the aggressor evokes it from others by treating them aggressively. In short, evocation—the ways in which features of personality elicit reactions in others—is the second key process by which personality can affect social interaction.

Evocation of Anger and Upset in Partners

There are at least two ways in which personality can play a role in evoking conflict in close relationships, after the initial selection of a partner has taken place. First, a person can perform actions that cause an emotional response in a partner. A dominant person, for example, might act in a condescending or high-handed manner, habitually evoking upset in the partner, or a husband low in conscientiousness might neglect personal grooming and consistently throw his clothes on the floor, both of which might upset his wife. In short, personality characteristics can evoke emotions in others through the actions performed.

A second form of evocation occurs when a person elicits actions from another that, in turn, upset the original elicitor. An aggressive man, for example, might elicit the silent treatment from his mate, which in turn upsets him because she won't speak to him. A condescending wife might undermine the self-esteem of her husband and then become angry because he lacks self-confidence. In sum, people's personality characteristics can upset others either directly by influencing how they act toward others or indirectly by eliciting actions from others that are upsetting.

To research these forms of evocation, it is necessary to design a study that assesses the personality characteristics of both persons involved. Such a study was carried out, with the goal of examining the role of five major personality dimensions, represented by the five-factor model of personality, on the evocation of anger and distress in a sample of married couples (Buss, 1991). The personality characteristics of both husbands and wives were assessed through three data sources—self-report, spouse-report, and independent reports by two interviewers. The instrument used to obtain a broad-gauge assessment of sources of anger and upset in close relationships was based on the acts that men and women perform that anger and upset one (Buss, 1989). A short version of this instrument is shown in the Exercise below.

Exercise

INSTRUCTIONS: We all do things that upset or anger other people from time to time. Think of a close romantic partner or close friend with whom you have been involved. Following is a list of things this person might have done that evoked anger or upset in you. Read the list, and simply place a check by the things your partner or close friend has done in the past year that have irritated, angered, annoyed, or upset you.

___ 1. He/she treated me as if I were stupid or inferior.
___ 2. He/she demanded too much of my time.
___ 3. He/she ignored my feelings.
___ 4. He/she slapped me.
___ 5. He/she saw someone else intimately.
___ 6. He/she did not help clean up.
___ 7. He/she fussed too much with his/her appearance.
___ 8. He/she acted too moody.
___ 9. He/she refused to have sex with me.

Exercise (*Continued*)

___ 10. He/she talked about members of the opposite sex as if they were sex objects.
___ 11. He/she got drunk.
___ 12. He/she did not dress well or appropriately for a social gathering.
___ 13. He/she told me that I was ugly.
___ 14. He/she tried to use me for sexual purposes.
___ 15. He/she acted selfishly.

These acts represent items from the larger instrument of 147 acts that one can do to upset or anger a member of the opposite sex. The acts correspond to the following factors: (1) condescending, (2) possessive/jealous, (3) neglecting/rejecting, (4) abusive, (5) unfaithful, (6) inconsiderate, (7) physically self-absorbed, (8) moody, (9) sexually withholding, (10) sexualizing of others, (11) abusive of alcohol, (12) disheveled, (13) insulting of partner's appearance, (14) sexually aggressive, and (15) self-centered. It turns out that the personality of the person we are close to is a reasonably good predictor of whether that person will perform these upsetting acts.

Source: Buss (1991).

After data were gathered on the personality characteristics of husbands and wives and the events that each partner performed that upset the other, statistical analyses were conducted to determine which personality traits predicted that the spouse would become upset. The results were similar for men and women, so we will use men's personality traits that upset women to highlight the results.

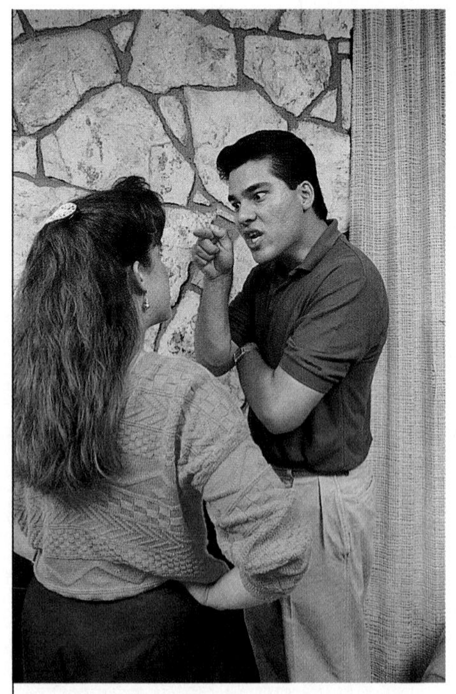

The strongest predictors of a wife's anger and dissatisfaction with marriage are the personality traits of disagreeableness and emotional instability on the part of the husband.

The husbands high on dominance tended to upset their partners by being condescending—treating their wives' opinions as stupid or inferior and placing more value on their own opinions. The husbands who scored low on conscientiousness, in contrast, tended to upset their wives by having extramarital affairs—seeing someone else intimately or having sex with another woman. The husbands low on openness tended to evoke upset in their wives by acting rejecting (ignoring the wife's feelings), abusive (slapping or hitting the wife), physically self-absorbed (focusing too much on his face and hair), sexually withholding (refusing the wife's sexual advances), and abusive of alcohol (getting drunk).

By far the strongest predictors of evoked anger and upset, however, were the personality characteristics of disagreeableness and emotional instability. Disagreeable husbands evoked anger and upset in their wives in the following ways: being condescending, such as treating them as if they were inferior; neglecting and rejecting them, such as failing to spend enough time with them and ignoring their feelings; abusing them, such as slapping, hitting, or spitting; committing infidelity, having extramarital sex with other women; abusing alcohol; insulting her appearance, such as calling her ugly; and exhibiting self-centeredness. Indeed, low agreeableness of the husband was a better predictor of evoking upset in the wife than any other personality variable in the study.

The emotionally unstable husbands also evoked anger and upset in their wives. In addition to being condescending, abusive, unfaithful, inconsiderate, and abusive of alcohol, these husbands also upset their wives by being moody (acting irritable) as well as jealous and possessive. For example, the emotionally unstable men tended to upset their wives by demanding too much attention, monopolizing the wife's time, being too dependent, and flying into jealous rages.

Several recent studies have confirmed the important role of agreeableness and emotional stability in evoking or diminishing conflict in interpersonal relationships. In one study that used both hypothetical and daily diary assessments of conflict, those high in agreeableness tended to evoke less interpersonal conflict (Jensen-Campbell & Graziano, 2001). One reason for this might be that highly agreeable individuals tend to use "compromise" in dealing with conflict when it arises, whereas those low in agreeableness are less willing to compromise and are more likely to use verbal insults and physical force to deal with conflict. The importance of low agreeableness in evoking conflict appears to extend to a wide variety of interpersonal relationships, including those in the workplace (Bono, Boles, Judge, & Lauver, 2002).

These links between personality and conflict show up at least as early as early adolescence—young teenagers low in agreeableness not only evoke more conflict, but also are more likely to become victimized by their peers in high school (Jensen-Campbell, Adams, Pery, Workman, Furdella, & Egan, 2002). Agreeable individuals also tend to use effective conflict resolution tactics, a path leading to harmonious social interactions (Jensen-Campbell, Gleason, Adams, & Malcolm, 2003). Yet another study revealed that those high in negative emotionality (high neuroticism) were also likely to experience greater conflict in all their relationships, whereas those high in positive emotionality (a close cousin of agreeableness) experienced less conflict in all of their relationships (Robins, Caspi, & Moffitt, 2002). Indeed, studies from the United States, Australia, the Netherlands, and Germany reveal that *agreeableness* and *emotional stability* are the traits most consistently conducive to evoking satisfaction in relationships (Barelds, 2005; Donnellan, Larsen-Rife, & Conger, 2005; Heaven et al., 2003; Neyer & Voigt, 2004; White, Hendrick, & Hendrick, 2004).

In summary, personality plays a key role in the process of evocation—in this case, the evocation of anger and upset. By far, the strongest predictors of this upset are low agreeableness and emotional instability. It would be premature to conclude from this study that this provides a recipe for choosing whom not to marry (in other words, avoid emotionally unstable and disagreeable people). But it does suggest that, if you marry someone with these personality attributes, your mate will be likely to behave in anger-evoking ways.

Application

Psychologist John Gottman has been conducting research on married persons for three decades. His main question has been "What distinguishes the happily married couple from the dissatisfied, unhappy couple?" After studying thousands of marital pairs, some of whom have been happily married for years, others of whom were applying for divorce, he has found many ways that the happy and unhappy couples differ. He distilled his research findings into an applied book on how to make marriage work (Gottman & Silver, 1999).

Application (*Continued*)

His seven principles of positive relationships are summarized below. Several of these principles concern behaviors related to evoking responses in the partner.

1. **Develop an empathic understanding of your partner (see Chapter 11 for a discussion of empathy). Get to know their "world," their preferences, and the important events in their life. As an example, once a day try to find out one important or significant event for your partner: what they are looking forward to or what important event happened to them. Trivial as it sounds, try asking, "How was your day?" each day.**
2. **Remain fond of each other and try to nurture your affection for your partner. Remember why you like this person, and tell them about it. As an example, keep a photo album together and go over it once in a while, reminding yourself of the fun times you had together and how much you enjoy being with this special person.**
3. **In times of stress, turn toward, rather than away, from each other. Also during the good times, do things together. In other words, don't take your partner for granted, and never ignore them, even in day-to-day life. Pay attention, stay connected, touch each other, and talk frequently.**
4. **Share power, even if you think you are the expert. Let your partner influence you. Ask them for help once in a while. You might be surprised to learn that your partner can be helpful in many ways. Ask for their opinion. Let them know that their views matter to you.**
5. **You will undoubtedly have arguments. However, try to argue only about the solvable problems. When arguing:**
   - **Start gently**
   - **Proceed with respect**
   - **If feelings get hurt, stop and try to repair those hurt feelings**
   - **Avoid being carried away by your emotions**
   - **Be willing to compromise**
6. **Realize that some problems may never be solved. For example, perhaps one of you is religious and the other is not, and both intend to stay this way. Avoid gridlock on such unsolvable problems and don't let them become permanent topics of argument. Accept the other's differences and agree to disagree on certain issues.**
7. **Become a "we" instead of "I" and "I." Make the relationship real and important and something to be considered besides your own wants and desires. Think about what is best for "us" rather than only what is best for "me."**

Source: Adapted from Gottman & Silver, 1999.

Personality also can evoke responses from others in a wide variety of social contexts outside of mating. Extraverted people tend to crack more jokes, evoking greater laughter from others than do introverts (Eysenck & Eysenck, 1985). Agreeable people tend to evoke more social support from their parents (Gallo & Smith, 1999). And aggressive people tend to evoke more hostility from strangers (Dodge & Coie, 1987). One's personality, in short, can create the social environment to which one is exposed through the process of evocation.

Evocation through Expectancy Confirmation

Expectancy confirmation is a phenomenon whereby people's beliefs about the personality characteristics of others cause them to evoke in others actions that are consistent with the initial beliefs. The phenomenon of expectancy confirmation has also been called self-fulfilling prophesy and behavioral confirmation. Can mere beliefs have such a powerful role in evoking behavior from others?

In a fascinating study of expectancy confirmation, Snyder and Swann (1978) led individuals to believe that they would be dealing with a hostile and aggressive individual and then introduced the two individuals. What they found was that people's beliefs led them to act in an aggressive manner toward the unspecting target. Then the behavior of the unspecting target was examined. The intriguing finding was that the unspecting target actually acted in a more hostile manner, behavior that was evoked by the person who was led to expect hostility. In this example, beliefs about the personality of the other actually created the behavior that confirmed those initial beliefs (Snyder & Cantor, 1998).

Expectancies about personality may have widespread evocation effects in everyday life. After all, we often hear information about a person's reputation prior to, or following, actual encounters with them. We hear that a person is smart, socially skilled, egocentric, or manipulative. These beliefs about the personality characteristics of others may have far-reaching effects on evoking behavior that confirm our initial beliefs. It is sometimes said that, in order to change your personality, you must move to a place where people don't already know you. Through the process of expectancy confirmation, people who already know you may unwittingly evoke in you behavior that confirms their beliefs, thereby constraining your ability to change.

Manipulation: Social Influence Tactics

Once social environments are selected, evocation does not exhaust the set of processes that link personality with the social world. **Manipulation,** or social influence, includes all the ways in which people intentionally try to change the behavior of others. No malicious intent need be implied by the term *manipulation,* although such intent is not excluded either. A parent might influence a child not to cross between parked cars, but we would not call this behavior malicious. Indeed, part of social living is that we influence others all the time. Thus, the term *manipulation* is used here descriptively, with no negative connotation.

From an evolutionary perspective (see Chapter 8), natural selection favors people who successfully manipulate objects in their environment. Some manipulable objects are inanimate, such as the raw materials used to build shelters, tools, clothing, and weapons. Other manipulable objects are alive, including predators and prey of different species as well as mates, parents, children, rivals, and allies of the same species. The manipulation of other people can be summarized as the various means by which we influence the psychology and behavior of other people.

The process of manipulation can be examined from two perspectives within personality psychology. First, we can ask, "Are some individuals consistently more manipulative than others?" Second, we can ask, "Given that all people attempt to influence others, do stable personality characteristics predict the sorts of tactics that are used?" Do extraverted people, for example, more often use the charm tactic, whereas introverts use the silent treatment tactic?

A Taxonomy of 11 Tactics of Manipulation

A **taxonomy** is simply a classification scheme—the identification and naming of groups within a particular subject field. Taxonomies of plants and animals, for example, have been developed to identify and name all the major plant and animal groups. The periodic table is a taxonomy of elements in the known universe. The Big Five personality traits that we examined in Chapter 3 is also an attempt to develop a taxonomy of the major dimensions of personality. In this section, we will look at the development of a taxonomy of tactics of manipulation—an attempt to identify and name the major ways in which people attempt to influence others in their social world.

A taxonomy of tactics of manipulation was developed through a two-step procedure: (1) nominations of acts of influence and (2) factor analysis of self-reports and observer-reports of the previously nominated acts (Buss, 1992; Buss et al., 1987). The act nomination procedure (see Chapter 2) was as follows: "We are interested in the things that people do to influence others in order to get what they want. Please think of your [romantic partner, close friend, mother, father, etc.]. How do you get this person to do something? What do you do? Please write down specific behaviors or acts that you perform in order to get this person to do things. List as many different sorts of acts as you can."

After this list was generated, the researchers converted it into a questionnaire that could be administered via self-report or observer report. You can see for yourself how this was done by taking the test in the Exercise below to find out what tactics of social influence you use.

INSTRUCTIONS: When you want your partner to do something for you, what are you likely to do? Look at each of the following items and *rate how likely you are to do each when you are trying to get your partner to do something.* None of them will apply to all situations in which you want your partner to do something, so rate how likely you are, in general, to do what is described. If you are extremely likely to do it, write a "7" in the blank next to the item. If you are not at all likely to do it, write a "1" in the blank next to the item. If you are somewhat likely to do it, write a "4" in the blank. Give intermediate ratings for intermediate likelihood of performing the behaviors.

___ 1. I compliment her/him so that she/he will do it.
___ 2. I act charming so she/he will do it.
___ 3. I try to be loving and romantic when I ask her/him.
___ 4. I give her/him a small gift or card before I ask.
___ 5. I don't respond to her/him until she/he does it.
___ 6. I ignore her/him until she/he does it.
___ 7. I am silent until she/he does it.
___ 8. I refuse to do something she/he likes until she/he does it.
___ 9. I demand that she/he do it.
___ 10. I yell at her/him until she/he does it.
___ 11. I criticize her/him for not doing it.

Exercise (*Continued*)

___ 12. I threaten her/him with something if she/he does not do it.
___ 13. I give her/him reasons that she/he should do it.
___ 14. I point out all the good things that will come from doing it.
___ 15. I explain why I want her/him to do it.
___ 16. I show her/him that I would be willing to do it for her/him.
___ 17. I pout until she/he does it.
___ 18. I sulk until she/he does it.
___ 19. I whine until she/he does it.
___ 20. I cry until she/he does it.
___ 21. I allow myself to be debased so that she/he will do it.
___ 22. I lower myself so that she/he will do it.
___ 23. I act humble so that she/he will do it.
___ 24. I act submissive so that she/he will do it.

You can find out your scores by simply adding up your scores in clusters of four: items 1–4 = charm tactic; items 5–8 = silent treatment tactic; items 9–12 = coercion tactic; items 13–16 = reason tactic; items 17–20 = regression tactic; items 21–24 = self-abasement tactic. The tactics you tend to use the most are those with the highest sums. The tactics you use the least are those with the lowest sums. This is an abbreviated version of the instrument used in the studies by Buss, 1992.

A large number of participants completed versions of an expanded instrument, consisting of 83 acts of influence or tactics. Factor analysis was then used to identify clusters of acts of influence, or tactics. In all, 11 tactics were discovered through this procedure, as shown in Table 15.5.

Table 15.5 Taxonomy of 11 Tactics of Manipulation

Tactic	Sample Act
Charm	I try to be loving when I ask her to do it.
Coercion	I yell at him until he does it.
Silent treatment	I don't respond to her until she does it.
Reason	I explain why I want him to do it.
Regression	I whine until she does it.
Self-abasement	I act submissive so that he will do it.
Responsibility invocation	I get her to make a commitment to doing it.
Hardball	I hit him so that he will do it.
Pleasure induction	I show her how much fun it will be to do it.
Social comparison	I tell him that everyone else is doing it.
Monetary reward	I offer her money so that she will do it.

Note: These tactics then formed the basis for subsequent analyses, such as whether there are sex differences in the tactics of manipulation and whether standard personality traits are associated with the tactics of manipulation that people use.

A Closer Look The Machiavellian Personality

The term *Machiavellian* originates from an Italian diplomat, Niccolo Machiavelli, who wrote a classic treatise, *The Prince,* in 1513 (Machiavelli,1966/1513). Machiavelli observed, in his diplomatic role, that leaders come and go, rising and falling as they gain and lose power. *The Prince* is a book of advice on acquiring and maintaining power, which Machiavelli wrote to ingratiate himself with a new ruler after the one that he had served had been overthrown. The advice is based on tactics for manipulating others and is entirely lacking in traditional values, such as trust, honor, and decency. One passage in the book, for example, notes that "men are so simple and so much inclined to obey immediate needs that a deceiver will never lack for victims for his deceptions" (Machiavelli, 1966/1513, p. 63). The adjective **Machiavellian** eventually came to be associated with a manipulative strategy of social interaction and with a personality style that uses other people as tools for personal gain.

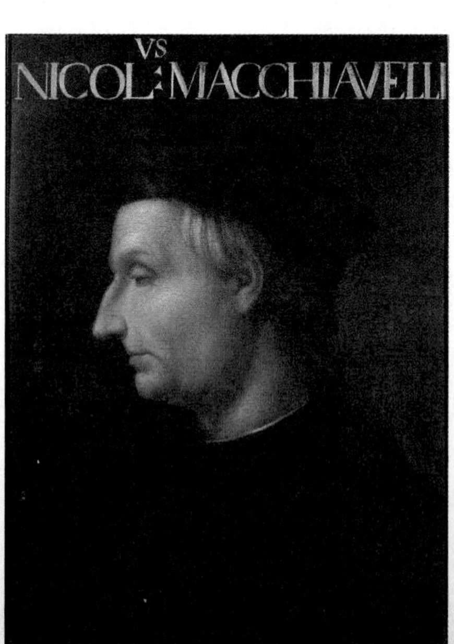

Niccolo Machiavelli, after whom the trait of Machiavellianism was named, wrote a book on strategies for manipulating others.

Intrigued by the possibility that an important personality type might be contained within this classic work, two psychologists—Richard Christie and Florence Geis—developed a self-report scale to measure individual differences in Machiavellianism (Christie & Geis, 1970). The following are some sample items from the test, with the Machiavellian direction noted in parentheses:

- *The best way to handle people is to tell them what they want to hear* (true).
- *Anyone who completely trusts anyone else is asking for trouble* (true).
- *Honesty is the best policy in all cases* (false).
- *Never tell anyone the real reason you did something unless it is useful to do so* (true).
- *Most people are basically good and kind* (false).
- *Most people who get ahead in the world lead clean, moral lives* (false).
- *The biggest difference between most criminals and other people is that criminals are stupid enough to get caught* (true).
- *It is wise to flatter important people* (true).

As you can see from these items the high scorer on the Machiavellianism scale (called a "high Mach") is manipulative, has a cynical worldview, treats other people as tools to be used for personal ends, does not trust other people, and lacks empathy. The low scorer on the Machiavellianism scale (called a "low Mach") is trusting, empathic, believes that things are clearly either right or wrong, and views human nature as basically good.

According to a review of the literature on Machiavellianism, high and low scorers represent two alternative strategies of social conduct (Wilson, Near, & Miller, 1996). The high Mach represents an exploitative social strategy—one that betrays friendship and uses other people opportunistically. Theoretically, this strategy works best in social situations when there is room for innovation, rather than those that are highly constrained by rules. For example, political consulting or the world of an independent entrepreneur might be relatively unconstrained, allowing much latitude for the high Mach to operate. The more structured world of universities, on the other hand, might allow fewer opportunities for the high Machs to ply their skills.

The low Mach, in contrast, represents a strategy of cooperation, sometimes called tit-for-tat. This strategy is based on reciprocity—you help me, and I'll help you in return, and we will both be better off as a result. This is a long-term social strategy, in contrast to the short-term strategy of the high Mach.

According to this view, the success of the high Mach should depend greatly on the context, rather than being uniform across contexts. One study examined this prediction in a real-world setting by studying the sales performance of stockbrokers from two different organizational contexts (Shultz, 1993). One organizational context, the NYNEX, is a highly structured stock brokerage and rule-bound, with little room for the salespeople to innovate or improvise. Employees are required to follow a two-volume manual of rules. The second organizational context, represented by stock brokerages such as Merrill Lynch and Shearson, Lehman, and Hutton, is more loosely structured and allows more opportunities for wheeling and dealing.

The sales success of stockbrokers who were high and low Machs was evaluated by the size of the commissions earned by the individuals in the two organizational contexts. In the loosely structured organizations, such as Merrill Lynch, the high Machs had more clients and earned fully twice as many commissions as the low Machs. On the basis of this impressive finding, one might be tempted to conclude that Machiavellianism is a successful strategy of social influence in general. However, in the more tightly structured organizations, the low Machs earned twice as much money on commissions as the high Machs. This study illustrates a key point about the Machiavellian social strategy of influence—its success is highly context-dependent. Thus, Machiavellianism is not a social strategy that works all the time. Social situations with lots of rules do not allow high Machs to con others, tell lies, and betray those who trust them with impunity. In these situations, the high Machs get caught, sustain damage to their reputations, and are often fired. In more fluid occupational contexts, high Machs succeed because they can wheel and deal, move quickly from one situation to another, and exploit the opportunities available in these less rule-bound settings.

A number of studies suggest that Machiavellianism is a social strategy in which practitioners are quick to betray others (Wilson et al., 1996). Is there direct evidence that high Machs betray more often than other people do? In one laboratory study, participants were given an opportunity to steal money in a worker-supervisor situation (Harrell & Hartnagel, 1976). The participants played the role of workers. They were supervised by a person who acted trustingly and who stated that he or she did not need to monitor the workers closely. In this study, the high Machs were far more likely to steal from the trusting supervisor than were the low Machs. A full 81 percent of the high Machs stole money, as contrasted with only 24 percent of the low Machs. Furthermore, the high Machs who did steal took a larger amount of money than those few low Machs who stole, they tended to conceal their theft, and they lied more often to the supervisor when questioned about the theft.

Not only do high Machs lie and betray others' trust more than low Machs, but there is also evidence that they make more believable liars (Exline et al., 1970; Geis & Moon, 1981). In one study, high and low Machs were instructed to cheat on a task and then to lie to the experimenter about having cheated (Exline et al., 1970). The experimenter then became increasingly suspicious and questioned the participants about whether they had cheated. The high Machs were able to maintain greater eye contact than the low Machs. Fewer of the high Machs than the low Machs confessed. Finally, when rated by judges who had no prior knowledge of the participants' scores on the Machiavellianism scale, the high Machs were judged to be better liars than the low Machs.

The manipulative tactics used by the high Machs extend to the romantic and sexual domains. High Machs, compared to their low Mach peers, are more likely to feign love in order to get sex (e.g., "I sometimes say 'I love you' when I don't really mean it to get someone to have sex with me"), get a partner drunk in order to induce the partner to have sex, and even express a willingness to use force to achieve sex with an unwilling partner (McHoskey, 2001). And as in other types of relationships, high Machs are more likely to cheat on their romantic partner and to be sexually unfaithful with other people. Interestingly, all of these links between Machiavellianism and specific tactics of manipulation are stronger for the male than for the female sample.

The Machiavellian strategy has many advantages, but it also has costs. By betraying, cheating, and lying, the high Mach runs the risk of retaliation and revenge by those who were exploited. Furthermore, the high Mach is more likely than the low Mach to incur damage to his or her reputation. Once people acquire reputations as exploitative, other people are more likely to avoid them, and refuse to interact with them. In short, the high Mach strategy seems most effective in contexts that are loosely structured and perhaps short-term, so that the manipulator can quickly escape to another social context before incurring the costs associated with reputational damage.

This in-depth discussion of the Machiavellian strategy also illustrates the three key processes by which personality affects social interaction, bringing us back full circle to the three central processes of personality and social interaction. First, the high Mach tends to *select* situations that are loosely structured, untethered by rules that would restrict the deployment of an exploitative strategy. Second, the high Mach tends to *evoke* specific reactions from others, such as anger and retaliation for having been exploited. Third, the high Mach tends to *manipulate* other people in predictable ways, using tactics that are exploitative, self-serving, and deceptive.

Sex Differences in Tactics of Manipulation

Do men and women differ in their usage of tactics of manipulations? Buss (1992) found that, by and large, the answer is no. Women and men equally performed almost all of the tactics of social influence. There was only one small exception: the regression tactic. In samples of dating couples and married couples, the women more than the men reported more frequent use of the regression tactic, including crying, whining, pouting, and sulking to get their way. The difference, however, was quite small, supporting the overall conclusion that men and women, in general, are similar in their performance of tactics of manipulation.

Personality Predictors of Tactics of Manipulation

The next interesting question is whether people with certain personality traits are more likely to use certain tactics of manipulation. A sample of more than 200 participants (Buss, 1992) rated each act of influence on the degree to which they used it in each of four relationships—spouse, friend, mother, and father. Then, correlations were computed between the personality traits of the participants and their use of each tactic of manipulation.

Those scoring relatively high in surgency (dominance, extraversion) tended to use coercion, such as demanding, threatening, cursing, and criticizing in order to get their way. The highly surgent people also tended to use responsibility invocation, getting others to make commitments to a course of action and saying that it was their duty to do it.

Those scoring low in surgency (relatively submissive individuals) used the self-abasement tactic as a means of influencing others. They lowered themselves, for example, or tried to look sickly to get others to do what they wanted. Interestingly, these submissive individuals also tended to use the hardball tactic more often than their surgent counterparts. That is, they used deception, lying, degradation, and even violence to get others to do what they wanted.

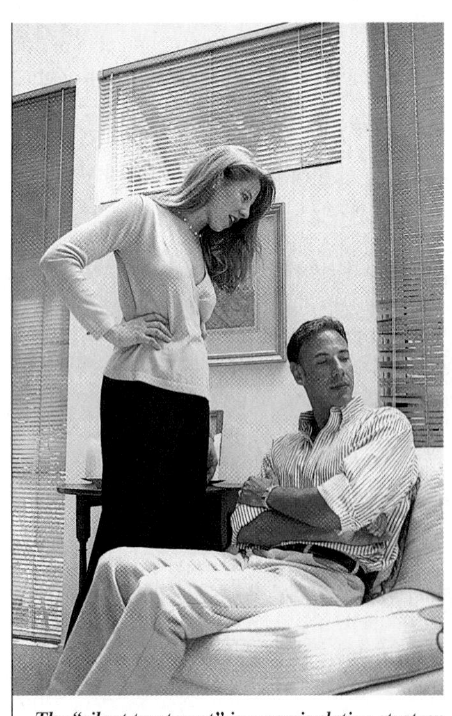

The "silent treatment" is a manipulation strategy often employed by persons high on the trait of disagreeableness.

The two primary tactics of influence used by highly agreeable people are pleasure induction and reason. That is, these agreeable individuals tell and show others how enjoyable the activity will be, explain the rationale for wanting others to engage in particular behaviors, and point out all the good things that will come from doing them.

Those who are disagreeable, in contrast, frequently use coercion and the silent treatment. Not only do they threaten, criticize, yell, and scream in order to get their way, they also give the stony silent look and refuse to speak to the other until he or she complies. Low-agreeable individuals are also likely to seek revenge on people whom they have perceived to have wronged them in some way, supporting the general use of cost-inflicting rather than benefit-bestowing tactics of manipulation (McCullough, Bellah, Kilpatrick, & Johnson, 2001). Interestingly, low-agreeable individuals tend to be more selfish in their use of collective resources, whereas high-agreeable individuals exercise more self-restraint when the group's resources are scarce or threatened (Koole, Jager, van den Berg, Vlek, & Hofstee, 2001).

The personality disposition of conscientiousness is associated with only one tactic of social influence—reason. Conscientious individuals explain why they want the other person to do something,

A Closer Look

Narcissism and Social Interaction

Narcissism is a personality dimension that involves, at the upper end, high levels of self-absorption and conceitedness, placing one's own wants and needs above those of others, displaying unusual grandiosity, showing a profound sense of entitlement, and lacking empathy for other people's feelings, needs, and desires (see Chapters 10 and 14; Raskin & Terry, 1988). Those high on narcissism tend to be *exhibitionistic* (e.g., flaunting money to impress others), *grandiose* (e.g., talking about how great they are), *self-centered* (e.g., taking the best piece of food for themselves), and *interpersonally exploitative* (e.g., using others for selfish ends) (Buss & Chiodo, 1991). Recently, personality psychologists have documented the impact of narcissism on social interaction, providing a fascinating illustration of the influence of personality on social selection, evocation, and manipulation.

In terms of *selection,* narcissists tend to choose people who admire them, who will reflect the extraordinarily positive view they hold about themselves. They don't want people around who will view them as anything other than as extraordinary, beautiful, or brilliant (Buss & Chiodo, 1991). In fact, because narcissists view themselves as "exceptional performers," they tend to select social situations in which they perceive that their "opportunity for glory" will be enhanced, and conversely avoid situations in which their self-perceived magnificence will not be noticed by others (Wallace & Baumeister, 2002). While they tend to appoint themselves to positions of power (Buss & Chiodo, 1991), they strenuously avoid social situations that don't afford the chance to show off their brilliance (Wallace & Baumeister, 2002). Life, however, sometimes has a way of crashing in, and narcissists are sometimes rejected. When they are rejected, narcissists tend to lash out with great anger at those they perceive to have wronged them. Interestingly, narcissists are highly selective in their social perceptions—they view themselves as victims of interpersonal transgressions far more frequently than those low on narcissism (McCullough, Emmons, Kilpatrick, & Mooney, 2003).

In the mating domain, the romantic partner selections of narcissists may be more precarious than those of others, since they score low on commitment to their partner, perhaps because they view themselves as "better" or more desirable than their partner (Campbell & Foster, 2002; Campbell, Rudich, & Sedikedes, 2002). Narcissists also are highly resistant to entertaining doubts about the commitment of their romantic partners (Foster & Campbell, 2005). When asked in an experiment to list possible reasons why their current romantic partner might be less committed than they are to the relationship, narcissists had great difficulty even completing the task! After the task, narcissists (compared with those low on narcissism) indicated substantially lower levels of their own commitment to their romantic partner and a greater willingness to accept a dating invitation from someone else. Narcissistic entitlement has also been linked to *an inability to forgive others,* a quality that could also impair the functioning of romantic relationships (Exline, Baumeister, Bushman, Campbell, & Finkel, 2004).

Narcissists also *evoke* predictable responses from others in their social environment. Because they are exhibitionistic and thrust themselves into the center of attention, narcissists sometimes split people in their evocations—some view them as brilliant, entertaining, and "not boring," whereas others view them as selfish and boorish (Campbell, Rudich, & Sedikedes, 2002). They sometimes evoke anger in others because of their self-aggrandizing actions, such as pulling rank on others to make a point.

Narcissists also use a predictable set of tactics of *manipulation.* They are highly exploitative of others and would be described as "users." They use friends ruthlessly for their wealth or connections. When in positions of power, they use their positions to exploit subordinates and show no hesitation in pulling rank to humiliate someone else in front of others. They react to failure with ferocious attempts to derogate other people, possibly in an attempt to transfer the blame for their failure onto others (South, Oltmanns, & Turkheimer, 2003). They also lash out in anger and aggression against others when confronted with their own failure, as described in Chapter 14. In sum, the personality dimension of narcissism shows many links to the social selections they make, the reactions they evoke from others, and the tactics of manipulation they use to enhance their self-centered goals.

provide logical explanations for wanting it done, and explain the underlying rationale for doing it. A recent study found that low-conscientious individuals are more likely to use criminal strategies in gaining resources, as indicated by arrest records and recidivism (being rearrested after being let out of prison) (Clower & Bothwell, 2001).

Emotionally unstable individuals use a wide variety of tactics to manipulate others—hardball and coercion, but also reason and monetary reward. The tactic most commonly used by emotionally unstable people, however, is regression. These people pout, sulk, whine, and cry to get their way. In a sense, this kind of behavior comes close to the core definition of emotional instability—the display of volatile emotions, some positive and some negative. But the fascinating part of these findings is that the emotional volatility is strategically motivated—it is used with the purpose of influencing others to get what they want.

What tactics do people high on intellect–openness use? Not surprisingly, these smart and perceptive people tend to use reason above all other tactics. They also use pleasure induction and responsibility invocation, however—findings that are not as intuitively obvious. Can you guess which tactic those *low* on intellect–openness use? They tend to use social comparison—saying that everyone else is doing it, comparing the partner with someone else who would do it, and telling others that they will look stupid if they do not do it.

In summary, these results provide strong evidence that personality dispositions are not static entities residing passively in the skulls of people. They have profound implications for social interaction—in this case, for the tactics people use to manipulate others in their social environment. In some cases, the links between personality dispositions and the tactics used are rather obvious and almost part of the definition—the use of regression by emotionally unstable people, for example, or the use of reason by agreeable people. In other cases, the results are not as intuitively obvious—the finding that submissive people tend to use the hardball tactic, for example, or the finding that those low on intellect–openness tend to use social comparison.

Panning Back: An Overview of Personality and Social Interaction

The most important message from this chapter is that personality does not reside passively within an individual, but rather reaches out and profoundly affects each person's social environment. The three processes by which personality can influence an individual's social environment—selection, evocation, and manipulation—are highlighted in Table 15.6.

These fundamental mechanisms operate in the physical as well as the social environment. Let's consider selection first. In the physical domain, an introvert is more likely to choose to live in a rural habitat, whereas an extravert is more likely to choose city living with all the opportunities for social interaction city life provides. In the social domain, an extravert is more likely to select a mate who is also extraverted, whereas an introvert is more likely to choose an introverted mate so that they can read books quietly side by side.

For the process of evocation, a loud, heavy person who treads heavily is more likely to evoke an avalanche while climbing a snowy mountain. In the social domain, narcissistic people evoke admiration from their followers and contempt from those who dislike their unbridled self-centeredness. For the process of manipulation,

Table 15.6 Causal Mechanisms That Create Links between Personality and Environment: Examples from the Physical and Social Domains

Mechanism	Physical Environment	Social Environment
Selection	Introvert selects rural habitat	Extravert chooses extraverted mate
	Avoidance of cold climates	Emotionally stable person chooses stable roommate
Evocation	Person who treads heavily elicits an avalanche	Disagreeable people evoke relationship conflict
	Clumsy person creates, elicits more noise and clatter	Narcissistic people evoke admiration from followers
Manipulation	Conscientious person creates clean, neat, uncluttered room	Disagreeable person uses "the silent treatment"
	Person high on openness creates stylish, colorful room with varied collection of books and CDs	Narcissists transfer blame to others

fascinating recent research has shown that personality affects how people mold and modify the rooms in which they live (Gosling, Ko, Mannarelli, & Morris, 2002). Conscientious individuals, for example, keep their rooms tidy, neat, and free of clutter. Those low on conscientiousness have more dirt, clutter, and mess in their rooms. Those high in openness decorate their rooms with stylish and unconventional objects and have many books and CDs that are highly varied in genre. Those low on openness have fewer and more conventional decorations, a narrower range of books, and a more delimited collection of CDs. In the social domain, disagreeable individuals are more likely than stable individuals to use "the silent treatment" as a tactic of manipulation. Those high in intellect–openness tend to use reason and rationality to get their way. And narcissists try to transfer blame for their failures onto others.

Personality, in short, affects the mates and friends a person chooses as well as the environments a person decides to enter or avoid (selection); the reactions elicited from others and from the physical environment (evocation); and the ways in which one's physical and social environments are altered once inhabited (manipulation). These three processes are shown in Figure 15.1.

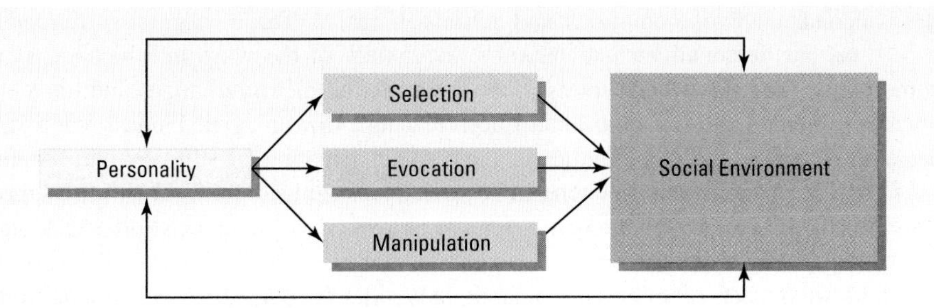

Figure 15.1

Personality and social interaction.

Further research is needed to determine whether the causal arrows run in both directions. Does the choice of a mate who is similar in personality, for example, create a social environment that reinforces that personality and makes it more stable over time? Does the conflict evoked by disagreeable people create a social environment in which they receive a lot of negative feedback, hence maintaining their disagreeable personality? Does the wide variety of manipulative tactics used by emotionally unstable individuals—from hardball to threats to sulking, whining, and pouting—create a social environment that is indeed rocked with greater turmoil, thus maintaining the personality disposition of neuroticism? Research within the next decade will undoubtedly answer these questions.

SUMMARY AND EVALUATION

Personality does not exist solely inside the heads of individuals. The personality characteristics we carry with us affect the outside world. Perhaps most important, personality affects the ways in which we interact with other people occupying our social world. Indeed, the reciprocal influences of personality and social interactions have brought the fields of personality psychology and social psychology closer together in recent years (Swann & Seyle, 2005).

This chapter described three key processes by which personality affects social interaction. First, we select people and environments, choosing the social situations to which we will expose ourselves. Personality plays a key role in the selection process. In selecting a mate, for example, people worldwide look for mates who are dependable, are emotionally stable, and have a pleasing disposition. Furthermore, we tend to select mates who are similar in personality to ourselves, in a process known as assortative mating. Complementary needs theory—the idea that opposites attract when it comes to human mating—has received no empirical support. Those who fail to get what they want—for example, ending up with mates who are emotionally unstable or disagreeable—tend to be unhappy with their marriages and tend to divorce more often than those who succeed in choosing what they want.

The process of selection extends far beyond the choice of romantic partners. The personality trait of shyness, for example, is linked with avoiding gynecological exams, entering risky sexual situations by failing to bring up the topic of contraception, and avoiding risky situations that involve gambling money. Similarly, high sensation-seeking heterosexual males tend to choose risky sexual situations, such as having unprotected sex and sex with a larger number of partners, compared with their less sensation-seeking peers.

Second, we evoke emotions and actions in others. These evocations are based, in part, on our personality characteristics. In a study of the ways in which men and women anger and upset their spouses, the strongest predictors of anger and upset are low agreeableness and low emotional stability. Those low on agreeableness, for example, tend to create a lot of conflict in their social situations, including with friends and romantic partners, and they tend to be socially victimized during their high school years. Furthermore, in a phenomenon known as expectency confirmation, our beliefs about the personality characteristics of others sometimes evoke in others precisely the behaviors we expect. A belief that someone is hostile, for example, tends to elicit hostile behavior from that person.

Manipulation is the third process and is defined as the ways in which people intentionally change and exploit others. Humans use a variety of tactics for influencing others, some of which are charm, silent treatment, coercion, reason, regression, and self-abasement. Men and women use these tactics approximately equally, with the small exception of regression, which is used slightly more often by women. However, personality characteristics play a key role in which tactics we use to influence others. Emotionally unstable people, for example, tend to use regression and the silent treatment. They also tend to use reason and monetary reward, though, suggesting some nonintuitive links between personality and tactics of manipulation. People high on intellect–openness tend to use reason, but they also use the social comparison tactic. Personality plays a key role in the tactics we use.

One personality trait linked with manipulation tactics is called Machiavellianism. The high Mach tends to tell people what they want to hear, to use flattery to get what he or she wants, and to rely heavily on lying and deception. In the mating domain, for example, high Machs are more likely to feign love in order to get sex, use drugs and alcohol to render a potential sex partner more vulnerable, and even express a willingness to use force to get sex. High Machs also betray the trust of others, sometimes feigning cooperation before defecting. They are also more likely than low Machs to steal and then to lie about stealing when they are caught. The success of the high Mach seems to depend heavily on context. In loosely structured social situations and work organizations, high Machs can wheel and deal, using their manipulative, conning strategies to great effect. In more tightly structured, rule-bound situations, however, low Machs outperform high Machs.

All three processes have been documented with the personality disposition of narcissism. Narcissists tend to select others who admire them and avoid others who are skeptical of their claims of greatness. They selectively enter social situations in which there are opportunities for glory and avoid situations in which their brilliance will not be seen by others. Narcissists evoke admiration and respect from those who fawn over them, while evoking anger and disgust from those who are victims of their scorn and conceit. In terms of manipulation, narcissists are highly interpersonally exploitative, using friends for wealth or connections and transferring blame to others when things go wrong. Examining all these processes with respect to narcissists creates a fascinating portrait of the ways in which personality is intimately connected with the social interactions we create and the social environments we inhabit.

In summary, personality is predictably and systematically linked with social interaction through the ways in which we select our partners and social worlds, the ways in which we evoke responses from people we have initially chosen, and the ways in which we influence those people to attain our desired ends.

KEY TERMS

16

Sex, Gender, and Personality

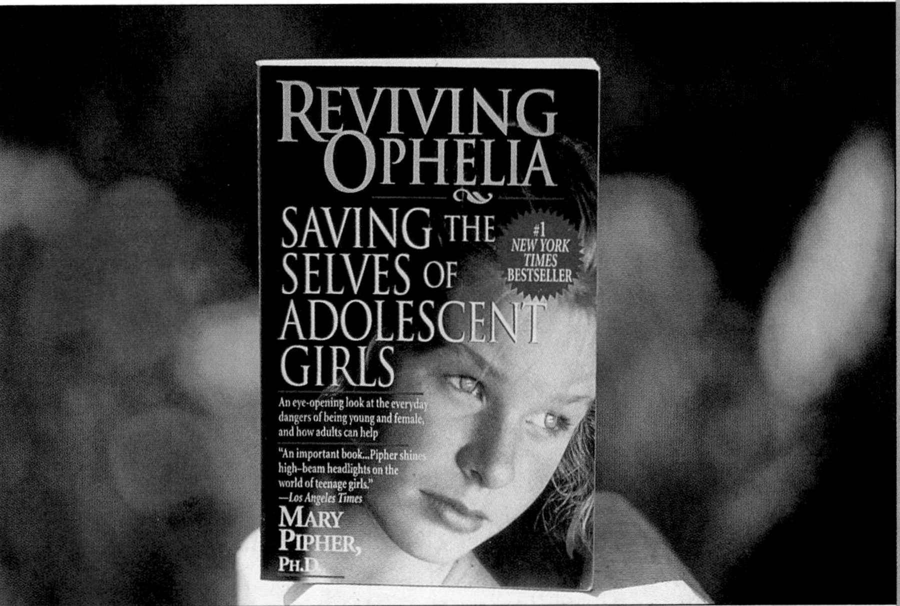

The popular book **Reviving Ophelia** *suggested that the differences in personality between adult men and women are the result of specific events that occur in adolescence.*

"Despite the advances of feminism, escalating levels of sexism and violence—from undervalued intelligence to sexual harassment in elementary school—cause girls to stifle their creative spirit and natural impulses, which ultimately destroys their self-esteem" (Pipher, 1994, bookjacket). This is a quotation from the book *Reviving Ophelia,* which remained on the best-seller list for an astonishing 135 weeks (Kling et al., 1999). The sentiment expresses widespread belief that women suffer lower self-esteem than men do and that this difference in adult personality is caused by destructive events during development.

Although we cannot know with certainty why *Reviving Ophelia* remained popular for so long, several possibilities warrant consideration. First, people are intrinsically fascinated with psychological **sex differences:** average differences between women and men in personality or behavior. The popular press and other mass media frequently pick up scientific findings of sex differences. Second, many people are concerned with the political implications of findings of sex differences. Will such findings be used to foster gender stereotypes? Will such findings be used to oppress women? And, third, people are concerned with the practical implications of sex differences for their everyday lives. Will knowledge of sex differences help us, for example, understand and communicate better with others?

This chapter focuses centrally on the scientific issues, but it also discusses the broader debate about the scientific findings. Are women and men basically different or basically the same when it comes to personality? Have the differences been exaggerated because of stereotypes people have about what women are like and what men are like? What theories provide compelling explanations for sex-linked features of personality? In this chapter, we will answer these questions by exploring what researchers have determined about sex differences. As used in this book, the term *sex differences* simply refers to an average difference between women and men on certain characteristics, such as height, body fat distribution, or personality characteristics, with no prejudgment about the cause of the difference.

We will begin by briefly sketching the history of the study of sex differences in personality. This background information will show you how complex this topic is: indeed, we will see that the very definition of **gender,** or social interpretations of what it means to be a man or a woman, can change over time. Next, we will look at some of the techniques psychologists use to tease out sex differences from research data. This will allow you to understand what sex differences really mean and what they imply in the real world.

After we have briefly explored this background of the study of sex and gender, we will see what the topic means to personality psychology by discussing sex differences in traits such as assertiveness, criminality, and sexuality. We will use these differences to explore the fascinating topic of **gender stereotypes:** beliefs about how men and women differ or are supposed to differ, in contrast to what the actual differences are. Finally, we will explore theories that attempt to explain the reasons for these sex differences. When you reach the end of the chapter, you should have a deeper understanding of what it means to be a woman or a man—how they are the same, as well as how they are different.

The Science and Politics of Studying Sex and Gender

Few topics generate as much controversy as the study of sex differences. This is especially true when it comes to examining the possibility that men and women differ. As noted in a recent discussion on gender, "public debates about the nature of women and men are frequently in the spotlight, whether in media reports on the latest sex difference findings or in highly publicized legal cases involving single-sex educational institutions or sexual harassment" (Deaux & LaFrance, 1998). Some worry that findings of sex differences might be used to support certain political agendas, such as excluding women from leadership roles. Some worry that findings of sex differences might be used to support the status quo, such as keeping men in power and women out of power. Some argue that findings of sex differences merely reflect gender stereotypes, rather than real differences. Some psychologists argue that any discovery of sex differences merely reflects the biases of the scientists, rather than any objective description of reality. Indeed, some psychologists such as Roy Baumeister have advocated stopping research on sex differences because findings of sex differences might conflict with ideals of egalitarianism (Baumeister, 1988), although he has since changed his views on this (personal communication, May 17, 2006).

Others argue, however, that both scientific psychology and social change will be impossible without coming to terms with the real sex differences that exist. Feminist psychologist Alice Eagly, for example, argues that sex differences exist, they are consistent across studies, and they should not be ignored merely because they are perceived to conflict with certain political agendas (Eagly, 1995). Indeed, Eagly argues that feminists who try to minimize these differences, or pretend that they do not exist, hamper the feminist agenda by presenting a dogma that is out of touch with reality. Still others, such as Janet Hyde, argue that sex differences have been exaggerated and that there is so much overlap between the sexes on most personality traits that the differences are minimal (Hyde, 2005; Hyde & Plant, 1995). We will examine these contrasting positions in more detail.

History of the Study of Sex Differences

The study of sex differences has a fascinating history within psychology. Prior to 1973, relatively little attention was paid to sex differences. Indeed, in psychology research, it was common practice to use participants of only one sex, most often males. And even when both men and women were studied, few articles actually analyzed or reported whether the effects differed for men and women.

All of this changed in the early 1970s (see Eagly, 1995; Hoyenga & Hoyenga, 1993). In 1974, Elenore Maccoby and Carol Jacklyn published a classic book, *The Psychology of Sex Differences,* in which they reviewed hundreds of studies and drew several key conclusions about how men and women differed. They concluded that women were slightly better than men at verbal ability. Men were slightly better than women in mathematical ability (e.g., geometry, algebra) and spatial ability (e.g., ability to visualize what a three-dimensional object would look like if it were rotated in space by 90 degrees). In terms of *personality* characteristics, they concluded that only one sex difference existed: men were more aggressive than women. With other aspects of personality and social behavior, they concluded that there was not enough evidence to determine whether men and women differed. Overall, they concluded that sex differences were few in number and trivial in importance.

The Psychology of Sex Differences set off an avalanche of research on the topic. The book itself was criticized on various grounds. Some argued that many more sex differences existed than were portrayed by Maccoby and Jacklyn (Block, 1983). Others challenged the conclusion that men were more aggressive than women (Frodi, Macauley, & Thome, 1977). Furthermore, the methods by which the authors drew their conclusions, although standard practice at that time, were crude by today's standards—the authors simply summarized the studies by counting how many reached statistical significance and then drew some interpretive conclusions. This method allows for the possibility of considerable subjectivity.

Following the publication of *The Psychology of Sex Differences,* psychology journals changed their reporting practices. They started to require authors to calculate and report sex differences, if members of both sexes were included. Furthermore, protests that many of the findings in psychology were based primarily on studies of men led to calls for the greater inclusion of women as participants. There followed an explosion of research on sex differences. Literally thousands of studies were conducted on the ways in which men and women differed. Indeed, by 1992, the federal government had required members of both sexes to be represented in all federally funded research (unless, of course, there was a legitimate reason to limit the research to one sex, such as studies of breast self-exam for breast cancer).

Since Maccoby and Jacklyn's early work, researchers have developed a more precise quantitative procedure for examining conclusions across studies and thus for determining sex differences, called meta-analysis. Recall that meta-analysis is a statistical method for summarizing the findings of large numbers of individual studies. Meta-analysis did not gain popularity until the mid-1980s. Meta-analysis allows researchers to calculate with greater objectivity and precision whether a particular difference—such as a sex difference—is consistent across studies. Furthermore, it allows researchers to estimate how large the difference actually is—called the effect size.

Calculation of Effect Size: How Large Are the Sex Differences?

The most commonly used statistic in meta-analysis is the **effect size,** or *d* statistic. The *d* statistic is used to express a difference in standard deviation units (see Chapter 2). A *d* of 0.50 means that the average difference between two groups is half a standard deviation. A *d* of 1.00 means that the difference between the groups is one full standard deviation. A *d* of 0.25 means that the difference between the groups is one-quarter of a standard deviation. An effect size can be calculated for each study of sex differences and then averaged across studies to give a more precise and objective assessment of whether the sexes differ and, if so, by how much.

Most meta-analyses have adopted a convention for interpreting effect sizes (Cohen, 1977):

d Score	Meaning
0.20 or −0.20	Small difference
0.50 or −0.50	Medium difference
0.80 or −0.80	Large difference

When comparing men to women, assume that positive *d* scores, such as .20 or .50, indicate that men score higher than women. Negative *d* scores, such as −.20 or −.50, indicate that women score higher than men. For example, a *d* score of −0.85 means that women score much higher on a particular trait.

To get a feel for various effect sizes, let's examine a few findings outside the realm of personality. Which sex can throw a ball farther, men or women? Although there are great individual differences within each sex, it is clear that men can, on average, throw farther than women. The *d* is approximately 2.00 (Ashmore, 1990). This means that the sexes differ, on average, by two full standard deviations, which is considered quite large. Which sex has a higher grade-point average in college? The *d* for grade-point average is −.04, which is very close to zero. This means that men and women are essentially the same in their grade-point average.

Which sex scores higher in verbal ability? It turns out that women are slightly better than men, but the *d* is only −0.11. Are men better at math? The *d* here also turns out to be quite small, only 0.15. These findings are in line with a vast literature that now documents that men and women are essentially the same (or do not differ by much) on most measures of cognitive ability (Hyde, 2005). About the only well-documented exception to this conclusion pertains to spatial rotation ability, such as the spatial ability involved in throwing a spear (or football) so that it correctly anticipates the trajectory of a moving object, such as an animal or a receiver. The *d* for this sort of spatial ability is 0.73, which comes close to the standard for "large" (Ashmore, 1990).

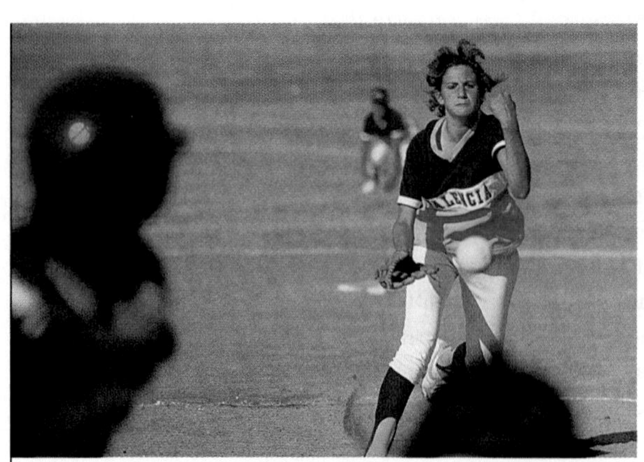

When it comes to who can throw a ball farther, the effect size for the difference between men and women is 2.00, in favor of the men. While this is a large difference in average ability, there will nevertheless be some women who can throw farther than most men because the distributions still overlap.

It is important to keep in mind that even large effect sizes for average sex differences do not necessarily have implications for any particular individual. Even with a *d* of 2.00 for throwing distance, some women can throw much farther than the average man and some men cannot throw as far as the average woman. This overlap in the distributions of the sexes must be kept in mind when evaluating effect sizes (see Figure 16.1).

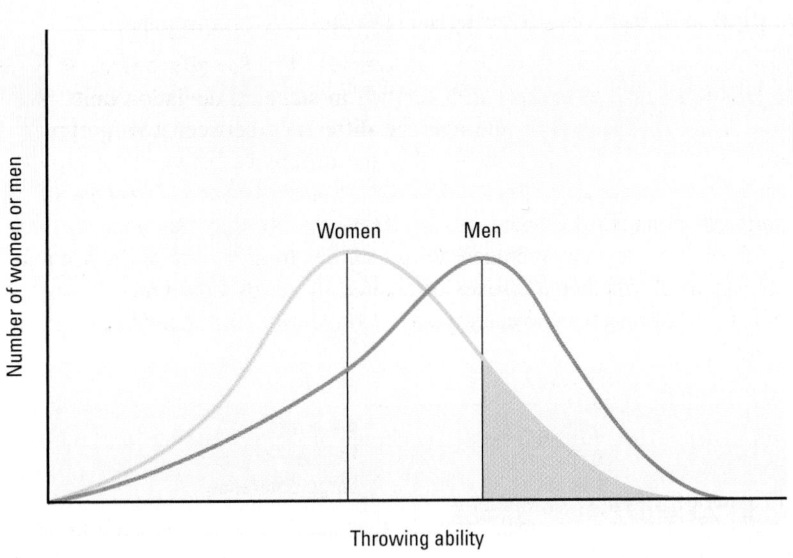

Figure 16.1

Overlap between the sexes in context of a mean difference. Even when one sex greatly exceeds the other in a particular ability, there is a large area of overlap. Women whose throwing ability falls in the shaded area exceed the throwing ability of the average man.

Minimalists and Maximalists

A central focus of the debate on sex differences follows from a consideration of effect sizes—on whether sex differences are small and relatively inconsequential or substantial and important. Those who describe sex differences as small and inconsequential, those who take the **minimalist** position, offer two arguments. The first is that, empirically, most findings of sex differences show small magnitudes of effect (Deaux, 1984; Hyde, 2005; Hyde & Plant, 1995). Minimalists tend to emphasize that the distributions of men and women on any given personality variable show tremendous overlap, which reflect their small magnitude of effect (review Figure 16.1). A second argument advanced by minimalists is that whatever differences exist do not have much practical importance for behavior in everyday life. If the sex differences are small and don't have consequences for people's lives, then perhaps we should concentrate on other psychological issues that are more important.

In contrast, those who take the **maximalist** position tend to argue that the magnitude of sex differences is comparable to the magnitude of many other effects in psychology and should not be trivialized (Eagly, 1995). Some sex differences tend to be small in magnitude, others are large in magnitude, and many are in the moderate range, according to this view. Furthermore, Eagly (1995) notes that even small sex differences can have large practical importance. A small sex difference in the proclivity to help other people, for example, could result in a large sex difference in the number of lives each sex aids over the long run in times of distress. As you read through this chapter, you should keep in mind the range of positions psychologists have taken on sex differences, from the minimalist stance to the maximalist stance.

Sex Differences in Personality

We begin by examining sex differences in temperament in children. The five-factor model of personality, discussed in detail in Chapter 3, provides a convenient framework for organizing a number of otherwise scattered findings about sex differences in personality (see Table 16.1). We examine sex differences in the personality characteristics that are subsumed by the five-factor model. Then we will move on to discuss sex differences in other domains of personality—such as sexuality, criminality and physical aggression, depression and psychopathy, and the interaction patterns of men and women in groups.

Temperament in Children

The importance of sex differences in temperament is aptly summarized by the authors of a recent meta-analysis: "The question of gender differences in temperament is arguably one of the most fundamental questions in gender differences research in the areas of personality and social behavior. Temperament reflects biologically based emotional and behavioral consistencies that appear early in life and predict—often in conjunction with other factors—patterns and outcomes in numerous other domains such as psychopathology and personality" (Else-Quest, Hyde, Goldsmith, & Van Hulle, 2006, p. 33). These authors conducted the most massive meta-analysis ever undertaken of sex differences in temperament in children ranging in age from 3 to 13.

The sex differences they discovered ranged from substantial to negligible. **Inhibitory control** showed the largest sex difference, with a $d = -.41$, which is considered in the moderate range. Inhibitory control refers to the ability to control

Table 16.1 Effect Sizes for Sex Differences in Personality: The Five-Factor Model

Dimension	Effect Size
Extraversion	
Gregariousness	−.15
Assertiveness	.50
Activity	.09
Agreeableness	
Trust	−.25
Tender-mindedness	−.97
Conscientiousness	
Order	−.13
Emotional Stability	
Anxiety	−.28
Impulsiveness	.06
Openness	
Ideas	.03

Note: Positive numbers mean men tend to score higher than women, and negative numbers mean women tend to score higher than men.

Adapted from Feingold, 1994.

inappropriate responses or behaviors. As the authors summarize, "these findings may represent an overall better ability of girls to regulate or allocate their attention" and suppress socially undesirable behavior (Else-Quest et al., 2006, p. 61). **Perceptual sensitivity**—the ability to detect subtle stimuli from the environment—also showed a sex difference favoring girls ($d = -.38$). Girls, on average, appear to be more sensitive than boys to subtle and low-intensity signals from their external worlds. Inhibitory control is related to the latter development of the personality trait of conscientiousness. Interestingly, the sex difference appears to fade, since adult men and women do not differ much in conscientiousness.

Surgency, a cluster including approach behavior, high activity, and impulsivity, showed the next largest sex difference ($d = +.38$), with boys scoring higher than girls. Perhaps the combination of high surgency and low inhibitory control accounts for the fact that boys tend to get into more disciplinary difficulties in school in the early years of their lives. Some subcomponents of surgency showed slightly smaller sex differences, such as activity level ($d = +.33$) and high-intensity pleasure ($d = +.30$), which is consistent with the finding that boys are more likely than girls to engage in rough-and-tumble play.

Perhaps the combination of low inhibitory control and high surgency accounts for another reliable gender difference—a difference in the domain of *physical aggressiveness.* Using an act frequency measure based on codings of actual behavior, Zakriski, Wright, and Underwood (2005) found a $d = +.60$, indicating that boys were more physically aggressive than girls (approximate age 13). The contexts in which this sex difference emerged, however, were quite specific, leading the authors to suggest that "gender differences in personality can be conceptualized as patterns of social adaptation that are complex and context-specific" (Zakriski et al., 2005, p. 844).

In contrast to inhibitory control and surgency, girls and boys showed virtually no difference in a variable called **negative affectivity,** which includes components such as anger, difficulty, amount of distress, and sadness. The only minor exception to this overall gender similarity occurred for the subcomponent of fearfulness ($d = -.12$), with girls being slightly more fearful than boys. This general lack of gender difference in negative affectivity is interesting, in that it is closely connected with emotional instability, which does show a moderate sex difference in adulthood (see next section on the five-factor model). Else-Quest and her colleagues speculate that gender stereotypes—beliefs that females are more emotional than males—may lead to the actual development of the gender difference in adulthood, given the negligible gender difference among children (Else-Quest et al., 2006).

In summary, meta-analysis of temperament in children between the ages of 3 and 13 suggest two gender differences of moderate magnitude. Girls show more inhibitory control and boys show higher levels of surgency. These are average sex differences, however, which means that the distributions overlap considerably. Contrary to gender stereotypes, there is little evidence that girls are more emotional than boys during this age range.

Five-Factor Model

As you may recall from Chapter 3, many personality psychologists argue for a taxonomy of personality that contains five fundamental factors. Therefore, the five-factor model provides a broad set of personality traits within which we can examine whether women and men differ.

Studies show that women naturally smile more than men. Researchers disagree, however, on what this sex difference means; some suggest smiling is a sign of agreeableness while others hold that smiling is a form of submissiveness or a way to ease tension in social situations.

Extraversion

Three facets of extraversion have been examined for sex differences—gregariousness, assertiveness, and activity. Women score slightly higher on gregariousness than men, but the difference is quite small. Similarly, men score very slightly higher on activity level. A recent study of personality in 50 different cultures revealed a relatively small gender difference (d = +.15) on extraversion (McCrae et al., 2005b). The only subscale of extraversion to show a substantial sex difference is assertiveness, with men scoring moderately higher than women. A related finding, emerging from a study of 127 samples in 70 countries (N = 77,528), is that men place a greater importance on the *value of power* than do women (Schwartz & Rubel, 2005). That is, men tend to value social status and dominance over other people more than women.

The medium-size sex difference in assertiveness (d = 0.50) may show up in social behavior in group contexts. A number of studies suggest that men interrupt others in conversation more than women do in a mixed-sex group (Hoyenga & Hoyenga, 1993). An important source of conflict between the sexes—unwanted interruptions of dialogue—may stem from this moderate sex difference in assertiveness.

Agreeableness

A study of 50 cultures revealed a small to medium gender difference (d = −.32) on agreeableness, indicating that women score higher than men (McCrae et al., 2005b). Two facets of agreeableness have been examined—trust and tender-mindedness. **Trust** is the proclivity to cooperate with others, giving others the benefit of the doubt, and viewing one's fellow human beings as basically good at heart. **Tender-mindedness** is a nurturant proclivity—having empathy for others and being sympathetic with those who are downtrodden. As you can see in Table 16.1, women score as more trusting than men. In contrast, women are substantially more tender-minded than men, with a large effect size of −.97, which is clearly well in the range considered to be large.

Another finding closely related to agreeableness pertains to *smiling* behavior. Meta-analyses of smiling show that women smile more often than men, with an effect size of −.60 (Hall, 1984). To the degree that smiling reflects an agreeable personality disposition, we can conclude that women are more agreeable than men. However, some researchers view smiling as a sign of submissiveness rather than agreeableness (Eagly, 1995). Furthermore, some argue that it is low-status people who do a lot of smiling. If this is correct, then smiling may be more a reflection of low status than of agreeableness.

Aggressiveness

Aggressiveness falls at the opposite end of agreeableness. It will probably not surprise you to find out that men are more physically aggressive than women. This shows up in personality tests, in aggressive fantasies, and in actual measures of behavior (Hyde, 1986). In general, the effect sizes for aggression are largest for projective tests, such as the TAT (d = .86), the next largest for peer report measures of aggression (d = .63), and the smallest for self-report measures of aggression (d = .40). Fantasy

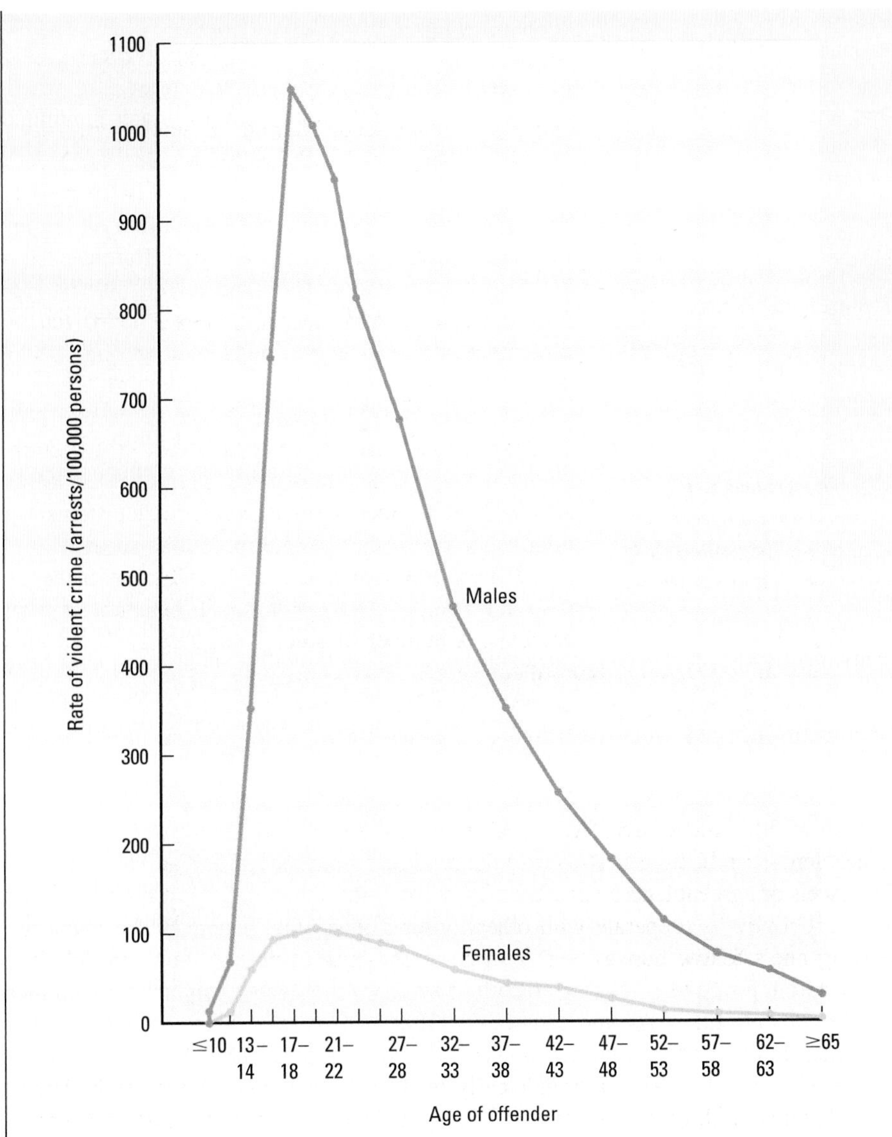

Figure 16.2

Arrest rates for violent crime in the United States as a function of age and gender.

measures of aggression, which assess how often men and women imagine showing aggression against others, show large sex differences, with an effect size of .84.

These sex differences can have profound consequences for everyday life. The effect size for violent crimes is especially striking. Worldwide, men commit roughly 90 percent of all homicides, and most of the victims of these homicides are other men (Daly & Wilson, 1988). Furthermore, men commit more violent crimes of all sorts, ranging from assaults to gang wars. Figure 16.2 shows the arrest rate for violent crimes within the United States as a function of age and gender. As you can see, men commit these crimes far more than women. Interestingly, the largest sex differences in violent crimes show up just after puberty, peaking in adolescence and the early twenties. After age 50, violent crimes of all sorts start to decline, and men and women become much more similar to each other in terms of criminal aggressiveness.

These findings are not limited to the United States. In all cultures for which there are data, the vast majority of killings and other violent crimes are committed by young men (Daly & Wilson, 1988). These findings lend credence to theories that offer evolutionary explanations for some of the sex differences.

Conscientiousness

The 50-culture study revealed a negligible sex difference ($d = -.14$) on overall levels of conscientiousness (McCrae et al., 2005b). Only one facet of conscientiousness has been scrutinized for sex differences—order. Women score slightly higher than men on order, with an effect size of only −.13. This is small enough to conclude that men and women are essentially the same on this dimension. Nonetheless, even very small effects can sometimes have large cumulative effects over time. For example, a small difference in order between marriage partners may result in a large number of arguments about housecleaning over the course of a year.

Emotional Stability

Emotional stability may be the most value-laden dimension of the five-factor model. As you will recall from Chapter 3, at one end of the dimension are those who are steady, calm, and stable. One can label this end "emotionally stable," as many have done. But psychologists could also just as easily have labeled this end of the dimension "emotionally constricted." The opposite end is characterized by volatility and changeability of mood. Although many have labeled this end of the dimension "emotionally unstable" or "neurotic," one could just as easily label it as "emotionally expressive." The important point to keep in mind is the psychological meaning of the dimension—the actual traits it includes—rather than the label given to either extreme.

The 50-culture study revealed that emotional stability shows the largest sex difference ($d = -.49$) in the five-factor model, indicating that women are moderately lower than men on this dimension (McCrae et al., 2005b). A study of 10 Arab countries—Kuwait, Saudi Arabia, Emirates, Oman, Egypt, Syria, Lebanon, Palestine (Nablus and Gaza), Jordan, and Iraq—found similar sex differences using a measure of anxiety, although effect sizes were not reported (Abdel-Khalek & Alansari, 2004). Two aspects of emotional stability have been examined in meta-analyses of sex differences—anxiety and impulsiveness. Men and women are virtually identical on impulsiveness, with a tiny effect size of .06. In contrast, women score higher on anxiety than men, with a small effect size of −.28. Thus, men and women differ in levels of anxiety, but the magnitude is properly considered to be just slightly greater than small. This difference may show up in such behaviors as women's slightly greater fear of spiders or snakes.

Openness to Experience

The 50-culture study revealed essentially no sex differences ($d = -.07$) in openness to experience (McCrae et al., 2005b). The facet of openness that has been examined via meta-analysis is the facet labeled ideas, which refers to the range of thoughts or concepts a person entertains. Men and women are virtually identical on this dimension, with an effect size of .03. A recent study verifies this lack of a sex difference. Botwin et al. (1997) examined sex differences in openness to experience using three data sources—self-report, spouse-report, and independent interviewer reports (one male and one female interviewer). Separate analyses of these three data sources yielded no sex differences in openness–intellect. Thus, it seems safe to conclude that men and women are identical on this dimension of personality.

Basic Emotions: Frequency and Intensity

Emotions are central to personality, so much so that we devoted an entire chapter to them (Chapter 13). Recent research conducted on a cross-cultural scale has revealed precisely where the sexes differ in their experiences of emotions and where the sexes are essentially the same. The most extensive study examined 2,199 Australians and an international sample of 6,868 participants drawn from 41 different countries (Brebner, 2003). Eight fundamental emotions were examined, four "positive" emotions (Affection, Joy, Contentment, Pride) and four "negative" emotions (Fear, Anger, Sadness, Guilt). Participants used rating scales to indicate (1) how frequently they experienced each emotion and (2) the intensity with which they experienced each emotion. The basic findings are summarized in Table 16.2.

As shown in Table 16.2, there are small, but statistically significant differences in the experience of emotions in this international sample. All point to women experiencing both positive emotions and negative emotions more frequently and intensely than do men. In the positive domain, affection and joy show the largest sex differences. Pride, in contrast, shows no sex difference in either frequency or intensity. In the negative domain, women experience fear and sadness more than men, especially in the reported intensity of the experience. Guilt, in contrast, shows a minimal sex difference in intensity and no sex difference in frequency—perhaps contradicting the stereotype that women are more guilt-prone than men. These results must be qualified in two ways. First, the effect sizes are generally small and should be interpreted in that light. Second, other research has documented that more specialized explorations of emotions reveal some reversals of these sex differences, such as men experiencing more intense jealousy in response to the sexual infidelity of a partner (see Chapter 8).

Table 16.2 Sex Differences in Experience of Emotions

Emotion	Frequency	Intensity
Positive Emotions	.20	.23
Affection	.30	.25
Joy	.16	.26
Contentment	.13	.18
Pride	ns	ns
Negative Emotions	.14	.25
Fear	.17	.26
Anger	.05	.14
Sadness	.16	.28
Guilt	ns	.07

Note: Entries in the table are effect sizes (*d*). The designation "ns" indicates that the sex difference was not significant. Positive values indicate that women report experiencing the emotion more frequently or intensely than do men.
Source: Brebner (2003).

It is interesting to note that one of the most common complaints that women express about men is that they don't express their emotions enough (Buss, 2003). Men, in contrast, often complain that women are too emotional. The recent international results point to one possible reason for these complaints—perhaps men don't express their emotions because they literally don't experience emotions as frequently or as intensely as do women. Knowledge of the actual sex differences in emotional experience may take men and women one step closer to understanding each other and perhaps ultimately help to reduce conflict between the sexes.

Other Dimensions of Personality

Several dimensions of personality are related to, but not directly subsumed by, the five-factor model of personality. We will examine three—self-esteem, sexuality and mating, and the people–things dimension.

Self-Esteem

A topic of major interest to women and men is self-esteem, or how good we feel about ourselves. This is reflected in the many popular books on the topic, such as *Schoolgirls: Young Women, Self-esteem, and the Confidence Gap* (Orenstein, 1994). Although researchers have explored many facets of self-esteem, such as esteem of one's athletic abilities and esteem of one's social skills, by far the most frequently measured component is **global self-esteem,** defined as "the level of global regard that one has for the self as a person" (Harter, 1993, p. 88). Global self-esteem can range from highly positive to highly negative and, as described in Chapter 14, reflects an overall evaluation of the self at the broadest level (Kling et al., 1999).

Global self-esteem is linked with many aspects of functioning and is commonly thought to be central to mental health. Those with high self-esteem appear to cope better with the stresses and strains of daily life. In laboratory studies, when faced with negative feedback about one's performance, those with high self-esteem perform better on cognitive tasks, whereas the performance of those with low self-esteem suffers. Those with high self-esteem tend to take credit for their successes but deny responsibility for their failures (Kling et al., 1999).

Meta-analyses have yielded an interesting pattern of sex differences (Feingold, 1994; Kling et al., 1999). The overall effect size is relatively small (d = .21), with males scoring slightly higher than females in self-esteem (Kling et al., 1999). The fascinating finding, however, emerged when the researchers analyzed sex differences in self-esteem according to the age of the participants. Young children (ages 7–10) showed only a slight sex difference in self-esteem (d = .16). As the children approached adolescence, however, the gap between the sexes widened. At ages 11–14, d was 0.23. And the sex difference peaked during the ages of 15–18 (d = 0.33). Females seem to suffer from lower self-esteem than males as they hit their mid- to late teens. The good news is that, in adulthood, the self-esteem gap starts to close. During the ages of 19–22, the effect size shrinks to 0.18. During the ages of 23–59, the sexes come even closer, with a d of 0.10. And, during older age, from 60 on up, the d is only −0.03, which means that the males and females are virtually identical in self-esteem.

The magnitudes of all these effects are relatively small, even during adolescence, when the gap between the sexes is the widest. The widespread fear that women's self-esteem is permanently decimated seems somewhat exaggerated in light of this empirical evidence. Nonetheless, even small differences in self-esteem can be extremely important to day-to-day well-being, so this sex difference should not be dismissed. It will be interesting for researchers to explore why females appear to lose self-esteem in adolescence relative to males and whether programs that attempt to raise self-esteem are successful.

Sexuality and Mating

As we saw in Chapter 3, individual differences in sexuality show some overlap with the five-factor model of personality, but not perfect overlap (Schmitt & Buss, 2000). Meta-analyses show profound sex differences in certain aspects of sexual desire, motivation, and attitudes. One of the largest sex differences pertains to attitudes toward casual sex, as noted in Chapter 8. Oliver and Hyde (1993) found an effect size of .81, with men having far more favorable attitudes toward casual sex. In another study, men stated that they would ideally liked to have more than 18 sex partners in their lifetimes, whereas women stated that they wanted to have only 4 or 5 (d = .87) (Buss & Schmitt, 1993).

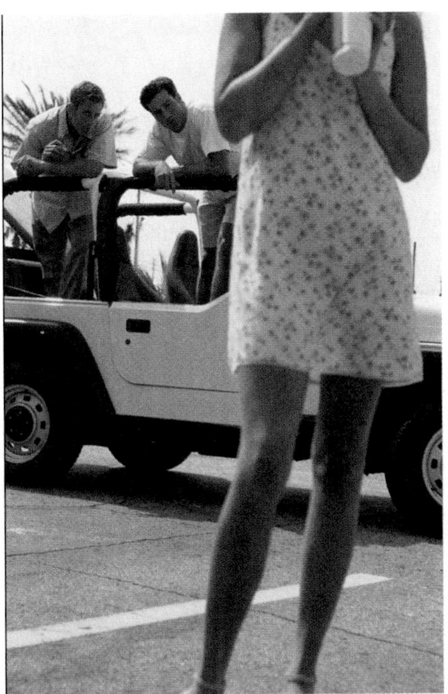

When it comes to attitudes about casual sex, men tend to be more interested in women than women are in men, on average.

Sex differences occur in other aspects of the mating domain, some following from the sex difference in attitudes toward casual sex. Can men and women be "just friends"? It turns out that men have more difficulty than do women in being friends with the opposite sex. Men are more likely than women to initiate friendship with someone of the opposite sex because they are sexually attracted to them; more likely to actually become sexually attracted to their opposite-sex friends; and more likely to dissolve such friendships if they do not result in sex (Bleske & Buss, 2001).

Men are more likely than women to be sexually aggressive in the sense of trying to force women to have sex when women express an unwillingness to have sex (Buss, 2003). Nonetheless, not all men are sexually aggressive. Recent studies have shown that men who indicate "hostile masculinity" (domineering and degrading attitudes toward women) and men who lack the personality disposition of empathy are most likely to report using sexual aggression (Wheeler, George, & Dahl, 2002). Furthermore, men who are narcissistic are especially likely to express rape-supportive beliefs and to lack empathy for rape victims (Bushman, Bonacci, Dijk, & Baumeister, 2003). So although the sexes can be said to differ overall in sexual aggression, it really appears to be limited to a subset of men—those who are narcissistic, lack empathy, and display hostile masculinity.

In summary, the major dimensions of personality vary from showing a large sex difference to showing a trivial sex difference. By far the largest sex differences show up on tender-mindedness, with women scoring substantially higher than men; physical aggressiveness, with men scoring higher than women; and attitudes toward casual sex, with men scoring higher than women. In the moderate range is assertiveness, with men scoring higher than women. In the small range of sex differences are the dimensions of trust and anxiety, with women scoring higher on both. The dimensions showing men and women to be virtually identical include gregariousness, activity level, order, impulsiveness, and the facet of openness to experience, labeled "ideas." There seems to be no support for the stereotypes that women are more gregarious than men or that men are more active and impulsive than women.

People–Things Dimension

Another dimension of personality has been labeled the **people–things dimension** (Little, 1972a, 1972b; Lippa, 1998). This refers to the nature of vocational interests.

A Closer Look Sex Differences in Depression

Depression is marked by characteristics such as low self-esteem, pessimism (expecting the worst to happen), and the perception that one has little control over one's life. It's one of the most common psychological maladies of modern humans, and there is evidence that the rate of depression is increasing. Five studies comprised of 39,000 individuals living in five areas of the world revealed that young people are more likely than older people to have experienced at least one major episode of depression (Nesse & Williams, 1994). Moreover, the incidence of depression appears to be higher in more economically developed cultures (Nesse & Williams, 1994).

Adult men and women differ in the incidence of depression and in the nature of their depressive symptoms, but the sexes don't start out different. In childhood, there are no sex differences in depression. After puberty, however, women show a depression rate two to three times that of men (Hoyenga & Hoyenga, 1993). Roughly 25 percent of all women have at least one depressive episode in their lifetimes. In contrast, only 10 percent of all men will have a depressive episode. The largest sex differences in depression show up between the ages of 18 and 44. After that, the sexes start to converge.

The following list contains some of the critical aspects of sex differences in depressive symptoms (Hoyenga & Hoyenga, 1993):

1. Depressed women more often than depressed men report excessive eating and weight gain as one of the symptoms (although loss of appetite is the most common symptom of depression in both sexes).
2. Women are more likely to cry when depressed and to confront their feelings directly; men are more likely to become aggressive when depressed.
3. Depressed women are more likely than men to seek treatment; depressed men are more likely simply to miss work.
4. Nervous activity (e.g., fidgeting) is more common in depressed women than in depressed men; inactivity is more common in depressed men than in depressed women.
5. Among depressed college students, men are more socially withdrawn, more likely to use drugs, and more likely to experience aches and pains; women are more likely to experience hurt feelings and a decline in self-esteem.
6. Before puberty, the rate of depression is the same in the sexes; only after puberty does the rate of depression in women more than double the rate in men.

People who score toward the "things" end of the dimension prefer vocations that deal with impersonal objects—machines, tools, or materials; examples include carpenters, auto mechanics, building contractors, tool makers, and farmers. Those scoring toward the "people" end of the dimension prefer social occupations, which involve thinking about others, caring for others, or directing others; examples include high school teachers, social workers, and religious counselors.

As you might imagine, there are strong sex differences in these occupational preferences. The correlation between sex and the people–things dimension is .56, or a *d* of roughly 1.35, which means that men are more likely to score at the things end of the dimension, and women are more likely to score at the people end (Lippa, 1998).

When girls are asked to describe themselves spontaneously, they are more likely than boys to make references to their close relationships. They are more likely to value personal qualities linked to group harmony, such as sensitivity to others. And they are more likely to identify their personal relationships as central to their identity as a person (Gabriel & Gardner, 1999).

Although these results are certainly not surprising in that they fit with our stereotypes of women and men, it is interesting that they were correctly identified nearly a century ago: "[Researchers] found as the greatest difference between men and women

7. Men are more likely to commit suicide "successfully," perhaps because men are more likely to use guns as the method; women are more likely to make nonfatal suicide attempts, perhaps because they use less lethal methods, such as overdosing on pills.

One clue to the sex difference in the nature and rate of depression comes from a large-scale study of 1,100 community-based adults (Nolen-Hoeksema, Larson, & Grayson, 1999). The researchers speculated that women's greater vulnerability to depressive symptoms may stem from factors such as their lower power in the workplace, their relative lack of control over important areas of their lives, their work overload, and their lower status in heterosexual relationships. Because they are searching for ways to control their lives, women may start to *ruminate.* **Rumination** involves repeatedly focusing on one's symptoms or distress (e.g., "Why do I continue to feel so bad about myself?" or "Why doesn't my boss like me?"). Because their ruminations fail to lead to efficacious solutions, according to this theory, women continue to ruminate, and rumination is a key contributor to women's greater experience of depressive symptoms. The research supported the importance of rumination. Women were found to ruminate substantially more than men, and rumination, in turn, contributed to the perseverance of the depressive symptoms.

Another theory is that the greater incidence of depression in women is caused by the fact that humans in the modern world live in isolated nuclear families, stripped of the extended kin and other social supports that characterize more traditional societies (Buss, 2000b).

Yet another theory is that women's greater depression is linked with entering mate competition and is caused by dissatisfaction with their physical appearance (Hankin & Abramson, 2001). Indeed, the onset of women's depression and the emergence of the sex difference appears around the age of 13, when heterosexual interactions start to increase. And it is well-documented that men place a greater value on physical appearance in their mate selections worldwide, suggesting that women are under increased pressure to compete in the realm of attractiveness (Buss, 2003). Furthermore, body dissatisfaction increases in women around puberty, as does the onset of eating disorders such as binging and purging and dissatisfaction with current weight (Hankin & Abramson, 2001). The final link is that a woman's dissatisfaction with her body and physical appearance is linked with increases in depression. If a woman's self-worth is in part tied up in her physical appearance because of its importance in what men want in a mate, then women's pubertal onset of depression could stem in part from the intensity of mate competition after women hit puberty.

Whatever their origins, sex differences in depression represent one of the largest and most consequential differences in personality.

that in the relative strength of the interest in things and their mechanisms [stronger in men] and the interest in persons and their feelings [stronger in women]" (Thorndike, 1911, p. 31).

Whatever the origins of these preferences, they are likely to have important consequences for the occupations women and men select and the pleasurable activities they pursue. Men, being more thing-oriented, are more likely to be found tinkering with engines or building wooden structures in their spare time. Women, being more people-oriented, are more likely to prefer planning weekend activities around other people.

Masculinity, Femininity, Androgyny, and Sex Roles

Women and men differ in a few dimensions: assertiveness, tender-mindedness, and anxiety, as well as in aggression, sexuality, and depression. But do these differences mean that there is such a thing as a masculine or feminine personality? This section explores the conceptions of masculinity and femininity and how the treatment of these topics has changed over time.

Starting in the 1930s, personality researchers began to notice that men and women differed in their responses to a number of personality items on large inventories. For example, when asked whether they preferred to take baths or showers, women indicated that they preferred baths, whereas men indicated that they preferred showers. Based on these sex differences, researchers assumed that the differences could be described by a single personality dimension, with *masculinity* at one end and *femininity* at the other end. A person who scored high on masculinity was assumed to score low on femininity, and vice versa. Researchers assumed that all people could be located on this single masculinity–femininity dimension. Items that showed large sex differences, such as "I enjoy reading *Popular Mechanics*" (men scored higher), and "I would enjoy the work of a librarian" (women scored higher), were used to construct a single scale of masculinity–femininity. But does a single scale with masculinity at one end and femininity at the other end really capture the important individual differences? Can't someone be both masculine *and* feminine? This question led to a new conception of sex-linked personality differences—androgyny.

The Search for Androgyny

In the early 1970s, with the rise of the feminist movement, researchers began to challenge the assumption of a single masculinity–femininity dimension. These new researchers, instead, started with the premise that masculinity and femininity are independent dimensions. Thus, one can be high on both masculinity and femininity, or low on both dimensions. Or one can be stereotypically masculine—high on masculinity, low on femininity. Or one can be stereotypically feminine—high on femininity, low on masculinity. This shift represented a fundamental change in thinking about masculinity, femininity, and sex roles.

Two major personality instruments were published in 1974 to assess people using this new conception of sex roles (Bem, 1974; Spence, Helmreich, & Stapp, 1974). The **masculinity** dimension contained items reflecting assertiveness, boldness, dominance, self-sufficiency, and instrumentality. Those who agreed with personality trait terms connoting these qualities scored high on masculinity. The **femininity** dimension contained items that reflected nurturance, expression of emotions, and empathy. Those who agreed with personality trait terms connoting these qualities scored high on femininity. Those who scored high on both dimensions were labeled **androgynous,** to reflect the notion that a single person could possess both masculine and feminine characteristics. Table 16.3 shows the four possible scores these instruments can yield.

The researchers who developed these questionnaires viewed the androgynous person as the most highly developed. Androgynous persons were presumed to embody the most valuable elements of both sexes, such as the assertiveness to take positive steps in one's job and interpersonal sensitivity to the feelings of others. Furthermore,

Table 16.3 Conception of Sex Roles Developed in the 1970s

	Low Masculinity	High Masculinity
Low Femininity	Undifferentiated	Masculine
High Femininity	Feminine	Androgynous

androgynous persons were presumed to be liberated from the shackles of traditional notions of sex roles. Before proceeding with our analysis, however, pause for a few minutes to determine where you are located on these measures. To find out, fill out the following Exercise.

Exercise

INSTRUCTIONS: Forty items follow. Each one contains a pair of statements describing contradictory characteristics; that is, you cannot be both at the same time, such as very artistic and not at all artistic. The letters form a scale between the two extremes. Select the letter that describes where you fall on the scale. For example, if you think that you are not at all aggressive, you would choose *A*. If you think you are very aggressive, you would choose *E*. If you are in between, you would choose *C*, or possibly *B* or *D*. Be sure to make a choice for every item. Mark your choice by drawing an *X* through the letter that you select.

1. Not at all aggressive	A.....B.....C.....D.....E	Very aggressive
2. Very whiny	A.....B.....C.....D.....E	Not at all whiny
3. Not at all independent	A.....B.....C.....D.....E	Very independent
4. Not at all arrogant	A.....B.....C.....D.....E	Very arrogant
5. Not at all emotional	A.....B.....C.....D.....E	Very emotional
6. Very submissive	A.....B.....C.....D.....E	Very dominant
7. Very boastful	A.....B.....C.....D.....E	Not at all boastful
8. Not at all excitable in a *major* crisis	A.....B.....C.....D.....E	Very excitable in a *major* crisis
9. Very passive	A.....B.....C.....D.....E	Very active
10. Not at all egotistical	A.....B.....C.....D.....E	Very egotistical
11. Not at all able to devote self completely to others	A.....B.....C.....D.....E	Able to devote self completely to others
12. Not at all spineless	A.....B.....C.....D.....E	Very spineless
13. Very rough	A.....B.....C.....D.....E	Very gentle
14. Not at all complaining	A.....B.....C.....D.....E	Very complaining
15. Not at all helpful to others	A.....B.....C.....D.....E	Very helpful to others
16. Not at all competitive	A.....B.....C.....D.....E	Very competitive
17. Subordinates oneself to others	A.....B.....C.....D.....E	Never subordinates onself to others
18. Very home-oriented	A.....B.....C.....D.....E	Very worldly
19. Very greedy	A.....B.....C.....D.....E	Not at all greedy
20. Not at all kind	A.....B.....C.....D.....E	Very kind
21. Indifferent to others' approval	A.....B.....C.....D.....E	Highly needful of other's approval
22. Very dictatorial	A.....B.....C.....D.....E	Not at all dictatorial
23. Feelings not easily hurt	A.....B.....C.....D.....E	Feelings easily hurt
24. Doesn't nag	A.....B.....C.....D.....E	Nags a lot
25. Not at all aware of feelings of others	A.....B.....C.....D.....E	Very aware of feelings of others
26. Can make decisions easily	A.....B.....C.....D.....E	Has difficulty making decisions

Exercise (*Continued*)

27.	Very fussy	A.....B.....C.....D.....E	Not at all fussy
28.	Gives up very easily	A.....B.....C.....D.....E	Never gives up easily
29.	Very cynical	A.....B.....C.....D.....E	Not at all cynical
30.	Never cries	A.....B.....C.....D.....E	Cries very easily
31.	Not at all self-confident	A.....B.....C.....D.....E	Very self-confident
32.	Does not look out only for self, principled	A.....B.....C.....D.....E	Looks out only for self, unprincipled
33.	Feels very inferior	A.....B.....C.....D.....E	Feels very superior
34.	Not at all hostile	A.....B.....C.....D.....E	Very hostile
35.	Not at all understanding of others	A.....B.....C.....D.....E	Very understanding of others
36.	Very cold in relations with others	A.....B.....C.....D.....E	Very warm in relations with others
37.	Very servile	A.....B.....C.....D.....E	Not at all servile
38.	Very little need for security	A.....B.....C.....D.....E	Very strong need for security
39.	Not at all gullible	A.....B.....C.....D.....E	Very gullible
40.	Goes to pieces under pressure	A.....B.....C.....D.....E	Stands up well under pressure

Source: Spence et al. (1974).

The enormous popularity of this new conception of sex roles is a testament to the influence of feminism in America. With the rise of the women's movement, traditional ideas about the roles of men and women were cast aside. Women started entering the workforce in record numbers. Some men opted for more nurturant roles. John Lennon, of former Beatles fame, decided to stay at home and raise his son, Sean, while his wife, Yoko Ono, went to work, overseeing a massive financial empire (Coleman, 1992). Many people applauded Lennon for taking on this new liberated role. This political movement reinforced the idea that men were supposed to become more nurturant, caring, and empathic. At the same time, women were supposed to become more assertive as they entered many professions traditionally reserved for men. The psychological trend toward changing the conceptualization and measurement of sex roles reflected this larger political movement.

The new androgynous conception of sex roles, however, was not without its critics. The new scales were criticized on several grounds. One criticism pertained to the items on the inventories and their correlations with each other. Researchers seemed to assume that masculinity and femininity were single dimensions. Other researchers argued, however, that both constructs were actually multidimensional, containing many facets.

Another criticism goes to the heart of the androgyny concept. It turns out that several studies have found that masculinity and femininity, indeed, consist of a single, bipolar trait. Those who score high on masculinity, for example, tend to score low on femininity. Those who score high on femininity tend to score low on masculinity (e.g., Deaux & Lewis, 1984).

In part as a response to these criticisms, the originators of the new conceptions of sex roles have changed their views. Janet Spence, author of one measure, no longer believes that her questionnaire assesses sex roles (Swann, Langlois, & Gilbert, 1999). Instead, she says that her scales really measure the personality characteristics of instrumentality and expressiveness. **Instrumentality** consists of personality traits that involve working with objects, getting tasks completed in a direct fashion, showing independence from others, and displaying self-sufficiency. **Expressiveness,** in contrast, is the ease with which one can express emotions, such as crying, showing empathy for the troubles of others, and showing nurturance to those in need.

Sandra Bem has also changed her views on sex roles. She now considers her measure (the Bem Sex Role Inventory; Bem, 1974) to assess **gender schemata,** or cognitive orientations that lead individuals to process social information on the basis of sex-linked associations (Hoyenga & Hoyenga, 1993). According to this new conception, the ideal is not to be androgynous but, rather, to be *gender-aschematic.* That is, the ideal is not to use gender and sex-linkage at all in one's processing of social information.

Although most researchers assume that masculinity, femininity, and "gender schema" are personality attributes absorbed from socialization, parents, the media, or the culture, recent studies have challenged this view. Cleveland and his colleagues (2001) found that sex-typed behaviors and attitudes themselves tend to show moderate heritability within sex. Among women, for example, 38 percent of the variance in proclivity to engage in sex-typical behaviors such as crying, expressing emotions, sensitivity to the feelings of others, taking risks, and even fighting was explained by genetic differences. Another study found moderate (roughly 50 percent) heritabilities for measures of "gender atypicality" in boys and girls—that is, masculinity in girls and femininity in boys (Knafo, Iervolino, & Plomin, 2005). These findings still leave large room for environmental influences to affect the adoption of sex roles, but they do suggest that genes also play a role, even within each gender, in the degree to which the sex roles are adopted.

The distinctions between what behavior is appropriate for a woman and what behavior is appropriate for a man in our culture—social roles—have changed dramatically in the past few decades.

In summary, the research measuring sex-related differences has encountered many difficulties and has produced dissatisfying results. The external validity of the measures is questionable. The assumption that masculinity and femininity are unidimensional traits, and that masculinity and femininity are independent of each other, no longer seems tenable.

The new research on masculinity and femininity is moving beyond these issues and beginning to explore the real-life consequences of masculinity and femininity. One study, for example, found that these dimensions affect sexual behavior and relationships (Udry & Chantala, 2004). Adolescent couples containing a highly masculine male and a highly feminine female tend to have sex sooner than other pairings. Couples in which both members are average for their sex tend to break up compared with other pairings. Future research can be expected to yield more interesting real-life consequences of masculinity and femininity.

Gender Stereotypes

Much of this chapter so far has been concerned with the ways in which men and women differ. An important related topic pertains to the *beliefs* that we hold about the ways in which the sexes differ, regardless of whether these beliefs are accurate reflections of the sex differences that empirically exist. The beliefs that we hold about men and women are sometimes called gender stereotypes.

Gender stereotypes have three components (Hoyenga & Hoyenga, 1993). The first is *cognitive* and deals with the ways in which we form **social categories.** For example, we may categorize all men into "cads" or "dads," those who play around and are reluctant to commit versus those who are faithful and invest heavily in their children. The second component of gender stereotypes is *affective*. You may feel hostile or warm toward someone, simply because you place that person in a particular social category. The third component of gender stereotypes is *behavioral*. For example, you may discriminate against someone simply because he belongs in a social category—in this case, "man." We will discuss all three components of gender stereotypes—cognitive, affective, and behavioral—in the following sections, in order to illuminate this form of social categorizing and show how it shows up in everyday life.

Content of Gender Stereotypes

Although there are some variations from culture to culture, it is remarkable that the content of gender stereotypes—the attributes that we believe that men and women possess—is highly similar across cultures. In the most comprehensive set of studies yet conducted, Williams and Best (1982, 1990) studied gender stereotypes in 30 countries around the world. In all these studies, men, compared with women, were commonly viewed as more aggressive, autonomous, achievement-oriented, dominant, exhibitionist, and persevering. Women, compared with men, were commonly seen as more affiliative, deferent, heterosexual, nurturant, and self-abasing. These general gender stereotypes have a common theme. Women in all 30 countries tend to be perceived as more *communal*—oriented toward the group. Men, in contrast, are perceived to be more *instrumental*—asserting their independence from the group. These stereotypes about the sexes correspond in many ways to the actual sex differences that have been discovered. Nonetheless, there is some evidence that people overestimate the magnitude of sex differences in personality, showing exaggerated beliefs about the size of sex differences that actually exist (Krueger, Hasman, Acevedo, & Villano, 2003).

Stereotypic Subtypes of Men and Women

In addition to general gender stereotypes, studies show that most people have more finely differentiated stereotypic views of each sex. Six and Eckes (1991) examined the structure of their participants' cognitive categories of men and women and came up with several subtypes, as shown in Figure 16.3. Men were viewed as falling into five subtypes. The playboy subtype, for example, includes males who are cool, casual, lady killers, and macho. The career man subtype includes men who are social climbers and managers. Stereotypes of women fell into a smaller number of subtypes. One might be called the "classically feminine" subtype, which includes housewives, secretaries, and maternal women. In the modern world, these women might be "soccer moms," highly devoted to their husbands and children. A second subtype is defined by short-term or overt sexuality. This subtype includes sex bombs, tarts, and vamps.

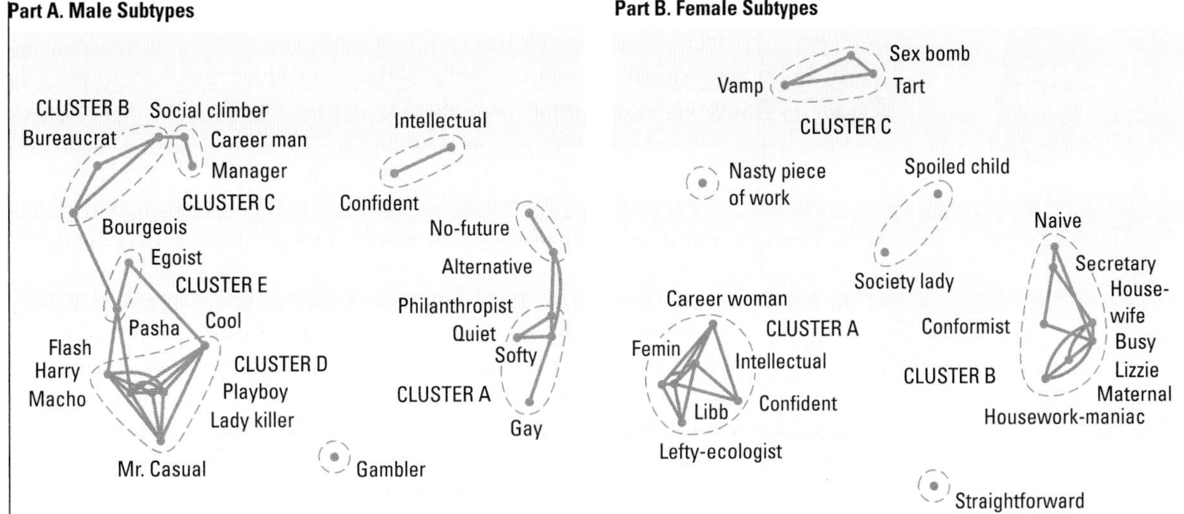

Figure 16.3

The structure of cognitive sexual categories. The structure of cognitive categories of various male and female subtypes, where distance between subtypes on the graphs is assumed to correspond to cognitive "distances" in people's stereotypic concepts. Some subtypes are closely related to each other, as indicated by the dotted lines that surround them to form the various clusters.

These two female subtypes correspond roughly to the "Madonna-whore" dichotomy, which is commonly made in everyday life (Buss, 2003). That is, these two stereotypes of women correspond to women who would make good mothers and women who give off the appearance of pursuing casual sex.

A third stereotype of women, however, involves a subtype that may have emerged relatively recently, perhaps over the past 20 or 30 years—the confident, intellectual, liberated career woman. Hillary Rodham Clinton would be a perfect illustration of this category—she scored at the top of her class in law school and developed an influential career in politics. Also included in this cluster are feminist, women's libber, and lefty-ecologist, perhaps suggesting that, in the minds of the subjects, these political orientations tended to go along with independent, confident, career women.

The key point is that, cognitively, most people do not hold only a single gender stereotype. Rather, cognitive categories are differentiated into subtypes of women and subtypes of men. It remains to be seen whether these stereotypical subtypes have any empirical basis. That is, are "playboy" men actually cooler, more casual, and more macho than other men? Are homemakers more naive, busy, and conformist than other women? Answers to these questions must await future research.

Prejudice and Gender Stereotypes

Categories of gender, and the stereotypes associated with them, are not merely cognitive constructions that rattle around inside people's heads. They have real-world consequences. Prejudiced behavior is one damaging consequence of gender stereotypes. These damaging effects can be found in many important activities: in legal decisions, in medical treatment, in car purchases, in check cashing, and in job hunting (Hoyenga & Hoyenga, 1993).

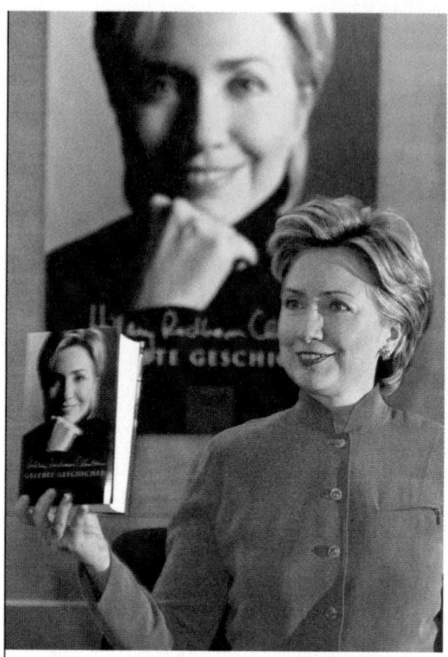

U.S. Senator and former First Lady Hillary Rodham Clinton illustrates a relatively new gender stereotype—women who are intellectual, assertive, liberated, and career-minded.

In wrongful death lawsuits, for example, the families of the victim receive more money if a man was killed than if a woman was killed (Goodman et al., 1991). In medicine, men are more likely to be recommended for coronary bypass surgery than women, even when they show the same amount of heart damage (Khan et al., 1990). A study in which men and women called car dealerships to request prices for particular cars found that the women were quoted higher prices than were the men for exactly the same car (Larrance et al., 1979).

Not all sex discrimination, however, favors men. In a study of book reviews published in the journal *Contemporary Psychology,* male authors were at the receiving end of more negative reviews (Moore, 1978). Interestingly, the male authors received more negative reviews than the women authors, whether the reviewer was a man or a woman. In another study of reviews by men and women of manuscripts submitted to refereed journals for publication, women were found to give more positive reviews to women authors than to men authors (Lloyd, 1990). Unlike the study of book authors, however, men reviewers did not show this bias.

In summary, gender stereotypes can have important consequences for men and women. These consequences can damage people where it counts most—in their health, their jobs, their chances for advancement, and their social reputations.

Theories of Sex Differences

So far in this chapter, we have seen that there are some differences in personality between the sexes but also many similarities. We have also seen that people hold stereotypes of sex differences that may go beyond the actual differences—stereotypes that can have lasting consequences for people's day-to-day lives. This section examines the major theories that have been proposed for explaining how sex differences arise. These include traditional theories of socialization and more complex theories of social roles and other notions of "gendered environments," hormonal theories, and, most recently, theories anchored in evolutionary psychology.

Both socialization and social learning theories hold that gender roles have their roots in early sex-differentiated learning experiences—in short, boys are encouraged in one direction, girls are encouraged in another direction.

Socialization and Social Roles

Socialization theory, the notion that boys and girls become different because boys are reinforced by parents, teachers, and the media for being "masculine," and girls for being "feminine," is probably the most widely held theory of sex differences in personality. The theory can be summarized as follows: Boys are given baseball bats and trucks. Girls are given dolls. Boys are praised for engaging in rough-and-tumble play. Girls are praised for being cute and obedient.

Boys are punished for crying. Girls are comforted when they cry. Over time, according to socialization theory, children learn the classes of behaviors deemed appropriate for their sex.

In Bandura's (1977) **social learning theory,** a variant of socialization theory, boys and girls also learn by observing the behaviors of others, called *models,* of their own sex. Boys watch their fathers, male teachers, and male peers. Girls watch their mothers, female teachers, and female peer models. Boys see their fathers work. Girls see their mothers cook. Over time, even in the absence of direct reinforcement, these models provide a guide to behaviors that are masculine or feminine.

Some empirical evidence exists to support socialization and social learning theories of sex differences. Studies of socialization practices have found that both mothers and fathers encourage dependency more in girls than in boys (Block, 1983). Furthermore, parents encourage girls to stay close to home, whereas boys are permitted or even encouraged to roam. Other studies suggest that fathers engage in more physical play with their sons than with their daughters (Fagot & Leinbach, 1987). Finally, it is clear that parents provide "gendered toys" to their children. Boys generally receive a greater variety of toys, more cars and trucks, more sports equipment, and more tools than girls do (Rheingold & Cook, 1975). Girls receive more dolls, pink clothing and furnishings, strollers, swings, and household appliances. There is considerable empirical evidence that is consistent with socialization and social learning theory.

Cross-cultural evidence for different treatment of boys and girls exists as well. In many cultures, fathers do not interact with their daughters as much as with their sons (Whiting & Edwards, 1988). Girls in most cultures tend to be assigned more domestic chores than boys. Boys are permitted in most cultures to stray farther from home than are girls (Hoyenga & Hoyenga, 1993). Finally, boys in most cultures are socialized to be more competitive than are girls (Low, 1989). In a large study of socialization practices across cultures, Low (1989) found that, in 82 percent of the cultures, the girls were trained to be more nurturant than the boys, and there were no cultures that showed the opposite pattern. Interestingly, in the majority of the cultures, the girls were socialized to be more sexually restrained than the boys—that is, the parents tried to teach their daughters to delay having sexual intercourse, whereas the boys were encouraged to have sexual intercourse (Low, 1989). In summary, the cross-cultural evidence tells us that patterns of socialization found in the United States are not unique.

One potential difficulty, however, pertains to the direction of effects—whether parents are socializing children in sex-linked ways or whether children are channeling their parents' behavior to correspond to their existing sex-linked preferences (e.g., Scarr & McCartney, 1983). Perhaps the interests of the children drive the parents' behavior, rather than the other way around. Parents may start out by giving a variety of toys to their children; however, if boys show no interest in dolls and girls show no interest in trucks, then over time parents may stop purchasing masculine toys for their daughters and feminine toys for their sons. The simple theory that the causal arrow runs one way—from parents to children—is at least open to question.

Another problem for traditional theories of socialization is that they provide no account of the origins of differential parental socialization practices. Why do parents want their boys and girls to grow up differently? Are these sex-linked socialization practices limited to America and other Western cultures, or are they seen universally? Ideally, a comprehensive theory of the origins of sex differences should be able to account for the origins of sex-linked socialization practices. In sum, parents undoubtedly treat boys and girls differently, supporting the theory of sex-linked socialization of personality, but the origins of these practices currently remain a mystery.

A theory closely related to traditional socialization theories is **social role theory** (Eagly, 1987; Eagly & Wood, 1999). According to social role theory, sex differences originate because men and women are distributed differently into different occupational and family roles. Men, for example, are expected to assume the breadwinning role. Women are expected to assume the homemaker role. Over time, children presumably learn the behaviors that are linked to these roles. Girls learn to be nurturing and emotionally supportive because these qualities are linked with the maternal role. Boys learn to be tough and aggressive because these are qualities expected of the breadwinner role.

Like more traditional socialization theories, there is some evidence supporting social role theory (Eagly, 1987, 1995). Men and women in America have assumed different occupation and family roles, with women found more often in domestic and child-caring roles, men more often in occupational roles. Another line of evidence supporting social role theory used an event-sampling procedure to explore how men's and women's behavior varied as a function of the social role to which they were assigned—a supervisor role, a co-worker role, or the role of someone being supervised by someone else. Social role assignment had a large impact on the dominant behaviors that were expressed. The men and women assigned to the supervisor role displayed significantly more dominance, whereas those assigned the supervisee role displayed significantly more submissiveness (Moskowitz, Suh, & Desaulniers, 1994). These findings are especially important in that the design of the study was within-subject. That is, when the roles were reversed, the people who formerly displayed dominance displayed submissiveness when they were put in a supervisee role, whereas the people who formerly were submissive became more dominant when they were assigned to the supervisor role.

Like socialization theory, however, social role theory fails to provide an account of the origins of sex-linked roles. Who assigns the different roles? Why should men and women passively accept the roles they are assigned? Why don't children follow the role of sitting quietly on airplanes or eating their spinach? Why do women assume domestic roles more than men? Are these roles found in all cultures?

Social role theory, however, is becoming increasingly testable, as family and occupational roles change. Women are assuming breadwinning roles more often than in the past, and men are assuming greater responsibility for domestic duties. With these changes, if social role theory is correct, sex differences should diminish as well. In other words, researchers 20 years from now should find smaller sex differences in assertiveness and tender-mindedness than they do today. If, on the other hand, sex differences persist, despite increased equality in role assignment, this will constitute empirical evidence against social role theory.

Hormonal Theories

Hormonal theories of sex differences argue that men and women differ not because of the external social environment but, rather, because the sexes have different underlying hormones. It is these physiological differences, not differential social treatment, that causes boys and girls to diverge over development. Thus, some studies have sought to identify links between hormones such as testosterone (present in greater amounts in men) and sex-linked behavior.

There is some evidence that hormonal influences on sex differences begin in utero. The hormonal bath that the developing fetus is exposed to, for example, might affect both the organization of the brain and consequently the gendered interests and activities of the individual. Some of the best evidence for this comes from a condition called congenital adrenal hyperplasia (CAH), in which the female fetus has an overactive adrenal gland. This results in the female being hormonally masculinized. Young girls with CAH show a marked preference for "male" toys, such as Lincoln logs and trucks (Berenbaum & Snyder, 1995). As adults, CAH females show superiority in traditionally masculine cognitive skills, such as spatial rotation ability and throwing accuracy, as well as preferring traditionally masculine occupations (Kimura, 2002). These findings suggest that fetal exposure to hormones can have lasting effects on gender-linked interests and abilities, although further research is needed in this area.

Men and women do differ in their levels of circulating hormones. Women's level of circulating testosterone typically falls between 200 and 400 picograms per milliliter of blood at the lowest part of the menstrual cycle and between 285 and 440 at the highest part of the menstrual cycle (just prior to ovulation) (Hoyenga & Hoyenga, 1993). Men, in contrast, have circulating testosterone levels ranging from 5,140 to 6,460 picograms per milliliter of blood. Following puberty, there is literally no overlap between the sexes in their levels of circulating testosterone. Men typically show more than 10 times the levels of women.

These sex differences in circulating testosterone have been linked with some of the traditional sex differences found in behavior, such as aggression, dominance, and career choice. In women, for example, high levels of testosterone are linked with pursuing a more masculine career and having greater success within the chosen career (Hoyenga & Hoyenga, 1993). In lesbian women, testosterone has been associated with erotic role identification, with more "masculine" lesbian partners having higher levels of testosterone than more "feminine" partners (Singh et al., 1999). Higher testosterone levels are associated with greater dominance and aggressiveness in both sexes. For example, in one study, female prison inmates who had more frequent disciplinary infractions also had higher testosterone (Dabbs & Hargrove, 1997). And Dabbs and colleagues (Dabbs, Hargrove, & Heusel, 1996) found that members of college fraternities who were more rambunctious tended to have higher average levels of testosterone than those in fraternities who were more well-behaved.

Testosterone is associated with dominance and aggressiveness, as well as with the massive buildup of muscular tissue. Here U.S. Olympic weightlifter Tim McRae rejoices after setting a new U.S. record in the snatch of 145 Kg, a feat no woman in his weight class is likely to ever match. Olympic athletes are tested to make sure their testosterone levels are within normal ranges for their sex.

Sexual desire has also been linked to levels of circulating testosterone. Women's testosterone levels peak just prior to ovulation. Interestingly, women report a peak in their sexual desire at precisely the same time. At this peak, women report more female-initiated sexual intercourse and more desire for sexual intercourse (Sherwin, 1988). Men with relatively high testosterone levels also report an increased level of sexual motivation (Dabbs & Dabbs, 2000). And weekly and seasonal changes in testosterone are correlated with parallel changes in sexual motivation (Hoyenga & Hoyenga, 1993).

These findings do not prove that the differences between men and women in sexuality, dominance, aggression, and career choices result from differences between the sexes in testosterone levels.

Correlation does not mean causation. Indeed, there is some evidence in nonhuman primates that rises in testosterone levels *follow* rises in status and dominance within the group, rather than lead to them (Sapolsky, 1987). Furthermore, sexual arousal itself can result in an increase in testosterone level (Hoyenga & Hoyenga, 1993). A study on sports fans found that those whose team had just won an event had higher levels of testosterone than those fans whose team had just lost (Bernhardt et al., 1998). These results suggest that the link between hormones and behavior is bidirectional. Higher testosterone may result from, as well as cause, behavior changes.

An additional limitation of hormonal theories of sex differences in personality is one shared with socialization theories—namely, neither of these theories identifies the *origins* of the differences. Precisely why do men and women differ so dramatically in their levels of circulating testosterone? Is this merely an incidental effect of being male versus being female? Or is there a systematic process that causes men and women to differ in testosterone precisely because testosterone differences lead to behavioral differences in dominance and sexuality? One theoretical perspective that argues for this possibility is evolutionary psychology.

Evolutionary Psychology Theory

According to the evolutionary psychology perspective (recall Chapter 8), men and women differ only in some domains of personality and show large similarities in most domains. In particular, the sexes are predicted to be essentially the same in all the domains in which the sexes have faced the same *adaptive problems* over human evolutionary history. Similarly, the sexes are predicted to differ only in the narrow domains in which men and women have confronted different adaptive challenges over human evolutionary history (Buss, 2004).

Adaptive problems are problems that need to be solved in order for an individual to survive and reproduce. For example, both sexes have similar taste preferences for sugar, salt, fat, and protein. That's why fast-food restaurants are so popular—they package food with concentrations of fat and sugar that both men and women desire. Food preferences reflect a solution to an important adaptive problem—getting enough calories and nutrients to survive. We prefer sweet and fatty foods because they are high in calories; in the past, finding such foods was key to an individual's survival.

In the domains of mating and sexuality, according to evolutionary psychologists, men and women have confronted somewhat different adaptive problems (Buss, 1995b). In order to reproduce, women must carry and gestate an embryo for nine months. Men, in contrast, can reproduce through a single act of sex. As a consequence, women have faced the adaptive problem of securing resources to carry them through harsh winters or droughts, when resources might be scarce and a woman's mobility might be restricted by the burden of pregnancy. The costs of making a poor choice of a mate, according to this logic, would have been more damaging to women than to men. Because of the heavy investment women require for reproduction, they are theorized to have evolved exacting mate preferences for men who showed signals of the ability and willingness to invest in them and their children.

This line of reasoning predicts that men will be more sexually wanton and more aggressive with other men about pursuing opportunities for sexual access to women. Because of women's heavy investment, they become the extraordinarily valuable reproductive resource over which men compete. Women, on the other hand, are predicted to be more selective about sex partners—being more discerning about who they are willing to have sex with. A woman who had made a hasty or poor mate choice in the past would have been faced with the difficulties of bearing and raising a child without the help of an investing man. A strategy of casual sex, in short, was more reproductively beneficial to ancestral men than to ancestral women.

Some of the empirical evidence for sex differences indeed corresponds to these predictions. Men clearly have a greater desire for sexual variety than women do (Buss, 2000a; Buss & Schmitt, 1993; Symons, 1979). Men desire a larger number of sex partners, seek sex after a shorter time period has elapsed in knowing a potential partner, and have more fantasies about casual sex than do women. Furthermore, men tend to take more risks to secure the resources and status that women find desirable in marriage partners (e.g., Byrnes, Miller, & Schafer, 1999). Thus, the findings that men are more aggressive, more willing to take physical risks, and more interested in casual sex are precisely the findings predicted by evolutionary psychology.

Despite this support, evolutionary psychology theory, like the other theoretical perspectives, leaves unanswered questions. What accounts for individual differences within each sex? Why are some women keenly interested in casual sex? Why are some men meek, dependent, and nurturing, whereas others are callous and aggressive? Some of these questions are beginning to be answered. It turns out, for example, that some women benefit greatly from pursuing a short-term sexual strategy, which can result in obtaining more and better resources, switching to a mate who is better than her regular mate, and possibly securing better genes for her offspring (Buss, 2003; Gangestad & Cousins, in press). Ultimately, a comprehensive theory of sex differences must account for these differences within each sex, as well as the average differences between the sexes.

An Integrated Theoretical Perspective

The theoretical accounts we have examined seem very different, but they are not necessarily incompatible. Indeed, to some extent, they operate at different levels of analysis. Evolutionary psychology suggests *why* the sexes differ, but it does not specify *how* they became different. Hormonal and socialization theories specify *how* the sexes became different but do not specify *why* the sexes are different.

An integrated theory of sex differences would take all of these levels of analysis into account, since they are clearly compatible with each other. Parents, for example, clearly have an interest in socializing boys and girls differently, and these socialization differences are, to some degree, universal (Low, 1989). Furthermore, there is a substantial body of evidence suggesting that both men and women change their behavior as a function of the roles they are assigned. Both sexes become more dominant when in supervisory roles; both become more submissive when being supervised. Socialization and social roles, in short, have to be central to any integrated theory of sex differences.

Men and women clearly differ in circulating testosterone levels, and these differences are linked with differences in sexuality, aggression, dominance, and career interests (Hoyenga & Hoyenga, 1993). Nonetheless, we cannot ignore the causal possibility, for which there is some evidence, that being in a dominant position actually causes testosterone to rise. Thus, social roles and hormones may be closely linked, and these links may be necessary for an integrated theory of sex differences.

These proximate paths—socialization and hormones—might provide the answers for *how* the sexes differ, whereas evolutionary psychology provides the answers for *why* the sexes differ. Are there evolutionary reasons that parents encourage greater aggressiveness and dominance in boys but more nurturance in girls? Are there evolutionary reasons for surges in testosterone when a person ascends a dominance hierarchy? At this point in the history of the science of sex differences, there are no answers to these questions. Nonetheless, it's a good bet that all three levels of analysis—current social factors, circulating hormones, and evolutionary processes—are needed for a complete understanding of gender and personality.

SUMMARY AND EVALUATION

The study of sex, gender, and personality has provoked heated debated over the past several decades. Perhaps in no other area of personality psychology do politics and values get intermingled with science. Some researchers, called minimalists, emphasize the great similarities between the sexes, pointing out that the effect size differences are small and the distributions overlapping. Other researchers, called maximalists, emphasize that sex differences are real and replicable and stress the effect size differences rather than the overlap of the distributions.

When we take a step back from these arguments, it is possible to gain a more accurate understanding of sex, gender, and personality. The past two decades have witnessed an explosion of research on sex differences, along with the development of meta-analytic statistical procedures, which allow for firm conclusions grounded in empirical data.

First, some sex differences are real and not artifacts of particular investigators or methods. There is some evidence that sex differences have remained relatively constant over generations and across cultures. Nonetheless, the magnitudes of sex differences vary tremendously. When questions about sex differences are posed, therefore, we must always ask the question "In what domains?"

The domains that show large and small sex differences are now fairly clear. Men score consistently higher on the personality attributes of assertiveness, aggressiveness (especially physical aggressiveness), and casual sexuality. Women consistently score higher on measures of anxiety, trust, and tender-mindedness (nurturance). Women are more likely than men to experience both positive emotions (e.g., affection, joy) and negative emotions (e.g., fear, sadness), although the magnitude of these differences is not large. Men are more likely to be sexually aggressive, trying to force women to have sex, although these findings appear to be limited to a subset of men—those who are narcissistic, lack empathy, and show hostile masculinity. Although no sex differences are reported in depression rates prior to puberty, at around age 13 women tend to show higher rates of depression than do men. This sex difference has been tied to theories of suggesting that women ruminate more than men and theories linked to the importance of physical appearance in the domain of mate competition. Men tend to score toward the things end of the people–things dimension, whereas women tend to score more toward the people end. Within each of these domains, however, there is overlap. Some women are more assertive, aggressive, and things-oriented than the majority of men. Some men are more anxious, tender-minded, and people-oriented than the majority of women.

In the 1970s, much attention was focused on the concept of androgyny. However, it became clear as more empirical evidence was gathered that masculinity and femininity were not independent, as the androgyny researchers had asserted. Those who score high on masculinity, or instrumentality, tend to score low on femininity, or expressiveness, and vice versa. Furthermore, many of the original androgyny researchers now believe that these dimensions capture the essence of sex differences. Men are more instrumental. Women are more expressive.

Another important topic during the past two decades has been that of gender stereotypes, or beliefs that people hold about each sex, regardless of their accuracy. Cross-cultural research has revealed some apparent universality of gender stereotypes. In all cultures, men are believed to be more aggressive, autonomous, dominant, achievement-oriented, and exhibitionistic, and women are believed to be more affiliative, deferent, nurturing, and self-abasing. These stereotypes about the sexes correspond in many ways to the actual sex differences that have been discovered. People also hold stereotypes about the subtypes within each sex. Men are viewed as playboys, career men, or losers. Women are viewed as feminists, housewives, or sex bombs.

Traditional theories of sex differences have emphasized social factors—socialization by parents, observational learning from social models, and social roles. There is clearly support for the importance of the social environment. Cross-cultural studies have revealed that boys are universally socialized more than girls to be achievement strivers, and girls are universally socialized to be more restrained than boys, especially in the sexual domain.

More recently, studies of hormones such as testosterone suggest that social factors do not tell the whole story. Testosterone, for example, has been implicated in the personality factors of dominance, aggression, and sexuality. Because men and women differ substantially in their levels of circulating testosterone, it is possible that some of the personality differences are caused by hormonal differences.

According to evolutionary psychologists, men and women differ only in domains in which the sexes have faced different adaptive problems over human evolutionary history. In all other domains, the sexes are the same or highly similar. Aggression and orientation toward casual sex are two domains in which the sexes should differ, according to this theory, and these predictions are empirically supported. What is needed is an integrative theory of sex, gender, and personality that takes into account all of these factors—social factors, physiological factors, and evolutionary factors.

KEY TERMS

Sex Differences 523
Gender 524
Gender Stereotypes 524
Effect Size 526
Minimalist 527
Maximalist 527
Inhibitory Control 528
Perceptual Sensitivity 529
Surgency 529
Negative Affectivity 529
Trust 530
Tender-Mindedness 530
Global Self-Esteem 534
People–Things Dimension 535
Rumination 537
Masculinity 538
Femininity 538
Androgynous 538
Instrumentality 541
Expressiveness 541
Gender Schemata 541
Social Categories 542
Socialization Theory 544
Social Learning Theory 545
Social Role Theory 546
Hormonal Theories 546
Adaptive Problems 548

Culture and Personality

17

17

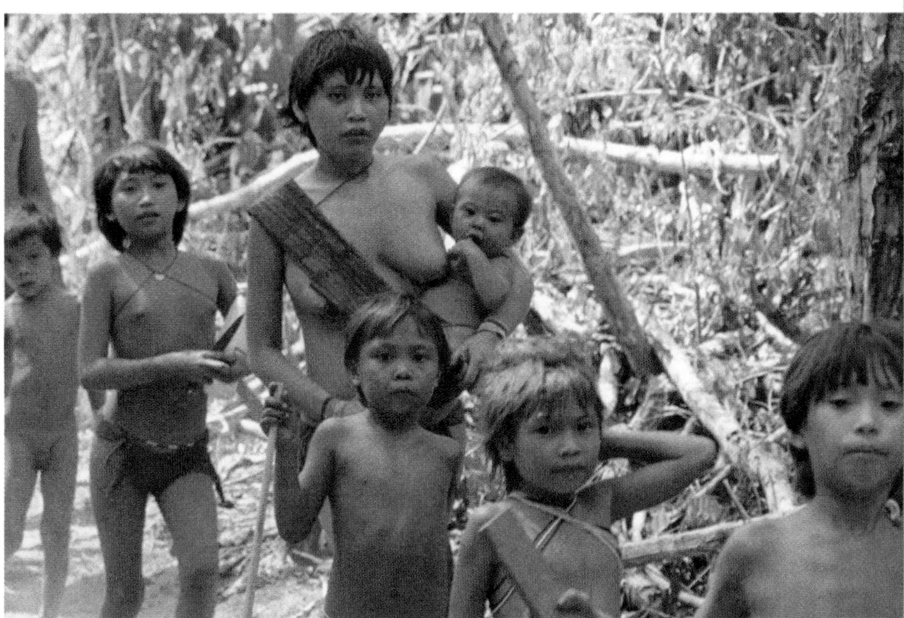

The Yanomamö Indian tribes are among the last truly traditional societies on earth, living a hunter-gatherer existence in the isolated jungles of Venezuela.

The Yanomamö Indians of Venezuela set up temporary shelters, from which they forage for food and hunt for game. When these shelters become depleted of food, they push on and settle elsewhere. On one particular day, the men gather at early dawn, preparing to raid a neighboring village. The group is tense. The men in the raiding party risk injury, and a fearful man might turn back, excusing himself from the raid by telling the others that he has a thorn in his foot. Men who do this too often, though, risk damaging their reputations. To a Yanomamö, few things can damage a reputation more than acts of cowardice (Chagnon, 1983).

But not all Yanomamö men are the same. There are at least two discernible groups that differ profoundly in personality. The lowland Yanomamö men are highly aggressive. They do not hesitate to hit their wives with sticks for "infractions" as minor as serving tea too slowly. They often challenge other men to club fights or ax fights. And they sometimes declare war on neighboring villages, attempting to kill the enemy men and capture their wives. These Yanomamö men shave the tops of their heads to reveal proudly the scars from club fights, sometimes painting the scars red to display them as symbols of courage and endurance. Indeed, one is not regarded as a true man until one has killed another man—acquiring the honor of being called an *unokai*. The men who are unokai have the most wives (Chagnon, 1988).

In the highlands reside a different group of Yanomamö. These people are more peaceful and dislike fighting. The high levels of agreeableness can be seen on their faces. These Yanomamö do not raid neighboring villages, do not engage in ax fights, and rarely engage in club fights. They stress the virtues of cooperation. Unfortunately, though, food resources are more plentiful in the lowlands, where the aggressive Yanomamö dominate.

How can we understand cultural differences in personality between the highland and lowland Yanomamö? Did those who were temperamentally more disposed to aggression drive those who were more agreeable up to the highlands and away from the food resources? Or did the two groups start out the same, and only subsequently did different cultural values take hold in one group, different from those that took hold in the other? These questions form the subject matter of this chapter. What is the effect of culture on personality? What is the effect of personality on culture? And, more generally, how can we understand patterns of cultural variation amid patterns of human universals?

There are several important reasons that personality psychologists explore personality across cultures (Church, 2000; Paunonen & Ashton, 1998). One reason is to discover whether concepts of personality in one culture, such as American culture, are also applicable in other cultures. A second reason is to find out whether cultures differ, on average, in the levels of particular personality traits. Are Japanese, for example, really more agreeable than Americans, or is this merely a stereotype? A third reason is to discover whether the factor structure of personality traits varies across cultures or is universal. Will the five-factor model of personality discovered in American samples, for example, be replicated in Holland, Germany, and the Philippines? A fourth reason is to discover whether certain features of personality are universal, corresponding to the human nature level of personality analysis (see Chapter 1).

In this chapter, we will explore which features of personality are common to everyone but differentially elicited only in some cultures; which features of personality are transmitted so that they become characteristic of some local groups but not others; and which features of personality are common to everyone in all cultures. We will start by examining just how different cultures can be.

Cultural Violations: An Illustration

Consider the following events:

1. One of your family members eats beef regularly. (your beef-eating family member)
2. A young married woman goes alone to see a movie without informing her husband. When she returns home, her husband says, "If you do it again, I will beat you black and blue." She does it again; he beats her black and blue. (the wife-beating husband)
3. A poor man goes to the hospital after being seriously hurt in an accident. The hospital refuses to treat him because he cannot afford to pay. (the refusing hospital)

Now examine each event and decide whether you think the behavior on the part of the person or institution in parentheses is wrong. If so, is it a serious violation, a minor offense, or not a violation at all?

If you are a Brahman Hindu, you are likely to believe that the first event—eating beef—is a serious violation but that the second event—the husband beating the wife for disobeying him—is not (Shweder, Mahapatra, & Miller, 1990). If you are an American, however, the odds are that your views are the reverse—unless you are a vegetarian, you see nothing wrong with eating beef, but you view it as very wrong for the husband to beat his wife. Both Brahman Hindus and Americans, however, agree that the hospital that denies treatment to the badly injured man is committing a serious violation.

This example highlights a fascinating question for personality psychologists. Some aspects of personality (including attitudes, values, and self-concepts) are highly variable across cultures. But other aspects of personality are universal—features that are shared by people everywhere. The central questions addressed by this chapter are "What are the ways in which people from different cultures differ in personality and what are the ways in which people from all cultures are the same?"

What Is Cultural Personality Psychology?

Before proceeding further, it is useful to briefly define culture. Let's start with an observation: "Humans everywhere show striking patterns of local within-group similarity in their behavior and thought, accompanied by profound intergroup differences" (Tooby & Cosmides, 1992, p. 6). These local within-group similarities and between-group differences can be of any sort—physical, psychological, behavioral, or attitudinal. These phenomena are often referred to as **cultural variations.**

Consider the example of eating beef. Beef eating is common among Americans but is rare and viewed with abhorrence among Hindus. Among Hindus, who form the majority religious group in India, the values and behaviors are shared for the most part. But they differ from the widely shared American attitudes toward beef eating. This difference—a local within-group similarity and between-group difference—is an example of a cultural variation.

Attaching the label of "culture" or "cultural variation" to phenomena such as these is best treated as a description, not an explanation. Labeling attitudes toward beef eating as "cultural" certainly describes the phenomenon. It tells us that we are dealing with a within-group similarity and a between-group difference. But it doesn't explain what has *caused* the cultural difference or *why* the groups differ. **Cultural personality psychology** generally has three key goals: (1) to discover the principles underlying the cultural diversity; (2) to discover how human psychology shapes culture; and (3) to discover how cultural understandings, in turn, shape our psychology (Fiske et al., 1997).

Three Major Approaches to Culture

Certain traits might be common to all people, but other traits display remarkable variation. Cultural variants are the personality attributes that vary from group to group. Psychologists have developed three major approaches to explaining and exploring personality across cultures: evoked culture, transmitted culture, and cultural universals.

Evoked Culture

Evoked culture is defined as cultural differences created by differing environmental conditions activating a predictable set of responses. Consider the physical examples of skin calluses and sweat. There are undoubtedly cultural differences in the thickness and distribution of calluses and in the amount people sweat. The traditional !Kung Bushmen of Botswana, for example, tend to have thicker calluses on their feet than most Americans, since they walk around without shoes. These differences can be thought of as aspects of evoked culture—different environments have different effects on people's callus-producing mechanisms and on sweat glands. People who live near the equator, for example, are exposed to more intense heat than those who live in more northern climates, such as Canada. The observation that residents of Zaire sweat more than residents of Canada is properly explained as an environmentally evoked difference that operates on sweat glands, which all humans possess.

Note that two ingredients are necessary to explain cultural variations: (1) a universal underlying mechanism (in this case, sweat glands possessed by all people), and (2) environmental differences in the degree to which the underlying mechanism is activated (in this case, differences in ambient temperature). Neither ingredient alone is adequate for a complete explanation.

The same explanatory logic applies to other environmentally triggered phenomena shared by members of one group but not by other groups. Drought, plentiful game, and poisonous snakes are all environmental events that affect some groups more than others. These events trigger the operation of mechanisms in some groups that lie dormant in others. In the next section, we will discuss several psychological examples of evoked culture and show how they may result in differences in personality traits among groups.

Evoked Cooperation

Whether someone is cooperative or selfish is a central part of personality, but these proclivities may differ from culture to culture. A concrete example of evoked culture is the patterns of cooperative food sharing found among different bands of hunter-gatherer tribes (Cosmides & Tooby, 1992). Different classes of food have different variances in their distribution. High-variance foods differ greatly in their availability from day to day. For example, among the Ache tribe of Paraguay, meat from hunting is a high-variance resource. On any given day, the probability that a hunter will come back with meat is only 60 percent. On any particular day, therefore, one hunter will be successful, whereas another hunter will come back empty-handed. Gathered food, on the other hand, is a lower-variance food resource. The yield from gathering depends more on the skill and effort a person expends than on luck. Under **high-variance conditions,** there are tremendous benefits to sharing. You share your meat today with an unlucky hunter, and next week he or she will share meat with you. The benefits of engaging in cooperative food sharing increase under conditions of high variance. In this

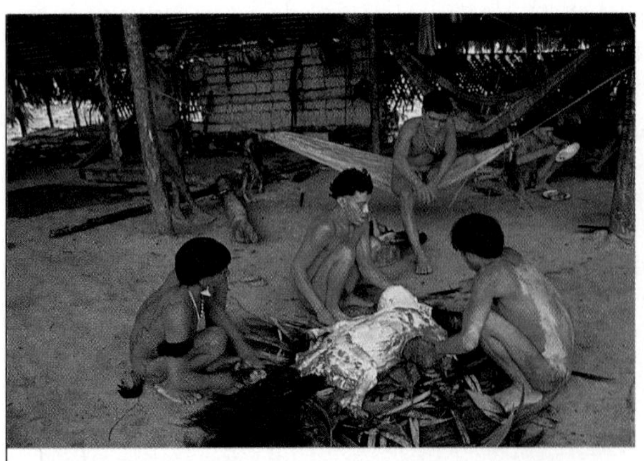

Yanomamö Indians butchering a giant anteater. In their culture, the successful hunter shares his catch with the whole tribe. The benefits of such cooperative food sharing are high in their environment (Chagnon, 1983).

example, the benefits of sharing are also increased by the fact that a large game animal contains more meat than one person, or even one family, can consume. Thus, the meat would spoil unless it were shared with others.

Kaplan and Hill (1985) found that, indeed, within the Ache tribe, meat is communally shared. Hunters deposit their kill with a "distributor," a person who allocates portions to various families, based on family size. In the same tribe, however, gathered food is not shared outside of the family. In short, cooperative sharing seems to be evoked by the environmental condition of high food variance.

Halfway around the world, in the Kalahari Desert, Cashden (1980) found that some San groups are more egalitarian than others. The degree of **egalitarianism** is closely correlated with the variance in food supply. The !Kung San's food supply is highly variable, and they share food and express egalitarian beliefs. To be called a "stinge" (stingy) is one of the worst insults, and the group imposes strong social sanctions for stinginess and gives social approval for food sharing. Among the Gana San, in contrast, food variance is low, and they show great economic inequality. The Gana San tend to hoard their food and rarely share it outside their extended families.

Environmental conditions can activate some behaviors, such as cooperation and sharing. Everyone has the capacity to share and cooperate, but cultural differences in the degree to which groups do share and cooperate depend, to some extent, on the external environmental conditions, such as variance in the food supply.

Early Experience and Evoked Mating Strategies

Another example of evoked culture comes from the work of Jay Belsky and his colleagues (Belsky, 2000; Belsky, Steinberg, & Draper, 1991). They argue that harsh, rejecting, and inconsistent child-rearing practices, erratically provided resources, and marital discord foster in children a personality of impulsivity and a mating strategy marked by early reproduction. In contrast, sensitive, supportive, and responsive child-rearing, combined with reliable resources and spousal harmony, foster in children a personality of conscientiousness and a mating strategy of commitment marked by delayed reproduction and stable marriage. Children in uncertain and unpredictable environments, in short, seem to learn that they cannot rely on a single mate and, so, opt for a sexual life that starts early and inclines them to seek immediate gratification from multiple mates. In contrast, children growing up in stable homes with parents who predictably invest in their welfare opt for a strategy of long-term mating because they expect to attract a stable, high-investing mate. The evidence from children of divorced homes supports this theory. Such children tend to be more impulsive, tend to reach puberty earlier, engage in sexual intercourse earlier, and have more sex partners than do their peers from intact homes.

The sensitivity of personality and mating strategies to early experiences may help explain the differences in the value placed on chastity across cultures. In China, for example, marriages are lasting, divorce is rare, and parents invest heavily in their children over extended periods. In Sweden, many children are born out of wedlock, divorce is common, and fewer fathers invest consistently over time. These cultural experiences may evoke in the two groups different mating strategies, with the Swedes more than the Chinese tending toward short-term mating and more frequent partner switching (Buss, 2003).

Although more evidence is needed to confirm this theory, this example illustrates how a consistent pattern of individual differences can be evoked in different cultures, producing a local pattern of within-group similarity and between-group differences. All humans presumably have within their mating menu a strategy of short-term mating, marked by frequent partner switching, and a strategy of long-term mating, marked by enduring commitment and love (Buss, 2003). These mating strategies may be differentially evoked in different cultures, resulting in enduring cultural differences in mating strategies. They exemplify the idea that an important component of human personality—the mating strategy pursued—may hinge on the particular cultural environment in which one is raised.

Honors, Insults, and Evoked Aggression

Why are people in some cultures prone to resort to aggression at the slightest provocation, whereas people in other cultures tend to resort to aggression only reluctantly as a last resort? Why do people in some cultures kill one another at relatively high rates, whereas people in other cultures kill one another at relatively low rates? Nisbett (1993) has proposed a theory to account for these cultural differences—a theory based on the notion of evoked culture.

Nisbett has proposed that the economic means of subsistence of a culture affects the degree to which the group develops what he calls a **culture of honor.** In cultures of honor, insults are viewed as highly offensive public challenges, which must be met with direct confrontation and physical aggression. The theory is that differences in the degree to which honor becomes a central part of the culture rests ultimately with economics—specifically, the manner in which food is obtained. In herding economies, one's entire stock could be lost suddenly to thieves. Cultivating a reputation as willing to respond with violent force—for example, by displaying physical aggression when publicly insulted—presumably deters thieves and others who might steal one's property. In more settled agricultural communities, the cultivation of an aggressive reputation is less important, since one's means of subsistence cannot be rapidly undermined.

Nisbett (1993) tested his theory by using homicide statistics from different regions within the United States and experiments in which subjects from the northern and southern United States were insulted. Interestingly, the southerners (historically using animal herding for subsistence) did not endorse more positive attitudes toward the use of violence in general, compared with the northerners (historically using farming or agriculture for subsistence). The southerners, however, were indeed more likely to endorse violence for the purposes of protection and in response to insults. Furthermore, the homicide rates in the South were far higher than those in the North, particularly for murders triggered by efforts to defend one's reputation.

Nisbett found a similar pattern in the laboratory, where the northern and southern participants were insulted by an experimenter. In this study, the experimenter intentionally bumped into the participants and then called them "an asshole." Subsequently, the participants were asked to complete a series of incomplete word stems, such as "h________." The southerners who had been insulted wrote down more aggressive words, such as *hate*, than did the northerners who had been insulted, suggesting that the insults had evoked in the southerners a higher level of aggression. In other studies, when southerners and northerners were threatened in a laboratory setting, southerners had higher elevations of testosterone and responded with greater aggression (Nisbett & Cohen, 1996).

Although more research is needed to confirm the hypothesis that these cultural differences in aggression and homicide ultimately stem from differences in the economic means of subsistence, the research done thus far provides a good illustration of evoked culture. Presumably, all humans have the capacity to develop a high sensitivity to public insults and a capacity to respond with violence. These capacities are evoked in certain cultures, however, and presumably lie dormant in others.

The concept of evoked culture provides one model for understanding and explaining cultural variations in personality traits, such as cooperativeness or aggression. It rests on the assumption that all humans have the same potentials or capabilities. The aspects of these potentials that get evoked depend on features of the social or physical environment. Evoked culture is one way to think about cultural variations; another way is transmitted culture.

Transmitted Culture

Transmitted culture consists of ideas, values, attitudes, and beliefs that exist originally in at least one person's mind that are transmitted to other people's minds through their interaction with the original person (Tooby & Cosmides, 1992). The view that it is wrong to eat beef, for example, is an example of transmitted culture. This value presumably originated in the mind of one person, who then transmitted it to others. Over time, the view that eating beef is a serious violation came to characterize Hindus. Although we do not know much about how culture is transmitted or why certain ideas spread but others do not, the discovery of large cultural differences in seemingly arbitrary values provides circumstantial evidence for the existence of transmitted culture. Whereas people in some cultures view the eating of beef as wrong, people in other cultures view the eating of pork as wrong. Others see nothing wrong with eating beef or pork, and still others eat no meat at all.

Cultural Differences in Moral Values

Cultures differ tremendously in their beliefs about what is morally right and wrong. As an example, consider whether you agree or disagree with the following statement: "It is immoral for adults to disobey their parents" (Rozin, 2003, p. 275). If you are a Hindu Indian, the odds are great that you will agree with this statement (80 percent of the Hindu women and 72 percent of the Hindu men). If you are an American, however, the odds are strong that you will disagree (only 13 percent of American women and 19 percent of American men agree). To get a concrete feel for these differences, complete the following exercise.

Exercise

Read each of the following items and decide whether the behavior described is wrong. Use the following four-point scale to indicate how serious the violation is (in parentheses is the person who committed the potential violation).

a: Not a violation
b: A minor offense
c: A somewhat serious offense
d: A very serious offense

___ 1. The day after his father's death, the eldest son had a haircut and ate chicken.
___ 2. One of your family members eats beef regularly.
___ 3. One of your family members eats dog meat regularly.
___ 4. A widow in your community eats fish two or three times a week.

Exercise (*Continued*)

___ 5. Six months after the death of her husband, a widow is wearing jewelry and brightly colored clothes.

___ 6. A woman cooks rice for her husband and his elder brother. Then she eats with them. (the woman)

___ 7. A woman cooks food for her family members and sleeps in the same bed with her husband during her menstrual period. (the woman)

___ 8. A man had a wife who was sterile. He wanted to have two wives. He asked his first wife and she said she did not mind, so he married a second woman and the three of them lived happily in the same house. (the man)

___ 9. A doctor's daughter meets a garbage man, falls in love with him, and decides to marry him. The doctor opposes the marriage and tries to stop it because the man is a garbage man. In spite of the opposition from the father, the girl marries the garbage man. (the daughter)

___ 10. A widow and an unmarried man loved each other. The widow asked him to marry her. (the widow)

___ 11. A brother and sister decide to get married and have children.

___ 12. The day after the birth of his first child, a man entered his temple (church) and prayed to God.

___ 13. A woman is playing cards at home with her friends. Her husband is cooking rice for them. (the husband)

___ 14. At night a wife asked her husband to massage her legs. (the wife)

Researchers interviewed Brahman Indian and American respondents about their reactions to the previous items (Shweder et al., 1990). To illustrate the cultural differences, consider the following responses from a Brahman to questions about the widow who eats fish two or three times a week (adapted from Shweder et al., 1990, p. 168):

Interviewer: Is the widow's behavior wrong?
Brahman: Yes. Widows should not eat fish, meat, onions or garlic, or any "hot" foods. They must restrict their diet to "cool" foods: rice, dhal, ghee, vegetables.
Interviewer: How serious is the violation?
Brahman: A very serious violation. She will suffer greatly if she eats fish.
Interviewer: Is it a sin?
Brahman: Yes. It is a great sin.
Interviewer: What if no one knew this had been done?
Brahman: It is [still] wrong. A widow should spend her time seeking salvation—seeking to be reunited with the soul of her husband. Hot foods will distract her. They will stimulate her sexual appetite. She will lose her sanctity. She will want sex and behave like a whore. . . . She will offend his spirit if she eats fish.

Now consider the responses from an American interviewee (Shweder et al., 1990, p. 168):

Interviewer: Is the widow's behavior wrong?
American: No. She can eat fish if she wants to.

Interviewer: How serious is the violation?
American: It's not a violation.
Interviewer: Is it a sin?
American: No.
Interviewer: What if no one knew this had been done?
American: It is not wrong, in private or public.

Americans and Brahman Indians disagree with one another not just about eating fish but about a host of other activities. The following are a few activities that Brahmans believe are wrong but that Americans believe are not wrong: a wife's eating with the husband's elder brother; eating beef; a wife's requesting a foot massage; addressing one's father by his first name; cutting one's hair and eating chicken after one's father's death; a widow's wearing bright clothes; a husband's cooking for the wife; and a widow's remarrying. In contrast, the following are a few examples of activities that Americans believe to be wrong but that Brahmans believe are not wrong: having unequal inheritance, with more going to males than females; beating a disobedient wife for going to the movies; and caning (beating with a stick) an errant child.

Source: Shweder et al., 1990.

Culturally variable views of morality are apparently transmitted to children early in life. American 5-year-old children, for example, make almost identical judgments about right and wrong as American adults, showing a correlation between the two groups of +.89 (Shweder et al., 1990).

Views of moral behavior—what is right and what is wrong—are presumed to be important psychological principles that guide behavior, and they are central to personality. Cultures clearly differ in their views of what is right and wrong, sometimes in seemingly arbitrary ways. Among the Semang of Malaysia, for example, it is considered sinful to comb one's hair during a thunderstorm, to watch dogs mate, to tease a helpless animal, to kill a sacred wasp, to have sexual intercourse during the daytime, to draw water from a fire-blackened vessel, or to act casually or informally with one's mother-in-law (Murdock, 1980).

There may also be universals in what is considered right and wrong. Both Brahman Indians and Americans, for example, agree about the following wrongs: ignoring an accident victim, breaking a promise, destroying another's picture, kicking a harmless animal, committing brother-sister incest, and stealing flowers (Shweder et al., 1990). Most cultures consider it wrong to kill without cause. Most cultures consider it wrong to commit incest or have sexual relations with a close genetic relative. But even these seeming universals are violated in some cultures. Among certain subcultures, for example, killing is viewed as justified if one has been publicly insulted (Nisbett, 1993). In certain royal dynasties, to take another example, incest between brother and sister was actively encouraged as a way to preserve the family's wealth and power. Statements about universality are always relative in the sense that there are always some cultural or subcultural exceptions.

The key point is that many moral values are specific to particular cultures and are likely to be examples of transmitted culture. They appear to be passed from one generation to the next, not through the genes but through the teachings of parents and

A Closer Look

Reaching across the Great Divide: The Psychology of Cross-Cultural Marriages

What happens when people from different cultures meet and fall in love? We might expect that the more differences between the cultures, the greater the potential difficulties in the marriage. Large cultural differences—such as those in language, religion, race, politics, and class—may create major divides that may separate a cross-cultural couple. There are also sociological and legal differences between cultures. For example, some countries (e.g., Germany) do not legally recognize arranged marriages, whereas in other countries (e.g., India) arranged marriages are still fairly common.

Sociologists Rosemary Breger and Rosanna Hill (1998) present a detailed look at cross-cultural marriages. Throughout the book, the emphasis is on how cultural differences create challenges in marriages. For example, many cultural rituals surround food and eating. In some cultures, men are served first and begin eating before women. A man from a different culture might politely wait and not touch his food until his wife begins to eat. If the wife comes from a culture in which men eat first, she might suspect that her husband is dissatisfied with the meal or that something is wrong because he is not eating before her. A polite social behavior in one culture can thus be seen as a signal of dissatisfaction in another.

There are many such small differences between cultures that pose daily challenges in cross-cultural marriages. For example, there are differences in conversational style, in privacy, in dress, in the use of space, in attention, in what counts as being polite, in role expectations for husbands and wives, in child-rearing beliefs and practices, and even in how a "good" marriage is defined. For example, in some cultures, the extended family becomes a large part of the couple's life, sometimes to the point of expecting to share sleeping space in their bedroom. In some cultures, you don't just marry the person; you marry his or her extended family as well.

According to Larsen & Prizmic-Larsen (1999), one of the largest challenges in cross-cultural marriages results from differences in native languages. They report a case where the wife, who was from Eastern Europe, said to the husband, "You are boring," when her real intent was to ask, "Are you bored?" Good communication is essential to any marriage. However, when one person has to conduct his or her marriage in a foreign language, there exists a minefield of potential misunderstandings between the spouses. Moreover, the presence of a heavy accent can lead to verbal misunderstandings, even when the content of a communication is accurate. Communicating in a foreign language also takes mental effort and, when tired or at times of strong emotion (ranging from anger to ecstasy), one may not be able to communicate very well in a second language.

Relationships that bridge two cultures bring unique challenges, as well as unique opportunities, to the couple.

In exploring the meaning of cross-cultural marriage, Larsen and Prizmic-Larsen (1999) suggest that psychologists consider the positive characteristics and possibilities, as well as the challenges. For example, cross-cultural couples have a wider choice of cultural models when it comes to gender roles, family relations, language use, child-rearing behaviors, and general lifestyle than do those in mono-cultural marriages. Although such choices have a high potential for conflict, they are also a source of diversity within the relationship. The couple can negotiate a new "culture of marriage" for their family by selecting and including the parts of their native cultures that they value and want to keep. Children of cross-cultural marriages, while shouldering their own unique difficulties, can nevertheless choose, and even alternate between, cultural identities.

There are at least two lines of inquiry that interest personality psychologists about cross-cultural marriages. One question concerns who is the most likely to marry outside of his or her own culture. Are some personality variables involved in being attracted to others who are very different from oneself? A second line of inquiry concerns process, what happens in cross-cultural marriages that might make them different from mono-cultural marriages. How do two people, who have more than their share of differences, come to accommodate and adapt to each other? Are there ways that people can emancipate themselves from cultural bonds and more easily function in a cross-cultural relation? How do people maintain their identities and sense of self, even when living in a foreign country and conducting their marriage in a foreign language?

Cross-cultural marriages have existed throughout history. However, the problems facing cross-cultural couples today are changing. In the past, the difficulties were most likely connected with social class differences (e.g., Romeo and Juliet), nonacceptance by one's extended family (e.g., King Edward VIII, who voluntarily abdicated the throne of England in order to marry Wallis Warfield Simpson, a twice-divorced American), religion, or race. Throughout much of the twentieth century, interracial (black-white) marriage was illegal in many U.S. jurisdictions, but today it is widely regarded as a matter of personal choice, and black-white couples are accepted at the highest levels of society.

In many ways, boundaries between cultures are becoming more permeable, especially in the European community. On the other hand, there are many wars and ethnic conflicts based on animosities associated with cultural differences. Those animosities may deter opportunities or even the acceptability of certain cultural combinations in marriage. A good example can be found in the countries of former Yugoslavia, where cross-cultural marriages between, say, Muslims and Serbs or between Serbs and Croats were once common and acceptable. However, the conflicts set in motion in 1991 with the breakup of former Yugoslavia, and continuing in Kosovo, Bosnia, and Montenegro, have resulted in a reversal of social diversity in this area of the world. A new term has even entered the English language: **Balkanization,** meaning social resegregation following a time of peaceful integration and social diversity. Balkanization in various countries around the world may make life difficult for cross-cultural marriages.

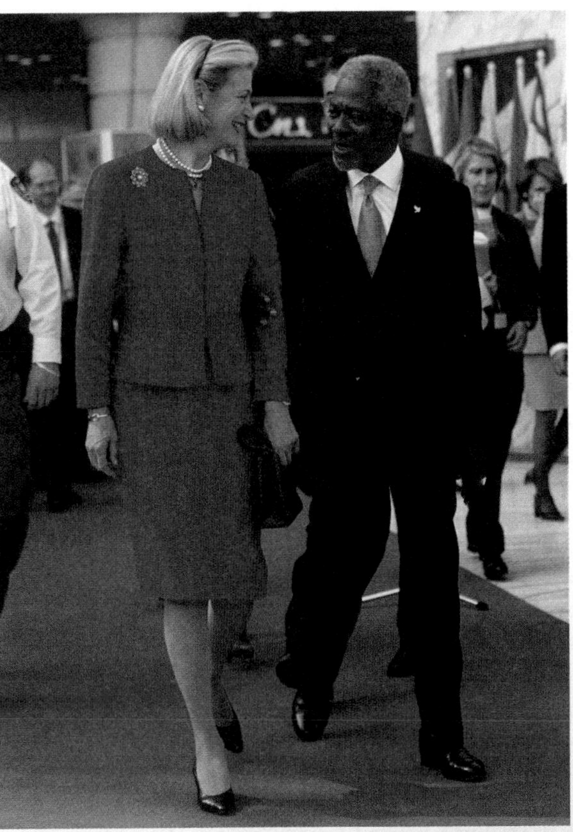

United Nations Secretary General Kofi Annan, born in Ghana, met Swedish attorney Nane Lagergren when they both worked for the U.N. High Commissioner for Refugees. They have been married since 1984.

teachers or through observations of the behavior of others within the culture. Now we turn to another possible example of transmitted culture—the self-concept.

Cultural Differences in Self-Concept

As we discussed in Chapter 14, the ways in which we define ourselves—our self-concepts—are the core components of human personality. These self-concepts influences our behavior. A woman who defines herself as conscientious, for example, may take pains to show up for classes on time, to return all phone calls from friends and family, and to remember to spell check her term paper before final printing. A man who defines himself as agreeable may ensure that the wishes of others are taken into account when deciding where to eat, may give more than his share in gifts to charity, and may wait until all others have feasted at the buffet table before helping himself. Our self-concepts, in short, affect how we present ourselves to others and how we behave in everyday life. Research has shown that self-concepts differ substantially from culture to culture.

Markus and Kitayama (1991, 1994, 1998) propose that each person has two fundamental "cultural tasks," which have to be confronted. The first is communion, or **interdependence.** This cultural task involves how you are affiliated with, attached to, or engaged in the larger group of which you are a member. Interdependence includes your relationships with other members of the group and your embeddedness within the group. The second task—agency, or **independence**—involves how you differentiate yourself from the larger group. Independence includes your unique abilities, your personal internal motives and personality dispositions, and the ways in which you separate yourself from the larger group.

According to Markus and Kitayama, people from different cultures differ profoundly in how they balance these two tasks. Western cultures, such as the United States and Western Europe, according to this theory, are characterized by independence. Independence is elaborated and supported by various cultural institutions and practices. Conversations emphasize individual choices (e.g., "Where do you want to eat tonight?"). The system of salaries puts a premium on individual merit—your salary is specifically pegged to *your* performance.

In contrast, many non-Western cultures, such as Japan and China, are characterized by interdependence. These cultures emphasize the fundamental interconnectedness among those within the group. The self is meaningful, according to this view, only with reference to the larger group of which the person is a part. The major cultural tasks in these cultures are to fit in and to promote harmony and group unity. Personal desires are to be constrained, rather than expressed in a selfish manner (e.g., "Where do *we* want to eat tonight?"). Interdependence is fostered by various cultural practices and institutions. Conversational scripts emphasize sympathy, deference, and kindness. Pay is often determined by seniority, rather than by individual performance.

To illustrate the contrasting orientations of independence and interdependence, consider the following descriptions, the first from an American student and the second from a Japanese student, in response to the instruction "describe yourself briefly":

> *I like to live life with a lot of positive energy. I feel like there is so much to do and see and experience. However, I also know the value of relaxation. I love the obscure. I play ultimate Frisbee, juggle, unicycle, and dabble on the recorder and concertina. I have a taste for the unique. I am very friendly and in most situations very self-confident. I'm almost always happy and when I am down, it is usually because of stress. (Markus & Kitayama, 1998, p. 63)*

> *I cannot decide quickly what I should do, and am often swayed by other people's opinions, and I cannot oppose the opinions of people who are supposed to be respected because of age or status. Even if I have displeasure, I compromise myself to the people around me without getting rid of the displeasure. When I cannot make a decision I often do it according to other people's opinions. Also, I am concerned about how other people think about me and often decide on that consideration. I try to have a harmless life. I calm down by being the same as others. (Markus & Kitayama, 1998, p. 64)*

Notice the different themes that run through the self-descriptions of these two individuals. The American student tends to use global and largely context-free trait descriptions, such as *friendly, self-confident,* and *happy.* The Japanese student tends to use self-descriptions that are embedded in a social context, such as responding to elders or those who are higher in status and even using the social group as a method of calming down. These illustrate the themes of independence and interdependence, which characterize the self-concepts of European Americans and Japanese, respectively. The independence theme is characterized by a self-view as autonomous, stable, coherent, and free from the influences of others. The interdependence theme is characterized by a self-view as connected, interpersonally flexible, and committed to being bound to others (Markus & Kitayama, 1998).

This fundamental distinction between independence and interdependence is similar to a distinction that many other cultural psychologists make. Triandis (1989, 1995), for example, coined the terms **individualism** (a sense of self as autonomous and independent, with priority given to personal goals) and **collectivism** (a sense of self as more connected to groups and interdependent, with priority given to group goals) to describe this distinction. According to Triandis (2001), in *individualist* societies, people tend to act independently of their groups, giving priority to personal goals rather than to group goals. They act according to their own attitudes and desires, rather than succumbing to the norms and attitudes of their in-group. In collectivist societies, in contrast, people are interdependent with others in the group, giving priority to the goals of their in-groups. People in collectivist societies tend to be especially concerned about social relationships. Finally, in collectivist societies, people tend to be more self-effacing, less likely to boast about their own personal accomplishments. As you can see, there is a lot of overlap between the independent-interdependent conception of cultural differences advanced by Markus and Kitayama and the individualistic-collectivistic conception of cultural differences advanced by Triandis.

Is there empirical evidence that the way in which we define ourselves—something so fundamental to personality—depends on the culture in which we reside? Using the Twenty Statements Test, researchers have discovered that North American participants tend to describe themselves using abstract internal characteristics, such as *smart, stable, dependable,* and *open-minded* (Rhee et al., 1995). Chinese participants, in contrast, more often describe themselves using social roles, such as "I am a daughter" or "I am Jane's friend" (Ip & Bond, 1995). Americans rarely describe themselves using social roles. These results support the suggestion that there are cultural differences in self-concept. Americans are more likely to have an independent, individualistic view of themselves than are Chinese, who tend to have an interdependent, collectivist view of themselves.

Another study administered the Twenty Statements Test to samples of Asians in Seoul, Korea; to Asian Americans in New York City; and to European Americans in New York City (Rhee et al., 1995). The study was designed to examine cultural differences in self-concept, but with an interesting twist: do Asians living in New York who self-identify as Asian differ in self-concept from Asians living in the same place who do not self-identify as Asian? In other words, do some people shift their self-concepts and adopt self-concepts similar to those of the adopted culture? The process of adapting to the ways of life in one's new culture is called **acculturation.**

The results were conclusive. The Asian Americans living in New York who did not self-identify as Asian described themselves using highly abstract and autonomous self-statements, similar to the responses of European Americans residing in New York. Interestingly, these Asian Americans used even more trait terms in their self-descriptions

A refugee family from Somalia experiences the Arizona State Fair. After entering a new culture, acculturation is the process of adopting the ways of life and beliefs common in that culture.

(45 percent) than did the European Americans (35 percent). Markus, Kitayama, and Heiman (1996) suggest that these "unidentified" Asian Americans may have been trying to achieve a culturally appropriate self-concept but overshot the mark.

In contrast, in the study, the New York–dwelling Asians who identified themselves as Asian used more socially embedded self-descriptions, much as the Chinese respondents did. They often referred to themselves by describing their role status (e.g., student) and their family status (e.g., son). Moreover, they were more likely to qualify their self-concepts with contextual information. In other words, rather than describing themselves as *reliable,* as a European American might, they described themselves as "reliable when I'm at home."

Another study asked Japanese and American college students to complete the Twenty Statements Test in four social contexts: alone, with a friend, in a classroom with other students, and in a professor's office (Cross et al., 1995). The Japanese college students tended to describe themselves in all four conditions using preferences (e.g., "I like frozen yogurt") and context-dependent activities (e.g., "I like to listen to rock music on the weekends"). The American students, as in previous studies, more often used abstract, context-independent trait terms, such as *friendly* and *assertive.* Furthermore, the Japanese students, but not the American students, tended to characterize themselves differently in different contexts. In the professor's office, for example, Japanese students described themselves as "good students," but they did not mention this role in the other three contexts. The American students' responses tended to be more constant across the four testing conditions.

Another study examined the frequency with which Japanese and European American students endorsed a variety of attributes as descriptive of themselves (Markus & Kitayama, 1998). A full 84 percent of the Japanese students described themselves as *ordinary,* whereas only 18 percent of the American students used this self-description. Conversely, 96 percent of the Americans described themselves as *special,* whereas only 55 percent of the Japanese described themselves with this term (see Table 17.1).

Table 17.1 Most Frequently Endorsed Attributes "I am"

European Americans		Japanese	
Attribute	**Percentage of Responses**	**Attribute**	**Percentage of Responses**
Responsible	100%	Happy	94%
Respectful	100	Fun-loving	94
Persistent	100	Relaxed	92
Cooperative	98	Direct	92
Special	96	Assertive	90
Happy	95	Laid-back	86
Unique	95	Calm	86
Reflective	95	Free-spirited	86
Fun-loving	93	Undisciplined	84
Sympathetic	93	Ordinary	84
Hardworking	93		
Ambitious	93		
Reliable	93		
Independent	93		

Source: Markus & Kitayama (1998), p. 79, Table 1.

This theme of standing out and being unique versus fitting in and going along with the group is seen in the folk sayings of American and Japanese cultures. In American culture, people sometimes say, "The squeaky wheel gets the grease," signifying that standing out and asserting oneself as an individual is the way to pursue one's interests. In Japan, it is sometimes said that "the nail that stands out gets pounded down," which suggests that the American social strategy would fail in Japan.

These cultural differences may be linked to the ways in which people process information. Japanese, compared with Americans, tend to explain events **holistically**—with attention to relationships, context, and the links between the focal object and the field as a whole (Nisbett et al., 2001). Americans, in contrast, tend to explain events **analytically**—with the object detached from its context, attributes of objects or people assigned to categories, and a reliance on rules about the categories to explain behavior. When watching animated scenes of fish swimming around, for example, the Japanese made more statements than did Americans about contextual information, linking the fish's behavior to their surroundings (Masuda & Nisbett, 2001). Thus, the cultural differences in the personality attributes of individualism–collectivism or independence–interdependence may be linked to underlying cognitive proclivities in the ways in which individuals *attend to,* and *explain,* events in their world.

In sum, there is empirical support for the claim that people in different cultures have different self-concepts. Presumably, these different self-concepts are transmitted through parents and teachers to children. The finding that Asian Americans who identify themselves as Americans show self-concepts more like those of European Americans than like native Asians suggests that differences in self-concept are transmitted by people in the social environment and do not represent genetic group differences.

Criticisms of the Interdependence–Independence and Collectivist–Individualist Concepts

Several authors have criticized the Markus-Kitayama theory that Western views of self are independent, whereas Asian views of self are interdependent, both on theoretical and evidentiary grounds. Matsumoto (1999) contends that the evidence for the theory comes almost exclusively from North America and East Asia (notably, Japan) and may not generalize to other cultures. Furthermore, there is far more overlap in the self-concepts of people from different cultures than Markus and Kitayama imply. Many individuals in collectivist cultures, for example, do use global traits (e.g., *agreeable, fun-loving*) when describing themselves, and many in individualist cultures use relational concepts (e.g., "I am the daughter of . . .") when describing themselves. The cultural differences may be more a matter of degree.

On theoretical grounds, Church (2000) notes that "attempts to characterize cultures of individuals in terms of such broad cultural dichotomies may be overly simplistic" (p. 688) in the sense that views of the self in all cultures appear to incorporate both independent and interdependent self-construals, and self-concepts in all cultures vary somewhat across social contexts. The differences between Japanese and American participants, in short, may reflect quantitative differences in degree, not qualitative differences of kind.

A recent meta-analysis of dozens of studies suggests even more caution in generalizing about cultural differences in individualism and collectivism (Oyserman, Coon, & Kemmelmeier, 2002a). It found that although European Americans tended to be somewhat more individualistic (valuing independence) and less collectivistic (valuing interdependence) than those from *some* other cultures, the effect sizes proved to be small and qualified by important exceptions. European Americans were *not* more individualistic than either African Americans or Latinos, for example. Nor were European Americans less collectivistic than Japanese or Koreans—two cultures presumed to anchor one end of the interdependence continuum. Indeed, the Chinese, rather than the Japanese or Koreans, stood out as being unusually collectivistic and nonindividualistic in self-concept.

Furthermore, characterizations such as independent–interdependent and individualistic–collectivistic have been criticized on the grounds that they are too general, conflating different kinds of social relationships and ignoring the context-specificity in which they are expressed (Fiske, 2002). Americans, for example, may be individualistic and independent at work and while playing computer games, but highly collectivistic and interdependent while with their families or in church. Future research must identify the specific contexts in which these cultural differences are, and are not, expressed.

Despite these criticisms, it's clear that there are real differences across cultures, albeit with important qualifications, and these must be explained. Most researchers have assumed that cultural differences in dimensions such as individualism–collectivism and independence–interdependence are instances of transmitted culture—ideas, attitudes, and self-concepts that are passed from one mind to another within a culture, down through the generations. Recently, a group of researchers has proposed a different explanation involving evolutionary psychology and evoked culture (Oyserman, Kemmelmeier, & Coon, 2003b). They hypothesize that humans have evolved psychological mechanisms for *both* types of self-concepts and that humans can switch from one mode to another depending on fitness advantages. Specifically, when one's group is low in mobility, limited in resources, and has many relatives in close proximity, it has paid fitness dividends to be highly collectivistic and interdependent. One's genetic relatives, often the recipients of these collectivist proclivities, tend to benefit. On the other hand, when mobility is high and people move frequently from place to place, when resources are relatively abundant, and when few genetic relatives live close by, it has paid fitness dividends to adopt a more individualistic and independent proclivity. This hypothesis is best summed up by its authors: "Thus, an evolutionary perspective suggests both the 'basicness' of independent and interdependent processing as well as the likelihood that all social systems are inhabited by individuals who can do both and draw on one or the other depending on their immediate contexts" (Oyserman et al., 2002b, p. 116). Future research will be needed to explore this fascinating fusion of evolutionary psychology and cultural psychology.

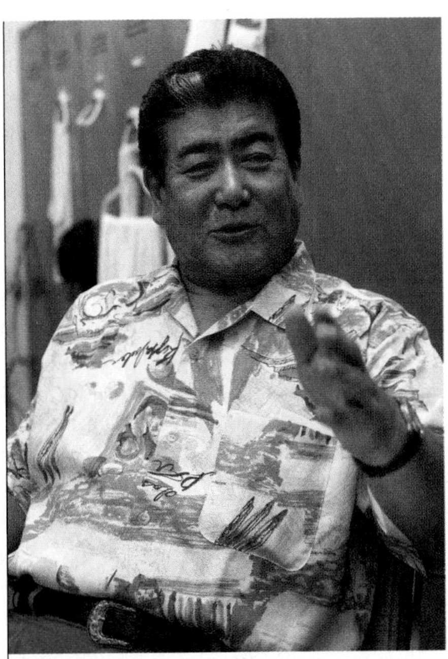

Toshiyuki Tanaka, an umpire in the Japanese baseball league, during an interview. In his culture, harmony is valued over conflict. To keep the peace during a heated game, Tanaka often plays the role of diplomat. He rarely penalizes a team or ejects a player or coach from the game, events that are fairly common in American baseball. Moreover, Tanaka sometimes admits it when he makes a mistake, which is practically unheard of among American umpires.

Cultural Differences in Self-Enhancement

Self-enhancement is the tendency to describe and present oneself using positive or socially valued attributes, such as *kind, understanding, intelligent,* and *industrious.* Tendencies toward self-enhancement tend to be stable over time and, hence, are enduring features of personality (Baumeister, 1997). Many studies have documented that North Americans tend to maintain a generally positive evaluation of themselves (Fiske et al., 1997). One study, for example, shows that the self-concepts of American adults contain more than four times as many positive attributes as negative ones (Herzog et al., 1995). In comparison with Americans, the Japanese tend to make far fewer spontaneous positive statements about themselves. The Japanese score lower than Americans on translations of self-esteem scales (Fiske et al., 1997). Furthermore, Japanese respondents tend to give more negative descriptions of themselves, such as "I think too much" and "I'm a somewhat selfish person" (Yeh, 1995). Even the positive self-descriptions of the Japanese respondents tend to be in the form of negations, such as "I'm not lazy." American respondents would express a similar sentiment with the phrase "I'm a hard worker."

Similar cultural differences have been discovered between Korean and American respondents (Ryff, Lee, & Na, 1995). Korean respondents are more likely to endorse negative statements about themselves, whereas American respondents are more likely to endorse positive statements. These differences in self-enhancement also show up in parents' self-descriptions of the quality of their parenting practices (Schmutte, Lee, & Ryff, 1995). Whereas American parents describe their parenting practices in generally glowing terms, Korean parents give mostly negative self-evaluations.

These cultural differences in self-enhancement also extend to evaluations of one's group, compared with evaluations of other groups. In one study, Heine and Lehman (1995) asked Japanese and Canadian students to compare their own university with a rival university within their own culture. The two pairs of universities used for the study were well matched in reputation—The University of British Columbia and Simon Fraser University in Canada, as well as Ritsumeikan and Doshisya in Japan. Among the Canadian respondents, there was a strong tendency toward in-group enhancement, with the rival university evaluated negatively by comparison. Among the Japanese respondents, there was no favoritism in the evaluation of one's own university in comparison with the rival university.

Psychologists have advanced two explanations for these cultural differences in self-enhancement. One explanation is that the Asians are engaging in impression management (see Chapter 4)—deep in their hearts, perhaps, they truly evaluate themselves positively, but to express these views publicly would damage their reputations. A second explanation is that these cultural differences accurately reflect the subjects' deep experiences. Asians, according to this view, due to profound cultural differences in values, truly evaluate themselves more negatively than do North Americans. There has been only one empirical test of these competing explanations (Fiske et al., 1997). When self-evaluations are made in conditions of total anonymity, where no one would be able to identify the respondent, researchers still found that the self-enhancement commonly seen among Americans does not occur among Asian respondents. This study supports the theory that these cultural differences reflect the actual subjective experiences of the respondent and are not merely surface differences due to impression management by the Asians.

It is important to recognize that these cultural differences are matters of degree, since people in all cultures appear to display a self-enhancement bias to some extent (Kurman, 2001). In a study of three cultures—Singaporeans, Druze Israelis, and Jewish Israelis—Kurman (2001) asked participants whether they considered themselves to be below average or above average for the sex and age group on six traits: intelligence, health, and sociability (agentic traits) and cooperation, honesty, and generosity (communal traits). Although the Singaporeans showed slightly more self-enhancement than the other two cultures, it only applied to the agentic traits, and people in *all* cultures showed a self-enhancement bias. On the communal traits, 85 percent of the participants in all three cultures viewed themselves as "above average" for their age and sex group. On the agentic traits, although the Druze and Jewish Israeli samples showed a self-enhancement level of 90 percent and 87 percent, respectively, the Singaporeans showed a self-enhancement level of nearly 80 percent. Thus, people across cultures show a self-enhancement bias, so the cultural differences must be interpreted within the context of this overall similarity. We must also recognize that there are tremendous individual differences *within* each culture—some individuals tend to be more individualistic and independent in self-concept, others more collectivistic and interdependent.

In sum, there appears to be a pervasive cultural difference in the degree to which people experience themselves. North Americans tend to experience themselves positively, expressing generally high levels of self-evaluation. Asians, in contrast, tend to self-enhance less and, instead, express negative or critical views of themselves. These views of self are core components of personality—they define the stable ways in which we think of ourselves, the ways in which we present ourselves to others, and the ways in which we behave in a variety of social settings.

Do Cultures Have Distinctive Personality Profiles?

People have long been fascinated with the question of whether cultures have distinctive personality profiles. Are people from the Mediterranean region of Europe really more emotionally expressive, or is this merely an incorrect stereotype? Are people from Scandinavia really more calm and stoic, or is this merely an incorrect stereotype?

Robert McCrae and 80 colleagues from around the world studied the personality profiles of 51 different cultures, using 12,156 participants (McCrae, Terracciano, et al., 2005a). They translated the Revised NEO Personality Inventory into the appropriate language for each culture, and then examined the aggregate Big Five personality scores for each culture. The largest difference they found across cultures centered on extraversion. As a general rule, Americans and Europeans scored higher than Asians and Africans. A few examples will illustrate these differences. With the cross-cultural average set to 50, the average extraversion score was 52.3 for Americans, 53.8 for Australians, 53.7 for the English, and 52.2 for Belgians. In contrast, the average extraversion scores were 46.5 for Ugandans, 47.0 for Ethiopians, and 46.6 for People's Republic Chinese.

It is important to bear in mind that these differences in average personalities are relatively small. Most of the differences in personality occur *within* cultures, not between cultures. Indeed, in examining the overall results, the most striking finding from this study is how similar the 51 cultures actually are in their overall scores on the five-factor model.

Personality Variations within Culture

Another dimension of transmitted culture pertains to **within-culture variations,** although these have not received the same degree of attention as cross-cultural variations. Within-culture variations can arise from several sources, including differences in growing up in various socioeconomic classes, differences in historical era, or differences in the racial context in which one grows up.

There is some evidence, for example, that **social class** within a culture can have an effect on personality (Kohn et al., 1990). Lower-class parents tend to emphasize the importance of obedience to authority, whereas higher-status parents tend to emphasize the importance of self-direction and nonconformity to the dictates of others. According to Kohn, these socialization practices stem from the sorts of occupations that parents expect their children to enter. Higher-status jobs (e.g., manager, start-up company founder, doctor, lawyer) often require greater self-direction, whereas lower-status jobs (e.g., factory worker, gas station employee) more often require the need to follow rules and permit less latitude for innovation. In studies of American, Japanese, and Polish men, Kohn and colleagues found that men from higher social classes in all cultures tended to be more self-directed, showed lower levels of conformity, and had greater intellectual flexibility than men from lower social classes.

These findings are correlational, so, of course, direction of effects cannot be unambiguously assumed. Perhaps people with personalities marked by self-direction and intellectual flexibility tend to gravitate toward the higher social classes. Or perhaps the socialization practices of higher-social-class parents tend to produce children with personalities that are different from the personalities of lower-social-class children. In either case, this example highlights the importance of intracultural differences. Not all people within a culture are alike in personality. Indeed, there is typically more variation among individuals within a culture than there is between cultures. This concept is illustrated in Figure 17.1, which shows the distribution of individualism–collectivism in two cultures. The shaded part shows the overlap between cultures. Consequently, even though cultures can differ in their average level on a particular trait, many individuals within the one culture can be higher (or lower) than many individuals in the other culture. This is why it is wise to treat individuals as individuals first, rather than members of some cultural group, because any individual may be far from his or her own group average.

Another type of intracultural variation pertains to the effects of **historical era** on personality. People who grew up during the Great Depression of the 1930s, for example, might be more anxious about job security, adopting a more conservative spending style. Those who came of age during the sexual revolution of the 1960s and 1970s, might show a greater openness to experimentation. Those growing up in the age of the Internet may spend more time interacting with others in distant places, expanding social horizons in ways that might influence personality development. Unfortunately, disentangling the effects of historical era on personality is an extremely difficult endeavor, since most currently used personality measures were not in use in earlier eras.

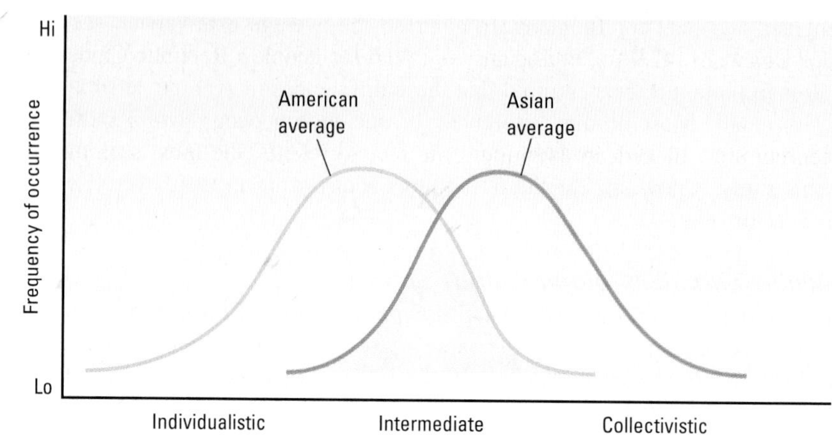

Figure 17.1

Individualism versus collectivism in American and Asian cultures. The distribution of two groups may be significantly different from each other in terms of the group mean yet have a high proportion of overlap. This means that many individuals from one group are higher (or lower) than many members of the other group, in a pattern opposite that of the mean difference. Asians score higher on collectivism than Americans do, yet there will always be some Americans who score higher than some Asians (those in the shaded area) on this measure.

Cultural Universals

A third approach to culture and personality is to attempt to identify features of personality that appear to be universal, or present in most or all human cultures. As described in Chapter 1, these universals constitute the human nature level of analyzing personality.

In the history of the study of personality and culture, the study of **cultural universals** has long been in disfavor. For most of the twentieth century, the focus was almost exclusively on cultural differences. This emphasis was fueled by anthropologists who reported on exotic cultures, which did everything differently than American culture did. Margaret Mead, for example, purported to discover cultures entirely lacking in sexual jealousy, cultures in which sex roles were reversed and adolescence was not marked with stress and turmoil (Mead, 1928, 1935). On sex roles, for example, Mead purported to discover "a genuine reversal of the sex-attitudes of our culture, with the woman the dominant, impersonal, managing partner, the man the less responsible and the emotionally dependent person" (Mead, 1935, p. 279). Human nature was presumed to be infinitely variable, infinitely flexible, and not constrained in any way by a universal human nature: "We are forced to conclude that human nature is almost unbelievably malleable, responding accurately and contrastingly to contrasting cultural conditions" (Mead, 1935, p. 280).

Over the past two decades, the pendulum has swung toward a more moderate view. Anthropologists who visited the islands Mead had visited failed to confirm Mead's findings (e.g., Freeman, 1983). In cultures in which sexual jealousy was presumed to be entirely absent, it turned out that sexual jealousy was the leading cause of spousal battering and spousal homicide. In cultures such as the Chambri, where the sex roles were presumed to be reversed, anthropologists instead found that wives were bought by men, men were stronger than women and sometimes beat them, and men were considered to be in charge (Brown, 1991; Gewertz, 1981). Furthermore, the Chambri considered men to be more aggressive than women and women to be more

Table 17.2 Culturally Universal Practices and Attitudes

Incest avoidance
Facial expressions of basic emotions
Favoritism toward in-group members
Favoritism toward kin over nonkin
Collective identities
Fear of snakes
Division of labor by sex
Revenge and retaliation
Self distinguished from others
Sanctions for crimes against the collectivity
Reciprocity in relationships
Envy, sexual jealousy, and love

Source: Brown, 1991.

submissive than men. Behavioral observations of social interactions among the Chambri confirmed these conceptions (Gewertz, 1981). All available evidence back to 1850, including some of Mead's recorded observations (as opposed to the inferences she made), suggest that the Chambri's sex roles are, in fact, strikingly similar to those of Western cultures. Brown (1991) has a list of practices and attitudes that are good candidates for cultural universals—see Table 17.2 (see also Pinker, 1997).

In this section, we will consider four examples of cultural universals—beliefs about the personality characteristics of men and women, the expression of emotion, the dimensions along which people describe and evaluate each other's personalities, and the possible universality of the five-factor model of personality traits.

Beliefs about the Personality Characteristics of Men and Women

In the most massive study undertaken to examine beliefs about the personality characteristics of men and women, Williams and Best (1990) examined 30 countries over a period of 15 years. These included Western European countries such as Germany, the Netherlands, and Italy; Asian countries such as Japan and India; South American countries such as Venezuela; and African countries such as Nigeria. In each country, university students were asked to examine 300 trait adjectives (e.g., *aggressive, emotional, dominant*) and to indicate whether each trait is more often linked with men, with women, or with both sexes. The responses of the subjects within each culture were then summed. When the results came in, the big shock was this: many of the trait adjectives were highly associated with one or the other sex, and there proved to be tremendous consensus across cultures. Table 17.3 shows sample trait adjectives most associated with men and with women across cultures.

How can we summarize and interpret these differences in beliefs about men and women? Williams and Best (1994) scored each of these adjectives on the following dimensions: *favorability* (how desirable is the trait?), *strength* (how much does the trait indicate power?), and *activity* (how much does the trait signify energy?). These dimensions originate from older classical work in the field that discovered three

Table 17.3 Pancultural Traits Linked with Men or Women

Traits Associated with Men		Traits Associated with Women	
Active	Loud	Affected	Modest
Adventurous	Obnoxious	Affectionate	Nervous
Aggressive	Opinionated	Appreciative	Patient
Arrogant	Opportunistic	Cautious	Pleasant
Autocratic	Pleasure-seeking	Changeable	Prudish
Bossy	Precise	Charming	Sensitive
Coarse	Quick	Dependent	Sentimental
Conceited	Reckless	Emotional	Softhearted
Enterprising	Show-off	Fearful	Timid
Hardheaded	Tough	Forgiving	Warm

Source: Adapted from Williams & Best, 1994.

universal semantic dimensions of *evaluation* (good–bad), *potency* (strong–weak), and *activity* (active–passive) (Osgood, Suci, & Tannenbaum, 1957). Overall, the traits ascribed to men and women turned out to be equally favorable. Some "masculine" traits, such as *serious* and *inventive,* were viewed as favorable, whereas others, such as *arrogant* and *bossy,* were viewed as unfavorable. Some "feminine" traits, such as *charming* and *appreciative,* were viewed as favorable, whereas others, such as *fearful* and *affected,* were viewed as unfavorable.

How can we interpret these cultural universals in beliefs about the personality characteristics of men and women? One interpretation is that these beliefs represent stereotypes based on the roles men and women assume universally. Williams and Best (1994), for example, argue that society assumes that men are stronger than women and therefore assigns men to roles and occupations such as soldier and construction worker. Over time, people may develop stereotypes about the "typical" personality characteristics of men and women. Thus, one interpretation is that these universal sex differences reflect stereotypes—mere beliefs about men and women rather than real or enduring differences.

A second possibility is that the traits ascribed to men and women in all 30 cultures reflect actual observations of real sex differences in personality. Studies of the five-factor model, for example, do find that women score lower on emotional stability, suggesting that they are more fearful and emotional. And does anyone really doubt that men are, on average, more physically aggressive or violent than women (see Chapter 16)? In short, the universal beliefs about the differences between men and women in personality may reflect actual differences in personality. Determining which interpretation is correct—the stereotype interpretation or the real difference interpretation—must await more extensive cross-cultural research.

Expression of Emotion

It is commonly believed that people in different cultures experience different emotions. As a consequence, personality psychologists have argued that different cultures have different words to describe emotional experience. The Tahitians, some have argued, do not experience the emotions of grief, longing, or loneliness, so they have no words in their language to express these emotions. For example, when a Tahitian boy dies in combat, according to legends reported by anthropologists, the parents smile and experience no grief, unlike the profound sadness felt by people in the modern Western world who experience similar events. Cultural variability in the presence or absence of emotion words has been interpreted by some personality psychologists to mean that cultures differ in the presence or absence of actual experiences of these emotions.

However, are emotions really this culturally variable? Or are there cultural universals in the experience of emotions? Psychologist Steven Pinker summarizes the evidence in this way: "Cultures surely differ in how often their members express, talk about, and act on various emotions. But that says nothing about what their people feel. The evidence suggests that the emotions of all normal members of our species are played on the same keyboard" (Pinker, 1997, p. 365).

The earliest evidence of cultural universals in emotions came from Charles Darwin. In gathering evidence for his book on emotions, *The Expression of Emotions in Man and Animals,* Darwin (1872/1965) asked anthropologists and travelers who interacted with peoples on five continents to give detailed information about how the natives expressed various emotions, such as grief, contempt, disgust, fear, and jealousy. He summarized the answers he received: "The same state of mind is expressed throughout the world with remarkable uniformity; and this fact is in itself interesting as evidence of the close similarity in bodily structure and mental disposition of all the races of mankind" (Darwin, 1872/1965, pp. 15, 17).

Darwin's methods, of course, were crude by today's scientific standards, but subsequent research over the past two decades has confirmed his basic conclusions. Psychologist Paul Ekman created a set of photographs of people expressing six basic emotions and then showed them to people in various cultures (Ekman, 1973). Some cultures in his study, such as the Fore foragers of New Guinea, had had almost no contact with Westerners. The Fore spoke no English, had seen no TV or movies, and had never lived with Caucasians. He also administered the tests to people in Japan, Brazil, Chile, Argentina, and the United States. Ekman asked each subject to label the emotion expressed in each photograph and to make up a story about what the person in the photograph had experienced. The six emotions—happiness, sadness, anger, fear, disgust, and surprise—were universally recognized by people in the various cultures. These findings have been subsequently replicated in other countries, such as Italy, Scotland, Estonia, Greece, Germany, Hong Kong, Sumatra, and Turkey (Ekman et al., 1987). And the research has extended to include the documentation of the universality of a seventh—the emotion of disgust (Ekman & Friesen, 1986).

In addition to finding that people of different cultures effortlessly recognized the emotions expressed on the faces in the photographs, Ekman reversed the procedure. He asked the Fore participants to act out scenarios, such as "Your child has died" and "You are angry and about to fight," and then photographed them.

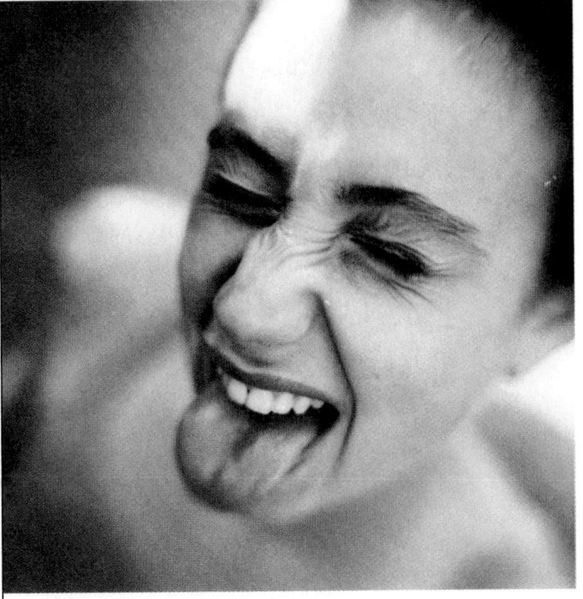

Disgust appears to be an emotion universally experienced by humans.

The emotions expressed in these photographs were easily recognized by facial expressions and were strikingly similar to the expressions of the same emotions seen in the photographs of the Caucasian participants. Further evidence for the universality, and possible innateness, of these basic emotions comes from the finding that children who are blind from birth display the same facial expressions of emotions that those with full sight display (Lazarus, 1991).

Pinker notes that whether a language has a word for a particular emotion or not matters little, if the question is whether people *experience* the emotion in the same way: Tahitians are said not to have a word for grief; however, "when a Tahitian woman says 'My husband died and I feel sick,' her emotional state is hardly mysterious; she is probably not complaining about acid indigestion" (Pinker, 1997, p. 367).

Another example is the German word *Schadenfreude:* "When English-speakers hear the word *Schadenfreude* for the first time, their reaction is not, 'Let me see . . . pleasure in another's misfortunes . . . what could that possibly be? I cannot grasp the concept; my language and culture have not provided me with such a category.' Their reaction is, 'You mean there's a word for it? Cool!'" (Pinker, 1997, p. 367). People universally may experience the emotion of pleasure in an enemy's misfortunes in the same way, even if all cultures do not have a single word in their lexicon to capture it.

The view that language is not necessary for people to experience emotions may be contrasted with what has been called the **Whorfian hypothesis of linguistic relativity,** which contends that language *creates* thought and experience. In the extreme view, the Whorfian hypothesis argues that the ideas that people can think and the emotions they feel are constrained by the words that happen to exist in their language and culture (Whorf, 1956).

The difference between *experiencing* an emotion and *expressing* that emotion in public may be critical to resolving this debate. Ekman (1973) performed an ingenious experiment to explore the difference between the experience of emotion and its expression in public. He secretly videotaped the facial expressions of Japanese and American students while they watched a graphic film of a primitive puberty rite involving genital mutilation. In one condition, an experimenter wearing a white lab coat was present in the room. In the other condition, the participants were alone. When the experimenter was present (a public context), the Japanese students smiled politely during the film, but the American students expressed horror and disgust. If this were the only condition run, we might conclude that Japanese and American students experience the emotion of disgust differently. However, when the students were filmed when they were alone in the room watching the film, both the Japanese and American faces showed equal horror. This result suggests that Japanese and American students experience this emotion in the same way, even if they differ in their expression of it in a more public setting.

In sum, there is evidence for cultural universals in the experience and expression of emotions, at least for the emotions of happiness, sadness, anger, fear, disgust, and surprise. People in all cultures studied so far can recognize and describe these emotions when presented photographs of others expressing them. Just as clearly, not all cultures have words corresponding to these emotions. The experience and expression of emotions appear to be more culturally universal than the language used to describe them.

Dimensions of Personality Description and Evaluation

In American culture, when we describe someone else, we often use trait terms. We might describe a woman as warm, intelligent, and assertive. We might even use slang terms, and describe her as cool, rad, fly, or zoned, sometimes modifying our opinion with the adjective *totally*. Although our intuitions tell us that people in different cultures use different terms to describe the personalities of others, there is some evidence for a universal map of personality descriptors.

A cultural anthropologist studied the similarity of 37 personality descriptors across several cultures, such as the A'ara of Santa Isabel in the Solomon Islands (White, 1980). Each participant was presented with a word in his or her own language, such as *warm, conscientious,* or *assertive,* and then was asked to select the five other words in the list that most closely matched the word in meaning. These data were then subjected to multidimensional scaling, a statistical procedure designed to identify the major dimensions in data sets, much like factor analysis (Chapter 3). Two clear dimensions emerged. The first was anchored by *dominance* at one end and *submissiveness* at the other. The second dimension, independent of the first, was anchored by *warmth* and *friendliness* at one end and *coldness* and *hostility* at the other. You may recall from Chapter 3 that these are precisely the two main dimensions of the circumplex model of interpersonal behavior (e.g., Wiggins, 1979).

The amazing similarity across cultures of this two-dimensional structure for evaluating and describing the personalities of others in languages as different as Oriya, A'ara, and English led one researcher to speculate that "these dimensions represent a universal conceptual schema produced by the interaction of innate psycholinguistic structures and fundamental conditions of human social life, for example, the potential for concord or discord in the goals and actions of multiple actors (solidarity/conflict), and for the asymmetrical influence of one actor upon another (dominance/submission)" (White, 1980, p. 759).

What are the implications of the discovery of universal dimensions for describing the personality characteristics of others? At this point, we can only speculate. Personality theorist Robert Hogan (1996) argues that these are universal dimensions because they describe the two most important tasks that humans have to accomplish in their interactions with others—getting along and getting ahead. Thus, our evaluations of others as dominant or submissive reflect our assessment of how well those others are succeeding in getting ahead. And evaluations of others as warm (agreeable) or cold (hostile) reflect our assessment of how well those others are succeeding in getting along with people in their social environment.

Another possible reason for the universality of these two dimensions of personality evaluation stems from an evolutionary perspective on solving social adaptive problems (Buss, 1996): "Over evolutionary time, those individuals who attended to and acted on individual differences in others that were adaptively consequential would have survived and reproduced more successfully than those who were oblivious to adaptively consequential differences in others" (p. 185). Natural selection, in short, produced "difference-detection mechanisms" designed to evaluate individual differences in others.

With respect to the dominance–submissiveness dimension, for example, it is an adaptive imperative for people to know how powerful or weak others are. Knowing the power or dominance of others provides valuable information about whom one can exploit with impunity (those who are submissive) or, in contrast, those to whom one must defer (those who are more dominant). Failure to evaluate accurately the dominance of others could lead to adaptive errors—yelling at someone who has more power, for example, could result in getting fired or ostracized from the group. Many social decisions, such as whom to befriend and whom to ignore, rest on an accurate evaluation of where others fall on the dominance–submissiveness dimension of personality.

The warm–cold, or agreeable–hostile, dimension of personality evaluation might affect adaptive decisions such as who will be a good friend or ally (someone who is agreeable and warm). It also might alert a person to those who are pursuing an aggressive social strategy—someone who is likely to interfere with a person's goals and aspirations.

Much more evidence is needed before we can conclude with certainty that these two dimensions—dominance and warmth—represent a universal map used to evaluate and describe the personality qualities of others around us. The available evidence, though, is consistent with this possibility. Future work in personality psychology will undoubtedly also be devoted to understanding why these dimensions of personality evaluation appear to be so important to people everywhere (MacDonald, 1998).

Five-Factor Model of Personality

Some personality psychologists have argued that universal dimensions of personality are not merely ways of evaluating other people; rather, they represent universal dimensions along which individuals differ. Most of this work has been devoted to exploring whether the five-factor model of personality is universal.

A fascinating question is whether there is a universal structure of personality, such as the five-factor model, or whether different factorial models exist in different cultures. To examine this issue, it is helpful to outline the conceptual positions that have been advanced.

According to some psychologists, even the concept of personality lacks universality. Hsu, for example, argues that ". . . the concept of personality is an expression of the Western ideal of individualism" (Hsu, 1985, p. 24). Shweder, a well-known cultural psychologist, argues that "the data gathered from . . . personality inventories lends illusory support to the mistaken belief that individual differences can be described in language consisting of context-free global traits, factors, or dimensions" (Shweder, 1991, pp. 275–276).

These views have been articulated even more recently: "Universal [personality] structure does not by itself imply that 'personality' as understood within a European-American framework is a universal aspect of human behavior . . . nor does it imply that the variability that appears as an obvious feature of human life is a function of an internal package of attributes called 'personality'" (Markus & Kitayama, 1998, p. 67). Finally, cultural anthropologist Lawrence Hirschfeld argues that "in many, perhaps most, cultures there is a marked absence of discourse that explains human behavior in terms of transsituationally stable motivational (or intentional) properties captured by explanations of trait and disposition" (Hirschfeld, 1995, p. 315).

What is reflected in all these quotations is a fundamental challenge to personality psychology—whether the core concept of traits is universal or, instead, is a local concept only applicable in Western cultures. The most extreme of these perspectives suggests that the very notion of personality, as an internal set of psychological characteristics, is an arbitrary construction of Western culture (Church, 2000). If this extreme position were really true, then any attempt to identify and measure personality traits in non-Western cultures would be doomed to failure (Church, 2000). At the other extreme is the position that personality traits are universal in their applicability and that precisely the same personality structure will emerge across cultures. As two personality researchers noted, "The most important dimensions . . . [of] personality judgment are the most invariant and universal dimensions" (Saucier & Goldberg, 2001, p. 851).

The first source of evidence bearing on this debate pertains to the existence of trait terms in other cultures. Many non-Western psychologists have, in fact, described traitlike concepts that are indigenous to non-Western cultures and that appear strikingly like those that appear in Western cultures. Following are some examples: the Filipino concepts of *pakikiramdam* (sensitivity, empathy) and *pakikisama* (getting along with others); the Korean concept of *chong* (human affection); the Japanese concept of *amae* (indulgent dependence); the Chinese concept of *ren qin* (being relationship-oriented); and the Mexican concept of *simpatico* (being harmonious and avoiding conflict) (Church, 2000). Many non-Western cultures, in short, appear to have traitlike concepts embedded in their languages in much the same way that the American culture and English language do.

A second source of evidence bearing on the debate concerns whether the same factor structure of personality traits is found across cultures. That is, do different cultures have roughly the same broad categories of traits? The trait perspective on personality, of course, does not require the existence of precisely the same traits in all cultures. Indeed, the trait perspective might be extremely useful even if cultures were to differ radically in terms of which trait dimensions they used. Nonetheless, the most powerful support for the trait perspective across cultures would occur if the structure of personality traits were found to be the same across cultures (Church, 2000).

Two approaches have been taken to exploring this issue. In the first approach, which can be labeled the "transport and test" strategy, psychologists have translated existing questionnaires into other languages and then have administered them to native residents in other cultures. This strategy has generated some findings supporting the five-factor model. The five-factor model (extraversion, agreeableness, conscientiousness, emotional stability, and openness) has now been replicated in France, Holland, and the Philippines and in languages from entirely different language families, such as Sino-Tibetan, Hamito-Semitic, Uralic, and Malayo-Polynesian (McCrae et al., 1998). More recently, the five-factor model has been replicated in Spain (Salgado, Moscoso, & Lado, 2003) as well as Croatia (Mlacic & Ostendorf, 2005). A study of 13 different countries—from Japan to Slovakia—also found support for the five-factor model (Hendriks et al., 2003).

Perhaps the most impressive was a massive study of 50 different cultures (McCrae, Terracciano, & 78 members of the Personality Profiles of Cultures Project, 2005b). This study, involving 11,985 participants, had college-age individuals rate someone they knew well using the Revised NEO Personality Inventory. Factor analyses of these observer-based ratings yielded the five-factor model, with only minor variations in factor structure across cultures. This study is extremely important in suggesting that cross-cultural evidence for the five-factor model is not limited to self-report data, but extends to observer-based data as well. Using the transport and test strategy, the five-factor structure of personality appears to be general across cultures. Table 17.4, for example, shows the factor structure from a Filipino sample. Nonetheless, a recent study conducted in Estonia found that the five-factor model was successfully replicated only among participants who were relatively high in general cognitive ability (Toomela, 2003). The Big-Five structure failed to emerge among those with relatively low levels of intellectual ability.

A more powerful test of generality, however, would come from studies that start out using indigenous personality dimensions first, then testing whether the five-factor structure still emerges. This approach has been tried in Dutch, German, Hungarian, Italian, Czech, and Polish (De Raad et al., 1998). In each case, the trait terms in the language were identified. Although the absolute numbers of personality trait terms varied from language to language—Dutch has 8,690 trait terms, whereas Italian has only 1,337 trait terms—the percentage of words in each language that constituted trait

Table 17.4 Factor Analysis of the Filipino NEO-PI-R

NEO-PI-R Facet Scale	N	E	O	A	C
N1: Anxiety	**76**	−08	00	00	06
N2: Angry hostility	**67**	−19	01	−44	−10
N3: Depression	**73**	−23	03	−02	−25
N4: Self-consciousness	**68**	−14	−15	22	−04
N5: Impulsiveness	**40**	20	04	−37	−47
N6: Vulnerability	**70**	−22	−23	04	−30
E1: Warmth	−21	**69**	17	28	08
E2: Gregariousness	−29	**65**	−02	07	04
E3: Assertiveness	−28	**42**	23	−29	35
E4: Activity	−15	**51**	10	−24	25
E5: Excitement seeking	−08	**51**	26	−29	−12
E6: Positive emotions	−16	**66**	14	15	01
O1: Fantasy	16	27	**47**	−06	−27
O2: Aesthetics	14	20	**65**	14	22
O3: Feelings	30	32	**53**	03	12
O4: Actions	−39	−03	**46**	01	04
O5: Ideas	−04	−01	**69**	01	30
O6: Values	−13	−06	**62**	−05	−16
A1: Trust	−20	41	09	**52**	−10
A2: Straightforwardness	−03	−22	−02	**57**	10
A3: Altruism	−12	27	13	**65**	31
A4: Compliance	−20	−10	−09	**75**	12
A5: Modesty	18	−27	−03	**55**	−13
A6: Tender-mindedness	22	27	09	**49**	20
C1: Competence	−38	22	16	−10	**69**
C2: Order	−04	−15	−08	10	**73**
C3: Dutifulness	−08	12	07	21	**69**
C4: Achievement striving	−12	06	01	11	**83**
C5: Self-discipline	−24	02	00	07	**81**
C6: Deliberation	−27	−20	03	24	**65**

Note: $N = 696$. Decimal points are omitted; loadings greater than 40 in absolute magnitude are given in boldface; N = Neuroticism, E = Extraversion, O = Openness, A = Agreeableness, C = Conscientiousness, L = Love, S = Submission.

terms was remarkably consistent, averaging 4.4 percent of all dictionary entries. You may recall the **lexical hypothesis** from Chapter 3, which states that the most important individual differences have been encoded within the natural language.

The next step in the De Raad et al., study was to reduce this list to a manageable number of several hundred trait terms, identified as indigenous to each culture, which could then be tested in each culture. Factor analyses of each sample within each culture showed that there was tremendous replicability of four of the five factors of the five-factor model: extraversion *(talkative, sociable versus shy, introverted),* agreeableness *(sympathetic, warm versus unsympathetic, cold),* conscientiousness *(organized, responsible versus disorganized, careless),* and emotional stability *(relaxed, imperturbable versus moody, emotional).*

Despite cross-cultural agreement on these four factors, this study found some differences in what constituted the fifth factor, as noted in Chapter 3. In some cultures, such as Polish and German, the fifth factor resembled the American fifth factor (openness–intellect), with *intelligent* and *imaginative* anchoring one end and *dull* and *unimaginative* anchoring the other end. One study conducted in the Philippines also found a replicated five-factor model, including the fifth factor resembling openness–intellect, although there are a few indigenous constructs that are less successfully subsumed by the Big Five such as social curiosity, obedience, and capacity for understanding (Katigbak, Church, Guanzon-Lapena, Carlota, & del Pilar, 2002). Other languages, however, revealed different fifth factors. In Dutch, for example, the fifth factor seemed more like a dimension of political orientation, ranging from *conservative* at one end to *progressive* at the other. In Hungarian, the fifth factor seemed to be one of truthfulness, with *just, truthful,* and *humane* anchoring one end and *greedy, hypocritical,* and *pretending* at the other (De Raad et al., 1998). The fifth factor, in summary, appeared to be somewhat variable across cultures.

Recent cross-cultural research using the lexical approach, as you may recall from Chapter 3, has found compelling evidence for *six* factors, rather than five (Ashton et al., 2004; Saucier, Georgiades, Tsaousis, & Goldberg, 2005). The new sixth factor—honesty–humility—represents a major discovery. By starting with the natural language within each culture, these researchers were able to capture an important dimension of personality that may have been bypassed using the "transport and test" research strategy.

Clearly, further indigenous tests are needed to determine whether the five-factor trait model of personality structure is universal or not. Based on the existing data, however, we can conclude that the truth is somewhere between the extreme positions outlined at the beginning of this section but closer to those that argue for universality. Trait terms appear to be present in all languages. Factor structures based on instruments developed in the United States, and then translated and transported to other cultures, show great similarity across cultures. Using the more rigorous standard of instruments developed indigenously, however, only four of the five factors emerge consistently across cultures. The fifth factor is somewhat variable across cultures and therefore may reflect an important lack of universality of personality trait structure.

SUMMARY AND EVALUATION

People living in different cultures differ in key personality traits, such as self-concept, the prevailing levels of aggressiveness, and the moral values they hold. The differences are called cultural variations—patterns of local within-group similarity and between-group difference.

There are two major approaches to examining cultural variations. The first, evoked culture, involves the capabilities present in all people that are elicited only in some cultural contexts. Evoked cooperation provides one example—people tend to share food when there is high variability in success at obtaining it. Presumably, all people have the capacity to cooperate and share, but these dispositions are evoked only in certain cultural circumstances. Evoked aggression provides a second example of evoked culture. All people have the capacity to be aggressive at times; however, if one grows up in a culture of honor, then aggression is more likely to be evoked in response to insults to one's honor than if one does not grow up in a culture of honor.

The second major way of conceptualizing cultural variants is called transmitted culture—representations originally in the mind of one or more persons that are transmitted to the minds of other people. Three examples of cultural variants that appear to be forms of transmitted culture are differences in moral values, self-concept, and levels of self-enhancement. Patterns of morality, such as whether it is considered appropriate to disobey one's parents or to eat beef, or wrong for a wife to go to the movies without her husband, are specific to certain cultures. These moral values appear to be transmitted from person to person within the culture. Cultural differences in self-concept are another example of transmitted culture. Many Asian cultures, for example, appear to foster self-concepts that are highly interdependent and contextual, emphasizing the embeddedness of the self within the group. European American culture, in contrast, appears to promote a self-concept that is more independent, stressing the separateness of the person from the group.

A related cultural difference pertains to the dimension of individualism versus collectivism. People in individualist cultures tend to be relatively autonomous, striving to behave in ways that are not yoked to their social group. They give personal priority to their own goals rather than to group goals. People in collectivist cultures, in contrast, give priority to in-group goals, focus more on behaving in ways that are sensitive to the social context, and are more self-effacing.

The cross-cultural work on interdependence–independence and collectivistic–individualistic has been criticized on several grounds. First, the magnitudes of effect are sometimes quite small. Second, the dichotomies may be overly simplistic because they ignore the context-specificity of the tendencies (e.g., Americans might be individualistic at work and collectivistic at home with their families) as well as individual differences within culture (e.g., some Koreans are more individualistic, others more collectivistic). Nonetheless, some cultural differences are real and must be explained. Most researchers have assumed that these differences are instances of transmitted culture. A recent alternative explanation proposes that all humans have evolved psychological mechanisms capable of acting both individualistically and collectively, as well as a switching mechanism that allows them to switch from one mode to the other, depending on the fitness advantages. This fascinating explanatory fusion of evolutionary psychology and cultural psychology holds much promise.

The culture in which we reside appears to have an effect on our self-concepts. Using a procedure known as the Twenty Statements Test, researchers have found that North Americans tend to describe themselves using abstract internal characteristics, such as "I am smart," "I am dependable," and "I am friendly." Asians, in contrast, tend to define themselves more often using social roles, such as "I am the son of . . ." or "I am Liu's friend." These differences in self-concept appear to be examples of transmitted culture, passed down from person to person through the generations. It's important to keep in mind that these cultural differences are a matter of degree, since even people in collectivist cultures use some global traits to describe themselves and people in individualist cultures use some relational terms to describe themselves.

Another reliable cultural difference pertains to self-enhancement, or the tendency to view oneself using positive or socially valued attributes. Korean and Japanese respondents are more likely than American respondents to endorse negative statements about themselves, such as "I am lazy" or "I am a somewhat selfish person." Americans, in contrast, tend to endorse more positive statements about themselves, such as "I'm a hard worker" or "I'm quite creative." These differences in self-enhancement also appear to be examples of transmitted culture.

In addition to cultural variations, some elements of personality appear to be culturally universal. One example of a cultural universal is people's beliefs about the personality traits that characterize men and women. Worldwide, people tend to regard men as having personalities that are more active, loud, adventurous, obnoxious, aggressive, opinionated, arrogant, coarse, and conceited. Women, in contrast, are regarded as having personalities that are more affectionate, modest, nervous, appreciative, patient, changeable, charming, fearful, and forgiving.

Another cultural universal appears to be the experience and recognition of specific emotional states, such as fear, anger, happiness, sadness, disgust, and surprise. People from Italy to Sumatra can recognize and describe these emotions when presented photographs of others expressing them, even if the photographs are of people from other cultures.

Finally, the dimensions used for personality evaluation of others appear to show some cultural universality. Strong evidence suggests that two key dimensions (dominance and warmth) are used for describing and evaluating the personality characteristics of others. Furthermore, there is some evidence that the structure of personality traits, as represented by the five-factor model of personality, may be universal, at least for four of the five traits—neuroticism, extraversion, agreeableness, and conscientiousness. There is also new evidence for the five-factor model using the "transport and test" strategy model of personality using observer-based data from 50 cultures. Nonetheless, studies that begin with the natural language within each culture, using the lexical strategy to identify important trait terms, have discovered a six-factor structure. In addition to the five major factors, the new honesty–humility factor is in contention for being a fundamentally important personality factor. This discovery attests to the importance of cross-cultural research, particularly research that uses a strategy that begins *within* each culture.

KEY TERMS

PART SIX

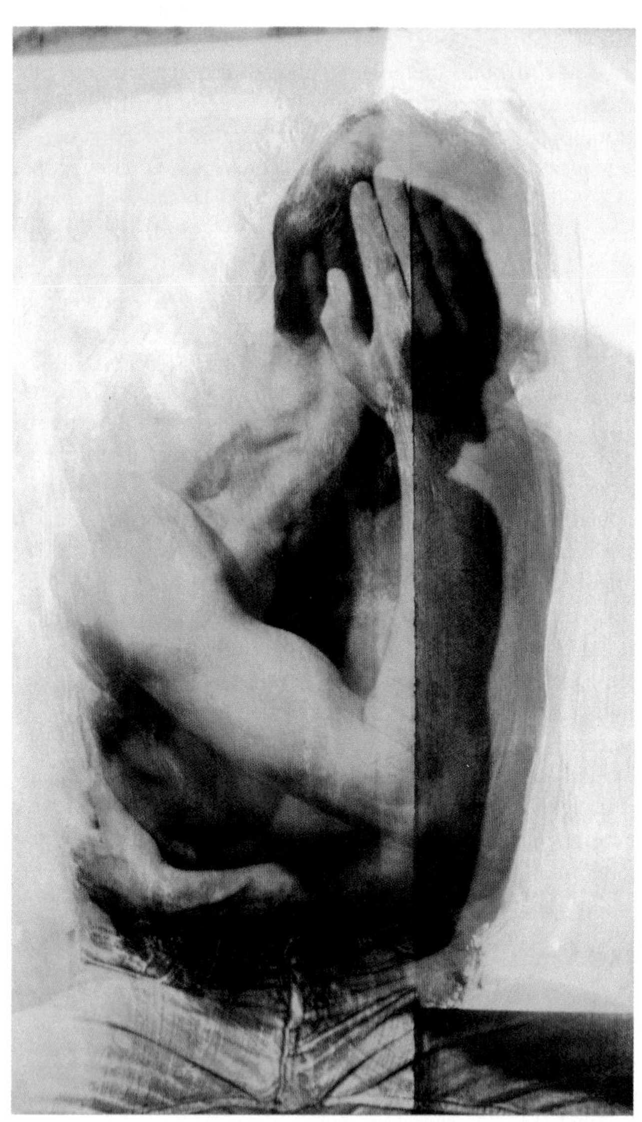

The Adjustment Domain

VI

This domain is different from the others discussed in the book so far. The first five domains each referred to a collection of specific explanations of personality. That is, each gave a perspective on, and a collection of knowledge about, the causes of personality and individual differences. In this last domain—the Adjustment Domain—we examine some of the consequences of personality. We focus on adjustment because, in many ways, personality functions to help us adjust to the challenges and demands of life, albeit in a unique way for each of us. We focus on two important outcomes in this domain: physical health and mental health.

Day by day, all of us are adjusting to the demands of life and reacting to life events. Some of us might even think there is too much stress in our lives. However, stress is not "out there" in our lives, but rather stress mostly refers to how we respond to life events. How we interpret some event will determine whether we feel it as stressful or not. The tendency to interpret events in a way that evokes a stress response is influenced by our personalities. Personality plays a key role in how we appraise and interpret events, cope, adapt, and adjust to the ebb and flow in our day-to-day lives. Moreover, some people display patterns of behavior, emotion, and interpersonal relations that create problems for themselves and those around them. These problematic personality profiles form the collection of personality disorders. These two areas—coping with stress and disorders of personality—define the adjustment domain because they refer to how effectively people interact with and cope with challenges from the environment.

Considerable evidence has been accumulating that personality is linked with important health outcomes, such as heart disease. Psychologists have developed several theories for how and why these relationships exist, as well as offering ways to change health-harming behavior patterns. Personality is also linked with a variety of health-related behaviors such as smoking, drinking, and risk-taking. Some research has even demonstrated that personality is correlated with how long we live (Peterson, 1995, 2000).

In addition to health and coping with stress, many of the important problems in living can be traced to personality. In this domain of knowledge there is the concept of disorder, the idea that certain personality profiles can be so abnormal or problematic so as to create clear difficulties in the person's life, particularly in terms of work and social relationships. Certain personality features that are related to poor adjustment and poor outcomes in life are described as personality disorders. We devote an entire chapter to the personality disorders, such as the antisocial personality and the narcissistic personality. We believe that an understanding of "normal" personality functioning can be enhanced by examining what can go wrong with personality. This is similar to the field of medicine, in which an understanding of normal physiological functioning is often illuminated by the study of disorders and disease. We begin our coverage of the adjustment domain with the topics of stress, coping, and health.

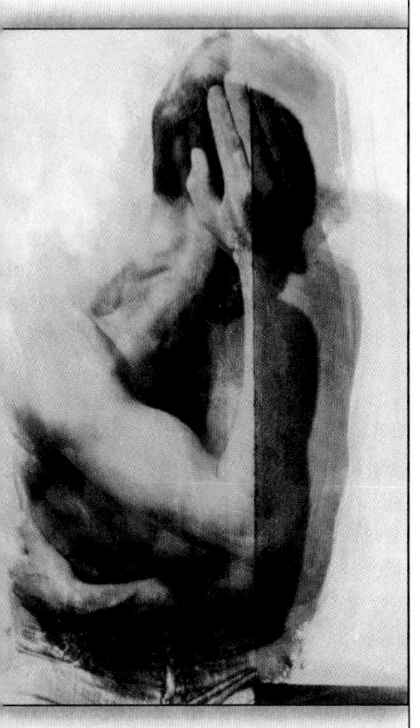

Stress, Coping, Adjustment, and Health

18

THE ADJUSTMENT DOMAIN

18

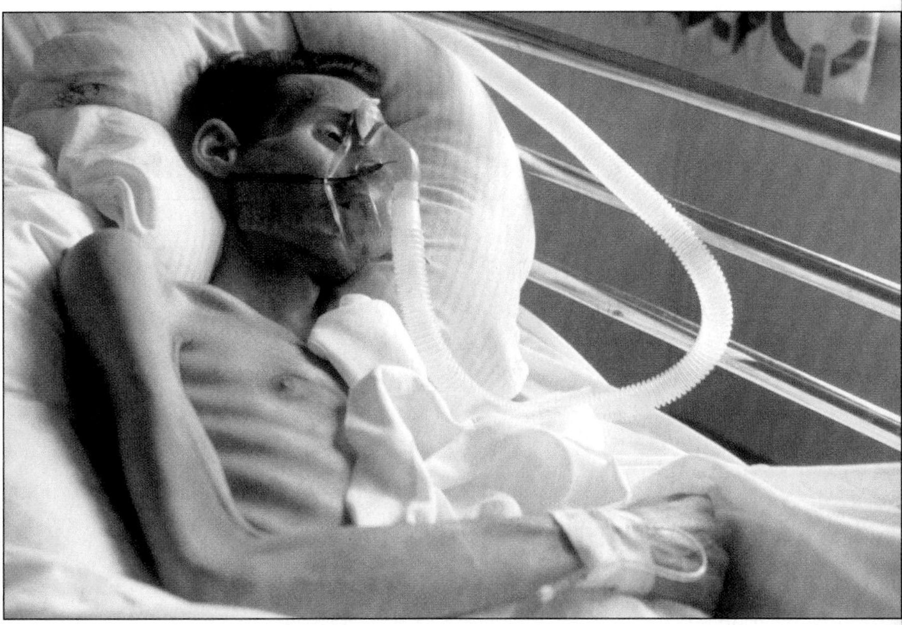

An AIDS patient in an advanced stage of the disease. Although AIDS is caused by a virus, its transmission from person to person occurs through specific behaviors.

For much of history, humans have been battling microbes in an effort to overcome disease and illness. The list of germ-borne illnesses is long, with many epidemics. For example, in 1520, the Spanish conquistadors landed in Mexico with several slaves brought from Spanish Cuba. One of the slaves had smallpox. The illness spread to the native Aztec tribes, who had no immunity to smallpox. It quickly killed half of the Aztec people, including their emperor, Cuitlahuac. Aided by the microbe that causes smallpox, the Spanish had no trouble conquering all of Mexico. Imagine how helpless the Aztecs must have felt as the mysterious disease killed *only* them, sparing the Spaniards, who had developed immunity. The Aztecs must have thought the Spaniards were invincible. The native population of Mexico, estimated at 20 million when the Spaniards arrived, fell to 1.6 million in less than 100 years (Diamond, 1999).

The world is currently experiencing another epidemic of an infectious disease: the HIV virus, which causes AIDS. The microbe that causes AIDS resides in bodily fluids and passes from person to person whenever bodily fluids containing the microbe are exchanged. A cure for AIDS has not yet been discovered, nor is there a vaccine that will prevent the spread of HIV. The explosive spread of this infectious disease has surprised even medical researchers. In some African countries, for example, the percentage of the adult population infected with HIV is huge; 37 percent of the population of Botswana, 38 percent of Swaziland, and 25 percent of Zimbabwe (Tarantola, Lamptev, & Moodie, 1999). South Africa, the largest country in Africa, with over 5,000,000 people, has an HIV infection rate of 22 percent, which translates into 1,100,000 people with the HIV virus living in this country alone. In 2005 in Africa 2.3 million people died from AIDS. Imagine living in a country in which one out of every three or four adults is carrying HIV.

The current epidemic of AIDS illustrates a very important distinction; while its cause is a virus, its transmission is through specific behaviors. For example, unsafe sex practices (e.g., not using condoms) greatly increase the likelihood of transmitting AIDS. Another high-risk behavior is the sharing of intravenous needles by drug addicts. While medical researchers search for a vaccination and cure, psychologists are searching for the best ways to change people's high-risk behavior.

This is only one example of the importance of behavior in understanding illness. In earlier centuries, most of the serious illnesses that afflicted humans were caused by microbe infection, including such diseases as tuberculosis, influenza, leprosy, polio, bubonic plague, cholera, smallpox, malaria, measles, rabies, and diphtheria. As modern medicine developed effective vaccines, these microbial diseases pretty much disappeared as major causes of death (at least in the United States). Today, many of the leading causes of death and disease are related not to microbes as much as to lifestyle factors, such as smoking, poor diet, inadequate exercise, and stress. In other words, now that we are curing microbe infections, psychological factors have emerged as important contributors to the development of illness.

The realization that psychological and behavioral factors can have important health consequences has given rise to the field of **health psychology.** Researchers in this area of psychology study the relationship between the mind and the body, as well as the ways in which these two components respond to challenges from the environment (e.g., stressful events, germs) to produce either illness or health. Many of the psychological variables of interest have to do with stable patterns of behavior—for example, whether a person copes well with stress, exercises some or not at all, sleeps seven to eight hours each night, drinks alcohol only in moderation, routinely wears a seat belt, keeps his or her weight at a desirable level, avoids drugs, practices safe sex, and avoids unnecessary risks. Researchers find that such behaviors are correlated with life expectancy. In fact, in the United States, researchers suggest that lifestyle contributes to more than half of all premature deaths—that is, death before age 65 (Taylor, 1991).

Personality can have an impact on health in many ways, and personality psychologists are developing new methodological approaches to the study of this link. Current research is based on detailed models of the mechanisms underlying the links between personality and health (Smith & Spiro, 2002). Life span studies show that personality can have life-long effects on health, though the effects differ depending on the traits being considered (Aldwin, Spiro, Levenson, & Cupertino, 2001) or the specific health outcomes under investigation, e.g., the cancer-prone personality characterized by being unassertive and emotionally inhibited, the coronary-prone personality characterized by being hostile and aggressive (Eysenck, 2000).

In this chapter, we will focus on a portion of the field of health psychology which concerns personality and individual differences. Some main research questions in this area are the following: "Are some people more likely than others to become ill?" "Do some people recover faster?" "Are some people more able than others to tolerate stress?" Understanding the nature and consequences of such differences between people is the focus of this chapter. We will begin by discussing various ways of thinking about how personality influences health. Within health psychology, several models have been applied to understanding the link between personality and illness.

Models of the Personality-Illness Connection

Researchers have proposed several ways of thinking about how personality can relate to health. These models can take the form of diagrams of key variables, with the causal relations among those variables depicted by arrows. Models are useful to researchers in guiding their thinking about specific variables, and especially in thinking about how those variables influence one another (Wiebe & Smith, 1997). In most of the models we will discuss, one variable—stress—will be important. **Stress** is the subjective feeling produced by events that are uncontrollable or threatening. It is important to realize that stress is a *response* to the perceived demands in some situation. Stress is not in the situation; stress refers to how people respond to a particular situation.

An early model of the personality health relationship, called the **interactional model,** is depicted in Figure 18.1(a). This model suggests that objective events happen to people, but personality factors determine the impact of those events by influencing people's ability to cope. In this model, personality has its effects on coping responses—that is, on how people respond to the event. It is called the interactional model because personality is assumed to moderate (influence) the relationship between stress and illness. In other words, events such as exposure to microbes or chronic stress cause illness, but personality factors make a person more or less vulnerable to those events. Personality influences how the person copes with stressful events. For example, if a person were infected with a cold virus but had a hard-driving, competitive personality, such that the person would not rest, would not take time off from work, and would not do other behaviors necessary to quickly recover from a cold, this person could become very ill, perhaps with the cold turning into pneumonia, because the person's personality influenced how well he or she coped with the viral infection. How a person copes can influence the degree, duration, and frequency of a stressful event.

Although the interactional model was useful in early research, health psychologists soon found its limitations. One problem was that researchers were unable to identify stable coping responses that were consistently adaptive or maladaptive (Lazarus, 1991). Subsequently, the interactional model was developed into a more complex and perhaps a more realistic model—the **transactional model,** depicted in Figure 18.1(b). In this model, personality has three potential effects: (1) it can influence coping, as in the interactional model; (2) it can influence how the person appraises or interprets the events; and (3) it can influence the events themselves. These last two processes deserve special attention.

In the transactional model, it is not the event itself that causes stress but, rather, how the event is appraised, or interpreted, by the person. You will recall from Chapter 12 that interpretation is important in determining behavior. An event, such as getting stuck in traffic on the way to a job interview, can happen to two people, yet the two people can interpret the event differently and, thus, experience it differently. One person might interpret getting stuck as a major frustration and, hence, might respond with a great deal of worry, stress, and anxiety. The other might interpret getting stuck in traffic as an opportunity to relax, enjoy some music on the radio, and do some planning on how to reschedule the job interview. This person does not experience the same level of stress.

The third point on the transactional model at which personality can have an impact consists of the events themselves. That is, people don't just respond to situations; they also create situations through their choices and actions, as we discussed

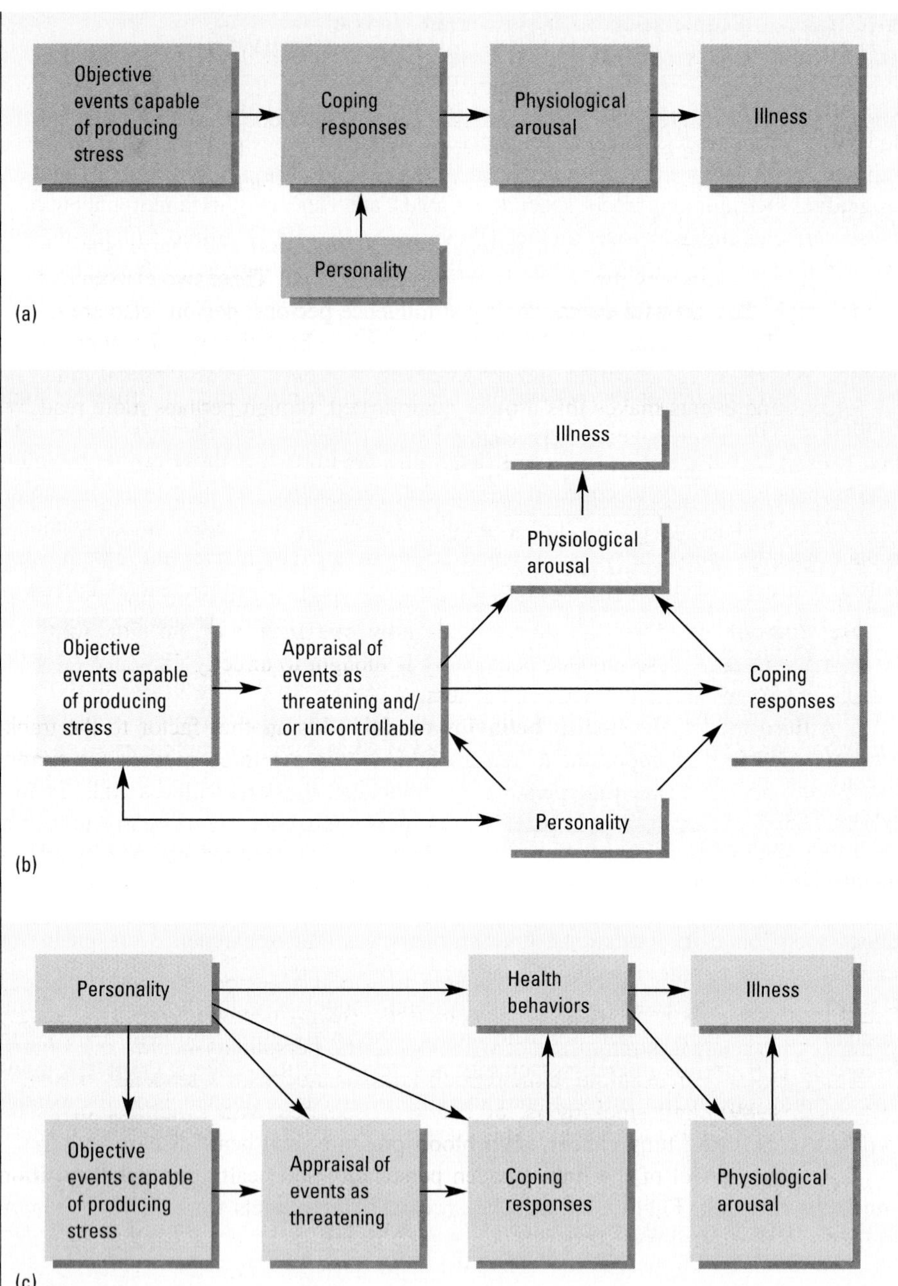

Figure 18.1

Three models specifying the role of personality in moderating the effects of stress on illness: (a) the interactional model, which specifies that personality influences how people cope; (b) the transactional model, which specifies that personality influences how people cope, as well as how they appraise and influence situations; and (c) the health behavior model, which specifies that personality influences how people cope, appraise, and influence situations, along with influencing the likely health behaviors that people practice.

in Chapter 4. People select to be in certain kinds of situations; they evoke certain responses from those situations, especially from the persons in the situations; and they manipulate the people in those situations, all in ways that may reflect their personalities. For example, a high-neuroticism person, someone who complains all the time, may create situations in which others frequently avoid him or her. Or a disagreeable person may create interpersonal situations in which he or she gets into a lot of arguments.

These two parts of the transactional model—appraisal and the person's influence on events—are why the model is called transactional. These two elements of the model imply that stressful events don't just influence persons; persons also are understood to influence events. And this influence comes about through the appraisal of events, as well as the selection and modification of events. This reciprocal influence of persons and events makes this a more complicated, though perhaps more realistic, model of how the process actually works.

The interactional and transactional models of personality and health are similar and were developed early on in research in this area. They are similar in that both posit a causal role for personality in coping with stress. However, the transactional model adds two additional roles for personality in influencing whether a stress response is evoked: first, personality influences the kinds of situations one encounters in life, and second, personality influences how one interprets the situations one encounters. In both these models, personality is thought to directly influence the relationship between stressful events and illness.

A third model, the **health behavior model,** adds another factor to the transactional model. It is important to realize that, so far, the three models are simply extensions of the theme that personality influences the stress-illness link. In this model, which is depicted in Figure 18.1(c), personality does not directly influence the relationship between stress and illness. Instead, in this model, personality affects health indirectly, through health-promoting or health-degrading behaviors. Everyone knows that poor health behaviors, such as eating too much fat, smoking, and practicing unsafe sex, increase the risk of developing certain illnesses. This model suggests that personality influences the degree to which a person engages in various health-promoting or health-degrading behaviors. Health behaviors are increasingly being acknowledged as important contributors to the personality-health link (Wiebe & Smith, 1997). For example, extraversion is associated with a tendency to smoke (Eysenck, 1989). And smoking is, of course, associated with a number of health problems, including lung cancer, high blood pressure, and heart disease.

A fourth model of the link between personality and health, the **predisposition model,** is shown in Figure 18.2(a). The previous three models were all variations on the same theme that personality influences the relationship between stress and illness either directly (interactional and transactional models) or indirectly (health behavior model). The fourth model is completely different and holds that personality and illness are both expressions of an underlying predisposition. This model is a very simple conception, suggesting that associations exist between personality and illness because of a third variable, which is causing them both. For example, enhanced sympathetic nervous system reactivity may be the cause of subsequent illnesses, *as well as* the cause of the behaviors and emotions that lead a person to be called neurotic. That is, an association can be found between disease and personality because of a predisposition that underlies both. The predisposition model has not been the topic of much systematic study, though it seems likely that this model will guide investigators interested in the genetic basis of illnesses. It may well turn out that some genetic

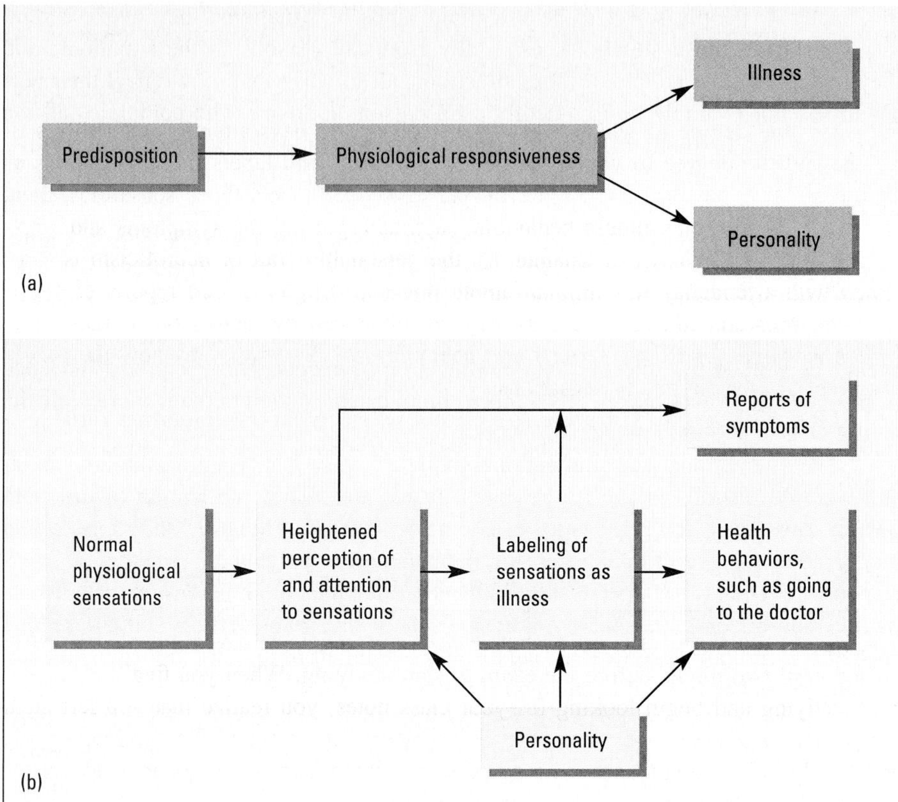

Figure 18.2

Additional models of the relationship between personality and health: (a) the predisposition model, which holds that personality and health are related due to a common predisposition; and (b) the illness behavior model, which specifies how personality might influence whether or not a person would seek medical attention or report illness symptoms.

predispositions are expressed both in terms of a stable individual difference and in terms of susceptibility to specific illnesses (Bouchard et al., 1990). For example, some researchers speculate that there is a genetic cause of novelty seeking (a trait like sensation seeking) and that this genetic sequence also causes, or makes a person more likely to develop an addiction to drugs (Cloninger, 1999). Consequently, the correlation between the novelty-seeking personality trait and addiction to drugs such as cocaine, meth, or heroin may be due to the fact that these two variables are both independently caused by a third variable—genes. This simple model may be useful as the human genome project (see Chapter 6) progresses from mapping the genome to understanding what specific genes control.

The final model for our consideration—called the **illness behavior model**—is not a model of illness per se but, rather, a model of illness behavior. Illness itself is defined as the presence of an objectively measurable abnormal physiological process, such as fever, high blood pressure, or a tumor. Illness behavior, on the other hand, is the action that people take when they think they have an illness, such as complaining to others about their symptoms, going to a doctor, taking the day off from school or work, or taking medication. Illness behaviors are related to actual illnesses, but not perfectly.

Some individuals may tough out an illness, stoically refusing to engage in illness behaviors (e.g., refusing to take the day off from work when ill). Alternatively, other people engage in all sorts of illness behaviors even in the absence of actual illness.

Figure 18.2(b) portrays the illness behavior model. It suggests that personality influences the degree to which a person perceives and pays attention to bodily sensations and the degree to which the person interprets and labels those sensations as an illness. The way in which a person perceives and labels those sensations, then, influences the person's illness behaviors, such as reporting the symptoms and going to a doctor. As discussed in Chapter 13, the personality trait of neuroticism is associated with a tendency to complain about physical symptoms. Self-reports of physical symptoms and illness behaviors may be influenced by factors other than actual illness, however, and these reports and behaviors are determined by how the person perceives and labels bodily sensations.

Most of the models of personality and illness contain one important variable—the concept of stress. Stress is an important but also a very much misunderstood phenomenon.

The Concept of Stress

Imagine that you have an important exam coming up in your chemistry class. You've waited until two nights before the exam to start studying. When you finally decide to start studying and begin looking for your class notes, you realize that you left them at your parents' home when you were visiting there last weekend. You go into a panic and finally call your parents, who agree to put them into overnight mail to you so you will have them the next day. You are pretty anxious now and cannot fall asleep for several hours after you go to bed, as you are worrying about this upcoming exam. The next day you are tired from not sleeping well. The class notes arrive, but you have other classes during the day, so you will have to study that night at your apartment. That night, as you are getting ready to study, your roommate reminds you of the party he had planned for this evening, about which you forgot. Now you have to go somewhere else to study, an unfamiliar environment, such as the library. You rush to the library and settle into a secluded area to study. Although it is quiet in the library, you are so tired and anxious that you cannot seem to concentrate on the material. At midnight, the library closes and you rush back to your apartment. The party is still going, and it continues until 2:00 A.M. Meanwhile, you are impatiently trying to study in your room but are distracted by the people and the music. Finally, you feel so overloaded you just give up and go to bed after the people leave. But even now you cannot sleep. You are anxious and frustrated and feeling totally unprepared for the important exam you have in the morning. In fact, you see that the exam will be held in just a few hours. Things are out of your control. You notice that

Studying for an exam can be stressful or not, depending on whether the situation controls you or you control the situation. Stress occurs when events seem uncontrollable and threatening. Taking control by keeping up with homework, planning each day, and preparing in a timely fashion can make studying less stressful.

you have a painful headache, and, even though you are lying in your bed, your heart is pounding and the palms of your hands are sweaty. You are not sure what to do. You want to study, but you also know it would be good to sleep a few hours. And you cannot seem to do either.

This is stress. It is a feeling of being overwhelmed by events that you cannot seem to control. Events that cause stress are called **stressors,** and they appear to have several common attributes:

1. Stressors are extreme, in the sense that they produce a state of feeling overwhelmed or overloaded, that one just cannot take it much longer.
2. Stressors often produce opposing tendencies, such as wanting and not wanting an activity or object—as in wanting to study but also wanting to put it off as long as possible.
3. Stressors are uncontrollable, outside our power to influence, such as an exam we cannot avoid.

Stress Response

When a stressor appears, people typically experience a pattern of emotional and physiological reactions, such as if someone were to startle you by honking an automobile horn as you walked in front of the car. You experience some startle, your heart beats faster and your blood pressure goes up, and your palms and soles of your feet begin to sweat. This pattern of reaction has commonly been called the fight-or-flight response. This physiological response is controlled by an increase of sympathetic nervous system activity (see Chapter 7 for more details on nervous system responses). The increase in heart rate and blood pressure prepares one for action, such as fighting or running away. The sweaty palms and feet are perhaps a preparation for holding a weapon or running away. This physiological response is usually very brief, and, if the stressor is as minor as someone honking a car horn to see you jump, then perhaps you return to your normal state in a minute or less.

If, however, a person is exposed to a particular stressor day in and day out, then this physiological fight-or-flight response is just the first step in a chain of events termed the **general adaptation syndrome (GAS)** by Hans Selye (1976), a pioneer in stress research. Selye proposed that the GAS followed a stage model, as depicted in Figure 18.3. The first stage, called the **alarm stage,** consists of the fight-or-flight response of the sympathetic nervous system and the associated peripheral nervous system reactions. These include the release of hormones, which prepare the body for challenge. If the stressor continues, then the next stage begins, the **resistance stage.** The body is using its resources at an above average rate, even though the immediate fight-or-flight response has subsided. At this point, stress is being resisted, but it is taking a lot of effort

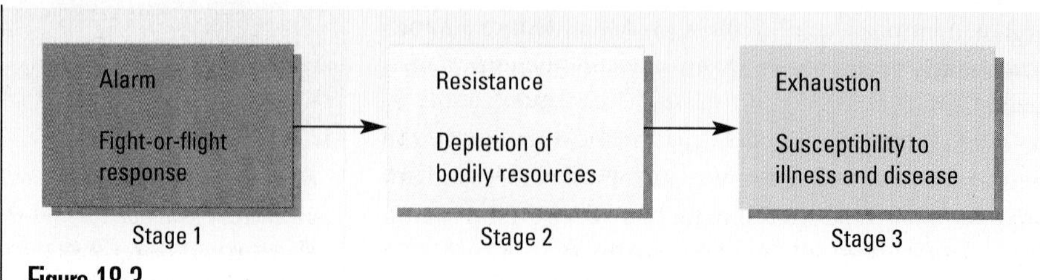

Figure 18.3

The three stages of the general adaptation syndrome proposed by Selye.

and energy. If the stressor remains constant, the person eventually enters the third stage, the **exhaustion stage.** Selye felt that this was the stage in which a person is most susceptible to illness and disease, as his or her physiological resources are depleted.

Major Life Events

What are some common stressors, events that are likely to evoke stress in most persons? Holmes and Rahe (1967) studied various **major life events,** those events that require people to make major adjustments in their lives. In their research, Holmes and Rahe wanted to estimate the potential stress value of a wide variety of life events. They started with a long list of events such as the death of a family member, loss of a job, or being put in jail. They then had a large number of subjects rate each of the events for how much stress each was likely to provoke. Each event was then associated with so many stress "points" and, by counting up the events a person had experienced, and adding up the stress points for all of those events, a good estimate of the amount of stress experienced by that person could be obtained.

In Table 18.1 we present a student version of the stressful event schedule based on the original Holmes and Rahe research. It has been modified for teaching purposes to apply to college-age adults and should be considered a rough indication of stress levels and health consequences. In this scale, the number following the event refers to the stress "points" associated with that event. You can see that death of a close family member, death of a friend, and divorce of parents are the events likely to evoke the most stress. Interestingly, getting married is also likely to be stressful, as are other "positive" events, such as starting college or making some major achievement. This highlights the fact that stress is the subjective response to an event and that, even though an event is positive, it may have the three characteristics associated with stressors: intensity, conflict, and uncontrollability.

If you take the Student Stress Test in Table 18.1 and turn out to have high levels of stress, there are several things you can do. First, monitor for early signs of stress, such as recurring stomachaches or headaches. Avoid negative thinking, pessimism, or catastrophizing. Arm your body against stress by eating nutritiously and getting enough sleep and exercise. Practice a relaxation technique regularly. Turn to friends and relatives for support when you need it.

In their initial research, Holmes and Rahe tallied up the stress points that each of the research participants had accumulated in the prior year. They found that the persons with the most stress points were also the most likely to have a serious illness during that year. This research was among the first systematic demonstrations that elevated stress—a psychological phenomenon—was associated with elevated risk for a number of illnesses. These findings persuaded medical researchers to take seriously the notion that factors other than microbes and organ malfunctions contribute to illness.

Other researchers have taken a more experimental approach to see if stress is related to susceptibility to disease. For example, Cohen, Tyrrell, and

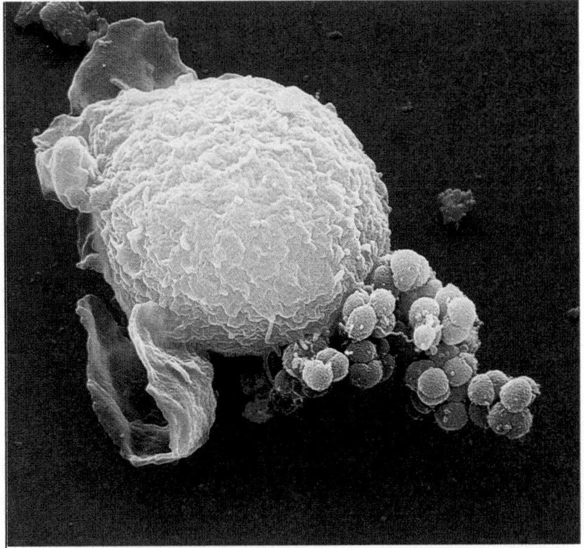

A macrophage white blood cell engulfing a cluster of Neisseria gonorrhoeae, the bacteria which cause the sexually transmitted disease gonorrhoea. The large white macrophages typically surround and destroy the bacteria, fulfilling their defensive role in the human immune system.

Table 18.1 The Student Stress Test

DIRECTIONS: On the list below, check off each event that has happened to you in the past year. To determine your stress score, add up the number of points corresponding to the events you have experienced in the past year. If your score is 300 or higher, you are at risk for developing a health problem from stress. If your score is between 150 and 300, you have a 50-50 chance of experiencing a health problem in the next few years if the stress persists. If your score is below 150, you have a relatively low risk of a serious health change due to stress (DeMeuse, 1985; Insel & Roth, 1985).

STUDENT STRESS SCALE

Event		Points
1. Death of a close family member	____	100
2. Death of a close friend	____	73
3. Divorce between parents	____	65
4. Jail term	____	63
5. Major personal injury or illness	____	63
6. Marriage	____	58
7. Fired from job	____	50
8. Failed important course	____	47
9. Change in health of a family member	____	45
10. Pregnancy	____	45
11. Sex problems	____	44
12. Serious argument with a close friend	____	40
13. Change in financial status	____	39
14. Change of major at college	____	39
15. Trouble with parents	____	39
16. New girl- or boyfriend	____	38
17. Increased workload	____	37
18. Outstanding personal achievement	____	36
19. First quarter/semester in college	____	35
20. Change in living conditions	____	31
21. Serious argument with instructor	____	30
22. Lower grades than expected	____	29
23. Change in sleeping habits	____	29
24. Change in social activities	____	29
25. Change in eating habits	____	28
26. Chronic car trouble	____	26
27. Change in number of family get-togethers	____	26
28. Too many missed classes	____	25
29. Change of college	____	24
30. Dropped more than one class	____	23
31. Minor traffic violations	____	20
TOTAL	____	

Source: From T. H. Holmes and R. H. Rahe, *Journal of Psychosomatic Research,* 1967, Vol. 11, pp. 213–217. Reprinted with permission from Elsevier.

Smith (1997) obtained reports of stressful life events for a group of volunteers and were able to score each participant along the lines of Holmes and Rahe's criteria for stressful points for various events. With the permission of the participants, these researchers then tried to infect half the participants with a cold by giving them nose drops containing the cold virus. The other half of the research participants were given plain nose drops; they served as the control group in this experiment. What happened? The participants with more negative life events in the previous year, who indicated they were experiencing a lot of life stress, were more likely to develop a cold after being given the cold virus than were the participants with fewer stressors in their lives, who were more resistant to the cold virus. The researchers interpreted this finding as consistent with the general adaptation syndrome: persons under chronic stress eventually deplete bodily resources and become vulnerable to microbial infections.

The relationship between increased stress and lowered resistance to viral and bacterial infection has been demonstrated repeatedly (e.g., Cohen et al., 1995). Currently, most researchers interpret such findings as illustrating the effects of stress on the immune system. That is, stress is thought to lower the functional ability of the immune system to mount an effective response to the presence of microbes, thereby leading to lowered immunity to infection and resulting illness (Marsland et al., 2001; Miller & Cohen, 2001).

Daily Hassles

Although the results on major life events are fascinating, researchers on stress have gone on to new questions. One new line of research starts with the observation that major life events are, thankfully, fairly infrequent in our lives. It seems that the major sources of stress in most people's lives are what are termed **daily hassles** (Delongis, Folkman, & Lazarus, 1988; Lazarus, 1991). While only minor, daily hassles can be chronic and repetitive. Examples of daily hassles are: having too much to do all the time, having to fight the crowds while shopping, getting stuck regularly in heavy traffic, having to wait in lines all the time, having an unpleasant boss at work, and having to worry over money. Such daily hassles can be chronically irritating, though they do not initiate the same general adaptation syndrome evoked by some major life events. The results of research on daily hassles have shown that, similar to major life events, persons with a lot of minor stress in their lives suffer more than expected from psychological and physical symptoms. The top 10 most common daily hassles are listed in Table 18.2.

Table 18.2 The 10 Most Commonly Experienced Daily Hassles

Hassles	Percentage*
Concerns about weight	52%
Health of a family member	48
Rising prices of common goods	43
Home maintenance	43
Too many things to do	39
Misplacing or losing things	38
Yard work or outside home maintenance	38
Property, investment, or taxes	37
Crime	37
Physical appearance	36

*Over a nine-month period, these percentages represent the average percentages of people indicating that the hassle was a significant source of stress.

Source: Adapted from Kanner et al., 1981, p. 14.

Varieties of Stress

Stress is a physical and psychological response to perceived demands and pressures. In the stress response, people mobilize physical and emotional resources to cope with the demands and pressures. A stress response that is frequent, extreme, or prolonged can place a large demand on, or even deplete, a person's physical, social, and psychological resources. Strong stressors also generate feelings of distress. Our bodies express this distress in a variety of ways, often in the form of irritability, anger, anxiety, depression, fatigue, tension headaches, stomachaches, hypertension, migraines, ulcers, or colitis. Eventually, stress can lead to even more serious illnesses, such as cancer, diabetes, or thyroid dysfunction.

Psychologists distinguish four varieties of stress:

- **Acute stress** is what most people associate with the term stress. Acute stress results from the sudden onset of demands and is experienced as tension headaches, emotional upsets, gastrointestinal disturbances, feelings of agitation, and pressure. September 11, 2001, was a day of acute stress for many people. Even for persons not directly involved in the terrible events of that day, many experienced the stress that comes from feeling that events are not under control (Peterson & Seligman, 2003).
- **Episodic acute stress** is more serious, in the sense that it refers to repeated episodes of acute stress, such as a weekend job that is stressful or having to meet a deadline each month. Episodic acute stress can lead to migraines, hypertension, stroke, anxiety, depression, or serious gastrointestinal distress.
- **Traumatic stress** refers to a massive instance of acute stress, the effects of which can reverberate for years or even a lifetime (e.g., Bunce, Larsen, & Peterson, 1995). Traumatic stress differs from acute stress mainly in terms of the symptoms associated with the stress response. This collection of

On September 11, 2001, many people in and around the World Trade Center in New York experienced traumatic stress. Many of these went on to develop posttraumatic stress disorder.

symptoms, called **posttraumatic stress disorder (PTSD),** is a syndrome that occurs in some persons following the experience of or witnessing life-threatening events, such as military combat, natural disasters, terrorist incidents, serious accidents, or violent personal assaults such as rape. Many persons in the United States experienced symptoms of PTSD after the September 11 terrorist tragedy. A recent study of refugees fleeing the war in Kosovo found that over 60 percent of them showed symptoms of PTSD (Ai, Peterson, Ubelhor, 2002). People who suffer from PTSD often relive the experience through nightmares or intense flashbacks, have difficulty sleeping, have physical complaints, have flattened emotions, and feel detached or estranged from others. These symptoms can be severe enough and last long enough to significantly impair the person's daily life, such as having trouble with personal relationships or difficulty holding down a job.

- **Chronic stress** is another serious form of stress. It refers to stress that does not end. Day in and day out, chronic stress grinds us down until our resistance is gone. Serious systemic illnesses, such as diabetes, decreased immune system functioning, or cardiovascular disease, can result from chronic stress.

Health psychologists believe that stress has **additive effects;** that is, the effects of stress add up and accumulate in a person over time. Stress affects each person differently. We each perceive demands and pressures differently and have different resources or coping skills. Such individual differences in the stress process form a core issue for psychologists who study personality and health.

Primary and Secondary Appraisal

Not all people respond to stressors in the same way. Two people can experience the same event, yet one is devastated and completely overwhelmed, whereas the other accepts the event as a challenge and is mobilized into positive action. Differences between people in how they respond to the same event are possible because stress is not "out there" in the environment. Rather, stress is in the *subjective reaction* of the person to potential stressors (Lazarus & Folkman, 1984). This is worth emphasizing, because many people refer to an event as stressful, as if stress were a characteristic of the event. Instead, stress is actually the response to that event. For example, two people are taking the same organic chemistry course; they take the same exam, and they both fail. One person may be very stressed by this event, whereas the other may take it in stride and not feel at all stressed by the failure. How can the same event happen to two people, yet one responds with stress and the other does not?

According to psychologist Richard Lazarus (1991), in order for stress to be evoked for a person, two cognitive events must occur. The first cognitive event, which Lazarus called **primary appraisal,** is for the person to perceive that the event is a threat to his or her personal goals. The second necessary cognitive event, **secondary appraisal,** is when the person concludes that he or she does not have the resources to cope with the demands of the threatening event. If either of these appraisals is absent—if the person does not perceive the event as threatening, or if the person feels he or she has plenty of resources for coping with the threat—then stress is not evoked. For example, if an event, such as an upcoming exam, is perceived as threatening to someone's goals, yet the person feels he or she has the resources demanded by that event (i.e., person has been studying and otherwise preparing for the exam), then the person might experience the event more as a challenge than as stress. Alternatively, the person might feel he or she does not have the resources demanded by the event (secondary appraisal) but might not think that the event is important to his or her long-term goals (primary appraisal) and, so, might not respond with stress.

What might lead some individuals to consistently avoid the stress response? What are some of the strategies that people use to overcome stress and the accompanying anxiety and feelings of being overwhelmed? Next we will consider several personality dimensions that have been associated with resistance to stress.

Coping Strategies and Styles

Everyone has unpleasant events happen in their lives. We all have temporary setbacks, losses, and frustrations in our day-to-day lives. However, some people seem better able to cope, to get over stressful events, or to somehow see such events as challenges rather than as sources of stress. One personality dimension that has been studied in relation to stress is one we are already familiar with from Chapter 12—attributional style.

Attributional Style

Recall that attributional style is a dispositional way of explaining the causes of bad events. One way to think about attributional style is in terms of the following question: "Where does the person typically place the blame when things go wrong?" You will also recall that the three important dimensions of attribution are external versus internal, unstable versus stable, and specific versus global. Various measures have been developed for assessing people's typical attributional style. Recall from Chapter 12 the Attributional Style Questionnaire (ASQ), developed by psychologist Chris Peterson and his colleagues (Peterson et al., 1982). However, another very useful technique for scoring attributional style is by analyzing the content of people's written or spoken explanations. People often spontaneously provide explanations for events in their everyday conversations or writings. It is possible to find these explanations in verbatim material and to rate them along the attributional dimensions of internality, stability, and globality. This technique for measuring attributional style was also developed by Peterson and his colleagues (Peterson et al., 1992), who called it the Content Analysis of Verbatim Explanations (CAVE).

Find a newspaper or magazine article in which a person is explaining an event—perhaps a story about an accident, a natural disaster, or some sporting event. Analyze the story, paying particular attention to quotes from various people, to find examples of each of the three dimensions of explanatory style:

- **Internal versus external**
- **Stable versus unstable**
- **Global versus specific**

Come up with a characterization of the views on this event in terms of how people attribute responsibility.

Following the events of September 11, 2001, the then mayor of New York City—Rudolph Giuliani—exhibited a public coping style that included making attributions for the events that were external, temporary, and specific.

The CAVE technique has the advantage of allowing the researcher to study participants who are either not available or not willing to participate in typical research, provided that such participants have made public some material containing causal explanations (Peterson, Seligman, & Vaillant, 1988). For example, presidential speeches, particularly State of the Union addresses, often contain explanations for a great many events. And movie stars often do interviews that contain explanations for events in their lives. Psychotherapy tapes can be analyzed with CAVE, as they often contain the persons' attributions for why things happened to them. Similarly, song lyrics, children's stories, descriptions of sports events, and myths and religious texts all contain explanations for events that can be rated for how internal, stable, and global they are.

Peterson, who has done a great deal of research on attributional style, now prefers the term *optimism* to refer to this individual difference construct (Peterson, 2000). Persons who make stable, global, and internal explanations for bad events are seen as pessimists, whereas persons who make unstable, specific, and external explanations for bad events are seen as optimists. Optimism/pessimism is viewed as a traitlike dimension along which people differ. Optimists believe that life events are unstable and specific and that what they do actually influences outcomes in life. Pessimists, on the other hand, believe that they are pretty helpless when it comes to bad events, that bad events have long-lasting causes that adversely affect many aspects of their lives (i.e., they blow things out of proportion). Consequently, pessimists believe that their behavior is not related to the outcomes in life.

Optimism has several different definitions, and distinctions can be made between the different underlying constructs (Peterson & Chang, 2003). For example, the optimism construct employed by Peterson and colleagues (e.g., Peterson & Steen, 2002) refers to the explanatory style for bad events being to blame them on stable,

A Closer Look

The Role of Positive Emotions in Coping with Stress

The vast majority of the research on personality and health focuses on negative emotions and how they contribute to stress and illness. However, in recent years, some researchers have taken an interest in the positive emotions, and positive appraisals, as well as how these can have a protective function (for a review, see Tedeschi, Park, & Calhoun, 1998). The general hypothesis is that positive emotions and positive appraisals may lead to a lowered impact of stress on health (Lyubomirsky, 2001).

Several decades ago, Lazarus, Kanner, and Folkman (1980) speculated that positive emotions played three important roles in the stress process: (1) they may sustain coping efforts, (2) they may provide a break from stress, and (3) they may give people time and opportunity to restore depleted resources, including the restoration of social relationships. However, no one in the health psychology research area gave serious attention to these ideas for almost two decades.

Recently, psychologist Barbara Fredrickson has led the way in the search for the effects of positive emotions on stress and illness. She has proposed a "broaden and build model" of positive emotions, suggesting that positive emotions broaden the scope of attention, cognition, and action. This helps the person see more options in stressful situations, think about alternatives, and try different ways of coping with the stress. The "build" part of her model suggests that positive emotions help a person build up reserves of energy, as well as build up social resources, especially in terms of how positive emotions help a person build a social support network. She proposes that positive emotions are important in facilitating adaptive coping and adjustment to stress (Fredrickson, 1998, 2000). In experimental research, Fredrickson and Levenson (1998) found that the experience of positive emotions, following a period of acute stress, facilitated recovery from that stress. Specifically, these researchers examined cardiovascular reactivity to anxiety and threat manipulations, and they found that the participants who underwent a positive emotion following this stress showed faster heart rate and blood pressure recovery than did the participants who did not get the positive mood induction.

Psychologists Susan Folkman and Judith Moskowitz (2000) have built on Fredrickson's ideas and have suggested several important mechanisms in determining whether people will experience positive emotions during periods of severe stress. They give examples of these positive coping mechanisms from their study of gay men who were caregivers of partners dying from AIDS. Caring for someone with a chronic debilitating disease, such as AIDS or Alzheimer's disease, can be extremely stressful and often leads the caregiver to suffer physical costs from the stress and strain. From their study of such caregivers, Folkman and Moskowitz have identified three coping mechanisms that are capable of generating positive emotion during stress, as opposed to coping strategies that mainly provide relief from negative emotions.

The first positive emotion coping strategy is called **positive reappraisal,** a cognitive process whereby a person focuses on the good in what is happening or has happened. Forms of this positive coping strategy include seeing opportunities for personal growth and seeing how one's own efforts can benefit other people. By changing how they interpret what is happening to them, people actually change the meaning of situations such that the adversity, in fact, gives them strength. In their study of AIDS caregivers, Folkman and Moskowitz found that the caregivers who were able to positively reappraise the situation (e.g., "I will emerge from this challenge a stronger and better person") showed better adjustment both during caregiving and even after the death of their partners (Moskowitz et al., 1996).

Folkman and Moskowitz caution that not all forms of positive reappraisal are adaptive. For example, if one fails at a goal, then devalues that goal, this may not lead to positive emotions. For example, imagine you want to go to Harvard Law School, but your application is rejected. You may cognitively reappraise the situation by saying, "Harvard Law School is really not so good." By lessening the significance of the goal, you may not feel as negative, but it does not necessarily produce happiness or the other positive emotions that Folkman and Moskowitz are talking about.

The second positive coping strategy identified by Folkman et al. (1997) is **problem-focused coping,** using thoughts and behaviors to manage or solve the underlying cause of the stress. It has typically been assumed that this strategy is useful in situations in which a person has some control over the outcomes. However, Folkman and Moskowitz note how this strategy can be useful in situations that, on the surface, appear uncontrollable. In the AIDS caregiver study, many of the caregivers were caring for partners who were dying, a situation that could not be stopped, reversed, or even slowed. However, even in these seemingly uncontrollable conditions, some caregivers were able to focus on the things they could control. For example, many created "to-do" lists of little things, such as getting prescriptions filled, administering medications, and changing their partners' bed linens. Keeping such lists, and ticking off the completed items, gave the caregivers opportunities to feel effective and in control in an otherwise overwhelming situation. And many reported that positive emotions accompanied such accomplishments, even minor ones. Many caregivers reported feeling energized and focused by their problem-directed actions. And they experienced the gratitude from their partners and others when tasks were completed. In short, focusing on solving problems, even little ones, can give a person a positive sense of control even in the most stressful and uncontrollable circumstances.

The third positive coping mechanism is called **creating positive events** and is defined as creating a positive time-out from the stress. This can be done in a number of ways. Often, all it takes is to pause and reflect on something positive, such as a compliment received, a pleasing or humorous memory, or a sunset. These sorts of time-outs can give a person a momentary respite from the chronic stress. Many of the AIDS caregivers took time to remember positive events or to plan positive events, such as taking their partners for scenic drives. Some tried to create positive events by infusing neutral events with positive meaning, trying to capture a few moments of happiness during an otherwise very stressful time. Some of the caregivers reported using humor to find some positive relief. It has long been thought that humor can be a tension reducer and that it may contribute to mental and physical health (Menninger, 1963). Folkman and Moskowitz note that humor can have the added benefit of generating positive emotional moments even during the darkest periods of stress. In this way, humor and positive emotions can provide a respite from stress and even help build and strengthen social bonds.

This focus on positive emotions and their role in health and illness is new, and the research is in very early stages. Many of the early findings are intriguing but also raise new questions for research. For example, do different kinds of positive emotions—such as excitement, happiness, or contentment—play different roles in the stress process? Are the positive emotions most helpful in coping with particular kinds of stress? For example, are positive emotions more helpful in chronic, long-term stress or in shorter, acute stress? And, finally, of particular interest to personality psychologists are questions about differences between people in the ability to generate positive emotions while coping with stress (Affleck & Tennen, 1996). Who are the people who can generate humor, for example, during periods of coping? Can people be taught different strategies for using positive emotions to cope? Are specific personality traits, such as extraversion or optimism, uniquely related to positive emotion coping styles? These important questions point the way for the personality researchers of the future, who will undertake the necessary studies to understand why it is that some people manage to survive disaster, hardship, and misfortune with some degree of positivity.

global, and internal causes. However, a slightly different definition of optimism is offered by Scheier and Carver (1985; Carver & Scheier, 2000). These researchers emphasize **dispositional optimism** as the expectation that good events will be plentiful in the future, and that bad events will be rare in the future. For example, optimists are likely to believe that they will achieve success in most areas of their lives. This definition emphasizes not explanatory style, but expectations for the future.

Another concept related to optimism, called **self-efficacy,** was developed by Bandura (1986). As discussed in Chapter 12, self-efficacy is the belief that one can do the behaviors necessary to achieve a desired outcome. Self-efficacy also is the confidence one has in one's ability to perform the actions needed to achieve a specific outcome. For example, someone's belief and confidence that he or she can climb Mt. Everest—this subjective feeling, the positive expectation about performing the behaviors necessary to climb the mountain—is self-efficacy.

Finally, a fourth concept related to optimism concerns perceptions of risk. Imagine being asked to estimate the probability of various events happening to you, using a scale from 0 to 100; 0 means "it will never happen to me" and 100 means "it is certain to happen to me." The events you are asked to estimate are such things as dying in a plane crash, being diagnosed with cancer, having a heart attack, and being hit by lightning. Optimists perceive that they are at lower risk for such negative events than the average person is. What is interesting, however, is that most people generally underestimate their risks, with the average person rating his or her risk as below what is the true probability. This has been referred to as the **optimistic bias,** and it may actually lead people in general to ignore or minimize the risks inherent in life or to take more risks than they should. Nevertheless, people differ dramatically from each other in their perceptions of the risks associated with everyday life, with pessimistic persons overestimating the risks, relative to optimistic persons.

Exercise

Before reading any further, please write a short answer to the following question: Define *health.* Now compare your answer to the points raised in the following discussion.

There are several ways to conceptualize and define *health.* For example, is health best measured by asking a person how he or she feels or by seeing how many times the person goes to the doctor? Would it be better to measure how many germs people have been exposed to or to assess the functioning of their immune system? Or is the best measure of health simply how long a person lives? Although there are many ways of thinking about health, they do not all necessarily correlate with each other. For example, women go to the doctor more frequently than men do, so do we conclude that men are healthier? On the other hand, women tend to live longer than men do, so should we then conclude that women are healthier? Obviously, how one interprets the results of this research depends on how health is defined in each study.

Many studies on personality and health focus on health as the absence of disease or on the length of the person's life. Psychologists focus on whether or not their participants are sick, or whether or not they are dead after a certain number of years. This view of health as the absence of disease may be only part of the picture when it comes to personality and health. Another part of the picture may have to do with quality of life. Is the person living well? How long a person lives or whether they are free from disease may not be a good measure of physical well-being. Physical wellness is something beyond normal health; it is an energetic life, a life of engagement with the events and activities of daily living, a satisfying career, rewarding friendships, and good relations with family members. In the future, psychologists interested in personality and health may begin to focus on what personality variables appear to promote not just physical health, but living well, living a high-quality life that is not only free from disease but that also includes enjoyment, satisfaction, engagement, and meaning. As such, the final word is not in on what is the best way to think about and measure health, so we should always qualify research findings by noting which measures of health were used.

Optimism and Physical Well-Being

Many theorists using the various optimism constructs have examined the correlation between this individual difference and physical health and well-being. Research on optimism and health has been reviewed in detail by Peterson and colleagues (Peterson & Bossio, 1991; Peterson & Seligman, 1987). As a summary, optimism in general has been shown to predict good health as measured by self-report, ratings of general health made by the participants' physicians, the number of visits to the doctor, survival time after heart attacks, immune system functioning, faster rehabilitation after breast cancer surgery, and longer life (Carver et al., 1993; Scheier & Carver, 1992; Scheier et al., 1999). Moreover, optimism is found to correlate with a number of positive health behaviors, such as exercising regularly, avoiding fatty foods, drinking only in moderation or not at all, and responding to a cold with appropriate action, (e.g., resting and taking fluids).

As with much personality research, the typical correlations between optimism and health or health behaviors tend to run between .20 and .30. Moreover, because this research is correlational, we cannot really know the causal mechanisms involved in the health-optimism link. For example, optimism may relate to a lower likelihood of becoming ill, to developing an illness of a lesser severity, to a faster recovery, or to a decreased likelihood of relapse.

As an in-depth example of research on optimism and health, let's look at a study by Peterson and colleagues (Peterson et al., 1998). This study examined more than 1,000 individuals over almost a 50-year period. The researchers found that the participants who scored in the more pessimistic direction were more likely to die an earlier death than the optimistic participants were. Similar findings, based on a much smaller sample, were mentioned in Chapter 12. Because Peterson and colleagues (1998) had such a large sample, the researchers were able to look at various causes of death to see where optimists and pessimists most differed. The researchers thought that the biggest differences might be in deaths due to cancer and heart disease, where they predicted that pessimists would have more of these lethal medical problems. This was not the case, however. The researchers found that the real difference between the optimists and pessimists, in terms of the causes of death, was in the frequency of accidents and violent deaths, with pessimists having more accidental deaths and deaths due to violent causes, resulting in a generally shorter life span, on average, than that of the optimists. This effect was especially strong for the men in this sample.

It seems that pessimists, especially male pessimists, have a habit of being in the wrong place at the wrong time. This research does not actually tell us specifically what the participants were doing when they accidentally or violently died. However, it seems likely that they were in the wrong situation, and moreover it is likely that pessimists, especially males, frequently choose to be in the wrong situation. An anecdote told by Peterson and Bossio (2001) is about a person who says, "I broke my nose in two places," and someone responds, "Well, I'd stay out of those two places if I were you." Pessimists, it appears, are frequently in those wrong places.

This result has recently been replicated, with pessimistic explanatory style correlating with the frequency of occurrence of accidents (Peterson et al., 2001). The link between pessimism and a greater likelihood of mishaps appeared to be due to a preference for potentially hazardous situations and activities on the part of pessimists. Perhaps pessimists are motivated to escape their gloomy moods by choosing exciting but risky situations and activities.

Because of optimism's obvious health benefits, psychologist Marty Seligman and his colleagues are attempting to develop therapeutic ways to increase people's level of optimism (2002; Seligman & Peterson, 2003). In particular, Seligman has introduced a "pessimism prevention" program for use in grade schools, the details of which can be found in Weissberg, Kumpfer, and Seligman (2003) as well as at Dr. Seligman's website at the University of Pennsylvania, http://www.psych.upenn.edu/seligman. The program teaches cognitive and social problem-solving skills that are based on optimistic principles. The program has been found to be effective at preventing symptoms of depression in low-income minority middle-school students (Cardemil, Reivich, & Seligman, 2002) and mainland Chinese adults (Yu & Seligman, 2002).

A Closer Look How Does Optimism Promote Health?

Is it possible to learn to be optimistic, and thereby avoid the health risks associated with pessimism? Is pessimism like smoking—once you overcome it, the health risk soon returns to normal levels? Psychologist Martin Seligman and colleagues have started a program to teach grade school children how to be optimistic. According to their evaluation of this program (Gillham et al., 1995), the results look promising. The children in this study who were taught to be more optimistic tended to have fewer episodes of depression than the ones who did not receive optimism training. The participants are still young, however, so future effects remain to be investigated. It will be interesting to see what happens to the trained optimists as they grow older. Will they have better physical health than the children who were not given the optimism training?

Psychologists might be able to teach specific skills if they knew exactly what it was about optimism that promotes better health. Psychologists have theorized about the possible mechanisms that link optimism to health. It is important to view these mechanisms not as competing hypotheses but, rather, with the view that two or more of these mechanisms may be operating to produce better health among optimists.

One mechanism is through the immune system. Seligman and his colleagues (Kamen-Siegel, Rodin, Seligman, & Dwyer, 1991), have shown that the immune systems of optimists respond better and with more strength to a challenge than the immune systems of pessimists. Other researchers have examined how optimism relates to the progression of HIV. Although results are mixed, there are suggestions in the literature that optimists have a longer survival time after the development of AIDS symptoms and that this may be due to stronger immune function among optimists (Peterson & Bossio, 2001).

Another way optimism may relate to better health is through an emotional mechanism. There is a very large literature on how optimists are resistant to depression. Other studies have linked depression to increased risk for disease and poor health. It could be that optimism is related to health indirectly, because it protects persons from depression and, hence, the debilitating health effects of this uncomfortable emotional condition.

Another mechanism through which optimism might be linked to health is through a cognitive process. Optimism may be related to an extensive set of beliefs about oneself and the world, and these beliefs may, in part, promote health or healthy behaviors. For example, Peterson and de Avila (1995) showed that optimism was related to the belief that one can maintain and promote one's own good health as well as the belief that one can reduce health risks. Other studies have shown that optimists see the world as less filled with hassles and therefore feel less stress than pessimists.

Another pathway through which optimism may influence health is through a mechanism that promotes social contact. Pessimists tend to be loners, and social isolation is a reliable predictor of poor health (Cobb, 1976) and general distress and dissatisfaction with life (Diener, 1996). A person's friends and family may provide the earliest medical feedback when things start going bad. For example, a friend might say, "You look stressed today," or a roommate might remark, "You are looking really tired these days. Is something wrong?" If pessimists are isolated and avoid social contact, then they may have less of this social feedback and, hence, not have this source of information about their health status.

A final and obvious way in which optimism and health might be related is through a direct behavioral mechanism. Optimism may set into motion certain behaviors that lead to benefits for health. For example, optimists engage in higher levels of problem-focused coping and lower levels of avoidance coping, such as ignoring problems (Scheier, Weintraub, & Carver, 1986). The answer to how optimism and health are linked could be as simple as that optimists act differently and take better care of their health than pessimists do. Or it could be that optimists are better at coping and, so, experience less stress than pessimists. Behavior—simply doing more of the right things (e.g., exercising, sleeping enough) and fewer of the wrong things (e.g., drinking, having unsafe sex)—may prove to be the most critical link in the connection between optimism and health.

You can see how complicated the link between optimism and health can be. Since most of the research on this topic is correlational, psychologists cannot pinpoint exactly which factors are responsible for the correlation. Nevertheless, psychologists speculate about what factors are behind this association, and future research will help determine the most effective components of the optimistic personality style in contributing to better health and a longer life.

Management of Emotions

Sometimes we have emotions, and sometimes emotions have us. Emotions, especially negative ones, can be particularly difficult to control. Nevertheless, we can try to inhibit the expression of negative emotions, especially under certain circumstances. Imagine that your school team just lost an important championship, and you are really unhappy, distressed, and in an irritable mood, angry at the referees and disappointed by your team. However, you have an important exam tomorrow, so you must inhibit your distracting unpleasant emotions and concentrate on studying. You can think of similar examples of **emotional inhibition,** such as controlling your anxiety or hiding the fact that you are disappointed. For example, have you ever received a gift you really didn't like? Perhaps you suppressed your disappointment and replaced it with some positive false emotions, smiled, and said, "Thanks a lot; I really wanted one of those."

We all have to cover up such disappointments once in a while. But what about people who routinely suppress their emotions, who keep everything inside? What are the consequences of chronically inhibiting one's emotions? Some theorists suggest that emotional inhibition leads to undesirable consequences. For example, Sigmund Freud (see Chapter 9) believed that most psychological problems were the result of inhibited negative emotions and motivations. That is, repression and the other defense mechanisms are ways of preventing an unacceptable emotion from surfacing and being directly experienced and expressed. The early psychoanalysts saw this suppression of emotion, the pushing of unacceptable desires or urges into the unconscious, as the root of all psychological problems. Psychoanalytic therapy, or the talking cure, was designed to bring unconscious emotion into conscious awareness, so that it could be experienced and expressed in a mature manner. Moreover, the therapeutic relationship was seen as a place to experience and express emotions that had long been inhibited. There are other therapies that might be called "expressive therapies" because their goal is to get the person to release inhibited emotions.

Other theorists see emotional inhibition more positively. From a developmental perspective, the ability to inhibit emotions is acquired at an early age, at around 3years, and is seen as a major developmental achievement. This is when children, though sad, are able to stop themselves from crying or when angry they can inhibit themselves from striking back (Kopp, 1989; Thompson, 1991). The ability to inhibit negative emotion is seen as a very useful skill to learn in childhood. Children need to learn to control temper outbursts, such as the urge to hit someone who takes a toy from them. We have all seen adults who don't do a very good job of controlling disappointment or frustration, and their behavior (e.g., an adult temper tantrum) is often seen as childish. Some people are, however, very good at inhibiting negative emotions, even strong emotions. As an example, perhaps you have seen the Miss America pageant on television. At the end, the judges narrow down the contest to two deserving women. And, while the camera is on both of them, the winner is announced. The woman who does *not* win graciously smiles and looks happy and excited for the winner. One wonders, however, if the runner-up is inhibiting herself from displaying the emotions she is really feeling at that moment. Is she really so happy about the other woman winning? Is she inhibiting the expression of her deep disappointment and sadness over her loss?

Which woman is genuinely happy? The woman on the left, Kelli Bradshaw from North Carolina, reacts to hearing her name called as the first runner-up (second place) in the Miss America Pageant in 1998. By implication, the woman on the right, Nicole Johnson from Virginia, simultaneously realizes that she is the next Miss America.

What do research psychologists know about the effects of chronically inhibited emotion? Surprisingly, there have been only a few well-done studies that directly address this question. For example, psychologists James Gross and Robert Levenson (1993, 1997; Gross, 2002) designed studies in which some of the participants were asked to suppress the expression of any emotions they were feeling while they watched a video designed to evoke the emotions of happiness (a comedy routine), then sadness (scenes from the funeral of a child, showing a distraught and highly emotional mother). Half of the participants were randomly assigned to the suppression condition, in which they were told, "If you have any feelings as you watch the [video,] please try your best not to let those feelings show. In other words, try to behave in a way that a person watching you would not know you were feeling anything at all." The other half of the participants were assigned to the no suppression condition, in which they were simply told to watch the video and were given no instructions to inhibit their emotions.

While the participants watched the videos, the researchers videotaped the participants, to determine how much the participants expressed their emotions while watching the video. The researchers also collected several physiological measures, such as those we discussed in Chapter 7. They also asked the participants to report on their feelings after each segment of the video.

Results showed that the participants who were instructed to suppress their emotions showed increased levels of physiological arousal, even before the video began, compared with the no-suppression participants. This widespread physiological arousal was interpreted as indicating that the participants were preparing for the effort necessary to suppress their emotions. The suppression participants also showed heightened physiological activity during the video, indicating increased sympathetic nervous system arousal, compared with the no-suppression participants. The researchers suggested that suppression of emotion takes effort and exerts physiological costs above and beyond the emotional arousal. The participants in the suppression condition showed less *outward* expression of emotion than did the control participants, as you would imagine. For example, the facial expressions of the suppression participants displayed little emotion, suggesting that they were, in fact, inhibiting the outward expression of their emotions, as instructed. As for the self-report, the suppression participants reported slightly less amusement in the amusement condition, but not less sadness in the sadness condition, compared with the no-suppression participants.

The researchers in this study suggest that hiding one's emotions, particularly negative emotions, is not likely to influence how one actually feels. Moreover, the inhibition of emotion appears to cause some increased physiological arousal, primarily in the sympathetic nervous system, the system associated with the fight-or-flight stress response. This study suggests that, at a physiological level, the inhibition of emotion is associated with a pattern of physiological arousal that looks much like a stress response. In other words, the inhibition of emotion seems to come with certain costs to the nervous system.

In addition to its effects on physiological arousal, the suppression of emotions also has other negative consequences. In a series of studies, Gross and John (2003) showed that the suppression of negative emotions, achieved by hiding one's feelings, was also associated with diminished positive emotions later in the experiment. Moreover, these researchers present a questionnaire for assessing whether someone uses suppression as a habitual style of coping with negative emotions. Butler et al. (2003) also showed that people who suppressed their negative emotions had worse interpersonal relations and lower levels of well-being than the more expressive persons. They argued that, by not expressing themselves, suppressors disrupt what is a normal form of communication. This has an inhibiting effect on the formation of relationships and reduces rapport between people.

In an interesting line of research on emotion, Gross and colleagues (Ochsner, Bunge, Gross, & Gabrieli, 2002) attempted to locate the emotional control center in the brain. They used fMRI to scan participants' brains while the participants tried to reinterpret a highly negative scene in unemotional terms. They found that several brain areas were associated with the successful regulation of negative emotions. These areas were mainly in the prefrontal cortex of the brain. This frontal part of the brain, which is also involved in planning and executive control, appears to be active when people are controlling their emotions. Interestingly, this is the area that was destroyed in the case of Phineas Gage, discussed in Chapter 7. Recall that Mr. Gage, after his accident, had difficulty controlling his negative emotions, took up cursing in public, was quick to anger, and frequently insulted people.

Sometimes it is necessary to inhibit feelings. Perhaps you do not want to hurt someone's feelings, perhaps you do not want to antagonize someone in a position of power, or perhaps you do not want to anger someone who is already acting aggressively (Larsen & Prizmic, 2004). For example, your boss may be upset with you for the wrong reason, and you may feel angry toward her. However, you cannot act out that anger because she is your boss and has a lot of power over you in terms of raises, workload, and working conditions. Quite simply, there are some situations in life in which it is wise to choose to hide feelings.

However, problems can arise when emotional inhibition becomes chronic, when a person routinely hides emotions. Someone who characteristically inhibits the free expression of emotion may suffer the effects of chronic sympathetic nervous system arousal. For example, Levy and colleagues (1985) have shown that people who keep their negative emotions to themselves are more likely than expressive persons to have

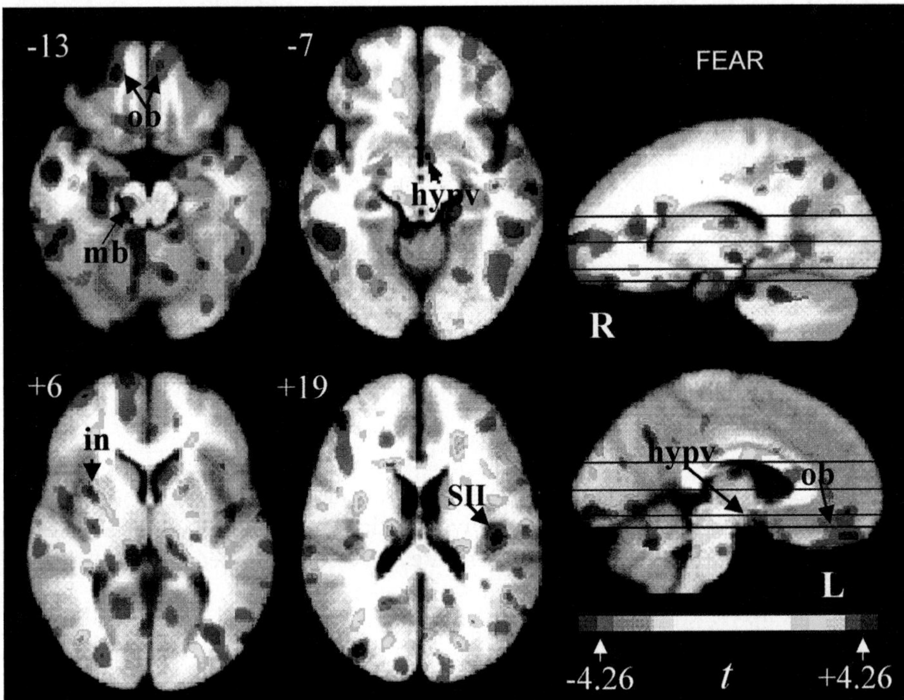

Example of an fMRI brain scan. Brighter colors, such as red, indicate areas with increased metabolic activity.

a higher mortality rate, a greater likelihood of recurrence of cancer after treatment, and a suppressed immune system. For example, cancer patients who express their negative emotions, and who emotionally fight their disease, sometimes live longer than patients who accept their situation, inhibit their emotions, and quietly accept their treatment (Levy, 1990, Levy & Heiden, 1990).

The importance of emotional expression was illustrated in a study done by Noller (1984) on emotional expressiveness in romantic relationships. Noller found that, the more people expressed their feelings to their partners, the fewer problems they reported in their relationships. Knowing how another feels allows you to adjust your behavior accordingly. If your partner never expresses how he or she feels, then it is difficult to know what makes him or her happy or sad.

Other studies suggest that emotional expressiveness is good for our psychological health and general adjustment. King and Emmons (1990) had participants keep daily records of how they were feeling each day for three consecutive weeks. The participants completed a questionnaire measure of emotional expressiveness. The researchers found that emotional expressiveness correlated with higher levels of happiness over the three weeks, as well as with lower levels of anxiety and guilt. A similar study by Katz and Campbell (1994) found that emotional expressiveness was correlated with higher self-esteem.

Disclosure

Related to emotional expressiveness is the topic of **disclosure,** or telling someone about a private aspect of oneself. Many theorists have suggested that keeping things to ourselves, not opening up to other people, may be a source of stress and ultimately may lead to psychological distress and physical disease. These theorists have further argued that being open to others with our feelings may be curative, that talk therapy may work in part because through it we uncover secrets and reveal what we have been keeping to ourselves.

Psychologist James Pennebaker has been a pioneer in researching the effects of disclosure. In a typical study, he asks participants to think of an upsetting or traumatic event that has happened to them, something they have not discussed with anyone. He asks them to write down these secrets. People write about many different unpleasant events, such as various embarrassing moments, sexual indiscretions, illegal or immoral behaviors, humiliations, and so on. It is interesting that *all* participants quickly come up with a secret that they have been keeping. This suggests that probably all of us have some secrets.

Pennebaker argues that *not* discussing traumatic, negative, or upsetting events can lead to problems. It takes physical energy, he says, to inhibit the thoughts and feelings associated with such events. In other words, it is not easy to keep a secret to ourselves, and keeping something in, especially if it is a major trauma, is upsetting and takes a lot of energy. Over time, this stress builds and, like all stress, can increase the likelihood of stress-related problems, such as trouble sleeping, irritability, physical symptoms (e.g., stomachaches and headaches), and even illness resulting from lowered immune system functioning. Telling the secret, according to Pennebaker, relieves this stress. Confronting the traumatic memory by telling someone or even writing about it releases the person from the work of keeping the secret.

Pennebaker and his colleagues have conducted many studies on the topic of disclosure. In one study (Pennebaker & O'Heeron, 1984), they contacted participants who had lost a spouse through accident or suicide. Clearly, such a sudden and complete loss of a loved one through an unexpected and traumatic death must have a huge impact on the surviving spouse (recall that death of a spouse was the most stressful life event on the Holmes and Rahe list). The survivors were asked how much they discussed the tragedy with friends, family, or other helping professionals, such as a priest, minister, or therapist. The researchers also did a thorough assessment of the participants' health since the death of the spouse. They discovered that, the more the participants had talked about the tragedy with others, the better their subsequent health. In other words, those who kept the trauma to themselves tended to suffer more health problems than those who disclosed their feelings to others.

In another study on this topic (Pennebaker, 1990), the participants were college students randomly assigned to one of two groups. One group was asked to recall and write about an experience that they found distressing. The other group was asked to write about a trivial topic, such as what they normally ate for breakfast. The students wrote about their assigned topic for 15 minutes each night for four consecutive nights. The participants writing about the traumatic event reported feeling more distress and discomfort while writing, and measures of blood pressure taken while writing suggested they were feeling more stress than was the trivial topic group. Six months later, the participants were contacted again and a health history was obtained. Students who had written about a trauma for those four days had had fewer illnesses in the subsequent six months, compared with the students who had written about trivial topics. Moreover, student records from the health services showed that the participants who had written about trauma had indeed gone to the campus health center less often than the participants who had written about trivial topics. Interestingly, just the act of writing about an upsetting event, even if no one ever reads the writing, may have a beneficial effect on health.

In another study by Pennebaker and colleagues (Pennebaker, Colder, & Sharp, 1990), the participants were just starting college. For three nights in a row, they were asked to write about their difficulties and their feelings about the challenges of leaving family and friends at home and starting an independent life at college. Other participants (the control group) wrote about trivial topics. Health measures were then obtained after the students had been in college for at least a semester: the students who had written about their feelings and problems had gone to the student health center fewer times during the subsequent semester than had those who had witten about trivial topics.

Other studies show that people who keep unpleasant information about themselves a secret are more likely to develop anxiety or depression than are those who tell someone (Larson & Chastain, 1990). Often, psychotherapists will ask their clients, especially those who have experienced a trauma or another extreme event, to talk or write about that trauma. Some psychologists even recommend keeping a diary of the events in one's life and how one is reacting to those events. Such a daily self-disclosure helps one put one's feelings into perspective and make some sense out of the events in one's life. The process provides insight into oneself and the events in one's life.

Exercise

Try conducting a small experimental test of Pennebaker's hypothesis that disclosing secrets, even in writing, is associated with better health. Keep a record of your health every day for two weeks. Record each day whether you have a stomachache, a headache, muscle aches, a sore throat, or a runny nose. After this baseline period of recording your health, try keeping a diary each day for two weeks, writing down and

Exercise (*Continued*)

describing all the stresses you experience each day and reflecting on how these make you feel. Pay attention to any difficulties, stress, or even embarassing or trying moments. When the two weeks are over, stop keeping the diary and begin recording your daily health again. Although this is not a true experiment (you are both the subject and the experimenter, which is not done in true experiments), you can nevertheless get a feel for how research on this topic is done, and you might see a change in your health for the better, as a function of keeping a diary.

How does disclosure work to promote healthy adjustment? Pennebaker's first theory of the mechanism concerned the relief that results from telling a secret. In other words, keeping the information inside takes effort and is stressful, and disclosing that information removes the effort and relieves the stress (Niederhoffer & Pennebaker, 2002). This explanation basically says that disclosure reduces the cost of having to inhibit this information. More recently, Pennebaker (2003a) has put forward a second explanation for how disclosure promotes adjustment. This explanation concerns how writing about an event allows a person to reinterpret and reframe the meaning of that event. In other words, a person writing or talking about a past traumatic event can try to better understand that event, can search for some positive meaning in the event (the silver lining that is in every cloud), and can integrate that event into her or his current situation. Both processes—relief from inhibition and reinterpretation of the event—may be occurring, and so both explanations may be correct. Indeed, Pennebaker (2003b) has speculated that this combination may be the basic ingredient that underlies most forms of successful talking therapy.

In summary, research on disclosure suggests that keeping traumatic events, and the feelings about those events, to ourselves can be stressful. Expressing our emotions in words can, in fact, produce some stress-reducing effects. Moreover, it appears that it does not matter how we put our feelings into words—whether we talk to a trusted friend or relative, go to a caring psychotherapist, go to confession at our church or have a talk with our minister or rabbi, have a discussion with our husband or wife, or write it in a diary. Whatever form it takes, the disclosure of traumatic events, and our reactions to them, is much better for our health than keeping it all to ourselves.

Type A Personality and Cardiovascular Disease

Cardiovascular disease is one of the most frequent causes of death and disability in the United States. Health professionals have been searching for the factors that put people at risk for this disease. Known risk factors for developing cardiovascular disease include high blood pressure, obesity, smoking, family history of heart disease, inactive lifestyle, and high cholesterol. In the 1970s, physicians began to consider a new risk factor, a specific personality trait. As mentioned in Chapter 13, this grew out of the observation by some physicians that the patients who had had heart attacks often behaved differently, and they seemed to have different personalities, compared with other patients. The heart attack patients were often more competitive and aggressive, more active and energetic in their actions and speaking, and more ambitious and driven (Friedman & Rosenman, 1974). They called this collection of behaviors the **Type A personality.**

Chapter 13 focused on the Type A personality dimension and emotion. Here we focus on Type A personality and health. Before examining some of the research findings on Type A, let us look at a few misconceptions. Although researchers often refer to Type A and Type B persons, it is not true that people come in these two distinct categories. Few variables are truly categorical, whereby people fall into distinct categories. Biological sex is an example of a categorical variable; blood type is another. However, very few personality traits are categorical. Instead, most are dimensional, ranging from one extreme to the other, with most people falling somewhere around the middle. The Type A/Type B distinction is like this, with Type As defining one end and Type Bs the other, and a large number of people in the middle, who are neither clearly A or B. Thus, the Type A personality variable is a trait, or disposition, as discussed in Chapter 3. It is distributed normally, as in Figure 18.4(a), not as a category variable. Psychologists describe normally distributed traits by reference to one end (e.g., Type A). However, by describing the characteristics of people at one end, e.g., Type A, it is implied that people at the low end (so-called Type B) have the opposite characteristics.

Another misconception is that Type A is a single trait; in actuality, Type A is a syndrome of several traits. More specifically, it is a collection of three subtraits, which together make up the Type A personality. One of these three subtraits is **competitive achievement motivation.** Type A persons like to work hard and achieve goals. They like recognition, power, and the defeat of obstacles. And they feel that they are at their best when competing with others. For example, a person who shows up at a charity bike-a-thon ready for the Tour de France bicycle race is exhibiting competitive achievement motivation. **Time urgency** is the second subtrait of the Type A behavior pattern. Type A persons hate wasting time. They are always in a hurry and feel under pressure to get the most done in the least amount of time. Often, they do two things at once, such as eat while reading a book. Red lights are their enemies, and they hate to wait in line for anything. The third subtrait of Type A is **hostility.** When blocked from attaining their goals, which is the definition of **frustration,** Type A persons can be hostile and aggressive. They get frustrated easily, and this frustration can make them act in an unfriendly or even malicious manner. The guy you see yelling at and pounding on a vending machine is perhaps displaying the hostile component of his Type A personality style.

Early studies of the Type A personality found that it was an independent risk factor for developing cardiovascular disease. An independent risk factor operates independently from other known risk factors, such as being overweight or smoking. Thus, for example, it is not true that Type A persons necessarily smoke more, and their smoking causes the heart disease. Instead, the Type A personality is independent of smoking, and someone who is Type A and smokes is at more of a risk for heart disease than someone who just smokes or who is just Type A. In fact, one study found that the Type A personality was a better predictor of heart disease than the person's history of smoking or the person's cholesterol level (Jenkins, Zyzanski, & Rosenman, 1976), although high cholesterol and smoking also contribute independently to heart disease.

Frequently doing two activities at once is a component of the Type A personality. Time urgency, however, is not the part of Type A that is most associated with heart disease.

Physicians conducted most of the early studies of Type A personality, and to measure this personality variable they developed a structured interview. Standard questions were asked, and the interviewer noted the participants' answers and how they reacted to the questions. In fact, the interviewer was very interested in the behavior of the participants. For example, what was the tempo of their speech? Did they frequently interrupt

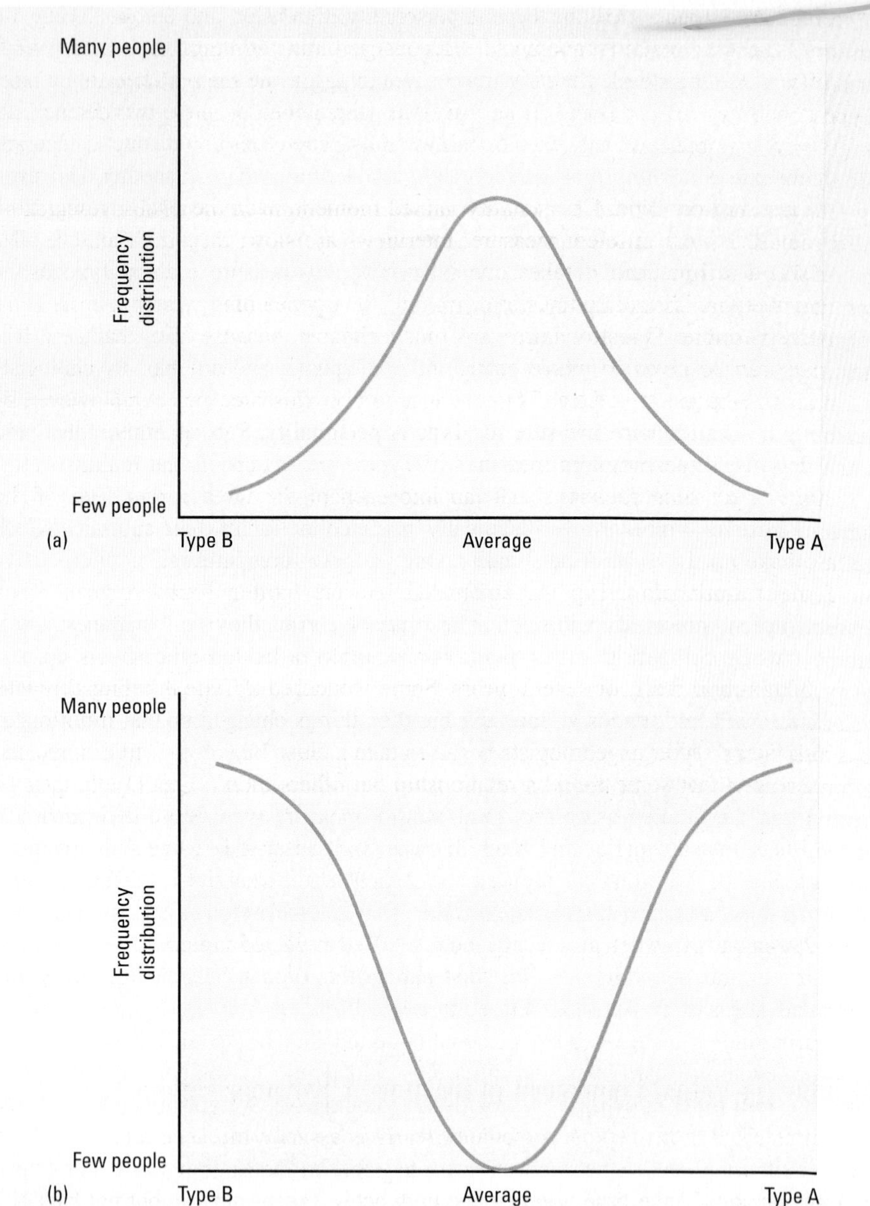

Figure 18.4

Type A and Type B are not really types at all and do not refer to categories of people. Rather, *Type A* refers to a normal distribution of people, anchored at one end by persons showing a lot of Type A behavior and at the other end by persons showing very little (a). Most people, however, are in the middle, or average, range. This is the case with almost all personality traits. A true type, or categorical variable, would be distributed as in (b), with most people at one end or the other and very few people in the middle. This is not the case with the Type A personality.

the interviewer or put words in the interveiwer's mouth? Did they fidget during the interview? Did they make frequent and vigorous gestures with their hands and heads? In one part of the interview, the interviewer tries to aggravate the participants by talking very slowly. Type A people are especially aggravated when other people talk slowly, and they interrupt, talk out of turn, or finish sentences for people in order to speed them up.

As research on Type A personality gained momentum in the 1980s, researchers tried to devise a more efficient measure. Interviews are slow; they can measure only one person at a time, and it takes one interviewer to measure each participant. In short, interviewing is a relatively expensive and time-consuming way to measure any personality variable. Questionnaires are much cheaper because they are generally faster, they can be given to whole groups of participants, and one person can assess 100 or more persons at a time. Thus, researchers in this area put some effort into developing a questionnaire measure for Type A personality. Subsequently, one of the most widely used questionnaire measures of Type A personality is the Jenkins Activity Survey. It contains questions that tap into each of the three components of the Type A syndrome—for example, "My work improves as the deadline approaches," "I have been told that I eat too fast," and "I enjoy a good competition."

Early researchers using the structured interview often found a relationship between Type A personality and risk for heart attack and cardiovascular disease. Later research, mostly using the Jenkins questionnaire, often failed to replicate this finding. This puzzled researchers for several years. Some wondered if Type A personality was a risk factor for heart attacks at one time but then things changed so that it no longer was a risk factor. Other psychologists began to take a close look at the studies, searching for a reason that some found a relationship but others didn't. Quickly the pattern emerged that the studies using the questionnaire measure were less likely to find a relationship between Type A and heart disease than the studies using the structured interview (Suls & Wan, 1989; Suls, Wan, & Costa, 1996). Researchers have concluded that the questionnaire measure taps into different aspects of Type A behavior than does the structured interview measures. Apparently, the structured interview gets more at the lethal component of Type A. But what part of the Type A behavior pattern is the most lethal, the part that is most related to heart disease?

Hostility: The Lethal Component of the Type A Behavior Pattern

You will recall that the Type A personality really is a syndrome, a collection of three subtraits, which often, but not always, occur together in the same persons. For example, a person could have time urgency and high achievement motive, but not have the hostility component. When the interview measures of Type A were developed by physicians, they tended to emphasize the assessment of hostility and aggression. For example, it assessed whether the participants got frustrated when the physicians talked slowly, whether they swore during the interview, or whether they actively gestured or pounded the table. Later, when questionnaire measures were developed, more of an emphasis was placed on the time urgency and achievement components. For example, did the participants say they were always in a hurry, that they worked better as deadlines got closer, or that they achieved more than their peers?

As researchers began to use the questionnaires more and more (because they were faster, easier, and cheaper to administer than the interviews), evidence began to accumulate, showing that general Type A personality did not predict heart disease. Researchers then compared the interviews with the questionnaires and learned that the interview method tapped more of the hostility component than the questionnaire method. As such, researchers began testing the hypothesis that it was really the more specific trait of hostility, rather than the general syndrome of Type A personality, that was the better predictor of heart disease.

What do researchers mean by the trait of hostility? People high in hostility are not necessarily violent or outwardly aggressive. They are not necessarily even assertive or demanding of others. Instead, such people are likely to react disagreeably to disappointments, frustrations, and inconveniences. Frustration can be understood as the subjective feeling that comes when you are blocked from an important goal. For example, you want a cold drink from the vending machine and it takes your money but does not give you the drink you request. This is frustrating. A hostile person reacts to such frustrations with disagreeable behavior, attacking the machine or swearing and kicking the garbage can as he or she sulks away. Hostile people are easily irritated, even by small frustrations, such as when they misplace their car keys or have to wait in line at the grocery store. In such situations, hostile people can become visibly upset, sometimes even becoming rude and uncooperative or even antagonistic.

Several studies have now established that hostility is a strong predictor of cardiovascular disease (Dembrowski & Costa, 1987; Helmers, Posluszny, & Krantz, 1994; Smith, 1992; Wiebe & Smith, 1997). In fact, psychologists Dembrowski and Costa have demonstrated that even a questionnaire measure of the specific trait of hostility is a better predictor of artery disease than are questionnaire measures of Type A. Recent studies have also shown that hostility is associated with systemic inflammation, as indicated by elevated blood **leukocyte** counts, also known as white blood cell counts (Surtees et al., 2003). Physicians have long known that chronic inflammation is related to risk for coronary disease, and so have recommended that persons at risk take an aspirin a day, because aspirin reduces inflammation. However, the Surtees et al. (2003) study is the first to establish a direct link between hostility and elevated white blood cell count. The correlation with hostility, while not large, was statistically significant and remained so even after accounting for known risk factors for chronic inflammation, such as age, sex, smoking history, and alcohol intake. Chronic inflammation may be the pathway whereby hostility is linked to the health endpoint of cardiovascular disease.

The good news about this research is that not everything about being Type A is bad for the heart and arteries. Given that hostility is apparently the lethal component, can we envision a "healthy" version of the Type A personality? It seems okay to strive for success and achievement, but don't be hostile and aggressive along the way. It's okay to strive to attain goals and even to be a workaholic, but don't get frustrated by the inevitable setbacks that come with everyday life. It's okay to be in a hurry and strive to get as much done as possible, but don't get frustrated and angry when you can't accomplish everything. And it's okay to enjoy a competition, as long as it's friendly, not hostile. And sometimes it may be good therapy to get into the longest and slowest line at the store and just try to relax, take it easy, and not feel hostile or angry in such situations (Wright, 1988).

It seems there may even be some benefits to being a nonhostile Type A person. In a longitudinal study of men, researchers discovered that, as expected, Type A men had more heart attacks than Type B men. However, after a heart attack, the Type A men were more likely to survive and to recover successfully from the heart attack than were the Type B men (Ragland & Brand, 1988). It appears that certain components of the Type A syndrome—such as striving and achievement motivation—help the Type A person develop and maintain a healthy post–heart attack regime of recovery and exercise.

Application

Models of health applied to Type A. Throughout this chapter, you should be able to make connections between the models covered in the beginning and the material in the rest of the chapter. For example, the work on appraisals and attributional style is an example of the transactional model of personality and health because this work stresses how the person influences the situation by construing or appraising it in certain ways. In this application, we will examine Type A and some examples of how it has been thought about in the ways suggested by the different models.

Early work on Type A conceived of this personality style as a specific pattern of action and emotion that occurred in response to specific events (e.g., frustration; Glass, 1977). This conception fits the interactional model because it assumes that Type A represents a style of responding to or coping with threats and challenges in the environment, and many researchers found this model useful. For example, Glass (1977) showed that Type A persons are sensitive to loss of control and that they cope by exerting vigorous attempts to regain control. The interaction between a category of events (i.e., loss of control) and health is moderated by the Type A person's coping style.

The majority of the research on Type A applies the transactional model. In this perspective, Type A persons are seen to create more severe, more frequent, or longer-lasting stressors in their lives by a particular pattern of thought and action, which evokes such stressors (Smith, 1989). The power of the transactional model is to guide researchers to look for the reciprocal influences of the Type A person's behavior in and way of thinking about the events in their lives. For example, how do Type A persons perceive certain situations, which in turn lead them to show larger cardiovascular responses? Type A persons are known to frequently interpret everyday events as competitions (Smith, 1989) and, so, to respond competitively.

The health behavior model has also been applied in research on Type A. Research with this model looks at the kinds of health behaviors the Type A person is more or less likely to engage in, compared with people low in Type A. Recall the study that found that, among men who had had a heart attack, those who were Type A were more likely to survive, especially after long-term follow-up (Ragland & Brand, 1988). The researchers found that the Type A person plunges into the problem of getting back into shape with the zeal, urgency, and competitiveness that they use to undertake other activities in their lives. Thus, a Type A person is more likely to take up an exercise program, to stick with it longer, to modify his diet, and in general to pursue his new program of health behavior with more vigor and enthusiasm than someone lower in Type A.

The predisposition model has also been applied to Type A behavior. Such persons are thought to be disposed to larger cardiovascular responses to stress than are persons low in Type A. It may turn out that a genetic basis is responsible for making some persons predisposed to such cardiovascular responses and predisposed to develop the hard-driving, competitive, and hostile personality that characterizes the Type A person (Wiebe & Smith, 1997).

Finally, the illness behavior model has also been applied to the Type A personality. Larsen and Kasimatis (1991) have shown that Type A persons are less likely to complain of various symptoms, including colds, muscle aches, and other minor, day-to-day physical symptoms. They hypothesize that Type As may relate to illness because the Type A person may not notice or communicate minor symptoms and thereby not take action to recover from illnesses.

Application (*Continued*)

In using the different models to think about how personality and health relate to each other, researchers develop ideas about which variables are important and how they specifically influence one another. The models themselves are not mutually exclusive. That is, they may all be correct, in the sense of leading researchers to find multiple connections and pathways between illness and personality.

How the Arteries Are Damaged by Hostile Type A Behavior

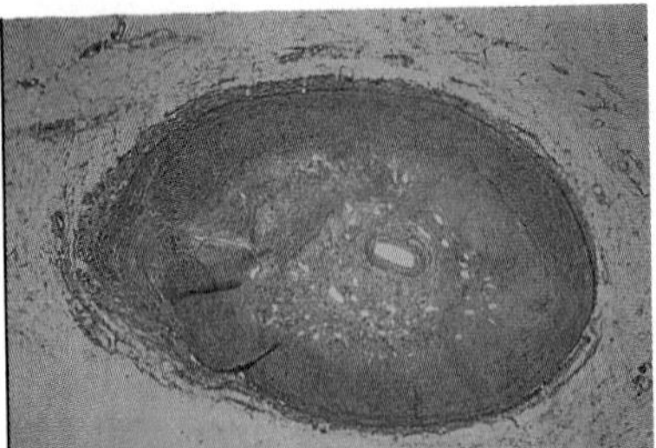

A cross-section of a human coronary artery, the artery that feeds the heart muscle itself, showing extreme arteriosclerosis. Here the artery diameter has narrowed dramatically by the buildup of plaque on the inside artery wall.

How does Type A behavior, particularly the hostility component, produce its toxic effects on the heart and arteries? Strong feelings of hostility and aggression produce the fight-or-flight response. Part of this response is an increase in blood pressure, accompanied by a constriction of the arteries, plus an increase in heart rate and in the amount of blood pumped out with each heartbeat. In short, the person's body suddenly pumps more blood through smaller arteries. These changes can produce wear and tear on the inside lining of the arteries, causing microscopic tears and abrasions. These abrasions then become sites at which cholesterol and fat can become attached. In addition to this mechanical wear and tear on the artery walls, stress hormones released into the blood during the fight-or-flight response may also lead to artery damage and subsequent buildup of fatty deposits on the artery walls. As these fat molecules build up on the inside of the arteries, the arteries become progressively narrower. This is called **arteriosclerosis,** or hardening or blocking of the arteries. When the arteries that feed the heart muscle itself become blocked, then the subsequent shortage of blood to the heart is called a heart attack.

In summary, research on the Type A personality has taken some interesting twists and turns. It all began with a couple of cardiologists noticing certain personality differences between heart attack patients and other medical patients. This led them to define the Type A personality as consisting of three characteristics: competitive achievement motivation, time urgency, and hostility. After several decades of research, psychologists have found that hostility is the most toxic component of the Type A personality, and most research on cardiovascular disease and personality today is focusing on specific traits. Understanding how hostility develops and is maintained, how exactly it damages the arteries, how it is evoked by specific situations, and how it can be overcome or managed are all important questions for future personality researchers.

SUMMARY AND EVALUATION

This chapter focused on the part of personality psychology related to physical adjustment and health. It began with several models of the personality and illness link. It then examined the concept of stress as the subjective reaction to extreme events, which often involve conflicting feelings, and over which one has little or no control. The stress response comes in four distinct varieties; acute, episodic acute, chronic, and traumatic. Traumatic stress can evolve into a disorder, called posttraumatic stress disorder, in which the person experiences nightmares or flashbacks, difficulties sleeping and other somatic problems, and feelings of being detached from reality or estranged from other people. It is important to realize that stress is not in the event but, rather, in how one appraises the event. Primary appraisal concerns an evaluation of how threatening the event is with respect to a person's goals and desires. Secondary appraisal concerns an evaluation of the person's own resources for meeting the challenge of the threatening event. Both of these appraisals are important for understanding how events come to elicit the stress response. Research is exploring the role of positive emotions in coping with chronic stress.

Much of the work on personality and stress began with a focus on major life events, such as losing a loved one or getting fired from one's job. Although serious, such events are relatively rare. More insidious are daily hassles, the relatively minor but frequent frustrations and disappointments of daily life. Stress researchers have begun to focus on these daily stressors in terms of their impact on health.

Personality psychologists have been concerned with understanding why some people appear more resistant to stress than others. That is, some people appear to take frustration and disappointment more in stride and to not suffer the deleterious health consequences often associated with chronic stress. One personality dimension in this regard is optimism, which has a wealth of findings associating it with stress resistance, good health, competent immune functioning, and longer life expectancy. Psychologists are developing grade school programs to train people to be more optimistic. Some related personality characteristics associated with generally better health prognosis are emotional expressivity and personal disclosure.

This chapter also focused on a specific disease, cardiovascular disease, one of the most common serious diseases in the United States. The chapter covered the history of the search for a personality dimension that might be a risk factor for developing heart disease. Type A personality provides an interesting example of progressive research, in which findings are gradually refined until the field becomes more and more certain about an effect. In the case of Type A personality, most researchers now agree that the hostility component is most associated with the tendency to develop heart disease. Fortunately, people can be competitive workaholics and strive to do more and more in less and less time, just as long as they do not have the hostile part of the Type A syndrome.

KEY TERMS

Health Psychology 588
Stress 589
Interactional Model 589
Transactional Model 589
Health Behavior Model 591
Predisposition Model 591
Illness Behavior Model 592
Stressors 594
General Adaptation Syndrome (GAS) 594
Alarm Stage 594
Resistance Stage 594
Exhaustion Stage 595
Major Life Events 595
Daily Hassles 597
Acute Stress 598
Episodic Acute Stress 598
Traumatic Stress 598
Posttraumatic Stress Disorder (PTSD) 599
Chronic Stress 599
Additive Effects 599
Primary Appraisal 599
Secondary Appraisal 599
Positive Reappraisal 602
Problem-Focused Coping 602
Creating Positive Events 603
Dispositional Optimism 603
Self-Efficacy 603
Optimistic Bias 604
Emotional Inhibition 607
Disclosure 610
Type A Personality 612
Competitive Achievement Motivation 613
Time Urgency 613
Hostility 613
Frustration 613
Leukocyte 616
Arteriosclerosis 618

Disorders of Personality

19

19

Kody Scott, a.k.a. "Monster," in Pelican Bay prison in 1993, photographed through Plexiglas. His autobiography, which he wrote while in solitary confinement, provides a real-life account of the mind of a person with antisocial personality disorder.

Kody Scott grew up in South Central Los Angeles. When he was 12 years old, he was initiated into the Eight-Tray Gangster CRIPS street gang. He shot his first victim the night he was initiated. He went on to earn the nickname "Monster" for particularly violent beatings he inflicted on people. For example, as a young teenager, Kody severely beat a victim who resisted when Kody attempted to mug him. Kody beat him far beyond what was necessary to make the victim submit. In fact, Kody seemed to enjoy hurting other people.

Kody's biological father was a professional football player, with whom his mother had had a brief affair. His mother had an unstable and violent marriage with Kody's stepfather, who left the home for good when Kody was 6. Kody's mother raised her six children in a two-bedroom house in a gang-infested ghetto neighborhood.

Kody was an intelligent and muscular boy, who enjoyed thrills and excitement. He might have gone on to become a professional athlete, or he could have succeeded in a career involving adventure and plenty of action, such as a policeman, a soldier, or maybe even an astronaut. Instead, Kody grew up to become Monster, a violent individual who feared nothing, had no feelings of guilt or remorse, and craved excitement.

Kody Scott was one of the most notorious gangbangers in South Central L.A. For the early part of his life, he aspired to be the most feared member of the CRIPS. To accomplish this goal, Kody killed many people and caused pain and suffering to countless others. Going out on gangbanging missions and maiming or killing rival gang members gave Kody the thrills and excitement he craved. He was sent to prison in 1993 to serve a seven-year sentence for shooting a drug dealer in the kneecaps. In prison, he was classed as a maximum threat to security and was housed away from other inmates. He wrote his autobiography, *Monster: The Autobiography of an L.A. Gang Member,* while in solitary confinement in San Quentin prison under the name Sanyika Shakur (1994).

The Building Blocks of Personality Disorders

Many of the topics we have covered in previous chapters come together in helping to describe and understand the various personality disorders. The symptoms of personality disorders can be seen as maladaptive variations within several of the domains we have covered. These include traits, emotions, cognitions, motives, interpersonal behavior, and self-concepts. The 10 personality disorders we present in this chapter are built on the foundation of these broader concepts, and so we briefly will discuss the relevance of each to this chapter.

Traits of personality describe consistencies in behavior, thought, or action and represent meaningful differences between persons, as we described in Chapter 3. Personality disorders can be thought of as maladaptive variations or combinations of normal personality traits. Widiger and colleagues describe how extremes on either end of specific trait dimensions can be associated with personality disorders (Widiger et al., 2002a, 2002b). For example, a person with extremely low levels of trust and extremely high levels of hostility might be disposed to paranoid personality disorder. A person very low on sociability but very high on anxiety might be prone to avoidant personality disorder. A person with the opposite combination—extremely high on sociability and low on anxiety—might be prone to histrionic personality disorder. Thus, the concept of traits, such as the five-factor model of traits, can be especially useful for describing personality disorders (Trull & McCrae, 2002).

Motivation is another basic building block of personality that is important to understanding personality disorders. Motives describe what people want and why they behave in particular ways. In the intrapsychic domain, Chapters 9 to 11, we discussed several different kinds of motives, ranging from the sexual and aggressive basis of Freud's theory to modern research on the need for intimacy, achievement, and power. A common theme in several personality disorders concerns maladaptive variations on these common motives, especially need for power and intimacy. One important variation concerns an extreme lack of motivation for intimacy, which is seen in certain personality disorders. Another theme is an exaggerated need for power over others, which, at an extremely high level, can result in a maladaptive personality disorder. Other motives can also be involved in personality disorders, such as the extreme need to be superior and receive the praise of others that is found in narcissistic personality disorder. The obsessive-compulsive personality disorder might be seen as having an extremely high motivation for order and devotion to detail.

Cognition also provides a building block for understanding personality disorders. As covered in Chapter 12, cognition consists of mental activity involved in perceiving, interpreting, and planning. These processes can become distorted in personality disorders. Some disorders involve routine and consistent misinterpretations of the intentions of others. Personality disorders typically involve an impairment of social judgment, such as when the paranoid thinks others are out to get her, or when the histrionic person thinks others actually like being with him. The person with a borderline personality disorder may misinterpret innocent comments as signs of abandonment or criticism or rejection. In various ways, each of the personality disorders involves some distortion in the perception of other persons and altered social cognition.

Emotion is another area that is important to understanding personality disorders. We discussed normal range individual differences in emotion in Chapter 13. With several personality disorders there is extreme variation in experienced emotions. Some disorders involve extreme volatility in emotions (e.g., borderline) whereas other disorders involve extremes of specific emotions, such as anxiety (avoidant personality disorder), fear (paranoid personality disorder), or rage (narcissistic personality disorder). Most personality disorders have an emotional core that is an important component to understanding that disorder.

The self-concept is another building block in personality disorders. As described in Chapter 14, the self-concept is the person's own collection of self-knowledge—one's understanding of oneself. With most personality disorders, there is some distortion in the self-concept. Most of us are able to build and maintain a stable and realistic image of ourselves; we know our own opinions, we know what we value, and we know what we want out of life. With many of the disorders, there is a lack of stability in the self-concept, such that the person may feel she or he has no "core" or has trouble making decisions or needs constant reassurance from others. Self-esteem is also an important part of the self, and some disorders are associated with extremely high (e.g., narcissism) or extremely low (e.g., dependent personality disorder) levels of self-esteem. The self provides an important perspective on understanding personality disorders.

Social relationships are frequently disturbed or maladaptive in personality disorders. Thus, the material we covered in the social and cultural domain, Chapters 15 through 17, is important for understanding and describing personality disorders. For example, a successful sexually intimate relationship with another person involves knowing when sexual behavior is appropriate and expected and when it is inappropriate and unwanted. Problems with intimacy, either staying too distant from others or becoming too intimate too quickly, are frequent features of several personality disorders. An important element of interpersonal skill involves empathy, knowing how the other person is feeling. Most personality disorders involve a deficit in empathy, such that the disordered person either misinterprets others or does not care about the feelings of others. Many disorders involve what might be called poor social skills, such as the schizoid person who stares at people without starting a conversation, or the histrionic person who behaves in an inappropriately flirtatious manner.

Biology can also form the building blocks of several of the personality disorders. The material covered in the biological domain, Chapters 6 through 8, is thus relevant. Some of the personality disorders have been found to have a genetic component. Others have been studied via physiological components, such as examining the brain functioning of antisocial persons. There has even been an evolutionary theory proposed to explain the existence of personality disorders (Millon, 2000a).

Most personality textbooks do not cover personality disorders. We feel, however, that knowing about how something can become broken can tell us about how it works normally. Plus, we believe that the concept of personality disorders really ties together all the different components and domains of personality. As such, it is a fitting topic with which to end this book because it applies much of what has come before to an understanding of how the human personality can become disordered.

The Concept of Disorder

Today, a psychological **disorder** is a pattern of behavior or experience that is distressing and painful to the person, that leads to disability or impairment in important life domains (e.g., problems with work, marriage or relationship difficulties), and that is associated with increased risk for further suffering, loss of function, death, or confinement (American Psychiatric Association, 1994). The idea that something can go wrong with a person's personality has a long history. Some of the earliest writings in medical psychiatry included classifications and descriptions of personality and mental disorders (e.g., Kraeplin, 1913; Kretschmer, 1925). A very early concept derived by French psychiatrist Philippe Pinel was *manie sans delire,* or madness without loss of reason. This was applied to individuals who demonstrated disordered behavior and emotions but who did not lose contact with reality (Morey, 1997). A related concept, popular in the early 1900s, was called moral insanity, to emphasize that the person did not suffer any impairment of intellect but, rather, was impaired in terms of feelings, temperament, or habits. An influential psychiatrist named Kurt Schneider (1958) proposed the term *psychopathic personality* to refer to behavior patterns that caused the person and the community to suffer. Schneider also emphasized statistical rarity along with behaviors that have an adverse impact on the person and the community in which that person lives. This definition highlights the notion that all forms of personality disorder involve impaired social relationships; other people suffer as much as or more than the person with the disorder.

A disorder is a conceptual entity that, although abstract, is nevertheless useful. It helps guide thinking about the distinction between what is normal and what is abnormal, or pathological. The field of **abnormal psychology** is the study of the various mental disorders, including thought disorders, emotional disorders, and personality disorders. In this chapter, we will focus on disorders of personality and the ways in which they affect functioning.

What Is Abnormal?

There are many ways to define **abnormal.** One simple definition is that whatever is different from normal is abnormal. This is a statistical definition, in the sense that researchers can statistically determine how often something occurs and, if it is rare, call it abnormal. In this sense, colorblindness or polydactyly (having more than 10 fingers) is considered abnormal. Another definition of abnormal is a social definition based on what society tolerates (Shoben, 1957). If we define the term in this sense, behaviors that society deems unacceptable are labeled as abnormal. In this sense, incest and child abuse are both considered abnormal. Both the statistical and the social definitions of abnormality suffer from changing times and changing social or cultural norms (Millon, 2000a, 2000b). Behaviors deemed offensive or socially inappropriate 20 years ago might be acceptable today. For example, 20 or 30 years ago, homosexuality was considered to be both rare and socially unacceptable, a form of abnormal behavior or even a mental illness. Today, homosexuality is not considered abnormal in itself (American Psychiatric Association, 1994) and is protected under civil rights laws in the United States. Thus, the statistical and social definitions of abnormality are always somewhat tentative because society changes.

Psychologists have consequently looked to other ways of identifying what is abnormal in behavior and experience. They have looked within persons, inquiring about subjective feelings, such as anxiety, depression, dissatisfaction, and feelings of loneliness. They have looked at how people think and experience themselves and their worlds. Psychologists have found that some people have disorganized thoughts, disruptive perceptions, or unusual beliefs and attitudes that do not match their circumstances. They have identified ways in which people fail to get along with one another and ways people have trouble living in the community. They have analyzed patterns of behavior that represent ineffective efforts at coping or that put people at higher risk for other problems, behaviors that harm more than help. From a psychological perspective, any of these may be considered abnormal.

Combining all these approaches to abnormality (statistical, social, and psychological), psychologists and psychiatrists have developed the field of **psychopathology,** or the study of mental disorders. The diagnosis of mental disorders is both a scientific discipline and an important part of the clinical work of many psychiatrists and psychologists. Knowing how to define and how to identify a disorder is the first step in devising treatment or in designing research on that disorder.

A system for diagnosing and describing mental disorders that is widely accepted is included in the *Diagnostic and Statistical Manual of Mental Disorders,* now in its fourth edition, commonly called the *DSM-IV,* published by the American Psychiatric Association (1994). This is a widely used manual for determining the nature and extent of psychological disorders, based on various symptoms and behaviors. This manual lists more than 200 mental disorders. Working through this manual often forms the basis of advanced or graduate-level courses in abnormal psychology.

To the student interested in mental disorders, there is a great number and variety for study. In this chapter, we will cover only the disorders of personality functioning. There are many other disorders, such as those that affect thought processes (e.g., schizophrenia), those that affect emotions (e.g., panic disorder), those that affect eating behavior (e.g., bulimia), those related to dysfunctional sexuality (e.g., pedophilia, or the sexual attraction to prepubescent children), and those that result from long-term substance abuse (e.g., cocaine-induced psychosis). Personality disorders represent only a small part of the list of possible psychopathologies.

What Is a Personality Disorder?

A **personality disorder** is an enduring pattern of experience and behavior that differs greatly from the expectations of the individual's culture *(DSM-IV).* As discussed in Chapter 3, traits are patterns of experiencing, thinking about, and interacting with oneself and the world. Traits are observed in a wide range of social and personal situations. For example, a person who is high on conscientiousness is hardworking and persevering. If a trait becomes maladaptive and inflexible and causes significant impairment or distress, then it is considered to be a personality disorder. For example, if someone were so conscientious that he or she checked the locks on the door 10 times each night and checked every appliance in the house 5 times before leaving in the morning, then we might consider the possibility of a disorder.

The essential features of a personality disorder, according to the American Psychiatric Association (1994), are presented in Table 19.1. A personality disorder is usually manifest in more than one of the following areas: in how people think, in how they feel, in how they get along with others, or in their ability to control their own behavior. The pattern is rigid and is displayed across a variety of situations, leading to distress or problems in important areas in life, such as at work or in relationships.

Table 19.1 General Criteria for Personality Disorders

1. An enduring pattern of inner experience and behavior that deviates markedly from the expectations of the individual's culture. This pattern is manifest in two or more of the following areas:
   - Cognition (i.e., ways of perceiving and interpreting the self, others, and events)
   - Affectivity (i.e., the range, intensity, ability, and appropriateness of emotional responses)
   - Interpersonal functioning
   - Impulse control
2. The enduring pattern is inflexible and pervasive across a broad range of personal and social situations.
3. The enduring pattern leads to clinically significant distress or impairment in social, occupational, or other important areas of functioning.
4. The pattern is stable and of long duration, and its onset can be traced back to adolescence or early adulthood.
5. The enduring pattern is not better accounted for as a manifestation or consequence of another mental disorder.
6. The enduring pattern is not due to the direct physiological effects of a substance (e.g., a drug of abuse, a medication) or a general medical condition, such as head trauma.

Source: American Psychiatric Association, 1994.

For example, an overly conscientious man might drive his wife crazy with his constant checking of his household appliances. The pattern of behavior that defines the personality disorder typically has a long history in the person's life and can often be traced back to manifestations in adolescence or even childhood. To be classed as a personality disorder, the pattern must not result from drug abuse, medication, or a medical condition, such as head trauma.

Varieties of Personality Disorder

The *DSM-IV* lists 10 personality disorders. These 10 disorders, in turn, fall into three groups. All of the personality disorders involve impaired social relations, or trouble getting along with others. The person with a personality disorder causes difficulties for other people. Personality disorders are unique in that, in addition to suffering themselves, persons with these disorders frequently make those around them uncomfortable as well.

Categories or Dimensions?

One way to view personality disorders is as distinct categories: people without a particular disorder are in one category, and people with the disorder are in another category. This **categorical view** is the dominant approach in psychiatry and clinical psychology today. A person either is diagnosed with the disorder or is not. For example, a study of more than 600 serious offenders in maximum security prisons in Canada concluded that antisocial personalities were a distinct category representing a segment of the prison population (Harris, Rice, & Quinsey, 1994). The categorical view holds that there is a qualitative break between people who are antisocial and people who are not. And this concept is applied to all the disorders, viewing disorders as distinct and qualitatively different from normal extremes on each trait.

In contrast to this categorical view is the dimensional view of personality disorders. In the **dimensional view,** each disorder is seen as a continuum, ranging from normality at one end to severe disability or disturbance at the other. According to this view, people with and without the disorder differ in degree only. For example, part of being an antisocial psychopath is a disregard for the rights of others, and there are degrees to which this lack of social caring manifests itself. For example, some people might simply be aloof and unconcerned about the feelings of others. Further out on this dimension, a person might lack a desire to help others, being both aloof and uncaring. Even further out on this dimension is the person who actively hurts or takes advantage of others. And, finally, at the greatest extreme is someone like "Monster," the person introduced at the start of this chapter, who takes pleasure in harming or terrorizing others, who is motivated to social crime because he or she enjoys seeing others suffer.

Research on American college students suggests that antisocial traits, such as impulsivity, quick temper, lack of remorse, manipulativeness, and callous social attitudes, are normally distributed. This implies that these traits are dimensions, which range from low to high, not distinct categories. Thus, the degree to which a given student exhibits antisocial personality traits varies according to where he or she falls on a continuum, ranging from highly agreeable and cooperative at one end to extremely uncaring and lacking in social interest at the other. The dimensional view implies that certain patterns of behavior, in various amounts, comprise the disorder, making the person a problem to themselves and to others. Modern theorists (e.g., Costa & Widiger, 1994; Widiger, 2000) argue that the dimensional view provides a more reliable and meaningful way to describe disorders as extreme forms of normal personality traits.

Culture, Age, and Gender: The Effect of Context

A person's social, cultural, and ethnic background must be taken into account whenever there is a question about personality disorders. Immigrants, for example, often have problems fitting into a new culture. Persons who originate in a different culture often have customs, habits, expressions, and values that are at odds with, or that create social problems within, a new culture. For example, the U.S. culture is very individualistic, and it values and rewards individuals for standing out from the crowd. To societies that are more collectivistic, which value fitting in with the group, efforts to stand out from the crowd might be interpreted as self-centered and individualistic in an unwanted sense. Indeed, the U.S. culture has been called a narcissistic culture; therefore, efforts to draw attention to the self are not socially abnormal in this society.

Before judging that a behavior is a symptom of a personality disorder, we must first become familiar with a person's cultural background, especially if it is different from the majority culture. A study of Third World immigrants to Norway (Sam, 1994) found that many exhibited adjustment problems, which might have appeared to be personality disorders. Many young male immigrants, for example, exhibited antisocial behaviors. These behaviors tended to diminish as the immigrants acculturated to their new social environment.

Age also is relevant to judgments about personality disorder. Adolescents, for example, often go through periods of instability, which may include identity crises (see Chapter 14), a symptom that is often associated with certain personality disorders. Most adolescents experiment with various identities yet do not have a personality disorder. For this reason, the American Psychiatric Association (1994) cautions against diagnosing personality disorders in persons under age 18. Also, adults who undergo severe loss, such as the death of a spouse or the loss of a job, sometimes undergo periods of instability or impulsive behavior, which may look like a personality disorder. For example, a person who has experienced such a traumatic event may become violent or may impulsively enter into sexual relationships. A person's age and life circumstances must therefore be considered, in order to make sure that the person is not simply going through a developmental stage or reacting to a traumatic life event.

Finally, gender is another context in which to frame our understanding of personality disorders. Certain disorders, such as the antisocial personality disorder, are diagnosed much more frequently in men than women. Other personality disorders are diagnosed more frequently in women than men. These gender differences may reflect underlying gender differences in how people cope. For example, in a study of more than 2,000 individuals, Huselid and Cooper (1994) found that males exhibit externalizing problems, such as fighting and vandalism, whereas females tend to exhibit relatively more internalizing problems, such as depression and self-harm. Similar findings were obtained by Kavanagh and Hops (1994). These differences in how men and women cope with problems most likely contribute to gender differences in the behaviors associated with the personality disorders. Psychologists need to be careful not to look for evidence of certain kinds of disorders just because of a person's gender. Particularly when a clinician is evaluating a specific case, social stereotypes about gender roles should not influence a diagnosis.

Exercise

In this chapter, you will read about specific personality disorders. For each, try to think of examples of how culture, gender, or age might influence whether a person's behavior is seen as evidence of a disorder. For example, are persons from low socioeconomic groups likely to be seen by others as having particular disorders? How does this correspond to the topic of stereotypes and prejudice? How does this fit with the use of "profiles" by police and other law enforcement agencies?

Specific Personality Disorders

The following sections describe specific personality disorders, including the criteria for diagnosing someone as possessing each disorder. We will focus this material on describing the characteristics of each personality disorder and by giving examples. A discussion of the causes of personality disorders is given in A Closer Look on the antisocial personality disorder, "Theories of the Psychopathic Mind" (pages 634–635), as well as in the last section of the chapter, "Causes of Personality Disorders."

The Erratic Cluster: Ways of Being Unpredictable, Violent, or Emotional

Persons who are diagnosed with disorders belonging to the erratic group tend to have trouble with emotional control and to have specific difficulties getting along with others. People with one of these disorders often appear dramatic and emotional and are unpredictable. This group consists of four disorders: *antisocial, borderline, histrionic,* and *narcissistic* personality disorders.

Antisocial Personality Disorder

The antisocial person shows a general disregard for others and cares very little about the rights, feelings, or happiness of other people. The antisocial person has also been referred to as a sociopath or a psychopath (Zuckerman, 1991). Adults with this disorder typically had a childhood that was fraught with behavioral problems. Such early childhood behavioral problems generally take the form of violating the rights of others (such as minor thefts) and breaking age-related social norms (such as smoking at an early age or fighting with other children). Other common childhood behavioral problems include behaving aggressively or cruelly toward animals, threatening and intimidating younger children, destroying property, lying, and breaking rules. Behavioral problems in childhood are often first noticed in school, but such children also come to the attention of the police and truant officers. Sometimes even very young children, during an argument with another child, use a weapon that can cause serious physical harm, such as a baseball bat or a knife.

Once childhood behavioral problems become an established pattern, the possibility of an **antisocial personality disorder** becomes more likely (American Psychiatric Association, 1994). As a child with behavioral problems grows up, the problems tend to worsen, as the child develops physical strength, cognitive power, and sexual maturity. Minor problems, such as lying, fighting, and shoplifting, evolve into more serious ones, such as breaking and entering and vandalism. Severe aggression, such as rape or cruelty to a theft victim, might also follow. Some children with these behavioral problems rapidly develop to a level of dangerous and even sadistic behavior. For example, we sometimes hear in the news about preteen children (usually male) who murder other children in cold blood and without remorse. In one study, children who grew into severe delinquency as teenagers were already identifiable by kindergarten teachers' ratings of impulsiveness and antisocial behavior at age 5 (Tremblay et al., 1994). Studies of children aged 6–13 also find that some children exhibit a syndrome of antisocial behaviors, including impulsivity, behavioral problems, callous social attitudes, and lack of feelings for others (Frick et al., 1994).

If a child exhibits no signs of conduct problems by age 16, it is unlikely that he or she will develop an antisocial personality as an adult. Moreover, even among children *with* conduct problems, the majority simply grow out of them by early adulthood (American Psychiatric Association, 1994). However, some children with conduct problems go on to develop full-blown antisocial personality disorder in adulthood. Children with earlier onset conduct problems (e.g., by age 6 or 7) are much more likely to grow into an antisocial personality disorder as an adult than are children who displayed a few conduct problems in high school (Laub & Lauritsen, 1994).

The antisocial adult continues with the same sorts of conduct problems started in childhood, but on a much grander scale. The term *antisocial* implies that the person has a *lack of concern for social norms*. Antisocial persons have very little respect for laws and may repeatedly engage in acts that are grounds for arrest, such as harassing others, fighting, destroying property, and stealing. "Cold-hearted" is a good description of their interactions with others. Antisocial persons can manipulate and deceive others in order to gain rewards or pleasure (e.g., money, power, social advantage, or sex).

Repeated lying is another feature of the antisocial personality. The pattern of lying starts early in life with minor deceptions and grows into a pattern of deceitfulness. Lying becomes a common part of social interaction for the antisocial personality. Some make a living conning others out of money. "Getting over" on people, especially authorities, through deception may even be pleasurable to the antisocial person.

Another common characteristic of the antisocial personality is *impulsivity,* which is often manifested as a failure to plan ahead. The antisocial person might start a chain of behavior without a clear plan or sequence in mind: For example, the person might enter a gas station and decide on the spot to rob the attendant, even though he or she has not planned a getaway. Prisoners with antisocial personalities often complain that their lack of planning led to their arrest, and they are often more remorseful about getting caught than about committing the crime.

A more common form of impulsivity is to simply make everyday decisions without much forethought or without considering consequences. For example, an antisocial man might leave his wife and baby for several days without calling to say where he is. This often results in trouble in relationships and trouble in employment settings. Generally, antisocial persons change jobs often, change relationships often, and move often.

Antisocial persons tend also to be *easily irritated* and to respond to even minor frustrations with aggression. Losing some coins in a vending machine might be all it takes for such a person to fly into a rage. Antisocial persons tend also to be *assaultive,* particularly to those around them, such as spouses or children. Fights and physical attacks are common. *Recklessness* is another characteristic, with antisocial persons showing little regard for their own safety and that of others. Driving while intoxicated or speeding is indicative of recklessness, as is having unprotected sex with multiple partners.

Irresponsibility is another key feature of the antisocial personality. Antisocial persons get bored easily and find monotony or routine to be stressful. An antisocial person may, for example, decide on the spur of the moment to abandon his or her job, with no plan for getting another right away. Repeated unexplained absences from work are a common sign of the antisocial character. Irresponsibility in financial matters is also common, with the antisocial person often running up unpayable debts, or borrowing money from one person to pay a debt owed to another, staying one step ahead of the bill collector. Such a person may squander the money needed to feed his or her children or gamble away the money needed to buy necessities.

Application

Kenneth Lay was the founder and former CEO of Enron, a large energy company that went bankrupt in 2001, creating $60 billion in investment losses and wiping out $2.1 billion in the pension plans of thousands of workers. Lay was charged with 11 counts of conspiracy, insider trading, securities fraud, and lying to auditors. Prosecuters charged that he knew his company was in deep trouble and was aware of fraudulent accounting practices, and that he hid losses from investors until the company collapsed. During this time, Lay began dumping his own stock before Enron collapsed, even while encouraging others, including company workers, to buy more. During his trial, Lay claimed he never knew of the accounting fraud. He portrayed himself as a trusting man who was let down by corrupt staff, especially former finance chief Andrew Fastow, now serving 10 years in prison for his role in the Enron collapse. At times during his trial, Lay became combative and hostile, insisting that others were responsible. At other times

he claimed that the collapse of Enron was the most painful experience of his life, even going so far as to say the experience was equivalent to the death of a loved one. In 2006 he was convicted and might have served up to 45 years in jail if he had not died suddenly of a heart attack before sentencing took place.

Kenneth Lay exhibited several characteristics consistent with the antisocial personality and psychopathy. He was a charming person who could convince others to buy his company's stock, even though he knew his company was in deep trouble and was secretly selling his own shares. Self-assured and confident, he used his personal charisma to dupe others out of billions of dollars. He repeatedly tried to shift the blame for his company's collapse onto others. When faced with evidence of his responsibility, he became combative and hostile and was easily irritated on the witness stand. He expressed no remorse for destroying the life savings of thousands of Enron workers. And finally, he tried to play the "poor me" card to garner sympathy from the jury by pointing out all the pain and suffering he had endured.

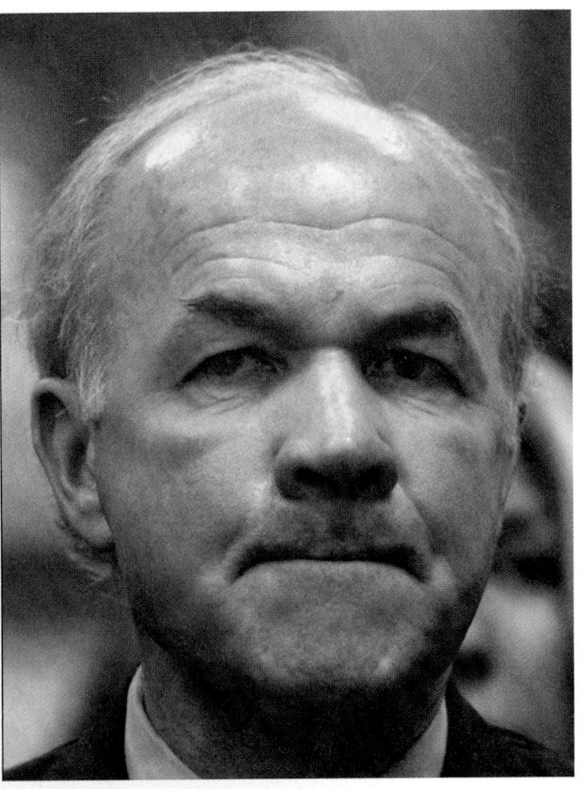

The *lack of remorse* and guilt feelings and indifference to the suffering of others is the hallmark of the antisocial mind. The antisocial person can be ruthless, without the normal levels of human compassion, charity, or social concern. See A Closer Look on pages 634–635 for current theories and research on how people become antisocial and the psychological forces that keep them that way. Table 19.2 summarizes the key characteristics of the antisocial personality disorder. Also included are typical beliefs or thoughts that someone with this disorder might have.

A concept related to antisocial personality disorder is *psychopathy,* which was a term coined toward the middle of the last century (Cleckley, 1941) to describe people who are superficially charming and intelligent, but are also deceitful, unable to feel remorse or care for others, impulsive, and lacking in shame, guilt, and fear. Psychopathy and antisocial personality are similar notions, but there are important distinctions so they should not be used interchangeably. The antisocial personality designation places emphasis on observable behaviors, such as chronic lying, repeated criminal behavior, and conflicts with authority. The psychopathy designation places emphasis on more subjective characteristics, such as the incapacity to feel guilt, a high degree of superficial charm, or having callous social attitudes. The distinction can get blurred, since the *DSM-IV* also includes a subjective criterion, "lack of remorse," in its definition of antisocial personality disorder. However, the concept of psychopathy is mainly a research construct, pioneered by the scientific work of psychologist Robert Hare. He developed a measure of the construct called the Psychopathy Checklist, which contains two major clusters of symptoms. One cluster

Table 19.2 Characteristics of Persons with Antisocial Personality Disorder

Fails to conform to social norms, e.g., breaks the law
Repeated lying or conning others for pleasure or profit
Impulsivity
Irritable and aggressive, e.g., frequent fights
Reckless disregard for safety of others and self
Irresponsible, e.g., truant from school, cannot hold a job
Lack of remorse, e.g., indifferent to pain of others, rationalizes having hurt or mistreated others

Typical Thoughts Associated with the Antisocial Personality
"Laws don't apply to me."
"I'll say whatever it takes to get what I want."
"I think I'll skip work today and go to the racetrack."
"That guy I beat up deserved every bit of it."
"She had it coming, she asked for it . . ."
"I'm the one you should feel sorry for here . . ."

refers to emotional and interpersonal traits, such as incapacity for fear, superficial charm, lack of empathy and care for others, being egocentric, and having callous social attitudes and shallow emotions. The second cluster assesses the social deviance associated with an antisocial lifestyle, such as being impulsive, displaying poor self-control, possessing a high need for excitement, and having early and chronic behavioral problems. The major distinction between psychopathy and antisocial personality disorder mainly lies in the first cluster of emotional and interpersonal traits that define psychopathy. Consequently, most extreme psychopaths would meet criteria for a diagnosis of antisocial personality disorder, but not all people with antisocial personality disorder are psychopaths (if they don't have the subjective characteristics of superficial charm, egocentricity, lack of empathy, and shallow emotions).

Exercise

For the next week, read through at least one newspaper or news magazine each day. Look for stories on persons who might be good examples of the antisocial personality disorder, such as murderers, white-collar criminals, and con artists. Clip the stories and bring them in for discussion. Look for evidence from the person's life and actual behaviors that match the characteristics of the antisocial personality listed in Table 19.2.

When evaluating the antisocial personality profile, it is good to keep in mind the social and environmental contexts in which some people live. Psychologists have expressed concern that the *antisocial* label is sometimes applied to people who live in settings where socially undesirable behaviors (such as fighting) are viewed as protective. For example, in a high-crime area, some of the antisocial attitudes may safeguard people against being victimized. Thus, the term *antisocial* should be used only when the behavior pattern is indicative of dysfunction and is not simply a response to the immediate social context. For example, youths who immigrate from war-ravaged countries, where aggressive behaviors are necessary to survive each day, should not be considered antisocial. The economic and social contexts must be taken into account when deciding whether undesirable behaviors are signs of dysfunction.

Borderline Personality Disorder

The lives of persons with **borderline personality disorder** are marked by *instability.* Their relationships are unstable, their behavior is unstable, their emotions are unstable, and even their images of themselves are unstable. Let's consider each of these, starting with relationships.

The relationships of borderline individuals tend to be intense, emotional, and potentially violent. They suffer from strong fears of abandonment. If such individuals sense separation or rejection in an important relationship, profound changes in their self-image and in how they behave may result, such as becoming very angry at other people. Borderline individuals show marked difficulties in their relationships. When others leave them, they feel strong abandonment fears and sometimes become angry or *aggressive.* Sometimes, in their efforts to manipulate people back into their relationships, they engage in *self-mutilating behavior* (burning or cutting themselves) or suicide attempts. A study of 84 hospital patients with a diagnosis of borderline personality disorder found that 72 percent had a history of attempting suicide (Soloff et al., 1994). In fact, among this sample, the average borderline patient had attempted suicide on at least three occasions. The relationships of borderline individuals are unpredictable and intense. They may go from idealizing the other to ridiculing the other. They are prone to sudden shifts in their views of relationships, behaving at one time in a caring manner and at another time in a punishing and cruel manner. They may go from being submissive to being an avenger for past wrongs. The movie *Fatal Attraction* contains a character with several features of the borderline personality disorder. See A Closer Look on page 637 for a discussion of how this personality disorder was portrayed in that Oscar-nominated movie from 1987.

Borderline persons also have *shifting views of themselves.* Their values and goals are shallow and change easily. Their opinions may change suddenly. They may experiment with different kinds of friends or with different sexual orientations. Usually, they view themselves as, at heart, evil or bad. Self-harming acts are common and increase when others threaten to leave or demand that the borderline person assume some new responsibilities.

Strong emotions are common in the borderline personality, including panic, anger, and despair. Mostly, these emotions are caused by interpersonal events, especially abandonment or neglect. When stressed by others, the borderline person may lash out, becoming bitter, sarcastic, or aggressive. Periods of anger are often followed by shame, guilt, and feelings of being evil or bad. Borderline persons often complain of feeling empty. They also have a way of undermining their own best efforts, such as dropping out of a training program just before finishing or destroying a caring relationship just when it starts going smoothly.

The borderline person is characterized by huge vacillations in both mood and feelings about the self and others. They can shift quickly from loving another to hating that same person. They are very demanding on their friends, relatives, lovers, and

A Closer Look

Theories of the Psychopathic Mind

Here we will compare two theories about the origins of psychopathy: a biological explanation and a social learning explanation. Many psychologists have argued that psychopathy is caused by a biological deficit or abnormality (e.g., Cleckley, 1988; Fowles, 1980; Gray, 1987a, 1987b). Research along these lines has focused on the idea that psychopaths are deficient in their abili... experience fear (Lykken, 198... why deficient in fear would he... well from psychopaths do no...ward (Newman, punishment a... may pursue a career 1987). Ps... lawlessness because, in in ...ey are simply not afraid of the ...ishment because they are insensitive to fear.

The theory of Jeffrey Gray (1990) has been influential on a number of researchers looking for a biological explanation of psychopathy. Recall from Chapter 7 that Gray proposed a system in the brain that is responsible for inhibiting behavior. The behavioral inhibition system (BIS) acts as a psychological brake, responsible for interrupting ongoing behavior when cues of punishment are present. According to Gray, the BIS is the part of the brain that is especially sensitive to signals of punishment coming from the environment. People who sense that a punishment is likely to occur typically stop what they are doing and look for ways to avoid the punishment. The BIS is thought to produce feelings of anxiety in the presence of cues for punishment, which in turn interrupts ongoing behavior. Gray (1990) holds that people differ greatly from each other in terms of the sensitivity of their BIS systems.

Researchers are beginning to examine the emotional lives of psychopaths, especially with respect to their ex... ence of anxiety and other nega... emotions. Psychologist Chris P...k and his colleagues are follow... an interesting line of research... study examined a group of pr...rs, all of whom were convic... sexual offenses (Patrick, ... & Lang, 1993). Even in this ...p of severe offenders, some individuals were more psychopathic than others, as measured by Hare's Psychopathy Checklist (Hare, Hart, & Harpur, 1991). Patrick and his colleagues had the prisoners look at unpleasant pictures (e.g., injured people, threatening animals) to try to bring about feelings of anxiety. While they were looking at the pictures, the prisoners were startled by random bursts of a loud noise. People typically blink their eyes when they are startled by a loud noise. Moreover, a person who is in an anxious or fearful state when startled will blink faster and harder than a person in a normal emotional state. This means that eye-blink speed when startled may be an objective physiological measure of how anxious or fearful a person is feeling. That is, the **eye-blink startle method** may allow researchers to measure how anxious persons are without actually having to ask them.

The results from this study of prisoners showed that the more psychopathic offenders displayed *less* of the eye-blink effect when startled, indicating that they were experiencing relatively *less* anxiety to the same unpleasant pictures. However, when *asked* about how distressing the pictures were, both the psychopaths and the nonpsychopaths reported that the pictures were distressing. Overall, these results suggest that psychopaths will say that they are feeling anxious or distressed, yet direct nervous system measures suggest that they are actually *experiencing* less anxiety than nonpsychopaths in the same situation.

In another study, Patrick, Cuthbert, and Lang (1994) again used a group of prisoners who differed from each other in terms of antisocial behaviors. This time, the prisoners were asked to imagine fearful scenes, such as having to undergo an operation. The low- and high-antisocial prisoners did not differ in terms of their self-reports of fear and anxiety—all reported more of these emotions in response to the fear images than in response to neutral images, such as walking across the yard. Large differences, however, were found in their *physiological* responses to the fear images. The less antisocial prisoners were

This is the kind of photo used in the study by psychologist Chris Patrick, who found that psychopaths did not exhibit the normal fear response to such threatening stimuli.

more aroused by the fear imagery than were the antisocial subjects. In other words, the antisocial prisoners displayed a deficit in fear responding, when their fear responses were assessed with physiological measures, which are less susceptible to being faked than the self-report measures. These results are consistent with the idea that the psychopath is deficient in the ability to experience fear and anxiety. In a review of the literature, Patrick (1994) argued that the core problem with psychopaths is a deficit in the fear response. Events that would be threatening or anxiety-provoking to a normal person do not elicit these feelings in a psychopath. As a consequence, the psychopath is not motivated to interrupt his or her ongoing behavior to avoid punishment or other unpleasant consequences.

Other researchers have deemphasized biological explanations for psychopathy and argue, instead, that the emotional unresponsiveness of the psychopath is learned (Levenson, Kiehl, & Fitzpatrick, 1995). The observed fearlessness of the psychopath may be the result of a desensitization process. If a person is repeatedly exposed to violence or other antisocial behavior (such as childhood abuse or gang activities), he or she may become desensitized to such behaviors. That is, the callous disregard for others—the hallmark of psychopathy—may result from desensitization, a well-known form of learning. A prospective study of more than 400 victims of childhood abuse found that, compared with a control group, the abused children had significantly higher rates of psychopathy 20 years later (Luntz & Widom, 1994). By being victims of abuse, the argument goes, people learn that abusing others is a means of achieving power and control and obtaining what they want. Many psychopaths are motivated by interpersonal dominance and appear to enjoy having power over others. This can sometimes be seen in board meetings of corporations, in police stations, in politics, and wherever else one person has an opportunity to bully others. The point of this research, however, is that people who grow up to be bullies were themselves frequently bullied and abused as children.

Levinson (1992) has used results such as these to argue for a social learning model of psychopathy. He holds that, at some point, people decide to engage in antisocial behavior because they have learned, from observing others, that this is one way to get what they want. And, because of desensitization, the repetition of antisocial behavior makes similar behaviors more likely in the future.

Psychologists are currently debating the relative merits of viewing psychopathy as biological or as learned. Whatever the cause of psychopathy, the frequency and severity of antisocial behaviors almost always decrease as a person ages. It has been said that the best therapy for the psychopath is to grow older while in prison. The incidence of antisocial behaviors dramatically decreases in persons age 40 and older (*DSM-IV*). It has been widely known that, among criminals, those who make it to their fourth decade are much less likely to be rearrested for antisocial acts than are those in their twenties or thirties. For example, a study of 809 male prison inmates aged 16–69 found that deviant social behaviors, impulsivity, and antisocial acts were much less prevalent in the older prisoners (Harpur & Hare, 1994). There was less of an age decline in antisocial beliefs and callous social attitudes. Thus, although older psychopaths still don't care much about other people or their feelings, they nevertheless are less likely to impulsively act out these beliefs or to engage in actual antisocial behaviors. Whether the reason is getting burned out or growing up, there is a definite decrease in the range and frequency of antisocial acts with middle age, even among the most hard-core criminals.

therapists because they are manipulative. For example, they may threaten or even try suicide when they don't get their way. They are very sensitive to cues that others may abandon or leave them.

Table 19.3 lists the major features of the borderline personality disorder, along with examples of beliefs and thoughts that persons with this disorder might commonly have. Persons with borderline personality disorder, compared with those without, have a higher incidence rate of childhood physical or sexual abuse, neglect, or early parental loss. Many researchers believe that borderline disorder is caused by an early loss of love from parents, as may happen in parental death, abuse, severe neglect, or parental drug or alcohol abuse (Millon et al., 2000). Early loss may affect a child's capacity to form relationships. Children in such circumstances may come to believe that others are not to be trusted. Although borderline persons have

Table 19.3 Characteristics of Borderline Personality Disorder
Instability of relationships, emotions, and self-image Fears of abandonment Aggressiveness Proneness to self-harm Strong emotions
Typical Thoughts or Beliefs Associated with the Borderline Personality "I'm nothing without you." "I'll just die if you leave me." "If you go, I'll kill myself." "I hate you, I hate you, I HATE YOU." "I love you so much that I'll do anything or be anything for you." "I feel empty inside, as if I don't know who I am."

difficulty with relationships, they may form stable relationships if given enough structure and support. If they find someone who is accepting and stable, who is diplomatic, who meets their expectations for commitment, and who is caring and can diffuse trouble as it occurs, then the borderline personality may experience a satisfying relationship.

Histrionic Personality Disorder

The hallmark of **histrionic personality disorder** is *excessive attention seeking* and *emotionality.* Often such persons are overly dramatic, preferring to be the center of attention. They may appear charming or even flirtatious. Many are inappropriately seductive or provocative. And this *sexually provocative* behavior is often undirected and occurs in inappropriate settings, such as in professional settings. Physical appearance is often very important to histrionic persons, and they work to impress others and obtain compliments. Often, however, they overdo it and appear gaudy or flamboyant (e.g., histrionic women may wear way too much makeup).

Histrionic individuals express their opinions frequently and dramatically. However, their *opinions are shallow* and easily changed. Such a person may say, for example, that some political official is a great and wonderful leader yet be unable to give any supporting details or actual examples of leadership. Such persons prefer impressions to facts and often act on intuition (Millon et al., 2000). They often *display strong emotions in public,* sometimes to the embarrassment of friends and family. They may throw temper tantrums over minor frustrations or cry uncontrollably over a sentimental little event. To others, their emotions appear insincere and exaggerated, to the point of being theatrical. Histrionic individuals are also highly *suggestible.* Because their opinions are not based on facts, they can be easily swayed. They take up whatever is popular at the time.

Socially, histrionic individuals are difficult to get along with, due to their *excessive need for attention.* They may become upset and act impulsively when not given the attention they think they deserve. Such persons may use suicidal gestures and threats to get attention from others and to manipulate others into caring for them. Their seductiveness may put them at risk for sexual victimization. Other social difficulties arise out of their shallow emotional style. That is, they crave excitement and

A Closer Look Fatal Attraction

The thriller *Fatal Attraction* stars Michael Douglas and Glenn Close. Douglas plays Dan, a rich and powerful lawyer who is happily married to a beautiful woman. The couple have a wonderful daughter whom they both love. At a business dinner, Dan meets Glenn Close's character, Alex, who is an attractive, intriguing, single woman who catches Dan's eye. Dan is with his wife, however, and nothing happens with Alex at the dinner. A few weeks later, Dan is on a business trip without his wife one weekend and he sees Alex again. They flirt for some time, and there is definitely some attraction between them. Dan does not know at this point, but it is a fatal attraction. During the weekend, Dan and Alex have sex several times, and they appear to enjoy each other very much. In one scene, Dan and Alex are together in bed after sex, and the camera turns to a pot of coffee that is boiling on the stove. This is a subtle visual hint of the dangerous consequences being set into motion with their adulterous affair.

After this weekend infidelity, Dan returns to his wife. Alex is upset that Dan just seems to want to forget about her. She feels she loves him, yet she hates him at the same time for leaving her. Over the next several weeks, she calls Dan at his home and even stalks him on several occasions. Finally, she confronts Dan and tells him she is pregnant with his baby and feels he should leave his wife for her. Dan, however, tells Alex to get an abortion and to forget about his ever leaving his wife. He makes it clear that he does not want to be a part of her life. She then alternates between extreme love and extreme hate for him. She wants Dan for herself and decides that the best way to get him is to destroy what is standing between her and Dan, which is his wife and child. The movie becomes a thriller when Alex begins terrorizing Dan and his family.

When this movie first came out, many reviewers referred to the Alex character incorrectly as a "psycho lover" or as "a nutcase." In fact, Alex exhibits several of the symptoms of borderline personality disorder. She exhibits the incredible relationship difficulties that are the hallmark of the borderline style. She vacillates between wanting to have and then wanting to destroy those she loves. She poses on the edge between destroying herself and harming those who are causing her emotional troubles. She becomes progressively angrier during the movie, and we don't know if she will direct this anger toward harming herself or harming others. All of this is triggered by feelings of abandoment, another hallmark of the borderline character. Being left out, left behind, or abandoned is a critical issue for persons with this disorder. Because they often define themselves in terms of their relationships ("I'm nothing without you"), they fear losing those relationships. However, because of their strong and unpredictable emotions, their relationships tend to be unstable and unsatisfying and end prematurely. They bring about that which they fear.

In the movie Fatal Attraction, *Glenn Close plays the character Alex, who has many of the characteristics of borderline personality disorder.*

novelty and, although they may start relationships or projects with great enthusiasm, their interest does not last long. They may forego long-term gains to make way for short-term excitement. Histrionic traits are maladaptive because they can interfere with relationships and cause difficulties with the individual being a productive member of society.

Table 19.4 lists the main characteristics of histrionic personality disorder along with typical beliefs and thoughts persons with this disorder might have. As with all personality disorder criteria, the standards for appropriate behavior differ greatly

Table 19.4 Characteristics of Histrionic Personality Disorder

Excessive attention seeking
Excessive and strong emotions
Sexual provocativeness
Shallow opinions
Suggestibility
Strong need for attention

Typical Thoughts or Beliefs Associated with the Histrionic Personality
"Hey, look at me!"
"I am happiest when I am the center of attention."
"Boredom is the pits."
"I usually go with my intuition; I don't have to think things through."
"I can amuse, impress, or entertain anyone, mainly because I am so interesting and exciting."
"If I feel like doing something, I go ahead and do it."

among cultures, generations, and genders. Therefore, we must ask whether specific behaviors cause social impairment or distress before concluding that those behaviors are signs or symptoms of histrionic personality disorder. For example, behavior that is considered seductive in one culture may be viewed as acceptable behavior in another. A woman from the southern coast of Italy may appear flirtatious in the United States, when, in fact, in her culture people are much more friendly and at ease with each other, and teasing flirtation is a common form of interaction. Consider also the culture of gender. The expression of histrionic personality disorder may depend on gender stereotypes. A male with this personality may behave in

Application

A case of histrionic personality disorder. **Roxann was a student who also worked in the evenings as a dancer at an adult club. She would tell people that this was temporary and that she was different from the other women who worked there. She readily admitted, however, that the job met her two most important needs: money and attention, "two things I cannot live without." Roxann decided to take some psychology courses for self-improvement. She typically showed up to classes dressed to kill and seemed out of place even among students her own age. Once she went to her professor's office yet did not seem to have any direct questions to discuss. Instead, she seemed just to want to talk about herself and her extracurricular job. After this meeting, she was overheard telling other students that she was on a first-name basis with her professor and that he was actually her good friend. In class, she frequently behaved in ways that drew attention to herself, such as sighing loudly when the professor made a point, or blurting out answers to rhetorical questions. Toward the end of the course, Roxann quit going to class and missed the final exam. She e-mailed the professor, saying that she had been experiencing a debilitating condition and frequently had to lie down to avoid fainting. She said she had been to several doctors but none were able to find any medical basis to her condition. The professor never heard from her again.**

a "hyper-macho" fashion and attempt to be the center of attention by boasting of his skills in seduction or how much influence and power he has in his workplace. A woman with the histrionic style may express it with hyperfemininity, seeking to be the center of attention by adorning herself with bright, sexy clothes and wearing lots of gaudy accessories and makeup.

Narcissistic Personality Disorder

The calling card of **narcissistic personality disorder** is a strong *need to be admired,* a strong sense of *self-importance,* and a *lack of insight into other people's feelings.* Narcissists see themselves in a very favorable light, inflating their accomplishments and undervaluing the work of others. Narcissists daydream about prosperity, victory, influence, adoration from others, and power. They routinely expect adulation from others, believing that homage is generally long overdue. They exhibit feelings of *entitlement,* believing that they should receive special privileges and respect, even though they have done nothing in particular to earn that special treatment.

A sense of *superiority* also pervades the narcissistic personality. They feel that they are special and should associate only with others who are similarly unique or gifted. Because they associate with special people, their own views of themselves are further enhanced. Such a person may insist on having the best lawyer or attending the best university, viewing him- or herself as unique, different from, and better than everyone else.

People with this personality expect a lot from those around them. They must receive regular praise from others and devoted admiration from those close to them. Many narcissistic persons prefer as friends those who are socially weak or unpopular, so that they will not compete with the narcissists for attention. The **narcissistic paradox** is that, although narcissists have high self-esteem, their *grandiose self-esteem is actually quite fragile.* That is, even though they appear self-confident and strong, they need to prop themselves up with admiration and attention from others. You might think that someone with truly high self-esteem would not have such an unreasonable need for praise and admiration from others. When narcissists show up at a party they expect to be welcomed with great fanfare. When they go to a restaurant or store, they assume that waiters or clerks will rush to their attention. Narcissists thus depend on others to verify their self-importance.

To say that the narcissist's self-esteem is vulnerable does not mean that they are covering up low self-esteem, but rather that they are exquisitely sensitive to criticism, that they can fly into a rage when they don't get what they think they deserve. Their self-esteem is full-blown and real; narcissists fully expect others to recognize how special, unique, and superior they are, even in the absence of any objective supportive evidence. Their vulnerability is exhibited as a thin-skinned, bristling kind of sensitivity, similar to childish temper tantrums and pouting. Such reactions indicate an inflated self-importance that knows no bounds.

Further making the narcissist socially difficult is an *inability to recognize the needs or desires of others.* In conversation, they tend to talk mostly about themselves—"I" this and "my" that. Narcissists use first-person pronouns *(I, me, mine)* more frequently in everyday conversation than does the average person (Raskin & Shaw, 1987). Psychologists Richard Robins and Oliver John (1997) have found that persons scoring high on a narcissism questionnaire evaluate their performances much more positively than those performances are evaluated by others, demonstrating the

Table 19.5 Characteristics of Narcissistic Personality Disorder

Need to be admired
Strong sense of self-importance
Lack of insight into other people's feelings and needs
Sense of entitlement
Sense of superiority
Self-esteem that is strong but paradoxically fragile
Envy of others

Typical Thoughts or Beliefs Associated with the Narcissistic Personality
"I'm special and deserve special treatment."
"The typical rules don't apply to me."
"If others don't give me the praise and recognition I deserve, they should be punished."
"Other people should do my bidding."
"Who are *you* to criticize *me?*"
"I have every reason to expect that I will get the best that life has to offer."

self-enhancement component of narcissism. People who are in a relationship with a narcissist often complain that narcissists are self-centered, emotionally cold, and unwilling to reciprocate in the normal give-and-take of a relationship.

A final social difficulty that creates problems for narcissists is the ease with which they become *envious of others*. When hearing of the success or accomplishment of acquaintances, narcissists may disparage that achievement. They may feel that they deserve the success more than the persons who worked to attain it. Narcissists may disdain others' accomplishments, particularly in public. A veneer of snobbery may hide strong feelings of envy and rage over the successes of others.

Table 19.5 lists the main characteristics of the narcissistic personality disorder, along with examples of some typical beliefs and thoughts persons with this disorder might have. Narcissists sometimes reach positions of high achievement, due primarily to their self-confidence and ambition. Nevertheless, their interpersonal lives are usually fraught with the problems that come with feelings of entitlement, an excessive need for praise and recognition, and an impaired recognition of others' needs. They have difficulty maintaining intimate relationships.

Exercise

Everyone knows someone who is a narcissist. Think of the most narcissistic person you know. List five of his or her characteristics or behaviors that make you think that this person is a narcissist. How do the acts and characteristics you have listed fit with the symptoms of the narcissistic personality disorder?

The Eccentric Cluster: Ways of Being Different

A second cluster of personality disorders contains traits that combine to make people ill-at-ease socially and just plain different. Most of the oddness in these disorders has to do with how the person interacts with others. Some people have no interest in others; some are extremely uncomfortable with others; and some are suspicious of others. When carried to extremes, these interpersonal styles form the three personality disorders known as the schizoid, schizotypal, and paranoid personalities.

Schizoid and **schizotypal personality disorders** both take their root from schizophrenia and are closely tied to the history of this diagnostic category. *Schizophrenia* as a term literally means a cutting of the mind off from itself and from reality. It is a serious mental illness that involves hallucinations, delusions, and perceptual aberrations. The personality disorders of schizoid and schizotypal exhibit some low-grade nonpsychotic symptoms of schizophrenia. For example, the schizotype is eccentric and is interested in odd and unusual beliefs, whereas the schizoid displays social apathy. Schizophrenics display both of these characteristics, *plus* delusions or hallucinations. Thus these personality disorders have much in common with this more severe mental illness. In the case of schizotypal disorders, persons are likely to possess the genotype that makes them vulnerable to schizophrenia. A large proportion of the family members of persons with schizophrenia exhibit odd and unusual behaviors that would contribute to a diagnosis of schizotypal personality disorder.

Schizoid Personality Disorder

The schizoid personality is split off (schism), or *detached, from normal social relations*. The schizoid person simply appears to have no need or desire for intimate relationships or even friendships. Family life usually does not mean much to such people, and they do not obtain satisfaction from being part of a group. They have few or no close friends, and they would rather spend time by themselves than with others. They typically choose hobbies that can be done and appreciated alone, such as stamp collecting. They also typically choose solitary jobs, often with mechanical or abstract tasks, such as machinists or computer programmers. Usually, the schizoid personality experiences *little pleasure* from bodily or sensory experiences, such as eating or having sex. The person's emotional life is typically constricted.

Application

The case of Roger, a schizoid research assistant. **Roger was an undergraduate who had volunteered to help out in the laboratory of one of his psychology professors. He was responsible, showing up on time and doing the work he was given. However, he seemed detached from the work, never getting too excited or appearing to be even interested, though he volunteered to work for several semesters. Roger often worked in the lab at night. On several occasions, some of the graduate students complained to the professor that Roger was "staring" at them. When pressed for details, these students said that, when they left their office doors open, they would sometimes turn around and find Roger standing in the doorway, looking at them. Several female graduate students complained that he was "spooky" and kept their office doors locked.**

Roger lived with his younger brother, who also went to the same university. The brother apparently handled all the daily chores, such as dealing with the landlord,

Application (*Continued*)

buying groceries, and arranging for utilities. Roger thus had a protected life and spent most of his time studying, reading, or exploring the Internet. In class, he never talked or participated in discussion. Outside of class, he appeared to have no friends, nor did he participate in any extracurricular activities. The professor he worked for thought he might be on medication but, after inquiring, learned that Roger took no medication. After graduating with a degree in psychology, Roger returned to live with his parents. He remodeled the space above his parents' garage and has been living there, rent-free, for the past 15 years. Every few years, he calls the psychology professor he used to work for. The conversations are always very short and never seem to have a point.

At best, the schizoid person appears indifferent to others, neither bothered by criticism nor buoyed by compliments. "Bland" would be one description of such a person's emotional life. Often, the schizoid person does not respond to social cues and, so, appears *inept* or *socially clumsy.* For example, such a person may walk into a room where there is another person and simply stare at that person, apparently not motivated to start a conversation. Sometimes the schizoid person is *passive* in the face of unpleasant happenings and does not respond effectively to important events. Such a person may appear directionless.

People from some cultures react to stress in a way that looks like schizoid personality disorder. That is, without actually having the disorder, some people under stress may appear socially numb and passive. For example, people who move out of extremely rural environments into large cities may react in a schizoid fashion for several weeks or months. Such a person, overwhelmed by noise, lights, and overcrowding, may prefer to be alone, have constricted emotions, and manifest other deficits in social skills. Also, people who immigrate from other countries are sometimes seen as cold, reserved, or aloof. For example, people who immigrated from Southeastern Asia during the 1970s and 1980s were sometimes seen as being hostile or cold by people in mainstream urban American culture. These are cultural differences and should not be interpreted as personality disorders.

The famous surrealist painter Salvador Dali displayed many of the characteristics associated with the schizotypal personality disorder.

Schizotypal Personality Disorder

Whereas the schizoid person is indifferent to social interaction, the schizotypal person is acutely uncomfortable in social relationships. Schizotypes are *anxious in social situations,* especially if those situations involve strangers. Schizotypal persons also feel that they are different from others or that they do not fit in with the group. Interestingly, when such persons have to interact with a group, they do not necessarily become less anxious as they become more familiar with the group. For example, while attending a group function, the schizotype will not become less anxious as time wears on but, instead, will become more and more tense. This is because schizotypes tend to be *suspicious of others* and are not prone to trust others or to relax in their presence.

Another characteristic of people with schizotypal personalities is that they are *odd* and *eccentric*. It is not unusual for them to harbor many superstitions such as believing in ESP and many other psychic or paranormal phenomena that are outside of the norms for their culture. They may believe in magic or that they possess some magical or extraordinary power, such as the ability to control other people or animals with their thoughts. They may have *unusual perceptions* that border on hallucinations, such as feeling that other people are looking at them or hearing murmurs that sound like their names.

Because of their suspiciousness of others, social discomfort, and general oddness, schizotypal persons have difficulty with social relationships. They often violate common social conventions in such ways as not making eye contact, dressing in unkempt clothing, and wearing clothing that does not go together. In many ways, the schizotype simply does not fit into the social group.

Because of their similarity in terms of avoiding social relations, the characteristics of schizoid and schizotypal personality disorders are presented together in Table 19.6. Some beliefs and thoughts, mostly concerned with other people, which characterize persons with these disorders are also listed.

Mason, Claridge, and Jackson (1995) published a questionnaire for assessing schizotypal traits and validated it in several British samples. One of the scales contains items that get at the presence of *unusual experiences:* "Are your thoughts sometimes so strong you can almost hear them? Have you sometimes had the feeling of gaining or losing energy when certain people look at you or touch you? Are you so good at controlling others that it sometimes scares you?" Another scale contains items that assess *cognitive disorganization:* "Do you ever feel that your speech is difficult to understand because the words are all mixed up and don't make any sense? Do you frequently have difficulty starting to do things?" Another set of items measures the

Table 19.6 Characteristics of Schizoid and Schizotypal Personality Disorders

Schizoid
Detached from normal social relationships
Pleasureless life
Inept or socially clumsy
Passive in the face of unpleasant events

Schizotypal
Anxious in social relations and avoids people
"Different" and nonconforming
Suspicious of others
Eccentricity of beliefs, such as in ESP or magic
Unusualness of perceptions and experiences
Disorganized thoughts and speech

Typical Thoughts or Beliefs Associated with the Schizoid and Schizotypal Personalities
"I hate being tied to other people."
"My privacy is more important to me than being close to others."
"It's best not to confide too much in others."
"Relationships are always messy."
"I manage best on my own and set my own standards."
"Intimate relations are unimportant to me."

A Closer Look

The Unabomber: Comorbidity of Personality Disorders

In 1996, Theodore Kaczynski was arrested for murder in a long line of bombings. He had been mailing bombs to unsuspecting university professors and scientists (hence his FBI code name—Unabomber) for 17 years. While many of his targets were computer scientists, he did injure one psychology professor with a mail bomb (Professor James McConnell at the University of Michigan). Police knew the bombs were all from the same person, but they had no idea of his motives or why he was targeting university professors. After a 17-year period of anonymous killing and maiming from a distance, he decided to make the nature of his grievances clear. He sent several taunting letters to the FBI, and a long rambling manifesto to the *Washington Post* and the *New York Times,* which published his diatribe against technology and modern society. This was his undoing. Kaczynski's brother recognized the nature of the complaints in the manifesto, and notified the police, who arrested Kaczynski at his isolated 10-by-12-foot shack in Montana.

A reporter—Maggie Scarf—writing in the *New Republic* magazine (June 10, 1996, p. 20), presented her view that Ted Kaczynski most likely had a narcissistic personality disorder. Scarf used the *DSM-IV* description of narcissistic disorder to explain Kaczynski's behavior. For example, as an undergraduate at Harvard, Kaczynski isolated himself so severely that none of his classmates can remember anything about him. He saw himself as a misunderstood genius whom the world would one day recognize. As a mathematics graduate student at the University of Michigan he isolated himself even more. In his isolation he probably nurtured fantasies of prestige and power and revenge on those who refused to praise him. As a promising young professor of mathematics at U.C. Berkeley he suddenly bolted from his faculty position in 1969. No one, apparently, was recognizing his superiority. People did not realize, as he did, that he possessed a phenomenal intellect and superior vision of how everything worked. His colleagues were fools, he must have concluded, because they could not see his obvious superiority. His students, however, complained loudly about his teaching style. In their course evaluations they indicated that his lectures were boring and useless and that he ignored questions from the students. They too must be fools, Kaczynski probably concluded.

In her article Scarf argued that when Kaczynski struck out at society, he was really saying, "I'm special and I deserve your respect." When he began taunting the police to try to capture him he was really saying, "I am so extraordinary that I operate with impunity; you haven't been able to catch me for 17 years and you never will." Finally, when he gave his manifesto to the world, he was really saying, "You had better realize you are dealing with someone unprecedented in the history of the human race. I am so clever and powerful and smart that I will tell you all the problems with the world and how to fix them, and if you ignore my commands you do so at your own risk." His entire ranting manifesto is easily located on the World Wide Web by entering "Unabomber" in a search engine.

Scarf is a journalist, not a psychologist, so her diagnosis is based on her speculation. Kaczynski certainly does have some features of the narcissistic personality disorder, but most narcissists are not serial murderers. What other possible clues might we have to his abnormal behavior? It turns out that the entire text of the court-appointed psychiatrist's

Former University of California at Berkeley math professor Theodore Kaczynski was convicted in several of the "Unabomber" attacks, which occurred over a 17-year period. Kaczynski displays characteristics associated with a number of personality disorders.

report on Ted Kaczynski is available on the Web at http://archive.abcnews.go.com/sections/living/InYourHead/kaczynskievaluation4.html. This report, prepared by government-appointed psychiatrist Sally Johnson, provides another perspective on Kaczynski. While at Harvard, Kaczynski was involved in a study by Henry Murray, whom we discussed in Chapter 11. Personality test results from his undergraduate days at Harvard indicate that he was extremely introverted and somewhat depressive, even at that early age. During his psychological evaluation 30 years later, the main finding was that he suffered from schizophrenia, paranoid type, which is a severe mental illness. However, he also had an IQ of 136, which puts him in the top 1 percent of the population. As for personality disorders the psychiatrist concluded that Kaczynski had paranoid personality disorder along with many features of the avoidant and antisocial personality disorders as well. The following is a quote from her official report:

Mr. Kaczynski is also diagnosed as suffering from a Paranoid Personality Disorder with Avoidant and Antisocial Features. Review of his developmental history, adolescence and early adult life draws a picture consistent with the symptomatology associated with this type of personality disorder. Consistent with this type of personality disordered function, Mr. Kaczynski historically has shown pervasive distrust of others such that their motives are interpreted as malevolent. Symptoms consistent with Paranoid Personality Disorders that are evident in Mr. Kaczynski's presentation include that he suspects, without sufficient basis, that others are exploiting, harming, or deceiving him; that he reads demeaning or threatening meanings into benign remarks or events; that he persistently bears grudges and is unforgiving of insults, injuries or slights; and that he perceives attacks on his character or reputation that are not apparent to others, and is quick to react angrily or to counterattack.

In addition to meeting the criteria for Paranoid Personality Disorder, Mr. Kaczynski also has features of two other personality disorder types. Support for Avoidant Personality Disorder Traits includes that he has demonstrated a pervasive pattern of social inhibition, feelings of inadequacy and hypersensitivity to negative evaluations, beginning in his early life. Consistent with this, he has shown restraint within intimate relationships because of his fear of being shamed or ridiculed; he has been preoccupied with being criticized or rejected in social situations; and is inhibited in new interpersonal situations because of feelings of inadequacy. Consistent with Antisocial Personality Disorder Traits is his pervasive pattern of disregard for and violation of the rights of others. This includes his failure to conform to social norms with respect to lawful behaviors, as indicated by repeatedly performing acts that are grounds for arrest. This description is based on his own account of his behavior in his writings and interviews. Also consistent with his Antisocial Personality Traits is the characteristic of deceitfulness, as indicated by his persistent and elaborate efforts to conceal his behaviors. He has demonstrated a reckless regard for the safety of others. He demonstrates a lack of remorse as indicated in his writings by being indifferent to having hurt, mistreated, or stolen from others. Mr. Kaczynski falls short of carrying a diagnosis of Antisocial Personality Disorder in that he does not have evidence of a conduct disorder before the age of 15. (Excerpted from the report of Sally C. Johnson, M.D., Chief Psychiatrist, Associate Warden of Health Services, Federal Correctional Institution, Butner, North Carolina, January, 1996.)

Kaczynski shows features of at least four different personality disorders, with the prominent personality disorder being paranoid personality disorder. This disorder occurred along with paranoid schizophrenia, which involves delusions and elaborate belief systems. The presence of two or more disorders in one person is called **comorbidity.** Comorbidity can occur when two or more personality disorders exist, or when two or more disorders of any type coexist in the same person. Comorbidity is fairly common, and it makes for difficulty in diagnosing disorders.

tendency to avoid people: "Are you much too independent to really get involved with people? Can you usually let yourself go and enjoy yourself at a party?" And, finally, there is a scale for assessing the *nonconformity* aspect of schizotypy: "Do you often feel like doing the opposite of what people suggest, even though you know they are right? Would you take drugs that might have strange or dangerous effects?"

Many famous persons have been odd or eccentric. Artists (e.g., Salvador Dali), writers (e.g., Tennessee Williams), musicians, film stars, and even politicians have exhibited some fairly eccentric behaviors. Can you think of examples of public figures who have displayed odd beliefs or actions recently? Would they fit the rest of the characteristics of the schizotypal personality?

Paranoid Personality Disorder

Whereas the schizotype is uncomfortable with others, the paranoid person is extremely *distrustful of others* and sees others as a constant threat. Such persons assume that others are out to exploit and deceive them, even though there is no good evidence to support this assumption. Paranoid persons feel that they have been injured by others and are preoccupied with doubts about the motivations of others.

People with this personality typically do not reveal personal information to others, fearing that the information will be used against them. Their reaction to others is "Mind your own business." The paranoid person often *misinterprets social events*. For example, someone makes an off-hand comment and the paranoid interprets it as a demeaning or threatening remark (e.g., wondering, "What did he mean by *that?*"). Paranoids are constantly on the lookout for hidden meanings and disguised motivations in the comments and behaviors of others.

The person with a **paranoid personality disorder** often holds *resentments toward others* for slights or perceived insults. Such a person is reluctant to forgive and forget even minor altercations. Paranoid persons often become involved in legal disputes, suing others for the slightest reasons. Sometimes paranoid persons plead with those in power to intervene on their behalf, such as writing to congresspersons or calling the local police chief day after day.

Pathological jealousy is a common manifestation of paranoid personality disorder. For example, a pathologically jealous woman suspects that her husband or partner is unfaithful, even though there is no objective evidence of infidelity. She may go to great lengths to find support for her jealous beliefs. She may restrict the activities of her partner or constantly question him as to his whereabouts. She may not believe her partner's accounts of how he spent his time or believe his claims of faithfulness.

People with paranoid personality disorder are at risk of harming those who threaten their belief systems. Their *argumentative and hostile nature* may provoke others to a combative response. This hostile response from others, in turn, validates the paranoids' original suspicion that others are out to get them. Their extreme suspiciousness and the unreasonableness of their beliefs make people with this disorder particularly difficult in social relations. Table 19.7 presents the main characteristics of the paranoid personality disorder, along with some examples of beliefs and thoughts commonly found among persons with this disorder.

The Anxious Cluster: Ways of Being Nervous, Fearful, or Distressed

The final cluster of personality traits consists of patterns of behavior that are geared toward avoiding anxiety. The disorders in this cluster, like all the other disorders, illustrate the **neurotic paradox:** Although a behavior pattern successfully solves one problem for the person, it may create or maintain another equally or more severe problem.

Table 19.7 Characteristics of Paranoid Personality Disorder

Is distrustful of others
Misinterprets social events as threatening
Harbors resentments toward others
Is prone to pathological jealousy
Is argumentative and hostile

Typical Thoughts or Beliefs Associated with the Paranoid Personality
"Get them before they get you."
"Other people always have ulterior motives."
"People will say one thing but do another."
"Don't let them get away with anything."
"I have to be on guard all the time."
"When people act friendly toward you, it is probably because they want something. Watch out!"

Avoidant Personality Disorder

The major feature of the **avoidant personality disorder** is a pervasive *feeling of inadequacy* and *sensitivity to criticism* from others. Clearly, no one likes to be criticized. However, avoidant persons will go to great lengths to avoid situations in which others may have opportunities to criticize their performance or character, such as in school, at work, or in other group settings. The main reason for this anxiety about performance is an extreme fear of criticism or rejection from others. Such persons may avoid making new friends or going to new places, through fear of criticism or disapproval. Friends may have to plead and promise lots of support and encouragement in order to get them involved in new activities.

Application

The case of Ellen, avoidant university student. **Ellen is a 21-year-old university student who has gone to the university's psychological clinic with the general complaint that she is uncomfortable in social settings. Because she is so shy and nervous, she keeps her contact with others to a minimum. She is worried about starting new classes next semester and having to be in rooms with total strangers. She is especially worried about her psychology courses, where "they might find out I am a nutcase." She adds, "They are going to think I am a dysfunctional idiot because I am so shy and I go into a panic at the thought of speaking up in a group of strangers." She adds that she is thinking of switching her major from psychology to computer science. Although she is curious about people, and therefore likes psychology, she neverthless feels awkward around them. Computers, she thinks, are much easier to get along with.**

Ellen reports that, as a child, she was teased mercilessly by the other children in her school. She remembers withdrawing from others at about this time in her life. She says that in grade school she would try to make herself small and inconspicuous, so others would not notice her. As a teenager, she took some jobs baby-sitting, but she has never held a real job. At the university, she apparently has no friends, or at least cannot name any. She says she is afraid others will not like her "when they find out what I am really like," so she avoids social contact. In fact, she never once makes eye contact with the interviewer at the clinic.

Application (*Continued*)

At the university, Ellen follows a pattern of letting work pile up, then works hard to get it all done. She tries to do a few errands each day, keeps her apartment neat, and goes to the grocery store twice a month. She describes her life as "not very happy, but at least predictable." She likes exploring the Internet on her home computer. She says she enjoys going to chat rooms on the Internet, but, when pressed on this, she confesses that she just watches and has never actually interacted with anyone over the Internet. She likes staying in the background, watching others interact: "When they don't even know I'm there, then I can be pretty sure they are not laughing at me."

Because avoidant persons fear criticism, they may *restrict their activities* to avoid potential embarrassments. For example, an avoidant man may cancel a blind date at the last minute because he can't find just the right clothes to wear. Avoidant individuals cope with anxiety by avoiding the risks of everyday social life. However, by avoiding the anxiety, they create other problems, often in the form of missed opportunities. In addition, avoidant individuals are typically seen by others as meek, quiet, shy, lonely, and solitary.

Avoidant persons are sensitive to what others think of them. Their feelings are easily hurt, and they appear vulnerable and inhibited in social interactions, withholding their own views, opinions, or feelings out of fear of being ridiculed. They typically have very *low self-esteem* and feel inadequate to many of life's day-to-day challenges. Because of their social isolation, they typically do not have many sources of social support. Even though they typically desire to be involved with others, and may even fantasize about relationships, they tend to avoid intimate contact out of their fear of rejection and criticism. The paradox is that, in avoidantly coping with their social anxiety, they shun the supportive relationships with caring others that could actually help boost their self-esteem. Table 19.8 presents the main features of the avoidant personality disorder, along with several examples of thoughts and beliefs that might occur in someone with this disorder.

Dependent Personality Disorder

Whereas the avoidant person avoids others to an extreme, the dependent person seeks out others to an extreme. The hallmark of the **dependent personality disorder** is an *excessive need to be taken care of,* to be nurtured, coddled, and told

Table 19.8 Characteristics of Avoidant Personality Disorder
Feelings of inadequacy Sensitive to criticism Activities are restricted to avoid embarrassment Low self-esteem
Typical Thoughts or Beliefs Associated with the Avoidant Personality "I am socially inept and undesirable." "I wish you would like me, but I think you really hate me." "I can't stand being criticized; it makes me feel so unpleasant." "I must avoid unpleasant situations at all costs." "I don't want to attract attention to myself." "If I ignore a problem, it will go away."

what to do. Dependent persons act in *submissive* ways, so as to encourage others to take care of them or take charge of the situation. Such individuals need lots of encouragement and advice from others and would much rather turn over responsibility for their decisions to someone else. Where should they live, what schools should they attend, what courses should they take, with whom should they make friends? The dependent personality has great difficulty making such decisions, and *seeks out reassurance from others.* However, such a person tends to seek advice about even minor decisions, such as whether to carry an umbrella today, what color clothes to wear, and what entree to order at a restaurant. The dependent person *rarely takes the initiative.*

Because of their fear of losing the help and advice of others, dependent persons *avoid disagreements* with those on whom they are dependent. Because of their extreme need for support, dependent personalities might even agree with decisions or opinions that they feel are wrong to avoid angering the persons on whom they depend.

Because of their low self-confidence and need for constant reassurance, dependent persons may *not work well independently.* They may wait for others to start projects or may need direction often during a task. They may demonstrate how inept they are, so as to trick others into assisting them. They may avoid becoming proficient at a task, so as to keep others from seeing that they are competent to work by themselves. It is too bad that a person who relies on others to solve problems may never learn the skills of living or working independently.

Persons with dependent personalities *may tolerate extreme circumstances to obtain reassurance and support from others.* Such people may submit to unreasonable demands, may tolerate abuse, or may stay in a distorted relationship. People who believe that they are unable to take care of themselves may tolerate a lot of abuse in order to maintain bonds with people who will take care of them. The unfortunate aspect of the dependent personality is that, by giving over responsibility and depending on other people, dependent persons may never discover that they can take care of themselves. Table 19.9 presents the main characteristics of the dependent personality disorder, along with associated beliefs and thoughts that persons with this disorder might have.

Table 19.9 Characteristics of Dependent Personality Disorder

Has an excessive need to be taken care of
Is submissive
Seeks reassurance from others
Rarely takes initiative and rarely disagrees with others
Does not work well independently
May tolerate abuse from others to obtain support

Typical Thoughts or Beliefs Associated with the Dependent Personality
"I am weak and need support."
"The worst possible thing would be to be abandoned and left alone."
"I must not offend those on whom I depend."
"I must be submissive to obtain their help."
"I need help making decisions."
"I hope someone will tell me what to do."

Application

Degrading and abusive relationships—the way out. A common tactic of keeping people in relationships is to convince them that no one else would want them. This is commonly seen in dysfunctional marriages, in which, for example, the husband degrades the wife constantly. This form of psychological abuse may take the form of constantly pointing out her shortcomings, insulting her appearance or abilities, or pointing to weaknesses. Often, men who are insecure in their relationships, who are worried that their mates will leave them, will try to lower the self-esteem of their partners, so that they will think they cannot do any better. Some men resort to physical abuse. Although the degradation and violence can go from female to male, the more common pattern is for the male to degrade the female.

After undergoing long periods of degradation and psychological abuse, many women do experience a decrease in self-esteem. A woman in this situation may begin to depend more and more on the man for reassurance. She will do whatever she can to avoid making him angry or starting him on one of his bouts of insulting her. She takes no initiative in any decisions about the relationship or the living arrangements and defers every decision to him. If he catches her taking the initiative, he may punish her by again going into a bout of degrading her. She tolerates it in order to obtain the minimal reassurance and support this relationship gives her. Moreover, she is firmly persuaded by him that she cannot find anyone better. Essentially, he psychologically batters her into dependency.

People who are in such abusive relationships, either psychologically or physically, need to realize that they do not have to tolerate such treatment, that they are not the degraded human beings their spouses are portraying them as. The first step is to be empowered to make their own decisions. Often, the first decision is to leave the abusive person and go to a safe place, such as a women's shelter or a protective relative. They have to realize that they can take the initiative. Often, once this first, most difficult decision is made, others come easier and they can get back on track toward taking care of their own lives.

Obsessive-Compulsive Personality Disorder

The obsessive-compulsive person is *preoccupied with order* and *strives to be perfect.* The high need for order can manifest itself in the person's attention to details, however trivial, and fondness for rules, rituals, schedules, and procedures. Such persons may, for example, plan out which clothes they will wear every day of the week or clean their apartments every Saturday and Wednesday from 5 until 7 P.M. People with **obsessive-compulsive personality disorder** *hold very high standards for themselves.* However, they may work so hard at being perfect that they are never satisfied with their work. For example, a student might never turn in a research paper because it is never quite perfect enough. The desire for perfection can actually stifle a person's productivity.

Another characteristic is a *devotion to work at the expense of leisure and friendships.* Obsessive-compulsive persons tend to work harder than they need to. They may work at night and on weekends and rarely take time off. In his book on adult personality development, George Vaillant (1977) saw it as a sign of positive mental adjustment when his adult subjects reported taking at least a one-week vacation each

Table 19.10 Characteristics of Obsessive-Compulsive Personality Disorder

Preoccupied with order
Perfectionistic
Devoted to work, seeking little leisure time or friendship
Frequently miserly or stingy
Rigid and stubborn

Typical Thoughts or Beliefs Associated with the Obsessive-Compulsive Personality
"I believe in order, rules, and high standards."
"Others are irresponsible, casual, and self-indulgent."
"Details are important; flaws and mistakes are intolerable."
"My way is the only right way to do things."
"If you can't do it perfectly, don't do it at all."
"I have only myself to depend on."

year. Obsessive-compulsives tend not to meet this criterion for adjustment. When they do take time off for recreation, they prefer serious tasks, such as stamp collecting or chess. For hobbies, they pick very demanding tasks or activities that require great attention to detail, such as cross-stitch sewing or computer programming. Even their play looks a lot like work.

The obsessive-compulsive person may also appear *inflexible* with regard to ethics and morals. Such persons set high principles for themselves and tend to follow the letter of the law. They are highly conscientious and expect others to be that way as well. There is usually only one right way to do something—their way. They often have trouble working with others because they are reluctant to delegate tasks; "If you want something done right, you have to do it yourself" is a common complaint from obsessive-compulsive persons. They become irritated when others don't take their work as seriously as they do.

A few other odd characteristics are often present in the obsessive-compulsive person. One is the preference to hang on to worn-out or useless things; many obsessive-compulsive people have trouble throwing things away. Many are *miserly or stingy,* hoarding their money and resources. And, finally, along with being inflexible, obsessive-compulsives can be frustratingly *stubborn.* They may stubbornly insist, for example, that they cannot complete their work because of the imperfections of others. As you might imagine, they often cause difficulties for others at the workplace. Table 19.10 presents the essential features of obsessive-compulsive personality disorder, along with some typical beliefs and thoughts that characterize persons with this disorder.

There is another disorder—obsessive-compulsive disorder (OCD)—that is often confused with obsessive-compulsive personality disorder (OCPD). OCD is an anxiety disorder that is, in several ways, more serious and debilitating than OCPD. In OCD there is a pattern of unwanted and intrusive thoughts that are recurrent and troubling to the person, such as the persistent thought that they may harm someone. In addition, OCD is characterized by the presence of ritualistic behaviors, such as frequent hand washing or the tendency to repeat actions a set number of times (e.g., having to touch an object three times before leaving a room, or repeating words to oneself three times). Obsessive-compulsive personality disorder, on the other hand, really involves a collection of traits, such as excessive need for order or extremely high conscientiousness. Nevertheless, people with OCPD are at risk for developing OCD as well as other kinds of anxiety disorders (Oltmanns & Emery, 2004).

Many of the characteristics of obsessive-compulsive personality can actually be adaptive in some respects. For example, wanting to perform a task as perfectly as possible is, up to a point, desirable and rewarded. Holding one's opinions firm is, up to a point, desirable and indicates character. Keeping everything neat and orderly is, up to a point, useful. How can one tell, however, when some of these characteristics and behaviors indicate an obsessive-compulsive personality? How can we tell the difference between a high level of conscientiousness and the disorder of obsessive-compulsiveness? We will turn to this topic next in our discussion of dimensional models of personality disorders.

Application

The case of Rita, an obsessive-compulsive personality. **Rita was a 39-year-old computer programmer who had been married for 18 years. She was always orderly and kept a very neat house. It was so neat, in fact, that she noticed when the books were in the wrong order on the bookshelves or if a knick-knack had been moved on a table or shelf. She vacuumed the house every day, whether it needed it or not. This resulted in the need for a new vacuum cleaner almost every year. Her husband thought this odd but concluded that she simply had a low threshold for what counted as dirty. She was constantly nagging him or angry at him because he did not seem to care as much as her that things be so neat, clean, and orderly. They did not have children because, according to Rita, children would be too much additional work for her, and she certainly could not count on her husband to do anything right in terms of taking care of children or the house. Besides, children would disrupt the order and neatness of her life.**

Over the years, Rita added to her list of things she needed to do each day but never took anything off the list. In addition to vacuuming, she added dusting each day. Then she added cleaning the sinks with strong cleaners each day. She had to get up earlier in the mornings to get all of this cleaning done before work.

Her boss often complained that she was slow. The boss did not appreciate the fact that Rita checked her work over and over again before turning it in. Rita also had difficulties working as part of a team because none of the other workers met her standards. They did not check their work often enough, she thought, and were sloppy and imprecise. Her boss eventually had to isolate her and give her independent work because she could not get along with her co-workers.

Before leaving the house each morning, Rita checked the windows and doors, the gas, the water faucets, and all the light fixtures. After a few months of this, one check was not sufficient, and she began to check everything twice. Her husband complained about this, so she started making him wait in the car while she checked each sink, light, door, window, and so on. Her husband dutifully waited each day, but, as the months went on, the wait grew longer and longer. He was now sitting in the car for an hour each morning, waiting for Rita to finish checking everything in the house. One morning, after checking the house thoroughly, she went outside to find that her husband had left without her. That afternoon, she received an e-mail from him, saying that he could not take it any longer and had decided to divorce her.

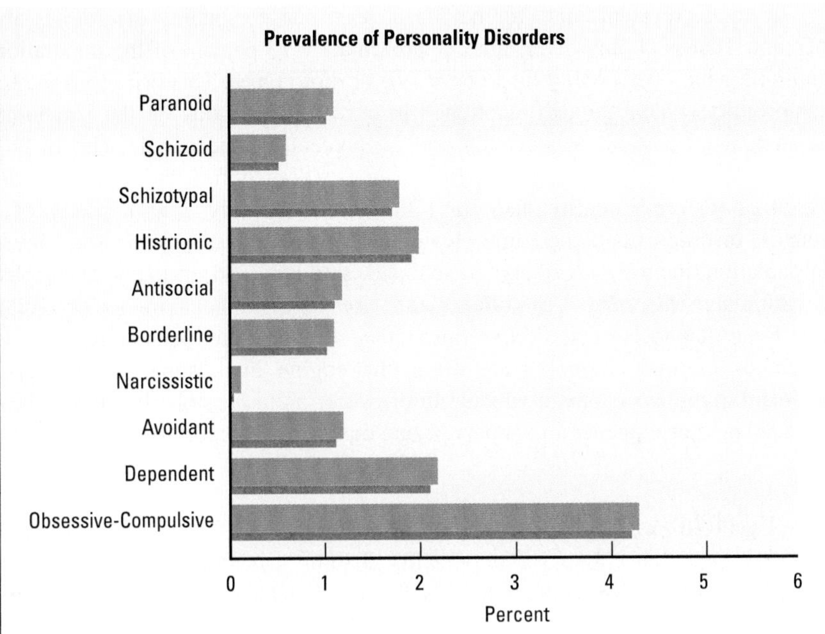

Figure 19.1

Estimates of the prevalence of personality disorders.

Source: Adapted from J. I. Mattia and M. Zimmerman, "Epidemiology." In W. J. Livesley (ed.), Handbook of Personality Disorders: Theory, Research, and Treatment. *New York: Guilford, 2001. Reprinted with permission.*

Prevalence of Personality Disorders

Figure 19.1 indicates the prevalence rates of the 10 personality disorders. **Prevalence** is a term that refers to the total number of cases that are present within a given population during a particular period of time. The data in Figure 19.1 are based on summaries of several community samples (Mattia & Zimmerman, 2001) and refer to prevalence rates at the time of sampling, e.g., at any given time, how many people are diagnosable with paranoid personality disorder? These results show that obsessive-compulsive personality disorder is the most common, at just over 4 percent prevalence rate. Next most common are the schizotypal, histrionic, and dependent personality disorders, approximately 2 percent prevalence each. The least common is narcissistic personality disorder, affecting only 0.2 percent of the population. However, these diagnoses were all based on interviews, and it may be that narcissists are least likely to admit to the more disordered features of their condition. In fact, Oltmanns and colleagues have shown that self-reports of narcissism correlate weakly with peer reports of narcissism, even though with most other personality traits there are modest to substantial correlations between self-report and peer report (Clifton, Turkheimer, & Oltmanns, in press; Klonsky, Oltmanns, & Turkheimer, 2002; Oltmanns, Friedman, Fiedler, & Turkheimer, in press). These findings suggest that, because the data in Figure 19.1 are based on self-report through structured interviews, they may actually underestimate the prevalence of some of the disorders, especially narcissism.

The total prevalence rate for having at least one personality disorder is about 13 percent. That is, at any given time, approximately 13 percent of the population is diagnosable with a personality disorder of one or more types. This brings up the issue of comorbidity, which we also mentioned in our A Closer Look on the Unabomber. A substantial proportion, between 25 and 50 percent, of the people who meet the criteria for a diagnosis on one personality disorder will also meet the criteria for diagnosis on another personality disorder (Oltmanns & Emery, 2004). Many of the personality disorders contain common features. For example, several disorders involve social isolation, including schizotypal, schizoid, avoidant, and, in many cases, obsessive-compulsive disorder. Uninhibited and irresponsible behavior is one of the criteria for a diagnosis of borderline, histrionic, and antisocial personality disorders. As such, differential diagnoses are often challenging in personality disorders. A **differential diagnosis** is one in which, out of two or more possible diagnoses, the clinician searches for evidence in support of one diagnostic category over all the others.

Gender Differences in Personality Disorders

The overall prevalence rate for personality disorders is fairly equal in men and women. There are a few specific disorders, however, that show a tendency to be more prevalent in men or in women. The one disorder with the most disparate gender distribution is antisocial personality disorder, which occurs in men with a prevalence rate of about 4.5 percent and in women at only about a 0.8 prevalence rate. As such, about one out of every 20 adult men have antisocial personality disorder, whereas it is less than one in a hundred for women (Oltmanns & Emery, 2004).

A few other personality disorders show tendencies to be more common among men or among women. Borderline and dependent personality disorders may be somewhat more prevalent in women than men, though the evidence is not strong. Paranoid and obsessive-compulsive personality disorder may be more common in men than women, but the difference is not large. One important issue concerns gender biases in diagnoses. For example, in dependent personality disorder, a few of the distinguishing traits might be viewed as traditionally feminine characteristics, such as putting others' needs ahead of one's own or being unassertive. Consequently, if the criteria for this disorder are based on feminine stereotypes, then it might be relatively easier for women than men to meet the criteria for this diagnosis, even if a particular woman is not suffering significant impairment from those particular traits. Clinicians need to be aware of how stereotypes affect the ways they diagnose their clients.

A related issue is gender differences in the manifestation of the different disorders. For example, in histrionic personality disorder a main issue concerns excessive attention seeking. A woman might pursue this through hyperfemininity, perhaps even being sexually seductive. A male might pursue this through hypermasculinity, perhaps through shows of strength and bragging about accomplishments. Each is engaging in excessive attention seeking but doing it in ways that are gender stereotyped.

Dimensional Model of Personality Disorders

As hinted at the beginning of this chapter, modern theorists are arguing for a dimensional, as opposed to a categorical, view of personality disorders. In the dimensional model of personality, the only distinctions made between normal personality traits and disorders are in terms of extremity, rigidity, and maladaptiveness. For example,

Widiger (1997) argues that disorders simply are maladaptive variants and combinations of normal-range personality traits. The personality traits most studied as sources of disorders are the five traits of the five-factor model, which we reviewed in Chapter 3. Costa and Widiger (1994) edited an influential book supporting the idea that the Big Five traits provide a useful framework for understanding disorders. Widiger (1997) presents data arguing that, for example, borderline personality disorder is extreme narcissism, and schizoid disorder is extreme introversion accompanied by low neuroticism (emotional stability). Extreme introversion accompanied by extremely high neuroticism, on the other hand, results in avoidant personality disorder. Histrionic disorder is characterized as extreme extraversion. Obsessive-compulsive disorder is a maladaptive form of extreme conscientiousness. Schizotypal personality disorder is a complex combination of introversion, high neuroticism, low agreeableness, and extreme openness.

The dimensional view is somewhat like chemistry: Add a little of this trait and some of that trait, amplify to extremely high (or low) levels, and the result is a specific disorder. Dimensional models may have certain advantages, such as accounting for why people in the same diagnostic category can be so different from each other in how they express the disorder. In addition, the dimensional model allows for a person to have multiple disorders of personality. And, finally, the dimensional model explicitly acknowledges that the distinction between what is normal and what is abnormal is more a matter of degree than a clear and qualitative break.

For now, however, the dominant model of personality disorders, as represented in the *DSM-IV,* is the categorical model. When the *DSM-IV* undergoes revision, and becomes *DSM-V,* it will be interesting to see if the dimensional model is given more recognition. At present, the *DSM-IV* only hints at the possibility of a dimensional view: "Only when personality traits are inflexible and maladaptive and cause significant functional impairment or subjective distress do they constitute Personality Disorders" (American Psychiatric Association, 1994, p. 630).

Causes of Personality Disorders

The material covered in this chapter so far has been mainly descriptive, drawing from and expanding on the diagnostic criteria in the *DSM-IV.* Abnormal psychology is a strongly descriptive science, and efforts are mainly to develop classification systems and taxonomies of disorders. This does not mean, however, that there are no attempts to understand how personality disorders develop or what causes one person to have a particular disorder. Researchers generally examine both biological and environmental factors that contribute to the development of personality disorders (Nigg & Goldsmith, 1994). For example, it is clear that persons who suffer with borderline personality disorder experienced poor attachment relationships in childhood (Kernberg, 1975, 1984; Nigg et al., 1994), and that many borderline persons were the target of sexual abuse in childhood (Westen et al., 1990). There is abundant evidence that most people with borderline personality disorder grew up in chaotic homes, with a lot of exposure to the impulsive behavior of adults (Millon, 2000b).

It appears that genetic factors play little role in borderline personality disorder. Instead most of the evidence implicates loss of, or neglect by, the parents in early childhood (Guzder et al., 1996).

Table 19.11 The Personality Disorders Described According to Unique Characteristics Associated with Self-Concept, Emotional Life, Behavior, and Social Relations

Specific Disorders	Self-Concept	Emotion
Antisocial Personality	Self as unfettered by rules	Lack of remorse, quick-tempered, easily irritated, aggressive
Borderline Personality	Self as vague, diffuse, changing, unstable, with no strong feeling of identity	Unstable, intense, with anger, shame, and guilt
Histrionic Personality	Self as desirable and charming	Flamboyant in public displays
Narcissistic Personality	Self as unique, admirable, special	Feelings of entitlement, vengeful when not recognized
Schizoid Personality	Self as loner, without ambition	Bland, taking little pleasure in life
Schizotypal Personality	Self as different from others, special	Uncomfortable, suspicious
Paranoid Personality	Self as victim	Feels threatened, argumentative, jealous
Avoidant Personality	Self as inadequate	Frequently embarrassed, fearing criticism and rejection
Dependent Personality	Self as needy, lacking self-direction	Meek, indecisive
Obsessive-Compulsive Personality	Self as rigid, with high standards and expectations	Easily irritated, stubborn, without much pleasure

When it comes to schizotypal personality disorder, the evidence is more in line with genetic causes. A variety of family, twin, and adoption studies suggest that schizotypal disorder is genetically similar to schizophrenia (Nigg & Goldsmith, 1994). Moreover, the first-degree relatives of persons with schizophrenia are much more likely to exhibit features of schizotypal personality disorder than persons in the general population. However, prevalence rates for paranoid and avoidant personality disorders were also elevated among the relatives of the schizophrenia patients, suggesting that these disorders may be genetically related to schizophrenia (Kendler et al., 1993).

Antisocial personality disorder also has several explanatory theories. For example, many antisocial persons were themselves abused and victimized as children (Pollock et al., 1990), leading to social learning and psychoanalytic theories of the cause of this disorder. A high proportion of antisocial persons also abuse multiple illegal drugs or alcohol, leading some researchers to propose that biological changes associated with drug abuse are responsible for antisocial behavior. There are also clear familial trends suggesting that antisocial personality disorder is due, in part, to genetic causes (Lykken, 1995). Others have proposed learning theories of antisocial personality disorder, due mainly to research showing that such persons are deficient in learning through punishment (e.g., Newman, 1987).

Behavior	Social Relations
Reckless, impulsive, irresponsible	Callous and indifferent to rights of others
Unpredictable, perhaps harmful to self or others	Intense, volatile, unstable, fearing abandonment
Attention-seeking, extravagant	Attention-seeking
Self-displaying, admiration-seeking	Envious, lacking in empathy
Passive	Detached, socially inept, having no or few friends
Odd, eccentric with unusual beliefs	Socially anxious, avoiding others
Distrustful, self-protective, resentful	Sensitive, prone to misinterpretations, with many enemies
Quiet, shy, solitary	Withdrawing, sensitive to criticism
Reassurance-seeking, rarely taking initiative	Submissive, needs nurturance, avoids conflict
Workaholic, likes repetition, details	No time for friends, others don't meet standards

Explanations of the other personality disorders also follow this pattern. There are biological explanations, learning explanations, psychodynamic explanations, and cultural explanations. There may be some truth to each of these views, that personality disorders, like normal-range personality variables, have multiple causes. Moreover, it is very difficult to separate biology from learning, to separate nature from nurture. For example, an individual's early experiences—such as with an abusive parent—may lead to neurological changes in certain brain centers, such as the abnormalities in the hypothalamus and pituitary functioning (e.g., Mason et al., 1994). Consequently, it does not make sense to speak of early childhood abuse as a strictly experiential or learning factor when biological changes can follow from such abusive experiences.

Clearly, biology and experience are tightly intermingled, making it difficult to attribute a disorder to only one kind of cause. Efforts to reduce the cause of personality disorders to one factor—say, genetics—is likely to be an oversimplification. Thus, we have to be comfortable with the notion that something as complicated as the human personality—and its disorders—has multiple causes. Table 19.11 (pages 656–657) presents all of the personality disorders along with descriptions of the self-concept, emotional life, behavior, and social relations of persons who have the disorder.

SUMMARY AND EVALUATION

We began this chapter with a discussion of how disorders of personality draw on almost all the other topics studied so far. The concept of disorder relies on making a distinction between what is normal and what is abnormal. There are several definitions of abnormality. One is statistical and relies on how frequently a condition appears among a population of people. Another definition is sociological and has to do with how much a society tolerates particular forms of behavior. A psychological definition emphasizes to what extent a behavior pattern causes distress for the person or for others. For example, is the behavior associated with disorganization in the person's own thoughts, emotions, or social relations? The hallmark of the psychological definition of abnormal is anything that prevents a person from having satisfying relationships or from carrying on productive work. Most of the personality disorders result in problems with relationships because they impair the person's ability to get along with others. Many of the disorders also impair the person's ability to engage in productive work. We saw that all of the personality disorders refer to symptoms that cause problems with relationships or with work, or both.

The study of abnormal psychology, also called psychopathology, has evolved into a distinct discipline within psychology and psychiatry. A major goal of this discipline is to develop reliable taxonomies for mental disorders. The most widely used system for classifying abnormal psychological conditions, at least in the United States, is the *Diagnostic and Statistical Manual of Mental Disorders*, fourth edition *(DSM-IV)*. This sourcebook is the major reference for diagnosing and describing all mental disorders, but in this chapter we focused only on the personality disorders.

Personality disorders are enduring patterns of experience and behavior that differ greatly from the norm and the expectations of the individual's social group. Disorders typically show up in abnormalities in how people think, in how they feel, in how they get along with others, or in their ability to control their own actions. The patterns are typically displayed across a variety of situations, leading to distress, either for themselves or others, in important areas in life, such as at work or in relations with others. Personality disorders typically have a long history in a person's life and can often be traced back to adolescence or childhood.

In this chapter, we covered the 10 personality disorders contained in the *DSM-IV*. We organized these 10 disorders into three clusters: the erratic cluster (disorders pertaining to ways of being unpredictable or violent), the eccentric cluster (disorders pertaining to ways of being odd), and the anxious cluster (disorders pertaining to ways of being nervous or distressed). Each disorder consists of a syndrome of behaviors and traits. Disorders are actually dimensions, and people range in the severity of the disorder from mild to severe, depending on the number and intensity of symptoms that they exhibit.

KEY TERMS

Disorder 624
Abnormal Psychology 624
Abnormal 624
Psychopathology 625
Personality Disorder 625
Categorical View 626
Dimensional View 627
Antisocial Personality Disorder 629
Borderline Personality Disorder 633
Eye-blink Startle Method 634
Histrionic Personality Disorder 636
Narcissistic Personality Disorder 639
Narcissistic Paradox 639
Schizoid Personality Disorder 641
Schizotypal Personality Disorder 641
Comorbidity 645
Paranoid Personality Disorder 646
Neurotic Paradox 646
Avoidant Personality Disorder 647
Dependent Personality Disorder 648
Obsessive-Compulsive Personality Disorder 650
Prevalence 653
Differential Diagnosis 654

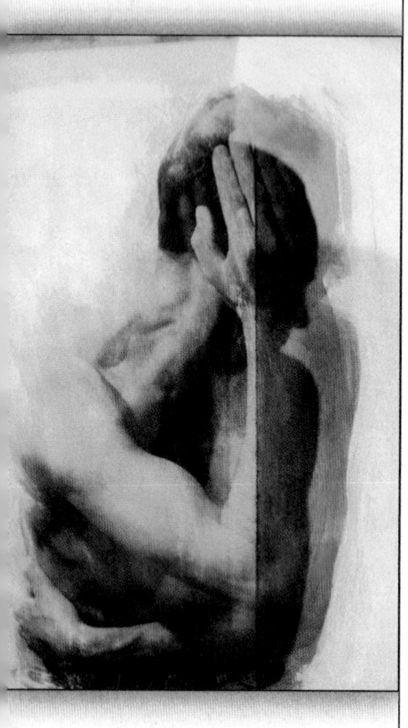

Summary and Future Directions

Current Status of the Field

Domains of Knowledge: Where We've Been, Where We're Going

- Dispositional Domain
- Biological Domain
- Intrapsychic Domain
- Cognitive/Experiential Domain
- Social and Cultural Domain
- Adjustment Domain

Integration: Personality in the New Millennium

20

20 CONCLUSION

After having read the first 19 chapters of this book, you should be able to provide answers the next time someone asks, "Why does that person behave in such a way?" Why do the things people do sometimes seem like a mystery. Personality psychology seeks to open this mystery to scientific investigation. If you are fascinated by the variety of human behavior, by the clever or silly things that people do, by the ways people solve or create problems for themselves, or by the variety of potential explanations for people's behavior, then you have something in common with personality psychologists—a deep curiosity about human nature.

Understanding the whole behind all the parts is the ultimate goal of personality psychology.

Although understanding the whole of human nature may seem like an impossible mission, this is the ultimate goal of personality psychology. Personality psychologists are motivated to understand the whole of personality. However, understanding the whole may be nearly impossible. Psychologist Charles Carver (1996) said that "personality is a topic that's just too large to hold in the mind at once" (p. 330). When confronted with a large and difficult task, it is sometimes useful to partition the task into smaller, more manageable domains. This is the approach taken by modern medical science. Medical researchers specialize—there are dermatologists who focus on the skin, heart specialists, lung specialists, and so on. This is the approach we have taken in this book, based on the assumption that progress can be made in understanding human personality by focusing on each of the major domains of functioning. Clearly, these domains of functioning are linked with one another, just as there are important connections between the heart and the skin (e.g., the heart pumps blood that nourishes skin cells). A full understanding of human personality will eventually require not merely understanding each domain of functioning, but also the ways in which the domains are connected and integrated with each other to form the whole functioning person.

Current Status of the Field

This is an exciting time for the field of personality psychology. Recent advances have led to a certain degree of consensus regarding the nature, structure, and development of personality, resulting in several decades of sustained growth (Robins, 2002). Recent evaluators have concluded that the field is thriving (Diener & Scollon, 2002; Funder, 2002). One hallmark that a field is hitting its stride is the existence of a handbook. Personality psychology has several handbooks (e.g., Hogan, Johnson, & Briggs, 1997; Pervin & John, 1999; Saklofske, 1995), as well as handbooks in personality disorders (e.g., Magnavita, 2003). Another indicator that a field is thriving is the existence of professional societies dedicated to its improvement. In personality psychology there are several societies, including the Society for Personality and Social Psychology and the recently formed Association for Research in Personality. This latter society, founded in 2001, is devoted especially to the interdisciplinary study of personality. It promotes scientific research on personality through an annual conference and through the official scientific journal of the association, the *Journal of Research in Personality.*

Personality psychologists doing research today typically focus on specific components of personality, such as self-esteem; specific traits, such as extraversion or agreeableness; or specific processes, such as the unconscious processing of information. This is the direction toward which the field of personality psychology has shifted over the past 100 years. The early personality theorists, such as Sigmund Freud, constructed theories about the whole person. These grand theories focused on universal properties of human nature, such as Freud's theory that all behavior is motivated by sexual or aggressive impulses or the theory that all persons go through specific stages of psychosexual development.

Starting about 50 years ago, personality psychologists began turning away from grand theories of personality. In their place, personality psychologists began constructing mini-theories of specific parts of personality. That is, they began to focus on distinct components of the whole person. This allowed psychologists to focus their research on very specific questions. For example, how do people develop and maintain self-esteem? In what ways do high and low self-esteem persons differ from each other? How might a person with low self-esteem increase self-esteem? Certainly, self-esteem is only part of personality, one little corner of the whole picture. Nevertheless, understanding self-esteem contributes to knowledge about the whole person.

The whole of personality is the sum of its parts and the connections among those parts. An understanding of the parts is required for an understanding of the whole. Most of the research in personality today is on specific parts of the proverbial elephant. When these parts are all put together—from the dispositional to the biological, to the intrapsychic, to the cognitive/experiential, to the social and cultural, to the adjustment domains—then we have the foundation for understanding the whole of personality.

To the extent that understanding the whole elephant requires understanding all of its parts, then the blind men, working together, could begin to assemble a reasonable understanding of the whole elephant. They could communicate to each other and work together to build a reasonable understanding of what a whole elephant is like. They could be systematic in their approach to the elephant, using diverse methods and approaches and communicating clearly with each other about how they see the elephant. Personality psychologists are like these blind men, in that they typically focus only on one domain of personality at a time. However, personality psychologists do an excellent job of working together and communicating with each other, and they have a wide variety of methods and approaches for observing and assessing personality. Many psychologists working in one domain are aware of what is going on in other domains. We can get an idea of the whole by knowing the diverse domains of knowledge about human nature.

All of the contemporary research and theorizing appears to fit into the six major domains of knowledge. Because they formed the basic structure of this book, let's briefly review each domain you have read about.

Domains of Knowledge: Where We've Been, Where We're Going

Each of the six domains of knowledge represents a specialty within the field of personality psychology. When any field of knowledge grows large and complex, workers in that field are forced to specialize. For example, there once was a time when the field of medicine was more simple and limited than it is now, and all doctors were general practitioners. The knowledge base of medicine was small enough so that each practitioner could generally master all of it. Today the field of medicine is so large and complicated that no one person can know it all, so doctors today are specialists. Personality psychology is much the same—a field in which people tend to specialize into the six domains of knowledge outlined in this book. In the remainder of this chapter, we will review the main features of each of these domains of knowledge, ending with some predictions about likely developments in each domain.

Dispositional Domain

The dispositional domain concerns the aspects of personality that are stable and that make people different from each other. For example, some people are outgoing and talkative; others are introverted and shy. Some are emotionally reactive and moody; others are calm and cool. Some people are conscientious and reliable; others are undependable. There are many ways in which people differ from one another, and many of these differences can be described as personality traits.

Major questions for psychologists working in this domain include the following: How many personality traits exist? How can we best discover and measure them? How do personality traits develop? How do traits interact with situations to produce behaviors?

It is likely that personality trait psychologists will continue to focus on the interaction of persons and situations. Psychologists have realized that behaviors always occur within a context. A formulation offered by psychologists Shoda and Mischel (1996) is the idea of if–then relations. Shoda and Mischel argue that personality is a specific pattern of if–then relationships. For example, if an adolescent is aggressive, it means that certain behaviors (e.g., verbal insults) are likely to occur if certain

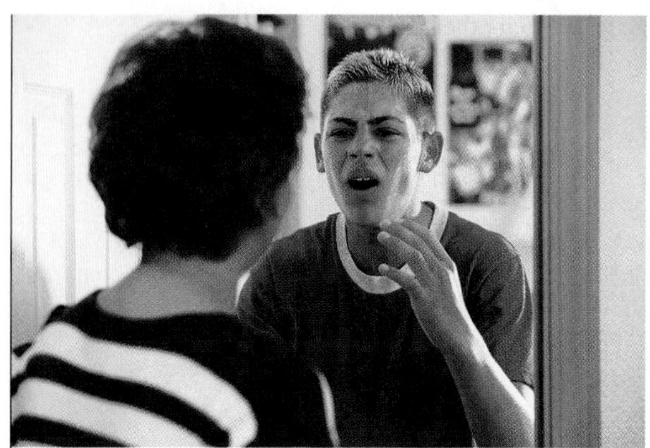

Personality psychologists will likely refine their understanding of the conditions or situations under which certain behaviors, such as arguing, will be evoked in people with certain traits, such as hostility.

situations are created (e.g., teased by a peer). Individual persons may be characterized by distinct profiles of if–then relationships. What are the conditions under which a particular person will become depressed, angry, or frustrated? Each person has a distinct psychological signature in terms of specific if–then relationships: The person will do behavior *A* when situation *Z* occurs, but behavior *B* when situation *Z* does not occur. Two people may be equally high on aggressiveness, but the situations that trigger their aggression may be different. This is the essence of person-by-situation interaction.

A major emphasis of the dispositional domain concerns the accurate measurement of traits and abilities. More than any other domain of knowledge about personality, the dispositional domain emphasizes quantitative techniques for measuring and studying personality. This trend will probably continue, with trait psychologists leading the way in developing new methods for measuring personality characteristics, as well as new statistics for evaluating personality research. Future developments in measurement theory are likely to have an impact on how measures of personality traits are developed and evaluated (West, 2002). For example, efforts are under way that will allow test makers to assess the accuracy and validity of individual items on a personality test. Other statistical developments are enabling personality researchers to examine causal connections between variables, even in the absence of experimental procedures. Continued progress in statistics, measurement, and testing will be a part of the dispositional domain of the future.

Different trait theories are associated with different procedures for identifying the most important individual differences. Some use the lexical strategy—starting with the thousands of trait terms embedded within language. Others use statistical techniques to identify important individual differences. The future will see cooperation among these researchers to test whether specific trait structures are found using different procedures. Indeed, the search will continue for other traits not yet identified by these strategies. For example, in the lexical approach, early researchers deleted adjectives related to sex or that were sex-linked (applied to one sex more than to the other). As a consequence of deleting these adjectives, researchers may have missed one or more traits related to sexuality or sex differences. The recent discovery of a possible sixth factor, *Honesty–Humility,* obtained from extensive cross-cultural research, represents an exciting new discovery in the dispositional domain.

Biological Domain

The core assumption of biological approaches to personality is that humans are biological systems. This domain concerns the factors within the body that influence or are related to personality as well as the evolutionary causal processes responsible for creating those bodily mechanisms. This domain is not any more fundamental than the other domains, nor is knowledge about this domain any closer to the truth about personality than is the knowledge in other domains. The biological domain simply contains the physical elements and biological systems that influence or are influenced by behaviors, thoughts, feelings, and desires. Biological processes may give rise to observable individual differences, or they may simply correlate with observable individual differences. In addition, biological differences between people may be the cause of personality differences (as in the biological theory of extraversion) or may be the result of personality differences (as in heart disease being the long-term consequence of the hostile Type A personality style).

One area of research that is likely to be active in the future concerns the psychology of approach and avoidance (Carver, Sutton, & Scheier, 1999). Many current researchers on biological bases of behavior recognize two tendencies that underlie human behavior and emotion: (1) the tendency to feel positive emotions and to approach and (2) the tendency to feel negative emotions and to avoid or withdraw (Davidson, 2000). Much of the research reviewed in Chapter 7 concerns examples of this theme. Some examples include the work on separate brain areas associated with positive and negative emotions, Gray's theory about behavioral approach and behavioral inhibition, and the work on sensitivity to reward and punishment. These areas of research will most likely further converge and the motives to approach and to avoid will become prominent themes in personality psychology.

Another major physical element within the body that influences personality is genes. Our genetic makeup contributes to whether we are tall or short, have blue eyes or brown eyes, or tend toward being skinny or overweight. It also appears that our genetic makeup influences behavior patterns associated with personality, such as how active we are, whether or not we are aggressive, and whether we like to be with others or prefer to spend time by ourselves. Understanding how genetics contributes to personality falls squarely within the biological domain.

Behavioral genetics research has come a long way from the simple nature versus nurture question. Most of the major personality traits are now known to show some moderate amount of heritability (in the range of .20 to .50). With 20 to 50 percent of the variance in these traits due to genetic differences, that leaves 50 to 80 percent due to either measurement error or the environment. The environment can be broken down into the shared and nonshared components. The shared environment is what siblings have in common, such as the same parents, the (presumably) same parental rearing style, the same schools and religious institutions, and so on. The nonshared environment consists of such chance factors as different friends or peers outside the family, different teachers, potentially different parental treatment, and random factors, such as accidents and illnesses. Researchers are pinpointing shared and nonshared environmental factors that appear important to personality. Thus, we will see the counterintuitive scenario in which genetics researchers will focus on a careful assessment of environmental characteristics.

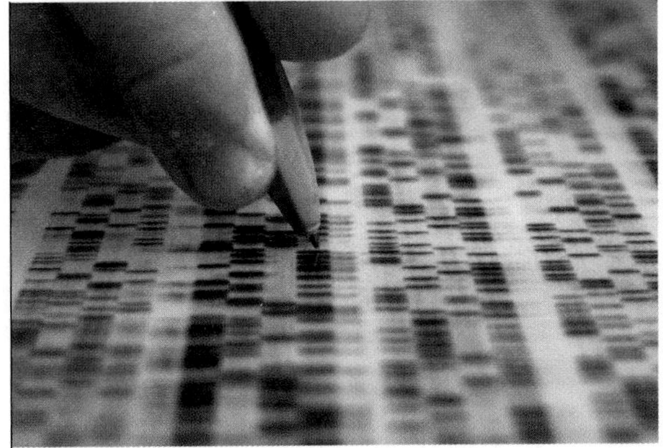

A technician works with DNA sequence information.

Other researchers will concentrate on genetics at the molecular level. The Human Genome Project, which began in the 1990s, is the largest and most expensive scientific project ever undertaken in the course of human history. The goal of this project is no less than to map the entire human genome, to use molecular techniques to learn what every strand of

DNA is responsible for. Twin and adoption studies, the primary methods of behavioral genetics, use indirect methods that only estimate the genetic component of traits by assessing the resemblance of relatives. Molecular genetic studies, on the other hand, are able to directly identify the DNA markers of genetic differences between individuals. As a consequence of these new techniques, "researchers are at the dawn of a new era which . . . will revolutionize genetic research on personality by identifying specific genes that contribute to genetic variation in behavioral dimensions and disorders" (Saudino & Plomin, 1996, p. 344). Already, researchers have begun to focus these molecular techniques on the search for genes related to alcoholism, certain cognitive abilities, criminality, and impulse control. It is likely that researchers will find that genes are responsible for synthesizing specific neurotransmitters, and those neurotransmitters are in turn related to specific traits. Personality psychologists may soon team with molecular geneticists to locate specific genes that will relate to personality dimensions (Plomin & Crabbe, 2000).

The biological domain also includes evolutionary thinking about personality. From the perspective of evolutionary psychology, personality can be analyzed at three levels—human nature, sex differences, and individual differences. At each of these levels, an evolutionary perspective poses two related questions: What adaptive problems have humans confronted over the long expanse of human evolutionary history? What psychological solutions have evolved in response to these adaptive problems?

Since adaptive problems tend to be specific—for example, the problem of food selection differs from the problem of mate selection—the psychological solutions also tend to be specific. Thus, an evolutionary perspective leads us to expect that personality will be quite complex, consisting of a large collection of evolved psychological mechanisms, each corresponding to a specific adaptive problem. Specific mate preferences, jealousy, fears and phobias, altruistic feelings toward kin, and dozens more all may be parts of evolved psychological mechanisms, according to the evolutionary perspective.

This perspective, however, does not claim that humans are optimally adapted, or even well adapted, to the conditions of modern living. Given the slow pace of evolution, we possess Stone-Age brains inhabiting a New-Age world of the Internet, global travel, and modern medical miracles. Thus, problems can arise when large discrepancies exist between the ancient world, in which our adaptations evolved, and the modern world, which we have created.

The evolutionary perspective will continue to gain in importance, although it probably will not supplant other perspectives. Instead, evolutionary psychology will add a new layer of questions and, hence, a necessary layer of insight when these questions are answered empirically. Perhaps most critically, an evolutionary perspective asks, "What is the adaptive function of each psychological mechanism?" Posing questions about adaptive function will likely result in the discovery that human personality is even more complex and contains even more psychological mechanisms than we are now aware of. Rather than being motivated merely by sex and aggression, as Freud envisioned, humans will be found to be motivated by a dozen or more drives. But it should not surprise us that human personality will turn out to be so complex. After all, if personality were really simple, consisting of a small number of easily understood psychological mechanisms, then this book would be a lot shorter than it is.

It is important to keep in mind that biology is not destiny. Rather, the biological domain, like all the other domains, includes one set of factors that influence or are related to personality. Personality is best thought of as multiply determined, as the collection of influences from all six of the broad domains considered in this book.

Intrapsychic Domain

The intrapsychic domain concerns the factors within the mind that influence behavior, thoughts, and emotions. The pioneer of this domain was Sigmund Freud, though new perspectives have advanced beyond his original ideas. This domain deals with the basic psychological mechanisms of personality, many of which operate outside the realm of conscious awareness. Theories within this domain often start with fundamental assumptions about the motivational system—for example, the sexual and aggressive forces that Freud presumed energized much of human activity. Although these fundamental assumptions often lie outside the realm of direct empirical testing, research has shown that motives, even those outside of awareness, can be powerful and that their manifestations in actual behavior can be studied empirically. The intrapsychic domain also includes defense mechanisms, such as repression, denial, and projection, some of which have been examined in laboratory studies.

In this book, the ideas and contributions of psychoanalysis were divided into two areas: classical psychoanalytic theory as put forward by Freud and his disciples and contemporary psychoanalytic theory consisting of extensions of and changes to these basic ideas. For example, newer views emphasize social crises rather than sexual conflict as the tasks of personality development. In addition, modern views in psychoanalysis emphasize the importance of internalized representations of important relationships. These views still retain the notion that childhood is crucial to understanding the adult personality, but the emphasis is now on relationships, such as the attachment between an infant and the primary caregiver.

A fundamental assumption of psychologists working in the intrapsychic domain is that there are areas of the mind that are outside of awareness. Within each person, there is a part of the mind that even the individual does not know about, called the unconscious. In classical psychoanalysis, the unconscious mind is thought to have a life of its own. It has its own motivation, its own will, and its own energy. It can interfere with the functions of the rest of the mind. In fact, it is thought to be the source of all psychological problems. Modern research on motives (e.g., the power motive, achievement motive, and intimacy motive) also draws on the notion that motive forces can operate outside of conscious awareness.

Psychologists will continue to be interested in the idea that people can have thoughts outside of awareness. Psychologists disagree about whether such thoughts are the result of a motivated unconscious, as Freud thought, or whether they are simply thoughts that are not accessible to immediate awareness. Many psychologists view the unconscious as an automatic information-processing mechanism, which can influence conscious awareness (e.g., Bargh & Chartrand, 1999). And they have developed impressive methods for studying the unconscious, such as priming and subliminal exposure. It seems likely that we are on the verge of learning a great deal about just how much cognitive activity occurs outside of awareness and the extent to which these unconscious thoughts influence behavior.

Another area likely to receive continued attention from both researchers and clinicians is the topic of repressed memories. Researchers can demonstrate false memories in the lab, such as by showing that subjects who learn a list of words sometimes falsely recall that a related word was on that list, when, in fact, it was not (Roediger

American actor Richard Gere, who often plays violent characters on film, leads a very different private life. As a practicing Buddhist, Gere believes in the principle of nonviolence. He is shown here speaking at an event for the National Day of Action for Tibet, 1998, in Washington, D.C. The development of the self and social identity, especially in complex and contradictory lives, will continue to fascinate personality psychologists.

& McDermott, 1995); many people in such false memory experiments are certain that the target word was on their list. Certainly, such experimental demonstrations of false memory are a long way from the issue of repressed or false childhood memories of traumatic events; however, traditional cognitive scientists are beginning to look seriously at how memory works, as well as at the processes that make it possible for people to recollect events that did not occur (Roediger, McDermott, & Robinson, 1998).

Cognitive/Experiential Domain

The cognitive/experiential domain concerns subjective experience and other mental processes, such as thoughts, feelings, beliefs, and desires about oneself and others. One of the central concepts in this domain is the self. Some aspects of the self describe how we view ourselves: our knowledge of ourselves, our images of past selves, and our images of possible future selves. Do we see ourselves as good or as evil? Are our past successes or past failures prominent in our self-views? Do we envision ourselves in a positive future? It is likely that psychologists will continue to focus their attention on self-concept and identity. Moreover, it is likely that psychologists will incorporate the idea that identity is like a story and that a narrative or case history approach to understanding will continue to be a part of personality psychology.

A modern metaphor that is informing personality psychology is the information-processing, or computer, metaphor. Humans take in sensory information; process it through an elaborate cognitive system, which selects and modifies from the vast array of information available; then store it in memories, which do not bear a one-to-one relationship with the original events. At every step along the way—from attention and perception to memory and recall—there are opportunities for personality to influence the process. Psychologists will continue to take seriously the notion that people construct their experiences. Understanding how this works, and what it says about personality, will be one objective in this domain (Pervin, 1999).

A somewhat different aspect of the cognitive/experiential domain pertains to the goals people strive for. Research within this tradition approaches personality through the personal projects that individuals are trying to accomplish (e.g., Little, 1999). Goal concepts will continue to be important within personality psychology. Goals have cognitive, emotional, and behavioral components. Goals are often individual expressions of social or institutional norms or standards, so the goal concept may be one route whereby psychologists can study relationships between individuals and broader social systems.

Yet another aspect of subjective experience entails emotions. Is a person habitually happy or sad? What makes a person angry or fearful? The joy, the sadness, feelings of triumph, and feelings of despair are essential elements in our subjective experience subsumed by the cognitive-experiential domain. If you want to learn what is important to a person, really important, ask about his or her emotions. When was the last time he or she was angry? What makes him or her sad? What does he or she fear? Emotions are likely to continue to be important concepts in personality.

Social and Cultural Domain

One of the novel features of this book is an emphasis on the social and cultural aspects of personality. Personality is not something that merely resides within the heads, nervous systems, and genes of individuals. Rather, personality affects, and is affected by, the significant others in our lives.

Humans are not passive recipients of their environments, and personality plays a key role in social interaction. We selectively enter some interpersonal environments and selectively avoid others. We actively choose our mates and friends. We evoke reactions from others, sometimes quite unintentionally. And we actively influence or manipulate those occupying our social worlds. Personality influences these processes of selection, evocation, and manipulation. Emotionally unstable individuals, for example, tend to choose similarly unstable persons as romantic partners; they evoke predictable forms of anger in those partners through their moodiness; and they more often use the "silent treatment" as a tactic for influencing those partners. Personality, in short, expresses itself through our social selections, evocations, and manipulations.

One important social sphere concerns relations between men and women. Personality may operate differently for men than for women in some domains. An essential part of our identity is gender. Much of what we call gender may have its origins in culture, in how society makes up different rules, roles, and expectations for men and women. Other aspects of gender may lie in evolved behavior patterns that represent adaptations to different pressures that faced men and women in the past. Whatever their origins, gender differences will continue to be a compelling interest of personality psychologists. In an effort to understand gender differences, it is likely that personality psychologists will enlist the help of specialists from other disciplines, such as anthropologists, animal behaviorists, sociologists, and biopsychologists.

Interacting with people from different cultures is a fact of daily life in many parts of the world. Understanding how people from different cultures are different from, or similar to, each other will continue to be an important part of personality psychology.

At the cultural level, it is clear that groups differ from one another. Some cultures are individualistic: People prefer to make their own decisions and to be responsible primarily for themselves. Other cultures are more collectivistic: People prefer to see themselves as part of a social group and do not think of their individual needs as more important than their group's needs. Personality differences among these groups may be instances of transmitted culture or evoked culture. Some psychologists assume that they are caused by transmitted culture—ideas, values, and representations passed on from parents and others to children within their culture, down the generations. Other psychologists, however, propose that these are instances of evoked culture. According to this view, everyone may have the evolved capacity to be individualistic and preoccupied with the self. And everyone may also have the evolved capacity to be communal and preoccupied with the greater good of the group. Which of these capacities any one individual displays may depend on whether one lives in a culture that is highly mobile, with few genetic kin in close proximity (evoking an individualistic proclivity), or highly stable, with many genetic kin in close proximity (evoking a collectivistic proclivity). This fascinating new direction represents a theoretical fusion of cultural psychology and evolutionary psychology.

The study of culture and cross-cultural differences and similarities will probably continue to grow in personality psychology. Our world is increasingly becoming a global community. Diversity is a fact of daily life in many areas. Many of us encounter persons from different cultures on a regular basis at our schools, jobs, and communities. Indeed, there is a growing interdependence among people from widely different backgrounds. An important goal of personality psychology will be to understand how cultures shape personality and how specific cultures are different from, or similar to, each other. It is of compelling importance that we seek to understand one another and the forces that shape differences between persons from different backgrounds.

Adjustment Domain

Personality plays a key role in how we cope, adapt, and adjust to the ebb and flow of events in our lives. Considerable evidence has accumulated, for example, that personality is linked with important health outcomes, such as heart disease. Personality is linked to a variety of health-related behaviors, such as smoking, drinking, and risk taking. Personality is even linked to how long we live (Peterson, 2000). Modeling how these processes work, and the role of personality in relation to health and well-being, will occupy personality psychologists of the future. There has been a shift toward looking at the role of positive emotions, and this emphasis on the positive in psychology is likely to be a part of personality psychology. In addition, there are several longitudinal studies that were started decades ago in various communities around the United States. Participants in this research are now well into adulthood, and researchers are beginning to learn about the long-term effects of specific lifestyle and personality factors on longevity and health.

Many of the important problems in coping and adjustment can be traced to personality disorders. An understanding of "normal" personality functioning can be deepened by examining disorders of personality, and vice versa. Psychologists have applied the trait approach to understanding personality disorders (Costa & Widiger, 2002; Widiger, 2000). This is likely to continue to sharpen our understanding of the nature of personality disorders.

Integration: Personality in the New Millennium

The domains of knowledge should be viewed as complementary, not as conflicting. People have many facets, and these facets can be observed and studied from many different perspectives. To say that people have evolved psychological mechanisms to solve social problems does not imply that the principles of psychoanalysis are wrong. Similarly, to say that a portion of the variance in personality traits is due to genetics does not in any way imply that people do not develop or change their personalities in adulthood.

The real action in personality research will occur at the boundaries of domains. Examples include collaborations between brain researchers using functional Magnetic Resonance Imaging (fMRI) technology to conduct brain scans and psychologists studying interpersonal dispositions (e.g., Aharon, Etcoff, Ariely, Chabris, O'Connor, & Breiter, 2001); collaborations between cultural and evolutionary psychologists to study the causal origins and nature of cultural differences (e.g., Oyserman et al., 2002a); and collaborations between dispositional researchers and cognitive psychologists to study the information-processing mechanisms underlying stable individual differences (e.g., Brendyl, Markman, & Messner, 2001). The most interesting work will happen as researchers expand the theories surrounding each domain and try to make connections between domains or between personality psychology and other scientific fields.

Progress in the new millennium will depend on researchers' willingness and ability to reach across domains. The most exciting progress will occur when researchers, perhaps working on multidisciplinary teams, combine different levels of analysis and different methods in approaching central questions of importance to the field. Building bridges that link domains of knowledge together in new and interesting ways will have the most impact on how human nature is understood.

If we look around the field of personality psychology today, we can find examples of bridges that are already being built between domains. For example, with regard to the topic of approach and avoidance motivation, psychologists are studying this phenomenon through brain activity, exploring the developmental course of these motives, examining cultural differences, and delving into how these traits contribute to disorders. It is likely that centers of research will be a model for progress, with groups of diverse scientists—such as trait psychologists, biological psychologists, cultural psychologists, and health psychologists—all working together on questions important to the field of personality psychology. It is not hard to imagine interesting possibilities. For example, it probably won't be long before psychologists interested in repressed memories approach the topic with functional MRI brain scans or before psychologists interested in self-esteem begin looking both at neurochemistry and at cultural influences. As we move forward in the new millennium, the possibilities for increasing our knowledge of human nature are especially exciting.

Glossary

a

abnormal Broadly defined, the term abnormal is based on current levels of societal tolerance. In this sense, behaviors that society deems unacceptable would be labeled as abnormal (e.g., incest and child abuse). Yet, because these tolerance levels (e.g., towards homosexuality) can change over time, psychologists have started directing their attention towards people's subjective views and experiences. Anxiety, depression, and feelings of loneliness may be linked to disorganized thought patterns, disruptive perceptions, or unusual beliefs. These may inhibit a person's ability to work or socialize, and may all be considered abnormal. 624

abnormal psychology Abnormal psychology is the study of the various mental disorders, including thought disorders (such as schizophrenia), emotional disorders (such as depression), and personality disorders (such as the antisocial personality). 624

acculturation Acculturation is the process of, after arriving in a new culture, adapting to the ways of life and beliefs common in that new culture. 565

achievement view of intelligence The achievement view of intelligence is associated with educational attainment—how much knowledge a person has acquired relative to others in their age cohort. 416

acquiescence Acquiescence (also known as yea saying) is a response set that refers to the tendency to agree with questionnaire items, regardless of the content of those items. 111

action tendencies Action tendencies are increases in the probabilities of certain behaviors that accompany emotions. The activity, or action tendency, associated with fear, for example, is to flee or to fight. 424

actometer An actometer is a mechanical motion-recording device, often in the form of a watch attached to the wrist. It has been used, for example, in research on the activity level of children during several play periods. Motoric movement activates the recording device. 145

acute stress Acute stress results from the sudden onset of demands or events that seem to be beyond the control of the individual. This type of stress is often experienced as tension headaches, emotional upsets, gastrointestinal disturbances, and feelings of agitation and pressure. 598

adaptations Adaptations are inherited solutions to the survival and reproductive problems posed by the hostile forces of nature. Adaptations are the primary product of the selective process. An adaptation is a "reliably developing structure in the organism, which, because it meshes with the recurrent structure of the world, causes the solution to an adaptive problem" (Tooby & Cosmides, 1992, p. 104). 10, 245

adaptive problem An adaptive problem is anything that impedes survival or reproduction. All adaptations must contribute to fitness during the period of time in which they evolve by helping an organism survive, reproduce, or facilitate the reproductive success of genetic relatives. Adaptations emerge from and interact with recurrent structures of the world in a manner that solves adaptive problems and hence aids in reproductive success. 248, 548

additive effect Health psychologists describe the effects of different kinds of stress adding up and accumulating in a person over time as being an additive effect. 599

adjacency In Wiggins circumplex model, adjacency indicates how close the traits are to each other on the circumference of the circumplex. Those variables that are adjacent or next to each other within the model are positively correlated. 81

adjustment domain Personality plays a key role in how we cope, adapt, and adjust to the ebb and flow of events in our day-to-day lives. In addition to health consequences of adjusting to stress, there are certain personality features that are related to poor social or emotional adjustment and that have been designated as personality disorders. 19

adoption studies Adoption studies examine the correlations between adopted children and their adoptive parents, with whom they share no genes. These correlations are then compared to the correlations between the adopted children and their genetic parents, who had no influence on the environments of the children. Differences in these correlations can indicate the relative magnitude of genetic and environment contributions to personality traits. 184

affect intensity Larsen and Diener (1987) describe high affect intensity individuals as people who typically experience their emotions strongly and are emotionally reactive and variable. Low affect intensity individuals typically experience their emotions only mildly and with only gradual fluctuations and minor reactions. 454

aggregation Aggregation refers to adding up or averaging several single observations, resulting in a better (i.e., more reliable) measure of a personality trait than a single observation of behavior. This approach implies that personality traits refer to average tendencies in behavior, how people behave on average. 101

Agreeableness Agreeableness is the second of the personality traits in the Five-Factor Model, a model which has proven to be replicable in studies using English language trait words as items. Some of the key adjective markers for Agreeableness are "good-natured," "cooperative," "mild/gentle," "not jealous." 86

alarm stage The alarm stage is the first stage in Seyle's general adaptation syndrome (GAS). The alarm stage consists of the flight or fight response of the sympathetic nervous system and the associated peripheral nervous system reactions. These include the release of hormones, which prepare our bodies for challenge. 594

alpha and beta press Murray introduced the notion that there is a real environment (what he called alpha press or objective reality) and a perceived environment (called beta press or reality-as-it-is-perceived). In any situation, what one person "sees" may be different from what another "sees." If two people walk down a street and a third person smiles at each of them, one person might "see" the smile as a sign of friendliness while the other person might "see" the smile as a smirk. Objectively (alpha press), it is the same smile; subjectively (beta press), it may be a different event for the two people. 356

alpha wave The alpha wave is a particular type of brain wave that oscillates 8 to 12 times a second. The amount of alpha wave present in a given time period is an inverse indicator of brain activity during that time period. The alpha wave is given off when the person is calm and relaxed. In a given time period of brain wave recording, the more alpha wave activity present the more we can assume that part of the brain was less active. 236

ambivalently attached Ambivalently attached infants, as determined by Ainsworth's strange situation paradigm, are very anxious about the mother leaving. They often start crying and protesting vigorously before the mother even gets out of the room. While the mother is gone these infants are difficult to calm. Upon her return, however, these infants behave ambivalently. Their behavior shows both anger and the desire to be close to the mother; they approach her but then resist by squirming and fighting against being held. 343

ambivalent relationship style In Hazan and Shaver's ambivalent relationship style, adults are vulnerable and uncertain about relationships. Ambivalent adults become overly dependant and demanding on their partners and friends. They display high levels of neediness in their relationships. They are high maintenance partners in the sense that they need constant reassurance and attention. 344

Americans with Disability Act (ADA) The ADA states that an employer cannot conduct a medical examination, or even make inquiries as to whether an applicant has a disability, during the selection process. Moreover, even if a disability is obvious, the employer cannot ask about the nature or severity of that disability. 122

amygdala The amygdala is a section of the limbic or emotional system of the brain that is responsible for fear. 475

anal stage The anal stage is the second stage in Freud's psychosexual stages of development. The anal stage typically occurs between the ages of 18 months and three years. At this stage, the anal sphincter is the source of sexual pleasure, and the child obtains pleasure from first expelling feces and then, during toilet training, from retaining feces. Adults who are compulsive, overly neat, rigid, and never messy are, according to psychoanalytic theory, likely to be fixated at the anal stage. 307

analytic To describe something analytically would be to explain the event with the object detached from its context, attributes of objects or people assigned to categories, and a reliance on rules about the categories to explain behavior. 567

androgynous In certain personality instruments, the masculinity dimension contains items reflecting assertiveness, boldness, dominance, self-sufficiency, and instrumentality. The femininity dimension contains items that reflect nurturance, expression of emotions, and empathy. Those persons who scored high on both dimensions are labeled androgynous, to reflect the notion that a single person can possess both masculine and feminine characteristics. 538

anterior cingulate Located deep toward the center of the brain, the anterior cingulate cortex most likely evolved early in the evolution of the nervous system. In experiments utilizing fMRI to trace increased activation of parts of the brain, the anterior cingulate cortex seems to be an area of the brain associated with affect, including social rejection. 443

antisocial personality disorder A person suffering from antisocial personality disorder has a general disregard for others and cares very little about the rights, feelings, or happiness of other people. Also referred to as a sociopath or psychopath, a person suffering from antisocial personality disorder is easily irritated, assaultive, reckless, irresponsible, glib or superficially charming, impulsive, callous, and indifferent to the suffering of others. 629

anxiety Anxiety is an unpleasant, high-arousal emotional state associated with perceived threat. In the psychoanalytic tradition, anxiety is seen as a signal that the control of the ego is being threatened by reality, by impulses from the id, or by harsh controls exerted by the superego. Freud identified three different types of anxiety: neurotic anxiety, moral anxiety, and objective anxiety. According to Rogers, the unpleasant emotional state of anxiety is the result of having an experience that does not fit with one's self-conception. 220, 297, 380

anxiety and impulsivity According to Gray's reinforcement sensitivity theory, people differ from each other in the relative sensitivity of their Behavioral Inhibition System (BIS) and the Behavioral Activation System (BAS). According to Gray, the BIS is responsible for the personality dimension of anxiety and the BAS is responsible for the personality dimension of impulsivity. 220, 297, 380

apperception The notion that a person's needs influenced how he or she perceives the environment, especially when the environment is ambiguous. The act of interpreting the environment and perceiving the meaning of what is going on in a situation is termed apperception. 356

aptitude view of intelligence The aptitude view of intelligence sees intelligence less as the product of education and more as an ability to become educated, as the ability or aptitude to learn. 416

archetypes According to Carl Jung, archetypes are the common symbols of core human feelings and experience that turn up in myths and stories across vastly different cultures. Jung felt that these are expressions of images of basic human needs and instincts with which we are all born. 291

arousal level versus arousability In Eysenck's original theory of extraversion, he held that extraverts had lower levels of cortical or brain arousal than introverts. More recent research on Eysenck's theory suggests that the difference between introverts and extraverts lies more in the arousability of their nervous systems, with extraverts showing less arousability or reactivity than introverts to the same levels of sensory stimulation. 215, 216

arteriosclerosis Arteriosclerosis is hardening or blocking of the arteries. When the arteries that feed the heart muscle itself become blocked, then the subsequent shortage of blood to the heart is called a heart attack. 618

ascending reticular activating system (ARAS) The ascending reticular activating system is a structure in the brainstem thought to control overall cortical arousal, and this was the structure Eysenck originally thought was responsible for differences between introverts and extraverts. 215

assortative mating Assortative mating refers to the phenomenon whereby people marry people who they are similar to. In addition to personality, people also show assortative mating on a number of physical characteristics, such as height and weight. 500

attachment Attachment in the human infant begins when he or she develops a preference for people over objects. Then the preference begins to narrow to familiar persons, so that the child prefers to see people he or she has seen before compared to strangers. Finally the preference narrows even further, so that the child prefers the mother or primary caretaker over anyone else. 342

attraction similarity theory The attraction similarity theory of attraction states that individuals are attracted to those whose personalities are similar to their own. In other words, "birds of a feather flock together" or "like attracts like." As of 2003, attraction similarity has been proven to be the dominant attraction theory except in biological sex choices, i.e., women tend to be attracted to men and vice versa. 499

autonomic nervous system (ANS) That part of the peripheral nervous system which connects to vital bodily structures associated with maintaining life and responding to emergencies (e.g., storing and releasing energy), such as the beating of the heart, respiration, and controlling blood pressure. There are two divisions of the ANS; the sympathetic and parasympathetic branches. 210

average tendencies Average tendency is the tendency to display a certain psychological trait with regularity. For example, on average, a high-talkative person will start more conversations than a low-talkative person. This idea explains why the principle of aggregation works when measuring personality. 6, 108

avoidantly attached Avoidantly attached infants in Ainsworth's strange situation avoided the mother when she returned. Infants in this group typically seemed unfazed when the mother left, and typically did not give her much attention when she returned. Avoidant children seem to be aloof from their mothers. Approximately 20 percent of the infants fall into this category. 343

avoidant personality disorder The major feature of the avoidant personality is a pervasive feeling of inadequacy and sensitivity to criticism from others. The avoidant personality will go to great lengths to avoid situations in which others may have opportunities to criticize their performance or character, such as school or work or other group settings. Such a person may avoid making new friends or going to new places because of fear of criticism or disapproval. 647

avoidant relationship style In Hazan and Shaver's avoidant relationship style, the adult has difficulty learning to trust others. Avoidant adults remain suspicious of the motives of others, and they are afraid of making commitments. They are afraid of depending on others because they anticipate being disappointed, let down, abandoned, or separated. 344

b

Balkanization Balkanization refers to social re-segregation following a time of peaceful integration and social diversity. The term is derived from breakup of Yugoslavia on the Balkan peninsula during the 1990s, where national groups split apart and re-segregated the formerly integrated countries in the Balkans. 563

Barnum statements Barnum statements are generalities or statements that could apply to anyone. A good example of these is the astrology columns published in daily newspapers. 116

behavioral activation system (BAS) In Gray's reinforcement sensitivity theory, the Behavioral Activation System (BAS) is the system that is responsive to incentives, such as cues for reward, and regulates approach behavior. When some stimulus is recognized as potentially rewarding, the BAS triggers approach behavior. This system is highly correlated with the trait of extraversion. 220

behavioral inhibition system In Gray's reinforcement sensitivity theory, the Behavioral Inhibition System (BIS) is responsive to cues for punishment, frustration, and uncertainty. The effect of BIS activation is to cease or inhibit behavior or to bring about avoidance behavior. This system is highly correlated with the trait of neuroticism. 220

belongingness needs At the third level of Maslow's motivation hierarchy are belongingness needs. Humans are a very social species, and most people possess a strong need to belong to groups. Being accepted by others and welcomed into a group represents a somewhat more psychological need than the physiological needs or the need for safety. 373

biological domain The core assumption of biological approaches to personality is that humans are, first and foremost, collections of biological systems, and these systems provide the building blocks (e.g., brain, nervous system) for behavior, thought, and emotion. Biological approaches typically refers to three areas of research within this general domain: the genetics of personality, the psychophysiology of personality, and the evolution of personality. 16

bipolarity In Wiggins circumplex model, traits that are bipolar are located at opposite sides of the circle and are negatively correlated with each other. Specifying this bipolarity is useful because nearly every interpersonal trait within the personality sphere has another trait that is its opposite. 81

blindsight Following an injury or stroke that damages the primary vision center in the brain, a person may lose some or all of their ability to see. In this kind of blindness the eyes still work to bring information into the brain, but the brain center responsible for object recognition fails. People who suffer this kind of "cortical" blindness often display an interesting capacity to make judgments about objects that they truly cannot see. This phenomenon is termed "blindsight." 294

bodily fluid theory The ancient idea that the amounts of four fluids (phlegm, blood, yellow bile, and black bile) present in the body were responsible for individual differences in personality. For example, an excess of phlegm was thought to make the person phlegmatic, that is, passive and lethargic. 207
borderline personality disorder The life of the borderline personality is marked by instability. Their relationships are unstable, their emotions are unstable, their behavior is unstable, and even their image of themselves is unstable. Persons with borderline personality disorder, compared to those without, have a higher incidence rate of childhood physical or sexual abuse, neglect, or early parental loss. 633
by-products of adaptations The evolutionary process produces mechanisms that are not adaptations, but rather are by-products of other adaptations. Our nose, for example, is clearly an adaptation designed for smelling. But the fact that we use our nose to hold up our eyeglasses is an incidental by-product. 248

C

cardiac reactivity The increase in blood pressure and heart rate during times of stress. Evidence suggests that chronic cardiac reactivity contributes to coronary artery disease. Also known as Cardiac Reactivity. 212
case study method In case studies, researchers examine the life of one person in particular depth. Case studies can give researchers insights into personality that can then be used to formulate a more general theory that is tested in a larger population. They can also provide in-depth knowledge of a particularly outstanding individual. Case studies can also be useful in studying rare phenomena, such as a person with a photographic memory or a person with multiple personalities—cases for which large samples would be difficult or impossible to obtain. 51
castration anxiety Freud argued that little boys come to believe that their fathers might make a preemptive Oedipal strike and take away what is at the root of the Oedipal conflict: the boy's penis. This fear of losing his penis is called castration anxiety; it drives the little boy into giving up his sexual desire for his mother. 308
categorical approach Emotion researchers who suggest emotions are best thought of as a small number of primary and distinct emotions (anger, joy, anxiety, sadness) are said to take the categorical approach. Emotion researchers who take the categorical approach have tried to reduce the complexity of emotions by searching for the primary emotions that underlie the great variety of emotion terms. An example of a categorical approach to emotion is that of Paul Ekman, who applies criteria of distinct and universal facial expressions, and whose list of primary emotions contains disgust, sadness, joy, surprise, anger, and fear. 425
categorical view In psychiatry and clinical psychology today, the categorical view is the dominant approach to viewing personality disorders in distinct categories. There is a qualitative distinction made in which people who have a disorder are in one category, while people who do not have the disorder are in another category. 626
causal attribution Causal attribution refers to a person's explanation of the cause of some event. 409
chronic stress Chronic stress refers to stress that does not end, like an abusive relationship that grinds the individual down until his or her resistance is eroded. Chronic stress can result in serious systemic diseases such as diabetes, decreased immune system functioning, or cardiovascular disease. 599
circadian rhythm Many biological processes fluctuate around an approximate 24- to 25-hour cycle. These are called circadian rhythms (circa 5 around; dia 5 day). Circadian rhythms in temporal isolation studies have been found to be as short as 16 hours in one person, and as long as 50 hours in another person (Wehr & Goodwin, 1981). 231
client-centered therapy In Rogers's client-centered therapy, clients are never given interpretations of their problem. Nor are clients given any direction about what course of action to take to solve their problem. The therapist makes no attempts to change the client directly. Instead, the therapist tries to create an atmosphere in which the client may change him or herself. 381
cognition Cognition is a general term referring to awareness and thinking as well as to specific mental acts such as perceiving, interpreting, remembering, believing, and anticipating. 393
cognitive approaches Differences in how people think form the focus of cognitive approaches to personality. Psychologists working in this approach focus on the components of cognition, such as how people perceive, interpret, remember, and plan, in their efforts to understand how and why people are different from each other. 392
cognitive/experiential domain This domain focuses on cognition and subjective experience, such as conscious thoughts, feelings, beliefs, and desires about oneself and others. This domain includes our feelings of self, identity, self-esteem, our goals and plans, and our emotions. 17
cognitive schema A schema is a way of processing incoming information and of organizing and interpreting the facts of daily life. The cognitive schema involved in depression, according to Beck, distorts the incoming information in a negative way that makes the person depressed. 447
cognitive social learning approach A number of modern personality theories have expanded on the notion that personality is expressed in goals and in how people think about themselves relative to their goals. Collectively these theories form an approach that emphasizes the cognitive and social processes whereby people learn to value and strive for certain goals over others. 412
cognitive triad According to Beck, there are three important areas of life that are most influenced by the depressive cognitive schema. This cognitive triad refers to information about the self, about the world, and about the future. 447
cognitive unconscious In the cognitive view of the unconscious, the content of the unconscious mind is assumed to operate just like thoughts in consciousness. Thoughts are unconscious because they are not in conscious awareness, not because they have been repressed or because they represent unacceptable urges or wishes. 330

cohort effects Cohort effects refers to personality change over time as a reflection of the social times in which an individual or group of individuals live. For example, American women's trait scores on assertiveness have risen and fallen depending on the social and historical cohort in which they have lived. Jean Twenge has posited that individuals internalize social change and absorb the cultural messages they receive from their culture, all of which, in turn, can affect their personalities. 159

collective unconscious According to Carl Jung, the collective unconscious is a prehistoric, inherited unconscious content that is passed on from previous generations and contains the collected primordial images common across the human species. 291

collectivism In collectivist societies, people are interdependent with others in the group, giving priority to the goals of their in-groups. People in collectivist societies tend to be especially concerned about social relationships. They focus more on context, features external to their own wishes and goals. In collectivist societies, people tend to be more self-effacing, less likely to boast or brag about their own personal accomplishments. 565

combinations of Big Five variables "Traits" are often examined in combinations. For example, two people high in extraversion would be very different if one was an extraverted neurotic and the other was extraverted but emotionally stable. 88

comorbidity Comorbidity is defined as the presence of two or more disorders of any type in one person. 227, 645

compatibility and integration across domains and levels In science, a theory that takes into account the principles and laws of other scientific domains that may affect the study's main subject. For example, a theory of biology that violated known principles of chemistry would be judged fatally flawed. 22

competitive achievement motivation Also referred to as the Need for Achievement, it is a subtrait in the Type A behavior pattern. The Type A person likes to work hard and achieve goals. They like recognition and overcoming obstacles and feel they are at their best when competing with others. 613

complementary needs theory The complementary needs theory of attraction postulates that people are attracted to people whose personality dispositions differ from theirs. In other words, "opposites attract." This is especially true in biological sex choices, i.e., women tend to be attracted to men and vice versa. Other than biological sex choices, the complementary needs theory of attraction has not received any empirical support. 499

comprehensiveness Comprehensiveness is one of the five scientific standards used in evaluating personality theories. Theories that explain more empirical data within a domain are generally superior to those that explain fewer findings. 21

conditional positive regard According to Rogers, people behave in specific ways to earn the love and respect and positive regard of parents and other significant people in their lives. Positive regard, when it must be earned by meeting certain conditions, is called conditional positive regard. 378

conditions of worth According to Rogers, the requirements set forth by parents or significant others for earning their positive regard are called conditions of worth. Children may become preoccupied with living up to these conditions of worth, rather than discovering what makes them happy. 378

confirmatory biases A confirmatory bias is the tendency to look only for evidence that confirms a previous hunch, and to not look for evidence that might disconfirm a belief. 327

Conscientiousness Conscientiousness is the third of the personality traits in the Five-Factor Model, a model which has proven to be replicable in studies using English language trait words as items. Some of the key adjective markers for Conscientiousness are "responsible," "scrupulous," "persevering," "fussy/tidy." 86

conscious The conscious mind is that part of the mind that contains all the thoughts, feelings, and images that a person is presently aware of. Whatever a person is currently thinking about is in his or her conscious mind. 289

conscious goals A person's awareness of what they desire and believe is valuable and worth pursuing. 395

consistency Trait theories assume there is some degree of consistency in personality over time. If someone is highly extraverted during one period of observation, trait psychologists tend to assume that she will be extraverted tomorrow, next week, a year from now, or even decades from now. 98

construct A construct is a concept or provable hypothesis that summarizes a set of observations and conveys the meaning of those observations, e.g., gravity. 403

construct validity Construct validity generally refers to whether a test measures what it claims to measure. It is often assessed by determining whether a test correlates with what it is supposed to correlate with, and does not correlate with what it is not supposed to correlate with. Construct validity is the broadest type of validity, subsuming face, predictive, convergent, and discriminant validity. 43

constructive memory It is accepted as fact that humans have a constructive memory; that is, memory contributes to or influences in various ways (adds to, subtracts from, etc.) what is recalled. Recalled memories are rarely distortion-free, mirror images of the facts. 326

content The content of emotional life refers to the characteristic or typical emotions a person is likely to experience over time. Someone whose emotional life contains a lot of pleasant emotions is someone who might be characterized as happy, cheerful, and enthusiastic. Thus the notion of content leads us to consider the *kinds* of emotions that people are likely to experience over time and across situations in their lives. 429

continuity Identity has an element of continuity because many of its aspects, such as gender, ethnicity, socio-economic status, educational level, and occupation, are constant. Having an identity means that others can count on you to be reliable in who you are and how you act. 482

contrast Identity contrast means that a person's social identity differentiates that person from other people. An identity is what makes a person unique in the eyes of others. The combination of characteristics that make up a person's identity differentiates him or her from everyone else. 483

convergent validity Convergent validity refers to whether a test correlates with other measures that it should correlate with. Convergent validity is high to the degree that alternative measures of the same construct correlate or converge with the target measure. 42

core conditions According to Carl Rogers, in client-centered therapy there are three core conditions that must be present in order for progress to occur. The three core conditions are: 1. an atmosphere of genuine acceptance on the part of the therapist; 2. the therapist must express unconditional positive regard for the client; and 3. the client must feel that the therapist understands him or her (empathic understanding). 381

correlation coefficient (its direction and magnitude) Researchers are interested in the direction (positive or negative) and the magnitude (size) of the correlation coefficient. Correlations around .10 are considered small; those around .30 are considered medium; and those around .50 or greater are considered large (Cohen & Cohen, 1975). 47

correlational method A correlation is a statistical procedure for determining whether there is a relationship between two variables. In correlational research designs, the researcher is attempting to directly identify the relationships between two or more variables, without imposing the sorts of manipulations seen in experimental designs. 47

cortisol Cortisol is a stress hormone that prepares the body to flee or fight. Increases in cortisol in the blood indicate that the animal has recently experienced stress. 239

counterbalancing In some experiments, manipulation is within a single group. For example, participants might get a drug and have their memory tested, then later take a sugar pill and have their memory tested again. In this kind of experiment, equivalence is obtained by counterbalancing the order of the conditions, with half the participants getting the drug first and sugar pill second, and the other half getting the sugar pill first and the drug second. 44

creating positive events Creating positive events is defined as creating a positive time-out from stress. Folkman and Moskowitz note that humor can have the added benefit of generating positive emotional moments even during the darkest periods of stress. 603

criterion validity Criterion validity or predictive validity refers to whether the test predicts criteria external to the test. Scales that successfully predict what they should predict have high criterion validity or predictive validity. 42

cross-cultural universality In the lexical approach, cross-cultural universality states that if a trait is sufficiently important in all cultures so that its members have codified terms within their own languages to describe the trait, then the trait must be universally important in human affairs. In contrast, if a trait term exists in only one or a few languages but is entirely missing from most, then it may be of only local relevance. 67

cultural context of intelligence The cultural context of intelligence looks at how the definition of intelligent behavior varies across different cultures. Because of these considerations, intelligence can be viewed as referring to those skills valued in a particular culture. 418

cultural personality psychology Cultural personality psychology generally has three key goals: (1) to discover the principles underlying the cultural diversity; (2) to discover how human psychology shapes culture; and (3) to discover how cultural understandings in turn shape our psychology (Fiske, Kitayama, Markus, & Nisbett, 1997). 555

cultural universals Cultural universals are features of personality that are common to everyone in all cultures. These universals constitute the human nature level of analyzing personality and define the elements of personality we share with all or most other people. 572

cultural variations Within-group similarities and between-group differences can be of any sort—physical, psychological, behavioral, or attitudinal. These phenomena are often referred to as cultural variations. Two ingredients are necessary to explain cultural variations: (1) a universal underlying mechanism and (2) environmental differences in the degree to which the underlying mechanism is activated. 555

culture Culture is a set of shared standards for many behaviors. It might contain different standards for males and females, such that girls should be ashamed if they engage in promiscuous sex, whereas boys might be proud of such behavior, with it being culturally acceptable for them to even brag about such behavior. 338

culture of honor Nisbett proposed that the economic means of subsistence of a culture affects the degree to which the group develops what he calls "a culture of honor." In cultures of honor, insults are viewed as highly offensive public challenges that must be met with direct confrontation and physical aggression. The theory is that differences in the degree to which honor becomes a central part of the culture rests ultimately with economics, and specifically the manner in which food is obtained. 558

d

D4DR gene The D4DR gene is located on the short arm of chromosome 11. This gene codes for a protein called a dopamine receptor. The function of this dopamine receptor is to respond to the presence of dopamine, which is a neurotransmitter. When the dopamine receptor encounters dopamine from other neurons in the brain, it discharges an electrical signal, activating other neurons. 198, 230

daily hassles The major sources of stress in most people's lives are what are termed daily hassles. While only minor, daily hassles can be chronic and repetitive, such as having too much to do all the time, having to fight the crowds while shopping, or having to worry over money. Such daily hassles can be chronically irritating though they do not initiate the same general adaptation syndrome evoked by some major life events. 597

deductive and inductive reasoning The deductive reasoning approach to scientific investigation is the top down, theory-driven method of empirical research. The inductive reasoning approach to scientific investigation is the bottom-up, data-driven method of empirical research. 251

defense mechanisms Strategies for coping with anxiety and threats to self-esteem. 298

defensive pessimism Individuals who use a defensive pessimism strategy have usually done well on important tasks but lack self-confidence in their ability to handle new challenges. A defensive pessimist controls anxiety by preparing for failure ahead of time; they set low expectations for their performance and often focus on worse-case outcomes. This strategy overcomes anticipatory anxiety and transforms it into motivation. 479

deliberation-without-awareness The notion that, when confronted with a decision, if a person can put it out of their conscious mind for a period of time, then their "unconscious mind" will continue to deliberate on it, helping them to arrive at a "sudden" and often correct decision sometime later. 295

denial When the reality of a particular situation is extremely anxiety-provoking a person may resort to the defense mechanism of denial. A person in denial insists that things are not the way they seem. Denial can also be less extreme, as when someone reappraises an anxiety-provoking situation so that it seems less daunting. Denial often shows up in people's daydreams and fantasies. 300

dependent personality disorder The dependent personality seeks out others to an extreme. The hallmark of the dependent personality is an excessive need to be taken care of, to be nurtured, coddled, and told what to do. Dependent persons act in submissive ways so as to encourage others to take care of them or take charge of the situation. Such individuals need lots of encouragement and advice from others, and would much rather turn over responsibility for their decisions to someone else. 648

depression Depression is a psychological disorder whose symptoms include a depressed mood most of the day; diminished interest in activities; change in weight, sleep patterns, and movement; fatigue or loss of energy; feelings of worthlessness; inability to concentrate; and recurrent thoughts of death and suicide. It is estimated that 20 percent of Americans are afflicted with depression at some time in their lives (American Psychiatric Association, 1994). 433

developmental crisis Erikson believed that each stage in personality development represented a conflict, or a developmental crisis, that needed to be resolved before the person advanced to the next stage of development. 334

diathesis-stress model of depression The diathesis-stress model suggests that a pre-existing vulnerability, or diathesis, is present among people who become depressed. In addition to this vulnerability, a stressful life event must occur in order to trigger the depression, such as the loss of a loved one or some other major negative life event. The events must occur together—something bad or stressful has to happen to a person who has a particular vulnerability to depression—in order for depression to occur. 446

differences between groups See group differences. 12

differential diagnosis A differential diagnosis is arrived at when, out of two or more possible diagnoses, the clinician searches for evidence in support of one diagnostic category over all the others. 654

differential gene reproduction According to modern evolutionary biologists, evolution operates by the process of differential gene reproduction. Differential gene reproduction is defined by reproductive success relative to others. The genes of organisms who reproduce more than others get passed down to future generations at a relatively greater frequency than the genes of those who reproduce less. Since survival is usually critical for reproductive success, characteristics that lead to greater survival get passed along. Since success in mate competition is also critical for reproductive success, qualities that lead to success in same-sex competition or to success at being chosen as a mate get passed along. Successful survival and successful mate competition, therefore, are both part of differential gene reproduction. 246

differential psychology Due to its emphasis on the study of differences between people, trait psychology has sometimes been called differential psychology in the interest of distinguishing this sub-field from other branches of personality psychology (Anastasi, 1976). Differential psychology includes the study of other forms of individual differences in addition to personality traits, such as abilities, aptitudes, and intelligence. 97

dimensional approach The dimensional approach to understanding the complexity of emotion has been based on empirical research rather than theoretical criteria. In this approach, researchers have gathered data by having subjects rate themselves on a wide variety of emotions, then apply statistical techniques (mostly factor analysis) to identify the basic dimensions underlying the ratings. Almost all the studies suggest that subjects categorize emotions using just two primary dimensions: how pleasant or unpleasant the emotion is, and how high or low on arousal the emotion is. 425

dimensional view The dimensional view approaches a personality disorder as a continuum that ranges from normality at one end to severe disability and disturbance at the other end. According to this view, people with and without the disorder differ in degree only. 627

directionality problem One reason why correlations can never prove causality is known as the directionality problem. If A and B are correlated, we do not know if A is the cause of B, or if B is the cause of A, or if some third, unknown variable is causing both B and A. 51

disclosure Disclosure refers to telling someone about some private aspect of ourselves. Many theorists have suggested that keeping things to ourselves may be a source of stress and ultimately may lead to psychological distress and physical disease. 610

discriminant validity Discriminant validity is often evaluated simultaneously with convergent validity. Whereas convergent validity refers to what a measure *should* correlate with, discriminant validity refers to what a measure *should not* correlate with. The idea behind discriminant validity is that part of knowing what a measure actually measures consists of knowing what it does *not* measure. 42

disorder A disorder is a pattern of behavior or experience that is distressing and painful to the person, leads to some disability or impairment in important life domains (e.g., work, marriage, or relationship difficulties), and is associated with increased risk for further suffering, loss of function, death, or confinement. 624

disparate impact Any employment practice that disadvantages people from a protected group. The Supreme Court has not defined the size of the disparity necessary to prove disparate impact. Most courts define disparity as a difference that is sufficiently large that it is unlikely to have occurred by chance. Some courts, however, prefer the 80 percent rule contained in the Uniform Guidelines on Employee Selection Procedures. Under this rule, adverse impact is established if the selection rate for any race, sex, or ethnic group is less than four-fifths (or 80 percent) of the rate for the group with the highest selection rate. 121

displacement Displacement is an unconscious defense mechanism that involves avoiding the recognition that one has certain inappropriate urges or unacceptable feelings (e.g., anger, sexual attraction) toward a specific other. Those feelings then get displaced onto another person or object that is more appropriate or acceptable. 300

dispositional domain The dispositional domain deals centrally with the ways in which individuals differ from one another. As such, the dispositional domain connects with all the other domains. In the dispositional domain, psychologists are primarily interested in the number and nature of fundamental dispositions, taxonomies of traits, measurement issues, and questions of stability over time and consistency over situations. 16

dispositional optimism The expectation that in the future good events will be plentiful and bad events will be rare. 603

distortion A defense mechanism in Roger's theory of personality, distortion refers to modifying the meaning of experiences to make them less threatening to the self-image. 380

dizygotic twins Dizygotic twins, or fraternal twins, are not genetically identical. They come from two eggs that were separately fertilized ("di" means two; so dizygotic means "coming from two fertilized eggs"). Such twins share only 50 percent of their genes with their co-twin, the same amount as ordinary brothers and sisters. Fraternal twins can be of the same sex or of the opposite sex. 182

domain of knowledge A specialty area of science and scholarship, where psychologists have focused on learning about some specific and limited aspect of human nature, often with preferred tools of investigation. 15

domain specific Adaptations are presumed to be domain-specific in the sense that they are "designed" by the evolutionary process to solve a specialized adaptive problem. Domain specificity implies that selection tends to fashion specific mechanisms for each specific adaptive problem. 249

dopamine Dopamine is a neurotransmitter that appears to be associated with pleasure. Dopamine appears to function something like the "reward system" and has even been called the "feeling good" chemical (Hamer, 1997). 229

dream analysis Dream analysis was a technique that Freud taught for uncovering the unconscious material in a dream by interpreting the content of a dream. Freud called dreams "the royal road to the unconscious." 311

dynamic Dynamic refers to the interaction of forces within a person. 354

e

effect size An effect size in meta-analysis indicates how large a particular difference is, or how strong a particular correlation is, as averaged over several experiments or studies. 526

effective polygyny Because female mammals bear the physical burden of gestation and lactation, there is a considerable sex difference in minimum obligatory parental investment. This difference leads to differences in the variances in reproduction between the sexes: most females will have some offspring, while a few males will sire many offspring, and some will have none at all. This is known as effective polygyny. 261

egalitarianism Refers to how much a particular group displays equal treatment of all individuals within that group. 557

ego The ego is the part of the mind that constrains the id to reality. According to Freud, it develops within the first two or three years of life. The ego operates according to the reality principle. The ego understands that the urges of the id are often in conflict with social and physical reality, and that direct expression of id impulses must therefore be redirected or postponed. 296

ego psychology Post-Freudian psychoanalysts felt that the ego deserved more attention and that it performed many constructive functions. Erikson emphasized the ego as a powerful and independent part of personality, involved in mastering the environment, achieving one's goals, and hence in establishing one's identity. The approach to psychoanalysis started by Erikson was called Ego Psychology. 332

electra complex Within the psychoanalytic theory of personality development, the electra complex is the female counterpart to the oedipal complex, which both refer to the phallic stage of development. 308

electrode A sensor usually placed on the surface of the skin and linked to a physiological recording machine (often called a polygraph) to measure physiological variables. 210

electrodermal activity Also known as galvanic skin response or skin conductance, it refers to the fact that electricity will flow across the skin with less resistance if that skin is made damp with sweat. Sweating on the palms of the hands is activated by the sympathetic nervous system, and so electrodermal activity is a way to directly measure changes in the sympathetic nervous system. 210

electroencephalograph (EEG) The brain spontaneously produces small amounts of electricity, which can be measured by electrodes placed on the scalp. This measure is called the electroencephalogram (EEG). EEGs can provide useful information about patterns of activation in different regions of the brain that may be associated with different types of information processing tasks. 236

emotion Emotions can be defined by their three components: (1) emotions have distinct subjective feelings or affects associated with them; (2) emotions are accompanied by bodily changes, mostly in the nervous system, and these produce associated changes in breathing, heart rate, muscle tension, blood chemistry, and facial and bodily expressions; (3) emotions are accompanied by distinct action tendencies or increases in the probabilities of certain behaviors. 424

emotional inhibition Emotional inhibition refers to the suppression of emotional expressions, and often is thought of as a trait, e.g., some people chronically suppress their emotions. 607

emotional intelligence Emotional intelligence is an adaptive form of intelligence consisting of the ability to: 1. know one's own emotions; 2. regulate those emotions; 3. motivate oneself; 4. know how others are feeling; and 5. influence how others are feeling. Goleman posited that emotional intelligence is more strongly predictive of professional status, marital quality, and salary than traditional measures of intelligence and aptitude. 381, 417

Emotional Stability Emotional Stability is the fourth of the personality traits in the Five-Factor Model, a model which has proven to be replicable in studies using English language trait words as items. Some of the key adjective markers for Emotional Stability are "calm," "composed," "not hypochondriacal," "poised." 87

emotional states Emotional states are transitory and depend more on the situation or circumstances a person is in than on the specific person. Emotions as states have a specific cause, and that cause is typically outside of the person (something happens in the environment). 425

emotional traits Emotional traits are stable personality traits that are primarily characterized by specific emotions. For example, the trait of neuroticism is primarily characterized by the emotions of anxiety and worry. 425

empathy In Rogers's client-centered therapy, empathy is understanding the person from his or her point of view. Instead of interpreting the meaning behind what the client says (e.g., "you have a harsh superego that is punishing you for the actions of your id."), the client-centered therapist simply listens to what the client says and reflects it back. 381

environment Environments can be physical, social, and intrapsychic (within the mind). Which aspect of the environment is important at any moment in time is frequently determined by the personality of the person in that environment. 10

environmentalist view Environmentalists believe that personality is determined by socialization practices, such as parenting style and other agents of society. 199

environmentality The percentage of observed variance in a *group* of individuals that can be attributed to environmental (nongenetic) differences is called environmentality. Generally speaking, the larger the heritability, the smaller the environmentality. And vice versa, the smaller the heritability, the larger the environmentality. 178

episodic acute stress Episodic acute stress refers to repeated episodes of acute stress, such as having to work at more than one job every day, having to spend time with a difficult in-law, or needing to meet a recurring monthly deadline. 598

equal environments assumption The equal environments assumption is that the environments experienced by identical twins are no more similar to each other than are the environments experienced by fraternal twins. If they are more similar, then the greater similarity of the identical twins could plausibly be due to the fact that they experience more similar environments rather than the fact that they have more genes in common. 183

Erikson's eight stages of development According to Erikson, there are eight stages of development: trust versus mistrust, autonomy versus shame and doubt, initiative versus guilt, industry versus inferiority, identity versus role confusion, intimacy versus isolation, generativity versus stagnation, and integrity versus despair. 333

esteem needs At the fourth level Maslow's motivation hierarchy are esteem needs. There are two types of esteem: esteem from others and self-esteem, the latter often depending on the former. People want to be seen by others as competent, as strong, and as able to achieve. They want to be respected by others for their achievements or abilities. People also want to feel good about themselves. Much of the activity of adult daily life is geared toward achieving recognition and esteem from others and bolstering one's own self-confidence. 373

eugenics Eugenics is the notion that the future of the human race can be influenced by fostering the reproduction of persons with certain traits, and discouraging reproduction among persons without those traits or who have undesirable traits. 175

evocation Evocation is a form of person-situation interaction discussed by Buss. It is based on the idea that certain personality traits may evoke consistent responses from the environment, particularly the social environment. 106, 506

evoked culture Evoked culture refers to a way of considering culture that concentrates on phenomena that are triggered in different ways by different environmental conditions. 556

evolutionary by-product Incidental effects evolved changes that are not properly considered adaptations. For example, our noses hold up glasses, but that is not what the nose evolved for. 248

evolutionary noise Random variations that are neutral with respect to selection. 248

evolutionary-predicted sex differences Evolutionary psychology predicts that males and females will be the same or similar in all those domains where the sexes have faced the same or similar adaptive problems (for example, both sexes have sweat glands because both sexes have faced the adaptive problem of thermal regulation) and different when men and women have faced substantially different adaptive problems (for example, in the physical realm, women have faced the problem of childbirth and have therefore, evolved adaptations that are lacking in men, such as mechanisms for producing labor contractions through the release of oxytocin into the bloodstream). 260

exhaustion stage The exhaustion stage is the third stage in Seyle's general adaptation syndrome (GAS). Selye felt that this was the stage where we are most susceptible to illness and disease, as our physiological resources are depleted. 595

expectancy confirmation Expectancy confirmation is a phenomenon whereby people's beliefs about the personality characteristics of others cause them to evoke in others actions that are consistent with the initial beliefs. The phenomenon of expectancy confirmation has also been called self-fulfilling prophesy and behavioral confirmation. 511

experience sampling In experience sampling, people answer some questions, for example about their mood or physical symptoms, every day for several weeks or longer. People are usually contacted electronically ("beeped") one or more times a day at random intervals to complete the measures. Although experience sampling uses self-report as the data source, it differs from more traditional self-report methods in being able to detect patterns of behavior over time. 29

experimental methods Experimental methods are typically used to determine causality—to find out whether one variable influences another variable. Experiments involve the manipulation of one variable (the independent variable) and random assignment of subjects to conditions defined by the independent variable. 44

explanatory style Whenever someone offers a cause for some event, that cause can be analyzed in terms of the three categories of attributions: internal-external, stable-unstable, and global-specific. The tendency a person has to employ certain combinations of attributions in explaining events (e.g., internal, stable, and global causes) is called their explanatory style. 409

expressiveness Expressiveness refers to the ease with which one can express emotions, such as crying, showing empathy for the troubles of others, and showing nurturance to those in need. 541

external locus of control Generalized expectancies that events are outside of one's control is called an external locus of control. 406

extreme responding Extreme responding is a response set that refers to the tendency to give endpoint responses, such as "strongly agree" or "strongly disagree" and avoid the middle part of response scales, such as "slightly agree," "slightly disagree," or "am indifferent." 111

eye-blink startle method People typically blink their eyes when they are startled by a loud noise. Moreover, a person who is in an anxious or fearful state when startled will blink faster and harder than a person in a normal emotional state. This means that eye-blink speed when startled may be an objective physiological measure of how anxious or fearful a person is feeling. The eye-blink startle method may allow researchers to measure how anxious persons are without actually having to ask them. 634

f

face validity Face validity refers to whether a test, on the surface, appears to measure what it is supposed to measure. Face validity is probably the least important aspect of validity. In fact, some psychologists might argue that face validity refers to the assumption of validity, not to evidence for real validity. 42

factor analysis Factor analysis is a commonly used statistical procedure for identifying underlying structure in personality ratings or items. Factor analysis essentially identifies groups of items that covary (i.e., go together or correlate) with each other, but tend not to covary with other groups of items. This provides a means for determining which personality variables share some common underlying property or belong together within the same group. 69

factor loadings Factor loadings are indexes of the how much of the variation in an item is "explained" by the factor. Factor loadings indicate the degree to which the item correlates with or "loads on" the underlying factor. 69

faking Faking involves the motivated distortion of answers on a questionnaire. Some people may be motivated to "fake good" in order to appear to be better off or better adjusted than they really are. Others may be motivated to "fake bad" in order to appear to be worse off or more maladjusted than they really are. 110

false consensus effect The false consensus effect refers to the tendency many people have to assume that others are similar to them, i.e., extraverts think that many other people are as extraverted as they are. To think that many other people share your own traits, preferences, or motivations is to display the false consensus effect. 305

false memories False memories are memories that have been "implanted" by well-meaning therapists or others interrogating a subject about some event. 324

false negative and false positive There are two ways for psychologists to make a mistake when making decisions about persons based on personality tests, e.g., when deciding whether or not to hire a person, to parole a person, or that the person was lying. For example, when trying to decide whether a person's answers are genuine or faked, the psychologist might decide that a person who was faking was actually telling the truth (called a false positive). Or they might conclude that a truthful person was faking. This is called a false negative. 110

family studies Family studies correlate the degree of genetic overlap among family members with the degree of personality similarity. They capitalize on the fact that there are known degrees of genetic overlap between different members of a family in terms of degree of relationship. 181

fear of success Horney coined the phrase "fear of success" to highlight a gender difference in response to competition and achievement situations. Many women, she argued, feel that if they succeed, they will lose their friends. Consequently, many women, she thought, harbor an unconscious fear of success. She held that men, on the other hand, feel that they will actually gain friends by being successful, and hence are not at all afraid to strive and pursue achievement. 339

femininity A psychological dimension containing traits such as nurturance, empathy, and expression of emotions (e.g., crying when sad). 538

field-dependent and field-independent In Witkin's rod and frame test, if a participant adjusts the rod so that it is leaning in the direction of the tilted frame, then that person is said to be dependent of the visual field, or field dependent. If a participant disregards the external cues and instead uses information from their bodies in adjusting the rod to upright, they are said to be independent of the field, or field independent; they appear to rely on their own sensations, not the perception of the field, to make the judgment. This individual difference may have implications in situations where people must extract information from complex sensory fields, such as in multimedia education. 396

five-factor model The Five-Factor Model of personality is a trait taxonomy that has its roots in the lexical hypothesis. The first psychologist to use the terms "Five-Factor Model" and "Big Five" was Warren Norman, based on his replications of the factor structure suggesting the following five traits: Surgency (or extraversion), Neuroticism (or emotional instability), Agreeableness, Conscientiousness, and Openness to Experience (or intellect). The Five Factor Model has been criticized by some for not being comprehensive and for failing to provide a theoretical understanding of the underlying psychological processes that generate the five traits. Nonetheless, the Five Factor Model remains heavily endorsed by many personality psychologists, and continues to be used in a variety of research studies and applied settings. 82

fixation According to Erikson, if a developmental crisis is not successfully and adaptively resolved, then personality development could become arrested and the person would continue to have a fixation on that crisis in development. According to Freud, if a child fails to fully resolve a conflict at a particular stage of development, he or she may get stuck in that stage, a phenomenon known as fixation. If a child is fixated at a particular stage, he or she exhibits a less mature approach to obtaining sexual gratification. 306, 334

flow A subjective state that people report when they are completely involved in an activity to the point of forgetting time, fatigue, and everything else but the activity itself. While flow experiences are somewhat rare, they occur under specific conditions; there is a balance between the person's skills and the challenges of the situation, there is a clear goal, and there is immediate feedback on how one is doing. 375

forced choice questionnaire In a forced-choice questionnaire format, test-takers are confronted with pairs of statements and are asked to indicate which statement in the pair is more true of them. Each statement in the pair is selected to be similar to each other in social desirability, forcing participants to choose between statements that are equivalently socially desirable (or undesirable), and differ in content. 113

free association In free association, patients relax, let their minds wander, and say whatever comes into their minds. Patients often say things that surprise or embarrass them. By relaxing the censor that screens everyday thoughts, free association allows potentially important material into conscious awareness. 310

free running Refers to a condition in studies of circadian rhythms, where participants are deprived from knowing what time it is, e.g., meals are served when the participant asks for them, not at pre-scheduled times. When a person is free-running in time, there are no time cues to influence their behavior or biology. 232

frequency-dependent selection In some contexts, two or more heritable variants can evolve within a population. The most obvious example is biological sex itself. Within sexually reproducing species, the two sexes exist in roughly equal numbers because of frequency-dependent selection. If one sex becomes rare relative to the other, evolution will produce an increase in the numbers of the rarer sex. Frequency-dependent selection, in this example, causes the frequency of men and women to remain roughly equal. Different personality extremes (e.g., introversion and extraversion) may be the result of frequency dependent selection. 272

frontal brain asymmetry Asymmetry in the amount of activity in the left and right part of the frontal hemispheres of the brain. Studies using EEG measures have linked more relative left brain activity with pleasant emotions and more relative right brain activity with negative emotions. 238

frustration Frustration is the high-arousal unpleasant subjective feeling that comes when a person is blocked from attaining an important goal. For example, a thirsty person who just lost his last bit of money in a malfunctioning soda machine would most likely feel frustration. 613

fully functioning person According to Rogers, a fully functioning person is on his or her way toward self-actualization. Fully functioning persons may not actually *be* self-actualized yet, but they are not blocked or sidetracked in moving toward this goal. Such persons are open to new experiences and are not afraid of new ideas. They embrace life to its fullest. Fully functioning individuals are also centered in the present. They do not dwell on the past or their regrets. Fully functioning individuals also trust themselves, their feelings, and their own judgments. 377

functional analysis In his book, *The Expression of the Emotions in Man and Animals,* Charles Darwin proposed a functional analysis of emotions and emotional expressions focusing on the "why" of emotions and expressions. Darwin concluded that emotional expressions communicate information from one animal to another about what is likely to happen. For instance, a dog baring its teeth, growling, and bristling the fur on its back is communicating to others that he is likely to attack. If others recognize the dog's communication, they may choose to back away to safety. 424

functional magnetic resonance imaging (fMRI) Functional magnetic resonance imaging (fMRI) is a non-invasive imaging technique used to identify specific areas of brain activity. As parts of the brain are stimulated, oxygenated blood rushes to the activated area, resulting in increased iron concentrations in the blood. The fMRI detects these elevated concentrations of iron and prints out colorful images indicating which part of the brain is used to perform certain tasks. 36, 212

functionality Functionality is the notion that our psychological mechanisms are designed to accomplish particular adaptive goals. 250

fundamental attribution error When bad events happen to others, people have a tendency to attribute blame to some characteristic of the person, whereas when bad events happen to onself, people have the tendency to blame the situation. 300

g

gender Gender refers to social interpretations of what it means to be a man or a woman. 524

gender differences The distinction between gender and sex can be traced back to Horney. Horney stressed the point that, while biology determines sex, cultural norms determine what is acceptable for typical males and females in that culture. Today we use the terms masculine and feminine to refer to traits or roles typically associated with being male or female in a particular culture, and we refer to differences in such culturally ascribed roles and traits as gender differences. Differences that are ascribed to being a man or a woman per se are, however, called sex differences. 339

gender identity disorder (GID) According to the *DSM-IV*, a diagnosis of gender identity disorder requires that two aspects be present simultaneously: (1) cross-gender indentification that is strong and persists over time, and (2) persistent psychological discomfort with one's biological sex. A recent study of twins has concluded that there is a strong heritable component in GID. 191

gender schemata Gender schemas are cognitive orientations that lead individuals to process social information on the basis of sex-linked associations (Hoyenga & Hoyenga, 1993). 541

gender stereotypes Gender stereotypes are the beliefs that we hold about how men and women differ or are supposed to differ, which are not necessarily based on reality. Gender stereotypes can have important real-life consequences for men and women. These consequences can damage people where it most counts—in their health, their jobs, their odds of advancement, and their social reputations. 524

general adaptation syndrome Seyle's general adaptation syndrome (GAS) has three stages: When a stressor first appears, people experience the alarm stage. If the stressor continues, then stage of resistance begins. If the stressor remains constant, the person eventually enters the third stage, the stage of exhaustion. 594

general intelligence Early on in the study of intelligence, many psychologists thought of intelligence in trait-like terms, as a property of the individual. Individuals were thought to differ from each other in how much intelligence they possessed. Moreover, intelligence was thought of as a single broad factor, often called "g" for general intelligence. This stands in contrast to those views of intelligence as consisting of many discrete factors, such as social intelligence, emotional intelligence, and academic intelligence. 416

generalizability Generalizability refers to the degree to which a measure retains its validity across different contexts, situations, and conditions. Greater generalizability is not always better; rather, what is important is to identify empirically the contexts in which the particular measure is and is not applicable. 43

generalized expectancies Rotter claimed that a person's expectations for reinforcement hold across a variety of situations, what he called generalized expectancies (Rotter, 1971, 1990). When people encounter a new situation, they base their expectancies about what will happen on their generalized expectancies about whether they have the abilities to influence events. 406

genes Genes are packets of DNA that are inherited by children from their parents in distinct chunks. They are the smallest discrete unit that is inherited by offspring intact, without being broken up. 246

genetic junk The 98% of the DNA in human chromosomes that are not protein-coding genes used to be called "genetic junk" because scientists believed that these parts were functionless residue. Recent studies have shown that these portions of DNA may affect everything from a person's physical size to personality, thus adding to the complexity of the human genome. 174

genital stage The genital stage is the final stage in Freud's psychosexual stage theory of development. This stage begins around age 12 and lasts through one's adult life. Here the libido is focused on the genitals, but not in the manner of self-manipulation associated with the phallic stage. People reach the genital stage with full psychic energy if they have resolved the conflicts at the prior stages. 309

genome Genome refers to the complete set of genes an organism possesses. The human genome contains somewhere between 30,000 and 80,000 genes. 174

genotype-environment correlation Genotype-environment correlation refers to the differential exposure of individuals with different genotypes to different environments. 196

genotype-environment interaction Genotype-environment interaction refers to the differential response of individuals with different genotypes to the same environments. 195

genotypic variance Genetic variance that is responsible for individual differences in the phenotypic expression of specific traits. 178

global self-esteem Although researchers have explored many facets of self-esteem, by far the most frequently measured component is global self-esteem, defined as "the level of global regard that one has for the self as a person" (Harter, 1993, p. 88). Global self-esteem can range from highly positive to highly negative, and reflects an overall evaluation of the self at the broadest level (Kling et al., 1999). Global self-esteem is linked with many aspects of functioning and is commonly thought to be central to mental health. 534

good theory A good theory is one that serves as a useful guide for researchers, organizes known facts, and makes predictions about future observations. 20

Griggs v. Duke Power Prior to 1964, Duke Power Company had used discriminatory practices in hiring and work assignment, including barring blacks from certain jobs. After passage of the Civil Rights Act of 1964, Duke Power instituted various requirements for such jobs, including passing certain aptitude tests. The effect was to perpetuate discrimination. In 1971 the Supreme Court ruled that the seemingly neutral testing practices used by Duke Power were unacceptable because they operated to maintain discrimination. This was the first legal case where the Supreme Court ruled that any selection procedure could not produce disparate impact for a group protected by the Act (e.g., racial groups, women). 119

group differences People in one group may have certain personality features in common, and these common features make them different from other groups. Examples of groups studied by personality psychologists include different cultures, different age groups, different political parties, and people from different socioeconomic backgrounds. The most common group difference studied by personality psychologists concerns differences between men and women. For example, in the realm of physical development, females go through puberty on average two years earlier than males. At the other end of life, men in the U.S. tend to die seven years earlier than women. These are sex differences in development. 12

h

happiness Researchers conceive of happiness in two complementary ways: in terms of a judgment that life is satisfying, as well as in terms of the predominance of positive compared to negative emotions in one's life (Diener, 2000). It turns out, however, that people's emotional lives and their judgments of how satisfied they are with their lives are highly correlated. People who have a lot of pleasant emotions relative to unpleasant emotions in their lives tend also to judge their lives as satisfying, and vice versa. 430

harm avoidance In Cloninger's tridimensional personality model, the personality trait of harm avoidance is associated with low levels of serotonin. People low in serotonin are sensitive to unpleasant stimuli or to stimuli or events that have been associated with punishment or pain. Consequently, people low in serotonin seem to expect harmful and unpleasant events will happen to them, and so they are constantly vigilant for signs of such threatening events. 229

health behavior model In the health behavior model, personality does not directly influence the relation between stress and illness. Instead, personality affects health indirectly, through health-promoting or health-degrading behaviors. This model suggests that personality influences the degree to which a person engages in various health-promoting or health-demoting behaviors. 591

health psychology Researchers in the area of health psychology study relations between the mind and the body, and how these two components respond to challenges from the environment (e.g., stressful events, germs) to produce illness or health. 508

heritability Heritability is a statistic that refers to the proportion of observed variance in a group of individuals that can be explained or "accounted for" by genetic variance (Plomin, DeFries, & McClearn, 1990). It describes the degree to which genetic differences between individuals cause differences in some observed property, such as height, extraversion, or sensation seeking. The formal definition of heritability is the proportion of phenotypic variance that is attributable to genotypic variance. 177

heuristic value Heuristic value is an evaluative scientific standard for assessing personality theories. Theories that steer scientists to important new discoveries about personality that were not known before are superior to those that fail to provide this guidance. 21

hierarchy of needs Murray believed that each person has a unique combination of needs. An individual's various needs can be thought of as existing at a different level of strength. A person might have a high need for dominance, an average need for intimacy, and a low need for achievement. High levels of some needs interact with the amounts of various other needs within each person. 354

high-variance conditions One key variable triggering communal food sharing is the degree of variability in food resources. Specifically, under high-variance conditions, there are substantial benefits to sharing. 556

historical era One type of intracultural variation pertains to the effects of historical era on personality. (People who grew up during the great economic depression of the 1930s, for example, might be more anxious about job security or adopting a more conservative spending style.) Disentangling the effects of historical era on personality is an extremely difficult endeavor since most currently used personality measures were not in use in earlier eras. 571

histrionic personality disorder The hallmark of the histrionic personality is excessive attention-seeking and emotionality. Often such persons are overly dramatic and draw attention to themselves, preferring to be the center of attention or the life of the party. They may appear charming or even flirtatious. Often they can be inappropriately seductive or provocative. 636

Hogan Personality Inventory (HPI) A questionnaire measure of personality based on the Big Five model but modified to emphasize the assessment of traits important in the business world, including the motive get along with others and the motive to get ahead of others. 130

holistic A way of processing information that involves attention to relationships, contexts, and links between the focal objects and the field as a whole. 567

hormonal theories Hormonal theories of sex differences argue that men and women differ not because of the external social environment, but rather because the sexes have different amounts of specific hormones. It is these physiological differences, not differential social treatment, which causes boys and girls to diverge over development. 546

hostile attributional bias A hostile attributional bias is the tendency to infer hostile intent on the part of others in the face of uncertain or unclear behavior from others. Essentially, people who are aggressive expect that others will be hostile toward them. 506

hostile forces of nature Hostile forces of nature are what Darwin called any event that impedes survival. Hostile forces of nature include food shortages, diseases, parasites, predators, and extremes of weather. 245

hostility Hostility is a tendency to respond to everyday frustrations with anger and aggression, to become irritable easily, to feel frequent resentment, and to act in a rude, critical, antagonistic, and uncooperative manner in everyday interactions (Dembrowski & Costa, 1987). Hostility is a subtrait in the Type A behavior pattern. 613

human nature Human nature is defined as the traits and mechanisms of personality that are typical of our species and are possessed by everyone or nearly everyone. 11

humanistic tradition Humanistic psychologists emphasize the role of choice in human life, and the influence of responsibility on creating a meaningful and satisfying life. The meaning of any person's life, according to the humanistic approach, is found in the choices that person makes and the responsibility they take for those choices. The humanistic tradition also emphasizes the human need for growth and realizing one's full potential. In the humanistic tradition it is assumed that, if left to their own devices, humans will grow and develop in positive and satisfying directions. 370

i

id The id is the most primitive part of the human mind. Freud saw the id as something we are born with and as the source of all drives and urges. The id is like a spoiled child: selfish, impulsive, and pleasure-loving. According to Freud, the id operates strictly according to the pleasure principle, which is the desire for immediate gratification. 295

id psychology Freud's version of psychoanalysis focused on the id, especially the twin instincts of sex and aggression, and how the ego and superego respond to the demands of the id. Freudian psychoanalysis can thus be called id psychology, to distinguish it from later developments that focused on the functions of the ego. 331

ideal self The self that a person wants to be. 470

identification Identification is a developmental process in children. It consists of wanting to become like the same-sex parent. In classic psychoanalysis, it marks the beginning of the resolution of the Oedipal or Electra conflicts and the successful resolution of the phallic stage of psychosexual development. Freud believed that the resolution of the phallic stage was both the beginning of the superego and morality, as well as the start of the adult gender role. 308

identity conflict According to Baumeister, an identity conflict involves an incompatibility between two or more aspects of identity. This kind of crisis often occurs when a person is forced to make an important and difficult life decision. Identity conflicts are "approach-approach" conflicts, in that the person wants to reach two mutually contradictory goals. Although these conflicts involve wanting two desirable identities, identity conflicts usually involve intense feelings of guilt or remorse over perceived unfaithfulness to an important aspect of the person's identity. 486

identity confusion Identity confusion refers to a period of a person not having a strong sense of who she or he really is in terms of values, careers, relationships, and ideologies. 335

identity crisis Erikson's term "identity crisis" refers to the desperation, anxiety, and confusion a person feels when he or she has not developed a strong sense of identity. A period of identity crisis is a common experience during adolescence, but for some people it occurs later in life, or lasts for a longer period. Baumeister suggests that there are two distinct types of identity crises, which he terms identity deficit and identity conflict. 332

identity deficit According to Baumeister, an identity deficit arises when a person has not formed an adequate identity and thus has trouble making major decisions. When people who have an identity deficit look toward their social identity for guidance in making decisions (e.g., "what would a person like me do in this situation?"), they find little in the way of a foundation upon which to base such life choices. Identity deficits often occur when a person discards old values or goals. 485

identity foreclosure Identity foreclosure occurs when a person does not emerge from a crisis with a firm sense of commitment to values, relationships, or career, but forms an identity without exploring alternatives. An example would be young people who accept the values of their parents or their cultural or religious group without question. 336

idiographic The study of single individuals, with an effort to observe general principles as they are manifest in a single life over time. 13

if . . . then . . . propositions A component of Walter Mischel's theory referring to the notion that, if situation A, the person does X, but if situation B, then the person does Y. Personality leaves its signature, Mischel argues, in terms of the specific situational ingredients that prompt behavior from the person. 415

illness behavior model The illness behavior model suggests that personality influences the degree to which a person perceives and pays attention to bodily sensations, and the degree to which a person will interpret and label those sensations as an illness. 592

imagination inflation effect An imagination inflation effect occurs when a memory is elaborated upon the imagination, leading the person to confuse the imagined event with events that actually happened. 325

implicit motivation Implicit motivation refers to motives as they are measured in fantasy-based (i.e., TAT) techniques, as opposed to direct self-report measures. The implied motives of persons scored, for example, from TAT stories, is thought to reveal their unconscious desires and aspirations, their unspoken needs and wants. McClelland has argued that implicit motives predict long-term behavioral trends over time, such as implicit need for achievement predicting long-term business success. 358

impulsivity A personality trait that refers to lowered self-control, especially in the presence of potentially rewarding activities, the tendency to act before one thinks, and a lowered ability to anticipate the consequences of one's behavior. 220

inclusive fitness theory Modern evolutionary theory, which is based on differential gene reproduction, is also called inclusive fitness theory (Hamilton, 1964). The "inclusive" part refers to the fact that the characteristics that affect reproduction need not affect the personal production of offspring; they can affect the survival and reproduction of genetic relatives as well. 246

independence Markus and Kitayama propose that each person has two fundamental "cultural tasks" that have to be confronted. One such task, agency or independence, involves how you differentiate yourself from the larger group. Independence includes your unique abilities, your personal internal motives and personality dispositions, and the ways in which you separate yourself from the larger group. 564

independence training McClelland believes that certain parental behaviors can promote high achievement motivation, autonomy, and independence in their children. One of these parenting practices is placing an emphasis on independence training. Training a child to be independent in different tasks promotes a sense of mastery and confidence in the child. 364

individual differences Every individual has personal and unique qualities which make them different from others. The study of all the ways in which individuals can differ from others, the number, origin, and meaning of such differences, is the study of individual differences. 12

individualism A sense of self as autonomous and independent, with priority given to personal goals. 565

influential forces Personality traits and mechanisms are influential forces in people's lives in that they influence our actions, how we view ourselves, how we think about the world, how we interact with others, how we feel, our selection of environments (particularly our social environment), what goals and desires we pursue in life, and how we react to our circumstances. Other influential forces include sociological and economic influences, as well as physical and biological forces. 9

information processing Information processing is the transformation of sensory input into mental representations and the manipulation of such representations. 393

infrequency scale A common method for detecting measurement technique problems is to use an infrequency scale embedded within a set of questionnaire items. The infrequency scale contains items that most or all people would answer in a particular way. If a participant answered more than one or two of these unlike the rest of the majority of the participants, a researcher could begin to suspect that the participant's answers do not represent valid information. Such a participant may be answering randomly, may have difficulty reading, or may be marking his or her answer sheet incorrectly. 109

inhibitory control The ability to control inappropriate responses or behaviors. 528

insight In psychoanalysis, through many interpretations, a patient is gradually led to an understanding of the unconscious source of his or her problems. This understanding is called insight. 313

inspection time Inspection time, a variable in intelligence research, refers to the time it takes a person to make a simple discrimination between two displayed objects or two auditory intervals that differ by only a few milliseconds. This variable suggests that brain mechanisms specifically involved in discriminations of extremely brief time intervals represent a sensitive indicator of general intelligence. 418

instincts Freud believed that there were strong innate forces that provided *all* the energy in the psychic system. He called these forces instincts. In Freud's initial formulation there were two fundamental categories of instincts: self-preservation instincts and sexual instincts. In his later formulations, Freud collapsed the self-preservation and sexual instincts into one, which he called the life instinct. 289

instrumentality Instrumentality refers to personality traits that involve working with objects, getting tasks completed in a direct fashion, showing independence from others, and displaying self-sufficiency. 541

integrity testing Because the private sector cannot legally use polygraphs to screen employees, some companies have developed and promoted questionnaire measures to use in place of the polygraph. These questionnaires, called integrity tests, are designed to assess whether a person is generally honest or dishonest. 115

interactional model The interactional model suggests that objective events happen to a person, but that personality factors determine the impact of those events by influencing the person's ability to cope. This is called the interactional model because personality is assumed to moderate (that is, influence) the relation between stress and illness. 589

interdependence Markus and Kitayama propose that each person has two fundamental "cultural tasks" that have to be confronted. The first is communion or interdependence. This cultural task involves how you are affiliated with, attached to, or engaged in the larger group of which you are a member. Interdependence includes your relationships with other members of the group and your embeddedness within the group. 564

internal locus of control An internal locus of control refers to the generalized expectancy that reinforcing events are under one's control, and that one is responsible for the major outcomes in life. 406

internalized In object relations theory, a child will create an unconscious mental representation of his or her mother. This allows the child to have a relationship with this internalized "object" even in the absence of the "real" mother. The relationship object internalized by the child is based on his or her developing relationship with the mother. This image then forms the fundamentals for how children come to view others with whom they develop subsequent relationships. 341

interpersonal traits Interpersonal traits pertain to what people do to and with each other. They include *temperament* traits, such as nervous, gloomy, sluggish, and excitable; *character* traits, such as moral, principled, and dishonest; *material* traits, such as miserly or stingy; *attitude* traits, such as pious or spiritual; *mental* traits, such as clever, logical, and perceptive; and *physical* traits, such as healthy and tough. 79

interpretation Interpretation is one of the three levels of cognition that are of interest to personality psychologists. Interpretation is the making sense of, or explaining, various events in the world. Psychoanalysts offer patients interpretations of the psychodynamic causes of their problems. Through many interpretations, patients are gradually led to an understanding of the unconscious source of their problems. 313, 394

inter-rater reliability Inter-rater reliability involves the use of multiple observers to gather information about a person's personality and then allows investigators to evaluate the degree of consensus among the observers. When different observers agree with one another, the degree of inter-rater reliability increases. When different raters fail to agree, the measure is said to have low inter-rater reliability. 30

intersexual selection In Darwin's intersexual selection, members of one sex choose a mate based on their preferences for particular qualities in that mate. These characteristics evolve because animals that possess them are chosen more often as mates, and their genes thrive. Animals that lack the desired characteristics are excluded from mating, and their genes perish. 245

intrapsychic domain This domain deals with mental mechanisms of personality, many of which operate outside the realm of conscious awareness. The predominant theory in this domain is Freud's theory of psychoanalysis. This theory begins with fundamental assumptions about the instinctual system—the sexual and aggressive forces that are presumed to drive and energize much of human activity. The intrapsychic domain also includes defense mechanisms such as repression, denial, and projection. 17

intrasexual competition In Darwin's intrasexual competition, members of the same sex compete with each other, and the outcome of their contest gives the winner greater sexual access to members of the opposite sex. Two stags locking horns in combat is the prototypical image of this. The characteristics that lead to success in contests of this kind, such as greater strength, intelligence, or attractiveness to allies, evolve because the victors are able to mate more often and hence pass on more genes. 245

j

job analysis When assisting a business in hiring for a particular job, a psychologist typically starts by analyzing the requirements of the job. The psychologist might interview employees who work in the job or supervisors who are involved in managing the particular job. The psychologist might observe workers in the job, noting any particular oral, written, performance, or social skills needed. He or she may also take into account both the physical and social aspects of the work environment in an effort to identify any special pressures or responsibilities associated with the job. Based on this job analysis, the psychologist develops some hypotheses about the kinds of abilities and personality traits that might best equip a person to perform well in that job. 124

k

kinesthetic figural aftereffect (KFA) In Petrie's kinesthetic figural aftereffect (KFA), subjects are blindfolded and presented with different sized wooden blocks. One block is a long wedge, and subjects can slide the fingers of one hand up and down the wedge. Using the other hand, participants are presented with wooden rectangular blocks of different size. Participants are asked to feel the width of a rectangular block with the other hand, and slide their other hand up the wooden wedge until they judge that the width of the wedge is equal to the width of the wooden block in their other hand. The KFA is a measure of individual differences in sensory reducing-augmenting. 400

l

latency stage The latency stage is the fourth stage in Freud's psychosexual stages of development. This stage occurs from around the age of six until puberty. Freud believed few specific sexual conflicts existed during this time, and was thus a period of psychological rest or latency. Subsequent psychoanalysts have argued that much development occurs during this time, such as learning to make decisions for oneself, interacting and making friends with others, developing an identity, and learning the meaning of work. The latency period ends with the sexual awakening brought about by puberty. 308

latent content The latent content of a dream is, according to Freud, what the elements of the dream actually represent. 311

learned helplessness Learned helplessness refers to the finding that animals (including humans), when subjected to unpleasant and inescapable circumstances, often become passive and accepting of their situation, in effect learning to be helpless. Researchers surmised that if people were in an unpleasant or painful situation, they would attempt to change the situation. However, if repeated attempts to change the situation failed, they would resign themselves to being helpless. Then, even if the situation did improve so that they could escape the discomfort, they would continue to act helpless. 407

leukocyte A leukocyte is a white blood cell. When there is an infection or injury to the body, or a systematic inflammation of the body occurs, there is an elevation in white blood cell counts. Surtees et al., in a 2003 study, have established a direct link between hostility and elevated white blood cell counts. 616

lexical approach The approach to determining the fundamental personality traits by analyzing language. For example, a trait adjective that has many synonyms probably represents a more fundamental trait than a trait adjective with few synonyms. 67

lexical hypothesis The lexical hypothesis—on which the lexical approach is based—states that important individual differences have become encoded within the natural language. Over ancestral time, the differences between people that were important were noticed and words were invented to communicate about those differences. 67, 581

libido Freud postulated that humans have a fundamental instinct toward destruction and that this instinct is often manifest in aggression toward others. The two instincts were usually referred to as libido, for the life instinct, and thanatos, for the death instinct. While the libido was generally considered sexual in nature, Freud also used this term to refer to any need-satisfying, life-sustaining, or pleasure-oriented urge. 289

life-outcome data (L-data) Life-outcome data, or L-data, refers to information that can be gleaned from the events, activities, and outcomes in a person's life that are available to public scrutiny. For example, marriages and divorces are a matter of public record. Personality psychologists can sometimes secure information about the clubs, if any, a person joins; how many speeding tickets a person has received in the last few years; whether they own a handgun. These can all serve as sources of information about personality. 38

Likert rating scale In using questionnaires, participants answer each item using the response options provided. These response options are in the form of various rating scales. One example is "true or false" as a rating scale. A common rating scale is called the Likert scale, and it provides numbers that are attached to descriptive phrases, such as 0 = disagree strongly, 1 = disagree slightly, 2 = neither agree nor disagree, 3 = agree slightly, 4 = strongly agree. 28

limbic system The limbic system is that part of the brain responsible for emotion and the "flight-fight" reaction. If some individuals have a limbic system that is easily activated, then we might expect such persons to have frequent episodes of emotion, particularly those emotions associated with flight (such as anxiety, fear, worry) and those associated with fight (such as anger, irritation, annoyance). Eysenck postulated that the limbic system was the source of the trait of neuroticism. 442

locus of control Locus of control is a concept that describes a person's perception of responsibility for the events in his or her life. It refers to whether people tend to locate that responsibility internally, within themselves, or externally, in fate, luck, or chance. Locus of control research started in the mid-1950s when Rotter was developing his social learning theory. 404

longitudinal study A longitudinal study examines individuals over time. Longitudinal studies have been conducted that have spanned as many as four and five decades of life and have examined many different age brackets. These studies are costly and difficult to conduct, but the information gained about personality development is valuable. 145

m

Machiavellianism Machiavellianism is a manipulative strategy of social interaction referring to the tendency to use other people as tools for personal gain. "High Mach" persons tend to tell people what they want to hear, use flattery to get what they want, and rely heavily on lying and deception to achieve their own ends. 514

major life events According to Holmes and Rahe, major life events require that people make major adjustments in their lives. Death or loss of a spouse through divorce or separation are the most stressful events, followed closely by being jailed, loosing a close family member in death, or being severely injured. 595

manifest content The manifest content of a dream is, according to Freud, what the dream actually contains. 311

manipulation Researchers conducting experiments use manipulation in order to evaluate the influence of one variable (the manipulated or independent variable) on another (the dependent variable). 44, 106, 511

manipulation in interpersonal interactions Manipulation is a form of person-situation interaction that can be defined as the various means by which people intentionally or purposefully alter, change, and exploit others. Manipulation differs from selection in that selection involves choosing existing environments, whereas manipulation entails altering those environments already inhabited. No evil or malicious intent need be implied by the term "manipulation," although such intent is not excluded either. 511

masculine and feminine Masculine and feminine refer to traits or roles typically associated with being male or female in a particular culture. 339

masculinity and femininity Traits that define the cultural roles associated with being male or female. Two major personality instruments were published in 1974 to assess people using this new conception of sex roles (Bem, 1974; Spence, Helmreich, & Stapp, 1974). The masculinity scales contained items reflecting assertiveness, boldness, dominance, self-sufficiency, and instrumentality. The femininity scales contained items that reflected nurturance, expression of emotions, and empathy. Masculinity and femininity are traits that refer to gender roles, as distinct from biological sex. 538

maximalist Those who describe sex differences as comparable in magnitude to effect sizes in other areas of psychology, important to consider, and recommend that they should not be trivialized. 527

mean level change Within a single group that has been tested on two separate occasions, any difference in group averages across the two occasions is considered a mean level change. 139

mean level stability Mean level stability refers to a population maintaining a consistent average level of a trait or characteristic over time. If the average level of liberalism or conservatism in a population remains the same with increasing age, we say that the population exhibits high mean level stability on that characteristic. If the average degree of political orientation changes, then we say that the population is displaying mean level change. 139

minimalist Those who describe sex differences as small and inconsequential. 527

modeling By seeing another person engage in a particular behavior with positive results, the observer is more likely to imitate that behavior. It is a form of learning whereby the consequences for a particular behavior are observed, and thus the new behavior is learned. 413

molecular genetics Molecular genetics techniques are designed to identify the specific genes associated with specific traits, such as personality traits. The most common method, called the association method, identifies whether individuals with a particular gene (or allele) have higher or lower scores on a particular trait measure. 198

monoamine oxidase (MAO) Monoamine oxidase (MAO) is an enzyme found in the blood that is known to regulate neurotransmitters, those chemicals that carry messages between nerve cells. MAO may be a causal factor in the personality trait of sensation seeking. 228

monozygotic twins Monozygotic twins are identical twins that come from a single fertilized egg (or zygote, hence monozygotic) that divides into two at some point during gestation. Identical twins are always the same sex because they are genetically identical. 182

mood induction In experimental studies of mood, mood inductions are employed as manipulations in order to determine whether the mood differences (e.g., pleasant versus unpleasant) effect some dependent variable. In studies of personality, mood effects might interact with personality variables. For example, positive mood effects might be stronger for persons high on extraversion, and negative mood effects might be stronger for persons high on neuroticism. 440

mood variability Mood variability refers to frequent fluctuations in a person's emotional life over time. 456

moral anxiety Moral anxiety is caused by a conflict between the id or the ego and the superego. For example, a person who suffers from chronic shame or feelings of guilt over not living up to "proper" standards, even though such standards might not be attainable, is experiencing moral anxiety. 298

moratorium In terms of identity development, a moratorium is the time taken to explore options before making a commitment to an identity. College can be considered a "time out" from life, in which students may explore a variety of roles, relationships, and responsibilities before having to commit to any single life path. 336

morningness–eveningness Refers to stable differences between persons in preferences for being active at different times of the day. The term "morningness–eveningness" was coined to refer to this dimension (Horne & Osterberg, 1976). Differences between morning-and evening-types of persons appear to be due to differences in the length of their underlying circadian biological rhythms. 231

motivated unconscious The motivated unconscious refers to the psychoanalytic idea that information that is unconscious (e.g., a repressed wish) can actually motivate or influence subsequent behavior. This notion was promoted by Freud, and formed the basis for his ideas about the unconscious sources of mental disorders and other problems with living. While many psychologists agree with the idea of the unconscious, there is less agreement today about whether information that is unconscious can have much of an influence on actual behavior. 292, 330

motives Motives refer to internal states that arouse and direct behavior toward specific objects or goals. A motive is often caused by a deficit, by the lack of something. Motives differ from each other in type, amount, and intensity, depending on the person and his or her circumstances. Motives are based on needs and propel people to perceive, think, and act in specific ways that serve to satisfy those needs. 352

multi-motive grid The multi-motive grid, designed to assess motives, uses 14 pictures representing achievement, power, or intimacy and a series of questions about important motivational states to elicit answers from test subjects. In theory, the motives elicited from the photographs would influence how the subject answers the test questions. 360

multiple intelligences Howard Gardner's theory of multiple intelligences includes several forms: interpersonal intelligence (social skills, ability to communicate and get along with others), intrapersonal intelligence (insight into oneself, one's emotions and motives), kinesthetic intelligence (the abilities of athletes, dancers, and acrobats), and musical intelligence. There are several other theories proposing multiple forms of intelligence. This position is in contrast to the theory of "g," or general intelligence, which holds that there is only one form of intelligence. 417

multiple social personalities Each of us displays different sides of ourselves to different people—we may be kind to our friends, ruthless to our enemies, loving toward a spouse, and conflicted toward our parents. Our social personalities vary from one setting to another, depending on the nature of relationships we have with other individuals. 31

Myers-Briggs Type Indicator (MBTI) One of the most widely used personality tests in the business world. The Myers-Briggs Type Indicator was developed by a mother-daughter team, Katherine Briggs and Isabel Myers, based on Jungian concepts. The test provides information about personality types by testing for eight fundamental preferences using questions in a "forced-choice" or either/or format. Individuals must respond in one way or another, even if their preferences might be somewhere in the middle. Although the test is not without criticism, it has great intuitive appeal. 125

n

narcissism Narcissism is a style of inflated self-admiration and the constant attempt to draw attention to the self and to keep others focused on oneself. Although narcissism can be carried to extremes, narcissistic tendencies can be found in normal range levels. 340, 517

narcissistic paradox The narcissistic paradox refers to the fact that, although a narcissistic person appears to have high self-esteem, they actually have doubts about their self-worth. While they appear to have a grandiose sense of self-importance, narcissists are nevertheless very fragile and vulnerable to blows to their self-esteem and cannot handle criticism well. They need constant praise, reassurance, and attention from others, whereas a person with truly high self-esteem would not need such constant praise and attention from others. 340, 639

narcissistic personality disorder The calling card of the narcissistic personality is a strong need to be admired, a strong sense of self-importance, and a lack of insight into other people's feelings. Narcissists see themselves in a very favorable light, inflating their accomplishments and undervaluing the work of others. Narcissists daydream about prosperity, victory, influence, adoration from others, and power. They routinely expect adulation from others, believing that homage is generally long overdue. They exhibit feelings of entitlement, even though they have done nothing in particular to earn that special treatment. 639

natural selection Darwin reasoned that variants that better enabled an organism to survive and reproduce would lead to more descendants. The descendants, therefore, would inherit the variants that led to their ancestors' survival and reproduction. Through this process, the successful variants were selected, and unsuccessful variants weeded out. Natural selection, therefore, results in gradual changes in a species over time, as successful variants increase in frequency and eventually spread throughout the gene pool, replacing the less successful variants. 244

naturalistic observation In naturalistic observation, observers witness and record events that occur in the normal course of the lives of their participants. For example, a child might be followed throughout an entire day, or an observer may record behavior in the home of the participant. Naturalistic observation offers researchers the advantage of being able to secure information in the realistic context of a person's everyday life, but at the cost of not being able to control the events and behavioral samples witnessed. 31

nature-nurture debate The nature-nurture debate is the ongoing debate as to whether genes or environments are more important determinants of personality. 179

need for achievement The need for achievement, according to McClelland, is the desire to do better, to be successful, and to feel competent. A person with a high need for achievement obtains satisfaction from accomplishing a task or from the anticipation of accomplishing a task. They cherish the process of being engaged in a challenging task. 360

need for intimacy McAdams defines the need for intimacy as the "recurrent preference or readiness for warm, close, and communicative interaction with others" (1990, p. 198). People with a high need for intimacy want more intimacy and meaningful human contact in their day-to-day lives than do those with a low need for intimacy. 368

need for power Winter defines the need for power as a preference for having an impact on other people. Individuals with a high need for power are interested in controlling situations and other people. 366

needs Needs refer to states of tension within a person; as a need is satisfied, the state of tension is reduced. Usually the state of tension is caused by the lack of something (for example, a lack of food causes a need to eat). 352

negative affectivity Includes components such as anger, sadness, difficulty, and amount of distress. 529

negative identity In resolving their identity crises, some people develop negative identities, identities founded on undersirable social roles, such as "gangstas," girlfriends of street toughs, or members of street gangs. 335

negligent hiring A charge sometimes brought against an employer for hiring someone who is unstable or prone to violence. Employers are defending themselves against such suits which often seek compensation for crimes committed by their employees. Such cases hinge on whether the employer should have discovered dangerous traits ahead of time, before hiring such a person into a position where he or she posed a threat to others. Personality testing may provide evidence that the employer did in fact try to reasonably investigate an applicant's fitness for the workplace. 119

neurotic anxiety Neurotic anxiety occurs when there is a direct conflict between the id and the ego. The danger is that the ego may lose control over some unacceptable desire of the id. For example, a man who worries excessively that he might blurt out some unacceptable thought or desire in public is beset by neurotic anxiety. 298

neurotic paradox The neurotic paradox refers to the fact that people with disorders or other problems with living often exhibit behaviors that exacerbate, rather than lessen, their problems. For example, borderline personality disordered persons, who are generally concerned with being abandoned by friends and intimate others, may throw temper tantrums or otherwise express anger and rage in a manner that drives people away. The paradox refers to doing behaviors that make their situation worse. 646

neuroticism Neuroticism is one of the "Big Five" dimensions of personality, and is present, in some form, in every major trait theory of personality. Different researchers have used different terms for neuroticism, such as emotional instability, anxiety-proneness, and negative affectivity. Adjectives useful for describing persons high on the trait of neuroticism include moody, touchy, irritable, anxious, unstable, pessimistic, and complaining. 442

neurotransmitter Neurotransmitters are those chemicals in the nerve cells that are responsible for the transmission of a nerve impulse from one cell to another. Some theories of personality are based directly on different amounts of neurotransmitters found in the nervous system. 228

neurotransmitter theory of depression According to the neurotransmitter theory of depression, an imbalance of the neurotransmitters at the synapses of the nervous system causes depression. Some medications used to treat depression target these specific neurotransmitters. Not all people with depression are treated successfully with drugs. That suggests that there may be varieties of depression; some are biologically based, while others are more reactive to stress, physical exercise, or cognitive therapy. 449

nomothetic The study of general characters of people as they are distributed in the population, typically involving statistical comparisons between individuals or groups. 13

noncontent responding Noncontent responding, also referred to as the concept of response sets, refers to the tendency of some people to respond to the questions on some basis that is unrelated to the question content. One example is the response set of acquiescence or yea saying. This is the tendency to simply agree with the questionnaire items, regardless of the content of those items. 111

nonshared environment Nonshared environment is a concept referring to features of the environment that siblings do not share. Some children might get special or different treatment from their parents, they might have different groups of friends, they might be sent to different schools, or one might go to summer camp while the other stays home each summer. These features are called "nonshared" because they are experienced differently by different siblings. 193

norepinephrine Norepinephrine is a neurotransmitter involved in activating the sympathetic nervous system for flight or fight. 229

novelty seeking In Cloninger's tridimensional personality model, the personality trait of novelty seeking is based on low levels of dopamine. Low levels of dopamine create a drive state to obtain substances or experiences that increase dopamine. Novelty and thrills and excitement can make up for low levels of dopamine, and so novelty seeking behavior is thought to result from low levels of this neurotransmitter. 229

O

objectifying cognitions Processing information by relating it to objective facts. This style of thinking stands in contrast to personalizing cognitions. 393

objective anxiety Objective anxiety (fear) occurs in response to some real, external threat to the person. For example, being confronted by a large, aggressive-looking man with a knife while taking a shortcut through an alley would elicit objective anxiety (fear) in most people. 298

objective self-awareness Objective self-awareness is seeing oneself as an object of others' attention. Often, objective self-awareness is experienced as shyness, and for some people this is a chronic problem. Although objective self-awareness can lead to periods of social sensitivity, this ability to consider oneself from an outside perspective is the beginning of a social identity. 469

object relations theory Object relations theory places an emphasis on early childhood relationships. While this theory has several versions that differ from each other in emphasis, all the versions have at their core a set of basic assumptions: that the internal wishes, desires, and urges of the child are not as important as his or her developing relationships with significant external others, particularly parents, and that the others, particularly the mother, become internalized by the child in the form of mental objects. 341

observer-report data (O-data) Observer-report data are the impressions and evaluations others make of a person whom they come into contact with. For every individual, there are dozens of observers who form such impressions. Observer-report methods capitalize on these sources and provide tools for gathering information about a person's personality. Observers may have access to information not attainable through other sources, and multiple observers can be used to assess each individual. Typically, a more valid and reliable assessment of personality can be achieved when multiple observers are used. 30

obsessive-compulsive personality disorder The obsessive-compulsive personality is preoccupied with order and strives to be perfect. The high need for order can manifest itself in the person's attention to details, however trivial, and fondness for rules, rituals, schedules, and procedures. Another characteristic is a devotion to work at the expense of leisure and friendships. Obsessive-compulsive persons tend to work harder than they need to. 650

Oedipal conflict For boys, the main conflict in the Freud's phallic stage is the Oedipal conflict. It is a boy's unconscious wish to have his mother all to himself by eliminating the father. (Oedipus is a character in a Greek myth who unknowingly kills his father and marries his mother). 308

Openness Openness is the fifth personality trait in the Five-Factor Model, a model which has proven to be replicable in studies using English language trait words as items. Some of the key adjective markers for Openness are "creative," "imaginative," "intellectual." Those who rate high on openness tend to remember their dreams more and have vivid, prophetic, or problem-solving dreams. 88

optimal level of arousal Hebb's believed that people are motivated to reach an optimal level of arousal. If they are underaroused relative to this level, an increase in arousal is rewarding; conversely, if they are overaroused, a decrease in arousal is rewarding. By optimal level of arousal Hebb meant a level that is "just right" for any given task. 224

optimistic bias Most people generally underestimate their risks, with the average person rating their risks as below what is the true average. This has been refereed to as the optimistic bias, and it may actually lead people in general to ignore or minimize the risks inherent in life or to take more risks than they should. 604

optimistic explanatory style An explanatory style that emphasizes external, temporary, and specific causes of events. 410

oral stage The oral stage is the first stage in Freud's psychosexual stages of development. This stage occurs during the initial 18 months after birth. During this time, the main sources of pleasure and tension reduction are the mouth, lips, and tongue. Adults who still obtain pleasure from "taking in," especially through the mouth (e.g., people who overeat or smoke or talk too much) might be fixated at this stage. 307

organized and enduring "Organized" means that the psychological traits and mechanisms for a given person are not simply a random collection of elements. Rather, personality is coherent because the mechanisms and traits are linked to one another in an organized fashion. "Enduring" means that the psychological traits are generally consistent over time, particularly in adulthood, and over situations. 8

orthogonality Discussed in terms of circumplex models, orthogonality specifies that traits that are perpendicular to each other on the model (at 90 degrees of separation, or at right angles to each other) are unrelated to each other. In general, the term "orthogonal" is used to describe a zero correlation between traits. 81

ought self A person's understanding of what others want them to be. 470

P

pain tolerance Pain tolerance is the degree to which people can tolerate pain, which shows wide differences between persons. Petrie believed that individual differences in pain tolerance originated in the nervous system. She developed a theory that people with low pain tolerance had a nervous system that amplified or augmented the subjective impact sensory input. In contrast, people who could tolerate pain well were thought to have a nervous system that dampened or reduced the effects of sensory stimulation. 399

paranoid personality disorder The paranoid personality is extremely distrustful of others and sees others as a constant threat. Such a person assumes that others are out to exploit and deceive them, even though there is no good evidence to support this assumption. Paranoid personalities feel that they have been injured by other persons and are preoccupied with doubts about the motivations of others. The paranoid personality often misinterprets social events and holds resentments toward others for slights or perceived insults. 646

parsimony The fewer premises and assumptions a theory contains, the greater its parsimony. This does not mean that simple theories are always better than complex ones. Due to the complexity of the human personality, a complex theory, that is, one containing many premises, may ultimately be necessary for adequate personality theories. 21

passive, reactive, and active forms of genotype-environment correlation Passive genotype-environment correlation occurs when parents provide both genes and environment to children, yet the children do nothing to obtain that environment. Reactive genotype-environment correlation occurs when parents (or others) respond to children differently, depending on their genotype. Active genotype-environment correlation occurs when a person with a particular genotype creates or seeks out a particular environment. 196

penis envy The female counterpart of castration anxiety, which occurs during the phallic stage of psychosexual development for girls around 3 to 5 years of age. 308

people-things dimension Brian Little's people-things dimension of personality refers to the nature of vocational interests. Those at the "things" end of the dimension like vocations that deal with impersonal tasks—machines, tools, or materials. Examples include a carpenter, auto mechanic, building contractor, tool maker, or farmer. Those scoring toward the "people" end of the dimension prefer social occupations that involve thinking about others, caring for others, or directing others. Examples include a high school teacher, social worker, or religious counselor. 535

percentage of variance Percentage of variance refers to the fact that individuals vary or are different from each other, and this variability can be partitioned into percentages that are related to separate causes or separate variables. An example is the percentages of variance in some trait that are related to genetics, the shared environment, and the unshared environment. Another example would be the percentage of variance in happiness scores that are related to various demographic variables, such as income, gender, and age. 177

perception Perception is one of the three levels of cognition that are of interest to personality psychologists. Perception is the process of imposing order on the information our sense organs take in. Even at the level of perception, what we "see" in the world can be quite different from person to person. 393

perceptual sensitivity The ability to detect subtle stimuli from the environment. 529

person-environment interaction A person's interactions with situations include perceptions, selections, evocations, and manipulations. *Perceptions* refer to how we "see" or interpret an environment. *Selection* describes the manner in which we choose situations—such as our friends, our hobbies, our college classes, and our careers. *Evocations* refer to the reactions we produce in others, often quite unintentionally. *Manipulations* refer to the ways in which we attempt to influence others. 9

person-situation interaction The person-situation interaction trait theory states that one has to take into account both particular situations (e.g., frustration) and personality traits (e.g., hot temper) when understanding a behavior. 101

personal construct A personal construct is a belief or concept that summarizes a set of observations or version of reality, unique to an individual, which that person routinely uses to interpret and predict events. 403

personal project A personal project is a set of relevant actions intended to achieve a goal that a person has selected. Psychologist Brian Little believes that personal projects make natural units for understanding the working of personality, because they reflect how people face up to the serious business of navigating through daily life. 411

personal unconscious According to Carl Jung, the personal unconscious developed from a person's own unique experiences. 291

personality The set of psychological traits and mechanisms within the individual that are organized and relatively enduring and that influence his or her interactions with, and adaptations to, the environment (including the intrapsychic, physical, and social environment). 4

personality coherence Personality coherence is defined as changes in the manifestations of personality variables over time, even as the underlying characteristics remain stable. The notion of personality coherence includes both elements of continuity and elements of change: continuity in the underlying trait but change in the outward manifestation of that trait. For example, an emotionally unstable child might frequently cry and throw temper tantrums, whereas as an adult such a person might frequently worry and complain. The manifestation might change, even though the trait stays stable. 139

personality-descriptive nouns As described by Saucier, personality-descriptive nouns differ in their content emphases from personality taxonomies based on adjectives and may be more precise. In Saucier's 2003 work on personality nouns, he discovered eight factors, including "Dumbell," "Babe/Cutie," "Philosopher," "Lawbreaker," "Joker," and "Jock." 90

personality development Personality development is the continuities, consistencies, and stabilities in people over time, and the ways in which people change over time. 138

personality disorder A personality disorder is an enduring pattern of experience and behavior that differs greatly from the expectations of the individual's culture. The disorder is usually manifest in more than one of the following areas: the way a person thinks, feels, gets along with others, or controls personal behavior. To be classed as a personality disorder, the pattern must NOT result from drug abuse, medication, or a medical condition such as head trauma. 625

personalizing cognition Processing information by relating it to a similar event in your own life. This style of processing information occurs when a person interprets a new event in a personally relevant manner. For example, they might see a car accident and start thinking about the time they were in a car accident. 393

personnel selection Employers sometimes use personality tests to select people especially suitable for a specific job. Alternatively, the employer may want to use personality assessments to de-select, or screen out, people with specific traits. In both cases an employer is concerned with selecting the right person for a specific position from among a pool of applicants. 118

perspective taking A final unfolding of the self-concept during the teen years involves perspective taking; the ability to take the perspectives of others, or to see oneself as others do, to step outside of one's self and imagine how one appears to other people. This is why many teenagers go through a period of extreme self-consciousness during this time, focusing much of their energy on how they appear to others. 469

pessimistic explanatory style The pessimistic explanatory style puts a person at risk for feelings of helplessness and poor adjustment, and emphasizes internal, stable, and global causes for bad events. It is the opposite of optimistic explanatory style. 410

phallic stage The phallic stage is the third stage in Freud's psychosexual stages of development. It occurs between three and five years of age, during which time the child discovers that he has (or she discovers that she does not have) a penis. This stage also includes the awakening of sexual desire directed, according to Freud, toward the parent of the opposite sex. 307

phenotypic variance Phenotypic variance refers to observed individual differences, such as in height, weight, or personality. 178

physiological needs At the base of Maslow's need hierarchy are the physiological needs. These include those needs that are of prime importance to the immediate survival of the individual (the need for food, water, air, sleep) as well as to the long-term survival of the species (the need for sex). 371

physiological systems Physiological systems are organ systems within the body. For example the nervous system (including the brain and nerves), the cardiac system (including the heart, arteries, and veins), and the musculoskeletal system (including the muscles and bones which make all movements and behaviors possible). 208

pleasure principle The pleasure principle is based on the desire for immediate gratification. The id operates according to the pleasure principle; therefore, it does not listen to reason, does not follow logic, has no values or morals (other than immediate gratification), and has very little patience. 296

positive illusions Some researchers believe that part of being happy is to have positive illusions about the self—an inflated view of one's own characteristics as a good, able, and desirable person—as this characteristic appears to be part of emotional well-being (Taylor, 1989; Taylor et al., 2000). 431

positive reappraisal Positive reappraisal refers to a cognitive process whereby a person focuses on the good in what is happening or has happened to them. Folkman and Moskowitz note that forms of this positive coping strategy include seeing opportunities for personal growth or seeing how one's own efforts can benefit other people. 602

positive regard According to Rogers, all children are born wanting to be loved and accepted by their parents and others. He called this in-born need the desire for positive regard. 377

positive self-regard According to Rogers, people who have received positive regard from others develop a sense of positive self-regard; they accept themselves, even their own weaknesses and shortcomings. A person with high positive self-regard would trust themselves, follow their own interests, and rely on their feelings to guide themselves to do the right thing. 378

possible selves The notion of possible selves can be viewed in a number of ways, but two are especially important. The first pertains to the desired self—the person we wish to become. The second pertains to our feared self—the sort of person we do not wish to become. 470

post modernism In personality psychology, post modernism is the notion that reality is a construct, that every person and culture has its own unique version of reality, and that no single version of reality is more valid or more privileged than another. 403

post-traumatic stress disorder (PTSD) Post-traumatic stress disorder or "PTSD" is a syndrome that occurs in some individuals after experiencing or witnessing life-threatening events, such as military combat, natural disasters, terrorist attacks, serious accidents, or violent personal assaults, e.g., rape. Those who suffer from PTSD often relive the trigger experience for years through nightmares or intense flashbacks; have difficulty sleeping; report physical complaints; have flattened emotions; and feel detached or estranged from others. These symptoms can be severe and last long enough to significantly impair the individual's daily life, health, relationships, and career. 599

power stress According to David McClelland, when people do not get their way, or when their power is challenged or blocked, they are likely to show strong stress responses or "power stress." This stress has been linked to diminished immune function and increased illness in longitudinal studies. 367

preconscious Any information that a person is not presently aware of, but that could easily be retrieved and made conscious, is found in the preconscious mind. 290

predictive validity Predictive validity refers to whether a test predicts some criteria external to the test. Scales that successfully predict what they

should predict have high predictive validity. 42
predisposition model In health psychology, the predisposition model suggests that associations may exist between personality and illness because a third variable is causing them both. 591
prefrontal cortex The prefrontal cortex of the brain has been found to be highly active in the control of emotions. Many people who have committed violent acts exhibit a neurological deficit in the frontal areas, portions of the brain assumed to be responsible for regulating negative emotions. 443
press Murray used the term press to refer to need-relevant aspects of the environment. A person's need for intimacy, for example, won't affect that person's behavior without an appropriate environmental press (such as the presence of friendly people). 356
prevalence Prevalence refers to the total number of cases that are present within a given population during a particular period of time. 653
prevention focus One focus of self-regulation where the person is concerned with protection, safety, and the prevention of negative outcomes and failures. Behaviors with a prevention focus are characterized by vigilance, caution, and attempts to prevent negative outcomes. 414
Price Waterhouse v. Hopkins A Supreme Court case in which Ann Hopkins sued her employer, Price Waterhouse, claiming that they had discriminated against her on the basis of sex in violation of Title VII of the Civil Rights Act, on the theory that her promotion denial had been based on sexual stereotyping. The Supreme Court accepted the argument that gender stereotyping does exist and that it can create a bias against women in the workplace that is not permissible under Title VII of the Civil Rights Act. By court order Ann Hopkins was made a full partner in her accounting firm. 120
primary appraisal According to Lazarus, in order for stress to be evoked for a person, two cognitive events must occur. The first cognitive event, called the primary appraisal, is for the person to perceive that the event is a threat to their personal goals. See also secondary appraisal. 599
primary process thinking Primary process thinking is thinking without the logical rules of conscious thought or an anchor in reality. Dreams and fantasies are examples of primary process thinking. Although primary process thought does not follow the normal rules of reality (e.g., in dreams people might fly or walk through walls), Freud believed there were principles at work in primary process thought and that these principles could be discovered. 296
priming Priming makes associated material more accessible to conscious awareness than material that is not primed. Research using subliminal primes demonstrates that information can get into the mind, and have some influence on it, without going through conscious experience. 330
private self-concept The development of an inner, private self-concept is a major but often difficult development in the growth of the self-concept. It may start out with children developing an imaginary friend, someone only they can see or hear. This imaginary friend may actually be children's first attempt to communicate to their parents that they know there is a secret part, an inner part, to their understanding of their self. Later children develop the full realization that only they have access to their own thoughts, feelings, and desires, and that no one else can know this part of themselves unless they choose to tell them. 467
problem-focused coping Problem-focused coping refers to thoughts and behaviors that manage or solve the underlying cause of stress. Folkman and Moskowitz note that focusing on solving problems, even little ones, can give a person a positive sense of control even in the most stressful and uncontrollable circumstances. 602
projection Projection is a defense mechanism based on the notion that sometimes we see in others those traits and desires that we find most upsetting in ourselves. We literally "project" (i.e., attribute) our own unacceptable qualities onto others. 304
projective hypothesis The idea that what a person "sees" in an ambiguous figure, such as an inkblot, reflects his or her personality is called the projective hypothesis. People are thought to project their own personalities into what they report seeing in such ambiguous stimulus. 312
projective techniques In projective techniques, a person is presented with an ambiguous stimulus and is then asked to impose some order on the stimulus, such as asking them what they see in an inkblot. What the person sees is interpreted to reveal something about his or her personality. The person presumably "projects" his or her concerns, conflicts, traits, and ways of seeing or dealing with the world onto the ambiguous stimulus. The most famous projective technique for assessing personality is the Rorschach inkblot test. 36
promotion focus One focus of self-regulation where the person is concerned with advancement, growth, and accomplishments. Behaviors with a promotion focus are characterized by eagerness, approach, and "going for the gold." 414
psychic energy According to Sigmund Freud, there is a source of energy, psychic energy, within each person that motivates them to do one thing and not another. In Freud's view, it is this energy that motivates all human activity. 288
psychoanalysis Psychoanalysis is a theory of personality and is also a method of psychotherapy (a technique for helping individuals who are experiencing some mental disorder or even relatively minor problems with living). Psychoanalysis can be thought of as a theory about the major components and mechanisms of personality, as well as a method for deliberately restructuring personality. 309
psychological mechanisms Psychological mechanisms are like traits, except that mechanisms refer more to the *processes* of personality. For example, most personality mechanisms involve some information-processing activity. A psychological mechanism may make people more sensitive to certain kinds of information from the environment (input), may make them more likely to think about specific options (decision rules), or may guide their behavior toward certain categories of action (outputs). 7

psychological traits Psychological traits are characteristics that describe ways in which people are unique or different from or similar to each other. Psychological traits include all sorts of aspects of persons that are psychologically meaningful and are stable and consistent aspects of personality. 6

psychological types A term growing out of Carl Jung's theory implying that people come in types or distinct categories of personality, such as "extraverted types." This view is not widely endorsed by academic or research-oriented psychologists, since most personality traits are normally distributed in the population and are best conceived as dimensions of difference, not categories. 126

psychopathology Psychopathology is the study of mental disorders that combines statistical, social, and psychological approaches to diagnosing individual abnormality. 625

psychopathy A term often used synonymously with the antisocial personality disorder. It is used to refer to individual differences in antisocial characteristics. 274

psychosexual stage theory According to Freud's psychosexual stage theory, all persons pass through a set series of stages in personality development. At each of the first three stages, young children must face and resolve specific conflicts, which revolve around ways of obtaining a type of sexual gratification. Children seek sexual gratification at each stage by investing libidinal energy in a specific body part. Each stage in the developmental process is named after the body part in which sexual energy is invested. 306

psychosocial conflicts As posited by Erik Erikson, psychosocial conflicts occur throughout a person's lifetime and contribute to the ongoing development of personality. He defined psychosocial conflicts as the crises of learning to trust our parents, learning to be autonomous from them, and learning from them how to act as an adult. 333

r

race or gender norming The Civil Rights Act of 1991 forbids employers from using different norms or cut-off scores for different groups of people. For example, it would be illegal for a company to set a higher threshold for women than men on their selection test. 122

random assignment Random assignment in an experiment is assignment that is conducted randomly. If an experiment has manipulation between groups, random assignment of participants to experimental groups helps ensure that each group is equivalent. 44

rank order Rank order refers to maintaining one's relative position within a group over time. Between ages 14 and 20, for example, most people become taller. But the rank order of heights tends to remain fairly stable because this form of development affects all people pretty much the same. The tall people at 14 fall generally toward the tall end of the distribution at age 20. The same can apply to personality traits. If people tend to maintain their position on dominance or extraversion relative to the other members of the group over time, then we say that there is high rank order stability to the personality characteristic. Conversely, if people fail to maintain their rank order, then we say that the group has displayed rank order instability or rank order change. 99

rationalization Rationalization is a defense mechanism that involves generating acceptable reasons for outcomes that might otherwise be unacceptable. The goal is to reduce anxiety by coming up with an explanation for some event that is easier to accept than the "real" reason. 301

reaction formation A defense mechanism that refers to an attempt to stifle the expression of an unacceptable urge; a person may continually display a flurry of behavior that indicates the opposite impulse. Reaction formation makes it possible for psychoanalysts to predict that sometimes people will do exactly the opposite of what you might otherwise think they would do. It also alerts us to be sensitive to instances when a person is doing something in excess. One of the hallmarks of reaction formation is excessive behavior. 301

reactively heritable Reactively heritable traits are secondary consequences of heritable traits. 272

reality principle In psychoanalysis, it is the counterpart of the pleasure principle. It refers to guiding behavior according to the demands of reality, and relies on the strengths of the ego to provide such guidance. 296

reciprocal causality The notion that causality can move in two directions; for example, helping others can lead to happiness, and happiness can lead one to be more helpful to others. 432

reducer-augmenter theory Petrie's reducer-augmenter theory refers to the dimension along which people differ in their reaction to sensory stimulation; some appear to reduce sensory stimulation, some appear to augment stimulation. 400

reinforcement sensitivity theory Reinforcement sensitivity theory is Gray's biological theory of personality. Based on recent brain function research with animals, Gray constructed a model of human personality based on two hypothesized biological systems in the brain: the Behavioral Activation System (which is responsive to incentives, such as cues for reward, and regulates approach behavior) and the Behavioral Inhibition System (which is responsive to cues for punishment, frustration, and uncertainty). 220

reliability Reliability is the degree to which an obtained measure represents the "true" level of the trait being measured. For example, if a person has a "true" IQ of 115, then a perfectly reliable measure of IQ will yield a score of 115 for that person. Moreover, a truly reliable measure of IQ would yield the same score of 115 each time it was administered to the person. Personality psychologists prefer reliable measures so that the scores accurately reflect each person's true level of the personality characteristic being measured. 41

repeated measurement Repeated measurement is a way to estimate the reliability of a measure. There are different forms of repeated measurement, and hence different versions of reliability. A common procedure is to repeat the same measurement over time, say at an interval of a month apart, for the same sample of persons. If the two tests are highly correlated between the first and second testing, yielding similar scores for most people, then the resulting

measure is said to have high test-retest reliability. 41
repression One of the first defense mechanisms discussed by Freud, refers to the process of preventing unacceptable thoughts, feelings, or urges from reaching conscious awareness. 299
resistance A psychoanalytic term, it refers to when a patient's defenses are threatened by a probing psychoanalyst, the patient may unconsciously set up obstacles to progress. This stage of psychoanalysis is called resistance. Resistance signifies that important unconscious material is coming to the fore. The resistance itself becomes an integral part of the interpretations the analyst offers to the patient. 313
resistance stage The resistance stage is the second stage in Seyle's general adaptation syndrome (GAS). Here the body is using its resources at an above average rate, even though the immediate fight or flight response has subsided. Stress is being resisted, but the effort is making demands on the person's resources and energy. 594
response sets The concept of response sets refers to the tendency of some people to respond to the questions on some basis that is unrelated to the question content. Sometimes this is referred to as non-content responding. One example is the response set of acquiescence or yea saying. This is the tendency to simply agree with the questionnaire items, regardless of the content of those items. 111
responsibility training Life experiences that provide opportunities to learn to behave responsibly, such as having younger siblings to take care of while growing up. Moderates the gender difference in impulsive behaviors associated with need for power. 366
restricted sexual strategy According to Gangestad and Simpson (1990), a woman seeking a high-investing mate would adopt a restricted sexual strategy marked by delayed intercourse and prolonged courtship. This would enable her to assess the man's level of commitment, detect the existence of prior commitments to other women and/or children, and simultaneously signal to the man the woman's sexual fidelity and, hence, assure him of his paternity of future offspring. 273
reward dependence (RFT) In Cloninger's tridimensional personality model, the personality trait of reward dependence is associated with low levels of norepinephrine. People high on this trait are persistent, they continue to act in ways that produced reward. They work long hours, put a lot of effort into their work, and will often continue striving after others have given up. 230
right to privacy Perhaps the largest issue of legal concern for employers using personality testing is privacy. The right to privacy in employment settings grows out of the broader concept of the right to privacy. Cases that charge an invasion-of-privacy claim against an employer can be based on the federal constitution, state constitutions and statutes, and common law. 123
rite of passage Some cultures and religions institute a rite of passage ritual, usually around adolescence, which typically is a ceremony that initiates a child into adulthood. After such ceremonies, the adolescent is sometimes given a new name, bestowing a new adult identity. 335
rod and frame test (RFT) Witkin devised an apparatus called the rod and frame test to research the cues that people use in judging orientation in space. The participant sits in a darkened room and is instructed to watch a glowing rod surrounded by a glowing square frame. The experimenter can adjust the tilt of the rod, the frame, and the participant's chair. The participant's task is to adjust the rod by turning a dial so that the rod is perfectly upright. To do this accurately, the participant has to ignore cues in the visual field in which the rod appears. This test measures the personality dimension of field dependence-independence. 395
rumination Rumination involves repeatedly focusing on one's symptoms or distress (e.g., "Why do I continue to feel so bad about myself" or "Why doesn't my boss like me?"). Because their ruminations fail to lead to efficacious solutions, according to this theory, women continue to ruminate. Rumination, according to this theory, is a key contributor to women's greater experience of depressive symptoms. 537

S

safety needs At the second to lowest level of Maslow's need hierarchy are the safety needs. These needs have to do with shelter and security, such as having a place to live and being free from the threat of danger. Maslow believed that building a life that was orderly, structured, and predictable also fell under safety needs. 371
schizoid personality disorder The schizoid personality is split off (schism) or detached from normal social relations. The schizoid person simply appears to have no need or desire for intimate relationships or even friendships. Family life usually does not mean much to such people, and they do not obtain satisfaction from being part of a group. They have few or no close friends, and they would rather spend time by themselves than with others. 641
schizotypal personality disorder Whereas the schizoid person is indifferent to social interaction, the schizotypal personality is acutely uncomfortable in social relationships. Schizotypes are anxious in social situations, especially if those situations involve strangers. Schizotypal persons also feel that they are different from others, or that they do not fit in with the group. They tend to be suspicious of others and are seen as odd and eccentric. 641
secondary appraisal According to Lazarus, in order for stress to be evoked for a person, two cognitive events must occur. The second necessary cognitive event, called the secondary appraisal, is when the person concludes that they do not have the resources to cope with the demands of the threatening event. See also primary appraisal. 599
secondary process thinking The ego engages in secondary process thinking, which refers to the development and devising of strategies for problem solving and obtaining satisfaction. Often this process involves taking into account the constraints of physical reality, about when and how to express some desire or urge. See also primary process thinking. 296
secure relationship style In Hazan and Shaver's secure relationship style, the adult has few problems developing

satisfying friendships and relationships. Secure people trust others and develop bonds with others. 344

securely attached Securely attached infants in Ainsworth's strange situation stoically endured the separation and went about exploring the room, waiting patiently, or even approaching the stranger and sometimes wanting to be held by the stranger. When the mother returned, these infants were glad to see her, typically interacted with her for a while, then went back to exploring the new environment. They seemed confident the mother would return. Approximately 66 percent of infants fall into this category. 343

selective breeding Selective breeding is one method of doing behavior genetic research. Researchers might identify a trait and then see if they can selectively breed animals to possess that trait. This can only occur if the trait has a genetic basis. For example, dogs that possess certain desired characteristics, such as a sociable disposition, might be selectively bred to see if this disposition can be increased in frequency among offspring. Traits that are based on learning cannot be selectively bred for. 180

selective placement If adopted children are placed with adoptive parents who are similar to their birth parents, this may inflate the correlations between the adopted children and their adoptive parents. In this case, the resulting inflated correlations would artificially inflate estimates of environmental influence since the correlation would appear to be due to the environment provided by the adoptive parent. There does not seem to be selective placement, and so this potential problem is not a problem in actual studies (Plomin et al., 1990). 185

self-actualization need Maslow defines self-actualization as becoming "more and more what one idiosyncratically is, to become everything that one is capable of becoming" (1970, p. 46). The pinnacle of Maslow's need hierarchy is the need for self-actualization. While Maslow was concerned with describing self-actualization, the work of Carl Rogers was focused on how people achieve self-actualization. 371, 373

self-attributed motivation McClelland argued that self-attributed motivation is primarily a person's self-awareness of his or her own conscious motives. These self-attributed motives reflect a person's conscious awareness about what is important to him or her. As such, they represent part of the individual's conscious self-understanding. McClelland has argued that self-attributed motives predict responses to immediate and specific situations and to choice behaviors and attitudes. See also implicit motivation. 359

self-complexity The view that each of us has many roles and many aspects to our self-concepts. However, for some of us, our self-concepts are rather simple, being made up of just a few large categories. Other people may have a more complex or differentiated self-concept. For people with high self-complexity, a failure in any one aspect of the self (such as a relationship that breaks apart) is buffered because there are many other aspects of the self that are unaffected by that event. However, if a person was low in self-complexity, the same event might be seen as devastating, since they define themselves mainly in terms of this one aspect. 478

self-concept The way a person sees, understands, and defines himself or herself is that person's self-concept. 463

self-efficacy Self-efficacy is a concept related to optimism developed by Bandura. This concept refers to the belief that one can behave in ways necessary to achieve some desired outcome. Self-efficacy also refers to the confidence one has in one's ability to perform the actions needed to achieve some specific outcome. 413, 603

self-enhancement Self-enhancement is the tendency to describe and present oneself using positive or socially valued attributes, such as kind, understanding, intelligent, and industrious. Tendencies toward self-enhancement tend to be stable over time, and hence are enduring features of personality (Baumeister, 1997). 569

self-esteem Self-esteem is defined as "the extent to which one perceives oneself as relatively close to being the person one wants to be and/or as relatively distant from being the kind of person one does not want to be, with respect to person-qualities one positively and negatively values" (Block & Robbins, 1993, p. 911). 153

self-esteem variability An individual difference characteristic referring to how much a person's self-esteem fluctuates or changes over time. It is uncorrelated with mean level of self-esteem. 479

self-fulfilling prophecy The tendency for a belief to become reality. For example, a person who thinks they are a "total failure" will often act like a total failure and may even give up trying to do better, thus creating a self-fulfilling prophecy. 448

self-guides The ideal self and the ought self act as self-guides, providing the standards that one uses to organize self-relevant information and motivate appropriate behaviors to bring the self in line with these self-guides. 470

self-handicapping Self-handicapping refers to situations in which people deliberately do things that increase the probability that they will fail. 479

self-report data (S-data) Information a person verbally reveals about themselves, often based on questionnaire or interview, is self-report data. Self-report data can be obtained through a variety of means, including interviews that pose questions to a person, periodic reports by a person to record the events as they happen, and questionnaires of various sorts. 26

self-schema The term self-schema (schemata is plural, schema is singular) is used to refer to the specific knowledge structure, or cognitive representation, of the self-concept. Self-schemas are the network of associated building blocks of the self-concept. 469

self-serving bias Self-serving bias refers to the common tendency for people to take credit for success, yet to deny responsibility for failure. 339

sensation seeking Sensation seeking is a dimension of personality postulated to have a physiological basis. It refers to the tendency to seek out thrilling and exciting activities, to take risks, and to avoid boredom. 223

sensory deprivation Often done in a sound-proof chamber containing water in which a person floats, in total darkness, such that sensory input is reduced to a minimum. Researchers used sensory deprivation chambers to see what happens when a person is deprived of sensory input. 223

separation anxiety Children experiencing separation anxiety react negatively to separation from their mother (or primary caretaker), becoming agitated and distressed when their mothers leave. Most primates exhibit separation anxiety. 343

serotonin Serotonin is a neurotransmitter that plays a role in depression and other mood disorders. Drugs such as Prozac, Zoloft, and Paxil block the re-uptake of serotonin, leaving it in the synapse longer, leading depressed persons to feel less depressed. 229

sex differences As used in this book, the phrase "sex differences" simply refers to an average difference between women and men on certain characteristics such as height, body fat distribution, or personality characteristics, with no prejudgment about the cause of the difference. 523

sexual selection Sexual selection is the evolution of characteristics because of their mating benefits, rather than because of their survival benefits. According to Darwin, sexual selection takes two forms: intrasexual competition and intersexual selection. 245

sexually dimorphic Species that show high variance in reproduction within one sex tend to be highly sexually dimorphic, or highly different in size and structure. The more intense the effective polygyny, the more dimorphic the sexes are in size and form (Trivers, 1985). 261

shared environment Shared environment refers to features of the environment that siblings share, for example, the number of books in the home, the presence or absence of a TV and VCR, quality and quantity of the food in the home, the values and attitudes of the parent, and the schools, church, synagogue, or temple the parents send the children to. 193

shyness Shyness is a tendency to feel tense, worried, or anxious during social interactions, or even when anticipating a social interaction (Addison & Schmidt, 1999). Shyness is a common phenomenon, and more than 90 percent of the population reports experiencing shyness at some point during their lives (Zimbardo, 1997). Some people, however, seem to be dispositionally shy—they tend to feel awkward in most social situations and so tend to avoid situations in which they will be forced to interact with people. 504

situational selection Situational selection is a form of interactionism which refers to the tendency to choose or select the situations in which one finds oneself. In other words, people typically do not find themselves in random situations in their natural lives. Instead, they select or choose the situations in which they will spend their time. 103, 496

situational specificity The view that behavior is determined by aspects of the situation, such as reward contingencies. 102

situationism Situationism is a theoretical position in personality psychology which states that situational differences, rather than underlying personality traits, determine behavior. The situationist position is that the situation, not personality traits, influences behavior; for example, how friendly a person will behave or how much need for achievement a person displays will depend on the situation, not the traits a person possesses. 101

social and cultural domain Personality affects, and is affected by, the social and cultural context in which it is found. Different cultures may bring out different facets of our personalities in manifest behavior. The capacities we display may depend to a large extent on what is acceptable in and encouraged by our culture. At the level of individual differences within cultures, personality plays itself out in the social sphere. One important social sphere concerns relations between men and women. 18

social anxiety Social anxiety is discomfort related to social interactions, or even to the anticipation of social interactions. Socially anxious persons appear to be overly concerned about what others will think. Baumeister and Tice propose that social anxiety is a species-typical adaptation that functions to prevent social exclusion. 253

social attention Social attention is the goal and payback for Surgent or Extraverted behavior. By being the center of attention, the Surgent or Extravert individual seeks to gain the approval of others and, in many cases, through tacit approval controls or directs others. 86

social categories The cognitive component that describes the ways individuals classify other people into groups, such as "cads" and "dads." This cognitive component is one aspect of stereotyping. 542

social class Variability between people based primarily on economic, educational, and employment variables. In terms of within-culture variation, social class can have an effect on personality (Kohn et al., 1990). For example, lower-class parents tend to emphasize the importance of obedience to authority, whereas higher-status parents tend to emphasize the importance of self-direction and not conforming to the dictates of others. 571

social comparison Social comparison is the evaluation of oneself or one's performance in terms of a comparison to some reference group. 467

social desirability Socially desirable responding refers to the tendency to answer items in such a way as to come across as socially attractive or likable. People responding in this manner want to make a good impression, to appear to be well adjusted, to be a "good citizen." 111

social identity Identity refers to the social aspects of the self, that part of ourselves we use to create an impression, to let other people know who we are and what can be expected from us. Identity is different from the self-concept because identity refers mainly to aspects of the self that are socially observable or publicly available outward, such as ethnicity or gender or age. Nevertheless, the social aspects of identity can become important aspects of the self-concept. 482

social learning theory A general theoretical view which emphasizes the ways in which the presence of others influence people's behavior, thoughts, or feelings. Often combined with learning principles, the emphasis is on how people acquire beliefs, values, skills, attitudes, and patterns of behavior through social experiences. 545

social power Horney, in reinterpreting Freud's concept of penis envy, taught that the penis was a symbol of social power rather than some organ that women actually desired. Horney wrote that girls realize, at an early age, that they are being denied social power because of their gender. She argued that girls did not really have a secret desire to become boys. Rather, she taught, girls desire the social power and preferences given to boys in the culture at that time. 338

social role theory According to social role theory, sex differences originate because men and women are distributed differentially into occupational and family roles. Men, for example, are expected to assume the bread-winning role. Women are expected to assume the housewife role. Over time, children presumably learn the behaviors that are linked to these roles. 546

socialization theory The socialization theory is the notion that boys and girls become different because boys are reinforced by parents, teachers, and the media for being "masculine," and girls for being "feminine." This is probably the most widely held theory of sex differences in personality. 544

sociosexual orientation According to Gangestad and Simpson's theory of sociosexual orientation, men and women will pursue one of two alternative sexual relationship strategies. The first mating strategy entails seeking a single committed relationship characterized by monogamy and tremendous investment in children. The second sexual strategy is characterized by a greater degree of promiscuity, more partner switching, and less investment in children. 70

specific expectancies Recent researchers have developed specific locus of control scales for specific categories of events. This approach is referred to as specific expectancies, where the emphasis is on locus of control in discrete areas of life, such as health locus of control. 406

spreading activation Roediger and McDermott applied the spreading activation model of memory to account for false memories. This model holds that mental elements (like words or images) are stored in memory along with associations to other elements in memory. For example, DOCTOR is associated with NURSE in most people's memories because of the close connection or similarity between these concepts. Consequently, a person recalling some medical event might falsely recall a nurse rather than a doctor doing something. 326

stability coefficients Stability coefficients are the correlations between the same measures obtained at two different points in time. Stability coefficients are also called test-retest reliability coefficients. 145

stage model of development A stage model of development implies that people go through stages in a certain order, and that there is a specific issue that characterizes each stage. 334

standards for evaluating theories The five scientific standards for evaluating personality theories are comprehensiveness, heuristic value, testability, parsimony, and compatibility and integration across domains and levels. 21

state levels A concept that can be applied to motives and emotions, state levels refer to a person's momentary amount of a specific need or emotion, which can fluctuate with specific circumstances. 359

statistical approach The statistical approach consists of having a large number of people rate themselves on certain items, and then employing a statistical procedure to identify groups or clusters of items that go together. The goal of the statistical approach is to identify the major dimensions or "coordinates" of the personality map. 67

statistically significant Refers to the probability of finding the results of a research study by chance alone. The generally accepted level of statistical significance is 5%, meaning that, if a study were repeated 100 times, the particular result reported would be found by chance only 5 times. 46

strange situation procedure The strange situation procedure was developed by Ainsworth and her colleagues for studying separation anxiety and for identifying differences between children in how they react to separation from their mothers. In this procedure, a mother and her baby come into a laboratory room. The mother sits down and the child is free to explore the room. After a few minutes an unfamiliar though friendly adult enters the room. The mother gets up and leaves the baby alone with this adult. After a few minutes, the mother comes back into the room and the stranger leaves. The mother is alone with the baby for several more minutes. All the while, the infant is being videotaped so that his or her reactions can later be analyzed. 343

stress Stress is the subjective feeling that is produced by uncontrollable and threatening events. Events that cause stress are called stressors. 589

stressors Events that cause stress are called stressors, and they appear to have several common attributes: (1) stressors are extreme in some manner, in the sense that they produce a state of feeling overwhelmed or overloaded, that one just cannot take it much longer; (2) stressors often produce opposing tendencies in us, such as wanting and not wanting some activity or object, as in wanting to study but also wanting to put it off as long as possible; and (3) stressors are uncontrollable, outside of our power to influence, such as the exam that we cannot avoid. 594

strong situation Certain situations that prompt similar behavior from everyone. 103

structured versus unstructured Self-report can take a variety of forms, ranging from open-ended questions to forced-choice true or false questions. Sometimes these are referred to as *unstructured* (open-ended, such as "Tell me about the parties you like the most") and *structured* ("I like loud and crowded parties"; answer true or false) personality tests. 26

style of emotional life Style of emotional life refers to how emotions are experienced. For example, saying that someone is high on mood variability is to say something about the style of his or her emotional life, that his or her emotions change frequently. Compare to the content of emotional life. 454

sublimation Sublimation is a defense mechanism which refers to the channeling of unacceptable sexual or aggressive instincts into socially desired activities. For Freud, sublimation is the most adaptive defense mechanism. A common example is going out to chop wood when you are angry rather than acting on that anger or even engaging in other less adaptive defense mechanisms such as displacement. 305

subliminal perception Perception that bypasses conscious awareness, usually achieved through very brief exposure times, typically less than 30 milliseconds. 330
superego The superego is that part of personality which internalizes the values, morals, and ideals of society. The superego makes us feel guilty, ashamed, or embarrassed when we do something wrong, and makes us feel pride when we do something right. The superego sets moral goals and ideals of perfection and is the source of our judgments that something is good or bad. It is what some people refer to as conscience. The main tool of the superego in enforcing right and wrong is the emotion of guilt. 297
Surgency or Extraversion Surgency or Extraversion is the first fundamental personality trait in the Five-Factor Model, a taxonomy which has proven to be replicable in studies using English language trait words as items. Some of the key adjective markers for Surgency or Extraversion are "talkative," "extraverted" or "extroverted," "gregarious," "assertive," "adventurous," "open," "sociable," "forward," and "outspoken." 86, 529
symbols Psychoanalysts interpret dreams by deciphering how unacceptable impulses and urges are transformed by the unconscious into symbols in the dream. (For example, parents may be represented as a king and queen; children may be represented as small animals.) 311
syndrome A collection of related traits. There is a consensus that Type A personality is actually not a single personality trait, but rather a syndrome or cluster of several different traits, which includes achievement striving and competitiveness, impatience, and hostility. 450
synonym frequency In the lexical approach, synonym frequency means that if an attribute has not merely one or two trait adjectives to describe it, but rather six, eight, or ten words, then it is a more important dimension of individual difference. 67

t

taxonomy A taxonomy is simply a technical name given to a classification scheme—the identification and naming of groups within a particular subject field. 512
telemetry Telemetry is the process by which electrical signals are sent from electrodes to a polygraph using radio waves instead of wires. 210
temperament Most researchers define temperament as those individual differences that emerge very early in life, are likely to have a heritable basis, and are often involved in behaviors linked with emotionality or arousability. 143
tender-mindedness Tender-mindedness is defined by a nurturant proclivity, having empathy for others, and being sympathetic with those who are downtrodden. 530
test data (T-data) A common source of personality-relevant information comes from standardized tests (T-data). In these measures, participants are placed in a standardized testing situation to see if different people react or behave differently to an identical situation. Taking an exam, like the Scholastic Aptitude Test, would be one example of T-data as a measure used to predict success in school. 32
testability Testability is the capacity to render precise predictions that scientists can test empirically. Generally, the testability of a theory is dependent upon the precision of its predictions. If it is impossible to test a theory empirically, the theory is generally discarded. 21
thanatos Freud postulated that humans have a fundamental instinct toward destruction and that this instinct is often manifest in aggression toward others. The two instincts were usually referred to as libido, for the life instinct, and thanatos, for the death instinct. While thanatos was considered to be the death instinct, Freud also used this term to refer to any urge to destroy, harm, or aggress against others or oneself. 289
thematic apperception technique The Thematic Apperception Technique (TAT), developed by Murray and Morgan, is a projective assessment technique which consists of a set of black and white ambiguous pictures. The person is shown each picture and is told to write a short story interpreting what is happening in each picture. The psychologist then codes the stories for the presence of imagery associated with particular motives. The TAT remains a popular personality assessment technique today. 356
theoretical approach The theoretical approach to identifying important dimensions of individual differences starts with a theory, which then determines which variables are important. The theoretical strategy dictates in a specific manner which variables are important to measure. 67
theoretical bridge A theoretical bridge refers to the connection between two different variables (for instance, dimensions of personality and physiological variables). 209
theoretical constructs Most personality traits refer to constructs, or what Allport called convenient fictions. For example, if someone asks you to show them your level of extraversion, there is nothing you could produce. Extraversion is a convenient fiction, a theoretical construct useful for explaining aspects of personality. Constructs are represented by observable measures, such as self-reports or observations of behavior. So, to explain how extraverted you are, you could produce scores on an extraversion scale. The construct, however, is always more than the observations. 43
theories versus beliefs Beliefs are often personally useful and crucially important to some people, but they are based on leaps of faith, not on reliable facts and systematic observations. Theories, on the other hand, are based on systematic observations, that can be repeated by others, and that yield similar conclusions. 20
third variable problem One reason why correlations can never prove causality is the third variable problem. It could be that two variables are correlated because some third, unknown variable is causing both. 51
time urgency Time urgency is a sub-trait in the Type A personality. Type A persons hate wasting time. They are always in a hurry and feel under pressure to get the most done in the least amount of time. Often they do two things at once, such as eat while reading a book. Waiting is stressful for them. 613
Title VII of the Civil Rights Act of 1964 A specific section of the Civil Rights Act of 1964 that requires employers to provide equal

employment opportunities to all persons, regardless of sex, race, color, religion, or national origin. 119

trait-descriptive adjectives Trait-descriptive adjectives are words that describe traits, attributes of a person that are reasonably characteristic of the individual and perhaps even enduring over time. 4

trait levels A concept that can be applied to motives and emotions, trait levels refer to a person's average tendency, or his or her set-point, on the specific motive or emotion. The idea is that people differ from each other in their typical or average amount of specific motives or emotions. 359

transactional model In the transactional model of personality and health, personality has three potential effects: (1) it can influence coping, as in the interactional model; (2) it can influence how the person appraises or interprets the events; and (3) it can influence exposure to the events themselves. 589

transference Transference is a term from psychoanalytic therapy. It refers to the patient reacting to the analyst as if he or she were an important figure from the patient's own life. The patient displaces past or present (negative and positive) feelings toward someone from his or her own life onto the analyst. The idea behind transference is that the interpersonal problems between a patient and the important people in his or her life will be reenacted in the therapy session with the analyst. This is a specific form of the mechanism of evocation, as described in the material on person-situation interaction. 314

transmitted culture Transmitted culture refers to representations originally in the mind of one or more persons that are transmitted to the minds of other people. Three examples of cultural variants that appear to be forms of transmitted culture are differences in moral values, self-concept, and levels of self-enhancement. Specific patterns of morality, such as whether it is considered appropriate to eat beef or wrong for a wife to go to the movies without her husband, are specific to certain cultures. These moral values appear to be transmitted from person to person within the culture. 559

traumatic stress A massive instance of acute stress, the effects of which can reverberate within an individual for years or even a lifetime is called traumatic stress. It differs from acute stress mainly in terms of its potential to lead to post-traumatic stress disorder. 598

tridimensional personality model Cloninger's tridimensional personality model ties three specific personality traits to levels of the three neurotransmitters. The first trait is called novelty seeking and is based on low levels of dopamine. The second personality trait is harm avoidance, which he associates with low levels of serotonin. The third trait is reward dependence, which Cloninger sees as related to low levels of norepinephrine. 229

trust Trust is defined by the proclivity to cooperate with others, giving others the benefit of the doubt, and viewing one's fellow human beings as basically good at heart. 530

twin studies Twin studies estimate heritability by gauging whether identical twins, who share 100 percent of their genes, are more similar to each other than fraternal twins, who share only 50 percent of their genes. Twin studies, and especially studies of twins reared apart, have received tremendous media attention. 182

type A personality In the 1960s, cardiologists Friedman and Rosenman began to notice that many of their coronary heart disease patients had similar personality traits—they were competitive, aggressive workaholics, were ambitious overachievers, were often hostile, were almost always in a hurry, and rarely relaxed or took it easy. Friedman and Rosenman referred to this as the Type A personality, formally defined as "an action-emotion complex that can be observed in any person who is aggressively involved in a chronic, incessant struggle to achieve more and more in less and less time, and if required to do so, against the opposing efforts of other things or other persons" (1974, p. 37). As assessed by personality psychologists, Type A refers to a syndrome of several traits: (1) achievement motivation and competitiveness; (2) time urgency; and (3) hostility and aggressiveness. 212, 612

Type 4 Dopamine Receptor Gene (DRD4) According to Schinka, Letsch, and Crawford, very specific types of repeated genetic codes on the Type 4 Dopamine Receptor Gene are associated with novelty seeking. 198

U

unconditional positive regard The receipt of affection, love, or respect without having done anything to earn it. For example, a parent's love for a child should be unconditional. 378

unconscious The unconscious mind is that part of the mind about which the conscious mind has no awareness. 290

Uniform Guidelines on Employee Selection Procedures The purpose of the guidelines is to provide a set of principles for employee selection that meet the requirements of all federal laws, especially those that prohibit discrimination on the basis of race, color, religion, sex, or national origin. They provide details on the proper use of personality tests and other selection procedures in employment settings. 119

unrestricted mating strategy According to Gangestad and Simpson (1990), a woman seeking a man for the quality of his genes is not interested in his level of commitment to her. If the man is pursuing a short-term sexual strategy, any delay on the woman's part may deter him from seeking sexual intercourse with her, thus defeating the main adaptive reason for her mating strategy. 273

V

validity Validity refers to the extent to which a test measures what it claims to measure. There are five types of validity: face validity, predictive validity, convergent validity, discriminant validity, and construct validity. 42

validity coefficients Validity coefficients are the correlations between a trait measure and measures of different criteria that should relate to the trait. An example might be the correlation between a self-report measure of agreeableness, and the person's roommate reports of how agreeable they are. 145

violation of desire According to the violation of desire theory of conflict between the sexes, break ups should occur more when one's desires are violated than when they are fulfilled (Buss, 1994). Following this theory, we would predict that people married to others who lack desired characteristics, such as dependability and emotional stability, will more frequently dissolve the marriage. 503

W

Ward's Cove Packing Co. v. Atonio Ward's Cove Packing Co. was a salmon cannery operating in Alaska. In 1974 the non-white cannery workers started legal action against the company, alleging that a variety of the company's hiring and promotion practices were responsible for racial stratification in the workplace. The claim was advanced under the disparate impact portion of Title VII of the Civil Rights Act. In 1989 the Supreme Court decided on the case in favor of Ward's Cove. The court decided that, even if employees can prove discrimination, the hiring practices may still be considered legal if they serve "legitimate employment goals of the employer." This decision allowed disparate impact if it was in the service of the company. This case prompted Congress to pass the Civil Rights Act of 1991, which contained several important modifications to Title VII of the original act. Most importantly, however, the new Act shifted the burden of proof onto the employer by requiring that they must prove a close connection between disparate impact and the ability to actually perform the job in question. 120

Whorfian hypothesis of linguistic relativity In 1956, Whorf proposed the theory that language creates thought and experience. According to this Whorfian hypothesis, the ideas that people can think and the emotions they feel are constrained by the words that happen to exist in their language and culture and with which they use to express them. 576

wish fulfillment If an urge from the id requires some external object or person, and that object or person is not available, the id may create a mental image or fantasy of that object or person to satisfy its needs. Mental energy is invested in that fantasy and the urge is temporarily satisfied. This process is called wish fulfillment, where something unavailable is conjured up and the image of it is temporarily satisfying. 296

within-culture variation Within-culture variations are variations within a particular culture that can arise from several sources, including differences in growing up in various socioeconomic classes, differences in historical era, or differences in the racial context in which one grows up. 571

within the individual The important sources of personality reside within the individual—that is, a person carries the sources of their personality inside themselves—and hence are stable over time and consistent over situations. 8

working models Early experiences and reactions of the infant to the parents, particularly the mother, become what Bowlby called "working models" for later adult relationships. These working models are internalized in the form of unconscious expectations about relationships. 344

X

xenophobia Xenophobia is the fear of strangers. Characteristics that were probably adaptive in ancestral environments, such as xenophobia, are not necessarily adaptive in modern environments. Some of the personality traits that make up human nature may be vestigial adaptations to an ancestral environment that no longer exists. 248

References

Abdel-Khalek, A. M., and Alansari, B. M. (2004). Gender differences in anxiety among undergraduates from ten Arab countries. *Social Behavior and Personality, 32,* 649–656.

Abe, J. A. A. (2005). The predictive validity of the Five-Factor Model of personality with preschool age children: A nine year follow-up study. *Journal of Research in Personality, 39,* 423–442.

Abelson, R. P. (1985). A variance explanation paradox: When a little is a lot. *Psychological Bulletin, 97,* 129–133.

Abrahamson, A. C., Baker, L. A., and Caspi, A. (2002). Rebellious teens? Genetic and environmental influences on the social attitudes of adolescents. *Journal of Personality and Social Psychology, 83,* 6, 1392–1408.

Adan, A. (1991). Influence of morningness-eveningness preference in the relationship between body temperature and performance: A diurnal study. *Personality and Individual Differences, 12,* 1159–1169.

Adan, A. (1992). The influence of age, work schedule and personality on morningness dimension. *International Journal of Psychophysiology, 12,* 95–99.

Addison, T. L., and Schmidt, L. A. (1999). Are women who are shy reluctant to take risks? Behavioral and psychophysiological correlates. *Journal of Research in Personality, 33,* 352–357.

Affleck, G., and Tennen, H. (1996). Construing benefits from adversity: Adaptational significance and dispositional underpinnings. *Journal of Personality, 64,* 899–922.

Aharon, I., Etcoff, N., Ariely, D., Chabris, C. F., O'Connor, E., and Breiter, H. C. (2001). Beautiful faces have variable reward value: fMRI and behavioral evidence. *Neuron, 32,* 537–551.

Ai, A. L., Peterson, C., and Ubelhor, D. (2002). War-related trauma and symptoms of posttraumatic stress disorder among adult Kosovar refugees. *Journal of Traumatic Stress, 15,* 157–160.

Aigner, M., Eher, R., Fruenhwald, S., Frottier, P., Gutierrez-Lobos, K., and Dwyer, S. M. (2000). Brain abnormalities and violent behavior. *Journal of Psychology and Human Sexuality, 11,* 57–64.

Ainsworth, M. D. (1979). Infant-mother attachment. *American Psychologist, 34,* 932–937.

Ainsworth, M. D., Bell, S. M., and Stayton, D. J. (1972). Individual differences in the development of some attachment behaviors. *Merrill-Palmer Quarterly, 18,* 123–143.

Ainsworth, M. D., and Bowlby, J. (1991). An ethological approach to personality development. *American Psychologist, 46,* 333–341.

Aldwin, C. M., Spiro, A. III, Levenson, M. R., and Cupertino, A. P. (2001). Longitudinal findings from the normative aging study: III. Personality, individual health trajectories, and mortality. *Psychology and Aging, 16,* 450–465.

Alexander, R. D., Hoodland, J. L., Howard, R. D., Noonan, K. M., and Sherman, P. W. (1979). Sexual dimorphisms and breeding systems in pinnepeds, ungulates, primates, and humans. In N. A. Chagnon and W. Irons (Eds.), *Evolutionary biology and human social behavior.* North Scituate, MA: Duxbury Press.

Algom, D., Chajut, E., and Lev, S. (2004). A rational look at the emotional Stroop phenomenon: A generic slowdown, not a Stroop effect. *Journal of Experimental Psychology: General, 133,* 323–338.

Allport, G. W. (1937). *Personality: A psychological interpretation.* New York: Holt, Rinehart and Winston.

Allport, G. W. (1961). *Pattern and growth in personality.* NY: Holt, Rinehart and Winston.

Allport, G. W., and Odbert, H. S. (1936). Trait-names: A psycho-lexical study. *Psychological Monographs, 47* (1, Whole No. 211).

Almagor, M., Tellegen, A., and Waller, N. G. (1995). The big seven model: A cross-cultural replication and further exploration of the basic dimensions of natural language trait descriptors. *Journal of Personality and Social Psychology, 69,* 300–307.

Alston, W. P. (1975). Traits, consistency and conceptual alternatives for personality theory. *Journal for the Theory of Social Behavior, 5,* 17–48.

Amelang, M., Herboth, G., and Oefner, I. (1991). A prototype strategy for the construction of a creativity scale. *European Journal of Personality, 5,* 261–285.

American Psychiatric Association. (1994). *Diagnostic and statistical manual of mental disorders* (4th ed.). Washington, DC: Author.

Anastasi, A. (1976). *Psychological testing.* New York: Macmillan.

Ando, J., Ono, Y., Yoshimura, K., Onoda, N., Shinohara, M., Kanba, S., and Asai, M. (2002). The genetic structure of Cloninger's seven-factor model of temperament and character in a Japanese sample. *Journal of Personality, 70, 5,* 583–610.

Andrews, J. D. W. (1967). The achievement motive in two types of organizations. *Journal of Personality and Social Psychology, 6,* 163–168.

Angier, N. (1996, January 2). Variant gene is connected to a love of the search for new thrills. *New York Times,* Section A, p. 1, col. 1.

Angier, N. (1999). *Woman: An intimate geography.* Boston: Houghton Mifflin.

Angleitner, A., and Demtroder, A. I. (1988). Acts and dispositions: A reconsideration of the act frequency approach. *European Journal of Psychology, 2,* 121–141.

Angleitner, A., Buss, D., M., and Demtroder, A. I. (1990). A cross-cultural comparison using the act frequency approach (AFA) in West Germany and the United States. *European Journal of Personality, 4,* 1–21.

Aron, A., Aron, E. N., Tudor, M., and Nelson, G. (2004). Close relationships as including other in the self. In H. T. Reis and C. E. Rustbult (Eds.), *Close relationships: Key readings* (pp. 365–379). Philadelphia: Taylor and Francis.

Aschoff, J. (1965). Circadian rhythms in man. *Science, 143,* 1427–1432.

Asendorpf, J. B., and Scherer, K. R. (1983). The discrepant repressor: Differentiation between low anxiety, high anxiety, and repression of anxiety by autonomic-facial-verbal patterns of behavior. *Journal of Personality and Social Psychology, 45,* 1334–1346.

Asendorpf, J. B., and Van Aken, M. A. G. (2003). Validity of five personality judgments in childhood: A 9-year longitudinal study. *European Journal of Personality, 32,* 649–656.

Ashmore, R. D. (1990). Sex, gender, and the individual. In L. A. Pervin (Ed.), *Handbook of personality: Theory and research* (pp. 486–526). New York: Guilford Press.

Ashton, M. C., Lee, K., and Goldberg, L. R. (2004). A hierarchical analysis of 1,710 English personality-descriptive adjectives. *Journal of Personality and Social Psychology, 87,* 707–721.

Ashton, M. C., and Lee, K. (2005). A defense of the lexical approach to the study of personality. *European Journal of Personality, 19,* 5–24.

Ashton, M. C., Lee, K., and Paunonen, S. V. (2002). What is the central feature of extraversion? Social attention versus reward sensitivity. *Journal of Personality and Social Psychology, 83,* 1, 245–252.

Ashton, M. C., Lee, K., Perugini, M., Szarota, P., de Vries, R. E., Di Blas, L., Boies, K., and De Raad, B. (2004). A six-factor structure of personality adjectives: Solutions from psycholexical studies in seven languages. *Journal of Personality and Social Psychology, 86,* 356–366.

Assor, A. (1989). The power motive as an influence on the evaluation of high and low status persons. *Journal of Research in Personality, 23,* 55–69.

Averill, J. R. (1975). A semantic atlas of emotional concepts. *Catalog of Selected Documents in Psychology, 5,* 30.

Azar, B. (2002). Searching for genes that explain our personalities. *American Psychological Association Monitor, 33,* p. 44.

Bailey, J. M., Dunne, M. P., and Martin, N. G. (2000). Genetic and environmental influences on sexual orientation and its correlates in an Australian twin sample. *Journal of Personality and Social Psychology, 78,* 524–536.

Bailey, J. M., Kirk, K. M., Zhu, G., Dunne, M. P., and Martin, N. G. (2000). Do individual differences in sociosexuality represent genetic or environmentally contingent strategies? Evidence from the Australian Twin Registry. *Journal of Personality and Social Psychology, 78,* 537–545.

Bailey, J. M., Pillard, R. C., Neale, M. C., and Agyei, Y. (1993). Heritable factors influence sexual orientation in women. *Archives of General Psychiatry, 50,* 217–223.

Bailey, S. L., and Heitkemper, M. M. (1991). Morningness-eveningness and early-morning salivary cortisol levels. *Biological Psychology, 32,* 181–192.

Baker, R. A. (1992). *Hidden memories.* Buffalo, NY: Prometheus Books.

Balay, J., and Shevrin, H. (1988). The subliminal psychodynamic activation method: A critical review. *American Psychologist, 43,* 161–174.

Bandura, A. (1977). *Social learning theory.* Englewood Cliffs, NJ: Prentice Hall.

Bandura, A. (1986). The explanatory and predictive scope of self-efficacy theory. *Journal of Social and Clinical Psychology, Special Issue: Self-efficacy theory in contemporary psychology, 4,* 359–373.

Bandura, A. (1989). Human agency in social cognitive theory. *American Psychologist, 44,* 1175–1184.

Bandura, A. (1997). *Self-efficacy: The exercise of control.* New York: Freeman.

Barelds, D. P. H. (2005). Self and partner personality in intimate relationships. *European Journal of Personality, 19,* 501–518.

Barenbaum, N. B., and Winter, D. G. (2003). Personality. In D. K. Freedheim (Ed.), *Handbook of psychology: History of psychology* (pp. 177–203). New York, NY: John Wiley and Sons, Inc.

Bargh, J. A. (2005). Bypassing the will: Toward demystifying the nonconscious control of social behavior. In R. R. Hassin, J. S. Uleman, and J. A. Bargh (Eds.), *The new unconscious* (pp. 37–60). New York: Oxford University Press.

Bargh, J. A., and Chartrand, T. L. (1999). The unbearable automaticity of being. *American Psychologist, 54,* 462–479.

Baron, M. (1993). Genetics and human sexual orientation. *Biological Psychology, 33,* 759–761.

Bar-On, R. (2001). Emotional intelligence and self-actualization. In J. Ciarrochi and J. P. Forgas (Eds.), *Emotional intelligence in everyday life: A scientific inquiry* (pp. 82–97). Philadelphia, PA: Psychology Press.

Baron, R. A. (1977). *Human aggression.* New York: Plenum Press.

Barrett, C., Frederick, D., and Haselton, M. G. (in press). Can cognitive manipulations of cognitive load be used to test evolutionary hypotheses? *Journal of Personality and Social Psychology.*

Barrick, M. R., and Mount, M. K. (1991). The big five personality dimensions and job performance: A meta-analysis. *Personnel Psychology, 44,* 1–25.

Barron, J. W., Eagle, M. N., and Wolitzky, D. L. (1992). *Interface of psychoanalysis and psychology.* Washington, DC: American Psychological Association.

Bass, E., and Davis, L. (1988). *The courage to heal: A guide for women survivors of child sexual abuse.* New York: Perennial Library/Harper and Row Publishers, Inc.

Bastone, L. M., and Wood, H. A. (1997). Individual differences in the ability to decode emotional facial expressions. *Psychology: A Journal of Human Behavior, 34,* 32–36.

Baumeister, R. F. (1986). *Identity: Cultural change and the struggle for self.* New York: Oxford University Press.

Baumeister, R. F. (1988). Should we stop studying sex differences altogether? *American Psychologist, 43,* 1092–1095.

Baumeister, R. F. (1991). The self against itself: Escape or defeat? In R. C. Curtis (Ed.), *The relational self: Theoretical convergences in psychoanalysis and social psychology* (pp. 238–256). New York: Guilford Press.

Baumeister, R. F. (1997). Identity, self-concept, and self-esteem: The self lost and found. In R. Hogan, J. Johnson, and S. Briggs (Eds.), *Handbook of personality psychology* (pp. 681–711). New York: Academic Press.

Baumeister, R. F. (2001, April). Violent pride. *Scientific American, 284,* 96–101.

Baumeister, R. F., Bushman, B. J., and Campbell, W. K. (2000). Self-esteem, narcissism, and aggression: Does violence result from low self-esteem or from threatened egotism? *Current Directions in Psychological Science, 9,* 26–29.

Baumeister, R. F., Campbell, J. D., Krueger, J. I., and Vohs, K. D. (2003). Does high self-esteem cause better performance, interpersonal success, happiness, or healthier lifestyles? *Psychological Science in the Public Interest, 4,* 1–44.

Baumeister, R. F., Dale, K., and Sommer, K. L. (1998). Freudian defense mechanisms and empirical findings in modern social psychology: Reaction formation, projection, displacement, undoing, isolation, sublimation, and denial. *Journal of Personality, 66,* 1061–1081.

Baumeister, R. F., and Leary, M. R. (1995). The need to belong: Desire for interpersonal attachments as a fundamental human motivation. *Psychological Bulletin, 117,* 497–529.

Baumeister, R. F., and Muraven, M. (1996). Identity as adaptation to social, cultural and historical context. *Journal of Adolescence, 19,* 405–416.

Baumeister, R. F., Tice, D. M., and Hutton, D. G. (1989). Self-presentational motivations and personality differences in self-esteem. *Journal of Personality, 57,* 547–579.

Baumeister, R. F., and Tice, D. M. (1990). Anxiety and social exclusion. *Journal of Social and Clinical Psychology, 9,* 165–195.

Baumeister, R. F., and Vohs, K. (2004). *Handbook of self-regulation.* New York: Guilford.

Beauducel, A., Debener, S., Brocke, B., and Kayser, J. (2000). On the reliability of augmenting/reducing: Peak amplitudes and principal components of auditory evoked potentials. *Journal of Psychophysiology, 14,* 226–240.

Beauregard, M., Levesque, J., and Bourgouin, P. (2001). Neural correlates of conscious self-regulation of emotion. *Journal of Neuroscience, 21,* RC165 (1–6).

Bechara, A., Damasio, A. R., Damasio, H., and Anderson, S. W. (1994). Insensitivity to future consequences following damage to human prefrontal cortex. *Cognition, 50,* 7–15.

Bechara, A., Dolan, S., Denbrug, N., Hindes, A., Anderson, S. W., and Nathan, P. E. (2001). Decision-making deficits, linked to a dysfunctional ventromedial prefrontal cortex, revealed in alcohol and stimulant abusers. *Neuropsychologica, 39,* 376–389.

Bechara, A., Tranel, D., and Damasio, H. (2000). Characterization of the decision-making deficit of patients with ventromedial prefrontal cortex lesions. *Brain, 123,* 2189–2202.

Beck, A. T. (1976). *Cognitive therapy and the emotional disorders.* New York: International Universities Press.

Belle, D., Doucet, J., Harris, J., Miller, J., and Tan, E. (2000). Who is rich? Who is happy? *American Psychologist, 55,* 116–117.

Belsky, J. (2000). Conditional and alternative reproductive strategies: Individual differences in susceptibility to rearing experience. In J. Rodgers, D. Rowe, and W. Miller (Eds.), *Genetic influences on human fertility and sexuality: Theoretical and empirical contributions from the biological and behavioral sciences* (pp. 127–146). Boston: Kluwer.

Belsky, J., Steinberg, L., and Draper, P. (1991). Childhood experience, interpersonal development, and reproductive strategy: An evolutionary theory of socialization. *Child Development, 62,* 647–670.

Bem, D. J. (1995). Exotic becomes erotic: A developmental theory of sexual orientation. *Psychological Review, 103,* 320–333.

Bem, S. L. (1974). The measurement of psychological androgyny. *Journal of Consulting and Clinical Psychology, 42,* 153–162.

Benjamin, J., Ebstein, R., and Belmaker, R. H. (in press). *Molecular genetics of human personality.* New York: American Psychiatric Press.

Benjamin, J., Li, L., Patterson, C., Greenberg, B. D., Murphy, D. L., and Hamer, D. H. (1996). Population and familial association between the D4 dopamine receptor gene and measures of novelty seeking. *Nature Genetics, 12,* 81–84.

Bentler, P. M., and Newcomb, M. D. (1978). Longitudinal study of marital success and failure. *Journal of Consulting and Clinical Psychology, 46,* 1053–1070.

Berenbaum, S. A., and Snyder, E. (1995). Early hormonal influences on childhood sex-typed activity and playmate preferences: Implications for the development of sexual orientation. *Developmental Psychology, 31,* 31–42.

Berman, S., Ozkaragoz, T., Yound, R. M., and Noble, E. P. (2002). D2 domapine receptor gene polymorphism discriminates two kinds of novelty seeking. *Personality and Individual Differences, 33,* 867–882.

Bernhardt, P. C., Dabbs, J. M., Jr., Fielden, J., and Lutter, C. (1998). Testosterone changes during vicarious experiences of winning and losing among fans at sporting events. *Physiology and Behavior, 65,* 59–62.

Berry, D. S., and Miller, K. M. (2001). When boy meets girl: Attractiveness and the Five-Factor Model in opposite-sex interactions. *Journal of Research in Personality, 35,* 62–77.

Birley, A. J., Gillespie, N. A., Heath, A. C., Sullivan, P. F., Boomsma, D. I., and Martin, N. G. (2006). Heritability and nineteen-year stability of long and short EPQ-R Neuroticism scales. *Personality and Individual Differences, 40,* 737–747.

Bjork, R. A., and Druckman, D. (1991). *In the mind's eye: Enhancing human performance.* Washington, DC: National Academy Press.

Black, J. (2000). Personality testing and police selection: Utility of the Big Five. *New Zealand Journal of Psychology, 29,* 2–9.

Bleske-Rechek, A. L., and Buss, D. M. (2001). Opposite-sex friendship: Sex differences and similarities in initiation, selection, and dissolution. *Personality and Social Psychology Bulletin, 27,* 10, 1310–1323.

Block, J. (1971). *Lives through time.* Berkeley, CA: Bancroft Books.

Block, J. (1977). Advancing the psychology of personality: Paradigmatic shift or improving the quality of research. In D. Magnusson and N. S. Endler (Eds.), *Personality at the crossroads* (pp. 37–63) Hillsdale, NJ: Erlbaum.

Block, J. (1989). Critique of the act frequency approach to personality. *Journal of Personality and Social Psychology, 56,* 234–245.

Block, J. (1995b). Going beyond the five factors given: Rejoinder to Costa and McCrae (1995) and Goldberg and Saucier (1995). *Psychological Bulletin, 117,* 226–229.

Block, J., and Robbins, R. W. (1993). A longitudinal study of consistency and change in self-esteem from early adolescence to early adulthood. *Child Development, 64,* 909–923.

Block, J. H. (1983). Differential premises arising from differential socialization of the sexes: Some conjectures. *Child Development, 54,* 1335–1354.

Block, J. H., and Block, J. (1980). *The California Child Q-Set.* Palo Alto, CA: Consulting Psychologists Press.

Blonigen, D. M., Carlson, S. R., Krueger, R. F., and Patrick, C. J. (2003). A twin study of self-reported psychopathic personality traits. *Personality and Individual Differences, 35,* 179–197.

Blonigen, D. M., Hicks, B. M., Krueger, R. F., Patrick, C. J., and Iacono, W. G. (2006). Continuity and change in psychopathic traits measures via normal-range personality: A longitudinal-biometric study. *Journal of Abnormal Psychology, 115,* 85–95.

Bochner, S. (1994). Cross-cultural differences in the self-concept: A test of Hofstede's individualism/collectivism distinction. *Journal of Cross-Cultural Psychology, 25,* 273–283.

Bolger, N., and Schilling, E. A. (1991). Personality and the problems of everyday life: The role of neuroticism in exposure and reactivity to daily stressors. *Journal of Personality, 59,* 355–386.

Bonanno, G. A. (1990). Repression, accessibility, and the translation of private experience. *Psychoanalytic Psychology, 7,* 453–473.

Bonanno, G. A., Wortman, C. B., Lehman, D. R., Tweed, R. G., Haring, M., Sonnega, J., Carr, D., and Nesse, R. M. (2002). Resilience to loss and chronic grief: A prospective study from preloss to 18-months postloss. *Journal of Personality and Social Psychology, 83,* 5, 1150–1164.

Bono, J. E., Boles, T. L., Judge, T. A., and Lauver, K. J. (2002). The role of personality in task and relationship conflict. *Journal of Personality, 70,* 311–344.

Boomsma, D. I., Koopmans, J. R., Van Doornen, L. J. P., and Orlebeke, J. M. (1994). Genetic and social influences on starting to smoke: A study of Dutch adolescent twins and their parents. *Addiction, 89,* 219–226.

Borkenau, P., Riemann, R., Angleitner, A., and Spinath, F. M. (2001). Genetic and environmental influences on observed personality: Evidence from the German observational study of adult twins. *Journal of Personality and Social Psychology, 80,* 4, 655–668.

Bornstein, R. F. (1999). Source amnesia, misattribution, and the power of unconscious perceptions and memories. *Psychoanalytic Psychology, 16,* 155–178.

Bornstein, R. F. (2005). The dependent patient: Diagnosis, assessment, and treatment. *Professional Psychology: Research and Practice, 36,* 82–89.

Bornstein, R. F., and Masling, J. M. (1998). *Empirical perspectives on the psychoanalytic unconscious.* Washington, DC: American Psychological Association.

Bornstein, R. F., and Masling, J. M. (1991). Perception without awareness and electodermal responding: A strong test of subliminal psychodynamic activation effects. *The Journal of Mind and Behavior, 12,* 33–48.

Botwin, M. D., and Buss, D. M. (1989). Structure of act-report data: Is the five-factor model of personality recaptured?

Journal of Personality and Social Psychology, 56, 988–1001.

Botwin, M., Buss, D. M., and Shackelford, T. (1997). Personality and mate preferences: Five factors in mate selection and marital satisfaction. *Journal of Personality, 65,* 107–136.

Bouchard, T. J. (1994). Genes, environment, and personality. *Science,* pp. 700–701.

Bouchard, T. J., and Loehlin, J. C. (2001). Genes, evolution, and personality. *Behavior Genetics, 31,* 243–273.

Bouchard, T. J., and McGue, M. (1990). Genetic and rearing environmental influences on adult personality: An analysis of adopted twins reared apart. *Journal of Personality, 58,* 263–292.

Bowlby, J. (1969a). *Attachment and loss: Vol. 1: Attachment.* New York: Basic Books.

Bowlby, J. (1969b). *Attachment and loss: Vol. 2: Separation, anger, and anxiety.* New York: Basic Books.

Bowlby, J. (1980). *Attachment and loss: Vol. 3: Loss, sadness, and depression.* New York: Basic Books.

Bowlby, J. (1988). *A secure base: Parent-child attachment and healthy human development.* New York: Basic Books.

Boyle, G. J. (1995). Myers-Briggs Type Indicatory (NBTI): Some psychometric limitations. *Australian Psychologist, 30,* 71–74.

Brand, C. R., and Egan, V. (1989). The "big five" dimensions of personality? Evidence from ipsative, adjectival self-attributions. *Personality and Individual Differences, 10,* 1165–1171.

Brand, M., Kalbe, E., Labudda, K., Fujiwara, E., Kessler, J., and Markowitsch, H. J. (2005). Decision-making impairments in patients with pathological gambling. *Psychiatry Research, 133,* 91–99.

Brase, G. L., Caprar, D. V., and Voracek, M. (2004). Sex differences in responses to relationship threats in England and Romania. *Journal of Social and Personal Relationships, 21,* 763–778.

Braun, K. A., Ellis, R., and Loftus, E. F. (2002). Make my memory: How advertising can change our memories of the past. *Psychology and Marketing, 19,* 1–23.

Brebner, J. (2003). Gender and emotions. *Personality and Individual Differences, 34,* 387–394.

Brebner, J., and Cooper, C. (1978). Stimulus- or response-induced excitation: A comparison of the behavior of introverts and extraverts. *Journal of Research in Personality, 12,* 306–311.

Breger, R., and Hill, R. (Eds.). (1998). *Cross-cultural marriage: Identity and choice.* New York: Berg.

Brendl, C. M., Markman, A. B., and Messner, C. (2001). How do indirect measures of evaluation work? Evaluating the inference of prejudice in the Implicit Association Test. *Journal of Personality and Social Psychology, 81,* 760–773.

Brennan, K. A., and Shaver, P. R. (1993). Attachment styles and parental divorce. *Journal of Divorce and Remarriage, 21,* 161–175.

Brennan, P. A., and Raine, A. (1997). Biosocial bases of antisocial behavior: Psychophysiological, neurological, and cognitive factors. *Clinical Psychology Review Special Issue: Biopsychosocial Conceptualizations of Human Aggression, 17,* 589–604.

Bretherton, I., and Main, M. (2000). Obituary: Mary Dinsmore Salter Ainsworth (1913–1999). *American Psychologist, 55,* 1148–1149.

Brickman, P., Coates, D., and Janoff-Bulman, R. J. (1978). Lottery winners and accident victims: Is happines relative? *Journal of Personality and Social Psychology, 36,* 917–927.

Brody, J. E. (1996, March 27). Personal health. *New York Times,* Section B.

Brose, L. A., Rye, M. S., Lutz-Zois, C., and Ross, S. R. (2005). Forgiveness and personality traits. *Personality and Individual Differences, 39,* 35–46.

Brown, D. E. (1991). *Human universals.* New York: McGraw-Hill.

Brown, J. D., and Dutton, K. A. (1995). The thrill of victory, the complexity of defeat: Self-esteem and people's emotional reactions to success and failure. *Journal of Personality and Social Psychology, 68,* 712–722.

Brown, J. D., and Smart, S. A. (1991). The self and social conduct: Linking self-representations to prosocial behavior. *Journal of Personality and Social Psychology, 60,* 368–375.

Bruce, J., Davis, E. P., and Gunnar, M. R. (2002). Individual differences in children's cortisol response to the beginning of a new school year. *Psychoneuroendocrinology, 27,* 635–650.

Bruch, M. A., and Hynes, M. J. (1987). Heterosexual anxiety and contraceptive behavior. *Journal of Research in Personality, 21,* 343–360.

Bruggemann, J. M., and Barry, R. J. (2002). Eysenck's P as a modulator of affective and electrodermal responses to violent and comic film. *Personality and Individual Differences, 32,* 1029–1048.

Buerkle, J. V. (1960). Self attitudes and marital adjustment. *Merrill-Palmer Quarterly, 6,* 114–124.

Bullock, W. A., and Gilliland, K. (1993). Eysenck's arousal theory of introversion-extraversion: A converging measures investigation. *Journal of Personality and Social Psychology, 64,* 113–123.

Bunce, S. C., Larsen, R. J., and Peterson, C. (1995). Life after trauma: Personality and daily life experiences of traumatized persons. *Journal of Personality, 63,* 165–188.

Burgess, E. W., and Wallin, P. (1953). *Engagement and marriage.* New York: Lippincott.

Burns, M. O., and Seligman, M. E. (1989). Explanatory style across the life span: Evidence for stability over 52 years. *Journal of Personality and Social Psychology, 56,* 471–477.

Burnstein, E., Crandall, C., and Kitayama, S. (1994). Some neo-Darwinian decision rules for altruism: Weighing cures for inclusive fitness as a function of the biological importance of the decision. *Journal of Personality and Social Psychology, 67,* 773–789.

Burt, S. A., McGue, M., Iacono, W., Comings, D., and MacMurray, J. (2002). An examination of the association between DRD4 and DRD2 polymorphisms and personality traits. *Personality and Individual Differences, 33,* 849–859.

Bush, G., Luu, P., and Posner, M. I. (2000). Cognitive and emotional influences in anterior cingulated cortex. *Trends in Cognitive Sciences, 4,* 215–222.

Bushman, B., and Baumeister, R. (1998). Threatened egotism, narcissism, self-esteem, and direct and displaced aggression: Does self-love or self-hate lead to violence? *Journal of Personality and Social Psychology, 75,* 219–229.

Bushman, B. J., and Baumeister, R. F. (2002). Does self-love or self-hate lead to violence? *Journal of Research in Personality, 36,* 543–545.

Bushman, B. J., Bonacci, A. M., van Dijk, M., and Baumeister, R. F. (2003). Narcissism, sexual refusal and aggression: Testing a narcissistic reactance model of sexual coercion. *Journal of Personality and Social Psychology, 84,* 5, 1027–1040.

Buss, 1995b in 1/e.

Buss, A. H. (1989). Personality as traits. *American Psychologist, 44,* 1378–1388.

Buss, D. M. (1981). Predicting parent-child interactions from children's activity level. *Developmental Psychology, 17,* 59–65.

Buss, D. M. (1984). Toward a psychology of person-environment (PE) correlation: The role of spouse selection. *Journal of Personality and Social Psychology, 47,* 361–377.

Buss, D. M. (1985). Human mate selection. *American Scientist, 73,* 47–51.

Buss, D. M. (1987). Selection, evocation, and manipulation. *Journal of Personality and Social Psychology, 53,* 1214–1221.

Buss, D. M. (1989). Sex differences in human mate preferences: Evolutionary hypotheses tested in 37 cultures. *Behavioral and Brain Sciences, 12,* 1–49.

Buss, D. M. (1990). The evolution of anxiety and social exclusion. *Journal of Social and Clinical Psychology, 9,* 196–201.

Buss, D. M. (1991a). Conflict in married couples: Personality predictors of anger and upset. *Journal of Personality, 59,* 663–688.

Buss, D. M. (1991b). Evolutionary personality psychology. *Annual Review of Psychology.* Palo Alto, CA: Annual Reviews, Inc.

Buss, D. M. (1992). Manipulation in close relationships: Five personality factors in interactional context. *Journal of Personality, 60,* 477–499.

Buss, D. M. (1993). Strategic individual differences: The role of personality in creating and solving adaptive problems. In J. Hettema and I. Deary (Eds.), *Social and Biological Approaches to Personality.* New York: Wiley (pp. 175–189).

Buss, D. M. (1995a). Evolutionary psychology: A new paradigm for psychological science. *Psychological Inquiry, 6,* 1–49.

Buss, D. M. (1995b). Psychological sex differences: Origins through sexual selection. *American Psychologist, 50,* 164–168.

Buss, D. M. (1996). Social adaptation and five major factors of personality. In J. S. Wiggins (Ed.), *The five-factor model of personality: Theoretical perspectives* (pp. 180–207). New York: Guilford Press.

Buss, D. M. (2000a). *The dangerous passion: Why jealousy is as necessary as love and sex.* New York: Free Press.

Buss, D. M. (2000b). The evolution of happiness. *American Psychologist, 55,* 15–23.

Buss, D. M. (2003). *The evolution of desire: Strategies of human mating* (Revised Edition). New York: Basic Books.

Buss, D. M. (2004). *Evolutionary psychology: The new science of the mind* (2nd ed.). Boston: Allyn and Bacon.

Buss, D. M. (2005). *The Handbook of evolutionary psychology.* New York: Wiley.

Buss, D. M. (2005). *The murderer next door: Why the mind is designed to kill.* New York: Penguin.

Buss, D. M., and Barnes, M. L. (1986). Preferences in human mate selection. *Journal of Personality and Social Psychology, 50,* 559–570.

Buss, D. M., and Chiodo, L. M. (1991). Narcissistic acts in everyday life. *Journal of Personality, 59,* 2, 179–215.

Buss, D. M., and Craik, K. H. (1983). The act frequency approach to personality. *Psychological Review, 90,* 105–126.

Buss, D. M., and Dentley, J. D. (in press). The evolution of aggression. In M./ Schaller, D. T. Kenrick, and J. A. Simpson (Eds.), *Evolution and social psychology.* New York: Psychology Press.

Buss, D. M., and Haselton, M. G. (2005). The evolution of jealousy. *Trends in Cognitive Science, 9,* 506–507.

Buss, D. M., and Schmitt, D. P. (1993) Sexual strategies theory: An evolutionary perspective on human mating. *Psychological Review, 100,* 204–232.

Buss, D. M., Abbott, M., Angleitner, A., Asherian, A., Biaggio, A., et al. (1990). International preferences in selecting mates: A study of 37 cultures. *Journal of Cross-Cultural Psychology, 21,* 5–47.

Buss, D. M., Block, J. H., and Block, J. (1980). Preschool activity level: Personality correlates and developmental implications. *Child Development, 51,* 401–408.

Buss, D. M., Gomes, M., Higgins, D. S., and Lauterbach, K. (1987). Tactics of manipulation. *Journal of Personality and Social Psychology, 52,* 1219–1229.

Buss, D. M., and Greiling, H. (1999). Adaptive individual differences. *Journal of Personality, 67,* 209–243.

Buss, D. M., Larsen, R. J., Semmelroth, J., and Westen, D. (1992). Sex differences in jealousy: Evolution, physiology, and psychology. *Psychological Science, 3,* 251–255.

Buss, D. M., Shackelford, T. K., Kirkpatrick, L. A., Choe, J., Hasegawa, M., Hasegawa, T., and Bennett, K. (1999). Jealousy and the nature of beliefs about infidelity: Tests of competing hypotheses about sex differences in the United States, Korea, and Japan. *Personal Relationships, 6,* 125–150.

Buss, K. A., Schumacher, J. R. M., Dolski, I., Kalin, N. H., Goldsmith, H. H., and Davidson, R. J. (2003). Right frontal brain activity, cortisol, and withdrawal behavior in 6-month-old infants. *Behavioral Neuroscience, 117,* 11–20.

Butler, A. C., Hokanson, J. E., and Flynn, H. A. (1994). A comparison of self-esteem lability and low trait self-esteem as vulnerability factors for depression. *Journal of Personality and Social Psychology, 66,* 166–177.

Butler, E. A., Egloff, B., Wilhelm, F. H., Smith, N. C., Erickson, E. A., and Gross, J. J. (2003). The social consequences of expressive suppression. *Emotion, 3,* 48–67.

Buunk, B., Angleitner, A., Oubaid, V., and Buss, D. M. (1996). Sexual and cultural differences in jealousy: Tests from the Netherlands, Germany, and the United States. *Psychological Science, 7,* 359–363.

Byrnes, J. P., Miller, D. C., and Schafer, W. D. (1999). Gender differences in risk taking: A meta-analysis. *Psychological Bulletin, 125,* 367–383.

Cafferty, T. P., Davis, K. E., Medway, F. J., O'Hearn, R. E., and Chappell, K. D. (1994). Reunion dynamics among couples separated during Operation Desert Storm: An attachment theory analysis. In: K. Bartholomew and D. Perlman (Eds.), *Attachment processes in adulthood* (pp. 309–330). Philadelphia, PA: Jessica Kingsley Publishers.

Campbell, J. B., and Hawley, C. W. (1982). Study habits and Eysenck's theory of extraversion-introversion. *Journal of Research in Personality, 16,* 139–146.

Campbell, W. K., and Foster, C. A. (2002). Narcissism and commitment in romantic relationships: An investment model analysis. *Personality and Social Psychology Bulletin, 28,* 4, 484–495.

Campbell, W. K., Rudich, E. A., and Sedikides, C. (2002). Narcissism, self-esteem, and the positivity of self-views: Two portraits of self-love. *Personality and Social Psychology Bulletin, 28,* 3, 358–368.

Canli, T., and Amin, Z. (2002). Neuroimaging of emotion and personality: Scientific evidence and ethical considerations. *Brain and Cognition, 50,* 414–431.

Canli, T., Zuo, Z., Kang, E., Gross, J., Desmond, J. E., and Gabrielil, J. D. (2001). An fMRI study of personality influences on brain reactivity to emotional stimuli. *Behavioral Neuroscience, 115,* 33–42.

Cann, A., Mangum, J. L., and Wells, M. (2001). Distress in response to relationship infidelity: The roles of gender and attitudes about relationships. *Journal of Sex Research, 38,* 185–190.

Cantor, N. (1990). From thought to behavior: "Having" and "doing" in the study of personality and cognition. *American Psychologist, 45,* 735–750.

Cantor, N., and Norem, J. K. (1989). Defensive pessimism and stress and coping. *Social Cognition, 7,* 91–112.

Cantor, N., Norem, J., Langston, C., Zirkel, S., Fleeson, W., and Cook Flannagan, C. (1991). Life tasks and daily life experience. *Journal of Personality, 59,* 425–451.

Cantor, N., and Zirkel, S. (1990). Personality, cognition, and purposive behavior. In L. A. Pervin (Ed.), *Handbook of personality: Theory and research* (pp. 135–164). New York: Guilford Press.

Caplan, S. E. (2002). Problematic Internet use and psychosocial well-being:

Development of a theory-based, cognitive-behavioral measurement instrument. *Computers in Human Behavior, 18,* 553–575.

Caprara, G. V., Barbaranelli, C., Consiglio, C., Picconi, L., and Zimbardo, P. G. (2003). Personalities of politicians and voters: Unique and synergistic relationships. *Journal of Personality and Social Psychology, 84,* 4, 849–856.

Caprara, G. V., and Perugini, M. (1994). Personality described by adjectives: Generalizability of the big five to the Italian lexical context. *European Journal of Psychology, 8,* 357–369.

Cardemil, E. V., Reivich, K. J., and Seligman, Martin E. P. (2002). The prevention of depressive symptoms in low-income minority middle school students. *Prevention and Treatment, 5,* np.

Carlo, G., Okun, M. A., Knight, G. P., and de Guzman, M. R. T. (2005). The interplay of traits and motives on volunteering: Agreeableness, extraversion and prosocial value motivation. *Personality and Individual Differences, 38,* 1293–1305.

Carter, R. (1999). *Mapping the mind.* University of California Press: Berkeley, CA.

Carver, C. S. (1996). Emergent integration in contemporary personality psychology. *Journal of Research in Personality, 30,* 319–334.

Carver, C. S., and Scheier, M. F. (2000). Autonomy and self regulation. *Psychological Inquiry, 11,* 284–291.

Carver, C. S., Pozo, C., Harris, S. D., Noriega, V., Scheier, M. F., Robinson, D. S., Ketcham, A. S., Moffat, F. L., and Clark, K. C. (1993). How coping mediates the effect of optimism on distress: A study of women with early stage breast cancer. *Journal of Personality and Social Psychology, 65,* 375–390.

Carver, C. S., Sutton, S. K., and Scheier, M. F. (1999). Action, emotion, and personality: Emerging conceptual integration. *Personality and Social Psychology Bulletin, 26,* 741–751.

Carver, C. S., and White, T. L. (1994). Behavioral inhibition, behavioral activation, and affective responses to impeding reward and punishments: The BIS/BAS scales. *Journal of Personality and Social Psychology, 67,* 319–333.

Cashden, E. (1980). Egalitarianism among hunters and gatherers. *American Anthropologist, 82,* 116–120.

Caspi, A., and Herbener, E. S. (1990). Continuity and change: Assortative mating and the consistency of personality in adulthood. *Journal of Personality and Social Psychology, 58,* 250–258.

Caspi, A., Elder, G. H., Jr., and Bem, D. J. (1987). Moving against the world: Life-course patterns of explosive children. *Developmental Psychology, 23,* 308–313.

Caspi, A., Harrington, H., Milne, B., Amell, J. W., Theodore, R. F., and Moffitt, T. E. (2003). Children's behavioral styles at age 3 are linked to their adult personality traits at age 26. *Journal of Personality, 71,* 495–513.

Caspi, A., Roberts, B. W., and Shiner, R. L. (2005). Personality development: Stability and change. *Annual Review of Psychology, 56,* 453–458.

Cassidy, J., and Shaver, P. (1999). *Handbook of attachment: Theory, research, and clinical applications.* New York: Guilford Press.

Cattell, R. B. (1943). The description of personality: Basic traits resolved into clusters. *Journal of Abnormal and Social Psychology, 38,* 476–507.

Cattell, R. B. (1967). *Objective personality and motivational tests: A theoretical introduction and practical compendium.* Champaign: University of Illinois Press.

Cattell, R. B. (1973). *Personality and mood by questionnaire.* San Francisco: Jossey-Bass.

Cattell, R. B. (1977). *Handbook of modern personality theory.* Washington, DC: Hemisphere.

Cattell, R. B. (1987). *Beyondism: Religion from science.* New York: Praeger.

Cattell, R. B., Eber, H. W., and Tatsouoka, M. M. (1970). *Handbook for the 16 PF.* Champaign, IL: Institute for Personality and Ability Testing.

Chagnon, N. (1983). *Yanomamö: The fierce people* (3rd ed.). New York: Holt, Rinehart and Winston.

Chagnon, N. (1988). Life histories, blood revenge, and warfare in a tribal population. *Science, 239,* 985–992.

Chamorro-Premuzic, T., and Furnham, A. (2003a). Personality predicts academic performance: Evidence from two longitudinal university samples. *Journal of Research in Personality, 37,* 319–338.

Chamorro-Premuzic, T., and Furnham, A. (2003b). Personality traits and academic examination performance. *European Journal of Personality, 17,* 237–250.

Charles, S. T., Reynolds, C. A. and Gatz, M. (2001). Age-related differences and change in positive and negative affect over 23 years. *Journal of Personality and Social Psychology, 80,* 1, 136–151.

Chavira, D. A., Stein, M. B., and Malcarne, V. L. (2002). Scrutinizing the relationship between shyness and social phobia. *Journal of Anxiety Disorders, 16,* 585–598.

Cheek, J. M. (1983). *The revised Cheek and Buss Shyness Scale.* Unpublished manuscript, Department of Psychology, Wellesley College, Wellesley, MA.

Cheek, J. M. (1989). *Conquering shyness.* New York: Dell.

Cheek, J. M., and Buss, A. H. (1981). Shyness and sociability. *Journal of Personality and Social Psychology, 41,* 330–339.

Cheek, J. M., and Krasnoperova, E. N. (1999). Varieties of shyness in adolescence and adulthood. In L. A. Schmidt and J. Schulkin (Eds.), *Extreme fear, shyness, and social phobia: Origins, biological mechanisms, and clinical outcomes* (pp. 224–250). London: Oxford University Press.

Cheek, J. M., and Melchior, L. A. (1990). Shyness, self-esteem, and self-consciousness. In H. Leitenberg (Ed.), *Handbook of social and evaluation anxiety* (pp. 47–82) New York: Plenum Press.

Cheng, H., and Furnham, A. (2003). Personality, self-esteem, and demographic predictions of happiness and depression. *Personality and Individual Differences, 34,* 921–942.

Chioqueta, A. P., and Stiles, T. C. (2005). Personality traits and the development of depression, hopelessness, and suicidal ideation. *Personality and Individual Differences, 38,* 1283–1291.

Chodorow, N. J. (1989). *Feminism and psychoanalytic theory.* New Haven, CT: Yale University Press.

Christ, S. E., White, D., Brunstrom, J. E., and Abrams, R. A. (2003). Inhibitory control following perinatal brain injury. *Neuropsychology, 17,* 171–178.

Christie, R., and Geis, F. L. (1970). *Studies in Machiavellianism.* (pp. 53–76) New York: Academic Press.

Chu, J. A. (1998). *Rebuilding shattered lives: The responsible treatment of complex post-traumatic and dissociative disorders.* New York: Wiley.

Church, A. T. (2000). Culture and personality: Toward an integrated cultural trait psychology. *Journal of Personality, 68,* 651–703.

Civil Service Reform Act of 1978. PL 95–454 (S 2640), U.S. Congress, October, 1978.

Clapper, R. L. (1990). Adult and adolescent arousal preferences: The revised reducer augmenter scale. *Personality and Individual Differences, 11,* 1115–1122.

Clapper, R. L. (1992). The reducer-augmenter scale, the revised reducer augmenter scale, and predicting late adolescent substance use. *Personality and Individual Differences, 13,* 813–820.

Claridge, G. S., Donald, J., and Birchall, P. M. (1981). Drug tolerance and personality: Some implications for Eysenck's theory. *Personality and Individual Differences, 2,* 153–166.

Clark, R. D. (1990). The impact of AIDS on gender differences in willingness to engage in casual sex. *Journal of Applied Social Psychology, 20,* 771–782.

Clark, R. D., and Hatfield, E. (1989). Gender differences in receptivity to sexual offers. *Journal of Psychology and Human Sexuality, 2,* 39–55.

Cleckley, H. (1988). *The mask of sanity.* Augusta, GA: Emily S. Cleckley.

Cleveland, H. H., Udry, J. R., and Chantala, K. (2001). Environmental and genetic influences on sex-types behaviors and attitudes of male and female adolescents. *Personality and Social Psychology Bulletin, 27,* 12, 1587–1598.

Clifton, A., Turkheimer, E., and Oltmanns, T. F. (in press). Contrasting perspectives on personality problems: Descriptions from the self and others. *Personality and Individual Differences.*

Clinton, W. J. (1995). Interview on MTV, August 9–16, 1995.

Cloninger, C. R. (1986). A unified biosocial theory of personality and its role in the development of anxiety states. *Psychiatric Developments, 3,* 167–226.

Cloninger, C. R. (1987). A systematic method for clinical description and classification of personality variants: A proposal. *Archives of General Psychiatry, 44,* 573–588.

Cloninger, C. R. (1999). *Personality and psychopathology.* Washington, DC: American Psychiatric Press.

Cloninger, C. R., Sigvardsson, S., and Bohman, M. (1988). Childhood personality predicts alcohol abuse in young adults. *Alcoholism Clinical and Experimental Research, 12,* 494–505.

Cloninger, C. R., Svrakic, D. M., and Przybeck, T. R. (1993). A psychobiological model of temperament and character. *Archives of General Psychiatry, 50,* 975–990.

Cloninger, C. R. Personal communication Oct. 2003.

Clower, C. E., and Bothwell, R. K. (2001). An exploratory study of the relationship between the Big Five and inmate recidivism. *Journal of Research in Personality, 35,* 231–237.

Cobb, S. (1976). Social support as a moderator of life stress. *Psychosomatic Medicine, 38,* 300–315.

Cohen, J. (1977). *Statistical power analysis for the behavioral sciences.* San Diego, CA: Academic Press.

Cohen, J., and Cohen, P. (1975). *Applied multiple regression/correlation analysis for the behavioral sciences.* Hillsdale, NJ: Lawrence Erlbaum.

Cohen, S., Doyle, W. J., Skoner, D. P., Fireman, P., Gwaltney, J. M., Jr., and Newsom, J. T. (1995). State and trait negative affect as predictors of objective and subjective symptoms of respiratory viral infections. *Journal of Personality and Social Psychology, 68,* 159–169.

Cohen, S., Tyrrell, D. A. J., and Smith, A. P. (1997). Psychological stress in humans and susceptibility to the common cold. In T. W. Moller (Ed.), *Clinical disorders and stressful life events* (pp. 217–235). Madison, CT: International Universities Press.

Coleman, R. (1992). *Lennon: The definitive biography.* New York: Perennial.

Collins, J. N. (1994). Some fundamental questions about scientific thinking. *Research in Science and Technological Education, 12,* 161–173.

Conley, J. J. (1984a). The hierarchy of consistency: A review and model of longitudinal findings on adult individual differences in intelligence, personality, and self-opinion. *Personality and Individual Differences, 5,* 11–25.

Conley, J. J. (1984b). Longitudinal consistency of adult personality: Self-reported psychological characteristics across 45 years. *Journal of Personality and Social Psychology, 47,* 1325–1333.

Conley, J. J. (1985). Longitudinal stability of personality traits: A multitrait-multimethod-multioccasion analysis. *Journal of Personality and Social Psychology, 49,* 1266–1282.

Conley, J. J., and Angelides, M. (1984). *Personality antecedents of emotional disorders and alcohol abuse in men: Results of a forty-five year prospective study.* Unpublished manuscript: Wesleyan University, Middletown, CT.

Connolly, I., and O'Moore, M. (2003). Personality and family relations of children who bully. *Personality and Individual Differences, 35,* 559–567.

Contrada, R. J., Leventhal, H., and O'Leary, A. (1990). Personality and health. In L. A. Pervin (Ed.), *Handbook of personality: Theory and research* (pp. 638–669). New York: Guilford Press.

Coolidge, F. L., Thede, L. L., and Young, S. E. (2002). The heritability of gender identity disorder in a child and adolescent twin sample. *Behavior Genetics, 32,* 251–257.

Cooper, M. L., Wood, P. K., Orcutt, H. K., and Albino, A. (2003). Personality and the predisposition to engage in risky or problem behaviors during adolescence. *Journal of Personality and Social Psychology, 84,* 2, 390–410.

Cooper, S. H. (1998). Changing notions of defense within psychoanalytic theory. *Journal of Personality, 66,* 947–965.

Corcoran, D. W. J. (1964). The relation between introversion and salivation. *American Journal of Psychology, 77,* 298–300.

Cosmides, L., and Tooby, J. (1992). Cognitive adaptations for social exchange. In J. Barkow, L. Cosmides, and J. Tooby (Eds.), *The adapted mind* (pp. 163–228). New York: Academic Press.

Costa, P. T., and McCrae, R. R. (1980). Influence of extraversion and neuroticism on subjective well-being: Happy and unhappy people. *Journal of Personality and Social Psychology, 38,* 668–678.

Costa, P. T., and McCrae, R. R. (1985). Hypochondriasis, neuroticism, and aging: When are somatic complaints unfounded? *American Psychologist, 40,* 19–28.

Costa, P. T., Jr., and McCrae, R. R. (1988). Personality in adulthood: A six-year longitudinal study of self-reports and spouse ratings on the NEO Personality Inventory. *Journal of Personality and Social Psychology, 54,* 853–863.

Costa, P. T., Jr., and McCrae, R. R. (1989). *The NEO-PI/NEO-FFI manual supplement.* Odessa, FL: Psychological Assessment Resources.

Costa, P. T., Jr., and McCrae, R. R. (1992). Trait psychology comes of age. In T. B. Sonderegger (Ed.), *Nebraska symposium on motivation: Psychology and aging* (pp. 169–204). Lincoln: University of Nebraska Press.

Costa, P. T., Jr., and McCrae, R. R. (1994). Set like plaster? Evidence for the stability of adult personality. In T. F. Heatherton and J. L. Weinberger (Eds.), *Can personality change?* Washington, DC: American Psychological Association.

Costa, P. T., Jr., and McCrae, R. R. (1995). Solid ground in the wetlands of personality: A reply to Block. *Psychological Bulletin, 117,* 216–220.

Costa, P. T., McCrae, R. R., and Zonderman, A. B. (1987). Environmental and dispositional influences on well-being: Longitudinal follow-up of an American national sample. *British Journal of Psychology, 78,* 299–306.

Costa, P. T., and Widiger, T. A. (1994). *Personality disorders and the five-factor model of personality.* Washington, DC: American Psychological Association.

Costa, P. T., and Widiger, T. A. (Eds.). (2002). *Personality disorders and the five-factor model of personality.* Washington, DC: American Psychological Association.

Coutts, L. M. (1990). Police hiring and promotion: Methods and outcomes. *Canadian Police College Journal, 14,* 98–122.

Craik, K. H. (1986). Personality research methods: An historical perspective. *Journal of Personality, 54,* 18–51.

Cramer, P. (2000). Defense mechanisms in psychology today: Further processes for adaptation. *American Psychologist, 55,* 637–646.

Cramer, P. (2002). Defense mechanisms, behavior, and affect in young adulthood. *Journal of Personality, 70,* 103–126.
Cramer, P., and Davidson, K. (1998). Defense mechanisms in contemporary personality research. *Special Issue of the Journal of Personality, 66.*
Crandall, J. E. (1991). A scale for social interest. *Individual Psychology: Journal of Adlerian Theory, Research and Practice, 47,* 106–114.
Crandall, V. C., Katkovsky, W., and Crandall, V. J. (1965). Children's belief in their own control of reinforcements in intellectual-academic achievement situations. *Child Development, 36,* 91–109.
Crandall, V., Dewey, R., Katkovsky, W., and Preston, A. (1964). Parents' attitudes and behaviors and grade-school children's academic achievements. *Journal of Genetic Psychology, 104,* 53–66.
Crocker, J., and Major, B. (1989). Social stigma and self-esteem: The self-protective properties of stigma. *Psychological Review, 96,* 608–630.
Cronbach, L. J., and Gleser, G. C. (1965). *Psychological tests and personnel decisions.* Urbana: University of Illinois Press.
Cronbach, L. J., and Meehl, P. E. (1955). Construct validity in psychological tests. *Psychological Bulletin, 52,* 281–302.
Crone, E. A., Vendel, I., and van der Molen, M. W. (2003). Decision-making in disinhibited adolescents and adults: Insensitivity to future consequences or driven by immediate reward? *Personality and Individual Differences, 35,* 1625–1641.
Cross, S. E., Kanagawa, C., Markus, H. R., and Kitayama, S. (1995). *Cultural variation in self-concept.* Unpublished manuscript, Iowa State University, Ames.
Crowne, D. P., and Marlowe, D. (1964). *The approval motive: Studies in evaluation dependence.* New York: Wiley.
Cruz, M., and Larsen, R. J. (1995). Personality correlates of individual differences in electrodermal lability. *Journal of Social Behavior and Personality, 23,* 93–104.
Csikszentmihalyi, M. (1999). If we are so rich, why aren't we happy? *American Psychologist, 54,* 821–827.
Csikszentmihalyi, M. (2000). Beyond boredom and anxiety (25th anniversary ed.). San Francisco: Jossey-Bass. (Original work published 1975.)
Csikszentmihalyi, M., Abuhamdeh, S., and Nakamura, J. (2005). Flow. In A. J. Elliot and C. S. Dweck (Eds.), *Handbook of competence and motivation* (pp. 598–608). New York: Guilford.
Cunningham-Williams, R. M., Grucza, R. A., Cottler, L. B., Womack, S. B., Books, S. J., Przybeck, T. R., Spitznagel, E. L., and Cloninger, C. R. (2005). Prevalence and predictors of pathological gambling: Results from the St. Louis personality, health, and lifestyle (SLPHL) study. *Journal of Psychiatric Research, 39,* 377–390.
Cutler, S. S., Larsen, R. J., and Bunce, S. C. (1996). Repressive coping style and the experience and recall of emotion: A naturalistic study of daily affect. *Journal of Personality, 65,* 379–405.
Dabbs, J. M., Jr., and Dabbs, M. G. (2000). *Heroes, rogues and lovers: Testosterone and behavior.* New York: McGraw-Hill.
Dabbs, J. M., Jr., and Hargrove, M. F. (1997). Age, testosterone, and behavior among female prison inmates. *Psychosomatic Medicine, 59,* 477–480.
Dabbs, J. M., Jr., Hargrove, M. F., and Heusel, C. (1996). Testosterone differences among college fraternities: Well-behaved vs. rambunctious. *Personality and Individual Differences, 20,* 157–161.
Dalgleish, T. (1995) Performance on the emotional Stroop task in groups of anxious, expert, and control subjects: A comparison of computer and card presentation formats. *Cognition and Emotion, 9,* 341–362.
Dallam, S. J., Gleaves, D. H., Cepeda-Benito, A., Silberg, J. L., Kraemer, H. C., and Spiegel, D. (2001). The effects of child sexual abuse: Comment on Rind, Tromovitch, and Bauserman (1998). *Psychological Bulletin, 127,* 715–733.
Daly, M., and Wilson, M. (1988). *Homicide.* New York: Aldine de Gruyter.
Daly, M., and Wilson, M. (1996). Evolutionary psychology and marital conflict: The relevance of stepchildren. In D. M. Buss and N. Malamuth (Eds.), *Sex, power, conflict: Evolutionary and feminist perspectives* (pp. 9–28). New York: Oxford University Press.
Damasio, A. R. (1994). *Descartes' error: Emotion, reason, and the human brain.* New York: Putnam.
Danner, D. D., Snowdon, D. A., and Friesen, W. V. (2001). Positive emotions in early life and longevity: Findings from the nun study. *Journal of Personality and Social Psychology, 80,* 804–813.
Darwin, C. (1859) *The origin of species.* London: Murray.
Darwin, C. (1872/1965). *The expression of the emotions in man and animals.* Chicago: University of Chicago Press.
Davidson, R. J. (1991). Cerebral asymmetry and affective disorders: A developmental approach. In D. Cicchetti and S. L. Toth (Eds.), *Internalizing and Externalizing Expressions of Dysfunction: Rochester Symposium and Developmental Psychopathology,* Vol. 2 (pp. 123–154). Hillsdale, NJ: Erlbaum.
Davidson, R. J. (1993). The neuropsychology of emotion and affective style. In M. Lewis and J. M. Haviland (Eds.), *Handbook of emotions* (pp. 143–154). New York: Guilford.
Davidson, R. J. (2000). Affective style, psychopathology, and resilience: Brain mechanisms and plasticity. *American Psychologist, 55,* 1196–1214.
Davidson, R. J. (2003). Affective neuroscience and psychophysiology: Toward a synthesis. *Psychophysiology, 40,* 655–665.
Davidson, R. J., Ekman, P., Saron, C. D., Senulis, J. A., and Friesen, W. V. (1990). Approach/withdrawal and cerebral asymmetry: Emotional expression and brain physiology. I. *Journal of Personality and Social Psychology, 58,* 330–341.
Davidson, R. J., Kabat-Zinn, J., Schumacher, J., Rosenkranz, M., Muller, D., Santorelli, S. F., Urbanowski, F., Harrington, A., Bonus, K., and Sheridan, J. F. (2003). Alterations in brain and immune function produced by mindfulness meditation. *Psychosomatic Medicine, 65,* 564–570.
Davidson, R. J., Scherer, K. R., and Goldsmith, H. H. (2003). *Handbook of affective sciences.* New York: Oxford University Press.
Davis, M. H., Luce, C., and Kraus, S. J. (1994). The heritability of characteristics associated with dispositional empathy. *Journal of Personality, 62,* 369–391.
Davis, M. H., Mitchell, K. V., Hall, J. A., Lothert, J., Snapp, T., and Meyer, M. (1999). Empathy, expectations, and situational preferences: Personality influences on the decision to participate in volunteer helping behaviors. *Journal of Personality, 67,* 469–503.
Davis, P. J. (1987). Repression and the inaccessibility of affective memories. *Journal of Personality and Social Psychology, 53,* 585–593.
Davis, P. J., and Schwartz, G. E. (1987). Repression and the inaccessibility of affective memories. *Journal of Personality and Social Psychology, 52,* 155–162.
De Gelder, B., Vroomen, J., and Pourtois, G. (2001). Covert affective cognition and affective blindsight. In B. De Gelder, E. De Haan, and C. A. Heywood, (Eds.), *Out of mind: Varieties of unconscious processes* (pp. 205–221). New York, NY: Oxford University Press.
De Raad, B. (1998). Five big, big five issues: Rationale, content, structure, status, and crosscultural assessment. *European Psychologist, 3,* 113–124.
De Raad, B., Perugini, M., Hrebickova, M., and Şzarota, P. (1998). Lingua Franca of personality: Taxonomies and structures

based on the psycholexical approach. *Journal of Cross-Cultural Psychology, 29,* 212–232.

De Vries, J., and Van Heck, G. L. (2002). Fatigue: Relationships with basic personality and temperament dimensions. *Personality and Individual Differences, 33,* 1311–1324.

DeAngelis, T. (1991). Honesty tests weigh in with improved ratings. *APA Monitor, 22,* 6.

Deaux, K. (1984). From individual differences to social categories: Analysis of a decade's research on gender. *American Psychologist, 39,* 105–116.

Deaux, K., and LaFrance, M. (1998). Gender. In D. T. Gilbert, S. T. Fiske, and G. Lindzey (Eds.), *The handbook of social psychology* (Vol. 1, 4th ed., pp. 788–827). Boston: McGraw-Hill.

Deaux, K., and Lewis, L. L. (1984). Structure of gender stereotypes: Interrelationships among components and gender label. *Journal of Personality and Social Psychology, 46,* 991–1004.

Deiner, C. I., and Dweck, C. S. (1978). An analysis of learned helplessness: Continuous changes in performance, strategy, and achievement cognitions following failure. *Journal of Personality and Social Psychology, 36,* 451–462.

Deiner, C. I., and Dweck, C. S. (1980). An analysis of learned helplessness (II): The processing of success. *Journal of Personality and Social Psychology, 39,* 940–952.

Delongis, A., Folkman, S., and Lazarus, R. S. (1988). The impact of daily stress on health and mood: Psychological and social resources as mediators. *Journal of Personality and Social Psychology, 54,* 986–995.

Dembrowski, T. M., and Costa, P. T. (1987). Coronary-prone behavior: Components of the Type A pattern and hostility. *Journal of Personality, 55,* 211–235.

Dembrowski, T. M., and MacDougall, J. M. (1985). Beyond global Type A: Relationships of paralinguistic attributes, hostility, and anger-in to coronary heart disease. In T. Field, P. McAbe, and N. Schneiderman (Eds.), *Stress and coping* (pp. 223–242). Hillsdale, NJ: Erlbaum.

Dembrowski, T. M., and Williams, R. B. (1989). Definition and assessment of coronary-prone behavior. In N. Schneiderman, P. Kaufman, and S. M. Weiss (Eds.), *Handbook of research methods in cardiovascular behavioral medicine.* New York: Plenum Press.

Demerath, P. (2001). The social cost of acting "extra": Students' moral judgments of self, social relations, and academic success in Papua New Guinea. *American Journal of Education, 108,* 3.

DeMeuse, K. (1985). The relationship between life events and indices of classroom performance. *Teaching of Psychology, 12,* 146–149.

DePaulo, B. M., Dull, W. R., Greenberg, J. M., and Swaim, G. (1989). Are shy people reluctant to ask for help? *Journal of Personality and Social Psychology, 56,* 834–844.

DePaulo, B. M., Kenny, D. A., Hoover, C. W., Webb, W., and Oliver, P. V. (1987). Accuracy of person perception: Do people know what kinds of impressions they convey? *Journal of Personality and Social Psychology, 52,* 303–315.

Depue, R. A. (1996). A neurobiological framework for the structure of personality and emotion: Implications for personality disorders. In J. Clarkin and M. Lenzenweger (Eds.), *Major theories of personality disorders* (pp. 347–390). New York: Guilford.

Depue, R. A., and Collins, P. F. (1999). Neurobiology of the structure of personality: Dopamine, facilitation of incentive motivation, and extraversion. *Behavioral and Brain Sciences, 22,* 491–517.

DeSteno, D. A., Bartlett, M. Y., Salovey, P., and Braverman, J. (2002). Sex differences in jealousy: Evolutionary mechanisms of experimental artifact? *Journal of Personality and Social Psychology, 83,* 1103–1116.

DeSteno, D. A., and Salovey, P. (1996). Evolutionary origins of sex differences in jealousy: Questioning the "fitness" of the model. *Psychological Science, 7,* 367–372.

Di Blas, L. (2005). Personality-relevant attribute-nouns: A taxonomic study in the Italian language. *European Journal of Personality, 19,* 537–557.

Diamond, J. (1999). *Guns, germs, and steel.* New York: Norton.

Diener, E. (1996). Traits can be powerful, but are not enough—Lessons from subjective well-being. *Journal of Research in Personality, 30,* 389–399.

Diener, E. (2000). Subjective well-being: The science of happiness and a proposal for a national index. *American Psychologist, 55,* 34–43.

Diener, E., and Biswas-Diener, R. (2002). Will money increase subjective well-being? A literature review and guide to needed research. *Social Indicators Research, 57,* 119–169.

Diener, E., Suh, E. M., Lucas, R. E., and Smith, H. L. (1999). Subjective well-being: Three decades of progress. *Psychological Bulletin, 125,* 276–302.

Diener, E., and Diener, M. (1995). Cross-cultural correlates of life satisfaction and self-esteem. *Journal of Personality and Social Psychology, 68,* 653–663.

Diener, E., and Larsen, R. J. (1984). Temporal stability and cross-situational consistency of affective, behavioral, and cognitive responses. *Journal of Personality and Social Psychology, 47,* 871–883.

Diener, E., and Scollon, C. N. (2002). Our desired future for personality psychology. *Journal of Research in Personality, 36,* 629–637.

Diener, E., and Seligman, M. E. P. (2002). Very happy people. *Psychological Science, 13,* 80–83.

Diener, E., Diener, M., and Diener, C. (1995). Factors predicting the subjective well-being of nations. *Journal of Personality and Social Psychology, 69,* 851–864.

Diener, E., Emmons, R. A., Larsen, R. J., and Griffin, S. (1985). The Satisfaction With Life Scale. *Journal of Personality Assessment, 49,* 71–75.

Diener, E., Horowitz, J., and Emmons, R. A. (1985). Happiness of the very wealthy. *Social Indicators Research, 16,* 263–274.

Diener, E., Larsen, R. J., and Emmons, R. A. (1984). Person X situation interactions: Choice of situations and congruence response models. *Journal of Personality and Social Psychology, 47,* 580–592.

Diener, E., Larsen, R. J., Levine, S., and Emmons, R. A. (1985). Intensity and frequency: Dimensions underlying positive and negative affect. *Journal of Personality and Social Psychology, 48,* 1253–1265.

Diener, E., Lucas, R. E., and Larsen, R. J. (2003). Measuring positive emotions. In C. R. Snyder, and S. J. Lopez (Eds.), *The handbook of positive psychological assessment* (pp. 201–218). Washington, DC: American Psychological Association.

Diener, E., Oishi, S., and Lucas, R. E. (2003). Personality, culture, and subjective well-being: Emotional and cognitive evaluations of life. *Annual Review of Psychology, 54,* 403–425.

Diener, E., Sandvik, E., Seidlitz, L., and Diener, M. (1993). The relationship between income and subjective well-being: Relative or absolute? *Social Indicators Research, 28,* 195–223.

Digman, J. M., and Inouye, J. (1986). Further specification of the five robust factors of personality. *Journal of Personality and Social Psychology, 50,* 116–123.

Dijksterhhuis, A., Bos, M. W., Nordgren, L. F., and van Baaren, R. B. (2006). On making the right chioice: The deliberation-without-attention effect. *Science, 311,* 1005–1007.

Dijkstra, P., and Buunk, B. P. (2001). Sex differences in the jealousy-evoking nature of a rival's body build. *Evolution and Human Behavior, 22,* 335–341.

Dill, K. E., Anderson, C. A., Anderson, K. B., and Deuser, W. E. (1999). Effects of aggressive personality on social expectations and social perceptions. *Journal of Research in Personality, 31,* 272–292.

Dixon, W. A., Mauzey, E. D., and Hall, C. R. (2003). Physical activity and exercise: Implications for counselors. *Journal of Counseling and Development, 81,* 502–505.

Dodge, K. A., and Coie, J. D. (1987). Social-information-processing factors in reactive and proactive aggression in children's peer groups. *Journal of Personality and Social Psychology, 53,* 1146–1158.

Donnellan, M. B., Larsen-Rife, D., and Conger, R. D. (2005). Personality, family history, and competence in early adult romantic relationships. *Journal of Personality and Social Psychology, 88,* 562–576.

Donohew, L., Zimmerman, R., Cupp, P. S., Novak, S., Colon, S., and Abell, R. (2000). Sensation seeking, impulsive decision-making, and risky sex: Implications for risk-taking and design interventions. *Personality and Individual Differences, 28,* 1079–1091.

Dubbert, Patricia M. (2002). Physical activity and exercise: Recent advances and current challenges. *Journal of Consulting and Clinical Psychology Special Issue: Behavioral medicine and clinical health psychology, 70,* 526–536.

Dudek, S. Z., and Hall, W. B. (1991). Personality consistency: Eminent architects 25 years later. *Creative Research Journal, 4,* 213–232.

Dudley, N. M., Orvis, K. A., Lebiecki, J. E., and Cortina, J. M. (2006). A meta-analytic investigation of conscientiousness in the prediction of job performance: Examining the intercorrelations and the incremental validity of narrow traits. *Journal of Applied Psychology, 91,* 40–57.

Dunbar, R. I. M. (1993). Coevolution of neocortical size, group size, and language in humans. *Behavioral and Brain Sciences, 16,* 681–735.

Dutton, D. G., Saunders, K., Starzomski, A., and Bartholomew, K. (1994). Intimacy-anger and insecure attachment as precursors of abuse in intimate relationships. *Journal of Applied Social Psychology, 24,* 1367–1386.

Dweck, C. S. (1999a). Caution—praise can be dangerous. *American Educator, 23,* 4–9.

Dweck, C. S. (1999b). *Self-theories: Their role in motivation, personality, and development.* Philadelphia: The Psychology Press.

Dweck, C. S., Chiu, C., and Hong, Y. (1995). Implicit theories and their role in judgments and reactions: A world from two perspectives. *Psychological Inquiry, 6,* 267–285.

Dweck, C. S. (2002). Beliefs that make smart people dumb. In R. J. Sternberg (Ed.), *Why smart people can be so stupid* (pp. 24–41). New Haven, CT: Yale University Press.

Dweck, C. S., and Molden, D. C. (2005). Self-theories: Their impact on competence motivation and acquisition. In A. J. Elliot and C. S. Dweck (Eds.), *Handbook of competence and motivation* (pp. 122–140). New York: Guilford.

Eagly, A. H. (1987). *Sex differences in social behavior: A social-role interpretation.* Hillsdale, NJ: Erlbaum.

Eagly, A. H. (1995). The science and politics of comparing women and men. *American Psychologist, 50,* 145–158.

Eagly, A., and Wood, W. (1999). A social role interpretation of sex differences in human mate preferences. *American Psychologist, 54,* 408–423.

Easterlin, R. A. (1974). Does economic growth improve the human lot: Some empirical evidence. In P. A. David and W. R. Levin (Eds.), *Nations and households in economic growth* (pp. 98–125). Palo Alto, CA: Stanford University Press.

Easterlin, R. A. (1995). Will raising the incomes of all increase the happiness of all? *Journal of Economic Behavior and Organization, 27,* 35–47.

Ebstein, R. P. (2006). The molecular genetic architecture of human personality: Beyond self-report questionnaires. *Molecular Psychiatry, 11,* 1–19.

Ebstein, R., Novick, O., Umansky, R., Priel, B., Osher, Y., Blaine, D., Bennett, E. R., Nemanov, L., Katz, M., and Belmaker, R. H. (1996). Dopamine D4 receptor (D4DR) exon III polymorphism associated with the human personality trait of novelty seeking. *Nature Genetics, 12,* 78–80.

Edwards, A. L. (1959). *Edwards Personal Preference Schedule.* New York: Psychological Corporation.

Egan, S., and Stelmack, R. M. (2003). A personality profile of Mount Everest climbers. *Personality and Individual Differences, 34,* 1491–1494.

Eisenberg, N., Guthrie, I. K., Cumberland, A., Murphy, B. C., Shepard, S. A., Zhou, Q., and Carlo, G. (2002). Prosocial development in early adulthood: A longitudinal study. *Journal of Personality and Social Psychology, 82,* 6, 993–1006.

Eisenberger, N. I., Lieberman, M. D., and Williams, K. D. (2003). Does rejection hurt? An fMRI study of social exclusion. *Science, 302,* 290–294.

Ekman, P. (1973). Cross-cultural studies of facial expression. In P. Ekman (Ed.), *Darwin and facial expression: A century of research in review* (pp. 169–222). New York: Academic Press.

Ekman, P. (1992a). An argument for basic emotions. *Cognition and Emotion, 6,* 169–200.

Ekman, P. (1992b). Facial expressions of emotion: New findings, new questions. *Psychological Science, 3,* 34–38.

Ekman, P., and Friesen, W. (1986). A new pan-cultural facial expression of emotion. *Motivation and Emotion, 10,* 159–168.

Ekman, P., Friesen, W. V., and Ellsworth, P. (1972). *Emotion in the human face: Guidelines for research and an integration of findings.* New York: Pergamon Press.

Ekman, P., Friesen, W. V., O'Sullivan, M., Chan, A., Diacoyanni-Tarlatzis, I., Heider, K., Krause, R., LeCompte, W., Pitcairn, T., Ricci-Bitti, P. E., Scherer, K., Tomita, M., and Tzavaras, A. (1987). Universals and cultural differences in the judgments of facial expressions of emotions. *Journal of Personality and Social Psychology, 53,* 712–717.

Elder, G. H., and Clipp, E. C. (1988). Wartime losses and social bonding: Influence across 40 years in men's lives. *Psychiatry, 51,* 117–198.

Elkins, I. J., King, S. M., McGue, M., and Iacono, W. G. (2006). Personality traits and the development of nicotine, alcohol, and illicit drug disorders: Prospective links from adolescence to young adulthood. *Journal of Abnormal Psychology, 115,* 26–39.

Elliot, A. J., and Reis, H. T. (2003). Attachment and exploration in adulthood. *Journal of Personality and Social Psychology, 85,* 317–331.

Elliot, A. J., and Dweck, C. S. (2005). *Handbook of competence and motivation.* New York: Guilford.

Ellis, B. J., Simpson, J. A., and Campbell, L. (2002). Trait-specific dependence in romantic relationships. *Journal of Personality, 70,* 611–660.

Ellis, L., and Bonin, S. L. (2003). Genetics and occupation-related preferences. Evidence from adoptive and non-adoptive families. *Personality and Individual Differences, 35,* 929–937.

Else-Quest, N. M., Hyde, J. S., Goldsmith, H. H., and Van Hulle, C. A. (2006). Gender differences in temperament: A meta-analysis. *Psychological Bulletin, 132,* 33–72.

Emmons, R. A. (1987). Narcissism: Theory and measurement. *Journal of*

Personality and Social Psychology, 52, 11–17.

Emmons, R. A. (1989). The personal striving approach to personality. In L. Pervin et al. (Eds.), *Goal concepts in personality and social psychology* (pp. 87–126). Hillsdale, NJ: Lawrence Erlbaum Associates, Inc.

Endler, N. S., and Magnusson, D. (1976). Toward an interactional psychology of personality. *Psychological Bulletin, 83,* 956–974.

Engelhard, I. M., van den Hout, M. A., and Kindt, M. (2003). The relationship between neuroticism, pre-traumatic stress, and post-traumatic stress: A prospective study. *Personality and Individual Differences, 35,* 381–388.

Entwisle, D. R. (1972). To dispel fantasies about fantasy-based measures of achievement motivation. *Psychological Bulletin, 77,* 377–391.

Epstein, S. (1979). The stability of behavior: I. On predicting most of the people much of the time. *Journal of Personality and Psychology, 37,* 1097–1126.

Epstein, S. (1980). The stability of behavior: II. Implications for psychological research. *American Psychologist, 35,* 790–806.

Epstein, S. (1983). Aggregation and beyond: Some basic issues on the prediction of behavior. *Journal of Personality, 51,* 360–392.

Erdelyi, M. H., and Goldberg, B. (1979). Let's not sweep repression under the rug: Toward a cognitive psychology of repression. In J. G. Kihlstrom and F. J. Evans (Eds.), *Functional disorders of memory* (pp. 355–402). Hillsdale, NJ: Erlbaum.

Erikson, E. H. (1963). *Childhood and society* (2nd ed.). New York: Norton. (Original work published 1950.)

Erikson, E. H. (1968). *Identity: Youth and crisis.* New York: Norton.

Erikson, E. H. (1975). *Life history and the historical moment.* New York: Norton.

Erikson, E. H. (1978). *Adulthood: Essays.* New York: Norton.

Exline, J. J., Baumeister, R. F., Bushman, B. J., Campbell, W. K., and Finkel, E. J. (2004). Too proud to let go: Narcissistic entitlement as a barrier to forgiveness. *Journal of Personality and Social Psychology, 87,* 894–912.

Exline, R. V., Thiabaut, J., Hickey, C. B., and Gumpart, P. (1970). Visual interaction in relation to expectations, and situational preferences: Personality influences on the decision to participate in volunteer helping behaviors. *Journal of Personality, 67,* 470–503.

Eysenck, H. J. (1967). *The biological basis of personality.* Springfield, IL: Charles C Thomas.

Eysenck, H. J. (1970). *The structure of human personality.* London, England: Methuen.

Eysenck, H. J. (Ed.). (1981). *A model for personality.* Berlin: Springer-Verlag.

Eysenck, H. J. (1985). *The decline and fall of the Freudian empire.* London: Viking Press.

Eysenck, H. J. (1989). Emotion, personality, and stress as determinants of disease. In K. V. Sudakov and D. Ganten (Eds.), *Perspectives in research in emotional stress* (pp. 177–190). London: Gordon and Breach.

Eysenck, H. J. (1990). Biological dimensions of personality. In L. Pervin (Ed.), *Handbook of personality theory and research* (pp. 244–276). New York: Guilford Press.

Eysenck, H. J. (1991). Biological dimensions of personality. In L. A. Pervin (Ed.), *Handbook of personality* (pp. 244–276). New York: Guilford.

Eysenck, H. J. (2000). Personality as a risk factor in cancer and coronary heart disease. In D. T. Kenny and J. G. Carlson (Eds.), *Stress and health: Research and clinical applications* (pp. 291–318). Amsterdam, Netherlands: Harwood Academic Publishers.

Eysenck, H. J., and Eysenck, M. W. (1985). *Personality and individual differences: A natural science approach.* New York: Plenum Press.

Eysenck, H. J., and Eysenck, S. B. (1967). On the unitary nature of extraversion. *Acta Psychologica, 26,* 383–390.

Eysenck, H. J., and Eysenck, S. B. G. (1972). *Manual of the Eysenck Personality Questionnaire.* San Diego: Educational and Industrial Testing Service.

Eysenck, H. J., and Eysenck, S. B. G. (1975). *Eysenck personality questionnaire manual.* San Diego: Educational and Industrial Testing Service.

Eysenck, H. J., and Gudjonsson, G. (1989). *Causes and cures of deliquency.* New York: Plenum Press.

Eysenck, S. B. G., Eysenck, H. J., and Barrett, P. (1985) A revised version of the Psychoticism scale. *Personality and Individual Differences, 6,* 21–29.

Fagot, B. I., and Leinbach, M. D. (1987). Socialization of sex roles within the family. In D. B. Carter (Ed.), *Current conceptions of sex roles and sex typing.* New York: Praetor.

Feingold, A. (1994). Gender differences in personality: A meta-analysis. *Psychological Bulletin, 116,* 429–456.

Fenichel, O. (1945). *The psychoanalytic theory of neurosis.* New York: Norton.

Fenigstein, A., and Peltz, R. (2002). Distress over the infidelity of a child's spouse: A crucial test of evolutionary and socialization hypotheses. *Personal Relationships, 9,* 301–312.

Figueredo, A. J., Sefcek, J. S., Vasquez, G., Brumbach, B. H., King, J. E., and Jacobs, W. J. (2005). Evolutionary personality psychology. In D. M. Buss (Ed.), *The handbook of evolutionary psychology* (pp. 851–877). New York: Wiley.

Figueredo, A. J., Vasquez, G., Brumbach, B. H., Sefcek, J. A., Kirsner, B. R., and Jacobs, W. J. (2005). The K-factor: Individual differences in life history strategy. *Personality and Individual Differences, 39,* 1349–1360.

Fineman, S. (1977). The achievement motive and its measurement: Where are we now? *British Journal of Psychology, 68,* 1–22.

Finger, F. W. (1982). Circadian rhythms: Implications for psychology. *New Zealand Psychologist, 11,* 1–12.

Fiske, A. P. (2002). Using individualism and collectivism to compare cultures: A critique of the validity and measurement of the constructs. *Psychological Bulletin, 128,* 78–88.

Fiske, A. P., Kitayama, S., Markus, H., and Nisbett, R. E. (1997). The cultural matrix of social psychology. In D. Gilbert, S. Fiske, and G. Lindzey (Eds.), *Handbook of social psychology* (3rd ed.). New York: McGraw-Hill.

Fiske, D. W. (1949). Consistency of the factorial structures of personality ratings from different sources. *Journal of Abnormal and Social Psychology, 44,* 329–344.

Fleeson, W., Malanos, A. B., and Achille, N. M. (2002). An intraindividual process approach to the relationship between extraversion and positive affect: Is acting extraverted as "Good" as being extraverted? *Journal of Personality and Social Psychology, 83,* 6, 1409–1422.

Fletcher, G. J. O., Tither, J. M., O'Loughlin, C., Friesen, M., and Overall, N. (2004). Warm and homely or cold and beautiful? Sex differences in trading off traits in mate selection. *Personality and Social Psychology Bulletin, 30,* 659–672.

Flett, G. L., Blankstein, K. R., and Hewitt, P. L. (1991). Factor structure of the Short Index of Self-Actualization. *Journal of Social Behavior and Personality Special Issue: Handbook of self-actualization, 6,* 321–329.

Floderus-Myrhed, B., Pedersen, N., and Rasmuson, I. (1980). Assessment of heritability for personality based on a short form of the Eysenck Personality Inventory: A study of 12,898 twin pairs. *Behavior Genetics, 10,* 153–162.

Flynn, F. J. (2005). Having an open mind: The impact of openness to experience on interracial attitudes and impression formation. *Journal of Personality and Social Psychology, 88,* 816–826.

Foa, U. G., and Foa, E. B. (1974). *Societal structures of the mind.* Springfield: Charles C Thomas.

Fodor, E. M. (1985). The power motive, group conflict, and physiological arousal. *Journal of Personality and Social Psychology, 49,* 1408–1415.

Folkman, S., and Moskowitz, J. T. (2000). Stress, positive emotion, and coping. *Current Directions in Psychological Science, 9,* 115–118.

Folkman, S., Moskowitz, J. T., Ozer, E. M., and Park, C. L. (1997). Positive meaningful events and coping in the context of HIV/AIDS. In B. H. Gottlieb (Ed.), *Coping with chronic stress* (pp. 293–314). New York: Plenum Press.

Fordyce, M. W. (1978). *Prospectus: The self-descriptive inventory.* (Unpublished manuscript, Edison Community College, Fort Myers, FL.)

Fordyce, M. W. (1988). A review of results on the happiness measures: A 60-second index of happiness and mental health. *Social Indicators Research, 20,* 355–381.

Foster, J. D., and Campbell, W. K. (2005). Narcissism and resistance to doubts about romantic partners. *Journal of Research in Personality, 39,* 550–557.

Fowles, D. C. (1980). The three arousal model: Implications of Gray's two-factor learning theory for heart rate, electrodermal activity, and psychopathy. *Psychophysiology, 17,* 87–104.

Fowles, D. C. (1987). Application of a behavioral theory of motivation to the concepts of anxiety and impulsivity. *Journal of Research in Personality, 21,* 417–435.

Fox, N. A., and Calkins, S. D. (1993). Multiple-measure approaches to the study of infant emotion. In M. Lewis and J. M. Haviland (Eds.), *Handbook of emotions* (pp. 167–185). New York: Guilford.

Fox, N. A., and Davidson, R. J. (1986). Taste-elicited changes in facial signs of emotion and the asymmetry of brain electrical activity in human newborns. *Neuropsychologia, 24,* 417–422.

Fox, N. A., and Davidson, R. J. (1987). Electroencephalogram asymmetry in response to the approach of a stranger and maternal separation. *Developmental Psychology, 23,* 233–240.

Fox, N. A., Bell, M. A., and Jones, N. A. (1992). Individual differences in response to stress and cerebral asymmetry. *Developmental Neuropsychology, 8,* 165–184.

Fraley, R. C. (2002a). Attachment stability from infancy to adulthood: Meta-analysis and dynamic modeling of developmental mechanisms. *Personality and Social Psychology Review, 6,* 123–151.

Fraley, R. C. (2002b). Introduction to the special issue: The psychodynamics of adult attachments—Bridging the gap between disparate research traditions. *Attachment and Human Development Special Issue: The psychodynamics of adult attachments—Bridging the gap between disparate research traditions, 4,* 131–132.

Fransella, F. (2003). *International handbook of personal construct psychology.* New York: John Wiley and Sons, Ltd.

Fransella, F., and Neimeyer, R. A. (2003). George Alexander Kelly: The man and his theory. In F. Fransella (Ed.), *International handbook of personal construct psychology* (pp. 21–31). New York: John Wiley and Sons, Ltd.

Fraser, S. (1995). *The bell curve wars: Race, intelligence, and the future of America.* New York: Basic Books.

Fredrickson, B. L. (1998). What good are positive emotions? *Review of General Psychology, 2,* 300–319.

Fredrickson, B. L. (2000). Cultivating positive emotions to optimize health and well-being. *Prevention and Treatment* (on-line), 2, available at *http://journals.apa.org/prevention.*

Fredrickson, B. L., and Levenson, R. W. (1998). Positive emotions speed recovery from the cardiovascular sequenlae of negative emotions. *Cognition and Emotion, 12,* 191–220.

Freeman, D. (1983). *Margaret Mead and Samoa: The making and unmaking of an anthropological myth.* Cambridge, MA: Harvard University Press.

Freshwater, S. M., and Golden, C. J. (2002). Personality changes associated with localized brain injury in elderly populations. *Journal of Clinical Geropsychology, 8,* 251–277.

Freud, A. (1936/1992). The ego and mechanisms of defense. In Vol. 2 of *The writings of Anna Freud.* New York: International Universities Press.

Freud, S. (1901/1960). The psychopathology of everyday life. In Vol. VI of James Strachey (Ed.), *The standard edition of the complete psychological works of Sigmund Freud.* London, Hogarth.

Freud, S. (1915/1957). The unconscious. In J. Strachey (Ed. and Trans.), *The standard edition of the complete psychological works of Sigmund Freud* (Vol. 14, pp. 166–204). London: Hogarth Press. (Original work published 1915.)

Freud, S. (1916/1947). *Leonardo da Vinci, a study in psychosexuality.* New York: Random House.

Freud, S. (1933). Introductory lectures on Psycho-analysis. London: Hogarth Press.

Freud, S. (1953). The interpretation of dreams. In J. Strachey (Ed. and Trans.), *The standard edition of the complete psychological works of Sigmund Freud* (Vols. 4–5). London: Hogarth Press. (Original work published 1900.)

Frick, P. J., O'Brien, B. S., Wootton, J. M., and McBurnett, K. (1994). Psychopathy and conduct problems in children. *Journal of Abnormal Psychology, 103,* 700–707.

Friedman, H. S., Tucker, J. S., Schwartz, J. E., Tomlinson-Keasey, C., and Martin, L. R., et al. (1995). Psychosocial and behavioral predictors of longevity. *American Psychologist, 50,* 69–78.

Friedman, M., and Rosenman, R. H. (1974). *Type A behavior and your heart.* New York: Knopf.

Frijda, N. H. (1986). *The emotions.* New York: Cambridge University Press.

Frodi, A., Macauley, J., and Thome, P. R. (1977). Are women always less aggressive than men? A review of the experimental literature. *Psychological Bulletin, 84,* 634–660.

Funder, D. C. (2002). Personality psychology: Current status and some issues for the future. *Journal of Research in Personality, 36,* 638–639.

Furmark, T. (2002). Social phobia: Overview of community surveys. *Acta Psychiatrica Scandinavica, 105,* 84–93.

Furnham, A. (1982). Psychotocism, social desirability, and situation selection. *Personality and Individual Differences, 3,* 43–51.

Furnham, A. (1996). The Big Five versus the big four: The relationship between the Myers-Briggs Type Indicator (MBTI) and the NEO-PI factor model of personality. *Personality and Individual Differences, 21,* 303–307.

Gable, S. L., and Nezlak, J. B. (1998). Level and instability of day-to-day psychological well-being and risk for depression. *Journal of Personality and Social Psychology, 74,* 129–138.

Gabriel, S., and Gardner, W. L. (1999). Are there "his" and "hers" types of interdependence? The implications of gender differences in collective versus relational interdependence for affect, behavior, and cognition. *Journal of Personality and Social Psychology, 77,* 642–655.

Gale, A. (1983). Electroencephalographic studies of extraversion-introversion: A case study in the psychophysiology of individual differences. *Personality and Individual Differences, 4,* 371–380.

Gale, A. (1986). Extraversion-introversion and spontaneous rhythms of the brain: Retrospect and prospect. In J. Strelau, F. Farley, and A. Gale (Eds.), *The biological basis of personality and behavior* (Vol. 2). Washington, DC: Hemisphere.

Gale, A. (1987). The psychophysiological context. In A. Gale and B. Christie (Eds.),

Psychophysiology and the electronic workplace (pp. 17–32). Chichester, England, UK: John Wiley and Sons.

Gallo, L. C., and Smith, T. W. (1999). Patterns of hostility and social support: Conceptualizing psychosocial risk factors as characteristics of the person and the environment. *Journal of Research in Personality, 33,* 281–310.

Gallup, G. G. (1977a). Self-recognition in primates: A comparative approach to the bidirectional properties of consciousness. *American Psychologist, 32,* 329–338.

Gallup, G. G. (1977b). Absences of self-recognition in a monkey (Macaca fascicularis) following prolonged exposure to a mirror. *Developmental Psychobiology, 10,* 281–284.

Gangestad, S. W., and Cousins, A. J. (in press). Adaptive design, female mate preferences, and shifts across the menstrual cycle. *Annual Review of Sex Research.*

Gangestad, S. W., and Simpson, J. A. (1990). Toward an evolutionary history of female sociosexual variation. *Journal of Personality, 58,* 69–96.

Garber, J., and Seligman, M. E. P. (1980). *Human helplessness: Theory and applications.* New York: Academic Press.

Gardner, H. (1983). *Frames of mind: The theory of multiple intelligences.* New York: Basic Books.

Gardner, H. (1999). *Intelligence reframed: Multiple intelligences for the 21st century.* New York: Basic Books.

Gardner, W. I., and Martinko, M. J. (1996). Using the Myers-Briggs Type Indicator to study managers: A literature review and research agenda. *Journal of Management, 22,* 45–83.

Gauguin, P. (1985). *Noa Noa: The Tahitian Journal.* Mineola, NY: Dover.

Geary, D. C., DeSoto, M/C., Hoard, M. K., Skaggs, S., and Cooper, M. L. (2001). Estrogens and relationship jealousy. *Human Nature, 12,* 299–320.

Geen, R. (1984). Preferred stimulation levels in introverts and extraverts: Effects on arousal and performance. *Journal of Personality and Social Psychology, 46,* 1303–1312.

Geer, J. H., and Head, S. (1990). The sexual response system. In J. T. Cacioppo and L. G. Tassinary (Eds.), *Principles of psychophysiology* (pp. 599–630). Cambridge, England: Cambridge University Press.

Geis, F. L., and Moon, T. H. (1981). Machiavellianism and deception. *Journal of Personality and Social Psychology, 41,* 766–775.

George, C., and Solomon, J. (1996). Representational models of relationships: Links between caregiving and attachment. *Infant Mental Health Journal, 17,* 198–216.

Gergen, K. J. (1992). Toward a postmodern psychology. In S. Kvale (Ed.), *Psychology and postmodernism* (pp. 17–30). London: Sage.

Gewertz, D. (1981). A historical reconsideration of female dominance among the Chambri of Papua New Guinea. *American Ethnologist, 8,* 94–106.

Gibbs, W. (2003). The unseen genome: Gems among the junk. *Scientific American, 289,* 49.

Gigy, L. L. (1980). Self-concept in single women. *Psychology of Women Quarterly, 5,* 321–340.

Gillham, J. E., Reivich, K. J., Jaycox, L. H., and Seligman, M. E. (1995). Prevention of depressive symptoms in schoolchildren: Two-year follow-up. *Psychological Science, 6,* 343–351.

Glass, D. C. (1977). *Behavior patterns, stress, and coronary disease.* Hillsdale, NJ: Erlbaum.

Glueck, S., and Glueck, E. (1956). *Physique and delinquency.* New York: Harper.

Goldberg, L. R. (1981). Language and individual differences: The search for universals in personality lexicons. In L. Wheeler (Ed.), *Review of personality and social psychology* (Vol. 2, pp. 141–165). Beverly Hills: Sage.

Goldberg, L. R. (1990). An alternative "description of personality": The big-five factor structure. *Journal of Personality and Social Psychology, 59,* 1216–1229.

Goldberg, L. R., and Saucier, G. (1995). So what do you propose we use instead? A reply to Block. *Psychological Bulletin, 117,* 221–225.

Golding, S. L. (1978). Toward a more adequate theory of personality: Psychological organizing principles. In H. London (Ed.), *Personality: A new look at metatheories* (pp. 69–96). New York: Wiley.

Goldsmith, H. H., and Rothbart, M. K. (1991). Contemporary instruments for assessing early temperament by questionnaire and in the laboratory. In J. Strelau and A. Angleitner (Eds.), *Explorations in temperament.* New York: Plenum Press.

Goldsmith, H. H., Aksan, N., and Essex, M. (2001). Temperament and socioemotional adjustment to kindergarten: A multi-informant perspective. In T. Wachs and G. A. Kohnstamm (Eds.), *Temperament in context* (pp. 103–138). Mahwah, NJ: Erlbaum.

Goleman, D. (1995). *Emotional intelligence: Why it can matter more than IQ.* New York: Bantam.

Gomez, R., Cooper, A., and Gomez, A. (2000). Susceptibility to positive and negative mood states: A test of Eysenck's, Ray's, and Newman's theories. *Personality and Individual Differences, 29,* 351–365.

Goodman, J., Lofts, E. F., Miller, M., and Greene, E. (1991). Money, sex, and death: Gender bias in wrongful death damage awards. *Law and Society Review, 25,* 263–285.

Gosling, S. D. (2001). From mice to men: What can we learn about personality from animal research? *Psychological Bulletin, 127,* 45–86.

Gosling, S. D., John, O. P., Craik, K. H., and Robins, R. W. (1998). Do people know how they behave? Self-reported act frequencies compared with on-line codings by observers. *Journal of Personality and Social Psychology, 74,* 1337–1349.

Gosling, S. D., Ko, S. J., Mannarelli, T., and Morris, M. E. (2002). A room with a cue: Personality judgments based on offices and bedrooms. *Journal of Personality and Social Psychology, 82,* 379–398.

Gottman, J. (1994). *Why marriages succeed or fail.* New York: Simon and Schuster.

Gottman, J., Levenson, R., and Woodin, E. (2001). Facial expressions during marital conflict. *Journal of Family Communication, 1, 3757.*

Gottman, J. M., and Silver, N. (1999). *The seven principles for making marriage work.* New York: Three Rivers Press.

Gough, H. G. (1957/1987). *California Psychological Inventory: Administrator's guide.* Palo Alto, CA: Consulting Psychologists Press.

Gough, H. G. (1980). *The Adjective Check List manual.* Palo Alto, CA: Consulting Psychologists Press.

Gough, H. G. (1996). *California psychological inventory manual* (3rd ed.). Palo Alto, CA: Consulting Psychologists Press.

Grano, N., Virtanen, M., Vahtera, J., Elovainio, M., and Kivimaki, M. (2004). Impulsivity as a predictor of smoking and alcohol consumption. *Personality and Individual Differences, 37,* 1693–1700.

Grant, H., and Higgins, E. T. (2003). Optimism, promotion pride, and prevention pride as predictors of quality of life. *Personality and Social Psychology Bulletin, 29,* 1521–1532.

Grant, J. D., and Grant, J. (1996) Officer selection and the prevention of abuse of force. In W. Geller and H. Toch (Eds.), *Police violence: Understanding and controlling police abuse of force* (pp. 150–164). New Haven, CT: Yale University Press.

Gray, J. (1990). Brain systems that mediate both emotion and cognition. *Motivation and Emotion, 4,* 269–288.

Gray, J. A. (1972). *The psychology of fear and stress.* New York: McGraw-Hill.

Gray, J. A. (1975). *Elements of a two-process theory of learning.* Oxford, England: Academic Press.

Gray, J. A. (1982). *The neuropsychology of anxiety.* Oxford, England: Oxford University Press.

Gray, J. A. (1987a). *The psychology of fear and stress.* Cambridge, England: Cambridge University Press.

Gray, J. A. (1987b). Perspectives on anxiety and impulsivity: A commentary. *Journal of Research in Personality, 21,* 493–509.

Gray, J. A. (1991). The neuropsychology of temperament. In J. Strelau and A. Angleitner (Eds.), *Explorations in temperament: International perspectives on theory and measurement* (pp. 105–128). New York: Plenum Press.

Graziano, W. G., (2003). Personality development: An introduction toward process approaches to long-term stability and change in persons. *Journal of Personality, 71,* 893–903.

Graziano, W. G., and Tobin, R. M. (2002). Agreeableness: Dimension of personality or social desirability artifact? *Journal of Personality, 70,* 695–727.

Greenberg, J. R., and Mitchell, S. (1983). *Object relations in psychoanalytic theory.* Cambridge, MA: Harvard University Press.

Greenwald, A. (1992). New look 3: Unconscious cognition reclaimed. *American Psychologist, 47,* 766–779.

Greiling, H., and Buss, D. M. (2000). Women's sexual strategies: The hidden dimension of extra-pair mating. *Personality and Individual Differences, 28,* 929–963.

Grigorenko, E. L. (2002). In search of the genetic engram of personality. In D. Cervone and W. Michele (Eds.), *Advances in personality science* (pp. 29–82). New York: Guilford Press.

Gross, J. J. (2002). Emotion regulation: Affective, cognitive, and social consequences. *Psychophysiology, 39,* 281–291.

Gross, J. J., and John, O. P. (2003). Individual differences in two emotion regulation processes: Implications for affect, relationships, and well-being. *Journal of Personality and Social Psychology, 85,* 348–362.

Gross, J. J., and Levenson, R. W. (1993). Emotional suppression: Physiology, self-report, and expressive behavior. *Journal of Personality and Social Psychology, 64,* 970–986.

Gross, J. J., and Levenson, R. W. (1997). Hiding feelings: The acute effects of inhibiting positive and negative emotions. *Journal of Abnormal Psychology, 106,* 95–103.

Grosskurth, P. (1991). *The secret ring: Freud's inner circle and the politics of psychoanalysis.* Reading, MA: Addison-Wesley.

Guzder, J., Paris, J., Zelkowitz, P., and Marchessault, K. (1996). Risk factors for borderline personality in children. *Journal of the American Academy of Child and Adolescent Psychiatry, 35,* 26–33.

Gyatso, T. (2003). A monk in the lab. *The New York Times,* April 26. Late Edition-Final, Section A, Page 19, Column 2.

Hacher, S. L., Nadeau, M. S., Walsh, L. K., and Reynolds, M. (1994). The teaching of empathy for high school and college students: Testing Rogerian methods with the Interpersonal Reactivity Index. *Adolescence, 29,* 961–974.

Hagerty, M. R. (1999). Testing Maslow's hierarchy of needs: National quality-of-life across time. *Social Indicators Research, 46,* 249–271.

Hair, E. C., and Graziano, W. G. (2003). Self-esteem, personality, and achievement in high school: A prospective longitudinal study in Texas. *Journal of Personality, 71,* 971–994.

Hall, J. A. (1984). *Nonverbal sex differences.* Baltimore: Johns Hopkins University Press.

Hamer, D. (1997). The search for personality genes: Adventures of a molecular biologist. *Current Directions in Psychological Science, 6,* 111–114.

Hamer, D., and Copeland, P. (1994). *The science of desire: The search for the gay gene and the biology of behavior.* New York: Simon and Schuster.

Hamilton, W. D. (1964). The evolution of social behavior. *Journal of Theoretical Biology, 7,* 1–52.

Hamm, A. O., Weike, A. I., Schupp, H. T., Treig, T., Dressel, A., and Kessler, C. (2003). Affective blindsight: Intact fear conditioning to a visual cue in a cortically blind patient. *Brain, 126* (2), 267–275.

Hampshire, S. (1953). Dispositions. *Analysis, 14,* 5–11.

Hampson, S. E., Severson, H. H., Burns, W. J., Slovic, P., and Fisher, K. J. (2001). Risk perception, personality factors and alcohol use among adolescents. *Personality and Individual Differences, 30,* 167–181.

Hampson, S. E., Goldberg, L. R., Vogt, T. M., and Dubanoski, J. P. (2006). Forty years on: Teachers' assessments of children's personality traits predict self-reported health behaviors and outcomes at midlife. *Health Psychology, 25,* 57–64.

Hankin, B. L., and Abramson, L. Y. (2001). Development of gender differences in depression: An elaborated cognitive vulnerability transactional stress theory. *Psychological Bulletin, 127,* 6, 773–796.

Hansen, C. H., Hansen, R. D., and Schantz, D. W. (1992). Repression at encoding: Discrete appraisals of emotional stimuli. *Journal of Personality and Social Psychology, 63,* 1026–1035.

Hansen, J., and Stansfield, C. (1982). Student-teacher cognitive styles and foreign language achievement: A preliminary study. *Modern Language Journal, 66,* 263–273.

Hansen, R. D., and Hansen, C. H. (1988). Repression of emotionally tagged memories: The architecture of less complex emotions. *Journal of Personality and Social Psychology, 55,* 811–818.

Hardaway, R. A. (1990). Subliminally activated symbiotic fantasies: Facts and artifacts. *Psychological Bulletin, 107,* 177–195.

Hare, R. D., Hart, S. D., and Harpur, T. J. (1991). Psychopathy and the DSM-IV criteria for antisocial personality disorder. *Journal of Abnormal Psychology Special Issue: Diagnosis, dimensions, and DSM-IV; The science of classification, 100,* 391–398.

Hargrave, G. E., and Hiatt, D. (1989). Use of the California Psychological Inventory in lay enforcement officer selection. *Journal of Personality Assessment, 53,* 267–277.

Haring, M. J., Stock, W. A., and Okun, M. A. (1984). A research systhesis of gender and social class as correlates of subjective well-being. *Human Relations, 37,* 645–657.

Harlow, H. F. (1958). The nature of love. *American Psychologist, 13,* 673–685.

Harlow, H. F., and Suomi, S. J. (1971). Production of depressive behaviors in young monkeys. *Journal of Autism and Childhood Schizophrenia, 1,* 246–255.

Harlow, H. F., and Zimmermann, R. R. (1959). Affectionate responses in the infant monkey. *Science, 130,* 421–432.

Harlow, R. E., and Cantor, N. (1994). The social pursuit of academics: Side-effects and "spillover" of strategic reassurance-seeking. *Journal of Personality and Social Psychology, 66,* 386–397.

Harpur, T. J., and Hare, R. D. (1994). Assessment of psychopathy as a function of age. *Journal of Abnormal Psychology, 103,* 604–609.

Harrell, W. A., and Hartnagel, T. (1976). The impact of Machiavellianism and the trustfulness of the victim on laboratory theft. *Sociometry, 39,* 157–165.

Harris, C. R. (2000). Psychophysiological responses to imagined infidelity: The specific innate modular view of jealousy reconsidered. *Journal of Personality and Social Psychology, 78,* 1082–1091.

Harris, G. T., Rice, M. E., and Quinsey, V. L. (1994). Psychopathy as a taxonomy: Evidence that psychopaths are a discrete class. *Journal of Consulting and Clinical Psychology, 62,* 387–397.

Harter, S. (1993). Causes and consequences of low self-esteem in children and adolescents. In R. Baumeister (Ed.), *Self-esteem: The puzzle of low self-regard* (pp. 87–111). New York: Plenum Press.

Hartshorne, H., and May, M. A. (1928). *Studies in the nature of character: Vol. 1. Studies in deceit.* New York: Macmillan.

Hazan, C., and Shaver, P. R. (1987). Romantic love conceptualized as an attachment process. *Journal of Personality and Social Psychology, 52,* 511–524.

Hazan, C., and Shaver, P. R. (1994). Attachment as an organizational framework for research on close relationships. *Psychological Inquiry, 5,* 1–22.

Heath, A. C., Bucholz, K. K., Dinwiddie, S. H., Madden, P. A. F., and Slutske, W. W. (1994). *Pathways from the genotype to alcoholism risk in women.* Paper presented at the annual meeting of the Behavioral Genetics Association, Barcelona, Spain.

Heatherton, T. E., and Polivy, J. (1991). Development and validation of a scale for measuring state self-esteem. *Journal of Personality and Social Psychology, 60,* 895–910.

Heaven, P. C. L., Crocker, D., Edwards, B., Preston, N., Ward, R., and Woodbridge, N. (2003). Personality and sex. *Personality and Individual Differences, 35,* 411–419.

Heaven, P. C. L., Da Silva, T., Carey, C., and Holen, J. (2004). Loving styles: Relationships with personality and attachment styles. *European Journal of Personality, 18,* 103–113.

Hebb, D. O. (1955). Drives and the CNS (conceptual nervous system). *Psychological Review, 62,* 243–259.

Heckhausen, H. (1982). The development of achievement motivation. In W. W. Hartup (Ed.), *Review of child development research* (Vol. 6, pp. 600–668). Chicago: University of Chicago Press.

Heine, S. J., and Lehman, D. R. (1995). Cultural variation in unrealistic optimism: Does the West feel more invulnerable than the East? *Journal of Personality and Social Psychology, 68,* 595–607.

Helmers, K. F., Posluszny, D. M., and Krantz, D. S. (1994). Associations of hostility and coronary artery disease: A review of studies. In A. W. Siegman and T. W. Smith (Eds.), *Anger, hostility, and the heart* (pp. 67–96). Hillsdale, NJ: Erlbaum.

Helson, R., and Picano, J. (1990). Is the traditional role bad for women? *Journal of Personality and Social Psychology, 59,* 311–320.

Helson, R., and Stewart, A. (1994). Personality change in adulthood. In T. F. Heatherton and J. L. Weinberger (Eds.), *Can personality change?* Washington, DC: American Psychological Association.

Helson, R., and Wink, P. (1992). Personality change in women from the early 40s to the early 50s. *Psychology and Aging, 7,* 46–55.

Henderson, L., and Zimbardo, P. (2001b). Shyness as a clinical condition: The Stanford model. In W. R. Crozier and L. E. Alden (Eds.), *International handbook of social anxiety: Concepts, research and interventions relating to the self and shyness* (pp. 431–447). New York: John Wiley.

Henderson, L. and Zimbardo, P. (2001a). Shyness, social anxiety, and social phobia. In S. G. Hofmann and P. M. DiBartolo (Eds.), *From social anxiety to social phobia: Multiple perspectives* (pp. 46–85). Needham Heights, MA: Allyn and Bacon.

Henderson, N. D. (1982). Human behavioral genetics. *Annual Review of Psychology, 33,* 403–440.

Hendriks, A. A. J., Perugini, M., Angleitner, A., Ostendorf, F., Johnson, J. A., De Fruyt, F., Hrebickova, M., Kreitler, S., Murakami, T., Bratko, D., Conner, M., Nagy, J., Rodrigues-Fornells, A., and Ruisel, I. (2003). The five-factor personality inventory: Cross-cultural generalizability across 13 countries. *European Journal of Personality, 17,* 347–373.

Herbert, T. B., and Cohen, S. (1993). Depression and immunity: A meta-analytic review. *Psychological Bulletin, 113,* 472–486.

Hernstein, R., and Murray, C. (1994). *The bell curve: Intelligence and class structure in American life.* New York: Free Press.

Herzog, A. R., Franks, X., Markus, H. R., and Holmberg, X. (1995). *The American self in its sociocultural variations.* Unpublished manuscript.

Herzog, T. R., and Weintraub, D. J. (1982). Roundup time at personality ranch: Branding the elusive augmenters and reducers. *Journal of Personality and Social Psychology, 42,* 729–737.

Herzog, T. R., Williams, D. M., and Weintraub, D. J. (1985). Meanwhile, back at personality ranch: The augmenters and reducers ride again. *Journal of Personality and Social Psychology, 48,* 1342–1352.

Higgins, E. T. (1987). Self-discrepancy: A theory relating self to affect. *Psychological Review, 94,* 319–340.

Higgins, E. T. (1996). The "self digest": Self-knowledge serving self-regulatory functions. *Journal of Personality and Social Psychology, 71,* 1062–1083.

Higgins, E. T. (1997). Beyond pleasure and pain. *American Psychologist, 52,* 1280–1300.

Higgins, E. T. (1999). Persons and situations: Unique explanatory principles or variability in general principles? In D. Cervone and Y. Shoda (Eds.), *The coherence of personality* (pp. 61–93). New York: Guilford Press.

Higgins, E. T., Friedman, R. S., Harlow, R. E., Idson, L. C., Ayduk, O. N., and Taylor, A. (2001). Achievement orientations from subjective histories of success: Promotion pride versus prevention pride. *European Journal of Social Psychology, 31,* 3–23.

Higgins, E. T., Shah, J., and Friedman, R. (1997). Emotional responses to goal attainment: Strength of regulatory focus as moderator. *Journal of Personality and Social Psychology, 72,* 515–525.

Hill, C. T., Rubin, Z., and Peplau, L. A. (1976). Breakups before marriage: The end of 103 affairs. *Journal of Social Issues, 32,* 147–168.

Hiroto, D. S. (1974). Locus of control and learned helplessness. *Journal of Experimental Psychology, 102,* 187–193.

Hiroto, D. S., and Seligman, M. E. P. (1975). Generality of learned helplessness in man. *Journal of Personality and Social Psychology, 102,* 311–327.

Hirschfeld, L. A. (1995). Anthropology, psychology, and the meaning of social causality. In D. Sperber, D. Premack, and A. J. Premack (Eds.), *Causal cognition: A multidisciplinary debate* (pp. 313–344). Oxford, England: Clarendon Press.

Hirsh, S. K., and Kummerow, J. M. (1990). *Introduction to type in organizations, Second edition.* Palo Alto, CA: Consulting Psychologists Press, Inc.

Hogan, J., and Holland, B. (2003). Using theory to evaluate personality and job performance relations. *Journal of Applied Psychology, 88,* 100–112.

Hogan, R. (1983). A socioanalytic theory of personality. In M. Page and R. Dienstbier (Eds.), *Nebraska Symposium on Motivation, 1982* (pp. 55–89). Lincoln: University of Nebraska Press.

Hogan, R. (1996). A socioanalytic perspective on the five-factor model. In J. S. Wiggins (Ed.), *The five-factor model of personality: Theoretical perspectives* (pp. 163–179). New York: Guilford Press.

Hogan, R. (2005). In defense of personality measurement: New wine for old whiners. *Human Performance, 18,* 331–341.

Hogan, R., Johnson, J., and Briggs, S. (Eds.). (1997). *Handbook of personality psychology.* San Diego, CA: Academic Press.

Hokanson, J. E., Burgess, M., and Cohen, M. F. (1963). Effect of displaced aggression on systolic blood pressure. *Journal of Abnormal and Social Psychology, 67,* 214–218.

Hollmann, E. (2001). *Paul Gaugin: Images from the South Seas.* New York: Prestel USA.

Holmes, D. (1990). The evidence for repression: An examination of sixty years of research. In J. Singer (Ed.), *Repression and dissociation: Implications for personality, theory, psychopathology, and health* (pp. 85–102). Chicago: University of Chicago Press.

Holmes, T. H., and Rahe, R. H. (1967). The Social Readjustment Rating scale. *Journal of Psychosomatic Research, 11,* 213–218.

Holroyd, K. A., and Coyne, J. (1987). Personality and health in the 1980s: Psychosomatic medicine revisited? *Journal of Personality, 55,* 359–375.

Hooper, C. J., Luciana, M., Conklin, H. M., and Yarger, R. S. (2004). Adolescents' performance on the Iowa Gambling Task: Implications for the development of decision making and ventromedial prefrontal cortex. *Developmental Psychology, 40*(6), 1148–1158.

Hooper, J. L., White, V. M., Macaskill, G. T., Hill, D. J., and Clifford, C. A. (1992). Alcohol use, smoking habits and the Junior Eysenck Personality Questionnaire in adolescent Australian twins. *Acta Genetica Med. Gemellol. 41,* 311–324.

Hormuth, S. E. (1986). The sampling of experiences in situ. *Journal of Personality, 54,* 262–293.

Horne, J. A., and Ostberg, O. (1976). A self-assessment questionnaire to determine morningness-eveningness in human circadian rhythms. *International Journal of Chronobiology, 4,* 97–110.

Horne, J. A., and Ostberg, O. (1977). Individual differences in human circadian rhythms. *Biological Psychology, 5,* 179–190.

Horney, K. (1937). *The neurotic personality of our time.* New York: Norton.

Horney, K. (1939). *New ways in psychoanalysis.* New York: Norton.

Horney, K. (1945). *Our inner conflicts: A constructive theory of neurosis.* New York: Norton.

Horney, K. (1950). *Neurosis and human growth: The struggle toward self-realization.* New York: Norton.

Hotard, S. R., McFatter, R. M., McWhirter, R. M., and Stegall, M. E. (1989). Interactive effects of extraversion, neuroticism, and social relationships on subjective well-being. *Journal of Personality and Social Psychology, 57,* 321–331.

Howard, A., and Bray, D. (1988). *Managerial lives in transition: Advancing age and changing times.* New York: Guilford Press.

Hoyenga, K. B., and Hoyenga, K. T. (1993). *Gender-related differences: Origins and outcomes.* Boston: Allyn and Bacon.

Hsu, F. K. K. (1985). The self in cross-cultural perspective. In J. J. Marsella, G. De Vos, and F. L. K. Hsu (Eds.), *Culture and self* (pp. 24–55). London: Tavistock. *http://www.courttv.com/trials/diallo*

Hudziak, J. J., van Beijhsterveldt, C. E. M., Bartels, M., Rietveld, J. J. J., Rettew, D. C., Derks, E. M., and Boomsma, D. I. (2003). *Behavior Genetics, 33,* 575–589.

Hunsley, J., Lee, C. M., and Wood, J. M. (2003). Controversial and questionable assessment techniques. In S. O. Lilienfeld, S. J. Lynn, and J. M. Lohr (Eds.), *Science and pseudoscience in clinical psychology* (pp. 39–76). New York: Guilford.

Huselid, R. F., and Cooper, M. L. (1994). Gender roles as mediators of sex differences in expressions of pathology. *Journal of Abnormal Psychology, 103,* 595–603.

Hyde, J. S. (1986). Gender differences in aggression. In J. S. Hyde and M. C. Linn (Eds.), *The psychology of gender: Advances through meta-analysis.* Baltimore: Johns Hopkins University Press.

Hyde, J. S. (2005). The gender similarities hypothesis. *American Psychologist, 60,* 581–592.

Hyde, J. S., and Plant, E. A. (1995). Magnitude of psychological gender differences: Another side to the story. *American Psychologist, 50,* 159–161.

Hyman, I. E., and Loftus, E. F. (2002). False childhood memories and eyewitness memory errors. In M. L. Eisen (Ed.), *Memory and suggestibility in the forensic interview* (pp. 63–84). Mahwah, NJ: Lawrence Erlbaum Associates, Publishers.

Ickes, W., Snyder, M., and Garcia, S. (1997). Personality influences on the choice of situations. In R. Hogan, J. A. Johnson, and S. Briggs (Eds.), *Handbook of personality psychology* (pp. 165–195). San Diego: Academic Press.

Immelman, A. (2002). The political personality of U.S. president George W. Bush. In L. O. Valenty and O. Feldman (Eds.), *Political leadership for the new century: Personality and behavior among American leaders* (pp. 81–103). Westport, CT: Praeger.

Inglehart, R. (1990). *Culture shift in advanced industrial society.* Princeton, NJ: Princeton University Press.

Insel, P., and Roth, W. (1985). *Core concepts in health* (4th ed.). Palo Alto, CA: Mayfield Publishing Co.

Ip, G. W. M., and Bond, M. H. (1995). Culture, values, and the spontaneous self-concept. *Asian Journal of Psychology, 1,* 30–36.

Ishihara, K., Miyake, S., Miyasita, A., and Miyata, Y. (1992). Morningness-eveningness preference and sleep habits in Japanese office workers of different ages. *Chronobiologia, 19,* 9–16.

Ishihara, K., Saitoh, T., and Miyata, Y. (1983). Short-term adjustment of oral temperature of 8-hour advanced-shift. *Japanese Psychological Research, 25,* 228–232.

Izard, C. E. (1977). *Human emotions.* New York: Plenum Press.

Izard, C. E., Libero, D. Z., Putnam, P., and Haynes, O. M. (1993). Stability of emotion experiences and their relations to traits of personality. *Journal of Personality and Social Psychology, 64,* 847–860.

Jackson, D. N. (1967). *Personality research form manual.* Goshen, NY: Research Psychologists Press.

Jackson, D. N., and Messick, S. (1967). *Problems in human assessment.* New York, McGraw-Hill.

Jacoby, L. L., Lindsay, D. S., and Toth, J. P. (1992). Unconscious influences revealed. *American Psychologist, 47,* 802–809.

Jacoby, R., and Glauberman, N. (1995). *The bell curve debate: History, documents, opinions.* New York: Random House.

James, W. (1884). What is an emotion? *Mind, 9,* 188–205.

Jamieson, J. (1992). The cognitive styles of reflection/impulsivity and field independence/dependence and ESL success. *Modern Language Journal, 76,* 491–501.

Jang, K. L., Livesley, W. J., Angleitner, A., Riemann, R., and Vernon, P. A. (2002). Genetic and environmental influences on the covariance of facets defining the domains of the five-factor model of personality. *Personality and Individual Differences, 33,* 83–101.

Jang, K. L., Livesley, W. J., Riemann, R., Vernon, P. A., Hu, Stella, Angleitner, A., Ando, J., Ono, Y., and Hamer, D. H. (2001). *Journal of Personality and Social Psychology, 81,* 2, 295–304.

Jang, K. L., Dick, D. M., Wolf, H., Livesley, W. J., and Paris, J. (2005). Psychosocial adversity and emotional instability: An application of gene-environment interaction models. *European Journal of Personality, 19,* 359–372.

Jenkins, C. D., Zyzanski, S. J., and Rosenman, R. H. (1976). Risk of new myocardial infarction in middle age men with manifest coronary heart disease. *Circulation, 53,* 342–347.

Jenkins, S. R. (1994). Need for power and women's careers over 14 years: Structural power, job satisfaction, and motive change. *Journal of Personality and Social Psychology, 66,* 155–165.

Jensen-Campbell, L. A., Adams, R., Perry, D. G., Workman, K. A., Furdella, J. Q., and Egan, S. K. (2002). Agreeableness, extraversion, and peer relations in early adolescence: Winning friends and deflecting aggression. *Journal of Research in Personality, 36,* 224–251.

Jensen-Campbell, L. A., Gleason, K. A., Adams, R., and Malcolm, K. T. (2003). Interpersonal conflict, agreeableness, and personality development. *Journal of Personality, 71,* 1059–1085.

Jensen-Campbell, L. A., and Graziano, W. G. (2001). Agreeableness as a moderator of interpersonal conflict. *Journal of Personality, 69,* 323–362.

John, O. P. (1990). The "big five" factor taxonomy: Dimensions of personality in the natural language and questionnaires. In L. A. Pervin (Ed.), *Handbook of personality* (pp. 66–100). New York: Guilford Press.

Johnson, R. E. (1970). Some correlates of extramarital coitus. *Journal of Marriage and the Family, 32,* 449–456.

Johnson, W., McGue, M., and Krueger, R. F. (2005). Personality stability in late adulthood: A behavior genetic analysis. *Journal of Personality, 73,* 523–551.

Johnson, W., McGue, M., Krueger, R. F., and Bouchard, T. J., Jr. (2004). Marriage and personality: A genetic analysis. *Journal of Personality and Social Psychology, 86,* 285–294.

Johnston, M. (1999). *Spectral evidence: The Ramona case: Incest, memory, and truth on trial in Napa Valley.* Boulder, CO: Westview Press.

Jones, A., and Crandall, R. (1986). Validation of a short index of self-actualization. *Personality and Social Psychology Bulletin, 12,* 63–73.

Judge, T., and Larsen, R. J. (2001). Dispositional sources of job satisfaction: A review and theoretical extension. *Organizational Behavior and Human Decision Processes, 86,* 67–98.

Jung, C. G. (1987). The association method: Lecture III. *American Journal of Psychology, 100,* 489–509.

Jung, I., Lee, H., and Cho, B. (2004). Persistent psychotic disorder in an adolescent with a past history of butane gas dependence. *European Psychiatry, 19,* 519–520.

Kagan, J. (1981). *The second year: The emergence of self-awareness.* Cambridge, MA: Harvard University Press.

Kagan, J. (1994). *Galen's prophecy: Temperament in human nature.* New York: Basic Books.

Kagan, J. (1999). Born to be shy? In R. Conlan (Ed.), *States of mind* (pp. 29–51). New York: Wiley.

Kagan, J., and Moss, H. (1962). *Birth to maturity: A study in psychological development.* New York: John Wiley.

Kagan, J., and Snidman, N. (1991). Infant predictors of inhibited and uninhibited profiles. *Psychological Science, 2,* 40–44.

Kamen-Siegel, L., Rodin, J., Seligman, M. E., and Dwyer, J. (1991). Explanatory style and cell-mediated immunity in elderly men and women. *Health Psychology, 10,* 229–235.

Kammrath, L. K., Mendoza-Denton, R., and Mischel, W. (2005). Incorporating if . . . then . . . personality signatures in person perception: Beyond the person-situation dichotomy. *Journal of Personality and Social Psychology, 88,* 605–618.

Kanner, Allen D., Feldman, S. Shirley, and Weinberger, Daniel A. (1991). Uplifts, hassles, and adaptational outcomes in early adolescents. In A. Monat and R. S. Lazarus (Eds.), *Stress and coping: An anthology* (3rd ed.) (pp. 158–181). New York: Columbia University Press.

Kaplan, H., and Hill, K. (1985). Food-sharing among Ache foragers: Tests of evolutionary hypotheses. *Current Anthropology, 26,* 223–246.

Katigbak, M. S., Church, A. T., Guanzon-Lapena, M. A., Carlota, A. J., and del Pilar, G. H. (2002). Are indigenous personality dimensions culture-specific? Philippine inventories and the five-factor model. *Journal of Personality and Social Psychology, 82,* 1, 89–101.

Katz, I. M., and Campbell, J. D. (1994). Ambivalence over emotional expression and well-being: Nomothetic and idiographic tests of the stress-buffering hypothesis. *Journal of Personality and Social Psychology, 67,* 513–524.

Kavanagh, K., and Hops, H. (1994). Good girls? Bad boys? Gender and development as contexts for diagnosis and treatment. *Advances in Clinical Child Psychology, 16,* 45–79.

Kelley, H. H. (1992). Common-sense psychology and scientific psychology. In M. R. Rosensweig and L. W. Porter (Eds.), *Annual Review of Psychology* (Vol. 43, pp. 1–23). Palo Alto, CA: Annual Reviews.

Kelly, E. L., and Conley, J. J. (1987). Personality and compatibility: A prospective analysis of marital stability and marital satisfaction. *Journal of Personality and Social Psychology, 52,* 27–40.

Kelly, G.A. (1955). *The psychology of personal constructs* (Vols. 1 and 2). London: Routledge.

Keltikangas-Järvinen, L., Elovainio, M., Kivimäki, M., Lichtermann, D., Ekelund, J., and Leena Peltonen, L. (2003). Association between the Type 4 dopamine receptor gene polymorphism and novelty seeking. *Psychosomatic Medicine, 65,* 471–476.

Kendler, K. S., McGuire, M., Gruenberg, A. M., O'Hare, A., Spellman, M., and Walsh, D. (1993). The Roscommon Family Study III: Schizophrenia-related personality disorders in relatives. *Archives of General Psychiatry, 50,* 781–788.

Kendler, R. S., Heath, A. C., Neale, M. C., Kessler, R. C., and Eaves, L. J. (1992). A population-based twin study of alcoholism in women. *Journal of the American Medical Association, 268,* 1877–1882.

Kenrick, D. T., and Luce, C. L. (2004). *The functional mind: Readings in evolutionary psychology.* Boston: Allyn and Bacon.

Kerkhof, G. A. (1985). Inter-individual differences in the human circadian system: A review. *Biological Psychology, 20,* 83–112.

Kernberg, O. (1975). *Borderline conditions and pathological narcissism.* New York: Jason Aronson.

Kernberg, O. F. (1984). *Severe personality disorders.* New Haven, CT: Yale University Press.

Kernis, M. H., Grannemann, B. D., and Barclay, L. C. (1992). Stability of self-esteem: Assessment, correlates, and excuse making. *Journal of Personality, 60,* 621–643.

Kernis, M. H., Grannemann, B. D., and Mathis, L. C. (1991). Stability of self-esteem as a moderator of the relation between level of self-esteem and depression. *Journal of Personality and Social Psychology, 61,* 80–84.

Ketelaar, T. (1995). *Emotion as mental representations of fitness affordances: I. Evidence supporting the claim that the negative and positive emotions map onto fitness costs and benefits.* Paper presented at the annual meeting of the Human Behavior and Evolution Society, Santa Barbara.

Khan, S. S., Nessim, S., Gray, R., Czer, L. S., Chaux, A., and Matloff, J. (1990). Increased mortality of women in coronary artery bypass surgery: Evidence for referral bias. *Annals of Internal Medicine, 112,* 561–567.

Kihlstrom, J. F. (1999). The psychological unconscious. In L. A. Pervin and O. P.

John (Eds.), *Handbook of personality: Theory and research* (pp. 424–442). New York: Guilford Press.

Kihlstrom, J. F. (2003). Freud is dead weight on psychology. In E. E. Smith, S. Noen-Hoeksema, B. L. Fredrickson, G. R. Loftus, D. J. Bem, and S. Maren, *Introduction to psychology* (p. 487). Belmont, CA: Wadsworth/Thomson Learning.

Kihlstrom, J. F. (2003). The fox, the hedgehog, and hypnosis. *International Journal of Clinical and Experimental Hypnosis Special Issue: University of Tennessee Conference on Brain Imaging and Hypnosis, Part I. Vol. 51,* 166–189.

Kihlstrom, J. F., Barnhardt, T. M., and Tataryn, D. J. (1992). The psychological unconscious: Found, lost, and regained. *American Psychologist, 47,* 788–791.

Kim, E. (2002). Agitation, aggression, and disinhibition syndromes after traumatic brain injury. *NeuroRehabilitation, 17,* 297–310.

Kim, K., Smith, P. K., and Palermiti, A. (1997). Conflict in childhood and reproductive development. *Evolution and Human Behavior, 18,* 109–142.

Kimura, D. (2002). Sex hormones influence human cognitive pattern. *Neuroendocrinology Letters, 23* (Suppl. 4): 67–77.

King, L. A. (1995). Wishes, motives, goals, and personal memories: Relations and correlates of measures of human motivation. *Journal of Personality, 63,* 985–1007.

King, L. A., and Emmons, R. A. (1990). Conflict over emotional expression: Psychological and physical correlates. *Journal of Personality and Social Psychology, 58,* 864–877.

Kintz, B. L., Delprato, D. J., Mettee, D. R., Parsons, D. E., and Schappe, R. H. (1965). The experimenter effect. *Psychological Bulletin, 63,* 223–232.

Kipnis, D. (1971). *Character structure and impulsiveness.* New York: Academic Press.

Kling, K. C., Hyde, J. S., Showers, C. J., and Buswell, B. N. (1999). Gender differences in self-esteem: A meta-analysis. *Psychological Bulletin, 125,* 470–500.

Klinger, E. (1977a). The nature of fantasy and its clinical uses. *Psychotherapy: Theory, Research, and Practice, 14,* 223–231.

Klinger, E. (1977b). *Meaning and void: Inner experience and the incentives in people's lives.* Minneapolis: University of Minnesota Press.

Klonsky, E. D., Oltmanns, T. F., and Turkheimer, E. (2002). Informant reports of personality disorder: Relation to self-reports and future research directions. *Clinical Psychology: Science and Practice, 9,* 300–311.

Kluckhohn, C., and Murray, H. A. (1948). *Personality in nature, society, and culture.* New York: Knopf.

Knafo, A., Iervolino, A. C., and Plomin, R. (2005). Masculine girls and feminine boys: Genetic and environmental contributions to atypical gender development in early childhood. *Journal of Personality and Social Psychology, 88,* 400–412.

Knutson, B., Wolkowitz, O. M., Cole, S. W., Chan, T., Moore, E. A., Johnson, R. C., Terpestra, J., Turner, R. A., and Reus, V. I. (1998). Selective alteration of personality and social behavior by serotonergic intervention. *American Journal of Psychiatry, 155,* 373–378.

Koenig, L. B., McGue, M., Krueger, R. F., and Bouchard, T. J., Jr. (2005). Genetic and environmental influences on religiousness ratings. *Journal of Personality, 73,* 471–488.

Koestner, R., and McClelland, D. C. (1990). Perspectives on competence motivation. In L. A. Pervin (Ed.), *Handbook of personality: Theory and research* (pp. 527–548). New York: Guilford Press.

Kofman, S. (1985). *The enigma of woman: Woman in Freud's writings.* Ithaca, NY: Cornell University Press.

Kohn, M. L., Naoi, A., Schoenbach, C., Schooler, C., and Slomczynski, K. M. (1990). Position in the class structure and psychological functioning in the United States, Japan, and Poland. *American Journal of Sociology, 95,* 964–1008.

Kohut, H. (1977). *The restoration of the self.* Madison, CT: International Universities Press.

Koole, S. L., Jager, W., van den Berg, A. E. Vlek, C. A. J., and Hofstee, W. K. B. (2001). On the social nature of personality: Effects of extraversion, agreeableness, and feedback about collective resource use on cooperation in a resource dilemma. *Personality and Social Psychology Bulletin, 27,* 3, 289–301.

Koopmans, J. R., and Boomsma, D. I. (1993). Bivariate genetic analysis of the relation between alcohol and tobacco use in adolescent twins. *Psychiatr. Genet., 3,* 172.

Kopp, C. B. (1989). Regulation of distress and negative emotions: A developmental view. *Developmental Psychology, 25,* 343–354.

Kosslyn, S. M., Cacioppo, J. T., Davidson, R. J., Hugdahl, K., Lovallo, W. R., Spiegel, D., and Rose, R. (2002). Bridging psychology and biology: The analysis of individuals in groups. *American Psychologist, 57,* 341–351.

Kosslyn, S. M., and Rosenberg, R. S. (2004). *Psychology: The brain, the person, the world.* Boston: Allyn and Bacon.

Kowalski, R. M., and Brown, K. J. (1994). Psychosocial barriers to cervical cancer screening: Concerns with self-presentation and social evaluation. *Journal of Applied Social Psychology, 24,* 941–958.

Kraeplin, E. (1913). *Psychiatrie: Ein Lehrbuch* (8th ed.). Leipzig: Barth.

Kretschmer, E. (1925). *Physique and character.* London: Kegan Paul.

Krueger, J. I., Hasman, J. F., Acevedo, M., and Villano, P. (2003). Perceptions of trait typicality in gender stereotypes: Examining the role of attribution and categorization processes. *Personality and Social Psychology Bulletin, 29,* 1, 108–116.

Krueger, R. F., Markon, K. E., and Bouchard, Jr., T. J. (2003). The extended genotype: The heritability of personality accounts for the heritability of recalled family environments in twins reared apart. *Journal of Personality, 71,* 5, 809–834.

Krug, S. E. (1981). *Interpreting 16 PF profile patterns.* Champaign, IL: Institute for Personality and Ability Testing.

Kuhn, M., and McPartland, T. S. (1954). An empirical investigation of self-attitudes. *American Sociological Review, 19,* 68–76.

Kurman, J. (2001). Self-enhancement: Is it restricted to individualistic cultures? *Personality and Social Psychology Bulletin, 27,* 12, 1705–1716.

Kwapil, T. R., Wrobel, M. J., and Pope, C. A. (2002). The five-factor personality structure of dissociative experiences. *Personality and Individual Differences, 32,* 431–443.

Kwon, P., Campbell, D. G., and Williams, M. G. (2001). Sociotropy and autonomy: Preliminary evidence for construct validity using TAT narratives. *Journal of Personality Assessment Special Issue: More data on the current Rorschach controversy, 77,* 128–138.

Kyl-Heku, L., and Buss, D. M. (1996). Tactics as units of analysis in and personality psychology: An illustration using tactics of hierarchy negotiation. *Personality Individual Differences, 21,* 497–517.

Lactic, B., and Ostendorf, F. (2005). Taxonomy and structure of Croatian personality-descriptive adjectives. *European Journal of Personality, 19,* 117–152.

LaHam, S. M., Gonsalkorale, K., and von Hipple, W. (2005). Darwinian grandparenting: Preferential investment in more certain kin. *Personality and Social Psychology Bulletin, 31,* 63–72.

Lajunen, T. (2001). Personality and accident liability: Are extraversion, neuroticism and psychoticism related to traffic and occupational fatalities? *Personality and Individual Differences, 31,* 1365–1373.

Lalumiere, M. L., Chalmers, L. J., Quinsey, V. L., and Seto, M. C. (1996). A test of the mate deprivation hypothesis of sexual coercion. *Ethology and Sociobiology, 17,* 299–318.

Lalumiere, M. L., Harris, G. T., and Rice, M. E. (2001). Psychopathy and developmental instability. *Evolution and Human Behavior, 22,* 75–92.

Langens, T. A. (2001) Predicting behavior change in Indian businessmen from a combination of need for achievement and self-discrepancy. *Journal of Research in Personality, 35,* 339–352.

Langevin, R., Bain, J., Wortzman, G., and Hucker, S. (1988). Sexual sadism: Brain, blood, and behavior. *Annals of the New York Academy of Science, 528,* 163–171.

Langford, P. H. (2003). A one-minute measure of the Big Five? Evaluating and abridging Shafer's (1999a) Big Five markers. *Personality and Individual Differences, 35,* 1127–1140.

Langner, C. A., and Winter, D. G. (2001). The motivational basis of concessions and compromise: Archival and laboratory studies. *Journal of Personality and Social Psychology, 81,* 711–727.

Lanning, K. (1994). Dimensionality of observer ratings on the California Adult Q-set. *Journal of Personality and Social Psychology, 67,* 151–160.

Larrance, D., Pavelich, S., Storer, P., Polizzi, M., Baron, B., Sloan, S., Jordan, R., and Reis, H. T. (1979). Competence and incompetence: Asymmetric responses to women and men on a sex-linked task. *Personality and Social Psychology Bulletin, 5,* 363–366.

Larsen, R. J. (1984). Theory and measurement of affect intensity as an individual difference characteristic. *Dissertation Abstracts International,* 45(7-B). (UMI No. 2297).

Larsen, R. J. (1985). Individual differences in circadian activity rhythm and personality. *Personality and Individual Differences, 6,* 305–311.

Larsen, R. J. (1987). The stability of mood variability: A spectral analytic approach to daily mood assessments. *Journal of Personality and Social Psychology, 52,* 1195–1204.

Larsen, R. J. (1989). A process approach to personality: Utilizing time as a facet of data. In D. Buss and N. Cantor (Eds.), *Personality psychology: Recent trends and emerging directions* (pp. 177–193). New York: Springer-Verlag.

Larsen, R. J. (1991). Personality and emotion. In V. Derlega, B. Winstead, and W. Jones (Eds.), *Contemporary research in personality* (pp. 407–432). Chicago: Nelson-Hall.

Larsen, R. J. (1992). Neuroticism and selective encoding and recall of symptoms: Evidence from a combined concurrent-retrospective study. *Journal of Personality and Social Psychology, 62,* 480–488.

Larsen, R. J. (2000a). Toward a science of mood regulation. *Psychological Inquiry, 11,* 129–141.

Larsen, R. J. (2000b). Maintaining hedonic balance. *Psycholôgical Inquiry, 11,* 218–225.

Larsen, R. J., Billings, D., and Cutler, S. (1996). Affect intensity and individual differences in cognitive style. *Journal of Personality, 64,* 185–208.

Larsen, R. J., Chen, B., and Zelenski, J. (2003). *Responses to punishment and reward in the emotion Stroop paradigm: Relations to BIS and BAS.* Manuscript submitted for publication.

Larsen, R. J., and Cowan, G. S. (1988). Internal focus of attention and depression: A study of daily experience. *Motivation and Emotion, 12,* 237–249.

Larsen, R. J., and Cutler, S. (1996). The complexity of individual emotional lives: A within-subject analysis of affect structure. *Journal of Social and Clinical Psychology, 15,* 206–230.

Larsen, R. J., and Diener, E. (1985). A multitrait-multimethod examination of affect structure: Hedonic level and emotional intensity. *Personality and Individual Differences, 6,* 631–636.

Larsen, R. J., and Diener, E. (1987). Affect intensity as an individual difference characteristic: A review. *Journal of Research in Personality, 21,* 1–39.

Larsen, R. J., and Diener, E. (1992). Problems and promises with the circumplex model of emotion. *Review of Personality and Social Psychology, 13,* 25–59.

Larsen, R. J., Diener, E., and Cropanzano, R. S. (1987). Cognitive operations associated with individual differences in affect intensity. *Journal of Personality and Social Psychology, 53,* 767–774.

Larsen, R. J., Diener, E., and Emmons, R. A. (1986). Affect intensity and reactions to daily life events. *Journal of Personality and Social Psychology, 51,* 803–814.

Larsen, R. J., Diener, E., and Lucas, R. (2002). Emotion: Models, measures, and individual differences. In R. Lord, R. Klimoski, and R. Kanfer (Eds.), *Emotions at work* (pp. 64–106). San Francisco: Jossey-Bass.

Larsen, R. J., and Fredrickson, B. L. (1999). Measurement issues in emotion research. In D. Kahneman, E. Diener, and N. Schwarz (Eds.), *Understanding quality of life: Scientific perspectives on enjoyment and suffering* (pp. 40–60). New York: Sage.

Larsen, R. J., and Kasimatis, M. (1990). Individual differences in entrainment of mood to the weekly calendar. *Journal of Personality and Social Psychology, 58,* 164–171.

Larsen, R. J., and Kasimatis, M. (1991). Day-to-day physical symptoms: Individual differences in the occurrence, duration, and emotional concomitants of minor daily illnesses. *Journal of Personality Special Issue: Personality and daily experience, 59,* 387–423.

Larsen, R. J., and Ketelaar, T. (1989). Extraversion, neuroticism, and susceptibility to positive and negative mood induction procedures. *Personality and Individual Differences, 10,* 1221–1228.

Larsen, R. J., and Ketelaar, T. (1991). Personality and susceptibility to positive and negative emotional states. *Journal of Personality and Social Psychology, 61,* 132–140.

Larsen, R. J., and Prizmic, Z. (2004). Affect regulation. In R. Baumeister and K. Vohs (Eds.), *Handbook of self-regulation research* (pp. 40–60). New York: Guilford.

Larsen, R. J., and Prizmic, Z. (in press). Multimethod measurement of emotion. In M. Eid and E. Diener (Eds.), *Handbook of measurement: A multimethod perspective.* Washington, DC: American Psychological Association.

Larsen, R. J., and Prizmic-Larsen, Z. (1999). Marrying a culture when you marry a person. *Contemporary Psychology, 44,* 538–540.

Larsen, R. J., and Zarate, M. A. (1991). Extending reducer/augmenter theory into the emotion domain: The role of affect in regulating stimulation level. *Personality and Individual Differences, 12,* 713–723.

Larson, D. G., and Chastain, R. L. (1990). Self-concealment: Conceptualization, measurement, and health implications. *Journal of Social and Clinical Psychology, 9,* 439–455.

Laub, J. H., and Lauritsen, J. L. (1994). The precursors of criminal offending across the life course. *Federal Probation, 58,* 51–57.

Lazarus, R. S. (1991). *Emotion and adaptation.* Oxford, England: Oxford University Press.

Lazarus, R. S., and Folkman, S. (1984). *Stress, appraisal and coping.* New York: Springer.

Lazarus, R. S., Kanner, A. D., and Folkman, S. (1980). Emotions: A cognitive-phenomenological analysis. In R. Plutchik and H. Kellerman (Eds.), *Theories of emotion* (pp. 189–217). New York: Academic Press.

Le Boeuf, B. J., and Reiter, J. (1988). Lifetime reproductive success in northern elephant seals. In T. H. Clutton-Brock (Ed.), *Reproductive success* (pp. 344–362). Chicago: University of Chicago Press.

Leary, M. R., and Kowalski, R. M. (1995). *Social anxiety.* New York: Guilford Press.

Lee, D., Kelley, K. R., and Edwards, J. K. (2006). A closer look at relationships among trait procrastination, neuroticism, and conscientiousness. *Personality and Individual Differences, 40,* 27–37.

Lee, K., Ogunfowora, B., and Ashton, M. C. (2005). Personality traits beyond the big five: Are they within the HEXACO space? *Journal of Personality, 73,* 1437–1463.

Lefkowitz, J., and Frazer, A. W. (1980). Assessment of achievement and power motivation of blacks and whites, using a black and white TAT, with black and white administrators. *Journal of Applied Psychology, 65,* 685–696.

Leiter, E. (1982). The effects of subliminal activation of aggressive and merging fantasies in differentiated and non-differentiated schizophrenics. *Psychological Research Bulletin, 22,* 1–21.

Lesch, K. P. (in press). Neuroticism and serotonin: A developmental perspective. In R. Plomin, J. C. DeFries, I. W. Craig, and P. McGuffin (Eds.), *Behavioral genetics in a postgenomic era.* Washington, DC: APA Books.

LeVay, S. (1991). A difference in hypothalamic structure between heterosexual and homosexual men. *Science,* pp. 1034–1037.

LeVay, S. (1993). *The sexual brain.* Cambridge, MA: MIT Press.

LeVay, S. (1996). *Queer science: The use and abuse of research into homosexuality.* Cambridge, MA: MIT Press.

Levinson, M. R. (1992). Rethinking psychopathy. *Theory and Psychology, 2,* 51–71.

Levenson, M. R., Kiehl, K. A., and Fitzpatrick, C. M. (1995). Assessing psychopathic attributes in a noninstitutionalized population. *Journal of Personality and Social Psychology, 68,* 151–158.

Levenson, R. W. (1983). Personality research and psychophysiology: General considerations. *Journal of Research in Personality, 17,* 1–21.

Levenson, R. W. (2003). Autonomic specificity and emotion. In R. J. Davidson, K. R. Scherer, and H. H. Goldsmith (Eds.), *Handbook of affective science* (pp. 212–224). New York: Oxford University Press.

Levesque, Johanne, Fanny, Eugene, and Joanette, Y. (2003). Neural circuitry underlying voluntary suppression of sadness. *Biological Psychiatry 53,* 502–510.

Levy, S. M. (1990). Psychosocial risk factors and cancer progression: Mediating pathways linking behavior and disease. In K. D. Craig and S. M. Weiss (Eds.), *Health enhancement, disease prevention, and early intervention: Biobehavioral perspectives* (pp. 348–369). New York: Springer.

Levy, S. M., and Heiden. L. A. (1990). Personality and social factors in cancer outcome. In H. S. Friedman (Ed.), *Personality and disease* (pp. 254–279). New York: John Wiley and Sons.

Levy, S. M., Herberman, R., Maluish, A., Achlien, B., and Lippman, M. (1985). Prognostic risk assessment in primary breast cancer by behavioral and immunological parameters. *Health Psychology, 4,* 99–113.

Lewis, M., and Ramsay, D. (2004). Development of self-recognition, personal pronoun use, and pretend play during the second year. *Child Development, 75,* 1821–1831.

Lillienfeld, S. O. (2002). When worlds collide: Social science, politics and the Rind et al. (1998) Child abuse meta-analysis. *American Psychologist, 57,* 177–187.

Linville, P. W. (1987). Self-complexity as a cognitive buffer against stress-related illness and depression. *Journal of Personality and Social Psychology, 52,* 663–676.

Lippa, R. (1998). Gender-related individual differences and the structure of vocational interests: The importance of the people-things dimension. *Journal of Personality and Social Psychology, 74,* 996–1009.

Lishman, W. A. (1972). Selective factors in memory. Part 1: Age, sex, and personality attributes. *Psychological Medicine, 2,* 121–138.

Little, A. C., Burt, D. M., and Perrett, D. I. (2006). Assortative mating for perceived facial personality traits. *Personality and Individual Differences, l 40,* 973–984.

Little, B. R. (1972a). *Person-thing orientation: A provisional manual for the T-P scale.* Oxford, England: Oxford University, Department of Experimental Psychology.

Little, B. R. (1972b). Psychological man as scientist, humanist, and specialist. *Journal of Experimental Research in Personality, 6,* 95–118.

Little, B. R. (1999). Personality and motivation: Personal action and the cognitive revolution. In L. A. Pervin and O. P. John (Eds.), *Handbook of personality: Theory and research* (pp. 501–524). New York: Guilford Press.

Little, B. R., Lecci, L., and Watkinson, B. (1992). Personality and personal projects: Linking big five and PAC units of analysis. *Journal of Personality, 60,* 501–525.

Lloyd, M. E. (1990). Gender factors in reviewer recommendations for manuscript publication. *Journal of Applied Behavior Analysis, 23,* 539–543.

Loehlin, J. C. (1992). *Genes and environment in personality development.* Newbury Park: Sage.

Loehlin, J. C., Neiderhiser, J. M., and Reiss, D. (2003). The behavior genetics of personality and the NEAD Study. *Journal of Research in Personality, 37,* 373–387.

Loehlin, J. C., and Nichols, R. C. (1976). *Heredity, environment and personality.* Austin: University of Texas Press.

Loftus, E. F. (1992). When a lie becomes memory's truth: Memory distortion after exposure to misinformation. *Current Directions in Psychological Science, 1,* 121–123.

Loftus, E. F. (1993). The reality of repressed memories. *American Psychologist, 48,* 518–537.

Loftus, E. F. (2000). Remembering what never happened. In E. Tulving (Ed.), *Memory, consciousness, and the brain: The Tallinn Conference* (pp. 106–118). Philadelphia, PA: Psychology Press.

Loftus, E. F. (2003). Memory in Canadian Courts of Law. *Canadian Psychology, 44,* 207–212.

London, H., and Exner, J. E., Jr. (Eds.). (1978). *Dimensions of personality.* New York: Wiley.

Lounsbury, J. W., Sundstrom, E., Loveland, James M., and Gibson, L. W. (2003). Intelligence, "Big Five" personality traits, and work drive as predictors of course grade. *Personality and Individual Differences, 35,* 1231–1239.

Low, B. (1989). Cross-cultural patterns in the training of children: An evolutionary perspective. *Journal of Comparative Psychology, 103,* 311–319.

Lowenstein, L. F. (2002). Ability and personality changes after brain injuries. *Criminal Lawyer, 120,* 5–8.

Lowry, P. E. (1997). The assessment center process; New directions. *Journal of Social Behavior and Personality, 12,* 53–62.

Lund, O. C. H., Tamnes, C. K., Moestue, C., Buss, D. M., and Vollrath, M. (in press). Tactics of hierarchy negotiation. *Journal of Research in Personality.*

Luntz, B. K., and Widom, C. S. (1994). Antisocial personality disorder in abused and neglected children grown up. *American Journal of Psychiatry, 151,* 670–674.

Luo, S., and Klohnen, E. C. (2005). Assortative mating and marital quality in newlyweds: A couple-centered approach. *Journal of Personality and Social Psychology, 88,* 304–326.

Lykken, D. T. (1982, September). Fearlessness. *Psychology Today,* pp. 6–10.

Lykken, D. T. (1995). *The antisocial personalities.* Hillsdale, NJ: Erlbaum.

Lynn, S. J., Lock, T., Loftus, E. F., Krackow, E., and Lilienfeld, S. O. (2003). The remembrance of things past: Problematic memory recovery techniques in psychotherapy. In S. O. Lilienfeld and S. J. Lynn (Eds.), *Science and pseudoscience in clinical psychology* (pp. 205–239). New York: Guilford Press.

Lytton, H., Martin, N. G., and Eaves, L. (1977). Environmental and genetical causes of variation in ethological aspects of behavior in two-year-old boys. *Social Biology, 24,* 200–211.

Lyubomirsky, S. (2001). Why are some people happier than others? The role of cognitive and motivational processes in well-being. *American Psychologist, 56,* 239–249.

Lyubomirsky, S., King, L., and Diener, E. (2005). The benefits of frequent positive affect: Does happiness lead to success? *Psychological Bulletin, 131,* 803–855.

Ma, V., and Schoeneman, T. J. (1997). Individualism versus collectivism: A comparison of Kenyan and American self-concepts. *Basic and Applied Social Psychology, 19,* 261–273.

MacAndrew, C., and Steele, T. (1991). Gray's behavioral inhibition system: A psychometric examination. *Personality and Individual Differences, 12,* 157–171.

Maccoby, E. E., and Jacklin, C. N. (1974). *The psychology of sex differences.* Stanford, CA: Stanford University Press.

MacDonald, G., and Leary, M. R. (2005). Why does social exclusion hurt? The relationship between social and physical pain. *Psychological Bulletin, 131,* 202–223.

MacDonald, K. (1998). Evolution, culture, and the five-factor model. *Journal of Cross-Cultural Psychology, 29,* 119–149.

MacGillivray, L., Nylander, P. P. S., and Corney, G. (1975). *Human multiple reproduction.* London: Saunders.

Machiavelli, N. (1966). *The Prince.* New York: Bantam. (Original work published 1513.)

Macmillan, M. B. (2000). Restoring Phineas Gage: A 150th retrospective. *Journal of the History of the Neurosciences, 9,* 42–62.

Magnavita, J. J. (2003). *Handbook of personality disorders: Theory and practice.* New York: Wiley.

Malcom, J. (1982). *Psychoanalysis: The impossible profession.* New York: Vintage.

Marangoni, C., Garcia, S., Ickes, W., and Teng, G. (1995). Empathic accuracy in a clinically relevant setting. *Journal of Personality and Social Psychology, 68,* 854–869.

Marcia, J. E. (1966). Development and validation of ego-identity status. *Journal of Personality and Social Psychology, 3,* 551–558.

Marcia, J. E. (2002). Identity and psychosocial development in adulthood. *Identity, 2,* 7–28.

Markey, C. N., Markey, P. M., and Tinsley, B. J. (2003). Personality, puberty, and preadolescent girls' risky behaviors: Examining the predictive value of the Five-Factor Model of personality. *Journal of Research in Personality, 37,* 405–419.

Markus, H. (1983). Self-knowledge: An expanded view. *Journal of Personality, 51,* 543–565.

Markus, H. R., and Kitayama, S. (1991). Culture and the self: Implications for cognition, emotion, and motivation. *Psychological Review, 98,* 224–253.

Markus, H. R., and Kitayama, S. (1994). A collective fear of the collective: Implications for selves and theories of selves. *Personality and Social Psychology Bulletin, 20,* 568–579.

Markus, H. R., and Kitayama, S. (1998). The cultural psychology of personality. *Journal of Cross-Cultural Psychology, 29,* 63–87.

Markus, H. R., Kitayama, S., and Heiman, R. J. (1996). Culture and "basic" psychological principles. In E. T. Higgins and A. W. Kruglanski (Eds.), *Social psychology: Handbook of basic principles* (pp. 857–913). New York: Guilford Press.

Markus, H., and Nurius, P. (1986). Possible selves. *American Psychologist, 41,* 954–969.

Markus, H., and Nurius, P. (1987). Possible selves: The interface between motivation and the self concept. In K. Yardley and T. Honness (Eds.), *Self and identity: Psychosocial perspectives,* (pp. 157–172). Chichester, England: John Wiley and Sons.

Marsh, Herbert W. (1996). Positive and negative global self-esteem: A substantively meaningful distinction or artifactors? *Journal of Personality and Social Psychology, 70,* 810–819.

Marsland, A. L., Cohen, S., Rabin, B. S., and Manuck, S. B. (2001). Associations between stress, trait negative affect, acute immune reactivity, and antibody response in hepatitis B injection in healthy young adults. *Health Psychology, 20,* 4–11.

Martin, M., Ward, J. C., and Clark, D. M. (1983). Neuroticism and the recall of positive and negative personality information. *Behavior Research and Therapy, 21,* 495–503.

Martin, N. G., Eaves, L. J., Heath, A. C., Jardine, R., Feingold, L. G., and Eysenck, H. J. (1986). Transmission of social attitudes. *Proceedings of the National Academy of Sciences, U.S.A., 83,* 4364–4368.

Maslow, A. H. (1968). *Toward a psychology of being* (2nd ed.). New York: Harper and Row. (Original work published 1954.)

Maslow, A. H. (1970). *Motivation and personality.* New York: Harper and Row. (Original work published 1954.)

Maslow, A. H. (1987). *Motivation and personality.* New York: Harper and Row. (Original work published 1954.)

Maslow, A. H., and Hoffman, E. (1996). *Future visions: The unpublished papers of Abraham Maslow.* Thousand Oaks, CA: Sage Publications, Inc.

Mason, A., and Blankenship, V. (1987). Power and affiliation motivation, stress, and abuse in intimate relationships. *Journal of Personality and Social Psychology, 52,* 203–210.

Mason, J., Southwick, S., Yehuda, R., Wang, S., Riney, S., Bremner, D., Johnson, D., Lubin, H., Blake, D., and Zhou, G. (1994). Elevation of serum free triiodothyronine, total triiodthyronine, thyroxine-binding globulin, and total thyroxine levels in combat-related posttraumatic stress disorder. *Archives of General Psychiatry, 51,* 629–641.

Mason, O., Claridge, G., and Jackson, M. (1995). New scales for the assessment of schizotypy. *Personality and Individual Differences, 18,* 7–13.

Masson, J. M. (1984). *The assault on truth: Freud's suppression of the seduction theory.* New York: Farrar, Straus and Giroux.

Masuda, T., and Nisbett, R. E. (2001). Attending holistically versus analytically: Comparing the context sensitivity of Japanese and Americans. *Journal of Personality and Social Psychology, 81,* 5, 922–934.

Matsumoto, D. (1999). Culture and self: An empirical assessment of Markus and Kitayama's theory of independent and interdependent self-construals. *Asian Journal of Social Psychology, 2,* 289–310.

Matthews, G. (2000). Attention, automaticity, and affective disorder. *Behavior Modification, 24,* 69–93.

Matthews, G., Derryberry, D., and Siegle, G. J. (2000). Personality and emotion: Cognitive science perspectives. In S. E. Hampson (Ed.), *Advances in personality psychology* (Vol. 1, pp. 199–237). Philadelphia: Taylor and Francis.

Matthews, G., and Gilliland, K. (1999). The personality theories of H. J. Eysenck and J. A. Gray: A comparative review. *Personality and Individual Differences, 26,* 583–626.

Matthews, G., and Oddy, K. (1993). Recovery of major personality dimensions from trait adjective data. *Personality and Individual Differences, 15,* 419–431.

Mattia, J. I., and Zimmerman, M. (2001). Epidemiology. In W. J. Livesley (Ed.), *Handbook of personality disorders: Theory, research and treatment.* New York: Guilford.

Maynard Smith, J. (1982). *Evolution and the theory of games.* Cambridge, England: Cambridge University Press.

McAdams, D. P. (1990). Motives. In V. Derlega, B. Winstead, and W. Jones (Eds.), *Contemporary research in personality* (pp. 175–204). Chicago: Nelson-Hall.

McAdams, D. P. (1992). The five-factor model in personality: A critical appraisal. *Journal of Personality, 60,* 329–361.

McAdams, D. P. (1999). Personal narratives and the life story. In L. A. Pervin and O. P. John (Eds.), *Handbook of personality: Theory and research* (2nd ed., 478–500). New York: Guilford Press.

McAdams, D. P., and Bryant, F. B. (1987). Intimacy motivation and subjective mental health in a nationwide sample. *Journal of Personality, 55,* 395–413.

McAdams, D. P., and Vaillant, G. E. (1982). Intimacy motivation and psychosocial adjustment: A longitudinal study. *Journal of Personality Assessment, 46,* 586–593.

McCarley, N. G., and Clarskadon, T. G. (1983). Test retest reliabilities of the scales and subscales of the Myers-Briggs Type Indicator and of criteria for clinical interpretive hypotheses involving them. *Research in Psychological Type, 6,* 24–36.

McClelland, D. C. (1958). Risk-taking in children with high and low need for achievement. In J. W. Atkinson (Ed.), *Motives in fantasy, action, and society* (pp. 306–327). Princeton, NJ: Van Nostrand.

McClelland, D. C. (1965). N achievement and entrepreneurship: A longitudinal study. *Journal of Personality and Social Psychology, 1,* 389–392.

McClelland, D. C. (1979). Inhibited power motivation and high blood pressure in men. *Journal of Abnormal Psychology, 88,* 182–190.

McClelland D. C. (1982). The need for power, sympathetic activation, and illness. *Motivation and Emotion, 6,* 31–41.

McClelland, D. C. (1985). How motives, skills, and values determine what people do. *American Psychologist, 40,* 812–825.

McClelland, D. C., and Jemmott, J. B. (1980). Power motivation, stress, and physical illness. *Journal of Human Stress, 6,* 6–15.

McClelland, D. C., and Pilon, D. A. (1983). Sources of adult motives in patterns of parent behavior in early childhood. *Journal of Personality and Social Psychology, 44,* 564–574.

McClelland, D. C., Alexander, C., and Marks, E. (1982). The need for power, stress, immune function, and illness among male prisoners. *Journal of Abnormal Psychology, 91,* 61–70.

McClelland, D. C., Koestner, R., and Weinberger, J. (1989). How do self-attributed and implicit motives differ? *Psychological Review, 96,* 690–702.

McCoul, M. D., and Haslam, N. (2001). Predicting high risk sexual behaviour in heterosexual and homosexual men: The roles of impulsivity and sensation seeking. *Personality and Individual Differences, 31,* 1303–1310.

McCrae, R. R., and Costa, P. T., Jr. (1985). Updating Norman's "adequate taxonomy": Intelligence and personality dimensions in natural language and questionnaires. *Journal of Personality and Social Psychology, 49,* 710–721.

McCrae, R. R., and Costa, P. T. (1989). Reinterpreting the Myers-Briggs Type Indicator from the perspective of the five-factor model of personality. *Journal of Personality, 57,* 17–40.

McCrae, R. R., and Costa, P. T. (1991). Adding liebe und arbeit: The full five-factor model and well-being. *Personality and Social Psychology Bulletin, 17,* 227–232.

McCrae, R. R., and Costa, P. T., Jr. (1997). Personality trait structure as a human universal. *American Psychologist, 52,* 509–516.

McCrae, R. R., and Costa, P. T., Jr. (1999). A five-factor theory of personality. In L. A. Pervin and O. John (Eds.), *Handbook of personality: Theory and research* (2nd ed.). New York: Guildford Press.

McCrae, R. R., and John, O. P. (1992). An introduction to the five-factor model and its applications. *Journal of Personality, 60,* 175–215.

McCrae, R. R., Costa, P. T., Jr., del Pilar, G. H., Rolland, J., and Parker, W. D. (1998). Cross-cultural assessment of the five-factor model: The Revised NEO Personality Inventory. *Journal of Cross-Cultural Psychology, 29,* 171–188.

McCrae, R. R., Costa, P. T., Jr., Terracciano, A., Parker, W. D., Mills, C. J., De Fruyt, F., and Mervielde, I. (2002) Personality trait development from age 12 to age 18: Longitudinal, cross-sectional, and cross-cultural analyses. *Journal of Personality and Social Psychology, 83,* 1456–1468.

McCrae, R. R., Terracciano, A., and 78 Members of the Personality Profiles of Cultures Project. (2005a). Personality profiles of cultures: Aggregate personality traits. *Journal of Personality and Social Psychology, 89,* 407–425.

McCrae, R. R., Terracciano, A., and 78 Members of the Personality Profiles of Cultures Project. (2005b). Universal features of personality traits from the observer's perspective: Data from 50 cultures. *Journal of Personality and Social Psychology, 88,* 547–561.

McCullough, M. E., Bellah, C. G., Kilpatrick, S. D., and Johnson, J. L. (2001). Vengefulness: Relationships with forgiveness, rumination, well-being, and the big five. *Personality and Social Psychology Bulletin, 27,* 5, 601–610.

McCullough, M. E., Emmons, R. A., Kilpatrick, S. D., and Mooney, C. N. (2003). Narcissists as "victims": The role of narcissism in the perception of transgressions. *Personality and Social Psychology Bulletin, 29,* 7, 885–893.

McDaniel, S. R., and Zuckerman, M. (2003). The relationship of impulsive sensation seeking and gender to interest and participation in gambling activities. *Personality and Individual Differences, 35,* 1385–1400.

McGuire, W. (1974). *The Freud/Jung Letters: The correspondence between Sigmund Freud and C. G. Jung* (R. Manheim and R. F. C. Hull, Translators). Princeton, NJ: Princeton University Press.

McHoskey, J. W. (2001). Machiavellianism and sexuality: On the moderating role of biological sex. *Personality and Individual Differences, 31,* 779–789.

McLoyd, V. S. (1998). Socioeconomic disadvantage and child development. *American Psychologist, 53,* 188–204.

Mead, M. (1928). *Coming of age in Samoa.* New York: Morrow.

Mead, M. (1935). *Sex and temperament in three primitive societies.* New York: Morrow.

Mealey, L. (1995). The sociobiology of sociopathy: An integrated evolutionary model. *Behavioral and Brain Sciences, 18,* 523–599.

Mecacci, L., Scaglione, M. R., and Vitrano, I. (1991). Diurnal and monthly variations of temperature and self-reported activation in relation to sex and circadian typology. *Personality and Individual Differences, 12,* 819–824.

Megargee, E. I. (1969). Influence of sex roles on the manifestation of leadership. *Journal of Applied Psychology, 53,* 377–382.

Menninger, K. (1963). *The vital valance: The life process in mental health and illness.* New York: Viking Press.

Messick, S. (1994). The matter of style: Manifestations of personality in cognition, learning, and teaching. *Educational Psychologist, 29,* 121–136.

Michalos, A. C. (1991). *Global report on student well-being. Vol. 1: Life satisfaction and happiness.* New York: Springer-Verlag.

Mikulincer, M., Florian, V. (1995). Appraisal and coping with a real-life stressful situation: The contribution of attachment styles. *Personality and Social Psychology Bulletin, 69,* 1203–1215.

Mikulincer, M., Florian, V., and Weller, A. (1993). Attachment styles, coping strategies, and posttraumatic psychological distress: The impact of the Gulf War in Israel. *Journal of Personality and Social Psychology, 64,* 817–826.

Milin, R., Loh, E. A., and Wilson, A. (1992). Drug preference, reported drug experience, and stimulus sensitivity. *American Journal on Addictions, 1,* 248–256.

Miller, D. T., and Prentice, D. A. (1994). Collective errors and errors about the collective. *Personality and Social Psychology Bulletin, 20,* 541–550.

Miller, G. E., and Cohen, S. (2001). Psychological interventions and the immune system: A meta-analytic review and critique. *Health Psychology, 20,* 47–63.

Miller, J. D., Lynam, D., Zimmerman, R. S., Logan, T. K., Leukefeld, C., and Clayton, R. (2004). The utility of the Five Factor Model in understanding risky sexual behavior. *Personality and Individual Differences, 36,* 1611–1626.

Miller, P. C., Lefcourt, H. M., and Ware, E. E. (1983). The construction and development of the Miller Marital Locus of Control scale. *Canadian Journal of Behavioral Science, 15,* 266–279.

Miller, T. W. K., Smith, T. W., Turner, C. W., Guajardo, M. L., and Hallet, A. J. (1996). A meta-analytic review of research on hostility and physical health. *Psychological Bulletin, 119,* 322–348.

Millon, T. (1990). *Toward a new personology: An evolutionary model.* New York: Wiley-Interscience.

Millon, T. (1999). Reflections on psychosynergy: A model for integrating science, theory, classification, assessment, and therapy. *Journal of Personality Assessment, 72,* 437–456.

Millon, T. (2000a). Reflections of the future of DSM Axis II. *Journal of Personality Disorders, 14,* 30–41.

Millon, T. (2000b). Sociocultural conceptions of the borderline personality. *Psychiatric Clinics of North America Special Issue: Borderline Personality Disorder, 23,* 123–136.

Millon, T., Davis, R., Millon, C., Escovar, L., and Meagher, S. (2000). *Personality disorders: Current concepts and classical foundations.* New York: Wiley.

Mischel, W. (1968). *Personality and assessment.* New York: Wiley.

Mischel, W. (1984). Convergences and challenges in the search for consistency. *American Psychologist, 39,* 351–364.

Mischel, W. (1990). Personality dispositions revisited and revised: A view after three decades. In L. Pervin (Ed.), *Handbook of personality: Theory and research* (pp. 111–134). New York, Guilford Press.

Mischel, W. (2000). A cognitive-affective system theory of personality: Reconceptualizing situations, dispositions, dynamics, and invariance in personality structure. In E. T. Higgins and A. W. Kruglanski (Eds.), *Motivational science: Social and personality perspectives* (pp. 150–176). New York: Pscychology Press.

Mischel, W. (2004). Toward an integrative science of the person. *Annual Review of Psychology, 55,* 1–22.

Mischel, W., and Peake, P. K. (1982). Beyond déjá vu in the search for cross-situational consistency. *Psychological Review, 89,* 730–755.

Mischel, W., Shoda, Y., and Mendoza-Denton, R. (2002). Situation-behavior profiles as a locus of consistency in personality. *Current Directions in Psychological Science, 11,* 50–54.

Mittler, P. (1971). *The study of twins.* Harmondsworth, England: Penguin Books.

Mlacic, B., and Ostendorf, F. (2005). Taxonomy and structure of Croatial personality-descriptive adjectives. *European Journal of Personality, 19,* 117–152.

Moffitt, T. E. (2005). The new look of behavioral genetics in developmental psychopathology: Gene-environment interplay in antisocial behaviors. *Psychological Bulletin, 131,* 533–554.

Monk, T. H., and Leng, V. C. (1986). Interactions between inter-individual and inter-task differences in the diurnal variation of human performance. *Chronobiology International, 3,* 171–177.

Monk, T. H., Leng, V. C., Folkard, S., and Weitzman, E. D. (1983). Circadian rhythms in subjective alertness and core body temperature. *Chronobiologia, 10,* 49–55.

Montemayor, R., and Eisen, M. (1977). The development of self-conceptions from childhood to adolescence. *Developmental Psychology, 13,* 314–319.

Moore, M. (1978). Discrimination or favoritism? Sex bias in book reviews. *American Psychologist, 33,* 936–938.

Moretti, R. J., and Rossini, E. D. (2004). The Thematic Apperception Test (TAT). In M. J. Hilsenroth and E. L. Segal (Eds.), *Comprehensive handbook of psychological assessment, Vol. 2: Personality assessment* (pp. 356–371). Hoboken, NJ: Wiley and Sons.

Morey, L. C. (1997). Personality diagnosis and personality disorders In R. Hogan, J. A. Johnson, and S. R. Briggs (Eds.), *Handbook of personality psychology* (pp. 919–946). San Diego: Academic Press, Inc.

Morgan, C. D., and Murray, H. A. (1935). A method of investigating fantasies. *Archives of Neurological Psychiatry, 34,* 289–306.

Moskowitz, D. S. (1993). Dominance and friendliness: On the interaction of gender and situation. *Journal of Personality, 61,* 387–409.

Moskowitz, D. S., Suh, E. J., and Desaulniers, J. (1994). Situational influences on gender differences in agency and communion. *Journal of Personality and Social Psychology, 66,* 753–761.

Moskowitz, J. T., Folkman, S., Collette, L., and Vittinghoff, E. (1996). Coping and mood during AIDS-related caregiving and bereavement. *Annals of Behavioral Medicine, 18,* 49–57.

Mower, O. H. (1960). *Learning theory and behavior.* New York: Wiley.

Mueller, C. M., and Dweck, C. S. (1998). Intelligence praise can undermine motivation and performance. *Journal of Personality and Social Psychology, 75,* 33–52.

Mufson, D. W., and Mufson, M. A. (1998). Predicting police officer performance using the Inwald Personality Inventory: An illustration from Appalachia. *Professional Psychology: Research and Practice, 29,* 59–62.

Multon, K. D., Brown, S. D., and Lent, R. W. (1991). Relation of the self-efficacy beliefs to academic outcomes: A meta-analytic investigation. *Journal of Counseling Psychology, 38,* 30–38.

Munafo, M. R., Clark, T. G., Moore, L. R., Payne, E., Walton, R., and Flint, J. (2003). Genetic polymorphisms and personality in healthy adults. A systematic review and meta-analysis. *Molecular Psychiatry, 8,* 471–484.

Murdock, G. P. (1980). *Theories of illness: A world survey.* Pittsburgh: University of Pittsburgh Press.

Murphy, K. R. (1995). Integrity testing. In N. Brewer and C. Wilson (Eds.), *Psychology and policing* (pp. 205–229). Hillsdale, NJ: Erlbaum.

Murphy, S. M., Vallacher, R. R., Shackelford, T. K., Bjorklund, D. F., and Yunger, J. L. (2006). Relationship experience as a predictor of romantic jealousy. *Personality and Individual Differences, 40,* 761–769.

Murray, G., Allen, N.B., and Trinder, J. (2002). Longitudinal investigation of mood variability and the neuroticism predicts variability in extended states of positive and negative affect. *Personality and Individual Differences, 33,* 1217–1228.

Murray, H. (1948). *Assessment of men: Selection of personnel for the Office of Strategic Services.* New York: Rinehart.

Murray, H. A. (1933). The effect of fear upon estimates of the maliciousness of other personalities. *Journal of Social Psychology, 4,* 310–329.

Murray, H. A. (1938). *Explorations in personality.* New York: Oxford University Press.

Murray, H. A. (1967). Autobiography (the case of Murr). In E. G. Boring and G. Lindzey (Eds.), *History of psychology in autobiography* (Vol. 5, pp. 285–310). New York: Appleton-Century-Crofts.

Murray, Henry A. (1962). Prospect for psychology. *Science, 136,* 483–488.

Murstein, B. I. (1976). *Who will marry whom? Theories and research in marital choice.* New York: Springer Publishing Company.

Myers, D. G. (1993). *The pursuit of happiness.* New York: Avon Books.

Myers, D. G. (2000). The funds, friends, and faith of happy people. *American Psychologist, 55,* 56–67.

Myers, D. G., and Diener, E. (1995). Who is happy? *Psychological Science, 6,* 10–19.

Myers, I. B., McCaulley, M. H., Quenk, N. L., and Hammer, A. L. (1998). *Manual: A guide to the development and use of the Myers-Briggs type indicator.* Palo Alto: Consulting Psychologists Press.

Nasby, W., and Read, N. W. (1997). The life voyage of a solo circumnavigator: Integrating theoretical and methodological perspectives. *Journal of Personality, 65,* 785–1068.

Nash, M. R. (1987). What, if anything, is regressed about hypnotic age regression: A review of the empirical literature. *Psychological Bulletin, 102,* 42–52.

Nash, M. R. (1988). Hypnosis as a window on regression. *Bulletin of the Menninger Clinic, 52,* 383–403.

Nash, M. R. (1999). The psychological unconscious. In V. J. Derlega, B. A. Winstead, and W. H. Jones (Eds.), *Personality: Contemporary theory and research* (pp. 197–228). Chicago: Nelson-Hall.

Neisser, U. (1998). *The rising curve: Long-term gains in IQ and related measures.* Washington, DC: American Psychological Association.

Nesse, R., and Williams, G. C. (1994). *Why we get sick.* New York: New York Times Books.

Newman, J. P. (1987). Reaction to punishment in extraverts and psychopaths: Implications for the impulsive behavior of disinhibited individuals. *Journal of Research in Personality, 21,* 464–480.

Newman, J. P., Widom, C. S., and Nathan, S. (1985). Passive avoidance and syndromes of disinhibition: Psychopathy and extraversion. *Journal of Personality and Social Psychology, 48,* 1316–1327.

Newman, P. R., and Newman, B. M. (1988). Differences between childhood and adulthood: The identity watershed. *Adolescence, 23,* 551–557.

Neyer, F. J., and Voigt, D. (2004). Personality and social network effects on romantic relationships: A dyadic approach. *European Journal of Personality, 18,* 279–299.

Niederhoffer, K. G., and Pennebaker, J. W. (2002). Sharing one's story: On the benefits of writing or talking about emotional experience. In C. R. Snyder and S. J. Lopez (Eds.), *Handbook of positive psychology* (pp. 573–583). London: Oxford University Press.

Niederle, M., and Vesterlund, L. (2005). Do women shy away from competition? Do men compete too much? Working paper # 11474, National Bureau of Economic Research, Cambridge, MA *http://www.nber.org/papers/w11474*

Nietzsche, F. (1891/1969). *Thus spoke Zarathustra: A book for everyone and no one.* Translated with an introduction by R. J. Hollingdale. New York: Penguin Books.

Nigg, J. T., and Goldsmith, H. H. (1994). Genetics of personality disorders: Perspectives from personality and psychopathology research. *Pathological Bulletin, 115,* 346–380.

Nisbett, R. E. (1993). Violence and U.S. regional culture. *American Psychologist, 48,* 441–449.

Nisbett, R., and Cohen, D. (1996). *Culture of honor.* Boulder, CO: Westview Press.

Nisbett, R. E., Peng, K., Choi, I., and Norenzayan, A. (2001). Culture and systems of thought: Holistic vs. analytic cognition. *Psychological Review, 108,* 291–310.

Nolen-Hoeksema, S., Larson, J., and Grayson, C. (1999). Explaining gender differences in depressive symptoms. *Journal of Personality and Social Psychology, 77,* 1061–1072.

Noller, P. (1984). *Nonverbal communication and marital interaction.* Oxford, England: Pergamon Press.

Norem, J. K. (1995). The power of negative thinking: Interview with psychology professor Julie Norem. *Men's Health, 10,* June, p. 46.

Norem, J. K. (1998). Why should we lower our defenses about defense mechanisms? *Journal of Personality Special Issue: Defense mechanisms in contemporary personality research, 66,* 895–917.

Norem, J. K. (2001). Defensive pessimism, optimism, and pessimism. In E. Change (Ed.), *Optimism and pessimism: Implications for theory, research, and practive* (pp. 77–100). Washington, DC: American Psychological Association.

Norem, J. K., and Cantor, N. (1986). Defensive pessimism: "Harnessing" anxiety as motivation. *Journal of Personality and Social Psychology, 51,* 1208–1217.

Norem, J. K., and Illingworth, K. S. S. (1993). Strategy-dependent effects of reflecting on self and tasks: Some implications of optimism and defensive pessimism. *Journal of Personality and Social Psychology, 65,* 822–835.

Norman, W. T. (1963). Toward an adequate taxonomy of personality attributes: Replicated factor structure in peer nomination personality ratings. *Journal of Abnormal Psychology, 66,* 574–583.

Norman, W. T. (1967). *2800 personality trait descriptors: Normative operating characteristics in a university population.* Ann Arbor: Department of Psychology, University of Michigan.

Nudelman, A. E. (1973). Bias in the Twenty-Statements Test: Administration time, incomplete protocols, and intelligence. *Psychological Reports, 33,* 524–526.

Oatley, K., and Johnson-Laird, P. N. (1987). Towards a cognitive theory of emotions. *Cognition and Emotion, 1,* 29–50.

Ochsner, K. N., Bunge, S. A., Gross, J. J., and Gabrieli, J. D. E. (2002). Rethinking feelings: An fMRI study of the cognitive regulation of emotion. *Journal of Cognitive Neuroscience, 14,* 1215–1229.

Office of Technology Assessment. (1983). Scientific Validity of Polygraph Testing: A Research Review and Evaluation, U.S. Congress, November, 1983.

Ofshe, R. J. (1992). Inadvertent hypnosis during interrogation: False confession due to dissociative states: Misidentified multiple personality and the satanic cult hypothesis. *International Journal of Clinical and Experimental Hypnosis, 40,* 125–156.

Oliver, M. B., and Hyde, J. S. (1993). Gender differences in sexuality: A meta-analysis. *Psychological Bulletin, 114,* 29–51.

Olson, J. (2002). *"I": The creation of a serial killer.* New York: St. Martin's Paperbacks.

Oltmanns, T. F., and Emery, R. E. (2004). *Abnormal psychology* (4th edition). Upper Saddle River, NJ: Prentice Hall.

Oltmanns, T. F., Friedman, J. N., Fiedler, E. R., and Turkheimer, E. (in press).

Perceptions of people with personality disorders based on thin slices of behavior. *Journal of Research in Personality.*

Olweus, D. (1978). *Bullies and whipping boys.* Washington, DC: Hemisphere.

Olweus, D. (1979). Stability of aggressive reaction patterns in males: A review. *Psychological Bulletin, 86,* 852–875.

Ones, D. S., and Viswesvaran, C. (1998). Integrity testing in organizations. *Monographs in Organizational Behavior and Industrial Relations, 23,* 243–276.

Oniszczenko, W., Zawadzki, B., Strelau, J., Reimann, R., Angleitner, A., and Spinath, F. M. (2003). Genetic and environmental determinants of temperament: A comprehensive study based on Polish and German samples. *European Journal of Personality, 17,* 207–220.

Orenstein, P. (1994). *Schoolgirls: Young women, self-esteem, and the confidence gap.* New York: Anchor Books.

Ortony, A., and Turner, T. J., (1990). What's basic about basic emotions. *Psychological Review, 97,* 315–331.

Osgood, C. E., Suci, G. J., and Tannenbaum, P. H. (1957). *The measurement of meaning.* Urbana: University of Illinois Press.

Osmon, D. C., and Jackson, R. (2002). Inspection time and IQ: Fluid or perceptual aspects of intelligence? *Intelligence, 30,* 119–128.

Ostendorf, F. (1990). *Language and personality structure: Towards the validity of the five-factor model of personality.* Regensburg, Germany: Roderer-Verlag.

Oughton, J. M., and Reed, W. M. (1999). The influence of learner differences on the construction of hypermedia concepts: A case study. *Computers in Human Behavior, 15,* 11–50.

Oyserman, D., Coon, H. M., and Kemmelmeier, M. (2002a). Rethinking individualism and collectivism: Evaluation of theoretical assumptions and meta-analyses. *Psychological Bulletin, 128,* 1, 3–72.

Oyserman, D., Coon, H. M., and Kemmelmeier, M. (2002b). Cultural psychology, a new look: Reply to Bond (2002), Fiske (2002), Kitayama (2002), and Miller (2002). *Psychological Bulletin, 128,* 1, 110–117.

Oyserman, D., and Markus, H. (1990). Possible selves in balance: Implications for delinquency. *Journal of Social Issues, 46,* 141–157.

Oyserman, D., and Saltz, E. (1993). Competence, delinquency, and attempts to attain possible selves. *Journal of Personality and Social Psychology, 65,* 360–374.

Ozer, D. J., and Benet-Martinez, V. (2006). *Annual Review of Psychology, 57,* 401–421.

Ozer, D. J., and Buss, D. M. (1991). Two views of behavior: Agreement and disagreement in married couples. In A. Stewart, J. Healy, and D. Ozer (Eds.), *Perspectives in personality psychology* (pp. 93–108). London: Jessica Kingsley Publishers.

Palys, T. S., and Little, B. R. (1983). Perceived life satisfaction and the organization of personal project systems. *Journal of Personality and Social Psychology, 44,* 1221–1230.

Panksepp, J. (2005). Why does separation distress hurt? Comment on MacDonald and Leary (2005). *Psychological Bulletin, 131,* 224–230.

Paradis, C. M., Horn, L., Lazar, R. M., and Schwartz, D. W. (1994). Brain dysfunction and violent behavior in a man with a congenital subarachnoid cyst. *Hospital and Community Psychiatry, 45,* 714–716.

Parkes, K. R., and Razavi, T. D. B. (2004). Personality and attitudinal variables as predictors of voluntary union membership. *Personality and Individual Differences, 37,* 333–347.

Patrick, C. J. (1994). Emotion and psychopathy: Startling new insights. *Psychophysiology, 31,* 319–330.

Patrick, C. J. (Ed.). (2005). *The handbook of psychopathy.* New York: Guilford.

Patrick, C. J., Bradley, M. M., and Lang, P. J. (1993). Emotion in the criminal psychopath: Startle reflex modulation. *Journal of Abnormal Psychology, 102,* 82–92.

Patrick, C. J., Cuthbert, B. N., and Lang, P. J. (1994). Emotion in the criminal psychopath: Fear image processing. *Journal of Abnormal Psychology, 103,* 523–534.

Patterson, C. H. (2000). *Understanding psychotherapy: Fifty years of client-centred theory and practice.* Ross-on-Wye, England: PCCS Books Ltd.

Patton, D., Barnes, G. E., and Murray, R. P. (1993). Personality characteristics of smokers and ex-smokers. *Personality and Individual Differences, 15,* 653–664.

Paulhus, D. L. (1984). Two component models of socially desirable responding. *Journal of Personality and Social Psychology, 46,* 598–609.

Paulhus, D. L. (1990). Measurement and control of response bias. In J. P. Robinson, P. R. Shaver, and L. Wrightsman (Eds.), *Measures of personality and social-psychological attitudes* (pp. 17–59). San Diego, CA: Academic Press.

Paulhus, D. L., Bruce, N. N., and Trapnell, P. D. (1995). Effects of self-presentation strategies on personality profiles and their structure. *Personality and Social Psychology Bulletin, 21,* 100–108.

Paulhus, D. L., Fridhandler, B., and Hayes, S. (1997). Psychological defense: Contemporary theory and research. In R. Hogan, J. Johnson, and S. Briggs (Eds.), *Handbook of personality psychology* (pp. 543–579). San Diego, CA: Academic Press.

Paunonen, S. V. (2002). *Design and construction of the Supernumerary Personality Inventory* (Research Bulletin 763). London, Ontario: University of Western Ontario.

Paunonen, S. V. (2003). Big five factors of personality and replicated predictions of behavior. *Journal of Personality and Social Psychology, 84,* 2, 411–424.

Paunonen, S. V., and Ashton, M. C. (1998). The structured assessment of personality across cultures. *Journal of Cross-Cultural Psychology, 29,* 150–170.

Paunonen, S. V., and Ashton, M. C. (2001a). Big five predictors of academic achievement. *Journal of Research in Personality, 35,* 78–90.

Paunonen, S. V., and Ashton, M. C. (2001b). Big five factors and facets and the prediction of behavior. *Journal of Personality and Social Psychology, 81,* 3, 524–539.

Paunonen, S. V., Haddock, G., Forsterling, F., and Keinonen, M. (2003). Broad versus narrow personality measures and the prediction of behaviour across cultures. *European Journal of Personality, 17,* 413–433.

Pedersen, N. L. (1993). Genetic and environmental change in personality. In T. J. Bouchard and P. Proping (Eds.), *Twins as a tool of behavioral genetics* (pp. 147–162). West Sussex, England: Wiley.

Pennebaker, J. W. (1990). *Opening up: The healing powers of confiding in others.* New York: Morrow.

Pennebaker, J. W. (2003a). The social, linguistic and health consequences of emotional disclosure. In J. Suls and K. A. Wallston (Eds.), *Social psychological foundations of health and illness* (pp. 288–313). Malden, MA: Blackwell Publishers.

Pennebaker, J. W. (2003b). Writing about emotional experiences as a therapeutic process. In P. Salovey and A. J. Rothman (Eds.), *Social psychology of health* (pp. 362–368). New York: Psychology Press.

Pennebaker, J. W., Colder, M., and Sharp, L. K. (1990). Accelerating the coping process. *Journal of Personality and Social Psychology, 58,* 528–537.

Pennebaker, J. W., and O'Heeron, R. C. (1984). Confiding in others and illness rates among spouses of suicide and accidental-death victims. *Journal of Abnormal Psychology, 93,* 473–476.

Pervin, L. A. (1999). Epilogue: Constancy and change in personality theory and research. In L. A. Pervin and O. P. John (Eds.), *Handbook of personality: Theory and research* (2nd ed.). (pp. 689–704). New York: Guilford.

Pervin, L. A., and John, O. P. (1999). *Handbook of personality* (2nd ed.). New York: Guilford.

Peterson, B. E., Winter, D. G., and Doty, R. M. (1994). Laboratory tests of a motivational-perceptual model of conflict escalation. *Journal of Conflict Resolution, 38,* 719–748.

Peterson, C. (1991). The meaning and measurement of explanatory style. *Psychological Inquiry, 2,* 1–10.

Peterson, C. (1995). Explanatory style and health. In G. M. Buchanan and M. E. P. Seligman (Eds.), *Explanatory style* (pp. 233–246). Hillsdale, NJ: Lawrence Erlbaum.

Peterson, C. (2000). The future of optimism. *American Psychologist, 55,* 44–55.

Peterson, C., and Bossio, L. M. (1991). *Health and optimism.* New York: Free Press.

Peterson, C., and Bossio, L. M. (2001). Optimism and physical well-being. In E. C. Chang (Ed.), *Optimism and pessimism: Implications for theory, research, and practice* (pp. 127–145). Washington, DC: American Psychological Association.

Peterson, C., and Chang, E. C. (2003). Optimism and flourishing. In C. L. Keyes and J. Haidt (Eds.), *Flourishing: Positive psychology and the life well-lived* (pp. 55–79). Washington, DC: American Psychological Association.

Peterson, C., and de Avila, M. E. (1995). Optimistic explanatory style and the perception of health problems. *Journal of Clinical Psychology, 51,* 128–132.

Peterson, C., and Seligman, M. E. (1984). Causal explanations as a risk factor for depression: Theory and evidence. *Psychological Review, 91,* 347–374.

Peterson, C., and Seligman, M. E. P. (1987). Explanatory style and illness. Special issue: Personality and physical health. *Journal of Personality, 55,* 237–265.

Peterson, C., and Seligman, M. E. P. (2003). Character strengths before and after September 11. *Psychological Science, 14,* 381–384.

Peterson, C., and Steen, T. A. (2002). Optimistic explanatory style. In C. R. Snyder and S. J. Lopez (Eds.), *Handbook of positive psychology* (pp. 244–256). London: Oxford University Press.

Peterson, C., and Ulrey, L. M. (1994). Can explanatory style be scored from TAT protocols? *Personality and Social Psychology Bulletin, 20,* 102–106.

Peterson, C., Maier, S. F., and Seligman, M. E. P. (1993). *Learned helplessness: A theory for the age of personal control.* New York: Oxford University Press.

Peterson, C., Schulman, P., Castellon, C., and Seligman, M. E. P. (1992). CAVE: Content analysis of verbatim explanations. In C. P. Smith (Ed.), *Motivation and personality: Handbook of thematic content analysis* (pp. 383–392). New York: Cambridge University Press.

Peterson, C., Seligman, M. E. P., and Vaillant, G. E. (1988). Pessimistic explanatory style is a risk factor for physical illness: A thirty-five-year longitudinal study. *Journal of Personality and Social Psychology, 55,* 23–27.

Peterson, C., Seligman, M. E. P., Yurko, K. H., Martin, L. R., and Friedman, H. S. (1998). Catastrophisizing and untimely death. *Psychological Science, 9,* 49–52.

Peterson, C., Semmel, A., von Baeyer, C., Abramson, L. Y., Metalsky, G. I., and Seligman, M. E. P. (1982). The Attributional Style Questionnaire. *Cognitive Therapy and Research, 6,* 287–299.

Peterson, J. B., Smith, K. W., and Carson, S. (2002). Openness and extraversion are associated with reduced latent inhibition: Replication and commentary. *Personality and Individual Differences, 33,* 1137–1147.

Petrie, A. (1967). *Individuality in pain and suffering.* Chicago: University of Chicago Press.

Petrill, S. A. (2002). The case for general intelligence: A behavioral genetic perspective. In R. J. Sternberg and E. L. Grigorenko (Eds.), *The general factor of intelligence: How general is it?* (pp. 281–298). Mahwah, NJ: Lawrence Erlbaum Associates, Publishers.

Pickering, A. D., Corr, P. J., and Gray, J. A. (1999). Interactions and reinforcement sensitivity theory: A theoretical analysis of Rusting and Larsen (1997). *Personality and Individual Differences, 26,* 357–365.

Pickering, A., Farmer, A., Harris, T., Redman, K., Mahmood, A., Sadler, S., and McGuffin, P. (2003). A sib-pair study of psychoticism, life events and depression. *Personality and Individual Differences, 34,* 613–623.

Piedmont, R. L. (2001). Cracking the plaster cast: Big five personality change during intensive outpatient counseling. *Journal of Research in Personality, 35,* 500–520.

Pietrzak, R., Laird, J. D., Stevens, D. A., and Thompson, N. S. (2002). Sex differences in human jealousy: A coordinated study of forced-choice, continuous rating-scale, and physiological responses on the same subjects. *Evolution and Human Behavior, 23,* 83–94.

Pincus, J. H. (2001). *Base instincts: What makes killers kill?* New York: Norton.

Pinker, S. (1997). *How the mind works.* New York: Norton.

Pipher, M. (1994). *Reviving Ophelia: Saving the selves of adolescent girls.* New York: Ballantine Books.

Pittenger, D. J. (2005). Cautionary comments regarding the Myers-Briggs Type Indicator. *Consulting Psychology Journal: Practice and Research, 57,* 210–221.

Plomin, R. (2002). Individual differences research in a postgenomic era. *Personality and Individual Differences, 33,* 909–920.

Plomin, R., and Crabbe, J. (2000). DNA. *Psychological Bulletin Special Issue: Psychology in the 21st Century, 126,* 806–828.

Plomin, R., and Daniels, D. (1987). Why are children in the same family so different from one another? *Behavioral and Brain Sciences, 10,* 1–16.

Plomin, R., and DeFries, G. E. (1985). *Origins of individual differences in infancy: The Colorado Adoption Project.* New York: Academic Press.

Plomin, R., DeFries, J. C., and Fulker, D. W. (1988). *Nature and nurture during infancy and early childhood.* New York: Cambridge University Press.

Plomin, R., DeFries, J. C., and Loehlin, J. C. (1977). Genotype-environment interaction and correlation in the analysis of human behavior. *Psychological Bulletin, 84,* 309–322.

Plomin, R., DeFries, J. C., and McClearn, G. E. (1990). *Behavioral genetics: A primer* (2nd ed.). New York: W. H. Freeman.

Plomin, R., DeFries, J. C., McClern, G. E., and McGuffin, P. (2001). *Behavioral genetics* (4th ed.). New York: Worth Publishers.

Plutchik, R. (1980). A general psychoevolutionary theory of emotion. In R. Plutchik and H. Kellerman (Eds.), *Emotion: Theory, research, and experience: Vol. 1: Theories of emotion* (pp. 3–31). New York: Academic Press.

Pollock, V. E., Briere, J., Schneider, L., Knop, J., Mednick, S., and Goodwin, D. W. (1990). Childhood antecedents of antisocial behavior: Parental alcoholism and physical abusiveness. *American Journal of Psychiatry, 147,* 1290–1293.

Post, J. M. (Ed.). (2003). *The psychological assessment of political leaders.* Ann Arbor: University of Michigan Press.

Price, M. E., Cosmides, L., and Tooby, J. (2002). Punitive sentiment as an anti-free rider psychological device. *Evolution and Human Behavior, 23,* 203–231.

Promislow, D. (2003). Mate choice, sexual conflict, and evolution of senescence. *Behavior Genetics, 33,* 191–201.

Rabbie, J. M., and Horwitz, M. (1969). Arousal of ingroup-outgroup bias by a chance win or loss. *Journal of Personality and Social Psychology, 13,* 269–277.

Ragland, D. B., and Brand, R. J. (1988). Type A behavior and mortality from coronary heart disease. *New England Journal of Medicine, 318,* 65–69.

Raine, A. (2002). Biosocial studies of antisocial and violent behavior in children and adults: A review. *Journal of Abnormal Child Psychology, 30,* 311–326.

Raine, A., and Brennan, P. A. (1997). *The biological basis of violence.* New York: Plenum Press.

Raine, A., Meloy, J. R., and Bihrle, S. (1998). Reduced prefrontal and increased subcortical brain functioning assessed using positron emission tomography in predatory and affective murderers. *Behavioral Sciences and the Law Special Issue: Impulsive aggression, 16,* 319–332.

Rammsayer, T. H., and Brandler, S. (2002). On the relationship between general fluid intelligence and psychophysical indicators of temporal resolution in the brain. *Journal of Research in Personality, 36,* 507–530.

Ramona v. Isabella, California Superior Court, Napa, C61898, 1994.

Raskin, J. D. (2001). The modern, the postmodern, and George Kelly's personal construct psychology. *American Psychologist, 56,* 368–369.

Raskin, R., and Hall, C. S. (1979). A narcissistic personality inventory. *Psychological Reports, 45,* 590.

Raskin, R., and Shaw, R. (1987). *Narcissism and the use of personal pronouns.* Unpublished manuscript.

Raskin, R., and Terry, H. (1988). A principle-components analysis of the narcissistic personality inventory and further evidence of its construct validity. *Journal of Personality and Social Psychology, 54,* 890–902.

Rawlings, D. (2003). Personality correlates of liking for "unpleasant" paintings and photographs. *Personality and Individual Differences, 34,* 395–410.

Regan, P. C., and Atkins, L. (2006). Sex differences and similarities in frequency and intensity of sexual desire. *Social Behavior and Personality, 34,* 95–102.

Renshon, S. A. (1998). Analyzing the psychology and performances of presidential candidates at a distance: Bob Dole and the 1996 presidential campaign. *Leadership Quarterly, 9,* 377–395.

Renshon, S. A. (2005). George W. Bush's cowboy politics: An inquiry. *Political Psychology, 26,* 585–614.

Revelle, W., Humphreys, M. S., Simon, L., and Gilliland, K. (1980). The interactive effect of personality, time of day, and caffeine: A test of the arousal model. *Journal of Experimental Psychology: General, 109,* 1–31.

Rhee, E., Uleman, J., Lee, H., and Roman, R. (1995). Spontaneous self-descriptions and ethnic identities in individualistic and collectivist cultures. *Journal of Personality and Social Psychology, 69,* 142–152.

Rheingold, H. L., and Cook, K. V. (1975). The contents of boys' and girls' rooms as an index of parents' behavior. *Child Development, 46,* 459–463.

Rhodenwalt, F., and Morf, C. (1998). On self-aggrandizement and anger: A temporal analysis of narcissism and affective reactions to success and failure. *Journal of Personality and Social Psychology, 74,* 672–685.

Richardson, J. A., and Turner, T. E. (2000). Field dependence revisited I: Intelligence. *Educational Psychology, 20,* 255–270.

Ridley, M. (1999). *Genome: The autobiography of a species in 23 chapters.* New York: HarperCollins.

Rind, B., Tromovitch, P., and Bauserman, R. (1998). A meta-analytic examination of assumed properties of child sexual abuse using college samples. *Psychological Bulletin, 124,* 22–53.

Ritts, V., and Patterson, M. L. (1996). Effects of social anxiety and action identification on impressions and thoughts in interaction. *Journal of Social and Clinical Psychology, 15,* 191–205.

Ritvo, L. B. (1990). *Darwin's influence on Freud: A tale of two sciences.* New Haven, CT: Yale University Press.

Roberts, B. W., and DelVecchio, W. F. (2000). The rank-order consistency of personality traits from childhood to old age: A quantitative review of the longitudinal studies. *Psychological Bulletin, 126,* 3–25.

Roberts, B. W., Caspi, A., and Moffitt, T. E. (2001). The kids are alright: Growth and stability in personality development from adolescence to adulthood. *Journal of Personality and Social Psychology, 81,* 4, 670–683.

Roberts, B. W., Caspi, A., and Moffitt, T. E. (2003). Work experiences and personality development in young adulthood. *Journal of Personality and Social Psychology, 84,* 5, 582–593.

Roberts, B. W., Walton, K. R., and Viechtbauer, W. (2006). Patterns of mean-level change in personality traits across the life course: A meta-analysis of longitudinal studies. *Psychological Bulletin, 132,* 1–25.

Roberts, J. E., and Monroe, S. M. (1992). Vulnerable self-esteem and depressive symptoms: Prospective findings comparing three alternative conceptualizations. *Journal of Personality and Social Psychology, 62,* 804–812.

Roberts, W. B., and Robins, R. W. (2004). Person-environment fit and its implications for personality development: A longitudinal study. *Journal of Personality, 72,* 89–110.

Robins, R. W. (2002). Overview of the proceedings of the 2002 meeting of the association for research in personality. *Journal of Research in Personality, 36,* 539–540.

Robins, R. W., and John, O. P. (1997). Self-perception, visual perspective, and narcissism: Is seeing believing? *Psychological Science, 8,* 37–42.

Robins, R. W., Caspi, A., and Moffitt, T. E. (2002). It's not just who you're with, it's who you are: Personality and relationship experiences across multiple relationships. *Journal of Personality, 70,* 925–964.

Robins, R. W., Fraley, R. C., Roberts, B. W., and Trzesniewski, K. H. (2001). A longitudinal study of personality change in young adulthood. *Journal of Personality, 69,* 4, 617–640.

Robins, R. W., Noftle, E. E., Trzesniewski, K. H., and Roberts, B. W. (2005). Do people know how their personality has changed? Correlates of perceived and actual personality change in young adulthood. *Journal of Personality, 73,* 489–521.

Roediger, H. L., and McDermott K. B. (1995). Creating false memories: Remembering words not presented in lists. *Journal of Experimental Psychology: Learning, Memory, and Cognition, 21,* 803–814.

Roediger, H. L., III, Balota, D. A., and Watson, J. M. (2001). Spreading activation and arousal of false memories. In Henry L. Roediger, III and James S. Nairne (Eds.), *The nature of remembering: Essays in honor of Robert G. Crowder,* 95–115. Washington, DC: American Psychological Association.

Roediger, H. L., McDermott, K. B., and Robinson, K. J. (1998). The role of associative processes in creating false memories. In M. A. Conway, S. E. Gathercole, and C. Cornoldi (Eds.), *Theories of memory II* (pp. 187–246). Hove, Sussex, England: Psychological Press.

Rogers, C. R. (1957). The necessary and sufficient conditions of therapeutic personality change. *Journal of Consulting Psychology, 21,* 95–103.

Rogers, C. R. (1975). Empathic: An unappreciated way of being. *The Counseling Psychologist, 5,* 2–10.

Rogers, C. R. (2002). *Carl Rogers: The quiet revolutionary, an oral history.* Roseville, CA, US: Penmarin Books.

Rogness, G. A., and McClure, E. B. (1996). Development and neurotransmitter-environment interactions. *Development and Psychopathology, 8,* 183–199.

Romero, E., Luengo, M. T., Carrillo-de-la-Pena, T., and Otero-Lopez, J. M. (1994). The act frequency approach to the study of impulsivity. *European Journal of Personality, 8,* 119–134.

Rosch, E. (1975). Cognitive reference points. *Cognitive Psychology, 7,* 532–547.

Rose, R. J. (1995). Genes and behavior. *Annual Review of Psychology, 46,* 625–654.

Rosen, D. H. (1993). *Transforming depression: Healing the soul through creativity.* New York: Penguin.

Rosenzweig, S. (1986). Idiodynamics vis-à-vis psychology. *American Psychologist, 41,* 241–245.

Rosenzweig, S. (1994). *The historic expedition to America (1909): Freud, Jung, and Hall the king-maker.* St. Louis, MO: Rana House.

Rosenzweig, S. (1997). "Idiographic" vis-à-vis "idiodynamic" in the historical perspective of personality theory: Remembering Gordon Allport, 1897–1997. *Journal of the History of the Behavioral Sciences, 33,* 405–419.

Ross, L., Greene, D., and House, P. (1977). The false consensus effect: An egocentric bias in social perception and attribution processes. *Journal of Experimental Social Psychology, 13,* 279–301.

Ross, S. R., Canada, K. E., and Rausch, M. K. (2002). Self-handicapping and the Five Factor Model of personality: Mediation between Neuroticism and Conscientiousness. *Personality and Individual Differences, 32,* 1173–1184.

Rothbart, M. K. (1981). Measurement of temperament in infancy. *Child Development, 52,* 569–578.

Rothbart, M. K. (1986). Longitudinal observation of infant temperament. *Developmental Psychology, 22,* 356–365.

Rotter, J. B. (1966). Generalized expectancies for internal versus external control of reinforcement. *Psychological Monographs: General and Applied 80*(1).

Rotter, J. B. (1971). Generalized expectancies for interpersonal trust. *American Psychologist, 26,* 443–452.

Rotter, J. B. (1982). *The development and application of social learning theory.* New York: Praeger.

Rotter, J. B. (1990). Internal versus external control of reinforcement: A case history of a variable. *American Psychologist, 45,* 489–493.

Rowe, D. C. (2001). *Biology and crime.* New York: Roxbury.

Rozin, P. (2003). Five potential principles for understanding cultural differences in relation to individual differences. *Journal of Research in Personality, 37,* 273–283.

Ruchkin, V. V., Koposov, R. A., Eisemann, M., and Hagglof, B. (2002). Alcohol use in delinquent adolescents from Northern Russia: The role of personality, parental rearing and family history of alcohol abuse. *Personality and Individual Differences, 32,* 1139–1148.

Rule, A. (2000). *The stranger beside me.* New York: Norton.

Runyon, W. M. (1983). Idiographic goals and methods in the study of lives. *Journal of Personality, 51,* 413–437.

Rusting, C. L., and Larsen, R. J. (1997). Extraversion, neuroticism, and susceptibility to positive and negative affect: A test of two theoretical models. *Personality and Individual Differences, 22,* 607–612.

Rusting, C. L., and Larsen, R. J. (1998a). Diurnal patterns of unpleasant mood: Associations with neuroticism, depression, and anxiety. *Journal of Personality, 66,* 85–103.

Rusting, C. L., and Larsen, R. J. (1998b). Personality and cognitive processing of affective information. *Personality and Social Psychology Bulletin, 24,* 200–213.

Rusting, C. L., and Larsen, R. J. (1999). Clarifying Gray's theory of personality: A response to Pickering, Corr, and Gray. *Personality and Individual Differences, 26,* 367–372.

Ryan, A. M., McFarland, L., Baron, H., and Page, R. (1999). An international look at selection practices: Nation and culture as explanations for variability in practice. *Personnel Psychology, 52,* 359–394.

Ryan, R. M., and Deci, E. L. (2000). Self-determination theory and the facilitation of intrinsic motivation, social development, and well-being. *American Psychologist, 55,* 68–78.

Ryff, C., Lee, Y., and Na, K. (1995). *Through the lens of culture: Psychological well-being at mid-life.* Unpublished manuscript, University of Michigan, Ann Arbor, Michigan.

Sagarin, B. J. (2005). Reconsidering evolved sex differences in jealousy: Comment on Harris (2003). *Personality and Social Psychology Review, 9,* 62–75.

Sagarin, B. J., Becker, D. V., Guadagno, R. E., Nicastle, L. D., and Millevoi, A. (2003). Sex differences (and similarities) in jealousy: The moderating influence of infidelity experience and sexual orientation. *Evolution and Human Behavior, 24,* 17–23.

Sagie, A., and Elizur, D. (1999). Achievement motive and entrepreneurial orientation: A structural analysis. *Journal of Organizational Behavior, 20,* 375–387.

Saklofske, D. H. (1995). *International handbook of personality and intelligence.* New York: Plenum.

Sakuta, A., and Fukushima, A. (1998). A study on abnormal findings pertaining to the brain in criminals. *International Medical Journal, 5,* 283–292.

Salgado, J. F., Moscoso, S., and Lado, M. (2003). Evidence of cross-cultural invariant of the Big Five personality dimensions in work settings. *European Journal of Personality, 17,* S67–S76.

Salovey, P., and Mayer, J. D. (1990). Emotional intelligence. *Imagination, Cognition, and Personality, 9,* 185–211.

Sam, D. L. (1994). The psychological adjustment of young immigrants in Norway. *Scandinavian Journal of Psychology, 35,* 240–253.

Sandvik, E., Diener, E., and Seidlitz, L. (1993). Subjective well-being: The convergence and stability of self-report and non-self-report measures. *Journal of Personality, 61,* 317–342.

Sapolsky, R. M. (1987). Stress, social status, and reproductive physiology in free-living baboons. In D. Crews (Ed.), *Psychobiology of reproductive behavior: An evolutionary perspective.* Englewood Cliffs, NJ: Prentice Hall.

Saroglou, V. (2002). Religion and the five factors of personality: A meta-analytic review. *Personality and Individual Differences, 32,* 15–25.

Satcher, D. (1996). Annual report of the surgeon general. Available at *http://www.surgeongeneral.gov/library/mentalhealth/home.html.*

Satterfield, J. H., and Schelle, A. M. (1984). Childhood brain function differences in delinquent and non-delinquent hyperactive boys. *Electroencephalography and Clinical Neurophysiology, 57,* 199–207.

Saucier, G., and Goldberg, L. R. (2001). Lexical studies of indigenous personality factors: Premises, products, and prospects. *Journal of Personality, 69,* 6, 847–880.

Saucier, G. (2003). Factor structure of English-Language personality Type-nouns. *Journal of Personality and Social Psychology, 85,* 4, 695–708.

Saucier, G., Georgiades, S., Tsaousis, I., and Goldberg, L. R. (2005). The factor structure of Greek personality adjectives. *Journal of Personality and Social Psychology, 5,* 856–875.

Saucier, G., and Goldberg, L. R. (1996). The language of personality: Lexical perspectives on the five-factor model. In J. S. Wiggins (Ed.), *The five-factor model of personality: Theoretical perspectives* (pp. 21–50). New York: Guilford Press.

Saucier, G., and Goldberg, L. R. (1998). What is beyond the big five? *Journal of Personality, 66*, 495–524.

Saudino, K. J., and Plomin, R. (1996). Personality and behavioral genetics: Where have we been and where are we going? *Journal of Research in Personality, 30*, 335–347.

Scarr, S. (1968). Environmental bias in twin studies. *Eugenics Quarterly, 15*, 34–40.

Scarr, S., and Carter-Saltzman, L. (1979). Twin method: Defense of a critical assumption. *Behavior Genetics, 9*, 527–542.

Scarr, S., and McCartney, K. (1983). How children make their own environments: A theory of genotype environment effects. *Child Development, 54*, 424–435.

Scealy, M., Phillips, J. G., and Stevenson, R. (2002). Shyness and anxiety as predictors of patterns of Internet usage. *CyberPsychology and Behavior, 5*, 507–515.

Schacter, D. L. (1997). *Searching for memory: The brain, the mind, and the past.* New York: Basic Books.

Scheier, M. F., and Carver, C. S. (1985). Optimism, coping, and health: Assessment and implications of generalized outcome expectancies. *Health Psychology, 4*, 219–247.

Scheier, M. F., and Carver, C. S. (1992). Effects of optimism on psychological and physical well-being: Theoretical overview and empirical update. *Cognitive Therapy and Research, 16*, 201–228.

Scheier, M. F., Matthews, K. A., Owens, J. F., Schulz, R., Bridges, M. W., Magovern, G. J., and Carver, C. S. (1999). Optimism and rehospitalization following coronary artery bypass graft surgery. *Archives of Internal Medicine, 159*, 829–835.

Scheier, M. F., Weintraub, J. K., and Carver, C. S. (1986). Coping with stress: Divergent strategies of optimists and pessimists. *Journal of Personality and Social Psychology, 51*, 1257–1264.

Schinka J. A., Letsch, E. A., and Crawford, F. C. (2002). DRD4 and novelty seeking: Results of meta-analyses. *American Journal of Medical Genetics, 114*, 643–648.

Schmalt, H. (1999). Assessing the achievement motive using the grid technique. *Journal of Research in Personality, 33*, 109–130.

Schmidt, L. A., and Fox, N. A. (1995). Individual differences in young adults' shyness and sociability: Personality and health correlates. *Personality and Individual Differences, 19*, 455–462.

Schmidt, L. A., and Fox, N. A. (2002). Individual differences in childhood shyness: Origins, malleability and developmental course. In D. Cervone and W. Mischel (Eds.), *Advances in personality science* (pp. 83–105). New York: Guilford Press.

Schmidt, L. A., Fox, N. A., Rubin, K. H., Hu, S., and Hamer, D. H. (2002). Molecular genetics of shyness and aggression in preschoolers. *Personality and Individual Differences, 33*, 227–238.

Schmitt, D. P., and Buss, D. M. (2000). Sexual dimensions of person description: Beyond or subsumed by the big five? *Journal of Research in Personality, 34*, 141–177.

Schmitt, D. P. and 118 Members of the International Sexuality Description Project (2003). Universal sex differences in the desire for sexual variety: Tests from 52 nations, 6 continents, and 13 islands. *Personality and Social Psychology, 85*, 85–104.

Schmitt, D. P., and Buss, D. M. (2001). Human mate poaching: Tactics and temptations for infiltrating existing relationships. *Journal of Personality and Social Psychology, 80*, 894–917.

Schmutte, P. S., Lee, Y. H., and Ryff, C. D. (1995). *Reflections on parenthood: A cultural perspective*. Unpublished manuscript, Madison: University of Wisconsin.

Schneider, K. (1958). *Psychopathic personalities.* London: Cassell.

Schultheiss, O. C., and Brunstein, J. C. (2001). Assessment of implicit motives with a research version of the TAT: Picture profiles, gender differences, and relations to other personality measures. *Journal of Personality Assessment Special Issue: More data on the current Rorschach controversy, 77*, 71–86.

Schutzwohl, A., and Koch, S. (in press). Sex differences in jealousy: The recall of cues to sexual and emotional infidelity in adaptively relevant and irrelevant context conditions. *Evolution and Human Behavior.*

Schwartz, C. E., Wright, C. I., Shin, L. M., Kagan, J., and Rauch, S. L. (2003). Inhibited and uninhibited infants "grown up": Adult amygdalar response to novelty. *Science, 300*, 1952–1953.

Schwartz, S. H., and Rubel, T. (2005). Sex differences in value priorities: Cross-cultural and multimethod studies. *Journal of Personality and Social Psychology, 89*, 1010–1028.

Schwerdtfeger, A., and Baltissen, R. (1999). Augmenters vs. reducers: Cortical and autonomic reactivity in response to increasing stimulus intensity. *Zeitschrift fuer Differentielle und Diagnostische Psychologie, 20*, 247–262.

Schwerdtfeger, A., and Baltissen, R. (2002). Augmenting-reducing paradox lost? A test of Davis et al.'s (1983) hypothesis. *Personality and Individual Differences, 32*, 257–271.

Scott, J. P., and Fuller, J. L. (1965). *Genetics and the social behavior of the dog.* Chicago: University of Chicago Press.

Scott, W. A., and Johnson, R. C. (1972). Comparative validities of direct and indirect personality tests. *Journal of Consulting and Clinical Psychology, 38*, 301–318.

Seal, D. W., Agosinelli, G., and Hannett, C. A. (1994). Extradyadic romantic involvement: Moderating effects of sociosexuality and gender. *Sex Roles, 31*, 1–22.

Segal, N. L. (1999). *Entwined lives: Twins and what they tell us about human behavior.* New York: Plume.

Seidlitz, L., and Diener, E. (1993). Review of the Satisfaction with Life Scale. *Psychological Assessment, 5*, 164–172.

Seligman, M. (2004) Web site: *http://www.psych.upenn.edu/seligman/*

Seligman, M. E. P. (1992). *Helplessness: On depression, development, and death.* New York: Freeman.

Seligman, M. E. P. (1994). *What you can change and what you can't.* New York: Knopf.

Seligman, M. E. P. (2002). Positive psychology, positive prevention, and positive therapy. In C. R. Snyder and S. J. Lopez (Eds.), *Handbook of positive psychology* (pp. 3–9) London: Oxford University Press.

Seligman, M. E. P., and Csikszentmihalyi, M. (2000). Positive psychology: An introduction. *American Psychologist, 55*, 5–14.

Seligman, M. E. P., and Peterson, C. (2003). Positive clinical psychology. In L. G. Aspinwall and U. M. Staudinger (Eds.), *A psychology of human strengths: Fundamental questions and future directions for a positive psychology* (pp. 305–317). Washington, DC: American Psychological Association.

Seligman, M., and Hager, J. (1972). *Biological boundaries of learning.* New York: Appleton-Century-Crofts.

Selye, H. (1976). *The stress of life.* New York: McGraw-Hill.

Shackelford, T. K., Buss, D. M., and Bennett, K. (2002). Forgiveness or breakup: Sex differences in responses to a partner's infidelity. *Cognition and Emotion, 16*, 299–307.

Shackelford, T. K., Goetz, A., Buss, D. M., Euler, H. A., and Hoier, S. (2005). When we hurt the ones we love: Predicting violence against women from men's mate retention. *Personal Relationships, 12*, 447–463.

Shackelford, T. K., Voracek, M., Schmitt, D. P., Buss, D. M., Weekes-Shackelford, V. A., and Michalski, R. L. (2004). Romantic jealousy in early adulthood and in later life. *Human Nature, 15,* 59–76.

Shafer, A. B. (2001). The Big Five and sexuality trait terms as predictors of relationships and sex. *Journal of Research in Personality, 35,* 313–338.

Shakur, S. (1994). *Monster: The autobiography of an L.A. gang member.* New York: Penguin.

Sheldon, K. M., and Kasser, T. (2001). Getting older, getting better? Personal strivings and psychological maturity across the life span. *Developmental Psychology, 37,* 491–501.

Sheldon, W. H., and Stevens, S. S. (1940). *The varieties of human physique.* New York: Harper.

Sheldon, W. H., and Stevens, S. S. (1942). *The varieties of temperament; a psychology of constitutional differences.* Oxford, England: Harper.

Sherwin, B. B. (1988). A comparative analysis of the role of androgen in human male and female sexual behavior: Behavioral specificity, critical thresholds, and sensitivity. *Psychobiology, 16,* 416–425.

Shevrin, H., and Dickman, S. (1980). The psychological unconscious: A necessary assumption for all psychological theory? *American Psychologist, 35,* 421–434.

Shiner, R. L., Masten, A. S., and Tellegen, A. (2002). A developmental perspective on personality in emerging adulthood: Childhood antecedents and concurrent adaptation. *Journal of Personality and Social Psychology, 83,* 5, 1165–1177.

Shiner, R. L., Masten, A. S., and Roberts, J. M. (2003). Childhood personality foreshadows adult personality and life outcomes two decades later. *Journal of Personality, 71,* 1145–1170.

Shneidman, E. S. (1981). *Endeavors in psychology: Selections from the personology of Henry A. Murray.* New York: Harper and Row.

Shoben, E. J. (1957). Toward a concept of the normal personality. *American Psychologist, 12,* 183–189.

Shoda, Y., and Mischel, W. (1996). Toward a unified, intra-individual dynamic conception of personality. *Journal of Research in Personality, 30,* 414–428.

Shoda, Y., Mischel, W., and Wright, J. C. (1994). Intra-individual stability in the organization and patterning of behavior: Incorportating psychological situations into the idiographic analysis of personality. *Journal of Personality and Social Psychology, 67,* 674–687.

Shultz, J. S. (1993). Situational and dispositional predictions of performance: A test of the hypothesized Machiavellianism X structure interaction among salespersons. *Journal of Applied Social Psychology, 23,* 478–498.

Shweder, R. A. (1991). *Thinking through cultures: Expeditions in cultural psychology.* Cambridge, MA: Harvard University Press.

Shweder, R. A., Mahapatra, M., and Miller, J. G. (1990). Culture and moral development. In J. W. Stigler, R. A. Shweder, and G. Herdt (Eds.), *Cultural psychology: Essays on comparative human development* (pp. 130–204). Cambridge, MA: Cambridge University Press.

Siegel, E. R. (1973). *Galen on psychology, psychopathology, and function and diseases of the nervous system.* Basel: Karger.

Siegel, J. (1997). Augmenting and reducing of visual evoked potentials in high- and low-sensation seeking humans, cats, and rats. *Behavior Genetics, 27,* 557–563.

Siegel, J. M. (1986). The Multidimensional Anger Inventory. *Journal of Personality and Social Psychology, 51,* 191–200.

Siegel, J., and Driscoll, P. (1996). Recent developments in an animal model of visual evoked potential augmenting/reducing and sensation seeking behavior. *Neuropsychobiology, 34,* 130–135.

Sigusch, V., and Schmidt, G. (1971) Lower-class sexuality: Some emotional and social aspects in West German males and females. *Archives of Sexual Behavior, 1,* 29–44.

Silas, F. A. (1984). Fit for the job? Testing grows—gripes too. *American Bar Association Journal,* July, p. 34.

Silverman, L. H. (1976). Psychoanalytic theory: "The reports of my death are greatly exaggerated." *American Psychologist, 31,* 621–637.

Silverman, L. H., and Weinberger, J. (1985). Mommy and I are one: Implications for psychotherapy. *American Psychologist, 40,* 1296–1308.

Silverthorne, C. (2001). Leadership effectiveness and personality: A cross cultural evaluation. *Personality and Individual Differences, 30,* 303–309.

Simonton, D. K. (1991). Emergence and realization of genius: The lives and works of 120 classical composers. *Journal of Personality and Social Psychology, 61,* 829–840.

Simpson, J. A., and Gangestad, S. W. (1991). Individual differences in sociosexuality: Evidence for convergent and discriminant validity. *Journal of Personality and Social Psychology, 60,* 870–883.

Simpson, J. A., and Rholes, W. S. (1998). *Attachment theory and close relationships.* New York: Guilford Press.

Simpson, J. A., Rholes, W. S., Orinea, M. M., and Grich, J. (2002). Working models of attachment, support giving, and support seeking in a stressful situation. *Personality and Social Psychology Bulletin, 28,* 598–608.

Singh, D., Vidaurri, M., Zambarano, R. J., and Dabbs, J. M., Jr. (1999). Behavioral, morphological, and hormonal correlates to erotic role identification among lesbian women. *Journal of Personality and Social Psychology, 76,* 1035–1049.

Singh, S. (1978). Achievement motivation and entrepreneurial success: A follow-up study. *Journal of Research in Personality, 12,* 500–503.

Six, B., and Eckes, T. (1991). A closer look at the complex structure of gender stereotypes. *Sex Roles, 24,* 64.

Slutske, W. S., Caspi, A., Moffitt, T. E., and Poulton, R. (2005). Personality and problem gambling. *Archives of General Psychiatry, 62,* 769–775.

Slutske, W. S., Eisen, S. A., True, W. R., Lyons, M. J., Goldberg, J., and Tsuang, M. T. (2005). Common genetic vulnerability for pathological gambling and alcohol dependence in men. *Archives of General Psychiatry, 57,* 666–673.

Smillie, L. D., Yeo, G. B., Furnham, A. F., and Jackson, C. J. (2006). Benefits of all work and no play: The relationship between neuroticism and performance as a function of resource allocation. *Journal of Applied Psychology, 91,* 139–155.

Smith, C. P., and Atkinson, J. W. (1992). *Motivation and personality: Handbook of thematic content analysis.* New York: Cambridge University Press.

Smith, G. M. (1967). Usefulness of peer ratings of personality in educational research. *Educational and Psychological Measurement, 27,* 967–984.

Smith, T. W. (1979). Happiness: Time trends, seasonal variations, intersurvey differences, and other mysteries. *Social Psychology Quarterly, 42,* 18–30.

Smith, T. W. (1989). Interactions, transactions, and the Type A pattern: Additional avenues in the search for coronary-prone behavior. In A. W. Siegman and T. M. Dembrowski (Eds.), *In search of coronary-prone behavior* (pp. 91–116). Hillsdale, NJ: Erlbaum.

Smith, T. W. (1992). Hostility and health: Current status of a psychosomatic hypothesis. *Health Psychology, 11,* 139–150.

Smith, T. W., Pope, M. K., Rhodewalt, F., and Poulton, J. L. (1989). Optimism, neuroticism, coping, and symptom reports: An alternative interpretation of the Life Orientation Test. *Journal of Personality and Social Psychology, 56,* 640–648.

Smith, T. W., and Spiro, A. III. (2002). Personality, health, and aging: Prolegomenon for the next generation. *Journal of Research in Personality, 36,* 363–394.

Snyder, M. (1983). The influence of individuals on situations: Implications for understanding the links between personality and social behavior. *Journal of Personality, 51,* 497–516.

Snyder, M., and Cantor, N. (1998). Understanding personality and social behavior: A functionalist strategy. In D. T. Gilbert, S. T. Fiske, and G. Lindzey (Eds.), *The handbook of social psychology* (Vol. 1, 4th ed., pp. 635–679). Boston: McGraw-Hill.

Snyder, M., and Gangestad, S. (1982). Choosing social situations: Two investigations of self-monitoring processes. *Journal of Personality and Social Psychology, 43,* 123–135.

Snyder, M., and Swann, W. B. (1978). Behavioral confirmation in social interaction: From social perception to social reality. *Journal of Experimental Social Psychology, 14,* 148–162.

Society for Industrial and Organizational Psychology, Inc. (1987). *Principles for the validation and use of personnel selection procedures.* (Third Edition). College Park, MD: Author.

Sokolowski, K., Schmalt, H., Langens, T. A., and Puca, R. M. (2000). Assessing achievement, affiliation, and power motives all at once: The Multi-Motive Grid (MMG). *Journal of Personality Assessment, 74,* 126–145.

Soloff, P. H., Lis, J. A., Kelly, T., and Cornelius, J. (1994). Risk factors for suicidal behavior in borderline personality disorder. *American Journal of Psychiatry, 151,* 1316–1323.

Somer, O., and Goldberg, L. R. (1999). The structure of Turkish trait-descriptive adjectives. *Journal of Personality and Social Psychology, 76,* 431–450.

South, S. C., Oltmanns, T. F., and Turkheimer, E. (2003). Personality and the derogation of others: Descriptions based on self- and peer report. *Journal of Research in Personality, 37,* 16–33.

Spangler, W. D. (1992). Validity of questionnaire and TAT measures of need for achievement: Two meta-analyses. *Psychological Bulletin, 112,* 140–154.

Spanos, N. P., and McLean, J. (1986). Hypnotically created false reports do not demonstrate pseudomemories. *British Journal of Experimental and Clinical Hypnosis, 3,* 167–171.

Spearman, C. (1910). Correlation calculated from faulty data. *British Journal of Psychology, 3,* 271–295.

Spence, J. T., Helmreich, R., and Stapp, J. (1974). The Personal Attributes Questionnaire: A measure of sex-role stereotypes and masculinity and femininity. *Journal Supplement Abstract Service Catalog of Selected Documents in Psychology, 4,* 42 (No. 617).

Spies, R. A., and Plake, B. S. (2005). *The Sixteenth Mental Measurements Yearbook.* Lincoln, NE: Buros Institute of Mental Measurements.

Spilker, B., and Callaway, E. (1969). Augmenting and reducing in averaged visual evoked responses to sine wave light. *Psychophysiology, 6,* 49–57.

Spinath, F. M., and O'Connor, T. G. (2003). A behavioral genetic study of the overlap between personality and parenting. *Journal of Personality, 71,* 5, 785–808.

Spinath, F. M., Wolf, H., Angleitner, A., Borkenau, P., and Riemann, R. (2002). Genetic and environmental influences on objectively assessed activity in adults. *Personality and Individual Differences, 33,* 633–645.

Spotts, E. L., Lichtenstein, P., Pedersen, N., Neiderhiser, J. M., Hansson, K., Cederblad, M., and Reiss, D. (2005). *European Journal of Personality, 19,* 205–227.

Spotts, E. L., Neiderhiser, J. M., Towers, H., Hansson, K., Lichtenstein, P., Cederblad, M., and Pedersen, N. L. (2004). Genetic and environmental influences on marital relationships. *Journal of Family Psychology, 18,* 107–119.

Srivastava, S., John, O. P., Gosling, S. D., and Potter, J. (2003). Development of personality in early and middle adulthood: Set like plaster or persistent change? *Journal of Personality and Social Psychology, 84,* 5, 1041–1053.

Stake, J. E., Huff, L., and Zand, D. (1995). Trait self-esteem, positive and negative events, and event specific shifts in self-evaluation and affect. *Journal of Research in Personality, 29,* 223–241.

Steel, P., and Ones, D. S. (2002). Personality and happiness: A national-level analysis. *Journal of Personality and Social Psychology, 83,* 3, 767–781.

Stein, A. A. (1976). Conflict and cohesion: A review of the literature. *Journal of Conflict Resolution, 20,* 143–172.

Stelmack, R. M. (1990). Biological basis of extraversion: Psychophysiological evidence. *Journal of Personality, 58,* 293–311.

Stelmack, R. M., and Stalkas, A. (1991). Galen and the humour theory of temperament. *Personality and Individual Differences, 12,* 255–263.

Sternberg, R. J. (1985). *Beyond IQ: A triarchic theory of human intelligence.* New York: Cambridge University Press.

Steward, H. (1980). Body type, personality, and psychotherapeutic treatment of male adolescents. *Adolescence, 15,* 927–932.

Stewart, A. J. (1982). The course of individual adaptation to life changes. *Journal of Personality and Social Psychology, 42,* 1100–1113.

Stewart, M. E., Ebmeier, K. P., and Deary, I. J. (2005). Personality correlates of happiness and sadness: EPQ-R and TPQ compared. *Personality and Individual Differences, 38,* 1085–1096.

Stocker, S. (1997). Don't be shy: Advice for becoming more outgoing. *Prevention,* p. 96.

Stoerig, P., and Cowey, A. (1997). Blindsight in man and monkey. *Brain, 120,* 535–559.

Stroop, J. R. (1935). Studies of interference in serial verbal reactions. *Journal of Experimental Psychology, 18,* 643–661.

Strout, S. L., Laird, J. D., Shafer, A., and Thompson, N. S. (2005). The effect of vividness of experience on sex differences in jealousy. *Evolutionary Psychology, 3,* 263–274.

Suls, J., and Wan, C. K. (1989). The relation between Type A behavior and chronic emotional distress: A meta-analysis. *Journal of Personality and Social Psychology, 57,* 503–512.

Suls, J., Wan, C. K., and Costa, P. T., Jr. (1996). Relationship of trait anger to resting blood pressure: A meta-analysis. *Health Psychology, 14,* 444–456.

Surtees, P., Wainwright, N., Khaw, K. T., Luben, R., Brayne, C., and Day, N. (2003). Inflammatory dispositions: A population-based study of the association between hostility and peripheral leukocyte counts. *Personality and Individual Differences, 35,* 1271–1284.

Sutton, S. K. (2002a). Incentive and threat reactivity: Relations with anterior cortical activity. In D. Cervone and W. Mischel (Eds.), *Advances in personality science* (pp. 127–150). New York: Guilford Press.

Sutton, S. K. (2002b). Incentive and threat reactivity: Relations with anterior cortical activity. In D. Cervone and W. Michele (Eds.), *Advances in personality science* (pp. 127–152). New York: Guilford Press.

Sutton, S. K., and Davidson, R. J. (1997). Prefrontal brain asymmetry: A biological substrate of the behavioral approach and inhibition systems. *Psychological Science, 8,* 210–214.

Sverko, B., and Fabulic, L. (1985). Stability of morningness-eveningness: Retest changes after seven years. *Revija za Psihologiju, 15,* 71–78.

Swanbrow, D. (1989, August). The paradox of happiness. *Psychology Today,* pp. 37–39.

Swann, W. B., Langlois, J. H., and Gilbert, L. A. (Eds.). (1999). *Sexism and stereotypes in modern society: The gender science of*

Janet Taylor Spence. Washington, DC: American Psychological Association.

Swann, W. R., Jr., and Selye, C. (2005). Personality psychology's comeback and its emerging symbiosis with social psychology. *Personality and Social Psychology Bulletin, 31,* 155–165.

Symons, D. (1979). *The evolution of human sexuality.* New York: Oxford.

Symons, D. (1992). On the use and misuse of Darwinism in the study of human behavior. In J. Barkow, L. Cosmides, and J. Tooby (Eds.), *The adapted mind* (pp. 137–159). New York: Oxford University Press.

Tarantolo, D., Lamptev, P. R., and Moodie, R. (1999). The global HIV/AIDS pandemic: Trends and patterns. In L. Gibney and R. J. DiClemente (Eds.), *Preventing HIV in developing countries: Biomedical and behavioral approaches* (pp. 9–41). New York: Kluwer Academic/Plenum Publishers.

Tate, R. L. (2003). Impact of pre-injury factors on outcome after severe traumatic brain injury: Does post-traumatic personality change represent an exacerbation of premorbid traits? *Neuropsychological Rehabilitation, 3,* 43–64.

Taylor, S. (1991). *Health psychology* (2nd ed.). New York: McGraw-Hill.

Taylor, S. E. (1989). *Positive illusions: Self-deception and the healthy mind.* New York: Basic Books.

Taylor, S. E., Kemeny, M. E., Reed, G. M., Bower, J. E., and Gruenewald, T. L. (2000). Psychological resources, positive illusions, and health. *American Psychologist, 55,* 99–109.

Tedeschi, R. G., Park, C. L., and Calhoun, L. (1998). Posttraumatic growth: Conceptual issues. In R. G. Tedeschi and P. L. Crystal (Eds.), *Posttraumatic growth: Positive changes in the aftermath of crisis* (pp. 1–22). Mahwah, NJ: Lawrence Erlbaum Associates, Inc.

Tellegen, A., Lykken, D. T., Bouchard, T. J., Wilcox, K., Segal, N., and Rich, S. (1988). Personality similarity in twins reared apart and together. *Journal of Personality and Social Psychology, 54,* 1031–1039.

Terman, L. M. (1938). *Psychological factors in marital happiness.* New York: McGraw-Hill.

Terracciano, A., McCrae, R. R., Hagemann, D., and Costa, P. T. (2003) Individual difference variables, affective differentiation, and the structures of affect. *Journal of Personality, 71,* 669–703.

Theakston, J. A., Stewart, S. H., Dawson, M. Y., Knowlden-Loewen, S. A. B., and Lehman, D. R. (2004). Big five personality domains predict drinking motives. *Personality and Individual Differences, 37,* 971–984.

Thomas, A. K., Bulevich, J. B., and Loftus, E. F. (2003). Exploring the role of repetition and sensory elaboration in the imagination inflation effect. *Memory and Cognition, 31,* 630–640.

Thompson, R. A. (1991). Emotional regulation and emotional development. *Educational Psychology Review, 3,* 269–307.

Thorndike, E. L. (1911). *Individuality.* Boston: Houghton Mifflin.

Thrash, T. M., and Elliot, A. J. (2002). Implicit and self-attributed achievement motives: Concordance and predictive validity. *Journal of Personality, 70,* 729–755.

Tice, D. M. (1991). Esteem protection or enhancement? Self-handicapping motives and attributions differ by trait self-esteem. *Journal of Personality and Social Psychology, 60,* 711–725.

Tice, D. M. (1993). The social motivations of people with low self-esteem. In R. F. Baumeister (Ed.), *Self-esteem: The puzzle of low self-regard* (pp. 37–53). New York: Plenum Press.

Tice, D. M., and Baumeister, R. F. (1990). Self-esteem, self-handicapping, and self-presentation: The strategy of inadequate practice. *Journal of Personality, 58,* 443–464.

Tice, D. M., and Bratslavsky, E. (2000). Giving in to feel good: The place of emotion regulation in the context of general self-control. *Psychological Inquiry, 11,* 149–159.

Tomarken, A. J., Davidson, R. J., and Henriques, J. B. (1990). Resting frontal brain asymmetry predicts affective responses to films. *Journal of Personality and Social Psychology, 59,* 791–801.

Tomkins, S. S. (1995). *Exploring affect: The selected writings of S. S. Tomkins.* E. V. Demos (Ed.). New York: Cambridge University Press.

Tooby, J., and Cosmides, L. (1990). On the universality of human nature and the uniqueness of the individual: The role of genetics and adaptation. *Journal of Personality, 58,* 17–68.

Tooby, J., and Cosmides, L. (1992). Psychological foundations of culture. In J. Barkow, L. Cosmides, and J. Tooby (Eds.), *The adapted mind* (pp. 19–136). New York: Oxford University Press.

Tooke, J., and Camie, L. (1991). Patterns of deception in intersexual and intrasexual mating strategies. *Ethology and Sociobiology, 12,* 345–364.

Toomela, A. (2003). Relationships between personality structure, structure of word meaning, and cognitive ability: A study of cultural mechanisms of personality. *Journal of Personality and Social Psychology, 85,* 4, 723–735.

Tremblay, R. E., Pihl, R. O., Vitaro, F., and Dobkin, P. L. (1994). Predicting early onset of male antisocial behavior from preschool behavior. *Archives of General Psychiatry, 51,* 732–739.

Triandis, H. C. (1989). The self and social behavior in differing contexts. *Psychological Review, 93,* 506–520.

Triandis, H. C. (1994). Cross-cultural industrial and organizational psychology. In Triandis H. C., Dunnette, M. D., Hough, L. M. (Eds.), *Handbook of industrial and organizational psychology* (Vol. 4, pp. 103–172). New York: Wiley.

Triandis, H. C. (1995). *Individualism and collectivism.* Boulder, CO: Westview Press.

Triandis, H. C. (2001). Individualism, collectivism and personality. *Journal of Personality, 69,* 907–924.

Trinkaus, E., and Zimmerman, M. R. (1982). Trauma among the Shanidar Neanderthals. *American Journal of Physical Anthropology, 57,* 61–76.

Trivers, R. (1985). *Social evolution.* Menlo Park, CA: Benjamin/Cummings.

Trivers, R. L. (1972). Parental investment and sexual selection. In B. Campbell (Ed.), *Sexual selection and the descent of man: 1871–1971* (pp. 136–179). Chicago: Aldine.

Trobst, K. K., Herbst, J. H., Masters, H. L., and Costa, P. T. (2002). Personality pathways to unsafe sex: Personality, condom use, and HIV risk behaviors. *Journal of Research in Personality, 36,* 117–133.

Trull, J. J., and McCrae, R. M. (2002). A five-factor perspective on personality disorder research. In P. T. Costa, Jr. and T. A. Widiger (Eds.), *Personality disorders and the five factor model of personality* (2nd ed.) (pp. 45–58). Washington, DC: American Psychological Association.

Trzesniewski, K. H., Donnellan, M. B., and Robins, R. W. (2003). Stability of self-esteem across the life span. *Journal of Personality and Social Psychology, 84,* 1, 205–220.

Tsai, A., Loftus, E., and Polage, D. (2000). Current directions in false-memory research. In D. F. Bjorklund (Ed.), *False-memory creation in children and adults: Theory, research, and implications* (pp. 31–44). Mahwah, NJ: Lawrence Erlbaum Associates, Publishers.

Tuerlinckz, F., De Boeck, P., and Lens, W. (2002). Measuring needs with the Thematic Apperception Test: A psychometric study. *Journal of Personality and Social Psychology, 82,* 448–461.

Tupes, E. C., and Christal, R. C. (1961). *Recurrent personality factors based on trait ratings.* USAF ASD Technical Report, No. 61–97, U.S. Air Force, Lackland Air Force Base, TX.

Twenge, J. M. (2000). The age of anxiety? Birth cohort change in anxiety and neuroticism, 1952–1993. *Journal of Personality and Social Psychology, 79,* 1007–1021.

Twenge, J. M. (2001a). Changes in women's assertiveness in response to status and roles: A cross-temporal meta-analysis, 1931–1993. *Journal of Personality and Social Psychology, 81,* 133–145.

Twenge, J. M. (2001b). Birth cohort changes in extraversion: A cross-temporal meta-analysis, 1966–1993. *Personality and Individual Differences, 30,* 735–748.

Twenge, J. M. (2006). *Generation me.* New York: Free Press.

Udry, J. R., and Chantala, K. (2004). Masculinity-femininity guides sexual union formation in adolescence. *Personality and Social Psychology Bulletin, 30,* 44–55.

U.S. Department of Health and Human Services. (2000). *Child maltreatment 1998: Reports from the states to the National Child Abuse and Neglect Data System.* Washington, DC: U.S. Government Printing Office.

Vaidya, J. G., Gray, E. K., Haig, J., and Watson, D. (2002). On the temporal stability of personality: Evidence for differential stability and the role of life experiences. *Journal of Personality and Social Psychology, 83,* 6, 1469–1484.

Vaillant, G. E. (1977). *Adaptation to life.* Boston: Little Brown.

Vaillant, G. E. (1994). Ego mechanisms of defense and personality psychopathology. *Journal of Abnormal Psychology, 103,* 44–50.

Van Beijsterveldt, C. E. M., Bartels, M., Hudziak, J. J., and Boomsma, D. I. (2003). Causes of stability of aggression form early childhood to adolescence: A longitudinal genetic analysis of Dutch twins. *Behavior Genetics, 33,* 591–605.

Vando, A. (1974). The development of the R-A scale: A paper-and-pencil measure of pain tolerance. *Personality and Social Psychology Bulletin, 1,* 28–29.

Vasquez, K., Durik, A. M., and Hyde, J. S. (2002). Family and work: Implications of adult attachment styles. *Personality and Social Psychology Bulletin, 28,* 874–886.

Vazire, S., and Gosling, S. D. (2003). The role of animal research in bridging psychology and biology. *American Psychologist, 58,* 407–408.

Veenhoven, R. (1988). The utility of happiness. *Social Indicators Research, 20,* 333–354.

Veenhoven, R. (1991a). Questions on happiness: Classical topics, modern answers, blind spots. In F. Strack and M. Argyle (Eds.), *Subjective well-being: An interdisciplinary perspective* (pp. 7–26). Oxford, England: Pergamon Press, Inc.

Veenhoven, R. (1991b). Is happiness relative? *Social Indicators Research, 24,* 1–34.

Veroff, J., Atkinson, J. W., Feld, S. C., and Gurin, G. (1960). The use of thematic apperception to assess motivation in a nationwide interview study. *Psychological Monography, 74,* 32.

Vidacek, S., Kaliterna, L., Radosevic-Vidacek, B., and Folkard, S. (1988). Personality differences in the phase of circadian rhythms: A comparison of morningness and extraversion. *Ergonomics, 31,* 873–888.

Vignoles, V. L., Regalia, C., Manzi, C., Golledtge, J., and Scabini, E. (2006). Beyond self-esteem: Influence of multiple motives on identity construction. *Journal of Personality and Social Psychology, 90,* 308–333.

Vitaro, F., Arsenault, L., and Tremblay, R. E. (1997). Dispositional predictors of problem gambling in male adolescents. *American Journal of Psychiatry, 154,* 1769–1770.

Vrij, A., van der Steen, J., and Koppelaar, L. (1995). The effects of street noise and field independence on police officers' shooting behavior. *Journal of Applied Social Psychology, 25,* 1714–1725.

Wachtel, P. L. (1973). Psychodynamics, behavior therapy, and the implacable experimenter: An inquiry into the consistency of personality. *Journal of Abnormal Psychology, 82,* 324–334.

Wagstaff, G. F., Vella, M., and Perfect, T. (1992). The effect of hypnotically elicited testimony on jurors' judgments of guilt and innocence. *Journal of Social Psychology, 132,* 591–595.

Wahba, M. A., and Bridwell, L. (1973). Maslow's need hierarchy theory: A review of research. *Proceedings of the Annual Convention of the American Psychological Association (1973),* 571–572.

Wallace, H. M., and Baumeister, R. F. (2002). The performance of narcissists rises and falls with perceived opportunity for glory. *Journal of Personality and Social Psychology, 82,* 5, 819–834.

Waller, N. (1994). The importance of nongenetic influences on romantic love styles. *Psychological Science, 9,* 268–274.

Wallston, B. S., and Wallston, K. (1978). Locus of control and health: A review of the literature. *Health Education Monographs, 6,* 107–117

Wallston, K. A., Wallston, B. S., Smith, S., and Dobbins, C. J. (1989). Perceived control and health. In M. Johnston and T. Marteau (Eds.), *Applications in health psychology* (pp. 5–25).

Watson, D. (2000). *Mood and temperament.* New York: Guilford Press.

Watson, D. (2003). To dream, perchance to remember: Individual differences in dream recall. *Personality and Individual Differences, 34,* 1271–1286.

Watson, D., and Clark, L. A. (1984). Negative affectivity: The disposition to experience aversive emotional states. *Psychological Bulletin, 96,* 465–490.

Watson, D., Klohnen, E. C., Casillas, A., Simms, E. N., Haig, J., and Berry, D. S. (2004). Match makers and deal breakers: Analyses of mating in newlywed couples. *Journal of Personality, 72,* 1029–1068.

Watson, D., and Pennebaker, J. W. (1989). Health complaints, stress, and distress: Exploring the central role of negative affectivity. *Psychological Review, 96,* 234–254.

Watson, D. C. (2001). Procrastination and the five-factor model: A facet level analysis. *Personality and Individual Differences, 30,* 149–158.

Watts, B. L. (1982). Individual differences in circadian activity rhythms and their effects on roomate relationships. *Journal of Personality, 50,* 374–384.

Wechsler, D. (1949). *The Wechsler Intelligence Scale for Children.* New York: Psychological Corporation.

Wehr, T. A., and Goodwin, F. K. (1981). Biological rhythms and psychiatry. In S. Arieti and H. K. Brodie (Eds.), *American handbook of psychiatry: Advances and new directions* (Vol. 7). New York: Basic Books.

Weinberger, D. S., Schwartz, G. E., and Davidson, R. J. (1979). Low-anxious, high-anxious, and repressive coping styles: Psychometric patterns and behavioral and physiological responses to stress. *Journal of Abnormal Psychology, 88,* 369–380.

Weinberger, J. (1992). Validating and demystifying subliminal psychodynamic activation. In R. F. Bornsteain and T. S. Pittman (Eds.), *Perception without awareness: Cognitive, clinical, and social perspectives* (pp. 170–188). New York: Guilford Press.

Weinberger, J. (2003). Freud's influence on psychology is alive and vibrant. In E. E. Smith, S. Noen-Hoeksema, B. L. Fredrickson, G. R. Loftus, D. J. Bem, and S. Maren, *Introduction to psychology* (p. 486). Belmont, CA: Wadsworth/Thomson Learning.

Weinberger, J., and Hardaway, R. (1990). Separating science from myth in subliminal psychodynamic activation. *Clinical Psychology Review, 10,* 727–756.

Weinberger, J., Kelner, S., and McClelland, D. (1997). The effects of subliminal symbiotic stimulation on free-response and self-reported mood. *Journal of Nervous and Mental Disease, 185,* 599–605.

Weinberger, J., and McClelland, D. C. (1990). Cognitive versus traditional motivational models: Irreconcilable or complementary? In E. T. Higgins and R. M. Sorrentino (Eds.), *Handbook of motivation and cognition* (Vol. 2, pp. 562–597). New York: Guilford Press.

Weinberger, J., and Silverman, L. H. (1990). Testability and empirical verification of psychoanalytic dynamic propositions through subliminal psychodynamic activation. *Psychoanalytic Psychology, 7,* 299–339.

Weinstock, L. M., and Whisman, M. A. (2006). Neuroticism as a common feature of the depressive and anxiety disorders: A test of the revised integrative hierarchical model in a national sample. *Journal of Abnormal Psychology, 115,* 68–74.

Weiskrantz, L. (1986). *Blindsight: A case study and its implications.* Oxford, Oxford University Press.

Weiss, A., King, J. E., and Enns, R. M. (2002). Subjective well-being is heritable and genetically correlated with dominance in chimpanzees *(Pan troglodytes). Journal of Personality and Social Psychology, 83,* 5, 1141–1149.

Weissberg, R. P., Kumpfer, K. L., and Seligman, M. E. P. (2003). Prevention that works for children and youth: An introduction. *American Psychologist Special Issue: Prevention that works for children and youth, 58,* 425–432.

Weller, H. G., Repman, J., Lan, W., and Rooze, G. (1995). Improving the effectiveness of learning through hypermedia-based instruction: The importance of learner characteristics. Special Issue: Hypermedia: Theory, research, and application. *Computers in Human Behavior, 11,* 451–465.

Wertsch, J., and Kanner, B. (1992). A socio-cultural approach to intellectual development. In R. Sternberg and C. A. Berg (Eds.), *Intellectual development* (pp. 328–349). New York: Cambridge University Press.

Wessman, A. E., and Ricks, D. F. (1966). *Mood and personality.* New York: Holt, Rinehart, and Winston.

West, S. G. (2002). Some methodological and training/funding perspectives on the future of personality research. *Journal of Research in Personality, 36,* 640–648.

Westen, D. (1990). Psychoanalytic approaches to personality. In L. A. Pervin (Ed.), *Handbook of personality: Theory and research* (pp. 21–65). New York: Guilford Press.

Westen, D. (1992). The cognitive self and the psychoanalytic self: Can we put our selves together? *Psychological Inquiry, 3,* 1–13.

Westen, D. (1998). The scientific legacy of Sigmund Freud: Toward a psychodynamically informed psychological science. *Psychological Bulletin, 124,* 333–371.

Westen, D., Ludolph, P., Misle, B., and Ruffins, S. (1990). Physical and sexual abuse in adolescent girls with borderline personality disorder. *American Journal of Orthopsychiatry, 60,* 55–66.

Wever, R. A. (1979). *The circadian system of man: Results of experiments under temporal isolation.* New York: Springer.

Whalen, P. J., Bush, G., and McNally, R. J. (1998). The emotional counting Stroop paradigm: A functional magnetic resonance imaging probe of the anterior cingulate affective division. *Biological Psychiatry, 44,* 1219–1228.

Wheeler, J. G., George, W. H., and Dahl, B. J. (2002). Sexually aggressive college males: Empathy as a moderator in the "Confluence Model" of sexual aggression. *Personality and Individual Differences, 33,* 759–775.

Wheeler, R. W., Davidson, R. J., and Tomarken, A. J. (1993). Frontal brain asymmetry and emotional reactivity: A biological substrate of affective style. *Psychophysiology, 30,* 82–89.

White, G. M. (1980). Conceptual universals in interpersonal language. *American Anthropologist, 82,* 759–781.

White, J. K., Hendrick, S. S., and Hendrick, C. (2004). Big five personality variables and relationship constructs. *Personality and Individual Differences, 37,* 1519–1530.

Whiting, B., and Edwards, C. P. (1988). *Children of different worlds.* Cambridge, MA: Harvard University Press.

Whorf, B. L. (1956). *Language, thought, and reality.* Cambridge, MA: MIT Press.

Wicker, F. W., Brown, G., Weihe, J. A., Hagen, A. S., and Reed, J. L. (1993). On reconsidering Maslow: An examination of the deprivation/domination proposition. *Journal of Research in Personality, 27,* 118–133.

Wickman, S. A., and Campbell, C. (2003). An analysis of how Carl Rogers enacted client-centered conversation with Gloria. *Journal of Counseling and Development, 81,* 178–184.

Widiger, T. A. (1997). Personality disorders as maladaptive variants of common personality traits: Implications for treatment. *Journal of Contemporary Psychotherapy Special Issue: Personality disorders, 27,* 265–282.

Widiger, T. A. (2000). Personality disorders in the 21st century. *Journal of Personality Disorders, 14,* 3–16.

Widiger, T. A., Costa, P. T., Jr., and McCrae, R. M. (2002a). A proposal for Axis II: Diagnosing personality disorders using the five-factor model. In P. T. Costa, Jr. and T. A. Widiger (Eds.), *Personality disorders and the five-factor model of personality* (2nd ed.) (pp. 431–456). Washington, DC: American Psychological Association.

Widiger, T. A., Trull, T. J., Clarkin, J. F., Sanderson, C., and Costa, P. T., Jr. (2002b). A description of the *DSM-IV* personality disorders with the five-factor model of personality. In P. T. Costa, Jr. and T. A. Widiger (Eds.), *Personality disorders and the five-factor model of personality* (2nd ed.) (pp. 89–102). Washington, DC: American Psychological Association.

Wiebe, D. J., and Smith, T. (1997). Personality and health: Progress and problems in psychosomatics. In R. Hogan, J. Johnson, and S. Briggs (Eds.), *Handbook of personality psychology* (pp. 892–918). San Diego, CA: Academic Press.

Wiederman, M. W., and Kendall, E. (1999). Evolution, gender, and sexual jealousy: Investigation with a sample from Sweden. *Evolution and Human Behavior, 20,* 121–128.

Wiggins, J. S. (1973). *Personality and prediction: Principles of personality assessment.* Menlo Park, CA: Addison-Wesley.

Wiggins, J. S. (1979). A psychological taxonomy of trait-descriptive terms: I. The interpersonal domain. *Journal of Personality and Social Psychology, 37,* 395–412.

Wiggins, J. S. (1996). *The five-factor model of personality: Theoretical perspectives.* New York: Guilford Press.

Wiggins, J. S. (2003). *Paradigms of personality assessment.* New York: Guilford.

Wiggins, J. S., Phillips, N., and Trapnell, P. (1989). Circular reasoning about interpersonal behaviour: Evidence concerning some untested assumptions underlying diagnostic classification. *Journal of Personality and Social Psychology, 56*(2), 296–305.

Willerman, L. (1979). Effects of families on intellectual development. *American Psychologist, 34,* 923–929.

Willerman, L., Loehlin, J. C., and Horn, J. M. (1992). An adoption and a cross-fostering study of the Minnesota Multiphasic Personality Inventory (MMPI) Psychopathic Deviate scale. *Behavior Genetics, 22,* 515–529.

Williams, D. E., and Page, M. M. (1989). A multi-dimensional measure of Maslow's hierarchy of needs. *Journal of Research in Personality, 23,* 192–213.

Williams, J. E., and Best, D. L. (1982). *Measuring sex stereotypes: A thirty-nation study.* Beverly Hills: Sage.

Williams, J. E., and Best, D. L. (1990). *Measuring sex stereotypes: A multi-nation study.* Newbury Park, CA: Sage.

Williams, J. E., and Best, D. L. (1994). Cross-cultural views of women and men. In W. J. Lonner and R. Malpass (Eds.), *Psychology and culture* (pp. 191–196). Boston: Allyn and Bacon.

Williams, J. M. G., Mathews, A., and MacLeod, C. (1996). The emotional Stroop task and psychopathology. *Psychological Bulletin, 120,* 3–24.

Williams, P. G., O'Brien, C. D., and Colder, C. R. (2004). The effects of neuroticism and extraversion on self-assessed health and health-relevant cognition. *Personality and Individual Differences, 37,* 83–94.

Wilson, D. S., Near, D., and Miller, R. R. (1996). Machiavellianism: A synthesis of the evolutionary and psychological literatures. *Psychological Bulletin, 119,* 285–299.

Wilson, M., and Daly, M. (1985). Competitiveness, risk-taking, and violence: The young male syndrome. *Ethology and Sociobiology, 6,* 59–73.

Winch, R. F. (1954). The theory of complementary needs in mate selection: An analytic and descriptive study. *American Sociological Review, 19,* 241–249.

Winter, D. G. (1973). *The power motive.* New York: Free Press.

Winter, D. G. (1988). The power motive in women—and men. *Journal of Personality and Social Psychology, 54,* 510–519.

Winter, D. G. (1993). Power, affiliation, and war: Three tests of a motivational model. *Journal of Personality and Social Psychology, 65,* 532–545.

Winter, D. G. (1998a). The contributions of David McClelland to personality assessment. *Journal of Personality Assessment, 71,* 129–145.

Winter, D. G. (1998b). A motivational analysis of the Clinton first term and the 1996 presidential campaign. *Leadership Quarterly, 9,* 367–376.

Winter, D. G. (1999). Linking personality and "scientific" psychology: The development of empirically derived Thematic Apperception Test measures. In Gieser and M. I. Stein (Eds.), *Evocative images: The Thematic Apperception Test and the art of projection* (pp. 107–124). Washington, DC: American Psychological Association.

Winter, D. G. (2002). The motivational dimensions of leadership: Power, achievement, and affiliation. In R. E. Riggio and S. E. Murphy (Eds.), *Multiple intelligences and leadership* (pp. 119–138). Mahwah, NJ: Lawrence Erlbaum Associates, Publishers.

Winter, D. G., and Barenbaum, N. B. (1985). Responsibility and the power motive in women and men. *Journal of Personality, 53,* 335–355.

Winter, D. G., John, O. P., Stewart, A. J., Klohnen, E. C., and Duncan, L. E. (1998). Traits and motives: Toward an integration of two traditions in personality research. *Psychological Review, 105,* 230–250.

Witkin, H. A. (1973). A cognitive-style perspective on evaluation and guidance. *Proceedings of the Invitational Conference on Testing Problems,* 21–27.

Witkin, H. A. (1977). Role of the field-dependent and field-independent cognitive styles in academic evolution: A longitudinal study. *Journal of Educational Psychology, 69,* 197–211.

Witkin, H. A., and Goodenough, D. R. (1977). Field dependence and interpersonal behavior. *Psychological Bulletin, 84,* 661–689.

Witkin, H. A., Dyk, R. B., Fattuson, H. F., Goodenough, D. R., and Karp, S. A. (1962). *Psychological differentiation: Studies of development.* New York: Wiley.

Witkin, H. A., Lewis, H. B., Hertzman, M., Machover, K., Meissner, P. B., and Wapner, S. (1954). *Personality through perception: An experimental and clinical study.* New York: Harper.

Witkin, H. A., Moore, C. A., Goodenough, D. R., and Cox, P. W. (1977). Field-dependent and field-independent cognitive styles and their educational implications. *Review of Educational Research, 47,* 1–64.

Woike, B. A. (1995). Most memorable experiences: Evidence for a link between implicit and explicit motives and social cognitive processes in everyday life. *Journal of Personality and Social Psychology, 68,* 1081–1091.

Wood, J. J., McLeod, B. D., Sigman, M., Hwang, W. C., and Chu, B. C. (2003). Parenting and childhood anxiety: Theory, empirical findings, and future directions. *Journal of Child Psychology and Psychiatry and Allied Disciplines, 44,* 134–151.

Wood, J. M., Nezworski, M. T., Lilienfeld, S. O., and Garb, H. N. (2003). What's Wrong with the Rorschach? Science Confronts the Controversial Inkblot Test. San Francisco: Jossey-Bass.

Wood, J. M., Nezworski, M. T., and Stejskal, J. W. (1996). The comprehensive system for the Rorschach: A critical examination. *Psychological Science, 7,* 3–10.

Wright, L. (1988). The Type A behavior pattern and coronary artery disease. *American Psychologist, 43,* 2–14.

Wu, K. D., and Clark, L. A. (2003). Relations between personality traits and self-reports of daily behavior. *Journal of Research in Personality, 37,* 231–256.

Yeh, C. (1995). *A cultural perspective on interdependence in self and morality: A Japan-U.S. comparison.* Unpublished manuscript, Department of Psychology, Stanford University, Stanford, CA.

Yik, M. S. M., and Russell, J. A. (2001). Predicting the big two of affect from the big five of personality. *Journal of Research in Personality, 35,* 247–277.

Yu, D. L., and Seligman, M. E. P. (2002). Preventing depressive symptoms in Chinese children. *Prevention and Treatment, 5,* np.

Zakriski, A. L., Wright, J. C., and Underwood, M. K. (2005). Gender similarities and differences in children's social behavior: Finding personality in contextualized patterns of adaptation. *Journal of Personality and Social Psychology, 88,* 844–855.

Zarevski, P., Bratko, D., Butkovic, A., and Lazic, A. (2002). Self-reports and peer-ratings of shyness and assertiveness. *Review of Psychology, 9,* 13–16.

Zeidner, M., Matthews, G., Roberts, R. D., and MacCann, C. (2003). Development of emotional intelligence: Towards a multi-level investment model. *Human Development, 46,* 69–96.

Zelenski, J. M., and Larsen, R. J. (1999). Susceptibility to affect: A comparison of three personality taxonomies. *Journal of Personality, 67,* 761–791.

Zelenski, J. M., and Larsen, R. J. (2000). The distribution of emotions in everyday life: A state and trait perspective from experience sampling data. *Journal of Research in Personality, 34,* 178–197.

Zentner, M. R. (2005). Ideal mate personality concepts and compatibility in close relationships: A longitudinal analysis. *Journal of Personality and Social Psychology, 89,* 242–256.

Zimbardo, P. G. (1977). *Shyness: What it is and what to do about it.* New York: Symphony.

Zinovieva, I. L. (2001). Why do people work if they are not paid? An example from Eastern Europe. In D. R. Denison (Ed.), *Managing organizational change in transition economies* (pp. 325–341). Mahwah, NJ: Lawrence Erlbaum Associates, Publishers.

Zuckerman, M. (1974). The sensation seeking motive. In B. Maher (Ed.), *Progress in experimental personality research* (Vol. 7, pp. 79–148). New York: Academic Press.

Zuckerman, M. (1978). Sensation seeking. In H. London and J. E. Exner (Eds.), *Dimensions of personality* (pp. 487–559). New York: Wiley Interscience.

Zuckerman, M. (1983). *Biological bases of sensation seeking, impulsivity, and anxiety.* Mahwah, NJ: Erlbaum.

Zuckerman, M. (1984). Sensation seeking: A comparative approach to a human trait. *Behavioral and Brain Sciences, 7,* 413–471.

Zuckerman, M. (1991). *Psychobiology of personality.* New York: Cambridge University Press.

Zuckerman, M. (1991). Sensation-seeking trait. *Encyclopedia of Human Biology, 6,* 809–817.

Zuckerman, M., and Haber, M. M. (1965). Need for stimulation as a source of stress response to perceptual isolation. *Journal of Abnormal Psychology, 70,* 371–377.

Zuckerman, M., Joireman, J., Kratl, M., and Kuhilan, D. M. (1999). Where do motivational and emotional traits fit within three factor models of personality? *Personality and Individual Differences, 26,* 487–504.

Zuckerman, M., and Kuhlman, D. M. (2000). Personality and risk-taking: Common biosocial factors. *Journal of Personality, 68,* 999–1029.

Zurbriggen, E. L., and Sturman, T. S. (2002). Linking motives and emotions: A test of McClelland's hypotheses. *Personality and Social Psychology Bulletin, 28,* 521–535.

Photo Credits

Chapter Openers

PO1, CO1, 1, 2, 3, 4, 5: © Royalty-Free/Corbis; PO2, CO2, 6, 7, 8: © Getty Images/Steve Allen; PO3, CO1, 2, 9, 10, 11: © Don Farrall/Getty Images; PO4, CO1, 2, 12, 13, 14: © Digital Vision/Getty Images; PO5, CO1, 2, 15, 16, 17: © Stockbyte/Punchstock Images; PO6, CO1, 2, 18, 19, 20: © Digital Vision/Getty Images

Chapter 1

Page 3: Chuck Savage/Corbis; p. 5: (clockwise from left) © Michael Newman/PhotoEdit; PhotoDisc/Getty; © PhotoDisc/Getty; © PhotoDisc/Getty; © PhotoDisc/Getty; © PhotoDisc/Getty; © PhotoDisc/Getty; © A. Ramey/PhotoEdit; © PhotoDisc/Getty; © PhotoDisc/Getty; p. 7: © Jose Jimenez/Primera Hora/Getty Images; p. 12: © Image Source/SuperStock; p. 17: (top) © AFP/Corbis, (bottom) Bettmann/Corbis; p. 19: (top) © Victor Englebert/Photo Researchers, (bottom) © PhotoDisc/Getty

Chapter 2

p. 25: (left) © Dennis Van Tine/Gamma, (right) © AFP/Corbis; p. 30: © Michael Newman/PhotoEdit; p. 33: Bonnie Kamin/PhotoEdit; p. 35: © Ariel Skelley/Corbis; p. 36: Dr. Scott T. Grafton/Visuals Unlimited; p. 37: Will & Deni McIntyre/Photo Researchers; p. 38: Mark Richards/PhotoEdit; p. 46: (left) © Robin L. Sachs/PhotoEdit, (right) © Jack Hollingsworth/Corbis; p. 51: Courtesy of Dodge Morgan; p. 53: © Bettmann/Corbis

Chapter 3

p. 61: © PhotoDisc/Getty; p. 73: © Randy J. Larsen, 1987; p. 77: Courtesy of the Cattell Family; p. 79: Courtesy of Krista Trobst

Chapter 4

p. 95: © Davis Barber/PhotoEdit; p. 96: Bob Daemmrich/The Image Works; p. 100: (left) © Michael S. Yamashita/Corbis, (right) © PhotoDisc/Getty; p. 104: (left) © Syracuse Newspapers/The Image Works, (right) © Michael Wickes/The Image Works; p. 109: © Ulrike Welsch/PhotoEdit; p. 112: © Gavin Wickham/Eye Ubiquitous/Corbis; p. 114: © Richard T. Nowitz/Photo Researchers; p. 125: PhotoDisc/Getty

Chapter 5

p. 137: © Kwame Zikomo/SuperStock; p. 139: (left) © PhotoDisc/Getty, (right) © Bob Daemmrich/The Image Works; p. 140: © Pierre Perrin/Gamma; p. 142: (left) © Wartenberg/Picture Press/Corbis, (right) David Katzenstein/Corbis; p. 160: © John Feingersh/Corbis; p. 161: (left) © PhotoDisc/Getty, (right) © PhotoDisc/Getty

Chapter 6

p. 173: © Kairos: Latin Stock/Science Photo Library/Photo Researchers; p. 176: (left) © Liaison/Getty, (right) © Liaison/Getty; p. 180: (left) © Randy Larsen, (right) © Randy Larsen; p. 181: © David Young-Wolff/PhotoEdit; p. 183: (left) © Tom Pettyman/PhotoEdit, (right) © Tony Freeman/PhotoEdit; p. 186: © Alvis Upitis/SuperStock; p. 191: © PhotoDisc/Getty; p. 197: © Jose Luis Pelaez, Inc./Corbis

Chapter 7

p. 205: © Royalty-Free/Corbis; p. 207: Phineas Gage-Reprinted with permission from Damasio H. Gravowski T, Frank R, Galaburda AM, Damasio AR: The return of Phineas Gage: Clues about the brain from a famous patient. Science, 264:1102-1105, © 1994. "Courtesy of Dr. Hanna Damasio, the Dana and David Dornsife Cognitive Neuroscience Imaging Center and Creativity Institute, University of Southern California"; p. 212: © Pete Saloutos/Corbis; p. 215: (left) © Pete Stone/Corbis, (right) © Richard Smith/Corbis; p. 224: © George Contorakes/Corbis; p. 226: © Stock4B/Corbis; p. 228: © John Bavosi/Science Photo Library/Photo Researchers; p. 240: © Eliana Aponte/Reuters/Corbis

Chapter 8

p. 243: © Giovanni Casselli; p. 246: © First Light/Corbis; p. 247: © AP Photo/Mohammed Ballas; p. 248: © Brian Haimer/PhotoEdit; p. 253: © Spencer Grant/PhotoEdit; p. 258: © 1988 Matsumoto and Paul Ekman, Ph.D.; p. 261: © Austrian Archives/Corbis; p. 272: © Steven Morris/Envision

Chapter 9

p. 285: Courtesy of Professor Ross E. Cheit; p. 287: © Keystone/Getty Images; p. 296: © Laura Dwight/Corbis; p. 305: © Reza Estakhrian/Getty; p. 312: © Laura Dwight/Corbis; p. 317: © PhotoFest

Chapter 10

p. 321: © Al Francis/AP Wide World Photos; p. 324: Courtesy of Elizabeth F. Loftus; p. 331: Reuters/Corbis; p. 336: (left) © Davis Turner/Corbis, (right) © Jahi Chikwendick-Pool/Getty Images; p. 338: © PhotoDisc/Getty; p. 342: © Rey Germain/Gamma; p. 345: © De Waele Tim/Photo News/Gamma

Chapter 11

p. 351: © Liaison/Getty Images; p. 357: Reproduced from the Collections of the Library of Congress; p. 361: © Justin Sullivan/Getty Images; p. 364: © Claro Cortes IV/Reuters/Corbis; p. 367: © A724/Gamma; p. 370: © Matthew Mendelsohn/Corbis; p. 373: © Photofest; p. 379: © Erich Lessing/Art Resource, NY

Chapter 12

p. 391: © Paul Fusco/Magnum Photos; p. 398: © The Californian, Richard D. Green/AP Photo; p. 399: © PhotoDisc/Getty

Chapter 13

p. 423: © Richard Lord/PhotoEdit; p. 426: (top left) © Spencer Grant/PhotoEdit, (top right) © Robert Hernandez/Photo Researchers, Inc., (bottom left) © Bill Bachmann/Photo Researchers, Inc., (bottom right) © Dinodia/The Image Works; p. 430: © Science Photo Library/Photo Researchers, Inc.; p. 433: © Kevin Dodge/Corbis; p. 442: © PhotoDisc/Getty; p. 453: © New Line/courtesy Everett Collection

Chapter 14

p. 463: © Michael Newman/PhotoEdit; p. 469: © Mark E. Gibson/Corbis; p. 484: © Photofest; p. 487: © Photofest

Chapter 15

p. 495: © Spencer Grant/PhotoEdit; p. 499: © Karim Shamsi-Basha/The Image Works; p. 505: © Michell D. Bridwell/PhotoEdit; p. 508: © Tony Freeman/PhotoEdit; p. 514:

© Archivo Iconográfico, S.A./Corbis; p. 516: © Michael Newman/PhotoEdit

Chapter 16

p. 523: © David Young-Wolff/PhotoEdit; p. 526: © Mark Richards/PhotoEdit; p. 530: © Photononstop/Envision; p. 535: © Superstock; p. 541: © PhotoDisc/Getty: p. 544 (top) © Robert Michael/GettyImages, (bottom) © Michell D. Bridwell/PhotoEdit; p. 547: © Kathy Willens/AP Photo

Chapter 17

p. 553: © John Maier/The Image Works; p. 556: © Victor Englebert/Photo Researchers, Inc.; p. 562: (top) © PhotoDisc/Getty, (center) © David Young-Wolff/PhotoEdit, (bottom) © Tom McCarthy/PhotoEdit; p. 563: © Javi Rodriguez/Cover/The Image Works; p. 566: © Christophe Calais/In Visu/Corbis; p. 569: © Itsuo Inouye/AP Photo; p. 575: © PhotoAlto/PunchStock

Chapter 18

p. 587: © A. Ramey/PhotoEdit; p. 593: © PhotoDisc/Getty; p. 595: © Juergen Berger: Max-Planck Institute/Science Photo Library/Photo Researchers, Inc.; p. 598: © Robert Stolarik/Gamma; p. 601: Henry Ray Abrams/AFP/Getty Images; p. 607: © Charles Rex Arbogast/AP Photo; p. 609: Phineas Gage-Reprinted with permission from Damasio H. Gravowski T, Frank R, Galaburda AM, Damasio AR: The return of Phineas Gage: Clues about the brain from a famous patient. Science, 264:1102-1105, © 1994. "Courtesy of Dr. Hanna Damasio, the Dana and David Dornsife Cognitive Neuroscience Imaging Center and Brain and Creativity Institute, University of Southern California"; p. 613: © PhotoDisc/Getty; p. 618: © Martin M. Rotker/Science Source/Photo Researchers, Inc.

Chapter 19

p. 621: © Susan Ragan/AP Photo; p. 631: © Ron Edmonds/AP Photo; p. 634: © PhotoDisc/Getty; p. 637: © Photofest; p. 642: © Photo B.D.V./Corbis; p. 644: © Reuters/Corbis

Chapter 20

p. 661: The Newark Museum/Art Resource, NY/Art © Romare Bearden Foundation/ Licensed by VAGA, New York, NY; p. 664: © PhotoDisc/Getty; p. 665: © John Griffin/ The Image Works; p. 668: © Mark Reinstein/The Image Works; p. 669: © Tom Carter/PhotoEdit

Name Index

Subject Index